Encyclopedia

of

Real Estate Formulas and Tables

Martin J. Miles

Prentice-Hall, Inc.
Englewood Cliffs, New Jersey

Prentice-Hall International, Inc., *London*
Prentice-Hall of Australia, Pty. Ltd., *Sydney*
Prentice-Hall of Canada, Ltd., *Toronto*
Prentice-Hall of India Private Ltd., *New Delhi*
Prentice-Hall of Japan, Inc., *Tokyo*
Prentice-Hall of Southeast Asia Pte. Ltd., *Singapore*
Whitehall Books, Ltd., *Wellington, New Zealand*

Library of Congress Cataloging in Publication Data

Miles, Martin J
    Encyclopedia of real estate formulas and tables.

    1. Real estate business--Problems, exercises, etc.
I. Title.
HF5695.5.R37M54   333.3'3   77-15508
ISBN 0-13-276220-X

Printed in the United States of America

To my parents
Mrs. Mary L. and the late Dr. Martin B. Miles

and

my children
Barbara and Martin

About the Author

Martin J. Miles is a real estate consultant and a mathematician. He holds a real estate license in Colorado and received his Bachelors and Masters degrees in Mathematics from the University of Colorado. He is the author and co-author of numerous mathematical articles published in the United States, Canada and Europe. Mr. Miles is also an active real estate investor.

ACKNOWLEDGEMENTS

The author would like to acknowledge his indebtedness to Dr. Edwin L. Crow, mathematical statistician with the National Center for Atmospheric Research, Mr. Thomas F. Hagerty, formerly with the Internal Revenue Service, Dr. Clyde W. Richey, Professor of Real Estate with the University of Colorado, Bradford M. Beeler MAI, and Kermit D. Glover for their important counsel and suggestions.

The author is equally indebted to Ms. Patricia Moreno for the excellent preparation of this lengthy and difficult manuscript, and to E. Dean Eicher for the clear and precise presentation of the many drawings.

How This Book Can Help You

This desk-top volume contains nearly every formula and table needed by the real estate professional. Whether you want to determine the capital gain on an installment sale, compute the rate of return, find the yield on a mortgage, or solve any other real estate problem, this book should provide the answer. And, except for one formula, only secondary school mathematics is required.

This encyclopedia solves two basic problems for the real estate professional: It eliminates the need to consult many different handbooks, and more importantly, it eliminates the need to adjust to the notations found in each. It is difficult enough to confidently use formulas from such diverse fields as finance, appraisal, investments, and taxes without the added burden of adjusting to the styles of different authors. The notation used in this book is as uniform as possible, and finally, it unifies the mathematics of real estate.

To make this encyclopedia thoroughly readable, every section follows the same format. Furthermore, each formula is used in at least one simple example. Hence, there is no doubt about its application. Frequently a graph of the formula or table is shown so that you can clearly see its behavior. For example, Figure 6-A can be used to quickly estimate the monthly payment for an amortized loan. If only an estimate is required, this figure alone can replace many pages of a table, and it helps you to understand the nature of these loans. In the same way, Figure 6-E can be used to quickly estimate the balance of a loan.

Here is a glimpse into *Encyclopedia of Real Estate Formulas and Tables:*

The first six chapters include all the formulas you will need for simple and compound interest, discount, annuities, bonds, notes, and mortgages. For example, you will find the relationship between interest and discount, the yield on purchased mortgages, the yield on wrap-around mortgages, the combination of interest rates and terms that result in a given monthly payment, balloon payments, etc.

The next four chapters provide the formulas you will need to evaluate almost every type of real property and investment. First, you will find the formulas for the capitalization rate and the rationale behind it. Next, you will find the formulas you need to determine the value of income property, including the rate of return and the Ellwood method. Also you will find a valuable formula that suggests the optimum holding period for an investment; so often an investor's yield is damped by holding a property too long. The chapter covering the cost approach provides you with a detailed look at depreciation and reproduction cost. You will find a formula that, based on these two phenomena, can be used to forecast property value.

The chapter covering the market approach shows you how location and spatial arrangements can influence value. This chapter also includes an important formula that determines a range of values within which a group of appraisers can be, say, 95% confident that the true value lies. By using this formula they can heighten the credibility of their appraisal.

The next four chapters deal with taxes. The formulas that correctly determine the amount of deduction, the basis, the capital gain, etc. can be found in a unique and painless way: To solve a given tax problem, you will find a diagram containing a set of simple questions. As you answer each question either "yes" or "no," follow to the right or left, respectively, and answer the next question. Continuing in this manner, you will arrive at the proper formula. Thus, almost all the effort, reading, and uncertainty is removed from your tax problem. For example, suppose you converted your personal residence to an income-producing property; Section 12.11 determines the basis of the converted property. Similarly, Section 13.10 determines the capital gain resulting from the sale of a personal residence after another has been purchased.

The final chapter allows you to convert most of the units used in real estate. Not only will you find the conversions for domestic and metric units, but also those peculiar to most foreign countries. For instance, you can determine how many Costa Rican varas equal one acre.

The appendix contains mathematical notes that will refresh you on some concepts used in this book. Remember, only one formula (i.e. multiple regression) requires more than secondary school mathematics.

Table 1 is extraordinarily complete. It lists all the values of compound interest and annuities for interest rates from 5% to 14%. The table spans 500 periods. Equally important, it can be used for both deposits and compounding whose frequencies are different (i.e. 1, 2, 4, and 12 times a year). For example, there are countless books from which you can compute the amount of an annuity on an annual basis. However, with this book, you can compute it when deposits are made, say, 12 times a year and compounding occurs 2 times a year.

Due to the scope of this book, and because all the mathematics of real estate is finally brought together, I believe you will find it an indespensible aid.

Martin J. Miles

Contents

Contents

FINANCE: SIMPLE INTEREST (SHORT-TERM DEBT)

Interest is consideration for the use of money. The amount of money borrowed is called the principal. Simple interest is interest paid on the principal only and is usually employed for short-term borrowing.

1.1.   Amount of Interest

Formulas:

$$I = prt = S - p$$

where

I   =   amount of interest
r   =   annual interest rate, expressed as a decimal
t   =   interest period, expressed as a fraction of a year
p   =   amount of principal
S   =   amount accumulated

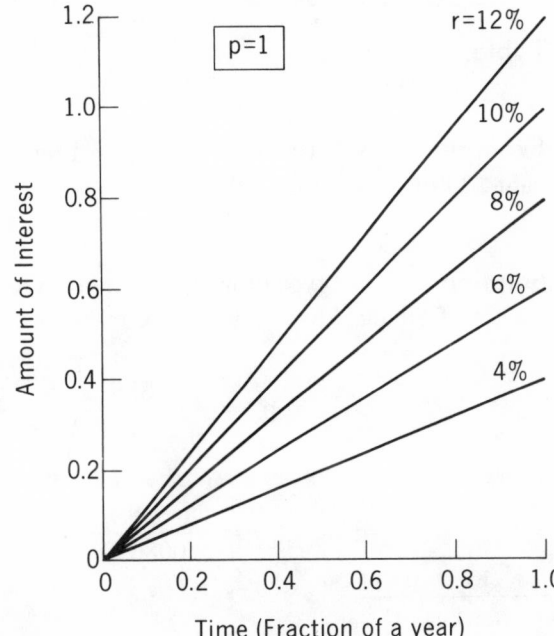

15

Table: Find t in Table 7.*

Example: What is the amount of interest on a construction loan of $220,000 at 7% ordinary simple interest from April 13 to November 24?

Solution: The information in this example (i.e., p, r, and t) suggests using the first formula. From Table 7, April 13 is the 103rd day of the year, and November 24 is the 328th day. Hence, the time interval is 225 days. Ordinary interest uses a 360-day year. Now,

$$I = \$220,000 \times .07 \times \left(\frac{225}{360}\right) = \$9,625.$$

1.2.   Amount of Principal

Formulas:

$$p = \frac{I}{rt} = \frac{S}{1 + rt}$$

where

p = amount of principal
I = amount of interest
r = annual interest rate, expressed as a decimal
t = interest period, expressed as a fraction of a year
S = amount accumulated

Table: 7

Example: What amount of principal must be loaned at exact simple interest of 7% to earn $39 of interest in 45 days?

Solution: The type of information given in this example (i.e., r, I, and t) suggests using the first formula. From Table 7, exact interest indicates a 365-day year. Now,

$$p = \frac{\$39}{.07 \times\left(\frac{45}{365}\right)} = \frac{\$39}{.07 \times 0.1233}$$

$$= \frac{\$39}{.008630} = \$4,519.12$$

*See Table 7, page 493.

1.3.   Amount of Time

Formulas:

$$t = \frac{I}{pr} = \frac{S - p}{pr}$$

where

t = interest period, expressed as a fraction of a year
I = amount of interest
p = amount of principal
r = annual interest rate, expressed as a decimal
S = amount accumulated

Table: 7

Example: How many days are required to earn $60 of interest on a principal amount of $10,000 at 7½% simple interest?

Solution: The information given in this example (i.e., I, p, and r) suggests using the first formula. Now,

$$t = \frac{\$60}{\$10,000 \times .075} = \frac{\$60}{\$750} = .08.$$

Since t is a fractional part of a year, to find the number of days required we must multiply t by the number of days in a year. Using Table 7, we see that for ordinary interest,

$$t \times 360 \text{ days} = .08 \times 360 \text{ days} = 28.8 \text{ days,}$$

and for exact interest

$$t \times 365 \text{ days} = .08 \times 365 \text{ days} = 29.2 \text{ days.}$$

1.4.   Rate of Interest

Formulas:

$$r = \frac{I}{pt} = \frac{S-p}{pt}$$

where

r = annual interest rate, expressed as a decimal
I = amount of interest
p = amount of principal
t = interest period, expressed as a fraction of a year
S = amount accumulated

Table: 7

Example: What annual interest rate must be charged to earn $500 of ordinary simple interest between March 15 and November 15 on a principal amount of $9,600?

Solution: The information in this example (i.e., I, t, and p) suggests using the first formula. From Table 7, March 15 is the 74th day of the year and November 15 is the 319th day of the year. Hence, there is a 245-day time interval. If ordinary interest is used, a year is said to have 360 days. Now,

$$r = \frac{\$500}{\$9,600 \times \left(\frac{245}{360}\right)} = \frac{\$500}{\$9,600 \times 0.680556}$$

$$= \frac{\$500}{\$6,533.33} = .0765 = 7.65\%.$$

1.5.   Amount Accumulated

Formulas:

$$S = p(1 + rt) = p + I$$

where

S = amount accumulated (principal + interest)
p = amount of principal
r = annual interest rate, expressed as a decimal
t = interest period, expressed as a fraction of a year
I = amount of interest

Table: 7

Example: On April 12, a commercial bank loaned $30,000 at ordinary simple interest of 6%. How much must be repaid when the debt is due February 2?

Solution: The type of information given in this example (i.e., p, r, and t) suggests using the first formula. From Table 7, April 12 is the 102nd day of the year, and there are 263 days remaining in the year. Also, February 2 is the 33rd day of the following year. The total time is 296 days. Since ordinary interest is specified, we must use a 360-day year. Now,

$$S = \$30,000 \left(1 + .06 \times \frac{296}{360} \right)$$

$$= \$30,000 \ (1 + .06 \times .82222)$$
$$= \$30,000 \times 1.04933$$
$$= \$31,480.$$

1.6. Present Value of an Interest-Bearing Debt*

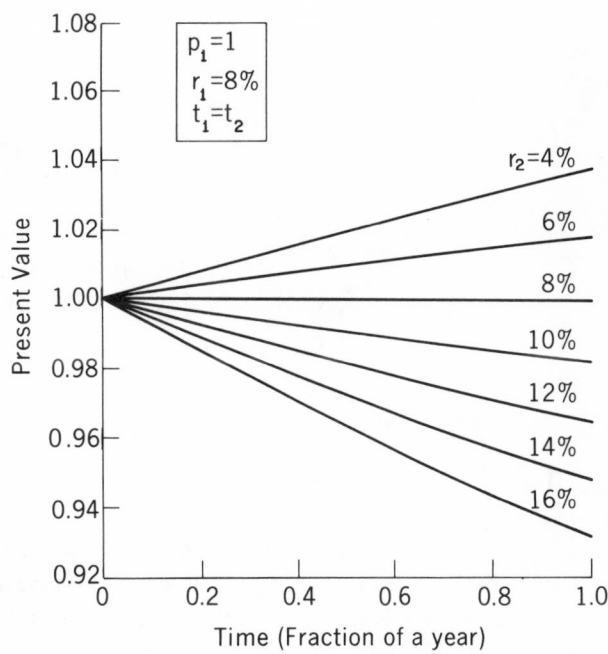

Time has value. An amount to be received in the future is worth less than if it were received immediately. However the figure shows that a debt to be paid in the future gains value if the interest rate it bears is larger than the interest rate currently being obtained.

Formula:

$$p_2 = p_1 \ \frac{1 + r_1 t_1}{1 + r_2 t_2}$$

where

p_1, p_2 = original and present value of the debt, respectively
r_1, r_2 = original and present annual interest rate, respectively, expressed as a decimal
t_1, t_2 = original and remaining interest period, respectively, expressed as a fraction of a year

Table: 7

---

*For a non-interest-bearing debt merely use $r_1 = 0$ in the formula.

Example: Mr. Madden signed a $3,000 note at 8% interest, due in 9 months. Two months later the holder sells the note to a third party who determines its worth (in terms of the present interest rate) at 6%. What is the present value of the note?

Solution: In this example,

$$p_1 = \$3,000, \; r_1 = 8\%, \; t_1 = 9/12, \; t_2 = 7/12, \text{ and } r_2 = 6\%.$$

Now,

$$p_2 = \$3,000 \times \frac{1 + .08 \times \dfrac{9}{12}}{1 + .06 \times \dfrac{7}{12}} = \$3,000 \times \frac{1 + .0600}{1 + .0350}$$

$$= \$3,000 \times \frac{1.0600}{1.0350} = \$3,072.46.$$

1.7.   Partial Payments

Non-scheduled partial payments are sometimes made on commercial paper. There are two methods used to compute interest on the balance of such loans: Merchant's Rule and United States Rule. Since there can be any number of partial payments at any time, the formulas that determine the balance must be general. The following parameters are needed to determine the balance when n partial payments are made:

p_o = amount of principal (amount borrowed)
r = annual interest rate, expressed as a decimal
t_o = date the loan starts, expressed as a fraction of a year
t_m = date the loan ends (maturity date), expressed as a fraction of a year
n = number of partial payments
p_i = amount of the ith partial payment
t_i = date the ith payment is made, expressed as a fraction of a year
B_i = loan balance after the ith partial payment
B_m = loan balance at maturity

Merchant's Rule.   This rule is used in commercial practices. It is the simpler of the two methods, but the balance after each partial payment (B_i) is not readily available. The principal and the partial payments earn interest from the time they are made until maturity.

Formula:

$$B_m = p_0 u_0 - \sum_{i=1}^{n} p_i u_i^*$$

where

$u_i = 1 + r(t_m - t_i)$ for $i = 0, 1, 2, \ldots, n.$

Table: 7

Example: On June 13, Bob Hall signed a 6-month $17,000 note, bearing exact interest at 6%. On August 12 he made a payment of $1,400, and on November 19 he made a payment of $5,000. What is the balance due at maturity?

Solution: In this example, $p_0 = \$17,000$, $p_1 = \$1,400$, and $p_2 = \$5,000$. From Table 7 we see that June 13, August 12, November 19, and December 13 (maturity date) are the 164th, 224th, 323rd, and 347th days of the year. Hence,

$$t_0 = \frac{164}{365} = .4493, \qquad t_1 = \frac{224}{365} = .6137,$$

$$t_2 = \frac{323}{365} = .8849, \text{ and } t_m = \frac{347}{365} = .9507.$$

Since there were two partial payments, n=2.

In accordance with the formula, it is convenient to first compute the u_i values:

$$u_0 = 1 + .06(.9507 - .4493) = 1 + .06 \times .5014$$
$$= 1.03008,$$

$$u_1 = 1 + .06(.9507 - .6137) = 1 + .06 \times .3370$$
$$= 1.02022, \text{ and}$$

$$u_2 = 1 + .06(.9507 - .8849) = 1 + .06 \times .0658$$
$$= 1.003948.$$

---

*The notation $\sum_{i=1}^{n}$ means to sum the values $p_i u_i$ from $i = 1$ to $i = n$

(See Appendix: Mathematical Notes)

Now using the formula, the balance due at maturity is

$$B_m = p_0 u_0 - \sum_{i=1}^{2} p_i u_i = p_0 u_0 - (p_1 u_1 + p_2 u_2)$$

$$= \$17{,}000 \times 1.03008 - (\$1{,}400 \times 1.02022$$
$$+ \$5{,}000 \times 1.003948)$$
$$= \$17{,}511.36 - (\$1{,}428.31 + \$5{,}019.74)$$
$$= \$17{,}511.36 - \$6{,}448.05$$
$$= \$11{,}063.31.$$

United States Rule.   This rule results from a U.S. Supreme Court decision and is used in government accounting. The formula is more difficult to compute than the Merchant's Rule, but the balance can be determined after each partial payment.

Formulas:

$$\mathbf{B_i = B_{i-1} \; v_i - p_i^* \quad for \; i = 1, 2, \ldots, n}$$

$$\mathbf{B_m = B_n v_m}$$

where

$B_0 = p_0 =$ amount of principal (amount borrowed)
$v_i = 1 + r(t_i - t_{i-1})$ for $i = 1, 2, \ldots, n$
$v_m = 1 + r(t_m - t_n)$

Table: 7

---

*This formula is valid only when the payment is greater than or equal to the interest on the balance. If the payment is less than the interest, the payment is not subtracted from the balance until it and the next payment exceed the accumulated interest. The following formula is general and determines the balance whether or not the previous payment exceeds the interest:

$$B_i = \begin{cases} B_{i-1} & \text{if } p_i < B_{i-1}(v_i-1) \text{ and} \\ & \quad p_{i-1} \geq B_{i-2}(v_{i-1}-1) \\ B_{i-1}v_i - p_i & \text{if } p_i \geq B_{i-1}(v_i-1) \text{ and} \\ & \quad p_{i-1} \geq B_{i-2}(v_{i-1}-1) \\ B_{i-2}(v_i + v_{i-1}-1) - (p_i + p_{i-1}) & \text{if } p_{i-1} < B_{i-2}(v_{i-1}-1) \text{ and} \\ & \quad p_i + p_{i-1} \geq B_{i-1}(v_i-1). \end{cases}$$

Example: Using the example from the Merchant's Rule (page 21), find the balance after each partial payment and also at maturity.

Solution: As shown in the example from the Merchant's Rule,

$$t_o = .4493, t_1 = .6137, t_2 = .8849, \text{ and } t_m = .9507.$$

The formula for the balance after the first partial payment is

$$B_1 = B_o v_1 - p_1$$

where

$$v_1 = 1 + r(t_1 - t_o) = 1 + .06(.6137 - .4493)$$
$$= 1 + .06 \times .1644 = 1.009864.$$

Now,

$$B_1 = \$17,000 \times 1.009864 - \$1,400$$
$$= \$15,767.69.$$

The formula for the balance after the second partial payment is

$$B_2 = B_1 v_2 - p_2$$

where

$$v_2 = 1 + r(t_2 - t_1) = 1 + .06 \times (.8849 - .6137)$$
$$= 1 + .06 \times .2712 = 1 + .016272$$
$$= 1.016272.$$

Now,

$$B_2 = \$15,767.69 \times 1.016272 - \$5,000$$
$$= \$11,024.26.$$

The formula for the balance due at maturity is

$$B_m = B_2 v_m$$

where

$$v_m = 1 + r(t_m - t_n) = 1 + .06(.9507 - .8849)$$
$$= 1 + .06 \times .06580 = 1.003948.$$

Now,

$$B_m = \$11,024.26 \times 1.003948 = \$11,067.78.$$

Notice that the balance due at maturity differs only slightly between the two rules.

1.8.   Rescheduled Payments (Equation of Value)

Sometimes it is desirable to reschedule the payments on one or more debts. Value can be preserved for both the lender and the borrower if they agree on a current interest rate. The following formula can be used for short-term debts to determine new payment dates or new amounts while still preserving value. (Note: there is a corresponding compound interest formula for long-term debts. See Section 3.8.)

Formula:

$$\sum_{i=1}^{n} p_i \, a_i * = \sum_{i=1}^{n'} p_i' \, a_i'$$

where

n, n' = number of new and old payments, respectively

p_i, p_i' = amount of the ith new and old payment, respectively

t_i, t_i' = date of the ith new and old payment, respectively, expressed as a fraction of a year

r = current (agreed upon) interest rate, expressed as a decimal

x = reference date (focal date) at which value is to be determined, expressed as a fraction of a year. This arbitrary date is often set to coincide with the last new payment.

$$a_i = \begin{cases} 1 + r(x - t_i) & \text{if } x \geq t_i \\ \dfrac{1}{1 + r(t_i - x)} & \text{if } x < t_i \end{cases}$$

$$a_i' = \begin{cases} 1 + r(x - t_i') & \text{if } x \geq t_i' \\ \dfrac{1}{1 + r(t_i' - x)} & \text{if } x < t_i' \end{cases}$$

Table: 7

---

*The notation $\sum_{i=1}^{n}$ means to sum the values $p_i \, a_i$ from $i = 1$ to $i = n$ (see Appendix: Mathematical Notes, Section A.1).

Example: Mr. Hall must make three payments on a debt. He owes $400 due April 30, $300 due September 3, and $600 due November 22. He wishes to arrange for only two payments, the second to be $200 more than the first.

He and the lender have agreed on new payment dates of July 14 and December 14, a focal date of October 31, and a current interest rate of 7%. What are the amounts of the two new payments that preserve the value of the original agreement?

Solution: From Table 7, we obtain the following day numbers:

$$\text{Apr. } 30 = 120\text{th day of the year: } t_1' = \frac{120}{365} = .3288.$$

$$\text{Sept. } 3 = 246\text{th day of the year: } t_2' = \frac{246}{365} = .6740.$$

$$\text{Nov. } 22 = 326\text{th day of the year: } t_3' = \frac{326}{365} = .8932.$$

$$\text{July } 14 = 195\text{th day of the year: } t_1 = \frac{195}{365} = .5342.$$

$$\text{Dec. } 14 = 348\text{th day of the year: } t_2 = \frac{348}{365} = .9534.$$

$$\text{Oct. } 31 = 304\text{th day of the year: } x = \frac{304}{365} = .8329.$$

We can now determine each a_i and a_i' :

$$a_1' = 1 + .07(.8329 - .3288) = 1.03529, \text{ (since } x > t_1')$$

$$a_2' = 1 + .07(.8329 - .6740) = 1.01112, \text{ (since } x > t_2')$$

$$a_3' = \frac{1}{1 + .07(.8932 - .8329)} = .995797, \text{ (since } x < t_3')$$

$$a_1 = 1 + .07(.8329 - .5342) = 1.02091, \text{ (since } x > t_1)$$

and

$$a_2 = \frac{1}{1 + .07(.9534 - .8329)} = .991636, \text{ (since } x < t_2).$$

Note that the original payments are

$$p_1' = \$400, \; p_2' = \$300, \; \text{and} \; p_3' = \$600.$$

Using these values in the basic formula, we have

$$p_1 \times 1.02090 + p_2 \times .991636$$
$$= \$400 \times 1.03529 + \$300 \times 1.01112$$
$$+ \$600 \times .995797.$$

There are two remaining unknown values (p_1 and p_2) in this equation; a solution cannot be found when the number of unknown values exceeds the number of equations. However, Mr. Hall asked that his second payment should be $200 greater than the first. This is the second equation:

$$p_2 = p_1 + \$200.$$

We can replace p_2 by (p_1 + $200) in the basic equation:

$$p_1 \times 1.02090 + (p_1 + \$200) \times .991636$$
$$= \$414.12 + \$303.34 + \$579.48$$
$$p_1 \times 1.02090 + p_1 \times .991636 + \$200 \times .991636$$
$$= \$1,296.94$$
$$p_1(1.02090 + .991636) + \$198.33 = \$1,296.94$$
$$p_1(2.01254) = \$1,098.61$$
$$p_1 = \frac{\$1,098.61}{2.01254} = \$545.88.$$

Now,

$$p_2 = p_1 + \$200 = \$545.88 + \$200 = \$745.88.$$

Mr. Hall's original payments totaled $1,300. His rescheduled payments total $1,291.76.

FINANCE: DISCOUNT (SHORT-TERM DEBT)

Discount is a charge for a debt before it is due; hence it is thought of as interest in advance. Discount is computed on the face value of a debt*. Since it is retained by the lender, the proceeds to the borrower are less than the face value of the debt.

2.1. Amount of Bank Discount

The amount of bank discount is the charge for credit based on the face value.

Formulas:

$$d = f(1 + rt)r't' = Sr't' = S - p$$

---

*The formulas in this chapter are general and define interest-bearing debt. For non-interest-bearing debt, merely use $r = 0$.

where

d = amount of bank discount
f = face value (amount loaned)
S = maturity value (face value plus interest, if any)
p = loan proceeds
r = annual interest rate, expressed as a decimal
r′ = annual discount rate, expressed as a decimal
t = interest period, expressed as a fraction of a year
t′ = discount period, expressed as a fraction of a year

Table: 7

Example: On April 3, Mr. J.A. Davis signed a $5,000 note with the AMT Company at 5% interest, due in 6 months. On June 10 the note is discounted at a bank which charges a 7% discount rate. What is the amount of discount?

Solution: The type of information given in this example (i.e., f, r, t, r′, and t′) suggests using the first formula. From Table 7, June 10 (discount date) is the 161st day of the year, and October 3 (maturity date) is the 276th day. Hence,

$$t' = \frac{276 - 161}{360} = \frac{115}{360} = .31944, \text{ and } t = \frac{6}{12} = \frac{1}{2}.$$

Now, the amount of discount is

$$d = \$5,000 \left(1 + .05 \times \frac{1}{2}\right) \times .07 \times .31944$$
$$= \$5,000 \times 1.025 \times .02236$$
$$= \$114.60.$$

2.2.   Face Value

The face value is the amount loaned.

Formulas:

$$f = \frac{p}{(1 + rt)(1 - r't')} = \frac{S}{1 + rt} = \frac{d}{(1 + rt) + r't'}$$

where

f = face value
p = proceeds (amount received)
r = annual interest rate, expressed as a decimal
r′ = annual discount rate, expressed as a decimal
t = interest period, expressed as a fraction of a year
t′ = discount period, expressed as a fraction of a year
S = maturity value (face value plus interest, if any)
d = amount of bank discount

Table: 7

Example: Consider a 180-day note, bearing 6% interest to yield proceeds of $4,189.85. If the note is discounted at 7% 36 days after the day of making, what is its face value?

Solution: The type of information given in this example (i.e., t, r, p, r′, and t′) suggests using the first formula.

The interest period is

$$t = \frac{180}{360} = \frac{1}{2},$$

and the discount period is

$$t' = \frac{180 - 36}{360} = 0.4.$$

Now,

$$f = \frac{\$4,189.85}{(1 + .06 \times \frac{1}{2})(1 - .07 \times .4)} = \frac{\$4,189.85}{(1.03)(.972)}$$

$$= \frac{\$4,189.85}{1.00116}$$

$$= \$4,185.$$

2.3.   Maturity Value

The maturity value is the amount loaned plus interest, if any.

Formulas:

$$S = f(1 + rt) = \frac{d}{r't'} = \frac{p}{(1 - r't')}$$

where

S = maturity value
f = face value (amount loaned)
r = annual interest rate, expressed as a decimal
t = interest period, expressed as a fraction of a year
d = amount of bank discount
r′ = annual discount rate, expressed as a decimal
t′ = discount period, expressed as a fraction of a year
p = proceeds (amount received)

Table: 7

Example: The proceeds of an interest-bearing note are $9,612. The note matures December 19 and is discounted August 10 at 7%. What is the maturity value?

Solution: The type of information given in this example (i.e., p, r′, and t′) suggests using the third formula. From Table 7, we see that December 19 is the 353rd day of the year, and August 10 is the 222nd day. Hence,

$$t' = \frac{353 - 222}{360} = \frac{131}{360} = .36389.$$

Now,

$$S = \frac{\$9,612}{1 - .07 \times .36389} = \frac{\$9,612}{.9745277}$$

$$= \$9,863.24.$$

2.4. Proceeds

The proceeds are the amount received by the borrower.

Formulas:

$$p = f(1 + rt)(1 - r't') = S(1 - r't') = d\ \frac{(1 - r't')}{r't'}$$

where

p = proceeds
f = face value (amount loaned)
S = maturity value (face value plus interest, if any)
r = annual interest rate, expressed as a decimal
r′ = annual discount rate, expressed as a decimal
t = interest period, expressed as a fraction of a year
t′ = discount period, expressed as a fraction of a year
d = amount of bank discount

Table: 7

Example: On April 28 a bank discounted a 6 month, $4,000 promissory note at 7%. The note is due July 3 and bears interest at 6%. What are the proceeds?

Solution: The type of information given in this example (i.e., f, r′, t, r, and t′) suggests using the first formula. From Table 7, April 28 is the 118th day of the year, and July 3 is the 184th day. Hence,

$$t' = \frac{184 - 118}{360} = \frac{66}{360} = .18333, \text{ and } t = \frac{6}{12} = \frac{1}{2}.$$

Now,

$$p = \$4,000(1 + .06 \times \frac{1}{2})(1 - .07 \times .18333)$$

$$= \$4,000(1 + .03)(1 - .01283)$$

$$= \$4,000 \times 1.03 \times .98717$$

$$= \$4,067.14.$$

2.5.   Rate of Bank Discount*

Formulas:

$$r' = \frac{d}{ft'(1 + rt)} = \frac{S - p}{St'}$$

where

r′ = annual discount rate, expressed as a decimal
d = amount of bank discount
f = face value (amount loaned)
r = annual interest rate, expressed as a decimal
t = interest period, expressed as a fraction of a year
t′ = discount period, expressed as a fraction of a year
S = maturity value (face value plus interest, if any)
p = proceeds (amount received)

Table: 7

Example: On April 13, Mr. DiScipio signed a $1,000 note that is discounted by $30 on March 23. The note bears 7% interest and matures September 23. What is the discount rate?

Solution: The type of information given in this example (i.e., f, d, r, t, and t′) suggests using the first formula. From Table 7, April 13 is the 103rd day of the year, May 23 is the 143rd day, and September 23 is the 266th day.
Hence,

$$t' = \frac{266 - 143}{360} = \frac{123}{360} = .34167,$$

and

$$t = \frac{266 - 103}{360} = \frac{163}{360} = .45278.$$

Now,

$$r' = \frac{\$30}{\$1,000 \times .34167(1 + .07 \times .45278)}$$

$$= \frac{\$30}{\$341.67(1 + .03169)} = \frac{\$30}{\$341.67 \times 1.03169}$$

$$= \frac{30}{\$352.50}$$

$$= .0851 = 8.51\%.$$

---

*See Section 2.6 for the relationship between the rate of bank discount and the rate of interest.

2.6. Relationship Between Bank Discount Rate and Its Equivalent Interest Rate

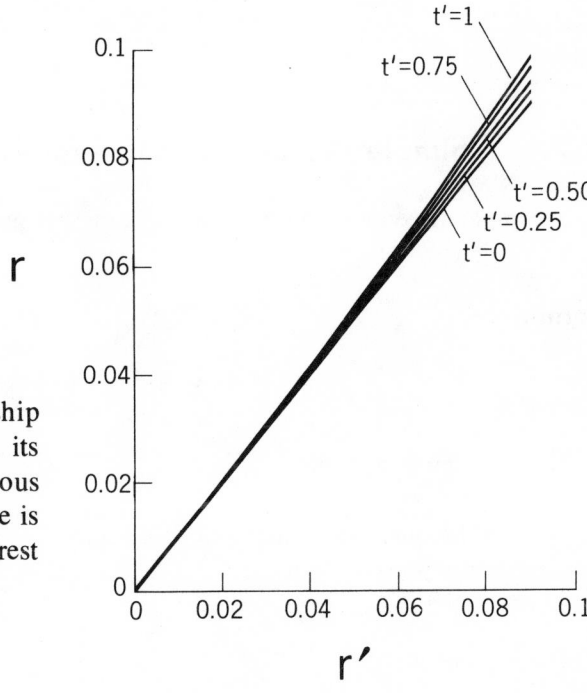

The figure shows the relationship between bank discount rate and its equivalent interest rate for various discount periods. The discount rate is always less than its equivalent interest rate.

Formulas:

$$r = \frac{r'}{1 - r't'} \quad \text{or} \quad r' = \frac{r}{1 + rt}$$

where

r = annual interest rate, expressed as a decimal
r' = annual discount rate, expressed as a decimal
t = interest period, expressed as a fraction of a year
t' = discount period, expressed as a fraction of a year

Table: Find t and t' in Table 7

Example: A bank discounts a note at 6%, due in 6 months. What interest rate is equivalent to this discount rate?

Solution: Since the note is due in 6 months,

$$t' = \frac{6}{12} = \frac{1}{2} .$$

Now,

$$r = \frac{.06}{1 - .06 \times \frac{1}{2}} = \frac{.06}{.97} = .06186 = 6.186\%.$$

2.7.   Simple Discount (Commercial)

Simple discount is the list price less the net price.

Formulas:

$$d = Sr' = S - p$$

where

d = simple discount
S = list price
r' = discount rate, expressed as a decimal
p = net price

Table: none

Example: A wholesaler lists end tables at $70 and grants a 30% discount to retailers. What is the amount of the discount and the net price to the retailer?

Solution: The information given in this example (i.e., S and r') suggests using the first formula:

The discount is

$$d = \$70 \times .30 = \$21.$$

The net price is

$$p = S - d = \$70 - \$21 = \$49.$$

2.8.   Chain Discount (Commercial)

A chain discount is two or more simple discounts that are applied successively.

Formulas:

$$D_n = \sum_{i=1}^{n} d_i = r'S = S - p^*$$

where

D_n = amount of the chain discount resulting from n simple discount amounts, d_i

$$d_i = \begin{cases} Sr_i' & \text{for } i = 1 \\ S(1 - r_1') \times (1 - r_2') \times \ldots \times (1 - r_{i-1}') \times r_i' & \\ & \text{for } i = 2, 3, \ldots, n \end{cases}$$

= amount of the ith simple discount

p = net price

S = list price (price to retail customers)

r_i' = rate of the ith simple discount, expressed as a decimal

r' = D_n/S = simple discount rate equivalent to chain discount rate

Table: none

Example: An apartment owner wants to buy new chairs for his furnished units. The chairs are listed by a wholesaler at $205 each. The simple discounts for quantity purchases are 15%, 5%, and 2%. What is the amount of the chain discount, what is the net price, and what is the equivalent simple discount rate?

Solution: First compute the amount of each simple discount:

$$d_1 = Sr_1' = \$205 \times .15 = \$30.75,$$
$$d_2 = S(1 - r_1') \times r_2' = \$205 \times (1 - .15) \times .05 = \$8.71,$$

and

$$d_3 = S(1 - r_1') \times (1 - r_2') \times r_3'$$
$$= \$205 \times (1 - .15) \times (1 - .05) \times .02 = \$3.31.$$

Now the amount of the chain discount is

$$D_3 = \sum_{i=1}^{3} d_i = d_1 + d_2 + d_3 = \$30.75 + \$8.71 + \$3.31 = \$42.77.$$

_____

*The symbol $\sum$ indicates the sum of each d_i. See Appendix: Mathematical Notes, Section A.1.

The net price is

$$p = S - D_3 = \$205 - \$42.77 = \$162.23.$$

The equivalent simple discount rate is

$$r' = \frac{D_3}{S} = \frac{\$42.77}{\$205} = .2086 = 20.86\%.$$

2.9.   Markup (Commercial)

When goods are resold at a profit, the markup can be computed on either the cost price or the selling price. Markup based on the cost price can be thought of as interest on the present value, and markup based on the selling price can be thought of as discount on the future value.

Formulas:

$$S = f(1 + r) = \frac{f}{1 - r'}$$

where
S = selling price
f = cost price
r = markup on cost price, expressed as a decimal
r' = markup on selling price, expressed as a decimal

Table: none

Example: Mr. Thomas paid $205 each for 100 chairs and plans to resell them for a profit. What is the selling price if he uses: (a) a markup of 20% on the cost price; or (b) a markup of 20% on the selling price?

Solution:

$$\text{(a) } S = \$205(1 + .20) = \$246.00$$

$$\text{(b) } S = \frac{\$205}{(1 - .20)} = \$256.25.$$

3

FINANCE: COMPOUND INTEREST
(LONG-TERM DEBT)

Interest is consideration for the use of principal. In compound interest, the amount of interest is added to the principal, thus forming a larger amount upon which interest will again be computed. This process is repeated each interest period. Hence the amount (principal + interest) grows in proportion to itself. Compound interest is generally employed in long-term debt.

3.1. Amount Accumulated at Interest Compounded Q Times a Year

An amount at compound interest increases with time and with the rate of interest. See Figure 3-A.

Interest can be computed any number of times a year. For a given rate of interest, the amount accumulated is larger for more frequent compounding. See Figure 3-B.

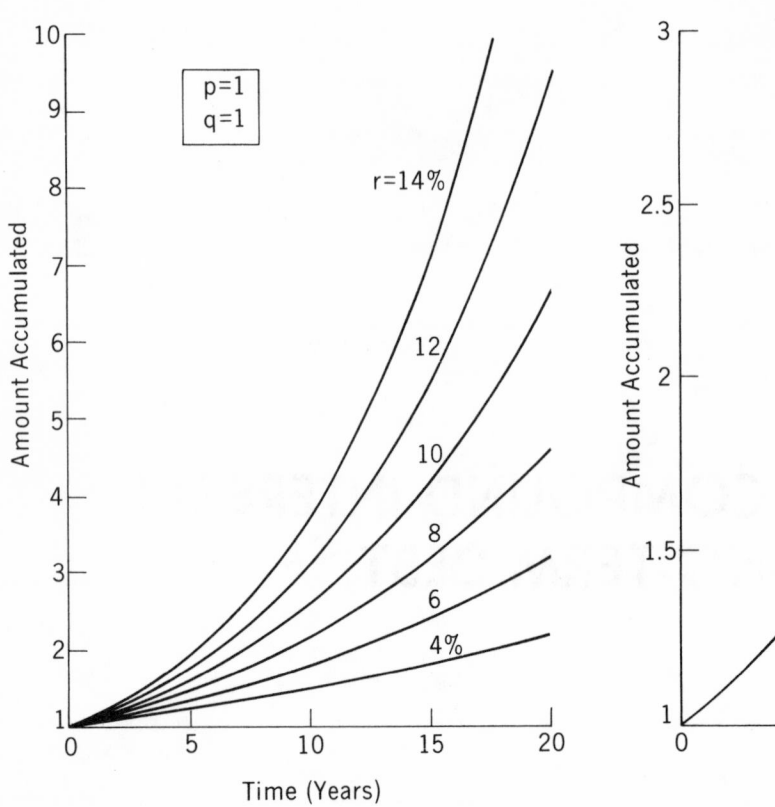

Figure 3-A

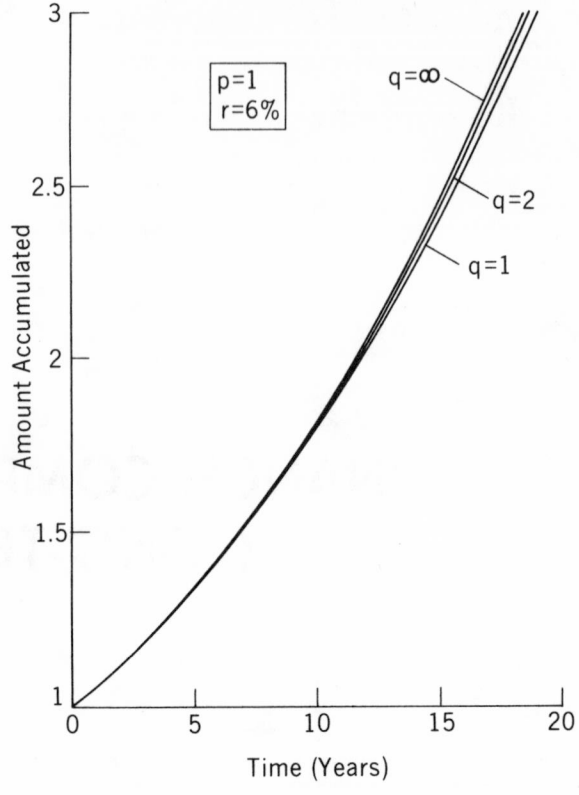

Figure 3-B

Formula:

$$S \;=\; p \cdot (1 + r/q)^m = p \cdot c(r,m,q)$$

where

        S   = amount accumulated
        p   = principal
        r   = annual interest rate, expressed as a decimal
        q   = number of interest periods per year
        n   = number of years
        m = nq = total number of periods
  c(r,m,q) = amount of 1 at compound interest

Table: Find c(r,m,q) in Table 1.*

---

*See Table 1, page 339.

Example 1:   An investor obtained a $50,000 loan for 3 years at 8% interest compounded quarterly. What is the total amount that he will owe?

Solution: In this example,

$$p = \$50,000, n = 3, r = 8\%, q = 4, \text{ and } m = nq = 12.$$

From Table 1,

$$c(r,m,q) = c(8,12,4) = 1.26824.$$

Now, he will owe

$$S = \$50,000 \times c(8,12,4) = \$50,000 \times 1.26824$$
$$= \$63,412.$$

Example 2:   Houses near the golf course have been increasing in value 11% annually. If this trend continues for 3 more years, how much will a $40,000 house be worth?

Solution: In this example,

$$r = 11\%, q = 1, n = 3, m = nq = 3, \text{ and } p = \$40,000.$$

From Table 1,

$$c(r,m,q) = c(11,3,1) = 1.367631.$$

A $40,000 house will be worth

$$S = \$40,000 \times 1.367631 = \$54,705.24.$$

3.2.   Present Value at Interest Compounded Q Times a Year

An amount to be received in the future is not as valuable as if it were received now.

Suppose $1, to be received 17 years hence, is judged to be the equivalent of 25¢ received now. This implies that money is worth 8½% per year. The figure illustrates this concept.

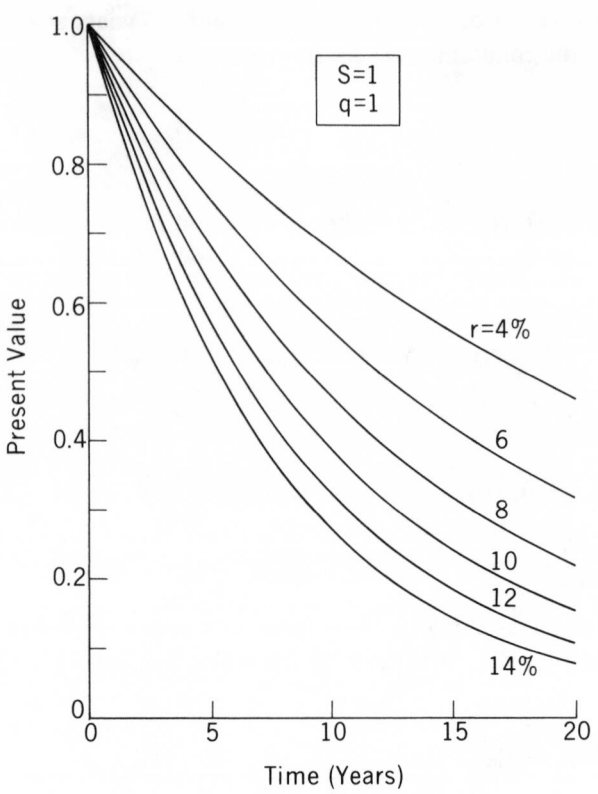

Formula:

$$p = \frac{S}{(1 + r/q)^m} = \frac{S}{c(r,m,q)}$$

where

  p   = present value
  S   = future amount
  r   = annual interest rate, expressed as a decimal
  q   = number of interest periods per year
  n   = number of years
  m   = nq = total number of periods
c(r,m,q) = amount of 1 at compound interest.

Table: Find c(r,m,q) in Table 1.

Example 1:   Dr. Johnson wants to accumulate $3,000 in 4 years. How much must he deposit at 6% interest compounded twice a year?

Solution: In this example,

$$S = \$3,000, n = 4, r = 6\%, q = 2, \text{ and } m = nq = 8.$$

From Table 1,

$$c(r,m,q) = c(6,8,2) = 1.26677.$$

Hence he must deposit

$$p = \frac{\$3,000}{1.26677} = \$2,368.23.$$

Example 2:   Houses along the lake have been increasing in value about 12% a year. If one of these houses is valued at $40,000 today, what was its value 2 years ago?

Solution: In this example,

$$r = 12\%, q = 1, S = \$40,000, n = 2, \text{ and } m = nq = 2.$$

From Table 1,

$$c(r,m,q) = c(12,2,1) = 1.254400.$$

Hence the value 2 years ago was

$$p = \frac{\$40,000}{1.254400} = \$31,887.76.$$

3.3.   Present Value of an Interest-Bearing Debt

A debt to be paid in the future is worth less to the lender than its face value unless it bears interest at a rate that equals or exceeds the prevailing rate. In the figure this concept is illustrated for an 8% loan.

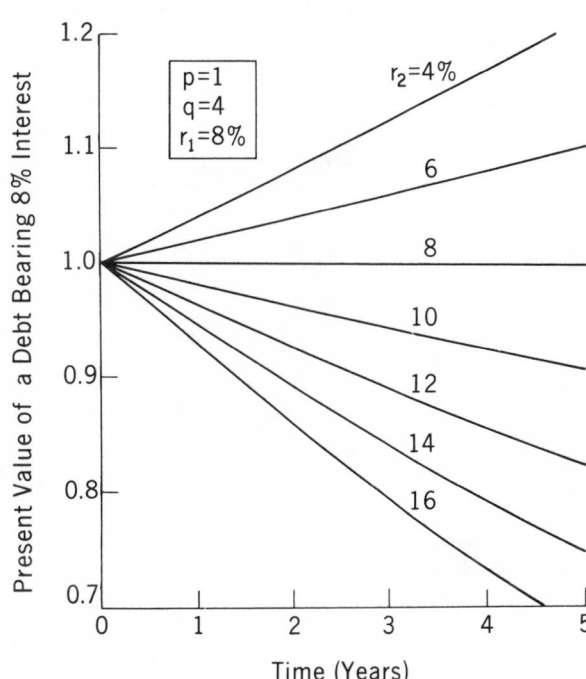

Formula:

$$p_2 = p_1 \cdot \frac{(1 + r_1/q)^m}{(1 + r_2/q)^m}$$

$$= p_1 \cdot \frac{c(r_1,m,q)}{c(r_2,m,q)}$$

where

p_1,p_2 = original and present value of debt, respectively

r_1,r_2 = original and present annual interest rate on debt, respectively, expressed as a decimal

n = number of years remaining on debt

q = number of interest periods per year

$m = nq$ = total number of interest periods

$c(r_1,m,q)$,

$c(r_2,m,q)$ = amount of 1 at compound interest

Table: Find $c(r_1,m,q)$ and $c(r_2,m,q)$ in Table 1.

Example: Mr. Madden has a $3,000 debt bearing 6% interest compounded quarterly, and due in 3 years. The present interest rate is considered to be 8%. What is the present value of the debt?

Solution: In this example,

p_1 = $3,000, r_1 = 6%, q = 4, n = 3, m = nq = 12, and r_2 = 8%.

From Table 1,

$$c(r_1,m,q) = c(6,12,4) = 1.19562 \text{ and,}$$

$$c(r_2,m,q) = c(8,12,4) = 1.26824.$$

Now,

$$p_2 = \$3,000 \times \frac{1.19562}{1.26824} = \$2,828.22.$$

3.4.   Amount of Interest

Formulas:

$$I = S - p = p\,[(1 + r/q)^m - 1] = p\,[c(r,m,q) - 1]$$

where

  I = amount of interest
  S = amount accumulated
  p = principal
  r = annual interest rate, expressed as a decimal
  q = number of interest periods per year
  n = number of years
  $m = nq$ = total number of periods
$c(r,m,q)$ = amount of 1 at compound interest

Table: Find $c(r,m,q)$ in Table 1.

Example: How much interest must be paid after 4 years on $4,000, at 7% interest compounded twice a year?

Solution: In this example,

  $n = 4$, $p = \$4,000$, $r = 7\%$, $q = 2$, and $m = nq = 8$.

From Table 1,

  $c(r,m,q) = c(7,8,2) = 1.316809$.

Now,

  $I = \$4,000 \times (1.316809 - 1) = \$4,000 \times .316809$
  $= \$1,267.24$.

3.5.   Amount of Time

The amount of time required to accumulate an amount of money decreases as either the interest rate or the frequency of compounding increases. The figure shows the amount of time required for a sum to double.

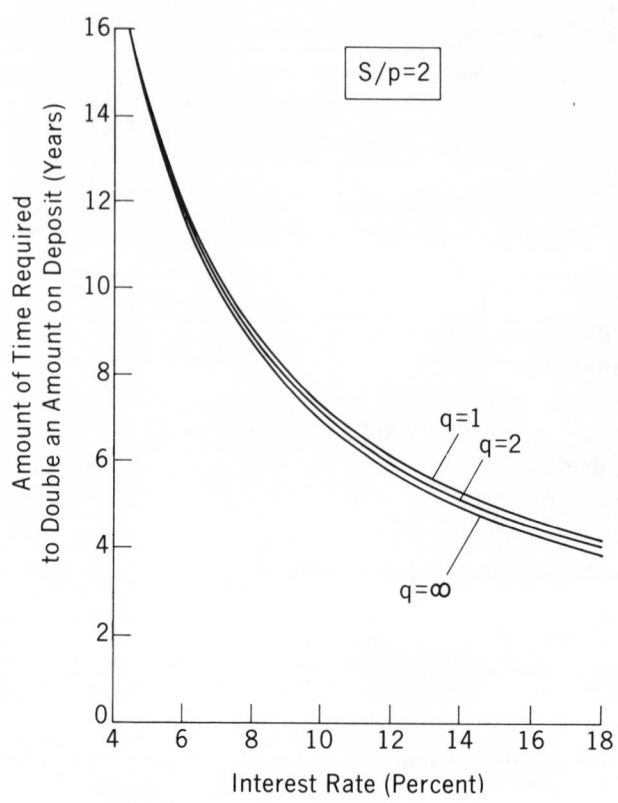

Formula:

$$n = \frac{1}{q} \cdot \frac{\log(S/p)*}{\log(1 + r/q)}$$

where

n = number of years
S = amount accumulated
p = principal
r = annual interest rate, expressed as a decimal
q = number of interest periods per year

Table: Use either a table or an electronic calculator to determine the logarithms.

Example: At 8% interest compounded quarterly, how long does it take for $3,000 to accumulate to $6,000?

*These logarithms can be either common or natural. See Section A.2, Example 2.

Solution: In this example,

$$r = 8\%, q = 4, p = \$3{,}000, \text{ and } S = \$6{,}000.$$

Now,

$$n = \frac{1}{4} \times \frac{\log(\$6{,}000/\$3{,}000)}{\log(1 + .08/4)} = \frac{1}{4} \times \frac{\log(2)}{\log(1.02)}.$$

From a table of common logarithms,

$$\log_{10}(2) = .30103, \text{ and } \log_{10}(1.02) = .008600.$$

Now,

$$n = \frac{.30103}{4 \times .008600} = 8.75 \text{ years.}$$

3.6.   Rate of Interest

This section gives the formula for the rate of interest required to accumulate a given amount.

Formula:

$$r = q \left[\left(\frac{S}{p} \right)^{\frac{1}{nq}} - 1 \right]$$

where

r   = annual interest rate, expressed as a decimal
q   = number of interest periods per year
S   = amount accumulated
p   = principal
n   = number of years

Table: Use an electronic calculator.*

Example 1: Mr. Chase hopes to receive \$5,400 by lending \$3,000 for 8 years. If the interest is to be compounded twice a year, what interest rate must he charge?

*See Section A.3.

Solution: In this example,

$$S = \$5,400, \ p = \$3,000, \ n = 8, \text{ and } q = 2.$$

Now,

$$r = 2\left[\left(\frac{\$5,400}{\$3,000}\right)^{\frac{1}{8\cdot2}} - 1\right] = 2\left[(1.8)^{\frac{1}{16}} - 1\right].$$

Using an electronic calculator,

$$1.8^{\frac{1}{16}} = 1.0374$$

(or form $1.8^{\frac{1}{16}} = e^{\frac{1}{16}\log_e(1.8)}$, and use tables).

Now,

$$r = 2(1.0374 - 1) = 2 \times .0374 = .0748 = 7.48\%.$$

Example 2:   Three years ago Evan Dutton paid \$32,000 for his house. If he sells it for \$40,000, what annual rate of interest has he achieved?

Solution: In this example,

$$n = 3, \ p = \$32,000, \ S = \$40,000, \text{ and } q = 1$$

Now the annual rate of interest is,

$$r = 1 \times \left[\left(\frac{\$40,000}{\$32,000}\right)^{\frac{1}{3\cdot1}} - 1\right] = \left[\left(1.25\right)^{\frac{1}{3}} - 1\right]$$
$$= 1.0772 - 1$$
$$= .0772 = 7.72\%.$$

3.7. Effective Rate of Interest

The annual rate of interest, r, is called the nominal (quoted) rate. If interest is compounded q times a year, r′ is the effective rate of interest. When compounding occurs annually (q = 1), the effective rate and the annual rate are equal. When q > 1, the effective rate exceeds the annual rate, as seen in the figure.

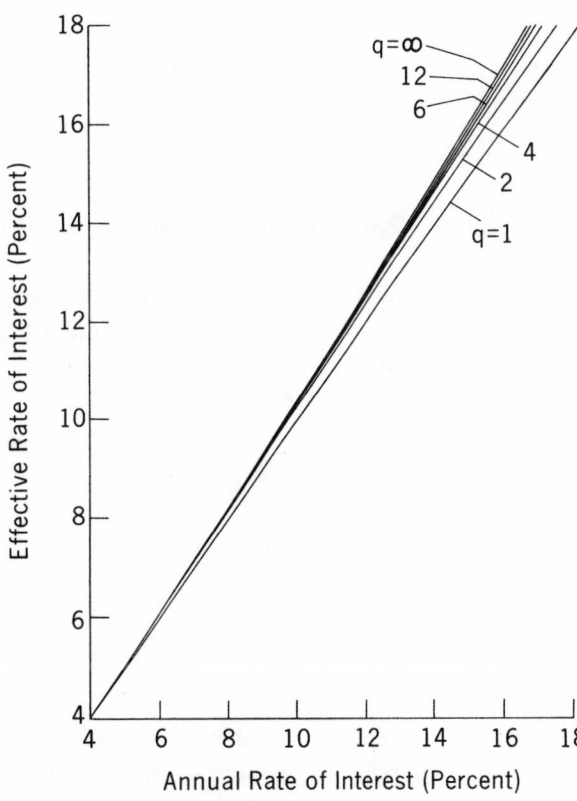

Formula:

$$r' = (1 + r/q)^q - 1 = c(r,q,q) - 1$$

where

  r′ = effective annual interest rate, expressed as a decimal
  r = annual interest rate, expressed as a decimal
  q = number of interest periods per year
  c(r,q,q) = amount of 1 at compound interest

Table: Find c(r,q,q) in Table 1.

Example: If interest is paid at 7% on a principal amount and compounded quarterly, what is the effective rate of interest?

Solution: In this example,

  r = 7%, and q = 4.

From Table 1,

  c(r,q,q) = c(7,4,4) = 1.0719.

Now,

$$r' = 1.0719 - 1 = .0719 = 7.19\%.$$

3.8.   Rescheduled Payments (Equation of Value)

Sometimes it is desirable to reschedule the payment of one or more debts. By using the present value concept, at the current interest rate, value can be preserved for both the lender and the borrower. The following equation can be solved for either an unknown payment or an unknown due date.

Formula:

$$\sum_{i=1}^{l} \frac{p_i}{c(r,m_i,q)} = \sum_{i=1}^{l'} \frac{p_i'}{c(r,m_i',q)} \; *\dagger$$

where

$$
\begin{aligned}
l, l' &= \text{number of new and old payments, respectively} \\
p_i, p_i' &= \text{amount of the ith new and old payment, respectively} \\
n_i, n_i' &= \text{number of years until the ith new and old payment, respectively, is due} \\
q &= \text{number of interest periods per year} \\
m_i, m_i' &= \text{total number of interest periods for the ith new and old payment, respec-} \\
&\quad \text{tively (i.e., } m_i = n_i q \text{ and } m_i' = n_i' q) \\
r &= \text{current (agreed upon) annual interest rate} \\
c(r,m_i,q), & \\
c(r,m_i',q) &= \text{amount of 1 at compound interest}
\end{aligned}
$$

Table: Find each $c(r,m_i,q)$ and $c(r,m_i',q)$ in Table 1.

Example 1: (Rescheduled Payments).   Mr. Hall has two payments, one of $4,000 due in 3 years and another of $6,000 due in 6 years. Instead, he wishes to pay $2,000 in 2 years, $4,000 in 4 years, and the balance in 8 years. He and the lender agree to a 7% interest

---

*A focal date is often used for equations of value involving compound interest, but it is not necessary and is, thus, omitted here.

†The notation $\sum_{i=1}^{l}$ means to sum the values $\frac{p_i}{c(r,m_i,q)}$ from $i=1$ to $i=l$. The same meaning is given to $\sum_{i=1}^{l'}$ (See Appendix: Mathematical Notes, Section A.1).

rate compounded annually. What balance due in 8 years will preserve value for both lender and borrower?

Solution: For the three new payments and the two old payments, the general formula becomes

$$\frac{p_1}{c(r,m_1,q)} + \frac{p_2}{c(r,m_2,q)} + \frac{p_3}{c(r,m_3,q)} = \frac{p_1'}{c(r,m_1',q)} + \frac{p_2'}{c(r,m_2',q)} \quad,$$

or

$$\frac{\$2,000}{c(7,2,1)} + \frac{\$4,000}{c(7,4,1)} + \frac{p_3}{c(7,8,1)} = \frac{\$4,000}{c(7,3,1)} + \frac{\$6,000}{c(7,6,1)} \quad.$$

This equation must be solved for p_3, the balance due in 8 years:

$$\frac{p_3}{c(7,8,1)} = \frac{\$4,000}{c(7,3,1)} + \frac{\$6,000}{c(7,6,1)} - \frac{\$2,000}{c(7,2,1)} - \frac{\$4,000}{c(7,4,1)} \quad,$$

and

$$p_3 = c(7,8,1)\left[\frac{\$4,000}{c(7,3,1)} + \frac{\$6,000}{c(7,6,1)} - \frac{\$2,000}{c(7,2,1)} - \frac{\$4,000}{c(7,4,1)}\right].$$

Each of the compound interest amounts can be found in Table 1. Now,

$$p_3 = 1.71819\left[\frac{\$4,000}{1.22504} + \frac{\$6,000}{1.50073} - \frac{\$2,000}{1.14490} - \frac{\$4,000}{1.31080}\right]$$

$$= 1.71819(\$3,265.20 + \$3,998.05 - \$1,746.88 - \$3,051.57)$$

$$= 1.71819 \times \$2,464.80$$

$$= \$4,234.99.$$

Example 2: (Rescheduled Due Dates).   Consider the same situation as in Example 1 except the last payment is known to be $4,500 and the due date (that preserves value) must be determined.

Solution: Since we must determine m_3, recall (Section 3.1) that

$$c(r,m_3,q) = (1 + r/q)^{m_3}.$$

Now the general equation is

$$\frac{p_1}{c(r,m_1,q)} \; + \; \frac{p_2}{c(r,m_2,q)} \; + \; \frac{p_3}{(1+r/q)^{m_3}} \; = \; \frac{p_1'}{c(r,m_1',q)} \; + \; \frac{p_2'}{c(r,m_2',q)} \;,$$

or

$$\frac{1}{(1+r/q)^{m_3}} \; = \; \frac{1}{p_3}\left[\frac{p_1'}{c(r,m_1',q)} \; + \; \frac{p_2'}{c(r,m_2',q)} \; - \; \frac{p_1}{c(r,m_1,q)} \; - \; \frac{p_2}{c(r,m_2,q)}\right].$$

The four terms in the bracket are the same as those in Example 1, and we found that value to be $2,464.80. Hence,

$$\frac{1}{(1.07)^{m_3}} \; = \; \frac{1}{p_3} \; \times \; \$2,464.80 \; = \; \frac{\$2,464.80}{\$4,500} \; = \; .54773.$$

Now,

$$(1.07)^{m_3} \; = \; \frac{1}{.54773} = 1.82571,$$

and

$$m_3 \; = \; \frac{\log(1.82571)*}{\log(1.07)} \; = \; \frac{.26143}{.029384} = 8.90 \text{ years.}$$

---

*See Appendix: Mathematical Notes, Section A.3.

4

FINANCE: ANNUITIES
(THE VALUE OF A
STREAM OF PAYMENTS)

An annuity is a stream of payments. The sum of an annuity is the total amount received. For an annuity with equal payments, the sum is merely the size of each payment multiplied by the number of payments. The straight line in the figure depicts the sum of an annuity of 1. The line is straight because equal amounts (i.e., $1) are being received at equal intervals.

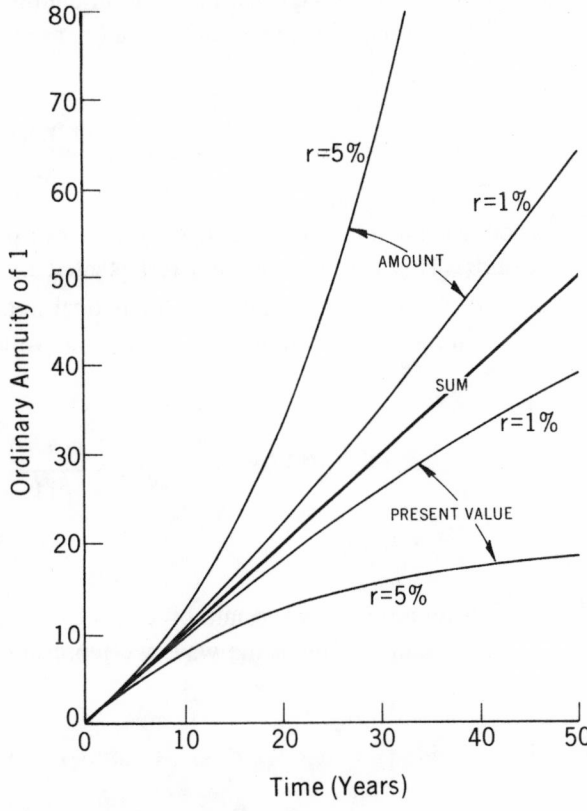

An important characteristic of an annuity is the amount of an annuity. The amount is derived from the assumption that each payment earns interest at a certain rate from the moment it is received and until the annuity is terminated. Hence, the amount of an annuity exceeds the sum of an annuity. The amount is shown in the figure for payments earning interest at the rates of 1% and 5%.

A second important characteristic of an annuity is the present value. The present value is derived from the assumption that payments not yet received are not worth face value because they cannot earn interest. We reason that if we could earn 5% on each payment, we are in fact penalized 5% each year that we must wait to receive a payment. Hence the present value of an annuity is less than the sum of the annuity. The present value is shown in the figure for payments that would have earned interest at the rate of 1% and 5%.

In summary, the sum of an annuity measures the payments, the amount measures the benefit from using the payments, and the present value measures the penalty for not being able to use the payments.

This chapter contains only annuities with equal periods, and, except for Sections 4.6 and 4.11, it contains only annuities with equal payments. In these two sections, we treat annuities whose payments change by either a fixed amount or a fixed percentage. For example, annuities that decrease by a fixed amount might result from properties subject to loss in value due to straight line depreciation, and annuities that increase by a fixed percentage might result from properties subject to an increase in value due to a fixed rate of inflation.

An ordinary annuity is one in which payments are received at the end of each period. Unless otherwise noted, assume that an annuity is an ordinary annuity.

The formula for the amount of an annuity of 1 is

$$\frac{(1 + r/q)^m - 1}{(r/q)}$$

where r is the interest rate, q is the number of periods per year, and m is the total number of periods. This formula is often represented by $s_{\overline{m}|r}^{(q)}$ (a notation peculiar to finance), but we will use the conventional mathematical notation, s(r,m,q).

Similarly, the formula for the present value of an annuity of 1 is

$$\frac{(1 + r/q)^m - 1}{(r/q)(1 + r/q)^m}$$

We will represent this formula by a(r,m,q) instead of $a_{\overline{m}|r}^{(q)}$.

Continuing in the same way, we represent the amount of 1 at compound interest by

$$c(r,m,q) = (1 + r/q)^m.$$

4.1. Present Value of an Ordinary Annuity When Payments and Interest Occur Q Times a Year

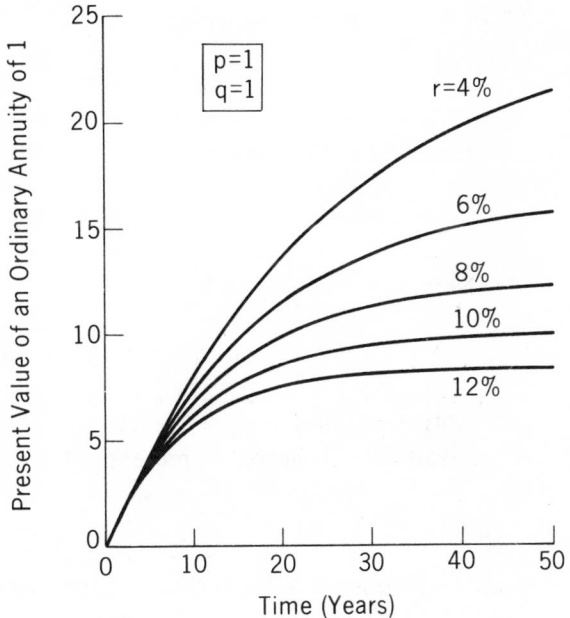

In an ordinary annuity, payments are received at the end of each period. Even though all payments may be equal, those that are received early are worth more to the recipient than are those received later. For instance, if money is currently worth a certain interest rate, r, the payment received in the first year has a present value that is $1/(1 + r)$ of its face value, and the payment received after n years has a present value that is $1/(1 + r)^n$ of its face value.

The present value of the total of these payments is the present value of the annuity and is depicted in the figure for several different interest rates. Notice in the figure that the present value of an annuity is greater for low interest rates (i.e., when interest rates are low, money has little value and there is only a small penalty for waiting to receive payments).

Formula:

$$A = p \cdot \frac{(1 + r/q)^m - 1}{(r/q)(1 + r/q)^m} = p \cdot a(r,m,q)$$

where

A = present value of the ordinary annuity
p = fixed payment deposited at the end of each period
r = annual interest rate, expressed as a decimal
q = number of periods per year
n = number of years
m = nq = total number of periods
$a(r,m,q)$ = present value of an annuity of 1

Table: Find $a(r,m,q)$ in Table 1.

Example: Suppose $75 is received quarterly for 20 years. If money is presently considered to be worth 6%, what is the present value of the annuity?

Solution: In this example,

$$p = \$75, \ q = 4, \ n = 20, \ m = nq = 80, \text{ and } r = 6\%.$$

From Table 1,

$$a(r,m,q) = a(6,80,4) = 46.4073.$$

Now,

$$A = \$75 \times 46.4073 = \$3,480.55.$$

Notice, the sum of money received is $p \cdot m = \$75 \times 80 = \$6,000$. However, because it is received over 20 years, its present value is only $3,480.55 at the present interest rate of 6%.

4.2.   Present Value of an Ordinary Annuity When Payments Occur U Times a Year and Interest Q Times

Formula:

$$A = p \cdot \frac{(1 + r/q)^m - 1}{(1 + r/q)^m \left[(1 + r/q)^t - 1 \right]} \quad = p \cdot a(r,m,q)/s(r,t,q)$$

where

$\quad\quad A$ = present value of the ordinary annuity
$\quad\quad p$ = fixed payment deposited at the end of each payment period
$\quad\quad r$ = annual interest rate, expressed as a decimal
$\quad\quad q$ = number of interest periods per year
$\quad\quad n$ = number of years
$\quad\quad m = nq$ = total number of interest periods
$\quad\quad u$ = number of payment periods per year
$\quad\quad t = q/u$
$\ a(r,m,q)$ = present value of an annuity of 1
$\ s(r,t,q)$ = amount of an annuity of 1*

Table: Find $a(r,m,q)$ and $s(r,t,q)$ in Table 1.

Example: Wayne Robinson will receive $1,000 at the end of each month for 13 years. If money is presently considered to be worth 6% when compounded quarterly, what is the present value of this annuity?

---

*If payment periods coincide with interest periods, set $s(r,t,q) = s(r,1,q) = 1$.

Solution:　　In this example,

$$p = \$1,000,\ u = 12,\ n = 13,\ r = 6\%,\ q = 4,$$
$$t = q/u = 1/3,\ \text{and}\ m = nq = 52.$$

From Table 1,

$$a(r,m,q) = a(6,52,4) = 35.928742,$$

and

$$s(r,t,q) = s(6,1/3,4) = 0.3316804.$$

Now,

$$A = \$1,000 \times 35.928742/0.3316804 = \$108,323.36.$$

If there had been twelve payment periods and twelve interest periods, then

$$A = \$108,140.44.$$

4.3.　Present Value of an Annuity Due

In an annuity due, payments are made at the beginning of each payment period (instead of at the end, as in an ordinary annuity). Real estate rent is a common example of the payment in an annuity due.

Formula:

$$A = p \cdot a(r,m,q)/a(r,t,q)$$

where

　　　　A　= present value of the annuity due
　　　　p　= fixed payment deposited at the beginning of each payment period
　　　　r　= annual rate of interest
　　　　q　= number of interest periods per year
　　　　n　= number of years
　　　　m　= nq = total number of interest periods
　　　　u　= number of payment periods per year
　　　　t　= q/u
　$a(r,m,q)$,
　　$a(r,t,q)$　= present value of an ordinary annuity of 1

Table:　　Find $a(r,m,q)$ and $a(r,t,q)$ in Table 1.

Example: The cash flow from an apartment complex is $1,500 per month. If this portion of the rent is promptly deposited at 6% interest compounded quarterly for 8 years, what is the present value of the cash flow (annuity due)?

Solution: In this example,

$$p = \$1{,}500,\ u = 12,\ r = 6\%,\ q = 4,\ n = 8,$$
$$t = q/u = 1/3,\ \text{and}\ m = nq = 32.$$

From Table 1,

$$a(r,m,q) = a(6,32,4) = 25.26714,\ \text{and}$$
$$a(r,t,q) = a(6,1/3,4) = 0.3300384.$$

Now the present value of the cash flow is,

$$A = \$1{,}500 \times 25.26714/0.3300384$$
$$= \$114{,}837.27.$$

4.4.   Present Value of a Deferred Ordinary Annuity

Deferred annuities do not begin until some future date. Because time has value, the present value of a deferred annuity is less than the present value of an annuity that is not deferred.

Formula:

$$A = p \cdot a(r,m,q)/\big[s(r,t,q) \cdot c(r,v,q) \big]$$

where

A = present value of the deferred ordinary annuity
p = fixed payment deposited at the end of each payment period
r = annual interest rate
n = number of years
q = number of interest periods per year
$m = nq$ = total number of interest periods
u = number of payment periods per year
$t = q/u$
v = number of interest periods that the ordinary annuity is deferred
$a(r,m,q)$ = present value of an annuity of 1
$s(r,t,q)$ = amount of annuity of 1
$c(r,v,q)$ = amount of 1 at compound interest

Table: Find a(r,m,q), s(r,t,q) and c(r,v,q) in Table 1.

Example: What is the present value of a trust fund that will begin in 3 years and from which $1,000 will be received monthly for 15 years? Assume that money is presently worth 6% when compounded quarterly.

Solution: In this example,

$$q = 4, \ v = 3 \times 4 = 12, \ p = \$1,000, \ u = 12,$$
$$t = q/u = 1/3, \ n = 15, \ m = nq = 60, \ \text{and} \ r = 6\%.$$

From Table 1,

$$a(r,m,q) = a(6,60,4) = 39.38027,$$
$$s(r,t,q) = s(6,1/3,4) = .03316804, \ \text{and}$$
$$c(r,v,q) = c(6,12,4) = 1.195618.$$

Now the present value of the trust fund is,

$$A = \$1,000 \times 39.38027/(0.3316804 \times 1.195618)$$
$$= \$39,380.27/0.396563$$
$$= \$99,303.94.$$

4.5.   Present Value of an Ordinary Annuity in Perpetuity

An annuity in perpetuity provides a constant stream of payments forever*.

Formula:

$$A = \frac{p}{(r/q) \cdot s(r,t,q)}$$

where

A = present value of the ordinary annuity in perpetuity
p = fixed payment deposited at the end of each period
r = annual interest rate, expressed as a decimal
q = number of interest periods per year
u = number of payment periods per year
t = q/u
s(r,t,q) = amount of an annuity of 1

_____

*The amount of an annuity in perpetuity is infinite because a constant amount is being supplied periodically, forever.

Table: Find s(r,t,q) in Table 1.

Example: Mary Good wants to donate $300 every year to her church, forever. If she can deposit a sum of money at 6% interest compounded quarterly, how large must the deposit be to supply $300 annually, forever?

Solution: In this example,

$$p = \$300, \ u = 1, \ r = 6\%, \ q = 4, \ \text{and} \ t = q/u = 4.$$

From Table 1,

$$s(r,t,q) = s(6,4,4) = 4.090904.$$

Hence, she must deposit

$$A = \frac{\$300}{(.06/4) \times 4.090904} = \frac{\$300}{.0613635} = \$4{,}888.90.$$

4.6.   Present Value of a Variable Annuity

Annuities can vary in any conceivable way. We include two important variable annuities—annuities in which the payment periods are equally spaced, but the payments vary.

Linear Annuity: The payment in each period is either decreased or increased by a *fixed amount* relative to the previous period. Since equal amounts are being added (or subtracted) at equal intervals, the payments are changing linearly. An income property that is depreciating according to straight line depreciation might generate an income stream that is declining linearly.

Exponential Annuity: The payment in each period is either decreased or increased by a *fixed percentage* of its previous value. Since the payment is changing in proportion to its value, the payments are changing exponentially (like an amount at compound interest). An income property that is increasing in value due to a fixed rate of inflation might generate an income stream that is increasing exponentially.

Formulas: Linear Annuity.

$$A = \begin{cases} \left[p + p'(m + 1 + \dfrac{q}{r})\right] \cdot a(r,m,q) - \dfrac{p' \cdot m \cdot q}{r} & \text{(ordinary annuity)} \\[2em] \left\{\left[p + p'(m + \dfrac{q}{r})\right] \cdot a(r,m,q) - \dfrac{p' \cdot m \cdot q}{r}\right\} \cdot (1 + r/q) & \text{(annuity due)} \\[2em] \left\{\left[p + p'(m + 1 + \dfrac{q}{r})\right] \cdot a(r,m,q) - \dfrac{p' \cdot m \cdot q}{r}\right\} \cdot \dfrac{1}{c(r,v,q)} & \text{(deferred annuity)} \end{cases}$$

Formulas: Exponential Annuity.

$$A = \begin{cases} p \cdot a(w,m,q) & \text{(ordinary annuity)} \\ p \cdot a(w,m,q) \cdot (1 + w/q) & \text{(annuity due)} \\ p \cdot a(w,m,q)/c(w,v,q) & \text{(deferred annuity)} \end{cases}$$

where

A	= present value of the annuity
p	= value of payment in the first period i.e. initial value
p′	= fixed amount of change of payment (positive or negative)
n	= number of years
q	= number of periods per year
m	= nq = total number of periods
r	= annual interest rate, expressed as a decimal
r′	= fixed rate of change of payment (positive, zero, or negative) , expressed as a decimal
w	= $q \cdot (r - r')/(q + r')$, an annual interest rate if r > r′
v	= number of payment periods the annuity is deferred
a(r,m,q), a(w,m,q)	= present value of an annuity of 1
c(r,v,q), c(w,v,q)	= amount of 1 at compound interest

Table: Find a(r,m,q) and c(r,v,q) in Table 1. Also find a(w,m,q) and c(w,v,q) in Table 1 if .05≤ w ≤ .1375.

Example 1: (Linear Annuity).   A tenant convinces the owner of a commercial building that the building is depreciating at the rate of 2.50% annually. Hence, they agree to a 10 year lease that calls for $100,000 at the beginning of the first year and decreases by $2,500 annually. If money is presently considered to be worth 5.75%, what is the present value of this variable annuity due?

Solution: In this example,

$$n = 10, \; p = \$100,000, \; p' = -\$2,500, \; q = 1,$$
$$m = nq = 10, \text{ and } r = 5.75\%.$$

From Table 1,

$$a(r,m,q) = a(5.75, 10, 1) = 7.44805.$$

Now, using the formula for the linear type of annuity due,

$$
\begin{aligned}
A = & \left\{ \left[\$100,000 - \$2,500(10 + 1/.0575) \right] \times 7.44805 \right. \\
& \left. + \$2,500 \times 10 \times 1/.0575 \right\} \cdot (1 + .0575/1) \\
= & \left[(\$100,000 - \$2,500 \times 27.39130) \times 7.44805 \right. \\
& \left. + \$434,782.60 \right] \times 1.0575 \\
= & (\$31,521.75 \times 7.44805 + \$434,782.60) \times 1.0575 \\
= & \$669,558.17 \times 1.0575 \\
= & \$708,057.76.
\end{aligned}
$$

Example 2: (Exponential Annuity).   The owner of a commercial property convinces his tenant that inflation will continue to be 4.70% annually. Hence, the owner and the tenant agree to a 10 year lease that calls for $100,000 rent at the beginning of the first year, and the rent is to be increased by compounding at the rate of 4.70% annually for the term of the lease. If money is thought to be worth 5.75%, what is the present value of this variable annuity due?

Solution: In this example,

$$
n = 10, \ p = \$100,000, \ q = 1, \ m = nq = 10,
$$
$$
r' = 4.70\%, \text{ and } r = 5.75\%.
$$

Now, using the formula for the exponential type of annuity due, first compute

$$
w = 1 \times \frac{.0575 - .0470}{1 + .0470} = \frac{.0105}{1.0470} = .0100 = 1\%.
$$

From Section 4.1,

$$
a(w,m,q) = a(1,10,1) = \frac{(1 + .01)^{10} - 1}{.01 \times (1 + .01)^{10}} = 9.47130.
$$

Now, using the formula for the exponential type of annuity due,

$$
\begin{aligned}
A = & \ \$100,000 \times 9.47130 \times (1 + .01/1) \\
= & \ \$947,130.00 \times 1.01 \\
= & \ \$956,601.30.
\end{aligned}
$$

If the rate of increase of the payments (4.70%) had been equal to the current interest rate (5.75%), there would have been no reason to discount future payments. Then the present value of the annuity would have been the sum of the annuity, $100,000 \times 10 = $1,000,000.

4.7. Amount of an Ordinary Annuity When Payments and Interest Occur Q Times a Year

In an ordinary annuity, payments are made at the end of each period. If the payments did not draw interest, the amount after n years would simply be the number of payments multiplied by the size of each payment. However, each payment is deposited at compound interest. The interest on the first payment is compounded for n − 1 years, the interest on the second payment is compounded for n − 2 years, etc. The figure shows how the amount of an ordinary annuity increases with the interest rate and with time.

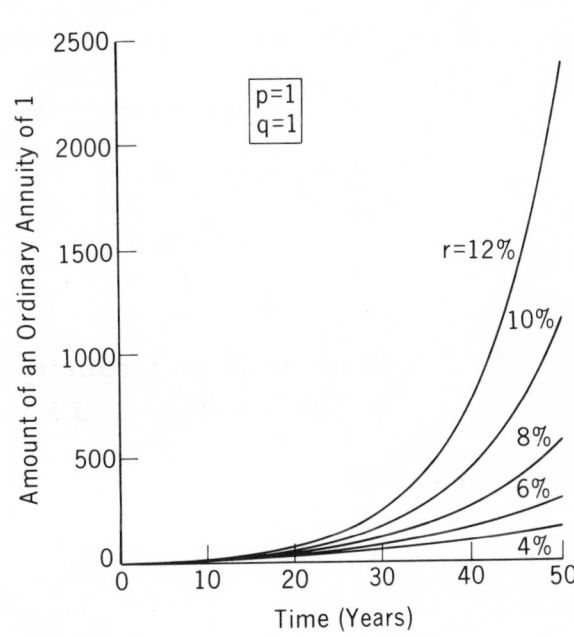

Formula:

$$S = p \cdot \frac{(1 + r/q)^m - 1}{(r/q)} = p \cdot s(r,m,q)$$

where

S = amount of the ordinary annuity
p = fixed payment deposited at the end of each period
r = annual interest rate, expressed as a decimal
q = number of periods per year
n = number of years
m = nq = total number of periods
$s(r,m,q)$ = amount of an annuity of 1

Table: Find $s(r,m,q)$ in Table 1.

Example: Bob Johnson has been depositing $1,000 at the end of each month to his retirement fund. If the deposits have drawn interest at 6% compounded monthly, how much will the fund be worth after 13 years?

Solution: In this example,

$$p = \$1,000, \ q = 12, \ r = 6\%, \ n = 13 \text{ and } m = nq = 156.$$

From Table 1,

$$s(r,m,q) = s(6,156,12) = 235.44733$$

Now the fund will be worth,

$$S = \$1,000 \times 235.44733 = \$235,447.33.$$

4.8.   Amount of an Ordinary Annuity When Payments Occur U Times a Year and Interest Q Times

Formula:

$$S = p \cdot \frac{(1 + r/q)^m - 1}{(1 + r/q)^t - 1} \ = p \cdot s(r,m,q)/s(r,t,q)$$

where

S	=	amount of the ordinary annuity
p	=	fixed payment deposited at the end of each period
r	=	annual interest rate expressed as a decimal
q	=	number of interest periods per year
n	=	number of years
m	= nq =	total number of interest periods
u	=	number of payment periods per year
t	= q/u	

s(r,m,q),
  s(r,t,q) = amount of an annuity of 1

Table: Find s(r,m,q) and s(r,t,q) in Table 1.

Example: Bob Johnson has been depositing $1,000 at the end of each month to his retirement fund. If the deposits have drawn interest at 6% compounded quarterly, how much will the fund be worth after 13 years?

Solution: In this example,

$$p = \$1,000, \ u = 12, \ r = 6\%, \ q = 4,$$
$$t = q/u = 1/3, \ n = 13, \text{ and } m = nq = 52.$$

From Table 1,

$$s(r,m,q) = s(6,52,4) = 77.924890, \text{ and}$$
$$s(r,t,q) = s(6,1/3,4) = 0.3316804.$$

Now, the fund will be worth

$$S = \$1,000 \times 77.924890/0.3316804$$
$$= \$234,939.67.$$

4.9.   Amount of an Annuity Due

In an annuity due, payments are made at the beginning of each payment period (instead of at the end, as in an ordinary annuity). Real estate rent is a common example of the payment in an annuity due.

Formula:

$$S = p \cdot s(r,m,q)/a(r,t,q)$$

where

S = amount of the annuity due
p = fixed payment deposited at the beginning of each period
r = annual interest rate
q = number of interest periods per year
n = number of years
m = nq = total number of interest periods
u = number of payment periods per year
t = q/u
$s(r,m,q)$ = amount of an ordinary annuity of 1
$a(r,t,q)$ = present value of an ordinary annuity of 1

Table: Find $s(r,m,q)$ and $a(r,t,q)$ in Table 1.

Example: The cash flow from an apartment building is $1,500 per month. If this portion of the rent is promptly deposited at 6% interest compounded quarterly, what is the amount of the annuity due after 8 years?

Solution: In this example,

$$p = \$1,500, u = 12, r = 6\%, q = 4,$$
$$t = q/u = 1/3, n = 8, \text{ and } m = nq = 32.$$

From Table 1,

$$s(r,m,q) = s(6,32,4) = 40.68829, \text{ and}$$
$$a(r,t,q) = a(6,1/3,4) = 0.3300384.$$

Now,

$$S = \$1,500 \times 40.68829/0.3300384$$
$$= \$184,925.25.$$

4.10.   Amount of a Deferred Annuity

Deferred annuities do not begin until some future date. They are distinguished from other annuities only by their delay. The amount of a deferred annuity equals the amount of an annuity that is not deferred and may be calculated from the formulas of Section 4.8 or of Section 4.9, depending on whether it is an ordinary annuity or an annuity due.

4.11.   Amount of a Variable Annuity

Annuities can vary in any conceivable way. We include two important variable annuities—annuities in which the payment periods are equally spaced, but the payments vary.

Linear Annuity: The payment in each period is either decreased or increased by a *fixed amount* relative to the previous period. Since equal amounts are being added (or subtracted) at equal intervals, the payments are changing linearly. An income property that is depreciating according to straight line depreciation might generate an income stream that is declining linearly.

Exponential Annuity: The payment in each period is either decreased or increased by a *fixed percentage* of its previous value. Since the payment is changing in proportion to its value, the payments are changing exponentially (like an amount at compound interest). An income property that is increasing in value due to a fixed rate of inflation might generate an income stream that is increasing exponentially.

Formulas: Linear Annuity.

$$S = \begin{cases} \left[p + p' \cdot (1 + \dfrac{q}{r}) \right] \cdot s(r,m,q) - \dfrac{p' \cdot m \cdot q}{r} & \text{(ordinary annuity)} \\[3ex] \left[(p + p' \cdot \dfrac{q}{r}) \cdot s(r,m,q) - \dfrac{p' \cdot m \cdot q}{r} \right] \cdot (1 + r/q) & \text{(annuity due)} \\[3ex] \left[p + p' \cdot (v + 1 + \dfrac{q}{r}) \right] \cdot s(r,m,q) - \dfrac{p' \cdot m \cdot q}{r} & \text{(deferred annuity)} \end{cases}$$

Formulas: Exponential Annuity.

$$
S = \begin{cases}
p \cdot s(w,m,q) \cdot c(r',m,q) & \text{(ordinary annuity)} \\
p \cdot s(w,m,q) \cdot c(r',m,q) \cdot (1 + w/q) & \text{(annuity due)} \\
p \cdot s(w,m,q) \cdot c(r',m + v,q) & \text{(deferred annuity)}
\end{cases}
$$

where

S = amount of the annuity

p = value of payment in the first period (i.e. initial value)

p' = fixed amount of change of payment (positive or negative)

n = number of years

q = number of periods per year

$m = nq$ = total number of periods

r = annual interest rate, expressed as a decimal

r' = fixed rate of change of payment (positive, zero, or negative), expressed as a decimal

$w = q \cdot (r - r')/(q + r')$, an annual interest rate if $r > r'$

v = number of payment periods the annuity is deferred

$s(r,m,q)$,

$s(w,m,q)$ = amount of an annuity of 1

$c(r',m,q)$,

$c(r',m + v,q)$ = amount of 1 at compound interest

Table: Find $s(r,m,q)$, $c(r',m,q)$, and $c(r',m + v,q)$ in Table 1. Also find $s(w,m,q)$ in Table 1 if $.05 \leq w \leq .1375$.

Example 1: (Linear Annuity).   Bill Thompson anticipates gradual retirement from his job. Hence, the amount he deposits to his retirement fund should also decrease. He will deposit $1,000 at the end of the first month and reduce this payment by $10 per month. If the deposits draw interest at 6% compounded monthly, what is the amount of the variable ordinary annuity after 5 years?

Solution: In this example,

$p = \$1,000$, $p' = -\$10$, $q = 12$, $r = 6\%$, $n = 5$ and $m = nq = 60$.

From Table 1,

$$s(r,m,q) = s(6,60,12) = 69.770030.$$

Now, using the formula for the ordinary linear annuity,

$$S = \left[\$1,000 - \$10 \times (1 + 12\,\tfrac{12}{.06})\right] \times 69.770030 + \frac{\$10 \times 60 \times 12}{.06}$$

$$= (\$1,000 - \$10 \times 201) \times 69.770030 + \frac{\$7200}{.06}$$

$$= -\$70,467.73 + \$120,000$$

$$= \$49,532.27.$$

Example 2: (Exponential Annuity).   Chet Winter anticipates that his income will continue to rise due to inflation. Hence the amount he deposits to his retirement fund should increase. He will deposit \$1,000 at the end of the first month and increase his payment 12% per year (i.e., a 1% increase each month). If the deposits draw interest at 6% compounded monthly, what is the amount of the ordinary variable annuity after 5 years?

Solution: In this example,

$$p = \$1,000, r' = 12\%, q = 12, r = 6\%, n = 5 \text{ and } m = nq = 60.$$

From Table 1,

$$c(r',m,q) = c(12,60,12) = 1.816697.$$

To compute $s(w,m,q)$, we must find

$$w = q \cdot \left(\frac{r - r'}{q + r'}\right) = 12 \times \left(\frac{.06 - .12}{12 + .12}\right) = -.05941.$$

Since w is negative, $s(w,m,q)$ is not available in Table 1, and must be computed by its formula (Section 4.7) and an electronic calculator:

$$s(-5.941,60,12) = \frac{(1 - .05941/12)^{60} - 1}{-.05941/12}$$

$$= \frac{.7424587 - 1}{-.0049508} = 52.02013.$$

Now, using the formula for the ordinary exponential annuity,

$$S = \$1,000 \times 1.816697 \times 52.02013$$
$$= \$94,504.81$$

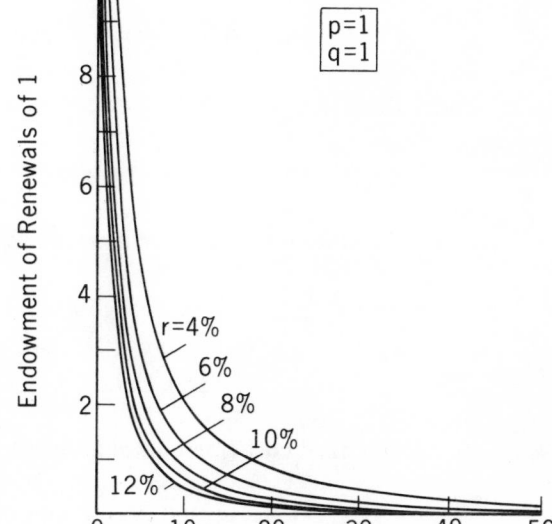

4.12. Capitalized Cost

The capitalized cost is the amount of money needed to acquire and retain an asset. Hence it is the sum of an initial investment and the amount, on deposit at compound interest, required to periodically renew the initial investment, forever.

The amount deposited is called the endowment of renewals. The figure shows that this amount can be less when interest rates are high or the period of renewal is extensive. For instance, an endowment of $2.08 deposited now at 4% interest compounded annually is sufficient to allow $1 to be withdrawn every 10 years, forever.

Formulas:

$$E = \frac{p}{(r/q) \cdot s(r,m,q)} \text{ , and } C = p + E$$

where

E = endowment of renewals
p = initial investment (and periodic investment)
C = capitalized cost
r = annual interest rate, expressed as a decimal
q = number of interest periods per year
n = number of years between renewals
m = nq = total number of interest periods between renewals
s(r,m,q) = amount of an annuity of 1.

Table: Find s(r,m,q) in Table 1.

Example: Mr. Morgan has given $1,500,000 to construct St. Joseph's hospital. He wants to establish an endowment fund that can supply the original amount ($1,500,000) every 50 years so that the hospital can be rebuilt every 50 years. How large must the endowment be if it draws interest at 6% compounded quarterly? Also, how much is the capitalized cost?

Solution: In this example,

$$p = \$1,500,000,\ n = 50,\ r = 6\%,\ q = 4,\ \text{and}\ m = nq = 200.$$

From Table 1,

$$s(r,m,q) = s(6,200,4) = 1242.8686.$$

Now, the endowment required for renewal is

$$E = \frac{\$1,500,000}{(.06/4) \times 1242.8686} = \frac{\$1,500,000}{18.64303}$$
$$= \$80,459.03.$$

The capitalized cost (total amount that Mr. Morgan must donate) is

$$C = \$1,500,000 + \$80,459.03 = \$1,580,459.03.$$

If \$80,459.03 is deposited under the stated conditions, it will equal \$1,580,459.03 after 50 years. Hence, \$1,500,000 can be withdrawn to rebuild the hospital, and \$80,459.03 will remain to again equal \$1,580,459.03 after another 50 years.

4.13.   Installments Required to Meet a Single Obligation

Installments placed at compound interest will accumulate to a sinking fund. In this section, assume the sinking fund is exactly sufficient to meet a single obligation. The figure shows the size of an installment required to accumulate a sinking fund of 1. For instance, 6¢ deposited annually at 12% interest will accumulate to about \$1 after 10 years.

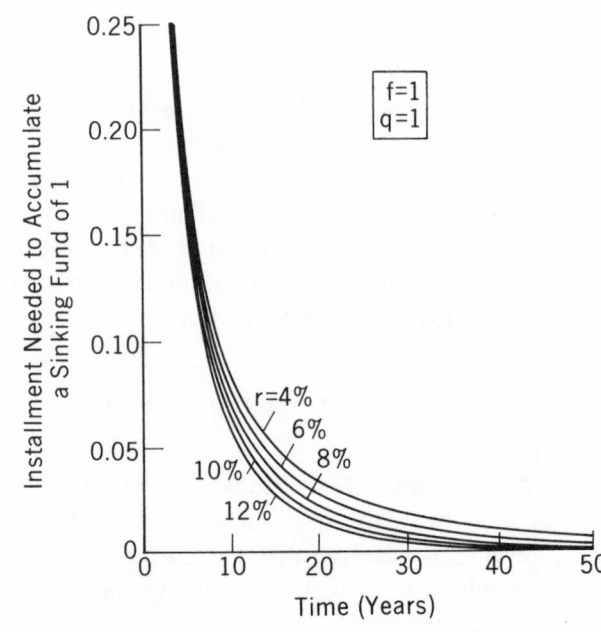

Formula:

$$p = \frac{f}{s(r,m,q)}$$

where

p = fixed installment deposited at the end of each period
f = amount of obligation or sinking fund
r = annual interest rate
q = number of periods per year
n = number of years
m = nq = total number of periods
$s(r,m,q)$ = amount of an annuity of 1

Table: Find $s(r,m,q)$ in Table 1.

Example: Mark Meredith needs to pay a balloon payment of $5,000 due in 4 years. Suppose he deposits a fixed sum at the end of each quarter, and these deposits are compounded quarterly at 6%. How large must each deposit be in order to meet the balloon payment?

Solution: In this example,

f = $5,000, n = 4, r = 6%, q = 4, and m = nq = 16.

From Table 1,

$$s(r,m,q) = s(6,16,4) = 17.93237.$$

Now,

$$p = \frac{\$5,000}{17.93237} = \$278.83.$$

4.14.   Installments Required to Meet Multiple Obligations

Installments placed at compound interest will accumulate to a sinking fund. The formula of this section determines the installments required to pay obligations of different amounts at different times. The fund will be exhausted after the final obligation is met.

Formula:

$$p = \frac{1}{a(r,m_k,q)} \cdot \sum_{i=1}^{k} \frac{f_i}{c(r,m_i,q)} \quad *$$

where

$p =$ fixed installment deposited at the end of each period
$k =$ number of obligations to be met by the sinking fund
$f_i =$ amount of the ith obligation
$r =$ annual interest rate
$q =$ number of periods per year
$m_i =$ number of periods until the ith obligation is due
$a(r,m_k,q) =$ present value of an annuity of 1
$c(r,m_i,q) =$ amount of 1 at compound interest

Table: Find $a(r,m_k,q)$ and each $c(r,m_i,q)$ in Table 1.

Example:

Mark Meredith must pay three separate debts: $30,000 due in 15 years, $30,000 due in 20 years, and $40,000 due in 25 years. He wants to make a fixed deposit each year at 5% interest compounded annually. How large must these deposits be in order to meet each debt and leave the sinking fund exhausted after the last debt is paid? The figure shows the amount of the sinking fund. It is exhausted after the last debt is paid.

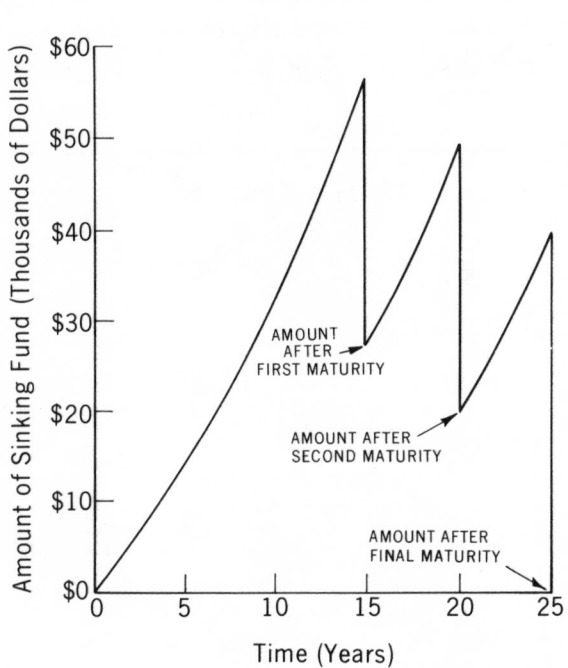

Solution: In this example,

$k = 3$, $q = 1$, $f_1 = \$30,000$, $m_1 = 15$, $f_2 = \$30,000$,
$m_2 = 20$, $f_3 = \$40,000$, $m_3 = 25$, and $r = 5\%$.

---

*The notation $\sum_{i=1}^{k}$ means to sum the values $\dfrac{f_i}{c(r,m_i,q)}$ from $i = 1$ to $i = k$. (See Appendix: Mathematical Notes).

From Table 1,

$$
\begin{aligned}
a(r,m_3,q) &= a(5,25,1) = 14.09395, \\
c(r,m_1,q) &= c(5,15,1) = 2.078928, \\
c(r,m_2,q) &= c(5,20,1) = 2.653298, \text{ and} \\
c(r,m_3,q) &= c(5,25,1) = 3.386355.
\end{aligned}
$$

Now, using the formula,

$$
\begin{aligned}
p &= \frac{1}{14.09395} \left(\frac{\$30{,}000}{2.078928} + \frac{\$30{,}000}{2.653298} + \frac{\$40{,}000}{3.386355} \right) \\
&= .07095242 \times (\$14{,}430.51 + \$11{,}306.68 + \$11{,}812.11) \\
&= .07095242 \times \$37{,}549.30 \\
&= \$2{,}664.21.
\end{aligned}
$$

The formula guarantees that the installment is the amount required to exactly meet the *total* debt, but one must verify that there are sufficient funds to meet the *individual* debts as they are due. To do this,

(1) determine p from the formula (as was just done).

(2) use this value to determine the amount of the sinking fund after the first debt is paid:

$$
F_1 = p \cdot s(r,m_1,q) - f_1{}^*.
$$

If $F_1 \geq 0$, there are sufficient funds to meet the first debt.

(3) use this value of F_1 to determine F_2:

$$
F_2 = p \cdot s(r,m_2 - m_1,q) + F_1 \cdot c(r,m_2 - m_1,q) - f_2.
$$

If $F_2 \geq 0$, there are sufficient funds to meet the second debt.

(4) continue in this way using (in general),

$$
\begin{aligned}
F_i &= p \cdot s(r,m_i - m_{i-1},q) + F_{i-1} \cdot c(r,m_i - m_{i-1},q) - f_i \\
&\quad \text{for } i = 2,3,\ldots,k.
\end{aligned}
$$

In our example, $F_1 = \$27{,}489.82$, $F_2 = \$19{,}806.19$, and $F_3 = \$0.00$. (See the figure.)

4.15. Term of an Annuity

Often the amount or the present value of an annuity is known, but the term is not known. The formulas in this section give the term, n, (in years) for both the amount and the present value. To find the term for the amount, S, of an annuity use formula (1), and to find

---

*Find each $s(r,m,q)$ in Table 1.

the term for the present value of an annuity, A, use formula (2). Then select the formula for Q that corresponds to the type of annuity. The definitions of the parameters for each type of annuity can be found in the appropriate sections of this chapter.

Formulas:

$$(1) \quad n = \frac{1}{q} \cdot \frac{\log\left[1 + (r/q) \cdot (S/p) \cdot Q\right]}{\log(1 + r/q)} \quad \text{(amount of an annuity)}$$

$$(2) \quad n = -\frac{1}{q} \cdot \frac{\log\left[1 - (r/q) \cdot (A/p) \cdot Q\right]}{\log(1 + r/q)} \text{(present value of an annuity)}$$

where

$$Q = \begin{cases} s(r,t,q) & \text{(Ordinary Annuity, Section 4.1, 4.2, 4.7, or 4.8)} \\ a(r,t,q) & \text{(Annuity Due, Section 4.3 or 4.9)} \\ s(r,t,q) \cdot c(r,v,q) & \text{(Deferred Annuity, Section 4.4 or 4.10)} \end{cases}$$

Table: Find $s(r,t,q)$, $a(r,t,q)$, and $c(r,v,q)$ in Table 1.

Example: Frank Tobin can deposit $1,000 at the end of each month to an account that draws 6% interest compounded quarterly. If he wants an account worth $235,000, how long must he make these deposits?

Solution: In this example we are to find the term for the amount of an ordinary annuity (see Section 4.8); hence we use Formula (1), and

$$Q = s(r,t,q).$$

The values are

$$p = \$1,000, \ u = 12, \ r = 6\%, \ q = 4,$$
$$t = q/u = 1/3, \text{ and } S = \$235,000.$$

From Table 1,

$$Q = s(r,t,q) = s(6, 1/3, 4) = 0.3316803.$$

The formula for n is

$$n = \frac{1}{4} \cdot \frac{\log\left[1 + (.06/4) \cdot (\$235,000/\$1,000) \cdot Q\right]}{\log(1 + .06/4)}$$

$$= \frac{1}{4} \cdot \frac{\log(1 + .015 \times 235 \times 0.3316803)}{\log(1.015)}$$

$$= \frac{1}{4} \cdot \frac{\log(2.1691735)}{\log(1.015)}.$$

From either an electronic calculator or tables we find,

$$n = \frac{1}{4} \cdot \frac{.33629429}{.00646605} = 13 \text{ years}.$$

4.16.   Interest Rate Required for an Ordinary Annuity

There is no formula that can express the interest rate for either the present value of an annuity or the amount of an annuity. However, the interest rate can be estimated easily from the tables if the number of annual interest periods and payment periods are equal.

Formula: none

Table: Find the interest rate in Table 1 in the following way:

(1) Divide either the present value (Section 4.1) or the amount (Section 4.7) of the annuity by the periodic payment, p.

(2) Locate the section of Table 1 that corresponds to q, the number of periods per year.

(3) Locate the row corresponding to m, the total number of periods of the annuity.

(4) Search this row until locating the value determined in step (1). Since this value undoubtedly lies between two consecutive tabular values, interpolate to determine the interest rate with more accuracy (see Appendix: Mathematical Notes, Section A.2).

Example: An ordinary annuity provides monthly payments of $1,500 for 90 months. If interest is compounded monthly, what interest rate renders a present value of $101,250?

Solution: Using the definitions of Section 4.1,

$$p = \$1,500, q = 12, m = 90, \text{ and } A = \$101,250.$$

Now,

(1)   Determine $\dfrac{A}{p} = a\,(r,90,12) = \dfrac{\$101,250}{\$1,500} = 67.50$

(2)   Locate the section of Table 1 corresponding to monthly payments, q = 12.

(3)   Locate the row corresponding to m = 90 periods.

(4)   The present value of 67.50 lies between the tabulated present values 67.514176 and 66.944162 that correspond to interest rates of 8% and 8.25%, respectively i.e., a(8,90,12) and a(8.25,90,12). Interpolation shows the interest rate is 8.0062%.

FINANCE:
FINANCIAL INSTRUMENTS

This chapter discusses several financial instruments that require formulas to determine value and yield. The yields of these instruments can be compared with the yields obtainable from real estate investments. Furthermore, some of these financial instruments are used by real estate investors as interim investments and means of raising capital.

5.1. Treasury Bills

Treasury bills have the shortest term of all government securities (91, 182, and 273 days). Although they do not bear interest, they are purchased at a price below their face value at maturity. This discounted price is equivalent to interest in advance. Treasury bills are often purchased as short-term investments for excess cash reserves. Because treasury bills have a secondary market, they can be converted to cash prior to maturity.

Formulas:

$$r' = \frac{S - p}{St'} \quad \text{and} \quad r = r' \cdot \frac{S}{p}$$

where

r′ = yield (bank discount rate)
S = selling price on the basis of 100 (S = 100 if the bill is held to maturity)
p = bid price on the basis of 100
t′ = time until maturity, expressed as a fraction of a 360-day year
r = interest rate equivalent to the bank discount rate, expressed as a decimal

Table: Find t′ in Table 7.

Example: A real estate investor has a short-term surplus of funds and chooses to invest in treasury bills. He bids 97.593 (on the basis of 100) for a 182-day $10,000 bill. (a) If held to maturity, what yield would the investor receive on a bank discount rate basis? (b) If held to maturity, what is the equivalent interest rate? (c) If he converts to cash after only 60 days and sells the bill for 98.730, what is the yield and the equivalent interest rate?

Solution: (a) In this case,

$$S = 100, \ p = 97.593, \text{ and } t' = \frac{182}{360}.$$

Now, the yield is

$$r' = \frac{100 - 97.593}{100 \times \left(\frac{182}{360}\right)} = \frac{2.407}{50.556} = .04761 = 4.761\%.$$

(b) Using the above result in the second basic formula, the equivalent interest rate if held to maturity is

$$r = .04761 \times \frac{100}{97.593} = .04761 \times 1.025 = .04879 = 4.879\%.$$

(c) After 60 days, S = 98.730, and $t' = \frac{60}{360}$.

Now, the yield if sold after 60 days is

$$r' = \frac{98.730 - 97.593}{98.730 \times \left(\frac{60}{360}\right)} = \frac{1.1370}{16.455} = .06910 = 6.910\%,$$

and the equivalent interest rate is

$$r = .06910 \times \frac{98.730}{97.593} = .06991 = 6.991\%.$$

In this example, the investor earns a higher interest rate by selling after 60 days (6.991%) than he would by holding to maturity (4.879%).

5.2.   Promissory Notes

A promissory note is a written promise to pay money. It may be interest bearing or non-interest bearing. Promissory notes may also be discounted. That is, there may be an initial charge for the note based on its maturity value. Discount can be considered interest in advance.

Formulas:

$$S = f(1 + rt), d = Sr't', \text{ and } p = S - d$$

where

S = amount at maturity
f = face value
r = interest rate, expressed as a decimal
t = interest period, expressed as a fraction of a year
d = amount of discount
r′ = discount rate, expressed as a decimal
t′ = discount period, expressed as a fraction of a year
p = proceeds

Table: Find t and t′ in Table 7.

Example: On August 26 a bank discounts a promissory note at 7%. The 6 month note has a face value of $4,000, bears interest at 6%, and is due December 4. What are the proceeds to the borrower?

Solution: In this example,

$$r' = 7\%, t = 1/2, f = \$4,000, \text{ and } r = 6\%.$$

To find the proceeds, we must first determine S and d:

$$S = \$4,000 (1 + .06 \times 1/2) = \$4,000 \times 1.03 = \$4,120.$$

From Table 7, August 26 is the 238th day of the year, and December 4 is the 338th day. Hence,

$$t' = \frac{338 - 238}{360} = \frac{100}{360} = .277778.$$

Now,

$$d = \$4,120 \times .07 \times .277778 = \$80.11.$$

The proceeds are

$$p = S - d = \$4,120.00 - \$80.11 = \$4,039.89.$$

5.3.   Certificates of Deposit

A certificate of deposit (CD) is a certificate issued by a bank in exchange for the deposit of money. At maturity the bank agrees to repay the deposited sum plus the accrued simple interest computed on a 360-day year. Certificates issued for large.deposits enjoy a secondary market.

Formula:

$$p = f \cdot \frac{(1 + r_1 t_1)}{(1 + r_2 t_2)}^{*}$$

where

p = purchase price (present value)
f = amount of deposit (face value)
r_1 = interest rate of CD, expressed as a decimal
r_2 = interest rate expected presently, expressed as a decimal
t_1 = original term of the CD, expressed as a fraction of a year
t_2 = remaining term of the CD, expressed as a fraction of a year

Table: Find t_1 and t_2 in Table 7.

Example: On March 11 a bank sells a \$1,000,000 negotiable CD which bears interest at 6.75% and matures December 6. (a) If the CD is repurchased on October 31, and the purchaser wants an interest rate of 5.1%, how much must he pay? (b) If the CD is held to maturity what will its value be?

Solution: (a) From Table 7, March 11 is the 70th day of the year, October 31 is the 304th day, and December 6 is the 340th day. Hence,

$$t_1 = \frac{340 - 70}{360} = \frac{270}{360} = .75,$$

---

*Also see Section 1.6.

and

$$t_2 = \frac{340 - 304}{360} = \frac{36}{360} = .10.$$

Now,

$$p = \$1,000,000 \left(\frac{1 + .0675 \times .75}{1 + .0510 \times .10} \right) = \$1,000,000 \left(\frac{1.050625}{1.005100} \right)$$

$$= \$1,045,294.$$

(b) If the CD is held to maturity, $t_2 = 0$ (i.e., there is no remaining term). Hence,

$$p = \$1,000,000 \left(\frac{1 + .0675 \times .75}{1 + .0510 \times 0} \right) = \$1,000,000 \left(\frac{1.050625}{1} \right)$$

$$= \$1,056,250.$$

5.4.   Commercial Paper

Commercial paper is a broad term referring to short-term negotiable notes issued by commercial organizations. The denominations are usually multiples of $100,000 and $250,000. Maturities vary from several days to 9 months. Commercial paper is often used by corporations to avoid bank restrictions on short-term loans.

Formulas:

$$\mathbf{S = f(1 + rt), \quad d = Sr't', \text{ and } p = S - d^*}$$

where

S = amount at maturity
f = face value
r = interest rate, expressed as a decimal
t = interest period, expressed as a fraction of a year
d = amount of bank discount
r′ = discount rate, expressed as a decimal
t′ = discount period, expressed as a fraction of a year
p = purchase price

Table: Find t or t′ in Table 7.

---

*Also see Section 2.3.

Example: The American Tire Company issued a $500,000 piece of non-interest bearing commerical paper to mature September 1. The entire issue was purchased by a brokerage firm on May 7. If the discount rate is 7%, what is the purchase price?

Solution: In this example,

$$f = \$500,000, \text{ and } r' = 7\%.$$

To find the purchase price, we must first determine the amount at maturity and the amount of bank discount. From Table 7, we see that May 7 is the 127th day of the year and September 1 is the 244th day. Hence,

$$t' = \frac{244 - 127}{360} = \frac{117}{360} = .325.$$

Now, since the paper does not bear interest, (i.e., r = 0) we have

$$S = f = \$500,000.$$

The amount of bank discount is

$$d = \$500,000 \times .07 \times .325 = \$11,375.$$

The purchase price is

$$p = \$500,000 - \$11,375 = \$488,625.$$

5.5.   Bonds (Present Value)

Bonds are issued by corporations and governmental agencies. The investor expects the issuing party to repay the principal on a future date and to pay periodic (usually semiannual) interest. Most bonds may be redeemed at maturity. However, some are callable (may be redeemed prior to maturity).

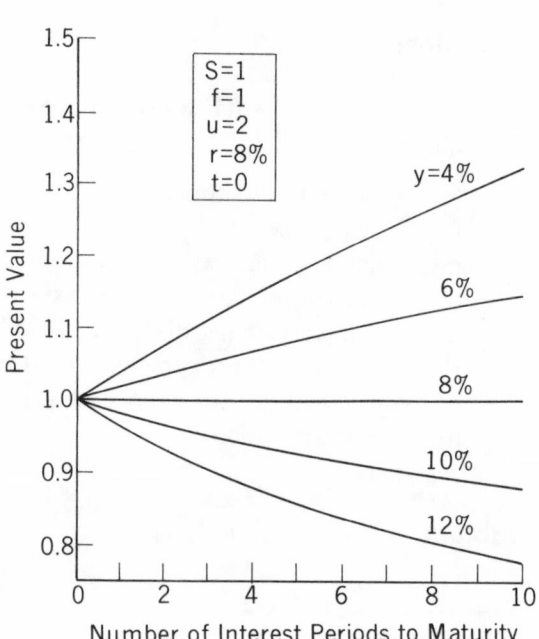

The first formula for the present value of a bond is very general (allowing: for a bond interest period that is different from the investor's interest period; for a redemption value that is different from face value; and for a purchase date that is different from the payment date). The second formula, although simplified, applies to many situations.* The figure shows the present value (purchase price) of an 8% bond for the simplified case (second formula) and for a variety of yields over the last 10 interest periods.

Formulas:

$$p = \left[f \cdot (r/u) \cdot a(y,k,u)/s(y,w,q) + \frac{S}{c(y,k,u)} \right] \cdot (1 + yt) \quad \textbf{(general)}$$

$$p = S \cdot \left[(r/u) \cdot a(y,k,u) + \frac{1}{c(y,k,u)} \right] \quad \textbf{(if } S = f, \, u = q, \text{ and } t = 0)$$

where

p = present value of the bond (purchase price)

S = redemption value (amount to be paid to the investor)

f = face value (value stated on the bond)

y = annual yield to investor, expressed as a decimal

k = number of bond interest periods to maturity (increase by 1 if there is a partial period)

u = number of bond interest periods per year

$c(y,k,u)$ = amount of 1 at compound interest

r = annual bond interest rate, expressed as a decimal

q = number of interest periods per year available to investor

w = q/u

$a(y,k,u)$ = present value of an annuity of 1

$s(y,w,q)$ = amount of an annuity of 1

t = time interval since last bond interest period, expressed as a fraction of a year (use ordinary interest and exact time as defined in Table 7)

Table: Find c(y,k,u), s(y,w,q), and a(y,k,u) in Table 1. Find t in Table 7.

Example: On October 7, Mr. Lynch purchased a $1,000 bond issued by the AMT Corporation, redeemable at $1050. The bond pays interest of 5% each January 1 and July 1. It has 37 complete interest periods remaining (i.e., k = 38). Mr. Lynch is accustomed to quarterly interest on his other assets. What is the value of the bond to Mr. Lynch if it is to yield 6%?

---

*Both formulas are derived from the simple concept that the present value of a bond is the sum of the present values to be received (i.e., the present value of its redemption value, S, plus the present value of its interest payments, f(r/u)).

Solution: In this example,

$$f = \$1,000, \ S = \$1,050, \ r = 5\%, \ u = 2, \ k = 38,$$
$$q = 4, \ w = q/u = 2, \ \text{and} \ y = 6\%.$$

The bond has been accruing interest from the last interest period to October 7. From Table 7, July 1 is the 182nd day of the year and October 7 is the 280th day. Hence,

$$t = \frac{280 - 182}{360} = .27222.$$

From Table 1,

$$c(y,k,u) = c(6,38,2) = 3.07478,$$
$$a(y,k,u) = a(6,38,2) = 22.49246, \ \text{and}$$
$$s(y,w,q) = s(6,2,4) = 2.01500.$$

Now, the value of the bond to Mr. Lynch is

$$p = \left[\$1,000(.05/2) \times 22.49246/2.01500 \ + \ \frac{1,050}{3.07478} \right] \times (1 + .06 \times 0.27222)$$
$$= \left[\$279.06 + \$341.49 \right] \times (1.016333)$$
$$= \$620.55 \times 1.016333$$
$$= \$630.69.$$

5.6.   Bonds (Estimated Yield)

The yield is the annual rate of return on invested capital. The yield on a bond can not be expressed explicitly (as can be seen from the formulas of Section 5.5). If the bond is held to maturity, the annual yield can be estimated by the "Bond Salesman's Method"*:

Formula:

$$y \approx \frac{\textbf{Average Annual Yield}}{\textbf{Average Annual Investment}} = \frac{\dfrac{\textbf{rkf} + (\textbf{S} - \textbf{p})}{\textbf{k}}}{\dfrac{\textbf{S} + \textbf{p}}{\textbf{2}}}$$

---

*The true yield can be found in the following way: (1) use this estimate of y (as a first estimate) in the formula of Section 5.5. The value of p thus determined is close to the actual purchase price, and (2) repeatedly select new values of y that render p as close as desired to the purchase price.

where

y = annual yield to investor, expressed as a decimal ($\approx$ indicates an approximation)

r = annual bond interest rate, expressed as a decimal

k = number of bond interest periods to maturity

f = face value (value stated on bond)

S = redemption value (amount to be paid to the investor)

p = present value of the bond (purchase price)

Example: A $1,000 bond bearing 6% interest has 20 remaining interest periods. It is presently selling at $930 and is redeemable at face value. What is the yield as estimated by the "Bond Salesman's Method?"

Solution: In this example,

$$f = \$1,000, r = .06, k = 20, p = \$930, \text{ and } S = \$1,000.$$

Now,

$$y \approx \frac{\dfrac{.06 \times 20 \times \$1,000 + (\$1,000 - \$930)}{20}}{\dfrac{\$1,000 + \$930}{2}}$$

$$\approx \frac{\dfrac{\$1,200 + \$70}{20}}{\$965} = \frac{\$63.50}{\$965} = .0658 = 6.58\%.$$

5.7. Bonds (Amortization of the Premium and Accumulation of the Discount)

The book value of a bond is its value as carried on the owner's books. When a bond is purchased at a premium (the amount that the purchase price exceeds the face value), the interest on the purchase price exceeds the interest on the face value. If the excess interest is successively applied to reduce the cost of the bond, its book value is thereby reduced. Finally at maturity, the book value is reduced sufficiently to equal the face value.

In the case of a bond purchased at a discount (the amount that the face value exceeds the purchase price), the interest on the face value exceeds the interest on the purchase price. If this excess interest is successively added to the purchase price, its book value is thereby increased. Finally at maturity, the book value is increased sufficiently to equal the face value.

Formula:

$$A_i = \left[p - f \cdot (r/u) \cdot a(y,i,u) \right] \cdot c(y,i,u)$$

where

A_i = book value after the ith interest period
p = purchase price
f = face (par) value
r = annual bond interest rate, expressed as a decimal
u = number of bond interest periods per year
y = annual yield to investor
$a(y,i,u)$ = present value of an annuity of 1
$c(y,i,u)$ = amount of 1 at compound interest

Table: Find $c(y,i,u)$ and $a(y,i,u)$ in Table 1.

Example: Ed Lowery bought a \$1,000 bond at 6% to yield 5%. The bond matures at par in 2 years, and interest is paid semi-annually. He paid \$1,018.81 for the bond. If Mr. Lowery applies the excess interest to reduce the premium, what is the book value after 2 interest periods?

Solution: In this example,

$$f = \$1,000, \; r = 6\%, \; y = 5\%, \; u = 2,$$
$$p = \$1,018.81, \text{ and } i = 2.$$

From Table 1,

$$c(y,i,u) = c(5,2,2) = 1.0506, \text{ and}$$
$$a(y,i,u) = a(5,2,2) = 1.9274.$$

Now, after two interest periods the book value is

$$
\begin{aligned}
A_2 &= \left[\$1,018.81 - \$1,000 \times (.06/2) \times 1.9274 \right] \times 1.0506 \\
&= (\$1,018.81 - \$57.82) \times 1.0506 \\
&= \$1,009.62.
\end{aligned}
$$

After four interest periods (at maturity),

$$A_4 = f = \$1,000.$$

5.8.   Bonds (Yield on Tax-Free Municipal Bonds)

Interest earned on municipal bonds is exempt from federal income tax and sometimes exempt from state and local tax. Because of this status, their effective yield should be compared with the yield from taxable investments.

Formula:

$$y' = \frac{y}{1 - z}$$

where

y′ = effective annual yield from municipal bonds by virtue of their tax-exempt status
y = annual contract yield from the tax-free municipal bond, expressed as a decimal
z = investor's federal tax rate, expressed as a decimal

Table: Find the federal tax rate using Table 8 and the example in Section 14.4.

Example: Mr. Morgan generally can earn 10% from his taxable investments, but good quality municipal bonds are available that yield 7%. Mr. Morgan estimates that his federal tax rate will be 42% (e.g., he is filing a married joint return, and his taxable income is $93,000). In view of this rate, what will be the effective yield to him?

Solution: In this example, y = .07, and z = .42. Now, the effective yield is

$$y' = \frac{.07}{1 - .42} = \frac{.07}{.58} = .1207 = 12.07\%.$$

5.9.   Mortgages (Yield)

New and existing mortgages are often traded. If there is no prepayment, the mortgage yield can be determined if either the purchase price or the discount from the loan balance is known. If there is prepayment, an electronic calculator must be used.

The figure can be used to quickly estimate the yield for loans with monthly payments. For instance, to find the yield from the figure, it is necessary to know only (1) the remaining number of payments and (2) the ratio of the purchase price to the monthly payment. (See Figure 5-A.)

Mortgage Yield and Purchase Price

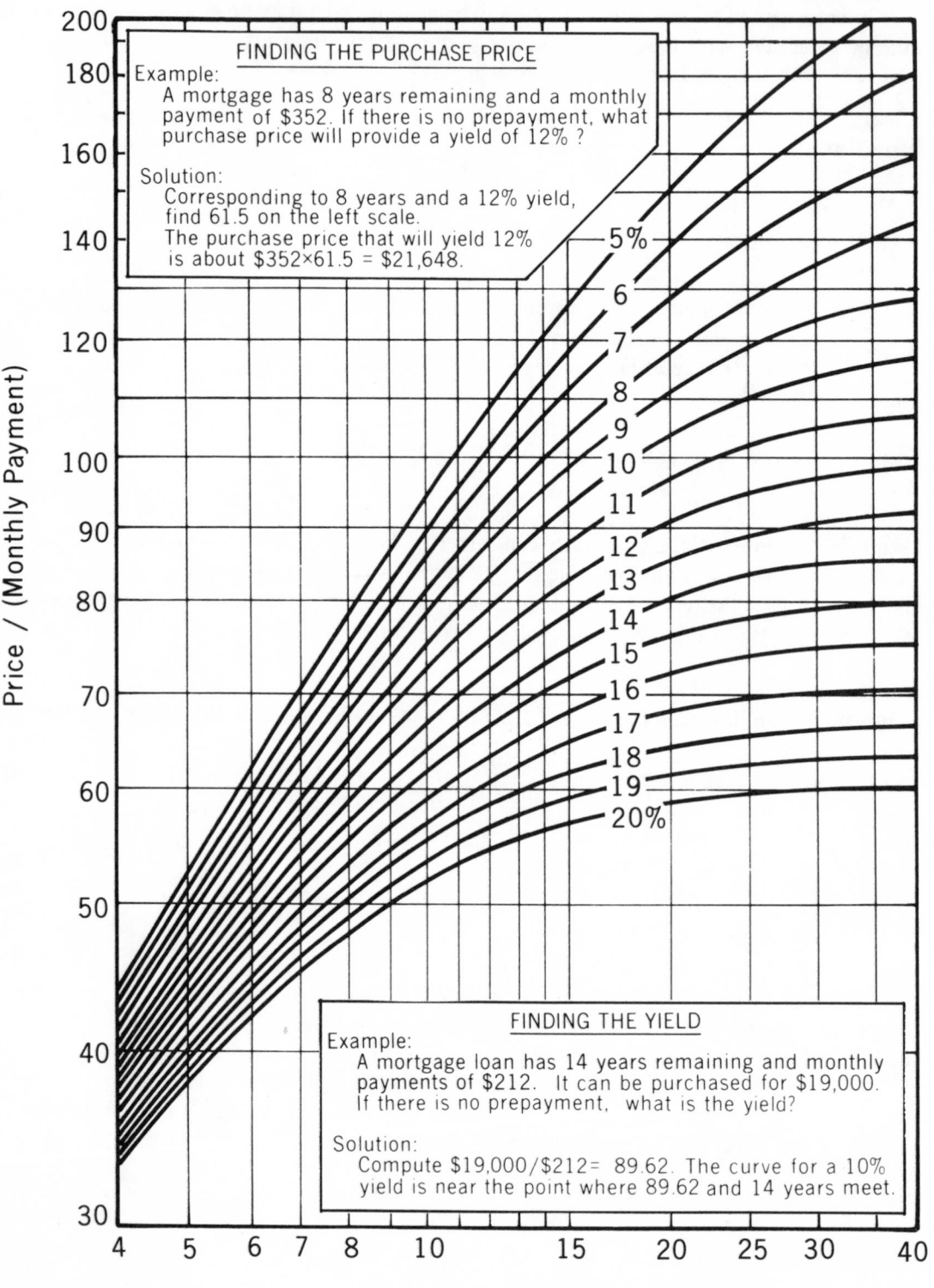

FINDING THE PURCHASE PRICE

Example:
A mortgage has 8 years remaining and a monthly payment of $352. If there is no prepayment, what purchase price will provide a yield of 12% ?

Solution:
Corresponding to 8 years and a 12% yield, find 61.5 on the left scale.
The purchase price that will yield 12% is about $352×61.5 = $21,648.

FINDING THE YIELD

Example:
A mortgage loan has 14 years remaining and monthly payments of $212. It can be purchased for $19,000. If there is no prepayment, what is the yield?

Solution:
Compute $19,000/$212= 89.62. The curve for a 10% yield is near the point where 89.62 and 14 years meet.

Price / (Monthly Payment)

Remaining Term (Years)

Figure 5-A

   There is no formula that states the mortgage yield, y, explicitly. However, it can be determined readily by locating a(y,k,q) in Table 1 and interpolating.*

   It is assumed that the mortgage will be held to maturity, at which time it will be fully amortized.

Formulas:

$$a(y,k,q) = \frac{p'}{g} = \frac{p'}{p} \cdot a(r,m,q) = (1 - r') \cdot a(r,k,q)$$

   where

   y = yield from mortgage
   k = remaining number of payment periods
   q = number of payment periods per year
   n = number of years
   m = nq = total number of periodic payments
   r = mortgage interest rate

a(y,k,q),
a(r,m,q),
   and
a(r,k,q) = present value of an annuity of 1
   g = amount of periodic loan payment
   p' = price of mortgage
   p = original amount of mortgage
   r' = discount rate on mortgage balance, expressed as a decimal

Table: Find a(y,k,q), a(r,m,q), or a(r,k,q) in Table 1.

Example: A loan has 84 remaining monthly payments of $324.43. If it can be purchased for $17,840, what is the yield?

Solution: Since this example involves monthly payments, the yield can be estimated from the figure or determined more accurately from Table 1.

   (1) To estimate the yield from the figure, find 7 years (i.e., 84 remaining monthly payments) on the bottom scale. Now find,

$$\frac{p'}{g} = \frac{\$17,840}{\$324.43} = 54.9887$$

on the side scale. The corresponding yield is about 12.5%..

   (2) To find the yield from Table 1, locate the section for monthly periods (i.e. q = 12) and the row corresponding to 84 periods (i.e. m = 84). Scan this row, and find the two

---

*See Appendix: Mathematical Notes, Section A.2.

consecutive interest rates whose values of a(y,84,12) bracket our value of $\frac{p'}{g}$ = 54.9887. Interpolation (Appendix: Mathematical Notes) shows that the exact yield is y = 12.99%.

5.10.   Mortgages (Purchase Price and Discount)

New and existing mortgages are often traded. Usually a buyer knows the yield he must have. He must then determine the purchase price (i.e., the discount from the loan balance) that will provide that yield.

The following formulas apply either to mortgages that are fully amortized (no prepayment) or to mortgages that are prepaid by a balloon payment.

Formulas:

$$p' = \begin{cases} g \cdot a(y,m-i,q) = p \cdot \dfrac{a(y,m-i,q)}{a(r,m,q)} & \text{(No prepayment)} \\[2em] g \cdot a(y,j-i,q) + \dfrac{B_j}{c(y,j-i,q)} \\[2em] p \cdot \dfrac{a(y,j-i,q)}{a(r,m,q)} + \dfrac{B_j}{c(y,j-i,q)} \end{cases} \text{(Prepayment)}*$$

and

$$r' = 1 - \frac{p'}{B_i}$$

where

p′ = purchase price that guarantees required yield
g = amount of periodic loan payment
y = yield from mortgage

---

*This formula for the purchase price contains the balloon implicitly:

$$p' = p \cdot \left[\frac{s(y,j-i,q) + a(r,k,q)}{c(y,j-i,q) \cdot a(r,m,q)} \right].$$

This formula is general, and also describes the case of no prepayment if k = 0. In this case j = m and a(r,k,q) = 0.

r = mortgage interest rate
q = number of payment periods per year
n = number of years (term of mortgage)
m = nq = total number of payment periods
i = number of payment periods before purchase
j = number of payment periods from inception until balloon
k = number of payment periods after balloon (until term)

$a(y,m-i,q)$,
$a(r,m,q)$,
$a(y,j-i,q)$,
and
$a(r,k,q)$ = present value of an annuity of 1
$s(y,j-i,q)$ = amount of an annuity of 1
$c(y,j-i,q)$ = amount of 1 at compound interest
p = original amount of mortgage
r' = discount rate on mortgage balance
B_i, B_j = balance of mortgage at time of purchase and at time of prepayment, respectively

Table: Find $a(y,m-i,q)$, etc., in Table 1.

Example 1: (No prepayment).   Eleven monthly payments of $324.43 have been made on a 5 year mortgage. The current balance is $13,523.14. If we insist upon a yield of 10%, what must the purchase price be? Express this price also in terms of the discount rate.

Solution: The information given suggests using the first equation for the purchase price with no prepayment. In this example,

$$i = 11, q = 12, n = 5, m = nq = 60, g = \$324.43,$$
$$B_i = \$13,523.14, \text{ and } y = 10\%.$$

From Table 1.

$$a(y,m-i,q) = a(10,49,12) = 40.0940.$$

Now, the purchase price must be

$$p' = \$324.43 \times 40.0940 = \$13,007.70.$$

At this price, the discount rate is

$$r' = 1 - \frac{\$13,007.70}{\$13,523.14} = 1 - .9619 = .0381 = 3.81\%.$$

Example 2: (Prepayment).   A 5 year mortgage has monthly payments of $324.43 and a current balance of $13,523.14 after 11 payments. After a total of 48 payment periods, the balance of $3,729.06 will be due. What purchase price will provide a 10% yield? At this price, what is the discount rate?

Solution: In this example,

$$n = 5, \ g = \$324.43, \ B_i = \$13,523.14, \ i = 11,$$
$$j = 48, \ B_j = \$3,729.06, \text{ and } y = 10\%.$$

From Table 1,

$$a(y, j - i, q) = a(10, 37, 12) = 31.99124, \text{ and}$$
$$c(y, j - i, q) = c(10, 37, 12) = 1.359417.$$

Now, the purchase price must be

$$p' = \$324.43 \times 31.99124 + \$3,729.06/1.359417$$
$$= \$10,378.92 + \$2,743.13$$
$$= \$13,122.05.$$

At this price, the discount rate is

$$r' = 1 - \frac{\$13,122.05}{\$13,523.14} = 1 - .9703 = .0297 = 2.97\%.$$

6

FINANCE: AMORTIZED LOANS

This chapter is devoted to loans in which the periodic payments reduce the principal. Each payment is at least large enough to pay the interest on the balance. Any excess is subtracted from the existing balance so as to reduce it further. Generally, this excess of payment is sufficient to extinguish the balance at the term of the loan. The payments dealt with in this chapter consist only of principal and interest (without taxes and insurance).

Payments made at fixed intervals of time constitute an annuity. Hence, the formulas concerning annuities (Chapter 4) are used extensively in this chapter. The notation $a(r,m,q)$ denotes the present value of an annuity of 1 for the interest rate r, the total number of periods m, and the number of periods per year, q*.

All periodic payments in this chapter are constant (level) payments except those of Section 6.16 which are constant principal payments.

The graphs included in this chapter are intended to illustrate the characteristics of mortgage loans. A few graphs, such as those of monthly payments and loan balances can be used in lieu of the formulas and tables to quickly estimate values.

---

*The notation $a(r,m,q)$ has been adopted in favor of $a_{\overline{m}|r/q}$. Whereas $a(r,m,q)$ is a standard mathematical notation for a function of three parameters (i.e., r, m, and q), the notation $a_{\overline{m}|r/q}$ is peculiar only to the mathematics of finance.

6.1.   Periodic Payment Required to Amortize

Loans can be amortized by many varying arrangements (see Sections 6.15 and 6.16). However, it is convenient to make equal payments at the end of equal periods. If the payments are large enough to amortize the loan at its term, such a schedule of payments constitutes an annuity whose present value is the amount borrowed (see Section 4.1). A portion of each payment pays the interest on the balance of the loan, and the remainder is subtracted from the balance (reducing it further). The figure illustrates the monthly payments for a $1,000 loan. It can be used to obtain a quick estimate of the monthly payment. (See Figure 6-A.)

Formula:

$$g = p/a(r,m,q)$$

where

g = amount of periodic payment
p = amount of the loan
r = annual interest rate
n = number of years
q = number of payment periods per year
$m = nq$ = total number of payments
$a(r,m,q)$ = present value of an annuity of 1

Table: If the payments are made monthly (i.e., $q = 12$), find g in Table 2. Generally, however, use Table 1 to determine $a(r,m,q)$.

Example: Mr. Scott obtained a $35,300 loan. The interest rate is 8.50%, and the term is 25 years. How much are the monthly payments?

Solution: We can determine the monthly payments in any of three ways:
(a) Quick estimate: From the figure we can estimate the monthly payment quickly by finding the payment for a $1,000 loan at 25 years and 8.50%. For a $1,000 loan, the payment is about $8. Hence, the payment for a $35,300 loan is about $8 × 35.3 = $282.40.
(b) Exact payment for multiples of $1,000: See Table 2.
(c) Exact payment for any amount: In the above example,

$p = \$35,300$, $r = 8.50\%$, $n = 25$, $q = 12$, and $m = nq = 300$.

From Table 1,

$$a(r,m,q) = a(8.50,300,12) = 124.1886.$$

MONTHLY PAYMENT

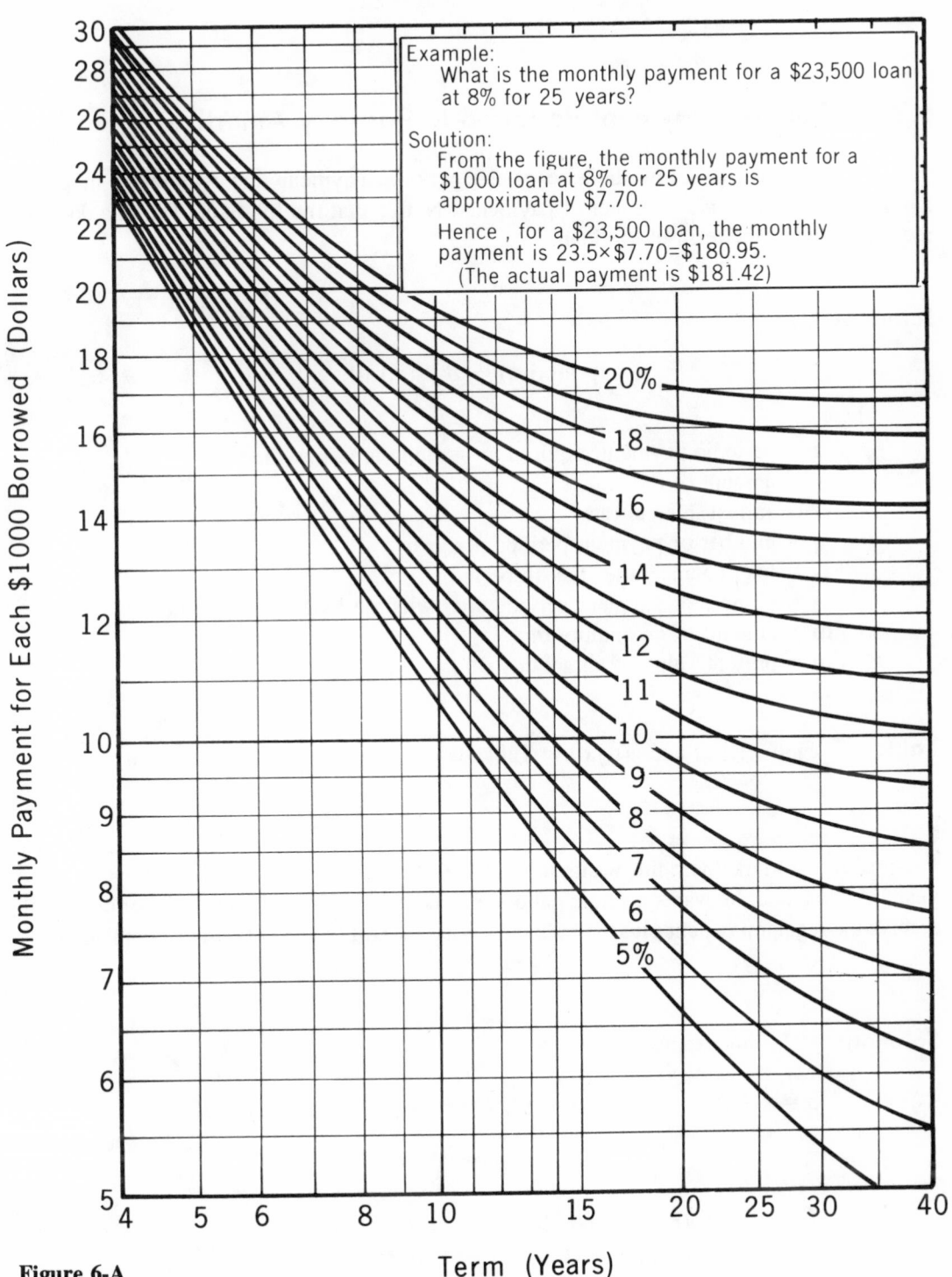

Example:
   What is the monthly payment for a $23,500 loan at 8% for 25 years?

Solution:
   From the figure, the monthly payment for a $1000 loan at 8% for 25 years is approximately $7.70.

   Hence , for a $23,500 loan, the monthly payment is 23.5×$7.70=$180.95.
   (The actual payment is $181.42)

Figure 6-A

Now,

$$g = \$35,300/124.1886 = \$284.25.$$

6.2.   Periodic Payment Required to Partially Amortize

We may wish to know the size of the periodic payment that will result in partial amortization after a given number of payments. Notice that the following formula does not require knowing the term of the loan.

Formula:

$$g = p/a(r,j,q) - B_j/s(r,j,q)$$

where

g = periodic payment required to partially amortize the loan
p = amount of the loan
r = annual interest rate
q = number of payment periods per year
B_j = loan balance after the jth period
j = number of payment periods after which a balance, B_j, remains
$s(r,j,q)$ = amount of an annuity of 1
$a(r,j,q)$ = present value of an annuity of 1

Table: Find $s(r,j,q)$ and $a(r,j,q)$ in Table 1.

Example: Mark Meredith wants to lend \$16,000 at 8% with monthly payments for 3 years. At this time, he wants a single balloon payment of \$5,000. (In the 36th period he will receive the regular payment plus the balloon.) What monthly payment will accomplish this?

Solution: In this example,

$$p = \$16,000, r = 8\%, q = 12, j = 3 \times q = 36, \text{ and } B_j = \$5,000.$$

From Table 1,

$$a(r,j,q) = a(8,36,12) = 31.91181, \text{ and}$$
$$s(r,j,q) = s(8,36,12) = 40.53556.$$

Now,

$$g = \$16,000/31.91181 - \$5,000/40.53556$$
$$= \$501.38 - \$123.35$$
$$= \$378.03.$$

6.3.   Monthly Payments for FHA Loans

For FHA loans, 1/2 of 1 percent of the loan amount, p, is charged to the borrower for the Mutual Mortgage Insurance Fund. Since this annual charge is paid monthly, the monthly payment is $\frac{.005}{12} \cdot$ p larger than the payment of a similar loan that is not insured.

Formulas:

$$g = p \cdot \left[\frac{1}{a(r,m,q)} + \frac{.005}{12} \right] \qquad \text{(periodic payment)}$$

$$a(r',m,q) = \frac{a(r,m,q)}{1 + (.005/12) \cdot a(r,m,q)} \qquad \text{(effective interest rate)}$$

where

   g = amount of the periodic payment
   p = amount of the loan
   r = quoted annual interest rate
   r′ = effective annual interest rate (by virtue of the insurance charge)
   q = number of payment periods per year
   n = number of years
   m = nq = total number of periods
a(r,m,q),
a(r′,m,q) = present value of an annuity of 1

Table: Find the monthly payment for FHA loans in Table 3.

Example: A $30,250 FHA loan for 25 years bears an interest rate of 8.50%. (a) How much is the monthly payment? (b) What is the effective interest rate created by the additional charge for insurance?

Solution: Since the loan amount is not a multiple of $1,000, the monthly payment is not listed in Table 3. In this example,

p = $30,250, n = 25, r = 8.50%, q = 12, and m = nq = 300.

From Table 1,

$$a(r,m,q) = a(8.5,300,12) = 124.18857.$$

(a) Now, the monthly payment is

$$g = \$30,250 \times \left(\frac{1}{124.18857} + \frac{.005}{12}\right)$$

$$= \frac{\$30,250}{124.18857} + \frac{\$30,250 \times .005}{12} = \$243.58 + \$12.60$$

$$= \$256.18.$$

(b) To find the effective interest rate, r', use the second basic formula:

$$a(r',300,12) = \frac{124.18857}{1 + (.005/12) \times 124.18857}$$

$$= \frac{124.18857}{1.0517452} = 118.079.$$

In Table 1, find the section corresponding to monthly payments ($q = 12$). Scan the row corresponding to 300 periods ($m = 300$). Our value of 118.079 lies between the values corresponding to interest rates of 9% and 9.25%, respectively. Interpolation (see Appendix: Mathematical Notes) shows the effective interest rate to be $r' = 9.11\%$.

6.4. Combinations of Interest Rates and Terms that Result in the Same Payment

Frequently a borrower will have a good idea of the amount of payment that he can afford. This section shows how the interest rate and term can be varied, and the payment will remain unchanged. For instance, the figure shows that a monthly payment of $8 for each $1,000 borrowed will result from either a 9% loan for 30 years or an 8% loan for 22.5 years. (See Figure 6-B.)

Formula:

$$n = -\frac{1}{q} \cdot \frac{\log\left[1 - (p/g)\cdot(r/q)\right]}{\log(1 + r/q)}$$

where

n = term of loan, expressed in years
q = number of payment periods per year
p = amount of the loan
g = amount of periodic payment
r = annual interest rate, expressed as a decimal

Monthly Payment for a $1000 Loan

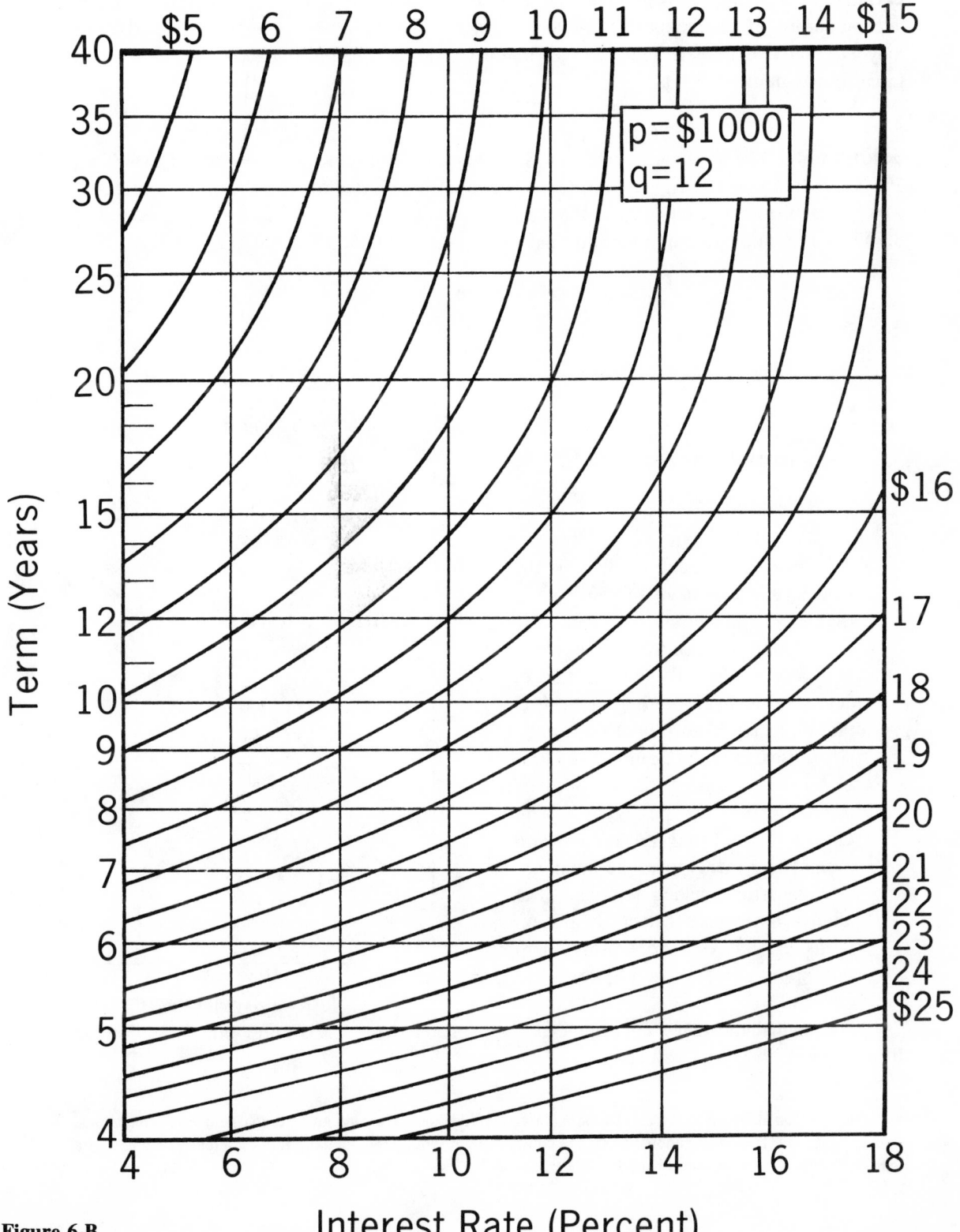

Figure 6-B

Interest Rate (Percent)

Table: None.

Example: Joanne Dugan feels she can spend $256 per month on the principal and interest portion of a home loan. The loan amount is $32,000. Several interest rates and terms may be available to her. Find several interest rates and terms that combine to provide monthly payments of $256.

Solution: The monthly payment of $256 for a $32,000 loan is $8.00 per $1,000 (i.e., 256/32 = 8). Using the figure, find the curve labeled $8.00. From any point on that curve we can read the term at the left and the interest rate at the bottom. For instance, 32 years and 8.75% will require the same monthly payment as 26 years and 8.50%, etc.

6.5.   Annual Mortgage Constant

The annual mortgage constant is the sum of the loan payments in a year, divided by the amount borrowed. The annual mortgage constant is a convenient way to view the annual rate of debt service, but more important, it is the mortgage capitalization rate*. Also, as seen in the figure, it is virtually independent of the number of payment periods per year. (The curves for annual payments and monthly payments form the boundary of the narrow shaded regions.) The annual mortgage constant always exceeds the interest rate (dashed line) but approaches it as the term increases.

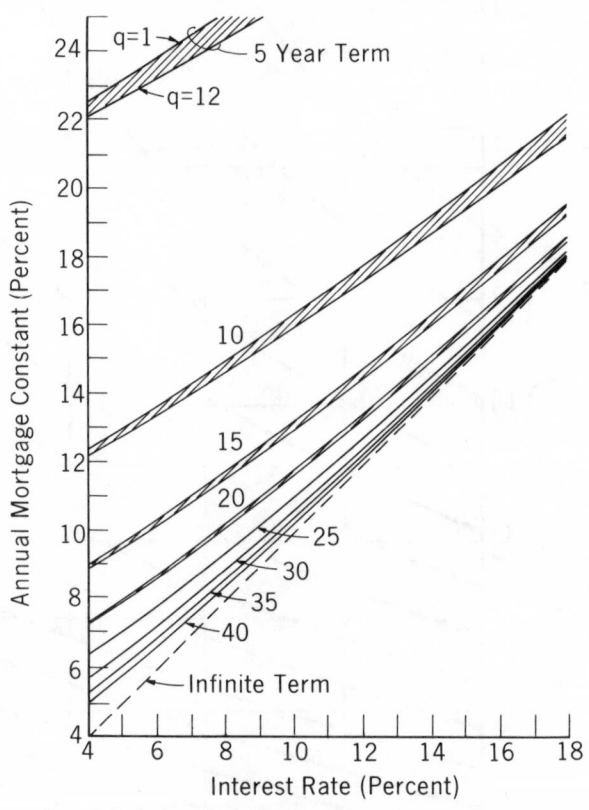

The annual mortgage constant can be estimated from the figure, but the following formulas give the exact value.

---

*The amount of annual interest is the annual return *on* the loan. The amount of annual principal is the annual return *of* the loan. Hence, the annual mortgage constant, representing the annual return on a loan and return of a loan, is the capitalization rate for the loan, see Section 7.7.

Formulas:

$$z_m = \frac{gq}{p} = q/a(r,m,q) = r \cdot \left[\frac{(1 + r/q)^m}{(1 + r/q)^m - 1} \right] \text{(complete amortization)}$$

$$z_m = r + q \cdot \left[\frac{1 - (B_j/p)}{s(r,j,q)} \right] \qquad \text{(partial amortization)}$$

where

z_m = annual mortgage constant
g = amount of the periodic payment
p = amount of the loan
q = number of payment periods per year
n = number of years
m = nq = total number of periods
r = annual interest rate, expressed as a decimal
B_j = loan balance after the jth period
$a(r,m,q)$ = present value of an annuity of 1
$s(r,j,q)$ = amount of an annuity of 1

Table: Find z_m in Table 4 if payments are monthly.

Example: An $83,000 loan is amortized by quarterly payments of $2,094.09. What is the annual mortgage constant?

Solution: From the information given (i.e., p = $83,000, q = 4, and g = $2,094.09), we must use the first formula:

$$z_m = \frac{\$2,094.09 \times 4}{\$83,000} = .1009 = 10.09\%.$$

6.6.   Annual Interest Rate and Annual Percentage Rate

The annual interest rate on an amortized loan is the annual rate at which interest is charged on the loan balance. However, due to initial finance charges sometimes imposed by the lender, the interest rate understates the cost of the loan. Finance charges might include points (i.e., 2 points is 2% of the loan amount), service charges, finder's fees, etc. These charges constitute a discount because they are deducted initially from the face value of the loan.

The annual percentage rate is the annual interest rate plus the annual rate resulting from the finance charges.

Formulas:

$$a(r,m,q) = \frac{p}{g} \qquad \text{(annual interest rate)}$$

$$a(r',m,q) = \frac{p'}{p} \cdot a(r,m,q) \quad \text{(annual percentage rate)}$$

where

r = annual interest rate
r' = annual percentage rate
n = number of years
q = number of periods per year
$m = nq$ = total number of periods
$a(r,m,q)$,
$a(r',m,q)$ = present value of an annuity of 1
g = amount of periodic payment
r'' = points, expressed as a decimal
c = finance charges, expressed in dollars
p' = amount received by the borrower (proceeds)
$p = \dfrac{p'}{1 - r''} + c$ = amount loaned (face value)

Table: Find $a(r,m,q)$ and $a(r',m,q)$ in Table 1.

Example 1: (Finding the annual interest rate).   A $35,000 loan has a term of 30 years and monthly payments of $260. What is the annual interest rate?

Solution: In this example,

$$p = \$35,000, \ n = 30, \ q = 12, \ m = nq = 360, \text{ and } g = \$260.$$

Now,

$$a(r,m,q) = a(r,360,12) = \frac{\$35,000}{\$260} = 134.6154.$$

Go to Table 1. Find the section dealing with monthly payments (i.e., $q = 12$), and find the row for $m = 360$ payments. Our value of $a(r,m,q) = 134.6154$ lies between the entries 136.2834 and 133.1097 that result from 8% and 8.25% interest rates, respectively. From interpolation (see Appendix: Mathematical Notes), the annual interest rate is 8.13%.

Example 2: (Finding the annual percentage rate).   Bob Hall needs to borrow $35,000 (net to him). For a 30 year loan with monthly payments at 8.13% interest, the lender will charge him 2 points and other charges totaling $163.06. How much must he borrow to net $35,000, and what is the annual percentage rate?

Solution: In this example,

$$p' = \$35,000, \; n = 30, \; q = 12, \; m = nq = 360, \; r = 8.13\%,$$
$$r'' = .02, \text{ and } c = \$163.06.$$

Now, the face value of the loan is

$$p = \frac{p'}{1 - r''} + c = \frac{\$35,000}{1 - .02} + \$163.06 = \$35,714.29 + \$163.06$$

$$= \$35,877.55.$$

Also,

$$a(r,m,q) = a(8.13,360,12) = 134.6154.$$

(This would usually be obtained from Table 1, but, in this case, it was found in Example 1.)
    Using the basic formula,

$$a(r',m,q) = \frac{\$35,000.00}{\$35,877.55} \times 134.61538 = 131.32274.$$

Go to Table 1. Find the section dealing with monthly payments (i.e., q = 12,) and find the row for m = 360 payments. Our value of a(r',m,q) = 131.32274 lies between the entries 133.10854 and 130.05364 that result from 8.25% and 8.50% interest rates, respectively. Interpolation (see Appendix: Mathematical Notes) shows the annual percentage rate to be 8.38%. The finance charges have increased the interest rate found in Example 1 by .25%.

6.7.   Number of Periods

The term of a loan is the stated period of indebtedness. Most loans are amortized at their term. Those that are not have a balance that is usually paid in a single payment called a balloon payment.
    The following formula can be used to determine the number of regular payments that will leave any desired balloon payment, B_j. If complete amortization is desired, set $B_j = \$0$.

Formula:

$$j = \frac{\log\left[\dfrac{1 - x \cdot (B_j/p)}{1 - x}\right]^{*}}{\log(1 + r/q)}$$

where

j = number of periods
B_j = balance desired after j payment periods
p = amount of loan
r = annual interest rate, expressed as a decimal
q = number of periods per year
g = amount of each periodic payment
x = $(p/g) \cdot (r/q) = r/z_m$
z_m = annual mortgage constant

Table: Use an electronic calculator to determine the logarithms.

Example 1: (Partial Amortization).   A \$45,000 loan has an interest rate of 8% and monthly payments of \$430.08. If there is to be a balloon payment (balance) of about \$22,500, how many periods of regular payments must there be?

Solution: In this example,

$$p = \$45,000, \ r = 8\%, \ q = 12, \ g = \$430.08, \ \text{and} \ B_j = \$22,500.$$

Determine,

$$x = (\$45,000/\$430.08) \cdot (.08/12)$$
$$= .69745.$$

Now, using the formula,

$$j = \frac{\log\left[\dfrac{1 - .69745(\$22,500/\$45,000)}{1 - .69745}\right]}{\log(1 + .08/12)}$$

$$= \frac{\log\left[\dfrac{1 - .69745 \times .5}{1 - .69745}\right]}{\log(1 + .0066667)}$$

---

*For more on logarithms see Appendix: Mathematical Notes.

$$= \frac{\log(2.1526194)}{\log(1.0066667)} = 115.44.*$$

Since we can't have fractional periods, choose $j = 115$. From Section 6.11, find the exact balance after 115 periods:

$$B_{115} = \$45,000 - \left[\$430.08 - (.08/12) \times \$45,000\right] \cdot s(8,115,12)$$
$$= \$45,000 - \$130.08 \times 172.066391$$
$$= \$22,617.60.$$

Example 2: (Complete Amortization)   Suppose the annual mortgage constant is 16%, and the interest rate is 8%. If payments are made monthly, what is the term required for complete amortization?

Solution: In this example,

$$z_m = 16\%, \; r = 8\%, \; q = 12, \; \text{and } B_j = \$0.$$

First determine x:

$$x = \frac{r}{z_m} = \frac{.08}{.16} = .50$$

Now, using the formula,

$$j = \frac{\log\left[\dfrac{1 - .50 \times 0}{1 - .5}\right]}{\log(1 + .08/12)} = \frac{\log\left[\dfrac{1}{1 - .5}\right]}{\log(1.0066667)}$$

$$= \frac{\log(2)}{\log(1.0066667)} = \frac{.3010305}{.0028851}$$

$$= 104.34 \text{ periods.}$$

Since j cannot be fractional, use $j = 104$.

6.8.   Amount of a Loan

For loans with monthly payments, the figure can be used to quickly estimate the original loan amount for each \$1 of monthly payment. (Multiply the value, thus determined, by the actual monthly payment.) To find the exact original amount, use one of the formulas. (See Figure 6-C.)

---

*The number of periods must be a whole number (i.e., 115 instead of 115.44). Hence we must be willing to slightly adjust one of the values g, p, or B_j (see Sections 6.2, 6.8, and 6.11, respectively). The interest rate is difficult to adjust because it cannot be expressed explicitly in a formula.

ORIGINAL LOAN AMOUNT

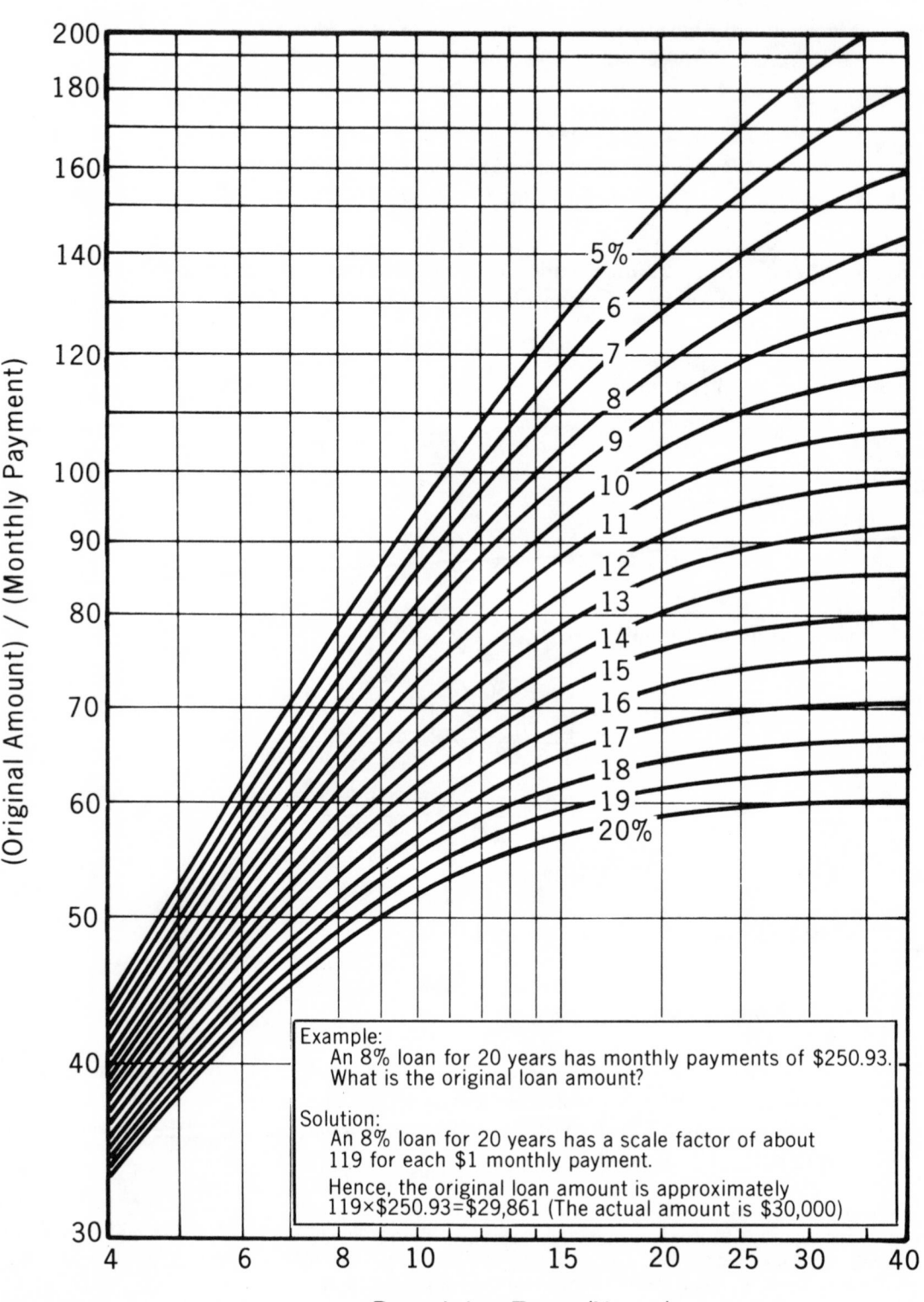

Figure 6-C   Remaining Term (Years)

Formulas:

$$p = g \cdot a(r,m,q) = B_j \cdot a(r,m,q)/a(r,k,q) = g \cdot a(r,j,q) + B_j /c(r,j,q)$$

where

      p = amount of loan
      g = amount of periodic payment
      r = annual interest rate
      q = number of periods per year
      n = term in years
      m = nq = total number of periods
      j = periods used
      k = periods remaining ($m = j + k$)
      B_j = remaining balance in the jth period
  $a(r,m,q)$,
  $a(r,k,q)$,
   $a(r,j,q)$ = present value of an annuity of 1
   $c(r,j,q)$ = amount of 1 at compound interest

Table: Find $a(r,m,q)$, $a(r,k,q)$, $a(r,j,q)$, and $c(r,j,q)$ in Table 1.

Example 1: (Periodic Payment Known).   Consider an existing loan at 8% with a term of 25 years and monthly payments of $270.14. What is the original amount of the loan?

Solution: Since the payments are made monthly, we can find the loan amount from Table 2. Also we can use the first formula. In this example,

      r = 8%, n = 25, q = 12, g = $270.14, and $m = nq = 300$.

From Table 1,

$$a(r,m,q) = a(8,300,12) = 129.5645.$$

Now,

$$p = g \cdot a(8,300,12) = \$270.14 \times 129.5645$$
$$= \$35,000.$$

Example 2: (Balance Known).   Consider an existing loan at 8% with monthly payments, a term of 25 years, and a balance of $22,265. If there are 10 years remaining, what is the amount of the loan?

Solution: In this example,

$$r = 8\%, \; q = 12, \; n = 25, \; m = nq = 300,$$
$$B_j = \$22{,}265, \text{ and } k = 10 \times 12 = 120.$$

We should use the second formula. From Table 1,

$$a(r,m,q) = a(8,300,12) = 129.5645, \text{ and}$$
$$a(r,k,q) = a(8,120,12) = 82.42148.$$

Now,

$$p = B_j \cdot a(r,m,q)/a(r,k,q)$$
$$= \$22{,}265 \times 129.5645/82.42148$$
$$= \$35{,}000.$$

Example 3: (Term Unknown).   Consider an existing loan at 8% with monthly payments of $270.14 and a balance of $22,265 after 180 payments. What is the amount of the loan?

Solution: In this example,

$$r = 8\%, \; q = 12, \; g = \$270.14, \; B_j = \$22{,}265, \text{ and } j = 180.$$

From Table 1,

$$c(r,j,q) = c(8,180,12) = 3.306921, \text{ and}$$
$$a(r,j,q) = a(8,180,12) = 104.6406.$$

Now, using the third formula,

$$p = \$270.14 \times 104.6406 + \$22{,}265/3.306921$$
$$= \$28{,}267.61 + \$6{,}732.85$$
$$= \$35{,}000.$$

Example 4: (Amount that Provides Given Payments and Given Balloon).   A lender can charge 8% interest. He wants to receive monthly payments of $100 for 3 years. He then wants to receive a balloon payment of $2,000. How large must the loan be?

Solution: In this example,

$$r = 8\%, \ q = 12, \ g = \$100, \ n = 3, \ j = 36, \ \text{and} \ B_j = \$2,000.$$

From Table 1,

$$a(r,j,q) = a(8,36,12) = 31.9118, \ \text{and}$$
$$c(r,j,q) = c(8,36,12) = 1.27024.$$

Now, using the third formula,

$$p = \$100 \times 31.9118 + \$2,000/1.27024$$
$$= \$3,191.18 + \$1,574.51$$
$$= \$4,765.69.$$

6.9. Amount of Principal and Interest in Each Payment

Constant periodic payments that amortize a loan consist of an amount (interest) that pays the interest on the loan balance and an amount (principal) that is subtracted from the loan balance (to reduce it further). From the lender's point of view, the interest portion is the return *on* his investment. It is the previous balance multiplied by the periodic interest rate. It decreases with time because the principal portion of the payment is continually reducing the balance. The principal portion is the return *of* his investment.* The figure shows the ratio of interest-to-principal for a 30 year loan with monthly payments. The higher the interest rate, the larger is the ratio of interest-to-principal.

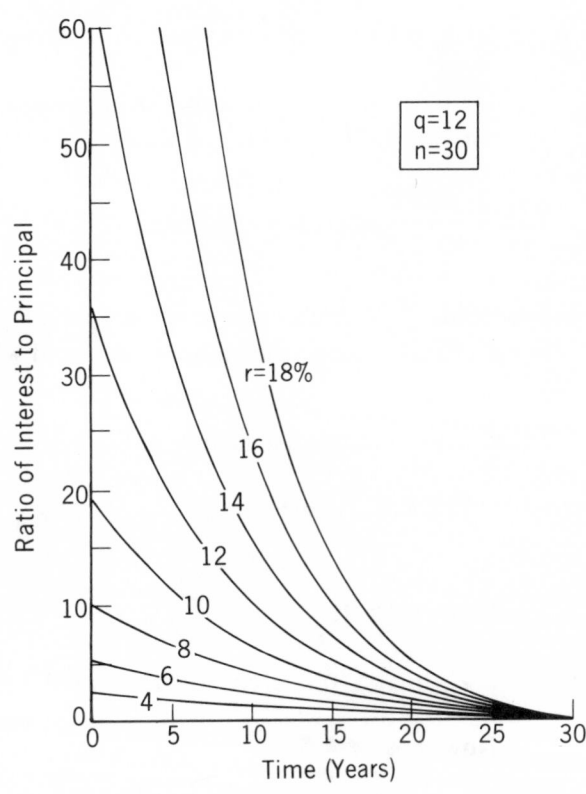

---

*The recapture rate is $p_j/B_{j-1} = 1/s(r, k+1, q)$

Formulas:

$$\mathbf{p_j} = \mathbf{g}/\mathbf{c(r,\ k+1,\ q)} = \left[\mathbf{g-(r/q)\cdot p}\right]\cdot\mathbf{c(r,\ j-1,\ q)} = \mathbf{B_{j-1}}/\mathbf{s(r,\ k+1,\ q)}$$
$$\mathbf{i_j} = \mathbf{g-p_j} = \mathbf{(r/q)\cdot g\cdot a(r,\ k+1,\ q)} = \mathbf{(r/q)\cdot B_{j-1}}$$
$$= \mathbf{g-\left[g-(r/q)\cdot p\right]\cdot c(r,\ j-1,\ q)}$$

$$\frac{\mathbf{i_j}}{\mathbf{p_j}} = \mathbf{c(r,k+1,q)} - 1$$

where

p_j = amount of the jth payment that is principal
i_j = amount of the jth payment that is interest
g = amount of each payment
B_{j-1} = balance remaining after $j-1$ payments
k = remaining number of periods
r = annual interest rate, expressed as a decimal
n = number of years
q = number of periods per year
m = nq = total number of periods
$a(r,k+1,q)$ = present value of an annuity of 1
$c(r,j-1,q)$
$c(r,k+1,q)$ = amount of 1 at compound interest
$s(r,k+1,q)$ = amount of an annuity of 1.

Table: Find $c(r,k+1,q)$, $c(r,j-1,q)$, $s(r,k+1,q)$ and $a(r,k+1,q)$ in Table 1.

Example: A 5 year loan at 8% has monthly payments of $324.43. What is the ratio of interest to principal on the 38th payment, and what is the amount of principal and interest?

Solution: In this example,

$$n = 5,\ r = 8\%,\ q = 12,\ g = \$324.43,\ m = nq = 60,$$
$$j = 38,\ \text{and}\ k = m - j = 22.$$

From Table 1,

$$c(r,k+1,q) = c(8,23,12) = 1.165120.$$

Now,

$$\frac{i_{38}}{p_{38}} = 1.165120 - 1 = .165120.$$

Notice from the formula that this ratio is independent of the amount of periodic payment and the term. Now, from the formula, the principal is

$$p_{38} = \$324.43/1.165120 = \$278.45,$$

and the interest is

$$i_{38} = \$324.43 - \$278.45 = \$45.98.$$

6.10.   Amount of Interest

Part of each payment is the interest owed on the previous remaining balance. The interest portion on each payment decreases in proportion to the balance. The following formulas can be used to compute the accumulating amount of interest.

Formulas:

$$I_j = g \cdot \left[j + a(r,k,q) - a(r,m,q) \right]$$
$$= g \cdot j - \left[g - (r/q) \cdot p \right] \cdot s(r,j,q) = g \cdot j - E_j{}^*$$

where

I_j = total amount of interest paid through the jth payment period
g = amount of each periodic payment
r = annual interest rate
q = number of periods per year
k = number of periods remaining
n = number of years
m = nq = total number of periods
p = amount of the loan
E_j = equity accumulated through the jth period
$a(r,k,q)$
    and
$a(r,m,q)$ = present value of an annuity of 1 (note: $a(r,0,q) = 0$)
$s(r,j,q)$ = amount of an annuity of 1

Table: Find $a(r,k,q)$, $a(r,m,q)$, and $s(r,j,q)$ in Table 1.

Example 1: (Interest from Beginning).   A 5 year loan at 8% interest has monthly payments of $324.43. How much total interest has been paid after the 40th payment? What is the total amount of interest paid on the loan at its term?

---

*At the term, j = m, k = 0, and a(r,k,q) = 0.

Finance: Amortized Loans

Solution: In this example,

$$n = 5, r = 8\%, q = 12, g = \$324.43, m = nq = 60, \text{ and } j = 40.$$

Hence there are $k = m - j = 20$ remaining periods.
From Table 1,

$$a(r,m,q) = a(8,60,12) = 49.31843, \text{ and}$$
$$a(r,k,q) = a(8,20,12) = 18.66590.$$

Now, using the first of the three formulas,

$$I_{40} = \$324.43 \left[40 + 18.66590 - 49.31843\right]$$
$$= \$324.43 \times 9.34747$$
$$= \$3,032.60.$$

The total amount of interest paid on a loan at its term is

$$I_m = g \cdot \left[m - a(r,m,q)\right].^*$$

In this example,

$$I_m = I_{60} = \$324.43 \times (60 - 49.31843)$$
$$= \$324.43 \times 10.68157$$
$$= \$3,465.42.$$

Example 2: (Interest Between Periods). A 5 year loan at 8% interest has monthly payments of \$324.43. How much interest must be paid between the 23rd and 40th payments?

Solution: This is the same loan as in Example 1. To find the interest paid between the 23rd and 40th payments, we must find I_{23} and I_{40}; then we simply evaluate $I_{40} - I_{23}$. From Example 1,

$$I_{40} = \$3,032.60.$$

Proceeding in the same way,

$$I_{23} = \$2,068.31.$$

Now, the interest paid between these periods is

$$I_{40} - I_{23} = \$3,032.60 - \$2,068.31$$
$$= \$964.29.$$

---

*This results from the basic formula since $a(r,0,q) = 0$.

6.11.   Loan Equity and Balance

The principal portion of each payment is subtracted from the previous balance, thus reducing it further. The equity is the difference between the original loan amount and the present balance.

Figure 6-D shows how equity is accumulated for a 30 year loan with monthly payments. Equity is accumulated relatively faster for loans with lower interest rates. For instance, the 4% loan is 50% equity after 231 payments but the 18% loan requires 314 payments before it is 50% equity.

Using an 8% interest loan with monthly payments, Figure 6-E shows that equity is accumulated relatively faster for loans with shorter terms. For instance, a 5 year loan is 50% equity when it is 55% through its term, but a 40 year loan must be 80% through its term before it is 50% equity.

Figure 6-F shows the balance for each $1 of monthly payment. To obtain a quick estimate of the balance, multiply the value obtained from the figure by the monthly payment. The following formulas can be used to find the exact balance and equity.*

Formulas:

$$B_j = g \cdot a(r,k,q) = p \cdot \frac{a(r,k,q)}{a(r,m,q)} = p - E_j$$

$$= p \cdot c(r,j,q) - g \cdot s(r,j,q)$$

$$E_j = p - g \cdot a(r,k,q) = p \cdot \frac{s(r,j,q)}{s(r,m,q)} = p - B_j$$

$$= \left[g - (r/q) \cdot p \right] \cdot s(r,j,q) = p \cdot \left(\frac{z_m - r}{q} \right) \cdot s(r,j,q)$$

where

B_j = balance after j payments
E_j = equity after j payments
g = amount of each periodic payment
p = amount of the loan
r = annual interest rate, expressed as a decimal
z_m = annual mortgage constant (mortgage capitalization rate)

---

*From the mortgagee's point of view, the balance is the reversion of his investment. This can be verified from the rate of return formula (Section 7.9 or 8.7).

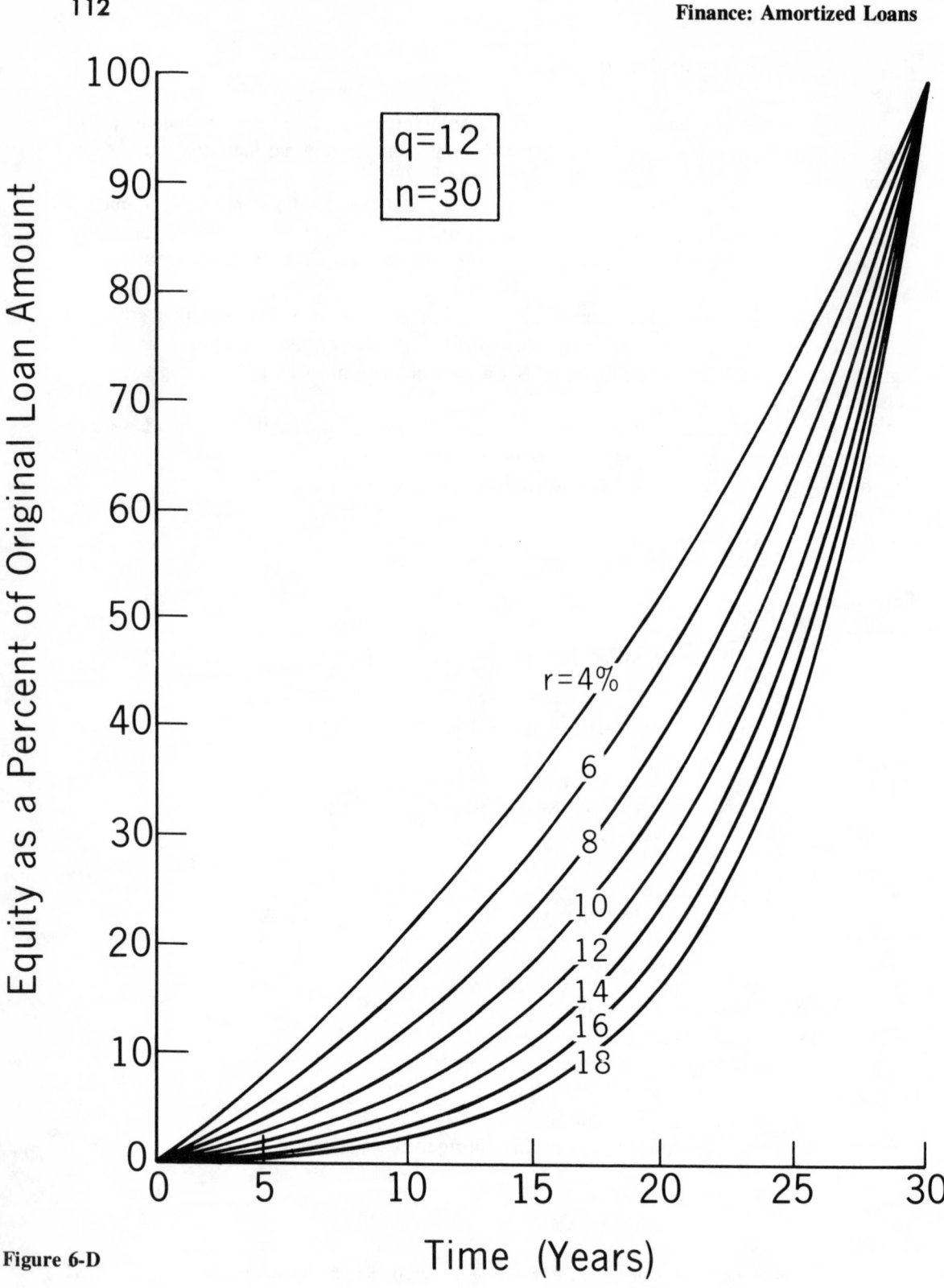

Figure 6-D

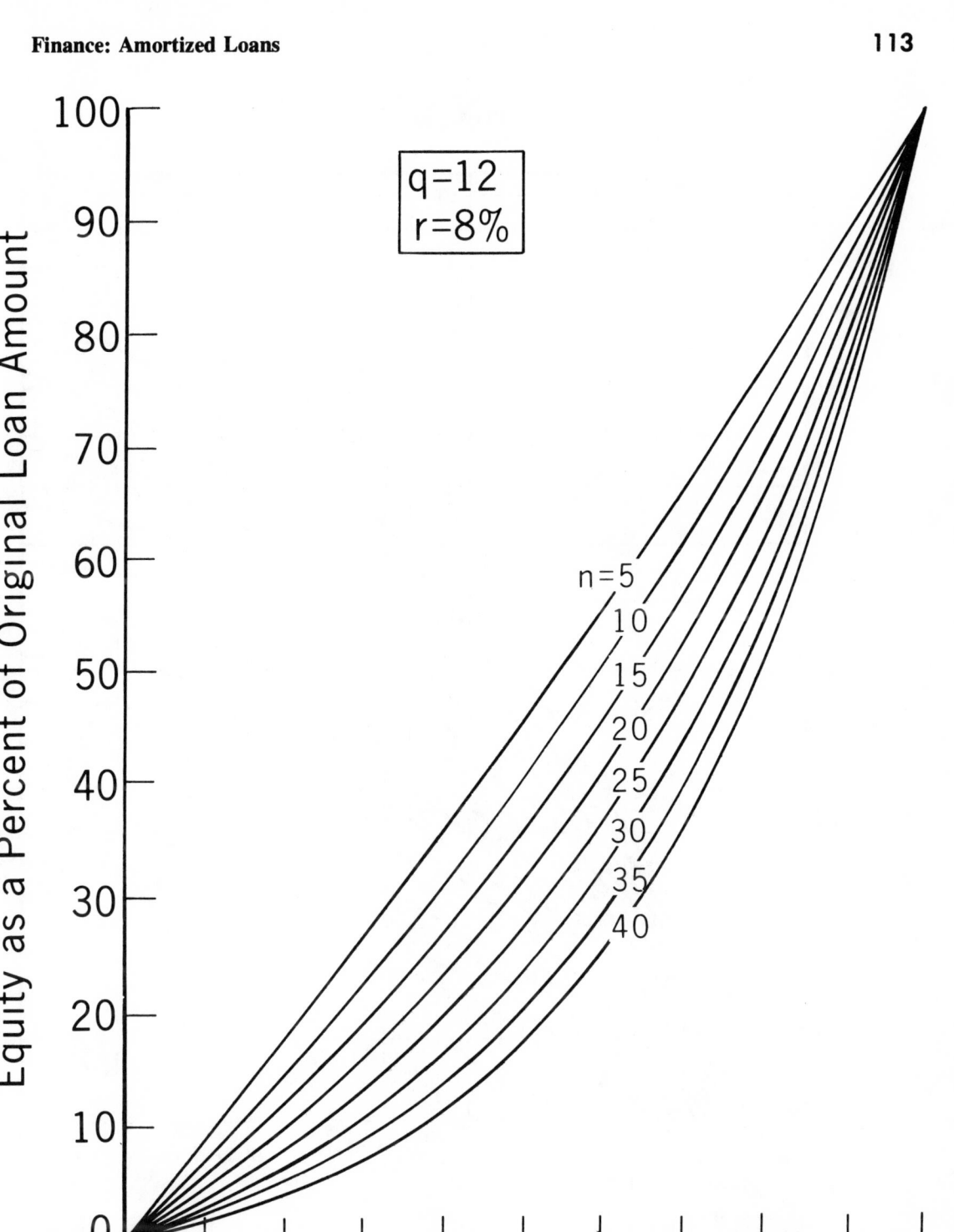

Figure 6-E

114 **Finance: Amortized Loans**

LOAN BALANCE

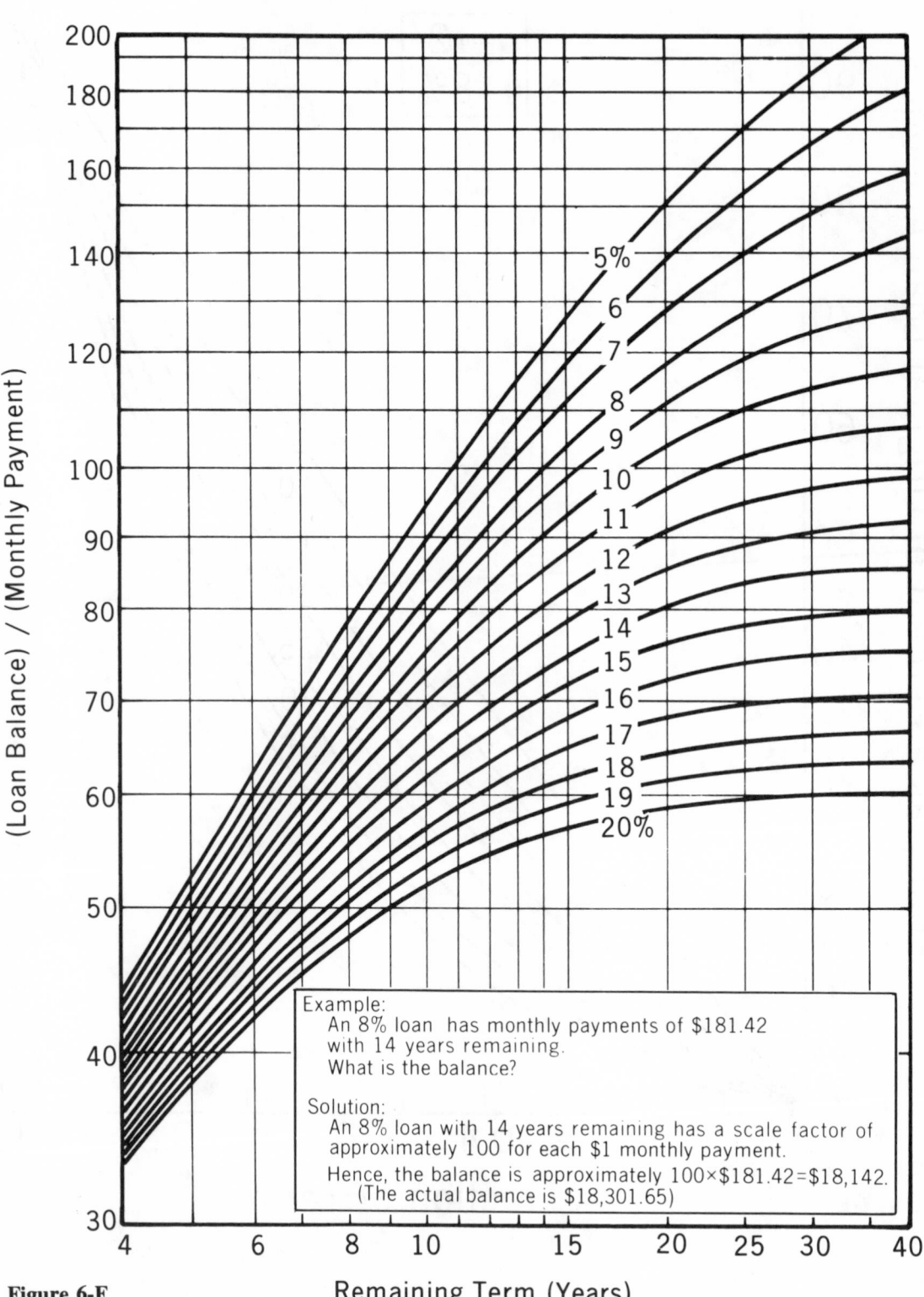

Figure 6-F

Remaining Term (Years)

$$n = \text{number of years}$$
$$q = \text{number of periods per year}$$
$$m = nq = \text{total number of periods}$$
$$j = \text{number of periods used}$$
$$k = \text{number of periods remaining } (m = j + k)$$

$$a(r,k,q),$$
$$a(r,m,q) = \text{present value of an annuity of 1}$$
$$s(r,j,q),$$
$$s(r,m,q) = \text{amount of an annuity of 1}$$
$$c(r,j,q) = \text{amount of 1 at compound interest}$$

Table: Find $a(r,k,q)$, $a(r,m,q)$, $s(r,j,q)$, $s(r,m,q)$, and $c(r,j,q)$ in Table 1.

Example 1: (Finding the Balance).   A 9% loan has monthly payments of $419.60. If there are 97 remaining payments, what is the balance?*

Solution: In this example,

$$r = 9\%, q = 12, g = \$419.60, \text{ and } k = 97.$$

Due to the information given, we must use the first formula. From Table 1,

$$a(r,k,q) = a(9,97,12) = 68.74287$$

Now, the balance is

$$B_j = \$419.60 \times 68.74287 = \$28{,}846.95.$$

This solution could have been estimated readily from Figure 6-F.

Example 2: (Finding the Equity).   A $50,000 loan at 9% interest has monthly payments of $419.60. What is the equity after 21 payments?**

Solution: In this example,

$$p = \$50{,}000, r = 9\%, q = 12, g = \$419.60, \text{ and } j = 21.$$

---

*Notice that in this example, neither the loan amount nor the term is required to determine the balance.

**Notice that the term of the loan is not given. However, the equity can still be determined by using the fourth formula. The term can be determined by finding, in Table 1, the value of j for which

$$s(r,j,q) = \frac{1}{(g/p) - (r/q)}.$$ In the above example, the term has 300 periods.

Due to the information given, we must use the fourth formula. From Table 1,

$$s(r,j,q) = s(9,21,12) = 22.65240.$$

Now,

$$\begin{aligned}
E_j = E_{21} &= \big[\$419.60 - (.09/12)\cdot\$50,000\big] \times 22.65240 \\
&= (\$419.60 - \$375.00) \times 22.65240 \\
&= \$44.60 \times 22.65240 \\
&= \$1,010.30.
\end{aligned}$$

6.12.   Balloon Payments

A balloon payment is generally a single payment equal to the loan balance. A balloon payment is required when a loan is amortized over a given period of time, but the balance is due in a single payment prior to that time.

Formulas:

$$B_j = p\cdot c(r,j,q) - g\cdot s(r,j,q) = g\cdot a(r,k,q)^*$$

where

j = payment period in which balloon payment is due
B_j = amount of balloon payment (loan balance) at the jth payment
g = amount of the periodic payment
r = annual interest rate
q = number of payment periods per year
n = number of years
$m = nq$ = number of payment periods required for amortization
$k = m - j$
p = amount of the loan
$a(r,k,q)$ = present value of an annuity of 1
$s(r,j,q)$ = amount of an annuity of 1
$c(r,j,q)$ = amount of 1 at compound interest

Table: Find $s(r,j,q)$, $a(r,k,q)$, and $c(r,j,q)$ in Table 1.

Example: A loan of \$15,000 at 9% has monthly payments of \$190.03. The balance is due in a single (balloon) payment after five years. What is the amount of the balloon payment?**

---

*Notice that, even though the term required for regular amortization might not be known, the balloon payment can be determined from the first formula.

**It is assumed that the last payment will contain the regular monthly payment of \$190.03 plus the balloon payment of \$9,152.37 (determined in the solution).

Solution: In this example,

$$p = \$15{,}000, \ r = 9\%, \ q = 12, \ g = \$190.03, \text{ and } j = 5 \times 12 = 60.$$

The type of information given suggests using the first formula. From Table 1,

$$s(r,j,q) = s(9,60,12) = 75.42414, \text{ and}$$
$$c(r,j,q) = c(9,60,12) = 1.565681.$$

Now,

$$\begin{aligned} B_j = B_{60} &= \$15{,}000 \times 1.565681 - \$190.03 \times 75.42414 \\ &= \$23{,}485.22 - \$14{,}332.85 \\ &= \$9{,}152.37. \end{aligned}$$

6.13. Refinancing

There are many reasons why a property owner might wish to obtain new financing. If he wishes to lower his payments, the profitability of refinancing can be evaluated*: Periodic payments constitute an annuity. Refinancing to obtain lower payments is profitable if the difference between the present values of the two annuities (existing payment and new payment) exceeds the costs of prepaying the existing loan and obtaining the new loan.

Formula:

$$R = g \cdot a(r,k,q) - g' \cdot a(r,m',q')$$

where

R = difference in the present value of the annuities created by the existing and new loans

g, g' = amount of periodic payment of the existing and new loans, respectively

r = present annual interest rate (not mortgage interest rate, but rate of return currently expected on investments. See Section 7.5)

k = number of payments remaining on the existing loan

m' = total number of payments on new loan

q, q' = number of periods per year for the existing and new loans, respectively

$a(r,k,q),$
$a(r,m',q')$ = the present value of an annuity of 1

---

*Combinations of interest rates and terms that provide a given payment can be found in Section 6.4.

Table: Find a(r,k,q) and a(r,m′,q′) in Table 1.

Example: Mr. Lynch has an existing loan of $21,000 at 7% for 30 years. His monthly payments are $139.71, and now, after 5 years, his loan balance is $19,768. Mr. Lynch obtains a new loan of $19,768 at 6% for 27 years. The monthly payment is $123.35, but the cost of obtaining the new loan is $500. Money is presently worth 5%. Is it profitable to obtain the new loan?

Solution: We will evaluate R since Mr. Lynch's refinancing is profitable if R > $500. In this example,

$$g = \$139.71, \; g' = \$123.35, \; r = 5\%, \; q = 12,$$
$$k = (30 - 5) \times q = 300, \; q' = 12, \; \text{and} \; m' = 27 \times q' = 324.$$

From Table 1,

$$a(r,k,q) = a(5,300,12) = 171.0600, \; \text{and}$$
$$a(r,m',q') = a(5,324,12) = 177.6076.$$

Now,

$$R = \$139.71 \times 171.0600 - \$123.35 \times 177.6076$$
$$= \$23,898.79 - \$21,907.90$$
$$= \$1,990.89.$$

Hence, refinancing will profit Mr. Lynch by $1,990.89 − $500 = $1,490.89. Notice, in this example, he will make 24 more payments by refinancing.

6.14.   Wrap-Around Mortgage

The wrap-around mortgage is a mortgage whose amount exceeds the balance on the existing first mortgage. It resembles a first mortgage due to the amount of its face value (often 70-75% of the present value of the property). However, it is a second mortgage because it does not replace the existing first mortgage.

A wrap-around mortgage might be considered desirable by a borrower when the present value of his property is large compared to the balance of his first mortgage. He receives from the lender the difference between the face value of the wrap-around mortgage and the balance of the first mortgage. However, he pays interest on the balance of the wrap-around mortgage.

The borrower benefits from the wrap-around mortgage because it frees some or all of his equity, and it can increase his rate of return on the first mortgage (i.e., the balance is now small compared to the original loan amount, but the amount of debt service remains the same).

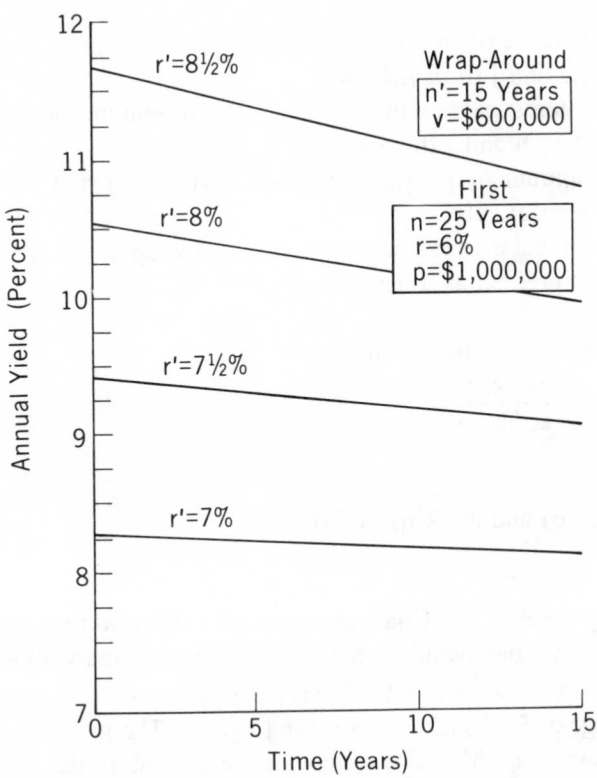

The lender of the wrap-around mortgage can benefit because he receives interest on an amount larger than he actually lends. Hence, his yield would be larger than with customary financing (provided only that the interest rate on the wrap-around mortgage is larger than the interest rate on the first mortgage). The figure illustrates the following example. It shows that the yield declines with time. For this reason, lenders of wrap-around mortgages are not adverse to prepayment.

Formulas:

$$v = p' - B_j = p' - g \cdot a(r,k,q)$$

$$y_j' = q \cdot \frac{i_{j+1}' - i_{j+1}}{B_{j'}' - B_j} = r' \cdot \frac{1 - \left(\frac{r}{r'}\right) \cdot w}{1 - w}$$

where

v = amount of cash received by the borrower

p, p' = face value of the first and wrap-around mortgage, respectively

y_j' = annual yield on the wrap-around mortgage during its jth payment period

j, j' = present payment periods of the first and wrap-around mortgage, respectively.

k, k' = remaining periods of the first and wrap-around mortgage, respectively

n, n' = number of years in the term of the first and wrap-around mortgage, respectively

$$q \;=\; \text{number of periods per year*}$$

$B_j, B'_{j'} \;=\;$ balance of the first and wrap-around mortgage, respectively, after their jth and j'th payments

$i_{j+1}, i'_{j'+1} \;=\;$ interest paid on the first and wrap-around mortgage, respectively, during the jth and j'th payments

$g, g' \;=\;$ amount of periodic payment on the first and wrap-around mortgage, respectively

$r, r' \;=\;$ annual interest rate on the first and wrap-around mortgage, respectively, expressed as a decimal

$a(r,k,q),$
$a(r',k',q) \;=\;$ present value of an annuity of 1

$$w \;=\; \frac{g \cdot a(r,k,q)}{g' \cdot a(r',k',q)}$$

Table: Find $a(r,k,q)$ and $a(r',k',q)$ in Table 1.

Example: Ten years ago Mr. Chase obtained a $1,000,000 first mortgage at 6% with a 25 year term. His monthly payments are $6,443. Now the fair market value of his property is $1,818.025, and his loan balance is $763,519. An insurance company grants him a 75% wrap-around mortgage of $1,363,519 at 8% for 15 years. The monthly payment is $13,030. Now, how much cash does Mr. Chase receive, and what is the yield to the insurance company initially and also at the last payment period?

Solution: In this example,

$$r = 6\%, \; q = 12, \; j = 10 \times q = 120, \; k = 12 \times 15 = 180,$$
$$g = \$6,443, \; B_{120} = \$763,519, \; p' = \$1,363,519,$$
$$r' = 8\%, \; k' = 15 \times q = 180, \; \text{and} \; g' = \$13,030.$$

From the first formula, Mr. Chase receives cash amounting to

$$v = p' - B_{120} = \$1,363,519 - \$763,519$$
$$= \$600,000.$$

To compute the initial yield to the insurance company, use the second yield formula. From Table 1,

$$a(r,k,q) = a(6,180,12) = 118.50351, \text{ and}$$
$$a(r',k',q) = a(8,180,12) = 104.64059.$$

---

*Must be the same for both mortgages in order to compute a yield during each period.

Now, evaluate

$$w = \frac{\$6{,}443 \times 118.50351}{\$13{,}030 \times 104.64059} = \frac{\$763{,}518.11}{\$1{,}363{,}466.80} = .559983.$$

The initial yield to the insurance company is

$$y_0 = .08 \times \left[\frac{1 - \left(\frac{.06}{.08}\right) \times .559983}{1 - .559983} \right] = .08 \times \left(\frac{.580013}{.440017}\right)$$
$$= .1054 = 10.54\%.$$

To determine the final yield (at the term), find

$$a(r,k,q) = a(6,1,12) = .0995025, \text{ and}$$
$$a(r',k',q) = a(8,1,12) = .0993377.$$

Now,

$$w = \frac{\$6{,}443 \times .0995025}{\$13{,}030 \times .0993377} = \frac{\$641.0946}{\$1{,}294.3702} = .49529,$$

and the final yield is

$$y_{180} = .08 \times \left[\frac{1 - \left(\frac{.06}{.08}\right) \times .49529}{1 - .49529} \right] = .08\left(\frac{.62853}{.50471}\right)$$
$$= .0996 = 9.96\%.$$

6.15. Amortization Using a Sinking Fund

Sometimes a borrower will make constant payments in the following manner: The interest portion of each payment pays the interest on the amount borrowed, but the principal portion, instead of directly reducing the amount of principal, is deposited in an interest-bearing (sinking) fund. When the amount of the fund equals the amount borrowed, the loan is paid.

Formulas:

$$i_j = p \cdot \left(\frac{r}{q}\right)$$
$$p_j = g - i_j = p \cdot s(r',t,q')/s(r',m',q')$$

where

i_j = interest portion of the jth payment*

p_j = principal portion of the jth payment

g = $i_j + p_j$ = amount of periodic payment

p = amount borrowed

r, r' = interest rate of loan and sinking fund, respectively

q, q' = number of periods per year for loan and sinking fund, respectively

t = q'/q

m, m' = total number of periods for the loan and sinking fund, respectively

Table: Find $s(r', t, q')$ and $s(r', m', q')$ in Table 1.

Example: Mr. Payne borrowed $52,185 from a building and loan association at 8% annual interest. His quarterly payments of $5,043.70 pay the interest on the loan, and the remainder is deposited into a sinking fund on which dividends are paid at the rate of 6% compounded monthly. When the amount of the fund equals the amount borrowed, the loan is considered to be paid. (a) What is the term of the sinking fund? (b) How much interest must Mr. Payne pay by the sinking fund method of amortization? (c) How much interest would he have paid by regular amortization?

Solution: In this example,

$$p = \$52,185, \ r = 8\%, \ q = 4, \ g = \$5,043.70,$$
$$r' = 6\%, \ q' = 12, \text{ and } t = q'/q = 3.$$

Since the principal is not reduced, the interest portion of the payment is constant:

$$i_j = p \cdot \left(\frac{r}{q}\right) = \$52,185 \times \left(\frac{.08}{4}\right) = \$1,043.70$$

Consequently, the principal portion is also constant:

$$p_j = g - i_j = \$5,043.70 - \$1,043.70 = \$4,000$$

(a) The deposits are made at the end of each period, so they constitute an ordinary annuity. The term of the sinking fund is the term of the amount of the ordinary annuity (see the first formula in Section 4.15):

$$m' = \frac{\log\left[1 + (r'/q') \cdot (p/p_j) \cdot s(r', t, q')\right]}{\log(1 + r'/q')}$$

---

*When the principal reduces the balance directly (as in the other loans discussed in this chapter) the interest and principal vary with the payment period (Section 6.9). With the sinking fund method, both remain constant.

$$= \frac{\log\left[1 + (.06/12)\cdot(\$52,185/\$4,000) \times 3.01503\right]}{\log(1 + .06/12)}$$

$$= \frac{\log(1.1966744)}{\log(1.005)} = \frac{.077976}{.002166}$$

$$= 36 \text{ (i.e., 36 monthly periods of the sinking fund} =$$
$$12 \text{ quarterly periods of the loan} = 3 \text{ years)}$$

(b) The total amount of interest paid on the loan is

$$I_{36} = i_j \cdot m = \$1,043.70 \times 12 = \$12,524.40.$$

The total amount of interest paid to Mr. Payne by the sinking fund is

$$p - q' \cdot p_j = \$52,185 - 12 \times \$4,000 = \$4,185.$$

Hence, the net amount of interest paid by the sinking fund method of amortization is

$$\$12,524.40 - \$4,185.00 = \$8,339.40.$$

(c) To determine the total amount of interest that would have been paid by regular amortization, we must first find the term required for regular amortization. From Section 6.7, $m = 11.7$ (say, $m = 12$).
Now, from Section 6.10,

$$I_m = g\cdot\left[m - a(r,m,q)\right].$$

From Table 1,

$$a(r,m,q) = a(8,12,4) = 10.57534.$$

Now, the amount of interest that would have been paid by regular amortization is

$$I_{12} = \$5,043.70 \times (12 - 10.57534)$$
$$= \$7,185.56.$$

6.16.   Constant Principal Payments

The amortization of a loan is usually accomplished by constant payments (payments in which the interest and the principal portions vary but always total the same amount).

In any amortized loan, the periodic payment (1) must at least pay the interest on the balance, and (2) the sum of the principal portions of the payments must equal the amount borrowed. Of course, the second criterion can be met in an infinite number of ways.

One type of non-constant payment is a payment that includes interest on the balance (as in constant payment amortization), but the principal portion of each payment is the same*. Amortization by constant principal payments and constant payments are compared in the figures. The monthly payments, monthly interest, and accumulated interest are compared in Figures 6-G, 6-H, and 6-I, respectively. Less interest is paid on a constant principal loan because the balance is reduced faster.

Formulas:

$$p_j = \frac{p}{m}$$

$$i_j = \frac{p}{m} \cdot \left(\frac{r}{q}\right) \cdot (m - j + 1)$$

$$g_j = i_j + p_j$$

$$= \frac{p}{m} \cdot$$

$$\left[\left(\frac{r}{q}\right) \cdot (m - j + 1) + 1\right]$$

$$g' = \frac{p}{m} \cdot \frac{r}{q}$$

$$G_j = j \cdot \left(\frac{p}{m}\right) \cdot$$

$$\left[\left(\frac{r}{q}\right) \cdot \left(\frac{2m - j + 1}{2}\right) + 1\right]$$

$$I_j = j \cdot \left(\frac{p}{m}\right) \cdot \left(\frac{r}{q}\right) \cdot$$

$$\left(\frac{2m - j + 1}{2}\right) **$$

$$B_j = \frac{p}{m} \cdot (m - j)$$

$$E = j \cdot \frac{p}{m}$$

where

p = amount of the loan
r = annual interest rate, expressed as a decimal
q = number of periods per year
n = number of years
m = nq = total number of payments
j = jth payment period
p_j = amount of the jth principal payment
i_j = amount of the jth interest payment
g_j = amount of the jth payment
g' = decrease in each payment relative to the previous one
G_j = total payment through the jth period
I_j = total interest paid through the jth period
B_j = balance after the jth period
E_j = equity after the jth period

---

*If the payment is considered to be an annuity (a variable annuity of the linear type), its present value and amount can be determined from Sections 4.6 and 4.11, respectively.

**The total interest paid on a constant principal loan is

$$I_m = p \cdot \left(\frac{r}{q}\right) \cdot \left(\frac{m + 1}{2}\right)$$

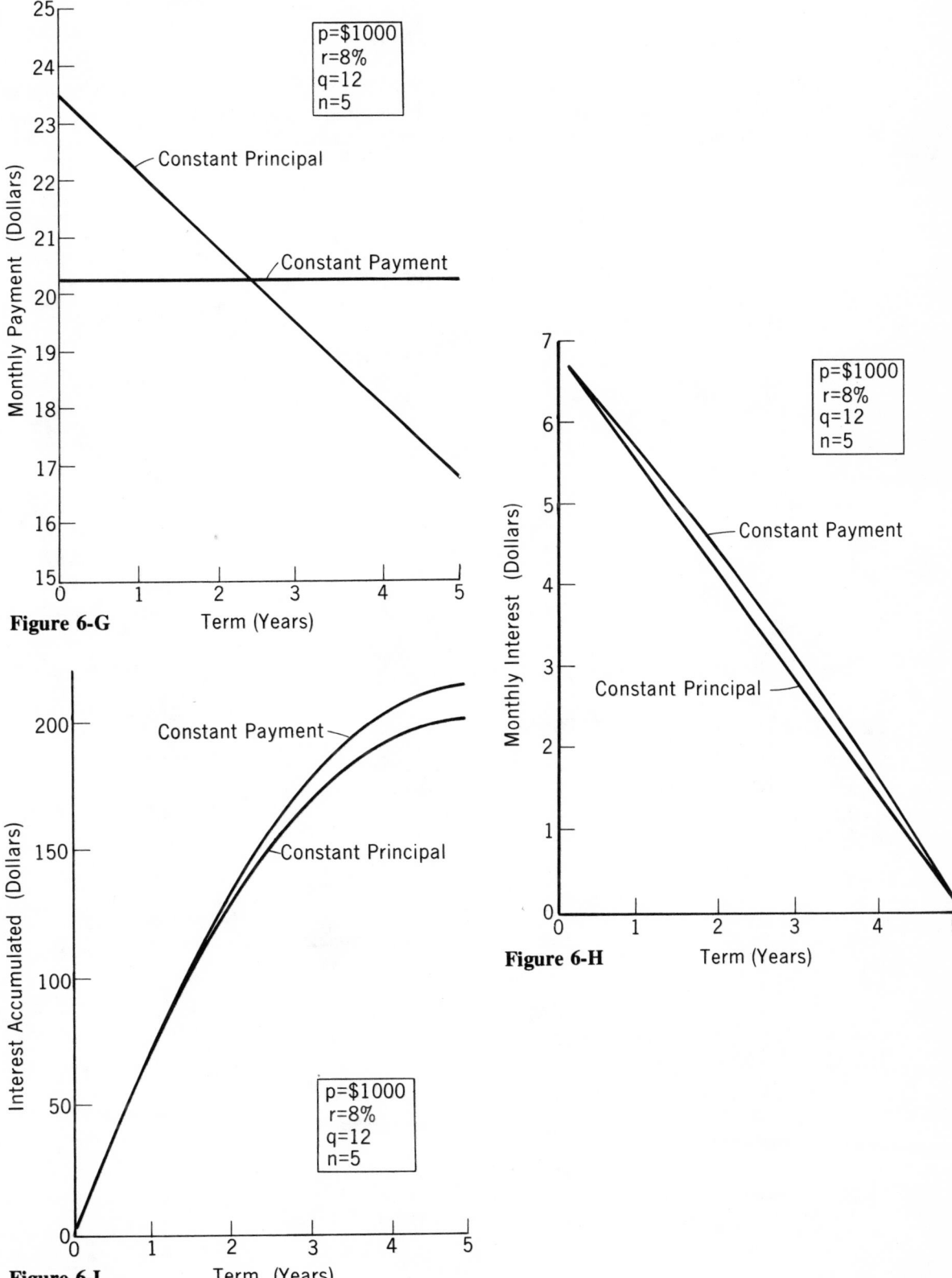

Figure 6-G

Figure 6-H

Figure 6-I

Table: none

Example: Consider a $1,000 constant principal loan at 8% that is amortized by monthly payments over 5 years. What is the amount of the 15th payment, and what is the total interest that has been paid through that payment?

Solution: In this example,

$$p = \$1,000, \ r = 8\%, \ q = 12, \ n = 5, \text{ and } m = nq = 60.$$

Now, the amount of the 15th payment is

$$g_j = \frac{p}{m} \cdot \left[\left(\frac{r}{q}\right) \cdot (m - j + 1) + 1 \right]$$

$$g_{15} = \frac{\$1,000}{60} \cdot \left[\left(\frac{.08}{12}\right) \cdot (60 - 15 + 1) + 1 \right]$$

$$= \$16.67 \left[.006667 \times (46) + 1 \right]$$

$$= \$16.67 \times 1.30667$$

$$= \$21.78.$$

The total interest paid through this payment is

$$I_j = j \cdot \left(\frac{p}{m}\right) \cdot \left(\frac{r}{q}\right) \ \left(\frac{2m - j + 1}{2}\right),$$

or

$$I_{15} = 15 \times \$16.67 \times .006667 \left(\frac{120 - 15 + 1}{2}\right)$$

$$= 1.6667 \times 53$$
$$= \$88.35.$$

INVESTMENTS AND VALUATION: RATES OF RETURN

This chapter explores the measures of value for real estate investments. It describes the income, the way in which it is distributed, and the rate at which it is distributed to investors.

The productive factors of real estate are labor, capital, entrepreneurship, and real estate. Real estate is fixed; however, labor, capital, and entrepreneurship are not, and they will relocate if their needs are not served.

The gross income that is produced by a real estate investment will be distributed first to labor (operating expenses), then to capital (debt service), and finally to entrepreneurship (cash flow). Each of these productive factors has absorbed some risk. Since the entrepreneur is served last, his risk is correspondingly greatest and his expected return must also be greatest.

Capitalization is the process through which income is converted to capital. The rate of capitalization provides a measure of the value of an investment. Whereas this chapter deals with the rate of return, Chapter 8 deals with value and assumes the rate of return is known.

Sinking funds and the present value of annuities are used extensively in this chapter. These concepts are discussed fully in Chapter 4.

7.1. Effective Gross Income

The effective gross income is the potential gross income less the possible vacancies and collection losses. The annual effective gross income is often used as a measure of income property value (Section 7.2).

Formula:

$$y = x_p + w = u \cdot \sum_{i=1}^{k} n_i \cdot (1 - a_i)(1 - c_i) \cdot y_i$$

where

y = annual effective gross income of the property
x_p = annual net operating income
w = annual operating expenses*
u = number of rental periods per year
y_i = amount of rent per period from the ith type of unit
n_i = number of rental units of the ith type
a_i = vacancy rate of the ith type of unit, expressed as a decimal
c_i = collection loss rate of the ith type of unit, expressed as a decimal
k = number of different types of units

Table: none

Example 1:   A 100 unit apartment building has annual net operating income of $120,820.00 and annual operating expenses of $60,411.20. What is the annual effective gross income?

Solution: In this example,

$$x_p = \$120,820.00, \text{ and } w = \$60,411.20.$$

Hence, the annual effective gross income is

$$\begin{aligned} y &= \$120,820.00 + \$60,411.20 \\ &= \$181,231.20. \end{aligned}$$

Example 2:   A 100 unit apartment building has 60 one-bedroom units and 40 two-bedroom units. The one-bedroom units rent for $150/mo., experience a 5% vacancy and a 6% collection loss. The two-bedroom units rent for $200/mo., experience an 8% vacancy and a 4% collection loss. What is the annual effective gross income?

Solution: In this example,

$$k = 2, n_1 = 60, n_2 = 40, y_1 = \$150, u = 12,$$
$$a_1 = .05, c_1 = .06, y_2 = \$200, a_2 = .08, \text{ and } c_2 = .04.$$

---

*The operating ratio is w/y.

Now,

$$
\begin{aligned}
y &= u \cdot \left[n_1 \cdot (1 - a_1)(1 - c_1) \cdot y_1 + n_2 \cdot (1 - a_2)(1 - c_2) \cdot y_2 \right] \\
  &= 12 \times \left[60 \cdot (1 - .05)(1 - .06) \times \$150 + 40 \times (1 - .08)(1 - .04) \times \$200 \right] \\
  &= 12 \cdot (\$8,037.00 + \$7,065.60) = 12 \times \$15,102.60 \\
  &= \$181,231.20.
\end{aligned}
$$

The annual potential gross income (achieved when $a_1 = c_1 = a_2 = c_2 = 0$) is $204,000. Hence, the effective gross income is 88.84% of the potential gross income.

7.2.   Gross Income Multiplier

The gross income multiplier is often the first measure of value for income property. This is a very rough measure because it doesn't account for the operating expenses. However, it is widely used because of its simplicity.

Formula:

$$
g = \frac{v_p}{y}
$$

where

g = gross income multiplier
v_p = present value or sale price of property
y = annual effective gross income

Table: none

Example: A 100 unit apartment complex is priced at $864,000. If the annual effective gross income is $144,000, what is the gross income multiplier?

Solution: In this example,

$$
v_p = \$864,000, \text{ and } y = \$144,000.
$$

Hence,

$$
g = \frac{\$864,000}{\$144,000} = 6.
$$

That is, the apartment is priced at "6 times gross."

7.3.   Net Operating Income

The annual net operating income is the annual effective gross income less the annual operating expenses. Operating expenses are the regularly recurring expenses such as taxes, management, maintenance, insurance, and utilities*.

The net operating income must first service debt. The remainder is available to the equity investor as cash flow. The net operating income is used with the property capitalization rate (Section 7.7) to determine the present value of income property.

Formula:

$$x_p = x_m + x_e = y - w$$

where

x_p = annual net operating income
x_m = annual debt service
x_e = annual cash flow
y = annual effective gross income (Section 7.1)
w = annual operating expenses**

Table: none

Example: A 20 unit apartment building has an annual effective gross income of $34,800. The annual taxes, insurance, utilities, and maintenance are $4,187, $506, $4,096, and $2,800, respectively. What is the annual net operating income?

Solution: In this example,

y = $34,800 and
w = $4,187 + $506 + $4,096 + $2,800 = $11,589.

Now, the annual net operating income is

$$x_p = \$34,800 - \$11,589 = \$23,211.$$

---

*The net operating income does not include non-recurring proceeds such as those resulting from sale, trade, refinancing, etc.

**The operating ratio is w/y.

7.4.   Cash Flow

The annual cash flow is the annual net operating income less the annual debt service. The cash flow is that portion of the net operating income available to the equity investor to do as he wishes since all prior obligations (operating expenses and debt service) have been met.

If the cash flow is computed before tax, it is called cash throw-off, and if it is computed after tax it is called net spendable income.

Cash flow can be regarded as return *on* the investor's equity. Any excess cash flow can then be regarded as return *of* his equity. Cash flow is used with the equity capitalization rate (Section 7.7) to determine the present value of the equity interest.

Formula:

$$x_e = x_p - x_m$$

where

x_e = annual cash flow (before tax)
x_p = annual net operating income of property
x_m = annual debt service

Table: none

Example: A 20 unit apartment building has an annual net operating income of $23,211. The first mortgage has monthly payments of $1,456 and the second mortgage has monthly payments of $106. What is the annual cash flow?

Solution: The annual net operating income is

$$x_p = \$23,211,$$

and the annual debt service is

$$x_m = 12 \times \$1,456 + 12 \times \$106 = \$18,744.$$

Now, the annual cash flow is

$$x_e = x_p - x_m = \$23,211 - \$18,744 = \$4,467.$$

7.5.   Interest Rate

The interest rate is the rate of return *on* invested capital (the recapture rate is the rate of return *of* invested capital).

If the invested capital is a mortgage loan, the lender's investment is the loan amount. Each payment of an amortized loan consists of an amount of interest and an amount of principal. The interest is the return on his investment, and the principal is the return of his investment.

If the invested capital is the original equity (down payment) in an income property, the interest on capital consists of some or all of the cash flow. Any excess cash flow can be regarded as a return of capital.

The property value is the sum of the mortgage amount and the investor's equity. Hence, the property interest rate can be thought of as the weighted average of the mortgage interest rate and the equity interest rate. This rate is known as the band of investment interest rate*.

A second method of determining the property interest rate is the component rate. It is the sum of four interest rates and is more abstract than the band of investment rate.

The interest rate is used to capitalize the non-depreciable portion of an investment**. The capitalization rate, which is the sum of the interest rate and the recapture rate, is used to capitalize the entire investment (non-depreciable and depreciable).

Formulas:

$$r_p = \begin{cases} t \cdot r_m + (1 - t) \cdot r_e & \text{(band of investment rate)} \\ r_1 + r_2 + r_3 + r_4 & \text{(component rate)} \\ \dfrac{x_p}{v_p} - r_p' & \end{cases}$$

$$r_e = \frac{r_p - t \cdot r_m}{1 - t} \qquad \text{(if } t < 1\text{)}$$

where

r_m, r_e, r_p = interest rate on mortgage, equity, and property, respectively

v_m, v_p = present value of mortgage and property, respectively

$t = \dfrac{v_m}{v_p}$ = loan-to-value ratio, expressed as a decimal

x_p = annual net operating income

r_p' = property recapture rate

r_1 = safe rate (such as that paid on government bonds and savings deposits)

r_2 = risk rate (for possible declining income)

r_3 = non-liquidity rate (real property is not readily transferred)

r_4 = management rate (for clerical duties)

---

*The weighted average can be generalized to include second mortgages as well.

**Sections 8.9, 8.10, and 8.11 describe interest rates associated with the value of leases.

Table: none

Example 1: (Band of investment rate).   A 20 unit apartment is priced at $227,000. A $170,000 first mortgage is available at 9%. Investors in similar properties currently obtain an 11% return on their equity. What is the property interest rate?

Solution: In this example,

$$v_p = \$227{,}000, \ v_m = \$170{,}000, \ r_m = 9\%, \text{ and } r_e = 11\%.$$

The loan-to-value ratio is

$$t = \frac{\$170{,}000}{\$227{,}000} = .75.$$

Now, the property interest rate is

$$
\begin{aligned}
r_p &= .75 \times .09 + (1 - .75) \times .11 \\
&= .0675 + .0275 \\
&= .095 = 9.50\%.
\end{aligned}
$$

Example 2: (Component rate).   Mr. Meredith is interested in buying a 120 unit apartment building. The current interest rate on long-term government bonds is 5.25%. The risk that the apartment income will decline is thought to be 3.50%. The penalty associated with the lack of liquidity is regarded as 0.75%. The nuisance of clerical duties such as mortgage and bill payments is worth about 0.50%. What is the property interest rate?

Solution: In this example,

$$r_1 = 5.25\%, \ r_2 = 3.50\%, \ r_3 = 0.75\%, \text{ and } r_4 = 0.50\%.$$

Now, the property interest rate is

$$
\begin{aligned}
r_p &= .0525 + .0350 + .0075 + .0050 = .1000 \\
&= 10.00\%.
\end{aligned}
$$

7.6.   Recapture Rate

The recapture rate is the rate of return *of* invested capital (the interest rate is the rate of return *on* invested capital).

If the invested capital is a mortgage loan, the capital is recaptured through the principal portion of the payments.

The equity investor in income property is generally concerned that depreciation of the improvement will cause a loss of his investment. Hence, he should provide for recapture of this portion of his investment. Actual recapture can come through cash flow that exceeds that which provides the interest on equity, through loan amortization, and through possible appreciation of the property value.

Generally, the period of recapture is taken to be the remaining economic life of the improvement. Then it is assumed that recapture comes from the excess cash flow which is periodically deposited in an interest-bearing account (a sinking fund, Section 4.13). The rate, r, at which these deposits draw interest varies widely. If they are not deposited ($r = 0$), recapture is called straight-line. If they are deposited at the safe rate ($r = r_1$ from Section 7.5), recapture is according to the Hoskold method. If they are deposited at the property interest rate ($r = r_p$, from Section 7.5), recapture is according to the Inwood method.

Formulas:

$$r_m' = \frac{q}{s(r_m, m, q)}$$

$$r_p' = \begin{cases} \dfrac{1}{s(r,k,1)} \quad * \\[2ex] \dfrac{x_p}{v_p} - r_p \\[2ex] t \cdot r_m' + (1-t) \cdot r_e' \end{cases}$$

(Band of Investment Rate)

$$r_e' = \frac{r_p' - t \cdot r_m'}{1 - t} \qquad \text{(if } t < 1)$$

where

r_m', r_e', r_p' = recapture rate of the mortgage, equity, and depreciable portion of the property, respectively

r_m, r_e, r_p = interest rate on the mortgage, equity, and property, respectively

t = loan-to-value ratio, expressed as a decimal

v_p = present value of the property

x_p = annual net operating income

r = interest rate of the sinking fund (recapture is straight-line when $r = 0$, Hoskold when $r = r_1$, and Inwood when $r = r_p$)**

q = number of mortgage interest periods per year

m = total number of mortgage interest periods

k = number of remaining years of recapture (usually the remaining economic life of the improvement)

$s(r_m, m, q)$,

$s(r, k, 1)$ = amount of an annuity of 1

---

*It is conventional to assume that deposits in a sinking fund are made annually. However, they are probably made q times a year. In that case,

$$r_p' = \frac{q}{s(r, k \cdot q, q)}$$

**For straight-line recapture, note that when $r = 0$, $s(r,k,1) = k$.

Table: Find $s(r_m,m,q)$ and $s(r,k,1)$ in Table 1.

Example: An apartment investor obtains a 70% first mortgage. It bears 8% interest and is to be amortized with constant monthly payments for 25 years. A market survey indicates the property interest rate is 10%. The building has a remaining economic life of 25 years. Determine (a) the mortgage recapture rate, (b) the property recapture rate using the Inwood sinking fund method, and (c) the resulting equity recapture rate.

Solution: In this example,

$$t = .7,\ r_m = 8\%,\ q = 12,\ m = 12 \times 25 = 300,$$
$$r_p = 10\%,\ \text{and}\ k = 25\ \text{years}:$$

(a) From Table 1,

$$s(r_m,m,q) = s(8,300,12) = 951.0264.$$

Now, the mortgage recapture rate is

$$r'_m = \frac{12}{951.0264} = .0126 = 1.26\%.$$

(b) Since the Inwood method of recapture is specified, $r = r_p = 10\%$. From Table 1,

$$s(r,k,1) = s(10,25,1) = 98.3471.$$

Now, the property recapture rate is

$$r'_p = \frac{1}{98.3471} = .01017 = 1.017\%.$$

(c) The equity recapture rate is

$$r'_e = \frac{.01017 - .7 \times .0126}{1 - .7}$$
$$= \frac{.00135}{.3}$$
$$= .0045 = .45\%.$$

7.7.   Capitalization Rate

Capitalization is the process of converting income into a capital value. The rate at which income is converted into the original investment is called the capitalization rate. It is the sum of the rate of return *on* the investment (interest rate) and the rate of return *of* the investment (recapture rate).

The capitalization rate for a mortgage loan is called the annual mortgage constant (Section 6.5). The payment on an amortized loan contains interest (return on investment) and principal (return of investment). The mortgage capitalization rate is also the ratio of the annual payment-to-loan amount. It is known and needn't be estimated.

The capitalization rate for the equity interest is the ratio of annual cash flow-to-original equity investment. The expected equity capitalization rate can be estimated from a market survey of annual cash flow and equity investments.

The property capitalization rate is the ratio of annual net operating income-to-present-property value. The expected property capitalization rate can be estimated from a market survey of annual net operating income and property values (direct comparison). This rate can also be obtained from the weighted average of the capitalization rates of the capital contributions, mortgage and equity (band of investment).

Another property capitalization rate, introduced by L.W. Ellwood, contains the weighted average plus a term that accounts for loan amortization and change in property value over the income projection period.

Formulas:

$$z_m = \begin{cases} r_m + r'_m \\[2mm] \dfrac{x_m}{v_m} \\[3mm] \dfrac{q}{a(r_m,m,q)} \end{cases}$$

$$z_p = \begin{cases} r_p + r'_p \; * & \\[2mm] \dfrac{x_p}{v_p} & \textbf{(Direct Comparison Rate)} \\[3mm] t \cdot z_m + (1-t) \cdot z_e & \textbf{(Band of Investment Rate)} \\[3mm] t \cdot z_m + (1-t) \cdot z_e + \left[\dfrac{1 - h - t \cdot \dfrac{s(r_m,j,q)}{s(r_m,m,q)}}{s(z_e,n,1)} \right]^{**} & \textbf{(Ellwood Rate)} \end{cases}$$

$$z_e = \begin{cases} r_e + r'_e \\[2mm] \dfrac{x_e}{v_e} & \textbf{(Direct Comparison Rate)} \\[3mm] \dfrac{z_p - t \cdot z_m}{1 - t} & \textbf{(if } t < 1) \end{cases}$$

---

*If the Inwood method of recapture is used, the property capitalization rate becomes $z_p = 1/a(r_p,k,1)$.

**Use this formula if recognizing mortgage amortization and change in property value at end of income projection period. The relationship between Ellwood's notation and that used here is listed in a footnote in Section 8.5.

where

z_m, z_e, z_p = capitalization rate for mortgage, equity, and property, respectively

r_m, r_e, r_p = interest rate for mortgage, equity, and property, respectively (Section 7.5)

r_m', r_e', r_p' = recapture rate for mortgage, equity, and property, respectively (Section 7.6)

x_m, x_e, x_p = annual mortgage payment, cash flow, and net operating income, respectively (Sections 6.1, 7.4, and 7.3)

v_m, v_e, v_p = loan amount, present value of equity, and present value of property, respectively

t = loan-to-value ratio, expressed as a decimal

h = forecast-to-current property value, expressed as a decimal

k = years remaining for recapture (usually the remaining useful life of the improvement)

n = number of years in income projection period

m = total number of mortgage interest periods

q = number of mortgage interest periods per year

j = nq = number of mortgage interest periods until end of income projection period

$s(r_m, j, q)$,
$s(r_m, m, q)$,
and $s(z_e, n, 1)$ = amount of an annuity of 1
$a(r_m, m, q)$,
$a(r_p, k, 1)$ = present value of an annuity of 1

Table: Find the amounts and present values of the annuities in Table 1.

Example 1: (Direct Comparison) Recent sales of six comparable income properties reveal the following ratios of annual net operating income-to-sale price: .124, .117, .112, .121, .115, and .126. (a) What is the average property capitalization rate, and (b) Using the method in Section 10.9, what are the upper and lower bounds within which the true property capitalization rate lies, with 95% certainty?

Solution: Let $n = 6$ be the number of samples, and identify the sample property capitalization rates by

$$z_{p1} = .124, \; z_{p2} = .117, \; z_{p3} = .112, \; z_{p4} = .121,$$
$$z_{p5} = .115, \text{ and } z_{p6} = .126.$$

(a) Now the average property capitalization rate is

$$z_p = \frac{1}{n} \sum_{i=1}^{n} z_{pi} = \frac{1}{6}(.124 + .117 + .112 + .121 + .115 + .126)$$

$$= \frac{1}{6} \times .715 = .119$$

(b) To find the bounds, first find the standard deviation of the 6 estimates:

$$s = \left(\frac{1}{n-1} \sum_{i=1}^{n} (z_{pi} - z_p)^2 \right)^{\frac{1}{2}}$$

$$= \left\{ \frac{1}{5} \left[(.124 - .119)^2 + (.117 - .119)^2 + (.112 - .119)^2 \right. \right.$$
$$\left. \left. + (.121 - .119)^2 + (.115 - .119)^2 + (.126 - .119)^2 \right] \right\}^{\frac{1}{2}}$$

$$= \left\{ \frac{1}{5} \left[.000025 + .000004 + .000049 + .000004 \right. \right.$$
$$\left. \left. + .000016 + .000049 \right] \right\}^{\frac{1}{2}}$$

$$= \left(\frac{1}{5} \times .000147 \right)^{\frac{1}{2}} = .00542.$$

From the table in Section 10.9, corresponding to n = 6 and 95%, find $t_6 = 1.050$. Now, the formula in that section says

$$
\begin{aligned}
Z_l &= z_p - 1.050 \times .00542 \\
&= .119 - .006 \\
&= .113, \text{ and} \\
Z_u &= z_p + 1.050 \times .00542 \\
&= .119 + .006 \\
&= .125.
\end{aligned}
$$

Hence, we are 95% certain that the true property capitalization rate is between 11.3% and 12.5%. For instance, if the annual net operating income of a comparable property is $20,000, we are 95% certain that the present value is greater than $\frac{\$20,000}{.125} = \$160,000$ and less than $\frac{\$20,000}{.113} = \$176,991$.

Example 2: (Band of Investment)   An apartment investor obtains a 75% first mortgage at 8% interest that is to be amortized with constant monthly payments for 25 years. A market survey indicates that the property interest rate is 10%. The improvement has a remaining useful life of 25 years. Determine (a) the mortgage capitalization rate (i.e., annual mortgage constant), (b) the property capitalization rate (using the Inwood method of recapture), and (c) the resulting equity capitalization rate.

Solution: In this example,

$t = .75$, $r_m = 8\%$, $q = 12$, $m = 12 \times 25 = 300$, $r_p = 10\%$, and $k = 25$ years.

(a) From Table 1,

$$a(r_m, m, q) = a(8, 300, 12) = 129.5645.$$

Now, the mortgage capitalization rate is

$$z_m = \frac{12}{129.5645} = .0926 = 9.26\%.$$

(b) Since the Inwood method of recapture is specified, $r = r_p = 10\%$. From the footnote on page 136 and Table 1,

$$a(r_p, k, l) = a(10, 25, 1) = 9.07704.$$

Now, the property capitalization rate is

$$z_p = \frac{1}{9.07704} = 0.1102 = 11.02\%.$$

(c) The resulting equity capitalization rate is

$$z_e = \frac{z_p - t \cdot z_m}{1 - t} = \frac{.1102 - .7 \times .0926}{1 - .7}$$

$$= \frac{.04538}{.3} = .1513$$

$$= 15.13\%.$$

Example 3: (Ellwood)   Consider the investment described in Example 2. A market survey indicates the equity capitalization rate to be 12%. Assume the property will be held for 10 years, and suppose at that time, the property value is only 80% of its current value. From these assumptions, determine Ellwood's version of the property capitalization rate.

Solution: In this example,

$$t = .75, r_m = 8\%, q = 12, m = 12 \times 25 = 300, z_m = 9.26\%, z_e = 12\%,$$
$$n = 10 \text{ years}, j = 12 \times 10 = 120, \text{ and } h = .80.$$

From Table 1,

$$s(r_m,j,q) = s(8,120,12) = 182.9460,$$
$$s(r_m,m,q) = s(8,300,12) = 951.0264, \text{ and}$$
$$s(z_e,n,1) = s(12,10,1) = 17.5487.$$

Now,

$$z_p = .75 \times .0926 + (1 - .75) \times .12 + \left(\frac{1 - .8 - .75 \times \dfrac{182.9460}{951.0264}}{17.5487} \right)$$

$$= .06945 + .03 + \left(\frac{.2 - .14428}{17.5487} \right)$$

$$= .09945 + .00318$$

$$= .10263 = 10.26\%.$$

7.8.   Reversion Necessary to Achieve a Given Equity Capitalization Rate

The return on and of an equity investment is determined by the cash flow (assumed to be constant over the years), loan amortization, and the amount of the reversion.

The following formula determines the ratio of forecast-to-current property value that will provide the desired equity capitalization rate. It assumes the loan is new.

The figure on page 141 shows the ratio that will result in a variety of different equity capitalization rates for holding periods of up to 20 years. For instance, a 14% equity capitalization rate will result from either a 5% property value increase after 10 years or a 25% property value increase after 17 years.

Formula:

$$h = \quad (1 - t) \cdot \left[1 - \frac{x_e}{v_e} \cdot a(z_e,n,1) \right] \cdot c(z_e,n,1) + t \cdot \frac{a(r_m,k,q)^*}{a(r_m,m,q)}$$

---

*In Section 7.7, one formula for the equity capitalization rate is $z_e = x_e/v_e$. However, that formula assumes no loan amortization and no change in property value. Since the above formula assumes both, do not substitute z_e for x_e/v_e in the formula.

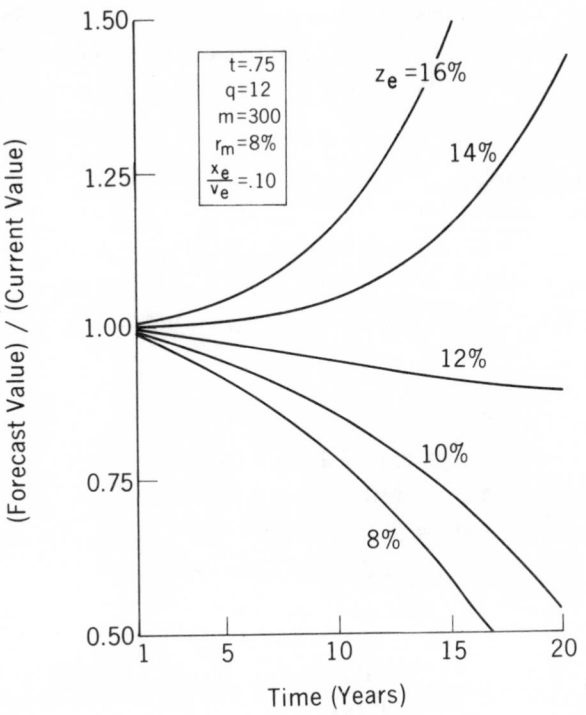

where

    h = forecast-to-current property value ratio

    t = loan-to-value ratio

    x_e = annual cash flow

    v_e = present value of equity

    z_e = equity capitalization rate

    n = number of years in income projection period

    r_m = mortgage interest rate

    q = number of loan interest periods per year

    m = total number of loan interest periods

    k = $m - nq$ = number of loan interest periods remaining at end of income projection period

$a(z_e,n,1),$

$a(r_m,k,q),$

    and

$a(r_m,m,q)$ = present value of an annuity of 1

 $c(z_e,n,1)$ = amount of 1 at compound interest

Table: Find $a(z_e,n,1)$, $a(r_m,k,q)$, $a(r_m,m,q)$, and $c(z_e,n,1)$ in Table 1.

Example: Michael Fenerty desires a 10% yield (equity capitalization rate) on his apartment investment. The property requires a $100,000 down payment. The 75% first mortgage bears an interest rate of 8% and has constant monthly payments for 25 years. The cash flow is $12,000 annually. If he holds the property for 5 years, what must the future property value be in order for him to achieve a 10% yield?

Solution: In this example,

$$z_e = 10\%, \ v_e = \$100,000, \ t = .75, \ r_m = 8\%,$$
$$q = 12, \ m = 25 \times 12 = 300, \ x_e = \$12,000,$$
$$n = 5 \text{ years, and } k = m - nq = 300 - 5 \times 12 = 240.$$

From Table 1,

$$c(z_e,n,l) = c(10,5,1) = 1.61051,$$
$$a(z_e,n,l) = a(10,5,1) = 3.79079,$$
$$a(r_m,k,q) = a(8,240,12) = 119.5543, \text{ and}$$
$$a(r_m,m,q) = a(8,300,12) = 129.5645.$$

Now,

$$h = (1 - .75) \cdot \left[1 - \frac{\$12,000}{\$100,000} \times 3.79079\right] \times 1.61051 + .75 \times \frac{119.5543}{129.5645}$$
$$= .25 \times (1 - .45489) \times 1.61051 + .75 \times .92274$$
$$= .219476 + .692055 = .911531.$$

Therefore if Mr. Fenerty can sell his apartment for 91% of its present value, he will still receive a 10% annual yield from his investment.

7.9.   Rate of Return

The rate of return is the rate of interest *on* an investment. The formula (Inwood method) implicitly assumes that income available for recapture of the investment is deposited in a sinking fund at a rate of interest equal to the rate of return*.

The formula is quite general. The income can change each year, resulting in a variable annuity. The summation portion of the formula expresses the present value of the variable annuity. The last (single) term expresses the present value of the reversion that is forecast to occur at the end of n years.

---

*The fact that the rate of return is the interest rate on the investment can be seen readily if periodic income is constant. In that case,

$$\sum_{j=1}^{n} \frac{x_j}{(1+r)^j} = x \cdot \sum_{j=1}^{n} \frac{1}{(1+r)^j} = x \cdot a(r,n,1).$$

See sections as 8.8.

Since the rate of return cannot be expressed explicitly from the formula, it must be determined by trial and error. That is, one can choose a rate that is, say, obviously too small and gradually increase it until the right side of the formula equals the left side. The rate that renders the right side equal to the left side is the rate of return on the investment. The formula can be used to find the rate of return on the mortgage, equity, property, developments, etc.

It is most important to be consistent when using the rate of return formula. For instance, if the rate of return on equity is to be determined, the annual income must be income to the equity investor (i.e., cash flow), the reversion must be reversion to the equity investor (i.e., the difference between property value and loan balance), and the present value of the investment must be the investor's present equity.

Formula:

$$
v = \begin{cases} \displaystyle\sum_{j=1}^{n} \frac{x_j}{(1+r)^j} + \frac{V}{(1+r)^n} & \text{*(Income received at end of each year)} \\[2em] \displaystyle\sum_{j=1}^{n} \frac{x_j}{(1+r)^{j-1}} + \frac{V}{(1+r)^n} & \text{(Income received at beginning of each year)} \end{cases}
$$

where

v = present value of investment (i.e., mortgage, equity, or property)
V = forecast reversion of investment
r = rate of return on investment (interest rate, Section 7.5)
x_j = annual income to investor in the jth year
n = number of years in the income projection period

Table: Find $(1 + r)^j = c(r,j,1)$ in Table 1.

Example 1: (Return on Mortgage, Property, and Equity). An investor is examining a $400,000 apartment building. The $300,000 first mortgage, with annual payments of $28,103.63, is amortized over 25 years. For the first five years, he projects the annual net operating income to be $36,000, $37,000, $38,000, $39,000 and $40,000. At the end of the five year period he expects to sell the property for $450,000 net. At that time the loan balance will be $275,925.42. If these expectations are realized, what is the rate of return on (a) the mortgage, (b) the property, and (c) the equity?

---

*
$$
\sum_{j=1}^{n} \frac{x_j}{(1+r)^j}
$$

is the present value of a variable annuity. If x_j is constant, see Section 4.1. If x_j changes by either a constant amount or a constant percentage, see Section 4.6.

Solution: (a) The rate of return on the mortgage is simply the contract interest rate on the mortgage. The annual payments are $x_j = \$28,103.63$, and the reversion (loan balance) after 5 years is $V = \$275,925.42$. The values of $c(r,j,1) = (1 + r)^j$ are found in Table 1. The formula is

$$\$300,000 = \left[\frac{\$28,103.63}{(1 + r)^1} + \frac{\$28,103.63}{(1 + r)^2} + \frac{\$28,103.63}{(1 + r)^3}\right.$$
$$\left. + \frac{\$28,103.63}{(1 + r)^4} + \frac{\$28,103.63}{(1 + r)^5}\right] + \frac{\$275,925.42}{(1 + r)^5} .$$

Figure 7-A on page 145 shows that when $r = 8\%$, the right side of the equation equals the left side. That is, the rate of return on the mortgage is in fact the rate of interest on the mortgage. From Sections 7.6 and 7.7, respectively, the mortgage recovery rate is

$$\frac{q}{s(r,m,q)} = \frac{1}{s(8,25,1)} = .0137 = 1.37\%,$$

and the mortgage capitalization rate (annual mortgage constant) is

$$\frac{q}{a(r,m,q)} = \frac{1}{a(8,25,1)} = .0937 = 9.37\%.$$

   (b) To determine the rate of return on the property, let $v = \$400,000$. The annual net operating income will be

$x_1 = \$36,000$, $x_2 = \$37,000$, $x_3 = \$38,000$, $x_4 = \$39,000$, and $x_5 = \$40,000$.

The total reversion will be $V = \$450,000$. Now,

$$\$400,000 = \left[\frac{\$36,000}{(1 + r)^1} + \frac{\$37,000}{(1 + r)^2} + \frac{\$38,000}{(1 + r)^3}\right.$$
$$\left. + \frac{\$39,000}{(1 + r)^4} + \frac{\$40,000}{(1 + r)^5}\right] + \frac{\$450,000}{(1 + r)^5} .$$

Figure 7-B on page 145 shows that the right side of the equation equals the left side when $r = 11.50\%$ (approximately). That is, the rate of return on the property is 11.50%.
   (c) To determine the rate of return on equity, let $v = \$100,000$. The annual cash flow will be

$$x_1 = \$36,000 - \$28,104 = \$7,896,*$$
$$x_2 = \$37,000 - \$28,104 = \$8,896,$$
$$x_3 = \$38,000 - \$28,104 = \$9,896,$$
$$x_4 = \$39,000 - \$28,104 = \$10,896, \text{ and}$$
$$x_5 = \$40,000 - \$28,104 = \$11,896.$$

---

*The annual mortgage payments and the loan balance are rounded to the nearer dollar.

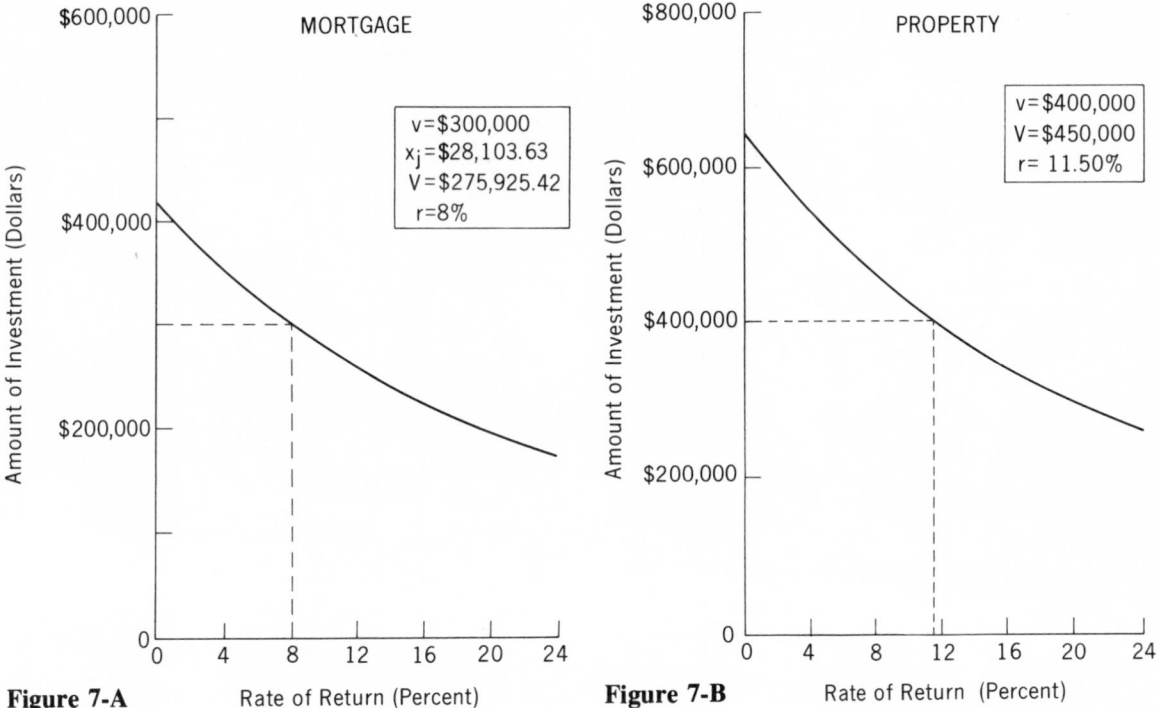

Figure 7-A — MORTGAGE

v=$300,000
x$_j$=$28,103.63
V=$275,925.42
r=8%

Figure 7-B — PROPERTY

v=$400,000
V=$450,000
r= 11.50%

The reversion to the equity investor will be the difference between the net sale price and the loan balance:

$$V = \$450,000 - \$275,925 = \$174,075.$$

Now,

$$\$100,000 = \left[\frac{\$7,896}{(1 + r)^1} + \frac{\$8,896}{(1 + r)^2} + \frac{\$9,896}{(1 + r)^3} + \frac{\$10,896}{(1 + r)^4} + \frac{\$11,896}{(1 + r)^5}\right] + \frac{\$174,075}{(1 + r)^5}.$$

Figure 7-C on page 146 shows that the right side of the equation equals the left side when r = 19.50% (approximately). That is, the rate of return on equity (equity interest rate) will be 19.50%.

Example 2: (Return on Equity After Taxes).   Consider the investment of Example 1, and determine the after-tax rate of return on equity. Assume the building, which represents 80% of the property value, has a remaining useful life of 40 years and will be depreciated by the straight-line method. Assume the investor's income tax rate is 40% each year, and the capital gain tax will be 25%. Use the present value, v_p, as the basis of the property since it is newly purchased.

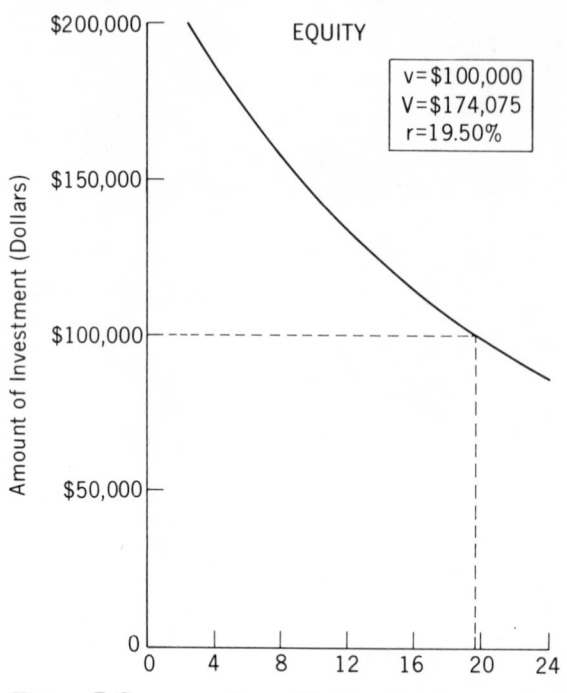

Figure 7-C   Rate of Return (Percent)

Solution: In this example, we will use the formula from this section. However, because we are using equity after taxes we define the parameters in the following way:

Use in the rate of return formula

$$v = v_e = \text{amount of equity investment}$$

$$x_j = x_{ej} - z_j \cdot (x_{pj} - i_j - d_j) = \text{annual cash flow after income taxes in the jth year (net spendable income)}$$

$$V = V_p - B_n - g \cdot (V_p - v_p + D_n) = \text{forecast reversion to equity investor after capital gain taxes in the nth year}$$

where

j = year within the projection period (not year of ownership, mortgage, depreciation, etc.)

x_{ej} = cash flow in jth year (Section 7.4)

x_{pj} = net operating income in jth year (Section 7.3)

i_j = amount of interest paid on mortgage in jth year (Section 6.9; but there j refers to payment period, not year)

d_j = amount of depreciation in jth year (Section 11.4)

k = useful life of depreciable property (Section 11.1)

z_j = investor's income tax bracket in jth year (Section 14.4)

g = capital gain tax rate for this property

v_p = present value of property (also the basis in this example)

V_p = forecast net receipts from disposition of property (after commission and expenses)

D_n = amount of depreciation accumulated over n years of ownership (Section 11.4)

B_n = loan balance after n years of debt (Section 6.11)

The table (below) lists the values that are required to evaluate each of the five x_j's.

Year j	x_{pj}	i_j	d_j	$x_{pj} - i_j - d_j$	$z_j \cdot (x_{pj} - i_j - d_j)$	x_{ej}	x_j
1	$36,000	$24,000	$8,000	$4,000	$1,600	$ 7,896	$6,296
2	$37,000	$23,672	$8,000	$5,328	$2,131	$ 8,896	$6,765
3	$38,000	$23,317	$8,000	$6,683	$2,673	$ 9,896	$7,223
4	$39,000	$22,934	$8,000	$8,066	$3,226	$10,896	$7,670
5	$40,000	$22,521	$8,000	$9,479	$3,792	$11,896	$8,104

In order to determine the reversion, we find that the loan balance is $B_5 = \$275,926$. The total depreciation is $D_5 = \$40,000$, and $g = .25$. Recall that, from the previous example, $V_p = \$450,000$ and $v_p = \$400,000$. Now, the forecast reversion is

$$V = \$450,000 - \$275,926 - .25 \times (\$450,000 - \$400,000 + \$40,000)$$
$$= \$450,000 - \$275,926 - \$22,500$$
$$= \$151,574.$$

The entire formula is

$$\$100,000 = \left[\frac{\$6,296}{(1 + r)^1} + \frac{\$6,765}{(1 + r)^2} + \frac{\$7,223}{(1 + r)^3} + \frac{\$7,670}{(1 + r)^4}\right.$$
$$\left. + \frac{\$8,104}{(1 + r)^5}\right] + \frac{\$151,574}{(1 + r)^5}.$$

Select a value of r that is clearly too small, and gradually increase it until the right side of the equation equals the left side. We find that $r = 14.75\%$ is the after-tax rate of return on equity.

8

INVESTMENTS AND VALUATION: INCOME APPROACH

The three approaches to real estate value are: income, cost, and market. The income approach utilizes the rate at which capital earns interest and the rate at which capital is returned. The periodic income, loan amortization, and change in property value can affect the return *on* and return *of* capital.

The first section of this chapter determines value simply by capitalizing the income at a capitalization rate that is derived from sampling the market. Any amortization or reversion is not explicitly accounted for but is implicit and embodied in the capitalization rate.

The components of property can be separated according to three different criteria: physical, financial, and legal. The next three sections (8.2, 8.3 and 8.4) utilize the physical separation of property into buildings and land. The following three sections (8.5, 8.6, and 8.7) utilize the financial separation of property into mortgage and equity. Three later sections (8.9, 8.10, and 8.11) utilize the legal separation of property into leased fee interest and leasehold interest. In all three separations, the property value is the sum of the values of the pair of components.

For instance, let v_p, v_b, v_l, v_m, v_e, v_f, and v_h denote the present value of the property, buildings, land, mortgage, equity, leased fee, and leasehold respectively. Then

$$v_p = \begin{cases} v_b + v_l & \textbf{(physical separation)} \\ v_m + v_e & \textbf{(financial separation)}* \\ v_f + v_h & \textbf{(legal separation)}. \end{cases}$$

---

*Another type of financial separation arises from the mortgage participation interest (Section 8.8).

Most of the present value formulas used in this chapter bear some resemblance to each other. This resemblance actually is more profound than might be realized. Usually the formulas consist of two types of terms. The first determines the present value of the income stream, and the second determines the present value of the reversion. The sum of the two terms is, of course, the present value of the investment (property, mortgage, equity, etc.).

The term expressing the present value of the reversion has the same form in Sections 8.4, 8.7, 8.8, and 8.9 and is explained in Section 3.2.

The term expressing the present value of the income stream can have several different formulas, depending upon the assumptions. For instance, the annual income can be treated as either constant or variable, and the recaptured income can be deposited in a sinking fund either at the interest rate of the investment or at an arbitrary interest rate. To see this, consider an income period of n years. Let x denote the constant amount of income each year, and let x_i denote the variable amount of income in the ith year. Let z denote the capitalization rate (Section 7.7), and let r denote the interest rate of the investment (Section 7.5).

If the income is assumed to be constant, and the recapture rate is arbitrary (i.e., because the interest rate of the sinking fund is arbitrary), the present value of the income stream is $\frac{x}{z}$ (see Sections 8.1 through 8.6).

If the annual income is assumed to be variable, but the income is deposited in a sinking fund at the interest rate of the investment, the present value of the income stream is $\sum_{i=1}^{n} \frac{x_i}{(1+r)^i}$. This formulation corresponds to the rate of return formula (Sections 7.9 and 8.7).

If the income is assumed to be constant, but the recaptured income is deposited in a sinking fund at the interest rate of the investment (this is called Inwood recapture), the capitalization rate is $\frac{1}{a(r,n,1)}$, and the present value of the income stream is $x \cdot a(r,n,1)$* (see Sections 8.8 through 8.11).

However, if the income is assumed to be variable and the income is deposited in a sinking fund at an arbitrary rate, the formula is unavailable.

The table below, formalizes the above observations.

Present Value of an Income Stream	Recapture Rate	
	Arbitrary Recapture	Inwood Recapture
Variable Income Stream	----	$\sum_{i=1}^{n} \frac{x_i}{(1+r)^i}$
Constant Income Stream	$\frac{x}{z}$	$x \cdot a(r,n,1)$

*$a(r,n,1)$ = present value of an annuity of 1. Note that $x \cdot \sum_{i=1}^{n} \frac{1}{(1+r)^i} = x \cdot a(r,n,1)$.

8.1.   Direct Capitalization (Sampling Method)

In direct capitalization, the present value of property is determined by the ratio of annual net operating income-to-property capitalization rate. The property capitalization rate can be determined in several ways (e.g., Section 8.5), but in this section we will use the property capitalization rate that is determined by a market survey of comparable investments: The ratios of annual net operating income-to-sale price are sampled and then averaged. This average rate is then used in the formula, below, to determine the present value of a comparable property. The method of Section 10.9 can be used to estimate the reliability of this rate.

Formula:

$$v_p = \frac{x_p}{z_p}$$

where

v_p = present value of the property
x_p = current annual net operating income from the property (Section 7.3)
z_p = property capitalization rate, expressed as a decimal (Section 7.7)

Table: none

Example: A property has a current annual net operating income of $27,900. The property capitalization rate, as determined by market samples, is 12%. What is the present value of the property?

Solution:

$$v_p = \frac{\$27,900}{.12} = \$232,500.$$

8.2.   Building Residual Technique

The building residual technique is the most commonly used of the residual appraisal techniques. It is used when the value of the building is difficult to determine, and the land value can be determined more accurately. The land is assumed to be vacant, and its value is determined by a market survey of recent comparable sales. The land is assumed to earn income at the property interest rate *. Any residual income is attributed to the building. This income is capitalized at the property capitalization rate to determine the value of the building.

---

*For non-depreciable assets such as land, the interest rate equals the capitalization rate because there is no reason to provide for recapture (i.e. capitalization rate = interest rate + recapture rate).

Formulas:

$$v_p = v_b + v_l = \frac{x_p - r_p \cdot v_l}{z_p} + v_l = \frac{x_p + r_p' \cdot v_l}{z_p}$$

where

v_p = present value of the property
v_b = present value of the building
v_l = present value of the land
x_p = annual net operating income from the property (Section 7.3)
r_p = property interest rate, expressed as a decimal (Section 7.5)
r_p' = $1/s(r,k,1)$ = property recapture rate, expressed as a decimal * (Section 7.6)
z_p = $r_p + r_p'$ = property capitalization rate, expressed as a decimal (Section 7.7)
r = interest rate of sinking fund
k = remaining useful life of building (Section 11.1)

Table: Find $s(r,k,1)$ in Table 1.

Example: An income property has an annual net operating income of $30,000. This income should remain constant for the remaining 20 years of useful life of the building. The property interest rate is 8%, and the property recapture rate is 2.44%. The present value of the land, as determined by a market survey, is $45,000. What is the present value of the property?

Solution: In this example,

$$x_p = \$30,000, \; r_p = 8\%, \; r_p' = 2.44\%, \text{ and } v_l = \$45,000.$$

Now,

$$z_p = .0800 + .0244 = .1044,$$

and

$$v_p = \frac{\$30,000 + .0244 \times \$45,000}{.1044}$$

$$= \frac{\$30,000 + \$1,098}{.1044} = \$297,900.$$

---

*Building residual technique equals the property residual technique (Section 8.4) if the Inwood method of recapture is used; i.e., if $r = r_p$.

8.3.   Land Residual Technique

The land residual technique can be used when the building is either new or nearly new and represents the highest and best use of the land. The building's value is determined from current reproduction cost new less accrued depreciation. The building earns income at the property capitalization rate.

The residual income attributable to the land is capitalized at the property interest rate.

Formulas:

$$v_p = v_b + v_l = v_b + \frac{x_p - z_p \cdot v_b}{r_p} = \frac{x_p - r_p' \cdot v_b}{r_p}$$

where

v_p = present value of the property
v_b = present reproduction cost of the building less accrued depreciation (Section 9.5)
v_l = present value of the land
x_p = annual net operating income (Section 7.3)
r_p = property interest rate, expressed as a decimal (Section 7.5)
r_p' = $1/s(r,k,1)$ = property recapture rate, expressed as a decimal (Section 7.6)
z_p = $r_p + r_p'$ = property capitalization rate, expressed as a decimal (Section 7.7)
k = remaining useful life of building (Section 11.1)
r = interest rate of sinking fund

Table: Find $s(r,k,1)$ in Table 1.

Example: An apartment building is five years old and is assumed to have a 35 year remaining useful life. The building is valued at $200,000 (reproduction cost new less accrued depreciation) and has an annual net operating income of $25,000. The interest rate on similar properties is 8%, and the recapture rate is 1%. What is the present value of the property?

Solution: In this example,

$$v_b = \$200,000, \; x_p = \$25,000, \; r_p = 8\%, \text{ and } r_p' = 1\%.$$

Now,

$$v_p = \frac{\$25,000 - .01 \times \$200,000}{.08}$$

$$= \frac{\$23,000}{.08} = \$287,500.$$

8.4.   Property Residual Technique

This technique is often used to determine property value when neither the present value of the land nor the present value of the building can be determined readily from the market*.

The property residual technique assumes that the present value of the reversion can be determined. The reversion is generally taken to be the land, and the date of reversion is the end of the useful life of the building. Because the present value of the income is unknown, the entire property is taken to be the residual.

Formula:

$$v_p = \frac{x_p}{z_p} + \frac{v_l}{c(r_p,k,1)}$$

where

v_p = present value of the property

v_l = present value of the land

x_p = annual net operating income (Section 7.3)

r_p = property interest rate (Section 7.5)

$r_p' = 1/s(r,k,1)$ = property recapture rate** (Section 7.6)

$z_p = r_p + r_p'$ = property capitalization rate, expressed as a decimal (Section 7.7)

r = interest rate of sinking fund

k = remaining income projection period (remaining useful life of the building or remaining term of the lease)

$c(r_p,k,1)$ = amount of 1 at compound interest

Table: Find $s(r,k,1)$ and $c(r_p,k,1)$ in Table 1.

Example: An income property has an annual net operating income of $30,000, and the building has a remaining useful life of 20 years. A market survey indicates that the land value is $75,000. The current interest rate on similar properties is 8%, and the property recapture rate is 3%. What is the value of the property?

Solution: In this example,

x_p = $30,000, k = 20 years, v_l = $75,000, r_p = 8%, and r_p' = 3%.

---

*This technique is also used to evaluate the leased fee interest under a long-term lease (Section 8.9). The entire property is considered to be the reversion, and the reversion date is the termination date of the lease.

**The property residual technique equals the building residual technique if the Inwood method of recapture is used; i.e., if $r = r_p$.

The property capitalization rate is

$$z_p = 8\% + 3\% = 11\%.$$

From Table 1,

$$c(r_p,k,1) = c(8,20,1) = 4.66096.$$

Now,

$$v_p = \frac{\$30,000}{.11} + \frac{\$75,000}{4.66096}$$

$$= \$272,727 + \$16,091$$
$$= \$288,818.$$

8.5.   Mortgage-Equity Method

The mortgage-equity method of income property appraisal uses a property capitalization rate that is derived from the financial components of the investment.

In its simple, band of investment form, this capitalization rate is the weighted average of the mortgage capitalization rate (i.e. annual mortgage constant) and the equity capitalization rate. In its more general form (developed by L.W. Ellwood), the property capitalization rate also accounts for loan amortization and a changed property value *. These two contributions are assumed to be deposited in a sinking fund at the equity capitalization rate throughout the income projection period. The income projection period is usually the estimated holding period.

The band of investment rate and the Ellwood rate are identical if the forecast property value equals the investor's original equity plus the equity accumulated by virtue of mortgage amortization during the estimated holding period.

---

*Relationship between Ellwood's notation and that used in this encyclopedia:

Ellwood		This Encyclopedia
R	=	z_p
f	=	z_m
Y	=	z_e
I	=	r_m
M	=	t

Ellwood		This Encyclopedia
P	=	$\dfrac{s(r_m,j,q)}{s(r_m,m,q)}$
s_n	=	$s(z_e,n,1)$
+ dep / − app	=	$1 - h$
C	=	$z_e - z_m + \dfrac{s(r_m,j,q)}{s(r_m,m,q)}\dfrac{1}{s(z_e,n,1)}$

Formula:

$$v_p = \frac{x_p}{z_p}$$

where

v_p = present value of property

x_p = annual net operating income (Section 7.3)

$$z_p = \begin{cases} t \cdot z_m + (1-t) \cdot z_e & \text{(Band of Investment Rate)} \\[2em] t \cdot z_m + (1-t) \cdot z_e + \left[\dfrac{1 - h - t \cdot \dfrac{s(r_m, j, q)}{s(r_m, m, q)}}{s(z_e, n, 1)} \right] & \text{(Ellwood Rate)} \end{cases}$$

= property capitalization rate

$z_m = \dfrac{q}{a(r_m, m, q)}$ = mortgage capitalization rate (Sections 6.5 and 7.7)

z_e = equity capitalization rate, expressed as a decimal (Section 7.7)

r_m = mortgage interest rate

t = loan-to-value ratio, expressed as a decimal

h = forecast-to-current property value ratio, expressed as a decimal

q = number of mortgage interest periods per year

m = total number of mortgage interest periods

n = number of years in income projection period

j = nq = number of mortgage interest periods in the income projection period

$s(r_m, j, q)$,

$s(r_m, m, q)$,

and $s(z_e, n, 1)$ = amount of an annuity of 1

$a(r_m, m, q)$ = present value of an annuity of 1

Table: Find $s(r_m, j, q)$, $s(r_m, m, q)$, $s(z_e, n, 1)$, and $a(r_m, m, q)$ in Table 1.

Example 1: (Band of Investment Rate).   An income property has an annual net operating income of \$30,000. It has a 70% loan at 8% interest with monthly payments for 25 years. If the equity capitalization rate is 11%, what is the present value of the property?

Solution: In this example,

$$x_p = \$30,000, \ t = .70, \ r_m = 8\%, \ q = 12,$$
$$m = 25 \times 12 = 300, \text{ and } z_e = 11\%.$$

To determine the property capitalization rate, we must first find the mortgage capitalization rate. From Table 1:

$$a(r_m, m, q) = (8, 300, 12) = 129.5645.$$

Now,

$$z_m = \frac{q}{a(r_m,m,q)} = \frac{12}{129.5645} = .09262.$$

The property capitalization rate in the band of investment form is

$$z_p = .70 \times .09261 + (1 - .70) \times .11$$
$$= .06483 + .03300$$
$$= .09783.$$

We can now determine the present value of the property:

$$v_p = \frac{\$30,000}{.09783} = \$306,654.$$

Example 2: (Ellwood Rate).   An income property has an annual net operating income of $30,000. It has a 70% loan at 8% interest with monthly payments for 25 years. The equity capitalization rate is 11%, and the income projection period is 10 years. What is the present value of the property, if at the end of the income projection period, the forecast property value is (a) 110% of the current value and (b) 90% of the current value?*

Solution: In this example,

$$x_p = \$30,000, \ t = .70, \ r_m = 8\%, \ q = 12,$$
$$m = 25 \times 12 = 300, \ z_e = 11\%, \ n = 10 \text{ years},$$
$$j = 10 \times 12 = 120, \text{ and } h = 1.10 \text{ and } .90.$$

We must first determine Ellwood's property capitalization rate, z_p. To do this, evaluate the annuities from Table 1:

$$a(r_m,m,q) = a(8,300,12) = 129.5645,$$
$$s(r_m,j,q) = s(8,120,12) = 182.9460,$$
$$s(r_m,m,q) = s(8,300,12) = 951.0264, \text{ and}$$
$$s(z_e,n,1) = s(11,10,1) = 16.7220.$$

Now,

$$z_p = .70 \times \frac{12}{129.5645} + (1 - .70) \times .11 + \left(\frac{1 - h - .70 \times \dfrac{182.9460}{951.0264}}{16.7220} \right)$$

---

*This example is also used in Section 8.6.

$$= .06483 + .03300 + \left(\frac{1 - h - .70 \times .192367}{16.7220} \right)$$

$$= .09783 + \left(\frac{.86534 - h}{16.7220} \right)$$

(a) If $h = 1.10$, then

$$z_p = .09783 + \left(\frac{.86534 - 1.10}{16.7220} \right) = .09783 - .014033$$

$$= .08380.$$

The present value of the property is

$$v_p = \frac{\$30,000}{.08380.} = \$357,995.$$

(b) If $h = .90$, then

$$z_p = .09783 + \left(\frac{.86534 - .90}{16.7220} \right) = .09783 - .00207$$

$$= .09576.$$

The present value of the property is

$$v_p = \frac{\$30,000}{.09576} = \$313,283.$$

8.6.   Mortgage-Equity Method (Property Residual Technique)

This method of determining present value assumes the annual net operating income will remain constant during the income projection period. It accounts for loan amortization and allows for an arbitrary property value at the end of the income projection period.

Formula:

$$v_p = \frac{x_p}{z_p} \cdot \left[\frac{c(z_e,n,1)}{c(z_e,n,1) + t \cdot \dfrac{a(r_m,k,q)}{a(r_m,m,q)} - h} \right] *$$

---

*This formula would resemble that of the property residual technique (Section 8.4) if there were no loan amortization and the reversion were the land. The results are identical to those of the mortgage-equity method using the band of investment rate (Section 8.5) if the forecast property value equals the loan balance.

where

v_p = present value of the property

x_p = annual net operating income

z_m = $q/a(r_m,m,q)$ = mortgage capitalization rate (i.e. annual mortgage constant)

z_e = equity capitalization rate

t = loan-to-value ratio, expressed as a decimal

z_p = $t \cdot z_m + (1 - t) \cdot z_e$ = property capitalization rate by band of investment method

q = number of mortgage interest periods per year

m = total number of mortgage interest periods

k = remaining number of mortgage interest periods

r_m = mortgage interest rate

n = number of years in income projection period (usually the intended holding period)

h = forecast-to-current property value ratio, expressed as a decimal

$c(z_e,n,1)$ = amount of 1 at compound interest

$a(r_m,k,q)$,

$a(r_m,m,q)$ = present value of an annuity of 1

Table: Find $c(z_e,n,1)$, $a(r_m,k,q)$, and $a(r_m,m,q)$ in Table 1.

Example: An income property has an annual net operating income of $30,000. It has a 70% loan at 8% interest with monthly payments for 25 years. The equity capitalization rate is 11%, and the income projection period is 10 years. What is the present value of the property if at the end of the income projection period, the forecast property value is (a) 110% of the current value and (b) 90% of the current value? *

Solution: In this example,

$$x_p = \$30,000, \, t = .70, \, r_m = 8\%, \, q = 12,$$
$$m = 25 \times 12 = 300, \, z_e = 11\%, \, n = 10,$$
$$k = 15 \times 12 = 180, \text{ and } h = 1.10 \text{ and } 0.09.$$

We should first evaluate the functions from Table 1:

$$c(z_e,n,1) = c(11,10,1) = 2.8394,$$
$$a(r_m,k,q) = a(8,180,12) = 104.6406, \text{ and}$$
$$a(r_m,m,q) = a(8,300,12) = 129.5645.$$

---

*This example is the same as Example 2 of Section 8.5.

Now, the property capitalization rate is

$$z_p = .70 \times \frac{12}{129.5645} + (1 - .70) \times .11 = .06483 + .03300$$

$$= .09783.$$

The formula for the present value of the property is

$$v_p = \frac{\$30,000}{.09783} \times \left(\frac{2.8394}{2.8394 + .70 \times \dfrac{104.6406}{129.5645} - h} \right)$$

$$= \$306,654 \times \left(\frac{2.8394}{3.4047 - h} \right)$$

(a) Now, if $h = 1.10$, the present value of the property is

$$v_p = \$306,654 \times \left(\frac{2.8394}{3.4047 - 1.10} \right)$$

$$= \$306,654 \times 1.2320$$

$$= \$377,798.$$

(b) If $h = .90$, the present value of the property is

$$v_p = \$306,654 \times \left(\frac{2.8394}{3.4047 - .90} \right)$$

$$= \$306,654 \times 1.1336$$

$$= \$347,623.$$

8.7.   Rate of Return Method (Variable Income)

The rate of return method to determine present value provides for a variable income stream. The amount of reversion is arbitrary. Section 7.9 contains a lengthy discussion of this method where it is assumed the present value is known, and the rate of return must be determined. On the other hand, this section assumes that the rate of return is known, and the present value is to be determined.

It is very important to be consistent when using these formulas. For instance, if the present value of equity interest is to be determined, the annual income must be income to the equity investor (i.e., cash flow), the reversion must be reversion to the equity investor (i.e., the difference between property value and loan balance), and the rate of return must be the rate of return on equity (i.e. the equity interest rate).

The first example determines the present value of property (i.e. land for development, a good example of variable income). The second example determines the future value of the reversion for a given present value, income, and rate of return.

Formula:

$$v = \begin{cases} \displaystyle\sum_{j=1}^{n} \frac{x_j}{(1+r)^j} + \frac{V}{(1+r)^n} & \text{(income received at the end of each year)} \\[3ex] \displaystyle\sum_{j=1}^{n} \frac{x_j}{(1+r)^{j-1}} + \frac{V}{(1+r)^n} & \text{(income received at the beginning of each year)} \end{cases}$$

where

v = present value of investment (i.e., mortgage, equity, or property)
V = future value of investment (reversion)
r = rate of return on investment, expressed as a decimal (investment interest rate)
x_j = annual net operating income on investment in the jth year
n = number of years in the income projection period

Table: Find $(1 + r)^j = c(r,j,1)$ in Table 1.

Example 1: (Present Value of Land for Development).

A 100 acre tract is scheduled for development over two years with sales over a 3-year period. In the first year, 50 acres will be developed at a cost of $120,000. In the second year, 30 acres will be developed at a cost of $80,000. The last 20 acres will be held for three years and sold for $140,000 net.

Each developed acre will sell for $9,000. The sales and promotional costs are projected to be $3,000 per acre. It is expected that 35 acres will be sold the first year, 28 acres the second year, and 17 acres the third year. If the developers want an 18% return on their investment, how much should they pay for the 100 acre tract?

Solution: Let d_j denote the cost of development in the jth year, and let s_j denote the net receipts from sales in the jth year. Now,

$$d_1 = \$120,000, \ d_2 = \$80,000, \text{ and } d_3 = \$0.$$

The net sales receipts from each acre are $9,000 - $3,000 = $6,000. Now,

$$s_1 = 35 \times \$6,000 = \$210,000, \ s_2 = 28 \times \$6,000 = \$168,000,$$
$$\text{and } s_3 = 17 \times \$6,000 = \$102,000.$$

Using the notation of the rate of return formula,

$$n = 3 \text{ years, } r = 18\%, \ V = \$140,000$$
$$x_1 = s_1 - d_1 = \$210,000 - \$120,000 = \$90,000,$$
$$x_2 = s_2 - d_2 = \$168,000 - \$80,000 = \$88,000, \text{ and}$$
$$x_3 = s_3 - d_3 = \$102,000 - \$0 = \$102,000.$$

Now, the price the developers can pay for the land and still receive their return of 18% is:

$$v = \sum_{j=1}^{3} \frac{x_j}{(1+r)^j} + \frac{V}{(1+r)^3}$$

$$= \left[\frac{\$90,000}{(1.18)^1} + \frac{\$88,000}{(1.18)^2} + \frac{\$102,000}{(1.18)^3} \right] + \frac{\$140,000}{(1.18)^3}$$

$$= \$76,271 + \$63,200 + \$62,080 + \$85,208$$

$$= \$286,759.$$

Example 2: (Future Value of Reversion).   For the next 3 years an income property is expected to have an annual cash flow of $10,000, $13,000, and $11,000. The present value of the equity is $120,000. If the equity investor is to realize a 12% rate of return on his equity, what must his reversion be after three years?

Solution: In this example,

$$n = 3 \text{ years, } x_1 = \$10,000, \ x_2 = \$13,000,$$
$$x_3 = \$11,000, \ v = \$120,000, \text{ and } r = .12.$$

To solve this problem, we must find V:

$$V = \left[v - \sum_{j=1}^{n} \frac{x_j}{(1+r)^j} \right] \cdot (1+r)^n.$$

Now,

$$V = \left\{ \$120,000 - \left[\frac{\$10,000}{(1.12)^1} + \frac{\$13,000}{(1.12)^2} + \frac{\$11,000}{(1.12)^3} \right] \right\} \cdot (1.12)^3$$

From Table 1,

$(1+r)^j = c(12,j,1) = 1.12000, \ 1.25440, \text{ and } 1.40493 \text{ for } j = 1, 2, \text{ and } 3, \text{ respectively.}$

Now, the future value of the reversion must be

$$V = \left[\$120,000 - (\$8,929 + \$10,364 + \$7,830) \right] \times 1.40493$$
$$= (\$120,000 - \$27,123) \times 1.40493$$
$$= \$92,877 \times 1.40493$$
$$= \$130,486.$$

In the case of the equity investor, the reversion is the difference between future property value and loan balance.

8.8.   Mortgage Participation Interest

Some mortgages are granted under the condition that the equity investor share some of the net operating income and/or some of the reversion with the mortgagee.

The participation interest rate, r_t, is the rate of return expected by the mortgagee in excess of the mortgage interest rate. It will probably be greater than the mortgage interest rate, r_m, because the amount of the participation is not guaranteed. On the other hand, it is probably less than the equity interest rate, r_e, because the mortgagee has less risk than the equity investor. Furthermore, the mortgage interest rate, r_m, should be smaller than it would be without participation.

Formulas:

$$v_t = x_t \cdot a(r_t,n,1) + \frac{V_t}{c(r_t,n,1)} \ ,$$

$$v_e = x_e \cdot a(r_e,n,1) + \frac{V_e}{c(r_e,n,1)} \ ,$$

$$v_m = \frac{x_m}{q} \cdot a(r_m,j,q) + \frac{V_m}{c(r_m,j,q)} \ ,$$

and

$$v_p = v_t + v_e + v_m \ ^*$$

where

v_t, v_e, v_m, v_p = present value of the mortgagee's participation interest, the equity interest, the mortgage, and the property, respectively

r_t, r_e, r_m = participation, equity, and mortgage interest rate, respectively

t_1, t_2 = fraction of the net operating income and reversion, respectively, that is claimed by the mortgagee

x_p = annual net operating income (Section 7.3)

$x_t = t_1 x_p$ = annual participation income

$x_m = q \cdot v_m / a(r_m,j,q)$ = annual debt service

$x_e = x_p - x_m - x_t$ = annual cash flow after participation income is deducted

V_p = property reversion (forecast value)

$V_m = v_m \cdot c(r,j,q) - \dfrac{x_m}{q} \cdot s(r,j,q)$ = mortgage reversion (i.e. balance, Section 6.11)

$V_t = t_2(V_p - V_m)$ = participation reversion

$V_e = (1 - t_2)(V_p - V_m)$ = equity reversion

n = number of years in income projection period

---

*Although it can be reasoned that this equation is valid by definition, it can be verified by the rate of return formula (Section 8.7) only when $r_t = r_e$, and $a(r_e,n,1) = a(r_m,j,q)/q$ (Section 6.5).

$$q = \text{mortgage interest periods per year}$$
$$j = nq = \text{number of mortgage interest periods}$$

$a(r_t, n, 1),$
$a(r_e, n, 1),$
$a(r_m, j, q) = \text{present value of an annuity of 1}$
$c(r_t, n, 1),$
$c(r_e, n, 1),$
$c(r_m, j, q) = \text{amount of 1 at compound interest}$
$s(r_m, j, q) = \text{amount of an annuity of 1}$

Table: Find the annuities in Table 1.

Example: A mortgagee grants a $245,000 loan at 8% with monthly payments for 25 years. He also obtains a participation interest for 10 years. At the end of 10 years it is assumed the property will be worth $297,500. The annual net operating income is $30,000. The equity and participation interest rates are thought to be 9% and 8.5%, respectively.

The mortgagee's participation is 10% of net operating income and 20% of the equity reversion. What is the present value of (a) the participation interest, (b) the equity interest, and (c) the property?

Solution: In this example,

$$v_m = \$245{,}000, \ r_m = 8\%, \ n = 10 \text{ years}, \ V_p = \$297{,}500,$$
$$x_p = \$30{,}000, \ r_e = 9\%, \ r_t = 8.5\%, \ t_1 = .10, \text{ and } t_2 = .20.$$

From Table 1,

$$a(r_e, n, 1) = a(9, 10, 1) = 6.41766,$$
$$a(r_t, n, 1) = a(8.5, 10, 1) = 6.56135,$$
$$c(r_e, n, 1) = c(9, 10, 1) = 2.36736, \text{ and}$$
$$c(r_t, n, 1) = c(8.5, 10, 1) = 2.26098.$$

All information required is now available except the cash flow (after the participation interest) and the reversions. From Section 6.1 the annual debt service is seen to be $x_m = \$22{,}691$. Also $x_t = .10 \times \$30{,}000 = \$3{,}000$. Now, the cash flow after the participation interest is

$$x_e = \$30{,}000 - \$22{,}691 - \$3{,}000 = \$4{,}309.$$

The reversion is the difference between the forecast value of the property, $297,500, and the loan balance.

From Section 6.11, the loan balance after 10 years will be $V_m = \$197{,}870$. Now,

$$V_t = .20(\$297{,}500 - \$197{,}870) = \$19{,}926,$$

and

$$V_e = (1 - .20)(\$297,500 - \$197,870) = \$79,704.$$

(a) The present value of the participation interest is

$$v_t = \$3,000 \times 6.56135 + \frac{\$19,926}{2.26098}$$

$$= \$19,684 + \$8,813$$
$$= \$28,497.$$

(b) The present value of the equity interest is

$$v_e = \$4,309 \times 6.41766 + \frac{\$79,704}{2.36736}$$

$$= \$27,654 + \$33,668$$
$$= \$61,322.$$

(c) The present value of the property is

$$v_p = \$28,497 + \$61,322 + \$245,000$$
$$= \$334,819.$$

8.9.   Leased Fee (Lessor's) Interest

The value of a lease to the lessor can be determined by a technique similar to the property residual technique (Section 8.4). The leased fee interest rate is proportional to the risk of collecting rent. Collection may be more difficult when contract rent exceeds economic rent *.

The property interest rate, which may differ from the leased fee interest rate, is used to discount the reversion.

The first formula should be used when the lease requires the payment of net operating income (net lease). (See Examples 1 and 2.) The second formula should be used when the lease requires the payment of gross income. In this case, the annual operating expenses are accounted for and treated as if they will change by a constant rate * *. (See Example 3.) Both formulas assume payments are made at the end of each year. If payments are made at the beginning see Section 4.3.

---

*If contract rent exceeds economic rent, the present value of the leasehold (lessee's) interest, v_h, actually belongs to the lessor. See Section 8.10. In this case, $v_h < 0$ and $v_p = v_f + v_h$. That is, the present value of the property equals the sum of the present values of the lessor's and lessee's interest.

* *The formulas of Section 4.6 can be used for other types of changes as well.

Formulas:[*]

$$
v_f = \begin{cases} x_c \cdot a(r_f, n, 1) + \dfrac{V}{c(r_p, n, 1)} & \text{(Net Rental)} \\[2em] y_c \cdot a(r_f, n, 1) - w \cdot a(r'', n, 1) + \dfrac{V}{c(r_p, n, 1)} & \text{(Gross Rental)} \end{cases}
$$

where

v_f = present value of the leased fee interest
y_c = annual contract gross rental
w = annual operating expenses in first year
x_c = annual contract net operating income
r_p = property interest rate (Section 7.5)
r_f = leased fee interest rate
r' = annual rate of change of operating expenses (positive, zero, or negative)
$r'' = \dfrac{r_f - r'}{1 + r'}$ (r_f and r' must be expressed as decimals. See Section 4.6)
V = forecast value of the reversion (usually the entire property) when the lease expires
n = remaining years of lease
$a(r_f, n, 1)$
$a(r'', n, 1)$ = present value of an ordinary annuity of 1. If rental is paid in advance, see Section 4.3
$c(r_p, n, 1)$ = amount of 1 at compound interest

Table: Find $a(r_f, n, 1)$, $a(r'', n, 1)$, and $c(r_p, n, 1)$ in Table 1.

Example 1: (Flat Net Rental).   A property is leased for 10 years and will net $15,000 per year (payable at the end of each year). The property value is expected to be worth $220,000 at the expiration of the lease. The property interest rate is 9%. The contract rental is slightly below the current economic rental; hence, the leased fee interest rate is 8%. What is the present value of the leased fee interest?

Solution: In this example,

$n = 10$ years, $x_c = \$15,000$, $V = \$220,000$, $r_p = 9\%$, and $r_f = 8\%$.

---

[*]The formulas in this section assume that rental payments are received but once a year, and interest on deposits is compounded but once a year. The formulas of Sections 3.2 and 4.2 are generalizations of those given here.

From Table 1,

$$a(r_f, n, 1) = a(8, 10, 1) = 6.7101, \text{ and}$$
$$c(r_p, n, 1) = c(9, 10, 1) = 2.3674.$$

Now, the present value of the leased fee interest is

$$\dot{v}_f = \$15,000 \times 6.7101 + \frac{\$220,000}{2.3674}$$

$$= \$100,652 + \$92,929$$
$$= \$193,581.$$

Example 2: (Stepped Net Rental).   A property is leased for 10 years. The lease calls for a step-up rental that will net $12,000 for each of the first four years and $17,000 for each of the next six years (payable at the end of each year). The property value is expected to be worth $220,000 at the expiration of the lease. The current return on similar leases is 8%. The property interest rate is 9%. What is the present value of the leased fee interest?

Solution: In this example, we must separate the first term of the first formula into two terms because of the two income streams. We will say that the two income streams are x_{c1} and x_{c2} and that they last for n_1 and n_2 years (i.e. $n = n_1 + n_2$). Furthermore, because the second income stream is delayed for 4 years, we must use the present value of a deferred ordinary annuity (Section 4.4 where we assume $q = 1$. Hence, $t = 1$). Let

$$n = 10 \text{ years, } x_{c1} = \$12,000, \, n_1 = 4 \text{ years,}$$
$$x_{c2} = \$17,000, \, n_2 = 6 \text{ years, } V = \$220,000,$$
$$r_f = 8\%, \text{ and } r_p = 9\%.$$

The formula is

$$v_f = x_{c1} \cdot a(r_f, n_1, 1) + x_{c2} \cdot \frac{a(r_f, n_2, 1)}{s(r_f, 1, 1) \cdot c(r_f, n_1, 1)} + \frac{V}{c(r_p, n, 1)} .$$

Now, from Table 1,

$$a(r_f, n_1, 1) = a(8, 4, 1) = 3.3121,$$
$$a(r_f, n_2, 1) = a(8, 6, 1) = 4.6229,$$
$$s(r_f, 1, 1) = 1,$$
$$c(r_f, n_1, 1) = c(8, 4, 1) = 1.3605, \text{ and}$$
$$c(r_p, n, 1) = c(9, 10, 1) = 2.3674.$$

Now, the present value of the leased fee interest is

$$v_f = \$12,000 \times 3.3121 + \$17,000 \times \frac{4.6229}{1 \times 1.3605} + \frac{\$220,000}{2.3674}$$

$$= \$39,745 + \$57,765 + \$92,929$$
$$= \$190,439.$$

Note that the sum of the payments in Examples 1 and 2 are equal. The value of the leased fee in the second example is lower than in the first because the lessor receives lower payments initially and must wait four years for the higher payments.

Example 3: (Flat Gross with Declining Net Rental).   A property is leased for 10 years with gross annual payments of $18,000 (payable at the end of each year). The operating expenses are currently $2,071 per year and are expected to increase by 5% each year (i.e., compounded annually). Hence, the net rental will decline. The property value is expected to be worth $220,000 at the expiration of the lease, and the property interest rate is 9%. The current return on similar leases is 8%. What is the present value of the leased fee interest?

Solution: The net operating income is the gross income less the operating expenses (Section 7.3). The gross annual income is a flat $18,000. However, the operating expenses will increase by 5% annually. Hence, the net operating income will constitute a declining annuity. In this case it is an annuity that declines exponentially (Section 4.6). Let

$$n = 10 \text{ years}, \ y_c = \$18,000, \ w = \$2,071, \ r' = 5\%,$$
$$V = \$220,000, \ r_p = 9\%, \text{ and } r_f = 8\%.$$

The interest rate that is used for the exponential annuity is

$$r'' = \frac{r_f - r'}{1 + r'} = \frac{.08 - .05}{1 + .05} = .02857.$$

From Table 1,

$$a(r'',n,1) = a(2.857,10,1) = 8.5930 \ *,$$
$$a(r_f,n,1) = a(8,10,1) = 6.7101, \text{ and}$$
$$c(r_p,n,1) = c(9,10,1) = 2.3674.$$

Now, the present value of the leased fee interest is

$$v_f = \$18,000 \times 6.7101 - \$2,071 \times 8.5930 + \frac{\$220,000}{2.3674}$$

$$= \$120,782 - \$17,796 + \$92,929$$
$$= \$195,915.$$

---

*This value is interpolated. See Appendix: Mathematical Notes, Section A.2.

In this example, the operating expenses have been designed so that the total net operating income over the 10 years is equal to that of Examples 1 and 2. The value of the leased fee is larger here because the net operating income is larger in the earlier years of the lease.

8.10. Leasehold (Lessee's) Interest

The lessee's interest in a property has a value that depends on both the contract rent and the economic rent. If the contract rent exceeds the economic rent, the value of the leasehold is negative and can be thought of as belonging to the lessor. If contract rent equals economic rent, the lessee's interest has no value. If contract rent is less than economic rent, the leasehold value belongs to the lessee.

Generally, the leasehold interest rate is rather high because the spread between contract and economic rent is uncertain.

Formulas:

$$v_h = v_p - v_f = (y_e - y_c) \cdot a(r_h,n,1) = (x_e - x_c) \cdot a(r_h,n,1) \; *$$

where

v_h, v_f, v_p = present value of the leasehold interest, leased fee interest, and property, respectively

y_e, y_c = annual economic and contract gross rent, respectively

x_e, x_c = annual economic and contract net rent, respectively

r_h = leasehold interest rate

n = number of years remaining on the lease

$a(r_h,n,1)$ = present value of an annuity of 1

Table: Find $a(r_h,n,1)$ in Table 1.

Example 1:   A lessee has a 20 year lease for gross rent of $15,000 per year. However, the current economic rent for comparable space is $18,000 per year. If the current leasehold interest rate is 12%, what is the present value of the lessee's interest?

Solution: In this example,

$$n = 20 \text{ years}, \; y_c = \$15,000, \; y_e = \$18,000, \text{ and } r_h = 12\%.$$

From Table 1,

$$a(r_h,n,1) = a(12,20,1) = 7.2414.$$

---

*The formulas in this section assume that rental payments are received but once a year, and interest on deposits is compounded but once a year. The formulas of Sections 3.2 and 4.2 are generalizations of those given here.

Now, since $y_e > y_c$, the value of the leasehold belongs to the lessee:

$$v_h = (y_e - y_c) \cdot a(r_h, n, 1) = (\$18,000 - \$15,000) \times 7.2414$$
$$= \$3,000 \times 7.2414$$
$$= \$21,724.$$

Example 2: (Leasehold Interest Rate Unknown).   A property is leased for 10 years to net $15,000 per year. The current net economic rent is $18,000 per year. The present value of the property is $211,000, and the present value of the leased fee (Example 1, Section 8.9) is $193,581. What is (a) the present value of the leasehold, and (b) the leasehold interest rate?

Solution: In this example,

$$n = 10 \text{ years}, \ x_c, = \$15,000, \ x_e = \$18,000,$$
$$v_p = \$211,000, \text{ and } v_f = \$193,581.$$

(a) From the formula, the present value of the leasehold is

$$v_h = v_p - v_f = \$211,000 - \$193,581 = \$17,419.$$

(b) To find the leasehold interest rate, use the formula and solve for the present value of an annuity of 1:

$$a(r_h, n, 1) = \frac{v_h}{x_e - x_c},$$

or

$$a(r_h, 10, 1) = \frac{\$17,419}{\$18,000 - \$15,000} = 5.8063.$$

From Table 1, corresponding to 10 periods, 5.8363 agrees very closely with an interest rate of 11.3%. * Hence, $r_h = 11.3\%$.

8.11.   Sandwich Lease Interest

Sometimes a property is leased, and the lessee, in turn, subleases the property. The original lessee becomes the owner of a sandwich leasehold. That is, he is simultaneously a lessor and a lessee.

---

*If the agreement is not close, use interpolation (See Appendix: Mathematical Notes, Section A.2).

The sandwich lease interest rate is related to the risk of the sublease. It is usually less than the rate applied to the leasehold interest and higher than the rate applied to the leased fee interest.

Formulas:

$$v_s = (y_{c2} - y_{c1}) \cdot a(r_s,n,1) = (x_{c2} - x_{c1}) \cdot a(r_s,n,1) \; *$$

where

v_s = present value of the sandwich lease interest

y_{c1}, y_{c2} = annual contract gross rent on original lease and sublease, respectively

x_{c1}, x_{c2} = annual contract net rent on original lease and sublease, respectively

r_s = sandwich lease interest rate, where $r_f < r_s < r_h$ (Sections 8.9 and 8.10)

n = remaining years of leases (assume they terminate simultaneously)

$a(r_s,n,1)$ = present value of an annuity of 1

Table: Find $a(r_s,n,1)$ in Table 1.

Example: A property is leased to gross $50,000 annually with 15 years remaining. The lessee subleases the property to gross $55,000 for the remaining 15 years. What is the present value of this sandwich lease if the sandwich lease interest rate is 10%?

Solution: In this example,

$$y_{c1} = \$50,000, \; y_{c2} = \$55,000, \; n = 15 \text{ years}, \text{ and } r_s = 10\%.$$

From Table 1,

$$a(r_s,n,1) = a(10,15,1) = 7.6061.$$

Now, the present value of the sandwich lease is

$$v_s = (\$55,000 - \$50,000) \times 7.6061$$

$$= \$5,000 \times 7.6061$$

$$= \$38,030.$$

---

*The formulas in this section assume that rental payments are received but once a year, and interest on deposits is compounded but once a year. The formulas of Sections 3.2 and 4.2 are generalizations of those given here.

8.12.   Air Rights

Air rights are rights granted for use of the space above the surface of the land. For instance, air rights might be granted for access, for transmission lines, etc. Often the cost of this access is $20 - 30\%$ of the land value. Hence, the value of the air rights is $70 - 80\%$ of the land value.

Formula:

$$v_a = v_l - (c + v_u + v_i - v_x)$$

where

v_a = value of air rights after granting interest
v_l = value of land prior to granting interest
v_u = economic value lost due to building modification to accommodate air rights
c = construction costs due to building modification
v_i = interest on investment for time required for building modification
v_x = value of savings on excavation not required due to air rights

Table: none

Example: On several acres of land there is a single large building. The land value is $600,000. Later, air rights are granted for elevated electric transmission lines. The building suffers a $40,000 loss in value due to modification to accommodate a power supply. The building also requires $30,000 of construction to accommodate a power pole. Since the lines are elevated, there is a $10,000 savings on excavation for underground lines. The time required to modify the building has cost about $60,000 in interest on the investment. What is the value of the air rights?

Solution: In this example,

$$v_l = \$600,000, \ v_u = \$40,000, \ c = \$30,000,$$
$$v_x = \$10,000, \text{ and } v_i = \$60,000.$$

Now, the value of the air rights is

$$v_a = \$60,000 - (\$40,000 + \$30,000 + \$60,000 - \$10,000)$$
$$= \$600,000 - \$120,000$$
$$= \$480,000.$$

The air rights represent about 80% of the value of the land, i.e.,

$$\frac{v_a}{v_l} = \frac{\$480,000}{\$600,000} = .8.$$

8.13.   Coal Seams

The following formula provides an indication of the present value of a coal seam. The formula depends upon the thickness, quality, accessibility, and depth of the coal seam. The value of each of these characteristics is weighted according to prevailing economic conditions. Other factors used in the formula are the fraction and weight of mineable coal and the current price of coal.

Formula:

$$v_c = (h_t \cdot c_t + h_q \cdot c_q + h_a \cdot c_a + h_d \cdot c_d) \cdot c_m \cdot p \cdot w$$

where

v_c = present value of coal seam (dollars/acre)

c_t, c_q, c_a, c_d = fractional contribution due to the average thickness (t) of the seam, the quality (q) of the coal, the access (a) of the seam to transportation, and the depth (d) of the seam from the surface, respectively

c_m = fraction of available coal that can be mined (i.e., for room and pillar system, $c_m = .65$. For long wall system, $c_m = .80$)

h_t, h_q, h_a, h_d = weights attached to the relative economic importance of the thickness (t), quality (q), accessibility (a), and depth (d), respectively. Each weight must be between 0 and 1, and $h_t + h_q + h_a + h_d = 1$. Weights will change with economic conditions

p = current royalties paid on coal (dollars/ton)

w = weight of available coal (tons/acre) (1 ft³ of anthracite = .043 to .056 tons and 1 ft³ of bituminous = .037 to .048 tons)

Table: See Tables that follow.

Thickness		Quality	
t (inches)	c_t	q(B.T.U./lb.)	c_q
72 in. and over	1.00	15,000	1.00
60	.90	14,500	.90
48	.70	14,000	.80
36	.50	13,500	.70
34	.40	13,000	.60
32	.35	12,500	.50
30	.30	12,000	.40
28	.25	11,500	.30
26	.20	11,000	.20
24	.10	10,500	.10

Access	
a (miles)	c_a
0	1.00
1	.90
2	.80
3	.70
4	.60
5	.50
7.5	.40
10	.30
12.5	.20
15	.10

Depth	
d(ft)	c_d
0	1.00
50	.90
100	.80
150	.70
200	.60
250	.50
300	.40
400	.30
500	.20
600	.10

Example: The Tobin Mine has a seam of very dense anthracite coal that averages 28 inches thick. The average thermal quality seems to be 11,500 B.T.U./lb. The seam is an average of 2 miles from a rail facility, and the average depth of this seam is 200 ft below the surface. Currently the relative importance of thickness, quality, accessibility, and depth is 35%, 35%, 15%, and 15%, respectively. If 65% of the seam can be mined and if coal brings royalties of $1.25/ton, what is the present value of the seam per acre?

Solution: In this example,

$$t = 28 \text{ in., } q = 11,500 \text{ B.T.U./lb, } a = 2 \text{ mi,}$$
$$d = 200 \text{ ft, } h_t = .35, h_q = .35, h_a = .15,$$
$$h_d = .15, c_m = .65, \text{ and } p = \$1.25/\text{ton.}$$

From each of the four tables in this section,

$$c_t = .25, c_q = .30, c_a = .80, \text{ and } c_d = .60.$$

Since the coal is described as very dense anthracite, 1 ft³ = .056 tons. The average thickness is 2.33 ft, and there are 43,560 ft²/acre. Hence, the volume of coal per acre is (2.33 ft) × (43,560 ft²/acre) = 101,640 ft³/acre. The weight of coal per acre is then

$$w = (101,640 \text{ ft}^3/\text{acre}) \times (.056 \text{ tons/ft}^3)$$
$$= 5,692 \text{ tons/acre.}$$

Now,

$$v_c = (.35 \times .25 + .35 \times .30 + .15 \times .80 + .15 \times .60) \times .65$$
$$\times (\$1.25/\text{ton}) \times (5,692 \text{ tons/acre})$$
$$= (.0875 + .105 + .12 + .09) \times \$4,624.75/\text{acre}$$
$$= .4025 \times \$4,624.75/\text{acre}$$
$$= \$1,861.46/\text{acre}.$$

8.14.   Optimum Holding Period

Due to the costs incurred when buying and selling properties, even good investments must be held for a minimum period of time before these costs are offset. Conversely, a good investment can be held so long that, due to appreciation, there is almost no leverage remaining to the equity investor. That is, the value has increased to the point that nearly all of the value is the investor's equity (initial and acquired during the holding period). There is some holding period between these extreme cases that, theoretically, is optimal in the following sense: If, over a given number of years, an investor repeatedly turned over a certain property* after this optimal period of time, his yield would be greater than if he repeatedly turned over the same property after any other holding period. For instance, after five years the yield might be greater if a property is turned over twice after each 2½ year period than it would be if turned over five times after each year. In both cases a five year investment period is used.

In the above discussion the yield is not defined. It might be defined as the present value of the investor's total profit (including accumulated cash flow, loan amortization, and capital gain) divided by the initial equity investment**. Either the before tax or after tax yield could be considered. In any case, let $z_1, z_2, \ldots, z_n$ denote the yield on an investment that is disposed of after the first, second, and nth year, respectively.

Suppose there is a type of investment that one would typically seek and could regularly obtain. The investment could be characterized by its yields $z_1, z_2, \ldots, z_n$. Suppose that over n years, this type of investment is acquired and disposed of annually for n years. Let w_1 describe the compound yield resulting at the end of n years. Now suppose this type of investment is acquired and disposed of every 2 years for n years. Let w_2 describe the compound yield resulting at the end of n years. Continue in this way until, finally, there is but a single turnover occurring at the end of the nth year. Let w_n describe the resulting compound yield (in this case, it is simply $w_n = z_n$).

---

*By a certain property we do not mean the same property in a physical sense, but a financial sense. Two properties are considered to be the same if they produce the same yield each year.

**In this case the formula for the yield is

$$z_i = \frac{v_{ei} - v_e'}{v_e'}$$

where

v_{ei} = present value of equity interest after i years, as determined in Section 8.7.
v_e' = initial equity investment.

As mentioned above, we generally expect w_1 and w_n to be smaller than some w_i for i between 1 and n. The largest value of w_i represents the maximum yield possible over n years, and the corresponding holding period, i, represents the optimal holding period for this type of investment (provided this type of investment will be repeatedly acquired and disposed of).

The above concept not only indicates (theoretically) the optimum holding period for a single investment program, but by comparing the maximum compound yields resulting from two different investment programs, it indicates the more profitable of the two. See Example 2.

Formula:

$$w_i = (1 + z_i)^{\frac{n}{i}} - 1$$

where

w_i = compound yield after n years if each holding period is i years ($i = 1, \ldots, n$)
z_i = yield on investment if property is held for i years, expressed as a decimal
n = number of years in projection period
i = holding period, expressed in years
n/i = number of turnovers in n years

Example 1:   Directors of the Eagle Corporation seek a certain type of investment and feel that it will generally be available to them (for example, surburban apartment complexes). They believe the yields over 5 years will be as shown in the table *. What is the optimal holding period if this type of investment will be repeatedly turned over?

Solution:

Year	Yield	Compound Yield
i	z_i	w_i
1	14%	92.5%
2	60	224
3	110	244
4	150	214
5	170	170

---

*For instance, suppose after 3 years the total discounted cash flow is $25,235, and the discounted gain to the corporation from the sale (including loan amortization) is $103,390. Since the initial equity investment was $61,250, the yield is

$$z_3 = \frac{\$25,235 + \$103,390 - \$61,250}{\$61,250} = \frac{\$67,375}{\$61,250} = 1.10 = 110\%.$$

The w_i's are determined in the following way:

$$w_1 = (1 + .14)^{\frac{5}{1}} - 1 = .925$$

$$w_2 = (1 + .60)^{\frac{5}{2}} - 1 = 2.24,$$

$$w_3 = (1 + 1.10)^{\frac{5}{3}} - 1 = 2.44,$$

$$w_4 = (1 + 1.50)^{\frac{5}{4}} - 1 = 2.14, \text{ and}$$

$$w_5 = (1 + 1.70)^{\frac{5}{5}} - 1 = 1.70.$$

Figure 8-A shows both z_i and w_i over the 5 year period. It is clear that the optimal holding period is about 2.7 years. That is, if this type of investment is continually acquired and disposed of every 2.7 years, it will yield about 245% on equity after 5 years.

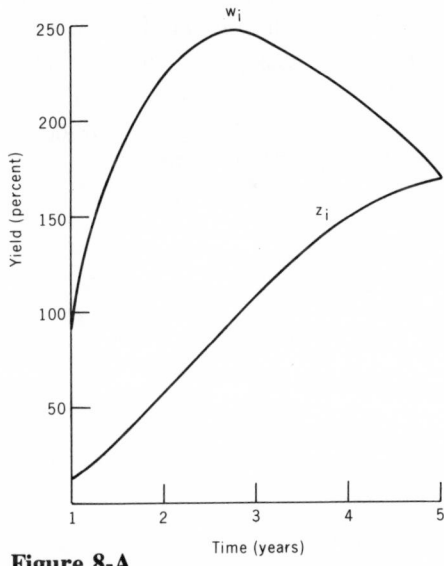

Figure 8-A

Example 2: An investor believes that two types of investments might be desirable. Both have essentially the same risk, liquidity, and management burden. The five yields for each are listed in the table. Which type of investment, if optimally traded, will provide the greater return (compound yield) over the five year period?

Solution: As in Example 1, compute the five w_i values for each case.

Year	Case 1		Case 2	
i	z_i	w_i	z_i	w_i
1	4 %	21.7%	8%	46.9%
2	60	224	50	176
3	97.5	211	90	194
4	110	153	112	156
5	115	115	125	125

Both the z_i and w_i curves are shown in Figure 8-B for each case. For Case 1, the optimal holding period is about 2.1 years and will provide a compound yield of about 225%. Conversely, for Case 2, the optimal holding period is about 2.9 years and will provide a compound yield of about 197%. From this data, Case 1 would provide the more profitable investment program.

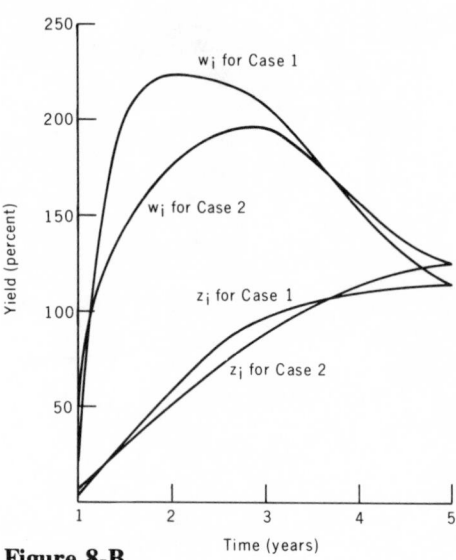

Figure 8-B

9

INVESTMENTS AND VALUATION: COST APPROACH

The cost approach is one of the three approaches to real estate value. The first two sections of this chapter deal with the floor area and volume of buildings. For instance, Section 9.1 contains formulas from which the area of even the most general shapes can be determined. Section 9.2 shows many different roof styles together with simple formulas needed to determine the volume beneath them. The subject of accrued depreciation is dealt with thoroughly in Sections 9.3 and 9.4. The first of these two sections discusses depreciation in general, and the second discusses the five categories of depreciation and how they can be applied to individual building components. Section 9.5 combines the reproduction cost and the accrued depreciation so that the present value of a building can be determined. Section 9.6 shows how to use the sinking fund method to determine the reserve for replacement of a depreciating asset. Section 9.7 shows how to forecast future value as it depends on the annual change in reproduction costs. Section 9.8 gives the formula for the forecast property value as it depends on changes in reproduction costs, physical and functional depreciation, and maintenance.

9.1.   Floor Area of a Building

The methods used to determine the floor area of buildings can also be used to determine the area of land.

The reproduction cost new of some buildings is often estimated by finding the floor area and then multiplying the area by the current reproduction cost, quoted on a square foot or square meter basis. This method of determining reproduction cost is usually applied to a single level of a building that has one or two levels. Sometimes, however, both levels of a two-level building are included as floor area. The outside dimensions of the walls at the first level are used. Generally only areas with both roof and foundation are included in the computation.

The area of most irregular shapes can be determined by partitioning them so that each component is either a rectangle or a triangle. The area is then the sum of the component areas. (Figure 9-A shows an example of components, and Figure 9-B shows the general triangle.) Some shapes are so irregular that their area must be obtained by partitioning into a field of parallel trapezoids. (See Figure 9-C.)

The floor area approach to determining the reproduction cost is frequently used because it is easier than the volume approach (Section 9.2); it is not as accurate, however.

The relationship between area and perimeter is a factor in cost. The more compact the building, the less expensive it is to construct. It should be noted that for all plane shapes with a given area, the circle has the least perimeter, and for all rectangles with a given area, the square has the least perimeter.

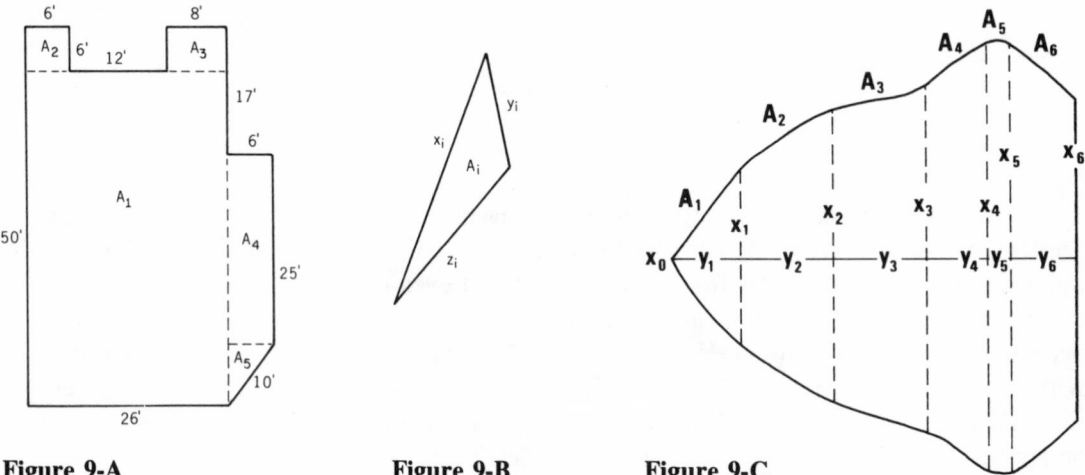

Figure 9-A   Figure 9-B   Figure 9-C

Formula:

$$A = A_1 + \ldots + A_i + \ldots + A_n$$

$$A_i = \begin{cases} x_i y_i & \text{if shape is a rectangle} \\ \dfrac{x_i y_i}{2} & \text{if shape is a right triangle} \\ \sqrt{p_i(p_i - x_i)(p_i - y_i)(p_i - z_i)} & \text{if shape is any triangle} \\ \dfrac{1}{2}(x_{i-1} + x_i)y_i & \text{if shape is partitioned into trapezoids} \end{cases}$$

where

A = area of building or land

A_i = area of the ith component

x_i, y_i = width and depth, respectively, of rectangle, right triangle, or trapezoid

x_i, y_i, z_i = three sides of any triangle

$$p_i = \frac{x_i + y_i + z_i}{2}$$

n = number of components

Table: If conversion of units is required, see the tables of Chapter 15.

Example 1: (Rectangles and Right Triangle).   Determine the area of Figure 9-A on page 180. The labelled dimensions are in feet.

Solution: Partition the shape into component shapes that are either rectangles or triangles. Label the component areas $A_1, \ldots, A_5$. These areas are

$$A_1 = 50' \times 26' = 1{,}300 \text{ ft}^2,$$
$$A_2 = 6' \times 6' = 36\text{ft}^2, \quad A_3 = 6' \times 8' = 48 \text{ ft}^2,$$

and

$$A_4 = 6' \times 25' = 150 \text{ ft}^2.$$

The fifth component is a right triangle, hence, its area is one half the area of a rectangle with the same dimensions:

$$A_5 = \frac{1}{2} \times 6' \times 10' = 30 \text{ ft}^2.$$

Now the area of the shape is

$$\begin{aligned} A &= A_1 + A_2 + A_3 + A_4 + A_5 \\ &= 1{,}300 + 36 + 48 + 150 + 30 \\ &= 1{,}564 \text{ ft}^2. \end{aligned}$$

Example 2: (General Triangle).   The ith component of a building or plot has a triangular shape with sides $x_i = 72$ ft, $y_i = 31$ ft, and $z_i = 49$ ft. See Figure 9-B on page 180. What is the area of the triangle?

Solution: Since the triangle is not a right triangle, its area must be determined from the general formula. First, determine

$$p_i = \frac{x_i + y_i + z_i}{2} = \frac{72 + 31 + 49}{2} = 76 \text{ ft.}$$

Now, the area is

$$A_i = \sqrt{76(76 - 72)(76 - 31)(76 - 49)}$$
$$= \sqrt{76 \times 4 \times 45 \times 27} = \sqrt{369,360}$$
$$= 607.75 \text{ ft}^2.$$

Example 3: (General Shape).   Determine the area of the general shape shown in Figure 9-C on page 180. The dimensions of the vertical lines (in yards) are

$$x_0 = 0, \ x_1 = 18, \ x_2 = 30, \ x_3 = 36, \ x_4 = 45,$$
$$x_5 = 45, \text{ and } x_6 = 33.$$

The widths of the sections (in yards) are

$$y_1 = 7.5, \ y_2 = 10, \ y_3 = 10, \ y_4 = 6.5,$$
$$y_5 = 2.5, \text{ and } y_6 = 7.$$

Solution: This general shape is partitioned into parallel trapezoids to approximate the irregular boundary. The trapezoids can be chosen as small as desired to increase accuracy. Determine the area of each component trapezoid by the formula:

$$A_1 = \frac{1}{2}(0 + 18) \times 7.5 = 67.5, \ A_2 = \frac{1}{2}(18 + 30) \times 10 = 240,$$

$$A_3 = \frac{1}{2}(30 + 36) \times 10 = 330, \ A_4 = \frac{1}{2}(36 + 45) \times 6.5 = 263.25,$$

$$A_5 = \frac{1}{2}(45 + 45) \times 2.5 = 112.5, \text{ and } A_6 = \frac{1}{2}(45 + 33) \times 7 = 273.$$

Now, the total area is

$$A = 67.5 + 240 + 330 + 263.5 + 112.5 + 273$$
$$= 1,286.55 \text{ yds}^2.$$

9.2.   Volume of a Building

The reproduction cost new of most buildings is estimated by first determining the volume, and then by multiplying the volume by the current reproduction cost new. This cost is quoted on a cubic foot or cubic meter basis.

The outside dimensions of the walls are used. The height of the walls is the vertical distance from the ground or basement to the bottom of the roof. If there is a basement, $6''$ is added to the depth below the finished basement surface. If there is no basement, the height is measured from grade level or one foot below the top of the first floor, whichever is lower. The volume of most buildings (i.e. the entire volume) can be computed from the formulas accompanying the roof shape in the figures.

The relationship between volume and surface area is a factor in cost. The more compact the building, the less material is used in construction. It should be noted that for all shapes with a given volume, the sphere has the least surface area, and for all rectangular solids with a given volume, the cube has the least surface area.

The volume of the building can be determined by partitioning the building into components, determining the volume of each component, and then summing the volumes. The building should be partitioned so that each component is a convex shape *. If this is done, no empty space will be included in the computation, and complicated roof lines will generally be avoided.

Six very common roof styles are shown on page 184. The formulas that accompany each figure can be used to compute the volume of the building.

Formula:

$$V = V_1 + \ldots + V_i + \ldots + V_n$$

where

V = volume of building

V_i = volume of the ith component. (See the appropriate figure for the volume formula)

n = number of components

A_i = base area of the ith component (Section 9.1)

x_i, y_i = length and width of the base of the ith component, if rectangular

w_i, r_i = height of the wall and roof, respectively

u_i = length of ridge on hip roof

t_i = length of ridge on roof that extends beyond the intersection of two connecting gable components

s_i = radius of base of dome roof

Table: If conversion of units is required, see Tables in Chapter 15.

Example 1: (Two Volume Components: Gable Roof and Pyramid Roof).   Determine the volume of the building shown in Figure 9-J. The dimensions are

$$y_1 = 100', \ x_1 = 60', \ w_1 = 70', \ r_1 = 80',$$
$$A_2 = 1000 \ \text{ft}^2, \ w_2 = 40', \ \text{and} \ r_2 = 60'.$$

---

*A convex shape is one in which every point in the figure can be reached from every other point in the figure by moving in a straight line and without leaving the figure. An egg and a solid cube are convex shapes. A donut or a u-shaped building are not convex shapes.

GABLE ROOF

SINGLE PITCH ROOF

$$V = xy\left(\frac{w+r}{2}\right)$$

The roof can have either one rectangular panel (single pitch)
or two rectangular panels (gable) with the same wall height, w.

Figure 9-D

CONNECTING GABLE ROOF

$$V = \frac{xt}{6}(r-w)$$

This formula determines the volume of the wedge only

Figure 9-E

CONE ROOF

PYRAMID ROOF

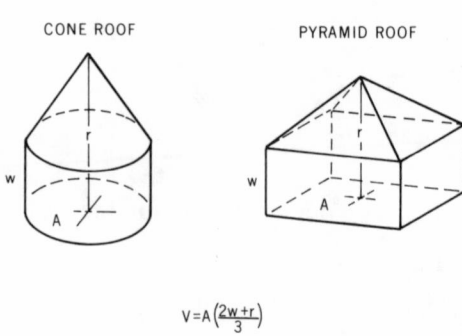

$$V = A\left(\frac{2w+r}{3}\right)$$

The base area, A, can be irregular, but
all wall heights ,w, must be the same.
The peak can lie anywhere above the base.

Figure 9-F

MANSARD ROOF

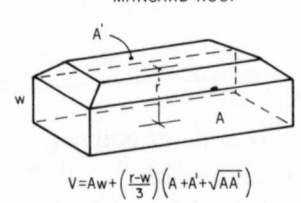

$$V = Aw + \left(\frac{r-w}{3}\right)\left(A + A' + \sqrt{AA'}\right)$$

The roof panels must all be trapezoids. The two bases,
whose areas are A and A', must be similar polygons.
(They need not be rectangles, as shown.)

Figure 9-G

HIP ROOF

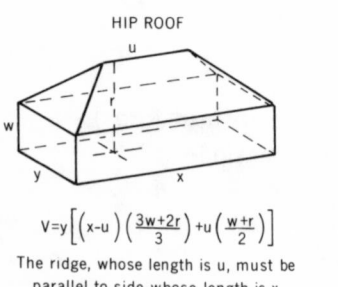

$$V = y\left[(x-u)\left(\frac{3w+2r}{3}\right) + u\left(\frac{w+r}{2}\right)\right]$$

The ridge, whose length is u, must be
parallel to side whose length is x.

Figure 9-H

DOME ROOF

$$V = 0.52360(3rs^2 + r^3)$$

Figure 9-I

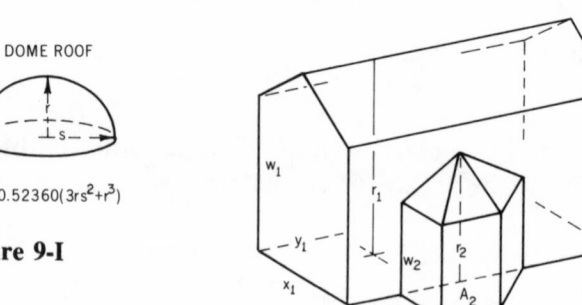

Figure 9-J

Solution: Partition the building into two convex components, and determine the volume of each. The first component has a gable roof, and the formula is given in Figure 9-D.

$$V_1 = x_1 y_1 \cdot \left(\frac{w_1 + r_1}{2} \right) = 100 \times 60 \left(\frac{70 + 80}{2} \right)$$

$$= 450,000 \text{ ft}^3.$$

The second component has a pyramid roof, and the formula is given in Figure 9-F.

$$V_2 = A_2 \left(\frac{2w_2 + r_2}{3} \right) = 1000 \left(\frac{2 \times 40 + 60}{3} \right)$$

$$= 1000 \times 46.667$$

$$= 46,667 \text{ ft}^3.$$

The volume of the building is

$$V = V_1 + V_2 = 450,000 + 46,667 = 496,667 \text{ ft}^3.$$

Example 2: (Connecting Gable Roof). A building has a connecting gable roof as shown in Figure 9-E. The values of the dimensions are

$$x = 20', w = 8', r = 13', \text{ and } t = 6'.$$

What is the volume of the wedge?

Solution: From the formula accompanying the figure of the connecting gable roof,

$$V = \frac{20 \times 6}{6} \times (13 - 8) = \frac{120}{6} \times 5 = 100 \text{ ft}^3.$$

Example 3: (Mansard Roof). A building has a mansard roof as shown in Figure 9-G. The base area at ground level is 1500 sq. ft. The area on top of the mansard roof is 1000 sq. ft. The wall height is 50 ft, and the top of the roof is 70 ft. What is the volume of the building?

Solution: In this example,

$$A = 1500 \text{ ft}^2, A' = 1000 \text{ ft}^2, w = 50 \text{ ft, and } r = 70 \text{ ft}.$$

Now, the volume of the building is

$$V = 1500 \times 50 + \left(\frac{70 - 50}{3}\right)(1500 + 1000 + \sqrt{1500 \times 1000})$$

$$= 75,000 + \frac{20}{3}(2500 + 1225)$$

$$= 99,833 \text{ ft}^3.$$

Example 4: (Hip Roof).   A building has a rectangular base and a hip roof as shown in Figure 9-H. The width is 30 ft., the length is 45 ft., the wall height is 15 ft., the roof height is 25 ft., and the length of the top ridge is 34 ft. What is the volume of the building?

Solution: In this example,

$$y = 30', x = 45', w = 15', r = 25', \text{ and } u = 34'.$$

Now, using the formula for a building with a hip roof, the volume of the building is

$$V = 30\left[(45 - 34)\left(\frac{3 \times 15 + 2 \times 25}{3}\right) + 34\left(\frac{15 + 25}{2}\right)\right]$$

$$= 30(11 \times 31.67 + 34 \times 20)$$
$$= 30(348.37 + 680)$$
$$= 30,851.10 \text{ ft}^3.$$

Example 5: (Dome Roof).   A building has a dome roof as shown in Figure 9-I. The width of the dome is 30 ft., and the height is 10 ft. What is the volume under the dome*?

Solution: In this example,

$$s = \frac{30}{2} = 15 \text{ ft, and } r = 10 \text{ ft.}$$

Now,

$$V = .52360(3rs^2 + r^3)$$
$$= .52360(3 \times 10 \times 15^2 + 10^3)$$
$$= .52360(6,750 + 1,000)$$
$$= .52360 \times 7,750$$
$$= 4,057.9 \text{ ft}^3.$$

---

*Only the volume inside the dome is to be determined.

9.3.   Accrued Depreciation (General Method)

Real estate appraisers generally agree that accrued depreciation or diminished utility can come from three sources:

1. *Physical Deterioration.* Accrued depreciation due to the damages of use and time. This form of depreciation begins the instant an improvement is constructed and continues forever. It can be categorized as:

   (a) Curable. The amount of curable physical deterioration is measured by the cost to cure.

   (b) Incurable. The amount of incurable physical deterioration is usually measured by the economic life of either the building as a whole or through a breakdown of principal components of the structure; i.e., floor, plumbing, lighting, heating, etc.

2. *Functional Obsolescence.*   Accrued depreciation due to the loss of appeal and utility. Value is lost in a rather unpredictable manner. It can be categorized as:

   (a) Curable.   The amount of curable functional obsolescence is measured by the cost to cure.

   (b) Incurable.   The amount of incurable functional obsolescence is measured by observation or by the loss of gross income in commercial properties.

3. *Economic Obsolescence.*   Accrued depreciation due to either unfavorable zoning or unfavorable supply and demand. Diminished utility results from causes external to the property and can be considered as "locational obsolescence." It is thought to be incurable since the property owner can not solve the problem.

There are three methods used to measure accrued depreciation:

1. *Comparable Sales Method.*   Assume the reproduction cost new for a building is known. Then the accrued depreciation can be estimated by a market survey of the sale price of similar properties. See Example 1.

2. *Comparable Income Method.*   Assume the reproduction cost new for a building is known. Then the accrued depreciation can be estimated by a market survey of the income from similar properties. See Example 2.

3. *Formula Method.* This method utilizes the life of an object as a basis to measure the accrued depreciation. See Example 3. The object can be the building itself or components of the building such as walls, floors, etc. (Section 9.4). The life can be considered to be the estimated physical life or the economic life. For instance, the physical life would describe physical depreciation only, whereas economic life would describe physical, functional, and economic depreciation. Although it is theoretically impossible to measure accrued depreciation by a formula, there are several formulas that plausibly describe it. Three of the formulas are, under certain conditions, approved by the Internal Revenue Service for depreciation (Section 11.4): straight line, sum of the years digits, and declining balance. The fourth formula describes exponential depreciation. According to this concept, the rate of decay is proportional to the amount of undecayed material. That is, newness vanishes in proportion to the amount present. Hence, the rate of exponential depreciation is highest when the building is new. (See Figures 9-K and 9-L on page 189.)

Formulas:

$$a_n = \frac{1}{k}$$

$$A_n = \frac{n}{k}$$
} **Straight Line***

$$a_n = \frac{2(k + 1 - n)}{k(k + 1)}$$

$$A_n = \frac{n(2k + 1 - n)}{k(k + 1)}$$
} **Sum of the Years Digits**

$$a_n = q(1 - q)^{n-1}$$

$$A_n = 1 - (1 - q)^n$$
} **Declining Balance**

$$a_n = \frac{te^{-nt}}{1 - e^{-kt}}$$

$$A_n = \frac{1 - e^{-nt}}{1 - e^{-kt}}$$
} **Exponential**

$$A_n = \frac{v_b' + v_l - v_p}{v_b'}$$
   Comparable Sales and Comparable Income

where

a_n = annual rate of depreciation in the nth year
A_n = fraction of accrued depreciation after n years
n = age of building
k = remaining economic life of depreciable asset
q = w/k = a parameter for the declining balance method. The values w = 1.25, 1.50, and 2.00 are used in depreciation for tax purposes
t = parameter for the exponential method. The value of t is at the user's discretion (probably $0 < t < .10$)
v_p = present value of the property
v_b' = reproduction cost new of the building
v_l = present value of the land, as if vacant and put to its highest and best use

---

*The straight line rate of depreciation is a special case of uniform rates given by

$$a_n = \frac{2n(1 - sk) \times sk^2}{k^2} \quad \text{and } A_n = \frac{n^2(1 - sk) + nsk^2}{k^2}.$$

The parameter s can have values between $\frac{1}{k}$ and $\frac{2}{k}$; it is assigned by the appraiser. The straight line rate is $s = \frac{1}{k}$. The sum of the years digits rate is close to the rate that results when $s = \frac{2}{k}$.

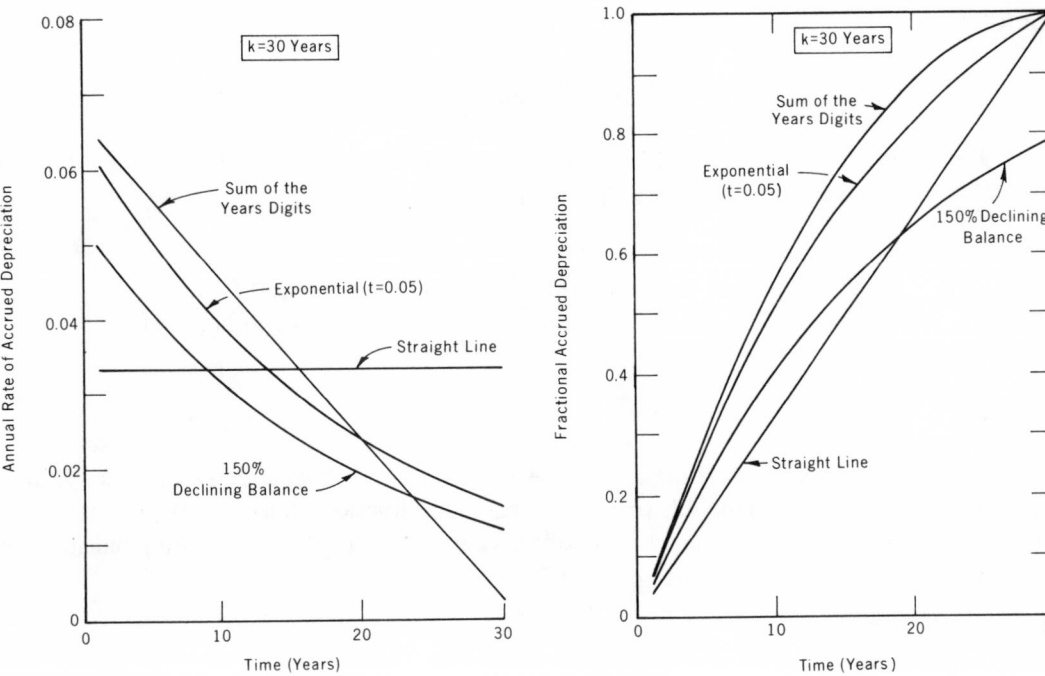

Figure 9-K   **Figure 9-L**

Table: Find a_n and A_n (for straight line, sum of the years digits, and declining balance) in Table 5.

Example 1: (Market Method).   A building would cost $200,000 to reproduce new. The land value, as if vacant, is thought to be $50,000. Similar properties are presently selling for $190,000. What is the fraction of accrued depreciation?

Solution: In this example,

$$v'_b = \$200{,}000, \ v_l = \$50{,}000, \text{ and } v_p = \$190{,}000.$$

Now, the fraction of accrued depreciation is

$$A_n = \frac{\$200{,}000 + \$50{,}000 - \$190{,}000}{\$200{,}000} = \frac{\$60{,}000}{\$200{,}000}$$

$$= .3 = 30\%.$$

Example 2: (Income Method).   A building would cost $200,000 to reproduce new. The land value, as if vacant, is thought to be $50,000. Similar properties are earning an annual net operating income of $22,800. The current property capitalization rate is 12%. What is the fraction of accrued depreciation?

Solution: In this example,

$$v_b' = \$200,000, \text{ and } v_l = \$50,000.$$

Using direct capitalization (Section 8.1), we see that $v_p = \$190,000$. Now, the fraction of accrued depreciation by the formula for the market method is

$$A_n = \frac{\$200,000 + \$50,000 - \$190,000}{\$200,000} = \frac{\$60,000}{\$200,000}$$

$$= .3 = 30\%.$$

Example 3: (Formula Method).   A building has a 25 year economic life. What is the rate of depreciation in the 4th year, and what is the fraction of accrued depreciation after the 8th year, for (a) straight line, (b) sum of the years digits, (c) 150% declining balance, and (d) exponential depreciation, using $t = .02$?

Solution: In this example,

$$k = 25 \text{ years}, n = 4 \text{ years}, \text{ and } n = 8 \text{ years}.$$

(a) For the straight line method,

$$a_4 = \frac{1}{25} = .04,$$

and

$$A_8 = \frac{8}{25} = .32.$$

(b) For the sum of the years digits method,

$$a_4 = \frac{2(25 + 1 - 4)}{25(25 + 1)} = \frac{2 \times 22}{25 \times 26} = .0677,$$

and

$$A_8 = \frac{8(2 \times 25 + 1 - 8)}{25(25 + 1)} = \frac{8 \times 43}{25 \times 26} = .529.$$

(c) For the declining balance method, we have $w = 1.50$. Therefore, $q = 1.50/25 = .06$.

Now,

$$a_4 = .06 \times (1 - .06)^{4-1} = .06 \times (.94)^3 = .0498,$$

and

$$A_8 = 1 - (1 - .06)^8 = 1 - (.94)^8 = .3904.$$

(d) For the exponential method, we have $t = .02$.
Now,

$$a_4 = \frac{.02 \times e^{-4 \times .02}}{1 - e^{-25 \times .02}} = \frac{.02 \times e^{-.08}}{1 - e^{-.5}} = \frac{.02 \times .92312}{1 - .60653}$$

$$= .0469,$$

and

$$A_8 = \frac{1 - e^{-8 \times .02}}{1 - e^{-25 \times .02}} = \frac{1 - e^{-.16}}{1 - e^{-.5}} = \frac{1 - .85214}{1 - .60653}$$

$$= .3758.$$

9.4. Accrued Depreciation (Breakdown Method)

Section 9.3 discusses accrued depreciation in general, describes the five categories of depreciation*, and provides some formulas that plausibly describe the rate and fraction of accrued depreciation after n years.

In this section, the accrued depreciation from each category is determined for individual building components. For instance, plumbing, roof, walls (etc.) each incur loss of value due to several categories of depreciation. The accrued depreciation for any category can be determined by summing the depreciation for each building component. The total accrued depreciation is then obtained by summing over each of the five categories of depreciation. Finally, the value of the property can be determined by using the total accrued depreciation $(v'_b \cdot A_n)$ in the formula of Section 9.5.

Formula:

$$v'_b \cdot A_n = P_c + P_i + F_c + F_i + E_i$$

where

v'_b = reproduction cost new of the improvement
A_n = fraction of accrued depreciation after n years

---

*The five categories are curable and incurable physical deterioration, curable and incurable functional obsolescence, and incurable economic obsolescence.

m   = number of building components considered in the breakdown method

P_{cj} = accrued curable physical deterioration of the jth building component

P_c = $\sum_{j=1}^{m} P_{cj}$ = total accrued curable physical deterioration

F_{cj} = accrued curable function obsolescence of the jth building component

F_c = $\sum_{j=1}^{m} F_{cj}$ = total accrued curable functional obsolescence

v'_j = reproduction cost new of the jth building component

P_{ij} = $(v'_j - P_{cj} - F_{cj}) \cdot A_{nj}$ = accrued incurable physical deterioration of the jth building component

P_i = $\sum_{j=1}^{m} P_{ij}$ = total accrued incurable physical deterioration

A_{nj} = $\dfrac{n}{k_j}$ = fraction of accrued depreciation of the jth building component after n years

n   = age of component, in years

k_j = physical life of the jth building component, in years

F_i = total accrued incurable functional obsolescence

   = $\begin{cases} g \cdot y_f & \text{(for income property)} \\ \text{an estimate} & \text{(for non-income property)} \end{cases}$

g   = gross income multiplier for this type of property (Section 7.2)

y_f = annual gross income thought to be lost due to incurable functional obsolescence

E_i = total accrued incurable economic obsolescence

   = $\begin{cases} g \cdot y_e & \text{(for income property)} \\ \text{an estimate} & \text{(for non-income property)} \end{cases}$

y_e = annual gross income thought to be lost due to accrued incurable economic obsolescence

Table: Find A_{nj} in Table 5.

Example: Consider a 10 year old apartment building. The table below lists the physical life, the cost new, the amount of curable physical deterioration, and the amount of curable functional obsolescence for three components of the building: the roof covering, the interior construction, and the heating. Only these three components are considered so that this example will be manageable. (Assume that, if all building components were considered, the total curable and incurable physical deterioration would be $11,000 and $45,000, respectively. Also assume the total curable functional obsolescence would be $6,000.)

Component	Component Number (j)	Phys. Life (k_j)	Cost New (v'_j)	Curable Physical Deterioration (P_{cj})	Curable Functional Obsolescence (F_{cj})
Roof Covering	1	20 yrs.	$ 700	$ 200	$ 0
Interior Const.	2	40 yrs.	$16,000	$ 800	$2,000
Heating	3	25 yrs.	$20,000	$1,300	$ 200

The reproduction cost new of the building is $200,000, and the gross income multiplier for buildings of this type is 5.5. The annual income that is thought to be lost due to incurable functional and economic obsolescence is $4,000 and $6,000, respectively. What is the total amount of accrued depreciation?

Solution: The values of k_j, v'_j, P_{cj}, and F_{cj} for three components are given in the table. The incurable physical deterioration for the three components for n = 10 years is computed in the footnote*.

Now, for the entire property,

$$P_c = \$11,000, \; P_i = \$45,000, \; F_c = \$6,000, \; v'_b = \$200,000,$$
$$g = 5.5, \; y_f = \$4,000, \text{ and } y_e = \$6,000.$$

The total incurable functional obsolescence is

$$F_i = 5.5 \times \$4,000 = \$22,000,$$

and the total economic obsolescence is

$$E_i = 5.5 \times \$6,000 = \$33,000.$$

---

*The fractional depreciation of each component is
$$A_{n1} = \frac{10}{20} = .50, \; A_{n2} = \frac{10}{40} = .25, \text{ and } A_{n3} = \frac{10}{25} = .40.$$

The incurable physical deterioration for each component can now be computed using the formula and the data in the table:
$$P_{i1} = (\$700 - \$200 - \$0) \times .50 = \$250,$$
$$P_{i2} = (\$16,000 - \$800 - \$2,000) \times .25 = \$3,300, \text{ and}$$
$$P_{i3} = (\$20,000 - \$1,300 - \$200) \times .40 = \$7,400.$$

For these three components the total incurable physical depreciation is
$$\$250 + \$3,300 + \$7,400 = \$10,950.$$

The total incurable physical depreciation for the entire building is given to be, $P_i = \$45,000$.

Now, the total accrued depreciation after 10 years is

$$v_b' A_{10} = P_c + P_i + F_c + F_i + E_i$$
$$= \$11,000 + \$45,000 + \$6,000$$
$$+ \$22,000 + \$33,000$$
$$= \$117,000.$$

9.5.   Reproduction Cost Approach to Value

The cost approach is one of three approaches to value. The cost approach is based on the concept that no knowledgeable buyer would pay more for a property than the cost to reproduce a new one of equal desirability.

The value of the building is determined by taking the reproduction cost new and subtracting the accrued depreciation. The value of the property is then obtained by adding the value of the land, as if vacant.

The accrued depreciation can be obtained either by the general method (Section 9.3) or by the breakdown method (Section 9.4).

Formula:

$$v_p = v_b' (1 - A_n) + v_l$$

where

v_p = present value of the property
v_b' = present reproduction cost new of building
v_l = present value of the land, as if vacant
A_n = fraction of accrued depreciation after n years
n   = age of building

Table: If the formulas of Section 9.3 are used to compute the accrued depreciation, find A_n in Table 5.

Example: It is estimated that the costs required to reproduce new a certain 10 year old building are $420,000. The estimated direct costs of $370,000 include the costs of the building components. The estimated indirect costs of $50,000 include consultation fees, insurance, taxes, tests, interim financing, etc. The accrued depreciation after 10 years is estimated to be 20% of the original value of the building. The value of the land, as if vacant, is estimated by a market survey to be $150,000. What is the present value of the building by the reproduction cost approach?

Solution: In this example,

n = 10 years, v_b' = $370,000 + $50,000 = $420,000, A_{10} = .20, and v_l = $150,000.

Now, the present value of the property is

$$v_p = \$420,000(1 - .20) + \$150,000$$
$$= \$420,000 \times .80 + \$150,000$$
$$= \$486,000.$$

9.6.　Reserve for Replacement

To replace a depreciable asset at the end of its useful life, a fixed sum of money can be deposited periodically in an interest-bearing account. At the end of the useful life, the amount on deposit should equal the replacement cost of the asset.

Section 4.13 introduces the sinking fund concept and Section 7.6 deals with the recapture rate of depreciable real estate through a sinking fund.

Formula:

$$p = \frac{v}{s(r,m,q)}$$

where

p = amount of periodic installment (reserve for replacement)
v = present value of asset to be replaced (if there will be some salvage value, reduce v accordingly)
r = interest rate of sinking fund
k = remaining useful life of asset (Section 11.1)
q = number of interest periods per year
$m = kq$ = total number of interest periods
$s(r,m,q)$ = amount of an annuity of 1

Table:　　Find $s(r,m,q)$ in Table 1.

Example:　　A refrigerator has an estimated useful life of 12 years. The replacement cost is $500 and it should have a 10% salvage value. Suppose quarterly deposits are made and interest is paid at 6% quarterly. How large must each deposit be in order to replace the asset after 12 years?

Solution:　　Notice that only 90% of v must be accumulated since there is a 10% salvage value. In this example,

$k = 12$ years, $v = \$500 \times .9 = \$450$, $q = 4$, $m = kq = 48$, and $r = 6\%$.

From Table 1,

$$s(r,m,q) = s(6,48,4) = 69.5652.$$

Now, the quarterly deposits that will accumulate to \$450 after 12 years are

$$p = \frac{\$450}{69.5652} = \$6.47.$$

9.7.   Compound Change of Reproduction Cost

The future replacement cost of land, a building, or any of its components can be forecast by estimating the annual rate of change of replacement cost.

Intuitively we know the change is compounded annually, but since the rates can vary, we need the following general formula.

Formula:

$$\mathbf{R_n = (1 + r_1) \cdot (1 + r_2) \cdot \ldots \cdot (1 + r_i) \cdot \ldots \cdot (1 + r_n)}$$

where

$R_n =$ fractional change in replacement cost after n years
$r_i \ =$ rate of change of replacement cost during the ith year, expressed as a decimal

Table: If all rates are equal, and denoted by r, find $R_n = (1 + r)^n = c(r,n,1)$ in Table 1.

Example: Suppose a certain model of a home presently costs \$50,000. How much will it cost in 4 years if (a) the replacement cost is estimated to decrease 2% next year, but to increase by 3, 7, and 9% over the following three years, and (b) the replacement cost is estimated to increase 5% annually?

Solution: (a) In the first case,

$$r_1 = - .02, \ r_2 = .03, \ r_3 = .07, \text{ and } r_4 = .09.$$

Now,

$$\begin{aligned} R_4 &= (1 - .02) \cdot (1 + .03) \cdot (1 + .07) \cdot (1 + .09) \\ &= .98 \times 1.03 \times 1.07 \times 1.09 \\ &= 1.177. \end{aligned}$$

Hence, a home that costs \$50,000 today will cost \$50,000 $\times$ 1.177 = \$58,850 in 4 years.

(b) In the second case,

$$r_1 = r_2 = r_3 = r_4 = .05.$$

Now, we can use the formula for the amount of 1 at compound interest.
From Table 1,

$$R_4 = c(5,4,1) = 1.2155.$$

Under these conditions, the \$50,000 home will cost \$50,000 $\times$ 1.2155 = \$60,775 in 4 years.

9.8.   Forecast Property Value

The future property value can be forecast if the annual rate of change of replacement cost, the rate of depreciation and the maintenance are estimated. The change in replacement cost can be somewhat difficult to estimate because it depends on economic forces external to the property. On the other hand, the rate of depreciation (Section 9.3) can usually be predicted more accurately. The effects of physical deterioration and functional obsolescence can be at least partially offset by the judicious application of maintenance. The effect of economic obsolescence is ignored in the following formulation. It is an important consideration, but it is assumed here to remain unchanged.

Figure 9-M shows a surface that describes the forecast property value through time and for different amounts of maintenance. Straight line depreciation is assumed for a building with a 20-year economic life. The figure shows the surface for four different annual rates of increase in replacement cost and land value (0, 2, 4, and 6%).

The figure for 6% shows that when no maintenance is applied to the building, the property value becomes the value of the land plus salvage value (both have inflated by 6% annually) at the end of the 20-year economic life of the building. If 50% of the maintenance required to keep the building in new condition is judiciously applied, the building has a value that exceeds salvage value until the 31st year.

Finally, if 100% of the maintenance required to keep the building in new condition is judiciously applied, the building doesn't depreciate at all, and the entire property value increases at the rate of 6% annually.

The following formula forecasts the future property value based on certain assumptions of replacement cost, depreciation, and maintenance.

Formula:

$$V_p = \begin{cases} \left[v_p - A_n \left(v_b - s - \dfrac{m_o}{a_o} \right) \right] \cdot R_n & \text{if } A_n \leq \dfrac{1}{1 - \dfrac{m_o}{a_o (v_b - s)}} \\[20pt] \left[v_p - (v_b - s) \right] \cdot R_n & \text{otherwise} \end{cases}$$

where

V_p = forecast property value after n years

v_p, v_b = present value of the property and building, respectively

m_o = present annual maintenance*

a_o = present annual rate of depreciation (use n = 0, Section 9.3)

A_n = fraction of accrued depreciation after n years (Section 9.3)

k = remaining economic life of building (Section 11.1)

s = estimated salvage value (Section 11.2)

r_i = annual rate of change of replacement cost in the ith year

R_n = cumulative change in replacement cost of property after n years (Section 9.7)

Table: Find A_n in Table 5.

Example: A property owner wants to predict the value of his property three years hence by the replacement cost approach.

The present value of the property is $200,000, and the building is thought to represent $160,000 of this value. The owner is contributing $1,000 annually to maintenance (a rate of $\dfrac{m_o}{v_p} = \dfrac{\$1,000}{\$200,000} = .005$) and plans to continue at this rate (i.e. $\dfrac{m_o}{V_p}$). Assume the building is actually depreciating according to the straight line rate. The remaining economic life of the building is 36 years at which time its scrap value is estimated to be $16,000 (i.e., 10% of its present value). If, over the next three years, the change in replacement cost is −1%, 3%, and 8%, what is the forecast value of the building?

Solution: In this example,

v_p = $200,000, v_b = $160,000, m_o = $1,000, k = 36 years (therefore a_o = 1/36 = .027778), s = $16,000, n = 3 years, r_1 = −.01, r_2 = .03, and r_3 = .08.

---

*The present annual maintenance required to keep the building in new condition is $m_o = (v_b - s)a_o$.

From Section 9.7, $R_3 = 1.10$. Now the forecast property value by the replacement cost method is

$$V_p = \left[\$200,000 - .083333(\$160,000 - \$16,000 - \frac{\$1,000}{.027778}) \right] \times 1.10$$

$$= (\$200,000 - .083333 \times \$108,000) \times 1.10$$

$$= \$191,000 \times 1.10$$

$$= \$210,000.$$

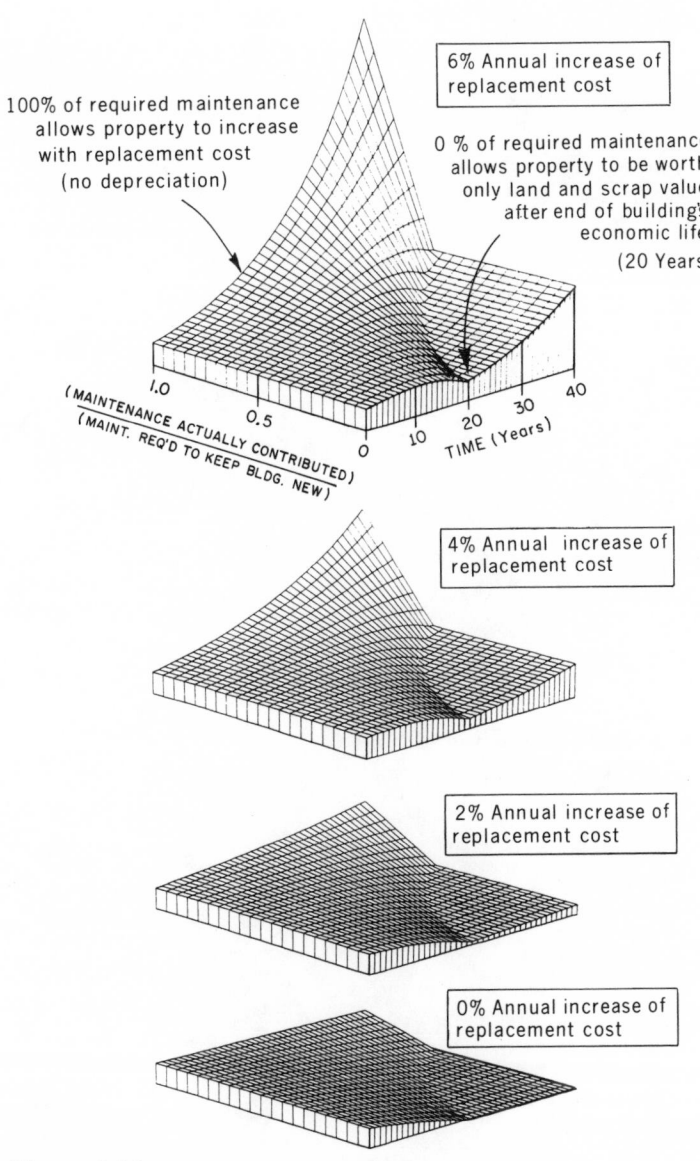

Figure 9-M

10

INVESTMENTS AND VALUATION: MARKET APPROACH

The market approach, together with the cost and the income approach, constitute the three approaches to real estate value. The market approach is fundamental and is accomplished by sampling the recent sales of similar properties. This approach is also required, in some way, to implement the other two approaches. For instance the market approach is often used to determine the capitalization rate which, in turn, is required to determine value by the income approach. Furthermore, the market approach is used to estimate the land value or reproduction cost new in the cost approach to value.

The first eight sections of this chapter deal with geometric or spatial influences on land value. The following three sections deal with statistics. For instance, the method of Section 10.9 provides a confidence interval for the estimates of several independent appraisals. The estimate may be of capitalization rates, land value, residential value, etc. Section 10.10 estimates sale price as it depends on the known value of a single characteristic such as floor area. Section 10.11 estimates sale price as it depends on more than one characteristic such as floor area and age.

10.1.   Land Area

The methods to determine land area are the same as those used to determine floor area in buildings. (See Section 9.1, Floor Area of a Building.)

10.2.   Land Value per Front Foot and per Square Foot

Often the value of land is known, but to compare its value with other parcels, it is necessary to convert the value to dollars per front foot or dollars per square foot.

Formulas:

$$u_a = \frac{v_l}{A_l} \text{ and } u_f = \frac{v_l}{w}$$

where

u_a, u_f = present value of land per square foot and per front foot, respectively
v_l = present value of land
A_l = area of land in square feet
w = width of frontage in feet

Table: Find conversion of units in the tables of Chapter 15.

Example: A rectangular lot 40 feet wide and 110 feet deep is valued at $25,000. What is the value of the lot (a) per square foot, and (b) per front foot?

Solution: In this example,

$$w = 40 \text{ ft and } v_l = \$25,000.$$

From Section 9.1,

$$A_l = 40 \times 110 = 4,400 \text{ ft}^2.$$

Now,

(a) the land value per square foot is

$$u_a = \frac{\$25,000}{4,400 \text{ ft}^2} = \$5.68/\text{ft}^2$$

(b) the land value per front foot is

$$u_f = \frac{\$25,000}{40 \text{ ft.}} = \$625/\text{front ft.}$$

10.3.   Land Value and Depth

The shape of a lot affects its utility, and hence, its value. Commercial usage generally favors frontage width over depth. This is particularly true of retail usage. On the other hand, land for warehouses can have unusual dimensions without adversely affecting its utility. Residential lots generally should not have extreme shapes.

There are many tables that are used to estimate lot value as a function of depth. Although the tabular values vary from city to city, the largest difference in value is caused by the intended use of the lot: commercial, residential, residential rental, etc. The formula, below, is generally representative of the depth tables.

Formula:

$$v_l = u_f \cdot w \cdot \sqrt{\frac{d}{d_s}}^{\,*}$$

where

v_l = present value of lot
u_f = front foot value of comparable lots that are d_s feet deep (Section 10.2)
w = width of frontage, in feet
d = depth of lot, in feet
d_s = depth of standard lot intended use, in feet

Table: Find conversion of units in the tables of Chapter 15.

Example: A lot in a retail location measures 40 feet wide and 130 feet deep. Comparable lots that are a standard 100 feet deep are presently valued at $1,100 per front foot. What is the present value of this lot?

Solution: In this example,

w = 40 ft, d = 130 ft, d_s = 100 ft, and u_f = $1,100/front foot.

Now,

$$v_l = \$1,100 \times 40 \sqrt{\frac{130}{100}} = \$44,000 \times 1.1402$$

$$= \$50,169.^{**}$$

---

*This formula is very representative of most tabular values when $d \le d_s$, however it overstates tabular values when $d > d_s$. The Davies rule which is frequently used is,

$$v_l = u_f \cdot w \cdot \left[\sqrt{1.45(\frac{d}{100} + .0352)} - .226 \right]$$

**The Davies rule evaluates the lot at $51,278.

10.4.   Value of Triangular Lots

If a lot is not located on a corner and has the shape of a right triangle, its value is given as a fraction of a comparable rectangular lot with the same width. The fraction is usually between .6 and .7 if the width is on the street (a delta triangle) and between .3 and .4 (i.e., $1 - .7$ and $1 - .6$) if the width is not on the street (a nabla triangle).

Formula:

$$v_l = u_f \cdot w \cdot t$$

where

v_l = present value of the (right) triangular lot
u_f = front foot value of comparable rectangular lots
w = width of lot, in feet
t = fraction such that $.6 \le t \le .7$ if width on street, and $.3 \le t \le .4$ if not

Table: Find the conversion of units in the tables of Chapter 15.

Example: A lot is shaped like a right triangle with its width of 25 feet on the street. Comparable rectangular lots are selling for $800/front foot. What is its value if we take $t = .65$?

Solution: In this example,

$$w = 25 \text{ ft.}, \ u_f = \$800/\text{front foot, and } t = .65.$$

Now,

$$v_l = (25 \text{ ft.}) (\$800/\text{front foot}) \times .65$$
$$= \$13,000.$$

10.5.   Site Coverage and Floor Area Ratios

Siting is a measure of the functional adequacy of improvements on a lot. The degree to which a site is being utilized can be determined by the ratio of ground floor area to site area and also by the ratio of total floor area to site area.

Triangular lots present an interesting example of site coverage (Section 10.6): the largest building with a rectangular base that can be situated on a triangular lot has a site coverage ratio of 1/2; the ratio is the same for all triangles.

Formulas:

$$s = \frac{A_b}{A_l} \quad \text{and } s' = \frac{A_b'}{A_l}$$

where

s	= site coverage ratio
s'	= floor area ratio
A_b	= ground floor area
A_b'	= total floor area
A_l	= area of land (site)

Table: Find the conversion of units in the tables of Chapter 15.

Example: A 3 story building has a ground floor area of 6,400 ft² and is located on an 8,000 ft² site. The total floor area is $3 \times 6,400$ ft² = 19,200 ft². Determine (a) the site coverage ratio, and (b) the floor area ratio.

Solution: In this example,

$$A_b = 6,400 \text{ ft}^2, \ A_l = 8,000 \text{ ft}^2, \text{ and } A_b' = 19,200 \text{ ft}^2.$$

(a) the site coverage ratio is

$$s = \frac{6,400}{8,000} = .8, \text{ and}$$

(b) the floor area ratio is

$$s' = \frac{19,200}{8,000} = 2.4.$$

10.6. Triangular Commercial Lots

The value of a triangular commercial lot can depend greatly upon the size of the largest rectangular building it can support. The largest such building has a rectangular base that is exactly 1/2 the area of the lot (i.e. the site coverage ratio is 1/2. See Section 10.5). This ratio is the same regardless of the

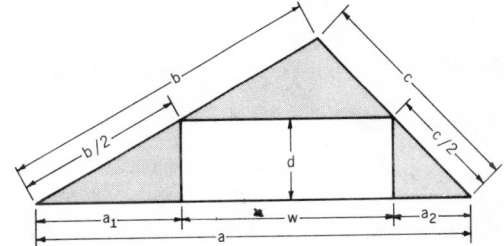

shape of the triangle. The figure shows the typical arrangement that results from maximizing the area of the rectangular base. The setback that is usually required does not alter the result since the setback leaves a smaller but similar triangle.

Formulas:

$$A_b = \frac{a^2 qp}{4(q - p)}$$

$$a_1 = \frac{aq}{2(q - p)}$$

$$a_2 = \frac{- ap}{2(q - p)}$$

$$d = \frac{aqp}{2(q - p)} = \frac{2A_b}{a}$$

$$w = \frac{a}{2}$$

where

A_b = maximum area of base of building

a = length of side of triangle on which building faces (this side must have acute angles at both ends)

b, c = length of other two sides of triangle

a_1, a_2 = distances from each corner of triangle to nearest side of building

$$s = \frac{a + b + c}{2}$$

$$p = \frac{4\sqrt{s(s - a)(s - b)(s - c)}}{c^2 - b^2 + a^2}$$

$$q = \frac{4\sqrt{s(s - a)(s - b)(s - c)}}{c^2 - b^2 - a^2}$$

d = depth of base of building

w = width of base of building

Table: Find conversion of units in the tables of Chapter 15.

Example: A triangular lot, as shown in the figure on page 205, has sides of 90, 60, and 120 feet. (a) what is the area of the base of the largest rectangular building, (b) what are its dimensions, and (c) how must it be situated on the lot?

Solution: In this example,

$$a = 120 \text{ ft}, b = 90 \text{ ft}, \text{ and } c = 60 \text{ ft}.$$

The building will border on side a since the triangle forms acute angles on each end of side a. We must first determine s, p, and q:

$$s = \frac{120 + 90 + 60}{2} = 135 \text{ ft},$$

$$p = \frac{4\sqrt{135(135 - 120)(135 - 90)(135 - 60)}}{60^2 - 90^2 + 120^2}$$

$$= \frac{4\sqrt{135 \times 15 \times 45 \times 75}}{3{,}600 - 8{,}100 + 14{,}400}$$

$$= \frac{10{,}457.04}{9{,}900}$$

$$= 1.05627,$$

and

$$q = \frac{10{,}457.04}{60^2 - 90^2 - 120^2} = \frac{10{,}457.04}{3{,}600 - 8{,}100 - 14{,}400}$$

$$= \frac{10{,}457.04}{-18{,}900}$$

$$= -.55328.$$

We can now answer each of the questions:

(a) The area of the base of the building is

$$A = \frac{120^2 \times (-.55328)(1.05627)}{4(-.55328 - 1.05627)} = \frac{-8{,}415.55}{4(-1.60955)}$$

$$= 1{,}307.13 \text{ ft}^2.$$

(b) The dimensions of the building are width,

$$w = \frac{a}{2} = 60 \text{ ft (along the side bordering a)},$$

and depth,

$$d = \frac{2A_b}{a} = \frac{2614.26 \text{ ft}^2}{120 \text{ ft}} = 21.79 \text{ ft}.$$

(c) The building is situated so that

$$a_1 = \frac{120 \times (-.55328)}{2(-.55328 - 1.05627)} = \frac{66.3936}{3.2191} = 20.62 \text{ ft,}$$

and

$$a_2 = \frac{-120 \times (1.05627)}{2(-.55328 - 1.05627)} = \frac{126.752}{3.2191} = 39.38 \text{ ft.}$$

That is, along side a, one corner of the building is 20.62 ft from the corner of the triangle, and the other corner of the building is 39.38 ft from the other corner of the triangle*. Any adjustment of these dimensions results in a rectangular base whose area is smaller than this one.

10.7.   Plant Coverage

The value of agricultural land depends upon its productivity. Although productivity can depend on many factors, the number of plants (crops, bushes, trees, etc.) is important. The number of plants in a given area is maximized if the plants are arranged so that each lies at an intersection in a grid of equilateral triangles. See Figure 10-A. The conventional arrangement locates plants at intersections of a grid of squares. See Figure 10-B.

If plants are arranged in the optimal way, a given area can support 15.5% more plants than in the conventional way. For instance, if the amount of plant separation is dictated by root size, the roots occupy 90.69% of the land in the optimal arrangement and 78.54% in the square conventional arrangement.

Formulas:

$$y = \sqrt{3}r = 1.73205r, \text{ and}$$

$$N = \frac{A_l}{2yr} ** \quad \text{(approx.)}$$

where

y = distance between rows
r = radius of circular space required by plant
N = number of plants per given area (approx.)
A_l = area to be planted

---

*The two corners of the building that do not touch side a, touch sides b and c at their midpoints.

**N cannot be determined precisely since the planting is affected by the shape of the boundary. The uncertainty is trivial if the planting area is large compared to the plant size.

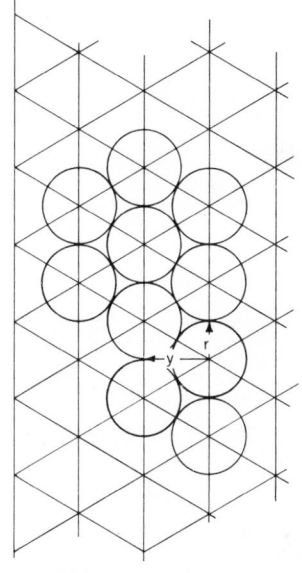

Figure 10-A

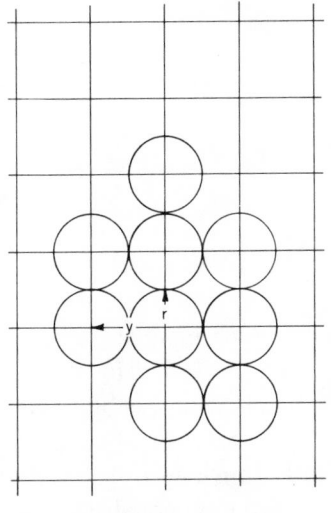

Figure 10-B

Table: Find conversion of units in the tables of Chapter 15.

Example: To allow room for root growth, each plant of a certain crop requires a circular area with a 10″ radius. If the crop is to be planted in the optimal way, (a) what is the distance between the rows, and (b) if 40 acres are to be planted, how many plants will there be?

Solution: In this example,

$$r = 10 \text{ in. and } A_l = 40 \text{ acres.}$$

(a) The distance between rows is

$$y = 1.73205 \times 10 \text{ in.} = 17.3205 \text{ in.}$$

(b) To determine the total number of plants, use the table of Section 15.2 to convert acres to square inches (since r is expressed in inches):

$$1 \text{ acre} = 6,272,640 \text{ in}^2.$$

Now,

$$A_l = 40 \times 6,272,640 \text{ in}^2 = 250,905,600 \text{ in}^2,$$

and

$$N = \frac{250{,}905{,}600 \text{ in}^2}{2 \times (17.3205 \text{ in}) \times (10 \text{ in/plant})}$$

$$= 724{,}302 \text{ plants (approx.)}$$

10.8   Effective Trading Region

The value of commercial property depends on the income it can generate. In turn, the potential income is affected by the accessibility of the property by customers. Although many factors affect the accessibility between two geographic locations, the following formulation assumes that accessibility depends only on the straight line distance between them and the propensity to gravitate from one to the other.*

Consider two commercial sites a and b (i.e. retail stores, shopping centers, towns, etc.). We ask: From which locations is a customer equally likely to gravitate to either site? In the narrowest sense, this question is answered by Reilly's Principle of Gravitation which determines a point on the straight line between a and b from which customers are equally likely to gravitate. In the broadest sense, this question is answered by the second formula, below, which defines a circle.** Customers located inside the circle will tend to gravitate to the site within the circle (call it b), and those located outside the circle will tend to gravitate to site a.

To be sure, this formulation portrays idealized situations. Rarely are two commercial sites unaffected by other such sites or by other aspects of accessibility. Nonetheless, these formulas do provide an estimate of the effective trading region about a site.

Formulas:

$$d_a = \frac{d}{1 + \sqrt{q}} \quad \textbf{(Effective Trading Distance, Reilly's Formula)}$$

$$\left. \begin{array}{l} \textbf{Center} = \dfrac{d}{1 - q} \\[2em] \textbf{Radius} = \dfrac{d\sqrt{q}}{1 - q} \end{array} \right\} \textbf{(Effective Trading Circle)}$$

where

- a, b = designation of two sites (designate the larger site as a)
- d_a = effective trading distance (or travel time) from site a to site b
- d = actual distance (or travel time) between sites a and b
- S_a, S_b = size of sites a and b, respectively (i.e., population, retail floor area, etc.) Take $S_a > S_b$
- $q = \dfrac{S_b}{S_a}$ = ratio of sizes of the two sites

---

*Here the propensity to gravitate concerns a customer's willingness to travel to a commercial site due to its size, selection of goods, bargains, etc.

**This circle is the locus of points in the plane for which the ratio of the distances (from the point to site a and from the point to site b) is a constant.

Table: none

Example 1: (Towns).   Towns a and b are 30 miles apart and have populations of 20,000 and 10,000, respectively. Determine the circle that defines the locations from which customers are equally likely to visit either town. This example is depicted in the figure.

Solution: In this example,

$$d = 30 \text{ mi, } S_a = 20,000, \text{ and } S_b = 10,000.$$

Now,

$$q = \frac{10,000}{20,000} = 0.5.$$

The center of the circle is

$$\frac{d}{1 - q} = \frac{30 \text{ miles}}{1 - .5}$$

$$= 60 \text{ miles from town a toward town b.}$$

The radius of the circle is

$$\frac{d\sqrt{q}}{1 - q} = \frac{30 \times \sqrt{.5}}{1 - .5}$$

$$= \frac{21.213}{.5}$$

$$= 42.43 \text{ miles.}$$

Example 2: (Retail Centers).   Department stores a and b have 250,000 ft^2 and 50,000 ft^2 of sales area, respectively. They are relatively isolated from other stores, and the travel time between them averages 10 minutes. Determine the circle that defines the locations from which customers are equally likely to visit either shopping center.

Solution: In this example,

$$S_a = 250,000 \text{ ft}^2, \ S_b = 50,000 \text{ ft}^2, \text{ and } d = 10 \text{ min.}$$

Now,

$$q = \frac{50,000}{250,000} = .2.$$

The center of the circle is

$$\frac{d}{1-q} = \frac{10 \text{ min.}}{1-.2} = 12.5 \text{ min.}$$

from shopping center a toward center b. The radius of the circle is

$$\frac{d\sqrt{q}}{1-q} = \frac{10 \text{ min.} \times .4472}{1-.2} = 5.59 \text{ min.}$$

10.9.   Value Estimate by Several Appraisers

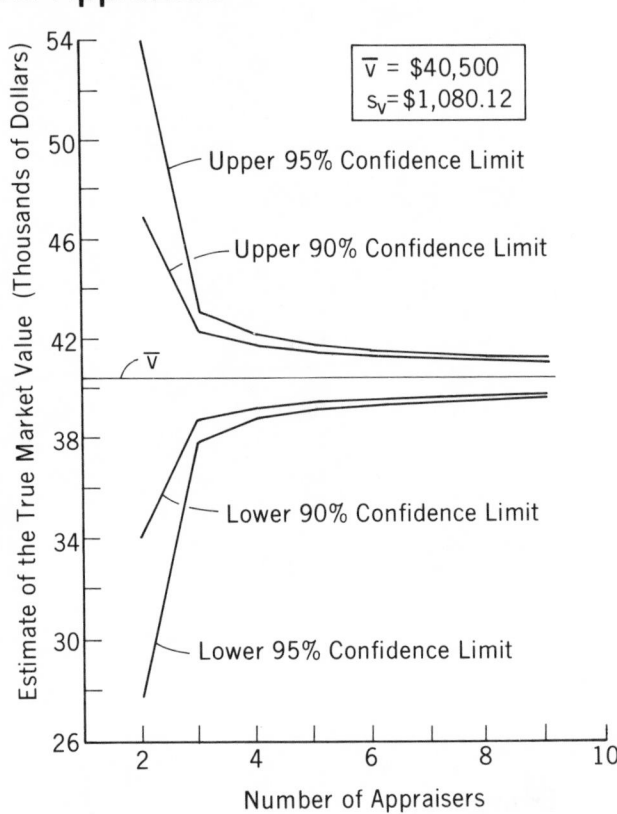

Suppose the market value of a property is estimated *independently* by several appraisers.* For example, suppose n appraisers independently estimate the value, and then the estimates are averaged. We might ask: How certain are we that this average value is within a given range of the true market value? The two formulas below give an upper and a lower value within which we can be, say, 95% certain that the true value lies.

The figure illustrates the 90% and 95% confidence limits for the example in this section. Notice that the confidence interval becomes smaller as more appraisers are used.

Formula:

$$V_l = \bar{v} - q_n s_v \text{ and } V_u = \bar{v} + q_n s_v$$

where

V_l, V_u = lower and upper estimate of market value, respectively
v_i = the ith independent estimate of market value
n = number of independent estimates

*Generally, an independent estimate is an estimate that is not influenced by other estimates.

$$\overline{v} = \frac{1}{n} \sum_{i=1}^{n} v_i = \text{average of n independent estimates of market value}$$

$$s_v = \sqrt{\frac{1}{n-1} \sum_{i=1}^{n} (v_i - \overline{v})^2} = \text{standard deviation of n independent estimates}$$

of market value

$q_n = $ factor that depends on n and the desired confidence level (e.g., 95%)

Table: Find q_n in the table, below.

Values of q_n

n	2	3	4	5	6	7	8	9	10
90%	6.311	1.686	1.177	.9534	.8226	.7345	.6698	.6198	.5797
95%	12.706	2.484	1.591	1.242	1.050	.9248	.8360	.7687	.7153

Example: Four Realtors independently (i.e., without communication) estimate the market value of a house at $41,000, $39,000, $41,500, and $40,500. To estimate the true market value, they will average their estimates. Both the Realtors and the owner would like to know how accurate the estimate is likely to be. Specifically, they would like to be 95% confident that the true market value lies within a certain range of values. What are these values?

Solution: In this example,

$$n = 4, \ v_1 = \$41,000, \ v_2 = \$39,000, \ v_3 = \$41,500, \text{ and } v_4 = \$40,500.$$

(a) Find the average of the estimates:

$$\overline{v} = \frac{1}{n} \sum_{i=1}^{n} v_i = \frac{1}{4}(\$41,000 + \$39,000 + \$41,500 + \$40,500)$$

$$= \$40,500.$$

(b) Find the standard deviation of the estimates:

$$s_v = \sqrt{\frac{1}{n-1} \sum_{i=1}^{n} (v_i - \overline{v})^2}$$

$$= \sqrt{\frac{1}{3}\left[(v_1 - \bar{v})^2 + (v_2 - \bar{v})^2 + (v_3 - \bar{v})^2 + (v_4 - \bar{v})^2\right]}$$

$$= \sqrt{\frac{1}{3}\left[(41{,}000 - 40{,}500)^2 + (39{,}000 - 40{,}500)^2 \atop + (41{,}500 - 40{,}500)^2 + (40{,}500 - 40{,}500)^2\right]}$$

$$= \sqrt{\frac{1}{3}\left[(500)^2 + (-1{,}500)^2 + (1{,}000)^2 + (0)^2\right]}$$

$$= \sqrt{\frac{1}{3}(250{,}000 + 2{,}250{,}000 + 1{,}000{,}000 + 0)}$$

$$= \sqrt{\frac{1}{3} \times 3{,}500{,}000} = \sqrt{1{,}166{,}666.67} = \$1{,}080.12.$$

(c) Go to the table to find q_4. Corresponding to the 95% confidence level and $n = 4$ samples, find $q_4 = 1.591$.

(d) Use the formulas to determine V_l and V_u, the lower and upper 95% confidence limits:

$$V_l = \$40{,}500 - 1.591 \times \$1{,}080.12 = \$38{,}781, \text{ and}$$
$$V_u = \$40{,}500 + 1.591 \times \$1{,}080.12 = \$42{,}218.$$

Hence, if the four Realtors arrive at their estimates independently, they can be 95% confident that the true market value of the house is between \$38,781 and \$42,218.

10.10.   Single Regression

Single regression analysis can be used to statistically estimate value as it depends on a single characteristic. For instance, if it is suspected that the value of single family residences depends largely on floor area, several samples of sale price and floor area can be obtained from recent comparable sales. This data can then be used in the formula, below, to estimate the sale price of a single family residence with a known floor area.*

The estimate is more accurate as more comparable samples are used. Although floor area is the characteristic used in this example, any reasonable characteristic can be used as long as it can be measured.

The floor area and its associated sale price are two numbers that define a point in the plane (two dimensions). Each sample then is a point in the plane. The formula, below, is the

---

*Actually the use of the formula is general and can be used to estimate the value of many phenomena, such as capitalization rates.

formula for the straight line that best fits the scattering of points*. (See Figure 10-C on page 216 which describes the following example.)

Formula:

$$v = b_1 + b_2x$$

where

v = estimated value of the sample
x = value of the characteristic of the sample to be tested
n = number of samples
v_i = value of the ith sample

$$\bar{v} = \frac{1}{n} \sum_{i=1}^{n} v_i = \text{average value}$$

x_i = value of the characteristic of the ith sample

$$\bar{x} = \frac{1}{n} \sum_{i=1}^{n} x_i = \text{average value of the characteristic}$$

$$s_x^2 = \frac{1}{n-1} \sum_{i=1}^{n} (x_i - \bar{x})^2 = \text{variance of the characteristic}$$

$$b_2 = \frac{\dfrac{1}{n-1} \sum_{i=1}^{n} (v_i - \bar{v}) \cdot (x_i - \bar{x})}{s_x^2}$$

$$b_1 = \bar{v} - b_2 \cdot \bar{x}$$

Table: none

Example: Brokers at the MJM Realty Co. know there is a relationship between recent sales price and floor area for comparable single family residences.

The company would like to estimate the sale price of other comparable residences based on the known floor area. They have collected five samples (this small sample size is used to provide a concise example).** The values are listed in the table.

---

*The best fitting straight line is the one that renders a minimum the sum of the squares of the vertical distance between the points and the line.

**To apply regression analysis in practice, the sample size should be at least 10 more than the number of characteristics (i.e., n ≥ 11). Furthermore, the sale price should be plotted against the characteristic to see if some correlation exists.

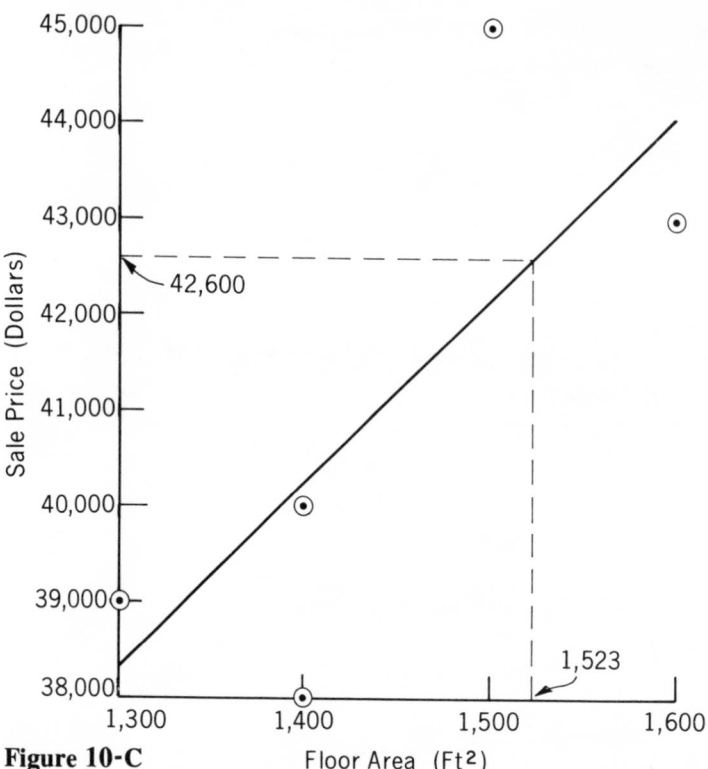

Figure 10-C   Floor Area (Ft²)

(a) Determine the single regression formula for this data, and (b) using the formula, estimate the sale price of a comparable residence with a floor area of 1,523 ft².

Sample, i	1	2	3	4	5
Sale Price, v_i	$40,000	$45,000	$43,000	$38,000	$39,000
Floor Area, x_i	1,400	1,500	1,600	1,400	1,300

Solution: (a) To determine the formula for v, we must first determine $\bar{v}$, $\bar{x}$, and s_x^2 :

(i) $\bar{v} = \dfrac{1}{5} \displaystyle\sum_{i=1}^{5} v_i = \dfrac{1}{5}(\$40,000 + \$45,000 + \$43,000 + \$38,000 + \$39,000)$

$= \$41,000,$

$\bar{x} = \dfrac{1}{5} \displaystyle\sum_{i=1}^{5} x_i = \dfrac{1}{5}(1,400 + 1,500 + 1,600 + 1,400 + 1,300)$ ft²

$= 1,440$ ft², and

$$s_x^2 = \frac{1}{4} \sum_{i=1}^{5} (x_i - \bar{x})^2$$

$$= \frac{1}{4} \left[(-40)^2 + (60)^2 + (160)^2 + (-40)^2 + (-140)^2 \right]$$

$$= 13{,}000.56 \text{ ft}^2.$$

(ii) Now we can evaluate the coefficients, b_2 and b_1.

$$b_2 = \frac{\dfrac{1}{4} \sum\limits_{i=1}^{5} (v_i - \bar{v})(x_i - \bar{x})}{s_x^2}$$

$$= \frac{1}{4s_x^2} \left[(40{,}000 - 41{,}000)(1{,}400 - 1{,}440) \right.$$

$$+ (45{,}000 - 41{,}000)(1{,}500 - 1{,}440)$$
$$+ (43{,}000 - 41{,}000)(1{,}600 - 1{,}440)$$
$$+ (38{,}000 - 41{,}000)(1{,}400 - 1{,}440)$$
$$\left. + (39{,}000 - 41{,}000)(1{,}300 - 1{,}440) \right]$$

$$= \frac{1}{4s_x^2} \left[(-1{,}000)(-40) + (4{,}000)(60) + (2{,}000)(160) \right.$$

$$\left. + (-3{,}000)(-40) + (-2{,}000)(-140) \right]$$

$$= \frac{1{,}000{,}000}{4 \times 13{,}000.56}$$

$$= \$19.22994/\text{ft}^2, \text{ and}$$

$$b_1 = \bar{v} - b_2\bar{x} = \$41{,}000 - \$19.22994/\text{ft}^2 \times 1{,}440 \text{ ft}^2$$
$$= \$13{,}308.89.$$

(iii) The regression formula for this example is

$$v = \$13{,}308.89 + (\$19.22994/\text{ft}^2)x.$$

(b) To determine the sale price, v, for a residence with a floor area of $x = 1{,}523 \text{ ft}^2$, we merely substitute this value in the above formula:

$$v = \$13{,}308.89 + (\$19.22994/\text{ft}^2)(1{,}523 \text{ ft}^2)$$
$$= \$42{,}596.09 \text{ (say, } \$42{,}600).$$

10.11.   Multiple Regression

Section 10.10 shows how to determine the statistical relationship between value and one characteristic of the property. This section shows how to determine the statistical relationship between value and more than one characteristic. For instance, if it is suspected that the sale price of single family residence depends on floor area, age, and the number of bedrooms, several samples of sale price and these three characteristics can be gathered from recent comparable sales. This data can then be used in the formula, below, to estimate the sale price of a single family residence with known floor area, age, and number of bedrooms. The estimate is more accurate as more comparable samples are used.

Formula:

$$v = b_1 + \sum_{k=2}^{m} b_k x_k$$

where

v = estimated value of the sample

m = number of characteristics

x_k = value of the kth characteristic of the sample to be tested

n = number of samples

x_{ki} = value of the kth characteristic of the ith sample

$$\bar{x}_k = \frac{1}{n} \sum_{i=1}^{n} x_{ki} = \text{ average value of the kth characteristic}$$

$$c_{kj} = \frac{1}{n-1} \sum_{i=1}^{n} (x_{ki} - \bar{x}_k)(x_{ji} - \bar{x}_j) = \text{ covariance of } x_k \text{ and } x_j$$

$$C = \begin{vmatrix} c_{22} & \cdots & c_{2m} \\ \vdots & & \vdots \\ c_{m2} & \cdots & c_{mm} \end{vmatrix}^* = \text{ determinant of covariances}$$

$$c^{kj} = \frac{A_{kj}}{C}$$

A_{kj} = cofactor of c_{kj}. That is,

$$A_{kj} = (-1)^{k+j} \times (\text{determinant with the kth row and jth column deleted})$$

---

*This array is called a determinant. See Appendix: Mathematical Notes, Section A.5.

$$b_k = \sum_{j=2}^{m} c_{1j} c^{kj} \quad (k = 2,3,\ldots,m)$$

$$b_1 = \bar{x}_1 - \sum_{k=2}^{m} \bar{x}_k b_k$$

Example: We suspect that floor area and age are two characteristics that significantly affect the sale price of single family residences. We sample five comparable single family residences and gather the following data. (This small sample size is used only to provide a concise example*).

Sample (i)	Sale Price (x_{1i})	Floor Area (x_{2i})	Age (x_{3i})
1	$40,000	1,400 ft²	10 yrs
2	45,000	1,500	6
3	43,000	1,600	9
4	38,000	1,300	7
5	46,000	1,500	4

(a) Find the multiple regression formula for this data, and (b) using this formula, what is the likely sale price for an 8 year old house with a floor area of 1,435 ft²?

Solution: For convenience, all units (such as dollars, ft², and years) shall be omitted until the end.

(a) To determine the multiple regression formula,

(i) first, find the average value of each characteristic:

$$\bar{x}_1 = \frac{1}{5} \sum_{i=1}^{5} x_{1i}$$

$$= \frac{1}{5}(40,000 + 45,000 + 43,000 + 38,000 + 46,000)$$

$$= 42,400,$$

$$\bar{x}_2 = \frac{1}{5} \sum_{i=1}^{5} x_{2i}$$

---

*To apply regression analysis in practice, the sample size should be at least 10 more than the number of characteristics (i.e., $n \geq m + 10$). Furthermore, the sale price should be plotted against each characteristic to see if some correlation exists.

$$= \frac{1}{5}(1,400 + 1,500 + 1,600 + 1,300 + 1,500)$$

$$= 1,460, \text{ and}$$

$$\bar{x}_3 = \frac{1}{5} \sum_{i=1}^{5} x_{3i} = \frac{1}{5}(10 + 6 + 9 + 7 + 4)$$

$$= 7.2.$$

(ii) Next, determine the c_{kj} values. These are the $m \times m = 9$ covariances:

$$c_{11} = \frac{1}{4} \sum_{i=1}^{5} (x_{1i} - \bar{x}_1)(x_{1i} - \bar{x}_1)$$

$$= \frac{1}{4}\Big[(40,000 - 42,400)(40,000 - 42,000)$$

$$+ (45,000 - 42,400)(45,000 - 42,400)$$

$$+ (43,000 - 42,400)(43,000 - 42,400)$$

$$+ (38,000 - 42,400)(38,000 - 42,400)$$

$$+ (46,000 - 42,400)(46,000 - 42,400)\Big]$$

$$= \frac{1}{4}\Big[(-2,400)(-2,400) + (2,600)(2,600) + (600)(600)$$

$$+ (-4,400)(-4,400) + (3,600)(3,600)\Big]$$

$$= 11,300,000,$$

$$c_{12} = \frac{1}{4} \sum_{i=1}^{5} (x_{1i} - \bar{x}_1)(x_{2i} - \bar{x}_2)$$

$$= \frac{1}{4}\Big[(40,000 - 42,400)(1,400 - 1,460)$$

$$+ (45,000 - 42,400)(1,500 - 1,460)$$

$$+ (43,000 - 42,400)(1,600 - 1,460)$$

$$+ (38,000 - 42,400)(1,300 - 1,460)$$

$$+ (46,000 - 42,400)(1,500 - 1,460)\Big]$$

$$= \frac{1}{4}\Big[(-2{,}400)(-60) + (2{,}600)(40) + (600)(140)$$
$$+ (-4{,}400)(-160) + (3{,}600)(40)\Big]$$
$$= 295{,}000,$$

$$c_{13} = \frac{1}{4} \sum_{i=1}^{5} (x_{1i} - \overline{x}_1)(x_{3i} - \overline{x}_3) = -4{,}850,$$

$$c_{21} = c_{12} = 295{,}000^*,$$

$$c_{22} = \frac{1}{4} \sum_{i=1}^{5} (x_{2i} - \overline{x}_2)(x_{2i} - \overline{x}_2) = 13{,}000,$$

$$c_{23} = \frac{1}{4} \sum_{i=1}^{5} (x_{2i} - \overline{x}_2)(x_{3i} - \overline{x}_3) = -15,$$

$$c_{31} = c_{13} = -4{,}850,$$

$$c_{32} = c_{23} = -15, \text{ and}$$

$$c_{33} = \frac{1}{4} \sum_{i=1}^{5} (x_{3i} - \overline{x}_3)(x_{3i} - \overline{x}_3) = 5.7.$$

(iii) We have evaluated each covariance. Hence,

$$C = \begin{vmatrix} c_{22} & c_{23} \\ c_{32} & c_{33} \end{vmatrix} = \begin{vmatrix} 13{,}000 & -15 \\ -15 & 5.7 \end{vmatrix}^{**}$$

$$= 13{,}000 \times 5.7 - (-15) \times (-15) = 73{,}875.$$

(iv) The cofactors of the c_{kj} are

$$A_{22} = (-1)^{2+2}c_{33} = 5.7, \quad A_{23} = (-1)^{2+3}c_{32} = 15,$$
$$A_{32} = A_{23} = 15, \text{ and } A_{33} = (-1)^{3+3}c_{22} = 13{,}000.$$

*The equation for c_{kj} is symmetric. Hence, $c_{kj} = c_{jk}$ for all k and j. (Likewise the A_{kj} and C_{kj}.)
**See Appendix: Mathematical Notes, Section A.5.

(v) The C^{kj} are now,

$$C^{22} = \frac{A_{22}}{C} = \frac{5.7}{73,875} = .00007715736,$$

$$C^{23} = \frac{A_{23}}{C} = \frac{15}{73,875} = .0002030457,$$

$$C^{32} = C^{32} = .0002030457, \text{ and}$$

$$C^{33} = \frac{A_{33}}{C} = \frac{13,000}{73,875} = .1759729.$$

(vi) We are now able to evaluate the coefficients, b_k:

$$b_2 = \sum_{j=2}^{3} c_{1j}C^{2j} = c_{12}C^{22} + c_{13}C^{23}$$

$$= 295,000 \times .00007715736 - 4,850 \times .0002030457$$
$$= 22.7614 - .9847716$$
$$= 21.77663,$$

$$b_3 = \sum_{j=2}^{3} c_{1j}C^{3j} = c_{12}C^{32} + c_{13}C^{33}$$

$$= 295,000 \times .0002030457 - 4,850 \times .1759729$$
$$= 59.898481 - 853.4685$$
$$= -793.5700, \text{ and}$$

$$b_1 = \bar{x}_1 - \sum_{k=2}^{3} \bar{x}_k b_k = 42,400 - (1,460 \times 21.77663 - 7.2 \times 793.5700)$$

$$= 16,319.80.$$

(vii) We can now write the multiple regression formula:

$$v = b_1 + b_2 x_2 + b_3 x_3$$
$$= \$16,319.80 + (\$21.77663/\text{ft}^2) \cdot x_2 - (\$793.5700/\text{yrs}) \cdot x_3.$$

(b) Using this formula, we can estimate the sale price of a single family residence with floor area $x_2 = 1,435$ ft² and age $x_3 = 8$ yrs:

$$v = \$16,319.80 + (\$21.77663/\text{ft}^2)(1,435 \text{ ft}^2) - (\$793.5700/\text{yrs})(8 \text{ yrs})$$
$$= \$41,200.7 \text{ (say, } \$41,200).$$

11

TAXES: DEDUCTIONS

Deductions reduce the ordinary income that is taxable. This chapter includes deductions related to real estate that can be expressed by formulas.

Generally, the tax regulations include so many exceptions and limitations that they are difficult to describe in words. Therefore, flow diagrams are used throughout the chapters on taxes. In most cases you merely answer the question (posed in a box), and flow to the right or left, depending on whether the answer is yes or no, respectively. When there are several questions in a box, all must be answered yes in order to flow to the right. Otherwise flow to the left. Finally, the box at the bottom of the chart contains the proper formula.

The diagram in Section 11.8 on page 237 is a simple example. (Recall that the notation "$h < v$" means "h is less than v.") If a deduction is subject to carryover, the first year deduction is denoted by d_1, and the carryover is denoted by d_i, meaning the deduction in the ith year (i = 2,3,. . .).

The four chapters on taxes include the rules from the Tax Reform Act of 1976.

[Note: *Although great effort has been made to use consistent notation throughout the four chapters on taxes, the large number of parameters makes total consistency very difficult. Therefore, the reader should assume that the notation is consistent within each section only. That is, "c" in Section 13.4 denotes capital gain or loss whereas "c" in Section 14.1 denotes capital gain after depreciation recapture.*]

11.1.   Useful Life

According to the Treasury, the useful life of a depreciable asset is "the period over which the asset may reasonably be expected to be useful to the taxpayer in his trade or business or in the production of his income."

In fact, the useful life of an asset can be determined either by the taxpayer's reasonable estimate or by the Treasury's class life system (generally not used for real property):

(1) *Taxpayer's reasonable estimate.*   This estimate is subjective and is affected by the taxpayer's goals. It needn't be related to the physical life of the property. Of course, the salvage value must be set to correspond to the useful life. Other effects on the useful life are: the age when acquired, the amount and type of use to which it will be subjected, the climate, the repair and maintenance policy, possible obsolescence, etc. An earlier estimate of useful life can be changed if there is good cause. At all times the estimate of useful life must be reasonable.

(2) *Class Life System.*   In this system, the Treasury has determined a guideline life for different types of depreciable property (mostly personal property). Furthermore, it has determined a range of lives, called the asset depreciation range, that is about 20% shorter and 20% longer than the guideline life. When the taxpayer elects to use the class life system, he can choose a useful life that falls anywhere within the asset depreciation range.

If the class life system is used, the salvage value must be zero. Its applicability to real property is questionable, and the Treasury has permitted its use for personal property even though the taxpayer's estimate of useful life is used for real property. The guideline life applies to property regardless of when it was placed into service. However, the asset depreciation range cannot be used for property placed into service before 1971.

The taxpayer can elect to use the system in one taxable year and not the next. If, for all assets placed into service during a given year, the cost of the used assets exceeds 10% of the cost of all assets, the class life system can be used only for the new assets. This system can't be used for those assets subject to special rapid amortization (Sections 11.15 and 11.16).

Formula: none

Table: Find the guideline life and the asset depreciation range for personal property in Table 6. Find the reasonable useful life and physical life of buildings in the table on page 225 in this section.

Example 1: (Taxpayer's Estimate).   Bill Pike bought a three year old apartment building. For the purpose of depreciation, what is the useful life?

Solution: From the table in this section a reasonable life would be $40 - 3 = 37$ years. The selection of a considerably shorter useful life would require a concomitantly large salvage value.

REASONABLE USEFUL AND PHYSICAL LIFE OF BUILDINGS

Building Type	Reasonable Useful Life (Years)	Physical Life (Years)
Apartments	40	50
Dwellings	45	60
Factories	45	50
Farm Buildings	30	60
Garages	45	60
Grain Elevators	60	75
Hotels	40	50
Loft Buildings	50	67
Machine Shops	45	60
Office Buildings	45	67
Stores	50	67
Theaters	40	50
Warehouses	60	75

Example 2: (Class Life System). Bill Pike bought some new office furniture. According to the class life system, what is the range of lives he can use for depreciation?

Solution: From Table 6, the shortest life is 8 years and the longest life is 12 years.

11.2. Salvage Value

Salvage value is the estimated value of depreciable property when it is no longer useful to the owner. This value depends on the owner's replacement policy rather than the physical life of the property. It can be the estimated sale price of the property at the end of its useful life.

If the property is to be removed instead of merely retired from service, the cost of removal can reduce salvage value (but not below zero).

The cost of demolishing depreciable real property can also reduce salvage value (but not below zero) if the owner did not intend to demolish it when he acquired it.

If the class life system (Section 11.1) is used for depreciation, salvage value is zero.

Although the salvage value is an estimate of the property value when it is disposed of, the Treasury requires that, when it is disposed of, the salvage value be readjusted to equal the amount realized upon disposition.

The following flow diagram can be used for real and personal property when the taxpayer estimates the useful life (Section 11.1).

Formula:

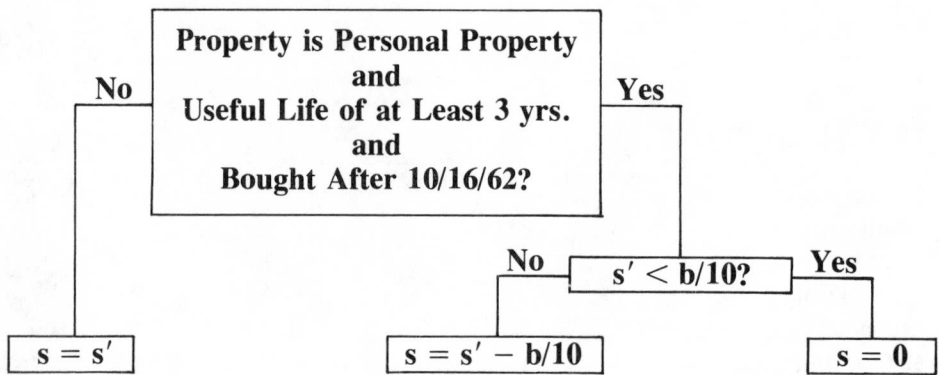

where

s = salvage value used for depreciation (Section 11.4)
s' = taxpayer's estimate of salvage value (less removal and demolition costs, if any)
b = basis of depreciable property (Chapter 12)

Example 1:   The United Parts Co. erected a new building at the cost of $500,000. The building has a 45-year useful life. The company estimates the salvage value to be $30,000. What is the salvage value to be used for depreciation?

Solution: In this example,

$$b = \$500,000, \text{ and } s' = \$30,000.$$

From the flow diagram (following no), the salvage value is

$$s = \$30,000.$$

Example 2:   Last year the United Parts Co. bought office desks for $500 each. The company estimates their useful life to be 8 years, at which time their salvage value is estimated to be $80. What is the salvage value to be used for depreciation?

Solution: In this example,

$$b = \$500, \text{ and } s' = \$80.$$

From the flow diagram (following yes, no), the salvage value used for depreciation is

$$s = \$80 - \$500/10 = \$30.$$

11.3. Allocation of Value Between Land and Buildings

Since buildings depreciate and land generally does not, it is necessary for tax purposes to estimate the portion of the property value that can be attributed to the buildings. If the allocation is not specified in a purchase contract, it can be determined either directly by an appraisal or indirectly by the assessment of real estate tax. If a tax assessment is used, the value of the building is estimated by the following formula.

Formula:

$$v_b = v_p \left(\frac{v_b'}{v_l' + v_b'} \right)$$

where

v_b = present value of the building*
v_p = present value of the property
v_l', v_b' = assessed value of the land and building, respectively

Example: Dan Miles is converting his home to rental property. He estimates the fair market value of his property to be $50,000. The assessed value of the building and land are $16,500 and $4,000, respectively. What is the estimated value of the building?

Solution: In this example,

$$v_p = \$50,000, \ v_b' = \$16,500, \text{ and } v_l' = \$4,000.$$

Now, the value of the building is estimated to be

$$v_b = \$50,000 \times \frac{\$16,500}{\$4,000 + \$16,500}$$

$$= \$50,000 \times .80488$$

$$= \$40,244.$$

---

*This is not necessarily the basis. The present owner may have claimed depreciation, thus reducing the basis.

11.4.   Types of Depreciation Allowance

Tangible personal property and improved real property will depreciate with time and use. To account for this presumed loss of value, the Treasury permits an annual deduction from ordinary income.

The annual deduction for depreciation depends on the basis of the property when acquired (Chapter 12), its useful life (Section 11.1), its estimated salvage value (Section 11.2), and the type of depreciation used by the taxpayer. The depreciation claimed reduces the basis of the property. However, in no case can this deduction be claimed after the adjusted basis becomes less than the salvage value.

If the class life system (Section 11.1) is not used, depreciation is claimed the month the property is put into use if that date falls in the first 15 days of the month. Otherwise depreciation is not claimed until the following month.

If the class life system is used, there are two possible definitions of the date an asset is placed into service:

(1) *Half-year Convention.*   Property placed into service during a taxable year is assumed to have been in service a half year.

(2) *Modified Half-year Convention.*   Property placed into service in the first half of the taxable year is assumed to be in service on the first day of the tax year. Similarly, property placed into service in the second half of the taxable year is assumed to be in service on the first day of the next tax year.

The same rules hold for property retired from use.

Although any method of depreciation used in accounting is acceptable, the straight line, declining balance (with different rates), and the sum-of-the-years digits are most often used. Graphs of these methods of depreciation are shown in the two figures of Section 9.3. The flow diagrams on pages 229 and 231 show which of these methods and rates are permitted. The formulas for each method determine the amount of depreciation that can be claimed.

Formulas:

$$d = \begin{cases} (b-s) \cdot a_n & \text{where } a_n = \dfrac{1}{k} & \text{(Straight line)} \\[2em] (b-s) \cdot a_n & \text{where } a_n = \dfrac{2(k+1-n)}{k(k+1)} & \text{(Sum of the years digits)} \\[2em] b \cdot a_n{}^* & \text{where } a_n = q(1-q)^{n-1} & \text{(Declining balance)} \end{cases}$$

$^*d = 0$ if $(1-q)^n < s/b$, because property can't be depreciated below salvage value.

DEPRECIATION ALLOWANCE FOR REAL PROPERTY

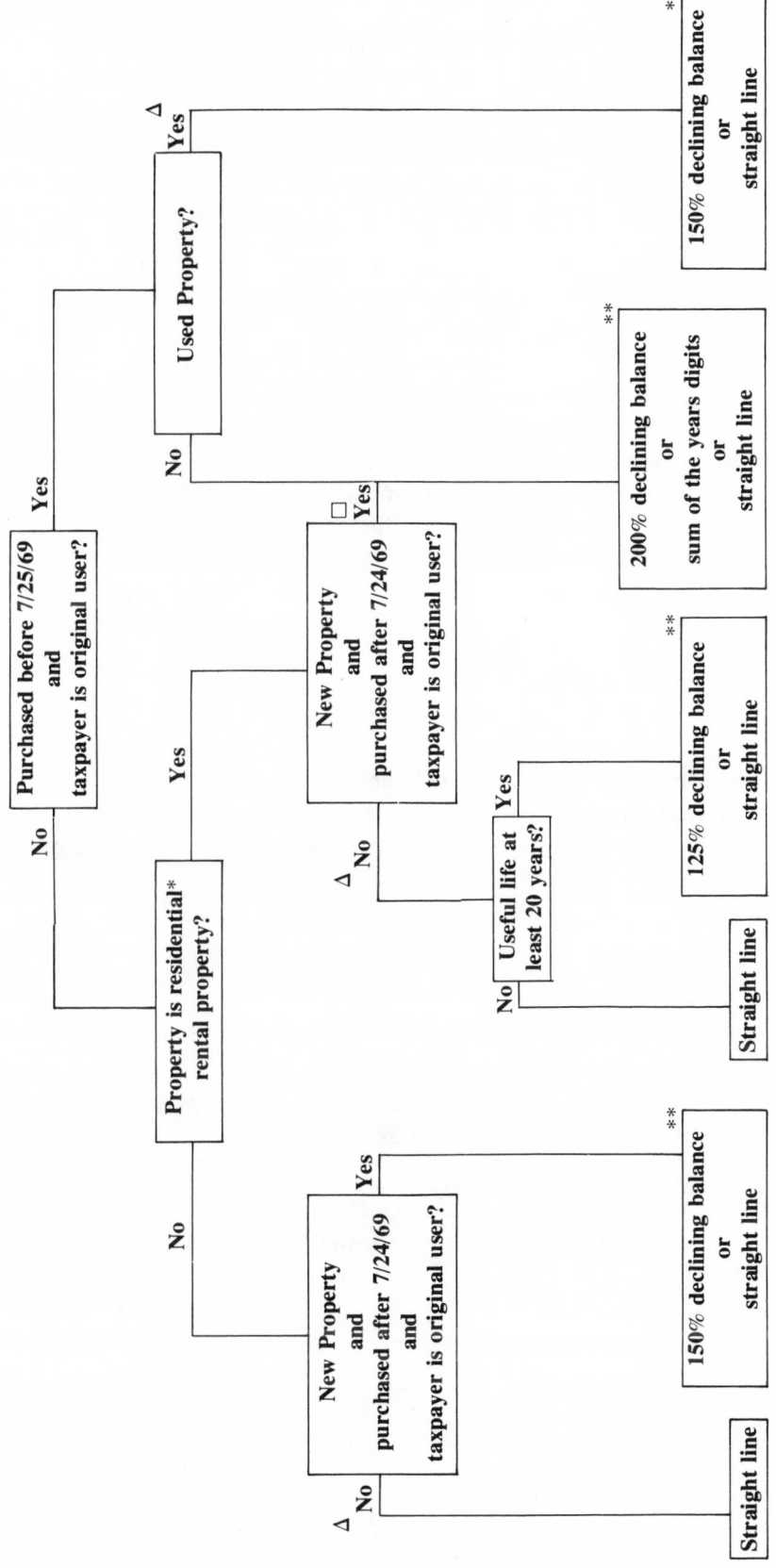

△Depreciation cannot be claimed on property acquired with the intent to demolish unless, prior to demolition, the building is used in trade or business or held for the production of income.

*Real property is considered to be residential rental property if, during the taxable year, at least 80% of the gross income is from dwelling units. A hotel or motel is not considered residential rental property if more than 50% of its dwelling units are occupied by transients.

**One can use any depreciation method, consistently applied, which during the first ⅔ of useful life will not yield more total depreciation than does the declining balance method.

□A residence converted to residential rental property does not qualify under the original user restriction.

$$D = \begin{cases} (b - s) \cdot A_n \text{ where } A_n = \dfrac{n}{k} & \textbf{(Straight line)} \\[2em] (b - s) \cdot A_n \text{ where } A_n = \dfrac{n(2k + 1 - n)}{k(k + 1)} & \textbf{(Sum of the years digits)} \\[2em] b \cdot A_n{}^* \quad \text{ where } A_n = 1 - (1 - q)^n & \textbf{(Declining balance)} \end{cases}$$

where

d =   depreciation allowance for the nth year**

D =   cumulative depreciation allowance through n years**†

a_n =   rate of depreciation allowance for the nth year

A_n=   fraction of cumulative depreciation allowance through n years

b =   basis of depreciable property when acquired (Chapter 12)

s =   salvage value of depreciable property (Section 11.2)

k =   useful life of depreciable property (Section 11.1)

q =   w/k. For 125, 150, and 200% declining balance, w = 1.25, 1.50, and 2.00, respectively

Table: Find a_n and A_n in Table 5.

Example 1: (Straight line).   Bob Good bought a used warehouse for $200,000 (consider the building only). He estimates the salvage value to be $20,000. If the remaining useful life of the warehouse is 40 years, how much depreciation can he claim over the first five years?

Solution: In this example,

$$b = \$200{,}000, \ s = \$20{,}000, \ k = 40 \text{ years, and } n = 5 \text{ years.}$$

---

* If property qualifies for additional first-year depreciation (Section 11.8), the basis used for regular depreciation must be reduced by the amount of additional first-year depreciation.

**The alternate notation $\bar{d}$ and $\overline{D}$ distinguishes straight line depreciation from the accelerated methods. This distinction is used when computing depreciation recapture and leasehold improvements by the lessee (Sections 14.1, 14.2, and 11.10).

†The following formulas for the depreciation between any two years, n and m (where m ≤ n), are more convenient for computation:

$$D_{mn} = \quad (b - s)\left(\frac{n - m}{k}\right) \qquad\qquad \text{(Straight line)}$$

$$D_{mn} = \quad (b - s)\left(\frac{n - m}{k}\right) \cdot \left[\frac{2k + 1 - (n + m)}{k + 1}\right] \qquad \text{(Sum of the years digits)}$$

$$D_{mn} = b\left[(1 - q)^m - (1 - q)^n\right] \qquad\qquad \text{(Declining balance)}$$

DEPRECIATION ALLOWANCE FOR TANGIBLE PERSONAL PROPERTY

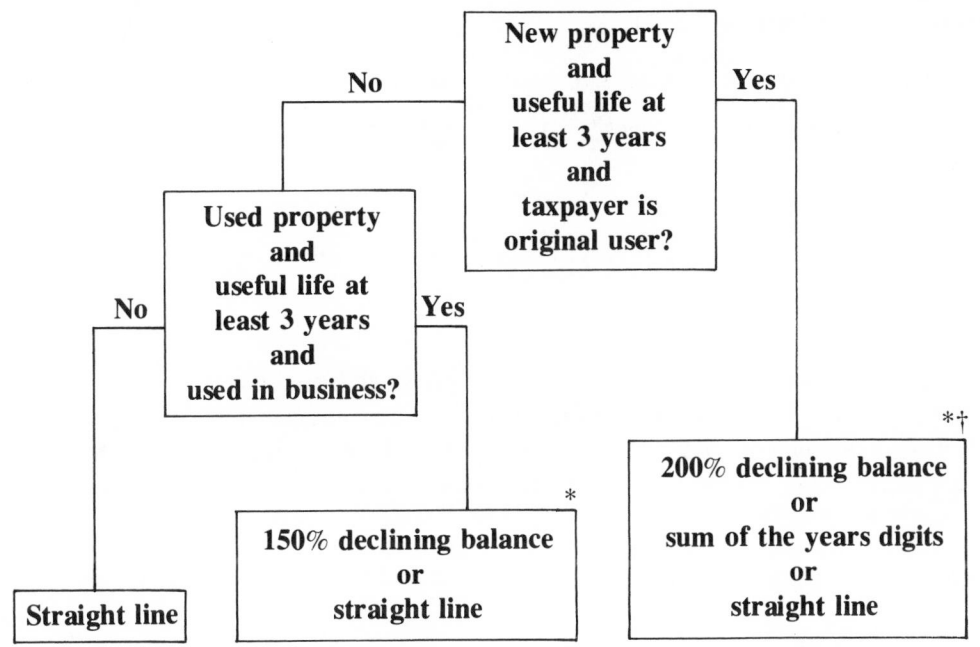

*One can use any depreciation method, consistently applied, which during the first ⅔ of useful life will not yield more total depreciation than does the declining balance method.

†If property qualifies for additional first-year depreciation (Section 11.8), the basis used for regular depreciation must be reduced by the amount of additional first-year depreciation.

From the flow diagram for real property (following no, no, no), Mr. Good can use only straight line depreciation.

From the formula (or Table 5), $A_5 = .125$. Now

$$D = (\$200,000 - \$20,000) \times .125 = \$22,500.$$

Example 2: (Sum of the Years Digits).   Five years ago Ms. Elliot bought a new apartment building for $200,000 (consider the building only, and consider her to be the original user). She estimated the useful life to be 38 years and the salvage value to be $20,000. How much depreciation can she claim in the fifth year?

Solution: In this example,

$$b = \$200,000, \ k = 38 \text{ years}, \ s = \$20,000, \text{ and } n = 5 \text{ years}.$$

From the flow diagram for real property (following yes, no), Ms. Elliot can use the sum of the years digits.

From the formula (or Table 5),

$$a_5 = \frac{2(38 + 1 - 5)}{38(38 + 1)} = \frac{2 \cdot 34}{38 \cdot 39} = .045884.$$

Now,

$$d = (\$200,000 - \$20,000) \times .045884 = \$8,259.$$

Example 3: (Declining Balance).   Two years ago Tom Grady bought a new commercial building for \$200,000 (consider the building only, and consider him to be the original user). He estimated the useful life to be 45 years and the salvage value to be \$20,000. How much depreciation can he claim in the second year if he sold the building October 13th?

Solution: In this example,

$$b = \$200,000, \ k = 45 \text{ years}, \ s = \$20,000, \text{ and } n = 2 \text{ years}.$$

From the flow diagram for real property (following no, no, yes), Mr. Grady can use either straight line or 150% declining balance depreciation. Suppose he chooses the declining balance method (in which case salvage value is not used).

From the formula (or Table 5),

$$q = 1.5/45 = .033333, \text{ and}$$

$$a_2 = .033333(1 - .033333)^{2-1} = .032222.$$

Now,

$$d = \$200,000 \times .032222 = \$6,444.$$

However, the building was owned by Mr. Grady for only 9 months of the second year (if he had sold on the 16th of October, he could have claimed 10 months). The depreciation that he can claim is

$$\frac{9}{12} \times \$6,444 = \$4,833.$$

11.5.   Composite Depreciation

   Composite depreciation considers the depreciable property to be depreciating as a unit. In this case a single basis, salvage value, and useful life are used for the entire property.

   On the other hand, component depreciation (Section 11.6) considers the components of a depreciable property to be depreciating independently. Each has its own basis, salvage value, and useful life.

Formula: Use the applicable formula from Section 11.4.

Table: Find a_n and A_n in Table 5.

Example: Three years ago Tom Hagerty bought a used $800,000 warehouse (including land). At that time the assessed value of the land was $132,000, and the assessed value of the warehouse was $108,000. The warehouse had a remaining useful life of 48 years. He estimated then, that the salvage value would be $60,000. How much depreciation can Mr. Hagerty claim in the third year?

Solution: From the flow diagram for real property in Section 11.4 (following no, no, no), Mr. Hagerty must use the straight line method of depreciation. He must first allocate the property between the land and the building (Section 11.3). In this example,

$$v_p = \$800,000, \ v'_l = \$132,000, \ v'_b = \$108,000,$$

$$k = 48 \text{ years}, \ s = \$60,000, \text{ and } n = 3 \text{ years}.$$

From Section 11.3, we find the value of the building is

$$v_b = \$360,000.$$

   Since the basis used for depreciation is determined when the property is acquired (and, hence is unadjusted), $b = v_b$. From Section 11.4,

$$a_3 = \frac{1}{48} = .020833.$$

Now the depreciation he can claim in the third year is

$$d = (\$360,000 - \$60,000) \times .020833 = \$6,250.$$

11.6.   Component Depreciation

Component depreciation separates the depreciable property into physical components, assigns a basis, a salvage value, and a useful life to each component, and depreciates each component separately (but by the same method). The depreciation allowance is then the sum of the depreciation allowances of the components.

The property needn't be new in order to use component depreciation although it is difficult to assign a basis and a useful life to older components. The class life system (Section 11.1) cannot be used with component depreciation.

Formulas:

$$d = \sum_{i=1}^{j} d_i, \text{ and } D = \sum_{i=1}^{j} D_i$$

where

d = depreciation allowance for the nth year for all j components combined
D = cumulative depreciation allowance through the nth year for all j components combined
d_i = depreciation allowance for the nth year for the ith component (Section 11.4)
D_i = cumulative depreciation allowance through n years for the ith component (Section 11.4)
b_i = basis of the ith component when acquired (Chapter 12)
s_i = salvage value of the ith component (Section 11.2)
a_{ni} = rate of depreciation for the nth year for the ith component
A_{ni} = fraction of cumulative depreciation through the nth year for the ith component
k_i = useful life of the ith component (Section 11.1)
q_i = w/k_i. For 125, 150, and 200% declining balance, w = 1.25, 1.50, and 2.00, respectively

Table: Find a_{ni} and A_{ni} in Table 5.

Example: The basis, salvage value, and useful life of the components of a new, first owner apartment building are listed in the following table. The value of the building is estimated to be $300,000. The salvage values are all estimated to be zero. Using 200% declining balance method (permitted according to the flow diagram on page 229), determine the depreciation allowed over the first 2 years.

Solution: Since the 200% declining balance method is specified, $q_i = 2/k_i$. To determine the depreciation over the first 2 years, find A_{2i} in Table 5 for each component. Then

Component	Number (i)	Basis (b_i)	Salvage Value (s_i)	Useful Life (k_i)
Shell	1	$130,000	$0	40 years
Heating	2	25,000	0	10
Electrical	3	55,000	0	10
Plumbing	4	45,000	0	12.5
Air Conditioning	5	25,000	0	12.5
Roof	6	20,000	0	10
		$300,000		

determine the cumulative depreciation, D, from Section 11.4 for each component. These values are listed in the following table:

Number (i)	Basis (b_i)	Fraction (A_{2i})	Cumulative Depreciation (D_i)
1	$130,000	.0975	$12,675
2	25,000	.3600	9,000
3	55,000	.3600	19,800
4	45,000	.2944	13,248
5	25,000	.2944	7,360
6	20,000	.3600	7,200
			$69,283

Now, the total depreciation claimed over the first two years is

$$D = \sum_{i=1}^{6} D_i = \$69,283.$$

11.7. Cross-Over Point from Declining Balance to Straight Line

It is permissible to switch from any depreciation method to the straight line method. Although the declining balance method permits a larger depreciation allowance than the straight line method in the earlier years, the allowance is smaller in later years. The general formula (formula 1), giving the year in which it becomes advantageous to cross over, cannot be solved explicitly for n, the year to cross-over. The taxpayer can, however, substitute likely values of n. By trial and error, he can determine the value of n that renders the right side of the formula equal to the left side. On the other hand, the formula can be solved for n if the salvage value is zero (Formula 2).

Formula 1:

$$s = b(1 - q)^{n-1} \left[1 - q - q(k - n) \right]^* \text{ (general)}$$

Formula 2:

$$n = k + 1 - \frac{1}{q} \text{ (specific, } s = 0\text{)}$$

where

n = number of years after which the rate of straight line depreciation exceeds that of declining balance

b = basis of depreciable property (Chapter 12)

s = salvage value of depreciable property (Section 11.2)

k = useful life of depreciable property (Section 11.1)

q = w/k. For 125, 150, and 200% declining balance, w = 1.25, 1.50, and 2.00, respectively

Table: The cross-over year is indicated in Table 5 for the special case in which s = 0.

Example: A new, first owner apartment building is assumed to have a useful life of 40 years. The building has an estimated value of $200,000 and a zero salvage value. When will the straight line method begin to provide more depreciation allowance (considering the adjusted basis) than the initially used 200% declining balance method?

Solution: In this example,

k = 40 years, b = $200,000, s = $0, and q = 2/40 = .05.

Now, from formula 2, the cross-over year is

$$n = 40 + 1 - \frac{1}{.05} = 41 - 20 = 21 \text{ years.}$$

---

*To derive the formula, one must use the adjusted basis (i.e. reduced by depreciation already claimed) less the salvage value. This basis for depreciation is then spread over the remaining useful life of k−n years. The following equation is then solved for n:

$$bq(1-q)^{n-1} = \left\{ b - s - b \left[1 - (1-q)^n \right] \right\} \cdot \frac{1}{k-n}$$

11.8.   Additional First-Year Depreciation

Up to 20% additional depreciation may be claimed on some personal property the year it is placed in service. This additional depreciation is generally available for personal property that is purchased (either new or used) and has a useful life of at least 6 years.

Wiring, heating systems and other items incorporated in a building are considered real property. On the other hand, items such as furniture and refrigerators that remain distinct from the improvements are considered personal property.

The full amount of additional depreciation is taken during the year the property is put into service providing regular depreciation is also allowed that year*. Regular depreciation is allowed along with the additional first year depreciation.

If personal property is traded, the additional first year depreciation is computed on the amount of cash given in the exchange.

Formula:

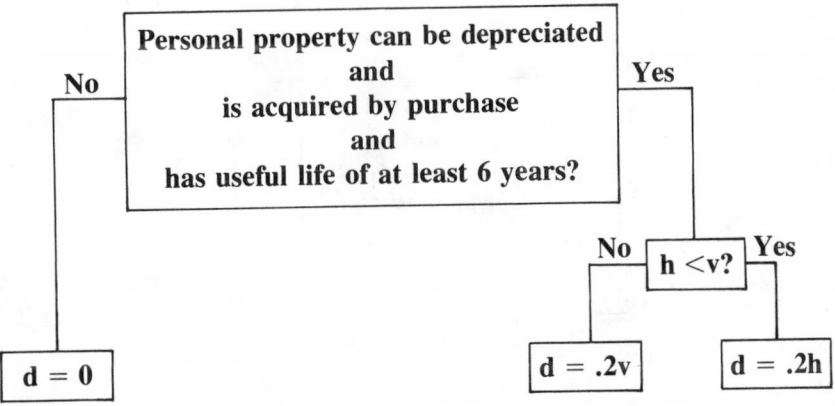

where

$d =$ additional first year depreciation

$v =$ cost of personal property

$h = \begin{cases} \$20,000 & \text{married joint return} \\ \$10,000 & \text{other returns} \end{cases}$

Example: Bob Madden has purchased $32,000 worth of slightly used furniture and $8,000 worth of new refrigerators for his apartment building. All items have a useful life of at least 6 years and are placed in service before December 16th. If Mr. Madden files a head of household return, what is his additional first year depreciation?

---

*Unless the half year convention of the class life system is used, depreciation must be deferred on property placed into service after December 15. Additional first year depreciation must also be deferred. See Section 11.4.

Solution: In this example,

$$v = \$32,000 + \$8,000 = \$40,000, \text{ and } h = \$10,000.$$

From the flow diagram (following yes, yes), we find the additional first year depreciation is

$$d = .2 \times \$10,000 = \$2,000.$$

11.9.   Business Lease

The cost of a business lease is deductible and is amortized over the term of the lease. If there is an option to renew the lease, the term over which the lease is amortized might include, not only the term of the lease, but the term of the renewal as well. Amortized deductions are computed by the straight line method.

Formula:

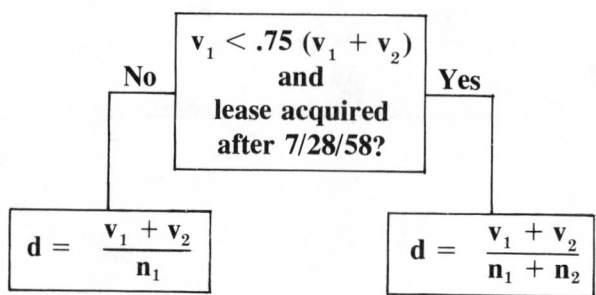

where

$d =$	annual deduction for cost of a business lease
$v_1, v_2 =$	cost of the lease and cost of renewals (if any), respectively
$n_1, n_2 =$	term of the lease and term of renewals (if any), respectively

Example: A 25-year business lease costs \$12,000 and two 5-year renewal options cost \$5,000 each. What is the annual deduction for the cost of the lease if it is acquired this year?

Solution: In this example,

$$v_1 = \$12,000, \ v_2 = \$5,000 + \$5,000 = \$10,000,$$
$$n_1 = 15 \text{ years, and } n_2 = 5 + 5 = 10 \text{ years.}$$

From the flow diagram (following yes), the annual deduction is

$$d = \frac{\$12,000 + \$10,000}{15 + 10} = \frac{\$22,000}{25} = \$880.$$

11.10.   Leasehold Improvements by Lessee

The cost of improvements made to a leasehold by a lessee can be deducted. Generally, the cost is either amortized over the remaining term of the lease or depreciated over the life of the improvements, whichever is shorter*. Amortization must be accomplished by the straight line method, but depreciation may be accomplished by one of the methods of Section 11.4.

If the lessee has renewal options on the lease, their terms can be used to determine the period of amortization or depreciation. A renewal period might be used if, when the improvement is completed, the remaining term of the original lease is less than 60% of the useful life of the improvement. See Treasury Regulations for exceptions and improvements begun before July 29, 1958.

Formula:

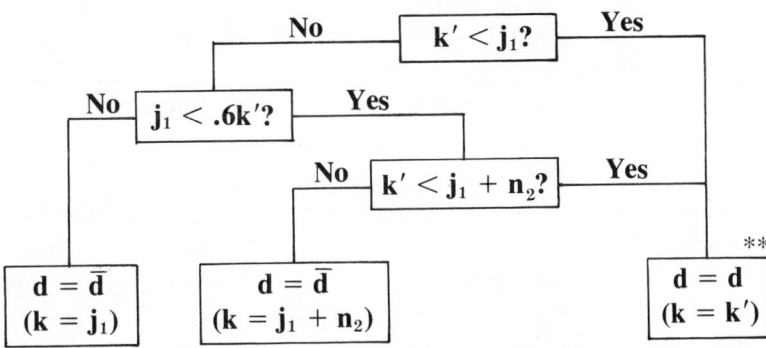

where

d = annual deduction for improvements
k' = actual useful life of the improvement (Section 11.1)
n_1, n_2 = original term of the lease and term of renewals, respectively
j_1 = remaining term of the lease when improvement completed
d = depreciation claimed, when shown on right side of equal sign (Section 11.4)
$\overline{d}$ = straight line depreciation claimed (i.e., amortization)
k = useful life of improvement to be used for depreciation or amortization
b = cost of improvement
s = salvage value (Section 11.2)

Example: Mr. Sullivan has a 10 year lease and a 4 year renewal option on a downtown building. With 6 years remaining on the original lease, he completed a $21,000 capital improvement that has a useful life of 15 years and no salvage value. How much of the capital improvement can he deduct each year?

---

*If the lease is cancelled, the unused depreciation allowance can be deducted immediately. Also if a renewal is obtained after some deduction has been claimed, the remaining deduction is claimed over the remaining term of the lease plus the term of the renewal.

**The d on the right of the equal sign indicates the deduction can be depreciated by any allowed method (Section 11.4).

Solution: In this example,

$$n_1 = 10 \text{ years}, n_2 = 4 \text{ years}, j_1 = 6 \text{ years},$$
$$b = \$21,000, k' = 15 \text{ years}, \text{ and } s = \$0.$$

From the flow diagram (following no,yes,no), Mr. Sullivan must amortize the capital improvement over the remaining term of the lease plus the term of the renewal (i.e., $k = j_1 + n_2 = 10$ years).

From Section 11.4, the annual deduction that he must claim is

$$d = \overline{d} = \$21,000 \times 1/10 = \$2,100.$$

11.11.   Investment Interest and "Points"

Interest paid on a business loan is always deductible from ordinary income. However, interest paid on a personal loan is deductible only if deductions are itemized.

The formulas of Sections 1.1, 3.4, 6.10, and 6.16 can be used to determine the amount of interest paid on simple interest loans, compound interest loans, constant payment amortized loans, and constant principal amortized loans, respectively.

"Points" are loan charges in addition to interest*. They are deductible if they are solely for the use of money and not for services performed by the lender**. Such services might include the settlement fee, property reports, mortgage preparation fee, and notary fee.

There is a limit to which interest is deductible for individuals. Generally, when the interest paid exceeds income from investments, some of the interest deduction can be carried over. Consult Treasury Regulations for the definition of terms such as investment interest and net investment income. The following formula determines the excess investment interest, if any, that must be carried over. It also determines one of the items of tax preference, p_1, used in Section 14.6.

Formula:

---

*State laws limit the amount of interest charged. Hence, in periods of tight money the charging of "points" is a frequently used method of obtaining the compensation dictated by supply and demand.

**Points are generally amortized over the term of the loan. However, points for home loans are currently deductible.

where

d_1 = investment interest deductible in the year incurred
d_i = investment interest deduction carried over to future years
I = amount of investment interest expense
X = net investment income
E = excess "out of pocket" expenses attributable to property subject to a net lease
C = excess of net long-term capital gains over net short-term capital gains in the taxable year attributable to property held for investment

$$h^* = \begin{cases} \$5,000 & \text{married, filing separately} \\ \$10,000 & \text{otherwise} \end{cases}$$

p_1 = an item of tax preference. Use the value determined here in Section 14.5

Example: Mr. Morgan has investment interest expenses of $73,000, net investment income of $13,000, and a net long-term capital gain of $19,000 from property held for investment. If he files a joint return, how much of the investment interest is deductible this year, and how much must be carried over?

Solution: In this example,

$I = \$73,000$, $X = \$13,000$, $C = \$19,000$, $E = \$0$, and $h = \$10,000$.

From the flow diagram (following no), the amount of investment interest that is currently deductible is

$$d_1 = \frac{1}{2}(\$73,000 + \$13,000 + \$0 + \$19,000 + \$10,000)$$

$$= \$57,500.$$

The amount of investment interest that must be carried over is

$$d_i = \$73,000 - \$57,500 = \$15,500.$$

The item of tax preference (Section 14.6) is

$$p_1 = \$0.$$

11.12. Real Estate Tax (Allocation Between Buyer and Seller)

Real estate tax is deductible. The seller of real property pays real estate tax from the beginning of the real property year (determined by state law) until the day before the sale. On

---

*For 50% owned corporations or partnerships use the lesser of $15,000 ($7,500 for married, filing separately) and the interest on the debt used to acquire the corporation or partnership.

the other hand, the buyer pays real estate tax from the day of the sale until the end of the real property year*.

The following formulas allocate the tax between buyer and seller.

Formula:

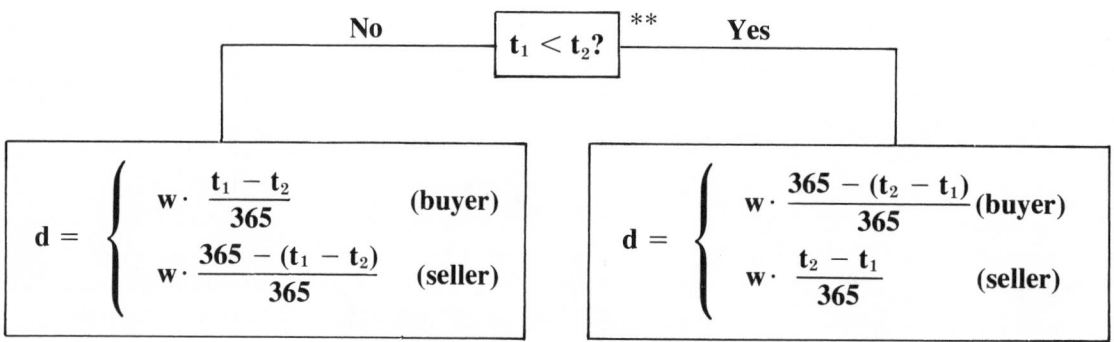

where

d = amount of real estate tax paid by buyer or seller

w = annual real estate tax

t_1 = day number (from January 1) on which real property year begins (determined by state law)

t_2 = day number of day of sale (from January 1)

Table: Find the day numbers, t_1 and t_2, in Table 7.

Example: In Grand County the real property year begins on April 1 and ends on March 31. On September 4 Bob Herman bought some land on which the annual real estate tax is $1,000. If this real property year does not include a leap year, how much of the tax is allocated to the seller and how much to Mr. Herman?

Solution: We have $w = \$1,000$, and, from Table 7, we find that

$$t_1 = 91, \text{ and } t_2 = 247.$$

---

*Seller's back taxes that are paid by the buyer are not deductible but add to the basis of the property.

**If the real property year includes February 28 in a leap year, use 366 instead of 365, and add 1 to either t_1 or t_2 if either falls after day 60 (i.e., February 28).

Since $t_1 < t_2$, the real estate tax deduction for the seller is

$$d = \$1,000 \times \frac{247 - 91}{365} = \$1,000 \times .42740 = \$427.40,$$

and the real estate tax deduction for the buyer is

$$d = \$1,000 \times \frac{365 - (247 - 91)}{365} = \$572.60.$$

11.13. Casualty and Theft Loss

Casualty and theft losses are deductible. The \$100 that must be subtracted from the loss of property held for personal use does not apply to property used for business or held for the production of income. If property qualifies as both types (personal and either business or income), the loss is to be allocated and treated separately. Casualty and theft losses that exceed taxable income can be carried back three years and forward five years.

Formula:

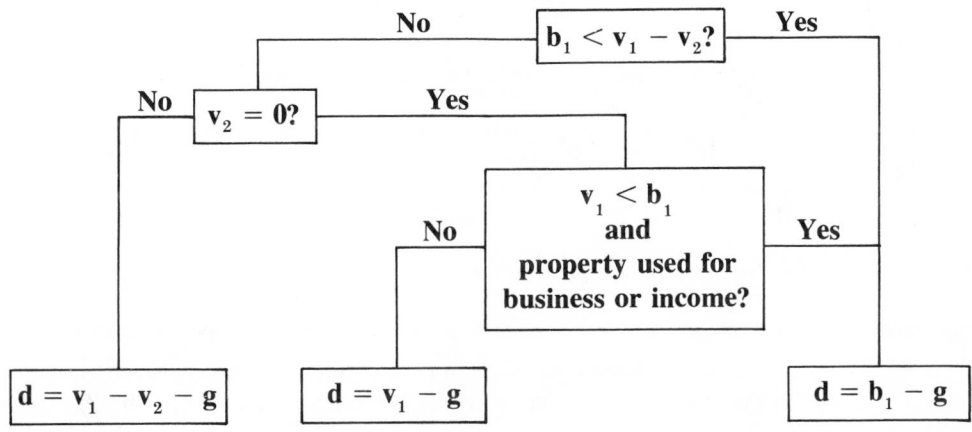

where

d = deduction for casualty and theft loss

v_1, v_2 = fair market value of property immediately prior to and immediately after casualty or theft, respectively

b_1, b_2 = basis of property immediately prior to and immediately after casualty or theft, respectively (b_2 is determined in Section 12.10)

g = insurance proceeds or other reimbursements

Example 1:   Fire in the Hotel Dante caused rather extensive damage. The fair market value just before the fire was estimated to be $880,000, and the adjusted basis was $530,000. Just after the fire, the hotel was valued at $750,000. The insurance company granted proceeds of $90,000. How much casualty loss can be deducted?

Solution: In this example,

$$v_1 = \$880,000, \ b_1 = \$530,000, \ v_2 = \$750,000, \text{ and } g = \$90,000.$$

From the flow diagram (following no,no), the deductible casualty loss is

$$d = \$880,000 - \$750,000 - \$90,000$$
$$= \$40,000.$$

Example 2:   Consider the situation of Example 1 except the hotel is completely destroyed, and the insurance proceeds are $400,000. How much casualty loss can be deducted?

Solution: In this example,

$$v_1 = \$880,000, \ b_1 = \$530,000 \ v_2 = \$0, \text{ and } g = \$400,000.$$

From the flow diagram (following yes), the deductible casualty loss is

$$d = \$530,000 - \$400,000 = \$130,000.$$

11.14.   Charitable Contributions

Charitable contributions made to qualified organizations or to the government are deductible from adjusted gross income to arrive at taxable income. The amount of the annual deduction is limited to a certain percentage of the donor's adjusted gross income* depending upon (A) the nature of the donee, (B) the nature of the gift, and (C) the order of deductibility. The amount of the donation that exceeds the annual limit can be carried forward for up to five years.**

---

*Adjusted gross income is gross income less expenses for business, travel, moving, IRA contributions, and operating loss deductions. See Treasury Regulations for details.

**Contributions for which the 20% limitation applies cannot be carried forward.

(A) Nature of the donee

If the donee is one of the following types of charities, the annual deduction is limited to 50% of the donor's adjusted gross income:

(1) all public charities,

(2) all private operating foundations,

(3) non-operating private foundations that distribute contributions to charities (1) or (2), above, within 2½ months following the year of receipt of the gift, or

(4) private foundations, the contributions to which are pooled in a common fund and the income and corpus of which are paid to public charities.

Donations are limited to 20% of adjusted gross income if they are given to certain non-operating private foundations, other organizations not qualifying for the 50% limitation, or for the use of any charitable organization.

(B) Nature of the gift

The annual deduction is also limited by the nature of the gift. Capital gain property is property that would result in a long-term capital gain if it were sold at its fair market value on the date it was contributed. Capital gain property may be subject to a reduced deduction if

(1) it is tangible personal property, the use of which by the charity is unrelated to its exempt purpose or function, or

(2) it is contributed to certain non-operating private foundations.

The annual deduction on capital gain property that is not (1) or (2) is limited to 30% of the donor's adjusted gross income.

(C) Order of deductibility

When several contributions are made in one year, they are deducted in the following order:

(1) gifts that qualify for the 50% limitation

(2) gifts that qualify for the 20% limitation, but only to the extent of the lesser of

(a) 20% of adjusted gross income or

(b) 50% of adjusted gross income less the contributions of (1), above.

(3) capital gain property to which the 30% limitation applies.

A charitable contribution can be an outright gift or a bargain sale to the charity (i.e., sold below its fair market value). If a deduction is allowed on the bargain sale, the transaction is considered to be both a sale and a gift (see Treasury Regulations). Hence, there is an allocation between the sale (Section 13.3) and the donation.

If the mortgage on the gift exceeds the adjusted basis, the gift is likely to be treated as a bargain sale.

The following flow diagram applies to appreciated property that is donated to charities qualifying for the 50% limitation.

Formula:

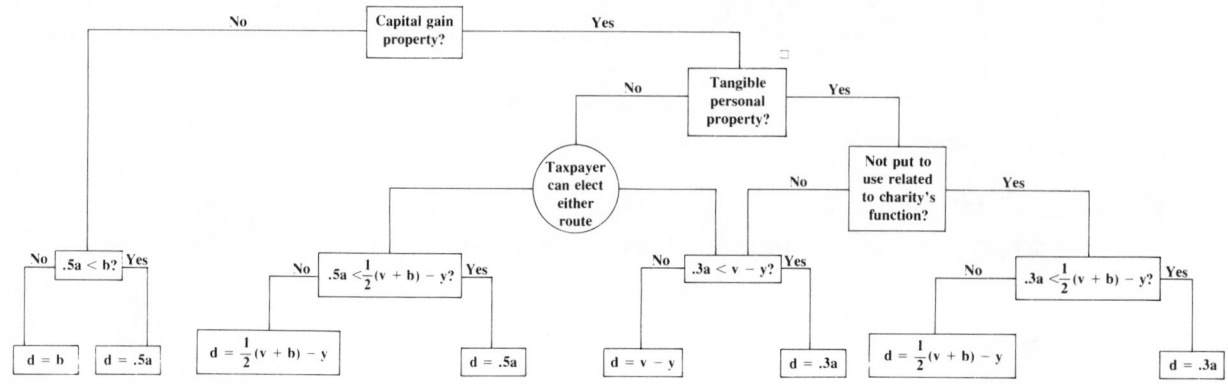

DEDUCTION FOR APPRECIATED PROPERTY CONTRIBUTED
TO CHARITIES QUALIFYING FOR THE 50% LIMITATION.

where

- d = amount of charitable deduction allowed in the first year
- v = fair market value of the contribution
- v' = sale price (if $v' \leq v$)
- b = basis of the contribution at the time of donation
- y = amount of contribution that is ordinary income (e.g., depreciation recapture)*
- p = amount of mortgage and other liens on contributed property
- a = taxpayer's adjusted gross income

Example 1:   Wayne Hanson has an adjusted gross income of $25,000. Last year he gave his alma mater stock (held for 3 months) worth $1,200 for which he paid $1,000 and land (held for investment for three years) worth $15,000 with a basis of $5,000. He also gave $2,500 cash to a charity that qualifies for the 20% limitation. What deductions can he claim on the gifts?

Solution: Since there are three gifts, it is convenient to use the subscripts 1, 2, and 3. In this example,

$$a = \$25{,}000, \; v_1 = \$1{,}200, \; b_1 = \$1{,}000, \; y_1 = \$0,$$
$$v_2 = \$15{,}000, \; b_2 = \$5{,}000, \; y_2 = \$0, \; v_3 = \$2{,}500,$$
$$b_3 = \$2{,}500, \text{ and } y_3 = \$0.$$

☐Securities are intangible personal property.

*Ordinary income property is property that, if sold at its fair market value on the date of contribution, would result in ordinary income or short-term capital gain. The amount of depreciation recapture (Sections 14.1 and 14.2) is an example of ordinary income.

Consider the gifts in order:

(1) The gifts to charities qualifying for the 50% limitation are considered first (identified by subscripts 1 and 2). The stock does not qualify for long-term gain. Therefore it is not capital gain property and $d = b_1 = \$1,000$ is deductible. The land is capital gain property. It is real property and since it is non-depreciable, none of its value is ordinary income. Mr. Hanson elects to deduct the lesser of 50% of his adjusted gross income and the value of his gift less 50% of its appreciation (expressible as $\frac{1}{2}(v + b)$). That is, he elects to deduct $10,000. The remaining $5,000 deduction for the gift of land can be carried over.

(2) The allowable contributions to the charity qualifying for the 50% limitation already exceed the limit (i.e., $.5a < v_1 + v_2$). Therefore, the contribution to the charity qualifying for the 20% limitation is not allowable.

Example 2: (Bargain Sale).   Mr. Post sold some land to his church for $300,000. The land was appraised at $400,000, and his basis was $280,000. Mr. Post had owned the land for five years and had paid the mortgage down to $240,000. If his adjusted gross income is $82,000, how much of the bargain sale is considered a charitable contribution? (His capital gain is treated in Section 13.3)

Solution: In this example,

$$v' = \$300,000, \ v = \$400,000, \ b = \$280,000,$$
$$p = \$240,000, \text{ and } a = \$82,000.$$

The charitable contribution is

$$v - v' = \$400,000 - \$300,000 = \$100,000.$$

See Treasury Regulations for annual deduction limitation.

Example 3: (Mortgage Exceeds Basis).   Wayne Hanson has an adjusted gross income of $25,000. He gave some land worth $15,000 to his alma mater. The mortgage is $11,000 and the basis is $5,000. How much is the charitable contribution?

Solution: In this example,

$$a = \$25,000, \ v = \$15,000, \ p = \$11,000, \text{ and } b = \$5,000.$$

The transaction will probably be considered a bargain sale for $11,000. The charitable contribution is

$$v - p = \$4,000.$$

See Treasury Regulations for annual deduction limitation.

11.15.   Facilities for Child Care, On-the-Job Training, and Pollution Control

The capital expenditures since 1972 used to acquire, construct, reconstruct, or rehabilitate facilities for child care or on-the-job training can be amortized over a 60-month period. Any other depreciation is disallowed if the 60-month amortization is elected. Once made, the election cannot be revoked*.

Child care facilities must be used primarily for the children of the taxpayer's employees. Similarly, on-the-job training facilities must be used primarily for training.

A certified pollution control facility is generally only tangible depreciable personal property. However, a building or structural component can qualify if its sole purpose is pollution control. If the 60-month amortization is used, regular depreciation (Section 11.4) cannot be used but the additional first year depreciation (Section 11.8) can be.

Formula:

$$d = \overline{d}$$

where

d = annual amortization deduction
$\overline{d}$ = straight line depreciation allowance (Section 11.4, where k = 5 yrs. and s = $0)

Example: The Alpine Ski Co. spent $80,000 to reconstruct a facility used exclusively for the care of employee's children. What is the annual amortization deduction?

Solution: From Section 11.4,

$$b = \$80,000, \ s = \$0, \ and \ k = 5 \ years.$$

Now the annual deduction is

$$d = \overline{d} = (\$80,000 - \$0) \times \frac{1}{5} = \$16,000.$$

11.16.   Rehabilitation Expenditures

Some capital expenditures for the rehabilitation of substandard properties rented to persons of moderate or low income may be amortized over 60 months, without salvage value.

---

*If this election is made, investment credit (Section 14.10) generally can't be used for the property. The amount that this deduction exceeds the otherwise allowable depreciation becomes an item of tax preference (Section 14.6). Also the total amount of the deduction is subject to depreciation recapture (Sections 14.1 and 14.2).

In order to qualify, (a) the expenditures for each two consecutive years must exceed $3,000/unit, and (b) the total expenditure must not exceed $20,000/unit. The expenditures that do not meet conditions (a) and (b) must be depreciated in the usual way (Section 11.4). Not qualified for rapid amortization are expenditures for new construction and for hotels and motels in which more than 50% of the units are rented on a transient basis.

The amount of rapid amortization (using 5 years) that exceeds straight line depreciation (using the useful life of the property) is subject to depreciation recapture (Section 14.1). See Treasury Regulations for precise definitions, rules, and time periods for which this amortization applies.

Formula:

$$d = \overline{d}$$

where

d = annual amortization deduction
$\overline{d}$ = straight line depreciation allowance (Section 11.4, where k = 5 yrs. and s = $0).

Example: The following rehabilitation expenditures were made on a single unit that qualifies for rapid amortization.

Year	Annual Expenditure	Running 2-year Sum	Cumulative Expenditure
1	$2,000	—	$ 2,000
2	2,500	$ 4,500	4,500
3	4,000	6,500	8,500
4	8,000	12,000	16,500
5	6,000	14,000	22,500

Which expenditures qualify for 60-month amortization, and which must be depreciated over the useful life of the unit?

Solution: The running sum over each two-year period (see the table) shows that the expenditures in years 2, 3, 4, and 5 all qualify for 60-month amortization according to the $3,000 minimum. (See Section 11.15 for an example of 60-month amortization.) However, the total expenditure of $22,500 exceeds the $20,000 maximum by $2,500. Hence, the last $2,500 expenditure must be depreciated over the useful life of the unit. (See Section 11.4 for examples of depreciation.)

11.17.   Amortization of a Purchased Life Estate

If a life estate is purchased during the life of the life tenant, the property must revert to the remainderman upon the death of the life tenant.* Hence, the property value is deductible by the purchaser. This value is amortized (by the straight line method) over the expected remaining life of the life tenant. Upon premature death of the life tenant, the unamortized amount can be deducted immediately.

Formula:

$$\mathbf{d} = \overline{\mathbf{d}}$$

where

$\underline{d}$ = annual amortization deduction
$\overline{d}$ = straight line depreciation allowance (Section 11.4 where s = $0)
k = life expectancy of the life tenant

Table: Find k in the table on page 251.

Example: Gerald Carter bought Mr. Adams' life estate for $208,000. He is 56 years old. How much can he deduct each full year that he owns the life estate?

Solution: In this example,

$$b = \$208{,}000 \text{ and } s = \$0.$$

From the table, Mr. Adams' life expectancy is 21 years. Hence k = 21 years. Using straight line depreciation, the amortization each 12 months is

$$\overline{D} = \frac{\$208{,}000}{21} = \$9{,}905.00.$$

---

*For more on life estates, see Section 12.4.

LIFE EXPECTANCY

Ages		Life Expectancy (k)	Ages		Life Expectancy (k)	Ages		Life Expectancy (k)
Male	Female		Male	Female		Male	Female	
6	11	65.0	41	46	33.0	76	81	9.1
7	12	64.1	42	47	32.1	77	82	8.7
8	13	63.2	43	48	31.2	78	83	8.3
9	14	62.3	44	49	30.4	79	84	7.8
10	15	61.4	45	50	29.6	80	85	7.5
11	16	60.4	46	51	28.7	81	86	7.1
12	17	59.5	47	52	27.9	82	87	6.7
13	18	58.6	48	53	27.1	83	88	6.3
14	19	57.7	49	54	26.3	84	89	6.0
15	20	56.7	50	55	25.5	85	90	5.7
16	21	55.8	51	56	24.7	86	91	5.4
17	22	54.9	52	57	24.0	87	92	5.1
18	23	53.9	53	58	23.2	88	93	4.8
19	24	53.0	54	59	22.4	89	94	4.5
20	25	52.1	55	60	21.7	90	95	4.2
21	26	51.1	56	61	21.0	91	96	4.0
22	27	50.2	57	62	20.3	92	97	3.7
23	28	49.3	58	63	19.6	93	98	3.5
24	29	48.3	59	64	18.9	94	99	3.3
25	30	47.4	60	65	18.2	95	100	3.1
26	31	46.5	61	66	17.5	96	101	2.9
27	32	45.6	62	67	16.9	97	102	2.7
28	33	44.6	63	68	16.2	98	103	2.5
29	34	43.7	64	69	15.6	99	104	2.3
30	35	42.8	65	70	15.0	100	105	2.1
31	36	41.9	66	71	14.4	101	106	1.9
32	37	41.0	67	72	13.8	102	107	1.7
33	38	40.0	68	73	13.2	103	108	1.5
34	39	39.1	69	74	12.6	104	109	1.3
35	40	38.2	70	75	12.1	105	110	1.2
						106	111	1.0
36	41	37.3	71	76	11.6	107	112	.8
37	42	36.5	72	77	11.0	108	113	.7
38	43	35.6	73	78	10.5	109	114	.6
39	44	34.7	74	79	10.1	110	115	.5
40	45	33.8	75	80	9.6	111	116	0

12

TAXES: BASIS OF PROPERTY

The basis of property is the amount of investment that a taxpayer has in the property, as determined by the Treasury. The basis is used to determine the amount of capital gain or loss to the taxpayer upon disposition of the property and to determine the amount of depreciation allowed on qualified depreciable property.

Since property may be acquired in a variety of ways, and since costs may have been incurred in acquisition, the basis is usually different from the cost. The unadjusted basis is determined by the means of acquisition, and the adjusted basis is determined by events during the holding period. For instance the basis can be adjusted by the cost of acquisition, the addition of capital improvements, depreciation (this lowers the basis), and selling costs. Other adjustments can result from casualty losses, partial divestiture, and the granting of easements.

All the sections of this chapter, except the last, are devoted to determining the basis of property when acquired. Hence, basis in this chapter implies unadjusted basis. The last section lists the events that adjust the basis after acquisition.

Many of the formulas for basis in this chapter are determined by flow diagrams. When there are many conditions that determine which formula is to be used, it is helpful to diagram the logic. Notations such as v_1 and v_2 refer to the value of property at two different times. Also v^+ and v^- are used to distinguish the value of property received and given, respectively.

12.1.   Basis of Property Acquired by Purchase

The basis of purchased property is the amount paid for the property. This amount is the sum of cash, the mortgage*, and the fair market value of other unlike property.

Formula:

$$b = v$$

where

b =   basis of the purchased property
v =   cost of the purchased property

Example: A property is purchased with a $15,000 down payment and a $45,000 purchase money mortgage. What is the (unadjusted) basis?

Solution: The basis is the sum of the two financial components.

$$b = \$15,000 + \$45,000 = \$60,000.$$

12.2.   Basis of Property Acquired by Inheritance

If the decedent died before 1977, and if an estate tax return is required, the executor can choose either the date of death or an alternate date upon which to determine the value of inherited property. The value determined on the valuation date becomes the basis to the beneficiary (less any depreciation claimed by the beneficiary).

However if the decedent dies after 1976, the valuation date is the death date. The basis to the beneficiary is generally the decedent's basis on the death date (except for regularly traded securities). However, for property owned by the decedent prior to 1977, there is a formula that adjusts the basis to the beneficiary uniformly from the decedent's basis to the fair market value on the valuation date (depending upon the percentage of the holding period that occurred before 1977). See Treasury Regulations concerning depreciation recapture.

The basis of property acquired by a survivor in joint ownership is treated in Section 12.3.

---

*The cost of securing a mortgage does not adjust the basis. However, this cost can be amortized (by the straight-line method) over the life of the mortgage if the purchased property is either income-producing or business property.

Formulas:

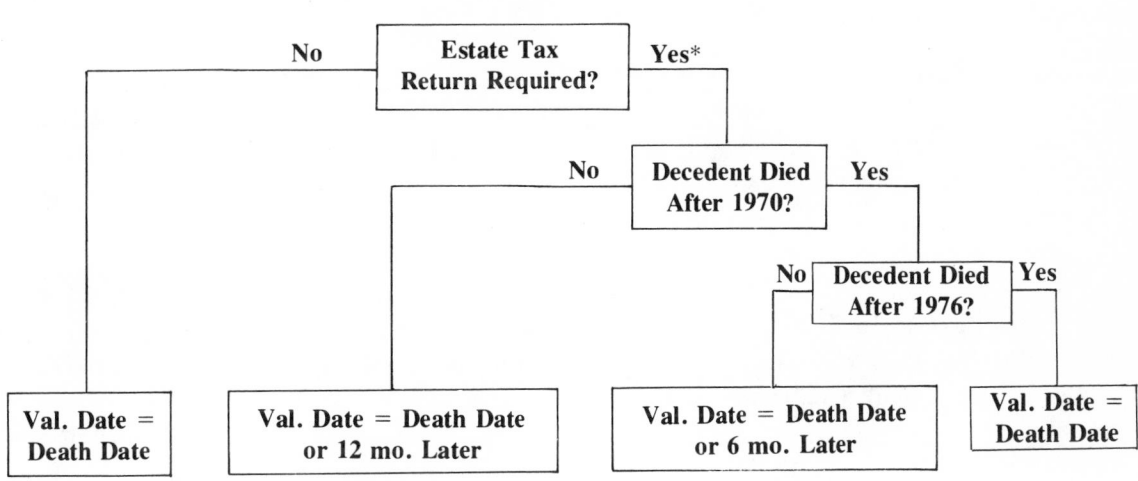

Use to Determine
Valuation Date

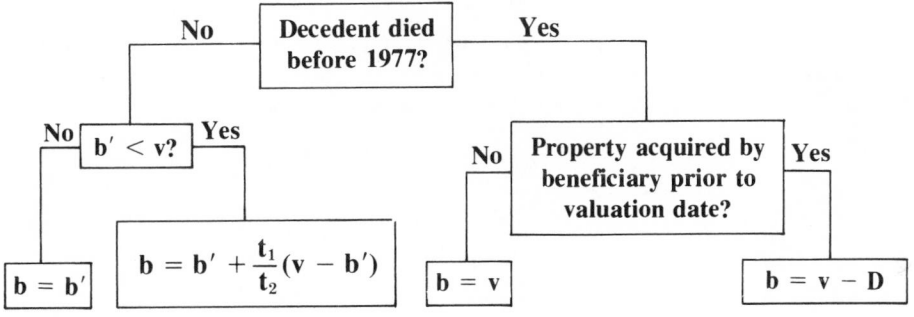

Use to Determine Basis

where

b = basis of inherited property

b′ = basis to decedent on valuation date (death date)

v = fair market value of inherited property on valuation date

D = amount of depreciation claimed (if any) between beneficiary's acquisition date
     and valuation date (Section 11.4)

t_1 = number of days property held by decedent

t_2 = number of days property held by decedent prior to 1977

---

*If the alternative valuation date is chosen and the property is distributed to the beneficiary after the death of
the decedent but before the alternate date, the valuation date is the date of distribution.

Table: Find D from Table 5 and Section 11.4. Find t_1 and t_2 in Table 7.

Example 1:   Jim Green's father died April 12, 1976 and left him a parcel of land valued then at $650,000. However, 6 months later the parcel was valued at $665,000. What is the beneficiary's basis?

Solution: Since the value is large enough to require the filing of an estate tax return, the executor can choose the valuation date to be either April 12, 1976 or October 12, 1976. If it benefits the beneficiary to have a large basis, the executor might choose October 12, 1976 to be the valuation date. Hence,

$$b = \$665,000.$$

Example 2:   Mr. James died October 13, 1978. He left his son an apartment that he acquired May 19, 1974. At the time of his death the adjusted basis was $180,000, and the fair market value was $240,000. What is his son's basis?

Solution: In this example,

$$b' = \$180,000, \text{ and } v = \$240,000.$$

Since Mr. James acquired the property prior to 1977 and the value exceeds the basis, we must determine t_1 and t_2. From Table 7, October 13 is the 286th day of the year, and May 19 is the 139th day. The holding period includes 1976, a leap year, hence,

$$t_1 = \underbrace{(365-139)}_{'74} + \underbrace{365}_{'75} + \underbrace{366}_{'76} = 957 \text{ days, and}$$

$$t_2 = \underbrace{(365-139)}_{'74} + \underbrace{365}_{'75} + \underbrace{366}_{'76} + \underbrace{365}_{'77} + \underbrace{286}_{'78} = 1,608 \text{ days.}$$

Now, the basis is

$$b = \$180,000 + \frac{957}{1,608}(\$240,000 - \$180,000)$$

$$= \$180,000 + \$35,709$$
$$= \$215,709.$$

12.3.   Basis of Property Acquired by a Survivor in Joint Ownership

Joint ownership enables each owner to possess an undivided interest in an entire property. Joint ownership can be either as tenants in common or as joint tenants:

1. *Tenants in Common.*   Each party has his own basis in the property. When one party dies the basis is transferred to the inheriting party (whoever he may be), and the basis is then determined by the rules of inheritance (Section 12.2). That is, there is no right of survivorship for the surviving joint owner.

2. *Joint Tenancy*   (called tenancy by the entirety if joint tenancy exists between spouses). When one party dies, ownership automatically passes to the other parties. That is, there is a right to survivorship, and the survivor's basis is determined by one of the following formulas. If the decedent died after 1976, the Treasury Regulations should be consulted for details.

Formula:

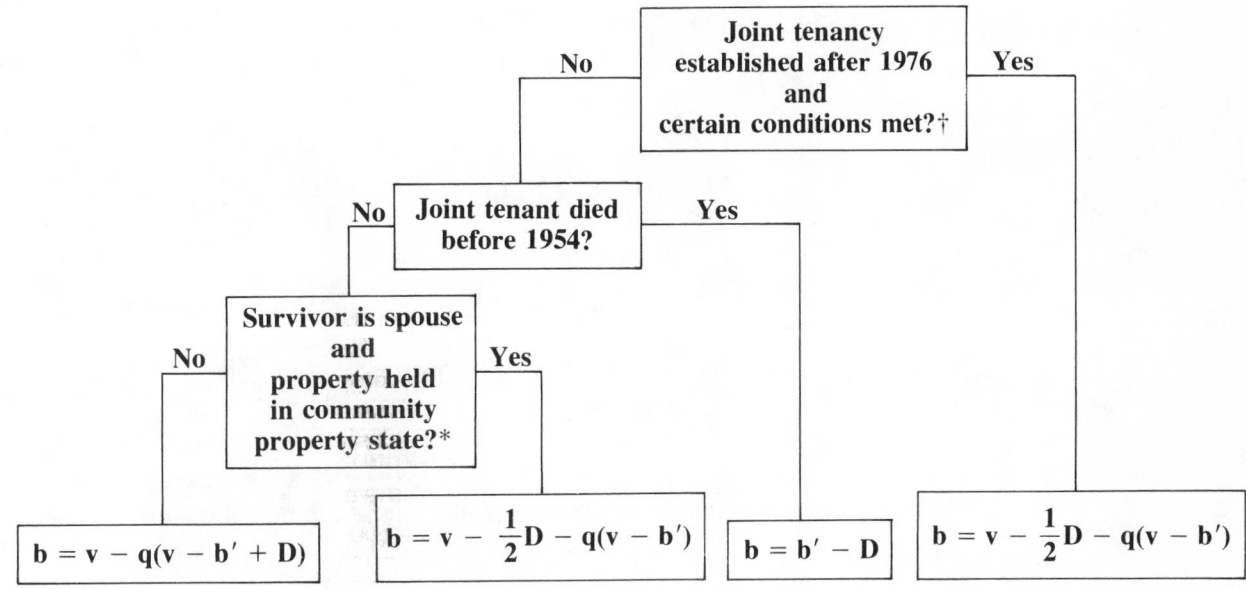

where

b = survivor's basis on valuation date**

v = fair market value of property on valuation date

b′ = basis of property before joint owner's death (not adjusted for depreciation)

q = survivor's fractional contribution to basis (i.e., $0 \leqslant q \leqslant 1$). Set q = 0 if survivor's contribution cannot be proved

D = total depreciation claimed on property until valuation date (Section 11.4)

---

*Community property states require that property acquired during marriage and income derived from it are owned equally by husband and wife. The community property states are Arizona, California, Idaho, Louisiana, Nevada, New Mexico, Texas, and Washington.

Separate property is property acquired by either spouse before marriage or through a gift or inheritance. Separate property does not generally become community property through marriage. However, in some states, the income derived from separate property does become community property.

†The conditions are: (1) The only survivor is a spouse. (2) The joint tenants did not inherit the interest. (3) For personal property, the creation of the joint interest was a completed gift for gift tax purposes. (4) For real property, the donor elected to treat the creation of the joint tenancy as a taxable gift at that time. It is considered a taxable gift only when the joint tenancy is terminated by other than the death of the spouse.

**If a uniform gift tax return is not required or if the tenancy was created after 1976, the valuation date is the date of death. Otherwise see the first flow diagram in Section 12.2.

Table: Find D from Table 5 and Section 11.4.

Example: In 1972 Mr. & Mrs. Howe bought an apartment and held it in joint tenancy. The basis was $180,000, and they have since claimed $24,000 in depreciation.

Mr. Howe died in 1976, and on the valuation date, the apartment was valued at $280,000. What is Mrs. Howe's basis if: (a) She has contributed everything to the basis, and the property is held in a community property state? (b) She has contributed ¼ to the basis, and the property is not held in a community property state? (c) She has contributed nothing to the basis, and the property is not held in a community property state?

Solution: In this example,

$$b' = \$180{,}000, \; D = \$24{,}000, \; \text{and} \; v = \$280{,}000.$$

Now,

(a) $q = 1$, and from the flow diagram (following no,no,yes), the basis is

$$b = \$280{,}000 - \frac{1}{2} \times \$24{,}000 - 1 \cdot (\$280{,}000 - \$180{,}000)$$

$$= \$168{,}000.$$

(b) $q = $ ¼, and from the flow diagram (following no,no,no), the basis is

$$b = \$280{,}000 - \frac{1}{4} \cdot (\$280{,}000 - \$180{,}000 + \$24{,}000)$$

$$= \$249{,}000.$$

(c) $q = 0$, and from the flow diagram (following no,no,no), the basis is

$$b = \$280{,}000 - 0 \cdot (\$280{,}000 - \$180{,}000 + \$24{,}000)$$
$$= \$280{,}000.$$

(Note: Comparing cases b and c, the basis is larger when Mrs. Howe has a smaller interest.)

12.4.   Basis of Property Acquired Through a Life Estate

A life estate is an interest in property held for life by a certain party (the life tenant). Sometimes there is a second party (the remainderman) that can inherit the property upon the death of the life tenant.

A third party (the purchaser) can also be involved in a life estate. He can purchase the property from either the life tenant or from both the life tenant and the remainderman, simultaneously. If he purchases the property from the life tenant alone, and there is a remainderman, the property will go to the remainderman upon the death of the life tenant. Hence, he amortizes the property value over the expected remaining life of the life tenant. The annual amortization is deductible from ordinary income. In the event the life tenant dies before expected, the full unamortized value is deducted that year. When the property is purchased from both parties simultaneously, the basis of the property is allocated between the life tenant and the remainderman according to a table based upon the age of the life tenant.

Formula:

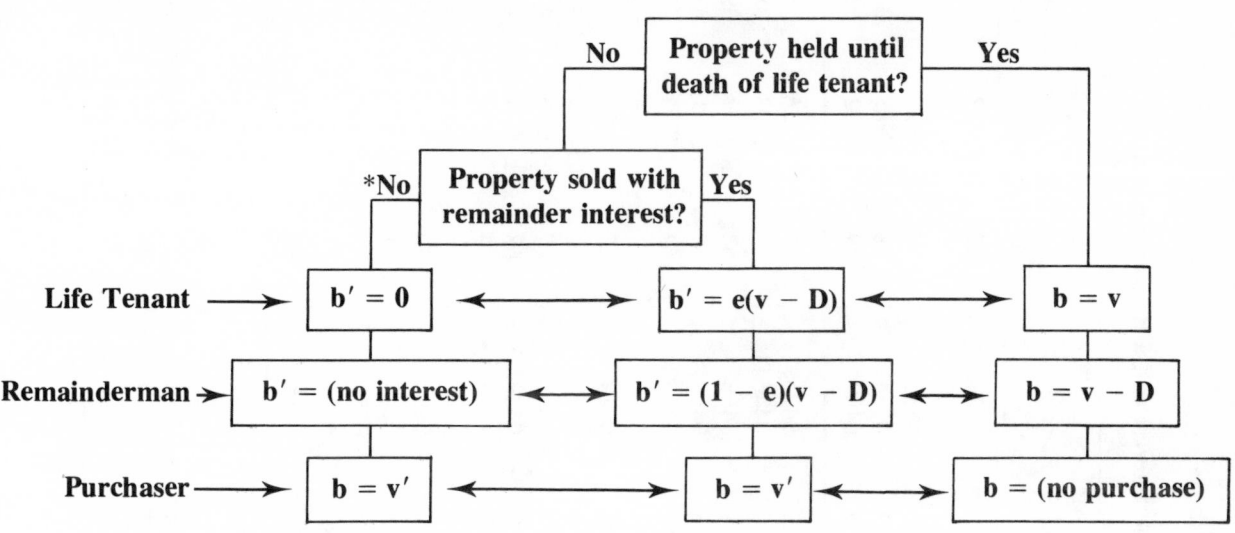

where

  b = basis of property when acquired by the life tenant, the remainderman, or the purchaser

  b' = basis of property when sold by the life tenant or remainderman

  v, v' = fair market value of the property at the time the property is included in the donor's estate and at the time of sale by the life tenant, respectively

  D = amount of depreciation claimed by the life tenant

  e = present value of a life interest (based upon the age of the life tenant at the time of sale)

Table: Find e in the table on pages 260 and 261.

---

*If the sale was made before 1969, see Treasury Regulations.

Present Value of a Life Interest and a Remainder Interest

Age	Female Life Estate (e)	Female Remainder (1 − e)	Male Life Estate (e)	Male Remainder (1 − e)	Age	Female Life Estate (e)	Female Remainder (1 − e)	Male Life Estate (e)	Male Remainder (1 − e)
0	0.95383	0.04617	0.93705	0.06295	55	0.69859	0.30141	0.61776	0.38224
1	.97370	.02630	.96217	.03783	56	.68612	.31388	.60466	.39534
2	.97372	.02628	.96170	.03830	57	.67320	.32680	.59131	.40869
3	.97308	.02692	.96053	.03947	58	.65988	.34012	.57778	.42222
4	.97217	.02783	.95905	.04095	59	.64622	.35378	.56417	.43583
5	.97110	.02890	.95732	.04268	60	.63226	.36774	.55052	.44948
6	.96989	.03011	.95540	.04460	61	.61803	.38197	.53687	.46313
7	.96853	.03147	.95331	.04669	62	.60352	.39648	.52321	.47679
8	.96703	.03297	.95105	.04895	63	.58871	.41129	.50954	.49046
9	.96541	.03459	.94861	.05139	64	.57355	.42645	.49585	.50415
10	.96365	.03635	.94598	.05402	65	.55803	.44197	.48212	.51788
11	.96176	.03824	.94316	.05684	66	.54211	.45789	.46836	.53164
12	.95975	.04025	.94019	.05981	67	.52583	.47417	.45458	.54542
13	.95764	.04236	.93708	.06292	68	.50924	.49076	.44077	.55923
14	.95543	.04457	.93391	.06609	69	.49241	.50759	.42689	.57311
15	.95314	.04686	.93069	.06931	70	.47540	.52460	.41294	.58706
16	.95076	.04924	.92746	.07254	71	.45823	.54177	.39889	.60111
17	.94829	.05171	.92419	.07581	72	.44088	.55912	.38474	.61526
18	.94572	.05428	.92089	.07911	73	.42341	.57659	.37051	.62949
19	.94303	.05697	.91751	.08249	74	.40587	.59413	.35624	.64376
20	.94021	.05979	.91403	.08597	75	.38833	.61167	.34194	.65806
21	.93724	.06276	.91046	.08954	76	.37073	.62927	.32761	.67239
22	.93412	.06588	.90678	.09322	77	.35307	.64693	.31327	.68673
23	.93085	.06915	.90292	.09708	78	.33546	.66454	.29895	.70105
24	.92739	.07261	.89884	.10116	79	.31811	.68189	.28481	.71519

Age				
25	.92375	.07625	.89445	.10555
26	.91993	.08007	.88972	.11028
27	.91591	.08409	.88465	.11535
28	.91168	.08832	.87925	.12075
29	.90725	.09275	.87353	.12647
30	.90259	.09741	.86750	.13250
31	.89773	.10227	.86117	.13883
32	.89265	.10735	.85451	.14549
33	.88733	.11267	.84752	.15248
34	.88176	.11824	.84020	.15980
35	.87593	.12407	.83255	.16745
36	.86985	.13015	.82455	.17545
37	.86349	.13651	.81622	.18378
38	.85687	.14313	.80755	.19245
39	.84998	.15002	.79854	.20146
40	.84281	.15719	.78923	.21077
41	.83536	.16464	.77960	.22040
42	.82764	.17236	.76967	.23033
43	.81962	.18038	.75944	.24056
44	.81131	.18869	.74891	.25109
45	.80269	.19731	.73808	.26192
46	.79374	.20626	.72695	.27305
47	.78448	.21552	.71552	.28448
48	.77488	.22512	.70385	.29615
49	.76498	.23502	.69198	.30802
50	.75476	.24524	.67997	.32003
51	.74423	.25577	.66785	.33215
52	.73339	.26661	.65560	.34440
53	.72220	.27780	.64320	.35680
54	.71062	.28938	.63060	.36940

		Age		
.30117	.69883	80	.27098	.72902
.28489	.71511	81	.25773	.74227
.26935	.73065	82	.24527	.75473
.25439	.74561	83	.23354	.76646
.23956	.76044	84	.22217	.77783
.22441	.77559	85	.21070	.78930
.21010	.78990	86	.19955	.80045
.19674	.80326	87	.18870	.81130
.18431	.81569	88	.17822	.82178
.17285	.82715	89	.16831	.83169
.16241	.83759	90	.15922	.84078
.15301	.84699	91	.15097	.84903
.14470	.85530	92	.14350	.85650
.13741	.86259	93	.13681	.86319
.13103	.86897	94	.13081	.86919
.12535	.87465	95	.12535	.87465
.11998	.88002	96	.11998	.88002
.11487	.88513	97	.11487	.88513
.10999	.89001	98	.10999	.89001
.10532	.89468	99	.10532	.89468
.10087	.89913	100	.10087	.89913
.09661	.90339	101	.09661	.90339
.09250	.90750	102	.09250	.90750
.08846	.91154	103	.08846	.91154
.08439	.91561	104	.08439	.91561
.08000	.92000	105	.08000	.92000
.07471	.92529	106	.07471	.92520
.06718	.93282	107	.06718	.93282
.05426	.94574	108	.05426	.94574
.02830	.97170	109	.02830	.97170

Example: Mrs. Adams inherited, as a life estate, a commercial building. Upon her death, the property is to be inherited by her daughter, Barbara. The building was worth $200,000 when it was included in the donor's estate. Mrs. Adams has just sold the property to a third party for $208,000. Mrs. Adams is 54 years old, and has claimed $18,000 worth of depreciation. What is the basis to each party if (a) Mrs. Adams and Barbara sold their interests simultaneously, and (b) Mrs. Adams sold her interest without her daughter's interest?

Solution: In this example,

$$v = \$200,000, \; v' = \$208,000, \text{ and } D = \$18,000.$$

(a) From the flow diagram (following no, yes), we see that we must determine e: From the table corresponding to a female at age 54, find $e = .71062$. Now the bases are

$$
\begin{aligned}
b' &= .71062(\$200,000 - \$18,000) \\
   &= \$129,333, && \text{(Life Tenant)} \\
b' &= (1 - .71062)(\$200,000 - \$18,000) \\
   &= \$52,667, \text{ and} && \text{(Remainderman)} \\
b &= \$208,000. && \text{(Purchaser)}
\end{aligned}
$$

(b) From the flow diagram (following no,no), the bases are

$$
\begin{aligned}
b' &= \$0, && \text{(Life Tenant)} \\
b' &= \text{(no interest)}, && \text{(Remainderman)}
\end{aligned}
$$

and

$$b = \$208,000 \qquad \text{(Purchaser)}.$$

12.5.   Basis of Property Acquired as a Gift

The basis of property acquired as a gift depends upon whether or not the donor's adjusted basis exceeds the fair market value of the gift when acquired. In the event the fair market value of the gift is less than the adjusted basis, the basis to the donee (for computing depreciation and capital gain), is the donor's basis. On the other hand, if the donee subsequently disposes of the property at a loss, the basis to the donee (for computing the loss) is the fair market value of the property when acquired.

If the fair market value of the gift exceeds the basis, some or all of the gift tax paid by the donor will add to the basis.

The following flow diagram can be used for property given after 1920. If the property was given before 1921, the basis to the donee is simply the fair market value at the time of the gift.

Formula:

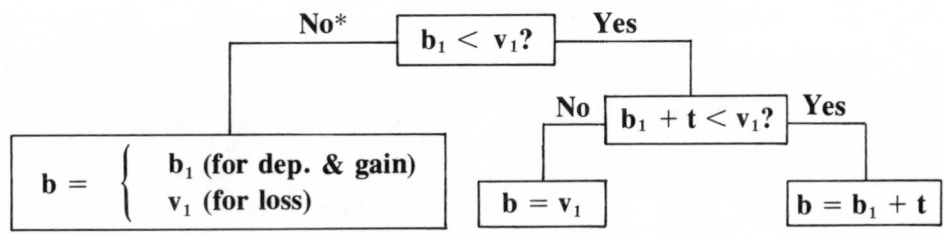

where

b = basis to the donee when gift acquired

b_1 = basis to the donor just prior to giving gift

v_1, v_2 = value of gift when acquired by donee and when disposed of by donee, respectively

t = amount of gift tax paid by donor. If gift is donated after 1976, include only the amount attributable to appreciation

Table: Find t in the table on page 264.

Example 1: Mr. Ramsdell gave his daughter Lynne an apartment house valued at $200,000. His basis at that time was $125,000, and his gift tax was $33,500. If Lynne later sold the apartment for $240,000, what was her basis (at the time of acquisition)?

Solution: In this example,

$$v_1 = \$200,000, \ b_1 = \$125,000, \ t = \$33,500, \text{ and } v_2 = \$240,000.$$

From the flow diagram (following yes), her basis was

$$b = \$125,000 \ + \$33,500 = \$158,500.$$

Example 2: Mr. Ramsdell gave his daughter Lynne an apartment house valued at $200,000. His basis was $215,000. What is her basis for (a) depreciation, (b) gain if she subsequently sells it for $230,000, and (c) loss if she subsequently sells it for $210,000?

---

*Basis is v_1 for computing depreciation, depletion, amortization, and gain. Basis is v_1 for computing loss. In the event $v_1 < v_2 < b_1$ there is neither a gain nor a loss.

FEDERAL GIFT TAXES
(for gifts made after 1941 and before 1977)

| If your taxable gift is | | | Your tax is | |
Over	But not over	This	Plus following percentage	Of the amount over
$ 0	$ 5,000	$ 0	2¼%	$ 0
5,000	10,000	112.50	5¼%	5,000
10,000	20,000	375	8¼%	10,000
20,000	30,000	1,200	10½%	20,000
30,000	40,000	2,250	13½%	30,000
40,000	50,000	3,600	16½%	40,000
50,000	60,000	5,250	18¾%	50,000
60,000	100,000	7,125	21%	60,000
100,000	250,000	15,525	22½%	100,000
250,000	500,000	49,275	24%	250,000
500,000	750,000	109,275	26¼%	500,000
750,000	1,000,000	174,900	27¾%	750,000
1,000,000	1,250,000	244,275	29¼%	1,000,000
1,250,000	1,500,000	317,400	31½%	1,250,000
1,500,000	2,000,000	396,150	33¾%	1,500,000
2,000,000	2,500,000	564,900	36¾%	2,000,000
2,500,000	3,000,000	748,650	39¾%	2,500,000
3,000,000	3,500,000	947,400	42%	3,000,000
3,500,000	4,000,000	1,157,400	44¼%	3,500,000
4,000,000	5,000,000	1,378,650	47¼%	4,000,000
5,000,000	6,000,000	1,851,150	50¼%	5,000,000
6,000,000	7,000,000	2,353,650	52½%	6,000,000
7,000,000	8,000,000	2,878,650	54¾%	7,000,000
8,000,000	10,000,000	3,426,150	57%	8,000,000
10,000,000	....	4,566,150	57¾%	10,000,000

Solution: In this example,

$$v_1 = \$200,000, \text{ and } b_1 = \$215,000.$$

(a) From the flow diagram (following no), her basis for depreciation is

$$b = \$215,000.$$

Of course, only that portion of the basis allocated to improvements is used for depreciation (Section 11.3).

(b) Since $v_2 = \$230{,}000$, there is a gain, and her basis for computing the gain is

$$b = \$215{,}000.$$

(c) Since $v_2 = \$210{,}000$ there is a loss, and her basis for computing the loss is

$$b = \$200{,}000.$$

In this event, there is neither a gain nor loss to be reported.

12.6.   Basis of Property Acquired by Repossession

Property can be financed either by a third party, such as a bank, that takes a mortgage or by the seller who takes a purchase money mortgage.

In the case of a defaulted third party mortgage, the basis to the buyer of the repossessed property is either the fair market value of the property or the amount paid, depending upon whether the buyer is or is not the creditor.

In the case of a defaulted purchase money mortgage, the basis of the property depends upon whether or not it is personal or real property.

The following rules, depicted by the flow diagram, do not apply to personal residences that qualify for deferred capital gain (Section 13.10).

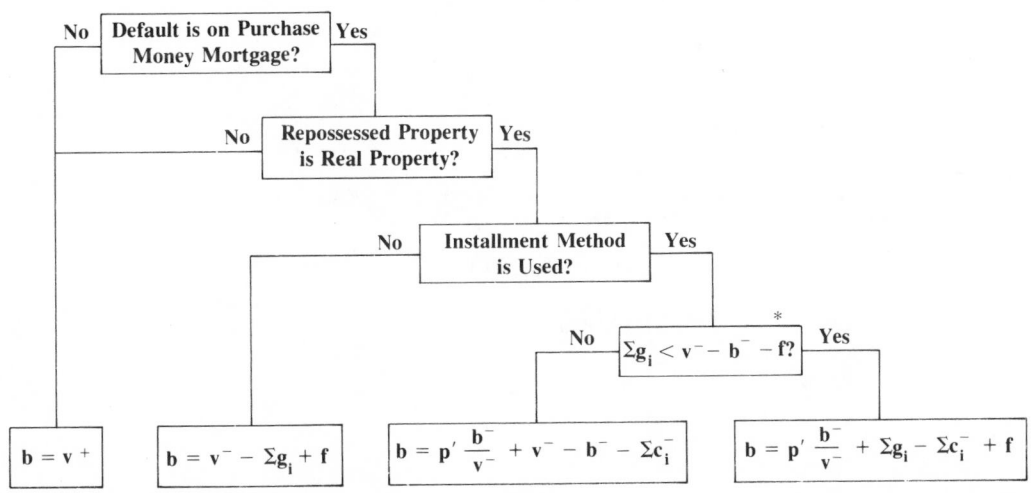

where

b = basis of repossessed property
b^- = basis of property when sold
v^- = value of property when sold

---

*The gain on repossession is the lesser of $(\sum g_i - \sum c_i)$ and $(v^- - b^- - f - \sum c_i^-)$.

$$v^+ = \begin{cases} \text{fair market value if personal property} \\ \text{fair market value if real property and buyer is creditor} \\ \text{sale price if real property and buyer is not creditor} \end{cases}$$

g_i = amount paid to seller by buyer in the ith year

c_i^- = capital gain reported by seller in the ith year

p' = balance of purchase money mortgage

f = cost of repossession

Example: Harry Lee sold his business building for $600,000. He took $150,000 in down payment and, beginning one year hence, is to be paid $30,000 annually on the $450,000 purchase money mortgage. The basis of the building is $500,000. Mr. Lee has been reporting his capital gain by the installment method, but after receiving two annual payments, the buyer defaulted, and Mr. Lee repossessed the building at a cost of $500. He had reported capital gain of $25,000, $5,000, and $5,000 for the three years. What is his basis of the repossessed building?

Solution: In this example,

$$v^- = \$600,000, \; g_1 = \$150,000, \; g_2 = \$30,000,$$

$$g_3 = \$30,000, \; p' = \$450,000 - \$30,000 - \$30,000 = \$390,000$$

$$b^- = \$500,000, \; f = \$500, \; c_1 = \$25,000,$$

$$c_2 = \$5,000, \text{ and } c_3 = \$5,000.$$

From the flow diagram (following yes,yes,yes,no),

$$b = \$390,000 \times \frac{\$500,000}{\$600,000} + \$600,000 - \$500,000$$

$$- (\$25,000 + \$5,000 + \$5,000)$$

$$= \$325,000 + \$100,000 - \$35,000$$

$$= \$390,000.$$

12.7.   Basis of Property Acquired After Involuntary Conversion

An involuntary conversion occurs when property is converted from one type to another against the wishes of the owner. For instance, if property is destroyed by a natural disaster, the property may be converted into cash received from an insurance company. Also governmental condemnation might cause property to be converted to cash or securities.

Formula:

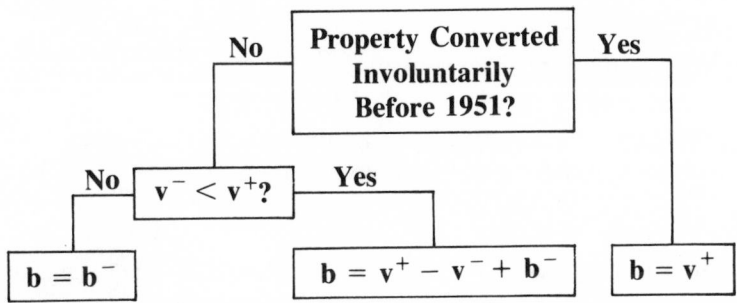

where

b = basis of property acquired after involuntary conversion
b^- = basis of property disposed of by involuntary conversion
v^- = value received for property disposed of by involuntary conversion
v^+ = value of property acquired after involuntary conversion

Example: Ed Lowery lost his warehouse in a fire last year. The basis of the warehouse was $470,000, and he received insurance proceeds of $510,000. He purchased another warehouse for $580,000. What is the basis of the new warehouse?

Solution: In this example,

$$b^- = \$470,000, \quad v^- = \$510,000, \text{ and } v^+ = \$580,000.$$

From the flow diagram (following no, yes), the basis of the new warehouse is

$$b = \$580,000 - \$510,000 + \$470,000$$
$$= \$540,000.$$

12.8.   Basis of Property Acquired by Exchange

When property is exchanged, some or all of the capital gain can be deferred. The amount of recognized gain depends on the amount of unlike property (boot) used in the exchange. For a personal residence see Section 12.13.

Formula:

$$b = b^- + u^- - u^+ + p^+ - p^- + c_1^-$$

where

b = basis of the property received
b^- = basis of the property given
u^-, u^+ = unlike property given and received, respectively
p^-, p^+ = mortgage on property given and received, respectively
c_1^- = recognized gain on property given (obtained from Section 13.5)

Example: Mr. Ahern wants to exchange his apartment for Mr. Hanson's small hotel. Mr. Ahern's apartment is valued at $230,000, has a $90,000 mortgage, and a basis of $110,000. Mr. Hanson's hotel is valued at $260,000, has a $160,000 mortgage, and a basis of $185,000. Since Mr. Ahern's equity is $230,000 − $90,000 = $140,000 and Mr. Hanson's equity is $260,000 − $160,000 = $100,000, Mr. Hanson will add $40,000 cash (unlike property) in order for the exchange to be equitable. What is (a) the basis of the hotel Mr. Ahern receives and (b) the basis of the apartment Mr. Hanson receives?

Solution: (a) From Mr. Ahern's point of view, the values in the exchange are

v^- = $230,000, p^- = $90,000, b^- = $110,000,
u^- = $0, v^+ = $260,000, p^+ = $160,000,
b^+ = $185,000, and u^+ = $40,000.

We must determine c_1^-, the amount of recognized gain on the apartment. From the flow diagram in Section 13.5 (following yes, no),

$$c_1^- = \$40,000.$$

Now, the basis of the hotel Mr. Ahern receives is,

$$\begin{aligned} b &= \$110,000 + \$0 - \$40,000 + \$160,000 \\ &\quad - \$90,000 + \$40,000 \\ &= \$180,000. \end{aligned}$$

(b) From Mr. Hanson's point of view, the values in the exchange are

v^- = $260,000, p^- = $160,000, b^- = $185,000,
u^- = $40,000, v^+ = $230,000, p^+ = $90,000,
b^+ = $110,000, and u^+ = $0.

Also, we must determine c_1^-, the amount of recognized gain on the hotel. From the flow diagram in Section 13.5 (following no, no),

$$c_1^- = \$30,000.$$

Now, from the formula, the basis of the apartment that Mr. Hanson receives is

$$\begin{aligned} b &= \$185,000 + \$40,000 - \$0 + \$90,000 \\ &\quad - \$160,000 + \$30,000 \\ &= \$185,000. \end{aligned}$$

12.9.   Basis of Property Acquired for Services Rendered

If property, instead of cash, is received for services rendered the basis of the property is its fair market value.

Formula:

$$b = v$$

where

$b =$ basis of property acquired for services rendered
$v =$ fair market value of property when services are rendered

Example: A real estate broker renders services worth $7,000. For these services, he receives $7,000 equity in a rental unit with a $21,000 mortgage. What is his basis?

Solution: The value of his services is $7,000, but the value of the property is $28,000 = $7,000 + $21,000. Hence, his basis is

$$b = v = \$28,000.$$

12.10.   Basis of Property Acquired by Casualty or Theft Loss

When property suffers a casualty or theft loss, there is often an insurance award and a deduction from ordinary income. The following formula determines the basis of the property.

Formula:

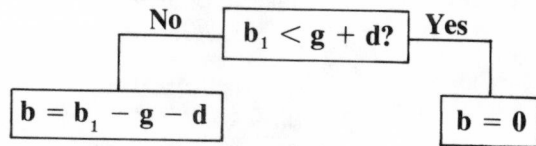

where

b = basis of property acquired after casualty or theft loss
b_1 = basis of property immediately prior to casualty or theft loss
g = insurance proceeds or other reimbursements
d = total amount that can be deducted from ordinary income, including carryover (Section 11.13)

Example: A fire damaged the Hotel Dante. The basis of the hotel just before the fire was $530,000. Insurance proceeds were $90,000, and the casualty deduction was $40,000. What is the basis of the hotel now?

Solution: In this example,

$$b_1 = \$530,000, \; g = \$90,000, \text{ and } d = \$40,000.$$

Now, the basis of the hotel is

$$b = \$530,000 - \$90,000 - \$40,000 = \$400,000.$$

12.11. Basis of a Personal Residence Converted to an Income-Producing Property

When a personal residence is converted to income-producing property, the fair market value should be noted at the time of conversion. The basis of the income-producing property is the lesser of the fair market value and the adjusted basis of the personal residence at that time.

Formula:

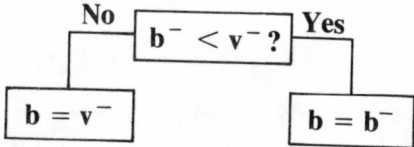

where

b = basis of the income-producing property at the time of conversion
b^- = adjusted basis of the personal residence at time of conversion
v^- = fair market value of the personal residence at the time of conversion

Example: Ms. Thomas decided to move to an apartment and rent her house to students. At the time of conversion, the house was appraised at $43,000, and her adjusted basis was $37,000. What is the basis of her house as an income-producing property?

Solution: In this example,

$$v^- = \$43,000, \text{ and } b^- = \$37,000.$$

From the flow diagram (following yes), the basis of the income-producing property is

$$b = \$37,000.$$

12.12.   Basis of Reinvestment in Qualified Low-Income Housing

If a qualified low-income housing project is sold either to the tenants or to a cooperative that benefits them, the gain realized from the sale can avoid tax. The proceeds must be reinvested in another qualified low-income housing project (Section 13.8)*.

Formula:

$$b = v^+ - c_i$$

where

b   = basis of reinvestment property
v^+ = cost of reinvestment property
c_i = gain from sale of previous property that is realized but not recognized due to reinvestment (Section 13.8)

Example: Mr. Rosenberg has sold a qualified low-income housing project and has a net realized gain of $280,000 that is not recognized because of his reinvestment in a second such project. The second project cost $400,000. What is his basis in this new property?

Solution: In this example,

$$c_i = \$280,000, \text{ and } v^+ = \$400,000.$$

Now, his basis is

$$b = \$400,000 - \$280,000 = \$120,000.$$

---

*According to sections 221(d)(3) or 236 of the National Housing Act, reinvestment must occur within a specified time, the rental proceeds must be limited, and the mortgage must be insured.

12.13. Basis of a Residence Acquired After the Sale of Old Residence

Some or all of the capital gain from the sale of an old residence can be deferred. A newly acquired residence must meet criteria concerning time and principal residence (see Section 13.10) for gain to be deferred. The following flow diagram determines the basis of the newly acquired residence (even if the criteria are not met).

Formula:

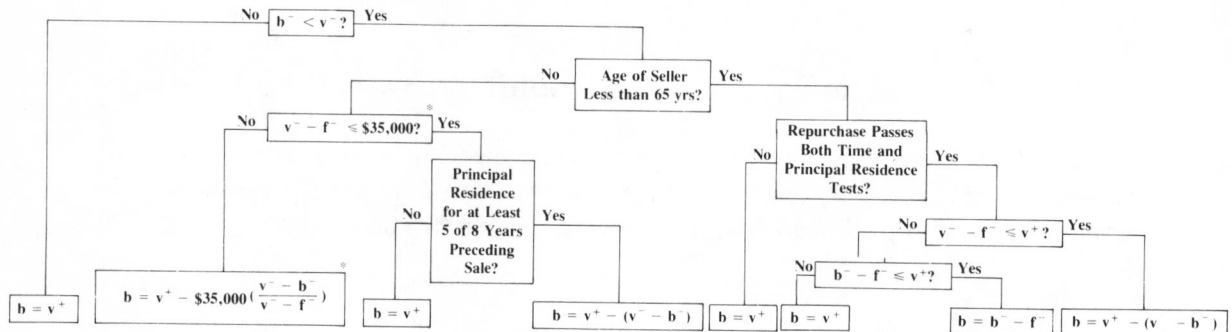

where

b = basis of newly acquired residence
b^- = basis of residence sold
v^- = sale price of residence sold, less selling expenses
v^+ = cost of newly acquired residence
f^- = fix-up costs on residence sold

Example: Phil Howard is 45 years old. He realized $50,000 on the sale of his home and bought another house for $53,000. His basis in the old house was $35,000, and he spent another $1,500 to get it into shape for sale. What is his basis in the newly acquired house if (a) he doesn't pass the time test, and (b) he passes both tests (Section 13.10)?

Solution: In this example,

$$v^- = \$50,000, \quad v^+ = \$53,000, \quad b^- = \$35,000, \quad \text{and} \quad f^- = \$1,500.$$

(a) From the flow diagram (following yes,yes,no), his basis is

_____

*The $35,000 limit is $20,000 for residences sold before 1977.

$$b = \$53,000.$$

(b) From the flow diagram (following yes,yes,yes,yes), his basis is

$$b = \$53,000 - (\$50,000 - \$35,000)$$
$$= \$38,000.$$

12.14. Adjustments to Basis

During the period of ownership, the unadjusted basis of property (basis when acquired) may change due to some additions and subtractions. The following is a partial list of some common additions and subtractions.

Additions to Basis:
1. Cost of capital improvements (i.e., generally improvements that have a useful life that exceeds one year).
2. Purchase commissions (selling commissions subtract from selling price).
3. Cost of exercised option (if not exercised, cost is a loss).
4. Title insurance.
5. Production costs of unharvested crops.
6. Demolition costs of property purchased with intent to demolish.
7. Interest equalization tax paid on foreign securities.
8. Excess of special assessment that exceeds condemnation award.
9. Tax payments buyer paid before taking title if property bought before 1954.
10. Deductible taxes, interest and carrying charges (provided property is unimproved and non-productive real property*).
11. Costs incurred on unimproved or developed real property up to the time work was completed, and personal property up to the time of installation or use (whichever is later).

Subtractions from Basis:
1. Depreciation and amortization on property used in business or the production of income except that amount that is taxed as a tax preference item (Section 14.6). Include the additional first year depreciation on personal property (Section 11.8).
2. Depletion.
3. Return of capital, such as dividends paid out of capital or depletion revenue.
4. Losses from casualty.
5. Insurance proceeds and other reimbursements to settle property damage.
6. Amortized premium of a bond bought at a premium. (Section 5.7)
7. Income not received due to cancellation of a business debt (up to the fair market value at the date of cancellation).
8. Payments received for granting an easement.

---

*Can be deducted or the election can be made to capitalize.

TAXES: CAPITAL GAINS AND LOSSES

The amount of *realized* gain or loss on the disposition of property depends upon the basis and the value received. However, the *recognized* gain is not determined so easily. It often depends upon the manner of disposition, the classification of the owner, the amount of depreciation recapture, etc.*

This chapter, like Chapters 11, 12, and 14, uses flow diagrams to arrive at the correct formula. At each box in the diagram a simple question must be answered either yes or no to determine the path to the next box. Finally, the correct formula to determine the recognized gain (and often the deferred gain) is given in the box at the bottom of the diagram. These formulas are not adjusted for depreciation recapture (determined in Sections 14.1 and 14.2).

13.1.   Property Disposed of by Sale

Most properties are disposed of by sale. The capital gain or loss that results is simply the difference between the amount realized from the sale and the adjusted basis.

Bargain and installment sales are discussed in Sections 13.3 and 13.4. The case of a personal residence that is sold and another residence acquired is discussed in Section 13.10.

---

*Property held by dealers, when sold or exchanged profitably, results in ordinary income to the dealer.

Formula:

$$c = v - b$$

where

c = recognized capital gain or loss
v = amount realized from sale of the property
b = adjusted basis of the property

Example: Don Burger sold his home for $63,000. He bought it 10 years ago when he was 33 years old. He had an adjusted basis of $31,000. Since he does not plan to purchase another home, what is his recognized capital gain?

Solution: In this example,

$$v = \$63{,}000, \text{ and } b = \$31{,}000.$$

His recognized capital gain is

$$c = \$63{,}000 - \$31{,}000 = \$32{,}000.$$

13.2.   Property Disposed of by Involuntary Conversion

An involuntary conversion occurs when a property is converted from one type to another against the wishes of the owner. For instance, property may be destroyed by fire, a natural disaster, or governmental condemnation. In any event, insurance proceeds, cash, or securities might be received in place of the property.

If the award exceeds the adjusted basis, a gain will be realized (in the year the proceeds are received)*. If a replacement property is purchased within a certain period of time**, and if the replacement property is a certain kind, some or all of the gain may be deferred. The replacement property must generally be related in use to the converted property. This requirement is not so strict for property used in trade or business or held for the production of income.

The following flow diagram defines the long-term gain or loss of a single asset. If conversion resulted from casualty or theft, it is assumed that the sum of all assets involuntarily converted from casualty or theft results in a gain.

---

*If the sum of all involuntary conversions from casualty or theft results in a loss, none of the conversions resulting from casualty or theft can be treated as a gain: the individual losses are deducted from ordinary income and the individual gains are added to ordinary income. If the sum is a gain, each is treated as a capital gain or loss.

**If the involuntary conversion occurred before 1970, the purchase must have occurred by the end of the first year after the gain. After 1969 and before 1975, the purchase must have occurred by the end of the second year after the gain. After 1974 the purchase must have occurred by the end of the third year. These deadlines can be extended by permission of the Treasury.

Formula:

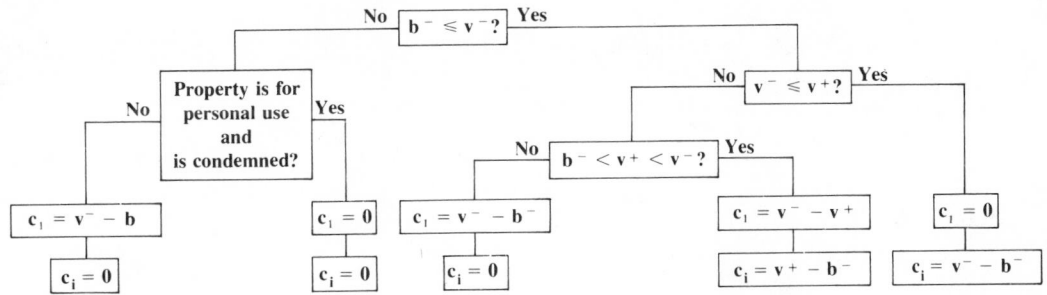

where

c_1 = capital gain upon involuntary conversion recognized in year of conversion

c_i = capital gain upon involuntary conversion deferred to the ith year (i = 2,3,. . .)

b^- = adjusted basis of property involuntarily converted

v^- = amount realized on property involuntarily converted

v^+ = cost of replacement property ($v^+ = 0$ if no replacement)

Example 1:   Ed Lowery lost his warehouse in a fire last year. The adjusted basis of the warehouse was $470,000, and the insurance proceeds were $510,000. This year he purchased another warehouse for $500,000. How much of the $40,000 capital gain is recognized in the year Mr. Lowery received the insurance proceeds, and how much is deferred?

Solution: In this example,

$$b^- = \$470,000, \ v^- = \$510,000, \text{ and } v^+ = \$500,000.$$

From the flow diagram (following yes, no, yes), the capital gain recognized in the year the insurance proceeds are received is

$$c_1 = \$510,000 - \$500,000 = \$10,000,$$

and the deferred capital gain is

$$c_i = \$500,000 - \$470,000 = \$30,000.$$

Example 2:   Consider the case of Example 1 except Mr. Lowery does not purchase another warehouse. How much capital gain is recognized?

Solution: In this example,

$$b^- = \$470,000, \quad v^- = \$510,000, \quad \text{and} \quad v^+ = \$0.$$

From the flow diagram (following yes,no,no)*, the gain in the year the insurance proceeds are received is

$$c_1 = \$510,000 - \$470,000 = \$40,000,$$

and the deferred capital gain is

$$c_i = \$0.$$

13.3.   Property Disposed of by Bargain Sale

A donation can be made to a qualified charity by selling appreciated property at a bargain price (i.e., a price below the fair market value). If a charitable deduction is allowed on the bargain sale (Section 11.14), part of the basis is allocated to the sale and part to the donation**. The formula below determines the amount of capital gain that is recognized from the sale.

Formula:

$$c = v' \left(\frac{v - b}{v}\right)$$

where

c =   recognized capital gain
b =   basis of property
v =   fair market value of property (if $b \leq v$)
v' =   sale price (if $v' \leq v$)

Example: Mr. Post sold some land to his church for $300,000. The land was appraised at $400,000, and his basis was $280,000. How much capital gain is recognized?

---

*The third box asks "$b^- < v^+ < v^-$?" This double inequality must be viewed in two parts: $v^+ < v^-$ is true, but $b^- < v^+$ is not true. Since both are not true, the answer is no.

**The allocation applies to real property, intangible personal property (such as securities), and tangible personal property that will be used by the charity as part of its normal function (i.e., paintings for an art museum). The allocation also is used for short and long-term capital gain and ordinary income (such as crops, business inventory items, etc.).

Solution: In this example,

$$v' = \$300,000, \; v = \$400,000, \text{ and } b = \$280,000.$$

Now, the recognized capital gain is

$$c = \$300,000 \left(\frac{\$400,000 - \$280,000}{\$400,000} \right)$$

$$= \$300,000 \left(\frac{\$120,000}{\$400,000} \right)$$

$$= \$90,000.$$

(The charitable deduction is treated in Example 2 of Section 11.14).

13.4.   Property Disposed of by Installment Sale

Sometimes when property is sold for a gain and payments are received over a period of years, only part of the gain needs to be reported each year. In the year of the sale, the amount received (including the amount of mortgage owed to a third party that exceeds the adjusted basis) cannot exceed 30% of the sale price. Also payments must be made over at least two taxable years (at any time during those years). Obviously the installment sale is most often used when the seller receives a purchase money mortgage.

Casual sellers may elect to use the installment method of reporting gain. However, if dealers once use this method, they must always do so unless they receive permission to cease from the Commissioner of the IRS.

The Treasury requires that at least 7% simple interest be charged on installments (after July 24, 1975). If this is not done, the Treasury will discount each installment at 7% from the time of the sale until the installment is due. The sale price is reduced due to the discounted installment, and the sale could retroactively be disqualified as an installment sale.

The gain reported on an installment sale is first treated as depreciation recapture, if any (Sections 14.1 and 14.2). Thereafter, the gain that exceeds depreciation recapture is treated as capital gain.

The following flow diagram applies to all real property or personal property sold for more than $1,000.

Formula:

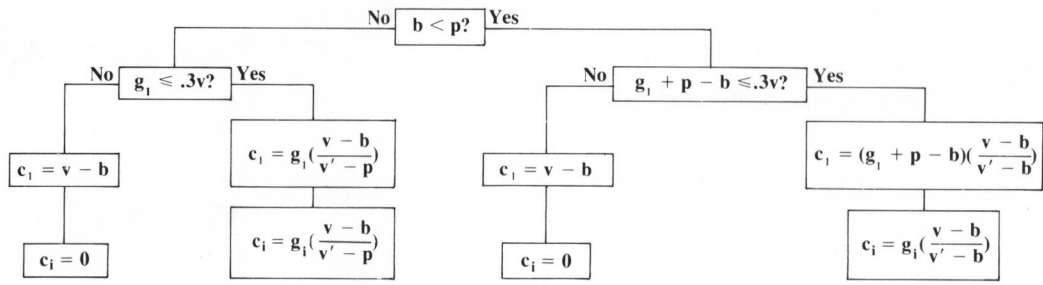

where

c_1 = recognized capital gain in year of sale

c_i = capital gain deferred to the ith year (i = 2,3,. . .)

g_i = amount received from buyer in ith year* (including down payment, when i = 1).

v' = sale price of property**

v = amount realized from sale of property (sale price less selling costs)

b = basis of property

p = amount of buyer's indebtedness that is payable to a third party (if only purchase money mortgage is given, p = $0)

Example 1: Stan Nicholas sold his home for $60,000 and paid a $3,000 sales commission. His basis was $54,000. The buyer obtained a $36,000 loan payable to a third party. He also is to pay Mr. Nicholas a down payment of $16,000 and $4,000 a year for two years at 8% interest, beginning one year hence. What is the recognized capital gain for each of the three installment years?

Solution: In this example,

$$v' = \$60,000, v = \$60,000 - \$3,000 = \$57,000,$$
$$b = \$54,000, p = \$36,000, g_1 = \$16,000,$$
$$g_2 = \$4,000, \text{ and } g_3 = \$4,000.$$

From the flow diagram (following no,yes), the recognized gain in the first year is

$$c_1 = \$16,000 \left(\frac{\$57,000 - \$54,000}{\$60,000 - \$36,000} \right) = \$16,000 \left(\frac{\$3,000}{\$24,000} \right)$$

$$= \$2,000.$$

---

*Must include liabilities of seller that are paid by the buyer (liens, taxes, etc.), payments to the seller on purchase money mortgage, demand notes, registered notes, bonds, readily marketable securities, etc. (it does not include interest paid to the seller on installments). These items are considered to be cash by the Treasury.

**The contract price is defined as the larger of $v' - b$ and $v' - p$.

The recognized gain in the second year is

$$c_2 = \$4,000 \; (\frac{\$57,000 - \$54,000}{\$60,000 - \$36,000}) \; = \$500.$$

Of course, $c_3 = \$500$ also. The interest paid to Mr. Nicholas is treated as ordinary income.

Example 2: In 1970 John Simonsen bought a new apartment building for $110,000. He sold the apartment for $120,000 in 1975 and paid $7,200 in selling commissions. Due mostly to depreciation, his basis has been reduced to $70,000. Since he claimed depreciation according to an accelerated method (200% declining balance), $12,000 of the gain is subject to recapture. The buyer obtained a $75,000 loan payable to a third party. He also gave Mr. Simonsen a down payment of $5,000 and will pay $40,000 at 8% interest in the following year. (a) What is the recognized gain in each of the two years, by virtue of the installment sale? (b) How much of the gain in each year is treated as ordinary income, by virtue of depreciation recapture?

Solution: In this example,

$v' = \$120,000$, $v = \$120,000 - \$7,200 = \$112,800$,
$b = \$70,000$, $y = \$12,000$ (i.e., depreciation recapture, Section 14.1)
$p = \$75,000$, $g_1 = \$5,000$, and $g_2 = \$40,000$.

(a) From the flow diagram (following yes,yes), the recognized capital gain in the first year is

$$c_1 = (\$5,000 + \$75,000 - \$70,000) \; (\frac{\$112,800 - \$70,000}{\$120,000 - \$70,000})$$

$$= \$10,000 \; (\frac{\$42,800}{\$50,000}) = \$10,000 \times .85600$$

$$= \$8,560.$$

The recognized capital gain in the second year is

$$c_2 = \$40,000 \times .85600 = \$34,240.$$

(b) From the flow chart on page 294 (following yes,no,yes,yes),* the amount of capital gain that is to be treated as ordinary income is the entire amount of the recaptured depreciation, $y = \$12,000$. This amount is to be deducted from the gain that is recognized first, and,

---

*As far as this diagram is concerned, c_2 refers to the total gain, $\$8,560 + \$34,240 = \$42,800$.

only after it is exhausted, will subsequently recognized gain be treated as capital gain: Since $c_1 < y^*$, all of c_1 is ordinary income, and the excess recaptured depreciation, $12,000 - \$8,560 = \$3,440$, is carried over. Hence, the amount of c_2 that is treated as ordinary income is $3,440, and the amount that is treated as capital gain is

$$\$34,240 - \$3,440 = \$30,800.$$

13.5.   Property Disposed of by Exchange

Some or all of the gain realized on the exchange of business or investment property of "like-kind" can be deferred**. The flow diagram determines the amount of realized capital gain that is recognized in the year of exchange and the remaining capital gain that is not recognized until there occurs a subsequent exchange of unlike property. Capital losses incurred from an exchange cannot be deducted. A transaction in which an old residence is traded for another residence is treated as a sale and purchase (Section 13.10).

Formula:

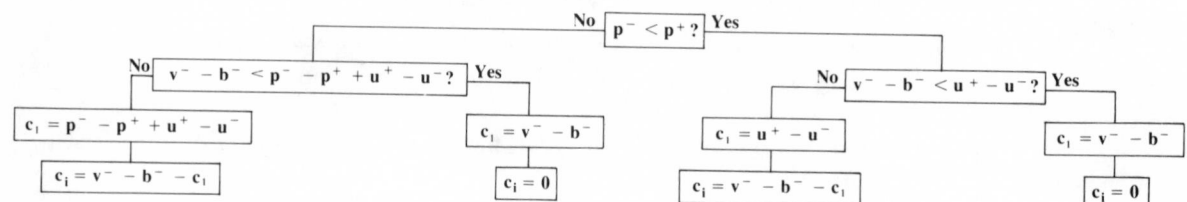

where

c_1 = recognized capital gain in the year of exchange

c_i = capital gain deferred to a subsequent year in which unlike property is exchanged (i = 2,3,. . .)

p^+, p^- = amount of mortgage on property acquired and disposed of, respectively

u^+, u^- = amount of unlike property (boot) acquired and disposed of, respectively

v^- = fair market value of property disposed of

b^- = basis of property disposed of

---

*The notations used in this or any section do not necessarily apply to another section.

**The exchange of real estate for real estate and personal property for personal property are exchanges of "like kind".

Example: Mr. Ammons wants to exchange his apartment for Mr. Martin's motel. Mr. Ammon's apartment is valued at $300,000, has a $200,000 mortgage, and a basis of $210,000. Mr. Martin's motel is valued at $275,000 and has a $185,000 mortgage. Because Mr. Ammon's equity is $10,000 greater than Mr. Martin's* he will not give any boot, but he will receive $10,000 cash from Mr. Martin in order to affect an equitable exchange. What is Mr. Ammon's recognized gain at the time of exchange, and what is the amount of gain that is deferred?

Solution: In this example,

$$v^- = \$300,000, \; p^- = \$200,000, \; b^- = \$210,000,$$
$$v^+ = \$275,000, \; p^+ = \$185,000, \; u^- = \$0, \text{ and } u^+ = \$10,000.$$

From the flow diagram (following no,no), Mr. Ammons' recognized capital gain at the time of exchange is

$$c_1 = \$200,000 - \$185,000 + \$10,000 - \$0$$
$$= \$25,000.$$

The capital gain that is deferred is

$$c_i = \$300,000 - \$210,000 - \$25,000$$
$$= \$65,000.$$

13.6.   Property Acquired by Repossession

When property is sold and foreclosure ensues, the repossession can result in a capital gain or loss to the seller. If the seller takes a purchase money mortgage, he might report his gain by the installment method. In this case, previously recognized gain must be determined from Section 13.4. If the repossessed property is financed by a third party (such as a bank), there can be a gain or loss on both the property and the debt. We consider only the case in which the creditor bids on the repossessed property; otherwise, the creditor would have only a bad debt loss (i.e., no capital gain or loss on the property).

The following flow diagram does not apply to personal residences on which gain is deferred (Section 13.10).

---

*$300,000 - $200,000 = $100,000, and $275,000 - $185,000 = $90,000.

Formula:

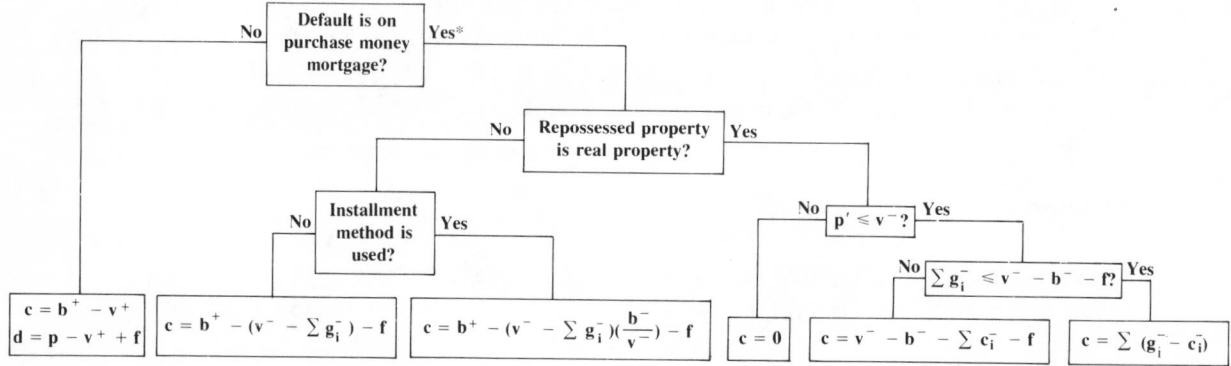

where

c = recognized capital gain or loss on property resulting from repossession
d = deduction for bad debt
v^- = amount realized on repossessed property at time of sale
v^+ = sale price of repossessed property at time of repossession
b^- = basis of repossessed property at time of sale
b^+ = fair market value of repossessed property at time of repossession
p = balance of mortgage owed to third party
p' = balance of purchase money mortgage
g_i^- = amount paid to seller by buyer in the ith year (including down payment when $i = 1$)
c_i^- = amount of recognized gain or loss by seller in the ith year
f = repossession cost incurred by seller

Example 1: (Installment Sale of Real Property).

John Henry sold a hotel for $400,000 and received a purchase money mortgage for $300,000. There was a $100,000 down payment, and, beginning one year hence, he was to receive $20,000 a year as payment for the purchase money mortgage. His basis was $240,000 and he chose to report his capital gain by the installment sale method. After making the first annual payment, the buyer defaulted. Mr. Henry then repossessed the hotel at a cost of $1,000. What is his capital gain upon repossession?

Solution:

In this example,

$$v^- = \$400,000, \ p = \$0, \ g_1^- = \$100,000,$$
$$g_2^- = \$20,000, \ p' = \$300,000 - \$20,000 = \$280,000,$$
$$b^- = \$240,000, \ \text{and} \ f = \$1,000.$$

---

*In the case of an installment sale, the gain must first counter depreciation recapture (this amount is treated as ordinary income), then the gain is treated as capital gain (see Example 2 of Section 13.4 and Sections 14.1 and 14.2).

From Section 13.4 (following no,yes in the flow diagram on page 280),* we find the reported gain from the sale in the first two years is

$$c_1^- = \$100,000 \left(\frac{\$400,000 - \$240,000}{\$400,000 - \$0} \right) = \$100,000 \times .40$$

$$= \$40,000,$$

and

$$c_2^- = \$20,000 \times .40 = \$8,000.$$

From the flow diagram in this section (following yes,yes,yes,yes), the capital gain upon repossession is

$$c = \sum_{i=1}^{2} (g_i^- - c_i^-)$$

$$= (\$100,000 - \$40,000) + (\$20,000 - \$8,000)$$

$$= \$72,000.$$

Example 2: (Installment Sale of Personal Property)   John Henry sold furniture for $20,000. His adjusted basis at the time of the sale was $15,000. He received $5,000 in the year of the sale and was to receive the balance with payments of $2,500 a year, beginning one year hence. The buyer defaulted after two payments, at which time the furniture had a fair market value of $16,000. If the cost of repossession was $700, what is Mr. Henry's recognized capital gain upon repossession?

Solution: In this example,

$$v^- = \$20,000, \; b^- = \$15,000, \; g_1^- = \$5,000,$$
$$g_2^- = \$2,500, \; g_3^- = \$2,500, \; b^+ = \$16,000,$$
and $f = \$700$.

From the flow diagram (following yes,no,yes), the recognized capital gain is

$$c = \$16,000 - \left[\$20,000 - (\$5,000 + \$2,500 + \$2,500) \right]$$

$$\times \frac{\$15,000}{\$20,000} - \$700$$

---

*For simplicity assume there were no selling costs, so $v' = v$. Also assume there was no depreciation recaptured by the seller (Sections 14.1 and 14.2).

$$= \$16,000 \ - \$10,000 \times \frac{\$15,000}{\$20,000} \ - \$700$$

$$= \$16,000 - \$7,500 - \$700$$

$$= \$7,800.$$

Example 3: (Third Party Mortgage). George Allen holds a $160,000 mortgage note on business property which is in default. The fair market value of the property is $150,000, and the cost of repossession is $1,000. What is the recognized capital gain or loss on the property and the bad debt deduction if Mr. Allen bids $140,000 for the property and buys it at that price?

Solution: In this example,

$$p = \$160,000, \ b^+ = \$150,000, \ f = \$1,000, \text{ and } v^+ = \$140,000.$$

From the flow diagram (following no), the recognized capital gain upon repossession is

$$c = \$150,000 - \$140,000 = \$10,000,$$

and the bad debt loss upon repossession is

$$d = \$160,000 - \$140,000 + \$1,000 = \$21,000.$$

13.7.   Property Disposed of by Casualty or Theft Loss

When property suffers a casualty or theft loss, the insurance proceeds can exceed the adjusted basis of the property and cause a capital gain.

Formula:

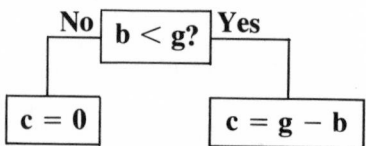

where

c = recognized capital gain or loss
b = basis of property immediately prior to casualty or theft loss
g = insurance proceeds or other reimbursements (reduce by $100 if property is for personal use)

Example: Hotel furniture was destroyed by fire. The basis just prior to the fire was $550. The insurance proceeds were $630. What is the recognized capital gain from the casualty?

Solution: In this example,

$$b = \$550, \text{ and } g = \$630.$$

The recognized capital gain is

$$c = \$630 - \$550 = \$80.$$

13.8.   Reinvestment in Qualified Low-Income Housing

Generally, qualified low-income housing is a rental or cooperative for low income families which has a mortgage insured under FHA 221 (d) (3) or 236 and has a limited return. For reinvestment to be in qualified low-income housing the property must be sold either to tenants or to a cooperative that benefits them. Also the capital gain realized on the sale must be reinvested in another qualified housing project (either by purchase, construction, or reconstruction) within the period beginning one full year before disposition and ending at the end of the taxable year following the year in which the capital gain is realized, i.e., if the gain is realized June 4, 1976, the reinvestment period is from June 4, 1975 through December 31, 1977.

Formula:

$$
\textbf{No } \boxed{v^+ < v^- - b^- ?} \textbf{ Yes}
$$

$$
\boxed{c = 0} \qquad \boxed{c = v^- - b^- - v^+}
$$

where

c = recognized capital gain on reinvestment
b^+, b^- = basis of property acquired and disposed of, respectively
v^+, v^- = value of property acquired and disposed of, respectively

Example: Mr. Rosenberg sold a qualified low-income housing for $600,000. His basis was $320,000. Mr. Rosenberg bought a second such property for $640,000. What is the recognized capital gain on the sale?

Solution: In this example,

$$v^- = \$600,000, \ b^- = \$320,000, \text{ and } v^+ = \$640,000.$$

From the flow diagram, the recognized capital gain is

$$c = \$0.$$

13.9.   Residence Acquired by Inheritance or Gift

Generally, the capital gain on a residence acquired by inheritance or gift is simply the amount realized less the basis. However, in the case of a loss, certain conditions must be met for the loss to be deductible.

Formula:

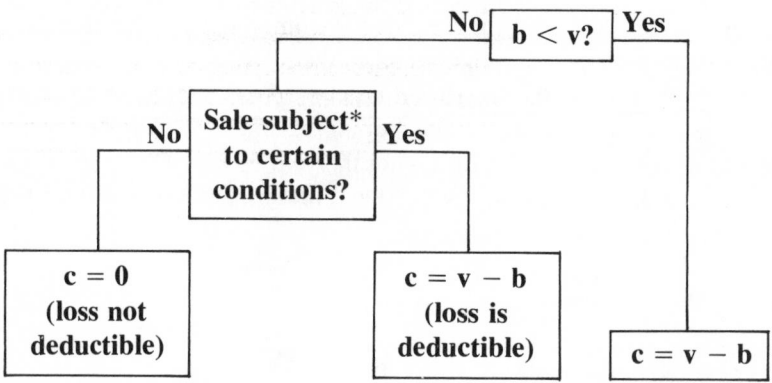

where

c = recognized capital gain or loss
v = amount realized from sale of property
b = basis of property

Example: Tom James realized \$37,000 on the sale of a house that was given to him by his father. He had lived in the house for three years and his basis was \$29,000. What is the recognized capital gain on the sale?

---

*The loss is deductible only if (1) the donee did not inhabit the residence, (2) shortly after acquiring the residence, the donee put it up for either sale or rent (simultaneously) with a real estate agent, and (3) the residence was rented prior to its sale.

Solution: In this example,

$$v = \$37{,}000, \text{ and } b = \$29{,}000.$$

From the flow diagram (following yes), Tom's capital gain is

$$c = \$37{,}000 - \$29{,}000 = \$8{,}000.$$

13.10. Residence Sold and Another Residence Acquired

Under certain conditions some or all of the capital gain realized on the sale of a principal residence can be deferred. This treatment of capital gain applies not only to single-family residences but to mobile homes, condominiums, trailers, houseboats, cooperative apartments in which there is stock ownership, and also the space in a multi-family building used by the owner.

Generally, in order to qualify for tax deferment the following two criteria must be met:

(1) Time. The newly acquired residence must be purchased either 18 months before or after the old residence is sold. If a new residence is constructed, it must be used either 18 months before or 24 months after the old residence is sold (see Treasury regulations for details).

(2) Principal Residence. There can be only one principal residence. Therefore, second homes such as summer cottages do not qualify.

Formula:

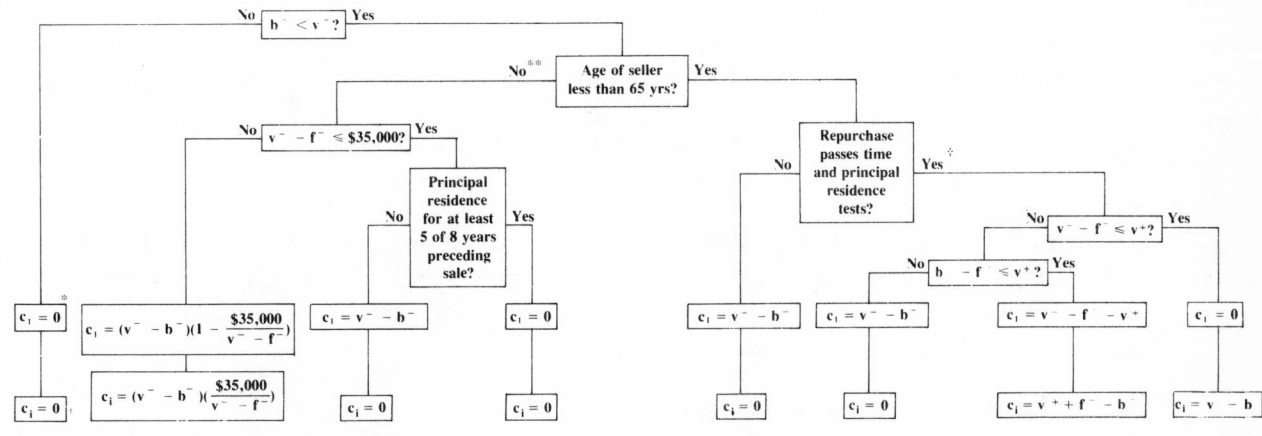

*The realized capital loss, $c_1 = v^- - b^-$, can't be deducted unless the residence had been either rented or acquired by gift or inheritance (see Section 13.9).

†Capital gain tax deferment is mandatory (not electable).

**If the election to exclude some or all of the capital gain has not been made before, another principal residence need not be acquired to defer capital gain tax. The gain is excludable (i.e. never recognized).

where

c_1 = capital gain recognized in year of sale
c_i = capital gain deferred (or excludable if 65 or over)
v^- = amount realized on sale of old residence (i.e., selling price less commission, legal fees, advertising, deed preparation, title service, etc.)
v^+ = cost of newly acquired residence (purchase price plus broker's commission, broker's fees, etc.)
b^- = basis of old residence
b^+ = basis of newly acquired residence at time of purchase
f^- = fix-up costs on old residence (fix-up costs that increase the basis should be added to b^-)*

Example 1: Pat Young is 35 years old and purchased a new principal residence 14 months after selling his old principal residence. The old residence sold for $52,000 and required $2,000 to fix-up for sale. His basis was $35,000. The newly acquired residence cost $64,000. How much of the capital gain is taxable in the year of the sale and how much is deferred?

Solution: In this example,

$$v^- = \$52,000, \ f^- = \$2,000, \ b^- = \$35,000, \text{ and } v^+ = \$64,000.$$

From the flow diagram (following yes,yes,yes,yes), the recognized capital gain in the year of the sale is

$$c_1 = \$0,$$

and the deferred capital gain is

$$c_i = \$52,000 - \$35,000 = \$17,000.$$

Example 2: Harry Withers is 77 years old. He spent $1,000 to fix up his principal residence and sold it for $41,000. His basis was $23,000. How much of the capital gain is taxable in the year of the sale, and how much is excludable?

Solution: In this example,

$$f^- = \$1,000, \ v^- = \$41,000, \text{ and } b^- = \$23,000.$$

---

*$v^- - f^-$ is called the adjusted sale price.

From the flow diagram (following yes,no,no), the capital gain recognized in the first year is

$$c_1 = (\$41,000 - \$23,000)(1 - \frac{\$35,000}{\$41,000 - \$1,000})$$

$$= \$18,000(1 - \frac{7}{8})$$

$$= \$2,250.$$

The amount of excludable capital gain is

$$c_i = (\$41,000 - \$23,000)(\frac{\$35,000}{\$40,000}) = \$18,000 \times \frac{7}{8}$$

$$= \$15,750.$$

14

TAXES:
SUMMARY CALCULATIONS

This chapter contains sections on depreciation recapture, net capital gain and loss, income tax computations, minimum and maximum tax computations, income averaging and investment credit.

As in the previous three chapters on taxes, flow diagrams are used to arrive at the proper formula. In this way, the chance for error is minimized.

14.1. Depreciation Recapture for Real Property

Improvements do, in fact, depreciate with use and time. The Treasury recognizes this and for certain properties grants a depreciation allowance during the holding period. The depreciation claimed is subtracted from the basis. Hence, when the property is disposed of a larger capital gain results than might be expected. The depreciation allowance could cause an unintentional advantage to the investor since the tax rate on capital gain is lower than the rate on ordinary income. Hence the Treasury, in the rules described by the following four flow diagrams, requires that a portion of the capital gain be treated as ordinary income (i.e., a fraction of the depreciation that exceeds straight line depreciation).

The rules for recapture have been revised several times. Thus, if a depreciable property has been held since 1969, there are three periods from which recapture is computed (see the accompanying flow charts: after 1975, after 1969 and before 1976, and before 1970). Depreciation claimed later is recaptured first and this procedure is described in the flow chart on page 295.

Formulas:

Depreciation Recaptured After 1975

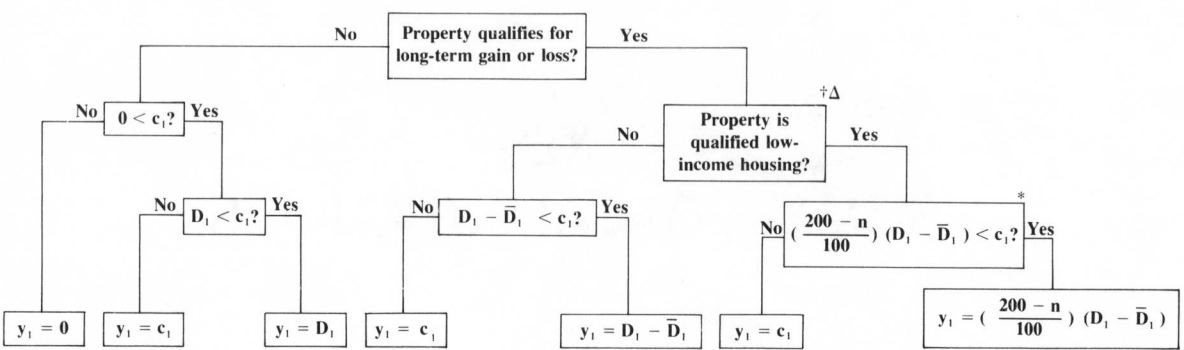

Depreciation Recaptured After 1969 and Before 1976

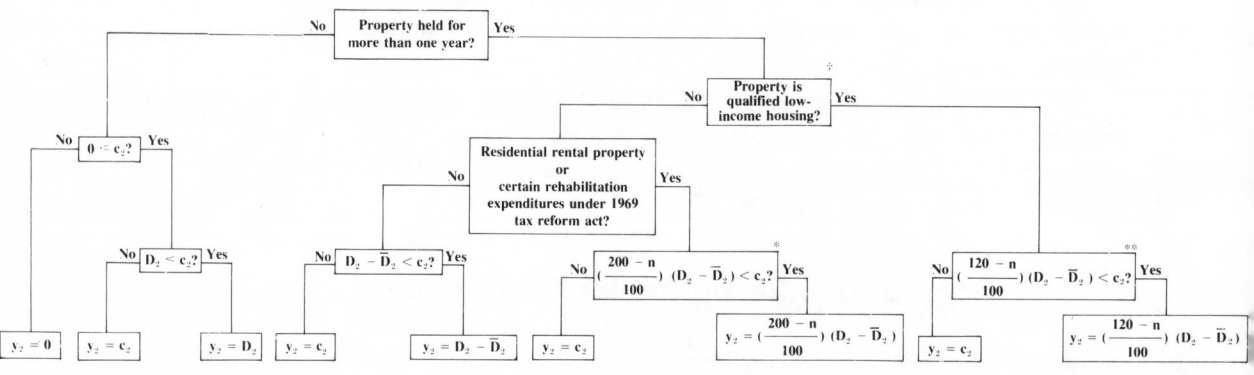

Depreciation Recaptured Before 1970

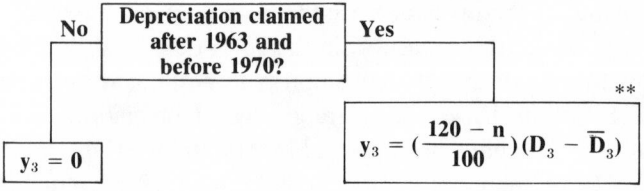

**Total Depreciation Recaptured, y,
and the Resulting Capital Gain, c**

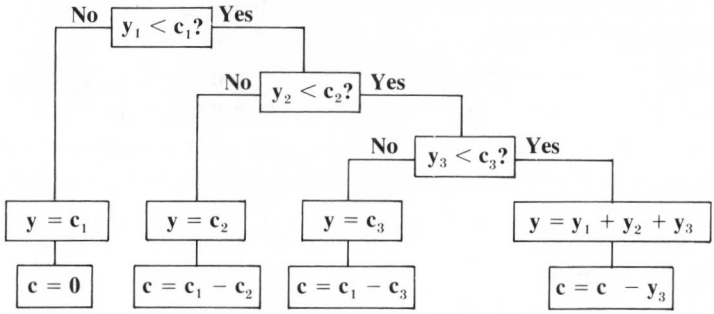

where

$$y = \text{total amount of capital gain that is treated as ordinary income (i.e.,}$$
depreciation recaptured)

c = total amount of capital gain that is treated as capital gain (after depreciation is recaptured)**

y_1, y_2, y_3 = capital gain treated as ordinary income during the time periods after 1975, after 1969 and before 1976, and before 1970, respectively

c_1 = capital gain before any depreciation is recaptured

$c_2 = c_1 - y_1$ = capital gain remaining after depreciation is recaptured from the period after 1975

$c_3 = c_2 - y_2$ = capital gain remaining after depreciation is recaptured from the period after 1969

n = number of full months the property was held

D_1, D_2, D_3 = depreciation claimed during each of the three time periods. If property qualifies for 5-year amortization, depreciation is straight line but is rapid depreciation because the short useful life of 5 years is used

$\overline{D}_1, \overline{D}_2, \overline{D}_3$ = straight line depreciation that could have been claimed during each of the three periods. If property qualifies for 5-year amortization, this value is computed from the actual useful life, not 5 years

---

†There are four types of qualified low-income housing: (1) property financed under sections 221 (d)(3) or 236 of the National Housing Act, (2) units occupied by those eligible for rent subsidies under section 8 of the Housing Act of 1937, (3) property having a mortgage or loan insured under Title V of the Housing Act of 1949, and (4) property qualified for rehabilitation expense deduction under section 197(k). (See Section 11.16.)

ΔAfter-1975 qualified low-income housing is treated in the same manner as the rehabilitation expenditures.

*If $n < 100$, set $n = 100$, and if $n > 200$, set $n = 200$.

**If $n < 20$, set $n = 20$, and if $n > 120$, set $n = 120$.

**The letter c that is used throughout Chapter 13 denotes capital gain or loss before depreciation recapture.

Table: Find D_1, D_2, D_3, $\overline{D}_1$, $\overline{D}_2$ and $\overline{D}_3$ from Table 5 and Section 11.4.

Example: On April 1, 1977 Ms. Moreno sold her apartment building for $200,000 (consider only the building). She had acquired the building new on April 1, 1969 and has since been claiming depreciation according to the 200% declining balance method using a basis of $180,000 and a useful life of 40 years. Because the depreciation allowance of $60,584 has lowered the basis to $119,416, her capital gain is $80,584. How much of the capital gain will be treated as ordinary income due to depreciation recapture?

Solution: In this example,

$$n = 8 \times 12 = 96 \text{ months, and } c_1 = \$80,584.$$

(1) Excess Depreciation
We must determine the depreciation claimed in excess of straight line during all three time periods. From either Section 11.4 or Table 5, the actual and straight line depreciation for each of the three periods is

$$D_1 = \$7,939, \overline{D}_1 = \$5,625, D_2 = \$45,895,$$
$$\overline{D}_2 = \$27,000, D_3 = \$6,750, \text{ and } \overline{D}_3 = \$3,375.$$

Now, the excess depreciation for each period is

$$D_1 - \overline{D}_1 = \$2,314, D_2 - \overline{D}_2 = \$18,895, \text{ and}$$
$$D_3 - \overline{D}_3 = \$3,375$$

(2) Period after 1975
From the flow chart for Depreciation Recaptured after 1975 (following yes,no,yes), the depreciation recaptured is

$$y_1 = D_1 - \overline{D}_1 = \$2,314.$$

(3) Period after 1969 and before 1976
Since the recaptured depreciation during this period is less than the capital gain (i.e., $y_1 < c_1$), the total depreciation recapture chart on page 295 indicates that y_2 and c_2 must also be determined. Now,

$$c_2 = c_1 - y_1 = \$78,270.$$

From the flow chart on page 294 (following yes,no,yes,yes), the depreciation recaptured after 1969 and before 1976 is

$$y_2 = (\frac{200 - 100}{100})(\$45,895 - \$27,000) = \$18,895^*.$$

(4) Period before 1970

Since the recaptured depreciation during this period is less than the remaining gain (i.e., $y_2 < c_2$), the chart on page 295 indicates that y_3 and c_3 must also be determined. Now,

$$c_3 = c_2 - y_2 = \$78,270 - \$18,895 = \$59,375.$$

From the chart for Before 1970 (following yes), the depreciation recaptured before 1970 is

$$y_3 = (\frac{120 - 96}{100})(\$6,750 - \$3,375) = \$810.$$

(5) Total Recaptured Depreciation

Now, the total amount of recaptured depreciation is

$$y = y_1 + y_2 + y_3 = \$22,019.$$

The remaining capital gain that is treated as capital gain is

$$c = c_3 - y_3 = \$59,375 - \$810 = \$58,565^{**}.$$

14.2.   Depreciation Recapture for Personal Property

Some gain on the disposition of depreciable personal property is treated as ordinary income and some is treated as a capital gain. The rationale for this treatment is discussed in Section 14.1.

The rules for recapturing some of the depreciation claimed are set forth in the following diagram. The rules for personal property are much less complex than those for real property.

Generally, only depreciation claimed after 1961 is subject to recapture. However, depreciation claimed after June 1963 for elevators and escalators and after 1969 for livestock is subject to recapture.

---

*Since $n < 100$, we must use $n = 100$ in this equation.

**This equation can also be written:

$$c = c_1 - (y_1 + y_2 + y_3).$$

Formula:

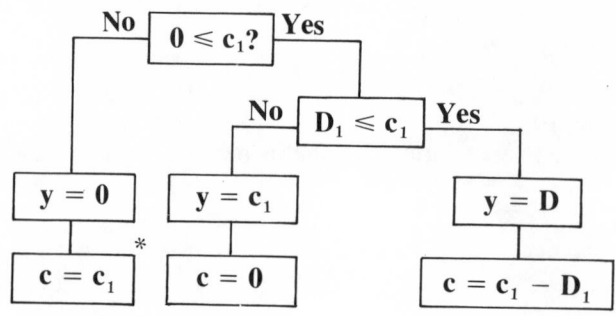

where

y = capital gain that is treated as ordinary income
c = capital gain that is treated as capital gain (after depreciation is recaptured)
c_1 = capital gain before any depreciation is recaptured
D_1 = depreciation claimed since 1961

Table: Find D_1 from Table 5 and Section 11.4.

Example: Herb Thomas sold tables from his motel for $18,000. He had claimed $5,000 depreciation since 1961. His adjusted basis of $16,000 gave him a capital gain of $2,000. How much of the capital gain must be treated as ordinary income?

Solution: In this example,

$$D_1 = \$5,000 \text{ and } c_1 = \$2,000.$$

From the flow diagram (following yes,no), the amount of capital gain that must be treated as ordinary income is

$$y = \$2,000.$$

The amount of the capital gain that will be treated as capital gain is

$$c = \$0.$$

---

*This is a capital loss.

14.3.   Net Capital Gains and Losses

Generally, a capital asset is any property you own and use for personal purposes or investment. Some exceptions are depreciable or real property used in trade or business.

The gain from the sale or exchange of property held for personal use is a capital gain. However, losses from the sale or exchange of such property are not deductible unless they result from casualty or theft (Section 11.13).

The gain or loss from the sale or exchange of investment property is generally a capital gain or loss.

If a capital asset is sold or exchanged, the holding period must be determined so that the gain or loss can be categorized as long-term or short-term. Generally, the holding period begins on the day after the day the property is acquired and includes the day the property is disposed of.

However,

(1) The holding period for new property acquired in a non-taxable exchange begins the day following the day the old property was acquired.

(2) The holding period for property received as a gift begins on the date the donor used.

(3) The holding period for property received from a decedent (through a will or otherwise) is always considered to be long-term.

(4) The holding period for real property purchased under an unconditional contract begins on the earlier of these two dates:

(a) the day after the day the title passes, or

(b) the day after the day on which delivery or possession was made and the burdens and privileges of ownership are assumed.

A gain or loss is considered long-term if:

$$
\text{in the tax year beginning} \quad
\begin{cases}
\text{before 1977 you held it over 6 months} \\
\text{or} \\
\text{in 1977 you held it over 9 months} \\
\text{or} \\
\text{after 1977 you held it over 12 months.}
\end{cases}
$$

Otherwise it is considered short-term.

The capital gain or loss from individual transactions are discussed in Chapter 13. The purpose of this section is to determine the net contribution of all capital gains and losses to the taxable income.

The capital gain or loss for all short term transactions must be added (call it C_s). Also the capital gain or loss for all long-term transactions must be added (call it C_l)*†. Notice from the flow diagram that some results are given as $C = \max(-x, -h, C_s + C_l)$. This means simply, that C, the net capital gain or loss, is equal to the largest of $-x$, $-h$, and $C_s + C_l$.

---

*In the case of investment interest (Section 11.11), if $I - X - E - h$ is positive, this amount is to be excluded from net long-term capital gain.

†If, for involuntary conversion (Section 13.2), the net is a loss, none of the individual gains can be included as capital gains (i.e., individual losses are deductible as casualty losses and individual gains are added to ordinary income).

Formula:

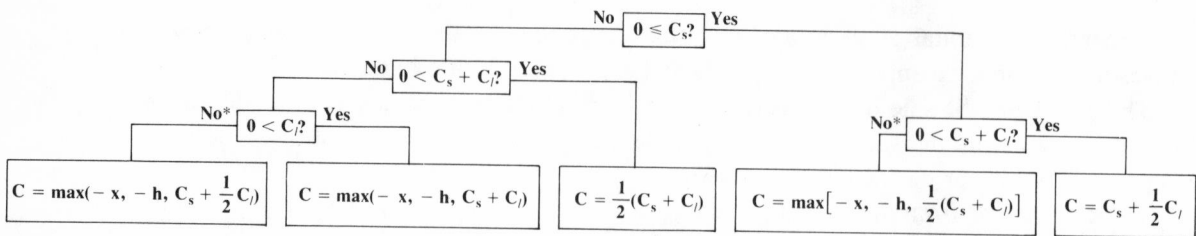

where

C = net capital gain or loss from the disposition of capital assets

C_s = net short-term capital gain or loss (if no short-term transactions, set $C_s = 0$)**

C_l = net long-term capital gain or loss (if no long-term transactions, set $C_l = 0$)†

$$h = \begin{cases} \$1,000 & \text{married single return} \\ \$2,000 & \text{other returns} \end{cases} \quad \text{For 1977}$$
$$\begin{cases} \$1,500 & \text{married single return} \\ \$3,000 & \text{other returns} \end{cases} \quad \text{After 1977}$$

x = adjusted taxable income (see the Treasury's instruction m)

Example 1:   In 1977, J.O. Smith, a single taxpayer, lost $8,000 on common stock he held for 3 months. In the same year, he had a long-term gain of $14,000 and a long-term loss of $10,000 on the sale of two duplexes. If his adjusted taxable income was $9,000, what is the net capital gain or loss?

Solution: In this example,

h = $2,000, C_s = − $8,000, C_l = $14,000 − $10,000 = $4,000, and x = $9,000.

From the flow diagram (following no,no,yes), the net capital loss is

$$C = \max(-\$9,000, -\$2,000, -\$4,000) = -\$2,000^{***}.$$

---

*If there is a long-term capital loss component carryover from years beginning before 1970, see part IV of Schedule D (Form 1040).

**Short-term losses, net short-term gain or loss from partnerships and fiduciaries and short-term capital loss carryover.

†Net section 1231 gain, long-term capital loss carryover, long-term gain from partnerships, fiduciaries, and electing small business corporations, and capital gain distributions for real estate investment trusts, investment companies and mutual funds.

***max(− $9,000, − $2,000, − $4,000) means choose the maximum of − $9,000, − $2,000, and − $4,000.

Example 2: (Short-term Gain).   Bill Gentry had an adjusted taxable income of $11,000 and will file a single (not head of household) return in 1977. He had a net short-term gain of $C_s = \$50,000$. What is the capital gain or loss if (a) the net long-term gain is $C_l = \$75,000$, and (b) the net long-term loss is $C_l = -\$75,000$?

Solution: In this example, $x = \$11,000$, $h = \$2,000$ and $C_s = \$50,000$. From the flow diagram:
(a) Following (yes,yes),

$$C = \$50,000 + \frac{1}{2} \times \$75,000 = \$87,500.$$

(b) Following (yes,no),

$$C = \max(-\$11,000, -\$2,000, -\$12,500) = -\$2,000.$$

Example 3: (Short-term Loss)   Jim Miller had an adjusted taxable income of $21,000 and will file a head of household return in 1977. He had a net short-term loss of $C_s = -\$50,000$. What is the capital gain or loss if (a) the net long-term gain is $C_l = \$75,000$, (b) the net long-term gain is $C_l = \$25,000$, and (c) the net long-term loss is $C_l = -\$75,000$?

Solution: In this example, $x = \$21,000$, $h = \$2,000$ and $C_s = -\$50,000$. From the flow diagram:
(a) Following (no,yes),

$$C = \frac{1}{2}(-\$50,000 + \$75,000) = \$12,500.$$

(b) Following (no,no,yes),

$$C = \max(-\$21,000, -\$2,000, -\$25,000) = -\$2,000.$$

(c) Following (no,no,no),

$$C = \max(-\$21,000, -\$2,000, -\$87,500) = -\$2,000.$$

14.4.   Income Tax Rates

Individuals computing tax according to the regular method and whose tax table income and exemptions do not exceed certain limits (described below) use the second set of four tables in Table 8. In this case tax is paid on an amount called *tax table income*.

Those individuals who exceed these limits or who compute their tax by other than the regular method [alternative method (Section 14.5), maximum tax on personal service income (Section 14.7), income averaging (Section 14.8), or foreign income exclusion] use the first set of four tables in Table 8. In this case tax is paid on an amount called *taxable income*. The taxpayer is free to use the method that results in the least tax.

Formula:

$$t = T(x)$$

where

t = amount of tax using the regular method.
x = taxable income or tax table income
$T(x)$ = amount of tax due on x
z = $\dfrac{T(x)}{x}$ = income tax rate

Table: 8.

Example: Evan Dutton is a bachelor whose tax table income is $9,000. (a) How much income tax must he pay using the regular method, and (b) what percent of his taxable income is this?

Solution: Since Mr. Dutton is single and not the head of a household, he must use table A in Table 8.

(a) From this table, he must pay $1,007. That is, his tax is

$$t = T(x) = T(\$9,000) = \$1,007$$

(b) The percent of tax is

$$z = \frac{T(x)}{x} = \frac{\$1,007}{\$9,000} = .1119 = 11.19\%.$$

14.5.   Alternative Tax Method

The alternative tax method can result in a lower amount of tax than is determined by the regular method (Section 14.4). This method usually results in less tax when the taxpayer is in the 50% tax bracket or higher (i.e., a taxable income exceeding $52,000 for joint returns, $38,000 for head of household and single returns, and $26,000 for married separate returns).

See Form 4726 for the alternative tax method if personal service (earned) income qualifies for the maximum tax (Sections 14.7).

Formula:

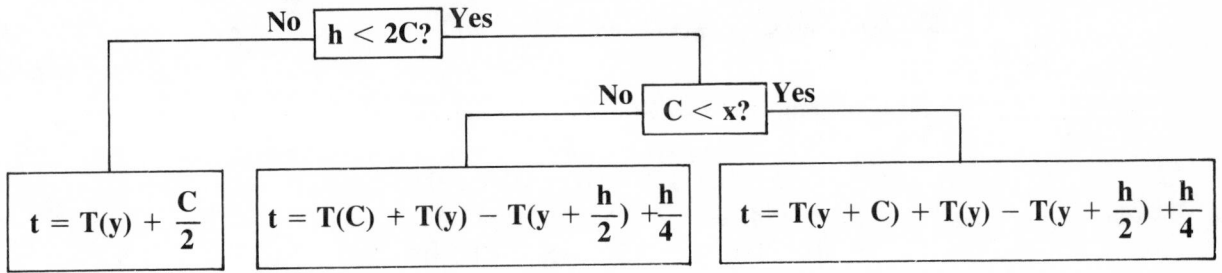

where

$t =$ amount of tax using the alternative method

$h = \begin{cases} \$25,000 \text{ for married separate returns} \\ \$50,000 \text{ for other returns} \end{cases}$

$C_l =$ net long-term capital gain or loss*

$C_s =$ net short-term capital gain or loss**

$C = \begin{cases} \dfrac{1}{2}(C_s + C_l) & \text{if } C_s < 0 \\ \\ \dfrac{1}{2}C_l & \text{if } C_s \geq 0 \end{cases}$

$y =$ taxable ordinary income

$x =$ taxable income

$T(y), T(C), \text{etc.} =$ tax on y, C, etc.

Table: Find $T(y)$, $T(C)$, $T(y + \dfrac{C}{2})$, and $T(y + C)$ from one of the first four tax tables in Table 8.

Example: Mr. & Mrs. Paul Wells have taxable income of $118,000 which includes $35,000 excludable capital gain and taxable ordinary income of $83,000. Their net long-term capital gain is $71,000, and their net short-term capital loss is $1,000. If they file a married joint return, what will their tax be according to the alternate tax method?

---

*Net section 1231 gain, long-term capital loss carryover, long-term gain from partnerships, fiduciaries, and electing small business corporations, and capital gain distributions for real estate investment trusts, investment companies and mutual funds.

**Short-term losses, net short-term gain or loss from partnerships and fiduciaries and short-term capital loss carryover.

Solution: In this example,

$$x = \$118,000, \; y = \$83,000, \; C_l = \$71,000, \; C_s = - \$1,000,$$

$$h = \$50,000, \text{ and } C = \frac{1}{2}(\$71,000 - \$1,000) = \$35,000.$$

From the flow diagram (following yes,yes), we have

$$\begin{aligned} t &= T(\$83,000 + \$35,000) + T(\$83,000) \\ &\quad - T(\$83,000 + \$25,000) + \$12,500 \\ &= T(\$118,000) + T(\$83,000) - T(\$108,000) + \$12,500. \end{aligned}$$

From the married joint return schedule in Table 8, the tax from the alternative tax method is

$$\begin{aligned} t &= \$54,356 + \$33,224 - 48,156 + \$12,500 \\ &= \$51,924 \end{aligned}$$

The regular tax method (Section 14.4) yields \$54,356 tax on tax table income of \$118,000. Therefore, the alternative tax method results in a saving of

$$\$54,356 - \$51,924 = \$2,432.$$

14.6. Minimum Tax on Preference Items

A minimum tax of 15% is imposed on several items whose sum exceeds a certain amount. This tax is in addition to the regular income tax. The items of preference are described briefly below. See the Treasury regulations for details.

Formula:

```
        No  ┌──────────────┐  Yes
    ┌───────│  h + A + L < P? │───────┐
    │       └──────────────┘        │
┌────────┐                  ┌──────────────────────────┐
│ t = 0  │                  │ t = .15[P − (h + A + L)]  │
└────────┘                  └──────────────────────────┘
```

where

$t =$ minimum tax

$$h = \begin{cases} \$10,000 & \text{married filing separate returns} \\ \$20,000 & \text{otherwise} \end{cases}$$

$A =$ income tax liability (Form 1040)

$L =$ operating loss carryover (Form 1040)

$p_1 = \frac{1}{2}$ (net long-term capital gain plus the net short-term capital loss less the amount used to offset excess investment interest). Computed in Section 11.11

$p_2 =$ depreciation subject to recapture on real property (Section 14.1)

$p_3 =$ depreciation subject to recapture on personal property subject to a net lease (Section 14.2)

$p_4 =$ amortization in excess of straight line depreciation (using the actual useful life) for expenditures and facilities qualifying for 60 month amortization (Sections 11.15 and 11.16)

$p_5 =$ amortization of railroad rolling stock

$p_6 =$ amount of percentage depletion that exceeds the basis

$p_7 =$ stock option price exceeded by the fair market value

$p_8 =$ itemized deductions that exceed 60% of adjusted gross income (see footnote, Section 11.14) except for medical and casualty loss deductions

$p_9 =$ some intangible drilling costs

$$P = \sum_{i=1}^{9} p_i = \text{sum of preference items}$$

Example: Mr. & Mrs. Thompson are filing a joint return. Their income tax liability is $10,000, and their operating loss carryover is $2,000. If the sum of their preference items is $44,000, what is the minimum tax (in addition to their regular tax)?

Solution: In this example,

$h = \$20,000$, $A = \$10,000$, $L = \$2,000$, and $P = \$44,000$.

From the flow diagram (following yes), the minimum tax is

$$t = .15\left[\$44,000 - (\$20,000 + \$10,000 + \$2,000)\right]$$
$$= .15(\$44,000 - \$32,000)$$
$$= \$1,800.$$

14.7. Maximum Tax on Personal Service (Earned) Income

The maximum tax shields income for personal service from being taxed at a rate higher than 50%. Personal service income generally includes wages, salaries, professional fees, tips, commissions, bonuses, pensions, annuities, and other compensation for services*. Personal service net income is personal service income less expenses attributable to earning the income. As defined in the following flow diagram, personal service income is reduced by the sum of preference items (Section 14.6), and it is further adjusted if net personal service income is less than adjusted gross income (see the footnote in Section 11.14).

The maximum tax on personal service income does not apply to

(a)   taxpayers filing single or head of household returns with personal service taxable income of $38,000 or less,

(b)   taxpayers filing married joint returns with personal service income of $52,000 or less,

(c)   married taxpayers filing separately, or

(d)   taxpayers using income averaging (Section 14.8).

Formula:

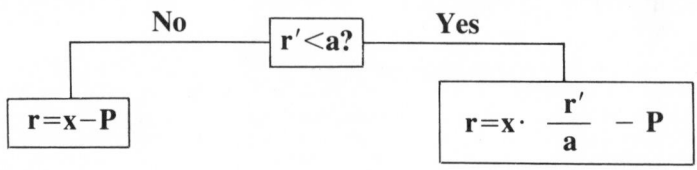

$$t = T(x) - \left[T(r) - T(h)\right] + \frac{1}{2}(r - h)$$

where

t   = maximum tax on personal service income
x   = taxable income
r' = personal service net income
a   = adjusted gross income
r   = personal service taxable income = $\begin{cases} x - P & \text{if } a \leq r' \\ x\left(\dfrac{r'}{a}\right) - P & \text{otherwise} \end{cases}$
P   = sum of preference items (Section 14.6)
h   = $\begin{cases} \$38,000 & \text{single or head of household return} \\ \$52,000 & \text{married joint return} \end{cases}$
$T(x), T(r), T(h)$ = tax on x, r, and h, respectively

Table: Find T(x), T(r), and T(h) in one of the first four tables of Table 8.

---

*Prior to 1977 personal service income was called earned income.

Example: Frank Tobin had taxable income of $120,000, adjusted gross income of $132,000, and personal service net income of $110,000. He also had $26,000 of preference items. If he files a head of household return, what is his tax by virtue of the maximum tax on personal service income?

Solution: In this example,

$$x = \$120,000, \ a = \$132,000, \ r' = \$110,000,$$
$$P = \$26,000, \text{ and } h = \$38,000.$$

Since $r' < a$,

$$r = \$120,000 \times \frac{\$110,000}{\$132,000} - \$26,000.$$

$$= \$74,000.$$

From schedule Z in Table 8,

$$T(x) = \$60,868, \ T(r) = \$31,358, \text{ and } T(h) = \$11,190.$$

Now, the maximum tax on personal service income is

$$t = \$60,868 - (\$31,358 - \$11,190) + \frac{1}{2}(\$74,000 - \$38,000)$$

$$= \$60,868 - \$20,168 + \$18,000$$

$$= \$58,700.$$

Without the maximum tax on personal service income, the tax would have been $60,868.

14.8.   Income Averaging

Income averaging can result in less tax than does the regular method during a year when taxable income is unusually large. Income averaging can be chosen by individuals who meet a residency test and a support test (see Treasury regulations). In order to use this method, the current adjusted taxable income must exceed, by the amount of $3,000, 30% of the total adjusted taxable income for the four preceding tax years.

If income averaging is used, the taxpayer cannot use the alternative tax method (Section 14.5), the maximum tax on personal service income (Section 14.7), limitation of tax from some distributions from an employee's trust, or the exclusion of income from sources outside the United States or within its possessions.

Formula:

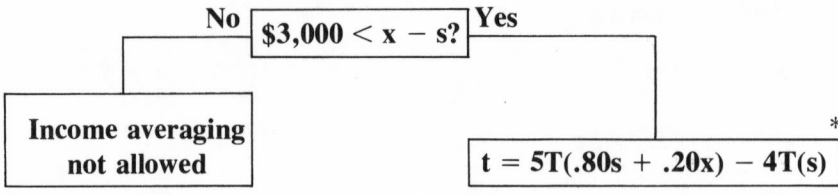

where

t = tax from income averaging
x = current year's taxable income
s = 30% of the sum of the adjusted taxable income from the four preceding tax years
T(.80s + .20x),T(s) = tax on the amounts .80s + .20x and s, respectively.

Table: Find T(.80s + .20x) and T(s) in one of the first four tables of Table 8.

Example: The Garnseys will file a joint return with two exemptions on this year's taxable income of $32,000. Their adjusted tax table income for the four preceding years was $18,000, $14,000, $22,000, and $19,000. (a) Can they use income averaging? (b) If so, what is their tax by income averaging? (c) What would the tax be by the regular method?

Solution: In this example,

x = $32,000, and s = .30($18,000 + $14,000 + $22,000 + $19,000) = $21,900.

(a) Since x − s = $32,000 − $21,900 = $10,100 (which is larger than $3,000), income averaging can be used.
(b) From schedule Y in Table 8,

$$T(.80s + .20x) = T(\$17,520 + \$6,400) = T(\$23,920)$$

---

*See Schedule G if you have current excess community income or you, as an owner-employee, receive premature or excessive distribution from a qualified employee pension plan or trust.

$$= \$4,610, \text{ and}$$

$$T(s) = T(\$21,900)$$

$$= \$4,016.$$

Now, the tax from income averaging is

$$t = 5 \times \$4,610 - 4 \times \$4,016 = \$23,050 - \$16,064$$
$$= \$6,986.$$

(c) The tax by the regular method (Section 14.4) is

$$t = T(\$32,000 + 2 \times \$750) = T(\$33,500) = \$7,242$$

since there are two exemptions.

14.9.   Investment Credit

The investment credit is a tax credit (credits reduce tax, not taxable income) that may be claimed for some tangible depreciable personal property. However, if the credit exceeds a certain allowable limit, the excess credit can be carried back three years and forward seven years.

The credit can be claimed only for the year the property was placed into service. The year it is placed in service is considered to be the earlier of (1) the taxable year in which depreciation is first taken, or (2) the taxable year in which the property is ready to be used for its purpose.

Buildings and their structural components do not qualify for the investment credit, but elevators and escalators bought for the taxpayer's original use do qualify. Property eligible for 60 month amortization generally does not qualify (Sections 11.15 and 11.16). Only 50% of the credit is available for pollution control facilities in place before 1976.

Property used in motels and hotels does qualify if more than one half of the units are used by people who normally stay less than 30 days*. Also qualifying are automobiles used for business and having a useful life of at least three years and many farm improvements.

See detailed tax guides or Treasury regulations for lists of qualifying property, credit limits, and carryover rules.

----

*Furniture, ranges, refrigerators, etc. used in rental property do not qualify.

Formula:

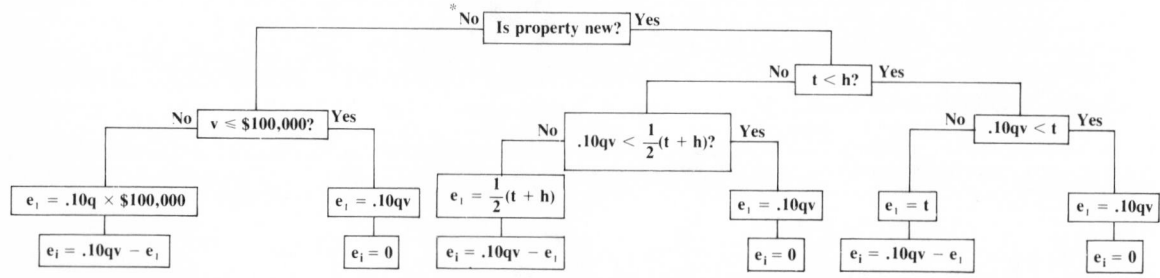

where

$e_1 =$ investment credit used in year property placed in service

$e_i =$ excess investment credit carried back 3 years or forward 7 years

$v =$ cost of qualified property including installation and freight cost. If used property is traded for other used property, the cost is the amount of cash paid

$k =$ estimated useful life of property (or the time used if property is disposed of prior to the end of its estimated useful life)

$$q = \begin{cases} 0 & \text{if } 0 < k \leq 3 \text{ yrs.} \\ \dfrac{1}{3} & \text{if } 3 < k \leq 5 \\ \dfrac{2}{3} & \text{if } 5 < k \leq 7 \\ 1 & \text{if } 7 < k \end{cases}$$

$t =$ income tax less credits for retirement income, foreign tax, minimum tax on preference items (Section 14.6), 10% tax on premature distributions from self-employed plan, tax on premature IRA distributions, tax on distributions from 10 year income averaging, and investment tax credit recapture

$$h = \begin{cases} \$12,500 & \text{married separate returns} \\ \$25,000 & \text{other returns} \end{cases}$$

Example 1:   Gerald Hart bought $400,000 worth of new furniture with a useful life of 8 years. His tax liability is $43,000. He will file a married joint return. What is the amount of investment credit that can be used this year and the amount that must be carried over?

---

*Reduce $100,000 to $50,000 if husband and wife file separate returns and both bought used property.

Solution: In this example,

$$v = \$400,000, \ k = 8 \text{ years, and } t = \$43,000.$$
$$\text{Also } q = 1, \text{ and } h = \$25,000.$$

From the flow diagram (following yes, no,no), the investment credit in the year the furniture is placed in service is

$$e_1 = \frac{1}{2}(\$43,000 + \$25,000) = \$34,000,$$

and the amount that must be carried over is

$$e_i = \$40,000 - \$34,000 = \$6,000.$$

Example 2:   Suppose Gerald Hart disposed of $60,000 worth of used furniture prior to the end of its remaining useful life of 6 years. Determine the amount of tax he must add in the year he disposed of the furniture if he did so after (a) 5½ years and (b) 4 years.

Solution: In this example,

$$v = \$60,000, \ k = 6 \text{ years, and } q = \frac{2}{3}.$$

From the flow diagram (following no,yes), the investment credit Mr. Hart claimed was

$$e_1 = .10(\frac{2}{3})\$60,000 = \$4,000.$$

(a) Now, k = 5½ years so that $q = \frac{2}{3}$.

The investment credit should have been

$$e_1 = .10(\frac{2}{3})\$60,000, = \$4,000.$$

This is the same amount computed on the useful life of 6 years, so no additional tax is due in the year of disposition.
  (b) In this case, k = 4 years, and $q = \frac{1}{3}$.

The investment credit should have been

$$e_1 = .10(\frac{1}{3})\$60,000 = \$2,000$$

instead of the $4,000 claimed. Thus, Gerald Hart must add $2,000 to his taxes in the year of disposition.

15

CONVERSION OF UNITS

This chapter illustrates the conversion of units of area, length, time, rates of pay, etc. Also for area and length, the foreign-U.S. conversions are given for most countries. Even though most of these countries long ago adopted the metric system, traditional units are frequently still in use.

Due to the wide range of values listed in the tables, it is convenient to use scientific notation. For example, the number 2,400 can also be written 2.4×10^3. That is,

$$2,400 = 2.4 \times 1000 = 2.4 \times 10 \times 10 \times 10 = 2.4 \times 10^3.$$

Similarly the number .0009384 can be written 9.384×10^{-4}. That is,

$$.0009384 = \frac{9.384}{10,000} = \frac{9.384}{10 \times 10 \times 10 \times 10} = \frac{9.384}{10^4} = 9.384 \times 10^{-4}.$$

15.1.   Angle

Table:

	Radians	Degrees	Minutes	Seconds
1 Radian =	1.0000×10^0	5.7296×10^1	9.5493×10^{-1}	1.5915×10^{-2}
1 Degree =	1.7453×10^{-2}	1.0000×10^0	6.0000×10^1	3.6000×10^3
1 Minute =	2.9089×10^{-4}	1.6667×10^{-2}	1.0000×10^0	6.0000×10^1
1 Second =	4.8481×10^{-6}	2.7778×10^{-4}	1.6667×10^{-2}	1.0000×10^0

Example 1:   How many radians are there in 4.7 degrees?

Solution: Since

$$1 \text{ degree} = 1.7453 \times 10^{-2} \text{ radians,}$$
$$4.7 \text{ degrees} = 4.7 \times 1.7453 \times 10^{-2} = 8.2029 \times 10^{-2}$$
$$= .082029 \text{ radians.}$$

Example 2:   How many degrees are there in 14 minutes?

Solution: Since

$$1 \text{ minute} = 1.6667 \times 10^{-2} \text{ degrees,}$$
$$14 \text{ minutes} = 14 \times 1.6667 \times 10^{-2} = 23.33 \times 10^{-2}$$
$$= .23333 \text{ degrees.}$$

15.2.   Area

Table 1:   For domestic conversions, see page 315.

Example 1:   A lot contains 5,200 sq. feet. What fraction of an acre is this?

Solution: Since

$$1 \text{ sq. foot} = 2.2956 \times 10^{-5} \text{ acres,}$$
$$5,200 \text{ sq. feet} = 5,200 \times 2.2956 \times 10^{-5}$$
$$= 11,937 \times 10^{-5} = .11937 \text{ acres.}$$

Example 2:   A parcel of land is priced at $6/square foot. What is the price per acre?

Solution: Since

$$1 \text{ acre} = 4.3650 \times 10^{4} \text{ sq. feet,}$$
$$\$6 \times 4.3560 \times 10^{4} = \$26.136 \times 10^{4}$$
$$= \$261,360/\text{acre.}$$

Example 3:   How many square yards are there in 3.25 acres?

	Sq. Inches	Sq. Links*	Sq. Feet	Sq. Yards	Sq. Rods*	Sq. Chains*	Acres	Sq. Miles	Sections	Sq. Cms	Sq. Meters	Hectares	Sq. Kms
1 sq. inch =	1.0000×10^{0}	1.5942×10^{-2}	6.9444×10^{-3}	7.7160×10^{-4}	2.5508×10^{-5}	1.5942×10^{-6}	1.5942×10^{-7}	2.4910×10^{-10}	2.4910×10^{-10}	6.4516×10^{0}	6.4516×10^{-4}	6.4516×10^{-8}	6.4516×10^{-10}
1 sq. link* =	6.2726×10^{1}	1.0000×10^{0}	4.3560×10^{-1}	4.8400×10^{-2}	1.6000×10^{-3}	1.0000×10^{-4}	1.0000×10^{-5}	1.5625×10^{-8}	1.5625×10^{-8}	4.0469×10^{2}	4.0469×10^{-2}	4.0469×10^{-6}	4.0469×10^{-8}
1 sq. foot =	1.4400×10^{2}	2.2956×10^{0}	1.0000×10^{0}	1.1111×10^{-1}	3.6731×10^{-3}	2.2957×10^{-4}	2.2956×10^{-5}	3.5870×10^{-8}	3.5870×10^{-8}	9.2903×10^{2}	9.2903×10^{-2}	9.2903×10^{-6}	9.2903×10^{-8}
1 sq. yard =	1.2960×10^{3}	2.0661×10^{1}	9.0000×10^{0}	1.0000×10^{0}	3.3058×10^{-2}	2.0661×10^{-3}	2.0661×10^{-4}	3.2283×10^{-7}	3.2283×10^{-7}	8.3613×10^{3}	8.3613×10^{-1}	8.3613×10^{-5}	8.3613×10^{-7}
1 sq. rod* =	3.9204×10^{4}	6.2500×10^{2}	2.7225×10^{2}	3.0250×10^{1}	1.0000×10^{0}	6.2500×10^{-2}	6.2500×10^{-3}	9.7656×10^{-6}	9.7656×10^{-6}	2.5293×10^{5}	2.5293×10^{1}	2.5293×10^{-3}	2.5293×10^{-5}
1 sq. chain* =	6.2726×10^{5}	1.0000×10^{4}	4.3560×10^{3}	4.8400×10^{2}	1.6000×10^{1}	1.0000×10^{0}	1.0000×10^{-1}	1.5625×10^{-4}	1.5625×10^{-4}	4.0469×10^{6}	4.0469×10^{2}	4.0469×10^{-2}	4.0469×10^{-4}
1 acre † =	6.2726×10^{6}	1.0000×10^{5}	4.3560×10^{4}	4.8400×10^{3}	1.6000×10^{2}	1.0000×10^{1}	1.0000×10^{0}	1.5625×10^{-3}	1.5625×10^{-3}	4.0469×10^{7}	4.0469×10^{3}	4.0469×10^{-1}	4.0469×10^{-3}
1 sq. mile =	4.0145×10^{9}	6.4000×10^{7}	2.7878×10^{7}	3.0976×10^{6}	1.0240×10^{5}	6.4000×10^{3}	6.4000×10^{2}	1.0000×10^{0}	1.0000×10^{0}	2.5900×10^{10}	2.5900×10^{6}	2.5900×10^{2}	2.5900×10^{0}
1 section =	4.0144×10^{9}	6.4000×10^{7}	2.7878×10^{7}	3.0976×10^{6}	1.0240×10^{5}	6.4000×10^{3}	6.4000×10^{2}	1.0000×10^{0}	1.0000×10^{0}	2.5900×10^{10}	2.5900×10^{6}	2.5900×10^{2}	2.5900×10^{0}
1 sq. cm =	1.5500×10^{-1}	2.4710×10^{-3}	1.0764×10^{-3}	1.1960×10^{-4}	3.9537×10^{-6}	2.4711×10^{-7}	2.4711×10^{-8}	3.8610×10^{-11}	3.8610×10^{-11}	1.0000×10^{0}	1.0000×10^{-4}	1.0000×10^{-8}	1.0000×10^{-10}
1 sq. meter =	1.5500×10^{3}	2.4710×10^{1}	1.0764×10^{1}	1.1960×10^{0}	3.9537×10^{-2}	2.4711×10^{-3}	2.4711×10^{-4}	3.8610×10^{-7}	3.8610×10^{-7}	1.0000×10^{4}	1.0000×10^{0}	1.0000×10^{-4}	1.0000×10^{-6}
1 hectare =	1.5500×10^{7}	2.4710×10^{5}	1.0764×10^{5}	1.1960×10^{4}	3.9537×10^{2}	2.4711×10^{1}	2.4711×10^{0}	3.8610×10^{-3}	3.8610×10^{-3}	1.0000×10^{8}	1.0000×10^{4}	1.0000×10^{0}	1.0000×10^{-2}
1 sq. km =	1.5500×10^{9}	2.4710×10^{7}	1.0764×10^{7}	1.1960×10^{6}	3.9537×10^{4}	2.4711×10^{3}	2.4711×10^{2}	3.8610×10^{-1}	3.8610×10^{-1}	1.0000×10^{10}	1.0000×10^{6}	1.0000×10^{2}	1.0000×10^{0}

*Surveyor's measure (in engineer's measure, 1 link = 12 inches, 1 chain = 100 links, and 1 mile = 52.8 chains.)

†If an acre is square, each of its sides are 208.81 ft, 69.57 yds, 316.23 links, 12.65 rods, 3.16 chains, .0395 mis., 63.62 ms, or .0636 kms.

Solution: Since

$$1 \text{ acre} = 4.8400 \times 10^3 \text{ sq. yards,}$$
$$3.25 \text{ acres} = 3.25 \times 4.8400 \times 10^3 = 15.730 \times 10^3$$
$$= 15,730 \text{ sq. yards.}$$

Table 2:

Foreign-U.S. Area Conversion

Country, Unit	U.S. Acres	Country, Unit	U.S. Acres
Afghanistan,		Czechoslovakia	
1 jerib =	.008907	1 jitro (in	
1 kubba =	.35583	Bohemia) =	1.422
		1 korec (in	
Argentina		Bohemia) =	.7111
1 cuadra =	4.17	1 merice (in	
1 manzana =	2.47	Bohemia) =	.4940
Austria			
1 joch,yoke =	1.422	Denmark	
		1 albrun =	.07314
Belgium		1 tönde hart	
1 roede (in		korn	7.0242
Flanders =	.02471	1 tönde (for	
		land) =	1.363
Brazil			
1 cuarta =	.92	Dominican Republic	
		1 tarea =	.15543
Bulgaria			
1 lekha =	.056776	Ecuador	
		1 caballería =	27.9
Chile		1 cantero =	.11
1 cuadra =	3.88	1 solar =	.43176
Columbia		Eqypt	
1 fanegada =	1.58	1 feddan =	1.0381
		1 renat kamel =	.04325
Costa Rica			
1 caballería =	111.824	El Salvador	
1 manzana =	1.727	1 caballería =	111.11
1 solar =	.21588	1 manzana =	1.73
Cuba		Finland	
1 caballería =	33.162	1 tunland,	
		tunnland =	1.22
Cyprus			
1 dönüm =	.3430		

Country, Unit	U.S. Acres	Country, Unit	U.S. Acres
France		Indonesia	
1 arpen, arpent =	.84	1 bouw =	1.7536
1 quarteron =	.26591	1 djung =	3.507
		1 paal carré =	561
Germany		Iran	
1 juchart (in		1 jerib =	.267300
Bavaria) =	.8419		
		Iraq	
Greece		1 donum =	.61775
1 stremma =	.247	1 mishara =	.61775
Guatemala		Israel	
1 caballería =	111.51	1 dönüm =	.24711
1 manzana =	1.744		
		Italy	
Haiti		1 giornata =	.9390
1 carreau de		1 quadrato =	1.248
terre =	3.188	1 tarola =	.009390
Honduras		Japan	
1 manzana =	1.727	1 chô carré =	2.4506
		1 tan =	.24506
Hong Kong		1 tsubo =	.0008170
1 dau chung =	.16667		
1 mu =	.208	Jordan	
		1 dönüm =	.24711
Hungary			
1 yock =	1.067	Lebanon	
		1 marasseh =	.01234
Iceland			
1 ferfathmur =	.87624	Libya	
1 tundagalatta =	.26257	1 dönüm =	.22709
		1 jabia =	.30271
India		1 sâa =	2.37
1 bigha =	.6250		
1 bigha (in		Macao	
Bengal) =	.3301	1 cheong =	.003136
1 bigha (in			
Bombay) =	1.3223	Malaya	
1 bigha (in		1 jemba =	.003306
Punjab) =	.33471	1 orlang =	1.3223
1 bigha (in			
United		Malta	
Provinces) =	.81136	1 modd =	4.444
1 ghamaon (in		1 siegh =	.04630
Punjab) =	1.3388		
1 kanal (in		Mexico	
Bombay) =	.66115	1 caballería =	105.75
1 marla (in		1 fanega =	8.81
United		1 manzana =	1.730
Provinces) =	.40558	1 sitiu =	4338.18

Country, Unit	U.S. Acres	Country, Unit	U.S. Acres
Morocco		Saudi Arabia	
1 aftari =	.2224	1 sq. baa =	.0006944
1 gouffa =	1.24	Somalia	
1 tarialte =	.89	1 darat =	1.977
Nepal		South Korea	
1 ropani =	.02324	1 chungbo =	2.45
Netherlands		1 tan =	.245
1 bunder =	2.471	Spain	
Nicaragua		1 aranzada =	1.105
1 caballería =	110.5	1 caballería =	95.48
1 estadal =	.0025496	1 celemín =	.133
1 manzana =	1.730	1 estadal =	.002762
Norway		1 fanegada =	1.59
1 maal =	.247104	1 yugada =	79.56
Pakistan		Sudan	
1 anna =	.0041663	1 kordofan =	1.796
1 bigha =	.33471	1 makhammus =	.798
1 ghumaon =	.669433	1 qada =	5.45
1 kanal =	.083679	Sweden	
1 marabba =	24.96	1 kappland =	.03812
Paraguay		1 tunland,	
1 cuadra =	1.85	tunnland =	1.22
1 legoa =	4.633		
Peru		Switzerland	
1 fanegada =	7.15045	1 juchart =	.89
1 topo =	.6687	Syria	
Philippines		1 dönüm =	.22709
1 balita =	.6907	1 kassabe =	.0058847
1 braza carrée = ·	.006907	Taiwan	
1 loan =	.06907	1 bin =	.00081694
Poland		Thailand	
1 morga =	1.384	1 ngan =	.40
1 vloka =	41.489	1 rai =	.40
Portugal		1 sq. sao =	.0132
1 alqueire			
carrée =	5.93	Turkey	
1 fanga carrée =	1.19440	1 djerib =	2.471
Puerto Rico		1 dönüm =	.618
1 caballería =	194.1	Union of South Africa	
1 cuerda =	.97	1 morgen (cape) =	2.1165

Country, Unit	U.S. Acres	Country, Unit	U.S. Acres
Uraguay		Yugoslavia	
1 cuadra =	1.82	1 dan oranja =	.889
1 suerte =	4921.6	1 dönüm =	.24711
		1 lanac =	1.771
USSR		1 motyka =	.19768
1 chast =	.009390	1 ralica, ralo =	.618
1 dessiatine =	2.70		
Venezuela			
1 area =	.13715		
1 fanegada =	1.73		
1 medio =	1.24		

15.3.   Density

Density is the weight of a substance per unit volume. When the weight is expressed in grams and the volume is expressed in cubic centimeters (or milliliters) the density is called the specific gravity.

Table:

	Pounds/in³	Pounds/ft³	gms/cm³	kgs/m³
1 pound/in³ =	1.000×10^0	1.728×10^3	2.768×10^1	2.768×10^4
1 pound/ft³ =	5.787×10^{-4}	1.000×10^0	1.602×10^{-2}	1.602×10^1
1 gm/cm³ =	3.613×10^{-2}	6.243×10^1	1.000×10^0	1.000×10^3
1 kg/m³ =	3.613×10^{-5}	6.243×10^{-2}	1.000×10^{-3}	1.000×10^0

Example: The specific gravity (i.e., the relative density expressed in gms/cm³) of Douglas-fir is listed as 0.46. What is the density in pounds/ft³?

Solution: Since

$$1 \text{ gm/cm}^3 = 6.243 \times 10^1 \text{ pounds/ft}^3$$
$$0.46 \text{ gm/cm}^3 = 0.46 \times 6.243 \times 10^1 = 2.87 \times 10^1$$
$$= 28.72 \text{ pounds/ft}^3.$$

15.4.   Flow

Table:

	ft³/min	yd³/min	gal/min	liter/min	miner's inch	pounds of water/min
1 ft³/min =	1.000×10^0	3.704×10^{-2}	7.482×10^0	2.832×10^1	8.333×10^{-1}	6.238×10^1
1 yd³/min =	2.700×10^1	1.000×10^0	2.020×10^2	7.644×10^2	2.250×10^1	1.684×10^3
1 gal/min =	1.337×10^{-1}	4.950×10^{-3}	1.000×10^0	3.785×10^0	1.114×10^{-1}	5.336×10^2
1 liter/min =	3.531×10^{-2}	1.308×10^{-3}	2.642×10^{-1}	1.000×10^0	2.943×10^{-2}	2.020×10^3
1 miner's inch* =	1.200×10^0	4.444×10^{-2}	8.978×10^0	3.398×10^1	1.000×10^0	7.485×10^1
1 pound of water/min† =	1.603×10^{-2}	5.937×10^{-4}	1.874×10^{-3}	4.951×10^{-4}	1.336×10^{-2}	1.000×10^0

Example: How many gallons per minute is equivalent to 7.9 cubic feet per minute?

Solution: Since

$$1 \text{ ft}^3/\text{min} = 7.482 \times 10^0 \text{ gal/min},$$
$$7.9 \text{ ft}^3/\text{min} = 7.9 \times 7.482 \times 10^0 = 59.10 \times 10^0$$
$$= 59.10 \text{ gals/min}.$$

15.5   Length

Table 1:   For domestic conversions, see page 321.

Example: How many feet are in 13.5 rods?

Solution: Since

$$1 \quad \text{rod} \ = 1.6500 \times 10^1 \text{ feet},$$
$$13.5 \text{ rods} = 13.5 \times 1.6500 \times 10^1 = 22.275 \times 10^1$$
$$= 222.75 \text{ feet}.$$

---

*Southern California miner's inch.

†Because the liquid is specified as water, this entry is given in weight per unit time. The other entries are given in volume per unit time.

	inches	links*	feet	yards	rods*	chains*	miles	cms.	meters	kms.
1 inch[+] =	1.0000×10^0	1.2626×10^{-1}	8.3333×10^{-2}	2.7778×10^{-2}	5.0505×10^{-3}	1.2626×10^{-3}	1.5783×10^{-5}	2.5400×10^0	2.5400×10^{-2}	2.5400×10^{-5}
1 link* =	7.9200×10^0	1.0000×10^0	6.6000×10^{-1}	2.2000×10^{-1}	4.0000×10^{-2}	1.0000×10^{-2}	1.25×10^{-4}	2.0117×10^1	2.0117×10^{-1}	2.0117×10^{-4}
1 foot =	1.2000×10^1	1.5152×10^0	1.0000×10^0	3.3333×10^{-1}	6.0606×10^{-2}	1.5152×10^{-2}	1.8939×10^{-4}	3.048×10^1	3.0480×10^{-1}	3.0480×10^{-4}
1 yard =	3.6000×10^1	4.5455×10^0	3.0000×10^0	1.0000×10^0	1.8182×10^{-1}	4.5455×10^{-2}	5.6818×10^{-4}	9.1440×10^1	9.1440×10^{-1}	9.1440×10^{-4}
1 rod* =	1.9800×10^2	2.5000×10^1	1.6500×10^1	5.5000×10^0	1.0000×10^0	2.5000×10^{-1}	3.1250×10^{-3}	5.0292×10^2	5.0292×10^0	5.0292×10^{-3}
1 chain* =	7.9200×10^2	1.0000×10^2	6.6000×10^1	2.2000×10^1	4.0000×10^0	1.0000×10^0	1.2500×10^{-2}	2.0117×10^3	2.0117×10^1	2.0117×10^{-2}
1 mile =	6.3360×10^4	8.0000×10^3	5.2800×10^3	1.7600×10^3	3.20000×10^2	8.0000×10^1	1.0000×10^0	1.6093×10^5	1.6093×10^3	1.6093×10^0
1 cm =	3.9370×10^{-1}	4.9710×10^{-2}	3.2808×10^{-2}	1.0936×10^{-2}	1.9884×10^{-3}	4.9710×10^{-4}	6.2137×10^{-6}	1.0000×10^0	1.0000×10^0	1.0000×10^{-5}
1 meter =	3.9370×10^1	4.9709×10^0	3.2808×10^0	1.0936×10^0	1.9884×10^{-1}	4.9710×10^{-2}	6.2137×10^{-4}	1.0000×10^2	1.0000×10^0	1.0000×10^{-3}
1 km =	3.9370×10^4	4.9709×10^3	3.2808×10^3	1.0936×10^3	1.9884×10^2	4.9710×10^1	6.2137×10^{-1}	1.00000×10^5	1.0000×10^3	1.0000×10^0

Table 2:

Foreign-U.S. Length Conversion

Country, Unit	U.S. Feet	Country, Unit	U.S. Feet
Afghanistan		**Ceylon**	
1 jerib (side of) =	144.9	1 guz =	3
		1 lasta =	2.152
Algeria		1 moolum =	1.5
1 nus =	.814	1 vilasti =	1.076
1 pik =	1.624		
1 rebia =	.407	**Chile**	
1 termin =	.203	1 braza =	5.486
		1 cuadra =	411.74
Argentina		1 legoa =	14,797
1 braza =	5.68	1 linia =	.00633
1 cuadra =	426.3	1 vara =	2.743
1 legua =	17054.4		
1 linea =	.006575	**Columbia**	
1 vara =	2.8418	1 braza =	5.25
		1 cuadra =	262.5
Austria		1 vara =	2.625
1 fuss =	1.037	1 yarda =	2.952
1 klafter =	6.222		
1 linie =	.00725	**Costa Rica**	
1 meile =	24,868.8	1 braza =	5.486
1 punkt =	.06	1 cuarta =	.6857
		1 mecate =	65.826
Belgium		1 tercia =	.9143
1 aune =	3.9367	1 vara =	2.74
1 perche =	21.33		
1 pied =	1.0658	**Cuba**	
		1 legua =	13,886
Brazil		1 vara =	2.782
1 braca =	7.22		
1 covado =	2.2467	**Curacao**	
1 legoa =	21648.0	1 vara =	2.78
1 milha =	6388.8		
1 passo =	5.4	**Cyprus**	
1 pé =	1.08	1 dhara =	2
1 hollegada =	.09	1 roupi =	.25
1 vara =	3.6092		
		Czechoslovakia	
Burma		1 latro =	6.289
1 kawtha =	16,800		
1 okthabak =	256.6	**Denmark**	
1 palgat =	1.08333	1 alen =	2.0594
1 taim =	1.5	1 fagn =	6.17
1 taing =	12,830	1 fod, fodder =	1.0295
		1 linje =	.00715

Country, Unit	U.S. Feet	Country, Unit	U.S. Feet
1 mil =	24,713	1 linie =	.00715
1 rode =	10.295	1 meile =	24,705
1 tomme =	.051509	1 stab =	3.2808
		1 strich =	.003281
Dominican Republic			
1 ona =	3.897	**Greece**	
1 vara =	2.742	1 daktylos =	.08333
		1 daktylos	
Ecuador		(royal) =	.032808
1 pie =	1	1 dira mimari =	2.4608
1 cuadra =	275.7	1 gramme (line) =	.006944
1 legua =	16,405	1 gramme	
1 milla =	4593.6	(royal) =	.003281
1 vara =	2.76	1 palame =	.32808
		1 stadion =	3278.88
Egypt			
1 diraa mimâri =	2.46	**Guatemala**	
1 quasaba =	11.65	1 braza =	5.486
		1 cuarta =	.6858
El Salvador		1 legua =	15,830
1 braza =	5.5	1 mecate =	66.15
1 legua =	13,121	1 tercia =	.9183
1 vara =	2.75	1 vara =	2.76
Ethiopia		**Hondurus**	
1 farsakh =	16,634	1 mecate =	65.62
1 gat =	.246	1 milla =	6,070
1 kend =	1.64	1 vara =	2.74
1 khalad =	213		
1 sinjer =	.75	**Hungary**	
1 tat =	.066	1 marok =	.34567
		1 meile =	27,407
Finland			
1 sjömil =	506.34	**Iceland**	
1 verste =	3,507	1 alin =	2.07
		1 fet =	1.035
France		1 ligne =	.00715
1 aune (metric) =	3.937	1 mila =	24,803
1 brasse =	5.331	1 sjomila =	6,086
1 encâblure =	656		
1 lieue =	13,123	**India**	
1 noeud de loch =	50.630	1 ady =	.8725
1 penche =	19.19	1 guz =	3
1 pied =	1.0656	1 moolum =	1.5
1 toise =	6.3944	1 niranja =	30
Germany		**Indonesia**	
1 fuss =	1.0295	1 deppa =	5.58
1 kette =	32.82	1 el =	2.257
1 klafter =	5.7		

Country, Unit	U.S. Feet	Country, Unit	U.S. Feet
1 kilam =	.6972	Mexico	
1 jengkal =	.66667	1 legua =	13,780.8
1 paal (Java) =	.4942	1 línea =	.006367
1 paal (Sumatra) =	6007	1 pulgada =	.076333
1 tjenghal =	12	1 vara =	2.75
		Morocco	
Iran		1 kala =	1.64
1 charac =	.853	1 tomini =	.23417
1 farsak			
(metric) =	32,808	Netherlands	
1 gareh		1 duim =	.032808
(metric) =	.32808	1 el =	3.2808
1 guz =	3.412	1 palm =	.32808
1 guz (metric) =	3.2808	1 roede =	32.808
1 ouroub =	.426	1 vadem =	6
Iraq		Nicaragua	
1 dhrâ =	244.4	1 mecate =	66
		1 milla =	6,122
Israel		1 tercia =	.9183
1 coudé =	1.4649	1 vara =	2.76
1 kaneh =	8.79		
1 reed =	8.79	Norway	
		1 alen =	2.0587
Italy			
1 miglio =	3,280.8	Pakistan	
1 palmo =	.32808	1 hath =	1.5
1 pie =	.919		
		Paraguay	
Japan		1 cuadra =	284.3
1 chô =	357.91	1 cuerda =	229.26
1 ken =	.016667	1 legua =	14,206
1 ri =	12.884	1 pié =	.9367
1 shaku =	.99419	1 vara =	2.84
Libya			
1 draarbi =	1.6083	Peru	
1 habl =	114.9	1 braza =	5.476
1 handaza =	2.2333	1 legua =	18,227
1 palmo =	.82	1 vara =	2.75
Malaya		Philippines	
1 depa =	6	1 braza =	5.486
1 ela =	3	1 vara =	2.743
1 hasta =	1.5		
1 jenghal =	.75	Poland	
1 jumba =	12	1 cal =	.0787
		1 lokiec =	1.890
Malta		1 sloppa =	.9475
1 canna =	6.82		

Country, Unit	U.S. Feet	Country, Unit	U.S. Feet
Portugal		Sweden	
1 braca =	7.2	1 abu =	1.948
1 covada =	2.17	1 fann =	5.84
1 estadio =	846	1 fötter =	9.74
1 legua =	20,328	1 nymil =	32,808
1 milha =	6,778	1 ref =	97.41
1 palmo =	.725	1 stang =	9.741
1 vara =	3.6	1 tum =	.9741
Rumania		Switzerland	
1 halibin =	2.3	1 aune =	1.97
		1 elle =	1.97
Salvador		1 fuss =	.9833
1 braza =	5.486	1 klafter =	5.91
1 vara =	2.743	1 perche =	9.84
		1 pied =	.9833
Saudi Arabia		1 staab =	2.937
1 barid =	63,360	1 strich =	9.833
1 covid,		1 toise =	5.91
covido =	1.5833		
1 farsakh,		Syria	
1 farsang =	15,845.3	1 dra maghmari =	2.4833
1 fitr =	.50		
1 marhala =	126,720	Thailand	
		1 ken =	3.2808
Somalia		1 keup =	.82
1 cubito =	1.8333	1 niu =	.82
1 top =	12.87	1 roeneng =	13,121
		1 sawk =	1.65
South Korea		1 sen =	131.2
1 ken =	5.965	1 sok =	1.64
1 liu =	12,883	1 wa,wah =	6.56
		1 yot,yote =	52,483
Spain			
1 braza =	5.486	Tunisia	
1 codo =	1.371	1 pic arabe =	1.617
1 cuarta =	.686	1 pic ture =	2.113
1 dedo =	.0571		
1 estadio =	565.534	Turkey	
1 legua =	18,285	1 arshin, zira,	
1 milla =	4,570	zirai =	3.28083
1 palmo =	.76	1 hatt =	.0011333
1 pié =	.915	1 nocktat, oka,	
1 pulgada =	.02979	oke =	.0011667
1 tereia =	.915	1 parmah,	
1 vara =	2.743	parmack =	.14417
Sudan			
1 rageil =	5.5		

Country, Unit	U.S. Feet	Country, Unit	U.S. Feet
Union of South Africa		1 sotka =	.07
1 elle =	2.247	1 totschka,	
1 feet (Cape) =	1.033	totska =	.008333
1 rood (Cape) =	12.396	1 verchok,	
		werchok =	.14583
Uruguay		1 verst, werst =	3500.64
1 cuadra =	282	Venezuela	
1 legua =	16,896	1 estadel =	10.71
1 vara =	2.82	1 milla =	6093.12
		1 vara =	2.782
USSR			
1 arshin,		Yugoslavia	
arsheen =	2.3333	1 hvat =	6.219
1 dium, duime =	.08333	1 palaz =	.11917
1 foot, stopa =	1	1 rif =	2.5492
1 liniya =	.008333	1 stopa =	1.03667
1 paletz =	.041667		
1 sagen,			
saschen =	7.0		

15.6.   Mass

Table:

		ounces (avdp)	pounds (avdp)	tons (short)
1 ounce (avdp)	=	1.0000×10^0	6.2500×10^{-2}	3.1250×10^{-5}
1 pound (avdp)	=	1.6000×10^1	1.0000×10^0	5.0000×10^{-4}
1 ton (short)	=	3.2000×10^4	2.0000×10^3	1.0000×10^0
1 ton (long)	=	3.5840×10^4	2.2400×10^3	1.1200×10^0
1 gram	=	3.5275×10^{-2}	2.2046×10^{-3}	1.1023×10^{-6}
1 kg	=	3.5275×10^1	2.2046×10^0	1.1023×10^{-3}
1 ton (metric)	=	3.52748×10^4	2.2046×10^3	1.1023×10^0

tons (long)	grams	kgs	tons (metric)
2.7900×10^{-5}	2.8350×10^1	2.8350×10^{-2}	2.8350×10^{-5}
4.4643×10^{-4}	4.5360×10^2	4.5360×10^{-1}	4.5360×10^{-4}
8.9286×10^{-1}	9.0719×10^5	9.0719×10^2	9.0719×10^{-1}
1.0000×10^0	1.0160×10^6	1.0160×10^3	1.0160×10^0
9.8421×10^{-7}	1.0000×10^0	1.0000×10^{-3}	1.0000×10^{-6}
9.8421×10^{-4}	1.0000×10^3	1.0000×10^0	1.0000×10^{-3}
9.8421×10^{-1}	1.0000×10^6	1.0000×10^3	1.0000×10^0

Example: How many kilograms are there in 52 pounds?

Solution: Since

$$1 \text{ pound} = 4.5360 \times 10^{-1} \text{ kg,}$$
$$52 \text{ pounds} = 52 \times 4.5360 \times 10^{-1} = 2.3587 \times 10^1$$
$$= 23.587 \text{ kgs.}$$

15.7.   Rates of Pay

The following table assumes 1 day = 8 hrs, 1 wk = 5 days, 1 mo.1/12 year, and 1 yr. = 52 wks.

Table:

	dols/hr	dols/day	dols/wk	dols/mo	dols/yr
1 dol/hr =	1.0000×10^0	8.0000×10^0	4.0000×10^1	1.7333×10^2	2.0800×10^3
1 dol/day =	1.2500×10^{-1}	1.0000×10^0	5.0000×10^0	2.1667×10^1	2.6000×10^2
1 dol/wk =	2.5000×10^{-2}	2.0000×10^{-1}	1.0000×10^0	4.3333×10^0	5.2000×10^1
1 dol/mo =	5.7694×10^{-3}	4.6154×10^{-2}	2.3077×10^{-1}	1.0000×10^0	1.2000×10^1
1 dol/yr =	4.8077×10^{-4}	3.8462×10^{-3}	1.9231×10^{-2}	8.3333×10^{-2}	1.0000×10^0

Example: What annual salary is equivalent to 7.50 dols/hr?

Solution: Since

$$1 \text{ dols/hr} = 2.0800 \times 10^3 \text{ dols/yr},$$
$$7.50 \text{ dols/hr} = 7.50 \times 2.0800 \times 10^3 = 15.600 \times 10^3$$
$$= 15,600 \text{ dols/yr}.$$

15.8.   Time

Table:

	secs.	mins.	hours	days	months†	years*
1 sec =	1.000×10^0	1.667×10^{-2}	2.778×10^{-4}	1.157×10^{-5}	3.858×10^{-7}	3.171×10^{-8}
1 min =	6.000×10^1	1.000×10^0	1.667×10^{-2}	6.944×10^{-4}	2.315×10^{-5}	1.0903×10^{-6}
1 hour =	3.600×10^3	6.000×10^1	1.000×10^0	4.167×10^{-2}	1.389×10^{-3}	1.142×10^{-4}
1 day =	8.640×10^4	1.440×10^3	2.400×10^1	1.000×10^0	3.333×10^{-2}	2.740×10^{-3}
1 month† =	2.592×10^6	4.320×10^4	7.200×10^2	3.000×10^{-1}	1.000×10^0	8.219×10^{-2}
1 year* =	3.154×10^7	5.256×10^5	8.760×10^3	3.650×10^2	1.217×10^1	1.000×10^0

---

*1 year = 365 days (leap year not included in Table).

†1 month = 30 days.

Example: How many days in 3.6 years?

Solution: Since

$$1 \text{ year} = 3.65 \times 10^2 \text{ days},$$
$$3.6 \text{ years} = 3.6 \times 3.65 \times 10^2 = 13.14 \times 10^2 = 1{,}314 \text{ days}.$$

15.9.   Volume

Table: (See page 330.)

Example: How many cubic yards are there in 34 cubic meters?

Solution: Since

$$1 \text{ cubic meter} = 1.3079 \times 10^0 \text{ cubic yards},$$
$$34 \text{ cubic meters} = 34 \times 1.3079 \times 10^0 = 44.4686 \times 10^0$$
$$= 44.4686 \text{ cu. yds.}$$

15.10.   Work and Energy

Table:

		BTUs (mean)	kilowatt -hrs.	horsepower -hrs.	foot-pounds	joules (abs.)
1 BTU (mean)	=	1.000×10^0	2.930×10^{-4}	3.929×10^{-4}	7.780×10^2	1.055×10^3
1 kilowatt-hr.	=	3.413×10^3	1.000×10^0	1.341×10^0	2.655×10^6	3.600×10^6
1 horsepower-hr.	=	2.545×10^3	7.457×10^{-1}	1.000×10^0	1.980×10^6	2.685×10^6
1 foot-pound	=	1.285×10^{-3}	3.766×10^{-7}	5.051×10^{-7}	1.000×10^0	1.356×10^0
1 joule (abs.)	=	9.480×10^{-4}	2.778×10^{-7}	3.725×10^{-7}	7.376×10^{-1}	1.000×10^0

Example: How many joules are there in 32 BTUs?

Solution: Since

$$1 \text{ BTU} = 1.055 \times 10^3 \text{ joules},$$
$$32 \text{ BTUs} = 32 \times 1.055 \times 10^3 = 33.760 \times 10^3$$
$$= 33{,}760 \text{ joules.}$$

	barrels (U.S. dry)	boardfeet	bushels	pecks	cu. ins.	cu. feet	cu. yards	cu. cms.	cu. meters
1 Barrel (U.S. dry) =	1.0000×10^{0}	4.9000×10^{1}	3.2810×10^{0}	1.3125×10^{1}	7.0560×10^{3}	4.0833×10^{0}	1.5123×10^{-1}	1.1563×10^{5}	1.1563×10^{-1}
1 Boardfoot =	2.0408×10^{-2}	1.0000×10^{0}	6.6964×10^{-2}	2.6786×10^{-1}	1.4400×10^{2}	8.3333×10^{-2}	3.0864×10^{-3}	2.3598×10^{3}	2.3598×10^{-3}
1 Bushel (U.S. dry) =	3.0479×10^{-1}	1.4933×10^{1}	1.0000×10^{0}	4.0000×10^{0}	2.1504×10^{3}	1.2444×10^{0}	4.6089×10^{-2}	3.5239×10^{4}	3.5239×10^{-2}
1 peck =	7.6191×10^{-2}	3.7333×10^{0}	2.5000×10^{-1}	1.0000×10^{0}	5.3760×10^{2}	3.111×10^{-1}	1.1523×10^{-2}	8.8098×10^{3}	8.8098×10^{-3}
1 cu. in. =	1.4172×10^{-4}	6.9444×10^{-3}	4.6503×10^{-4}	1.860×10^{-3}	1.0000×10^{0}	5.7870×10^{-4}	2.1433×10^{-5}	1.6387×10^{1}	1.6387×10^{-5}
1 cu. ft. =	2.4490×10^{-1}	1.2000×10^{1}	8.0357×10^{-1}	3.214×10^{0}	1.7280×10^{3}	1.0000×10^{0}	3.7037×10^{-2}	2.8317×10^{4}	2.8317×10^{-2}
1 cu. yd. =	6.6124×10^{0}	3.2400×10^{2}	2.1696×10^{1}	8.679×10^{1}	4.6656×10^{4}	2.7000×10^{1}	1.0000×10^{0}	7.6456×10^{5}	7.6456×10^{-1}
1 cu. cm. =	8.6483×10^{-6}	4.2376×10^{-4}	2.8378×10^{-5}	1.1351×10^{-4}	6.1023×10^{-2}	3.5314×10^{-5}	1.3079×10^{-6}	1.0000×10^{0}	1.0000×10^{-6}
1 cu. meter =	8.6483×10^{0}	4.2376×10^{2}	2.8378×10^{1}	1.3209×10^{2}	6.1023×10^{4}	3.5314×10^{1}	1.3079×10^{0}	1.0000×10^{6}	1.0000×10^{0}

APPENDIX: MATHEMATICAL NOTES

A.1.   Summation

When n numbers (say a_1, a_2, . . ., a_n) are to be added, we can write

$$a_1 + a_2 + \ldots + a_n.$$

However, it is more convenient to write

$$\sum_{i=1}^{n} a_i.$$

The symbol "$\sum$" is the greek equivalent of "s" and is used in mathematics to indicate summation. Hence, $\sum_{i=1}^{n} a_i$ means: add all of the numbers a_i, starting with $i = 1$ and ending with $i = n$. Sometimes when a summation is known or understood only Σa_i is used.

Example 1:   If we are asked to find the sum of the first 100 integers, we could write

$$1 + 2 + 3 + \ldots + 100,$$

or we can write

$$\sum_{i=1}^{100} i^*.$$

Example 2:   If $a_i = (1 + r)^i$, (for $i = 1,2,3,\ldots$) the sum of the first 4 values can be written

$$\sum_{i=1}^{4} (1 + r)^i$$

to represent

$$(1 + r)^1 + (1 + r)^2 + (1 + r)^3 + (1 + r)^4.$$

A.2.   Interpolation

Often it is necessary to know a value that is not listed in a table. If the formula from which the table is derived is known, the unknown value can theoretically be determined. However, often either the formula is not known or it is quite complicated. In either event the unknown value can be estimated by using the nearest tabulated values. If the unknown value lies beyond the table it can sometimes be estimated by *extrapolation*. On the other hand, if the unknown value lies between two listed values, it can be estimated by *interpolation*.

By interpolating we imply that the formula is a straight line**. This assumption is of course usually not true, but it generally provides a good estimate of the true value.

As an example, the figure shows a portion of a curve, some of whose values might be listed in a table. Consider the listed values y_1 and y_2 corresponding to x_1 and x_2. Also consider a straight line through the points $P_1 = (x_1,y_1)$ and $P_2 = (x_2,y_2)$. The straight line, although not identical to the curve, can be used to approximate values on the curve between x_1 and x_2.

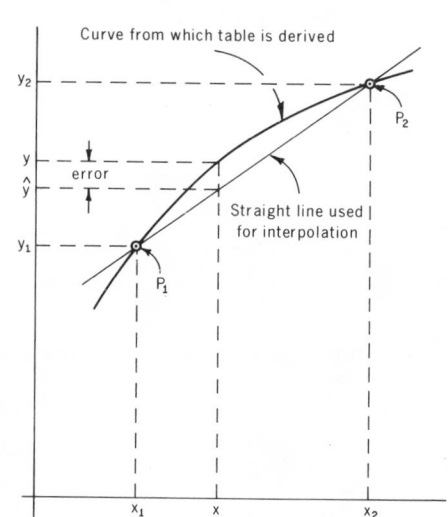

---

*The sum of the first n integers is $\dfrac{n(n + 1)}{2}$.

**The word interpolation usually refers to linear interpolation although it needn't be so restrictive.

For instance, the value on the curve corresponding to x is y and the value on the straight line corresponding to x is $\hat{y}$. Therefore, $\hat{y}$ is the estimate of y obtained by using linear interpolation.

The following formula determines the estimate of y.

Formula:

$$\hat{y} = \left(\frac{x_2 - x}{x_2 - x_1}\right) \cdot y_1 + \left(\frac{x - x_1}{x_2 - x_1}\right) \cdot y_2$$

where

$\hat{y}$ = estimate of y using linear interpolation
y = nonlisted value, to be estimated by $\hat{y}$
x_1, x_2 = first and second listed parameter values that straddle x
x = nonlisted parameter value (between x_1 and x_2)
y_1, y_2 = first and second listed value corresponding to x_1 and x_2, respectively

Example: Find the present value of an annuity of 1 corresponding to q = 1, r = 5%, and m = 20.25 (see Table 1).

Solution: Since m = 20.25 is the non-listed parameter value (i.e. x = 20.25), we will interpolate. Let

$$x_1 = 20 \text{ and } x_2 = 21$$

be the nearest listed values that straddle x.

The present values of an annuity of 1 corresponding to x_1 and x_2 (obtained from Table 1) are

$$y_1 = a(5,20,1) = 12.46221, \text{ and } y_2 = a(5,21,1) = 12.82115.$$

Now, using the formula, the estimate of y is

$$\hat{y} = \left(\frac{21 - 20.25}{21 - 20}\right) \times 12.46221 + \left(\frac{20.25 - 20}{21 - 20}\right) \times 12.842115$$

$$= .75 \times 12.46221 + .25 \times 12.842115$$

$$= 9.34666 + 3.21053$$

$$= 12.55719$$

(Note: The actual value using the formula in Section 4.1 is y = 12.55842.)

A.3.   Logarithms

The logarithm of x to the base b is written, $\log_b x$. The base b and the argument x must both be positive. When b = 10, the logarithm is called the common logarithm and when $b = e = 2.71828\cdots$ it is called the natural logarithm. Both logarithms are listed extensively in tables and are available from electronic calculators.

Example 1:   The value of $\log_{10} 0.64030 = -.19362$.

The base of a logarithm can be changed from b to c by using the following formula:

$$\log_b x = A \cdot \log_c x \quad \text{where } A = \frac{1}{\log_c b}.$$

Because of this property, the ratio of two logarithms is independent of the base, as seen in the following example.

Example 2:   The bases of two logarithms can be changed from b to c without changing the value of their ratio:

$$\frac{\log_b x_1}{\log_b x_2} = \frac{A \cdot \log_c x_1}{A \cdot \log_c x_2} = \frac{\log_c x_1}{\log_c x_2}.$$

The following are three frequently used formulas of logarithms:

$$\log_b(x_1 \cdot x_2) = \log_b x_1 + \log_b x_2 \qquad\qquad \text{where } x_1, x_2 > 0.$$

$$\log_b\left(\frac{x_1}{x_2}\right) = \log_b x_1 - \log_b x_2$$

$$\log_b x^p = p \cdot \log_b x \qquad\qquad\qquad \text{where } x > 0.$$

A.4.   Exponents

Exponents and logarithms are inverse functions of each other*. For instance, an exponential function, plotted on a logarithmic scale, will appear as a straight line.

Formulas:

$$\text{If } b^y = x, \text{ then } y = \log_b x \qquad \text{for } b > 0,$$
$$\text{and}$$
$$b^y = c^{y \log_c b}.$$

---

*Just as the square and the square root are inverse functions of each other.

Example 1:   If $(1.07)^y = 1.82571$, find y.

Solution: In this example,

$$b = 1.07, \text{ and } x = 1.82571.$$

From the first formula,

$$y = \log_{1.07}(1.82571).$$

However, since the logarithm to the base 1.07 is not listed in tables, the formula of Section A.3 can be used to change the base to 10 (whose logarithm is listed):

$$y = \log_{1.07}(1.82571) = \frac{\log_{10}(1.82571)}{\log_{10}(1.07)}$$

$$= \frac{.261432}{.0293838} = 8.89715.$$

Example 2:   Determine the value of $1.8^{\frac{1}{16}}$.

Solution: In this example,

$$b = 1.8, \text{ and } y = \frac{1}{16}.$$

Using the second formula with $c = e = 2.71828 \ldots$ (the base of the natural logarithm),

$$1.8^{\frac{1}{16}} = e^{\frac{1}{16}\log_e(1.8)}$$

From a table of natural logarithms or an electronic calculator,

$$\log_e 1.8 = 0.587787.$$

Then

$$1.8^{\frac{1}{16}} = e^{\frac{0.587787}{16}} = e^{0.114904}.$$

From a table of e^x or an electronic calculator,

$$1.8^{\frac{1}{16}} = e^{0.114904} = 1.037420.$$

The following are frequently used rules of exponents:

$$b^x \cdot b^y = b^{x+y},$$

and

$$\frac{b^x}{b^y} = b^x \cdot b^{-y} = b^{x-y}.$$

A.5.   Determinants

A determinant is a square array of numbers that has a value. A determinant with n elements (i.e., numbers) on each side of the array is a determinant of order n. Let C be the value of an n $\times$ n determinant, and let c_{kj} denote the element in the kth row and jth column:

Formula:

$$C = \begin{vmatrix} c_{11} & c_{12} & \ldots & c_{1n} \\ c_{21} & c_{22} & \ldots & c_{2n} \\ \cdot & \cdot & & \cdot \\ \cdot & \cdot & & \cdot \\ \cdot & \cdot & & \cdot \\ c_{n1} & c_{n2} & \ldots & c_{nn} \end{vmatrix} \quad *$$

Example 1:   Consider the following 3 $\times$ 3 determinant:

$$C = \begin{vmatrix} 5 & 3 & 1 \\ 9 & -1 & 0 \\ -2 & 4 & 2 \end{vmatrix}$$

The elements are $c_{11} = 5$, $c_{22} = -1$, $c_{32} = 4$, etc. The cofactor of the element c_{kj} is

$$A_{kj} = (-1)^{k+j} \times \text{(The determinant remaining after the kth row and jth column are deleted).}$$

Example 2:   Using the determinant in Example 1, the cofactor of c_{11} is

$$A_{11} = (-1)^{1+1} \times \begin{vmatrix} -1 & 0 \\ 4 & 2 \end{vmatrix} = \begin{vmatrix} -1 & 0 \\ 4 & 2 \end{vmatrix},$$

---

*Note that the determinant of Section 10.11 doesn't contain the usual first row and first column.

The cofactor of c_{22} is

$$A_{22} = (-1)^{2+2} \times \begin{vmatrix} 5 & 1 \\ -2 & 2 \end{vmatrix} = \begin{vmatrix} 5 & 1 \\ -2 & 2 \end{vmatrix},$$

the cofactor of c_{32} is

$$A_{32} = (-1)^{3+2} \times \begin{vmatrix} 5 & 1 \\ 9 & 0 \end{vmatrix} = - \begin{vmatrix} 5 & 1 \\ 9 & 0 \end{vmatrix}, \text{ etc.}$$

Now that the elements c_{kj} and their cofactors A_{kj} are defined, the determinant C can be evaluated. The value of the determinant is

$$C = \sum_{j=1}^{n} c_{kj}A_{kj} \qquad \begin{array}{l} \text{(a single value of k can be} \\ \text{chosen arbitrarily as long as} \\ 1 \le k \le n). \end{array}$$

Example 3: The value of the determinant in Example 1 is, using $k = 1$:

$$C = \begin{vmatrix} 5 & 3 & 1 \\ 9 & -1 & 0 \\ -2 & 4 & 2 \end{vmatrix} = c_{11}A_{11} + c_{12}A_{12} + c_{13}A_{13}$$

$$= 5 \times (-1)^{1+1} \begin{vmatrix} -1 & 0 \\ 4 & 2 \end{vmatrix} + 3 \times (-1)^{1+2} \begin{vmatrix} 9 & 0 \\ -2 & 2 \end{vmatrix} + 1 \times (-1)^{1+3} \begin{vmatrix} 9 & -1 \\ -2 & 4 \end{vmatrix}^{*}$$

$$= 5[-1 \times 2 - 0 \times 4] - 3[9 \times 2 - 0 \times (-2)] + 1[9 \times 4 - (-1) \times (-2)]$$
$$= 5(-2) - 3(18) + 1(34)$$
$$= -10 - 54 + 34$$
$$= -30.$$

---

*Although we can evaluate these 2×2 determinants using the concept of the sum of products of elements and their cofactors, it is convenient to simply note that for any 2×2 determinant,

$$\begin{vmatrix} c_{11} & c_{12} \\ c_{21} & c_{22} \end{vmatrix} = c_{11}c_{22} - c_{12}c_{21}.$$

Table 1

ANNUITIES

This table lists values of the three functions needed to solve interest problems covering a year or more. The functions are:

compound interest,

$$c(r,m,q) = (1 + r/q)^m,$$

the present value of an annuity of 1,

$$a(r,m,q) = \frac{(1 + r/q)^m - 1}{(r/q)(1 + r/q)^m},$$

and the amount of an annuity of 1,

$$s(r,m,q) = \frac{(1 + r/q)^m - 1}{(r/q)}.$$

where

r = annual interest rate, expressed as a decimal

q = number of interest periods per year

$m = nq$ = total number of interest periods, and n is the number of years

This table lists the letter **m** only because it occurs most often in the formulas. If your problem uses different notation such as s(r,t,q) in Section 4.2, treat the **t** as **m** and locate the value of **t** in the column labeled **m**. In the same way a(r,m,q), a(r,t,q), and a(y,k,u) etc. are treated identically; the difference is a notational difference only.

This table is first divided according to the four values of **q** (i.e. q=1,2,4,12). In each of these sections the interest rate goes from r=5% through 13.75% in increments of ¼%. As an example, the value of a(5,20,1) is 12.4622103.

Further explanation of compound interest can be found in the introduction to Chapter 3, and further explanation of the present value of an annuity and the amount of an annuity can be found in the introduction to Chapter 4.

Table 1

M	C(5.00,M,1)	A(5.00,M,1)	S(5.00,M,1)	M	C(5.25,M,1)	A(5.25,M,1)	S(5.25,M,1)	M	C(5.50,M,1)	A(5.50,M,1)	S(5.50,M,1)
1/12	1.0040741	.0811519	.0814825	1/12	1.0042731	.0810466	.0813929	1/12	1.0044717	.0809417	.0813036
1/4	1.0122722	.2424691	.2454447	1/4	1.0128742	.2421067	.2452236	1/4	1.0134752	.2417456	.2450032
1/2	1.0246951	.4819985	.4939015	1/2	1.0259142	.4811360	.4936043	1/2	1.0271319	.4802770	.4933078
1	1.0500000	.9523810	1.0000000	1	1.0525000	.9501188	1.0000000	1	1.0550000	.9478673	1.0000000
2	1.1025000	1.8594104	2.0500000	2	1.1077563	1.8528444	2.0525000	2	1.1130250	1.8463197	2.0550000
3	1.1576250	2.7232480	3.1525000	3	1.1659135	2.7105410	3.1602563	3	1.1742414	2.6979334	3.1680250
4	1.2155063	3.5459505	4.3101250	4	1.2271239	3.5254547	4.3261797	4	1.2388247	3.5051501	4.3422664
5	1.2762816	4.3294767	5.5256313	5	1.2915479	4.2997194	5.5532929	5	1.3069600	4.2702845	5.5810910
6	1.3400956	5.0756921	6.8019128	6	1.3593542	5.0353028	6.8448415	6	1.3789428	4.9955303	6.8880510
7	1.4071004	5.7863734	8.1420085	7	1.4307203	5.7343115	8.2041957	7	1.4546792	5.6829971	8.2669938
8	1.4774554	6.4632128	9.5491089	8	1.5058331	6.3935957	9.6349160	8	1.5346865	6.3345660	9.7215730
9	1.5513282	7.1078217	11.0265643	9	1.5848893	7.0293546	11.1407491	9	1.6190943	6.9521952	11.2562595
10	1.6228946	7.7217349	12.5778925	10	1.6660960	7.6268405	12.7256304	10	1.7081445	7.5376258	12.8753538
11	1.7103394	8.3064142	14.2067872	11	1.7555711	8.1984232	14.3937344	11	1.8020924	8.0925363	14.5834983
12	1.7958563	8.8632516	15.9171265	12	1.8478438	8.7395945	16.1494055	12	1.9012075	8.6185178	16.3855907
13	1.8853491	9.3935730	17.7129829	13	1.9440556	9.2537715	17.9972493	13	2.0057739	9.1170785	18.2867931
14	1.9799316	9.8981409	19.5986520	14	2.0463605	9.7423007	19.9421049	14	2.1160915	9.5896479	20.2925720
15	2.0789282	10.3796580	21.5785636	15	2.1544259	10.2064615	21.9890654	15	2.2324765	10.0375809	22.4086635
16	2.1828746	10.8377696	23.6574918	16	2.2675333	10.6474694	24.1434913	16	2.3552627	10.4621620	24.6411400
17	2.2920183	11.2740682	25.8403664	17	2.3855788	11.0664792	26.4110246	17	2.4848022	10.8646086	26.9964027
18	2.4066192	11.6895869	28.1323847	18	2.5118742	11.4645883	28.7976034	18	2.6214663	11.2460745	29.4812049
19	2.5269502	12.0853208	30.5390039	19	2.6437476	11.8428393	31.3094776	19	2.7656469	11.6076535	32.1026711
20	2.6532977	12.4622103	33.0659541	20	2.7825443	12.2022226	33.9532251	20	2.9177575	11.9503825	34.8683180
21	2.7859626	12.8211527	35.7192518	21	2.9283279	12.5436794	36.7357695	21	3.0782342	12.2752441	37.7860755
22	2.9252607	13.1630026	38.5052144	22	3.0823309	12.8681039	39.6643974	22	3.2475370	12.5831697	40.8643097
23	3.0715238	13.4885739	41.4304752	23	3.2442059	13.1763458	42.7467792	23	3.4261516	12.8750424	44.1118467
24	3.2251000	13.7986418	44.5019789	24	3.4145267	13.4692121	45.9909841	24	3.6145899	13.1516989	47.5379983
25	3.3863549	14.0939446	47.7270989	25	3.5937893	13.7474700	49.4055108	25	3.8133924	13.4139326	51.1525882
26	3.5556727	14.3751853	51.1134528	26	3.7824633	14.0118480	52.9993001	26	4.0231289	13.6624954	54.9659806
27	3.7334563	14.6430336	54.6691255	27	3.9810426	14.2630384	56.7817633	27	4.2444010	13.8980999	58.9891095
28	3.9201291	14.8981272	58.4025829	28	4.1900473	14.5016992	60.7628059	28	4.4778431	14.1214217	63.2335106
29	4.1161356	15.1410736	62.3227120	29	4.4100248	14.7284553	64.9528532	29	4.7241245	14.3331011	67.7113536
30	4.3219424	15.3724510	66.4388476	30	4.6315511	14.9439005	69.3628780	30	4.9839513	14.5337452	72.4354781
31	4.5380395	15.5928105	70.7607900	31	4.8852325	15.1485991	74.0044291	31	5.2580686	14.7239291	77.4194294
32	4.7649415	15.6026766	75.2988265	32	5.1417072	15.3430870	78.8896617	32	5.5472624	14.9041982	82.6774980
33	5.0031886	16.0025494	80.0637710	33	5.4116469	15.5278736	84.0313689	33	5.8523518	15.0750593	88.2247604
34	5.2533480	16.1929040	85.0669596	34	5.6957583	15.7034129	89.4430158	34	6.1742417	15.2370325	94.0771223
35	5.5160154	16.3741943	90.3203075	35	5.9947857	15.8702545	95.1387741	35	6.5136250	15.3905522	100.2513640
36	5.7918162	16.5468517	95.8363229	36	6.3095119	16.0287454	101.1335598	36	6.8720854	15.5360384	106.7651890
37	6.0814070	16.7112873	101.6281391	37	6.6407613	16.1793305	107.4430717	37	7.2500501	15.6731985	113.6372744
38	6.3854773	16.8676927	107.7095460	38	6.9894012	16.3224043	114.0838330	38	7.6488029	15.8047379	120.8873245
39	6.7047512	17.0170408	114.0950234	39	7.3563448	16.4583414	121.0732342	39	8.0694870	15.9286615	128.5361274
40	7.0399887	17.1590363	120.7997745	40	7.7425529	16.5874978	128.4295790	40	8.5133088	16.0461247	136.6056144
41	7.3919882	17.2943679	127.8397633	41	8.1490369	16.7102116	136.1721319	41	8.9815408	16.1574641	145.1189232
42	7.7615876	17.4232078	135.2317515	42	8.5768614	16.8268044	144.3211689	42	9.4755255	16.2629992	154.1004640
43	8.1496670	17.5459120	142.9933350	43	9.0271466	16.9375814	152.8980303	43	9.9967794	16.3630324	163.5759895
44	8.5571503	17.6627733	151.1430060	44	9.5010718	17.0428327	161.9251769	44	10.5464968	16.4578506	173.5726690
45	8.9850073	17.7740693	159.7001563	45	9.9988781	17.1428339	171.4262487	45	11.1265541	16.5477257	184.1191050
46	9.4342582	17.8800665	168.6651642	46	10.5243717	17.2378469	181.4261267	46	11.7385146	16.6329153	195.2457199
47	9.9059711	17.9810157	178.1194224	47	11.0774242	17.3281206	191.9509984	47	12.3841329	16.7136638	206.9842346
48	10.4012697	18.0771578	188.0253935	48	11.6589924	17.4138913	203.0284258	48	13.0653602	16.7902027	219.3683675
49	10.9213332	18.1687217	198.4266632	49	12.2710895	17.4953836	214.6874182	49	13.7838495	16.8627514	232.4336277
50	11.4673998	18.2559254	209.3479964	50	12.9153217	17.5728111	226.9585077	50	14.5419613	16.9315179	246.2174773

Table 1 341

M	C(5.75,M,1)	A(5.75,M,1)	S(5.75,M,1)	M	C(6.00,M,1)	A(6.00,M,1)	S(6.00,M,1)	M	C(6.25,M,1)	A(6.25,M,1)	S(6.25,M,1)
1/12	1.0046698	.0808371	.0812146	1/12	1.0048676	.0807329	.0811258	1/12	1.0050648	.0806290	.0810374
1/4	1.0140750	.2413858	.2447833	1/4	1.0146738	.2410273	.2445641	1/4	1.0152716	.2406701	.2443455
1/2	1.0283482	.4794213	.4930120	1/2	1.0295630	.4785690	.4927169	1/2	1.0307764	.4777200	.4924225
1	1.0575000	.9456265	1.0000000	1	1.0600000	.9433962	1.0000000	1	1.0625000	.9411765	1.0000000
2	1.1183063	1.8398359	2.0575000	2	1.1236000	1.8333927	2.0600000	2	1.1289063	1.8269896	2.0625000
3	1.1826089	2.6854240	3.1758063	3	1.1910160	2.6730119	3.1836000	3	1.1994629	2.6606961	3.1914063
4	1.2506089	3.4850345	4.3584151	4	1.2624770	3.4651056	4.3746160	4	1.2744293	3.4453610	4.3908691
5	1.3225189	4.2411674	5.6090240	5	1.3382256	4.2123638	5.6370930	5	1.3540812	4.1838692	5.6652985
6	1.3985637	4.9561867	6.9315429	6	1.4185191	4.9173243	6.9753185	6	1.4387112	4.8789357	7.0193796
7	1.4789811	5.6323278	8.3301066	7	1.5036303	5.5823814	8.3938377	7	1.5286307	5.5331160	8.4580908
8	1.5640225	6.2717048	9.8090877	8	1.5938481	6.2097938	9.8974679	8	1.6241701	6.1488150	9.9867215
9	1.6533538	6.8763166	11.3731102	9	1.6894790	6.8016923	11.4913160	9	1.7250807	6.7282965	11.6108916
10	1.7490562	7.4480535	13.0270641	10	1.7908477	7.3600870	13.1807949	10	1.8335358	7.2736908	13.3365723
11	1.8496269	7.9887031	14.7761203	11	1.8982986	7.8868746	14.9716426	11	1.9481318	7.7870031	15.1701081
12	1.9559805	8.4999556	16.6257472	12	2.0121965	8.3838439	16.8699412	12	2.0698900	8.2701206	17.1182399
13	2.0684493	8.9834096	18.5817277	13	2.1329283	8.8526830	18.8821377	13	2.1992581	8.7248194	19.1881299
14	2.1873852	9.4405764	20.6501770	14	2.2609040	9.2949839	21.0150659	14	2.3357118	9.1527712	21.3873880
15	2.3131598	9.8728855	22.8375622	15	2.3965582	9.7122490	23.2759699	15	2.4827562	9.5555494	23.7240997
16	2.4461665	10.2816684	25.1507220	16	2.5403517	10.1058953	25.6725281	16	2.6379285	9.9346347	26.2068560
17	2.5868211	10.6682633	27.5968885	17	2.6927728	10.4772597	28.2128798	17	2.8027990	10.2914209	28.8447845
18	2.7355633	11.0338187	30.1837096	18	2.8543392	10.8276035	30.9056526	18	2.9779740	10.6272196	31.6475835
19	2.8928582	11.3794976	32.9192729	19	3.0255995	11.1581165	33.7599917	19	3.1640973	10.9432655	34.6255575
20	3.0591975	11.7063807	35.8121311	20	3.2071355	11.4699212	36.7855912	20	3.3618534	11.2407205	37.7896548
21	3.2351014	12.0154900	38.8713287	21	3.3995636	11.7640766	39.9927267	21	3.5719693	11.5206781	41.1515083
22	3.4211197	12.3077920	42.1064301	22	3.6035374	12.0415817	43.3922903	22	3.7952174	11.7841677	44.7234775
23	3.6178341	12.5842005	45.5275498	23	3.8197497	12.3033790	46.9958278	23	4.0324184	12.0321578	48.5186949
24	3.8275596	12.8455796	49.1453739	24	4.0489347	12.5503575	50.8155774	24	4.2844446	12.2655603	52.5511133
25	4.0453465	13.0927467	52.9712435	25	4.2918707	12.7833561	54.8645121	25	4.5522224	12.4852332	56.8355579
26	4.2784827	13.3264744	57.0170900	26	4.5493830	13.0031662	59.1563828	26	4.8367363	12.6919842	61.3877803
27	4.5244954	13.5474935	61.2955727	27	4.8223460	13.2105341	63.7057658	27	5.1390323	12.8865733	66.2245166
28	4.7845539	13.7564951	65.8200681	28	5.1116867	13.4061643	68.5281117	28	5.4602218	13.0697161	71.3635488
29	5.0597715	13.9541325	70.6047220	29	5.4183879	13.5907210	73.6397984	29	5.8014857	13.2420857	76.8237707
30	5.3507084	14.1410236	75.6644936	30	5.7434912	13.7648311	79.0581864	30	6.1640785	13.4043160	82.6252563
31	5.6583741	14.3177528	81.0152019	31	6.0881007	13.9290860	84.8016775	31	6.5493334	13.5570033	88.7893349
32	5.9837306	14.4848726	86.6735761	32	6.4533867	14.0840434	90.8897782	32	6.9586668	13.7007090	95.3386683
33	6.3277951	14.6429056	92.6573067	33	6.8405899	14.2302296	97.3431649	33	7.3935835	13.8359614	102.2973351
34	6.6916434	14.7923457	98.9851018	34	7.2510253	14.3681411	104.1837548	34	7.8556824	13.9632578	109.6909185
35	7.0764129	14.9336602	105.6767452	35	7.6860868	14.4982463	111.4347801	35	8.3466626	14.0830661	117.5466009
36	7.4833066	15.0672910	112.7531581	36	8.1472520	14.6209871	119.1208669	36	8.8683290	14.1958269	125.8932635
37	7.9135967	15.1933558	120.2364647	37	8.6360871	14.7367803	127.2681190	37	9.4225995	14.3010543	134.7615925
38	8.3688285	15.3131497	128.1500614	38	9.1542524	14.8460191	135.9042061	38	10.0115120	14.4018398	144.1841920
39	8.8493247	15.4261463	136.5186899	39	9.7035075	14.9490747	145.0584585	39	10.6372315	14.4958492	154.1957041
40	9.3588896	15.5329988	145.3685146	40	10.2857180	15.0462969	154.7619660	40	11.3020585	14.5843287	164.8329356
41	9.8983143	15.6340414	154.7272042	41	10.9028611	15.1380159	165.0476840	41	12.0068431	14.6676034	176.1349941
42	10.4558811	15.7295900	164.6240185	42	11.5570327	15.2245433	175.9505450	42	12.7589645	14.7459797	188.1434312
43	11.0676692	15.8199433	175.0898996	43	12.2504547	15.3061729	187.5075778	43	13.5563998	14.8197456	200.9023957
44	11.7040602	15.9053837	186.1575688	44	12.9854820	15.3831820	199.7580324	44	14.4036747	14.8891723	214.4587954
45	12.3770437	15.9861784	197.8616290	45	13.7646109	15.4558321	212.7435144	45	15.3039044	14.9545151	228.8624702
46	13.0887237	16.0625801	210.2386727	46	14.5904875	15.5243699	226.5081253	46	16.2603984	15.0160142	244.1663746
47	13.8413253	16.1348275	223.3273964	47	15.4659168	15.5890282	241.0986128	47	17.2766733	15.0738958	260.4267730
48	14.6372015	16.2031466	237.1687218	48	16.3938718	15.6500266	256.5645296	48	18.3564654	15.1283725	277.7034464
49	15.4788406	16.2677509	251.8059233	49	17.3775041	15.7075723	272.9584014	49	19.5037445	15.1796447	296.0599118
50	16.3688740	16.3288425	267.2847639	50	18.4201544	15.7618606	290.3359055	50	20.7227286	15.2279009	315.5636563

Table 1

M	C(6.50,M,1)	A(6.50,M,1)	S(6.50,M,1)	M	C(6.75,M,1)	A(6.75,M,1)	S(6.75,M,1)	M	C(7.00,M,1)	A(7.00,M,1)	S(7.00,M,1)
1/12	1.0052617	.0805254	.0809491	1/12	1.0054581	.0804222	.0808612	1/12	1.0056541	.0803194	.0807735
1/4	1.0158683	.2403141	.2441275	1/4	1.0164639	.2399594	.2439100	1/4	1.0170585	.2396059	.2436932
1/2	1.0319884	.4768744	.4921288	1/2	1.0331989	.4760320	.4918358	1/2	1.0344080	.4751930	.4915435
1	1.0650000	.9389671	1.0000000	1	1.0675000	.9367681	1.0000000	1	1.0700000	.9345794	1.0000000
2	1.1342250	1.8206264	2.0650000	2	1.1395563	1.8143027	2.0675000	2	1.1449000	1.8080182	2.0700000
3	1.2079496	2.6484755	3.1992250	3	1.2164763	2.6363491	3.2070563	3	1.2250430	2.6243160	3.2149000
4	1.2854664	3.4257986	4.4071746	4	1.2975884	3.4064161	4.4235325	4	1.3107960	3.3872113	4.4399430
5	1.3700867	4.1556794	5.6936410	5	1.3862432	4.1277902	5.7221210	5	1.4025517	4.1001974	5.7507390
6	1.4591423	4.8410136	7.0637276	6	1.4798146	4.8035506	7.1083642	6	1.5007304	4.7665397	7.1532907
7	1.5539865	5.4845198	8.5228699	7	1.5797021	5.4365813	8.5881787	7	1.6057815	5.3892894	8.6540211
8	1.6549957	6.0887510	10.0768565	8	1.6863320	6.0295844	10.1678808	8	1.7181862	5.9712985	10.2598026
9	1.7625704	6.6561042	11.7318522	9	1.8001594	6.5850907	11.8542128	9	1.8384592	6.5152322	11.9779888
10	1.8771375	7.1888302	13.4944225	10	1.9216701	7.1054714	13.6543721	10	1.9671514	7.0235815	13.8164480
11	1.9991514	7.6890425	15.3715600	11	2.0513829	7.5929475	15.5760422	11	2.1048520	7.4986743	15.7835993
12	2.1290962	8.1587253	17.3707114	12	2.1898512	8.0495995	17.6274251	12	2.2521916	7.9426863	17.8884513
13	2.2674875	8.5997421	19.4998077	13	2.3376662	8.4773766	19.8172763	13	2.4098450	8.3576507	20.1406429
14	2.4148742	9.0138423	21.7672952	14	2.4954586	8.8781045	22.1549425	14	2.5785342	8.7454680	22.5504879
15	2.5718410	9.4026688	24.1821694	15	2.6639021	9.2534937	24.6504011	15	2.7590315	9.1079140	25.1290220
16	2.7390107	9.7677642	26.7540104	16	2.8437155	9.6051463	27.3143031	16	2.9521638	9.4466486	27.8880536
17	2.9170464	10.1105767	29.4930210	17	3.0356663	9.9345633	30.1580186	17	3.1583152	9.7632230	30.8402173
18	3.1066544	10.4324664	32.4100674	18	3.2405737	10.2431506	33.1936849	18	3.3799323	10.0590869	33.9990325
19	3.3085869	10.7347102	35.5167218	19	3.4593125	10.5322254	36.4342586	19	3.6165275	10.3355952	37.3789648
20	3.5233451	11.0185072	38.8253087	20	3.6928161	10.8030215	39.8935711	20	3.8698845	10.5940142	40.9954924
21	3.7526820	11.2849833	42.3489538	21	3.9420811	11.0566946	43.5863871	21	4.1405624	10.8355273	44.8651768
22	3.9966063	11.5351956	46.1016358	22	4.2081716	11.2943275	47.5284682	22	4.4304018	11.0612405	49.0057392
23	4.2563857	11.7701367	50.0982421	23	4.4922232	11.5169344	51.7366399	23	4.7405299	11.2721874	53.4361410
24	4.5330508	11.9907387	54.3546279	24	4.7954483	11.7254655	56.2288630	24	5.0723670	11.4693340	58.1766708
25	4.8276991	12.1978767	58.8876787	25	5.1191410	11.9208108	61.0243113	25	5.4274327	11.6535832	63.2490378
26	5.1414996	12.3923725	63.7153778	26	5.4648830	12.1038040	66.1434523	26	5.8073529	11.8257787	68.6764705
27	5.4756970	12.5749977	68.8568774	27	5.8335491	12.2752262	71.6081354	27	6.2138676	11.9867090	74.4838234
28	5.8316173	12.7464767	74.3325744	28	6.2273137	12.4358091	77.4416045	28	6.6488384	12.1371112	80.6976910
29	6.2106725	12.9074898	80.1641917	29	6.6476574	12.5862380	83.6689982	29	7.1142571	12.2776741	87.3465294
30	6.6143662	13.0586759	86.3748642	30	7.0963743	12.7271551	90.3166556	30	7.6122551	12.4090412	94.4607865
31	7.0443000	13.2006346	92.9892304	31	7.5753795	12.8591616	97.4130299	31	8.1451129	12.5318142	102.0730416
32	7.5021795	13.3339292	100.0335304	32	8.0867176	12.9828212	104.9884094	32	8.7152708	12.6465553	110.2181545
33	7.9893212	13.4590885	107.5357099	33	8.6325711	13.0986616	113.0751270	33	9.3253398	12.7537900	118.9334253
34	8.5091595	13.5766089	115.5255310	34	9.2152696	13.2071771	121.7076981	34	9.9781136	12.8540093	128.2587651
35	9.0622549	13.6869567	124.0346905	35	9.8373003	13.3088310	130.9229678	35	10.6765815	12.9476723	138.2368787
36	9.6513015	13.7905697	133.0969454	36	10.5013181	13.4040571	140.7602681	36	11.4239422	13.0352077	148.9134602
37	10.2786361	13.8878589	142.7482469	37	11.2101571	13.4932620	151.2615862	37	12.2236182	13.1170166	160.3374024
38	10.9467474	13.9792102	153.0268830	38	11.9668427	13.5768262	162.4717433	38	13.0792715	13.1934734	172.5610206
39	11.6582860	14.0649861	163.9736304	39	12.7746046	13.6551065	174.4385860	39	13.9948205	13.2649284	185.6402920
40	12.4160746	14.1455269	175.6319163	40	13.6368904	13.7284370	187.2131906	40	14.9744579	13.3317088	199.6351125
41	13.2231194	14.2211520	188.0479909	41	14.5573805	13.7971307	200.8500810	41	16.0226699	13.3941204	214.6095704
42	14.0026222	14.2921615	201.2711104	42	15.5400037	13.8614807	215.4074614	42	17.1442568	13.4524490	230.6322403
43	14.9979926	14.3588371	215.3537326	43	16.5889539	13.9217618	230.9474651	43	18.3443548	13.5069617	247.7764972
44	15.9728622	14.4214433	230.3517252	44	17.7087083	13.9782312	247.5364190	44	19.6284597	13.5579081	266.1208520
45	17.0110982	14.4802284	246.3245874	45	18.9040461	14.0311299	265.2451273	45	21.0024518	13.6055216	285.7493117
46	18.1168196	14.5354257	263.3356856	46	20.1800692	14.0806838	284.1491735	46	22.4726235	13.6500202	306.7517635
47	19.2944129	14.5872542	281.4525051	47	21.5422239	14.1271042	304.3292427	47	24.0457071	13.6916076	329.2243870
48	20.5485497	14.6359194	300.7469180	48	22.9963240	14.1705894	325.8714666	48	25.7289066	13.7304744	353.2700941
49	21.8842054	14.6816145	321.2954677	49	24.5485759	14.2113250	348.8677906	49	27.5299301	13.7667985	378.9990008
50	23.3066788	14.7245207	343.1796731	50	26.2056048	14.2494848	373.4163665	50	29.4570252	13.8007463	406.5289309

Table 1

M	C(7.25,M,1)	A(7.25,M,1)	S(7.25,M,1)	M	C(7.50,M,1)	A(7.50,M,1)	S(7.50,M,1)	M	C(7.75,M,1)	A(7.75,M,1)	S(7.75,M,1)
1/12	1.0058497	.0802168	.0806861	1/12	1.0060449	.0801146	.0805989	1/12	1.0062397	.0800128	.0805120
1/4	1.0176521	.2392537	.2434770	1/4	1.0182446	.2389027	.2432613	1/4	1.0188361	.2385529	.2430463
1/2	1.0356158	.4743573	.4912518	1/2	1.0369221	.4735247	.4909609	1/2	1.0380270	.4726955	.4906706
1	1.0725000	.9324009	1.0000000	1	1.0750000	.9302326	1.0000000	1	1.0775000	.9280742	1.0000000
2	1.1502563	1.8017724	2.0725000	2	1.1556250	1.7955652	2.0750000	2	1.1510063	1.7893961	2.0775000
3	1.2336498	2.6123752	3.2227563	3	1.2422969	2.6005257	3.2306250	3	1.2509842	2.5887666	3.2385063
4	1.3230894	3.3681820	4.4564061	4	1.3354691	3.3493263	4.4729219	4	1.3479355	3.3306419	4.4894905
5	1.4190134	4.0728970	5.7794955	5	1.4356293	4.0458849	5.8083910	5	1.4524005	4.0191572	5.8374260
6	1.5218919	4.7299739	7.1985089	6	1.5433015	4.6938464	7.2440203	6	1.5649616	4.6581505	7.2898265
7	1.6322291	5.3426330	8.7204008	7	1.6590491	5.2966013	8.7873219	7	1.6862461	5.2511838	8.8547881
8	1.7505657	5.9138769	10.3526299	8	1.7834778	5.8573036	10.4463710	8	1.8169301	5.8015627	10.5410341
9	1.8774817	6.4465053	12.1031956	9	1.9172387	6.3788870	12.2298488	9	1.9577422	6.3123552	12.3579643
10	2.0135991	6.9431285	13.9806773	10	2.0610316	6.8640810	14.1470875	10	2.1094673	6.7864085	14.3157065
11	2.1595850	7.4061804	15.9942764	11	2.2156089	7.3154241	16.2081191	11	2.2729510	7.2263652	16.4251738
12	2.3161550	7.8379304	18.1538614	12	2.3817796	7.7352783	18.4237280	12	2.4491047	7.6346777	18.6981248
13	2.4840762	8.2404946	20.4700164	13	2.5604131	8.1258403	20.8055076	13	2.6369103	8.0136220	21.1472294
14	2.6641717	8.6158458	22.9540925	14	2.7524441	8.4891537	23.3659207	14	2.8434258	8.3653104	23.7861397
15	2.8573242	8.9658235	25.6182642	15	2.9588774	8.8271197	26.1183647	15	3.0637913	8.6917034	26.6295655
16	3.0644302	9.2921432	28.4755884	16	3.1807932	9.1415067	29.0772421	16	3.3012352	8.9946203	29.6933569
17	3.2865550	9.5964039	31.5400686	17	3.4193526	9.4339598	32.2580352	17	3.5570809	9.2757497	32.9945920
18	3.5249375	9.8800969	34.8267235	18	3.6758041	9.7060091	35.6773879	18	3.8327547	9.5366587	36.5516729
19	3.7804954	10.1446125	38.3516610	19	3.9514894	9.9590782	39.3531920	19	4.1297931	9.7788016	40.3844276
20	4.0545813	10.3912470	42.1321564	20	4.2478511	10.1944914	43.3046814	20	4.4498521	10.0035281	44.5142207
21	4.3485385	10.6212094	46.1867378	21	4.5664399	10.4134803	47.5525325	21	4.7947156	10.2120911	48.9640728
22	4.6638075	10.8356264	50.5352763	22	4.9089229	10.6171910	52.1189724	22	5.1663061	10.4056530	53.7587885
23	5.0019336	11.0355491	55.1990838	23	5.2770922	10.8066893	57.0278954	23	5.5666948	10.5852928	58.9250946
24	5.3653738	11.2219572	60.2010174	24	5.6728741	10.9829668	62.3049875	24	5.9981137	10.7520118	64.4917894
25	5.7535054	11.3957643	65.5655912	25	6.0983396	11.1469459	67.9778616	25	6.4629675	10.9067395	70.4899031
26	6.1705345	11.5578222	71.3190965	26	6.5557151	11.2994845	74.0762012	26	6.9638475	11.0503383	76.9528706
27	6.6180055	11.7089251	77.4897310	27	7.0473937	11.4413809	80.6319163	27	7.5035457	11.1836086	83.9167181
28	7.0978109	11.8498136	84.1077365	28	7.5759483	11.5733798	87.6793101	28	8.0850704	11.3072934	91.4202637
29	7.6124022	11.9811782	91.2055474	29	8.1441444	11.6961652	95.2552583	29	8.7118634	11.4220820	99.5053342
30	8.1643014	12.1036627	98.8179496	30	8.7549552	11.8103863	103.3994027	30	9.3868173	11.5286144	108.2169976
31	8.7562132	12.2178673	106.9822510	31	9.4115769	11.9166384	112.1543579	31	10.1142957	11.6274844	117.6038149
32	9.3910387	12.3243518	115.7384642	32	10.1174451	12.0154776	121.5659348	32	10.8981536	11.7192430	127.7181106
33	10.0718890	12.4236380	125.1295029	33	10.8762535	12.1074210	131.6833799	33	11.7427605	11.8044019	138.6162642
34	10.8021009	12.5162126	135.2013918	34	11.6919725	12.1929497	142.5596334	34	12.6528244	11.8834356	150.3590247
35	11.5852532	12.6025292	146.0034928	35	12.5688705	12.2725114	154.2516059	35	13.6334183	11.9567848	163.0118491
36	12.4251841	12.6830109	157.5887460	36	13.5115357	12.3465222	166.8204764	36	14.6900082	12.0248583	176.6452674
37	13.3260099	12.7580522	170.0139301	37	14.5249009	12.4153695	180.3320121	37	15.8284839	12.0880355	191.3352756
38	14.2921457	12.8280207	183.3399401	38	15.6142685	12.4794135	194.8569131	38	17.0551914	12.1466687	207.1637595
39	15.3283262	12.8932594	197.6320857	39	16.7853386	12.5389893	210.4711816	39	18.3769687	12.2010846	224.2189509
40	16.4356299	12.9540880	212.9604120	40	18.0442390	12.5944086	227.2565202	40	19.8011838	12.2515867	242.5959196
41	17.6315031	13.0108046	229.4000419	41	19.3975570	12.6459615	245.3007592	41	21.3357755	12.2984563	262.3971034
42	18.9097870	13.0636873	247.0315449	42	20.8523737	12.6939177	264.6983162	42	22.9892981	12.3419548	283.7328790
43	20.2807466	13.1129952	265.9413319	43	22.4163018	12.7385281	285.5506899	43	24.7709688	12.3823247	306.7221771
44	21.7511007	13.1589698	286.2220785	44	24.0975244	12.7800261	307.9669917	44	26.6907188	12.4197909	331.4931459
45	23.3280555	13.2018367	307.9731793	45	25.9048387	12.8186290	332.0645161	45	28.7592496	12.4545623	358.1838347
46	25.0193396	13.2418058	331.3012348	46	27.8477017	12.8545386	357.9693549	46	30.9880914	12.4868327	386.9431143
47	26.8332417	13.2790730	356.3205743	47	29.9362793	12.8879429	385.8170565	47	33.3896685	12.5167821	417.9312056
48	28.7786517	13.3138210	383.1538160	48	32.1815002	12.9190166	415.7533358	48	35.9773678	12.5445774	451.3208741
49	30.8651040	13.3462200	411.9324677	49	34.5951127	12.9479224	447.9348360	49	38.7656138	12.5703734	487.2982419
50	33.1028240	13.3764289	442.7975717	50	37.1897462	12.9748116	482.5299488	50	41.7699489	12.5943141	526.0638557

Table 1

M	C(8.00,M,1)	A(8.00,M,1)	S(8.00,M,1)	M	C(8.25,M,1)	A(8.25,M,1)	S(8.25,M,1)	M	C(8.50,M,1)	A(8.50,M,1)	S(8.50,M,1)
1/12	1.0064340	.0799112	.0804254	1/12	1.0066280	.0798100	.0803390	1/12	1.0068215	.0797091	.0802529
1/4	1.0194265	.2382043	.2428318	1/4	1.0200160	.2378570	.2426180	1/4	1.0206044	.2375109	.2424047
1/2	1.0392305	.4718694	.4903811	1/2	1.0404326	.4710465	.4900921	1/2	1.0416333	.4702268	.4898039
1	1.0800000	.9259259	1.0000000	1	1.0825000	.9237875	1.0000000	1	1.0850000	.9216590	1.0000000
2	1.1664000	1.7832647	2.0800000	2	1.1718063	1.7771709	2.0825000	2	1.1772250	1.7711143	2.0850000
3	1.2597120	2.5770970	3.2464000	3	1.2684803	2.5655159	3.2543063	3	1.2772891	2.5540224	3.2622250
4	1.3604890	3.3121268	4.5061120	4	1.3731299	3.2937791	4.5227865	4	1.3858587	3.2755967	4.5395141
5	1.4693281	3.9927100	5.8666010	5	1.4864131	3.9665396	5.8959164	5	1.5036567	3.9406421	5.9253728
6	1.5868743	4.6228797	7.3359290	6	1.6090422	4.5880273	7.3823295	6	1.6314675	4.5535872	7.4290295
7	1.7138243	5.2063701	8.9228034	7	1.7417882	5.1621500	8.9913717	7	1.7701422	5.1185135	9.0604970
8	1.8509302	5.7466389	10.6366276	8	1.8854857	5.6925173	10.7331599	8	1.9206043	5.6391830	10.8306393
9	1.9990046	6.2468879	12.4875578	9	2.0410383	6.1824640	12.6186455	9	2.0830557	6.1190626	12.7512436
10	2.1539250	6.7100814	14.4865625	10	2.2094239	6.6350707	14.6596838	10	2.2609834	6.5613481	14.8350993
11	2.3316390	7.1389643	16.6454875	11	2.3917014	7.0531831	16.8691077	11	2.4531670	6.9689844	17.0960828
12	2.5181701	7.5360780	18.9771265	12	2.5890168	7.4394301	19.2608091	12	2.6616862	7.3446861	19.5492498
13	2.7196237	7.9037759	21.4952966	13	2.8026106	7.7962403	21.8498259	13	2.8879296	7.6909549	22.2109360
14	2.9371936	8.2442370	24.2149203	14	3.0338260	8.1258570	24.6524365	14	3.1334036	8.0100967	25.0988656
15	3.1721691	8.5594787	27.1521139	15	3.2841167	8.4303529	27.6862625	15	3.3997429	8.3042366	28.2322692
16	3.4259426	8.8513691	30.3242831	16	3.5550563	8.7116424	30.9703792	16	3.6887210	8.5753332	31.6320121
17	3.7000181	9.1216381	33.7502257	17	3.8483484	8.9714942	34.5254355	17	4.0022623	8.8251919	35.3207331
18	3.9960195	9.3718871	37.4502438	18	4.1658372	9.2115419	38.3737839	18	4.3424546	9.0554764	39.3229954
19	4.3157011	9.6035992	41.4462633	19	4.5095187	9.4332951	42.5396211	19	4.7115633	9.2677202	43.6654500
20	4.6609572	9.8181474	45.7619643	20	4.8815540	9.6381479	47.0491398	20	5.1120461	9.4633366	48.3770133
21	5.0338337	10.0168031	50.4229215	21	5.2842822	9.8273884	51.9306938	21	5.5465701	9.6436282	53.4890594
22	5.4365404	10.2007437	55.4567552	22	5.7202355	10.0022063	57.2149761	22	6.0180285	9.8097956	59.0356205
23	5.8714637	10.3710589	60.8932957	23	6.1921550	10.1637010	62.9352116	23	6.5295609	9.9629452	65.0536580
24	6.3411808	10.5287583	66.7647593	24	6.7030078	10.3128878	69.1273666	24	7.0845736	10.1040970	71.5832189
25	6.8484752	10.6747762	73.1059401	25	7.2560059	10.4507046	75.8303743	25	7.6867624	10.2341908	78.6677925
26	7.3963532	10.8099779	79.9544153	26	7.8546264	10.5780181	83.0863602	26	8.3401372	10.3540929	86.3545549
27	7.9880615	10.9351648	87.3507685	27	8.5026331	10.6956288	90.9410066	27	9.0490488	10.4646017	94.6946921
28	8.6271064	11.0510785	95.3388300	28	9.2041003	10.8042760	99.4436397	28	9.8182180	10.5664532	103.7437409
29	9.3172749	11.1584060	103.9659364	29	9.9634386	10.9046429	108.6477399	29	10.6527665	10.6603255	113.5619589
30	10.0626569	11.2577833	113.2832113	30	10.7854222	10.9973607	118.6111785	30	11.5582517	10.7468438	124.2147254
31	10.8676695	11.3497994	123.3458682	31	11.6752196	11.0830122	129.3966007	31	12.5407031	10.8265642	135.7729771
32	11.7370830	11.4349994	134.2135377	32	12.6384252	11.1621360	141.0718203	32	13.6086628	10.9000776	148.3136802
33	12.6760497	11.5138884	145.9506207	33	13.6810953	11.2352295	153.7102455	33	14.7632292	10.9678134	161.9203430
34	13.6901336	11.5869343	158.6266704	34	14.8097856	11.3027524	167.3913408	34	16.0181037	11.0302428	176.6835722
35	14.7853443	11.6545682	172.3168041	35	16.0315929	11.3651293	182.2011264	35	17.3796425	11.0877814	192.7016758
36	15.9681719	11.7171928	187.1021484	36	17.3541994	11.4227522	198.2327194	36	18.8569121	11.1408123	210.0813183
37	17.2456256	11.7751785	203.0703203	37	18.7859208	11.4759836	215.5869187	37	20.4597496	11.1896888	228.9382304
38	18.6252757	11.8288690	220.3159459	38	20.3357593	11.5251580	234.3728395	38	22.1983283	11.2347362	249.3979800
39	20.1152978	11.8785824	238.9412216	39	22.0134594	11.5705848	254.7085988	39	24.0857287	11.2762546	271.5968083
40	21.7245216	11.9246133	280.7810410	40	23.8295698	11.6125495	276.7220583	40	26.1330157	11.3145203	295.6825370
41	23.4624833	11.9672346	280.7810410	41	25.7955093	11.6513159	300.5516281	41	28.3543220	11.3497883	321.8155527
42	25.3394820	12.0066987	304.2435243	42	27.9236389	11.6871278	326.3471374	42	30.7644394	11.3822934	350.1698747
43	27.3666405	12.0432395	329.5830062	43	30.2273391	11.7202105	354.2707763	43	33.3794167	11.4122520	380.9343141
44	29.5559718	12.0770736	356.9496468	44	32.7210946	11.7507718	384.4981154	44	36.2166672	11.4398636	414.3137308
45	31.9204495	12.1084015	386.5056186	45	35.4205849	11.7790040	417.2192099	45	39.2950839	11.4653120	450.5303980
46	34.4740855	12.1374088	418.4260681	46	38.3427831	11.8050845	452.6397948	46	42.6351660	11.4887668	489.8254819
47	37.2320123	12.1642674	452.9001536	47	41.5060627	11.8291774	490.9825779	47	46.2591551	11.5103842	532.4606479
48	40.2105733	12.1891365	490.1321659	48	44.9303129	11.8514341	532.4886406	48	50.1911833	11.5303080	578.7198030
49	43.4274192	12.2121634	530.3427392	49	48.6370637	11.8719945	577.4189536	49	54.4574339	11.5486710	628.9109863
50	46.9016127	12.2334846	573.7701584	50	52.6496215	11.8909880	626.0560173	50	59.0863158	11.5655954	683.3684202

Table 1

M	C(8.75,M,1)	A(8.75,M,1)	S(8.75,M,1)	M	C(9.00,M,1)	A(9.00,M,1)	S(9.00,M,1)	M	C(9.25,M,1)	A(9.25,M,1)	S(9.25,M,1)
1/12	1.0070146	.0796086	.0801670	1/12	1.0072073	.0795083	.0800814	1/12	1.0073996	.0794084	.0799960
1/4	1.0211918	.2371660	.2421919	1/4	1.0217782	.2368222	.2419798	1/4	1.0223636	.2364797	.2417682
1/2	1.0428327	.4694103	.4895164	1/2	1.0440307	.4685968	.4892295	1/2	1.0452272	.4677865	.4889432
1	1.0875000	.9195402	1.0000000	1	1.0900000	.9174312	1.0000000	1	1.0925000	.9153318	1.0000000
2	1.1826563	1.7650945	2.0875000	2	1.1881000	1.7591112	2.0900000	2	1.1935563	1.7531641	2.0925000
3	1.2861387	2.5426416	3.2701563	3	1.2950290	2.5312947	3.2781000	3	1.3039602	2.5200587	3.2860563
4	1.3986758	3.2575776	4.5562949	4	1.4115816	3.2397199	4.5731290	4	1.4245765	3.2220217	4.5900165
5	1.5210599	3.9150138	5.9549707	5	1.5386240	3.8896513	5.9847106	5	1.5563499	3.8645507	6.0145930
6	1.6541527	4.5195530	7.4760307	6	1.6771001	4.4859186	7.5233346	6	1.7003122	4.4526780	7.5709428
7	1.7988910	5.0754510	9.1301834	7	1.8280391	5.0329528	9.2004347	7	1.8575911	4.9910096	9.2712550
8	1.9562940	5.5866216	10.9290744	8	1.9925626	5.5348191	11.0284738	8	2.0294183	5.4837617	11.1288461
9	2.1274697	6.0566635	12.8853684	9	2.1718933	5.9952469	13.0210364	9	2.2171395	5.9347933	13.1582644
10	2.3136233	6.4888860	15.0128381	10	2.3673637	6.4176577	15.1929297	10	2.4222249	6.3476369	15.3754039
11	2.5160654	6.8863320	17.3264615	11	2.5804264	6.8051905	17.5602934	11	2.6462807	6.7255258	17.7976287
12	2.7362211	7.2517995	19.8425269	12	2.8126648	7.1607253	20.1407198	12	2.8910616	7.0714195	20.4439094
13	2.9756404	7.5878616	22.5787480	13	3.0658046	7.4869039	22.9533846	13	3.1584848	7.3880270	23.3349710
14	3.2360090	7.8968842	25.5543884	14	3.3417270	7.7861504	26.0191892	14	3.4506447	7.6778279	26.4934558
15	3.5191598	8.1810430	28.7903974	15	3.6424825	8.0606884	29.3609162	15	3.7698293	7.9430919	29.9441005
16	3.8270863	8.4423384	32.3095572	16	3.9703059	8.3125582	33.0033987	16	4.1185385	8.1858965	33.7139298
17	4.1619563	8.6826100	36.1366434	17	4.3276334	8.5436314	36.9737046	17	4.4995033	8.4081432	37.8324683
18	4.5261275	8.9035494	40.2985997	18	4.7171204	8.7556251	41.3013380	18	4.9157074	8.6115727	42.3319716
19	4.9221636	9.1067121	44.8247272	19	5.1416613	8.9501148	46.0184584	19	5.3704103	8.7977782	47.2476790
20	5.3528530	9.2935284	49.7468909	20	5.6044108	9.1285457	51.1601197	20	5.8671733	8.9682181	52.6180893
21	5.8212276	9.4653135	55.0997438	21	6.1088077	9.2922437	56.7645305	21	6.4098868	9.1242271	58.4852626
22	6.3305850	9.6232767	60.9209714	22	6.7186004	9.4424254	62.8733382	22	7.0025013	9.2670271	64.8951493
23	6.8845112	9.7685303	67.2515564	23	7.2578745	9.5802068	69.5319387	23	7.6505604	9.3977364	71.8979507
24	7.4869059	9.9020969	74.1360676	24	7.9110832	9.7066118	76.7898132	24	8.3582373	9.5173789	79.5485111
25	8.1420102	10.0249166	81.6229735	25	8.6230807	9.8225796	84.7008964	25	9.1313742	9.6268914	87.9067484
26	8.8544361	10.1378544	89.7649837	26	9.3991579	9.9289721	93.3239770	26	9.9760264	9.7271317	97.0381226
27	9.6291992	10.2417052	98.6194198	27	10.2450822	10.0265799	102.7231350	27	10.8988088	9.8188849	107.0141490
28	10.4717542	10.3372002	108.2486190	28	11.1671396	10.1161284	112.9682171	28	11.9058486	9.9028695	117.9129578
29	11.3880327	10.4250116	118.7203732	29	12.1721821	10.1982829	124.1353567	29	13.0083414	9.9797432	129.8199064
30	12.3844855	10.5057578	130.1084059	30	13.2676785	10.2736540	136.3075388	30	14.2116129	10.0501082	142.8282477
31	13.4681280	10.5800072	142.4928914	31	14.4617696	10.3428019	149.5752173	31	15.5261871	10.1145155	157.0398607
32	14.6465892	10.6482825	155.9610194	32	15.7633288	10.4062402	164.0369869	32	16.9623594	10.1734696	172.5660478
33	15.9281658	10.7110644	170.6076086	33	17.1820284	10.4644406	179.8003157	33	18.5313777	10.2274321	189.5284072
34	17.3218803	10.7687948	186.5357744	34	18.7284110	10.5178354	196.9823441	34	20.2455301	10.2768257	208.0597849
35	18.8375448	10.8218803	203.8576547	35	20.4139680	10.5668215	215.7107551	35	22.1182417	10.3220373	228.3053151
36	20.4858300	10.8706945	222.6951995	36	22.2512251	10.6117628	236.1247231	36	24.1641790	10.3634209	250.4235567
37	22.2783401	10.9155812	243.1810295	37	24.2538354	10.6529934	258.3759482	37	26.3993656	10.4013005	274.5877357
38	24.2276949	10.9568562	265.4593696	38	26.4366806	10.6908196	282.6297836	38	28.8413069	10.4359730	300.9871013
39	26.3476182	10.9948103	289.6870645	39	28.8159818	10.7255226	309.0664641	39	31.5091278	10.4677099	329.8284082
40	28.6530348	11.0297106	316.0346826	40	31.4094202	10.7573602	337.8824459	40	34.4237221	10.4967596	361.3375360
41	31.1601753	11.0618029	344.6877174	41	34.2362680	10.7865690	369.2918661	41	37.6079164	10.5233498	395.7612591
42	33.8866906	11.0913130	375.8478927	42	37.3175321	10.8133660	403.5281341	42	41.0866487	10.5476886	433.3691746
43	36.8517761	11.1184487	409.7345833	43	40.6761100	10.8379505	440.8456662	43	44.8871637	10.5699666	474.4558232
44	40.0763065	11.1434011	446.5863594	44	44.3369599	10.8605050	481.5217762	44	49.0392263	10.5903585	519.3429869
45	43.5829833	11.1663459	486.6626659	45	48.3272863	10.8811973	525.8587361	45	53.5733548	10.6090238	568.3822133
46	47.3964944	11.1874445	530.2456492	46	52.6757421	10.9001810	574.1860224	46	58.5310751	10.6261087	621.9575681
47	51.5436876	11.2068455	577.6421436	47	57.4176489	10.9175972	626.8627645	47	63.9451996	10.6417471	680.4886432
48	56.0537603	11.2246855	629.1858312	48	62.5852373	10.9335754	684.2804134	48	69.8601305	10.6560614	744.4338427
49	60.9584643	11.2410901	685.2395915	49	68.2179086	10.9482344	746.8656506	49	76.3221926	10.6691638	814.2939733
50	66.2923300	11.2561748	746.1980558	50	74.3575204	10.9616829	815.0835593	50	83.3819954	10.6811568	890.6161659

Table 1

M	C(9.50,M,1)	A(9.50,M,1)	S(9.50,M,1)	M	C(9.75,M,1)	A(9.75,M,1)	S(9.75,M,1)	M	C(10.00,M,1)	A(10.00,M,1)	S(10.00,M,1)
1/12	1.0075915	.0793088	.0799109	1/12	1.0077830	.0792095	.0798260	1/12	1.0079741	.0791106	.0797414
1/4	1.0229479	.2361383	.2415572	1/4	1.0235313	.2357981	.2413468	1/4	1.0241137	.2354591	.2411369
1/2	1.0464225	.4669793	.4886577	1/2	1.0476163	.4661752	.4883727	1/2	1.0480088	.4653741	.4880885
1	1.0950000	.9132420	1.0000000	1	1.0975000	.9111617	1.0000000	1	1.1000000	.9090909	1.0000000
2	1.1990250	1.7472530	2.0950000	2	1.2045063	1.7413774	2.0975000	2	1.2100000	1.7355372	2.1000000
3	1.3129324	2.5089068	3.2940250	3	1.3219456	2.4978382	3.3020063	3	1.3310000	2.4868520	3.3100000
4	1.4376610	3.2044811	4.6069574	4	1.4533353	3.1870963	4.6239519	4	1.4641000	3.1698654	4.6410000
5	1.5742387	3.8397088	6.0446183	5	1.5922917	3.8151219	6.0747872	5	1.6105100	3.7907868	6.1051000
6	1.7237914	4.4198254	7.6188571	6	1.7475402	4.3873548	7.6670789	6	1.7715610	4.3552607	7.7156100
7	1.8875516	4.9496122	9.3426485	7	1.9179254	4.9087516	9.4146191	7	1.9487171	4.8684188	9.4871710
8	2.0668690	5.4334358	11.2302001	8	2.1049231	5.3838283	11.3325445	8	2.1435888	5.3349262	11.4358881
9	2.2632216	5.8752838	13.2970691	9	2.3101531	5.8167000	13.4374676	9	2.3579477	5.7590238	13.5794769
10	2.4762276	6.2787980	15.5602907	10	2.5353930	6.2111162	15.7476207	10	2.5937425	6.1445671	15.9374246
11	2.7136592	6.6473041	18.0385183	11	2.7825938	6.5704931	18.2830137	11	2.8531167	6.4950610	18.5311671
12	2.9714569	6.9838394	20.7521775	12	3.0536967	6.8979436	21.0656075	12	3.1384284	6.8136918	21.3842838
13	3.2537453	7.2911775	23.7236344	13	3.3516517	7.1963040	24.1195042	13	3.4522712	7.1033562	24.5227122
14	3.5628511	7.5718516	26.9773797	14	3.6784377	7.4681585	27.4711559	14	3.7974983	7.3666875	27.9749834
15	3.9013219	7.8281750	30.5402307	15	4.0370854	7.7158620	31.1495936	15	4.1772482	7.6060795	31.7724817
16	4.2719475	8.0622603	34.4415527	16	4.4307012	7.9415599	35.1866790	16	4.5949730	7.8237086	35.9497299
17	4.6777825	8.2760368	38.7135002	17	4.8626946	8.1472072	39.6173802	17	5.0544703	8.0215533	40.5447029
18	5.1221719	8.4712665	43.3912827	18	5.3368073	8.3345851	44.4800748	18	5.5599173	8.2014121	45.5991732
19	5.6087782	8.6495584	48.5134545	19	5.8571460	8.5053168	49.8168821	19	6.1159091	8.3649201	51.1590905
20	6.1416121	8.8123821	54.1222327	20	6.4282177	8.6608809	55.6740281	20	6.7275000	8.5135637	57.2749996
21	6.7250653	8.9610796	60.2638449	21	7.0549690	8.8026249	62.1022458	21	7.4002500	8.6486943	64.0024995
22	7.3639465	9.0968763	66.9889101	22	7.?428284	8.9317767	69.1572148	22	8.1402750	8.7715403	71.4027495
23	8.0635214	9.2208916	74.3528566	23	8.4977542	9.0494549	76.9000432	23	8.9543025	8.8832184	79.5430244
24	8.8205559	9.3341476	82.4163780	24	9.3262853	9.1566787	85.3977974	24	9.8497327	8.9847440	88.4973269
25	9.6683637	9.4375777	91.2459339	25	10.2355981	9.2543769	94.7240827	25	10.8347060	9.0770400	98.3470596
26	10.5868583	9.5320344	100.9142976	26	11.2335689	9.3433958	104.9596808	26	11.9181766	9.1609455	109.1817655
27	11.5926098	9.6182963	111.5011559	27	12.3283419	9.4245065	116.1932497	27	13.1099942	9.2372231	121.0999421
28	12.6939078	9.6970742	123.0937657	28	13.5309039	9.4984113	128.5220915	28	14.4209936	9.3065665	134.2099363
29	13.8998290	9.7690176	135.7876735	29	14.8501671	9.5657507	142.0529954	29	15.8630930	9.3696059	148.6309300
30	15.2203127	9.8347192	149.6875025	30	16.2980584	9.6271077	156.9031625	30	17.4494023	9.4269145	164.4940230
31	16.6662425	9.8947208	164.9078152	31	17.8871191	9.6830138	173.2012209	31	19.1943425	9.4790131	181.9434253
32	18.2495355	9.9495167	181.5740577	32	19.6311132	9.7339534	191.0883399	32	21.1137768	9.5263756	201.1377679
33	19.9832414	9.9995586	199.8235932	33	21.5451467	9.7803675	210.7194531	33	23.2251545	9.5694323	222.2515447
34	21.8816493	10.0452590	219.8068345	34	23.6457985	9.8226583	232.2645998	34	25.5476699	9.6085749	245.4766992
35	23.9604060	10.0869945	241.6884339	35	25.9512639	9.8611921	255.9103983	35	28.1024369	9.6441590	271.0243691
36	26.2366446	10.1251091	265.6488898	36	28.4815121	9.8963026	281.8616621	36	30.9126806	9.6765081	299.1268060
37	28.7291258	10.1599170	291.8855344	37	31.2584595	9.9282939	310.3431742	37	34.0039487	9.7053165	330.0394867
38	31.4583928	10.1917050	320.6146602	38	34.3061593	9.9574432	341.6016338	38	37.4043436	9.7326514	364.0434354
39	34.4469401	10.2207352	352.0730529	39	37.6510099	9.9840029	375.9077931	39	41.1447779	9.7569558	401.4477789
40	37.7193994	10.2472468	386.5199930	40	41.3219833	10.0082031	413.5588029	40	45.2592557	9.7790507	442.5925569
41	41.3027423	10.2714582	424.2393924	41	45.3508767	10.0302534	454.8807863	41	49.7851813	9.7991370	487.8518126
42	45.?265028	10.2935692	465.5421347	42	49.7725872	10.0503448	500.2316630	42	54.7636994	9.8173973	537.6369939
43	49.5230206	10.3137618	510.7686376	43	54.6254144	10.0686513	550.0042502	43	60.2400694	9.8339975	592.4006934
44	54.2277076	10.3322025	560.2916582	44	59.9513924	10.0853315	604.6296646	44	66.2640763	9.8490887	652.6407628
45	59.3793398	10.3490434	614.5193658	45	65.7966531	10.1005298	664.5810570	45	72.8904840	9.8628079	718.9048091
46	65.0203771	10.3644232	673.8987056	46	72.2118268	10.1143780	730.3777101	46	80.1795324	9.8752799	791.7953231
47	71.1973129	10.3784687	738.9190827	47	79.2524799	10.1269959	802.5895369	47	88.1974856	9.8866181	871.9748555
48	77.9610577	10.3912956	810.1163956	48	86.9795967	10.1384928	881.8420168	48	97.0172342	9.8969255	960.1723411
49	85.3673581	10.4030097	888.0774532	49	95.4601074	10.1489684	968.8216136	49	106.7189576	9.9062959	1057.1895753
50	93.4772572	10.4137075	973.4448114	50	104.7674679	10.1585133	1064.2817210	50	117.3908534	9.9148145	1163.9085330

Table 1

347

M	C(10.25,M,1)	A(10.25,M,1)	S(10.25,M,1)	M	C(10.50,M,1)	A(10.50,M,1)	S(10.50,M,1)	M	C(10.75,M,1)	A(10.75,M,1)	S(10.75,M,1)
1/12	1.0081648	.0790119	.0796570	1/12	1.0083552	.0789136	.0795729	1/12	1.0085451	.0788155	.0794890
1/4	1.0246951	.2351212	.2409276	1/4	1.0252755	.2347845	.2407188	1/4	1.0258549	.2344490	.2405106
1/2	1.0500000	.4645761	.4878049	1/2	1.0511898	.4637811	.4875219	1/2	1.0523783	.4629891	.4872396
1	1.1025000	.9070295	1.0000000	1	1.1050000	.9049774	1.0000000	1	1.1075000	.9029345	1.0000000
2	1.2155063	1.7297320	2.1025000	2	1.2210250	1.7239614	2.1050000	2	1.2265563	1.7182253	2.1075000
3	1.3400956	2.4759473	3.3180063	3	1.3492326	2.4651235	3.3260250	3	1.3584110	2.4543795	3.3340563
4	1.4774554	3.1527867	4.6581019	4	1.4909021	3.1358583	4.6752576	4	1.5044402	3.1190786	4.6924673
5	1.6288946	3.7667000	6.1355573	5	1.6474468	3.7428582	6.1661597	5	1.6661676	3.7192583	6.1969075
6	1.7958563	4.3235374	7.7644520	6	1.8204287	4.2921794	7.8136064	6	1.8452806	4.2611813	7.8630751
7	1.9799316	4.8286053	9.5603083	7	2.0115737	4.7893026	9.6340351	7	2.0436482	4.7505023	9.7083557
8	2.1828746	5.2867169	11.5402399	8	2.2227889	5.2391879	11.6456088	8	2.2633404	5.1923271	11.7520039
9	2.4066192	5.7022375	13.7231145	9	2.4561818	5.6463239	13.8683977	9	2.5066495	5.5912660	14.0153443
10	2.6532977	6.0791270	16.1297337	10	2.7140808	6.0147727	16.3245795	10	2.7761143	5.9514818	16.5219938
11	2.9252607	6.4209769	18.7830314	11	2.9990593	6.3482106	19.0386603	11	3.0745466	6.2767330	19.2981082
12	3.2250999	6.7310448	21.7082921	12	3.3139606	6.6499644	22.0377197	12	3.4050604	6.5704135	22.3726548
13	3.5556727	7.0122855	24.9333921	13	3.6619264	6.9230447	25.3516803	13	3.7711044	6.8355878	25.7777152
14	3.9201291	7.2673791	28.4890648	14	4.0464287	7.1701762	29.0136067	14	4.1764981	7.0750229	29.5488196
15	4.3219424	7.4987566	32.4091939	15	4.4713037	7.3938246	33.0600354	15	4.6254717	7.2912170	33.7253177
16	4.7649415	7.7086228	36.7311363	16	4.9407906	7.5962213	37.5313391	16	5.1227099	7.4864262	38.3507894
17	5.2533480	7.8989776	41.4960778	17	5.4595736	7.7793858	42.4721297	17	5.6734012	7.6626873	43.4734992
18	5.7918161	8.0716350	46.7494258	18	6.0328289	7.9451456	47.9317033	18	6.2832918	7.8218396	49.1469004
19	6.3854773	8.2282403	52.5412419	19	6.6662759	8.0951543	53.9645322	19	6.9587457	7.9655436	55.4301922
20	7.0399887	8.3702860	58.9267192	20	7.3662349	8.2309089	60.6308081	20	7.7068108	8.0952990	62.3889378
21	7.7615876	8.4991256	65.9667079	21	8.1398895	8.3537637	67.9970429	21	8.5352930	8.2124596	70.0957487
22	8.5571503	8.6159870	73.7282955	22	8.9943569	8.4649445	76.1367325	22	9.4523370	8.3182479	78.6310417
23	9.4342582	8.7219837	82.2854458	23	9.9387644	8.5655607	85.1310894	23	10.4690170	8.4137679	88.0838786
24	10.4063697	8.8181258	91.7197040	24	10.9823347	8.6566160	95.0698538	24	11.5944363	8.5000161	98.5528956
25	11.4673998	8.9053295	102.1209737	25	12.1354798	8.7390190	106.0521884	25	12.8408382	8.5778927	110.1473319
26	12.6428083	8.9844258	113.5883735	26	13.4097052	8.8135918	118.1876682	26	14.2212283	8.6482101	122.9881701
27	13.9386961	9.0561686	126.2311818	27	14.8177242	8.8810786	131.5973734	27	15.7500103	8.7117021	137.2093984
28	15.3674125	9.1212413	140.1698779	28	16.3735853	8.9421526	146.4150976	28	17.4431365	8.7690313	152.9594087
29	16.9425723	9.1802642	155.5372904	29	18.0928117	8.9974231	162.7886829	29	19.3182736	8.8207957	170.4025452
30	18.6791859	9.2337998	172.4798627	30	19.9925570	9.0474418	180.8814946	30	21.3949880	8.8675356	189.7208188
31	20.5938025	9.2823581	191.1590487	31	22.0917754	9.0927075	200.8740515	31	23.6949493	8.9097387	211.1158068
32	22.7046673	9.3264019	211.7528512	32	24.4114119	9.1336719	222.9658270	32	26.2421563	8.9478453	234.8107561
33	25.0318957	9.3663509	234.4575184	33	26.9746101	9.1707438	247.3772388	33	29.0631881	8.9822531	261.0529124
34	27.5976650	9.4025858	259.4894141	34	29.8069442	9.2042930	274.3518489	34	32.1874808	9.0133211	290.1161005
35	30.4264256	9.4354520	287.0870791	35	32.9366733	9.2346543	304.1587931	35	35.6476350	9.0413735	322.3035813
36	33.5451343	9.4652626	317.5135047	36	36.3950240	9.2621306	337.0954664	36	39.4797558	9.0667029	357.9512164
37	36.9835105	9.4923017	351.0586390	37	40.2165015	9.2869960	373.4904904	37	43.7238295	9.0895737	397.4309722
38	40.7743204	9.5168269	388.0421495	38	44.4392342	9.3094987	413.7065919	38	48.4241412	9.1102246	441.1548017
39	44.9536882	9.5390720	428.8164698	39	49.1053538	9.3298631	458.1462261	39	53.6297364	9.1288710	489.5789429
40	49.5614412	9.5592490	473.7701580	40	54.2614159	9.3482924	507.2515799	40	59.3949331	9.1457074	543.2086793
41	54.6414890	9.5775501	523.3315993	41	59.9588646	9.3649705	561.5129959	41	65.7798884	9.1609096	602.6036124
42	60.2422416	9.5941498	577.9730883	42	66.2545454	9.3800638	621.4718605	42	72.8512264	9.1746362	668.3835008
43	66.4170714	9.6092061	638.2153299	43	73.2112727	9.3937229	687.7264059	43	80.6827333	9.1870305	741.2347272
44	73.2248212	9.6228627	704.6324012	44	80.8984563	9.4060840	760.9376786	44	89.3561271	9.1982216	821.9174605
45	80.7303654	9.6352496	777.8572224	45	89.3927943	9.4172706	841.8361349	45	98.9619108	9.2083265	911.2735376
46	89.0052278	9.6464849	858.5875878	46	98.7790377	9.4273942	931.2289292	46	109.6003162	9.2174506	1010.2354983
47	98.1282637	9.6566757	947.5928157	47	109.1508366	9.4365559	1030.0079668	47	121.3823502	9.2256890	1119.8358145
48	108.1864107	9.6659190	1045.7210794	48	120.6116745	9.4448469	1139.1588034	48	134.4309528	9.2331278	1241.2181646
49	119.2755179	9.6743029	1153.9074901	49	133.2759003	9.4523502	1259.7704779	49	148.8822803	9.2398445	1375.6491175
50	131.5012584	9.6819074	1273.1830080	50	147.2698699	9.4591404	1393.0463782	50	164.8871254	9.2459092	1524.5313977

Table 1

M	C(11.00,M,1)	A(11.00,M,1)	S(11.00,M,1)	C(11.25,M,1)	A(11.25,M,1)	S(11.25,M,1)	C(11.50,M,1)	A(11.50,M,1)	S(11.50,M,1)
1/12	1.0087346	.0787178	.0794054	1.0089237	.0786204	.0793220	1.0091125	.0785233	.0792389
1/4	1.0264333	.2341145	.2403030	1.0270108	.2337813	.2400959	1.0275873	.2334491	.2398893
1/2	1.0535654	.4622000	.4869580	1.0547512	.4614140	.4866769	1.0559356	.4606309	.4863956
1	1.1100000	.9009009	1.0000000	1.1125000	.8988764	1.0000000	1.1150000	.8968610	1.0000000
2	1.2321000	1.7125233	2.1100000	1.2376563	1.7068552	2.1125000	1.2432250	1.7012206	2.1150000
3	1.3676310	2.4437147	3.3421000	1.3768926	2.4331283	3.3501563	1.3861959	2.4226194	3.3582250
4	1.5180704	3.1024457	4.7097310	1.5317930	3.0859580	4.7270188	1.5456084	3.0696138	4.7444209
5	1.6850582	3.6958970	6.2278014	1.7041197	3.6727712	6.2588418	1.7233534	3.6498778	6.2900293
6	1.8704146	4.2305379	7.9125506	1.8958332	4.2002438	7.9629615	1.9215390	4.1702940	8.0133826
7	2.0761602	4.7121963	9.7832741	2.1091144	4.6743764	9.8587947	2.1425160	4.6370350	9.9349216
8	2.3045378	5.1461228	11.8594343	2.3463898	5.1005631	11.9679091	2.3889053	5.0556368	12.0774396
9	2.5580369	5.5370475	14.1639720	2.6103586	5.4836522	14.3142999	2.6636294	5.4310644	14.4663430
10	2.8394210	5.8092320	16.7220090	2.9040240	5.8280020	16.9246575	2.9699468	5.7677707	17.1299724
11	3.1517573	6.2065153	19.5614300	3.2307267	6.1375299	19.8286815	3.3114907	6.0697495	20.0999192
12	3.4984506	6.4923561	22.7131873	3.5941834	6.4157572	23.0594081	3.6923121	6.3405825	23.4114100
13	3.8832602	6.7498704	26.2116379	3.9985291	6.6658492	26.6535916	4.1169280	6.5834821	27.1037221
14	4.3104410	6.9818652	30.0949180	4.4483636	6.8906509	30.6521206	4.5903748	6.8013292	31.2206501
15	4.7845895	7.1906696	34.4053590	4.9488045	7.0927199	35.1004842	5.1182679	6.9967078	35.8110249
16	5.3109943	7.3791618	39.1899485	5.5055450	7.2743550	40.0492887	5.7068687	7.1719353	40.9292928
17	5.8950927	7.5487944	44.5008428	6.1249188	7.4376225	45.5548336	6.3631586	7.3290899	46.6361615
18	6.5435529	7.7016166	50.3959356	6.8139722	7.5843798	51.6797524	7.0949218	7.4700358	52.9993200
19	7.2633437	7.8392942	56.9394885	7.5805440	7.7162964	58.4937246	7.9108378	7.5964447	60.0942418
20	8.0623116	7.9633281	64.2028322	8.4333552	7.8348732	66.0742686	8.8205842	7.7098159	68.0050797
21	8.9491658	8.0750704	72.2651438	9.3821077	7.9414590	74.5076238	9.8349513	7.8114940	76.8256638
22	9.9335741	8.1757391	81.2143096	10.4375948	8.0372665	83.8897315	10.9659708	7.9026852	86.6606152
23	11.0262672	8.2664316	91.1478837	11.6118242	8.1233857	94.3273263	12.2270574	7.9844711	97.6265859
24	12.2391563	8.3481366	102.1741509	12.9181544	8.2007961	105.9391506	13.6331690	8.0578216	109.8536433
25	13.5854638	8.4217447	114.4133075	14.3714468	8.2703785	118.8573050	15.2009834	8.1236068	123.4868123
26	15.0798649	8.4880583	127.9987713	15.9882346	8.3329245	133.2287518	16.9490965	8.1826070	138.6877957
27	16.7386500	8.5478002	143.0786362	17.7869110	8.3891456	149.2169864	18.8982426	8.2355220	155.6368923
28	18.5799015	8.6016218	159.8172862	19.7879385	8.4396815	167.0038974	21.0715405	8.2829793	174.5351349
29	20.6236907	8.6501097	178.3971876	22.0140816	8.4851069	186.7918359	23.4947677	8.3255420	195.6066754
30	22.8922966	8.6937926	199.0208783	24.4906657	8.5259388	208.8059174	26.1968660	8.3637148	219.1014431
31	25.4104493	8.7331465	221.9131749	27.2458656	8.5626416	233.2965832	29.2092826	8.3979505	245.2981091
32	28.2055987	8.7686004	247.3236242	30.3110255	8.5956329	260.5424498	32.5683501	8.4286552	274.5073917
33	31.3082145	8.8005409	275.5292229	33.7210159	8.6252880	290.8534743	36.3137103	8.4561930	307.0757418
34	34.7521181	8.8293161	306.8374374	37.5146302	8.6519443	324.5744902	40.4897870	8.4808905	343.3894521
35	38.5748511	8.8552398	341.5895556	41.7350261	8.6759050	362.0891204	45.1461125	8.5030408	383.8792391
36	42.8180848	8.8785944	380.1644067	46.4302165	8.6974427	403.8241465	50.3379155	8.5229066	429.0253516
37	47.5280741	8.8996346	422.9824915	51.6536159	8.7168024	450.2543630	56.1267758	8.5407234	479.3632671
38	52.7561623	8.9185897	470.5105656	57.4646477	8.7342044	501.9079789	62.5813550	8.5567026	535.4900429
39	58.5593401	8.9356664	523.2667279	63.9294205	8.7498467	559.3726265	69.7782108	8.5710337	598.0713979
40	65.0008675	8.9510508	581.8260680	71.1214804	8.7639071	623.3020471	77.8027051	8.5836867	667.8496087
41	72.1509630	8.9649106	646.8269356	79.1226469	8.7765457	694.4235274	86.7500162	8.5954141	745.6523138
42	80.0875689	8.9773970	716.9778935	88.0239447	8.7879063	773.5461743	96.7262680	8.6057526	832.4023299
43	88.8972015	8.9886459	799.0654674	97.9266385	8.7981180	861.5701190	107.8497889	8.6150247	929.1285979
44	98.6758937	8.9987801	887.9626689	108.9433853	8.8072971	959.4967575	120.2525146	8.6233406	1036.9783868
45	109.5302420	9.0079100	986.6385326	121.1995162	8.8155479	1068.4401428	134.0815538	8.6307987	1157.2309014
46	121.5785686	9.0161351	1096.1688046	134.8344618	8.8229644	1189.6396590	149.5009325	8.6374876	1291.3124552
47	134.9522112	9.0235452	1217.7473732	150.0033387	8.8296309	1324.4741208	166.6935397	8.6434867	1440.8133876
48	149.7969544	9.0302209	1352.6995944	166.8787143	8.8356233	1474.4774595	185.8632968	8.6488670	1607.5069273
49	166.2746194	9.0362350	1502.4965388	185.6525697	8.8410097	1641.3561738	207.2375760	8.6536923	1793.3702242
50	184.5648276	9.0416532	1668.7711582	206.5384838	8.8458514	1827.0087435	231.0698972	8.6580200	2000.6078001

Table 1

M	C(11.75,M,1)	A(11.75,M,1)	S(11.75,M,1)	C(12.00,M,1)	A(12.00,M,1)	S(12.00,M,1)	C(12.25,M,1)	A(12.25,M,1)	S(12.25,M,1)
1/12	1.0093008	.0784265	.0791559	1.0094888	.0783300	.0790733	1.0096764	.0782338	.0789908
1/4	1.0281628	.2331181	.2396833	1.0287373	.2327882	.2394779	1.0293109	.2324594	.2392730
1/2	1.0571187	.4598507	.4861168	1.0583005	.4590735	.4858377	1.0594810	.4582991	.4855592
1	1.1175000	.8948546	1.0000000	1.1200000	.8928571	1.0000000	1.1225000	.8908686	1.0000000
2	1.2488063	1.6956193	2.1175000	1.2544000	1.6900510	2.1200000	1.2600063	1.6845155	2.1225000
3	1.3955410	2.4121873	3.3663063	1.4049280	2.4018313	3.3744000	1.4143570	2.3915505	3.3825063
4	1.5595171	3.0534115	4.7618472	1.5735194	3.0373493	4.7793260	1.5876158	3.0214258	4.7968633
5	1.7427603	3.6272138	6.3213643	1.7623417	3.6047762	6.3528474	1.7820987	3.5825620	6.3844790
6	1.9475346	4.1406835	8.0641246	1.9738227	4.1114073	8.1151890	2.0004058	4.0824606	8.1665777
7	2.1763700	4.6001642	10.0116592	2.2106814	4.5637565	10.0890117	2.2454555	4.5278045	10.1669835
8	2.4320934	5.0113326	12.1880292	2.4759632	4.9676398	12.2996931	2.5205238	4.9245475	12.4124389
9	2.7178644	5.3792686	14.6201226	2.7730788	5.3282498	14.7756563	2.8292879	5.2779933	14.9329627
10	3.0372135	5.7085177	17.3379870	3.1058482	5.6502230	17.5487351	3.1758757	5.5928671	17.7622506
11	3.3940861	6.0031479	20.3752005	3.4785500	5.9376991	20.6545833	3.5649205	5.8733782	20.9381264
12	3.7928912	6.2657990	23.7692866	3.8959760	6.1943742	24.1331333	4.0016232	6.1232768	24.5030468
13	4.2385559	6.5027284	27.5621777	4.3634931	6.4235484	28.0291093	4.4918221	6.3459036	28.5046701
14	4.7365862	6.7138509	31.8007336	4.6871123	6.6281682	32.3926024	5.0420703	6.5442349	32.9964922
15	5.2931351	6.9027749	36.5373198	5.4735658	6.8106645	37.2797147	5.6597239	6.7209219	38.0385625
16	5.9150785	7.0718343	41.8304549	6.1303937	6.9739861	42.7532805	6.3530401	6.8783269	43.6982864
17	6.6101002	7.2231180	47.7455334	6.8660409	7.1196305	48.8836741	7.1312875	7.0185540	50.0513264
18	7.3867869	7.3584948	54.3556336	7.6899658	7.2496701	55.7497150	8.0048702	7.1434780	57.1826139
19	8.2547344	7.4796374	61.7424205	8.6127617	7.3657769	63.4396808	8.9854668	7.2547688	65.1874841
20	9.2246657	7.5880424	69.9971549	9.6462931	7.4694436	72.0524425	10.0861865	7.3539143	74.1729510
21	10.3085639	7.6850492	79.2218206	10.8038483	7.5620032	81.6987356	11.3217443	7.4422399	84.2591375
22	11.5193202	7.7718561	89.5303846	12.?003101	7.6446457	9?.5025839	12.7086580	7.5209264	95.5808818
23	12.8733991	7.8495356	101.0502048	13.5523473	7.7184337	104.6028940	14.2654686	7.5910258	108.2895398
24	14.3870235	7.9190475	113.9236038	15.1786290	7.7843158	118.1552413	16.0129886	7.6534751	122.5550085
25	16.0763812	7.9812506	128.3096273	17.0000644	7.8431391	133.3338703	17.9745797	7.7091092	138.5679970
26	17.9653560	8.0369133	144.3860085	19.0400722	7.8956599	150.3339347	20.1764657	7.7586719	156.5425767
27	20.0762853	8.0867233	162.3513645	21.3248808	7.9425535	169.3740069	22.6460827	7.8028257	176.7190423
28	22.4354665	8.1312960	182.4276499	23.8838665	7.9844228	190.6988877	25.4224728	7.8421610	199.3671250
29	25.0713906	8.1711821	204.8628987	26.7499305	8.0218060	214.5827543	28.5367258	7.8772036	224.7895979
30	28.0172790	8.2068744	229.9342894	29.9599222	8.0551840	241.3326848	32.0324747	7.9084219	253.3263236
31	31.3093093	8.2388138	257.9515684	33.5551129	8.0849857	271.2926070	35.9564528	7.9362333	285.3587983
32	34.9881532	8.2673949	289.2608777	37.5817264	8.1115944	304.8477199	40.3611183	7.9610096	321.3152511
33	39.0992612	8.2929708	324.2490309	42.0915336	8.1353521	342.4294463	45.3053553	7.9830821	361.6763694
34	43.6934243	8.3158575	363.3482920	47.1425176	8.1565644	384.5209799	50.8552613	8.0027457	406.9817247
35	48.8274017	8.3363378	407.0417164	52.7996197	8.1755039	431.6634975	57.0850308	8.0202634	457.8369860
36	54.5646214	8.3546647	455.8691181	59.1355741	8.1924142	484.4631173	64.0779471	8.0358694	514.9220169
37	60.9759644	8.3710646	510.4337395	66.2318430	8.2075127	543.5986914	71.9274956	8.0497723	578.9999640
38	68.1406403	8.3857402	571.4097040	74.1796642	8.2209935	609.8305344	80.7386139	8.0621580	650.9274597
39	76.1471655	8.3988726	639.5503442	83.0812239	8.2330299	684.0101986	90.6290941	8.0731920	731.6660735
40	85.0944575	8.4106243	715.6975097	93.0509708	8.2437767	767.0914225	101.7311581	8.0830218	822.2951676
41	95.0930562	8.4211403	800.7919672	104.2170873	8.2533720	860.1423932	114.1932250	8.0917789	924.0263257
42	106.2264903	8.4305506	895.8850234	116.7231378	8.2619393	964.3594805	128.1818951	8.0995803	1038.2195507
43	118.7528030	8.4389714	1002.1515138	130.7299143	8.2695887	1081.0826183	143.8841772	8.1065303	1166.4014458
44	132.7062573	8.4465069	1120.9043167	146.4175040	8.2764185	1211.8125326	161.5099889	8.1127219	1310.2856230
45	148.2992426	8.4532500	1253.6105741	163.9876045	8.2825165	1358.2300366	181.2943626	8.1182378	1471.7956120
46	165.7244036	8.4592841	1401.9098167	183.6661171	8.2879611	1522.2176411	203.5035955	8.1231517	1653.0905746
47	185.1970210	8.4646838	1567.6342203	205.7060512	8.2928224	1705.8837582	228.4327860	8.1275293	1856.5941701
48	206.9576710	8.4695157	1752.8312413	230.3907773	8.2971639	1911.5898094	256.4158023	8.1314293	2085.0269561
49	231.2751974	8.4738395	1959.7889123	258.0376706	8.3010383	2141.9805867	287.8267381	8.1349036	2341.4427585
50	258.4500331	8.4777088	2191.0641097	289.0021911	8.3044985	2400.0182573	323.0855136	8.1379987	2629.2694966

Table 1

M	C(12.50,M,1)	A(12.50,M,1)	S(12.50,M,1)	M	C(12.75,M,1)	A(12.75,M,1)	S(12.75,M,1)	M	C(13.00,M,1)	A(13.00,M,1)	S(13.00,M,1)
1/12	1.0098636	.0781379	.0789086	1/12	1.0100504	.0780423	.0788267	1/12	1.0102368	.0779470	.0787450
1/4	1.0298836	.2321317	.2390686	1/4	1.0304553	.2318051	.2388647	1/4	1.0310260	.2314795	.2386614
1/2	1.0606602	.4575277	.4852814	1/2	1.0618380	.4567591	.4850041	1/2	1.0630146	.4559933	.4847275
1	1.1250000	.8888889	1.0000000	1	1.1275000	.8869180	1.0000000	1	1.1300000	.8849558	1.0000000
2	1.2656250	1.6790123	2.1250000	2	1.2712563	1.6735414	2.1275000	2	1.2769000	1.6681024	2.1300000
3	1.4238281	2.3813443	3.3906250	3	1.4333414	2.3712119	3.3987563	3	1.4428970	2.3611526	3.4069000
4	1.6018066	3.0056394	4.8144531	4	1.6160925	2.9899884	4.8320977	4	1.6304736	2.9744713	4.8497970
5	1.8020325	3.5605683	6.4162598	5	1.8221442	3.5387924	6.4481901	5	1.8424352	3.5172313	6.4802706
6	2.0272865	4.0538385	8.2182922	6	2.0544676	4.0255365	8.2703344	6	2.0819518	3.9975498	8.3227058
7	2.2806973	4.4923009	10.2455788	7	2.3164123	4.4572385	10.3248020	7	2.3526055	4.4226104	10.4046575
8	2.5657845	4.8820453	12.5262761	8	2.6117548	4.8401229	12.6412143	8	2.6584442	4.7987703	12.7572630
9	2.8865076	5.2284647	15.0920606	9	2.9447536	5.1797099	15.2529691	9	3.0040419	5.1316551	15.4157072
10	3.2473210	5.5364308	17.9785682	10	3.3202096	5.4808957	18.1977226	10	3.3945674	5.4262435	18.4197492
11	3.6532362	5.8101607	21.2258892	11	3.7435364	5.7480228	21.5179323	11	3.8359612	5.6869411	21.8143166
12	4.1099907	6.0534762	24.8791254	12	4.2208373	5.9849426	25.2614586	12	4.3345231	5.9176470	25.6501777
13	4.6236270	6.2697566	28.9890161	13	4.7589940	6.1950710	29.4823059	13	4.8980111	6.1218115	29.9847008
14	5.2015804	6.4620059	33.6126431	14	5.3657657	6.3814377	34.2412999	14	5.5347526	6.3024881	34.8827119
15	5.8517779	6.6328941	38.8142235	15	6.0499009	6.5467297	39.6070356	15	6.2542704	6.4623788	40.4174645
16	6.5832502	6.7847948	44.6660014	16	6.8212632	6.6933301	45.6569665	16	7.0673255	6.6038751	46.6717349
17	7.4061565	6.9198176	51.2492516	17	7.6909743	6.8233526	52.4782297	17	7.9860779	6.7290930	53.7390604
18	8.3319260	7.0398378	58.6554081	18	8.6715735	6.9386720	60.1692040	18	9.0242680	6.8399053	61.7251383
19	9.3734168	7.1465225	66.9873341	19	9.7771991	7.0409507	68.8407776	19	10.1974228	6.9379693	70.7494062
20	10.5450939	7.2413534	76.3607508	20	11.0237920	7.1316636	78.6179767	20	11.5230878	7.0247516	80.9468291
21	11.8632306	7.3256474	86.9058447	21	12.4293255	7.2121185	89.6417688	21	13.0210892	7.1015501	92.4699168
22	13.3461344	7.4005755	98.7690753	22	14.0240645	7.2834754	102.0710943	22	14.7133308	7.1695133	105.4910060
23	15.0144012	7.4671782	112.1152097	23	15.8008578	7.3467631	116.0851588	23	16.6266288	7.2296578	120.2048368
24	16.8912014	7.5263806	127.1296109	24	17.6154671	7.4028941	131.8860166	24	18.7880905	7.2828830	136.8314056
25	19.0026016	7.5790050	144.0208123	25	20.0869392	7.4526777	149.7014837	25	21.2305423	7.3299850	155.6195562
26	21.3779267	7.6257822	163.0234139	26	22.6460239	7.4968317	169.7884229	26	23.9905128	7.3716681	176.8500985
27	24.0501676	7.6673620	184.4013406	27	25.5356470	7.5359926	192.4364468	27	27.1092795	7.4085559	200.8406113
28	27.0564385	7.7043218	208.4515082	28	28.7914420	7.5707251	217.9720938	28	30.6334858	7.4411999	227.9498908
29	30.4384934	7.7371749	235.5079468	29	32.4623508	7.6015301	246.7635358	29	34.6158390	7.4700884	258.5833766
30	34.2433050	7.7663777	265.9464401	30	36.6013006	7.6288515	279.2258866	30	39.1158981	7.4956534	293.1992156
31	38.5237182	7.7923357	300.1897452	31	41.2679664	7.6530834	315.8271872	31	44.2009648	7.5182774	332.3151137
32	43.3391830	7.8154095	338.7134633	32	46.5296321	7.6745750	357.0951536	32	49.9470902	7.5382986	376.5160785
33	48.7565808	7.8359196	382.0526463	33	52.4621602	7.6936364	403.6247857	33	56.4402120	7.5560164	426.4631687
34	54.8511534	7.8541507	430.8092271	34	59.1510856	7.7105423	456.0869459	34	63.7774395	7.5716960	482.9033307
35	61.7075476	7.8703562	485.6603805	35	66.6928491	7.7255364	515.2380316	35	72.0685067	7.5855716	546.6808203
36	69.4209911	7.8847611	547.3679282	36	75.1961873	7.7388349	581.9308806	36	81.4374126	7.5978510	618.7493270
37	78.0986150	7.8975654	616.7889192	37	84.7837012	7.7506296	657.1270680	37	92.0242762	7.6087177	700.1867395
38	87.8609418	7.9089470	694.8875342	38	95.5936231	7.7610906	741.9107692	38	103.9874321	7.6183343	792.2110157
39	98.8435596	7.9190640	782.7484760	39	107.7818101	7.7703686	837.5043924	39	117.5057983	7.6268445	896.1984479
40	111.1990045	7.9280569	881.5920356	40	121.5239909	7.7785974	945.2862025	40	132.7815521	7.6343756	1013.7042462
41	125.0988801	7.9360506	992.7910402	41	137.0182998	7.7858957	1066.8101934	41	150.0431539	7.6410404	1146.4857983
42	140.7362401	7.9431561	1117.8899203	42	154.4881330	7.7923687	1203.8284931	42	169.5487639	7.6469388	1296.5289522
43	158.3282702	7.9494721	1258.6261604	43	174.1853700	7.7981097	1358.3166261	43	191.5901032	7.6521579	1466.0777161
44	178.1193040	7.9550863	1416.9544306	44	196.3940047	7.8032015	1532.5019961	44	216.4968167	7.6567769	1657.6678193
45	200.3842170	7.9600767	1595.0737346	45	221.4342403	7.8077175	1728.8960008	45	244.6414029	7.6608645	1874.1646360
46	225.4322441	7.9645126	1795.4579516	46	249.6671059	7.8117229	1950.3302410	46	276.4447853	7.6644818	2118.8060389
47	253.6112747	7.9684557	2020.8901957	47	281.4996620	7.8152753	2199.9973470	47	312.3826074	7.6676831	2395.2508241
48	285.3126840	7.9719606	2274.5014704	48	317.3908689	7.8184260	2481.4970089	48	352.9923464	7.6705160	2707.6334315
49	320.9767696	7.9750761	2559.8141544	49	357.8582047	7.8212204	2798.8878778	49	398.8813514	7.6730230	3060.6257779
50	361.0988658	7.9778454	2880.7909239	50	403.4851258	7.8236988	3156.7460825	50	450.7359272	7.6752416	3459.5071293

Table 1

351

M	C(13.25,M,1)	A(13.25,M,1)	S(13.25,M,1)	M	C(13.50,M,1)	A(13.50,M,1)	S(13.50,M,1)	M	C(13.75,M,1)	A(13.75,M,1)	S(13.75,M,1)
1/12	1.0104229	.0778520	.0786635	1/12	1.0106086	.0777573	.0785822	1/12	1.0107939	.0776629	.0785012
1/4	1.0315958	.2311551	.2384586	1/4	1.0321646	.2308318	.2382564	1/4	1.0327325	.2305095	.2380547
1/2	1.0641898	.4552304	.4844516	1/2	1.0653638	.4544703	.4841762	1/2	1.0665365	.4537130	.4839015
1	1.1325000	.8830022	1.0000000	1	1.1350000	.8810573	1.0000000	1	1.1375000	.8791209	1.0000000
2	1.2825563	1.6626951	2.1325000	2	1.2882250	1.6573192	2.1350000	2	1.2939063	1.6519744	2.1375000
3	1.4524950	2.3511657	3.4150563	3	1.4621354	2.3412504	3.4232250	3	1.4718184	2.3314061	3.4314063
4	1.6449505	2.9590867	4.8675512	4	1.65?3237	2.9438329	4.8853?04	4	1.6741934	2.9287086	4.9032246
5	1.8629065	3.4958823	6.5125017	5	1.8835593	3.4747427	6.5448840	5	1.9043950	3.4538098	6.5774180
6	2.1097416	3.9698740	8.3754082	6	2.1378399	3.9425046	8.4284434	6	2.1662493	3.9154372	8.4818130
7	2.3892824	4.3884097	10.4851498	7	2.4264482	4.3546296	10.5662832	7	2.4641086	4.3212634	10.6480623
8	2.7058623	4.7579776	12.8744322	8	2.7540187	4.7177353	12.9927315	8	2.8029235	4.6780338	13.1121708
9	3.0643890	5.0843070	15.5802944	9	3.1258113	5.0376522	15.7467502	9	3.1883255	4.9916781	15.9150943
10	3.4704206	5.3724565	18.6446834	10	3.5477958	5.3195174	18.8725615	10	3.6267202	5.2674093	19.1034198
11	3.9302513	5.6268931	22.1151040	11	4.0257482	5.5678567	22.4203573	11	4.1253943	5.5098104	22.7301400
12	4.4510096	5.8515613	26.0453553	12	4.5703592	5.7866579	26.4471055	12	4.6926360	5.7229102	26.8555342
13	5.0407683	6.0499437	30.4963649	13	5.1873577	5.9794343	31.0174648	13	5.3378734	5.9102507	31.5481702
14	5.7086702	6.2251159	35.5371332	14	5.8876510	6.1492813	36.2048225	14	6.0718310	6.0749457	36.8860436
15	6.4650689	6.3797933	41.2458033	15	6.6824839	6.2989263	42.0924736	15	6.9067078	6.2197325	42.9578746
16	7.3216906	6.5163737	47.7108723	16	7.5846193	6.4307720	48.7749575	16	7.8553801	6.3470176	49.8645824
17	8.2918146	6.6369746	55.0325629	17	8.6085429	6.5469357	56.3595768	17	8.9366323	6.4589165	57.7209625
18	9.3904800	6.7434654	63.3243775	18	9.7706962	6.6492826	64.9681197	18	10.1654193	6.5572893	66.6575948
19	10.6347186	6.8374971	72.7148575	19	11.0897401	6.7394560	74.7388158	19	11.5631644	6.6437708	76.8230141
20	12.0438188	6.9205272	83.3495761	20	12.5868551	6.8189040	85.8285560	20	13.1530996	6.7197985	88.3861785
21	13.6396248	6.9938430	95.3933950	21	14.2860805	6.8889022	98.4154110	21	14.9616507	6.7856360	101.5392781
22	15.4468751	7.0585810	109.0330198	22	16.2?47014	6.9505746	112.7014915	22	17.0189777	6.8453943	116.5009288
23	17.4935861	7.1157448	124.4798949	23	18.4036861	7.0049115	128.9161929	23	19.3569734	6.8970499	133.5198066
24	19.8114862	7.1662206	141.9734910	24	20.8881837	7.0527855	147.3198789	24	22.0208323	6.9424615	152.8787300
25	22.4365082	7.2107908	161.7849673	25	23.7080885	7.0949652	168.2080626	25	25.0485967	6.9823837	174.8996122
26	25.4093455	7.2501464	184.2214755	26	26.9085804	7.1321279	191.9161511	26	28.4923925	7.0174802	199.9483089
27	28.7760838	7.2848975	209.6308210	27	30.5413523	7.1648704	218.8248315	27	32.4106652	7.0483342	228.4412014
28	32.5889149	7.3155828	238.4069048	28	34.6644348	7.1937184	249.3661838	28	36.8671317	7.0754587	260.8518667
29	36.9069461	7.3426780	270.9958197	29	39.3441335	7.2191352	284.0306186	29	41.9363623	7.0993042	297.7189984
30	41.7971165	7.3666030	307.9027658	30	44.6555916	7.2415288	323.3747521	30	47.7026121	7.1202675	339.6553607
31	47.3352344	7.3877290	349.6998823	31	50.6840964	7.2612588	368.0303437	31	54.2617213	7.1386967	387.3579728
32	53.6071530	7.4063832	397.0351167	32	57.5264495	7.2786422	418.7144402	32	61.7227080	7.1548982	441.6196941
33	60.7101008	7.4228549	450.6422698	33	65.2925201	7.2939578	476.2408696	33	70.2095803	7.1691413	503.3424021
34	68.7541891	7.4373995	511.3523705	34	74.1070104	7.3074518	541.5334098	34	79.6633976	7.1816627	573.5519824
35	77.8641192	7.4502424	580.1065597	35	84.1114568	7.3193408	615.6404201	35	90.8445148	7.1926705	653.4153800
36	88.1811150	7.4615827	657.9706789	36	95.4665035	7.3298157	699.7518769	36	103.3357494	7.2023477	744.2599949
37	99.8651128	7.4715962	746.1517939	37	108.3544814	7.3390447	795.2183804	37	117.5444149	7.2108551	847.5957442
38	113.0972402	7.4804381	846.0169067	38	122.9823364	7.3471759	903.5728618	38	133.7067720	7.2183342	965.1401591
39	128.0826246	7.4882456	959.1141469	39	139.5849519	7.3543400	1026.5551982	39	152.0914531	7.2249091	1098.8469311
40	145.0535723	7.4951396	1087.1967715	40	158.4289204	7.3606520	1166.1401501	40	173.0040280	7.2306894	1250.9383843
41	164.2731707	7.5012270	1232.2503438	41	179.6168246	7.3662132	1324.5690705	41	196.7920818	7.2357709	1423.9424122
42	186.0393658	7.5066022	1396.5235145	42	204.0920960	7.3711130	1504.3858951	42	223.8509931	7.2402381	1620.7344940
43	210.6895818	7.5113485	1582.5628803	43	231.6445290	7.3754299	1708.4779911	43	254.6305047	7.2441654	1844.5854871
44	238.6059514	7.5155395	1793.2524621	44	262.9165404	7.3792334	1940.1225201	44	289.6421991	7.2476179	2099.2159918
45	270.2212400	7.5192402	2031.8584135	45	298.4102734	7.3825845	2203.0390605	45	329.4630015	7.2506531	2388.8581909
46	306.0255543	7.5225079	2302.0796535	46	338.6956603	7.3855370	2501.4493339	46	374.7698517	7.2533214	2718.3261924
47	346.5739403	7.5253933	2608.1052078	47	384.4195745	7.3881383	2840.1449942	47	426.3007064	7.2556672	3093.0960441
48	392.4949874	7.5279411	2954.6791481	48	436.3162171	7.3904302	3224.5645687	48	484.9170535	7.2577294	3519.3967505
49	444.5005733	7.5301908	3347.1741355	49	495.2189064	7.3924496	3660.8807858	49	551.5931485	7.2595423	4004.3138040
50	503.3968993	7.5321773	3791.6747088	50	562.0734589	7.3942287	4156.0996922	50	627.4372064	7.2611361	4555.9069524

M	C(5.00,M,2)	A(5.00,M,2)	S(5.00,M,2)	M	C(5.25,M,2)	A(5.25,M,2)	S(5.25,M,2)	M	C(5.50,M,2)	A(5.50,M,2)	S(5.50,M,2)
1/6	1.0041239	.1642791	.1649566	1/6	1.0043279	.1641620	.1648725	1/6	1.0045317	.1640450	.1647884
1/2	1.0124228	.4908161	.4969135	1/2	1.0130400	.4903668	.4967611	1/2	1.0136567	.4899183	.4966090
1	1.0250000	.9756098	1.0000000	1	1.0262500	.9744214	1.0000000	1	1.0275000	.9732360	1.0000000
2	1.0506250	1.9274242	2.0250000	2	1.0531891	1.9239186	2.0262500	2	1.0557563	1.9204243	2.0275000
3	1.0768906	2.8550236	3.0756250	3	1.0808353	2.8491289	3.0794391	3	1.0847895	2.8422621	3.0832563
4	1.1038129	3.7619742	4.1525156	4	1.1092072	3.7506738	4.1602743	4	1.1146213	3.7394279	4.1680458
5	1.1314082	4.6458285	5.2563285	5	1.1383229	4.6291583	5.2694815	5	1.1452733	4.6125819	5.2826671
6	1.1596934	5.5081254	6.3877367	6	1.1682049	5.4851726	6.4078054	6	1.1767684	5.4623668	6.4279404
7	1.1886858	6.3493906	7.5474301	7	1.1983703	6.3192912	7.5760103	7	1.2091295	6.2894081	7.6047088
8	1.2184029	7.1701372	8.7361159	8	1.2303406	7.1320742	8.7748806	8	1.2423806	7.0943144	8.8138383
9	1.2488630	7.9708655	9.9545188	9	1.2626371	7.9240675	10.0052212	9	1.2765460	7.8776783	10.0562188
10	1.2800845	8.7520639	11.2033818	10	1.2957813	8.6958026	11.2678583	10	1.3116510	8.6400762	11.3327648
11	1.3120867	9.5142087	12.4834663	11	1.3297955	9.4477979	12.5636395	11	1.3477214	9.3820693	12.6444159
12	1.3448888	10.2577646	13.7955530	12	1.3647027	10.1805583	13.8934351	12	1.3847838	10.1042037	13.9921373
13	1.3785110	10.9831850	15.1404418	13	1.4005261	10.8945757	15.2581378	13	1.4228653	10.8070109	15.3769211
14	1.4129738	11.6909122	16.5189528	14	1.4372899	11.5903295	16.6586659	14	1.4619941	11.4910081	16.7997864
15	1.4482982	12.3813777	17.9319267	15	1.4750188	12.2682870	18.0959538	15	1.5021990	12.1566989	18.2617805
16	1.4845056	13.0550027	19.3802248	16	1.5137380	12.9289033	19.5709726	16	1.5435094	12.8045731	19.7639795
17	1.5216183	13.7121977	20.8647305	17	1.5534737	13.5726219	21.0847106	17	1.5859559	13.4351077	21.3074889
18	1.5596587	14.3533636	22.3863487	18	1.5942523	14.1998752	22.6381843	18	1.6295597	14.0487666	22.8934449
19	1.5986502	14.9788913	23.9460074	19	1.6361015	14.8110843	24.2324366	19	1.6743829	14.6460016	24.5230146
20	1.6386164	15.5891623	25.5446576	20	1.6790491	15.4066594	25.8685381	20	1.7204284	15.2272521	26.1973975
21	1.6795819	16.1845486	27.1832741	21	1.7231242	15.9870007	27.5475872	21	1.7677402	15.7929461	27.9178259
22	1.7215714	16.7654132	28.8628559	22	1.7683562	16.5524976	29.2707114	22	1.8163531	16.3434999	29.6855662
23	1.7646107	17.3321105	30.5844273	23	1.8147755	17.1035300	31.0390675	23	1.8663028	16.8793186	31.5019192
24	1.8087260	17.8849058	32.3490380	24	1.8624134	17.6404677	32.8538431	24	1.9176261	17.4007967	33.3682220
25	1.8539441	18.4243764	34.1577740	25	1.9113017	18.1636713	34.7162565	25	1.9703608	17.9083179	35.2858481
26	1.9002927	18.9506111	36.0117081	26	1.9614734	18.6734927	36.6275582	26	2.0245457	18.4022559	37.2562089
27	1.9478000	19.4640109	37.9120008	27	2.0129621	19.1702725	38.5890316	27	2.0802208	18.8829741	39.2807547
28	1.9964950	19.9648886	39.8598008	28	2.0658023	19.6543459	40.6019937	28	2.1374268	19.3508264	41.3609754
29	2.0464074	20.4535499	41.8562958	29	2.1200296	20.1260374	42.6677960	29	2.1962061	19.8061571	43.4984023
30	2.0975676	20.9302926	43.9027032	30	2.1756804	20.5856637	44.7878257	30	2.2566027	20.2493013	45.6946083
31	2.1500068	21.3954074	46.0002708	31	2.2327920	21.0335335	46.9635061	31	2.3186583	20.6805852	47.9512101
32	2.2037569	21.8491779	48.1502767	32	2.2914028	21.4699474	49.1962981	32	2.3824214	21.1003262	50.2698684
33	2.2588509	22.2918809	50.3540345	33	2.3515522	21.8951984	51.4877009	33	2.4479380	21.5088333	52.6522897
34	2.3153221	22.7237863	52.6128854	34	2.4132804	22.3095721	53.8392531	34	2.5152563	21.9064071	55.1002277
35	2.3732052	23.1451573	54.9282075	35	2.4766290	22.7133468	56.2525335	35	2.5844258	22.2933402	57.6154840
36	2.4325353	23.5562510	57.3014127	36	2.5416405	23.1067935	58.7291625	36	2.6554975	22.6699175	60.1999098
37	2.4933487	23.9573181	59.7339480	37	2.6083586	23.4901763	61.2708030	37	2.7285237	23.0364161	62.8554073
38	2.5556824	24.3486030	62.2272957	38	2.6768280	23.8637528	63.8791616	38	2.8035581	23.3931057	65.5839310
39	2.6195745	24.7303444	64.7829791	39	2.7470947	24.2277738	66.5559896	39	2.8806560	23.7402488	68.3874891
40	2.6850638	25.1027750	67.4025536	40	2.8192060	24.5824836	69.3030843	40	2.9598740	24.0781010	71.2681451
41	2.7521904	25.4661220	70.0876175	41	2.8932101	24.9281204	72.1222903	41	3.0412705	24.4069110	74.2280191
42	2.8209952	25.8206068	72.8398079	42	2.9691569	25.2649163	75.0155004	42	3.1249055	24.7269207	77.2692896
43	2.8915201	26.1664457	75.6608031	43	3.0470973	25.5930975	77.9846573	43	3.2106404	25.0383656	80.3941951
44	2.9638081	26.5038494	78.5523232	44	3.1270836	25.9128843	81.0317546	44	3.2991385	25.3414750	83.6050354
45	3.0379033	26.8330238	81.5161313	45	3.2091695	26.2244914	84.1588381	45	3.3898648	25.6364721	86.9041739
46	3.1138509	27.1541696	84.5540345	46	3.2934097	26.5281281	87.3680076	46	3.4830861	25.9235738	90.2940387
47	3.1916971	27.4674825	87.6678854	47	3.3798622	26.8239981	90.6614178	47	3.5788709	26.2029915	93.7771248
48	3.2714896	27.7731537	90.8595926	48	3.4685836	27.1123002	94.0412801	48	3.6772899	26.4749309	97.3559957
49	3.3532768	28.0713694	94.1310727	49	3.5596339	27.3932280	97.5098637	49	3.7784154	26.7395921	101.0332856
50	3.4371087	28.3623117	97.4843489	50	3.6530743	27.6669700	101.0694976	50	3.8823218	26.9971700	104.8117009
51	3.5230364	28.6461577	100.9214577	51	3.7489675	27.9337101	104.7225719	51	3.9890856	27.2478540	108.6940227
52	3.6111124	28.9230807	104.4444941	52	3.8473779	28.1936274	108.4715394	52	4.0987855	27.4918287	112.6831083
53	3.7013902	29.1932495	108.0556065	53	3.9483716	28.4468964	112.3189173	53	4.2115021	27.7292737	116.7818938
54	3.7939249	29.4568287	111.7569966	54	4.0520163	28.6936871	116.2672889	54	4.3273184	27.9603636	120.9933959
55	3.8887720	29.7139792	115.5509215	55	4.1583818	28.9341662	120.3193053	55	4.4463196	28.1852688	125.3207143
56	3.9859924	29.9648578	119.4356946	56	4.2675393	29.1684923	124.4776870	56	4.5685934	28.4041545	129.7670340
57	4.0856492	30.2096194	123.4258870	57	4.3795622	29.3968256	128.7452263	57	4.6942298	28.6171820	134.3356274
58	4.1877832	30.4484072	127.5113291	58	4.4945257	29.6193185	133.1247885	58	4.8233211	28.8245080	139.0298572
59	4.2924778	30.6813729	131.6991124	59	4.6125070	29.8361204	137.6193142	59	4.9559624	29.0262852	143.8531782
60	4.3997898	30.9086564	135.9915902	60	4.7335853	30.0473767	142.2318212	60	5.0922514	29.2226620	148.8091407
61	4.5097845	31.1303905	140.3913800	61	4.8578479	30.2532295	146.9654066	61	5.2322883	29.4137829	153.9013920
62	4.6225291	31.3467283	144.9011645	62	4.9853603	30.4538168	151.8232485	62	5.3761762	29.5997888	159.1336803
63	4.7380923	31.5577837	149.5236936	63	5.1162260	30.6492733	156.8086068	63	5.5240211	29.7808163	164.5098565
64	4.8565447	31.7636914	154.2617859	64	5.2505269	30.8397304	161.9248347	64	5.6759316	29.9569988	170.0338776
65	4.9779585	31.9645770	159.1183306	65	5.3883533	31.0253159	167.1753617	65	5.8320198	30.1284660	175.7098092
66	5.1024072	32.1605629	164.0962889	66	5.5297975	31.2061543	172.5637149	66	5.9924003	30.2953441	181.5418290
67	5.2299674	32.3517687	169.1986961	67	5.6749547	31.3823672	178.0935124	67	6.1571913	30.4577558	187.5342293
68	5.3607166	32.5383107	174.4286635	68	5.8239223	31.5540728	183.7684672	68	6.3265141	30.6158207	193.6914206
69	5.4947345	32.7203034	179.7893801	69	5.9768002	31.7213864	189.5923994	69	6.5004932	30.7696552	200.0179347
70	5.6321029	32.8978599	185.2841146	70	6.1336912	31.8844203	195.5691897	70	6.6792568	30.9193724	206.5184279
71	5.7729054	33.0710799	190.9162175	71	6.2947006	32.0432841	201.7028809	71	6.8629363	31.0650827	213.1976847
72	5.9172281	33.2400780	196.6891229	72	6.4599365	32.1980844	207.9975815	72	7.0516671	31.2068931	220.0606210
73	6.0651588	33.4049541	202.6063510	73	6.6295099	32.3489251	214.4575181	73	7.2455879	31.3449081	227.1122881
74	6.2167878	33.5658089	208.6715098	74	6.8035345	32.4959075	221.0870279	74	7.4448416	31.4792293	234.3578761
75	6.3722074	33.7227404	214.8882976	75	6.9821273	32.6391304	227.8905624	75	7.6495747	31.6099555	241.8027177
76	6.5315126	33.8758443	221.2605050	76	7.1654081	32.7786898	234.8726897	76	7.8599381	31.7371830	249.4522924
77	6.6948005	34.0252139	227.7920176	77	7.3535001	32.9146794	242.0380978	77	8.0760864	31.8610054	257.3122305
78	6.8621705	34.1709404	234.4868181	78	7.5465295	33.0471907	249.3915979	78	8.2981787	31.9815137	265.3883168
79	7.0337247	34.3131126	241.3489886	79	7.7446259	33.1763125	256.9381273	79	8.5263786	32.0987968	273.6864955
80	7.2095678	34.4518172	248.3827133	80	7.9479223	33.3021315	264.6827532	80	8.7608541	32.2129409	282.2128742
81	7.3898070	34.5871387	255.5922811	81	8.1565552	33.4247323	272.6306755	81	9.0017775	32.3240301	290.9737282
82	7.5745522	34.7191597	262.9820882	82	8.3705648	33.5441971	280.7872307	82	9.2493264	32.4321461	299.9755058
83	7.7639160	34.8479607	270.5566404	83	8.5903948	33.6606062	289.1578955	83	9.5036829	32.5373685	309.2248322
84	7.9580139	34.9736202	278.3205564	84	8.8153926	33.7740377	297.7482903	84	9.7650342	32.6397746	318.7285151
85	8.1569628	35.0962148	286.2785703	85	9.0473098	33.8845678	306.5641830	85	10.0335726	32.7394400	328.4935493
86	8.3608884	35.2158193	294.4355346	86	9.2843017	33.9922707	315.6114928	86	10.3094959	32.8364380	338.5271219
87	8.5699106	35.3325067	302.7964230	87	9.5285277	34.0972187	324.8962945	87	10.5930070	32.9308399	348.8366178
88	8.7841584	35.4463480	311.3663336	88	9.7786516	34.1994823	334.4248222	88	10.8843147	33.0227152	359.4296248
89	9.0037623	35.5574126	320.1504919	89	10.0353412	34.2991301	344.2034738	89	11.1836334	33.1121316	370.3139395
90	9.2288564	35.6657684	329.1542542	90	10.2987689	34.3962291	354.2388150	90	11.4911833	33.1991548	381.4975728
91	9.4595778	35.7714814	338.3831106	91	10.5691116	34.4908444	364.5375839	91	11.8071908	33.2838490	392.9887561
92	9.6960672	35.8746160	347.8426884	92	10.8465508	34.5830396	375.1066955	92	12.1318886	33.3662764	404.7959469
93	9.9384689	35.9752351	357.5387556	93	11.1312727	34.6728766	385.9532463	93	12.4655155	33.4464977	416.9278355
94	10.1869306	36.0734001	367.4772245	94	11.4234686	34.7604157	397.0845190	94	12.8083712	33.5245720	429.3933510
95	10.4416039	36.1691708	377.6641552	95	11.7233347	34.8457157	408.5079877	95	13.1605459	33.6005567	442.2016681
96	10.7026440	36.2626057	388.1057591	96	12.0310724	34.9288338	420.2313224	96	13.5224609	33.6745077	455.3622140
97	10.9702101	36.3537616	398.8084031	97	12.3468879	35.0098259	432.2623946	97	13.8943286	33.7464795	468.8846750
98	11.2444653	36.4426943	409.7786131	98	12.6709937	35.0887463	444.6092825	98	14.2764265	33.8165251	482.7790035
99	11.5255770	36.5294578	421.0230785	99	13.0036073	35.1656480	457.2802762	99	14.6690242	33.8846959	497.0554262
100	11.8137164	36.6141052	432.5486555	100	13.3449520	35.2405827	470.2838835	100	15.0724224	33.9510423	511.7244504

Table 1

M	C(5.75,M,2)	A(5.75,M,2)	S(5.75,M,2)	M	C(6.00,M,2)	A(6.00,M,2)	S(6.00,M,2)	M	C(6.25,M,2)	A(6.25,M,2)	S(6.25,M,2)
1/6	1.0047353	.1639283	.1647045	1/6	1.0049386	.1638117	.1646207	1/6	1.0051418	.1636954	.1645371
1/2	1.0142731	.4894707	.4964570	1/2	1.0148892	.4890241	.4963052	1/2	1.0155048	.4885783	.4961536
1	1.0287500	.9720535	1.0000000	1	1.0300000	.9708738	1.0000000	1	1.0312500	.9696970	1.0000000
2	1.0583266	1.9169414	2.0287500	2	1.0609000	1.9134697	2.0300000	2	1.0634766	1.9100092	2.0312500
3	1.0887535	2.8354230	3.0870766	3	1.0927270	2.8286114	3.0909000	3	1.0967102	2.8218271	3.0947266
4	1.1200551	3.7282362	4.1758300	4	1.1255088	3.7170984	4.1836270	4	1.1305824	3.7060141	4.1914368
5	1.1522567	4.5960984	5.2958851	5	1.1592741	4.5797072	5.3091358	5	1.1653256	4.5634077	5.3224192
6	1.1853841	5.4397068	6.4481418	6	1.1940523	5.4171914	6.4684099	6	1.2027733	5.3948195	6.4887448
7	1.2194639	6.2597393	7.6335259	7	1.2298739	6.2302830	7.6624622	7	1.2403599	6.2010371	7.6915180
8	1.2545235	7.0568547	8.8529898	8	1.2667701	7.0196922	8.8923360	8	1.2791212	6.9828239	8.9318780
9	1.2905910	7.8316935	10.1075132	9	1.3047732	7.7861089	10.1591061	9	1.3190937	7.7409201	10.2109992
10	1.3276955	8.5848783	11.3981042	10	1.3439164	8.5302028	11.4638793	10	1.3603154	8.4760438	11.5300929
11	1.3658667	9.3170141	12.7257997	11	1.3842339	9.2526241	12.8077957	11	1.4028253	9.1888909	12.8904083
12	1.4051354	10.0286893	14.0916665	12	1.4257609	9.9540040	14.1920296	12	1.4466635	9.8801367	14.2932336
13	1.4455331	10.7204756	15.4968019	13	1.4685337	10.6349553	15.6177905	13	1.4918718	10.5504355	15.7398971
14	1.4870921	11.3929289	16.9423349	14	1.5125897	11.2960731	17.0863242	14	1.5384928	11.2004223	17.2317689
15	1.5298460	12.0465895	18.4294271	15	1.5579674	11.9379351	18.5989139	15	1.5865707	11.8307126	18.7702617
16	1.5738291	12.6819825	19.9592731	16	1.6047064	12.5611020	20.1568813	16	1.6361510	12.4419031	20.3568323
17	1.6190767	13.2996184	21.5331022	17	1.6528476	13.1661185	21.7615878	17	1.6872807	13.0345727	21.9929834
18	1.6656251	13.8999936	23.1521789	18	1.7024331	13.7535131	23.4144354	18	1.7400083	13.6092826	23.6802641
19	1.7135119	14.4835904	24.8178040	19	1.7535061	14.3237991	25.1168684	19	1.7943835	14.1665771	25.4202723
20	1.7627753	15.0508777	26.5313159	20	1.8061112	14.8774749	26.8703745	20	1.8504580	14.7069838	27.2146559
21	1.8134551	15.6023112	28.2940912	21	1.8602946	15.4150241	28.6764857	21	1.9082848	15.2310146	29.0651139
22	1.8655920	16.1383341	30.1075464	22	1.9161034	15.9369166	30.5367803	22	1.9679187	15.7391657	30.9733987
23	1.9192277	16.6593770	31.9731383	23	1.9735865	16.4436084	32.4528837	23	2.0294162	16.2319183	32.9413174
24	1.9744055	17.1658586	33.8923661	24	2.0327941	16.9355421	34.4264702	24	2.0928354	16.7097389	34.9707335
25	2.0311697	17.6581857	35.8667716	25	2.0937779	17.4131477	36.4592643	25	2.1582365	17.1730802	37.0635690
26	2.0895658	18.1367541	37.8979413	26	2.1565913	17.8768424	38.5530423	26	2.2256814	17.6223908	39.2218055
27	2.1496408	18.6019481	39.9875071	27	2.2212890	18.3270315	40.7096335	27	2.2952340	18.0580362	41.4474869
28	2.2114430	19.0541415	42.1371479	28	2.2879277	18.7641082	42.9309226	28	2.3669600	18.4805490	43.7427209
29	2.2750220	19.4936977	44.3485909	29	2.3565655	19.1884546	45.2186502	29	2.4409275	18.8902294	46.1096809
30	2.3404289	19.9209698	46.6236129	30	2.4272625	19.6004413	47.5754157	30	2.5172065	19.2874951	48.5506085
31	2.4077162	20.3363011	48.9640418	31	2.5000803	20.0004285	50.0026782	31	2.5958692	19.6727226	51.0678150
32	2.4769380	20.7400254	51.3717580	32	2.5750828	20.3887655	52.5027586	32	2.6769901	20.0462764	53.6636842
33	2.5481500	21.1324670	53.8486960	33	2.6523352	20.7657918	55.0078413	33	2.7605461	20.4095105	56.3406743
34	2.6214093	21.5139412	56.3968460	34	2.7319053	21.1318367	57.7301766	34	2.8469163	20.7597677	59.1013204
35	2.6967748	21.8847545	59.0182554	35	2.8133625	21.4872201	60.4620819	35	2.9358824	21.1003308	61.9482367
36	2.7743071	22.2452048	61.7150302	36	2.8982783	21.8322525	63.2759443	36	3.0276287	21.4306723	64.8841191
37	2.8540685	22.5955819	64.4893373	37	2.9852267	22.1672354	66.1742227	37	3.1222421	21.7509550	67.9117478
38	2.9361229	22.9361671	67.3434058	38	3.0747835	22.4926616	69.1594493	38	3.2199122	22.0615321	71.0339899
39	3.0205365	23.2672341	70.2795287	39	3.1670270	22.8082151	72.2342328	39	3.3204313	22.3626973	74.2533021
40	3.1073769	23.5890489	73.3000652	40	3.2620378	23.1147720	75.4012598	40	3.4241948	22.6547372	77.5742334
41	3.1967140	23.9018701	76.4074420	41	3.3598989	23.4124000	78.6632976	41	3.5312009	22.9379270	80.9984282
42	3.2886195	24.2059491	79.6041560	42	3.4606959	23.7013592	82.0231965	42	3.6415509	23.2125353	84.5296201
43	3.3831673	24.5015301	82.8927755	43	3.5645168	23.9819021	85.4638925	43	3.7553494	23.4788221	88.1711800
44	3.4804334	24.7888507	86.2759428	44	3.6714523	24.2542739	89.0484092	44	3.8727040	23.7370396	91.9265294
45	3.5804958	25.0681416	89.7563761	45	3.7815958	24.5187125	92.7198615	45	3.9937260	23.9874533	95.7992334
46	3.6834351	25.3396273	93.3368720	46	3.8950437	24.7754490	96.5014574	46	4.1185300	24.2302374	99.7929595
47	3.7893338	25.6035259	97.0203070	47	4.0118950	25.0247078	100.3965011	47	4.2472341	24.4656848	103.9114895
48	3.8982772	25.8600495	100.8096409	48	4.1322519	25.2667065	104.4083961	48	4.3799601	24.6939974	108.1587235
49	4.0103526	26.1094041	104.7079180	49	4.2562194	25.5016569	108.5406480	49	4.5168339	24.9153914	112.5386836
50	4.1256503	26.3517902	108.7182707	50	4.3839060	25.7297640	112.7968675	50	4.6579849	25.1300765	117.0555175
51	4.2442627	26.5874023	112.8439210	51	4.5154232	25.9512272	117.1807735	51	4.8035470	25.3382560	121.7135024
52	4.3662853	26.8164300	117.0881837	52	4.6508859	26.1662400	121.6961967	52	4.9536578	25.5401270	126.5170494
53	4.4918160	27.0390571	121.4544690	53	4.7904125	26.3749903	126.3470826	53	5.1084596	25.7358807	131.4707072
54	4.6209557	27.2554625	125.9462850	54	4.9341249	26.5776604	131.1374951	54	5.2680990	25.9257025	136.5791668
55	4.7538082	27.4656202	130.5672407	55	5.0821486	26.7744276	136.0716199	55	5.4327271	26.1097324	141.8472658
56	4.8904802	27.6702991	135.3210489	56	5.2346131	26.9654637	141.1537686	56	5.6024998	26.2882639	147.2799928
57	5.0310815	27.8690635	140.2115290	57	5.3916515	27.1509358	146.3883816	57	5.7775779	26.4613468	152.8824926
58	5.1757251	28.0622732	145.2426105	58	5.5534010	27.3310055	151.7800331	58	5.9581272	26.6291848	158.6600705
59	5.3245272	28.2500833	150.4183356	59	5.7200032	27.5058305	157.3334341	59	6.1443187	26.7919368	164.6181977
60	5.4776073	28.4326447	155.7428627	60	5.8916031	27.6755636	163.0534371	60	6.3363286	26.9497569	170.7625164
61	5.6350885	28.6101042	161.2204700	61	6.0683512	27.8403530	168.9450402	61	6.5343389	27.1027945	177.0988451
62	5.7970973	28.7826044	166.8555585	62	6.2504018	28.0003428	175.0133914	62	6.7385370	27.2511947	183.6331840
63	5.9637639	28.9502837	172.6526559	63	6.4379128	28.1556726	181.2637932	63	6.9491163	27.3950979	190.3717210
64	6.1352221	29.1132770	178.6164197	64	6.6310512	28.3064782	187.7017070	64	7.1662762	27.5346404	197.3208373
65	6.3116097	29.2717152	184.7516418	65	6.8299828	28.4528915	194.3327582	65	7.3902223	27.6699543	204.4871135
66	6.4930685	29.4257256	191.0632515	66	7.0348822	28.5950403	201.1627410	66	7.6211668	27.8011678	211.8773358
67	6.6797442	29.5754319	197.5563200	67	7.2459287	28.7330488	208.1976232	67	7.8593282	27.9284051	219.4985025
68	6.8717869	29.7209545	204.2360642	68	7.4633066	28.8670377	215.4435519	68	8.1049322	28.0517868	227.3578307
69	7.0693507	29.8624102	211.1078511	69	7.6872058	28.9971240	222.9068585	69	8.3582114	28.1714296	235.4627630
70	7.2725946	29.9999127	218.1772018	70	7.9178219	29.1234213	230.5940642	70	8.6194055	28.2874469	243.8209743
71	7.4816817	30.1335725	225.4497964	71	8.1553566	29.2460401	238.5118862	71	8.8887619	28.3999485	252.4403798
72	7.6967800	30.2634969	232.9314780	72	8.4000173	29.3650875	246.6672428	72	9.1665357	28.5090410	261.3291416
73	7.9180624	30.3897904	240.6282580	73	8.6520178	29.4806675	255.0672601	73	9.4529999	28.6148276	270.4956773
74	8.1457067	30.5125545	248.5463204	74	8.9115784	29.5928810	263.7192779	74	9.7483959	28.7174090	279.9486673
75	8.3798958	30.6318877	256.6920272	75	9.1789227	29.7018262	272.6308562	75	10.0530332	28.8168811	289.6970631
76	8.6208178	30.7478860	265.0719230	76	9.4542935	29.8075983	281.8097819	76	10.3671905	28.9133392	299.7500964
77	8.8686665	30.8606425	273.6927408	77	9.7379223	29.9102896	291.2640754	77	10.6911652	29.0068744	310.1172869
78	9.1236405	30.9702479	282.5614071	78	10.0300599	30.0099899	301.0019977	78	11.0252641	29.0975752	320.8084521
79	9.3859451	31.0767902	291.6850475	79	10.3309637	30.1067843	311.0320576	79	11.3698037	29.1855274	331.8337163
80	9.6557911	31.1803550	301.0709927	80	10.6408906	30.2007634	321.3630194	80	11.7251100	29.2708145	343.2035199
81	9.9333950	31.2810255	310.7267837	81	10.9601173	30.2920033	332.0039100	81	12.0915197	29.3535171	354.9286299
82	10.2189802	31.3788826	320.6601788	82	11.2889208	30.3805857	342.9640273	82	12.4693797	29.4337135	367.0201496
83	10.5127708	31.4740050	330.8791589	83	11.6275385	30.4665081	354.2529481	83	12.8590478	29.5114798	379.4895293
84	10.8150181	31.5664690	341.3919348	84	11.9764161	30.5500855	365.8805366	84	13.2608931	29.5868895	392.3485772
85	11.1259499	31.6563490	352.2069529	85	12.3357086	30.6311510	377.8569527	85	13.6752960	29.6600140	405.6094702
86	11.4458210	31.7437171	363.3329028	86	12.7057799	30.7098553	390.1926613	86	14.1026476	29.7309227	419.2847662
87	11.7748883	31.8286436	374.7787238	87	13.0869523	30.7862673	402.8984412	87	14.5433567	29.7996826	433.3874151
88	12.1134164	31.9111967	386.5536121	88	13.4795619	30.8604537	415.9853944	88	14.9978366	29.8663589	447.9307719
89	12.4616771	31.9914427	398.6670285	89	13.8839487	30.9324793	429.4649563	89	15.4665190	29.9310147	462.9286005
90	12.8199503	32.0694461	411.1287056	90	14.3004672	31.0024071	443.3489050	90	15.9498478	29.9937112	478.3951276
91	13.1885239	32.1452696	423.9486559	91	14.7294812	31.0702982	457.6493722	91	16.4482805	30.0545078	494.3449753
92	13.5676939	32.2189741	437.1371798	92	15.1713656	31.1362118	472.3788534	92	16.9622893	30.1134621	510.7932558
93	13.9577651	32.2906188	450.7048737	93	15.6265066	31.2002056	487.5502190	93	17.4923608	30.1706300	527.7555451
94	14.3590509	32.3602613	464.6626388	94	16.0953018	31.2623356	503.1767256	94	18.0389971	30.2260654	545.2479059
95	14.7718736	32.4279575	479.0216897	95	16.5781608	31.3226559	519.2720274	95	18.6027157	30.2798210	563.2869030
96	15.1965650	32.4937619	493.7935633	96	17.0755057	31.3812193	535.8501882	96	19.1840506	30.3319476	581.8896187
97	15.6334662	32.5577272	508.9901283	97	17.5877708	31.4380770	552.9256939	97	19.7835322	30.3824947	601.0736694
98	16.0829284	32.6199049	524.6235945	98	18.1154040	31.4932786	570.5134647	98	20.4017882	30.4315100	620.8572216
99	16.5453126	32.6803450	540.7065229	99	18.6588661	31.5468725	588.6288687	99	21.0393441	30.4790400	641.2590098
100	17.0209903	32.7390960	557.2518355	100	19.2186321	31.5989053	607.2877348	100	21.6968236	30.5251297	662.2983538

Table 1

M	C(6.50,M,2)	A(6.50,M,2)	S(6.50,M,2)	M	C(6.75,M,2)	A(6.75,M,2)	S(6.75,M,2)	M	C(7.00,M,2)	A(7.00,M,2)	S(7.00,M,2)
1/6	1.0053447	.1635793	.1644535	1/6	1.0055475	.1634633	.1643701	1/6	1.0057500	.1633476	.1642868
1/2	1.0161201	.4881335	.4960022	1/2	1.0167350	.4876895	.4958510	1/2	1.0173495	.4872464	.4956999
1	1.0325000	.9685230	1.0000000	1	1.0337500	.9673519	1.0000000	1	1.0350000	.9661836	1.0000000
2	1.0660563	1.9065598	2.0325000	2	1.0686391	1.9031215	2.0337500	2	1.0712250	1.8996943	2.0350000
3	1.1007013	2.8150700	3.0985563	3	1.1047056	2.8083400	3.1023891	3	1.1087179	2.8016370	3.1062250
4	1.1364759	3.6949831	4.1992593	4	1.1419894	3.6840049	4.2070947	4	1.1475230	3.6730792	4.2149429
5	1.1734114	4.5471991	5.3357353	5	1.1805316	4.5310809	5.3490841	5	1.1875863	4.5150524	5.3624559
6	1.2115473	5.3725899	6.5091467	6	1.2203745	5.3505015	6.5296157	6	1.2292553	5.3285530	6.5501522
7	1.2509226	6.1719999	7.7206939	7	1.2615622	6.1431695	7.7499903	7	1.2722793	6.1145440	7.7794075
8	1.2915775	6.9462469	8.9716165	8	1.3041399	6.9099584	9.0115524	8	1.3168090	6.8739555	9.0516868
9	1.3335538	7.6961229	10.2631940	9	1.3481546	7.6517131	10.3156923	9	1.3628974	7.6076865	10.3684958
10	1.3768943	8.4223951	11.5967478	10	1.3936548	8.3692509	11.6638469	10	1.4105988	8.3166053	11.7313932
11	1.4216434	9.1258064	12.9736421	11	1.4406907	9.0633624	13.0575018	11	1.4599697	9.0015510	13.1419919
12	1.4678468	9.8070764	14.3952855	12	1.4893140	9.7348125	14.4931925	12	1.5110687	9.6633343	14.6019816
13	1.5155518	10.4669021	15.8631323	13	1.5395783	10.3843410	15.9875065	13	1.5639561	10.3027385	16.1130303
14	1.5643072	11.1059584	17.3786841	14	1.5915391	11.0126636	17.5270848	14	1.6186945	10.9205203	17.6769864
15	1.6155835	11.7246992	18.9434913	15	1.6452536	11.6204726	19.1186239	15	1.6753488	11.5174109	19.2956809
16	1.6681725	12.3243576	20.5591548	16	1.7007809	12.2084378	20.7638775	16	1.7339360	12.0941168	20.9710297
17	1.7223881	12.9049468	22.2273273	17	1.7581822	12.7772071	22.4646583	17	1.7946756	12.6513206	22.7050158
18	1.7783658	13.4672608	23.9497154	18	1.8175209	13.3274071	24.2228406	18	1.8574892	13.1896817	24.4996913
19	1.8361626	14.0118749	25.7280812	19	1.8788622	13.8596441	26.0403614	19	1.9225013	13.7098374	26.3571805
20	1.8958379	14.5393461	27.5642438	20	1.9422738	14.3745046	27.9192236	20	1.9897889	14.2124033	28.2796818
21	1.9574527	15.0502142	29.4600818	21	2.0078255	14.8725558	29.8614974	21	2.0594315	14.6979742	30.2694707
22	2.0210699	15.5450016	31.4175344	22	2.0755897	15.3543466	31.8693230	22	2.1315116	15.1671248	32.3289022
23	2.0867546	16.0242146	33.4386043	23	2.1456408	15.8204079	33.9449126	23	2.2061145	15.6204105	34.4604137
24	2.1545742	16.4883435	35.5253589	24	2.2180562	16.2712531	36.0905534	24	2.2833285	16.0583676	36.6665282
25	2.2245978	16.9378629	37.6799231	25	2.2929156	16.7073790	38.3086096	25	2.3632450	16.4815146	38.9498567
26	2.2968973	17.3732329	39.9045309	26	2.3703015	17.1292663	40.6015252	26	2.4459586	16.8903523	41.3131017
27	2.3715464	17.7948987	42.2014282	27	2.4502992	17.5373797	42.9718267	27	2.5315671	17.2853645	43.7590603
28	2.4486217	18.2032917	44.5729746	28	2.5329967	17.9321690	45.4221258	28	2.6201720	17.6670188	46.2906274
29	2.5282019	18.5988297	47.0215963	29	2.6184854	18.3140692	47.9551226	29	2.7118780	18.0357670	48.9107993
30	2.6103684	18.9819174	49.5497982	30	2.7058593	18.6835010	50.5736079	30	2.8067937	18.3920454	51.6226773
31	2.6952054	19.3529466	52.1601666	31	2.7962158	19.0408716	53.2804672	31	2.9050315	18.7362757	54.4294710
32	2.7827996	19.7122970	54.8553720	32	2.8926556	19.3865747	56.0786830	32	3.0067076	19.0688655	57.3345025
33	2.8732406	20.0603361	57.6381716	33	2.9902827	19.7209913	58.9713385	33	3.1119424	19.3902082	60.3412101
34	2.9666209	20.3974199	60.5114122	34	3.0912047	20.0444897	61.9616212	34	3.2208603	19.7006842	63.4531525
35	3.0630361	20.7238934	63.4780331	35	3.1955329	20.3574266	65.0528259	35	3.3335905	20.0006611	66.6740128
36	3.1625848	21.0400904	66.5410692	36	3.3033821	20.6601466	68.2483588	36	3.4502661	20.2904938	70.0076033
37	3.2653688	21.3463346	69.7036539	37	3.4148713	20.9529834	71.5517409	37	3.5710254	20.5705254	73.4578694
38	3.3714932	21.6429390	72.9690227	38	3.5301232	21.2367597	74.9666122	38	3.6960113	20.8410873	77.0288948
39	3.4810668	21.9302073	76.3405159	39	3.6492648	21.5102875	78.4967354	39	3.8253717	21.1024999	80.7249061
40	3.5942014	22.2084332	79.8215827	40	3.7724275	21.7753688	82.1460002	40	3.9592597	21.3550723	84.5502778
41	3.7110130	22.4779014	83.4157841	41	3.8997469	22.0317957	85.9184277	41	4.0978338	21.5991037	88.5095376
42	3.8316209	22.7388876	87.1267971	42	4.0313634	22.2798507	89.8181746	42	4.2412580	21.8348828	92.6073714
43	3.9561486	22.9916587	90.9584180	43	4.1674219	22.5198072	93.8495380	43	4.3897020	22.0626887	96.8486294
44	4.0847234	23.2364733	94.9145666	44	4.3080724	22.7519296	98.0169599	44	4.5433416	22.2827910	101.2383314
45	4.2174769	23.4735819	98.9992900	45	4.4534698	22.9764736	102.3250323	45	4.7023586	22.4954502	105.7816730
46	4.3545449	23.7032270	103.2167670	46	4.6007745	23.1936867	106.7785022	46	4.8669411	22.7009181	110.4840316
47	4.4960676	23.9256436	107.5713119	47	4.7591518	23.4038081	111.3822766	47	5.0372841	22.8994378	115.3509727
48	4.6421898	24.1410592	112.0673795	48	4.9197732	23.6070695	116.1414285	48	5.2135890	23.0912442	120.3882568
49	4.7930610	24.3496941	116.7095694	49	5.0858156	23.8036948	121.0612017	49	5.3960646	23.2765645	125.6018458
50	4.9488355	24.5517618	121.5026304	50	5.2574618	23.9939007	126.1470173	50	5.5849269	23.4556178	130.9979104
51	5.1096726	24.7474657	126.4514659	51	5.4349012	24.1778967	131.4044791	51	5.7803993	23.6286163	136.5828372
52	5.2757370	24.9370161	131.5611385	52	5.6183291	24.3558855	136.8393803	52	5.9827133	23.7957645	142.3632365
53	5.4471985	25.1205492	136.8368755	53	5.8079477	24.5280634	142.4577094	53	6.1921083	23.9572604	148.3459494
54	5.6242324	25.2983987	142.2840740	54	6.0039654	24.6946200	148.2656571	54	6.4088320	24.1132951	154.5380581
55	5.8070200	25.4706041	147.9083064	55	6.2065998	24.8557388	154.2696822	55	6.6331412	24.2640532	160.9468901
56	5.9957481	25.6373889	153.7153264	56	6.4160725	25.0115974	160.4762228	56	6.8653011	24.4097132	167.5800313
57	6.1906099	25.7989239	159.7110745	57	6.6326150	25.1623675	166.8922953	57	7.1055866	24.5504476	174.4453324
58	6.3918048	25.9553742	165.9016844	58	6.8564657	25.3082152	173.5249103	58	7.3542822	24.6864228	181.5509190
59	6.5995384	26.1069000	172.2934892	59	7.0878714	25.4493013	180.3813760	59	7.6116821	24.8177998	188.9052012
60	6.8140234	26.2536562	178.8930276	60	7.3270971	25.5857812	187.4692475	60	7.8780909	24.9447341	196.5168833
61	7.0354792	26.3957929	185.7070510	61	7.5743763	25.7178050	194.7963346	61	8.1538241	25.0673759	204.3949742
62	7.2641322	26.5334566	192.7425201	62	7.8300115	25.8455190	202.3707109	62	8.4392080	25.1858705	212.5487983
63	7.5002165	26.6667851	200.0066624	63	8.0942744	25.9690631	210.2007224	63	8.7345802	25.3003579	220.9880062
64	7.7439736	26.7959177	207.5068789	64	8.3674562	26.0885737	218.2949968	64	9.0402905	25.4109739	229.7225865
65	7.9956527	26.9209887	215.2508525	65	8.6498578	26.2041826	226.6642529	65	9.3567007	25.5178491	238.7628770
66	8.2555114	27.0421169	223.2465052	66	8.9417905	26.3160170	235.3123107	66	9.6841852	25.6211103	248.1195777
67	8.5238156	27.1594353	231.5020166	67	9.2435759	26.4242002	244.2541012	67	10.0231317	25.7208795	257.8037629
68	8.8008396	27.2730608	240.0258322	68	9.5555466	26.5288515	253.4976772	68	10.3739413	25.8172749	267.8268947
69	9.0868668	27.3831097	248.8266718	69	9.8780463	26.6300861	263.0532238	69	10.7370293	25.9104105	278.2008360
70	9.3821900	27.4896946	257.9135386	70	10.2114304	26.7280156	272.9312701	70	11.1128253	26.0003966	288.9378653
71	9.6871112	27.5929246	267.2957286	71	10.5560662	26.8227478	283.1427005	71	11.5043363	26.0873397	300.0506935
72	10.0019423	27.6929052	276.9828398	72	10.9123334	26.9143873	293.6987666	72	11.9043363	26.1713427	311.5524647
73	10.3270050	27.7897387	286.9847821	73	11.2806246	27.0030348	304.6111000	73	12.3522260	26.2525050	323.4568010
74	10.6626331	27.8835241	297.3117876	74	11.6613457	27.0887882	315.8917247	74	12.7522226	26.3309227	335.7777891
75	11.0091687	27.9743575	307.9744207	75	12.0549161	27.1717419	327.5530704	75	13.1985504	26.4066886	348.5300117
76	11.3669667	28.0623317	318.9835893	76	12.4617696	27.2519874	339.6079865	76	13.6604997	26.4798924	361.7285621
77	11.7363931	28.1475368	330.3505560	77	12.8823543	27.3296129	352.0697561	77	14.1386172	26.5506207	375.3890618
78	12.1178259	28.2300598	342.0869491	78	13.3171337	27.4047042	364.9521104	78	14.6334688	26.6189572	389.5276790
79	12.5116552	28.3099863	354.2047750	79	13.7665870	27.4773408	378.2692441	79	15.1456402	26.6849828	404.1611478
80	12.9182840	28.3873950	366.7164302	80	14.2312093	27.5476119	392.0358311	80	15.6757376	26.7487756	419.3067880
81	13.3381282	28.4623680	379.6347142	81	14.7115126	27.6155895	406.2670404	81	16.2243684	26.8104112	434.9825256
82	13.7716174	28.5349811	392.9728424	82	15.2090262	27.6813406	420.9785531	82	16.7922420	26.8699625	451.2069140
83	14.2191950	28.6053086	406.7444598	83	15.7212971	27.7449486	436.1865793	83	17.3799705	26.9275000	467.9991560
84	14.6813188	28.6734224	420.9636548	84	16.2518908	27.8064799	451.9078763	84	17.9882695	26.9830918	485.3791265
85	15.1584617	28.7393921	435.6449736	85	16.8003922	27.8660023	468.1597672	85	18.6178589	27.0368037	503.3673959
86	15.6511117	28.8032653	450.8034352	86	17.3674054	27.9235815	484.9601594	86	19.2694839	27.0886992	521.9852548
87	16.1597728	28.8651674	466.4545469	87	17.9535553	27.9792807	502.3275648	87	19.9439159	27.1388398	541.2547388
88	16.6849654	28.9251016	482.6143197	88	18.5594878	28.0331615	520.2811201	88	20.6419529	27.1872849	561.1986547
89	17.2272268	28.9831492	499.2992851	89	19.1858705	28.0852832	538.8406079	89	21.3644213	27.2340917	581.8406076
90	17.7871117	29.0393697	516.5265119	90	19.8333937	28.1357032	558.0264785	90	22.1121760	27.2793156	603.2050289
91	18.3651928	29.0938206	534.3136236	91	20.5027707	28.1844771	577.8598721	91	22.8861022	27.3230102	625.3172049
92	18.9620616	29.1465574	552.6788164	92	21.1947392	28.2316586	598.3626429	92	23.6871158	27.3652273	648.2033071
93	19.5783286	29.1976343	571.6408779	93	21.9100617	28.2772998	619.5573821	93	24.5161648	27.4060167	671.8904229
94	20.2146242	29.2471035	591.2192065	94	22.6495263	28.3214508	641.4674438	94	25.3742306	27.4454268	696.4065878
95	20.8715995	29.2950155	611.4338307	95	23.4139478	28.3641604	664.1169700	95	26.2623287	27.4835041	721.7808184
96	21.5499265	29.3414193	632.3054302	96	24.2041685	28.4054756	687.5309178	96	27.1815102	27.5202938	748.0431470
97	22.2502991	29.3863625	653.8553568	97	25.0210592	28.4454419	711.7350863	97	28.1328630	27.5558394	775.2246572
98	22.9734338	29.4298911	676.1056559	98	25.8655199	28.4841034	736.7561455	98	29.1175132	27.5901830	803.3575203
99	23.7200705	29.4720495	699.0790897	99	26.7384812	28.5215027	762.6216654	99	30.1366262	27.6233653	832.4750335
100	24.4909727	29.5128808	722.7991602	100	27.6409050	28.5576810	789.3601467	100	31.1914081	27.6554254	862.6116597

Table 1

355

M	C(7.25,M,2)	A(7.25,M,2)	S(7.25,M,2)	M	C(7.50,M,2)	A(7.50,M,2)	S(7.50,M,2)	M	C(7.75,M,2)	A(7.75,M,2)	S(7.75,M,2)
1/6	1.0059524	.1632321	.1642037	1/6	1.0061545	.1631167	.1641206	1/6	1.0063565	.1630016	.1640377
1/2	1.0179637	.4868043	.4955491	1/2	1.0185774	.4863630	.4953984	1/2	1.0191909	.4859226	.4952479
1	1.0362500	.9650181	1.0000000	1	1.0375000	.9638554	1.0000000	1	1.0387500	.9626955	1.0000000
2	1.0738141	1.8962780	2.0362500	2	1.0764063	1.8928727	2.0375000	2	1.0790016	1.8894783	2.0387500
3	1.1127398	2.7949607	3.1100641	3	1.1167715	2.7883110	3.1139063	3	1.1208129	2.7816879	3.1177516
4	1.1530766	3.6622057	4.2228039	4	1.1586504	3.6513841	4.2306777	4	1.1642444	3.6406141	4.2385644
5	1.1948757	4.4991129	5.3758805	5	1.2020998	4.4832618	5.3893281	5	1.2093588	4.4674985	5.4028088
6	1.2381899	5.3067434	6.5707562	6	1.2471785	5.2850716	6.5914280	6	1.2562215	5.2635365	6.6121676
7	1.2830743	6.0861215	7.8089461	7	1.2939477	6.0579004	7.8386065	7	1.3049001	6.0298787	7.8683891
8	1.3295857	6.8382355	9.0920204	8	1.3424708	6.8027955	9.1325542	8	1.3554650	6.7676329	9.1732892
9	1.3777832	7.5640391	10.4216061	9	1.3928134	7.5207668	10.4750250	9	1.4079892	7.4778656	10.5287542
10	1.4277279	8.2644527	11.7993894	10	1.4450439	8.2127872	11.8678385	10	1.4625488	8.1616035	11.9367434
11	1.4794830	8.9403645	13.2271172	11	1.4992331	8.8797949	13.3128824	11	1.5192226	8.8198349	13.3992922
12	1.5331143	9.5926316	14.7066002	12	1.5554543	9.5226939	14.8121155	12	1.5780924	9.4535113	14.9185148
13	1.5886697	10.2220811	16.2397145	13	1.6137839	10.1423556	16.3675698	13	1.6392435	10.0635488	16.4966072
14	1.6462797	10.8295113	17.8284041	14	1.6743008	10.7396198	17.9813537	14	1.7027642	10.6508291	18.1358508
15	1.7059573	11.4156925	19.4746838	15	1.7370870	11.3152962	19.6556545	15	1.7687463	11.2162013	19.8386150
16	1.7677982	11.9813679	21.1806411	16	1.8022278	11.8701650	21.3927415	16	1.8372853	11.7604826	21.6073613
17	1.8318809	12.5272549	22.9484393	17	1.8699114	12.4049783	23.1949693	17	1.9084801	12.2844598	23.4446466
18	1.8982866	13.0540457	24.7803203	18	1.9399293	12.9204611	25.0647807	18	1.9824337	12.7888903	25.3531266
19	1.9670995	13.5624084	26.6786069	19	2.0126766	13.4173119	27.0047100	19	2.0592530	13.2745033	27.3355603
20	2.0384069	14.0529876	28.6457064	20	2.0881520	13.8962042	29.0173866	20	2.1390490	13.7420008	29.3948133
21	2.1122991	14.5264054	30.6841132	21	2.1664577	14.3577872	31.1055386	21	2.2219372	14.1920585	31.5338623
22	2.1888699	14.9832622	32.7964123	22	2.2478399	14.8026864	33.2719963	22	2.3080372	14.6253271	33.7557994
23	2.2682165	15.4241372	34.9852823	23	2.3319886	15.2315050	35.5196961	23	2.3974737	15.0424328	36.0638367
24	2.3504393	15.8495896	37.2534988	24	2.4194382	15.6448241	37.8516847	24	2.4903758	15.4439786	38.4613103
25	2.4356428	16.2601588	39.6039391	25	2.5101671	16.0432040	40.2711229	25	2.5868778	15.8305450	40.9516861
26	2.5239348	16.6563656	42.0395808	26	2.6042984	16.4271845	42.7812900	26	2.6871194	16.2026908	43.5385639
27	2.6154274	17.0387123	44.5635157	27	2.7015596	16.7972863	45.3855884	27	2.7912452	16.5609538	46.2256833
28	2.7102367	17.4076837	47.1789431	28	2.8032831	17.1540109	48.0875480	28	2.8994060	16.9058520	49.0169285
29	2.8084828	17.7637479	49.8891798	29	2.9084062	17.4978418	50.8908310	29	3.0117580	17.2378840	51.9163345
30	2.9102903	18.1073562	52.6976626	30	3.0174714	17.8292451	53.7992372	30	3.1284636	17.5575297	54.9260925
31	3.0157883	18.4389445	55.6079528	31	3.1306266	18.1486700	56.8167086	31	3.2496916	17.8652513	58.0565561
32	3.1251106	18.7589331	58.6237411	32	3.2480251	18.4565494	59.9473352	32	3.3756171	18.1614934	61.3062476
33	3.2383959	19.0677280	61.7488517	33	3.3693260	18.7533006	63.1953602	33	3.5064223	18.4466844	64.6818647
34	3.3557877	19.3657206	64.9872476	34	3.4961945	19.0393259	66.5651863	34	3.6422961	18.7212365	68.1882870
35	3.4774350	19.6532889	68.3430353	35	3.6273018	19.3150129	70.0613807	35	3.7834351	18.9855465	71.8305831
36	3.6034921	19.9307975	71.8204704	36	3.7633256	19.5807353	73.6886325	36	3.9300432	19.2399967	75.6140182
37	3.7341186	20.1985983	75.4239624	37	3.9044503	19.8368533	77.4520081	37	4.0823324	19.4849547	79.5440614
38	3.8694804	20.4570309	79.1580811	38	4.0508672	20.0837141	81.3564584	38	4.2405228	19.7207746	83.6263930
39	4.0097491	20.7064231	83.0275615	39	4.2027747	20.3216521	85.4073256	39	4.4048430	19.9477975	87.8669166
40	4.1551025	20.9470910	87.0373106	40	4.3603788	20.5509900	89.6101003	40	4.5755307	20.1663514	92.2717596
41	4.3057250	21.1793400	91.1924131	41	4.5238930	20.7720385	93.9704791	41	4.7528325	20.3767522	96.8472903
42	4.4618075	21.4034644	95.4981381	42	4.6935390	20.9850974	98.4943721	42	4.9370048	20.5793042	101.6001228
43	4.6235480	21.6197485	99.9599456	43	4.8695467	21.1904553	103.1879110	43	5.1283137	20.7743001	106.5371275
44	4.7911517	21.8284666	104.5834937	44	5.0521547	21.3883907	108.0574577	44	5.3270359	20.9620217	111.6654412
45	4.9648309	22.0298833	109.3746453	45	5.2416105	21.5791717	113.1096124	45	5.5334585	21.1427405	116.9924771
46	5.1448060	22.2242541	114.3394762	46	5.4381709	21.7630571	118.3512228	46	5.7478800	21.3167177	122.5259356
47	5.3313032	22.4118254	119.4842822	47	5.6421023	21.9402960	123.7893937	47	5.9706104	21.4842048	128.2738156
48	5.5245651	22.5928351	124.8155875	48	5.8536811	22.1111286	129.4314960	48	6.2019715	21.6454438	134.2444259
49	5.7248305	22.7675128	130.3401525	49	6.0731941	22.2757866	135.2851771	49	6.4422979	21.8006679	140.4463975
50	5.9323556	22.9360799	136.0649831	50	6.3009389	22.4344932	141.3583712	50	6.6919370	21.9501015	146.8886954
51	6.1474035	23.0987502	141.9973387	51	6.5372241	22.5874633	147.6593102	51	6.9512495	22.0939605	153.5806323
52	6.3702469	23.2557300	148.1447422	52	6.7823700	22.7349044	154.1965343	52	7.2206104	22.2324530	160.5318818
53	6.6011684	23.4072183	154.5149892	53	7.0367089	22.8770163	160.9789043	53	7.5004091	22.3657790	167.7524923
54	6.8404607	23.5534073	161.1161575	54	7.3005855	23.0139916	168.0156133	54	7.7910499	22.4941314	175.2529013
55	7.0884274	23.6944823	167.9566182	55	7.5743595	23.1460460	175.3161988	55	8.0929531	22.6176957	183.0439513
56	7.3453829	23.8306223	175.0450457	56	7.8583959	23.2732684	182.8905562	56	8.4065551	22.7366505	191.1369044
57	7.6116530	23.9619998	182.3904286	57	8.1530857	23.3959213	190.7489521	57	8.7323091	22.8511678	199.5434594
58	7.8875755	24.0887814	190.0020816	58	8.4588264	23.5141411	198.9020378	58	9.0706860	22.9614130	208.2757685
59	8.1735001	24.2111281	197.8896571	59	8.7760324	23.6280678	207.3608642	59	9.4221751	23.0675456	217.3464546
60	8.4697895	24.3291947	206.0631572	60	9.1051336	23.7379159	216.1368967	60	9.7872844	23.1697190	226.7686297
61	8.7768193	24.4431312	214.5329466	61	9.4465761	23.8437744	225.2420303	61	10.1665417	23.2680809	236.5559141
62	9.0919790	24.5530820	223.3097760	62	9.8008228	23.9458066	234.6886064	62	10.5604952	23.3627734	246.7224558
63	9.4246720	24.6591865	232.4047450	63	10.1683536	24.0441510	244.4894292	63	10.9697144	23.4539335	257.2829509
64	9.7663164	24.7615793	241.8294170	64	10.5496669	24.1389407	254.6577828	64	11.3947908	23.5416929	268.2526653
65	10.1203453	24.8603901	251.5957334	65	10.9452794	24.2303043	265.2074497	65	11.8363389	23.6261785	279.6474561
66	10.4872079	24.9557444	261.7160787	66	11.3557274	24.3183656	276.1527291	66	12.2949971	23.7075124	291.4837950
67	10.8673692	25.0477630	272.2032866	67	11.7815671	24.4032439	287.5084564	67	12.7714282	23.7858121	303.7787921
68	11.2613113	25.1365626	283.0706557	68	12.2233759	24.4850544	299.2900235	68	13.2663211	23.8611910	316.5502203
69	11.6695338	25.2222558	294.3319670	69	12.6817525	24.5639078	311.5133994	69	13.7803910	23.9337559	329.8165414
70	12.0925544	25.3049513	306.0015008	70	13.1573182	24.6399112	324.1951519	70	14.3143811	24.0036177	343.5969324
71	12.5309095	25.3847540	318.0940553	71	13.6507176	24.7131674	337.3524701	71	14.8690634	24.0708714	357.9113135
72	12.9851550	25.4617650	330.6249648	72	14.1626196	24.7837758	351.0031878	72	15.4452396	24.1356163	372.7803769
73	13.4558669	25.5360820	343.6101198	73	14.6937178	24.8518321	365.1658073	73	16.0437427	24.1979459	388.2256166
74	13.9436420	25.6077993	357.0659866	74	15.2447322	24.9174285	379.8595251	74	16.6654377	24.2579503	404.2693592
75	14.4490991	25.6770078	371.0096287	75	15.8164097	24.9806540	395.1042574	75	17.3112234	24.3157163	420.9347969
76	14.9728789	25.7437952	385.4587277	76	16.4095250	25.0415942	410.9206670	76	17.9820333	24.3713274	438.2460203
77	15.5156458	25.8082463	400.4316066	77	17.0248822	25.1003318	427.3301921	77	18.6788371	24.4248639	456.2280536
78	16.0780879	25.8704427	415.9472524	78	17.6633153	25.1569463	444.3550743	78	19.4026220	24.4764033	474.9068907
79	16.6609186	25.9304634	432.0253403	79	18.3255896	25.2115145	462.0183896	79	20.1544944	24.5260202	494.3095328
80	17.2648769	25.9883845	446.6862589	80	19.0129030	25.2641100	480.3440791	80	20.9354811	24.5737858	514.4640272
81	17.8907287	26.0442793	465.9511358	81	19.7258869	25.3148051	499.3569822	81	21.7467310	24.6197697	535.3995083
82	18.5392676	26.0982189	483.8418645	82	20.4653076	25.3636676	519.0828591	82	22.5894168	24.6640382	557.1462392
83	19.2113161	26.1502702	502.3811321	83	21.2330679	25.4107640	539.5484767	83	23.4647567	24.7066553	579.7356560
84	19.9077263	26.2005033	521.5924482	84	22.0293080	25.4561580	560.7815446	84	24.3740160	24.7476826	603.2004127
85	20.6293814	26.2489793	541.5001745	85	22.8554070	25.4999114	582.8108525	85	25.3185091	24.7871794	627.5744287
86	21.3771964	26.2957567	562.1295558	86	23.7124848	25.5420082	605.6662595	86	26.2996014	24.8252028	652.8929379
87	22.1521198	26.3408490	583.5067522	87	24.6017029	25.5827308	629.3787443	87	27.3187109	24.8618078	679.1925393
88	22.9551341	26.3844623	605.6588720	88	25.5242668	25.6219092	653.9804473	88	28.3773110	24.8970472	706.5112502
89	23.7872578	26.4265016	628.6140062	89	26.4814268	25.6596715	679.5047141	89	29.4769318	24.9309720	734.8885612
90	24.6495459	26.4670703	652.4012639	90	27.4744803	25.6960660	705.9861409	90	30.6191629	24.9636313	764.3654930
91	25.5430919	26.5062199	677.0508098	91	28.5047733	25.7311508	733.4606212	91	31.8056555	24.9950722	794.9846559
92	26.4690290	26.5439999	702.5939017	92	29.5737023	25.7649646	761.9653945	92	33.0381246	25.0253403	826.7903113
93	27.4285313	26.5804583	729.0629307	93	30.6827162	25.7975563	791.5390968	93	34.3183519	25.0544792	859.8284359
94	28.4223155	26.6156413	756.4914619	94	31.8333180	25.8289699	822.2218130	94	35.6481881	25.0825312	894.1467878
95	29.4531426	26.6495535	784.9142775	95	33.0270675	25.8592481	854.0551310	95	37.0295536	25.1095366	929.7949759
96	30.5208190	26.6823580	814.3674201	96	34.2655825	25.8884319	887.0821985	96	38.4644506	25.1355346	966.8245313
97	31.6271987	26.7139764	844.8882391	97	35.5505418	25.9165609	921.3477810	97	39.9549481	25.1605628	1005.2889819
98	32.7736847	26.7444887	876.5154378	98	36.8836872	25.9436731	956.8983228	98	41.5032023	25.1846574	1045.2439300
99	33.9617307	26.7739336	909.2891224	99	38.2668254	25.9698054	993.7820100	99	43.1114514	25.2078530	1086.7471324
100	35.1928435	26.8023484	943.2508532	100	39.7018314	25.9949932	1032.0488354	100	44.7820202	25.2301834	1129.8585838

M	C(8.00,M,2)	A(8.00,M,2)	S(8.00,M,2)	M	C(8.25,M,2)	A(8.25,M,2)	S(8.25,M,2)	M	C(8.50,M,2)	A(8.50,M,2)	S(8.50,M,2)
1/6	1.0065582	.1628867	.1639549	1/6	1.0067597	.1627720	.1638722	1/6	1.0069611	.1626574	.1637897
1/2	1.0198039	.4854831	.4950976	1/2	1.0204166	.4850445	.4949474	1/2	1.0210289	.4846067	.4947975
1	1.0400000	.9615385	1.0000000	1	1.0412500	.9603842	1.0000000	1	1.0425000	.9592326	1.0000000
2	1.0816000	1.8860947	2.0400000	2	1.0842016	1.8827219	2.0412500	2	1.0868063	1.8793598	2.0425000
3	1.1248640	2.7750910	3.1216000	3	1.1289249	2.7685204	3.1254516	3	1.1329955	2.7619758	3.1293063
4	1.1698586	3.6298952	4.2464640	4	1...54930	3.6192273	4.2543764	4	1.1811478	3.6086099	4.2623018
5	1.2166529	4.4518223	5.4163226	5	1.2239821	4.4362327	5.4298695	5	1.23'3466	4.4207289	5.4434196
6	1.2653190	5.2421369	6.6329755	6	1.2744714	5.2208717	6.6538516	6	1.2836788	5.1997400	6.6747962
7	1.3159318	6.0020547	7.8982945	7	1.3270433	5.9744266	7.9283230	7	1.3382352	5.9469928	7.9584750
8	1.3685691	6.7327449	9.2142263	8	1.3817839	6.6981288	9.2553663	8	1.3951102	6.6637821	9.2967102
9	1.4233118	7.4353316	10.5827953	9	1.4387824	7.3931609	10.6371501	9	1.4544024	7.3513497	10.6918204
10	1.4802443	8.1108958	12.0061071	10	1.4981322	8.0606588	12.0759326	10	1.5162145	8.0108870	12.1462228
11	1.5394541	8.7604767	13.4863514	11	1.5599302	8.7017131	13.5740648	11	1.5806536	8.6435367	13.6624372
12	1.6010322	9.3850738	15.0258055	12	1.6242773	9.3173715	15.1339950	12	1.6478314	9.2503949	15.2430908
13	1.6650735	9.9856478	16.6268377	13	1.6912787	9.9086401	16.7582723	13	1.7178642	9.8325131	16.8909222
14	1.7316764	10.5631229	18.2919112	14	1.7610440	10.4764851	18.4495510	14	1.7908734	10.3908999	18.6087864
15	1.8009435	11.1183874	20.0235876	15	1.8336870	11.0218344	20.2105950	15	1.8669855	10.9265226	20.3996598
16	1.8729812	11.6522956	21.8245312	16	1.9093266	11.5455793	22.0442820	16	1.9463324	11.4403095	22.2666454
17	1.9479005	12.1656688	23.6975124	17	1.9880864	12.0485755	23.9536087	17	2.0290516	11.9331506	24.2129778
18	2.0259165	12.6592970	25.6454129	18	2.0700949	12.5316452	25.9416950	18	2.1152862	12.4058998	26.2420293
19	2.1068492	13.1339394	27.6712294	19	2.1554863	12.9955776	28.0117899	19	2.2051859	12.8593763	28.3573156
20	2.1911231	13.5903263	29.7780786	20	2.2444001	13.4411309	30.1672763	20	2.2989063	13.2943658	30.5625015
21	2.2787681	14.0291599	31.9692017	21	2.3369817	13.8690333	32.4116764	21	2.3966098	13.7116219	32.8614078
22	2.3699188	14.4511153	34.2479698	22	2.4333821	14.2799840	34.7486581	22	2.4984658	14.1118675	35.2580177
23	2.4647155	14.8568417	36.6178886	23	2.5337592	14.6746545	37.1820402	23	2.'.46505	14.4957962	3'.7564834
24	2.5633042	15.2469631	39.0826041	24	2.6382767	15.0536898	39.7157994	24	2.7153482	14.8640731	40.3611339
25	2.66'9363	15.6220799	41.6459083	25	2.7471056	15.4177093	42.3540761	25	2.8307505	15.2173363	43.0764821
26	2.7724698	15.9827692	44.3117446	26	2.8604238	15.7673078	45.1011818	26	2.9510574	15.5561979	45.9072326
27	2.8833686	16.3295857	47.0842144	27	2.9784162	16.1030567	47.9616055	27	3.0764773	15.8812449	48.8582900
28	2.9987033	16.6630632	49.9675830	28	3.1012759	16.4255047	50.9400217	28	3.2072276	16.1930407	51.9347674
29	3.1186515	16.9837146	52.9662863	29	3.2292035	16.7351785	54.0412976	29	3.3435348	16.4921254	55.1419950
30	3.2433975	17.2920333	56.0849378	30	3.3624082	17.0325844	57.2705012	30	3.4856350	16.7790172	58.4855298
31	3.3731334	17.5884935	59.3283353	31	3.5011075	17.3182083	60.6329094	31	3.6337745	17.0542131	61.9711648
32	3.5080588	17.8735515	62.7014687	32	3.6455282	17.5925170	64.1340169	32	3.7882099	17.3181900	65.6049393
33	3.6483811	18.1476457	66.2095275	33	3.7959062	17.8559587	67.7795451	33	3.9492088	17.5714053	69.3931492
34	3.7943163	18.4111977	69.8579086	34	3.9524874	18.1089640	71.5754513	34	4.1170502	17.8142976	73.3423581
35	3.9460890	18.6646132	73.6522249	35	4.1155275	18.3519462	75.5279367	35	4.2920249	18.0472879	77.4594083
36	4.1039326	18.9082819	77.5983139	36	4.2852930	18.5853024	79.6434661	36	4.4744359	18.2707798	81.7514331
37	4.2680809	19.1425788	81.7022465	37	4.4620613	18.8094141	83.9287591	37	4.6645994	18.4851604	86.2258690
38	4.4368135	19.3678642	85.9703364	38	4.6461213	19.0245474	88.3908204	38	4.8628449	18.6908014	90.8904635
39	4.6163660	19.5844848	90.4091498	39	4.8377739	19.2313541	93.0369418	39	5.0695158	18.8880589	95.7533134
40	4.8010206	19.7927739	95.0255158	40	5.0373320	19.4298718	97.8747156	40	5.2849702	19.0772747	100.8228292
41	4.9930615	19.9930518	99.8265364	41	5.2451220	19.6205252	102.9120477	41	5.5095815	19.2587767	106.1077995
42	5.1927839	20.1856267	104.8195979	42	5.4614833	19.8036256	108.1571696	42	5.7437387	19.4328793	111.6173809
43	5.'004953	20.3707949	110.0123818	43	5.6867694	19.9794724	113.6186529	43	5.9878476	19.5998842	117.3611196
44	5.6165151	20.5488413	115.4128771	44	5.9213487	20.1483528	119.3054223	44	6.2423311	19.7600808	123.3489672
45	5.8411757	20.7200397	121.0293922	45	6.1656043	20.3105429	125.2267710	45	6.5076302	19.9137466	129.5912983
46	6.0748227	20.8846535	126.8705679	46	6.4189355	20.4663077	131.3923753	46	6.7842045	20.0611478	136.0989285
47	6.3178156	21.0429361	132.9453906	47	6.6847728	20.6159018	137.8123108	47	7.0725332	20.2025399	142.8831330
48	6.5705283	21.1951309	139.2632062	48	6.9605041	20.7595695	144.4970686	48	7.3731158	20.3381677	149.9556662
49	6.8333494	21.3414720	145.8337345	49	7.2476249	20.8975458	151.4575727	49	7.6864732	20.4682664	157.3287820
50	7.1066834	21.4821846	152.6670839	50	7.5465894	21.0300560	158.7051976	50	8.0131484	20.5930613	165.0152552
51	7.3909507	21.6174852	159.7737673	51	7.8578262	21.1573167	166.2517870	51	8.3537072	20.7172686	173.0284036
52	7.6865887	21.7475819	167.1647180	52	8.1820240	21.2795358	174.1096732	52	8.7087397	20.8275958	181.3821107
53	7.9940523	21.8726749	174.8513067	53	8.5195325	21.3969131	182.2916973	53	9.0788612	20.9377418	190.0908505
54	8.3138144	21.9929566	182.8453590	54	8.8709632	21.5096405	190.8112298	54	9.4647128	21.0433974	199.1697116
55	8.6463669	22.1086122	191.1591733	55	9.2368905	21.6179020	199.6821930	55	9.8669630	21.1447457	208.6344244
56	8.9922216	22.2198194	199.8055403	56	9.6179122	21.7218747	208.9190835	56	10.2863090	21.2419623	218.5013874
57	9.3519105	22.3267494	208.7977619	57	10.0146521	21.8217284	218.5369957	57	10.7234771	21.3352156	228.7876964
58	9.7259869	22.4295667	218.1496724	58	10.4277554	21.9176203	228.5516468	58	11.1792249	21.4246673	239.5111735
59	10.,1150264	22.5284296	227.8756593	59	10.8579004	22.0097251	238.9794022	59	11.6543419	21.5104722	250.6903984
60	10.5196274	22.6234900	237.9906857	60	11.3057887	22.0981754	249.8373026	60	12.1496515	21.5927791	26?.3447403
61	10.9404125	22.7148942	248.5103103	61	11.7721525	22.1831216	261.1430913	61	12.6560117	21.6717305	274.4943918
62	11.3780290	22.8027829	259.4507256	62	12.2577538	22.2647026	272.9152439	62	13.2043172	21.7474633	287.1604035
63	11.8331502	22.8872912	270.8287547	63	12.7633862	22.3430518	285.1729977	63	13.7655006	21.8201087	300.3647206
64	12.3064762	22.9685492	282.6619049	64	13.2893758	22.4182970	297.9363839	64	14.3505344	21.8897925	314.1302213
65	12.7987353	23.0466820	294.9683815	65	13.8380832	22.4905613	311.2262597	65	14.9604321	21.9566535	328.4807557
66	13.3106847	23.1218096	307.7671163	66	14.4089042	22.5599629	325.0643429	66	15.5962505	22.0207535	343.4411878
67	13.8431121	23.1940477	321.0778010	67	15.0032715	22.6266150	339.4732471	67	16.2590911	22.0822576	359.0374383
68	14.3968365	23.2635074	334.9209131	68	15.6221564	22.6906267	354.4765186	68	16.9501025	22.1412542	375.2965295
69	14.9727100	23.3302956	349.3177496	69	16.2665704	22.7521024	370.0986750	69	17.6704819	22.1978458	392.2466320
70	15.5716184	23.3945150	364.2904596	70	16.9375664	22.8111428	386.3652453	70	18.4214774	22.2521303	409.9171139
71	16.1944831	23.4562644	379.8620780	71	17.6362410	22.8678442	403.3028117	71	19.2043901	22.3042017	428.3385912
72	16.8422625	23.5156388	396.0565612	72	18.3637359	22.9222994	420.9390527	72	20.0205767	22.3541503	447.5429814
73	17.5159530	23.5727296	412.8988236	73	19.1212401	22.9745972	439.3027887	73	20.8714512	22.4020626	467.5635581
74	18.2165911	23.6276247	430.4147766	74	19.9100628	23.0248233	458.4240287	74	21.7584879	22.4481072	488.4350093
75	18.9452547	23.6804083	448.6313677	75	20.7312783	23.0730596	478.3340199	75	22.6832237	22.4921072	510.1934973
76	19.7030649	23.7311618	467.5766224	76	21.5864436	23.1193849	499.0652983	76	23.6472607	22.5343954	532.8767209
77	20.4911875	23.7799633	487.2796873	77	22.4768844	23.1638751	520.6517419	77	24.6522692	22.5749596	556.5239816
78	21.3108350	23.8268878	507.7708748	78	23.4040559	23.2066027	543.1286262	78	25.6999907	22.6138701	581.1762508
79	22.1632684	23.8720075	529.0817099	79	24.3694732	23.2476377	566.5326821	79	26.7922403	22.6511943	606.8762415
80	23.'-97992	23.9153918	551.2449783	80	25.3747139	23.2870470	590.9021553	80	27.9309105	22.6869970	633.6684818
81	23.9717911	23.9571075	574.2947774	81	26.4214209	23.3248950	616.2768692	81	29.1179782	22.7213400	661.5993923
82	24.9306628	23.9972188	598.2665666	82	27.51:3045	23.3612437	642.6982901	82	30.3554881	22.7542830	690.7173665
83	25.9278893	24.0357873	623.1972313	83	28.6461458	23.3961525	670.2095946	83	31.6455964	22.7858830	721.0728546
84	26.9650049	24.0728724	649.1251206	84	29.8277993	23.4296782	698.8557404	84	32.9905342	22.8161947	752.7184510
85	28.0436051	24.1085311	676.0901255	85	31.0581960	23.4618758	728.6835397	85	34.3925319	22.8452707	785.7089852
86	29.1653493	24.1428184	704.1337305	86	32.3393466	23.4927979	759.7417358	86	35.8543188	22.8731613	820.1016171
87	30.3319632	24.1757869	733.2990798	87	33.6733447	23.5224950	792.0810824	87	37.3781273	22.8999149	855.9559359
88	31.5452418	24.2074874	763.6310430	88	35.0623702	23.5510156	825.7544271	88	38.9666977	22.9255779	893.3340632
89	32.8070514	24.2379687	795.1762848	89	36.5086929	23.5784064	860.8167972	89	40.6227824	22.9501946	932.3007609
90	34.1193335	24.2672776	827.9833362	90	38.0146765	23.6047120	897.3254902	90	42.3492506	22.9738078	972.9235433
91	35.4841068	24.2954592	862.1026697	91	39.5827819	23.6299755	935.3401667	91	44.1490938	22.9964553	1015.2727940
92	36.9034711	24.3225569	897.5867765	92	41.2155717	23.6542382	974.9229480	92	46.0254303	23.0181854	1059.4218878
93	38.3796100	24.3486124	934.4902476	93	42.9157140	23.6775397	1016.1385203	93	47.9815111	23.0390202	1105.4473180
94	39.9147944	24.3736658	972.8698576	94	44.6859872	23.6999180	1059.0542343	94	50.0207253	23.0590185	1153.4288291
95	41.5113861	24.3977556	1012.7846519	95	46.5292842	23.7214099	1103.7402215	95	52.1466061	23.0781952	1203.4495544
96	43.1718416	24.4209188	1054.2960381	96	48.4488172	23.7420503	1150.2695061	96	54.3628369	23.0965571	1255.5961605
97	44.8987152	24.4431912	1097.4678796	97	50.4471226	23.7618730	1198.7181229	97	56.6732575	23.1142351	1309.9589974
98	46.6946628	24.4646069	1142.3665949	98	52.5280664	23.7809105	1249.1652455	98	59.0818709	23.1311608	1366.6322549
99	48.5624504	24.4851989	1189.0612587	99	54.6948492	23.7991937	1301.6933119	99	61.5928504	23.1473964	1425.7141258
100	50.5049484	24.5049990	1237.6237091	100	56.9510117	23.8167527	1356.3881611	100	64.2105466	23.1629702	1487.3069762

Table 1 357

M	C(8.75,M,2)	A(8.75,M,2)	S(8.75,M,2)	M	C(9.00,M,2)	A(9.00,M,2)	S(9.00,M,2)	M	C(9.25,M,2)	A(9.25,M,2)	S(9.25,M,2)
1/6	1.0071622	.1625431	.1637073	1/6	1.0073631	.1624290	.1636250	1/6	1.0075639	.1623150	.1635428
1/2	1.0216408	.4841699	.4946477	1/2	1.0222524	.4837339	.4944981	1/2	1.0228636	.4832987	.4943487
1	1.0437500	.9580838	1.0000000	1	1.0450000	.9569378	1.0000000	1	1.0462500	.9557945	1.0000000
2	1.0894141	1.8760085	2.0437500	2	1.0920250	1.8726678	2.0450000	2	1.0946391	1.8693376	2.0462500
3	1.1370759	2.7554572	3.1331641	3	1.1411661	2.7489644	3.1370250	3	1.1452661	2.7424971	3.1408891
4	1.1860230	3.5980428	4.2702400	4	1.1925186	3.5875257	4.2781911	4	1.1982347	3.5770582	4.2861552
5	1.2387465	4.4053105	5.4570630	5	1.2461819	4.3899767	5.4707097	5	1.2535530	4.3747271	5.4843999
6	1.2929417	5.1787406	6.6958095	6	1.3022601	5.1578725	6.7168917	6	1.3116345	5.1371346	6.7380429
7	1.3495079	5.9197515	7.9887512	7	1.3608618	5.8927009	8.0191518	7	1.3722976	5.8658395	8.0496774
8	1.4085488	6.6297020	9.3382590	8	1.4221006	6.5958861	9.3800136	8	1.4357663	6.5623317	9.4219750
9	1.4701728	7.3098941	10.7468079	9	1.4860951	7.2687905	10.8021142	9	1.5021705	7.2280351	10.8577413
10	1.5344929	7.9615752	12.2169807	10	1.5529694	7.9127182	12.2882094	10	1.5716459	7.8643107	12.3599118
11	1.6016270	8.5859403	13.7514736	11	1.6228530	8.5289169	13.8411788	11	1.6443345	8.4724594	13.9315578
12	1.6716982	9.1841345	15.3531006	12	1.6958814	9.1185808	15.4640318	12	1.7203850	9.0537247	15.5758923
13	1.7449349	9.7572546	17.0247987	13	1.7721961	9.6828524	17.1599133	13	1.7999528	9.6092948	17.2962773
14	1.8211715	10.3063517	18.7696337	14	1.8519449	10.2228253	18.9321094	14	1.8832006	10.1403057	19.0962301
15	1.9008477	10.8324327	20.5908052	15	1.9352824	10.7395457	20.7840543	15	1.9702987	10.6478429	20.9794308
16	1.9840098	11.3364225	22.4916529	16	2.0223702	11.2340150	22.7193367	16	2.0614625	11.1329442	22.9497295
17	2.0708102	11.8193653	24.4756627	17	2.1133768	11.7071914	24.7417069	17	2.1567659	11.5966014	25.0111545
18	2.1614082	12.2820266	26.5464729	18	2.2084788	12.1599918	26.8550837	18	2.2565163	12.0397624	27.1679204
19	2.2559698	12.7252950	28.7078811	19	2.3078603	12.5932936	29.0635625	19	2.3608802	12.4633333	29.4244367
20	2.3546685	13.1499832	30.9638509	20	2.4117140	13.0079364	31.3714228	20	2.4700709	12.8681799	31.7853169
21	2.4576852	13.5568701	33.3185194	21	2.5202412	13.4047239	33.7831368	21	2.5843117	13.2551302	34.2553878
22	2.5652090	13.9467019	35.7762046	22	2.6336520	13.7844248	36.3033780	22	2.7038361	13.6249751	36.8396995
23	2.6774368	14.3201934	38.3414136	23	2.7521664	14.1477749	38.9370300	23	2.8288885	13.9784708	39.5435356
24	2.7945747	14.6780297	41.0188504	24	2.8760138	14.4954784	41.6891983	24	2.9597246	14.3163401	42.3724241
25	2.9168374	15.0208667	43.8134751	25	3.0054345	14.8282090	44.5652102	25	3.0966119	14.6392737	45.3321487
26	3.0444490	15.3493334	46.7302625	26	3.1406790	15.1466114	47.5706446	26	3.2398302	14.9479318	48.4287606
27	3.1776436	15.6640320	49.7747115	27	3.2820096	15.4513028	50.7113236	27	3.3896723	15.2429456	51.6685908
28	3.3166655	15.9655396	52.9523551	28	3.4297000	15.7428735	53.9933332	28	3.5464447	15.5249181	55.0582631
29	3.4617697	16.2544092	56.2690207	29	3.5840365	16.0218885	57.4230332	29	3.7104677	15.7944259	58.6047078
30	3.6132221	16.5311705	59.7307903	30	3.7453181	16.2888885	61.0070697	30	3.8820769	16.0520200	62.3151755
31	3.7713005	16.7963310	63.3440124	31	3.9138575	16.5443909	64.7523878	31	4.0616229	16.2982270	66.1972524
32	3.9362949	17.0503770	67.1153129	32	4.0899810	16.7888909	68.6662453	32	4.2494730	16.5335503	70.2588753
33	4.1085078	17.2937744	71.0516079	33	4.2740302	17.0228621	72.7562263	33	4.4460111	16.7584710	74.5083483
34	4.2882551	17.5269695	75.1601157	34	4.4663615	17.2467580	77.0302565	34	4.6516391	16.9734490	78.9543594
35	4.4758662	17.7503899	79.4483708	35	4.6673478	17.4610124	81.4966181	35	4.8667774	17.1789238	83.6059985
36	4.6716854	17.9644454	83.9242370	36	4.8773785	17.6660406	86.1639659	36	5.0918659	17.3753154	88.4727759
37	4.8760716	18.1695286	88.5959224	37	5.0968605	17.8622398	91.0413444	37	5.3273647	17.5630255	93.5646418
38	5.0893997	18.3660154	93.4719940	38	5.3262192	18.0499902	96.1382049	38	5.5737553	17.7424377	98.8920065
39	5.3120610	18.5542662	98.5613937	39	5.5658991	18.2296557	101.4644241	39	5.8315415	17.9139190	104.4657618
40	5.5444636	18.7346263	103.8734547	40	5.8163645	18.4015844	107.0303232	40	6.1012503	18.0778198	110.2973033
41	5.7870339	18.9074264	109.4179184	41	6.0781010	18.5661095	112.8466877	41	6.3834331	18.2344753	116.3985536
42	6.0402167	19.0729834	115.2049523	42	6.3516155	18.7235497	118.9247887	42	6.6786669	18.3842058	122.7819867
43	6.3044761	19.2316009	121.2451690	43	6.6374382	18.8742103	125.2764042	43	6.9875552	18.5273174	129.4606536
44	6.5802970	19.3835697	127.5496451	44	6.9361229	19.0183830	131.9138424	44	7.3107297	18.6641026	136.4482088
45	6.8681850	19.5291686	134.1299421	45	7.2482484	19.1563474	138.8499653	45	7.6488509	18.7948412	143.7589385
46	7.1686681	19.6686645	140.9981271	46	7.5744196	19.2883707	146.0982137	46	8.0026103	18.9198005	151.4077894
47	7.4822973	19.8023133	148.1667951	47	7.9152685	19.4147088	153.6726334	47	8.3727310	19.0392358	159.4103997
48	7.8096478	19.9303600	155.6490924	48	8.2714556	19.5356065	161.5879019	48	8.7599698	19.1533914	167.7831307
49	8.1513199	20.0530396	163.4587402	49	8.6436711	19.6512981	169.8593575	49	9.1651184	19.2625008	176.5431005
50	8.5079401	20.1705768	171.6100601	50	9.0326363	19.7620078	178.5030286	50	9.5890051	19.3667869	185.7082189
51	8.8801625	20.2831874	180.1180003	51	9.4391049	19.8679500	187.5356649	51	10.0324966	19.4664630	195.2972240
52	9.2686696	20.3910777	188.9981628	52	9.8638647	19.9693302	196.9747698	52	10.4964996	19.5617328	205.3297206
53	9.6741739	20.4944457	198.2668324	53	10.3077386	20.0663446	206.8386344	53	10.9819627	19.6527912	215.8262202
54	10.0974190	20.5934809	207.9410064	54	10.7715868	20.1591815	217.1463730	54	11.4898785	19.7396244	226.8081829
55	10.5391811	20.6883650	218.0384254	55	11.2563082	20.2480205	227.9179598	55	12.0212854	19.8230101	238.2980614
56	11.0002703	20.7792718	228.5776065	56	11.7628421	20.3330340	239.1742680	56	12.5772698	19.9025186	250.3193468
57	11.4815321	20.8663663	239.5778768	57	12.2921700	20.4143866	250.9371101	57	13.1589685	19.9785124	262.8966166
58	11.9838492	20.9498138	251.0594089	58	12.8453176	20.4922360	263.2292800	58	13.7675708	20.0511469	276.0555851
59	12.5081426	21.0297618	263.0432581	59	13.4233569	20.5667320	276.0745976	59	14.4043210	20.1205705	289.8231559
60	13.0553738	21.1063586	275.5514006	60	14.0274080	20.6380220	289.4979545	60	15.0705208	20.1869252	304.2274769
61	13.6265464	21.1797447	288.6067744	61	14.6565413	20.7062042	303.5253625	61	15.7675324	20.2503467	319.2979977
62	14.2207078	21.2500548	302.2333708	62	15.3182602	20.7715226	318.1840038	62	16.4967808	20.3109646	335.0655301
63	14.8449513	21.3174178	316.4560286	63	16.0076028	20.8339930	333.5022640	63	17.2597569	20.3689028	351.5623109
64	15.4944179	21.3819572	331.3009799	64	16.7279449	20.8937732	349.5098868	64	18.0580207	20.4242799	368.8220678
65	16.1722987	21.4437913	346.7953978	65	17.4800724	20.9509791	366.2378318	65	18.8932041	20.4772090	386.8800884
66	16.8798367	21.5030336	362.9676965	66	18.2673341	21.0057216	383.7185342	66	19.7670148	20.5277983	405.7732926
67	17.6183296	21.5597927	379.8475332	67	19.0893641	21.0581068	401.9858683	67	20.6812392	20.5761513	425.5403074
68	18.3891315	21.6141726	397.4658628	68	19.9483855	21.1082362	421.0752324	68	21.6377466	20.6223668	446.2215466
69	19.1936560	21.6662732	415.8549943	69	20.8460628	21.1562069	441.0236178	69	22.6384923	20.6665394	467.8592931
70	20.0333785	21.7161899	435.0486503	70	21.7841357	21.2021118	461.8696807	70	23.6855226	20.7087593	490.4977855
71	20.9098388	21.7640162	455.0820288	71	22.7644218	21.2460400	483.6538163	71	24.7809780	20.7491128	514.1833081
72	21.8245442	21.8098340	475.9918676	72	23.7888207	21.2880766	506.4182381	72	25.9270983	20.7876825	538.9642861
73	22.7794724	21.8537332	497.8165118	73	24.8593177	21.3283000	530.2070588	73	27.1262266	20.8245472	564.8913844
74	23.7760743	21.8957923	520.5959842	74	25.9779870	21.3667971	555.0663765	74	28.3808145	20.8597822	592.0176109
75	24.8162776	21.9360884	544.3720586	75	27.1469964	21.4036336	581.0443634	75	29.6934272	20.8934597	620.3984255
76	25.9019897	21.9746955	569.1883362	76	28.3686112	21.4388688	608.1913598	76	31.0667482	20.9256485	650.0918527
77	27.0352018	22.0116843	595.0903259	77	29.6451987	21.4726161	636.5599711	77	32.5085823	20.9564143	681.1586009
78	28.2179919	22.0471227	622.1255277	78	30.9792327	21.5048958	666.2051698	78	34.0068761	20.9858201	713.6621862
79	29.4525290	22.0810756	650.3435196	79	32.3732931	21.5357854	697.1844025	79	35.5796942	21.0139261	747.6690624
80	30.7410772	22.1136054	679.7960486	80	33.8300966	21.5653449	729.5577006	80	37.2252550	21.0407895	783.2487565
81	32.0859993	22.1447716	710.5371257	81	35.3524509	21.5936315	763.3877972	81	38.9469231	21.0664655	820.4740116
82	33.4897618	22.1746315	742.6231250	82	36.9432312	21.6207000	798.7402381	82	40.7482283	21.0910065	859.4209346
83	34.9549388	22.2032397	776.1128868	83	38.6057602	21.6466029	835.6835593	83	42.6328234	21.1144626	900.1691529
84	36.4842174	22.2306488	811.0678256	84	40.3430194	21.6713903	874.2893195	84	44.6045914	21.1368818	942.8019763
85	38.0804019	22.2569091	847.5520430	85	42.1584553	21.6951103	914.6323389	85	46.6675538	21.1583099	987.4065677
86	39.7464195	22.2820686	885.6324450	86	44.0555587	21.7178089	956.7907902	86	48.8259282	21.1787909	1034.0741215
87	41.4853254	22.3061735	925.3788645	87	46.0380871	21.7395301	1000.8463800	87	51.0841274	21.1983664	1082.9000497
88	43.3003084	22.3292680	966.8641898	88	48.1098011	21.7603159	1046.8844671	88	53.4467682	21.2170766	1133.9841770
89	45.1946968	22.3513945	1010.1644982	89	50.2747421	21.7802066	1094.9942682	89	55.9186813	21.2349597	1187.4309453
90	47.1719648	22.3725935	1055.3591950	90	52.5371055	21.7992407	1145.2690103	90	58.5049203	21.2520523	1243.3496266
91	49.2357383	22.3929040	1102.5311599	91	54.9012753	21.8174552	1197.8061159	91	61.2107729	21.2683893	1301.8545469
92	51.3898019	22.4123631	1151.7668982	92	57.3718327	21.8348854	1252.7073911	92	64.0417711	21.2840041	1363.0653197
93	53.6381057	22.4310066	1203.1567000	93	59.9535651	21.8515650	1310.0792238	93	67.0037030	21.2989287	1427.1070908
94	55.9847728	22.4488686	1256.7948057	94	62.6514756	21.8675263	1370.0327809	94	70.1026243	21.3131935	1494.1107938
95	58.4341066	22.4659818	1312.7795785	95	65.4707920	21.8828003	1432.6842645	95	73.3448707	21.3266277	1564.2134181
96	60.9905988	22.4823708	1371.2136851	96	68.4169776	21.8974165	1498.1550565	96	76.7370709	21.3398592	1637.5582888
97	63.6589375	22.4980865	1432.2042839	97	71.4957416	21.9114034	1566.5720341	97	80.2861605	21.3523146	1714.2953597
98	66.4440160	22.5131368	1495.8632214	98	74.7130500	21.9247879	1638.0677757	98	83.9993954	21.3642195	1794.5615202
99	69.3509417	22.5275562	1562.3072374	99	78.0751372	21.9375961	1712.7808257	99	87.8843674	21.3755981	1878.5809156
100	72.3850454	22.5413712	1631.6581792	100	81.5885184	21.9498527	1790.8559630	100	91.9490194	21.3864737	1966.4652831

Table 1

M	C(9.50,M,2)	A(9.50,M,2)	S(9.50,M,2)	M	C(9.75,M,2)	A(9.75,M,2)	S(9.75,M,2)	M	C(10.00,M,2)	A(10.00,M,2)	S(10.00,M,2)
1/6	1.0077644	.1622013	.1634607	1/6	1.0079647	.1620878	.1633787	1/6	1.0081648	.1619744	.1632969
1/2	1.0234745	.4828645	.4941995	1/2	1.0240850	.4824311	.4940504	1/2	1.0246951	.4819985	.4939015
1	1.0475000	.9546539	1.0000000	1	1.0487500	.9535161	1.0000000	1	1.0500000	.9523810	1.0000000
2	1.0972563	1.8660181	2.0475000	2	1.0998766	1.8627090	2.0487500	2	1.1025000	1.8594104	2.0500000
3	1.1493759	2.7360554	3.1447563	3	1.1534955	2.7296391	3.1486266	3	1.1576250	2.7232480	3.1525000
4	1.2039713	3.5666400	4.2941322	4	1.2097285	3.5562709	4.3021221	4	1.2155063	3.5459505	4.3101250
5	1.2611599	4.3595609	5.4981035	5	1.2687027	4.3444776	5.5116506	5	1.2762816	4.3294767	5.5256213
6	1.3210650	5.1165259	6.7592634	6	1.3305520	5.0960454	6.7805533	6	1.3400956	5.0756921	6.8019128
7	1.3838156	5.8391656	8.0803284	7	1.3954164	5.8126774	8.1111052	7	1.4071004	5.7863734	8.1420085
8	1.4495468	6.5290363	9.4641440	8	1.4634429	6.4959975	9.5065216	8	1.4774575	6.4632128	9.5491089
9	1.5184003	7.1876242	10.9136908	9	1.5347858	7.1475542	10.9699646	9	1.5513282	7.1078217	11.0265643
10	1.5905243	7.8163477	12.4320911	10	1.6096066	7.7688241	12.5047503	10	1.6288946	7.7217349	12.5778925
11	1.6660742	8.4165610	14.0226155	11	1.6880749	8.3612148	14.1143569	11	1.7103394	8.3064142	14.2067872
12	1.7452128	8.9895571	15.6886897	12	1.7703686	8.9260690	15.8024318	12	1.7958563	8.8632516	15.9171265
13	1.8281104	9.5365700	17.4339025	13	1.8566740	9.4646665	17.5728004	13	1.8856491	9.3935730	17.7129829
14	1.9149456	10.0587780	19.2620128	14	1.9471869	9.9782279	19.4294744	14	1.9799316	9.8986409	19.5986320
15	2.0059055	10.5573060	21.1769584	15	2.0421122	10.4679169	21.3766613	15	2.0789282	10.3796580	21.5785636
16	2.1011860	11.0332277	23.1828640	16	2.1416652	10.9348433	23.4187735	16	2.1828746	10.8377696	23.6574918
17	2.2009924	11.4875682	25.2840500	17	2.2460714	11.3800651	25.5604387	17	2.2920183	11.2740662	25.8403664
18	2.3055395	11.9213061	27.4850424	18	2.3555674	11.8045913	27.8065101	18	2.4066192	11.6895869	28.1323847
19	2.4150526	12.3353758	29.7905819	19	2.4704013	12.2093838	30.1620775	19	2.5269502	12.0853209	30.5390039
20	2.5297676	12.7306690	32.2056345	20	2.5908333	12.5953600	32.6324787	20	2.6532977	12.4622103	33.0659541
21	2.6499316	13.1080372	34.7354022	21	2.7171365	12.9633946	35.2233121	21	2.7859626	12.8211527	35.7192518
22	2.7758034	13.4682933	37.3853338	22	2.8495969	13.3143214	37.9404485	22	2.9252607	13.1630026	38.5052144
23	2.9076045	13.8122132	4C.1611371	23	2.9885147	13.6489358	40.7900454	23	3.0715238	13.4885739	41.4304751
24	3.0457676	14.1405376	43.0687911	24	3.1342048	13.9679960	43.7785601	24	3.2250999	13.7986418	44.5019989
25	3.1924415	14.4539394	46.1145587	25	3.2869973	14.2722250	46.9127649	25	3.3863549	14.0939446	47.7270989
26	3.3419875	14.7531970	49.3050003	26	3.4472384	14.5623123	50.1997622	26	3.5556727	14.3751853	51.1134538
27	3.5007319	15.0388516	52.6469878	27	3.6152913	14.8389152	53.6470006	27	3.7334563	14.6430336	54.6691265
28	3.6670167	15.3115528	56.1477197	28	3.7915367	15.1026605	57.2622919	28	3.9201291	14.8981272	58.4025828
29	3.8412000	15.5718881	59.8147364	29	3.9763742	15.3541459	61.0538287	29	4.1161356	15.1410736	62.3227120
30	4.0236570	15.8204183	63.6559364	30	4.1702224	15.5939412	65.0302028	30	4.3219424	15.3724510	66.4388476
31	4.2147807	16.0576785	67.6795934	31	4.3735207	15.8225900	69.2004252	31	4.5380395	15.5928105	70.7607899
32	4.4149828	16.2841800	71.8943740	32	4.5867299	16.0406102	73.5739459	32	4.7649415	15.8026767	75.2988294
33	4.6246945	16.5004105	76.3093568	33	4.8103329	16.2484960	78.1606758	33	5.0031885	16.0025492	80.0637709
34	4.8443674	16.7068358	80.9340513	34	5.0448361	16.4467185	82.9710088	34	5.2533480	16.1929040	85.0669595
35	5.0744749	16.9039005	85.7784187	35	5.2907725	16.6357268	88.0158454	35	5.5160154	16.3741943	90.3203074
36	5.3155125	17.0920291	90.8528936	36	5.5486976	16.8159943	93.3066179	36	5.7918161	16.5468517	95.8363228
37	5.5679993	17.2716268	96.1684060	37	5.8191966	16.9877943	98.8553155	37	6.0814070	16.7112873	101.6281390
38	5.8324793	17.4430805	101.7364053	38	6.1028825	17.1516513	104.6745122	38	6.3854773	16.8678927	107.7095459
39	6.1095220	17.6067594	107.5688846	39	6.4003980	17.3078916	110.7773946	39	6.7047512	17.0170407	114.0950232
40	6.3997243	17.7630162	113.6784066	40	6.7124174	17.4568692	117.1777926	40	7.0399887	17.1590863	120.7997744
41	6.7037112	17.9121873	120.0781309	41	7.0396477	17.5989218	123.8902100	41	7.3919882	17.2943679	127.8397631
42	7.0221375	18.0545941	126.7818422	42	7.3828306	17.7343712	130.9298578	42	7.7615876	17.4232076	135.2317513
43	7.3556890	18.1905433	133.8039797	43	7.7427436	17.8635244	138.3126883	43	8.1496669	17.5459120	142.9933388
44	7.7050843	18.3203277	141.1596687	44	8.1202023	17.9866740	146.0554319	44	8.5571503	17.6627733	151.1430058
45	8.0710758	18.4442269	148.8647530	45	8.5160622	18.1040992	154.1756342	45	8.9850078	17.7740698	159.7001561
46	8.4544519	18.5625078	156.9358288	46	8.9312202	18.2160660	162.6916964	46	9.4342582	17.8800557	168.6851639
47	8.8560383	18.6754251	165.3902806	47	9.3666172	18.3228281	171.6229166	47	9.9059711	17.9810157	178.1194221
48	9.2767002	18.7832220	174.2463190	48	9.8232398	18.4246275	180.9895538	48	10.0412697	18.0771578	188.0253932
49	9.7173434	18.8861308	183.5230191	49	10.3021227	18.5216949	190.8127736	49	10.9213332	18.1687217	198.4266629
50	10.1789172	18.9843731	193.2403626	50	10.8043512	18.6142502	201.1148963	50	11.4673998	18.2559254	209.3479961
51	10.6624158	19.0781605	203.4192798	51	11.3310633	18.7025031	211.9192475	51	12.0407698	18.3389766	220.8153959
52	11.1688806	19.1676960	214.0816956	52	11.8834527	18.7866538	223.2503108	52	12.6428083	18.4180730	232.8561657
53	11.6994024	19.2531694	225.2505761	53	12.4627710	18.8668928	235.1337635	53	13.2749487	18.4934028	245.4989740
54	12.2551264	19.3347679	236.9499785	54	13.0703311	18.9434009	247.5965345	54	13.9386961	18.5651455	258.7739227
55	12.8372424	19.4126663	249.2051025	55	13.7075097	19.0163546	260.6668656	55	14.6356310	18.6334719	272.7126188
56	13.4470114	19.4870323	262.0423449	56	14.3757508	19.0859162	274.3743753	56	15.3674125	18.6985447	287.3482498
57	14.0857444	19.5580260	275.4893563	57	15.0765687	19.1522443	288.7501261	57	16.1357831	18.7605188	302.7156623
58	14.7548173	19.6258005	289.5751007	58	15.8115514	19.2154892	303.8266947	58	16.9425723	18.8195417	318.8514454
59	15.4556711	19.6905017	304.3299180	59	16.5823645	19.2757942	319.6382461	59	17.7897009	18.8757540	335.7940177
60	16.1898155	19.7522689	319.7855891	60	17.3907548	19.3332960	336.2206106	60	18.6791859	18.9292895	353.5837186
61	16.9588317	19.8112352	335.9754046	61	18.2385541	19.3881249	353.6113654	61	19.6131452	18.9802757	372.2629045
62	17.7643702	19.8675277	352.9342264	62	19.1276836	19.4404052	371.8499195	62	20.5938025	19.0288340	391.8760498
63	18.6081841	19.9212675	370.6986126	63	20.0601582	19.4902552	390.9776031	63	21.6234926	19.0750800	412.4698523
64	19.4920729	19.9725704	389.3067967	64	21.0380909	19.5377881	411.0377613	64	22.7046673	19.1191238	434.0933449
65	20.4179463	20.0215469	408.7988696	65	22.0636978	19.5831114	432.0758521	65	23.8399006	19.1610703	456.7980122
66	21.3877998	20.0683025	429.2168159	66	23.1393031	19.6263279	454.1395500	66	25.0318957	19.2010193	480.6379128
67	22.4037192	20.1129380	450.6046147	67	24.2673441	19.6675356	477.2788530	67	26.2834905	19.2390660	505.6698085
68	23.4678959	20.1555494	473.0083339	68	25.4503771	19.7068277	501.5461971	68	27.5976650	19.2753010	531.9532990
69	24.5826209	20.1962285	496.4762298	69	26.6910830	19.7442934	526.9965743	69	28.9775482	19.3098105	559.5509639
70	25.7502954	20.2350630	521.0588508	70	27.9922733	19.7800175	553.6876573	70	30.4264256	19.3426766	588.5285122
71	26.9734345	20.2721365	546.8091462	71	29.3568966	19.8140811	581.6799306	71	31.9477469	19.3771089	618.9549378
72	28.2266067	20.3075289	573.7825807	72	30.7880454	19.8465612	611.0368273	72	33.5451343	19.4037883	650.9026847
73	29.5967696	20.3413164	602.0372533	73	32.2889026	19.8775356	641.8248726	73	35.2223910	19.4321794	684.4478190
74	31.0026161	20.3735717	631.6340228	74	33.8630495	19.9070623	674.1138352	74	36.9835105	19.4592184	719.6702100
75	32.4752404	20.4043644	662.6366399	75	35.5130732	19.9352203	707.9768847	75	38.8326601	19.4849699	756.6537205
76	34.0178143	20.4337608	695.1118793	76	37.2451745	19.9620694	743.4907579	76	40.7743204	19.5094952	795.4864066
77	35.6336605	20.4618241	729.1296936	77	39.0074332	19.9876705	780.7359324	77	42.8130364	19.5328525	836.2607269
78	37.3262594	20.4886149	764.7633541	78	40.9850945	20.0120815	819.7968091	78	44.9536882	19.5550977	879.0737633
79	39.0992567	20.5141908	802.0896135	79	42.9621428	20.0353578	860.7619036	79	47.2013726	19.5762835	924.0274515
80	40.9564714	20.5386070	841.1888702	80	45.0565473	20.0575521	903.7240464	80	49.5614413	19.5964605	971.2288241
81	42.9015038	20.5619160	882.1453415	81	47.2530540	20.0787148	948.7805937	81	52.0395133	19.6156766	1020.7902654
82	44.9397442	20.5841680	925.0472453	82	49.5575404	20.0988937	996.0336477	82	54.6414890	19.6339777	1072.8297787
83	47.0743987	20.6054110	969.9869895	83	51.9725266	20.1181346	1045.5902881	83	57.3735634	19.6514074	1127.4712677
84	49.3104152	20.6256907	1017.0613716	84	54.5061873	20.1364812	1097.5628147	84	60.2422416	19.6680070	1184.8448311
85	51.6526599	20.6450508	1066.3717868	85	57.1633639	20.1539749	1152.0690020	85	63.2543537	19.6838162	1245.0870728
86	54.1061613	20.6635330	1118.0244467	86	59.9500779	20.1706555	1209.2323659	86	66.4170714	19.6988726	1308.3414265
87	56.6762039	20.6811770	1172.1306080	87	62.8726442	20.1865606	1269.1824438	87	69.7379250	19.7132120	1374.7584979
88	59.3603236	20.6980210	1228.8068119	88	65.9376856	20.2017265	1332.0550880	88	73.2248212	19.7268686	1444.4964228
89	62.1883190	20.7141012	1288.1751355	89	69.1521478	20.2161873	1397.9927736	89	76.8860623	19.7398748	1517.7212440
90	65.1422642	20.7294523	1350.3634545	90	72.5233150	20.2299760	1467.1449214	90	80.7303654	19.7522617	1594.6073063
91	68.2365217	20.7441072	1415.5057187	91	76.0588266	20.2431237	1539.6682363	91	84.7668837	19.7640588	1675.3376717
92	71.4777565	20.7580975	1483.7422404	92	79.7666944	20.2556603	1615.7270629	92	89.0052279	19.7752941	1760.1045554
93	74.8729499	20.7714535	1555.2199969	93	83.6553208	20.2676141	1695.4937573	93	93.4554893	19.7859944	1849.1097832
94	78.4294151	20.7842038	1630.0929468	94	87.7335176	20.2790122	1779.1490781	94	98.1282637	19.7961851	1942.5652725
95	82.1548123	20.7963759	1708.5223619	95	92.0105266	20.2898806	1866.8825957	95	103.0346769	19.8053906	2040.6935362
96	86.0571659	20.8079961	1790.6771741	96	96.4960398	20.3002437	1958.8931224	96	108.1864108	19.8151339	2143.7282131
97	90.1448812	20.8190894	1876.7343400	97	101.2002218	20.3101251	2055.3891622	97	113.5957313	19.8239370	2251.9146239
98	94.4267631	20.8296796	1966.8792212	98	106.1337326	20.3195472	2156.5893840	98	119.2755179	19.8323210	2365.5103552
99	98.9120344	20.8397896	2061.3059844	99	111.3077520	20.3285313	2262.7231165	99	125.2392938	19.8403057	2484.7858731
100	103.6103560	20.8494411	2160.2180187	100	116.7340050	20.3370977	2374.0308686	100	131.5012585	19.8479102	2610.0251668

Table 1   **359**

M	C(10.25,M,2)	A(10.25,M,2)	S(10.25,M,2)	M	C(10.50,M,2)	A(10.50,M,2)	S(10.50,M,2)	M	C(10.75,M,2)	A(10.75,M,2)	S(10.75,M,2)
1/6	1.0083648	.1618613	.1632152	1/6	1.0085645	.1617483	.1631336	1/6	1.0087641	.1616356	.1630522
1/2	1.0253048	.4815669	.4937528	1/2	1.0259142	.4811360	.4936043	1/2	1.0265233	.4807061	.4934560
1	1.0512500	.9512485	1.0000000	1	1.0525000	.9501188	1.0000000	1	1.0537500	.9489917	1.0000000
2	1.1051266	1.8561222	2.0512500	2	1.1077563	1.8528444	2.0525000	2	1.1103891	1.8495769	2.0537500
3	1.1617643	2.7168820	3.1563766	3	1.1659135	2.7105410	3.1602563	3	1.1700725	2.7042249	3.1641391
4	1.2213047	3.5356785	4.3181409	4	1.2271239	3.5254547	4.3261697	4	1.2329639	3.5152786	4.3342115
5	1.2838966	4.3145574	5.5394456	5	1.2915479	4.2997194	5.5532936	5	1.2992357	4.2849619	5.5671754
6	1.3496963	5.0554642	6.8233422	6	1.3593542	5.0353628	6.8448415	6	1.3690696	5.0153850	6.8664111
7	1.4189682	5.7602520	8.1730385	7	1.4307203	5.7343115	8.2041957	7	1.4426571	5.7085504	8.2354807
8	1.4915852	6.4306796	9.5919067	8	1.5058331	6.3983957	9.6349160	8	1.5201999	6.3663586	9.6781378
9	1.5680290	7.0684230	11.0834919	9	1.5848893	7.0293546	11.1407491	9	1.6019107	6.9906132	11.1963377
10	1.6483904	7.6750753	12.6515209	10	1.6680960	7.6288405	12.7256384	10	1.6880133	7.5830255	12.8002483
11	1.7328705	8.2521525	14.2999113	11	1.7556711	8.1984232	14.3937344	11	1.7787441	8.1452200	14.4882617
12	1.8216801	8.8010963	16.0327818	12	1.8478438	8.7395945	16.1494055	12	1.8743516	8.6787378	16.2670057
13	1.9150412	9.3232783	17.8544618	13	1.9448556	9.2537715	17.9972493	13	1.9750980	9.1850418	18.1413573
14	2.0131870	9.8200032	19.7695030	14	2.0469605	9.7423007	19.9421048	14	2.0812595	9.6655201	20.1164553
15	2.1163629	10.2925119	21.7826900	15	2.1544259	10.2064615	21.9890654	15	2.1931272	10.1214900	22.1977147
16	2.2248265	10.7419852	23.8990529	16	2.2675333	10.6474694	24.1434913	16	2.3110078	10.5542017	24.3908419
17	2.3388488	11.1695460	26.1238793	17	2.3865788	11.0664792	26.4110246	17	2.4352244	10.9648414	26.7018496
18	2.4587148	11.5762625	28.4627282	18	2.5118742	11.4645883	28.7976034	18	2.5661177	11.3545352	29.1370741
19	2.5847240	11.9631510	30.9214430	19	2.6437476	11.8428393	31.3094776	19	2.7040466	11.7243513	31.7031918
20	2.7171911	12.3311781	33.5061669	20	2.7825443	12.2022226	33.9532251	20	2.8493891	12.0753037	34.4072384
21	2.8564471	12.6812634	36.2233580	21	2.9266279	12.5436794	36.7357694	21	3.0025437	12.4083547	37.2566274
22	3.0028400	13.0142815	39.0798051	22	3.0823809	12.8681039	39.6643973	22	3.1639305	12.7244172	40.2591711
23	3.1567356	13.3310644	42.0826451	23	3.2442059	13.1763458	42.7467782	23	3.3339917	13.0243580	43.4231016
24	3.3185183	13.6324037	45.2393807	24	3.4145267	13.4692122	45.9909841	24	3.5131938	13.3089993	46.7570933
25	3.4875923	13.9190523	48.5578989	25	3.5937893	13.7474700	49.4055107	25	3.7020279	13.5791215	50.2702871
26	3.6673827	14.1917263	52.0464912	26	3.7824633	14.0118480	52.9993000	26	3.9010119	13.8354652	53.9723150
27	3.8553360	14.4511071	55.7138739	27	3.9810426	14.2630384	56.7817633	27	4.1106913	14.0787333	57.8733269
28	4.0529220	14.6978426	59.5692100	28	4.1900473	14.5016992	60.7628059	28	4.3316402	14.3095927	61.9840183
29	4.2606343	14.9325495	63.6221320	29	4.4100248	14.7284553	64.9528532	29	4.5644667	14.5286764	66.3156593
30	4.4789918	15.1558140	67.8827662	30	4.6415511	14.9439005	69.3628780	30	4.8098068	14.7365849	70.8801259
31	4.7085401	15.3681941	72.3617580	31	4.8852325	15.1485991	74.0044291	31	5.0683339	14.9338884	75.6899327
32	4.9496528	15.5702203	77.0702981	32	5.1417072	15.3430870	78.8896616	32	5.3407568	15.1211278	80.7582656
33	5.2035327	15.7623024	82.0201509	33	5.4116469	15.5278737	84.0313689	33	5.6278225	15.2988164	86.0990234
34	5.4702138	15.9452056	87.2236836	34	5.6957583	15.7034429	89.4430157	34	5.9303180	15.4674414	91.7268460
35	5.7505622	16.1191017	92.6938974	35	5.9947846	15.8702545	95.1387740	35	6.2490726	15.6274652	97.6571639
36	6.0452786	16.2845200	98.4444597	36	6.3095119	16.0287454	101.1335597	36	6.5849602	15.7793264	103.9062365
37	6.3550991	16.4418740	104.4897382	37	6.6407613	16.1793305	107.4430716	37	6.9389018	15.9234414	110.4911967
38	6.6807979	16.5915567	110.8448373	38	6.9894012	16.3221043	114.0838328	38	7.3118678	16.0602054	117.4300985
39	7.0231888	16.7339421	117.5256353	39	7.3563448	16.4583414	121.0732341	39	7.7048807	16.1899932	124.7419663
40	7.3831272	16.8693861	124.5488241	40	7.7425529	16.5874978	128.4295789	40	8.1190180	16.3131608	132.4468470
41	7.7615125	16.9982270	131.9319513	41	8.1490369	16.7102117	136.1721318	41	8.5554153	16.4300459	140.5658651
42	8.1592900	17.1207867	139.6934638	42	8.5768614	16.8268044	144.3211687	42	9.0152688	16.5409688	149.1212803
43	8.5774536	17.2373714	147.8527539	43	9.0271466	16.9375814	152.8980301	43	9.4998395	16.6462337	158.1365492
44	9.0170481	17.3482724	156.4302075	44	9.5010718	17.0428327	161.9251766	44	10.0104559	16.7461293	167.6363887
45	9.4791719	17.4537669	165.4472556	45	9.9998781	17.1428339	171.4262484	45	10.5485179	16.8409293	177.6468446
46	9.9649794	17.5541183	174.9264275	46	10.5248716	17.2378469	181.4261265	46	11.1155007	16.9308938	188.1953625
47	10.4756846	17.6495774	184.8914069	47	11.0774274	17.3281206	191.9509981	47	11.7129589	17.0162693	199.3108632
48	11.0125635	17.7403828	195.3670915	48	11.6589924	17.4138913	203.0284255	48	12.3425305	17.0972900	211.0238221
49	11.5769573	17.8267613	206.3796550	49	12.2710894	17.4953837	214.6874179	49	13.0059415	17.1741779	223.3663526
50	12.1702764	17.9089287	217.9566123	50	12.9153216	17.5728111	226.9585073	50	13.7050108	17.2471439	236.3722941
51	12.7940031	17.9870903	230.1268887	51	13.5933760	17.6463763	239.8738290	51	14.4416551	17.3163861	250.0773049
52	13.4496957	18.0614415	242.9208918	52	14.3070283	17.7162720	253.4672050	52	15.2178941	17.3821002	264.5189600
53	14.1389926	18.1321679	256.3705875	53	15.0581473	17.7826813	267.7742333	53	16.0358559	17.4444604	279.7368541
54	14.8636160	18.1994462	270.5095801	54	15.8487000	17.8457779	282.8323805	54	16.8977832	17.5036398	295.7727101
55	15.6253763	18.2634447	285.3731961	55	16.6807567	17.9057272	298.6810805	55	17.8060390	17.5598005	312.6704932
56	16.4261769	18.3243231	300.9985724	56	17.5564965	17.9626862	315.3618373	56	18.7631136	17.6130966	330.4765323
57	17.2680184	18.3822337	317.4247492	57	18.4782125	18.0168040	332.9183338	57	19.7716310	17.6636741	349.2396459
58	18.1530044	18.4373210	334.6927677	58	19.4483187	18.0682223	351.3965463	58	20.8343562	17.7116717	369.0112769
59	19.0833458	18.4897227	352.8457720	59	20.4693554	18.1170759	370.8448650	59	21.9542028	17.7572211	389.8456330
60	20.0613673	18.5395697	371.9291177	60	21.5439966	18.1634925	391.3142204	60	23.1342412	17.8004471	411.7998358
61	21.0895124	18.5869867	391.9904852	61	22.6750564	18.2075938	412.8582170	61	24.3777067	17.8414682	434.9340770
62	22.1703499	18.6320031	413.0799975	62	23.8654969	18.2494993	435.5332734	62	25.6880084	17.8803968	459.3117837
63	23.3065803	18.6749983	435.2503474	63	25.1184355	18.2893067	459.3987703	63	27.0687388	17.9173398	484.9997921
64	24.5010426	18.7158120	458.5569278	64	26.4371533	18.3271323	484.5172058	64	28.5236836	17.9523984	512.0685309
65	25.7567210	18.7546377	483.0579703	65	27.8251039	18.3630710	510.9543591	65	30.0568316	17.9856687	540.5922145
66	27.0767530	18.7915667	508.8146913	66	29.2859218	18.3972071	538.7794630	66	31.6723863	18.0172419	570.6490461
67	28.4644365	18.8267013	535.8914443	67	30.8234327	18.4296600	568.0653848	67	33.3477770	18.0472041	602.3214323
68	29.9232389	18.8601201	564.3558808	68	32.4416630	18.4604845	598.8888175	68	35.1686713	18.0756391	635.6962093
69	31.4568049	18.8919098	594.2791198	69	34.1448503	18.4897715	631.3304805	69	37.0589874	18.1026231	670.8648806
70	33.0689662	18.9221146	625.7359247	70	35.9374549	18.5175977	665.4753307	70	39.0509079	18.1282307	707.9238680
71	34.7637507	18.9509152	658.8048909	71	37.8241713	18.5440358	701.4127856	71	41.1498942	18.1525321	746.9747759
72	36.5453929	18.9782784	693.5686415	72	39.8099403	18.5691551	739.2369569	72	43.3617011	18.1755939	788.1246702
73	38.4183443	19.0043076	730.1140345	73	41.8999621	18.5930215	779.0468972	73	45.6923925	18.1974794	831.4863712
74	40.3872845	19.0290679	768.5323788	74	44.0997102	18.6156974	820.9468593	74	48.1483586	18.2182485	877.1787637
75	42.4571328	19.0526211	808.9196532	75	46.4149449	18.6372422	865.0465695	75	50.7363329	18.2379583	925.3271223
76	44.6330608	19.0750260	851.3767960	76	48.8517096	18.6577123	911.4615144	76	53.4634108	18.2566627	976.0634552
77	46.9205052	19.0963386	896.0098568	77	51.4164454	18.6771613	960.3132440	77	56.3370691	18.2744130	1029.5268659
78	49.3251811	19.1166123	942.9303620	78	54.1158087	18.6956402	1011.7296894	78	59.3651866	18.2912579	1085.8639350
79	51.8530966	19.1358975	992.2555431	79	56.9569887	18.7131973	1065.8454981	79	62.5560653	18.3072435	1145.2291216
80	54.5905678	19.1542426	1044.1086398	80	59.9471254	18.7298787	1122.8023868	80	65.9184539	18.3224138	1207.7851869
81	57.3042344	19.1716993	1098.6192076	81	63.0943494	18.7457280	1182.7495122	81	69.4615708	18.3368102	1273.7036408
82	60.2410765	19.1882933	1155.9234421	82	66.4003028	18.7607867	1245.8438316	82	73.1951302	18.3504723	1343.1652116
83	63.3284316	19.2040802	1216.1645185	83	69.8931599	18.7750942	1312.2506644	83	77.1293684	18.3634376	1416.3603417
84	66.5740138	19.2191048	1279.4929502	84	73.5625508	18.7886681	1382.1438244	84	81.2750028	18.3757415	1493.4897102
85	69.9859320	19.2333934	1346.0669639	85	77.4245848	18.8016039	1455.7063752	85	85.6436071	18.3874178	1574.7647822
86	73.5727110	19.2469854	1416.0528959	86	81.4893755	18.8138754	1533.1309600	86	90.2469510	18.3984985	1660.4083893
87	77.3433124	19.2599144	1489.6256069	87	85.7675677	18.8255349	1614.6203355	87	95.0977246	18.4090140	1750.6553403
88	81.3071572	19.2722138	1566.9689193	88	90.2703650	18.8366127	1700.3879074	88	100.2092273	18.4189931	1845.7530649
89	85.4741490	19.2839133	1648.2760765	89	95.0095592	18.8471379	1790.6582681	89	105.5954733	18.4284632	1945.9622923
90	89.8546991	19.2950424	1733.7502255	90	99.9975610	18.8571382	1885.6678273	90	111.2712300	18.4374502	2051.5577656
91	94.4597525	19.3056289	1823.6049246	91	105.2474330	18.8666396	1985.6653883	91	117.2520586	18.4459789	2162.8289956
92	99.3008148	19.3156993	1918.0646771	92	110.7729232	18.8756671	2090.9128213	92	123.5543568	18.4540725	2280.0810542
93	104.3899816	19.3252782	2017.3654919	93	116.5885017	18.8842443	2201.6857445	93	130.1954035	18.4617532	2403.6354110
94	109.7399681	19.3343912	2121.7554735	94	122.7093980	18.8923936	2318.2742462	94	137.1934064	18.4690422	2533.8308144
95	115.3641415	19.3430594	2231.4954416	95	129.1516414	18.9001364	2440.9836443	95	144.5675520	18.4753594	2671.0242208
96	121.2765538	19.3513050	2346.8595831	96	135.9321026	18.9074930	2570.1352857	96	152.3380579	18.4825237	2815.5917728
97	127.4919771	19.3591486	2468.1361368	97	143.0685380	18.9144827	2706.0673884	97	160.5262286	18.4886013	2967.9298308
98	134.0259410	19.3666099	2595.6281140	98	150.5796363	18.9211237	2849.1359264	98	169.1545133	18.4946650	3128.4560593
99	140.8947705	19.3737074	2729.6540550	99	158.4850672	18.9274335	2999.7155627	99	178.2465684	18.5002752	3297.6105727
100	148.1156274	19.3804589	2870.5488254	100	166.3055332	18.9334285	3158.2006299	100	187.8273215	18.5055993	3475.8571411

M	C(11.00,M,2)	A(11.00,M,2)	S(11.00,M,2)	M	C(11.25,M,2)	A(11.25,M,2)	S(11.25,M,2)	M	C(11.50,M,2)	A(11.50,M,2)	S(11.50,M,2)
1/6	1.0089634	.1615230	.1629708	1/6	1.0091625	.1614106	.1628896	1/6	1.0093615	.1612985	.1628084
1/2	1.0271319	.4802770	.4933078	1/2	1.0277402	.4798487	.4931598	1/2	1.0283482	.4794213	.4930120
1	1.0550000	.9478673	1.0000000	1	1.0562500	.9467456	1.0000000	1	1.0575000	.9456265	1.0000000
2	1.1130250	1.8463197	2.0550000	2	1.1156641	1.8430727	2.0562500	2	1.1183063	1.8398359	2.0575000
3	1.1742414	2.6979334	3.1680250	3	1.1784202	2.6916665	3.1719141	3	1.1826089	2.6854240	3.1758063
4	1.2388247	3.5051501	4.3422664	4	1.2447063	3.4950689	4.3503342	4	1.2506089	3.4850345	4.3584151
5	1.3069600	4.2702845	5.5810910	5	1.3147210	4.2556865	5.5950405	5	1.3275189	4.2411674	5.6090740
6	1.3788428	4.9955303	6.8880510	6	1.3886741	4.9757979	6.9097616	6	1.3985637	4.9561667	6.9315429
7	1.4546792	5.6829671	8.2668938	7	1.4667870	5.6575601	8.2984356	7	1.4789611	5.6323278	8.3301066
8	1.5346865	6.3345660	9.7215730	8	1.5492938	6.3030155	9.7652227	8	1.5640225	6.2717048	9.8090877
9	1.6190943	6.9521952	11.2562595	9	1.6364415	6.9140975	11.3145164	9	1.6539538	6.8763166	11.3731102
10	1.7081445	7.5376258	12.8753538	10	1.7284914	7.4926367	12.9509580	10	1.7490562	7.4480535	13.0270641
11	1.8020924	8.0925363	14.5834983	11	1.8257190	8.0403661	14.6794494	11	1.8496269	7.9887031	14.7761203
12	1.9012075	8.6185178	16.3855907	12	1.9284157	8.5589265	16.5051684	12	1.9559805	8.4999556	16.6257472
13	2.0057739	9.1170785	18.2867981	13	2.0368891	9.0498712	18.4335841	13	2.0684493	8.9834096	18.5817276
14	2.1160915	9.5896479	20.2925720	14	2.1514641	9.5146710	20.4704732	14	2.1873852	9.4405764	20.6501770
15	2.2324765	10.0375809	22.4086635	15	2.2724840	9.9547181	22.6219373	15	2.3131598	9.8728855	22.8375622
16	2.3552627	10.4621620	24.6411400	16	2.4003112	10.3713307	24.8944213	16	2.4461665	10.2816884	25.1507220
17	2.4848021	10.8646086	26.9964027	17	2.5353287	10.7657569	27.2947325	17	2.5869211	10.6682633	27.5968885
18	2.6214663	11.2460745	29.4812048	18	2.6779409	11.1391781	29.8300612	18	2.7355633	11.0338187	30.1837096
19	2.7656469	11.6076535	32.1026711	19	2.8285751	11.4927130	32.5080022	19	2.8928582	11.3794976	32.9192729
20	2.9177575	11.9503825	34.8683180	20	2.9876825	11.8274206	35.3365773	20	3.0591975	11.7063807	35.8121311
21	3.0782342	12.2752441	37.7860755	21	3.1557396	12.1443035	38.3242598	21	3.2351014	12.0154900	38.8713286
22	3.2475370	12.5831697	40.8643097	22	3.3332500	12.4443110	41.4799994	22	3.4211197	12.3077920	42.1064300
23	3.4261516	12.8750424	44.1118467	23	3.5207453	12.7283418	44.8132493	23	3. 78341	12.5842005	45.5275498
24	3.6145899	13.1516989	47.5379983	24	3.7187872	12.9972467	48.3339946	24	3.8258596	12.8455796	49.1453839
25	3.8173924	13.4139326	51.1525082	25	3.9279690	13.2518312	52.0527818	25	4.0458465	13.0927467	52.9712435
26	4.0231289	13.6624954	54.9659805	26	4.1489172	13.4928579	55.9807508	26	4.2784827	13.3264744	57.0170900
27	4.2444010	13.8980999	58.9891095	27	4.3822938	13.7210489	60.1296680	27	4.5244954	13.5474935	61.2955726
28	4.4778431	14.1214217	63.2335105	28	4.6287979	13.9370877	64.5119619	28	4.7846539	13.7564951	65.8200681
29	4.7241245	14.3331011	67.7113536	29	4.8891677	14.1416215	69.1407597	29	5.0597715	13.9541325	70.6047220
30	4.9839513	14.5337452	72.4354780	30	5.1641834	14.3352630	74.0299275	30	5.3507084	14.1410236	75.6644935
31	5.2580686	14.7239291	77.4194293	31	5.4546487	14.5185922	79.1941109	31	5.6583741	14.3177523	81.0152019
32	5.5472624	14.9041982	82.6774979	32	5.7614939	14.6921583	84.6487796	32	5.9837306	14.4848726	86.6735760
33	5.8523618	15.0750693	88.2247603	33	6.0855779	14.8564812	90.4102735	33	6.3277951	14.6429056	92.6573006
34	6.1742417	15.2370326	94.0771222	34	6.4278916	15.0120532	96.4958514	34	6.6916434	14.7923457	98.9851017
35	6.5138250	15.3905522	100.2513639	35	6.7894606	15.1593403	102.9237430	35	7.0764128	14.9336602	105.6767451
36	6.8720854	15.5360684	106.7651889	36	7.1713677	15.2987837	109.7132036	36	7.4833066	15.0672910	112.7531579
37	7.2500501	15.6739985	113.6372743	37	7.5747571	15.4308012	116.8845713	37	7.9135967	15.1936558	120.2364645
38	7.6488028	15.8047379	120.8873244	38	8.0008372	15.5557881	124.4593284	38	8.3668285	15.3131497	128.1500613
39	8.0694870	15.9286615	128.5361272	39	8.4508843	15.6741189	132.4601657	39	8.8498247	15.4261463	136.5186898
40	8.5133030	16.0461247	136.6056142	40	8.9262466	15.7861481	140.9110500	40	9.3586896	15.5329988	145.3685145
41	8.9815408	16.1574641	145.1189230	41	9.4283479	15.8922112	149.8372966	41	9.8968412	15.6340414	154.7272040
42	9.4755255	16.2629992	154.1004638	42	9.9586925	15.9926260	159.2656445	42	10.4658811	15.7295900	164.6240183
43	9.9966794	16.3630324	163.5759933	43	10.5188690	16.0876932	169.2243370	43	11.0678692	15.8199433	175.0898993
44	10.5464968	16.4578506	173.5726687	44	11.1105553	16.1776977	179.7432060	44	11.7040602	15.9053837	186.1575586
45	11.1265541	16.5477257	184.1191655	45	11.7355241	16.2629091	190.8537613	45	12.3770437	15.9861785	197.8616288
46	11.7385146	16.6329154	195.2457196	46	12.3956473	16.3435826	202.5892854	46	13.0887237	16.0625801	210.2386724
47	12.3841329	16.7136638	206.9842342	47	13.0929025	16.4199598	214.9849327	47	13.8413253	16.1348275	223.3273961
48	13.0652602	16.7902027	219.3683671	48	13.8293782	16.4922697	228.0778352	48	14.6372015	16.2031466	237.1687214
49	13.7838495	16.8627514	232.4336273	49	14.6072808	16.5607287	241.9072134	49	15.4788406	16.2677509	251.8059229
50	14.5419612	16.9315179	246.2174768	50	15.4289403	16.6255419	256.5144942	50	16.3688730	16.3288425	267.2847605
51	15.3417691	16.9966994	260.7594381	51	16.2968182	16.6869036	271.9434345	51	17.3100842	16.3866123	283.6536374
52	16.1855664	17.0584829	276.1012072	52	17.2135142	16.7449975	288.2402527	52	18.3054140	16.4412409	300.9637215
53	17.0757726	17.1170454	292.2867736	53	18.1817744	16.7999976	305.4537669	53	19.3579753	16.4928992	319.2691355
54	18.0149401	17.1725548	309.3625462	54	19.2044992	16.8520688	323.6355413	54	20.4710589	16.5417487	338.6271108
55	19.0057618	17.2251705	327.3774862	55	20.2847523	16.9013669	342.8400406	55	21.6481448	16.5879420	359.0981697
56	20.0510787	17.2750431	346.3832480	56	21.4257696	16.9480396	363.1247929	56	22.8929131	16.6316236	380.7463145
57	21.1538880	17.3223157	366.4343266	57	22.6309692	16.9922269	384.5505625	57	24.2092556	16.6729301	403.6392276
58	22.3173518	17.3671239	387.5882146	58	23.9039612	17.0340061	407.1815316	58	25.6012378	16.7119907	427.8484832
59	23.5448062	17.4095961	409.9055664	59	25.2485590	17.0736672	431.0854928	59	27.0733619	16.7489274	453.4497710
60	24.8397705	17.4498542	433.4503726	60	26.6687904	17.1111642	456.3340518	60	28.6300802	16.7838557	480.5231329
61	26.2059579	17.4880134	458.2901431	61	28.1689099	17.1466643	483.0028422	61	30.2663098	16.8168848	509.1532130
62	27.6472856	17.5241833	484.4961010	62	29.7534111	17.1802739	511.1717521	62	32.0171976	16.8481180	539.4295228
63	29.1678863	17.5584676	512.1433866	63	31.4270405	17.2120936	540.9251632	63	33.8581865	16.8776529	571.4467204
64	30.7721200	17.5909646	541.3112729	64	33.1948115	17.2422188	572.3522037	64	35.8050322	16.9055820	605.3049069
65	32.4645860	17.6217674	572.0833929	65	35.0620196	17.2707397	605.5470152	65	37.8638215	16.9319924	641.1099390
66	34.2501389	17.6509643	604.5479796	66	37.0342582	17.2977417	640.6090348	66	40.0409911	16.9569668	678.9737606
67	36.1338965	17.6786392	638.7981185	67	39.1174353	17.3233058	677.6432930	67	42.3433483	16.9805833	719.0147518
68	38.1212609	17.7048712	674.9320150	68	41.3177910	17.3475084	716.7607283	68	44.7780908	17.0029156	761.3581001
69	40.2179302	17.7297532	713.0532759	69	43.6419167	17.3704222	758.0785193	69	47.3528310	17.0240337	806.1361909
70	42.4299164	17.7533040	753.2712061	70	46.0967746	17.3921157	801.7204360	70	50.0756188	17.0440035	853.4890219
71	44.7635618	17.7756436	795.7011225	71	48.6897181	17.4126539	847.8172106	71	52.9549569	17.0628875	903.5646407
72	47.2255577	17.7968186	840.4646843	72	51.4285148	17.4320984	896.5069288	72	55.9998775	17.0807446	956.5196076
73	49.8229634	17.8168897	887.6902419	73	54.3213687	17.4505073	947.9354435	73	59.2198704	17.0976309	1012.5194851
74	52.5632263	17.8359144	937.5132053	74	57.3769457	17.4679359	1002.2568123	74	62.6520130	17.1135989	1071.7393555
75	55.4542038	17.8539473	990.0764316	75	60.6043989	17.4844364	1059.6337580	75	66.2259512	17.1286988	1134.3643685
76	58.5041850	17.8710401	1045.5306354	76	64.0133964	17.5000581	1120.2381570	76	70.0332434	17.1429775	1200.5903198
77	61.7219152	17.8872418	1104.0348204	77	67.6141499	17.5148479	1184.2515534	77	74.0608952	17.1564799	1270.6242632
78	65.1165205	17.9025989	1165.7567356	78	71.4174469	17.5288501	1251.8657033	78	78.3193967	17.1692482	1344.6851584
79	68.6980346	17.9171055	1230.8733561	79	75.4346772	17.5421066	1323.2831492	79	82.8227620	17.1813222	1423.0045551
80	72.4764266	17.9309525	1299.5713907	80	79.6677878	17.5546571	1398.7178264	80	87.5390708	17.1927396	1505.8273171
81	76.4626300	17.9440312	1372.0478173	81	84.1597584	17.5665393	1478.3957042	81	92.6212124	17.2035363	1593.4123879
82	80.6680747	17.9564227	1448.5104473	82	88.8924771	17.5777887	1562.5554526	82	97.9469321	17.2137459	1686.0336003
83	85.1048188	17.9681779	1529.1785220	83	93.8940180	17.5884390	1651.4492075	83	103.5788807	17.2234004	1783.9805324
84	89.7855838	17.9793155	1614.2833408	84	99.1755565	17.5985221	1745.3432255	84	109.5346663	17.2325299	1887.5594131
85	94.7237909	17.9898725	1704.0689246	85	104.7541816	17.6080683	1844.5187820	85	115.8329097	17.2411639	1997.0940794
86	99.9335994	17.9998792	1798.7927155	86	110.6466403	17.6171061	1949.2729636	86	122.4933020	17.2493267	2112.9269891
87	105.4299474	18.0093641	1898.7263150	87	116.8704758	17.6256625	2059.9195679	87	129.5366668	17.2570466	2235.4202911
88	111.2285945	18.0183546	2004.1562624	88	123.4444401	17.6337634	2176.7900436	88	136.9850252	17.2643466	2364.9569579
89	117.3461672	18.0268764	2115.3848569	89	130.3881898	17.6414328	2300.2344837	89	144.8616642	17.2712498	2501.9419831
90	123.8002064	18.0349540	2232.7310242	90	137.7225255	17.6486937	2430.6226735	90	153.1912098	17.2777776	2646.8036473
91	130.6092178	18.0426104	2356.5312306	91	145.4694176	17.6555680	2568.3451990	91	161.9997044	17.2839504	2799.9948571
92	137.7927248	18.0498677	2487.1404484	92	153.6520723	17.6620762	2713.8146166	92	171.3146874	17.2897876	2961.9945615
93	145.3713247	18.0567466	2624.9331732	93	162.2950014	17.6682377	2867.4666889	93	181.1652820	17.2953079	3133.3092490
94	153.3667475	18.0632669	2770.3044979	94	171.4240952	17.6740714	3029.7616903	94	191.5822857	17.3005271	3314.4745309
95	161.8019186	18.0694473	2923.6712454	95	181.0667006	17.6795942	3201.1857856	95	202.5982671	17.3054630	3506.0568166
96	170.7010242	18.0753055	3085.4731640	96	191.2517025	17.6848229	3382.2524862	96	214.2476675	17.3101305	3708.6550838
97	180.0895805	18.0808583	3256.1741882	97	202.0096108	17.6897731	3573.5041887	97	226.5669084	17.3145442	3922.9027513
98	189.9945075	18.0861216	3436.2637687	98	213.3726514	17.6944598	3775.5137995	98	239.5945056	17.3187179	4149.4696597
99	200.4442054	18.0911105	3626.2582762	99	225.3748631	17.6988968	3988.8864509	99	253.3711897	17.3226647	4389.0641653
100	211.4686367	18.0958394	3826.7024815	100	238.0521991	17.7030976	4214.2613139	100	267.9400331	17.3263969	4642.4353550

Table 1

M	C(11.75,M,2)	A(11.75,M,2)	S(11.75,M,2)	C(12.00,M,2)	A(12.00,M,2)	S(12.00,M,2)	C(12.25,M,2)	A(12.25,M,2)	S(12.25,M,2)
1/6	1.0095602	.1611865	.1627275	1.0097588	.1610747	.1626466	1.0099572	.1609631	.1625658
1/2	1.0289558	.4789947	.4928644	1.0295630	.4785690	.4927169	1.0301699	.4781441	.4925696
1	1.0587500	.9445100	1.0000000	1.0600000	.9433962	1.0000000	1.0612500	.9422850	1.0000000
2	1.1209516	1.8366092	2.0587500	1.1236000	1.8333927	2.0600000	1.1262516	1.8301861	2.0612500
3	1.1868075	2.6792059	3.1797016	1.1910160	2.6730119	3.1836000	1.1952345	2.6668421	3.1875016
4	1.2565324	3.4750469	4.3665090	1.2624770	3.4651056	4.3746160	1.2684426	3.4552104	4.3827360
5	1.3303537	4.2267267	5.6230414	1.3382256	4.2123638	5.6370930	1.3461347	4.1980761	5.6511786
6	1.4085120	4.9366958	6.9533951	1.4185191	4.9173243	6.9753185	1.4285854	4.8980713	6.9973133
7	1.4912620	5.6072688	8.3619071	1.5036303	5.5823814	8.3938377	1.5160863	5.5576643	8.4258987
8	1.5788737	6.2406317	9.8531691	1.5938481	6.2097938	9.8974679	1.6089466	6.1791890	9.9419850
9	1.6716325	6.8388493	11.4320428	1.6894790	6.8016923	11.4913160	1.7074946	6.7648424	11.5509316
10	1.7698409	7.4038718	13.1036753	1.7906477	7.3600870	13.1807949	1.8120786	7.3166948	13.2584262
11	1.8738191	7.9375413	14.8735163	1.8982986	7.8868746	14.9716426	1.9230684	7.8366971	15.0705048
12	1.9839060	8.4415974	16.7473353	2.0121965	8.3838439	16.6699412	2.0408564	8.3266875	16.9935732
13	2.1004604	8.9176835	18.7312413	2.1329283	8.8526830	18.8821377	2.1653588	8.7883981	19.0344296
14	2.2233625	9.3673516	20.8317017	2.2609040	9.2949839	21.0150659	2.2985177	9.2234612	21.2002684
15	2.3545144	9.7920676	23.0555642	2.3965582	9.7122490	23.2759699	2.4393019	9.6334145	23.4988061
16	2.4928421	10.1932162	25.4100786	2.5403517	10.1058953	25.6725281	2.5887091	10.0197074	25.9381079
17	2.6392966	10.5721050	27.9029207	2.6927728	10.4772597	28.2128798	2.7472675	10.3837055	28.5268170
18	2.7943553	10.9299693	30.5422173	2.8543392	10.8276035	30.9056526	2.9155377	10.7266954	31.2740846
19	2.9585236	11.2679757	33.3365726	3.0255995	11.1581015	33.7599917	3.0941144	11.0498896	34.1896223
20	3.1323369	11.5872262	36.2950962	3.2071355	11.4699212	36.7855912	3.2836289	11.3544308	37.2837366
21	3.3163617	11.8887615	39.4274331	3.3995636	11.7640766	39.9927267	3.4847511	11.6413953	40.5673655
22	3.5111979	12.1735645	42.7437948	3.6035374	12.0415841	43.3922903	3.6981921	11.9117977	44.0521166
23	3.7174808	12.4425639	46.2549928	3.8197497	12.3033790	46.9956277	3.9247064	12.1665938	47.7503088
24	3.9358828	12.6960365	49.9724736	4.0489346	12.5503575	50.8155774	4.1650947	12.4066844	51.6750152
25	4.1671159	12.9366106	53.9083564	4.2918707	12.7833562	54.8645120	4.4202067	12.6329182	55.8401099
26	4.4119340	13.1632686	58.0754723	4.5493830	13.0031662	59.1563828	4.6909444	12.8460948	60.2603166
27	4.6711351	13.3773493	62.4874063	4.8223459	13.2105341	63.7057657	4.9782647	13.0469681	64.9512610
28	4.9455643	13.5795507	67.1585415	5.1116867	13.4061643	68.5281117	5.2831835	13.2362479	69.9295258
29	5.2361162	13.7705320	72.1041058	5.4183879	13.5907210	73.6397984	5.6067784	13.4146034	75.2127092
30	5.5437380	13.9509157	77.3402220	5.7434912	13.7648311	79.0581863	5.9501936	13.5826652	80.8194877
31	5.8694327	14.1212899	82.8839601	6.0881007	13.9290860	84.8016775	6.3146430	13.7410272	86.7696813
32	6.2142618	14.2822101	88.7533927	6.4533867	14.0840434	90.8897781	6.7014149	13.8902495	93.0843243
33	6.5793497	14.4342008	94.9676545	6.8405899	14.2302209	97.3431648	7.1118765	14.0308593	99.7857391
34	6.9658865	14.5777575	101.5470042	7.2510253	14.3681411	104.1837547	7.5474790	14.1633539	106.8976157
35	7.3751323	14.7133483	108.5128908	7.6860868	14.4982464	111.4347800	8.0097621	14.2882016	114.4450946
36	7.8084214	14.8414151	115.8880231	8.1472520	14.6209871	119.1208668	8.5003600	14.4058436	122.4548567
37	8.2671661	14.9623756	123.6964445	8.6360871	14.7367803	127.2681188	9.0210070	14.5166960	130.9552166
38	8.7528621	15.0766239	131.9636106	9.1542524	14.8460192	135.9042059	9.5735437	14.6211505	139.9762237
39	9.2670928	15.1845326	140.7164727	9.7035075	14.9490747	145.0584583	10.1599233	14.7195765	149.5497674
40	9.8115345	15.2864535	149.9835655	10.2857180	15.0462969	154.7619658	10.7822186	14.8123218	159.7096906
41	10.3879621	15.3827188	159.7951000	10.9028610	15.1380159	165.0476838	11.4426294	14.8997143	170.4919092
42	10.9982549	15.4736423	170.1830621	11.5570327	15.2245433	175.9505448	12.1434905	14.9820629	181.9343586
43	11.6444024	15.5595204	181.1813170	12.2504547	15.3061729	187.5075775	12.8872293	15.0596588	194.0780291
44	12.3285110	15.6406332	192.8257194	12.9854819	15.3831820	199.7580322	13.6766252	15.1327763	206.9653084
45	13.0528110	15.7172451	205.1542304	13.7646109	15.4558321	212.7435141	14.5143184	15.2016737	220.6419336
46	13.8196637	15.7896058	218.2070414	14.5904875	15.5243699	226.5081250	15.4033204	15.2665948	235.1562520
47	14.6315689	15.8579511	232.0267051	15.4659168	15.5890282	241.0986125	16.3467738	15.3277690	250.5595725
48	15.4911736	15.9225040	246.6582741	16.3938718	15.6500266	256.5645292	17.3480137	15.3854124	266.9063463
49	16.4012801	15.9834794	262.1494447	17.3775041	15.7075723	272.9584010	18.4105796	15.4397290	284.2543600
50	17.3648553	16.0410624	278.5507278	18.4201543	15.7618606	290.3359051	19.5382276	15.4909108	302.6649396
51	18.3850405	16.0954445	295.9155830	19.5253656	15.8130761	308.7560594	20.7349440	15.5391385	322.2031672
52	19.4651616	16.1468283	314.3006235	20.6968854	15.8613925	328.2814230	22.0049593	15.5845628	342.9381112
53	20.6087399	16.1953514	333.7657852	21.9386985	15.9069741	348.9783804	23.3527501	15.6274043	364.9430705
54	21.8195034	16.2411820	354.3745251	23.2550204	15.9499755	370.9170069	24.7831198	15.6677544	388.2958336
55	23.1013992	16.2844694	376.1940285	24.6503217	15.9905430	394.1720273	26.3010859	15.7057756	413.0789534
56	24.4586064	16.3253548	399.2954277	26.1293410	16.0288041	418.8223490	27.9120274	15.7416024	439.3800393
57	25.8955495	16.3639715	423.7540340	27.6971014	16.0649190	444.9516899	29.6216391	15.7753616	467.2920668
58	27.4169131	16.4004453	449.6495836	29.3589275	16.0999842	472.6487913	31.4359645	15.8071723	496.9137059
59	29.0276567	16.4348952	477.0664966	31.1204862	16.1311134	502.0077188	33.3614173	15.8371447	528.3496704
60	30.7330315	16.4674335	506.0941533	32.9876909	16.1614277	533.1281820	35.4048042	15.8653918	561.7110877
61	32.5385971	16.4981662	536.8271849	34.9669524	16.1900261	566.1158729	37.6533484	15.8920064	597.1156919
62	34.4502397	16.5271936	569.3657820	37.0649696	16.2170058	601.0828254	39.8747160	15.9170849	634.6892403
63	36.4741913	16.5546103	603.8160217	39.2888677	16.2424583	638.1477949	42.3170424	15.9407161	674.5639563
64	38.6170500	16.5805056	640.2902130	41.6461998	16.2664701	677.4366626	44.9089612	15.9629833	716.8809986
65	40.8850017	16.6049639	678.9072630	44.1449718	16.2891227	719.0828624	47.6598351	15.9839654	761.7899599
66	43.2878426	16.6280651	719.7930648	46.7933701	16.3104931	763.2278342	50.5787877	16.0037366	809.4495949
67	45.8310033	16.6498844	763.0809074	49.6012903	16.3306539	810.0215043	53.6767385	16.0223666	860.0283237
68	48.5235748	16.6704929	808.9119107	52.5773677	16.3496735	859.6227946	56.9644387	16.0399214	913.7051211
69	51.3743348	16.6899577	857.4354855	55.7320098	16.3676165	912.2001623	60.4535106	16.0564631	970.6695599
70	54.3925770	16.7083428	908.8098204	59.0755304	16.3845439	967.9321721	64.1562881	16.0720500	1031.1230704
71	57.5881409	16.7257075	963.2023974	62.6204862	16.4005131	1027.0081025	68.0858308	16.0867373	1095.2793586
72	60.9714442	16.7421086	1020.7905382	66.3777154	16.4155784	1089.6285887	72.2561197	16.1005770	1163.3652193
73	64.5535165	16.7575996	1081.7619824	70.3603783	16.4297909	1156.0063040	76.6818071	16.1136179	1235.6213391
74	68.3460356	16.7722310	1146.3154989	74.5820010	16.4431990	1226.3666823	81.3785678	16.1259061	1312.3031462
75	72.3613652	16.7860506	1214.6615346	79.0569211	16.4558481	1300.9486833	86.3630050	16.1374852	1393.6817139
76	76.6125954	16.7991032	1287.0228998	83.8003363	16.4677812	1380.0056044	91.6527391	16.1483959	1480.0447190
77	81.1135854	16.8114316	1363.6354952	88.8283565	16.4790389	1463.8059407	97.2664694	16.1586770	1571.6974581
78	85.8790086	16.8230759	1444.7490806	94.1580579	16.4896593	1552.6342973	103.2240406	16.1683646	1668.9639275
79	90.9244003	16.8340741	1530.6280892	99.8075414	16.4996786	1646.7923552	109.5465131	16.1774932	1772.1879681
80	96.2562088	16.8444619	1621.5524895	105.7959939	16.5091308	1746.5998966	116.2562371	16.1860949	1881.7344812
81	101.9218486	16.8542734	1717.8186983	112.1437535	16.5180479	1852.3958904	123.3769316	16.1942001	1997.9907183
82	107.9097572	16.8635404	1819.7405464	118.8728787	16.5264603	1964.5396440	130.9337687	16.2018376	2121.3676499
83	114.2494555	16.8722931	1927.6503042	126.0047215	16.5343965	2083.4120227	138.9534620	16.2090342	2252.3014186
84	120.9616110	16.8805602	2041.8997596	133.5650048	16.5418835	2209.4167442	147.4643616	16.2158155	2391.2548806
85	128.0681056	16.8883686	2162.8613706	141.5789051	16.5489467	2342.9817489	156.4965537	16.2222054	2538.7192421
86	135.5921068	16.8957436	2290.9294762	150.0736394	16.5556101	2484.5606540	166.0819676	16.2282265	2695.2157958
87	143.5581431	16.9027095	2426.5215831	159.0780577	16.5618963	2634.6342933	176.2544882	16.2339002	2861.2977635
88	151.9921840	16.9092887	2570.0797862	168.6227412	16.5678267	2793.7123511	187.0500756	16.2392463	3037.5522516
89	160.9217249	16.9155029	2722.0719103	178.7401057	16.5734214	2962.3350923	198.5068927	16.2442839	3224.6023272
90	170.3758762	16.9213723	2882.9936351	189.4645120	16.5786994	3141.0751980	210.6654399	16.2490308	3423.1092199
91	180.3854589	16.9269160	3053.3695113	200.8323828	16.5836787	3330.5397100	223.5686981	16.2535037	3633.7746598
92	190.9831047	16.9321521	3233.7549703	212.8823257	16.5883761	3531.3720928	237.2622809	16.2577184	3857.3433579
93	202.2033621	16.9370976	3424.7380749	225.6552653	16.5928077	3744.2544185	251.7945956	16.2616899	4094.6056387
94	214.0828096	16.9417082	3626.9414370	239.1945812	16.5969884	3969.9096838	267.2170146	16.2654322	4346.4002343
95	226.6601747	16.9461806	3841.0242466	253.5462561	16.6009324	4209.1042650	283.5840567	16.2689585	4613.6172489
96	239.9764600	16.9503504	4067.6844213	268.7590315	16.6046502	4462.6505212	300.9535880	16.2722811	4897.2013056
97	254.0750770	16.9542835	4307.6608813	284.8845734	16.6081634	4731.4095526	319.3869870	16.2754123	5198.1548858
98	269.0019878	16.9580009	4561.7359582	301.9776478	16.6114749	5016.2941260	338.9494400	16.2783626	5517.5418728
99	284.8058546	16.9615121	4830.7379460	320.0963067	16.6145990	5318.2717739	359.7100932	16.2811426	5856.4913128
100	301.5381985	16.9648284	5115.5438006	339.3020851	16.6175462	5638.3680805	381.7423364	16.2837621	6216.2014060

Table 1

M	C(12.50,M,2)	A(12.50,M,2)	S(12.50,M,2)	M	C(12.75,M,2)	A(12.75,M,2)	S(12.75,M,2)	M	C(13.00,M,2)	A(13.00,M,2)	S(13.00,M,2)
1/6	1.0101553	.1608517	.1624852	1/6	1.0103533	.1607404	.1624046	1/6	1.0105511	.1606294	.1623242
1/2	1.0307764	.4777200	.4924225	1/2	1.0313826	.4772968	.4922756	1/2	1.0319884	.4768744	.4921288
1	1.0625000	.9411765	1.0000000	1	1.0637500	.9400705	1.0000000	1	1.0650000	.9389671	1.0000000
2	1.1289063	1.8269896	2.0625000	2	1.1315641	1.8238031	2.0637500	2	1.1342250	1.8206264	2.0650000
3	1.1994293	2.6606961	3.1914063	3	1.2037013	2.6545740	3.1953141	3	1.2079496	2.6484755	3.1992250
4	1.2744293	3.4453610	4.3908691	4	1.2804372	3.4355572	4.3990153	4	1.2864664	3.4257986	4.4071746
5	1.3540812	4.1838692	5.6652985	5	1.3620651	4.1697365	5.6794526	5	1.3700867	4.1556794	5.5936410
6	1.4387112	4.8789357	7.0193796	6	1.4488968	4.8599168	7.0415177	6	1.4591423	4.8410136	7.0637276
7	1.5286307	5.5331160	8.4580908	7	1.5412639	5.5087349	8.4904144	7	1.5539365	5.4845198	8.5228699
8	1.6241701	6.1488150	9.9867215	8	1.6395195	6.1186697	10.0316783	8	1.6549957	6.0887510	10.0768565
9	1.7256607	6.7282965	11.6108916	9	1.7440389	6.6920515	11.6711978	9	1.7625704	6.6561042	11.7318522
10	1.8335358	7.2736908	13.3365723	10	1.8552213	7.2310707	13.4152367	10	1.8771375	7.1888302	13.4944225
11	1.9481318	7.7870031	15.1701081	11	1.9734917	7.7377868	15.2704580	11	1.9991514	7.6890425	15.3715600
12	2.0699900	8.2701206	17.1182399	12	2.0993018	8.2141357	17.2439497	12	2.1290962	8.1587253	17.3707114
13	2.1992581	8.7248194	19.1881299	13	2.2331323	8.6619372	19.3432515	13	2.2674875	8.5997421	19.4998077
14	2.3367118	9.1527712	21.3873880	14	2.3754945	9.0829021	21.5763638	14	2.4148742	9.0138423	21.7672952
15	2.4827562	9.5555494	23.7240997	15	2.5269322	9.4796389	23.9518783	15	2.5718410	9.4026689	24.1821693
16	2.6379285	9.9346347	26.2068560	16	2.6830242	9.8506594	26.4788105	16	2.7390107	9.7677642	26.7540103
17	2.8027990	10.2914209	28.8447845	17	2.8593857	10.2003848	29.1668347	17	2.9170464	10.1105767	29.4930210
18	2.9779740	10.6272197	31.6475835	18	3.0416791	10.5291514	32.0262204	18	3.1066544	10.4324664	32.4100674
19	3.1640973	10.9432656	34.6255575	19	3.2355781	10.8392152	35.0678920	19	3.3085869	10.7347102	35.5167218
20	3.3618534	11.2407205	37.7896548	20	3.4418462	11.1287570	38.3034701	20	3.5236451	11.0185072	38.8253087
21	3.5719693	11.5206781	41.1515082	21	3.6612639	11.4018867	41.7453163	21	3.7528320	11.2849683	42.3489538
22	3.7952173	11.7841677	44.7234775	22	3.8945695	11.6586479	45.4065802	22	3.9968063	11.5351958	46.1016358
23	4.0324184	12.0321578	48.5186949	23	4.1429547	11.9000215	49.3012497	23	4.2563857	11.7701367	50.0984215
24	4.2844446	12.2655603	52.5511133	24	4.4070660	12.1269297	53.4442004	24	4.5330508	11.9907387	54.3546278
25	4.5572224	12.4852332	56.8355579	25	4.6880186	12.3402395	57.8512724	25	4.8276991	12.1978767	58.8876786
26	4.8367363	12.6919842	61.3877802	26	4.9850798	12.5407657	62.5392910	26	5.1414996	12.3923725	63.7153777
27	5.1390323	12.8865734	66.2245165	27	5.3047934	12.7292744	67.5261708	27	5.4756970	12.5749977	68.8568773
28	5.4602218	13.0697161	71.3635488	28	5.6429740	12.9064859	72.8309642	28	5.8316173	12.7464767	74.3325743
29	5.8014857	13.2420857	76.8237706	29	6.0027136	13.0730773	78.4739382	29	6.2106725	12.9074898	80.1641917
30	6.1640785	13.4043160	82.6252563	30	6.3853866	13.2296849	84.4766518	30	6.6143662	13.0586759	86.3748641
31	6.5493334	13.5570033	88.7893348	31	6.7924549	13.3769070	90.8620383	31	7.0443000	13.2006346	92.9892303
32	6.9586668	13.7007090	95.3386682	32	7.2254740	13.5153063	97.6544933	32	7.5021795	13.3339292	100.0335303
33	7.3935834	13.8359614	102.2973350	33	7.6860979	13.6454113	104.8799072	33	7.9898211	13.4590885	107.5357097
34	7.8556824	13.9632578	109.6909164	34	8.1760867	13.7677192	112.5660051	34	8.5091595	13.5766089	115.5255309
35	8.3468626	14.0830661	117.5466008	35	8.6973122	13.8826972	120.7421518	35	9.0622549	13.6869567	124.0346904
36	8.8683290	14.1958270	125.8932634	36	9.2517658	13.9907847	129.4394640	36	9.6513014	13.7905697	133.0969453
37	9.4225995	14.3019548	134.7615923	37	9.8415659	14.0923946	138.6912298	37	10.2786360	13.8878589	142.7482467
38	10.0115120	14.4018398	144.1841919	38	10.4689657	14.1870150	148.5327957	38	10.9467474	13.9792102	153.0268828
39	10.6372315	14.4958492	154.1957039	39	11.1353623	14.2777109	159.0017614	39	11.6582860	14.0649861	163.9736302
40	11.3020585	14.5843287	164.8329354	40	11.8463054	14.3621254	170.1381237	40	12.4160746	14.1455269	175.6319161
41	12.0084371	14.6676035	176.1349938	41	12.6015074	14.4414810	181.9844291	41	13.2231194	14.2211520	188.0479907
42	12.7589644	14.7459797	188.1434310	42	13.4043535	14.5160808	194.5859365	42	14.0826222	14.2921615	201.2711101
43	13.5163997	14.8197456	200.9023954	43	14.2594129	14.5862100	207.9807900	43	14.9979926	14.3588317	215.3537323
44	14.4036747	14.8891723	214.4587951	44	15.1684504	14.6521363	222.2502028	44	15.9728621	14.4214433	230.3517249
45	15.3039044	14.9545151	228.8624698	45	16.1354392	14.7141116	237.4186553	45	17.0110982	14.4802284	246.3245870
46	16.2603984	15.0160143	244.1663742	46	17.1640734	14.7723729	253.5540924	46	18.1168195	14.5354257	263.3356852
47	17.2766733	15.0738958	260.4267726	47	18.2563821	14.8271425	270.7181658	47	19.2944128	14.5872542	281.4525047
48	18.3564664	15.1283725	277.7034459	48	19.4222486	14.8786299	288.9764489	48	20.5485497	14.6359194	300.7469175
49	19.5037445	15.1796447	296.0599113	49	20.6604170	14.9270316	308.3986976	49	21.8842054	14.6816145	321.2954672
50	20.7227285	15.2279009	315.5636558	50	21.9775186	14.9725327	329.0591145	50	23.3066787	14.7245207	343.1796726
51	22.0178990	15.2733185	336.2863843	51	23.3785854	15.0153068	351.0366331	51	24.8216129	14.7648081	366.4863513
52	23.3940177	15.3160645	358.3042833	52	24.8689702	15.0555176	374.4152185	52	26.4350177	14.8026367	391.3079641
53	24.8561438	15.3562960	381.6983010	53	26.4543670	15.0933185	399.2841887	53	28.1532938	14.8381566	417.7429818
54	26.4098528	15.3941609	406.5544449	54	28.1408329	15.1288541	425.7385557	54	29.9832579	14.8715085	445.8962757
55	28.0602561	15.4297985	432.9640977	55	29.9349111	15.1622600	453.8793987	55	31.9321697	14.9028243	475.8795336
56	29.8140221	15.4633398	461.0243538	56	31.8431553	15.1936639	483.8141997	56	34.0077607	14.9322299	507.8117033
57	31.6773985	15.4949080	490.8383760	57	33.8731564	15.2231853	515.6573550	57	36.2182652	14.9598403	541.8194641
58	33.6572359	15.5246193	522.5157745	58	36.0325701	15.2509385	549.5305114	58	38.5724524	14.9857656	578.0377293
59	35.7608132	15.5525829	556.1730104	59	38.3296465	15.2770280	585.5630815	59	41.0796618	15.0101085	616.6101817
60	37.9958640	15.5789015	591.9338236	60	40.7731614	15.3015539	623.8927280	60	43.7400399	15.0329657	657.6898435
61	40.3706055	15.6036720	629.9296876	61	43.3724505	15.3246100	664.6658894	61	46.5755795	15.0544279	701.4386834
62	42.8937684	15.6269854	670.3002231	62	46.1374442	15.3462844	708.0383399	62	49.6221621	15.0745602	748.0332628
63	45.5746289	15.6489275	713.1940615	63	49.0787063	15.3666598	754.1757841	63	52.8476027	15.0935025	797.6554250
64	48.4230432	15.6695788	758.7686903	64	52.2074738	15.3858142	803.2544904	64	56.2826368	15.1112700	850.5030276
65	51.4494804	15.6890153	807.1917335	65	55.5357003	15.4038206	855.4619642	65	59.9410721	15.1279530	906.7857245
66	54.6650761	15.7073085	858.6412169	66	59.0761012	15.4207479	910.9975465	66	63.8372418	15.1436179	966.7267966
67	58.0816404	15.7245257	913.3062930	67	62.8422026	15.4356669	970.0737056	67	67.9866625	15.1583266	1030.5640384
68	61.7117461	15.7407301	971.3879364	68	66.6483930	15.4516200	1032.9159682	68	72.4057956	15.1721377	1098.5507010
69	65.5687302	15.7559812	1033.0996824	69	71.1099781	15.4656827	1099.7643613	69	77.1121723	15.1851058	1170.9564986
70	69.6667758	15.7703353	1098.6684126	70	75.6432392	15.4789027	1170.8743393	70	82.1244635	15.1972625	1248.0686302
71	74.0209493	15.7838450	1168.3351885	71	80.4654957	15.4913304	1246.5175785	71	87.4625537	15.2087159	1330.1931325
72	78.6472587	15.7965600	1242.3561378	72	85.5951710	15.5030133	1326.9830742	72	93.1476197	15.2194516	1417.6556862
73	83.5627123	15.8085270	1321.0033965	73	91.0518632	15.5139960	1412.5782453	73	99.2022150	15.2295320	1510.8033058
74	88.7853819	15.8197901	1404.5661088	74	96.8564195	15.5243206	1503.6301085	74	105.6503509	15.2389972	1610.0055208
75	94.3344602	15.8303907	1493.3514907	75	103.0310162	15.5340264	1600.4865280	75	112.5176323	15.2478847	1715.6558797
76	100.2303725	15.8403677	1587.6859590	76	109.5992435	15.5431506	1703.5175442	76	119.8312784	15.2562297	1828.1735120
77	106.4947708	15.8497579	1687.9163315	77	116.5861953	15.5517279	1813.1167808	77	127.6203115	15.2640655	1948.0047903
78	113.1506940	15.8585956	1794.4111023	78	124.0185663	15.5597912	1929.7029831	78	135.9156317	15.2714230	2075.6251018
79	120.2223124	15.8669135	1907.5617963	79	131.9247488	15.5673713	2053.7215483	79	144.7501478	15.2783314	2211.5407335
80	127.7265256	15.8747422	2027.7844086	80	140.3349518	15.5744921	2185.6462971	80	154.1589074	15.2848183	2356.2908313
81	135.7200585	15.8821103	2155.5209343	81	149.2813047	15.5811959	2325.9812487	81	164.1792364	15.2909092	2510.4497887
82	144.2025622	15.8890450	2291.2409928	82	158.7979879	15.5874932	2475.2625534	82	174.8508868	15.2966283	2674.6290251
83	153.2152223	15.8955717	2435.4435549	83	168.9213596	15.5934131	2634.0605413	83	186.2161944	15.3019984	2849.4799119
84	162.7911737	15.9017146	2588.6587772	84	179.6900963	15.5989782	2802.9819010	84	198.3202471	15.3070408	3035.6961063
85	172.9656607	15.9074961	2751.4499509	85	191.1453400	15.6042099	2982.6719973	85	211.2110631	15.3117754	3234.0163534
86	183.7759735	15.9129375	2924.4155730	86	203.3308554	15.6091279	3173.8173373	86	224.9397822	15.3162210	3445.2274165
87	195.2619718	15.9180588	3108.1915465	87	216.2931975	15.6137513	3377.1481927	87	239.5608681	15.3203953	3670.1671987
88	207.4658451	15.9228789	3303.4535183	88	230.0816888	15.6180976	3593.4413901	88	255.1323245	15.3243148	3909.7280068
89	220.4324604	15.9274154	3510.9193633	89	244.7493092	15.6221834	3823.5232789	89	271.7159256	15.3279952	4164.8603914
90	234.2094892	15.9316851	3731.3518237	90	260.3523968	15.6260243	4068.2728881	90	289.3774608	15.3314508	4436.5763170
91	248.8475823	15.9357036	3965.5613129	91	276.9498621	15.6296351	4328.6252850	91	308.1869958	15.3346956	4725.9537779
92	264.4005562	15.9394857	4214.4088951	92	294.6054159	15.6330295	4605.5751471	92	328.2191505	15.3377424	5034.1407737
93	280.9255909	15.9430454	4478.8094513	93	313.3865111	15.6362204	4900.1805629	93	349.5533953	15.3406032	5362.3599242
94	298.4834404	15.9463957	4759.7350422	94	333.3649012	15.6392201	5213.5670741	94	372.2743661	15.3432894	5711.9133195
95	317.1386554	15.9495489	5058.2184826	95	354.6169137	15.6420401	5546.9319753	95	396.4721999	15.3458116	6084.1876856
96	336.9598214	15.9525166	5375.3571380	96	377.2237420	15.6446910	5901.5488890	96	422.2428929	15.3481799	6480.6598855
97	358.0198102	15.9553097	5712.3169594	97	401.2717555	15.6471631	6278.7726310	97	449.6886809	15.3504037	6902.9027784
98	380.3960484	15.9579386	6070.3367696	98	426.8528300	15.6495258	6680.0443865	98	478.9184452	15.3524917	7352.5914593
99	404.1708015	15.9604128	6450.7328181	99	454.0646979	15.6517282	7106.8972165	99	510.0481442	15.3544523	7831.5099045
100	429.4314766	15.9627414	6854.9036195	100	483.0013224	15.6537985	7560.9619144	100	543.2012736	15.3562932	8341.5580487

Table 1

M	C(13.25,M,2)	A(13.25,M,2)	S(13.25,M,2)
1/6	1.0107487	.1605186	.1622439
1/2	1.0325938	.4764528	.4919822
1	1.0662500	.9378664	1.0000000
2	1.1368891	1.8174597	2.0662500
3	1.2122080	2.6424006	3.2031391
4	1.2925167	3.4160850	4.4153470
5	1.3781460	4.1416975	5.7078638
6	1.4694481	4.8222251	7.0860097
7	1.5667991	5.4604690	8.5554579
8	1.6705995	6.0590565	10.1222570
9	1.7812767	6.6204516	11.7928565
10	1.8992863	7.1469652	13.5741332
11	2.0251140	7.6407645	15.4734196
12	2.1592779	8.1038823	17.4985336
13	2.3023300	8.5382249	19.6578115
14	2.4548594	8.9455802	21.9601415
15	2.6174938	9.3276251	24.4150009
16	2.7909028	9.6859321	27.0324947
17	2.9758001	10.0219761	29.8233974
18	3.1729468	10.3371406	32.7991975
19	3.3831546	10.6327227	35.9721444
20	3.6072886	10.9099392	39.3552989
21	3.8462714	11.1699313	42.9625875
22	4.1010869	11.4137691	46.8088589
23	4.3727839	11.6424563	50.9099458
24	4.6624808	11.8569344	55.2827297
25	4.9713702	12.0580862	59.9452106
26	5.3007235	12.2467397	64.9165808
27	5.6518964	12.4236715	70.2173042
28	6.0263345	12.5896098	75.8692006
29	6.4255792	12.7452378	81.8955352
30	6.8512738	12.8911961	88.3211144
31	7.3051707	13.0280854	95.1723882
32	7.7891383	13.1564693	102.4775590
33	8.3051687	13.2768763	110.2666973
34	8.8553861	13.3898019	118.5718659
35	9.4420555	13.4957110	127.4272521
36	10.0675916	13.5950397	136.8693075
37	10.7345696	13.6881965	146.9368992
38	11.4457348	13.7755654	157.6714687
39	12.2040147	13.8575057	169.1172036
40	13.0125307	13.9343547	181.3212183
41	13.8746109	14.0064288	194.3337490
42	14.7938039	14.0740246	208.2083599
43	15.7738934	14.1374205	223.0021638
44	16.8189138	14.1968774	238.7760571
45	17.9331668	14.2526400	255.5949709
46	19.1212391	14.3049379	273.5281377
47	20.3880212	14.3539863	292.6493769
48	21.7387276	14.3999871	313.0373981
49	23.1789183	14.4431298	334.7761253
50	24.7145217	14.4835918	357.9550441
51	26.3518588	14.5215398	382.6695658
52	28.0976694	14.5571299	409.0214245
53	29.9591400	14.5905087	437.1190939
54	31.9439330	14.6218136	467.0782339
55	34.0602186	14.6511687	499.0221670
56	36.3167081	14.6787089	533.0823855
57	38.7226900	14.7045335	569.3990936
58	41.2880682	14.7287538	608.1217836
59	44.0234027	14.7514688	649.4098518
60	46.9399531	14.7727726	693.4332545
61	50.0497250	14.7927527	740.3732076
62	53.3655193	14.8114914	790.4229327
63	56.9009850	14.8290658	843.7884520
64	60.6706752	14.8455483	900.6894370
65	64.6901075	14.8610065	961.3601123
66	68.9758271	14.8755044	1026.0502197
67	73.5454757	14.8891014	1095.0260468
68	78.4178634	14.9018536	1168.5715225
69	83.6130469	14.9138135	1246.9893859
70	89.1524112	14.9250302	1330.6024328
71	95.0587585	14.9355500	1419.7548441
72	101.3564012	14.9454162	1514.8136025
73	108.0712628	14.9546694	1616.1700038
74	115.2309840	14.9633476	1724.2412666
75	122.8650367	14.9714866	1839.4722506
76	131.0048454	14.9791199	1962.3372873
77	139.6839164	14.9862789	2093.3421327
78	148.9379755	14.9929931	2233.0260401
79	158.8051168	14.9992902	2381.9640250
80	169.3259558	15.0051959	2540.7691417
81	180.5433003	15.0107347	2710.0950975
82	192.5048271	15.0159299	2890.6388978
83	205.2582719	15.0208013	3083.1437250
84	218.8566325	15.0253705	3288.4019969
85	233.3553844	15.0296558	3507.2586294
86	248.8157117	15.0336749	3740.6145137
87	265.2997526	15.0374442	3989.4302254
88	282.8759613	15.0409793	4254.7299781
89	301.6163871	15.0442948	4537.6058393
90	321.5984727	15.0474043	4839.2222264
91	342.9043716	15.0503205	5160.8206992
92	365.6217862	15.0530556	5503.7250707
93	389.8442296	15.0556207	5869.3468570
94	415.6714098	15.0580265	6259.1910865
95	443.2096407	15.0602827	6674.8624963
96	472.5722794	15.0623988	7118.0721370
97	503.8801930	15.0643834	7590.6444165
98	537.2622558	15.0662447	8094.5246094
99	572.8558803	15.0679903	8631.7868652
100	610.8075823	15.0696275	9204.6427455

M	C(13.50,M,2)	A(13.50,M,2)	S(13.50,M,2)
1/6	1.0109461	.1604079	.1621637
1/2	1.0331989	.4760320	.4918358
1	1.0675000	.9367681	1.0000000
2	1.1395563	1.8143027	2.0675000
3	1.2164763	2.6363491	3.2070563
4	1.2985884	3.4064161	4.4235325
5	1.3862432	4.1277902	5.7221210
6	1.4798146	4.8035505	7.1083642
7	1.5797021	5.4365813	8.5881787
8	1.6863320	6.0295844	10.1678808
9	1.8001594	6.5850907	11.8542128
10	1.9216701	7.1054744	13.6543721
11	2.0513829	7.5929475	15.5760422
12	2.1898512	8.0495995	17.6274251
13	2.3376662	8.4773766	19.8172763
14	2.4954586	8.8781045	22.1549424
15	2.6639021	9.2534937	24.6504011
16	2.8437155	9.6051463	27.3143031
17	3.0356663	9.9345633	30.1580186
18	3.2405737	10.2431506	33.1936849
19	3.4593125	10.5322254	36.4342586
20	3.6928160	10.8030215	39.8935710
21	3.9420811	11.0566946	43.5863871
22	4.2081716	11.2943275	47.5284682
23	4.4922232	11.5169344	51.7366398
24	4.7954483	11.7254655	56.2288620
25	5.1191410	11.9208108	61.0243113
26	5.4646830	12.1038040	66.1434523
27	5.8335491	12.2752262	71.6081353
28	6.2273137	12.4358091	77.4416844
29	6.6476574	12.5862380	83.6689982
30	7.0963942	12.7271551	90.3166555
31	7.5753795	12.8591617	97.4130298
32	8.0867176	12.9828212	104.9884093
33	8.6325711	13.0986616	113.0751269
34	9.2152696	13.2071771	121.7076980
35	9.8373003	13.3088310	130.9229676
36	10.5013181	13.4040572	140.7602680
37	11.2101571	13.4932620	151.2615860
38	11.9668427	13.5769262	162.4717431
39	12.7746045	13.6551065	174.4385858
40	13.6368904	13.7284370	187.2131903
41	14.5573805	13.7971307	200.8500807
42	15.5400036	13.8614807	215.4074611
43	16.5889539	13.9217618	230.9474648
44	17.7087083	13.9782312	247.5364187
45	18.9040461	14.0311299	265.2451269
46	20.1800692	14.0806838	284.1491730
47	21.5422239	14.1271042	304.3292422
48	22.9963240	14.1705895	325.8714661
49	24.5485758	14.2113260	348.8677901
50	26.2056047	14.2494848	373.4163659
51	27.9744830	14.2852317	399.6219706
52	29.8627606	14.3187182	427.5964536
53	31.8784970	14.3500887	457.4592143
54	34.0302955	14.3794729	489.3377113
55	36.3273405	14.4070003	523.3680068
56	38.7794360	14.4327872	559.6953473
57	41.3970479	14.4569435	598.4747833
58	44.1913486	14.4795724	639.8718312
59	47.1742647	14.5007704	684.0631798
60	50.3585275	14.5206280	731.2374445
61	53.7577282	14.5392300	781.5959720
62	57.3863748	14.5566557	835.3537002
63	61.2599551	14.5729796	892.7400750
64	65.3950021	14.5882713	954.0000301
65	69.8091647	14.6025960	1019.3950322
66	74.5212833	14.6160150	1089.2041969
67	79.5514700	14.6285655	1163.7254802
68	84.9211942	14.6403611	1243.2769502
69	90.6533748	14.6513922	1328.1981444
70	96.7724776	14.6617257	1418.6515192
71	103.3046199	14.6714058	1515.6239968
72	110.2776817	14.6804738	1618.9286167
73	117.7244622	14.6889684	1729.2062984
74	125.6676214	14.6969259	1846.9277236
75	134.1501859	14.7043803	1972.5953451
76	143.2053234	14.7113632	2106.7455310
77	152.8716828	14.7179047	2249.9508544
78	163.1905214	14.7240325	2402.8225372
79	174.2058816	14.7297728	2566.0130586
80	185.9647784	14.7351502	2740.2189401
81	198.5174012	14.7401875	2926.1837187
82	211.9172027	14.7449063	3124.7011199
83	226.2217452	14.7493268	3336.6184456
84	241.4917131	14.7534677	3562.8401909
85	257.7924037	14.7573468	3804.3319040
86	275.1933910	14.7609806	4062.1243077
87	293.7689449	14.7643840	4337.3176996
88	313.5983487	14.7675734	4631.0866435
89	334.7662372	14.7705606	4944.6849922
90	357.3629582	14.7733589	5279.4512294
91	381.4849579	14.7759802	5636.8141877
92	407.2351926	14.7784358	6018.2991456
93	434.7235682	14.7807361	6425.5343382
94	464.0674090	14.7828910	6860.2579064
95	495.3919592	14.7849096	7324.3253154
96	528.8309164	14.7868005	7819.7172746
97	564.5270033	14.7885719	8348.5481910
98	602.6325761	14.7902313	8913.0751943
99	643.3102750	14.7917858	9515.7077704
100	686.7337186	14.7932419	10159.0180453

M	C(13.75,M,2)	A(13.75,M,2)	S(13.75,M,2)
1/6	1.0111433	.1602974	.1620837
1/2	1.0338037	.4756121	.4916895
1	1.0687500	.9356725	1.0000000
2	1.1422266	1.8111556	2.0687500
3	1.2207546	2.6303210	3.2109766
4	1.3046915	3.3967916	4.4317312
5	1.3943784	4.1139570	5.7364127
6	1.4902419	4.7849890	7.1307911
7	1.5926960	5.4128552	8.6210330
8	1.7021939	6.0003324	10.2137290
9	1.8192197	6.5500186	11.9159229
10	1.9442911	7.0643449	13.7351426
11	2.0779611	7.5455859	15.6794336
12	2.2208209	7.9958698	17.7573947
13	2.3735023	8.4171881	19.9782156
14	2.5366806	8.8114041	22.3517179
15	2.7110774	9.1802611	24.8883985
16	2.8974640	9.5253905	27.5994759
17	3.0966646	9.8483186	30.4969399
18	3.3095603	10.1504736	33.5936045
19	3.5370926	10.4331917	36.9031648
20	3.7802677	10.6977232	40.4402574
21	4.0401611	10.9452381	44.2205251
22	4.3179222	11.1768309	48.2606862
23	4.6147793	11.3935260	52.5786083
24	4.9320454	11.5962817	57.1933877
25	5.2711235	11.7859945	62.1254331
26	5.6335133	11.9635037	67.3965506
27	6.0209173	12.1295941	73.0300699
28	6.4347485	12.2850003	79.0508872
29	6.8771375	12.4304096	85.4856357
30	7.3499407	12.5664652	92.3627731
31	7.8552491	12.6937686	99.7127138
32	8.3952975	12.8128829	107.5679629
33	8.9724742	12.9243348	115.9632603
34	9.5893318	13.0286114	124.9357345
35	10.2485983	13.1261917	134.5250662
36	10.9531894	13.2174993	144.7736645
37	11.7062212	13.3029140	155.7268540
38	12.5110239	13.3828435	167.4330752
39	13.3711568	13.4576313	179.9440991
40	14.2904239	13.5276083	193.3152560
41	15.2728905	13.5930838	207.6056798
42	16.3229017	13.6543474	222.8785703
43	17.4451012	13.7116701	239.2014720
44	18.6444519	13.7653053	256.6465733
45	19.9262580	13.8154904	275.2910252
46	21.2961882	13.8624471	295.2172832
47	22.7603012	13.9063833	316.5134714
48	24.3250719	13.9474931	339.2737076
49	25.9974206	13.9859585	363.5988445
50	27.7847432	14.0219494	389.5962650
51	29.6949443	14.0556252	417.3810083
52	31.7364718	14.0871347	447.0759526
53	33.9183542	14.1166173	478.8124244
54	36.2502411	14.1442033	512.7307786
55	38.7424451	14.1700148	548.9810196
56	41.4059882	14.1941659	587.7234648
57	44.2526949	14.2167634	629.1294530
58	47.2950196	14.2379073	673.3821029
59	50.5465522	14.2576910	720.6771225
60	54.0216277	14.2762021	771.2236748
61	57.7356146	14.2935224	825.2453024
62	61.7049381	14.3097286	882.9809170
63	65.9471526	14.3248923	944.6858551
64	70.4810193	14.3390805	1010.6330077
65	75.3265894	14.3523560	1081.1140270
66	80.5052924	14.3647775	1156.4406164
67	86.0400313	14.3764000	1236.9459089
68	91.9552835	14.3872749	1322.9859402
69	98.2772092	14.3974502	1414.9412234
70	105.0337673	14.4069709	1513.2184328
71	112.2548388	14.4158792	1618.2522001
72	119.9723590	14.4242145	1730.5070390
73	128.2204587	14.4320136	1850.4793993
74	137.0356152	14.4393109	1978.6998567
75	146.4568018	14.4461389	2115.7354792
76	156.5257198	14.4525276	2262.1922858
77	167.2868630	14.4585054	2418.7180015
78	178.7878348	14.4640986	2586.0048685
79	191.0794985	14.4693320	2764.7927034
80	204.2162140	14.4742288	2955.8722019
81	218.2560787	14.4788106	3160.0884159
82	233.2611842	14.4830976	3378.3444946
83	249.2978906	14.4871089	3611.6056788
84	266.4371206	14.4908621	3860.9035694
85	284.7546776	14.4943739	4127.3406900
86	304.3315564	14.4976598	4412.0953626
87	325.2543509	14.5007343	4716.4269190
88	347.6155876	14.5036110	5041.6812700
89	371.5141592	14.5063027	5389.2968575
90	397.0557577	14.5088213	5760.8110167
91	424.3533411	14.5111770	6157.8667744
92	453.5276333	14.5133827	6582.2201155
93	484.7076581	14.5154458	7035.7477488
94	518.0313096	14.5173762	7520.4554068
95	553.6459622	14.5191824	8038.4867164
96	591.7091221	14.5208724	8592.1326786
97	632.3891243	14.5224537	9183.8418007
98	675.8659596	14.5239333	9816.2309249
99	722.3316556	14.5253177	10492.0968015
100	771.9919570	14.5266131	11214.4284571

Table 1

M	C(5.00,M,4)	A(5.00,M,4)	S(5.00,M,4)	M	C(5.25,M,4)	A(5.25,M,4)	S(5.25,M,4)	M	C(5.50,M,4)	A(5.50,M,4)	S(5.50,M,4)
1/3	1.0041494	.3305823	.3319540	1/3	1.0043560	.3304461	.3318855	1/3	1.0045625	.3303101	.3318171
1	1.0125000	.9876543	1.0000000	1	1.0131250	.9870450	1.0000000	1	1.0137500	.9864365	1.0000000
2	1.0251563	1.9631154	2.0125000	2	1.0264223	1.9613029	2.0131250	2	1.0276891	1.9594935	2.0137500
3	1.0379707	2.9265337	3.0376563	3	1.0399941	2.9229394	3.0395473	3	1.0418198	2.9190524	3.0414391
4	1.0509453	3.8780580	4.0756270	4	1.0535427	3.8721178	4.0794413	4	1.0561448	3.8661922	4.0832588
5	1.0640822	4.8178350	5.1265723	5	1.0673704	4.8089997	5.1329840	5	1.0706668	4.8001896	5.1394037
6	1.0773832	5.7460099	6.1906544	6	1.0813797	5.7337443	6.2003544	6	1.0853885	5.7215187	6.2100705
7	1.0908505	6.6627258	7.2680376	7	1.0955728	6.6465089	7.2817341	7	1.1003126	6.6303514	7.2954589
8	1.1044861	7.5681243	8.3588881	8	1.1099522	7.5474466	8.3773068	8	1.1154419	7.5268571	8.3957715
9	1.1182922	8.4623450	9.4633742	9	1.1245203	8.4367167	9.4872590	9	1.1307792	8.4112031	9.5112133
10	1.1322708	9.3455259	10.5816664	10	1.1392796	9.3144643	10.6117792	10	1.1463274	9.2835542	10.6419925
11	1.1464242	10.2176034	11.7139372	11	1.1542326	10.1808408	11.7510588	11	1.1620894	10.1440732	11.7883199
12	1.1607545	11.0793120	12.8603614	12	1.1693820	11.0359934	12.9052915	12	1.1780681	10.9929205	12.9504093
13	1.1752639	11.9301847	14.0211159	13	1.1847301	11.8800675	14.0746734	13	1.1942666	11.8302545	14.1284775
14	1.1899547	12.7705527	15.1963799	14	1.2002797	12.7132067	15.2594035	14	1.2106877	12.6562314	15.3227440
15	1.2048292	13.6005459	16.3863346	15	1.2160333	13.5355525	16.4596332	15	1.2273347	13.4710050	16.5334318
16	1.2198895	14.4202923	17.5911638	16	1.2319938	14.3472450	17.6757165	16	1.2442105	14.2747275	17.7607664
17	1.2351382	15.2299183	18.8110534	17	1.2481637	15.1484219	18.9077103	17	1.2613184	15.0675487	19.0049770
18	1.2505774	16.0295489	20.0461915	18	1.2645458	15.9392197	20.1558740	18	1.2786616	15.8496165	20.2662954
19	1.2662096	16.8193076	21.2967689	19	1.2811430	16.7197726	21.4204199	19	1.2962432	16.6210767	21.5449570
20	1.2820372	17.5993161	22.5629785	20	1.2979580	17.4902136	22.7015629	20	1.3140665	17.3820732	22.8412001
21	1.2980627	18.3696949	23.8450158	21	1.3149937	18.2506735	23.9995209	21	1.3321349	18.1327479	24.1552666
22	1.3142835	19.1305629	25.1430785	22	1.3322530	19.0012817	25.3145146	22	1.3504518	18.8732409	25.4874016
23	1.3307171	19.8820374	26.4573670	23	1.3497388	19.7421658	26.6467676	23	1.3690205	19.6036901	26.8378533
24	1.3473511	20.6242345	27.7880840	24	1.3674541	20.4734517	27.9965064	24	1.3878445	20.3242319	28.2068738
25	1.3641929	21.3572686	29.1354351	25	1.3854020	21.1952639	29.3639606	25	1.4069274	21.0350007	29.5947183
26	1.3812454	22.0612530	30.4996780	26	1.4035854	21.9077250	30.7493626	26	1.4262726	21.7361289	31.0016457
27	1.3985109	22.7962092	31.8808734	27	1.4220074	22.6109562	32.1529480	27	1.4458839	22.4277474	32.4279183
28	1.4159923	23.5025178	33.2793843	28	1.4406713	23.3050770	33.5749554	28	1.4657648	23.1099851	33.8738022
29	1.4336922	24.2000176	34.6953766	29	1.4595801	23.9902056	35.0156267	29	1.4859190	23.7829692	35.3395670
30	1.4516134	24.8889062	36.1290688	30	1.4787371	24.6664583	36.4752068	30	1.5063504	24.4468254	36.8254860
31	1.4697585	25.5692901	37.5806822	31	1.4981455	25.3339502	37.9539439	31	1.5270628	25.1016773	38.3318365
32	1.4881305	26.2412742	39.0504447	32	1.5178087	25.9927948	39.4520894	32	1.5480599	25.7476472	39.8588992
33	1.5067321	26.9049621	40.5335712	33	1.5377299	26.6431040	40.9698981	33	1.5693457	26.3848554	41.4069591
34	1.5255663	27.5604564	42.0453034	34	1.5579126	27.2849886	42.5076280	34	1.5909242	27.0134209	42.9763048
35	1.5446359	28.2078582	43.5708696	35	1.5783602	27.9185575	44.0655406	35	1.6127994	27.6334608	44.5672290
36	1.5639438	28.8472074	45.1155055	36	1.5990762	28.5439186	45.6439008	36	1.6349754	28.2450908	46.1800284
37	1.5834931	29.4787826	46.6794493	37	1.6200641	29.1611781	47.2429770	37	1.6574563	28.8484249	47.8150038
38	1.6032868	30.1025013	48.2629425	38	1.6413274	29.7704411	48.8630411	38	1.6802463	29.4435758	49.4724601
39	1.6233279	30.7185198	49.8662292	39	1.6628698	30.3718110	50.5043685	39	1.7033497	30.0306543	51.1527064
40	1.6435195	31.3269331	51.4895571	40	1.6846950	30.9653903	52.1672384	40	1.7267708	30.6097699	52.8560561
41	1.6641647	31.9278352	53.1331766	41	1.7068036	31.5512798	53.8519334	41	1.7505139	31.1810308	54.5828269
42	1.6849668	32.5213187	54.7973413	42	1.7292085	32.1295790	55.5587400	42	1.7745834	31.7445433	56.3333407
43	1.7060289	33.1074753	56.4823080	43	1.7519043	32.7003865	57.2879484	43	1.7989840	32.3004126	58.1079242
44	1.?73542	33.6863953	58.1883369	44	1.7748981	33.2637991	59.0399528	44	1.8237200	32.8487424	59.9069081
45	1.7489461	34.2581682	59.9156911	45	1.7981936	33.8199127	60.8147503	45	1.8487961	33.3896404	61.7306281
46	1.7708080	34.8228822	61.6646393	46	1.8217949	34.3688319	62.6129444	46	1.8742171	33.9231911	63.5794243
47	1.7929431	35.3806244	63.4354452	47	1.8457060	34.9106201	64.4347393	47	1.8999876	34.4495103	65.4536414
48	1.8153549	35.9314809	65.2283883	48	1.8699308	35.4453992	66.2804453	48	1.9261124	34.9686908	67.3536269
49	1.8360468	36.4755367	67.0437431	49	1.8944737	35.9732503	68.1503761	49	1.9525964	35.4808294	69.2797413
50	1.8610224	37.0128757	68.8817899	50	1.9193387	36.4942631	70.0448498	50	1.9794446	35.9860216	71.2323378
51	1.8842852	37.5435810	70.7428123	51	1.9445300	37.0085262	71.9641885	51	2.0066620	36.4843616	73.2117824
52	1.9078387	38.0677343	72.6270075	52	1.9700519	37.5161270	73.9087185	52	2.0342536	36.9759424	75.2184444
53	1.9316867	38.5854166	74.5349362	53	1.9959089	38.0171519	75.8787704	53	2.0622246	37.4608506	77.2526980
54	1.9558328	39.0967077	76.4668259	54	2.0221052	38.5116860	77.8746793	54	2.0905802	37.9391918	79.3149226
55	1.9802807	39.6016866	78.4224557	55	2.0486453	38.9998134	79.8967844	55	2.1193257	38.4110400	81.4055028
56	2.0050342	40.1004313	80.4027364	56	2.0755333	39.4816172	81.9454297	56	2.1484664	38.8764882	83.5248285
57	2.0300971	40.5930185	82.4077706	57	2.1027751	39.9571792	84.0209635	57	2.1780078	39.3356234	85.6732949
58	2.0554733	41.0795245	84.4378677	58	2.1303747	40.4265604	86.1237386	58	2.2079554	39.7885311	87.8513027
59	2.0811668	41.5600242	86.4923411	59	2.1583352	40.8899004	88.2541127	59	2.2383148	40.2352958	90.0592581
60	2.1071814	42.0345078	88.5745078	60	2.1866634	41.3472068	90.4124479	60	2.2690916	40.6760008	92.2975729
61	2.1335211	42.5033005	90.6816992	61	2.2153633	41.7986114	92.5991113	61	2.3002916	41.1107283	94.5666645
62	2.1601901	42.9662227	92.8152103	62	2.2444400	42.2441569	94.8144747	62	2.3319206	41.5395593	96.8669562
63	2.1871925	43.4234298	94.9754004	63	2.2738983	42.6839303	97.0589146	63	2.3639846	41.9625739	99.1988768
64	2.2145324	43.8749924	97.1625929	64	2.3037432	43.1180064	99.3328129	64	2.3964893	42.3796510	101.5628614
65	2.2422141	44.3209802	99.3771253	65	2.3339798	43.5464592	101.6365561	65	2.4294411	42.7914683	103.9593507
66	2.2702417	44.7614619	101.6193394	66	2.3646133	43.9693613	103.9705359	66	2.4628459	43.1975026	106.3887918
67	2.2986198	45.1965056	103.8895812	67	2.3956488	44.3867847	106.3351492	67	2.4967100	43.5980297	108.8516377
68	2.3273525	45.6261784	106.1882009	68	2.4270917	44.7988005	108.7307980	68	2.5310398	43.9931243	111.3483477
69	2.3564444	46.0505465	108.5155534	69	2.4589473	45.2054786	111.1578897	69	2.5658416	44.3826599	113.8793875
70	2.3859000	46.4696756	110.8719979	70	2.4912210	45.6068882	113.6168370	70	2.6011219	44.7673094	116.4452297
71	2.4157321	46.8836302	113.2578978	71	2.5239183	46.0030075	116.1080580	71	2.6368873	45.1465444	119.0463510
72	2.4459203	47.2924743	115.6736216	72	2.5570447	46.3941740	118.6319763	72	2.6731445	45.5206357	121.6832383
73	2.4764709	47.6962709	118.1195418	73	2.5906059	46.7801841	121.1890210	73	2.7099003	45.8896530	124.3563828
74	2.5074505	48.0950824	120.5960361	74	2.6246076	47.1611934	123.7796269	74	2.7471614	46.2536651	127.0662831
75	2.5387936	48.4889702	123.1034866	75	2.6590556	47.5372668	126.4042345	75	2.7849349	46.6127399	129.8134445
76	2.5705285	48.8779953	125.6422802	76	2.6939557	47.9084681	129.0632901	76	2.8232277	46.9669444	132.5983794
77	2.6026501	49.2622176	128.2128087	77	2.7293139	48.2748606	131.7572458	77	2.8620471	47.3163447	135.4216071
78	2.6351934	49.6416964	130.8154688	78	2.7651361	48.6365064	134.4865596	78	2.9014002	47.6610058	138.2836542
79	2.6681333	50.0164902	133.4506621	79	2.8014285	48.9934672	137.2516957	79	2.9412945	48.0009922	141.1850544
80	2.7014849	50.3866570	136.1187954	80	2.8381973	49.3456035	140.0531242	80	2.9817373	48.3363671	144.1263489
81	2.7352535	50.7522538	138.8202804	81	2.8754486	49.6935753	142.8913215	81	3.0227362	48.6671932	147.1080862
82	2.7694442	51.1133371	141.5555339	82	2.9131889	50.0368418	145.7667701	82	3.0642988	48.9935322	150.1308224
83	2.8040622	51.4699626	144.3249780	83	2.9514245	50.3756602	148.6799589	83	3.1064329	49.3154448	153.1951213
84	2.8391130	51.8221853	147.1290403	84	2.9901519	50.7100913	151.6313834	84	3.1491464	49.6329912	156.3015542
85	2.8746019	52.1700595	149.9681533	85	3.0294078	51.0401888	154.6215453	85	3.1924471	49.9462305	159.4507005
86	2.9105344	52.5136390	152.8427552	86	3.0691688	51.3650099	157.6509531	86	3.2363433	50.2552212	162.6431477
87	2.9469161	52.8529768	155.7532896	87	3.1094505	51.6976100	160.7201219	87	3.2808430	50.5600209	165.8794910
88	2.9837526	53.1881253	158.7002058	88	3.1502632	52.0050438	163.8295735	88	3.3259546	50.8606665	169.1603340
89	3.0210495	53.5191361	161.6839593	89	3.1916104	52.3183653	166.9798366	89	3.3716865	51.1572740	172.4862886
90	3.0588126	53.8460603	164.7050078	90	3.2335002	52.6276277	170.1714470	90	3.4180472	51.4498387	175.8579750
91	3.0970478	54.1689484	167.7638204	91	3.2759399	52.9328836	173.4049472	91	3.4650453	51.7384352	179.2760222
92	3.1357609	54.4878503	170.8608682	92	3.3189366	53.2341849	176.6808872	92	3.5126897	52.0231173	182.7410765
93	3.1749579	54.8028151	173.9966230	93	3.3624977	53.5315829	179.9998238	93	3.5609892	52.3039382	186.2537572
94	3.2146448	55.1138915	177.1715869	94	3.4066305	53.8251281	183.3623215	94	3.6099528	52.5809501	189.8147464
95	3.2548279	55.4211274	180.3862318	95	3.4513425	54.1148704	186.7689520	95	3.6595896	52.8542048	193.4246991
96	3.2955133	55.7245703	183.6410597	96	3.4966414	54.4008591	190.2202945	96	3.7099090	53.1237532	197.0842887
97	3.3367072	56.0242669	186.9365729	97	3.5425348	54.6831428	193.7169358	97	3.7609202	53.3896456	200.7941977
98	3.3784160	56.3202636	190.2732801	98	3.5890306	54.9617696	197.2594706	98	3.8126329	53.6519315	204.5551179
99	3.4206462	56.6126060	193.6516961	99	3.6361366	55.2367868	200.8485012	99	3.8650566	53.9106599	208.3677508
100	3.4634043	56.9013393	197.0723423	100	3.?838609	55.5082411	204.4846378	100	3.9182011	54.1658791	212.2328074

Table 1

M	C(5.00,M,4)	A(5.00,M,4)	S(5.00,M,4)	M	C(5.25,M,4)	A(5.25,M,4)	S(5.25,M,4)	M	C(5.50,M,4)	A(5.50,M,4)	S(5.50,M,4)
101	3.5066968	57.1865080	200.5357466	101	3.7322115	55.7761788	208.1684986	101	3.9720764	54.4176366	216.1510085
102	3.5505305	57.4681560	204.0424434	102	3.7811968	56.0406453	211.9007102	102	4.0266924	54.6659794	220.1230849
103	3.5949122	57.7463269	207.5929740	103	3.8308250	56.3016857	215.6819070	103	4.0820594	54.9109537	224.1497773
104	3.6398486	58.0210636	211.1878861	104	3.8811046	56.5593443	219.5127321	104	4.1381878	55.1526054	228.2318367
105	3.6853467	58.2924085	214.8277347	105	3.9320441	56.8136649	223.3938367	105	4.1950878	55.3909795	232.3700245
106	3.7314135	58.5604035	218.5130814	106	3.9836522	57.0646909	227.3258808	106	4.2527703	55.6261203	236.5651123
107	3.7780562	58.8250898	222.2444949	107	4.0359376	57.3124648	231.3095330	107	4.3112459	55.8580718	240.8178927
108	3.8252819	59.0865085	226.0225511	108	4.0889093	57.5570288	235.3454706	108	4.3705255	56.0868772	245.1291285
109	3.8730979	59.3446997	229.8478330	109	4.1425762	57.7984244	239.4343799	109	4.4306202	56.3125793	249.4996541
110	3.9215116	59.5997034	233.7209309	110	4.1969476	58.0366928	243.5769561	110	4.4915413	56.5352200	253.9302743
111	3.9705305	59.8515590	237.6424426	111	4.2520325	58.2718745	247.7739037	111	4.5533000	56.7548409	258.4218156
112	4.0201622	60.1003051	241.6129731	112	4.3078404	58.5040094	252.0259362	112	4.6153078	56.9714830	262.9751156
113	4.0704142	60.3459804	245.6331353	113	4.3643808	58.7331369	256.3337766	113	4.6793766	57.1851857	267.5910234
114	4.1212944	60.5886226	249.7035495	114	4.4216633	58.9592962	260.6981574	114	4.7437180	57.3959918	272.2704000
115	4.1728106	60.8282692	253.8248439	115	4.4796977	59.1825255	265.1198208	115	4.8089441	57.6039377	277.0141180
116	4.2249707	61.0649573	257.9976544	116	4.5384937	59.4028629	269.5995184	116	4.8750671	57.8090631	281.8230621
117	4.2777828	61.2987232	262.2226251	117	4.5980614	59.6203459	274.1380121	117	4.9420993	58.0114062	286.6981292
118	4.3312551	61.5296032	266.5004079	118	4.6584110	59.8350114	278.7360735	118	5.0100531	58.2110049	291.6402285
119	4.3853958	61.7576328	270.8316630	119	4.7195526	60.0468959	283.3944845	119	5.0789414	58.4076963	296.6502817
120	4.4402132	61.9828472	275.2170588	120	4.7814967	60.2560354	288.1140371	120	5.1487768	58.6021172	301.7292231
121	4.4957159	62.2052812	279.6572721	121	4.8442539	60.4524655	292.8955339	121	5.2195725	58.7937038	306.8779999
122	4.5519124	62.4249690	284.1529860	122	4.9078347	60.6662214	297.7397877	122	5.2913416	58.9826918	312.0975724
123	4.6088113	62.6419447	288.7049003	123	4.9722501	60.8673376	302.6476225	123	5.3640976	59.1691164	317.3889140
124	4.6664214	62.8562417	293.3137116	124	5.0375108	61.0658483	307.6198725	124	5.4378539	59.3530125	322.7530116
125	4.7247517	63.0678930	297.9801330	125	5.1036282	61.2617874	312.6573833	125	5.5126244	59.5344143	328.1909855
126	4.7838111	63.2769314	302.7048847	126	5.1706133	61.4551880	317.7610115	126	5.5884230	59.7133557	333.7034399
127	4.8436087	63.4833890	307.4886057	127	5.2384776	61.6460832	322.9316248	127	5.6652638	59.8898700	339.2919129
128	4.9041538	63.6872978	312.3323044	128	5.3072326	61.8345053	328.1701024	128	5.7431612	60.0639901	344.9571767
129	4.9654557	63.8986892	317.2364582	129	5.3766900	62.0204864	333.4773350	129	5.8221297	60.2357485	350.7003379
130	5.0275239	64.0875943	322.2019140	130	5.4474617	62.2040581	338.8542250	130	5.9021839	60.4051774	356.5224676
131	5.0903680	64.2840437	327.2294379	131	5.5189596	62.3852517	344.3016867	131	5.9833390	60.5723081	362.4246515
132	5.1539976	64.4780679	332.3198059	132	5.5913960	62.5640979	349.8206464	132	6.0656069	60.7371720	368.4079905
133	5.2184226	64.6696967	337.4736035	133	5.6647831	62.7406272	355.4120424	133	6.1490120	60.8997998	374.4736003
134	5.2836528	64.8589597	342.6922260	134	5.7391333	62.9148695	361.0768254	134	6.2335609	61.0602221	380.6226124
135	5.3496985	65.0458861	347.9758789	135	5.8144595	63.0868546	366.8159588	135	6.3192724	61.2184678	386.8561733
136	5.4165697	65.2305048	353.3255774	136	5.8907742	63.2566115	372.6304182	136	6.4061624	61.3745675	393.1754457
137	5.4842768	65.4128442	358.7421471	137	5.9680907	63.4241693	378.5211925	137	6.4942471	61.5285499	399.5816081
138	5.5528303	65.5929326	364.2264239	138	6.0464219	63.5895564	384.4892831	138	6.5835430	61.6804438	406.0758552
139	5.6222407	65.7707976	369.7792542	139	6.1257811	63.7528009	390.5357050	139	6.6740667	61.8302775	412.6593982
140	5.6925187	65.9464668	375.4014949	140	6.2061820	63.9139305	396.6614861	140	6.7658352	61.9780789	419.3334649
141	5.7636552	66.1199672	381.0940136	141	6.2876382	64.0729728	402.8676682	141	6.8588654	62.1238756	426.0993001
142	5.8357211	66.2913256	386.8576888	142	6.3701634	64.2299546	409.1553063	142	6.9531748	62.2676948	432.9581655
143	5.9086676	66.4605685	392.6934099	143	6.4537718	64.3849027	415.5254697	143	7.0487809	62.4095633	439.9113403
144	5.9825260	66.6277220	398.6020776	144	6.5384776	64.5384435	421.9792415	144	7.1457017	62.5495076	446.9601212
145	6.0573076	66.7928118	404.5846035	145	6.6242951	64.6888030	428.5177191	145	7.2439551	62.6875537	454.1058229
146	6.1330239	66.9558635	410.6419111	146	6.7112389	64.8378068	435.1420141	146	7.3435595	62.8237275	461.3497780
147	6.2096867	67.1169022	416.7749350	147	6.7993240	64.9848802	441.8532531	147	7.4445334	62.9580542	468.6933374
148	6.2873078	67.2759528	422.9846217	148	6.8865651	65.1300484	448.6525170	148	7.5468957	63.0905590	476.1378708
149	6.3658991	67.4330398	429.2719295	149	6.9789775	65.2733358	455.5411421	149	7.6506656	63.2212666	483.6847666
150	6.4454729	67.5881875	435.6378286	150	7.0705766	65.4147670	462.5201196	150	7.7558622	63.3502013	491.3354321
151	6.5260413	67.7414197	442.0833015	151	7.1633779	65.5543659	469.5906962	151	7.8625053	63.4773873	499.0912943
152	6.6076168	67.8927602	448.6093427	152	7.2573972	65.6921564	476.7540741	152	7.9706148	63.6028481	506.9537996
153	6.6902120	68.0422323	455.2169595	153	7.3526506	65.8281618	484.0114713	153	8.0802107	63.7266072	514.9244144
154	6.7738397	68.1898591	461.9071715	154	7.4491541	65.9624052	491.3641219	154	8.1913136	63.8486878	523.0046251
155	6.8585127	68.3356633	468.6810112	155	7.5469243	66.0949095	498.8132760	155	8.3039442	63.9691125	531.1959387
156	6.9442441	68.4796674	475.5395238	156	7.6459776	66.2256972	506.3602003	156	8.4181234	64.0879038	539.4998829
157	7.0310471	68.6218938	482.4837679	157	7.7463311	66.3547906	514.0061779	157	8.5333726	64.2050839	547.9180063
158	7.1189352	68.7623642	489.5148150	158	7.8480017	66.4822116	521.7525090	158	8.6512133	64.3206746	556.4518789
159	7.2079219	68.9011005	496.6337502	159	7.9510067	66.6079918	529.6005107	159	8.7701675	64.4346975	565.1030922
160	7.2980209	69.0381239	503.8416721	160	8.0553637	66.7321227	537.5515174	160	8.8907573	64.5471739	573.8732598
161	7.3892462	69.1734557	511.1396930	161	8.1610903	66.8546553	545.6068811	161	9.0130052	64.6581247	582.7640171
162	7.4815118	69.3071157	518.5289792	162	8.2682046	66.9756006	553.7679715	162	9.1369341	64.7675706	591.7770223
163	7.5751319	69.4391256	526.0105510	163	8.3767248	67.0949790	562.0361761	163	9.2625669	64.8755320	600.9139564
164	7.6698210	69.5695088	533.5856829	164	8.4866693	67.2128108	570.4129009	164	9.3899272	64.9820291	610.1765233
165	7.7655938	69.6982803	541.2555039	165	8.5980569	67.3291162	578.8995703	165	9.5190387	65.0870817	619.5664505
166	7.8627650	69.8254620	549.0211977	166	8.7109064	67.4439148	587.4976271	166	9.6499255	65.1907095	629.0854892
167	7.9610495	69.9510736	556.8839227	167	8.8252370	67.5572262	596.2085335	167	9.7826120	65.2929317	638.7354147
168	8.0605627	70.0751344	564.8450122	168	8.9410683	67.6690697	605.0337705	168	9.9171229	65.3937674	648.5180267
169	8.1613197	70.1976635	572.9055749	169	9.0584198	67.7794642	613.9748388	169	10.0534833	65.4932354	658.4351496
170	8.2633362	70.3186801	581.0668946	170	9.1773115	67.8884286	623.0332585	170	10.1917187	65.5913542	668.4886329
171	8.3665279	70.4382026	589.3302308	171	9.2977637	67.9959813	632.2105701	171	10.3318549	65.6881423	678.6803516
172	8.4712107	70.5562494	597.6968587	172	9.4197969	68.1021407	641.5083338	172	10.4739179	65.7836175	689.0122065
173	8.5771009	70.6728390	606.1680695	173	9.5434317	68.2069248	650.9281307	173	10.6179342	65.8777978	699.4861243
174	8.6843146	70.7879891	614.7451703	174	9.6685393	68.3103515	660.4715625	174	10.7639308	65.9707007	710.1040586
175	8.7928686	70.9017176	623.4294850	175	9.7955908	68.4124382	670.1402517	175	10.9119349	66.0623435	720.8679894
176	8.9027794	71.0140421	632.2223536	176	9.9241580	68.5132024	679.9358426	176	11.0619740	66.1527432	731.7799243
177	9.0140642	71.1249798	641.1251330	177	10.0544125	68.6126612	689.8600005	177	11.2140761	66.2419169	742.8418982
178	9.1267400	71.2345480	650.1391972	178	10.1863767	68.7108316	699.9144130	178	11.3682597	66.3298810	754.0559744
179	9.2408242	71.3427634	659.2659372	179	10.3200729	68.8077301	710.1007897	179	11.5245384	66.4166521	765.4242440
180	9.3563345	71.4496429	668.5067614	180	10.4555238	68.9033733	720.4208626	180	11.6830464	66.5022462	776.9488274
181	9.4732887	71.5552029	677.8630959	181	10.5927526	68.9977775	730.8763064	181	11.8436883	66.5866793	788.6318738
182	9.5917048	71.6594596	687.3363846	182	10.7317825	69.0909587	741.4691390	182	12.0065390	66.6699673	800.4755621
183	9.7116011	71.7624293	696.9280895	183	10.8728371	69.1829327	752.2009215	183	12.1716289	66.7521255	812.4821012
184	9.8329962	71.8641277	706.6396906	184	11.0153405	69.2737152	763.0735586	184	12.3389888	66.8331695	824.6537300
185	9.9559086	71.9645705	716.4726368	185	11.1599168	69.3633216	774.0888991	185	12.5086499	66.9131141	836.9927188
186	10.0803575	72.0637734	726.4285954	186	11.3063907	69.4517671	785.2489159	186	12.6803438	66.9919745	849.5013687
187	10.2063619	72.1617515	736.5085528	187	11.4547871	69.5390669	796.5552066	187	12.8550027	67.0697562	862.1820125
188	10.3339415	72.2585220	746.7153147	188	11.6051312	69.6252357	808.0099937	188	13.0317590	67.1465008	875.0370152
189	10.4631157	72.3540938	757.0492562	189	11.7574485	69.7102881	819.6151249	189	13.2109457	67.2221956	888.0687742
190	10.5939047	72.4484877	767.5123719	190	11.9117650	69.7942387	831.3725735	190	13.3925962	67.2968638	901.2797199
191	10.7263285	72.5417162	778.1062766	191	12.0681070	69.8771018	843.2843385	191	13.5767444	67.3705739	914.6723161
192	10.8604076	72.6337938	788.8326051	192	12.2265009	69.9588913	855.3524455	192	13.7634246	67.4431755	928.2490604
193	10.9961627	72.7247346	799.6930126	193	12.3869737	70.0396213	867.5789463	193	13.9526717	67.5148463	942.0124850
194	11.1336147	72.8145527	810.6891753	194	12.5495512	70.1193054	879.9659200	194	14.1445209	67.5855451	955.9651567
195	11.2727849	72.9032619	821.8227900	195	12.7142656	70.1979572	892.5154728	195	14.3390081	67.6552849	970.1096777
196	11.4136947	72.9908760	833.0955749	196	12.8811403	70.2755901	905.2297384	196	14.5361695	67.7240788	984.4486857
197	11.5563659	73.0774084	844.5092696	197	13.0502053	70.3522172	918.1108787	197	14.7360418	67.7919396	998.9848552
198	11.7008205	73.1628725	856.0656355	198	13.2214893	70.4278517	931.1610840	198	14.9386624	67.8588800	1013.7208970
199	11.8470807	73.2472815	867.7664560	199	13.3950213	70.5025063	944.3825733	199	15.1440690	67.9249125	1028.6595593
200	11.9951692	73.3306483	879.6135367	200	13.5708310	70.5761937	957.7775946	200	15.3522999	67.9900493	1043.8036283

Table 1

M	C(5.75,M,4)	A(5.75,M,4)	S(5.75,M,4)	M	C(6.00,M,4)	A(6.00,M,4)	S(6.00,M,4)	M	C(6.25,M,4)	A(6.25,M,4)	S(6.25,M,4)
1/3	1.0047689	.3301742	.3317487	1/3	1.0049752	.3300384	.3316804	1/3	1.0051814	.3299028	.3316121
1	1.0143750	.9858287	1.0000000	1	1.0150000	.9852217	1.0000000	1	1.0156250	.9846154	1.0000000
2	1.0289566	1.9576870	2.0143750	2	1.0302250	1.9558834	2.0150000	2	1.0314941	1.9540828	2.0156250
3	1.0437479	2.9157727	3.0433316	3	1.0456784	2.9122004	3.0452250	3	1.0476112	2.9086354	3.0471191
4	1.0587518	3.8602812	4.0870795	4	1.0613636	3.8543846	4.0909034	4	1.0639802	3.8485026	4.0947304
5	1.0739713	4.7914047	5.1458313	5	1.0772340	4.7826450	5.1522669	5	1.0806049	4.7739102	5.1587105
6	1.0894097	5.7093331	6.2198026	6	1.0934433	5.6971872	6.2295509	6	1.0974893	5.6850008	6.2393154
7	1.1050699	6.6142532	7.3092123	7	1.1098449	6.5982140	7.3229942	7	1.1146376	6.5822334	7.3368047
8	1.1209553	7.5063494	8.4142822	8	1.1264926	7.4859251	8.4328391	8	1.1320538	7.4655837	8.4514423
9	1.1370690	8.3858035	9.5352375	9	1.1433900	8.3605173	9.5593317	9	1.1497421	8.3353439	9.5834961
10	1.1534144	9.2527946	10.6723066	10	1.1605408	9.2221846	10.7027217	10	1.1677068	9.1917233	10.7332382
11	1.1699947	10.1074993	11.8257210	11	1.1779489	10.0711178	11.8632625	11	1.1859523	10.0349275	11.9009450
12	1.1868134	10.9500917	12.9957157	12	1.1956182	10.9075052	13.0412114	12	1.2044828	10.8651594	13.0868973
13	1.2033739	11.7807435	14.1825291	13	1.2135524	11.7315322	14.2368296	13	1.2233028	11.6826185	14.2913801
14	1.2211795	12.5996239	15.3864030	14	1.2317557	12.5433815	15.4503820	14	1.2424169	12.4875013	15.5146829
15	1.2387340	13.4068997	16.6075825	15	1.2502321	13.3432330	16.6821378	15	1.2618297	13.2800013	16.7570998
16	1.2565409	14.2027354	17.8463165	16	1.2689955	14.1312640	17.9323698	16	1.2815458	14.0603089	18.0189295
17	1.2746036	14.9872931	19.1028573	17	1.2880203	14.9076493	19.2013554	17	1.3015699	14.8286119	19.3004753
18	1.2929260	15.7607325	20.3774609	18	1.3073406	15.6725609	20.4893757	18	1.3219070	15.5850048	20.6020452
19	1.3115118	16.5232114	21.6703869	19	1.3269507	16.4261684	21.7967164	19	1.3425618	16.3299395	21.9239521
20	1.3303648	17.2748849	22.9818987	20	1.3468550	17.1686388	23.1236671	20	1.3635393	17.0633260	23.2665139
21	1.3494888	18.0159063	24.3122635	21	1.3670578	17.9001367	24.4705221	21	1.3848446	17.7854277	24.6300532
22	1.3688877	18.7464264	25.6617523	22	1.3875637	18.6208244	25.8375799	22	1.4064828	18.4964211	26.0148978
23	1.3885655	19.4665941	27.0306400	23	1.4083772	19.3308614	27.2251436	23	1.4284591	19.1964762	27.4213805
24	1.4085261	20.1765561	28.4192054	24	1.4295028	20.0304054	28.6335208	24	1.4507787	19.8857612	28.8498396
25	1.4287736	20.8764570	29.8277315	25	1.4509454	20.7196112	30.0630236	25	1.4734472	20.5644418	30.3006183
26	1.4493123	21.5664395	31.2565052	26	1.4727095	21.3986317	31.5139690	26	1.4964698	21.2326811	31.7740655
27	1.4701461	22.2466439	32.7058174	27	1.4948002	22.0676175	32.9866785	27	1.5198521	21.8906399	33.2705353
28	1.4912795	22.9172091	34.1759635	28	1.5172222	22.7267167	34.4814787	28	1.5435998	22.5384762	34.7903874
29	1.5127166	23.5782714	35.6672430	29	1.5399805	23.3760756	35.9987009	29	1.5677186	23.1763458	36.3339872
30	1.5344619	24.2299657	37.1799596	30	1.5630802	24.0158380	37.5386814	30	1.5922142	23.8044020	37.9017058
31	1.5565198	24.8724246	38.7144243	31	1.5865264	24.6461458	39.1017616	31	1.6170925	24.4227958	39.4939199
32	1.5788948	25.5057790	40.2709414	32	1.6103243	25.2671387	40.6882802	32	1.6423596	25.0316759	41.1110124
33	1.6015914	26.1301580	41.8498362	33	1.6344792	25.8789544	42.2986123	33	1.6680214	25.6311885	42.7533720
34	1.6246143	26.7456887	43.4514275	34	1.6589964	26.4817285	43.9330915	34	1.6940843	26.2214779	44.4213934
35	1.6479681	27.3524965	45.0760418	35	1.6838813	27.0755946	45.5920879	35	1.7205543	26.8026860	46.1154777
36	1.6716576	27.9507052	46.7240099	36	1.7091395	27.6606843	47.2759662	36	1.7474380	27.3749523	47.8360320
37	1.6956877	28.5404364	48.3956676	37	1.7347766	28.2371274	48.9851088	37	1.7747417	27.9384146	49.5834700
38	1.7200632	29.1218074	50.0913553	38	1.7607983	28.8050516	50.7198954	38	1.8024721	28.4932082	51.3582118
39	1.7447891	29.6949455	51.8114185	39	1.7872103	29.3645829	52.4806837	39	1.8306357	29.0394666	53.1606838
40	1.7698705	30.2599586	53.5562077	40	1.8140184	29.9158452	54.2678939	40	1.8592394	29.5773209	54.9913195
41	1.7953124	30.8169647	55.3260782	41	1.8412287	30.4589608	56.0819124	41	1.8882900	30.1069006	56.8505589
42	1.8211200	31.3660774	57.1213905	42	1.8688471	30.9940500	57.9231410	42	1.9177945	30.6283329	58.7388468
43	1.8472985	31.9074084	58.9425105	43	1.8968798	31.5212316	59.7919882	43	1.9477601	31.1417432	60.6566434
44	1.8738535	32.4410680	60.7698091	44	1.9253330	32.0406222	61.6888380	44	1.9781938	31.6472548	62.6044034
45	1.9007902	32.9671650	62.6636628	45	1.9542130	32.5523372	63.6142010	45	2.0091031	32.1449894	64.5825972
46	1.9281140	33.4858066	64.5644528	46	1.9835262	33.0564898	65.5684140	46	2.0404953	32.6350664	66.5917003
47	1.9558306	33.9970908	66.4925668	47	2.0132791	33.5531919	67.5519402	47	2.0723781	33.1176039	68.6321956
48	1.9839457	34.5011443	68.4483974	48	2.0434782	34.0425536	69.5652193	48	2.1047590	33.5927177	70.7045737
49	2.0124649	34.9980474	70.4323431	49	2.0741305	34.5246834	71.6086976	49	2.1376458	34.0605220	72.8093326
50	2.0413941	35.4879087	72.4448081	50	2.1052424	34.9996881	73.6828281	50	2.1710465	34.5211294	74.9469785
51	2.0707392	35.9708280	74.4862022	51	2.1368211	35.4676730	75.7880705	51	2.2049691	34.9746504	77.1180250
52	2.1005060	36.4469038	76.5569414	52	2.1688730	35.9287417	77.9248916	52	2.2394218	35.4211943	79.3229942
53	2.1307008	36.9162330	78.6574474	53	2.2014065	36.3829969	80.0937649	53	2.2744128	35.8608682	81.5624159
54	2.1613296	37.3789111	80.7881482	54	2.2344276	36.8305388	82.2951714	54	2.3099505	36.2937779	83.8368287
55	2.1923987	37.8350325	82.9494778	55	2.2679440	37.2714668	84.5295990	55	2.3460043	36.7200275	86.1467791
56	2.2239145	38.2846901	85.1418766	56	2.3019631	37.7058786	86.7975430	56	2.3827004	37.1397194	88.4928226
57	2.2558832	38.7279754	87.3657910	57	2.3364926	38.1338706	89.0995061	57	2.4199300	37.5529545	90.8755229
58	2.2883116	39.1649789	89.6216743	58	2.3715400	38.5555375	91.4359967	58	2.4577415	37.9598321	93.2954530
59	2.3212060	39.5957894	91.9099859	59	2.4071131	38.9709729	93.8075367	59	2.4961437	38.3604501	95.7531944
60	2.3545734	40.0204948	94.2311919	60	2.4432198	39.3802689	96.2146518	60	2.5351459	38.7549047	98.2493381
61	2.3884204	40.4391815	96.5857653	61	2.4798681	39.7835161	98.6578716	61	2.5747576	39.1432908	100.7844840
62	2.4247539	40.8519350	98.9741757	62	2.5170661	40.1808041	101.1377396	62	2.6149882	39.5257017	103.3592416
63	2.4575810	41.2588392	101.3969396	63	2.5548221	40.5722207	103.6548057	63	2.6558473	39.9022293	105.9742297
64	2.4929097	41.6599770	103.8545206	64	2.5931444	40.9578529	106.2096278	64	2.6973450	40.2729643	108.6300771
65	2.5287443	42.0554302	106.3474293	65	2.6320416	41.3377862	108.8027723	65	2.7394910	40.6379956	111.3274220
66	2.5650905	42.4452392	108.8761736	66	2.6715222	41.7121046	111.4348138	66	2.7822955	40.9974110	114.0669130
67	2.6019682	42.8296037	111.4412686	67	2.7115950	42.0808912	114.1063361	67	2.8257689	41.3512970	116.8492085
68	2.6393715	43.2084818	114.0432369	68	2.7522690	42.4442278	116.8179311	68	2.8699215	41.6997386	119.6749774
69	2.6773125	43.5819907	116.6826084	69	2.7935530	42.8021949	119.5702001	69	2.9147640	42.0428195	122.5448989
70	2.7157989	43.9502065	119.3599209	70	2.8354563	43.1548718	122.3637531	70	2.9603072	42.3806223	125.4596630
71	2.7548385	44.3132042	122.0757198	71	2.8779981	43.5023367	125.1992094	71	3.0065620	42.7132281	128.4199702
72	2.7944393	44.6710527	124.8305583	72	2.9211580	43.8446667	128.0771975	72	3.0535396	43.0407169	131.4265322
73	2.8346093	45.0238400	127.6249975	73	2.9649753	44.1819377	130.9983555	73	3.1012511	43.3631694	134.4800718
74	2.8753569	45.3716229	130.4596069	74	3.0094500	44.5142243	133.9633308	74	3.1497082	43.6806572	137.5813229
75	2.9166901	45.7144773	133.3349637	75	3.0545917	44.8416003	136.9727808	75	3.1989224	43.9932624	140.7310311
76	2.9586175	46.0524732	136.2516538	76	3.1004106	45.1641382	140.0273725	76	3.2489055	44.3010584	143.9299535
77	3.0011477	46.3856789	139.2102714	77	3.1469167	45.4819096	143.1277831	77	3.2996697	44.6040843	147.1788590
78	3.0442892	46.7141628	142.2114190	78	3.1941205	45.7949848	146.2746998	78	3.3512270	44.9025172	150.4785288
79	3.0880508	47.0379917	145.2557082	79	3.2420323	46.1034333	149.4688203	79	3.4035899	45.1963246	153.8297557
80	3.1324415	47.3572315	148.3437590	80	3.2906628	46.4073235	152.7108526	80	3.4567710	45.4856119	157.2333456
81	3.1774704	47.6719472	151.4762005	81	3.3400227	46.7067226	156.0015154	81	3.5107831	45.7704487	160.6901167
82	3.2231465	47.9822030	154.6536709	82	3.3901231	47.0016972	159.3415282	82	3.5655391	46.0509033	164.2008997
83	3.2694793	48.2880621	157.8768174	83	3.4409749	47.2923125	162.7316612	83	3.6213522	46.3270433	167.7665388
84	3.3164780	48.5895868	161.1462967	84	3.4925895	47.5786330	166.1726362	84	3.6779358	46.5989349	171.3878910
85	3.3641524	48.8868385	164.4627747	85	3.5449784	47.8607221	169.6652257	85	3.7354035	46.8666436	175.0658268
86	3.4125121	49.1798778	167.8269271	86	3.5981531	48.1386425	173.2102041	86	3.7937692	47.1302337	178.8012303
87	3.4615669	49.4687643	171.2394392	87	3.6521254	48.4124557	176.8083572	87	3.8530469	47.3897686	182.5949995
88	3.5113270	49.7535569	174.7010061	88	3.7069072	48.6822223	180.4604825	88	3.9132507	47.6453106	186.4480464
89	3.5618023	50.0343137	178.2123331	89	3.7625109	48.9480023	184.1673898	89	3.9743953	47.8969212	190.3612972
90	3.6130032	50.3110917	181.7741354	90	3.8189485	49.2098545	187.9299006	90	4.0364953	48.1446609	194.3356924
91	3.6649401	50.5839475	185.3871386	91	3.8762327	49.4678366	191.7488491	91	4.0995654	48.3885892	198.3721876
92	3.7176236	50.8529365	189.0520787	92	3.9343762	49.7220068	195.6250819	92	4.1636211	48.6287607	202.4717531
93	3.7710645	51.1181136	192.7697023	93	3.9933919	49.9724205	199.5594581	93	4.2286777	48.8652452	206.6353742
94	3.8252735	51.3795328	196.5407668	94	4.0532928	50.2191335	203.5528500	94	4.2947508	49.0980876	210.8640519
95	3.8802618	51.6372474	200.3660403	95	4.1140921	50.4622005	207.6061428	95	4.3618563	49.3273478	215.1588028
96	3.9360406	51.8913098	204.2463022	96	4.1758035	50.7016754	211.7202349	96	4.4300103	49.5530089	219.5205590
97	3.9926212	52.1417718	208.1823428	97	4.2384406	50.9376112	215.8960384	97	4.4992292	49.7753412	223.9506694
98	4.0500151	52.3886845	212.1749640	98	4.3020172	51.1700603	220.1344790	98	4.5695297	49.9941821	228.4498986
99	4.1082341	52.6320981	216.2249791	99	4.3665474	51.3990742	224.4364962	99	4.6409286	50.2096562	233.0194282
100	4.1672899	52.8720622	220.3332131	100	4.4320457	51.6247036	228.8030436	100	4.7134431	50.4218154	237.6603568

Table 1

367

M	C(5.75,M,4)	A(5.75,M,4)	S(5.75,M,4)	M	C(6.00,M,4)	A(6.00,M,4)	S(6.00,M,4)	M	C(6.25,M,4)	A(6.25,M,4)	S(6.25,M,4)
101	4.2271947	53.1086257	224.5005031	101	4.4985263	51.8469986	233.2350893	101	4.7870906	50.6307105	242.3737999
102	4.2879607	53.3418368	228.7276978	102	4.5660042	52.0660085	237.7336157	102	4.8618889	50.8363919	247.1603905
103	4.3496001	53.5717430	233.0156585	103	4.6344943	52.2817818	242.2996199	103	4.9378559	51.0389089	252.0227794
104	4.4121256	53.7983911	237.3652586	104	4.7040117	52.4943663	246.9341142	104	5.0150099	51.2383103	256.9606354
105	4.4755499	54.0218273	241.7773842	105	4.7745719	52.7038091	251.6381259	105	5.0933695	51.4346440	261.9756453
106	4.5398859	54.2420972	246.2529341	106	4.8461905	52.9101568	256.4126978	106	5.1729534	51.6279572	267.0690148
107	4.6051468	54.4592455	250.7928200	107	4.9188833	53.1134550	261.2588883	107	5.2527808	51.8182963	272.2419561
108	4.6713458	54.6733166	255.3979668	108	4.9926666	53.3137487	266.1777716	108	5.3358711	52.0057071	277.4957489
109	4.7384964	54.8843540	260.0693126	109	5.0675566	53.5110825	271.1704382	109	5.4192441	52.1902347	282.8316200
110	4.8066123	55.0924008	264.8078090	110	5.1435599	53.7055000	276.2379948	110	5.5039198	52.3719234	288.2508640
111	4.8757073	55.2974992	269.6144212	111	5.2207235	53.8970443	281.3815647	111	5.5899185	52.5508169	293.7547838
112	4.9457956	55.4996911	274.4901285	112	5.2990343	54.0857580	286.6022882	112	5.6772610	52.7269582	299.3447023
113	5.0168914	55.6990178	279.4359242	113	5.3785198	54.2716827	291.9013225	113	5.7659582	52.9003896	305.0219633
114	5.0890092	55.8955197	284.4528156	114	5.4591976	54.4548598	297.2798424	114	5.8560614	53.0711528	310.7879315
115	5.1621637	56.0892369	289.5418248	115	5.5410856	54.6353299	302.7390400	115	5.9475624	53.2392889	316.6439929
116	5.2363698	56.2802089	294.7039885	116	5.6242019	54.8131329	308.2801256	116	6.0404931	53.4048383	322.5915553
117	5.3116427	56.4684746	299.9403584	117	5.7085649	54.9883082	313.9043275	117	6.1348758	53.5678408	328.6320484
118	5.3879975	56.6540723	305.2520010	118	5.7941934	55.1608948	319.6128924	118	6.2307332	53.7283356	334.7669241
119	5.4654500	56.8370398	310.6399986	119	5.8811063	55.3309309	325.4070858	119	6.3280884	53.8863612	340.9976573
120	5.5440158	57.0174145	316.1054485	120	5.9693229	55.4984540	331.2881921	120	6.4269648	54.0419556	347.3257457
121	5.6237111	57.1952330	321.6494644	121	6.0588627	55.6635015	337.2575150	121	6.5273861	54.1951563	353.7527105
122	5.7045519	57.3705316	327.2731754	122	6.1497457	55.8261099	343.3163777	122	6.6293765	54.3460001	360.2800966
123	5.7865548	57.5433460	332.9777273	123	6.2419919	55.9863151	349.4661234	123	6.7329605	54.4945231	366.9094732
124	5.8697366	57.7137114	338.7642822	124	6.3356217	56.1441529	355.7081153	124	6.8381630	54.6407612	373.6424337
125	5.9541140	57.8816625	344.6340187	125	6.4306561	56.2996580	362.0437370	125	6.9450093	54.7847495	380.4805967
126	6.0397044	58.0472335	350.5881328	126	6.5271159	56.4528650	368.4743931	126	7.0535251	54.9265226	387.4256060
127	6.1255252	58.2104582	356.6278372	127	6.6250226	56.6038079	375.0015090	127	7.1637364	55.0661146	394.4791312
128	6.2145940	58.3713698	362.7543624	128	6.7243980	56.7525201	381.6265316	128	7.2756698	55.2035589	401.6428676
129	6.3039283	58.5300010	368.9689563	129	6.8252640	56.8990346	388.3509296	129	7.3893522	55.3388888	408.9185374
130	6.3945477	58.6863842	375.2728951	130	6.9276429	57.0433838	395.1761936	130	7.5043108	55.4721357	416.3078896
131	6.4864694	58.8405513	381.6674328	131	7.0315596	57.1855998	402.1038365	131	7.6220735	55.6033346	423.8127003
132	6.5797124	58.9925336	388.1539022	132	7.1370309	57.3257141	409.1353940	132	7.7411684	55.7325140	431.4347738
133	6.6742957	59.1423622	394.7336145	133	7.2440864	57.4637577	416.2724250	133	7.8621241	55.8597061	439.1759421
134	6.7702387	59.2900674	401.4079102	134	7.3527477	57.5997613	423.5165113	134	7.9849698	55.9849414	447.0380663
135	6.8675609	59.4356795	408.1781490	135	7.4630369	57.7337550	430.8692590	135	8.1097349	56.1082500	455.0230361
136	6.9662821	59.5792281	415.0457099	136	7.5749845	57.8657685	438.3322979	136	8.2364496	56.2296615	463.1327710
137	7.0664224	59.7207425	422.0119920	137	7.6886092	57.9958310	445.9072824	137	8.3651441	56.3492052	471.3692206
138	7.1680022	59.8602513	429.0784144	138	7.8039384	58.1239714	453.5958916	138	8.4958495	56.4669097	479.7343646
139	7.2710422	59.9977832	436.2464166	139	7.9209975	58.2502181	461.3998300	139	8.6285971	56.5828034	488.2302141
140	7.3755635	60.1333661	443.5174588	140	8.0398124	58.3745991	469.3208275	140	8.7634189	56.6969142	496.8588112
141	7.4815872	60.2670275	450.8930223	141	8.1604096	58.4971420	477.3606399	141	8.9003474	56.8092693	505.6222301
142	7.5891350	60.3987949	458.3746095	142	8.2828158	58.6178739	485.5210495	142	9.0394153	56.9198959	514.5225775
143	7.6982288	60.5286949	465.9637445	143	8.4070580	58.7368216	493.8038653	143	9.1806562	57.0288206	523.5619928
144	7.8088909	60.6567540	473.6619734	144	8.5331639	58.8540114	502.2109233	144	9.3241039	57.1360695	532.7426489
145	7.9211437	60.7829984	481.4708642	145	8.6611613	58.9694694	510.7440871	145	9.4697930	57.2416685	542.0667528
146	8.0350101	60.9074538	489.3920079	146	8.7910787	59.0832211	519.4052484	146	9.6177585	57.3456428	551.5365459
147	8.1505134	61.0301454	497.4270181	147	8.9229449	59.1952917	528.1963272	147	9.7680360	57.4480175	561.1543044
148	8.2676770	61.1510984	505.5775315	148	9.0567891	59.3057061	537.1192721	148	9.9206616	57.5488172	570.9223404
149	8.3865249	61.2703373	513.8452085	149	9.1926409	59.4144887	546.1760612	149	10.0756719	57.6480662	580.8430020
150	8.5070812	61.3878864	522.2317334	150	9.3305305	59.5216638	555.3687021	150	10.2331043	57.7457883	590.9186739
151	8.6293705	61.5037697	530.7388145	151	9.4704885	59.6272550	564.6992327	151	10.3929965	57.8420069	601.1517782
152	8.7534177	61.6180108	539.3681850	152	9.6125458	59.7312857	574.1697212	152	10.5553871	57.9367453	611.5447748
153	8.8792481	61.7306330	548.1216027	153	9.7567340	59.8337790	583.7822670	153	10.7203150	58.0300261	622.1001619
154	9.0068872	61.8416591	557.0008507	154	9.9030850	59.9347765	593.5390010	154	10.8878108	58.1218719	632.8204770
155	9.1363612	61.9511119	566.0077380	155	10.0516313	60.0342440	603.4420861	155	11.0579422	58.2123046	643.7082969
156	9.2676964	62.0590136	575.1440992	156	10.2024058	60.1322601	613.4937174	156	11.2307225	58.3013461	654.7662391
157	9.4009196	62.1653861	584.4117957	157	10.3554419	60.2288276	623.6961232	157	11.4062025	58.3890177	665.9969616
158	9.5360578	62.2702513	593.8127153	158	10.5107735	60.3239681	634.0515650	158	11.5844245	58.4753405	677.4031641
159	9.6731386	62.3736303	603.3487731	159	10.6684351	60.4177026	644.5623385	159	11.7654311	58.5603352	688.9875886
160	9.8121900	62.4755444	613.0219117	160	10.8284616	60.5100518	655.2307736	160	11.9492659	58.6440224	700.7530197
161	9.9532402	62.5760142	622.8341017	161	10.9908885	60.6010363	666.0592352	161	12.1359732	58.7264220	712.7022856
162	10.0963181	62.6750622	632.7873419	162	11.1557705	60.6906761	677.0501238	162	12.3255978	58.8075540	724.8382588
163	10.2414526	62.7727026	642.8836600	163	11.3230882	60.7789912	688.2058756	163	12.5181853	58.8884378	737.1638567
164	10.3886735	62.8689613	653.1251126	164	11.4929345	60.8660012	699.5289838	164	12.7137819	58.9660926	749.6820419
165	10.5380107	62.9638558	663.5137861	165	11.6653285	60.9517253	711.0218983	165	12.9124348	59.0435373	762.3958239
166	10.6894946	63.0574056	674.0517968	166	11.8403084	61.0361826	722.6872268	166	13.1141916	59.1197906	775.3082586
167	10.8431561	63.1496297	684.7412914	167	12.0179130	61.1193917	734.5275352	167	13.3191008	59.1948707	788.4224502
168	10.9990264	63.2405468	695.5844475	168	12.1981817	61.2013712	746.5454482	168	13.5272118	59.2687958	801.7415510
169	11.1571375	63.3301756	706.5834739	169	12.3811545	61.2821391	758.7436300	169	13.7385744	59.3415835	815.2687627
170	11.3175213	63.4185341	717.7406114	170	12.5668718	61.3617134	771.1247844	170	13.9532397	59.4132515	829.0073372
171	11.4802107	63.5056406	729.0581327	171	12.7553749	61.4401117	783.6916562	171	14.1712590	59.4838168	842.9605768
172	11.6452387	63.5915126	740.5383434	172	12.9467055	61.5173514	796.4470311	172	14.3926850	59.5532966	857.1318359
173	11.8126390	63.6761677	752.1835821	173	13.1409061	61.5934497	809.3937366	173	14.6175707	59.6217074	871.5245208
174	11.9824457	63.7596231	763.9962211	174	13.3380197	61.6684233	822.5346426	174	14.8459702	59.6890657	886.1420915
175	12.1546934	63.8418958	775.9786668	175	13.5380900	61.7422890	835.8726623	175	15.0779385	59.7553878	900.9880617
176	12.3294171	63.9230026	788.1333601	176	13.7411616	61.8150360	849.4107522	176	15.3135313	59.8206895	916.0660002
177	12.5066524	64.0029601	800.4627772	177	13.9472787	61.8867616	863.1519136	177	15.5523052	59.8849866	931.3795315
178	12.6864356	64.0817844	812.9694296	178	14.1564879	61.9574006	877.0991923	178	15.7958178	59.9482945	946.9323367
179	12.8688031	64.1594917	825.6558652	179	14.3653352	62.0269957	891.2556802	179	16.0426274	60.0106284	962.7281544
180	13.0537921	64.2360978	838.5246683	180	14.5843578	62.0955622	905.6245154	180	16.2932935	60.0720034	978.7707819
181	13.2414404	64.3116183	851.5784604	181	14.8031333	62.1631155	920.2088832	181	16.5478762	60.1324341	995.0640754
182	13.4317861	64.3860686	864.8199008	182	15.0251803	62.2296704	935.0120164	182	16.8054368	60.1919351	1011.6119516
183	13.6248680	64.4594638	878.2516369	183	15.2505260	62.2952448	950.0371967	183	17.0690373	60.2505207	1028.4183883
184	13.8207255	64.5318189	891.8765549	184	15.4793163	62.3598441	965.2877547	184	17.3357411	60.3082050	1045.4874257
185	14.0193984	64.6031486	905.6972804	185	15.7115061	62.4234918	980.7670710	185	17.6066120	60.3650019	1062.8231667
186	14.2209273	64.6734675	919.7166788	186	15.9471787	62.4861988	996.4785771	186	17.8817153	60.4209249	1080.4297788
187	14.4253531	64.7427899	933.9376061	187	16.1863864	62.5479791	1012.4257558	187	18.1611171	60.4759876	1098.3114941
188	14.6327176	64.8111299	948.3629592	188	16.4291822	62.6088464	1028.6121422	188	18.4448846	60.5302032	1116.4726112
189	14.8430629	64.8785015	962.9956768	189	16.6756199	62.6688142	1045.0413243	189	18.7330859	60.5835847	1134.9174958
190	15.0564319	64.9449183	977.8387397	190	16.9257542	62.7278957	1061.7169442	190	19.0257904	60.6361449	1153.6505817
191	15.2728681	65.0103939	992.8951716	191	17.1796405	62.7861042	1078.6426984	191	19.3230683	60.6878965	1172.6763720
192	15.4924156	65.0749416	1008.1680397	192	17.4373351	62.8434524	1095.8223389	192	19.6249913	60.7388520	1191.9994404
193	15.7151191	65.1385746	1023.6604553	193	17.6988951	62.8999531	1113.2596740	193	19.9316318	60.7890235	1211.6244317
194	15.9410239	65.2013058	1039.3755744	194	17.9643786	62.9556188	1130.9585691	194	20.2430635	60.8384231	1231.5560634
195	16.1701761	65.2631480	1055.3165983	195	18.2338442	63.0104619	1148.9229477	195	20.5593614	60.8870627	1251.7991270
196	16.4026224	65.3241139	1071.4867744	196	18.5073519	63.0644945	1167.1567920	196	20.8806014	60.9349541	1272.3584884
197	16.6384101	65.3842158	1087.8893968	197	18.7849622	63.1177285	1185.6641439	197	21.2068608	60.9821086	1293.2390898
198	16.8775873	65.4434660	1104.5278069	198	19.0667366	63.1701759	1204.4491061	198	21.5382180	61.0285377	1314.4459506
199	17.1202026	65.5018765	1121.4053942	199	19.3527377	63.2218482	1223.5158427	199	21.8747527	61.0742525	1335.9841686
200	17.3663055	65.5594593	1138.5255967	200	19.6430287	63.2727568	1242.8685803	200	22.2165457	61.1192640	1357.8589213

Table 1

M	C(6.50,M,4)	A(6.50,M,4)	S(6.50,M,4)	M	C(6.75,M,4)	A(6.75,M,4)	S(6.75,M,4)	M	C(7.00,M,4)	A(7.00,M,4)	S(7.00,M,4)
1/3	1.0053876	.3297673	.3315439	1/3	1.0055937	.3296319	.3314757	1/3	1.0057996	.3294966	.3314076
1	1.0162500	.9840098	1.0000000	1	1.0168750	.9834050	1.0000000	1	1.0175000	.9828010	1.0000000
2	1.0327641	1.9522852	2.0162500	2	1.0340348	1.9504905	2.0168750	2	1.0353063	1.9486988	2.0175000
3	1.0495465	2.9050777	3.0490141	3	1.0514841	2.9015272	3.0509098	3	1.0534241	2.8979840	3.0528063
4	1.0666016	3.8426349	4.0985605	4	1.0692279	3.8367816	4.1023939	4	1.0718590	3.8309425	4.1062304
5	1.0839339	4.7652004	5.1651622	5	1.0872711	4.7565154	5.1716218	5	1.0906166	4.7478551	5.1780894
6	1.1015478	5.6730139	6.2490960	6	1.1056188	5.6609862	6.2588929	6	1.1097024	5.6489976	6.2687060
7	1.1194480	6.5663113	7.3506438	7	1.1242761	6.5504474	7.3645117	7	1.1291221	6.5346414	7.3784083
8	1.1376390	7.4453248	8.4700918	8	1.1432483	7.4251480	8.4887878	8	1.1488818	7.4050530	8.5075305
9	1.1561256	8.3102827	9.6077308	9	1.1625406	8.2853330	9.6320361	9	1.1689872	8.2604943	9.6564122
10	1.1749127	9.1614098	10.7638554	10	1.1821585	9.1312433	10.7945767	10	1.1894445	9.1012229	10.8253995
11	1.1940050	9.9989272	11.9387691	11	1.2021074	9.9631157	11.9767352	11	1.2102598	9.9274918	12.0148439
12	1.2134076	10.8230526	13.1327741	12	1.2223930	10.7811833	13.1788426	12	1.2314393	10.7395497	13.2251037
13	1.2331255	11.6340001	14.3461817	13	1.2430209	11.5856750	14.4012356	13	1.2529895	11.5376410	14.4565430
14	1.2531637	12.4319804	15.5793071	14	1.2639968	12.3768162	15.6442565	14	1.2749168	12.3220059	15.7095325
15	1.2735277	13.2172009	16.8324709	15	1.2853268	13.1548285	16.9082533	15	1.2972279	13.0928805	16.9844494
16	1.2942225	13.9898656	18.1059985	16	1.3070167	13.9199297	18.1935801	16	1.3199294	13.8504968	18.2816772
17	1.3152536	14.7501753	19.4002210	17	1.3290726	14.6723340	19.5005967	17	1.3430281	14.5950828	19.6016066
18	1.3366265	15.4983274	20.7154746	18	1.3515007	15.4122523	20.8296693	18	1.3665311	15.3268627	20.9446347
19	1.3583466	16.2345165	22.0521010	19	1.3743072	16.1398916	22.1811700	19	1.3904454	16.0460567	22.3111658
20	1.3804198	16.9589339	23.4104477	20	1.3974987	16.8554558	23.5554772	20	1.4147782	16.7528813	23.7016112
21	1.4028516	17.6717676	24.7908675	21	1.4210815	17.5591452	24.9529759	21	1.4395368	17.4475492	25.1163894
22	1.4256479	18.3732031	26.1937191	22	1.4450622	18.2511569	26.3740573	22	1.4647287	18.1302695	26.5559262
23	1.4488147	19.0634225	27.6193670	23	1.4694476	18.9316848	27.8191196	23	1.4903615	18.8012476	28.0206549
24	1.4723580	19.7426051	29.0681817	24	1.4942446	19.6009193	29.2885672	24	1.5164428	19.4606856	29.5110164
25	1.4962838	20.4109276	30.5405397	25	1.5194599	20.2590478	30.7828118	25	1.5429805	20.1087820	31.0274592
26	1.5205984	21.0685634	32.0368034	26	1.5451008	20.9062548	32.3022717	26	1.5699822	20.7457317	32.5704297
27	1.5453081	21.7156836	33.5574218	27	1.5711744	21.5427213	33.8473726	27	1.5974574	21.3717264	34.1404224
28	1.5704194	22.3524561	35.1027299	28	1.5976880	22.1686258	35.4185470	28	1.6254129	21.9869547	35.7378798
29	1.5959387	22.9790466	36.6731493	29	1.6246490	22.7841434	37.0162350	29	1.6538576	22.5916017	37.3632927
30	1.6218727	23.5956178	38.2690880	30	1.6520649	23.3894465	38.6408839	30	1.6828001	23.1858493	39.0171503
31	1.6482281	24.2023300	39.8909606	31	1.6799435	23.9347046	40.2929488	31	1.7122491	23.7698765	40.6999504
32	1.6750118	24.7993407	41.5391888	32	1.7082924	24.5700844	41.9728924	32	1.7422135	24.3438590	42.4121996
33	1.7022308	25.3868051	43.2142006	33	1.7371200	25.1457499	43.6811849	33	1.7727022	24.9079695	44.1544131
34	1.7298920	25.9648759	44.9164313	34	1.7664339	25.7118622	45.4183049	34	1.8037245	25.4623779	45.9271153
35	1.7580028	26.5337032	46.6463233	35	1.7962425	26.2685759	47.1847388	35	1.8352897	26.0072510	47.7308398
36	1.7865703	27.0934349	48.4043261	36	1.8265541	26.8160589	48.9809813	36	1.8674073	26.5427528	49.5661295
37	1.8156021	27.6442164	50.1908964	37	1.8573772	27.3544525	50.8075353	37	1.9000869	27.0690445	51.4335368
38	1.8451056	28.1861908	52.0064985	38	1.8887204	27.8839115	52.6649125	38	1.9333383	27.5862846	53.3336237
39	1.8750886	28.7194989	53.8516041	39	1.9205926	28.4045842	54.5536329	39	1.9671718	28.0946286	55.2669621
40	1.9055588	29.2442794	55.7266926	40	1.9530026	28.9156163	56.4742255	40	2.0015973	28.5942295	57.2341339
41	1.9365241	29.7606685	57.6322514	41	1.9859595	29.4201512	58.4272280	41	2.0366253	29.0852399	59.2357313
42	1.9679926	30.2688005	59.5687755	42	2.0194725	29.9153300	60.4131875	42	2.0722662	29.5678013	61.2723566
43	1.9999725	30.7688074	61.5367681	43	2.0535511	30.4022913	62.4326600	43	2.1085309	30.0420662	63.3446228
44	2.0324720	31.2608191	63.5367406	44	2.0882048	30.8811716	64.4862112	44	2.1454302	30.5081722	65.4531537
45	2.0654997	31.7449634	65.5692126	45	2.1234433	31.3521048	66.5744160	45	2.1829752	30.9662626	67.5985839
46	2.0990641	32.2213662	67.6347123	46	2.1592764	31.8152229	68.6978593	46	2.2211773	31.4164743	69.7815591
47	2.1331739	32.6901512	69.7337764	47	2.1957142	32.2706556	70.8571356	47	2.2600479	31.8589424	72.0027364
48	2.1678379	33.1514403	71.8669503	48	2.2327668	32.7185304	73.0528498	48	2.2995987	32.2938013	74.2627843
49	2.2030653	33.6053533	74.0347882	49	2.2704448	33.1589727	75.2856166	49	2.3398417	32.7211806	76.5623830
50	2.2388651	34.0520082	76.2378535	50	2.3087585	33.5921059	77.5560614	50	2.3807889	33.1412094	78.9022247
51	2.2752467	34.4915210	78.4767186	51	2.3477188	34.0180513	79.8648200	51	2.4224527	33.5540142	81.2830137
52	2.3122194	34.9240059	80.7519653	52	2.3873366	34.4369282	82.2125388	52	2.4648457	33.9597191	83.7054664
53	2.3497930	35.3495753	83.0641847	53	2.4276229	34.8488538	84.5998754	53	2.5079805	34.3584463	86.1703121
54	2.3879771	35.7683398	85.4139777	54	2.4685890	35.2539435	87.0274983	54	2.5518701	34.7503158	88.6782925
55	2.4267818	36.1804081	87.8019549	55	2.5102465	35.6523107	89.4960873	55	2.5965278	35.1354455	91.2301627
56	2.4662170	36.5858875	90.2287369	56	2.5526069	36.0440671	92.0063338	56	2.6419671	35.5139513	93.8266905
57	2.5062930	36.9848831	92.6949536	57	2.5956821	36.4293223	94.5589407	57	2.6882015	35.8859472	96.4686576
58	2.5470203	37.3774988	95.2012466	58	2.6394843	36.8081842	97.1546228	58	2.7352450	36.2515452	99.1568591
59	2.5884093	37.7638364	97.7482669	59	2.6840252	37.1807589	99.7941071	59	2.7831118	36.6108552	101.8921041
60	2.6304710	38.1439965	100.3368762	60	2.7293185	37.5471507	102.4781326	60	2.8318163	36.9639855	104.6752160
61	2.6732161	38.5180777	102.9673472	61	2.7753757	37.9074623	105.2074511	61	2.8813731	37.3110423	107.5070322
62	2.7166459	38.8861773	105.6403734	62	2.8222102	38.2617945	107.9828269	62	2.9317971	37.6521300	110.3884053
63	2.7608015	39.2483910	108.3570193	63	2.8698350	38.6102466	110.8050371	63	2.9831035	37.9873513	113.3202024
64	2.8056646	39.6048128	111.1178208	64	2.9182635	38.9529161	113.6748721	64	3.0353079	38.3168072	116.3033060
65	2.8512566	39.9555353	113.9234854	65	2.9675092	39.2898991	116.5931355	65	3.0884257	38.6405968	119.3386138
66	2.8975896	40.3006498	116.7747421	66	3.0175859	39.6212898	119.5606447	66	3.1424732	38.9588174	122.4270396
67	2.9446752	40.6402458	119.6723316	67	3.0665076	39.9471811	122.5782306	67	3.1974665	39.2715651	125.5695128
68	2.9925264	40.9744116	122.6170070	68	3.1202887	40.2676643	125.6467382	68	3.2534221	39.5789337	128.7669792
69	3.0411549	41.3032340	125.6095334	69	3.1729436	40.5828290	128.7670269	69	3.3103570	39.8810159	132.0204014
70	3.0905737	41.6267985	128.6506883	70	3.2264870	40.8927636	131.9399705	70	3.3682883	40.1779026	135.3307584
71	3.1407955	41.9451492	131.7412620	71	3.2809340	41.1975494	135.1664575	71	3.4272333	40.4696832	138.6990467
72	3.1918334	42.2584888	134.8820575	72	3.3362997	41.4972882	138.4473915	72	3.4872099	40.7564454	142.1262800
73	3.2437007	42.5667786	138.0738909	73	3.3925998	41.7920404	141.7836912	73	3.5482361	41.0382756	145.6134899
74	3.2964109	42.8701389	141.3175917	74	3.4493499	42.0819150	145.1762910	74	3.6103302	41.3152585	149.1617260
75	3.3499775	43.1686483	144.6140025	75	3.5080661	42.3669724	148.6261410	75	3.6735110	41.5874777	152.7720562
76	3.4044147	43.4623846	147.9639801	76	3.5672647	42.6472992	152.1342071	76	3.7377974	41.8550149	156.4455672
77	3.4597364	43.7514239	151.3683948	77	3.6274623	42.9229740	155.7014718	77	3.8032098	42.1179508	160.1833646
78	3.5159571	44.0358415	154.8281312	78	3.6886758	43.1940740	159.3289342	78	3.8697650	42.3763644	163.9865735
79	3.5730914	44.3157112	158.3440883	79	3.7509222	43.4606751	163.0176099	79	3.9374859	42.6303336	167.8563385
80	3.6311542	44.5911057	161.9171798	80	3.8142190	43.7228520	166.7685321	80	4.0063919	42.8799347	171.7938244
81	3.6901604	44.8620967	165.5483339	81	3.8785839	43.9806781	170.5827511	81	4.0765038	43.1252430	175.8002164
82	3.7501255	45.1287544	169.2384944	82	3.9440350	44.2342255	174.4613050	82	4.1478426	43.3663321	179.8767202
83	3.8110651	45.3911482	172.9886199	83	4.0105908	44.4835653	178.4053701	83	4.2204299	43.6032748	184.0245628
84	3.8729949	45.6493464	176.7996850	84	4.0782693	44.7287674	182.4159607	84	4.2942874	43.8361423	188.2449926
85	3.9359311	45.9034159	180.6726799	85	4.1470901	44.9699003	186.4942300	85	4.3694374	44.0650048	192.5392800
86	3.9998899	46.1534227	184.6086109	86	4.2170723	45.2070317	190.6413202	86	4.4459026	44.2899310	196.9087174
87	4.0648881	46.3994320	188.6085009	87	4.2882354	45.4402278	194.8583924	87	4.5237059	44.5109887	201.3546200
88	4.1309426	46.6415075	192.6733890	88	4.3605993	45.6695541	199.1466288	88	4.6028707	44.7282444	205.8783258
89	4.1980704	46.8797121	196.8043316	89	4.4341845	45.8950747	203.5072272	89	4.6834209	44.9417635	210.4811965
90	4.2662890	47.1141079	201.0024020	90	4.5090113	46.1168528	207.9414116	90	4.7653808	45.1516485	215.1646175
91	4.3356162	47.3447556	205.2686910	91	4.5851009	46.3349505	212.4504230	91	4.8487750	45.3578480	219.9299983
92	4.4060700	47.5717152	209.6043072	92	4.6624745	46.5494289	217.0355259	92	4.9336285	45.5605386	224.7787733
93	4.4776686	47.7950457	214.0103772	93	4.7411537	46.7603480	221.6979983	93	5.0199670	45.7597431	229.7124018
94	4.5504308	48.0148052	218.4880459	94	4.8211607	46.9677670	226.4391521	94	5.1078165	45.9555214	234.7323688
95	4.6243753	48.2310506	223.0384766	95	4.9025178	47.1717438	231.2603127	95	5.1972032	46.1479326	239.8401853
96	4.6995213	48.4438382	227.6628519	96	4.9852478	47.3723356	236.1628305	96	5.2881543	46.3370345	245.0373865
97	4.7758886	48.6532233	232.3623732	97	5.0693738	47.5695986	241.1480783	97	5.3806970	46.5228840	250.3255429
98	4.8534968	48.8592603	237.1382618	98	5.1549195	47.7635881	246.2174521	98	5.4748592	46.7055371	255.7062399
99	4.9323661	49.0620028	241.9917586	99	5.2419088	47.9543583	251.3723716	99	5.5706692	46.8850488	261.1810991
100	5.0125170	49.2615034	246.9241246	100	5.3303660	48.1419627	256.6142804	100	5.6681560	47.0614730	266.7517683

Table 1 369

M	C(6.50,M,4)	A(6.50,M,4)	S(6.50,M,4)	M	C(6.75,M,4)	A(6.75,M,4)	S(6.75,M,4)	M	C(7.00,M,4)	A(7.00,M,4)	S(7.00,M,4)
101	5.0939704	49.4578139	251.9366417	101	5.4203159	48.3264538	261.9446464	101	5.7673487	47.2348629	272.4199243
102	5.1767475	49.6505854	257.0306121	102	5.5117837	48.5078832	267.3649623	102	5.8682773	47.4052707	278.1872729
103	5.2608696	49.8410680	262.2073596	103	5.6047951	48.6863019	272.8767461	103	5.9709721	47.5727476	284.0555502
104	5.3463587	50.0281112	267.4682292	104	5.6993760	48.8617597	278.4815412	104	6.0754641	47.7373441	290.0265224
105	5.4332371	50.2121636	272.8145879	105	5.7955530	49.0343058	284.1809172	105	6.1817848	47.8991096	296.1019385
106	5.5215272	50.3932729	278.2478249	106	5.8933529	49.2039885	289.9764702	106	6.2899660	48.0580930	302.2837713
107	5.6112520	50.5714862	283.7693521	107	5.9928033	49.3708553	295.8698231	107	6.4000404	48.2143420	308.5737373
108	5.7024348	50.7468499	289.3806041	108	6.0939318	49.5349530	301.8626264	108	6.5120411	48.3679037	314.9737777
109	5.7950994	50.9194095	295.0830389	109	6.1967669	49.6963274	307.9565582	109	6.6260018	48.5188243	321.4858188
110	5.8892698	51.0892098	300.8781383	110	6.3013374	49.8550239	314.1533251	110	6.7419569	48.6671492	328.1118206
111	5.9849704	51.2562950	306.7674081	111	6.4076724	50.0110868	320.4546625	111	6.8599411	48.8129230	334.8537775
112	6.0822262	51.4207085	312.7523784	112	6.5158019	50.1645599	326.8623349	112	6.9799901	48.9561897	341.7137166
113	6.1810623	51.5824930	318.8346046	113	6.6257561	50.3154860	333.3781368	113	7.1021399	49.0969923	348.6937087
114	6.2815046	51.7416905	325.0156669	114	6.7375657	50.4639076	340.0038929	114	7.2264274	49.2353733	355.7958486
115	6.3835790	51.8983425	331.2971715	115	6.8512621	50.6098661	346.7414586	115	7.3528898	49.3713742	363.0222760
116	6.4873122	52.0524895	337.6807506	116	6.9668772	50.7534024	353.5927207	116	7.4815654	49.5050361	370.3751658
117	6.5927310	52.2041717	344.1680628	117	7.0844432	50.8945568	360.5595979	117	7.6124928	49.6363991	377.8567312
118	6.6998629	52.3534285	350.7607938	118	7.2039932	51.0333687	367.6440411	118	7.7457112	49.7655028	385.4692240
119	6.8087357	52.5002987	357.4606567	119	7.3255606	51.1698770	374.8480343	119	7.8812614	49.8923861	393.2149355
120	6.9193776	52.6448203	364.2693924	120	7.4491794	51.3041200	382.1735949	120	8.0191835	50.0170870	401.0961969
121	7.0318175	52.7870311	371.1887700	121	7.5748843	51.4361352	389.6227744	121	8.1595192	50.1396433	409.1153803
122	7.1460846	52.9269678	378.2205876	122	7.7027105	51.5659596	397.1976587	122	8.3023108	50.2600917	417.2748995
123	7.2622084	53.0646670	385.3666721	123	7.8326937	51.6936296	404.9003692	123	8.4476012	50.3784685	425.5772102
124	7.3802193	53.2001643	392.6288805	124	7.9643704	51.8191809	412.7330629	124	8.5954342	50.4948093	434.0248114
125	7.5001479	53.3334950	400.0090999	125	8.0992776	51.9426487	420.6979334	125	8.7458543	50.6091492	442.6202456
126	7.6220253	53.4646938	407.5092477	126	8.2359529	52.0640676	428.7972110	126	8.8989068	50.7215226	451.3660999
127	7.7458832	53.5937946	415.1312730	127	8.3749347	52.1834715	437.0331639	127	9.0545376	50.8319632	460.2650067
128	7.8717538	53.7208311	422.8771562	128	8.5162617	52.3008939	445.4080986	128	9.2130938	50.9405044	469.3196443
129	7.9995698	53.8458362	430.7489100	129	8.6599736	52.4163677	453.9243603	129	9.3743229	51.0471787	478.5327381
130	8.1296644	53.9688426	438.7485798	130	8.8061106	52.5299252	462.5843339	130	9.5383736	51.1520184	487.9070610
131	8.2617715	54.0898820	446.8782443	131	8.9547138	52.6415983	471.3904445	131	9.7052951	51.2550550	497.4454346
132	8.3960253	54.2089859	455.1400157	132	9.1058246	52.7514181	480.3451583	132	9.8751378	51.3563194	507.1507297
133	8.5324607	54.3261854	463.5360410	133	9.2594853	52.8594154	489.4509328	133	10.0479527	51.4558421	517.0258675
134	8.6711132	54.4415109	472.0685017	134	9.4157392	52.9656206	498.7104682	134	10.2237919	51.5536532	527.0738202
135	8.8120188	54.5549923	480.7396149	135	9.5746298	53.0700633	508.1262073	135	10.4027082	51.6497820	537.2976121
136	8.9552141	54.6666590	489.5516336	136	9.7362016	53.1727727	517.7008371	136	10.5847556	51.7442575	547.7003203
137	9.1007363	54.7765403	498.5068477	137	9.9005000	53.2737777	527.4370387	137	10.7699888	51.8371081	558.2850759
138	9.2486233	54.8846645	507.6075840	138	10.0675710	53.3731066	537.3375388	138	10.9584636	51.9283618	569.0550648
139	9.3989134	54.9910597	516.8562072	139	10.2374612	53.4707870	547.4051098	139	11.1502368	52.0180460	580.0135284
140	9.5516457	55.0957537	526.2551206	140	10.4102184	53.5668465	557.6425710	140	11.3453659	52.1061877	591.1637652
141	9.7068600	55.1987737	535.8067663	141	10.5858908	53.6613119	568.0527894	141	11.5439098	52.1928134	602.5091311
142	9.8645964	55.3001463	545.5136263	142	10.7645277	53.7542096	578.6386802	142	11.7459282	52.2779493	614.0530409
143	10.0248961	55.3998979	555.3782227	143	10.9461791	53.8455665	589.4032080	143	11.9514820	52.3616210	625.7989691
144	10.1878007	55.4980546	565.4031188	144	11.1308959	53.9354057	600.3493871	144	12.1605329	52.4438535	637.7504511
145	10.3533525	55.5946416	575.5909919	145	11.3187298	54.0237548	611.4802831	145	12.3734440	52.5246718	649.9110840
146	10.5215944	55.6896843	585.9442720	146	11.5097334	54.1106378	622.7990129	146	12.5899793	52.6041000	662.2845280
147	10.6925703	55.7832071	596.4658664	147	11.7039601	54.1960790	634.3087462	147	12.8103039	52.6821622	674.8745073
148	10.8663246	55.8752346	607.1584368	148	11.9014644	54.2801022	646.0127063	148	13.0344842	52.7588817	687.6848111
149	11.0429024	55.9657905	618.0247614	149	12.1023016	54.3627311	657.9141708	149	13.2625877	52.8342818	700.7192954
150	11.2223496	56.0548984	629.0676638	150	12.3065280	54.4439888	670.0164724	150	13.4946830	52.9083851	713.9818830
151	11.4047127	56.1425814	640.2900133	151	12.5142006	54.5238981	682.3230004	151	13.7308399	52.9812138	727.4765660
152	11.5900393	56.2288624	651.6947261	152	12.7253778	54.6024812	694.8372010	152	13.9711296	53.0527900	741.2074059
153	11.7783775	56.3137638	663.2847654	153	12.9401185	54.6797602	707.5625788	153	14.2156244	53.1231351	755.1785356
154	11.9697761	56.3973075	675.0631428	154	13.1584830	54.7557568	720.5026974	154	14.4643978	53.1922704	769.3941600
155	12.1642849	56.4795154	687.0329189	155	13.3805323	54.8304923	733.6611804	155	14.7175248	53.2602166	783.8585578
156	12.3619546	56.5604087	699.1972039	156	13.6063289	54.9039875	747.0417128	156	14.9750815	53.3269942	798.5760826
157	12.5623363	56.6400086	711.5591585	157	13.8359357	54.9762630	760.6480418	157	15.2371454	53.3926233	813.5511640
158	12.7659824	56.7183356	724.1219948	158	14.0694171	55.0473392	774.4839775	158	15.5037954	53.4571236	828.7683094
159	12.9744459	56.7954102	736.8889772	159	14.3068366	55.1172358	788.5533946	159	15.7751119	53.5205146	844.2921048
160	13.1852806	56.8712524	749.8634231	160	14.5482665	55.1859725	802.8602332	160	16.0511763	53.5828154	860.0672167
161	13.3995415	56.9458818	763.0487038	161	14.7937685	55.2535686	817.4084096	161	16.3320719	53.6440446	876.1183930
162	13.6172840	57.0193179	776.4482452	162	15.0434133	55.3200429	832.2022691	162	16.6178832	53.7042207	892.4504649
163	13.8385649	57.0915797	790.0655292	163	15.2972709	55.3854140	847.2456814	163	16.9086961	53.7633619	909.0683481
164	14.0634415	57.1626861	803.9040941	164	15.5554123	55.4497003	862.5429523	164	17.2045983	53.8214859	925.9770442
165	14.2919725	57.2326554	817.9675356	165	15.8179099	55.5129198	878.0983646	165	17.5056788	53.8786102	943.1816425
166	14.5242170	57.3015059	832.2595081	166	16.0848372	55.5750901	893.9162745	166	17.8120281	53.9347520	960.6873213
167	14.7602356	57.3692555	846.7837252	167	16.3562688	55.6362288	910.0011117	167	18.1237386	53.9899283	978.4993494
168	15.0000894	57.4359218	861.5430927	168	16.6322808	55.6963528	926.3573805	168	18.4409041	54.0441556	996.6230880
169	15.2439408	57.5015221	876.5440501	169	16.9129506	55.7554791	942.9896613	169	18.7636199	54.0974502	1015.0639921
170	15.4915532	57.5660734	891.7878909	170	17.1983566	55.8136242	959.9026118	170	19.0919832	54.1498282	1033.8276120
171	15.7432910	57.6295925	907.2794442	171	17.4885789	55.8708044	977.1009684	171	19.4260929	54.2013053	1052.9195952
172	15.9991195	57.6920959	923.0227352	172	17.7835986	55.9270356	994.5895473	172	19.7660496	54.2518971	1072.3456882
173	16.2591052	57.7535999	939.0218546	173	18.0837986	55.9823338	1012.3732459	173	20.1119554	54.3016188	1092.1117377
174	16.5233156	57.8141205	955.2809939	174	18.3839627	56.0367142	1030.4570445	174	20.4639147	54.3504853	1112.2236932
175	16.7918195	57.8736733	971.8042754	175	18.6992764	56.0901922	1048.8460071	175	20.8220332	54.3985114	1132.6876078
176	17.0646866	57.9322738	988.5960949	176	19.0148267	56.1427827	1067.5452835	176	21.1854187	54.4457114	1153.5096410
177	17.3419877	57.9899373	1005.6607815	177	19.3357019	56.1945005	1086.5601102	177	21.5571811	54.4920997	1174.6960597
178	17.6237950	58.0466788	1023.0027692	178	19.6619919	56.2453601	1105.8958121	178	21.9344317	54.5376901	1196.2532408
179	17.9101817	58.1025130	1040.6265642	179	19.9937880	56.2953756	1125.5578040	179	22.3182843	54.5824964	1218.1876726
180	18.2012221	58.1574543	1058.5367459	180	20.3311831	56.3445612	1145.5515919	180	22.7088543	54.6265321	1240.5059569
181	18.4969920	58.2115172	1076.7379681	181	20.6742719	56.3929305	1165.8827751	181	23.1062592	54.6698104	1263.2148111
182	18.7975681	58.2647156	1095.2349601	182	21.0231502	56.4404971	1186.5570469	182	23.5108188	54.7123444	1286.3210704
183	19.1030286	58.3170633	1114.0325282	183	21.3779159	56.4872743	1207.5801971	183	23.9220546	54.7541468	1309.8316891
184	19.4134528	58.3685739	1133.1355068	184	21.7386662	56.5332753	1228.9581130	184	24.3408905	54.7952303	1333.7537437
185	19.7289214	58.4192610	1152.5490097	185	22.1055082	56.5785129	1250.6967812	185	24.7686526	54.8356072	1358.0944343
186	20.0495164	58.4691375	1172.2779311	186	22.4785387	56.6229998	1272.8022894	186	25.2000691	54.8752896	1382.8610869
187	20.3753211	58.5182164	1192.3276420	187	22.8578640	56.6667484	1295.2808281	187	25.6410703	54.9142895	1408.0611560
188	20.7064200	58.5665106	1212.7027685	188	23.2435905	56.7097710	1318.1386921	188	26.0897890	54.9526187	1433.7022262
189	21.0428993	58.6140326	1233.4091886	189	23.6358261	56.7520796	1341.3822825	189	26.5463603	54.9902888	1459.7920152
190	21.3848465	58.6607947	1254.4520879	190	24.0346806	56.7936862	1365.0181086	190	27.0109216	55.0273107	1486.3383755
191	21.7323502	58.7068091	1275.8369344	191	24.4402659	56.8346023	1389.0527892	191	27.4836127	55.0636960	1513.3492971
192	22.0855009	58.7520876	1297.5692846	192	24.8526953	56.8748394	1413.4930551	192	27.9645760	55.0994555	1540.8329099
193	22.4443903	58.7966422	1319.6547855	193	25.2720846	56.9144087	1438.3457504	193	28.4539560	55.1346000	1568.7974858
194	22.8091116	58.8404843	1342.0991758	194	25.6985510	56.9533214	1463.6178350	194	28.9519003	55.1691401	1597.2514419
195	23.1797597	58.8836254	1364.9082874	195	26.1322141	56.9915884	1489.3163860	195	29.4585585	55.2030861	1626.2033421
196	23.5564308	58.9260767	1388.0880471	196	26.5731952	57.0292203	1515.4466000	196	29.9740833	55.2364482	1655.6619007
197	23.9392228	58.9678491	1411.6444779	197	27.0216178	57.0662277	1542.0217952	197	30.4986298	55.2692366	1685.6359840
198	24.3282352	59.0089536	1435.5837007	198	27.4776076	57.1026209	1569.0434130	198	31.0323558	55.3014610	1716.1346137
199	24.7235690	59.0494008	1459.9119359	199	27.9412923	57.1384103	1596.5210207	199	31.5754220	55.3331312	1747.1669695
200	25.1253270	59.0892013	1484.6355049	200	28.4128016	57.1736057	1624.4623129	200	32.1279919	55.3642567	1778.7423915

Table 1

M	C(7.25,M,4)	A(7.25,M,4)	S(7.25,M,4)	M	C(7.50,M,4)	A(7.50,M,4)	S(7.50,M,4)	M	C(7.75,M,4)	A(7.75,M,4)	S(7.75,M,4)
1/3	1.0060055	.3293615	.3313395	1/3	1.0062113	.3292265	.3312714	1/3	1.0064171	.3290916	.3312034
1	1.0181250	.9821977	1.0000000	1	1.0187500	.9815951	1.0000000	1	1.0193750	.9809933	1.0000000
2	1.0365785	1.9469099	2.0181250	2	1.0378516	1.9451240	2.0187500	2	1.0391254	1.9433410	2.0193750
3	1.0553665	2.8944481	3.0547035	3	1.0573113	2.8909193	3.0566016	3	1.0592584	2.8873977	3.0585004
4	1.0744950	3.8251178	4.1100700	4	1.0771359	3.8193073	4.1139128	4	1.0797816	3.8135109	4.1177588
5	1.0939702	4.7392194	5.1845650	5	1.0973322	4.7306084	5.1910497	5	1.1007023	4.7220217	5.1975404
6	1.1137985	5.6370479	6.2785353	6	1.1179071	5.6251370	6.2883809	6	1.1220285	5.6132647	6.2982428
7	1.1339860	6.5188930	7.8923337	7	1.1386679	6.5032020	7.4062880	7	1.1437678	6.4875681	7.4202712
8	1.1545395	7.3850392	8.5263198	8	1.1602217	7.3651063	8.5451559	8	1.1659283	7.3452538	8.5640390
9	1.1754656	8.2357659	9.6808593	9	1.1819758	8.2111473	9.7053776	9	1.1885181	8.1866377	9.7299672
10	1.1967709	9.0713477	10.8563249	10	1.2041379	9.0416169	10.8873534	10	1.2115457	9.0120296	10.9184853
11	1.2184624	9.8920543	12.0530958	11	1.2267155	9.8568019	12.0914913	11	1.2350194	9.8217335	12.1300310
12	1.2405470	10.6981503	13.2715582	12	1.2497164	10.6559835	13.3182068	12	1.2589479	10.6160478	13.3650503
13	1.2630319	11.4898959	14.5121051	13	1.2731486	11.4424377	14.5679231	13	1.2833400	11.3952644	14.6239932
14	1.2859244	12.2675466	15.7751370	14	1.2970201	12.2134358	15.8410717	14	1.3082047	12.1596708	15.9073382
15	1.3092317	13.0313534	17.0610614	15	1.3213392	12.9702438	17.1380918	15	1.3335511	12.9095483	17.2155428
16	1.3329516	13.7815625	18.3702931	16	1.3461143	13.7131227	18.4594310	16	1.3593887	13.6451730	18.5490940
17	1.3571215	14.5184152	19.7032547	17	1.3713540	14.4423290	19.8055453	17	1.3857269	14.3668160	19.9084827
18	1.3817193	15.2421522	21.0603762	18	1.3970665	15.1581144	21.1768993	18	1.4125753	15.0747428	21.2942095
19	1.4067630	15.9530040	22.4420955	19	1.4232619	15.8607258	22.5739662	19	1.4399440	15.7692143	22.7067848
20	1.4322606	16.6512010	23.8488585	20	1.4499480	16.5504057	23.9972280	20	1.4678429	16.4504861	24.1467268
21	1.4582203	17.3369685	25.2811191	21	1.4771346	17.2273921	25.4471761	21	1.4962823	17.1188092	25.6145717
22	1.4846505	18.0105276	26.7393393	22	1.5048308	17.8919186	26.9243106	22	1.5252728	17.7744296	27.1108540
23	1.5115598	18.6720959	28.2239899	23	1.5330464	18.5442146	28.4291414	23	1.5548250	18.4175888	28.6361268
24	1.5389568	19.3218667	29.7355497	24	1.5617910	19.1845051	29.9621879	24	1.5849497	19.0485237	30.1909517
25	1.5668504	19.9601097	31.2745065	25	1.5910746	19.8130111	31.5239789	25	1.6155581	19.6674665	31.7759014
26	1.5952496	20.5869709	32.8413570	26	1.6209073	20.4299496	33.1150535	26	1.6469615	20.2746453	33.3915595
27	1.6241635	21.2026724	34.4366066	27	1.6512993	21.0355333	34.7359607	27	1.6788713	20.8702835	35.0385210
28	1.6536015	21.8074131	36.0607701	28	1.6822611	21.6299714	36.3872600	28	1.7113995	21.4546006	36.7173923
29	1.6835730	22.4013879	37.7143715	29	1.7133035	22.2134689	38.0695211	29	1.7445578	22.0278118	38.4287918
30	1.7140877	22.9847886	39.3979445	30	1.7459373	22.7862271	39.7833246	30	1.7783587	22.5901281	40.1733497
31	1.7451556	23.5578034	41.1120322	31	1.7785737	23.3484438	41.5292620	31	1.8128143	23.1417565	41.9517083
32	1.7767865	24.1206172	42.8571878	32	1.8120238	23.9003129	43.3079356	32	1.8479376	23.6829003	43.7645227
33	1.8089908	24.6734117	44.6339794	33	1.8459992	24.4420249	45.1199594	33	1.8837414	24.2137588	45.6124603
34	1.8417787	25.2163650	46.4429651	34	1.8806117	24.9737668	46.9659587	34	1.9202389	24.7345273	47.4962017
35	1.8751610	25.7496526	48.2847439	35	1.9158732	25.4957220	48.8465704	35	1.9574435	25.2453997	49.4164406
36	1.9091483	26.2734464	50.1599049	36	1.9517958	26.0080707	50.7624436	36	1.9953690	25.7465581	51.3738842
37	1.9437516	26.7879154	52.0690531	37	1.9883920	26.5109996	52.7142394	37	2.0340293	26.2381932	53.3692532
38	1.9789821	27.2932257	54.0128047	38	2.0256743	27.0046524	54.7026314	38	2.0734386	26.7204838	55.4032824
39	2.0148511	27.7895403	55.9917868	39	2.0636557	27.4892293	56.7283058	39	2.1136115	27.1936076	57.4767210
40	2.0513703	28.2770193	58.0066380	40	2.1023493	27.9646877	58.7919615	40	2.1545627	27.6577389	59.5903325
41	2.0885514	28.7558201	60.0580083	41	2.1417683	28.4317916	60.8943108	41	2.1963073	28.1130486	61.7448952
42	2.1264064	29.2260970	62.1465597	42	2.1819265	28.8901022	63.0360791	42	2.2388608	28.5597043	63.9412026
43	2.1649475	29.6880020	64.2729661	43	2.2228376	29.3399776	65.2180056	43	2.2822387	28.9978706	66.1800634
44	2.2041872	30.1416840	66.4379136	44	2.2645158	29.7815731	67.4408432	44	2.3264571	29.4277087	68.4623021
45	2.2441381	30.5872492	68.6421008	45	2.3069755	30.2150411	69.7053590	45	2.3715322	29.8493771	70.7887592
46	2.2848131	31.0249619	70.8862388	46	2.3502313	30.6405311	72.0123345	46	2.4174806	30.2630308	73.1602914
47	2.3262253	31.4548429	73.1710519	47	2.3942981	31.0581901	74.3625658	47	2.4643193	30.6688224	75.5777720
48	2.3683882	31.8770710	75.4972772	48	2.4391912	31.4681620	76.7568639	48	2.5120655	31.0669012	78.0420914
49	2.4113152	32.2917824	77.8656654	49	2.4849260	31.8705885	79.1960551	49	2.5607368	31.4574138	80.5541569
50	2.4550203	32.6991110	80.2769806	50	2.5315184	32.2656083	81.6809811	50	2.6103511	31.8405040	83.1148937
51	2.4995175	33.0991883	82.7320009	51	2.5789844	32.6533579	84.2124995	51	2.6609266	32.2163130	85.7252448
52	2.5448213	33.4921432	85.2315184	52	2.6273403	33.0339709	86.7914839	52	2.7124821	32.5849790	88.3861714
53	2.5909462	33.8781025	87.7763397	53	2.6766030	33.4075768	89.4188242	53	2.7650364	32.9466379	91.0986535
54	2.6379071	34.2571910	90.3672858	54	2.7257893	33.7743105	92.0954271	54	2.8186090	33.3014228	93.8636899
55	2.6857191	34.6295307	93.0051929	55	2.7779166	34.1342925	94.8222164	55	2.8732195	33.6494644	96.6822989
56	2.7343978	34.9952420	95.6909120	56	2.8300025	34.4876491	97.6001330	56	2.9286882	33.9908909	99.5555184
57	2.7839587	35.3544427	98.4253098	57	2.8830652	34.8345022	100.4301355	57	2.9853354	34.3258280	102.4844066
58	2.8344180	35.7072488	101.2092685	58	2.9371225	35.1749714	103.3312005	58	3.0434821	34.6543990	105.4700420
59	2.8857918	36.0436865	104.0436865	59	2.9921936	35.5091744	106.2503230	59	3.1024495	34.9767250	108.5135240
60	2.9380968	36.3941305	106.9294783	60	3.0482972	35.8372264	109.2425166	60	3.1625595	35.2929246	111.6159736
61	2.9913498	36.7284278	109.8675751	61	3.1054528	36.1592407	112.2908138	61	3.2238341	35.6031142	114.7785330
62	3.0455680	37.0567737	112.8589249	62	3.1636800	36.4753283	115.3962665	62	3.2862959	35.9074082	118.0023671
63	3.1007689	37.3792744	115.9044929	63	3.2229990	36.7855983	118.5599465	63	3.3499678	36.2059185	121.2886630
64	3.1569704	37.6960338	119.0052619	64	3.2834302	37.0901578	121.7829455	64	3.4149735	36.4987551	124.6386308
65	3.2141905	38.0071541	122.1622323	65	3.3449945	37.3891120	125.0663758	65	3.4810366	36.7860259	128.0535043
66	3.2724477	38.3127358	125.3764227	66	3.4077132	37.6825639	128.4113703	66	3.5484817	37.0678366	131.5345410
67	3.3317608	38.6128774	128.6488704	67	3.4716078	37.9706149	131.8190835	67	3.6172336	37.3442909	135.0830227
68	3.3921489	38.9076757	131.9806312	68	3.5387005	38.2533643	135.2906913	68	3.6873175	37.6154908	138.7002563
69	3.4536316	39.1972260	135.3727801	69	3.6030136	38.5309097	138.8273918	69	3.7587592	37.8815360	142.3875737
70	3.5162287	39.4816216	138.8264118	70	3.6705701	38.8033470	142.4304054	70	3.8315852	38.1425246	146.1463330
71	3.5799604	39.7609543	142.3426405	71	3.7393933	39.0707700	146.1009755	71	3.9059222	38.3985527	149.9779182
72	3.6448471	40.0353143	145.9226008	72	3.8095069	39.3332712	149.8403688	72	3.9814975	38.6497144	153.8837404
73	3.7109100	40.3047899	149.5674480	73	3.8809352	39.5909411	153.6498757	73	4.0583390	38.8961024	157.8652378
74	3.7781702	40.5694683	153.2783580	74	3.9537027	39.8438685	157.5308109	74	4.1372751	39.1378074	161.9238768
75	3.8466496	40.8294348	157.0565262	75	4.0278346	40.0921409	161.4845136	75	4.2174348	39.3749184	166.0611519
76	3.9163701	41.0847733	160.9031778	76	4.1033565	40.3358438	165.5123482	76	4.2991476	39.6075226	170.2785969
77	3.9873543	41.3355662	164.8195479	77	4.1802945	40.5750614	169.6157047	77	4.3824436	39.8357058	174.5777344
78	4.0596251	41.5818943	168.8069022	78	4.2586762	40.8098762	173.7959992	78	4.4673535	40.0595220	178.9601780
79	4.1332058	41.8238373	172.8665273	79	4.3385251	41.0403693	178.0546742	79	4.5539084	40.2791436	183.4275314
80	4.2081202	42.0614731	176.9997331	80	4.4198725	41.2666202	182.3931994	80	4.6421404	40.4945615	187.9814399
81	4.2843923	42.2948784	181.2078533	81	4.5027451	41.4887069	186.8130718	81	4.7320819	40.7058849	192.6235803
82	4.3620470	42.5241286	185.4922456	82	4.5871716	41.7067062	191.3158169	82	4.8237660	40.9131919	197.3556621
83	4.4411091	42.7492976	189.8542926	83	4.6731810	41.9206932	195.9029885	83	4.9172264	41.1165585	202.1794281
84	4.5216042	42.9704580	194.2954017	84	4.7603032	42.1307418	200.5761696	84	5.0124977	41.3160599	207.0966455
85	4.6035582	43.1876813	198.8170058	85	4.8500682	42.3369244	205.3369727	85	5.1095148	41.5117693	212.1091522
86	4.6869977	43.4010375	203.4205640	86	4.9410070	42.5393123	210.1670410	86	5.2086136	41.7037590	217.2187670
87	4.7719496	43.6105954	208.1075618	87	5.0333509	42.7379753	215.1280480	87	5.3095305	41.8920996	222.4273807
88	4.8584411	43.8164228	212.8795113	88	5.1280319	42.9329819	220.1616989	88	5.4124027	42.0768604	227.7369112
89	4.9465004	44.0185859	217.7379525	89	5.2241825	43.1243994	225.2897308	89	5.5172680	42.2581095	233.1493138
90	5.0361557	44.2171500	222.6844529	90	5.3221359	43.3122939	230.5139132	90	5.6241650	42.4359137	238.6665818
91	5.1274360	44.4121793	227.7206086	91	5.4219259	43.4967302	235.8360491	91	5.7331332	42.6103384	244.2907468
92	5.2203708	44.6037366	232.8480446	92	5.5235870	43.6777720	241.2579750	92	5.8442127	42.7814478	250.0238900
93	5.3149900	44.7918837	238.0684154	93	5.6271543	43.8554817	246.7815621	93	5.9574443	42.9493051	255.8680927
94	5.4113242	44.9766813	243.3834055	94	5.7326634	44.0299207	252.4087164	94	6.0728698	43.1139770	261.8255370
95	5.5094045	45.1581891	248.7947297	95	5.8401509	44.2011491	258.1413798	95	6.1905316	43.2755089	267.8984068
96	5.6092624	45.3364657	254.3041342	96	5.9496537	44.3692261	263.9815307	96	6.3104732	43.4339756	274.0889384
97	5.7109303	45.5115685	259.9133962	97	6.0612097	44.5342097	269.9311844	97	6.4327386	43.5894304	280.3994116
98	5.8144409	45.6835541	265.6243270	98	6.1748574	44.6961568	275.9923941	98	6.5573729	43.7419305	286.8321502
99	5.9198277	45.8524779	271.4387679	99	6.2906360	44.8551232	282.1672515	99	6.6844220	43.8915320	293.3895232
100	6.0271246	46.0183945	277.3585956	100	6.4085854	45.0111639	288.4578975	100	6.8139327	44.0382902	300.0739452

Table 1   371

M	C(7.25,M,4)	A(7.25,M,4)	S(7.25,M,4)	M	C(7.50,M,4)	A(7.50,M,4)	S(7.50,M,4)	M	C(7.75,M,4)	A(7.75,M,4)	S(7.75,M,4)
101	6.1363662	46.1813574	283.3857201	101	6.5287464	45.1643326	294.8664729	101	6.9459526	44.1822589	306.8878779
102	6.2475878	46.3414192	289.5220863	102	6.6511604	45.3146823	301.3952192	102	7.0805305	44.3234913	313.8338305
103	6.3608254	46.4986315	295.7696741	103	6.7753696	45.4622649	308.0463796	103	7.2177158	44.4620392	320.9143610
104	6.4761153	46.6530451	302.1304995	104	6.9029172	45.6071312	314.8222492	104	7.3575590	44.5979539	328.1320767
105	6.5934949	46.8047097	308.6066148	105	7.0323469	45.7493312	32?.7251664	105	7.5001117	44.7312852	335.4896357
106	6.7130020	46.9536744	315.2001097	106	7...42034	45.8889141	328.7575133	106	7.6454264	44.8620824	342.9897474
107	6.8346752	47.0999871	321.9131117	107	7.2985322	46.0259279	335.9217167	107	7.79?5565	44.9903935	350.6351738
108	6.9585536	47.2436951	328.74778E8	108	7.4353797	46.1604200	343.2202489	108	7.9445567	45.1162659	358.4287303
109	7.0843774	47.3848448	335.7063405	109	7.5747930	46.2924368	350.6556286	109	8.0984824	45.2397458	366.3732870
110	7.2130872	47.5234817	342.7910179	110	7.7168204	46.4220239	358.2304216	110	8.2553905	45.3608788	374.4717694
111	7.3438244	47.6596505	350.0041051	111	7.8615108	46.5492259	365.9472420	111	8.4153387	45.4797094	382.7271599
112	7.4769312	47.7933952	357.3479295	112	8.0089141	46.6740668	373.8087528	112	8.5783859	45.5962814	391.1424987
113	7.6124506	47.9247590	364.8248608	113	8.1590813	46.7966496	381.8176069	113	8.7445921	45.7106378	399.7208846
114	7.7504263	48.0537841	372.4373114	114	8.3120640	46.9169567	389.9767482	114	8.5140186	45.8228207	408.4654767
115	7.8903028	48.1805124	380.1877376	115	8.4679152	47.0350495	398.2888122	115	9.0867277	45.9328713	417.3794954
116	8.0333254	48.3049845	388.0786404	116	8.6265887	47.1509688	406.7567275	116	9.2627831	46.0408302	426.4662231
117	8.1795403	48.4272408	396.1125658	117	8.7384391	47.2647547	415.3834161	117	9.4422495	46.1467372	435.7290062
118	8.3277944	48.5473206	404.2921060	118	8.8532223	47.3764463	424.1718522	118	9.6251931	46.2506312	445.1712557
119	8.4787357	48.6652627	412.6199005	119	9.1210952	47.4860622	433.1250775	119	9.8116812	46.3525505	454.7964488
120	8.6324128	48.7811052	421.0986362	120	9.2921157	47.5937004	442.2461727	120	10.0017825	46.4525327	464.6081300
121	8.7888753	48.8948854	429.7310490	121	9.4663429	47.6993378	451.5382885	121	10.1955671	46.5506145	474.6099125
122	8.9481736	49.0066400	438.5199242	122	9.6438368	47.8030309	461.0046314	122	10.3931062	46.6468322	484.8054796
123	9.1103593	49.1164052	447.4680979	123	9.8246588	47.9048157	470.6484682	123	10.5944726	46.7412210	495.1985858
124	9.2754845	49.2242162	456.5784572	124	10.0088711	48.0047270	480.4731270	124	10.7997405	46.8338158	505.7930584
125	9.4436027	49.3301080	465.8539417	125	10.1965375	48.1027905	490.4819982	125	11.?°89855	46.9246507	516.5927989
126	9.6147660	49.4341147	475.2975444	126	10.3877226	48.1990670	500.6785356	126	11.2222846	47.0137591	527.6017844
127	9.7890357	49.5362698	484.9123124	127	10.5824924	48.2935627	511.0662582	127	11.4397163	47.1011739	538.8240690
128	9.9664619	49.6356063	494.7013481	128	10.7809141	48.3863192	521.6487505	128	11.6613609	47.1869272	550.2637853
129	10.1471041	49.7351566	504.6678100	129	10.9830562	48.4773696	532.4296646	129	11.8872997	47.2710506	561.9251482
130	10.3310203	49.8319525	514.8149141	130	11.1889885	48.5667422	543.4127209	130	12.1176162	47.3535750	573.8124459
131	10.5182701	49.9270251	525.1459344	131	11.3987821	48.6544708	554.6017094	131	12.3523950	47.4345310	585.9300620
132	10.7069137	50.0204053	535.6642045	132	11.6125092	48.7405849	566.0004914	132	12.5917226	47.5139483	598.2824570
133	10.9030128	50.1121231	546.3731182	133	11.8302038	48.8251140	577.6130007	133	12.8356872	47.5918560	610.8741790
134	11.1006299	50.2022080	557.2761310	134	12.0520608	48.9080873	589.4432445	134	13.0843787	47.6682831	623.7098669
135	11.3018288	50.2906893	568.3767609	135	12.2780370	48.9895336	601.4953053	135	13.3378885	47.7432574	636.7942456
136	11.5066745	50.3775954	579.6785897	136	12.5082502	49.0694808	613.7733423	136	13.5963101	47.8168068	650.1321341
137	11.7152329	50.4629543	591.1852642	137	12.7427799	49.1479586	626.2815925	137	13.8597306	47.8889582	663.7284442
138	11.9275715	50.5467937	602.9004971	138	12.5817070	49.2249881	639.0243723	138	14.1282711	47.9597383	677.5881828
139	12.1437588	50.6291405	614.8280686	139	13.2251140	49.3006010	652.0060793	139	14.4020063	48.0291731	691.7164539
140	12.3633644	50.7100214	626.9718274	140	13.4730849	49.3748239	665.2311933	140	14.6810452	48.0972881	706.1184602
141	12.5879594	50.7894624	639.3356918	141	13.7257052	49.4476799	678.7042762	141	14.9654904	48.1641085	720.7995054
142	12.8161162	50.8674891	651.9236512	142	13.9830622	49.5191950	692.4299835	142	15.2554468	48.2296589	735.7649958
143	13.0484083	50.9441268	664.7397674	143	14.2452446	49.5893938	706.4130457	143	15.5510211	48.2939633	751.0204426
144	13.2849107	51.0194002	677.7881757	144	14.5123430	49.6583007	720.6582903	144	15.8523221	48.3570456	766.5714637
145	13.?256997	51.0933335	69..0730864	145	14.7844494	49.7259393	735.1706333	145	16.1594609	48.4189288	782.4237859
146	13.7708530	51.1659501	704.5987861	146	15.0616578	49.7923331	749.9550827	146	16.4725504	48.4796359	798.5832457
147	14.0204497	51.2372751	718.3696391	147	15.3440630	49.8575049	765.0167405	147	16.7917061	48.5391891	815.0557971
148	14.2745704	51.3073297	732.3900888	148	15.6317651	49.9214772	780.3608044	148	17.1170454	48.5976104	831.8475032
149	14.5332970	51.3761372	746.6646592	149	15.9248607	49.9842721	795.9925695	149	17.4486882	48.6549213	848.9645486
150	14.7967130	51.4437198	761.1979562	150	16.2234518	50.0459112	811.9174302	150	17.7867565	48.7111429	866.4132368
151	15.0649034	51.5100992	775.9946692	151	16.5276416	50.1064159	828.1408820	151	18.1313749	48.7662959	884.1999933
152	15.3379548	51.5752970	791.0595726	152	16.8375348	50.1658070	844.6685236	152	18.4826703	48.8204006	902.3313682
153	15.6159552	51.6393341	806.3975273	153	17.1532386	50.2241051	861.5060584	153	18.8407720	48.8734770	920.8140384
154	15.8989944	51.7022311	822.0134825	154	17.4748618	50.2813301	878.6592970	154	19.2058120	48.9255446	939.6548105
155	16.1871627	51.7640085	837.9124769	155	17.8025155	50.3375020	896.1341589	155	19.5779246	48.9766225	958.8606224
156	16.4805560	51.8246860	854.0995406	156	18.1363127	50.3926400	913.9366744	156	19.9572469	49.0267297	978.4385470
157	16.7792661	51.8842834	870.5801966	157	18.4763685	50.4467631	932.0729870	157	20.3439185	49.0758844	998.3957939
158	17.0833903	51.9428198	887.3594627	158	18.8229004	50.4998902	950.5493556	158	20.7380820	49.1241049	1018.7397124
159	17.3930362	52.0003441	904.4426530	159	19.1757279	50.5520395	969.3721560	159	21.1398323	49.1714088	1039.4777944
160	17.7082753	52.0567849	921.8358797	160	19.5352728	50.6032289	988.5478840	160	21.5494675	49.2178137	1060.6176767
161	18.0292378	52.1122503	939.5441550	161	19.9015692	50.6534762	1008.0831568	161	21.9669884	49.2633365	1082.1671442
162	18.3550178	52.1667284	957.5733029	162	20.2747135	50.7027988	1027.9847160	162	22.3925988	49.3079941	1104.1341326
163	18.6847206	52.2202366	975.9294106	163	20.6548643	50.7512135	1048.2594295	163	22.8264555	49.3518030	1126.5267315
164	19.0274537	52.2727922	994.6181312	164	21.0421430	50.7987372	1068.9142938	164	23.2687180	49.3947791	1149.3531869
165	19.3723263	52.3244122	1013.6455849	165	21.4366832	50.8453862	1089.9564368	165	23.7195494	49.4369384	1172.6219050
166	19.7234497	52.3751133	1033.0179111	166	21.8386210	50.8911765	1111.3931201	166	24.1791157	49.4782966	1196.3414544
167	20.0809372	52.4249118	1052.7413608	167	22.2480952	50.9361243	1133.2317411	167	24.6475861	49.5188684	1220.5205701
168	20.4449042	52.4738237	1072.8222980	168	22.6652470	50.9802447	1155.4798363	168	25.1251331	49.5586691	1245.1681562
169	20.8154681	52.5218649	1093.2672022	169	23.0902203	51.0235531	1178.1450832	169	25.6119325	49.5977134	1270.2932892
170	21.1927484	52.5690509	1114.0826702	170	23.5231610	51.0660644	1201.2353036	170	26.1081637	49.6360156	1295.9052217
171	21.5766670	52.6153968	1135.2754187	171	23.9642213	51.1077933	1224.7584655	171	26.6140094	49.6735898	1322.0133854
172	21.9676477	52.6609177	1156.8522857	172	24.4135504	51.1487541	1248.7226868	172	27.1296558	49.7104499	1348.6273948
173	22.3651168	52.7056282	1178.8202334	173	24.8713045	51.1889611	1273.1362372	173	27.6552929	49.7466093	1375.7570506
174	22.7715026	52.7495427	1201.1863501	174	25.3376414	51.2284281	1298.0075417	174	28.1911157	49.7820815	1403.4123435
175	23.1842361	52.7926755	1223.9578527	175	25.8127222	51.2671686	1323.3451831	175	28.7373170	49.8168794	1431.6034577
176	23.6044504	52.8350403	1247.1420889	176	26.2967108	51.3051962	1349.1579093	176	29.2940865	49.8510160	1460.3407747
177	24.0322811	52.8766510	1270.7465393	177	26.7897741	51.3425239	1375.4546161	177	29.8616758	49.8845037	1489.6348773
178	24.4678662	52.9175210	1294.7788203	178	27.2920824	51.3791646	1402.2443902	178	30.4402458	49.9173550	1519.4965531
179	24.9113462	52.9576633	1319.2466865	179	27.8038089	51.4151309	1429.5364725	179	31.0300255	49.9495818	1549.9367988
180	25.???8644	52.9970911	134...1580327	180	28.3251303	51.4504352	1457.3402024	180	31.6312323	49.9811962	1580.9668243
181	25.8225663	53.0358169	1369.5208971	181	28.8562265	51.4850898	1485.6654117	181	32.2440874	50.0122096	1612.5980566
182	26.2906003	53.0738533	1395.3434634	182	29.3978608	51.5191065	1514.5216382	182	32.8688160	50.0426336	1644.8421440
183	26.7671174	53.1112125	1421.6340637	183	29.9484798	51.5524972	1543.9189190	183	33.5056499	50.0724793	1677.7109606
184	27.2522714	53.1479067	1448.4011811	184	30.5100138	51.5852733	1573.8673988	184	34.1543219	50.1017577	1711.2168105
185	27.7462189	53.1839477	1475.6534525	185	31.0820765	51.6174462	1604.3774125	185	34.8165715	50.1304797	1745.3714323
186	28.2491191	53.2193470	1503.3996714	186	31.6648655	51.6490269	1635.4594891	186	35.4911426	50.1586557	1780.1880039
187	28.7611344	53.2541162	1531.6487905	187	32.2585917	51.6800264	1667.1243545	187	36.1787835	50.1862962	1815.6791465
188	29.2824299	53.2882663	1560.4099249	188	32.6634301	51.7104554	1699.3829362	188	36.8797474	50.2134114	1851.8579300
189	29.8131740	53.3218086	1589.6923548	189	33.4796194	51.7403243	1732.2463663	189	37.5942925	50.2400112	1888.7376775
190	30.3535377	53.3547536	1619.5055288	190	34.1073623	51.7696435	1765.7259857	190	38.3226820	50.2661054	1926.3319700
191	30.9036956	53.3871122	1649.8590665	191	34.7468753	51.7984231	1799.8333480	191	39.0651839	50.2917036	1964.6546520
192	31.4633251	53.4188948	1680.7627621	192	35.3983792	51.8266729	1834.5802233	192	39.8220719	50.3168153	2003.7198359
193	32.0341069	53.4501115	1712.2265872	193	36.0620938	51.8544029	1869.9786025	193	40.5935245	50.3414497	2043.5419078
194	32.6147251	53.4807725	1744.2606942	194	36.7382632	51.8816225	1906.0407014	194	41.3801260	50.3656159	2084.1355323
195	33.2058670	53.5108876	1776.8754193	195	37.4271056	51.9083411	1942.7789646	195	42.1818659	50.3893228	2125.5156583
196	33.8077234	53.5404667	1810.0812863	196	38.1288639	51.9345679	1980.2060702	196	42.9991396	50.4125791	2167.6975242
197	34.4204883	53.5695192	1843.8890097	197	38.8437801	51.9603121	2018.3349341	197	43.8322479	50.4353933	2210.6966638
198	35.0443597	53.5980544	1878.3094980	198	39.5721009	51.9855824	2057.1787142	198	44.6814977	50.4577739	2254.5289117
199	35.6795387	53.6260817	1913.3538577	199	40.3140778	52.0103876	2096.7508151	199	45.5472017	50.4797292	2299.2104094
200	36.3262304	53.6536100	1949.0333964	200	41.0599668	52.0347363	213?.0648929	200	46.4296788	50.5012671	2344.7576112

M	C(8.00,M,4)	A(8.00,M,4)	S(8.00,M,4)	M	C(8.25,M,4)	A(8.25,M,4)	S(8.25,M,4)	M	C(8.50,M,4)	A(8.50,M,4)	S(8.50,M,4)
1/3	1.0066227	.3289569	.3311355	1/3	1.0068283	.3288223	.3310676	1/3	1.0070337	.3286878	.3309997
1	1.0200000	.9803922	1.0000000	1	1.0206250	.9797918	1.0000000	1	1.0212500	.9791922	1.0000000
2	1.0404000	1.9415609	2.0200000	2	1.0416754	1.9397838	2.0206250	2	1.0428516	1.9380095	2.0212500
3	1.0612080	2.8838833	3.0604000	3	1.0631599	2.8803760	3.0623004	3	1.0651143	2.8768759	3.0642016
4	1.0824322	3.8077287	4.1216080	4	1.0850876	3.8019606	4.1254603	4	1.0877480	3.7962065	4.1293158
5	1.1040808	4.7134595	5.2040402	5	1.1074676	4.7049216	5.2105460	5	1.1103626	4.6964078	5.2170638
6	1.1261624	5.6014309	6.3081210	6	1.1303091	5.5896353	6.3180155	6	1.1334684	5.5778779	6.3279264
7	1.1486857	6.4719911	7.4342834	7	1.1536217	6.4564706	7.4483246	7	1.1585759	6.4410065	7.4623949
8	1.1716594	7.3254814	8.5829691	8	1.1774151	7.3057887	8.6019463	8	1.1831956	7.2861753	8.6209707
9	1.1950926	8.1622367	9.7546284	9	1.2016993	8.1379436	9.7793614	9	1.2083385	8.1137579	9.8041664
10	1.2189944	8.9825050	10.9497210	10	1.2264844	8.9532822	10.9810607	10	1.2340157	8.9241204	11.0125049
11	1.2433743	9.7868480	12.1687154	11	1.2517806	9.7521442	12.2075451	11	1.2602386	9.7176209	12.2465206
12	1.2682418	10.5753412	13.4120897	12	1.2775986	10.5348627	13.4593257	12	1.2870186	10.4946104	13.5067592
13	1.2936066	11.3483737	14.6803315	13	1.3039491	11.3017638	14.7369243	13	1.3143678	11.2554325	14.7937778
14	1.3194788	12.1062498	15.9739382	14	1.3308430	12.0531672	16.0408734	14	1.3422981	12.0004235	16.1081456
15	1.3458683	12.8492635	17.2924169	15	1.3582917	12.7893861	17.3717164	15	1.3708219	12.7299129	17.4504437
16	1.3727857	13.5777093	18.6392853	16	1.3863064	13.5107274	18.7300081	16	1.3999519	13.4442231	18.8212656
17	1.4002414	14.2918719	20.0120710	17	1.4148990	14.2174916	20.1163145	17	1.4297009	14.1436701	20.2212175
18	1.4282462	14.9920312	21.4123124	18	1.4440813	14.9099734	21.5312135	18	1.4600820	14.8285632	21.6509184
19	1.4568112	15.6784620	22.8405586	19	1.4738655	15.5884614	22.9752947	19	1.4911088	15.4992051	23.1110004
20	1.4859474	16.3514333	24.2973698	20	1.5042639	16.2532384	24.4491602	20	1.5227948	16.1558923	24.6021092
21	1.5156663	17.0112092	25.7833172	21	1.5352894	16.9045814	25.9534241	21	1.5551542	16.7989154	26.1249040
22	1.5459797	17.6580482	27.2989835	22	1.5669547	17.5427619	27.4887135	22	1.5882012	17.4285585	27.6800582
23	1.5768993	18.2922041	28.8449632	23	1.5992732	18.1680460	29.0556682	23	1.6219505	18.0451001	29.2682594
24	1.6084373	18.9139256	30.4218625	24	1.6322582	18.7806941	30.6549414	24	1.6564170	18.6488129	30.8902100
25	1.6406060	19.5234565	32.0302997	25	1.6659235	19.3809618	32.2871995	25	1.6916158	19.2399636	32.5466269
26	1.6734181	20.1210358	33.6709057	26	1.7002832	19.9690991	33.9531230	26	1.7275627	19.8188138	34.2382427
27	1.7068865	20.7068978	35.3443238	27	1.7353515	20.5453513	35.6534062	27	1.7642734	20.3856194	35.9658054
28	1.7410242	21.2812723	37.0512103	28	1.7711431	21.1099584	37.3887577	28	1.8017642	20.9406310	37.7300788
29	1.7758447	21.8443847	38.7922345	29	1.8076730	21.6631558	39.1599008	29	1.8400517	21.4840940	39.5318429
30	1.8113616	22.3964555	40.5680792	30	1.8449562	22.2051741	40.9675738	30	1.8791528	22.0162487	41.3718906
31	1.8475888	22.9377015	42.3794408	31	1.8830084	22.7362391	42.8125300	31	1.9190848	22.5373305	43.2510474
32	1.8845405	23.4683348	44.2270296	32	1.9218455	23.2565723	44.6955304	32	1.9598653	23.0475696	45.1701321
33	1.9222314	23.9885635	46.1115702	33	1.9614835	23.7663905	46.6173839	33	2.0015124	23.5471918	47.1299974
34	1.9606760	24.4985917	48.0338016	34	2.0019391	24.2659052	48.5788675	34	2.0440446	24.0364179	49.1315099
35	1.9998896	24.9986193	49.9944777	35	2.0432291	24.7553276	50.5808066	35	2.0874805	24.5154643	51.1755545
36	2.0398873	25.4888425	51.9943372	36	2.0853707	25.2348586	52.6240357	36	2.1318395	24.9845423	53.2630350
37	2.0806851	25.9694534	54.0342546	37	2.1283815	25.7046992	54.7094065	37	2.1771411	25.4438607	55.3948745
38	2.1222988	26.4406406	56.1149396	38	2.1722746	26.1650451	56.8377880	38	2.2234053	25.8936213	57.5720156
39	2.1647448	26.9025888	58.2372384	39	2.2170826	26.6166883	59.0100674	39	2.2706527	26.3340233	59.7954209
40	2.2080397	27.3554792	60.4019832	40	2.2628100	27.0580167	61.2271500	40	2.3189401	26.7652615	62.0660736
41	2.2522005	27.7994894	62.6100229	41	2.3094804	27.4910145	63.4899500	41	2.3681808	27.1875265	64.3849777
42	2.2972445	28.2347936	64.8622233	42	2.3571135	27.9152623	65.7994404	42	2.4185046	27.6010052	66.7531585
43	2.3431894	28.6615623	67.1594678	43	2.4057289	28.3309367	68.1565539	43	2.4698978	28.0058802	69.1716631
44	2.3900531	29.0799631	69.5022657	44	2.4553471	28.7382111	70.5622828	44	2.5223832	28.4023307	71.6415609
45	2.4378542	29.4901599	71.8927103	45	2.5059886	29.1372552	73.0176299	45	2.5759838	28.7905319	74.1639441
46	2.4866113	29.8923136	74.3305645	46	2.5576746	29.5282353	75.5236185	46	2.6307235	29.1706554	76.7399279
47	2.5363435	30.2865819	76.8171758	47	2.6104267	29.9113145	78.0812931	47	2.6866263	29.5428695	79.3706514
48	2.5870704	30.6731196	79.3535193	48	2.6642667	30.2865623	80.6917198	48	2.7437172	29.9073385	82.0572777
49	2.6388118	31.0520780	81.9405897	49	2.7192172	30.6544052	83.3559865	49	2.8020211	30.2642238	84.8009949
50	2.6915880	31.4236059	84.5794015	50	2.7753017	31.0147264	86.0752037	50	2.8615641	30.6136830	87.6030160
51	2.7454198	31.7878498	87.2709895	51	2.8325417	31.3677663	88.8505048	51	2.9223723	30.9558707	90.4645801
52	2.8003282	32.1449499	90.0164093	52	2.8909628	31.7136718	91.6830465	52	2.9844727	31.2909383	93.3869524
53	2.8563348	32.4950489	92.8167375	53	2.9505889	32.0525872	94.5740093	53	3.0478928	31.6190338	96.3714252
54	2.9134614	32.8382803	95.6730723	54	3.0114448	32.3846537	97.5245983	54	3.1126605	31.9403024	99.4193180
55	2.9717307	33.1747875	98.5865337	55	3.0735559	32.7100097	100.5360431	55	3.1783045	32.2548861	102.5319785
56	3.0311653	33.5046936	101.5582868	56	3.1369480	33.0287909	103.6095990	56	3.2463541	32.5629239	105.7107830
57	3.0917886	33.8281310	104.5894297	57	3.2016475	33.3411301	106.7465470	57	3.3153392	32.8645522	108.9571312
58	3.1536244	34.1452205	107.6812583	58	3.2676815	33.6471575	109.9481945	58	3.3857901	33.1599042	112.2724763
59	3.2166969	34.4561044	110.8348427	59	3.3350774	33.9470006	113.2158760	59	3.4577382	33.4491106	115.6582665
60	3.2810308	34.7608687	114.0515305	60	3.4038634	34.2407844	116.5509535	60	3.5312151	33.7322993	119.1160046
61	3.3466514	35.0596928	117.3325703	61	3.4740681	34.5286314	119.9548169	61	3.6062539	34.0095954	122.6472197
62	3.4135844	35.3526400	120.6792217	62	3.5457208	34.8106615	123.4288850	62	3.6828863	34.2811215	126.2534731
63	3.4818561	35.6398431	124.0928062	63	3.6188512	35.0869923	126.9746057	63	3.7611476	34.5469978	129.9363594
64	3.5514932	35.9214148	127.5746623	64	3.6934901	35.3577389	130.5934570	64	3.8410720	34.8073418	133.6975071
65	3.6225231	36.1974585	131.1261555	65	3.7696683	35.6230142	134.2869471	65	3.9226948	35.0622686	137.5385791
66	3.6949736	36.4681035	134.7486786	66	3.8474177	35.8829288	138.0566153	66	4.0060521	35.3118909	141.4612739
67	3.7688730	36.7334348	138.4436522	67	3.9267707	36.1375910	141.9040302	67	4.0911807	35.5563192	145.4673624
68	3.8442505	36.9935635	142.2125253	68	4.0077603	36.3871069	145.8308037	68	4.1781183	35.7956613	149.5585067
69	3.9211355	37.2485917	146.0567758	69	4.0904024	36.6315806	149.8385640	69	4.2669033	36.0300233	153.7366250
70	3.9995582	37.4986193	149.9779113	70	4.1747853	36.8711139	153.9289844	70	4.3575750	36.2595088	158.0035282
71	4.0795494	37.7437444	153.9774695	71	4.2609003	37.1058066	158.1037697	71	4.4501734	36.4842191	162.3611032
72	4.1611404	37.9840631	158.0570189	72	4.3487711	37.3357565	162.3646600	72	4.5447396	36.7042537	166.8112767
73	4.2443532	38.2196697	162.2181593	73	4.4384565	37.5610598	166.7134311	73	4.6413154	36.9197009	171.3560163
74	4.3292505	38.4506563	166.4625225	74	4.5300079	37.7818099	171.1518956	74	4.7399433	37.1306829	175.9973317
75	4.4158355	38.6771143	170.7917729	75	4.6234393	37.9980091	175.6819035	75	4.8406671	37.3372660	180.7372750
76	4.5041522	38.8991317	175.2076084	76	4.7187977	38.2100175	180.3053427	76	4.9435313	37.5395505	185.5779420
77	4.5942352	39.1167958	179.7117608	77	4.8161229	38.4176534	185.0241404	77	5.0485313	37.7376260	190.5214733
78	4.6861199	39.3301919	184.3059958	78	4.9154554	38.6210934	189.8402633	78	5.1556637	37.9315799	195.5700546
79	4.7798423	39.5394038	188.9922067	79	5.0168363	38.8204222	194.7557188	79	5.2654258	38.1214981	200.7259183
80	4.8754392	39.7445136	193.7719580	80	5.1203090	39.0157229	199.7725555	80	5.3773161	38.3074645	205.9913441
81	4.9729479	39.9456015	198.6473972	81	5.2259153	39.2070769	204.8928645	81	5.4915840	38.4895613	211.3686601
82	5.0724069	40.1427466	203.6203452	82	5.3337998	39.3945640	210.1187798	82	5.6082802	38.6678691	216.8602442
83	5.1738550	40.3360261	208.6927521	83	5.4437074	39.5782624	215.4524796	83	5.7274561	38.8424665	222.4685244
84	5.2773321	40.5255158	213.8666071	84	5.5559839	39.7582485	220.8961870	84	5.8491646	39.0134312	228.1959805
85	5.3828788	40.7112900	219.1439393	85	5.6705760	39.9345497	226.4521709	85	5.9734593	39.1808384	234.0451451
86	5.4905364	40.8934215	224.5268180	86	5.7875317	40.1073826	232.1227469	86	6.1003954	39.3447622	240.0186044
87	5.6003471	41.0719819	230.0173544	87	5.9068995	40.2766762	237.9102786	87	6.2300288	39.5052751	246.1189998
88	5.7123540	41.2470411	235.6177015	88	6.0287293	40.4425486	243.8171781	88	6.3624169	39.6624481	252.3490205
89	5.8266011	41.4186677	241.3300555	89	6.1530718	40.6050061	249.8459074	89	6.4976182	39.8163506	258.7114454
90	5.9431331	41.5869291	247.1566567	90	6.2799790	40.7643053	255.9989792	90	6.6355926	39.9670508	265.2090636
91	6.0619958	41.7518913	253.0997698	91	6.4095035	40.9203236	262.2789582	91	6.7767011	40.1146152	271.8447562
92	6.1832357	41.9136189	259.1617856	92	6.5416995	41.0731891	268.6884617	92	6.9207060	40.2591092	278.6214573
93	6.3069004	42.0721754	265.3450213	93	6.6766221	41.2229654	275.2301612	93	7.0677710	40.4005965	285.5421633
94	6.4330384	42.2276230	271.6519218	94	6.8143274	41.3697105	281.9067833	94	7.2179651	40.5391398	292.6099343
95	6.5616992	42.3800225	278.0849602	95	6.9548729	41.5134991	288.7211107	95	7.3713428	40.6740003	299.8278954
96	6.6929332	42.5294338	284.6466594	96	7.0983172	41.6543776	295.6759836	96	7.5279838	40.8076379	307.1992382
97	6.8267919	42.6759155	291.3395926	97	7.2447200	41.7924091	302.7743008	97	7.6879535	40.9377116	314.7272220
98	6.9633277	42.8195250	298.1663685	98	7.3941423	41.9276513	310.0190208	98	7.8513255	41.0650787	322.4151755
99	7.1025943	42.9603186	305.1297122	99	7.5466465	42.0601605	317.4131631	99	8.0181631	41.1897955	330.2664979
100	7.2446461	43.0983516	312.2323064	100	7.7022961	42.1899919	324.9598096	100	8.1885491	41.3119173	338.2846610

M	C(8.00,M,4)	A(8.00,M,4)	S(8.00,M,4)	M	C(8.25,M,4)	A(8.25,M,4)	S(8.25,M,4)	M	C(8.50,M,4)	A(8.50,M,4)	S(8.50,M,4)
101	7.3895391	43.2336780	319.4769525	101	7.8611559	42.3171997	332.6621057	101	8.3625557	41.4314979	346.4732101
102	7.5373298	43.3663510	326.8664916	102	8.0232923	42.4418368	340.5232616	102	8.5402600	41.5485904	354.8357658
103	7.6880764	43.4964226	334.4038214	103	8.1887727	42.5639552	348.5465539	103	8.7217406	41.6632464	363.3760258
104	7.8418380	43.6239437	342.0918979	104	8.3576661	42.6836059	356.7353268	104	8.9070775	41.7755167	372.0977664
105	7.9986747	43.7489644	349.9337358	105	8.5300430	42.8008386	365.0929927	105	9.0963529	41.8854508	381.0048439
106	8.1586482	43.8715337	357.9324106	106	8.7.59751	42.9157022	373.6233073	106	9.2896504	41.9930975	390.1011969
107	8.3218212	43.9916997	366.0910588	107	8.8855359	43.0282447	382.3290108	107	9.4870555	42.0985043	399.3908°73
108	8.4882576	44.1095095	374.4128800	108	9.0688000	43.1385128	391.2145466	108	9.6886554	42.2017178	408.8779028
109	8.6580228	44.2250094	382.9011376	109	9.2558440	43.2465527	400.2833467	109	9.8945394	42.3027836	418.5665583
110	8.8311832	44.3382445	391.5591604	110	9.4467458	43.3524092	409.5391907	110	10.1047983	42.4017465	428.4610977
111	9.0078069	44.4492593	400.3903436	111	9.6415850	43.4561266	418.9859365	111	10.3195253	42.4986502	438.5658960
112	9.1879630	44.5580973	409.3981504	112	9.8404426	43.5577481	428.6275215	112	10.5388152	42.5935375	448.8854213
113	9.3717223	44.6648013	418.5861135	113	10.0434018	43.6573159	438.4679641	113	10.7627650	42.6864505	459.4242365
114	9.5591567	44.7694130	427.9578357	114	10.2505469	43.7548717	448.5113659	114	10.5914738	42.7774301	470.1870016
115	9.7503399	44.8719736	437.5169925	115	10.4619645	43.8504560	458.7619128	115	11.2250426	42.8665166	481.1784754
116	9.9453467	44.9725231	447.2673323	116	10.6777425	43.9441088	469.2238773	116	11.4635748	42.9537494	492.4035160
117	10.1442536	45.0711011	457.2126790	117	10.8979709	44.0358690	479.9016198	117	11.7071757	43.0391671	503.8670927
118	10.3471387	45.1677462	467.3569326	118	11.1227416	44.1257740	490.7995907	118	11.9559532	43.1228074	515.5742685
119	10.5540814	45.2624962	477.7040712	119	11.3521481	44.2138639	501.9223323	119	12.2100172	43.2047074	527.5302217
120	10.7651631	45.3553285	488.2581527	120	11.5862862	44.3001729	513.2744804	120	12.4694801	43.2849032	539.7402399
121	10.9804663	45.4464593	499.0233157	121	11.8252533	44.3847377	524.8607665	121	12.7344565	43.3634303	552.2097190
122	11.2000757	45.5357444	510.0037821	122	12.0691492	44.4675935	536.6860199	122	13.0050637	43.4403234	564.9441755
123	11.4240772	45.6232788	521.2038577	123	12.3180754	44.5487751	548.7551690	123	13.2814213	43.5156166	577.9492393
124	11.6525587	45.7090969	532.6279349	124	12.5721357	44.6283160	561.0732444	124	13.5636516	43.5893431	591.2306606
125	11.8856099	45.7932322	544.2804936	125	12.8314360	44.7062496	573.6453601	125	13.°.18791	43.6615354	604.7943122
126	12.1233221	45.8757179	556.1661035	126	13.0960843	44.7826083	586.4768161	126	14.1462316	43.7322256	618.6461913
127	12.3657885	45.9565861	568.2894256	127	13.3661911	44.8574240	599.5729004	127	14.4469390	43.8014449	632.7924229
128	12.6131043	46.0358688	580.6552141	128	13.6418688	44.9307277	612.9390015	128	14.7533343	43.8692239	647.2392619
129	12.8653664	46.1135968	593.2683184	129	13.9232323	45.0025501	626.5809603	129	15.0673533	43.9355926	661.9930963
130	13.1226737	46.1898008	606.1336048	130	14.2103990	45.0729211	640.5041926	130	15.3675346	44.0005802	677.0604496
131	13.3851272	46.2645106	619.2563505	131	14.5034885	45.1418700	654.7145916	131	15.7145197	44.0642157	692.4479341
132	13.6528297	46.3377555	632.6414657	132	14.8025229	45.2094256	669.2180801	132	16.0484532	44.1265270	708.1625038
133	13.9258863	46.4095642	646.2943154	133	15.1079270	45.2756161	684.0207030	133	16.3894829	44.1875417	724.2109570
134	14.2044041	46.4799649	660.2202017	134	15.4195280	45.3404689	699.1286300	134	16.7377594	44.2472868	740.6004399
135	14.4884921	46.5489852	674.4246058	135	15.7375558	45.4040112	714.5481560	135	17.0934368	44.3057888	757.3381993
136	14.7782620	46.6166522	688.9130979	136	16.0621429	45.4662693	730.2857138	136	17.4566723	44.3630735	774.4316360
137	15.0738272	46.6829923	703.6913599	137	16.3934246	45.5272694	746.3478566	137	17.8276266	44.4191562	791.6883083
138	15.3753038	46.7480317	718.7651871	138	16.7315389	45.5870368	762.7412812	138	18.2064636	44.4740918	809.7159349
139	15.6828098	46.8117958	734.1404909	139	17.0766269	45.6455964	779.4728202	139	18.5933510	44.5278745	827.9223085
140	15.9964660	46.8743096	749.8233007	140	17.4288324	45.7020725	796.5494471	140	18.9884597	44.5605380	846.5157495
141	16.3163954	46.9355976	765.8197667	141	17.7883020	45.7591893	813.9782795	141	19.3919645	44.6321058	865.5042092
142	16.6427233	46.9956839	782.1361621	142	18.1551858	45.8142699	831.7665815	142	19.8040437	44.6826005	884.8961737
143	16.9755777	47.0545921	798.7788854	143	18.5296305	45.8682375	849.9217673	143	20.2248796	44.7320446	904.7002174
144	17.3150893	47.1123452	815.7544631	144	18.9118102	45.9211146	868.4514037	144	20.6546583	44.7804598	924.9250970
145	17.°13911	47.1689659	833.0695524	145	19.3018663	45.9729230	887.3632139	145	21.0935698	44.8278675	945.5797941
146	18.0146189	47.2244763	850.7309434	146	19.6999673	46.0236845	906.6650803	146	21.5418082	44.8742890	966.6733252
147	18.3749113	47.2788984	868.7455623	147	20.1062791	46.0734202	926.3650476	147	21.9995716	44.9197444	988.2153133
148	18.7424095	47.3322533	887.1204736	148	20.5209711	46.1221509	946.4713267	148	22.4670625	44.9642540	1010.2147050
149	19.1172577	47.3845621	905.8628831	149	20.9442162	46.1698967	966.9922978	149	22.9444876	45.0078374	1032.6817675
150	19.4996028	47.4358452	924.9801408	150	21.3761906	46.2166778	987.9365140	150	23.4320579	45.0505140	1055.6262551
151	19.8895949	47.4861227	944.4797436	151	21.8170746	46.2625134	1009.3127046	151	23.9295892	45.0923026	1079.0583130
152	20.2873868	47.5354144	964.3693385	152	22.2670517	46.3074228	1031.1297792	152	24.4385014	45.1332216	1102.9883022
153	20.6931345	47.5837396	984.6567253	153	22.7263097	46.3514242	1053.3968309	153	24.9578196	45.1732892	1127.4268036
154	21.1069972	47.6311173	1005.3498598	154	23.1950398	46.3945374	1076.1231406	154	25.4881733	45.2125231	1152.3846232
155	21.5291372	47.6775659	1026.4568570	155	23.6734375	46.4367788	1099.3181804	155	26.0297970	45.2509406	1177.8727965
156	21.9597199	47.7231039	1047.9859942	156	24.1617021	46.4781666	1122.9916179	156	26.5829301	45.2885588	1203.9025935
157	22.3989143	47.7677489	1069.9457141	157	24.6600373	46.5187168	1147.1533200	157	27.1478174	45.3253941	1230.4855236
158	22.8468926	47.8115185	1092.3446284	158	25.1686605	46.5584500	1171.8133573	158	27.7247085	45.3614830	1257.6333410
159	23.3038304	47.8544299	1115.1915210	159	25.6877539	46.5973791	1196.9820078	159	28.3130586	45.3967814	1285.3580405
160	23.7699071	47.8964999	1138.4953515	160	26.2175639	46.6355214	1222.6697617	160	28.9155281	45.4313649	131° 6719081
161	24.2453052	47.9377450	1162.2652565	161	26.7583011	46.6728930	1248.8873256	161	29.°9831	45.4652288	1342.5804362
162	24.7372113	47.9781814	1186.5105537	162	27.3101911	46.7095094	1275.6456267	162	30.1574952	45.4983881	1372.1174193
163	25.2248155	48.0178249	1211.2407750	163	27.8734638	46.7453858	1302.9558178	163	30.7983420	45.5308573	1402.2944471
164	25.7293118	48.0566911	1236.4655906	164	28.4433540	46.7805372	1330.8292816	164	31.4528067	45.5626510	1433.0732564
165	26.2439981	48.0947952	1262.1949024	165	29.0351013	46.8149783	1359.2776355	165	32.1211789	45.5937831	1464.5260672
166	26.7637760	48.1321521	1288.4388005	166	29.6339502	46.8487234	1388.3127368	166	32.8037539	45.6242674	1496.6472420
167	27.3041516	48.1687766	1315.2075735	167	30.2451505	46.8817865	1417.9466870	167	33.5008337	45.6541174	1529.4509960
168	27.8502346	48.2046829	1342.5117281	168	30.8669567	46.9141815	1448.1918375	168	34.2127264	45.6833463	1562.9516297
169	28.4072393	48.2398852	1370.3619627	169	31.5056289	46.9459219	1479.0607942	169	34.9397469	45.7119670	1597.1645561
170	28.9753841	48.2743973	1398.7692020	170	32.1554325	46.9770208	1510.5664231	170	35.6822165	45.7399922	1632.1043029
171	29.5548918	48.3082326	1427.7445661	171	32.8183383	47.0074913	1542.7218556	171	36.4404636	45.7674342	1667.7865194
172	30.1459896	48.3414045	1457.2994778	172	33.4955227	47.0373461	1575.5404939	172	37.2148234	45.7943052	1704.2269083
173	30.7489094	48.3739260	1487.4454874	173	34.1853679	47.0665975	1609.0360166	173	38.0056384	45.8206171	1741.4418064
174	31.3638876	48.4058098	1518.1943768	174	34.8914617	47.0952578	1643.2223845	174	38.8132582	45.8463815	1779.4444044
175	31.9911653	48.4370684	1549.5582644	175	35.6110981	47.1233389	1678.1138462	175	39.6380400	45.8716098	1818.2607031
176	32.6309986	48.4677142	1581.5494297	176	36.3455770	47.1508526	1713.7249444	176	40.4803483	45.8963131	1857.8987637
177	33.2836084	48.4977590	1614.1804183	177	37.0952045	47.1778103	1750.0765214	177	41.3405557	45.9205025	1898.3790914
178	33.9492806	48.5272147	1647.4640267	178	37.8602931	47.2042231	1787.1657259	178	42.2190426	45.9441885	1939.7196472
179	34.6282662	48.5560928	1681.4133073	179	38.6411617	47.2301023	1825.0260191	179	43.1161972	45.9673816	1981.9386897
180	35.°°08315	48.5844047	1716.0415735	180	39.4381356	47.2554585	1863.6671808	180	44.0324164	45.9900921	2025.0548869
181	36.0272481	48.6121615	1751.3624050	181	40.2515472	47.2803022	1903.1053164	181	44.9681052	46.0123301	2069.0873033
182	36.7477293	48.6393740	1787.3896532	182	41.0817345	47.3046439	1943.3568876	182	45.9235775	46.0341054	2114.0554086
183	37.4827490	48.6660530	1824.1374463	183	41.9290462	47.3284938	1984.4385990	183	46.8995556	46.0554275	2159.9790861
184	38.2324040	48.6922088	1861.6201952	184	42.7938327	47.3518616	2026.3676451	184	47.8961712	46.0763060	2206.8786417
185	38.9970520	48.7178517	1899.8525992	185	43.6764555	47.3747572	2069.1614779	185	48.9139648	46.0967501	2254.7748129
186	39.7769931	48.7429919	1938.8496512	186	44.5772824	47.3971902	2112.8379334	186	49.9533866	46.1167688	2303.6887777
187	40.5725329	48.7676391	1978.6266443	187	45.4966889	47.4191698	2157.4152158	187	51.0146961	46.1363709	2353.6421643
188	41.3839836	48.7918031	2019.1991772	188	46.4350581	47.4407053	2202.9119047	188	52.0989626	46.1555661	2404.6570604
189	42.2116533	48.8154932	2060.5831608	189	47.3927812	47.4618055	2249.3469628	189	53.2060655	46.1743600	2456.7560229
190	43.0558965	48.8387188	2102.7948241	190	48.3702573	47.4824794	2296.7397440	190	54.3365944	46.1927637	2509.9620885
191	43.9170145	48.8614890	2145.8507206	191	49.3678938	47.5027355	2345.1100012	191	55.4913492	46.2107846	2564.2987829
192	44.7953548	48.8838128	2189.7677351	192	50.3861066	47.5225822	2394.4778951	192	56.6705404	46.2284304	2619.7901321
193	45.6912569	48.9056988	2234.5630898	193	51.4253201	47.5420279	2444.8640017	193	57.8747894	46.2457091	2676.4606725
194	46.6050871	48.9271557	2280.2543517	194	52.4859673	47.5610806	2496.2893218	194	59.1046286	46.2626282	2734.3354619
195	47.5371888	48.9481918	2326.8594388	195	53.5684904	47.5797483	2548.7752891	195	60.3606020	46.2791953	2793.4400905
196	48.4879326	48.9688155	2374.3966276	196	54.6733405	47.5980387	2602.3437795	196	61.6432648	46.2954177	2853.8006925
197	49.4576913	48.9890348	2422.8845602	197	55.8009782	47.6159596	2657.0171200	197	62.9531842	46.3113025	2915.4439573
198	50.4468451	49.0088577	2472.3422515	198	56.9518733	47.6335182	2712.8180982	198	64.2909393	46.3268568	2978.3971415
199	51.4557820	49.0282918	2522.7890966	199	58.1265057	47.6507221	2769.7699716	199	65.6571218	46.3420875	3042.6880808
200	52.4848976	49.0473449	2574.2448786	200	59.°253649	47.6675783	282°.8964773	200	67.0523356	46.3570012	3108.3452026

Table 1

M	C(8.75,M,4)	A(8.75,M,4)	S(8.75,M,4)	M	C(9.00,M,4)	A(9.00,M,4)	S(9.00,M,4)	M	C(9.25,M,4)	A(9.25,M,4)	S(9.25,M,4)
1/3	1.0072391	.3285534	.3309319	1/3	1.0074444	.3284192	.3308641	1/3	1.0076497	.3282851	.3307964
1	1.0218750	.9785933	1.0000000	1	1.0225000	.9779951	1.0000000	1	1.0231250	.9773977	1.0000000
2	1.0442285	1.9362381	2.0218750	2	1.0455063	1.9344695	2.0225000	2	1.0467848	1.9327039	2.0231250
3	1.0670710	2.8733828	3.0661035	3	1.0690301	2.8698969	3.0680063	3	1.0709917	2.8664180	3.0699098
4	1.0904132	3.7904664	4.1331745	4	1.0930833	3.7847402	4.1370364	4	1.0957583	3.7790280	4.1409014
5	1.1142660	4.6879182	5.2235877	5	1.1176777	4.6794525	5.2301197	5	1.1210978	4.6710108	5.2366598
6	1.1386405	5.5661584	6.3378537	6	1.1428254	5.5544768	6.3477974	6	1.1470231	5.5428328	6.3577575
7	1.1635483	6.4255985	7.4764943	7	1.1685390	6.4102463	7.4906228	7	1.1735481	6.3949496	7.5047807
8	1.1890009	7.2666407	8.6400426	8	1.1948311	7.2471846	8.6591619	8	1.2006864	7.2278066	8.6783287
9	1.2150103	8.0896790	9.8290435	9	1.2217148	8.0657062	9.8539930	9	1.2284522	8.0418391	9.8790151
10	1.2415887	8.8950987	11.0440538	10	1.2492034	8.8662163	11.0757078	10	1.2568602	8.8374725	11.1074673
11	1.2687484	9.6832770	12.2856425	11	1.2773105	9.6491113	12.3249113	11	1.2859251	9.6151228	12.3643275
12	1.2965023	10.4545830	13.5543909	12	1.3060500	10.4147788	13.6022218	12	1.3156621	10.3751964	13.6502526
13	1.3248633	11.2093779	14.8508932	13	1.3354361	11.1635979	14.9082718	13	1.3460868	11.1180905	14.9659147
14	1.3530447	11.9480150	16.1757565	14	1.3654834	11.8959392	16.2437079	14	1.3772150	11.8441936	16.3120014
15	1.3834600	12.6708404	17.5296012	15	1.3962058	12.6121655	17.6091913	15	1.4090631	12.5538850	17.6892165
16	1.4137232	13.3781924	18.9130612	16	1.4276215	13.3126313	19.0053981	16	1.4416477	13.2475357	19.0982796
17	1.4446484	14.0704024	20.3267844	17	1.4597429	13.9976834	20.4330196	17	1.4749858	13.9255083	20.5399273
18	1.4762501	14.7477944	21.7714329	18	1.4925872	14.6676611	21.8927625	18	1.5090949	14.5881572	22.0149131
19	1.5085431	15.4106856	23.2476829	19	1.5261704	15.3228959	23.3853497	19	1.5439927	15.2358287	23.5240080
20	1.5415424	16.0593866	24.7562260	20	1.5605092	15.9637124	24.9115200	20	1.5795975	15.8688612	25.0680007
21	1.5752637	16.6942009	26.2977685	21	1.5956207	16.5904277	26.4720292	21	1.6162280	16.4875858	26.6476982
22	1.6097226	17.3154260	27.8730321	22	1.6315221	17.2033523	28.0676499	22	1.6536033	17.0923258	28.2639262
23	1.6449353	17.9233526	29.4827547	23	1.6682314	17.8027895	29.6991720	23	1.6918429	17.6833972	29.9175295
24	1.6809182	18.5182656	31.1276900	24	1.7057666	18.3890362	31.3674034	24	1.7309667	18.2611091	31.6093724
25	1.7176883	19.1004434	32.8086082	25	1.7441463	18.9623326	33.0731700	25	1.7709953	18.8257633	33.3403391
26	1.7552627	19.6701586	34.5262065	26	1.7833896	19.5231126	34.8173163	26	1.8119496	19.3776550	35.1113345
27	1.7936591	20.2276782	36.2815592	27	1.8235159	20.0715038	36.6007059	27	1.8538509	19.9170727	36.9232941
28	1.8328954	20.7732631	38.0752183	28	1.8645450	20.6078276	38.4242218	28	1.8967212	20.4442983	38.7771350
29	1.8729900	21.3071687	39.9081138	29	1.9064973	21.1323498	40.2887658	29	1.9405829	20.9596074	40.6738563
30	1.9139616	21.8296453	41.7811037	30	1.9493934	21.6453298	42.1952640	30	1.9854589	21.4632693	42.6144392
31	1.9558296	22.3409372	43.6950654	31	1.9932548	22.1470218	44.1446575	31	2.0313726	21.9555473	44.5998981
32	1.9966133	22.8412842	45.6508949	32	2.0381030	22.6376742	46.1379123	32	2.0783481	22.4356986	46.6312707
33	2.0423330	23.3309203	47.6495083	33	2.0838603	23.1175298	48.1760153	33	2.1264099	22.9069748	48.7096189
34	2.0870090	23.8100749	49.6918413	34	2.1308495	23.5868262	50.2599756	34	2.1755832	23.3666217	50.8360288
35	2.1326624	24.2789724	51.7789503	35	2.1787936	24.0457958	52.3908251	35	2.2258935	23.8158795	53.0116120
36	2.1793143	24.7378323	53.9115126	36	2.2278164	24.4946658	54.5696187	36	2.2773673	24.2549830	55.2375055
37	2.2269868	25.1868695	56.0908270	37	2.2779423	24.9336585	56.7974351	37	2.3300314	24.6841617	57.5148728
38	2.2757022	25.6262943	58.3178138	38	2.3291960	25.3629910	59.0753774	38	2.3839134	25.1036401	59.8449043
39	2.3254032	26.0563125	60.5935160	39	2.3816029	25.7828764	61.4045734	39	2.4390414	25.5136372	62.2288177
40	2.3763531	26.4771254	62.9189092	40	2.4351890	26.1935222	63.7861763	40	2.4954442	25.9143675	64.6678591
41	2.4283358	26.8889300	65.2953523	41	2.4899807	26.5951317	66.2213652	41	2.5531514	26.3060403	67.1633033
42	2.4814557	27.2919193	67.7236881	42	2.5460053	26.9879039	68.7113460	42	2.6121930	26.6888604	69.7164547
43	2.5357375	27.6862819	70.2051438	43	2.6032904	27.3720331	71.2573512	43	2.6726000	27.0630279	72.3286477
44	2.5912068	28.0722024	72.7408813	44	2.6618644	27.7477097	73.8606417	44	2.7344039	27.4287383	75.0012477
45	2.6478894	28.4498617	75.3320881	45	2.7217564	28.1151195	76.5225061	45	2.7976369	27.7861828	77.7356516
46	2.7058120	28.8194365	77.9799775	46	2.7829959	28.4744445	79.2442625	46	2.8623323	28.1355483	80.5332885
47	2.7650016	29.1811000	80.6857895	47	2.8456133	28.8258626	82.0272584	47	2.9285237	28.4770172	83.3956208
48	2.8254861	29.5350214	83.4507912	48	2.9096396	29.1695478	84.8728717	48	2.9962458	28.8107682	86.3241446
49	2.8872936	29.8813665	86.2762772	49	2.9751065	29.5056702	87.7825113	49	3.0655340	29.1369757	69.3203904
50	2.9504531	30.2202975	89.1635708	50	3.0420464	29.8343963	90.7576178	50	3.1364245	29.4558100	92.3859244
51	3.0149943	30.5519731	92.1140239	51	3.1104924	30.1558888	93.7996642	51	3.2089543	29.7674380	95.5223489
52	3.0809473	30.8765486	95.1290282	52	3.1804785	30.4703069	96.9101567	52	3.2831614	30.0720225	98.7313033
53	3.1483430	31.1941760	98.2099655	53	3.2520393	30.7778062	100.0906352	53	3.3590845	30.3697227	102.0144646
54	3.2172130	31.5050040	101.3583085	54	3.3252102	31.0785391	103.3426745	54	3.4367633	30.6606941	105.3735491
55	3.2875895	31.8091782	104.5755215	55	3.4000274	31.3726544	106.6678847	55	3.5162385	30.9450689	108.8103125
56	3.3595056	32.1068411	107.8631110	56	3.4765280	31.6602977	110.0679121	56	3.5975515	31.2230558	112.3265510
57	3.4329947	32.3991319	111.2226166	57	3.5547459	31.9416114	113.5444401	57	3.6807449	31.4947399	115.9241024
58	3.5080915	32.6831872	114.6556113	58	3.6347318	32.2167349	117.0991900	58	3.7653621	31.7602834	119.6048473
59	3.5848310	32.9621404	118.1637028	59	3.7165132	32.4858043	120.7339218	59	3.8529477	32.0198249	123.3707094
60	3.6632492	33.2351221	121.7485338	60	3.8001348	32.7489528	124.4504350	60	3.9420471	32.2735002	127.2236571
61	3.7433828	33.5022602	125.4117830	61	3.8856378	33.0063108	128.2505698	61	4.0432069	32.5214419	131.1657041
62	3.8252693	33.7636797	129.1551657	62	3.9730647	33.2580057	132.1362077	62	4.1264748	32.7637795	135.1989111
63	3.9089470	34.0195030	132.9804350	63	4.0624586	33.5041621	136.1092723	63	4.2218996	33.0006397	139.3253859
64	3.9944552	34.2698501	136.8893920	64	4.1538640	33.7449018	140.1717310	64	4.3195310	33.2321463	143.5472854
65	4.0818339	34.5148380	140.8838372	65	4.2473259	33.9803440	144.3255949	65	4.4194201	33.4584203	147.8666164
66	4.1711241	34.7545815	144.9656712	66	4.3428907	34.2106054	148.5729208	66	4.5216192	33.6795800	152.2862365
67	4.2623674	34.9891929	149.1367952	67	4.4406058	34.4357999	152.9158115	67	4.6261817	33.8957416	156.8078565
68	4.3556067	35.2187821	153.3991626	68	4.5405194	34.6560390	157.3564173	68	4.7331621	34.1070163	161.4340374
69	4.4508856	35.4434565	157.7547693	69	4.6426811	34.8714318	161.8969367	69	4.8426165	34.3135162	166.1671996
70	4.5482487	35.6633213	162.2056549	70	4.7471414	35.0820849	166.5396178	70	4.9546020	34.5153488	171.0098161
71	4.6477416	35.8784796	166.7539036	71	4.8539521	35.2881026	171.2867592	71	5.0691772	34.7126194	175.9644161
72	4.7494110	36.0890322	171.4016453	72	4.9631660	35.4895869	176.1407112	72	5.1864019	34.9054313	181.0335952
73	4.8533044	36.2950772	176.1510563	73	5.0748730	35.6866375	181.1038773	73	5.3063294	35.0938852	186.2199971
74	4.9594704	36.4967116	181.0043606	74	5.1890211	35.8793521	186.1787145	74	5.4290465	35.2780797	191.5263346
75	5.0679588	36.6940297	185.9638310	75	5.3057741	36.0678260	191.3677356	75	5.5545932	35.4581108	196.9553310
76	5.1788204	36.8871239	191.0317898	76	5.4251540	36.2521526	196.6735096	76	5.6830432	35.6340729	202.5099742
77	5.2921071	37.0760845	196.2106102	77	5.5472199	36.4324231	202.0986636	77	5.8144635	35.8060578	208.1930174
78	5.4078719	37.2610001	201.5027173	78	5.6720324	36.6087267	207.6458835	78	5.9489230	35.9741555	214.0074809
79	5.5261691	37.4419573	206.9105892	79	5.7996531	36.7811508	213.3179159	79	6.0864918	36.1384537	219.9564039
80	5.6470541	37.6190408	212.4367584	80	5.9301453	36.9497808	219.1175690	80	6.2272420	36.2990385	226.0428958
81	5.7705834	37.7923335	218.0838125	81	6.0635736	37.1147000	225.0477144	81	6.3712469	36.4559996	232.2701377
82	5.8968149	37.9619166	223.8543959	82	6.2000040	37.2759902	231.1112879	82	6.5185820	36.6094012	238.6413847
83	6.0258077	38.1278694	229.7512108	83	6.3395041	37.4337313	237.3112919	83	6.6693242	36.7593414	245.1599667
84	6.1576223	38.2902698	235.7770186	84	6.4821429	37.5880012	243.6507960	84	6.8235524	36.9058927	251.8292910
85	6.2923203	38.4491937	241.9346409	85	6.6279917	37.7388765	250.1329389	85	6.9813470	37.0491315	258.6526433
86	6.4299648	38.6047155	248.2269612	86	6.7771209	37.8864318	256.7609300	86	7.1427907	37.1891328	265.6341903
87	6.5706203	38.7569081	254.6569259	87	6.9296062	38.0307402	263.5380510	87	7.3079677	37.3259697	272.7769810
88	6.7143526	38.9058428	261.2275462	88	7.0855223	38.1718730	270.4676571	88	7.4769644	37.4597139	280.0849487
89	6.8612290	39.0515093	267.9418988	89	7.2449465	38.3099003	277.5531794	89	7.6498692	37.5904351	287.5619131
90	7.0113184	39.1942158	274.8031278	90	7.4079578	38.4448902	284.7981260	90	7.8267725	37.7182016	295.2117324
91	7.1646910	39.3337892	281.8144462	91	7.5746369	38.5769097	292.2060838	91	8.0077666	37.8430804	303.0385548
92	7.3214186	39.4703748	288.9791373	92	7.7450662	38.7060242	299.7807207	92	8.1929462	37.9651366	311.0463214
93	7.4815747	39.6040365	296.3005559	93	7.9193302	38.8322975	307.5257869	93	8.3824081	38.0844341	319.2392676
94	7.6452341	39.7348369	303.7821306	94	8.0975151	38.9557922	315.4451171	94	8.5762513	38.2010049	327.6216757
95	7.8124736	39.8628373	311.4273647	95	8.2797092	39.0765694	323.5426323	95	8.7745771	38.3150007	336.1979269
96	7.9833715	39.9880977	319.2398383	96	8.4660027	39.1946889	331.8223415	96	8.9774892	38.4263905	344.9725040
97	8.1580077	40.1106766	327.2232098	97	8.6564878	39.3102092	340.2883442	97	9.1850936	38.5352625	353.9499932
98	8.3364641	40.2306316	335.3812175	98	8.8512587	39.4231874	348.9448319	98	9.3974989	38.6416738	363.1350868
99	8.5188243	40.3480187	343.7176816	99	9.0504120	39.5336797	357.7960907	99	9.6148161	38.7456800	372.5325857
100	8.7051736	40.4628929	352.2365059	100	9.2540463	39.6417405	366.8465027	100	9.8371587	38.8473353	382.1474017

Table 1

375

M	C(8.75,M,4)	A(8.75,M,4)	S(8.75,M,4)	M	C(9.00,M,4)	A(9.00,M,4)	S(9.00,M,4)	M	C(9.25,M,4)	A(9.25,M,4)	S(9.25,M,4)
101	8.8955992	40.5753080	360.9416795	101	9.4622624	39.7474235	376.1005490	101	10.0646430	38.9466931	391.9845604
102	9.0901905	40.6853167	369.8372787	102	9.6751633	39.8507809	385.5628114	102	10.2973878	39.0438051	402.0492034
103	9.2890384	40.7929705	378.9274692	103	9.8928544	39.9518640	395.2379747	103	10.5355149	39.1387221	412.3465912
104	9.4922361	40.8983197	388.2165076	104	10.1154437	40.0507227	405.1308291	104	10.7791487	39.2314938	422.8821061
105	9.6998788	41.0014138	397.7087437	105	10.3432411	40.1474061	415.2462728	105	11.0284165	39.3221687	433.6612549
106	9.9120636	41.1023010	407.4086225	106	10.5737596	40.2419619	425.5893139	106	11.2834487	39.4107940	444.6896714
107	10.1288900	41.2010285	417.3206881	107	10.8137142	40.3344371	436.1650735	107	11.5443784	39.4974163	455.9731200
108	10.3504595	41.2976425	427.4495762	108	11.0570227	40.4248773	446.9787877	108	11.8113422	39.5820807	467.5174985
109	10.5763758	41.3921884	437.8000356	109	11.3058057	40.5133275	458.0358104	109	12.0844795	39.6648315	479.3288406
110	10.8082449	41.4847104	448.3769114	110	11.5601864	40.5998313	469.3416161	110	12.3639330	39.7457119	491.4133201
111	11.0446753	41.5752517	459.1851564	111	11.8202906	40.6844315	480.9018025	111	12.6493490	39.8247642	503.7772531
112	11.2862776	41.6638549	470.2298317	112	12.0862471	40.7671702	492.7220931	112	12.9423757	39.9020298	516.4271021
113	11.5331649	41.7505614	481.5161093	113	12.3581877	40.8480882	504.8083402	113	13.2416692	39.9775489	529.3694789
114	11.7854529	41.8354143	493.0492742	114	12.6362469	40.9272257	517.1665279	114	13.5478828	40.0513612	542.6111481
115	12.0432597	41.9184458	504.8347271	115	12.9205624	41.0046217	529.8027748	115	13.8611776	40.1235051	556.1590309
116	12.3067060	41.9997023	516.8779867	116	13.2112751	41.0803146	542.7233372	116	14.1817173	40.1940185	570.0202085
117	12.5750152	42.0792193	529.1846927	117	13.5085288	41.1543419	555.9346123	117	14.5096695	40.2629380	584.2019258
118	12.8510133	42.1570342	541.7606079	118	13.8124707	41.2267402	569.4431411	118	14.8452057	40.3302998	598.7115954
119	13.1321292	42.2331833	554.6116212	119	14.1232513	41.2975455	583.2556118	119	15.1885010	40.3961391	613.5568010
120	13.4193946	42.3077023	567.7437504	120	14.4410244	41.3667926	597.3788631	120	15.5397351	40.4604903	628.7453021
121	13.7129438	42.3806261	581.1631450	121	14.7659475	41.4345160	611.8198875	121	15.8999915	40.5233870	644.2850372
122	14.0129145	42.4519889	594.8760888	122	15.0981813	41.5007492	626.5858350	122	16.2667580	40.5848620	660.1841287
123	14.3194470	42.5218240	608.8890032	123	15.4378904	41.5655248	641.6840163	123	16.6429268	40.6449476	676.4508867
124	14.6326849	42.5901641	623.2084502	124	15.7852429	41.6288752	657.1219007	124	17.0277945	40.7036751	693.0938134
125	14.9527748	42.6570414	637.8411351	125	16.1404109	41.6908314	672.9071496	125	17.4215622	40.7610753	710.1216079
126	15.2798668	42.7224870	652.7939099	126	16.5035701	41.7514244	689.0475605	126	17.8244358	40.8171780	727.5431701
127	15.6141139	42.7865316	668.0737767	127	16.8749005	41.8106840	705.5511306	127	18.2366259	40.8720127	745.3676059
128	15.9556726	42.8492052	683.6878906	128	17.2545857	41.8686396	722.4260310	128	18.6583479	40.9256080	763.6042318
129	16.3047030	42.9105372	699.6435632	129	17.6428139	41.9253199	739.6806168	129	19.0899222	40.9779920	782.2625797
130	16.6613683	42.9705563	715.9482662	130	18.0397772	41.9807530	757.3234307	130	19.5312743	41.0291919	801.3524019
131	17.0258358	43.0292906	732.6096345	131	18.4456722	42.0349662	775.3632079	131	19.9829350	41.0792346	820.8836762
132	17.3982759	43.0867675	749.6354703	132	18.8603998	42.0879865	793.8088801	132	20.4450404	41.1281462	840.8666112
133	17.7788632	43.1430141	767.0337462	133	19.2850656	42.1398401	812.6695799	133	20.9178320	41.1759523	861.3116516
134	18.1677759	43.1980566	784.8126094	134	19.7189795	42.1905527	831.9546454	134	21.4015558	41.2226779	882.2294836
135	18.5651959	43.2519208	802.9803853	135	20.1626566	42.2401493	851.6736250	135	21.6964678	41.2683474	903.6310404
136	18.9713096	43.3046320	821.5455812	136	20.6163164	42.2886546	871.8362816	136	22.4023237	41.3129846	925.5275083
137	19.3863070	43.3562148	840.5168908	137	21.0801935	42.3360925	892.4525079	137	22.9208889	41.3566129	947.9300319
138	19.8103825	43.4066934	859.9031978	138	21.5544876	42.3824866	913.5327814	138	23.4509345	41.3992551	970.8512209
139	20.2437346	43.4560914	879.7135803	139	22.0394664	42.4278597	935.0872690	139	23.9932314	41.4409335	994.3021554
140	20.6865663	43.5044319	899.9573149	140	22.5353515	42.4723044	957.1267326	140	24.5480810	41.4816699	1018.2953927
141	21.1390849	43.5517377	920.6438812	141	23.0423969	42.5156327	979.6620841	141	25.1157554	41.5214856	1042.8434727
142	21.6015024	43.5980307	941.7829861	142	23.5608508	42.5580760	1002.7044810	142	25.6965572	41.5604013	1067.9592291
143	22.0740353	43.6433328	963.3844685	143	24.0909700	42.5995683	1026.2653319	143	26.2907901	41.5984374	1093.6557663
144	22.5569048	43.6876552	985.4585038	144	24.6330168	42.6401813	1050.3563019	144	26.8987646	41.6356139	1119.9465764
145	23.0503371	43.7310485	1000.0154086	145	25.1872567	42.6798809	1074.9893187	145	27.5207985	41.6719500	1146.8453410
146	23.5545632	43.7735031	1031.0657457	146	25.7539730	42.7187128	1100.1765784	146	28.1572170	41.7074649	1174.3661395
147	24.0698193	43.8150489	1054.6203089	147	26.3334347	42.7566874	1125.9305514	147	28.8083526	41.7421770	1202.5233565
148	24.5963466	43.8557053	1078.6901282	148	26.9259398	42.7938263	1152.2639388	148	29.4745458	41.7761046	1231.3317092
149	25.1343917	43.8954945	1103.2864748	149	27.5317734	42.8301479	1179.1899286	149	30.1561447	41.8092654	1260.8062550
150	25.6842065	43.9344259	1128.4208664	150	28.1512383	42.8656704	1206.7217020	150	30.8535055	41.8416766	1290.9623997
151	26.2460485	43.9725269	1154.1050729	151	28.7846412	42.9004111	1234.8729404	151	31.5669928	41.8733552	1321.8159052
152	26.8201808	44.0098122	1180.3511214	152	29.4322956	42.9343874	1263.6575816	152	32.2969796	41.9043179	1353.3828980
153	27.4068723	44.0462994	1207.1713022	153	30.0945223	42.9676760	1293.0898772	153	33.0438472	41.9345807	1385.6298770
154	28.0063976	44.0820056	1234.5781745	154	30.7716490	43.0001135	1323.1843994	154	33.8079862	41.9641595	1418.7237248
155	28.6190375	44.1169473	1262.5845721	155	31.4640111	43.0318958	1353.9560485	155	34.5897959	41.9930698	1452.5317109
156	29.2450790	44.1511411	1291.2036096	156	32.1719514	43.0629708	1385.4200596	156	35.3896849	42.0213266	1487.1215088
157	29.8843151	44.1846029	1320.4486886	157	32.8958203	43.0933778	1417.5920110	157	36.2080713	42.0489448	1522.5111077
158	30.5385454	44.2173484	1350.3335037	158	33.6359762	43.1231079	1450.4878312	158	37.0453830	42.0759387	1558.7192630
159	31.2065761	44.2493930	1380.8720491	159	34.3927857	43.1521837	1484.1238075	159	37.9020075	42.1023225	1595.7646460
160	31.8892200	44.2807515	1412.0786252	160	35.1666234	43.1806198	1518.5165932	160	38.7785426	42.1281099	1633.6667035
161	32.5867967	44.3114388	1443.9678452	161	35.9578724	43.2084301	1553.6832166	161	39.6752964	42.1533145	1672.4456240
162	33.2995328	44.3414692	1476.5546719	162	36.7669245	43.2356285	1589.6410890	162	40.5927876	42.1779494	1712.1205424
163	34.0280623	44.3708567	1509.8542747	163	37.5941803	43.2622283	1626.4080135	163	41.5314958	42.2020276	1752.7133300
164	34.7724262	44.3996151	1543.8823219	164	38.4400494	43.2882429	1664.0021939	164	42.4919116	42.2255614	1794.2448258
165	35.5330730	44.4277579	1578.6547631	165	39.3049505	43.3136849	1702.4422433	165	43.4745371	42.2485634	1836.7367374
166	36.3103590	44.4552982	1614.1878361	166	40.1893119	43.3385662	1741.7471938	166	44.5004831	42.2710455	1880.2112745
167	37.1046481	44.4822490	1650.4981951	167	41.0935714	43.3629019	1781.9365057	167	45.5084831	42.2930194	1924.6911603
168	37.9163122	44.5086229	1687.6028431	168	42.0181768	43.3867011	1823.0300771	168	46.5608668	42.3144967	1970.1996434
169	38.7457316	44.5344322	1725.5191554	169	42.9635858	43.4099766	1865.0482539	169	47.6375868	42.3354885	2016.7605102
170	39.5932944	44.5596890	1764.2648863	170	43.9302664	43.4327400	1908.0118397	170	48.7392060	42.3560059	2064.3980971
171	40.4593978	44.5844051	1803.8581814	171	44.9183974	43.4550024	1951.9421061	171	49.8663002	42.3760595	2113.1373031
172	41.3444471	44.6085922	1844.3175792	172	45.9293681	43.4767750	1996.8608035	172	51.0194584	42.3956599	2163.0036033
173	42.2488569	44.6322615	1895.6620262	173	46.9627789	43.4980684	2042.7901717	173	52.1992834	42.4148172	2214.0230617
174	43.1730506	44.6554241	1927.9108893	174	48.0194414	43.5188933	2089.7529506	174	53.4063918	42.4335416	2266.2223451
175	44.1174611	44.6780908	1971.0839337	175	49.0998789	43.5392600	2137.7723920	175	54.6414146	42.4518427	2319.6287369
176	45.0825306	44.7002724	2015.2013948	176	50.2046261	43.5591785	2186.8722709	176	55.9049973	42.4697302	2374.2701515
177	46.0687109	44.7219791	2060.2639254	177	51.3342302	43.5786587	2237.0768970	177	57.1978004	42.4872134	2430.1751488
178	47.0754640	44.7432211	2106.3526363	178	52.4892504	43.5977102	2288.4111273	178	58.5204995	42.5043014	2487.3729491
179	48.1052616	44.7640084	2153.4291003	179	53.6702586	43.6163425	2340.9003777	179	59.8737861	42.5210032	2545.8934487
180	49.1585861	44.7843507	2201.5333619	180	54.8778394	43.6345648	2394.5706363	180	61.2583674	42.5373275	2605.7672407
181	50.2339302	44.8042576	2250.6939480	181	56.1125908	43.6523861	2449.4484756	181	62.6749671	42.5532828	2667.0256021
182	51.3327974	44.8237383	2300.9278782	182	57.3717241	43.6698152	2505.5610064	182	64.1243257	42.5688775	2729.7005692
183	52.4557023	44.8428020	2352.2606756	183	58.6660643	43.6868609	2562.9361905	183	65.6072008	42.5841198	2793.8248949
184	53.6031708	44.8614576	2404.7163779	184	59.9860508	43.7035314	2621.6022548	184	67.1243673	42.5990175	2859.4320957
185	54.7757402	44.8797139	2458.3195487	185	61.3357369	43.7198351	2681.5883056	185	68.6766183	42.6135785	2926.5564630
186	55.9739595	44.8975794	2513.0952889	186	62.7157910	43.7357801	2742.9240426	186	70.2647651	42.6278104	2995.2330813
187	57.1982899	44.9150622	2569.0692464	187	64.1269963	43.7513741	2805.6398336	187	71.8893378	42.6417206	3065.4978463
188	58.4496047	44.9321711	2626.2676383	188	65.5697515	43.7666251	2869.7667299	188	73.5520856	42.6553164	3137.3874841
189	59.7281898	44.9489105	2684.7172430	189	67.0450709	43.7815404	2935.3364814	189	75.2529776	42.6686049	3210.9395698
190	61.0347439	44.9652977	2744.4454327	190	68.5535850	43.7981275	3002.3815523	190	76.9932027	42.6815931	3286.1925474
191	62.3698789	44.9813311	2805.4801766	191	70.0960407	43.8103937	3070.9351373	191	78.7736706	42.6942877	3363.1857501
192	63.7342200	44.9970213	2867.8500556	192	71.6732016	43.8243459	3141.0311780	192	80.5953117	42.7066953	3441.9594207
193	65.1284061	45.0123756	2931.5842756	193	73.2858486	43.8379911	3212.7043796	193	82.4590783	42.7188225	3522.5547324
194	66.5530900	45.0274012	2996.7126817	194	74.9347802	43.8513360	3285.9902292	194	84.3659445	42.7306757	3605.0138107
195	68.0089388	45.0421051	3063.2657717	195	76.6208128	43.8643873	3360.9250084	195	86.3169069	42.7422609	3689.3797551
196	69.4966344	45.0564943	3131.2747105	196	78.3447811	43.8771514	3437.5458212	196	88.3129854	42.7535843	3775.6966620
197	71.0168732	45.0705755	3200.7713449	197	80.1075386	43.8896346	3515.8906022	197	90.3552232	42.7646517	3864.0096475
198	72.5703674	45.0843552	3271.7882181	198	81.9099583	43.9018432	3595.9981409	198	92.4446877	42.7754690	3954.3648706
199	74.1578441	45.0978399	3344.3585855	199	83.7529323	43.9137830	3677.9080991	199	94.5824711	42.7860447	4046.8095584
200	75.7800470	45.1110360	3418.5164296	200	85.5373733	43.9254602	3761.6610314	200	96.7696908	42.7963756	4141.3920295

Table 1

M	C(9.50,M,4)	A(9.50,M,4)	S(9.50,M,4)	M	C(9.75,M,4)	A(9.75,M,4)	S(9.75,M,4)	M	C(10.00,M,4)	A(10.00,M,4)	S(10.00,M,4)
1/3	1.0078548	.3281512	.3307287	1/3	1.0080599	.3280173	.3306611	1/3	1.0082648	.3278836	.3305935
1	1.0237500	.9768010	1.0000000	1	1.0243750	.9762050	1.0000000	1	1.0250000	.9756098	1.0000000
2	1.0480641	1.9309411	2.0237500	2	1.0493441	1.9291812	2.0243750	2	1.0506250	1.9274242	2.0250000
3	1.0729556	2.8629462	3.0718141	3	1.0749219	2.8594814	3.0737191	3	1.0768906	2.8560236	3.0755250
4	1.0984383	3.7733296	4.1447696	4	1.1011231	3.7676400	4.1486410	4	1.1038129	3.7619742	4.1525156
5	1.1245262	4.6625930	5.2432079	5	1.1279630	4.6541989	5.2497642	5	1.1314082	4.6458285	5.2563285
6	1.1512337	5.5312264	6.3677341	6	1.1554571	5.5196573	6.3777272	6	1.1595934	5.5081254	6.3877767
7	1.1785755	6.3797083	7.5189678	7	1.1836214	6.3645220	7.5331843	7	1.1886958	6.3493906	7.5474301
8	1.2065667	7.2085063	8.6975433	8	1.2124721	7.1892833	8.7168056	8	1.2184029	7.1701372	8.7361159
9	1.2352226	8.0180769	9.9041099	9	1.2420261	7.9944193	9.9292778	9	1.2458630	7.9708655	9.9545188
10	1.2645591	8.8088664	11.1393325	10	1.2723005	8.7803971	11.1713039	10	1.2800845	8.7520639	11.2033818
11	1.2945924	9.5813102	12.4038917	11	1.3033129	9.5476726	12.4436045	11	1.3120367	9.5142087	12.4834663
12	1.3253390	10.3359342	13.6984841	12	1.3350811	10.2966908	13.7469173	12	1.3448988	10.2577646	13.7955530
13	1.3568158	11.0728539	15.0238231	13	1.3676237	11.0278860	15.0819984	13	1.3785110	10.9831350	15.1404418
14	1.3899402	11.7927755	16.3806389	14	1.4009595	11.7416825	16.4496221	14	1.4129738	11.6909122	16.5189526
15	1.4220299	12.4959956	17.7696791	15	1.4351079	12.4384942	17.8505817	15	1.4482982	12.3813777	17.9319267
16	1.4559031	13.1829017	19.1917090	16	1.4700887	13.1187253	19.2856896	16	1.4845056	13.0550027	19.3802248
17	1.4903784	13.8538722	20.6475121	17	1.5059221	13.7827703	20.7557783	17	1.5216183	13.7121977	20.8647305
18	1.5257749	14.5092769	22.1378905	18	1.5426289	14.4310143	22.2617004	18	1.5596587	14.3533636	22.3863487
19	1.5620121	15.1494768	23.6636654	19	1.5802305	15.0638334	23.8043293	19	1.5985502	14.9788913	23.9460074
20	1.5991098	15.7748247	25.2256774	20	1.6187486	15.6815945	25.3845599	20	1.6386164	15.5891623	25.5446576
21	1.6370887	16.3856652	26.8247873	21	1.6582056	16.2846560	27.0033085	21	1.6795819	16.1845486	27.1832741
22	1.6759696	16.9823347	28.4618760	22	1.6986244	16.8733677	28.6615142	22	1.7215714	16.7654132	28.8628559
23	1.7157738	17.5651621	30.1378455	23	1.7400284	17.4480709	30.3601386	23	1.7646107	17.3321105	30.5844273
24	1.7565235	18.1344685	31.8536194	24	1.7824416	18.0090991	32.1001669	24	1.8087260	17.8849858	32.3490330
25	1.7982409	18.6905675	33.6101428	25	1.8258886	18.5567777	33.8826085	25	1.8539441	18.4243764	34.1577639
26	1.8409491	19.2337656	35.4083837	26	1.8703946	19.0914242	35.7084971	26	1.9002927	18.9506111	36.0117080
27	1.8846717	19.7643620	37.2493328	27	1.9159855	19.6133488	37.5788917	27	1.9478000	19.4640109	37.9120007
28	1.9294326	20.2826491	39.1340045	28	1.9626876	20.1228543	39.4948772	28	1.9964950	19.9648686	39.8598008
29	1.9752566	20.7889124	41.0634371	29	2.0105281	20.6202360	41.4575648	29	2.0464074	20.4535499	41.8562958
30	2.0221690	21.2834309	43.0386937	30	2.0595348	21.1057826	43.4680930	30	2.0975676	20.9302926	43.9027032
31	2.0701955	21.7664771	45.0608627	31	2.1097359	21.5797755	45.5276277	31	2.1500068	21.3954074	46.0002708
32	2.1193626	22.2383171	47.1310582	32	2.1611607	22.0424898	47.6373637	32	2.2037569	21.8491780	48.1502775
33	2.1696975	22.6992108	49.2504208	33	2.2133390	22.4941939	49.7985244	33	2.2598509	22.2918809	50.3540345
34	2.2212278	23.1494123	51.4201183	34	2.2678014	22.9351496	52.0123634	34	2.3153221	22.7237863	52.6128853
35	2.2739820	23.5891695	53.6413461	35	2.3230790	23.3656128	54.2801648	35	2.3732052	23.1451573	54.9282075
36	2.3279890	24.0187248	55.9153281	36	2.3797041	23.7858331	56.6032438	36	2.4325353	23.5562511	57.3014127
37	2.3832788	24.4383148	58.2433171	37	2.4377094	24.1960543	58.9829479	37	2.4933347	23.9573181	59.7339480
38	2.4398817	24.8481707	60.6265959	38	2.4971285	24.5965142	61.4206572	38	2.5556824	24.3486030	62.2272967
39	2.4978288	25.2485184	63.0664776	39	2.5579960	24.9874453	63.9177858	39	2.6195745	24.7303444	64.7829791
40	2.5571523	25.6395764	65.5643064	40	2.6203472	25.3690741	66.4757818	40	2.6850638	25.1027750	67.4025536
41	2.6178846	26.0215662	68.1214587	41	2.6842181	25.7416220	69.0961290	41	2.7521904	25.4661220	70.0876174
42	2.6800594	26.3946925	70.7393433	42	2.7496460	26.1053052	71.7803471	42	2.8209952	25.8206068	72.8398079
43	2.7437108	26.7591622	73.4194028	43	2.8166686	26.4603346	74.5299931	43	2.8915201	26.1664457	75.6608030
44	2.8088739	27.1151767	76.1631136	44	2.8853249	26.8069160	77.3466617	44	2.9638081	26.5038494	78.5523231
45	2.8755847	27.4629321	78.9719875	45	2.9556547	27.1452505	80.2319866	45	3.0379033	26.8330238	81.5161312
46	2.9438798	27.8026193	81.8475722	46	3.0276988	27.4755344	83.1876412	46	3.1138509	27.1541896	84.5540345
47	3.0137970	28.1344272	84.7914521	47	3.1014909	27.7979591	86.2153400	47	3.1916971	27.4674325	87.6678854
48	3.0853347	28.4585370	87.8052491	48	3.1770980	28.1127118	89.3168389	48	3.2714896	27.7731537	90.8595825
49	3.1586523	28.7751277	90.8906237	49	3.2545397	28.4199749	92.4939369	49	3.3532768	28.0713695	94.1310721
50	3.2336703	29.0843738	94.0492760	50	3.3338691	28.7199267	95.7484766	50	3.4371087	28.3623117	97.4843489
51	3.3104700	29.3864457	97.2829463	51	3.4151322	29.0127411	99.0823457	51	3.5230364	28.6461577	100.9214576
52	3.3890936	29.6815099	100.5934163	52	3.4983760	29.2985880	102.4974779	52	3.6111124	28.9230807	104.4444940
53	3.4695846	29.9697288	103.9825100	53	3.5836489	29.5776332	105.9958539	53	3.7013902	29.1932495	108.0556064
54	3.5519872	30.2512614	107.4520946	54	3.6710004	29.8500385	109.5795028	54	3.7939249	29.4568287	111.7569965
55	3.6363469	30.5262626	111.0040818	55	3.7604810	30.1159619	113.2505032	55	3.8897720	29.7139793	115.5509215
56	3.7227102	30.7948841	114.6404288	56	3.8521427	30.3755577	117.0109842	56	3.9850924	29.9648578	119.4398945
57	3.8111246	31.0572739	118.3631390	57	3.9460387	30.6289764	120.8631291	57	4.0856422	30.2096174	123.4256693
58	3.9016368	31.3135764	122.1742635	58	4.0422234	30.8763650	124.8091657	58	4.1877832	30.4484072	127.5113290
59	3.9943027	31.5639330	126.0759023	59	4.1407526	31.1178670	128.8513891	59	4.2924778	30.6813729	131.6991123
60	4.0891674	31.8084816	130.0702050	60	4.2416835	31.3536225	132.9921417	60	4.3997898	30.9086565	135.9915901
61	4.1852351	32.0473568	134.1593723	61	4.3450745	31.5837681	137.2338252	61	4.5097345	31.1303906	140.3913798
62	4.2857094	32.2806904	138.3456074	62	4.4509857	31.8084374	141.5788997	62	4.6225291	31.3467283	144.9011643
63	4.3874950	32.5086109	142.6313668	63	4.5594785	32.0277608	146.0298864	63	4.7380923	31.5577287	149.5236934
64	4.4916980	32.7312439	147.0188518	64	4.6705157	32.2418653	150.5893638	64	4.8565446	31.7636915	154.2617058
65	4.5963758	32.9487120	151.5105597	65	4.7844620	32.4508752	155.2599796	65	4.9779583	31.9645770	159.1183304
66	4.7075872	33.1611350	156.1089355	66	4.9010833	32.6549117	160.0444416	66	5.1024072	32.1605630	164.0962887
67	4.8193924	33.3686301	160.8165228	67	5.0205472	32.8540932	164.9455248	67	5.2299674	32.3517687	169.1986959
68	4.9330530	33.5713114	165.6359152	68	5.1429230	33.0485352	169.9660720	68	5.3607166	32.5383110	174.4286633
69	5.0510120	33.7692908	170.5697692	69	5.2682818	33.2383504	175.1089960	69	5.4947345	32.7203034	179.7893799
70	5.1705940	33.9626772	175.6208002	70	5.3966961	33.4236489	180.3772768	70	5.6321029	32.8976570	185.2841144
71	5.2938051	34.1515772	180.7917942	71	5.5282406	33.6045383	185.7739729	71	5.7729054	33.0710800	190.9162173
72	5.4195330	34.3360950	186.0855993	72	5.6629915	33.7811234	191.3022135	72	5.9172281	33.2400780	196.6891227
73	5.5482469	34.5163321	191.5051323	73	5.8010269	33.9535067	196.9652050	73	6.0651588	33.4049542	202.6063508
74	5.6800178	34.6923879	197.0533792	74	5.9424269	34.1217881	202.7662318	74	6.2167877	33.5658089	208.6715096
75	5.8149182	34.8643593	202.7333969	75	6.0872736	34.2860653	208.7086587	75	6.3722074	33.7227404	214.8882973
76	5.9530225	35.0323412	208.5483151	76	6.2356509	34.4464335	214.7959323	76	6.5315126	33.8758443	221.2605047
77	6.0944068	35.1964261	214.5013376	77	6.3876448	34.6029857	221.0315832	77	6.6948004	34.0252140	227.7920174
78	6.2391489	35.3567044	220.5957444	78	6.5433437	34.7558128	227.4192280	78	6.8621705	34.1709404	234.4868178
79	6.3873287	35.5132643	226.8348933	79	6.7028377	34.9050033	233.9625717	79	7.0337247	34.3131125	241.3469883
80	6.5390278	35.6661923	233.2222220	80	6.8662194	35.0506439	240.6654094	80	7.2095678	34.4518172	248.3827130
81	6.6943297	35.8155724	239.7612498	81	7.0335835	35.1923189	247.5316287	81	7.3898070	34.5871387	255.5922808
82	6.8533200	35.9614871	246.4555795	82	7.2040271	35.3316109	254.5652122	82	7.5745522	34.7191597	262.9820878
83	7.0160864	36.1040167	253.3088995	83	7.3806496	35.4671003	261.7702393	83	7.7639160	34.8479607	270.5566400
84	7.1827184	36.2432398	260.3249059	84	7.5605529	35.5993658	269.1508888	84	7.9580139	34.9736202	278.3205560
85	7.3533080	36.3792330	267.5077043	85	7.7448414	35.7284840	276.7114418	85	8.1569643	35.0962148	286.2785699
86	7.5279490	36.5120713	274.8610123	86	7.9336219	35.8545298	284.4562832	86	8.3600884	35.2158194	294.4355342
87	7.7067378	36.6418279	282.3889613	87	8.1270039	35.9775764	292.3899051	87	8.5699106	35.3325067	302.7964226
88	7.8897729	36.7685742	290.0956992	88	8.3250997	36.0976951	300.5169090	88	8.7841583	35.4463480	311.3663331
89	8.0771550	36.8923802	297.9854720	89	8.5280240	36.2149555	308.8420087	89	9.0037623	35.5574127	320.1504915
90	8.2689874	37.0133340	306.0626270	90	8.7358946	36.3294258	317.3700327	90	9.2288564	35.6657685	329.1542538
91	8.4653758	37.1314422	314.3316144	91	8.9488320	36.4411722	326.1059272	91	9.4595778	35.7714814	338.3831101
92	8.6664285	37.2468300	322.7969903	92	9.1669598	36.5502596	335.0547592	92	9.6960672	35.8746160	347.8426879
93	8.8722562	37.3595409	331.4634188	93	9.3904044	36.6567513	344.2217190	93	9.9384689	35.9752351	357.5387551
94	9.0829723	37.4696370	340.3356750	94	9.6192955	36.7607090	353.6121234	94	10.1869306	36.0734001	367.4772240
95	9.2986929	37.5771790	349.4186473	95	9.8537658	36.8621931	363.2314189	95	10.4416039	36.1691709	377.6641546
96	9.5195368	37.6822262	358.7173402	96	10.0939514	36.9612623	373.0851847	96	10.7026440	36.2626057	388.1057584
97	9.7456258	37.7848363	368.2368770	97	10.3399915	37.0579742	383.1791361	97	10.9702101	36.3537617	398.8084024
98	9.9770845	37.8850660	377.9825028	98	10.5920287	37.1523848	393.5191276	98	11.2444653	36.4426943	409.7786125
99	10.2140402	37.9829704	387.9595873	99	10.8502094	37.2445489	404.1111563	99	11.5255770	36.5294579	421.0230778
100	10.4566237	38.0786036	398.1736275	100	11.1146833	37.3345200	414.9613658	100	11.8137164	36.6141052	432.5486548

Table 1

M	C(9.50,M,4)	A(9.50,M,4)	S(9.50,M,4)	C(9.75,M,4)	A(9.75,M,4)	S(9.75,M,4)	C(10.00,M,4)	A(10.00,M,4)	S(10.00,M,4)
101	10.7049665	38.1720182	408.6302512	11.3856037	37.4223502	426.0760491	12.1090593	36.6966880	444.3623711
102	10.9592115	38.2632656	419.3352196	11.6631278	37.5080905	437.4616528	12.4117858	36.7772566	456.4714304
103	11.2194927	38.3523962	430.2944311	11.9474165	37.5917906	449.1247806	12.7220804	36.8558601	468.8832162
104	11.4859557	38.4394590	441.5139239	12.2386348	37.6734990	461.0721971	13.0401324	36.9325465	481.6052966
105	11.7587472	38.5245021	452.9998796	12.5369515	37.7532633	473.3108319	13.3661357	37.0073624	494.6454290
106	12.0380174	38.6075723	464.7586267	12.8425397	37.8311295	485.8477824	13.7002891	37.0803536	508.0115648
107	12.3239203	38.6887153	476.7966441	13.1555756	37.9071429	498.6903232	14.0427964	37.1515644	521.7118539
108	12.6166134	38.7679759	489.1205644	13.4762438	37.9813475	511.8456998	14.3930863	37.2210385	535.7546503
109	12.9162580	38.8453977	501.7371778	13.8047273	38.0537865	525.3221436	14.7537129	37.2888180	550.1485166
110	13.2230191	38.9210234	514.6534358	14.1412175	38.1245017	539.1269709	15.1225558	37.3549444	564.9022295
111	13.5370658	38.9948946	527.8764549	14.4859097	38.1935343	553.2680884	15.5006196	37.4194580	580.0247852
112	13.8585711	39.0670521	541.4135207	14.8390037	38.2609243	567.7539981	15.8881351	37.4823980	595.5254049
113	14.1877122	39.1375357	555.2720919	15.2007044	38.3267107	582.5930018	16.2853385	37.5438029	611.4135400
114	14.5246704	39.2063840	569.4598041	15.5712216	38.3909318	597.7937062	16.6924720	37.6037102	627.6988785
115	14.8696313	39.2736352	583.9844744	15.9507701	38.4536244	613.3649278	17.1097838	37.6621563	644.3913505
116	15.2227850	39.3393262	598.8541057	16.3395702	38.5148258	629.3156980	17.5375284	37.7191769	661.5011343
117	15.5843262	39.4034932	614.0768907	16.7378472	38.5745706	645.6552681	17.9758666	37.7748067	679.0386627
118	15.9544539	39.4661717	629.6612169	17.1458322	38.6328938	662.3931153	18.4253657	37.8290797	697.0146292
119	16.3333722	39.5273960	645.6156708	17.5637619	38.6898293	679.5389475	18.8859999	37.8820290	715.4399950
120	16.7212898	39.5872000	661.9490430	17.9918786	38.7454099	697.1027093	19.3581499	37.9336868	734.3259949
121	17.1184204	39.6456166	678.6703328	18.4304306	38.7996680	715.0945879	19.8421036	37.9840847	753.6841448
122	17.5249829	39.7026780	695.7887532	18.8796723	38.8526350	733.5250185	20.3381562	38.0332533	773.5262484
123	17.9412013	39.7584156	713.3137362	19.3398644	38.9043417	752.4046908	20.8465101	38.0812228	793.8644046
124	18.3673048	39.8128602	731.2549374	19.8112736	38.9548180	771.7445552	21.3673771	38.1280222	814.7110148
125	18.8035283	39.8660407	749.6222422	20.2941733	39.0040932	791.5558288	21.9019598	38.1736802	836.0787902
126	19.2501121	39.9179995	768.4257705	20.7883438	39.0521959	811.8500021	22.4495190	38.2182246	857.9807599
127	19.7073022	39.9687321	787.6758025	21.2955719	39.0991541	832.6388459	23.0107570	38.2616825	880.4302790
128	20.1753507	40.0182975	807.3831848	21.8143515	39.1449948	853.9344178	23.5860259	38.3040805	903.4410360
129	20.6545152	40.0667131	827.5585354	22.3463836	39.1897448	875.7490693	24.1756766	38.3454444	927.0270619
130	21.1450600	40.1140054	848.2130506	22.8910767	39.2334299	898.0954529	24.7800685	38.3857994	951.2027384
131	21.6472551	40.1602007	869.3581106	23.4494407	39.2760756	920.9865295	25.3995702	38.4251702	975.9828069
132	22.1613775	40.2053242	891.0053658	24.0206172	39.3177065	944.4355762	26.0345595	38.4635806	1001.3823771
133	22.6877102	40.2494000	913.1667432	24.6061197	39.3583468	968.4561934	26.6854234	38.5010543	1027.4169366
134	23.2265433	40.2924551	935.8544534	25.2058939	39.3980200	993.0623132	27.3525590	38.5376139	1054.1023600
135	23.7781731	40.3345105	959.0809967	25.8202876	39.4367493	1018.2692071	28.0363730	38.5732819	1081.4549191
136	24.3429053	40.3755902	982.8591704	26.4495571	39.4745569	1044.0884946	28.7372823	38.6080799	1109.4912921
137	24.9210493	40.4157170	1007.2020757	27.0943675	39.5114650	1070.5381517	29.4557144	38.6420292	1138.2285744
138	25.5129242	40.4549128	1032.1231250	27.7547927	39.5474948	1097.6325192	30.1921072	38.6751504	1167.6842868
139	26.1188562	40.4931993	1057.6360493	28.4313158	39.5826673	1125.3873119	30.9469099	38.7074639	1197.8763560
140	26.7391790	40.5305976	1083.7549055	29.1243291	39.6170028	1153.8186276	31.7205827	38.7389891	1228.8233080
141	27.3742345	40.5671281	1110.4940865	29.8342346	39.6505214	1182.9429567	32.5135972	38.7697454	1260.5438886
142	28.0243726	40.6028115	1137.8683190	30.5614441	39.6832423	1212.7771913	33.3264372	38.7997516	1293.0574559
143	28.6899515	40.6376669	1165.8926916	31.3063793	39.7151847	1243.3386354	34.1595981	38.8290260	1326.3839231
144	29.3713378	40.6717137	1194.5826431	32.0694723	39.7463670	1274.6450146	35.0135881	38.8575863	1360.5455212
145	30.0685077	40.7049707	1223.9539809	32.8511657	39.7768073	1306.7144869	35.8883278	38.8854501	1395.5571092
146	30.7830436	40.7374561	1254.0228380	33.6519128	39.8065233	1339.5656526	36.7861510	38.9126342	1431.4460370
147	31.5141409	40.7691879	1284.8059916	34.4721782	39.8355322	1373.2175654	37.7058047	38.9391553	1468.2321880
148	32.2626018	40.8001835	1316.3200725	35.3124375	39.8638509	1407.6897436	38.6484499	38.9650295	1505.9379927
149	33.0288385	40.8304601	1348.5826743	36.1731782	39.8914957	1443.0021811	39.6146611	38.9902728	1544.5864425
150	33.8132735	40.8600343	1381.6115128	37.0548994	39.9184826	1479.1753593	40.6050276	39.0149003	1584.2011037
151	34.6163387	40.8889224	1415.4247863	37.9581126	39.9448275	1516.2302587	41.6201533	39.0389271	1624.8061313
152	35.4394768	40.9171403	1450.0411250	38.8833416	39.9705454	1554.1883713	42.6606572	39.0623679	1666.4262846
153	36.2801406	40.9447035	1485.4796017	39.8311230	39.9956514	1593.0717129	43.7271736	39.0852370	1709.0863418
154	37.1417939	40.9716274	1521.7597423	40.8020067	40.0201600	1632.9028359	44.8203529	39.1075483	1752.8141153
155	38.0239115	40.9979267	1558.9015382	41.7965556	40.0440854	1673.7048426	45.9408618	39.1293154	1797.6344583
156	38.9269794	41.0236158	1596.9254478	42.8153466	40.0674415	1715.5013982	47.0893833	39.1505516	1843.5533300
157	39.8514952	41.0487090	1635.8524272	43.8589707	40.0902419	1758.3167448	48.2663179	39.1712698	1890.6647133
158	40.7979682	41.0732200	1675.7039224	44.9280331	40.1124997	1802.1757155	49.4732833	39.1914828	1938.9313312
159	41.7669199	41.0971624	1716.5018906	46.0231539	40.1342279	1847.1037486	50.7101154	39.2112027	1988.4046145
160	42.7588843	41.1205493	1758.2688105	47.1449683	40.1554391	1893.1269025	51.9778683	39.2304417	2039.1147299
161	43.7744078	41.1433937	1801.0276948	48.2941269	40.1761455	1940.2718708	53.2773150	39.2492114	2091.0925982
162	44.8110500	41.1657081	1844.8021026	49.4712962	40.1963593	1988.5659977	54.6092479	39.2675233	2144.3699133
163	45.8783837	41.1875049	1889.6161526	50.6771591	40.2160920	2038.0372940	55.9794749	39.2853885	2198.9791611
164	46.9679953	41.2087960	1935.4945363	51.9124148	40.2353552	2088.7144531	57.3738411	39.3028181	2254.9536402
165	48.0834852	41.2295932	1982.4625315	53.1777800	40.2541601	2140.6263679	58.8081871	39.3198226	2312.3274813
166	49.2254679	41.2499070	2030.5460167	54.4739883	40.2725175	2193.6046479	60.2783918	39.3364122	2371.1356684
167	50.3945728	41.2697513	2079.7714847	55.8017918	40.2904381	2248.2788362	61.7853516	39.3525973	2431.4140601
168	51.5914439	41.2891343	2130.1660575	57.1619605	40.3079322	2304.0804280	63.3293854	39.3683876	2493.1994117
169	52.8167407	41.3080677	2181.7575014	58.5552833	40.3250101	2361.2423885	64.9123530	39.3837928	2556.5293971
170	54.0711383	41.3265619	2234.5742421	59.9825683	40.3416816	2419.7976718	66.5350659	39.3988222	2621.4426321
171	55.3553278	41.3446270	2288.6453804	61.4446434	40.3579564	2479.7802401	68.1994675	39.4134851	2687.9786979
172	56.6700169	41.3622730	2344.0007087	62.9423566	40.3738440	2541.2248835	69.9044542	39.4277904	2756.1781654
173	58.0159298	41.3795096	2400.6707251	64.4765765	40.3893535	2604.1672401	71.6520656	39.4417467	2826.0826196
174	59.3938081	41.3963464	2458.6866549	66.0481931	40.4044939	2668.6438167	73.4433672	39.4553626	2897.7346852
175	60.8044111	41.4127926	2518.0804600	67.6581178	40.4192741	2734.6920098	75.2794514	39.4686465	2971.1780524
176	62.2485158	41.4288572	2578.8848741	69.3072844	40.4337026	2802.3501478	77.1614377	39.4816063	3046.4575038
177	63.7269181	41.4445492	2641.1333899	70.9965495	40.4477878	2871.6574120	79.0904736	39.4942500	3123.6189415
178	65.2404324	41.4598781	2704.8603080	72.7271928	40.4615378	2942.6540105	81.0677355	39.5065354	3202.7094151
179	66.7898927	41.4748494	2770.1007404	74.4999181	40.4749605	3015.3812543	83.0944288	39.5186199	3283.7771505
180	68.3761526	41.4894944	2836.8906330	76.3150537	40.4890641	3089.8811725	85.1717896	39.5303609	3366.8715794
181	70.0000862	41.5037601	2905.2667856	78.1760526	40.5008557	3166.1970261	87.3010843	39.5418155	3452.0433693
182	71.6625883	41.5177144	2975.2668719	80.0815946	40.5133430	3244.3730787	89.4836114	39.5529907	3539.3444533
183	73.3645748	41.5313449	3046.9294602	82.0335827	40.5255331	3324.4546726	91.7207017	39.5636934	3628.8280647
184	75.1063834	41.5446593	3120.2940049	84.0331515	40.5374332	3406.4882553	94.0137193	39.5745301	3720.5487664
185	76.8907743	41.5576647	3195.4010183	86.0814594	40.5490501	3490.5214066	96.3640022	39.5849075	3814.5624856
186	78.7169302	41.5703685	3272.2917926	88.1796949	40.5603306	3576.6028660	98.7731638	39.5950317	3910.9265479
187	80.5864572	41.5827775	3351.0087227	90.3290750	40.5714612	3664.7825610	101.2424929	39.6049089	4009.6997117
188	82.5003856	41.5948987	3431.5951800	92.5308462	40.5822684	3755.1115360	103.7735552	39.6145453	4110.9422046
189	84.4597698	41.6067386	3514.0955656	94.7862856	40.5928184	3847.6424822	106.3678941	39.6239466	4214.7157598
190	86.4656893	41.6183039	3598.5553354	97.0967013	40.6031175	3942.4287678	109.0270915	39.6331187	4321.0836539
191	88.5192494	41.6296009	3685.0210247	99.4634334	40.6131714	4039.5254691	111.7527687	39.6420670	4430.1107453
192	90.6215816	41.6406358	3773.5402741	101.8878546	40.6229861	4138.9889025	114.5465880	39.6507971	4541.8635141
193	92.7738442	41.6514147	3864.1618557	104.3713711	40.6325673	4240.8767571	117.4102527	39.6593142	4656.4101020
194	94.9772230	41.6619435	3956.9356999	106.9154232	40.6419205	4345.2481282	120.3455090	39.6676236	4773.8203547
195	97.2329320	41.6722281	4051.9129228	109.5214867	40.6510511	4452.1635514	123.3541467	39.6757304	4894.1658637
196	99.5422142	41.6822741	4149.1458549	112.1910729	40.6599645	4561.6850381	126.4360004	39.6836394	5017.5200104
197	101.9063417	41.6920070	4248.6880690	114.9257303	40.6686657	4673.8761110	129.5989504	39.6913555	5143.9580108
198	104.3266174	41.7016723	4350.5944108	117.7270450	40.6771600	4788.8018413	132.6389242	39.6988834	5273.5569612
199	106.8043745	41.7110352	4454.9210281	120.5966417	40.6854521	4906.5288863	136.1598973	39.7062277	5406.3958853
200	109.3409784	41.7201809	4561.7254027	123.5361849	40.6935469	5027.1255281	139.5638947	39.7133929	5542.5557826

Table 1

M	C(10.25,M,4)	A(10.25,M,4)	S(10.25,M,4)	M	C(10.50,M,4)	A(10.50,M,4)	S(10.50,M,4)	M	C(10.75,M,4)	A(10.75,M,4)	S(10.75,M,4)
1/3	1.0084697	.3277500	.3305260	1/3	1.0086745	.3276165	.3304585	1/3	1.0088793	.3274832	.3303910
1	1.0256250	.9750152	1.0000000	1	1.0262500	.9744214	1.0000000	1	1.0268750	.9738284	1.0000000
2	1.0519066	1.9256699	2.0256250	2	1.0531891	1.9239186	2.0262500	2	1.0544723	1.9221700	2.0268750
3	1.0788617	2.8525728	3.0775316	3	1.0809353	2.8491289	3.0794391	3	1.0828112	2.8456921	3.0813473
4	1.1065076	3.7563171	4.1563934	4	1.1092072	3.7506738	4.1602743	4	1.1119118	3.7450440	4.1641585
5	1.1348618	4.6374817	5.2629010	5	1.1383239	4.6291583	5.2694815	5	1.1417944	4.6208584	5.2760702
6	1.1639427	5.4966305	6.3977628	6	1.1682049	5.4851726	6.4070054	6	1.1704801	5.4737514	6.4178646
7	1.1937687	6.3343137	7.5617055	7	1.1988703	6.3192912	7.5760103	7	1.2039905	6.3043227	7.5903447
8	1.2243590	7.1510676	8.7554742	8	1.2303406	7.1320742	8.7748806	8	1.2363478	7.1131566	8.7943352
9	1.2557332	7.9474151	9.9798332	9	1.2626371	7.9240675	10.0052212	9	1.2695746	7.9008220	10.0306830
10	1.2879114	8.7238660	11.2355664	10	1.2957813	8.6956026	11.2678583	10	1.3036944	8.6678729	11.3002576
11	1.3209141	9.4809175	12.5234778	11	1.3297955	9.4477979	12.5636395	11	1.3387312	9.4148489	12.6039520
12	1.3547625	10.2190543	13.8443919	12	1.3647027	10.1805583	13.8934351	12	1.3747096	10.1422752	13.9426832
13	1.3894783	10.9387488	15.1991545	13	1.4005261	10.8945757	15.2581378	13	1.4116549	10.8506636	15.3173929
14	1.4250837	11.6404620	16.5886328	14	1.4372899	11.5903295	16.6586639	14	1.4495932	11.5405124	16.7290478
15	1.4616015	12.3246430	18.0137165	15	1.4750188	12.2682870	18.0959538	15	1.4885510	12.2123066	18.1786410
16	1.4990550	12.9917299	19.4753180	16	1.5137380	12.9289033	19.5709726	16	1.5285558	12.8665189	19.6671919
17	1.5374683	13.6421498	20.9743731	17	1.5534737	13.5726223	21.0847106	17	1.5696357	13.5036094	21.1957477
18	1.5768659	14.2763192	22.5118414	18	1.5942523	14.1998752	22.6381843	18	1.6118197	14.1240262	22.7653834
19	1.6172731	14.8946439	24.0887073	19	1.6361015	14.8110843	24.2324366	19	1.6551373	14.7282057	24.3772031
20	1.6587157	15.4975200	25.7059804	20	1.6790491	15.4066595	25.8685381	20	1.6998192	15.3165728	26.0323404
21	1.7012203	16.0853333	27.3646952	21	1.7231242	15.9870007	27.5475872	21	1.7452964	15.8895414	27.7319596
22	1.7448141	16.6584602	29.0659165	22	1.7683562	16.5524976	29.2707114	22	1.7922013	16.4475144	29.4772560
23	1.7895250	17.2172678	30.8107306	23	1.8147755	17.1035300	31.0390675	23	1.8403667	16.9908844	31.2694573
24	1.8353816	17.7621136	32.6002556	24	1.8624134	17.6404677	32.8538431	24	1.8698265	17.5200335	33.1098239
25	1.8824132	18.2933466	34.4356371	25	1.9113017	18.1636713	34.7162584	25	1.9406156	18.0353339	34.9996505
26	1.9305500	18.8113069	36.3180503	26	1.9614734	18.6734921	36.6275582	26	1.9927607	18.5371481	36.9402661
27	1.9801229	19.3163260	38.2487004	27	2.0129621	19.1702725	38.5890316	27	2.0463253	19.0258289	38.9330357
28	2.0306636	19.8087274	40.2288233	28	2.0658023	19.6543459	40.6019937	28	2.1013203	19.5017202	40.9793610
29	2.0829045	20.2888262	42.2598869	29	2.1200296	20.1260374	42.6677960	29	2.1577933	19.9651566	43.0806814
30	2.1362789	20.7559299	44.3425914	30	2.1756804	20.5856637	44.7878256	30	2.2157840	20.4164641	45.2384747
31	2.1910211	21.2133381	46.4788703	31	2.2327920	21.0335335	46.9635061	31	2.2753332	20.8559602	47.4542587
32	2.2471660	21.6583430	48.6698914	32	2.2914028	21.4699474	49.1962901	32	2.3364328	21.2839539	49.7295919
33	2.3047496	22.0922295	50.9170573	33	2.3515522	21.8951984	51.4877009	33	2.3992758	21.7007464	52.0660747
34	2.3638088	22.5152757	53.2218069	34	2.4132804	22.3095721	53.8392531	34	2.4637563	22.1066307	54.4653504
35	2.4243814	22.9277521	55.5856157	35	2.4766290	22.7133468	56.2525335	35	2.5299697	22.5018923	56.9291047
36	2.4865062	23.3299228	58.0099971	36	2.5416405	23.1067935	58.7291625	36	2.5979627	22.8868093	59.4590765
37	2.5502229	23.7220454	60.4965033	37	2.6083586	23.4901763	61.2708030	37	2.6677829	23.2616524	62.0570392
38	2.6155724	24.1043709	63.0467262	38	2.6769280	23.8637528	63.8791616	38	2.7394796	23.6266852	64.7248221
39	2.6825964	24.4771441	65.6622996	39	2.7470947	24.2277738	66.5559896	39	2.8131031	23.9821646	67.4643017
40	2.7513379	24.8406036	68.3448950	40	2.8192060	24.5824836	69.3030843	40	2.8887053	24.3283404	70.2774048
41	2.8218410	25.1949822	71.0962329	41	2.8932101	24.9281204	72.1222903	41	2.9663392	24.6654563	73.1661101
42	2.8941506	25.5405067	73.9180739	42	2.9691569	25.2649164	75.0155004	42	3.0460596	24.9937403	76.1324493
43	2.9683133	25.8773983	76.8122245	43	3.0470973	25.5930975	77.9846573	43	3.1279224	25.3134503	79.1785088
44	3.0443763	26.2058729	79.7805378	44	3.1270366	25.9128843	81.0317545	44	3.2119863	25.6247842	82.3064313
45	3.1223884	26.5261405	82.8249141	45	3.2091695	26.2244914	84.1588381	45	3.2963074	25.9279700	85.5184166
46	3.2023996	26.8384063	85.9473025	46	3.2934102	26.5281281	87.3680076	46	3.3869495	26.2232209	88.8167241
47	3.2844611	27.1428703	89.1497021	47	3.3798622	26.8239981	90.6614178	47	3.4779737	26.5107447	92.2036735
48	3.3686254	27.4397273	92.4341633	48	3.4685836	27.1123002	94.0412800	48	3.5714443	26.7907435	95.6816472
49	3.4549465	27.7291674	95.8027887	49	3.5596339	27.3932280	97.5098636	49	3.6674268	27.0634142	99.2530915
50	3.5434795	28.0113759	99.2577351	50	3.6530743	27.6669700	101.0694975	50	3.7659889	27.3289487	102.9205184
51	3.6342811	28.2865334	102.8012146	51	3.7489675	27.9337101	104.7225718	51	3.8671999	27.5875337	106.6865073
52	3.7274096	28.5548163	106.4354957	52	3.8473779	28.1936274	108.4715393	52	3.9711309	27.8393512	110.5537072
53	3.8229245	28.8163961	110.1629053	53	3.9483716	28.4468964	112.3189173	53	4.0778550	28.0845781	114.5248391
54	3.9208869	29.0714405	113.9858298	54	4.0520163	28.6936871	116.2672888	54	4.1874474	28.3233871	118.6026931
55	4.0213596	29.3201126	117.9067167	55	4.1583818	28.9341653	120.3193052	55	4.2999850	28.5559460	122.7901455
56	4.1244070	29.5625717	121.9280763	56	4.2675393	29.1684923	124.4776869	56	4.4155471	28.7824185	127.0901255
57	4.2300949	29.7989730	126.0524832	57	4.3795622	29.3968257	128.7452262	57	4.5342150	29.0029639	131.5056726
58	4.3384911	30.0294679	130.2825781	58	4.4945257	29.6193185	133.1247884	58	4.6560720	29.2177372	136.0398876
59	4.4493649	30.2542039	134.6210692	59	4.6125070	29.8361204	137.6193141	59	4.7812039	29.4266895	140.6959596
60	4.5636876	30.4733249	139.0707341	60	4.7335853	30.0473767	142.2318211	60	4.9098988	29.6305680	145.4771635
61	4.6806321	30.6869713	143.6344217	61	4.8578419	30.2532295	146.9654064	61	5.0416469	29.8289159	150.3866822
62	4.8005733	30.8952298	148.3150537	62	4.9853603	30.4538168	151.8232453	62	5.1771412	30.0220727	155.4285092
63	4.9235879	31.0983837	153.1156270	63	5.1162260	30.6492734	156.8086006	63	5.3162769	30.2101743	160.6056504
64	5.0497549	31.2964131	158.0392149	64	5.2505269	30.8397304	161.9248346	64	5.4591518	30.3933529	165.9219272
65	5.1791549	31.4894948	163.0889698	65	5.3883532	31.0253159	167.1753615	65	5.6058665	30.5717375	171.3810790
66	5.3118707	31.6777524	168.2681247	66	5.5297975	31.2061543	172.5637147	66	5.7565242	30.7454534	176.9869455
67	5.4479874	31.8613064	173.5799954	67	5.6749547	31.3823672	178.0935123	67	5.9112308	30.9146229	182.7434697
68	5.5875921	32.0402744	179.0279827	68	5.8239223	31.5540728	183.7684670	68	6.0700951	31.0793650	188.6547004
69	5.7307741	32.2147709	184.6155748	69	5.9768002	31.7213864	189.5923892	69	6.2332289	31.2397955	194.7247955
70	5.8776252	32.3849076	190.3463489	70	6.1336912	31.8844204	195.5691894	70	6.4007469	31.3960272	200.9580244
71	6.0282393	32.5507935	196.2239741	71	6.2947006	32.0432841	201.7026807	71	6.5727670	31.5481702	207.3587713
72	6.1827130	32.7125348	202.2522135	72	6.4590365	32.1980844	207.9975813	72	6.7494101	31.6963313	213.9315383
73	6.3411450	32.8702350	208.4349264	73	6.6295098	32.3489251	214.4575178	73	6.9309005	31.8406127	220.6809484
74	6.5036368	33.0239952	214.7760714	74	6.8035345	32.4959076	221.0870277	74	7.1170508	31.9811221	227.6117489
75	6.6702925	33.1739136	221.2797083	75	6.9821273	32.6391304	227.8905621	75	7.3083369	32.1179521	234.7288146
76	6.8412188	33.3200868	227.9500008	76	7.1654081	32.7786898	234.8726894	76	7.5047485	32.2512011	242.0371515
77	7.0165250	33.4626071	234.7912196	77	7.3535001	32.9146795	242.0380975	77	7.7064386	32.3809627	249.5419000
78	7.1963235	33.6015670	241.8077446	78	7.5465294	33.0471907	249.3915976	78	7.9135491	32.5073283	257.2483386
79	7.3807292	33.7370549	249.0040680	79	7.7443258	33.1763125	256.9381270	79	8.1262257	32.6303866	265.1618877
80	7.5697604	33.8691561	256.3847973	80	7.9479223	33.3021315	264.6827529	80	8.3446181	32.7502244	273.2881134
81	7.7633381	33.9979600	263.9546577	81	8.1565592	33.4247323	272.6306751	81	8.5688797	32.8669257	281.6327315
82	7.9527865	34.1235442	271.7184958	82	8.3715648	33.5441971	280.7872004	82	8.7991683	32.9805728	290.2016111
83	8.1663329	34.2459907	279.6812823	83	8.5903948	33.6606062	289.1578952	83	9.0356460	33.0912456	299.0007794
84	8.3761080	34.3653779	287.8481152	84	8.8158926	33.7740377	297.7482899	84	9.2784789	33.1990219	308.0364254
85	8.5907457	34.4817822	296.2242231	85	9.0473098	33.8845678	306.5641825	85	9.5278381	33.3039775	317.3149043
86	8.8108836	34.5952782	304.8149688	86	9.2848017	33.9922707	315.6114923	86	9.7838987	33.4061862	326.8427424
87	9.0365525	34.7059385	313.6258524	87	9.5285277	34.0972187	324.8962940	87	10.0468410	33.5057200	336.6266411
88	9.2682270	34.8138340	322.6625149	88	9.7785516	34.1994823	334.4248217	88	10.3168498	33.6026498	346.6734821
89	9.5057253	34.9190338	331.9307419	89	10.0353412	34.2991301	344.2034733	89	10.5941152	33.6970408	356.9903319
90	9.7493095	35.0216052	341.4364671	90	10.2987689	34.3962291	354.2388145	90	10.8783320	33.7889625	367.5844471
91	9.9991355	35.1216138	351.1857766	91	10.5691116	34.4908445	364.5375834	91	11.1712006	33.8784784	378.4632791
92	10.2553634	35.2191238	361.1849121	92	10.8465508	34.5830397	375.1066950	92	11.4714267	33.9655615	389.6344798
93	10.5181571	35.3141954	371.4402755	93	11.1312727	34.6728767	385.9532457	93	11.7797212	34.0505431	401.1059064
94	10.7876848	35.4068957	381.9584326	94	11.4234686	34.7604157	397.0845184	94	12.0963013	34.1332130	412.8856277
95	11.0641193	35.4972780	392.7461174	95	11.7233347	34.8457157	408.5079870	95	12.4213894	34.2137193	424.9819289
96	11.3476373	35.5854021	403.8102367	96	12.0310722	34.9288338	420.2313217	96	12.7552142	34.2921186	437.4033183
97	11.6384205	35.6713244	415.1578740	97	12.3468879	35.0098259	432.2623939	97	13.0980106	34.3684661	450.1585325
98	11.9366551	35.7550999	426.7962946	98	12.6709937	35.0887463	444.6092818	98	13.4500192	34.4428154	463.2565420
99	12.2425318	35.8367824	438.7329496	99	13.0036072	35.1656480	457.2802754	99	13.8114889	34.5152189	476.7065626
100	12.5562467	35.9164240	450.9754815	100	13.3449519	35.2405827	470.2838827	100	14.1826726	34.5857275	490.5180515

Table 1 379

M	C(10.25,M,4)	A(10.25,M,4)	S(10.25,M,4)	C(10.50,M,4)	A(10.50,M,4)	S(10.50,M,4)	C(10.75,M,4)	A(10.75,M,4)	S(10.75,M,4)
101	12.8780005	35.9940758	463.5317282	13.6952569	35.3136007	483.6288346	14.5638320	34.6543908	504.7007242
102	13.2079993	36.0697875	476.4097287	14.0547574	35.3847510	497.3240915	14.9552350	34.7212570	519.2645561
103	13.5464543	36.1436076	489.6177280	14.4236948	35.4540814	511.3788489	15.3571569	34.7863732	534.2197911
104	13.8935822	36.2155833	503.1641823	14.8023168	35.5216384	525.8025437	15.7698805	34.8497852	549.5769480
105	14.2495052	36.2857606	517.0577645	15.1908776	35.5874673	54?.6042605	16.1936960	34.9115378	565.3460285
106	14.6147514	36.3541847	531.3073698	15.?896381	35.6516125	555.7957381	16.6289016	34.9716739	581.5405245
107	14.9892544	36.4208991	545.9221211	15.9988561	35.7141169	571.3853763	17.0759033	35.0302363	598.1694261
108	15.3733540	36.4859467	560.9113755	16.4188364	35.7750226	587.3842424	17.5347156	35.0872660	615.2452295
109	15.7672962	36.5493691	576.2847295	16.8498308	35.8343704	603.8030788	18.0059610	35.1428032	632.7799450
110	16.1713332	36.6112070	592.0520257	17.2921389	35.8922001	620.6520096	18.4896712	35.1968369	650.7859061
111	16.5857236	36.6714998	608.2233589	17.7460575	35.9485507	637.9450485	18.9857865	35.2495551	669.2757773
112	17.0107328	36.7302862	624.8090825	18.2119916	36.0034598	655.6911060	19.4970564	35.3008449	688.2625638
113	17.4465328	36.7876038	641.8198152	18.6899537	36.0569645	673.9029976	20.0210398	35.3507923	707.7596203
114	17.8937027	36.8434894	659.2664480	19.1805650	36.1091006	692.5929513	20.5591053	35.3994326	727.7800601
115	18.3522289	36.8979787	677.1601507	19.6840548	36.1599032	711.7735163	21.1116312	35.4467998	748.3397653
116	18.8225047	36.9511066	695.5123796	20.2007613	36.2094063	731.4575711	21.6790063	35.4929274	769.4513985
117	19.3043314	37.0029071	714.3348844	20.7310312	36.2576431	751.6583324	22.2616296	35.5378477	791.1304028
118	19.7995177	37.0534134	733.6397158	21.2752208	36.3046462	772.3893636	22.8599109	35.5815924	813.3920324
119	20.3068804	37.1026578	753.4392335	21.8335954	36.3504469	793.6645844	23.4742710	35.6241923	836.2519433
120	20.8272442	37.1506718	773.7461139	22.4068299	36.3950362	815.4982798	24.1051420	35.6656772	859.7262143
121	21.3609423	37.1974862	794.5733581	22.9950091	36.4385639	837.9051096	24.7529677	35.7060764	883.8313564
122	21.9083165	37.2431310	815.9343004	23.5988281	36.4809392	860.9001188	25.4182037	35.7454185	908.5843241
123	22.4697171	37.2876354	837.8426169	24.2180921	36.5222307	884.4987469	26.1013180	35.7837305	934.0025278
124	23.0455036	37.3310278	860.3123340	24.8538170	36.5624659	908.7168391	26.8027996	35.8210401	960.1038458
125	23.6360446	37.3733360	883.3578375	25.5062297	36.6016720	933.5706561	27.?231159	35.8573732	986.9066367
126	24.2417183	37.4145872	906.9930822	26.1757683	36.6398753	959.0768059	28.2627996	35.8927554	1014.4297525
127	24.8629123	37.4548078	931.2356004	26.8628622	36.6771014	985.2526541	29.0223624	35.9272115	1042.6925522
128	25.5000244	37.4940234	956.0985127	27.5680329	36.7133753	1012.1155363	29.8023384	35.9607660	1071.7149145
129	26.1534625	37.5322593	981.5985371	28.2916937	36.7487214	1039.6835692	30.6032762	35.9934422	1101.5172529
130	26.8236450	37.5695398	1007.7519996	29.0343507	36.7831633	1067.9752629	31.4257392	36.0252632	1132.1205291
131	27.5110009	37.6058889	1034.5756447	29.7965024	36.8167243	1097.0096136	32.2703060	36.0562515	1163.5462683
132	28.2159703	37.6413298	1062.0866456	30.5788606	36.8494269	1126.8061160	33.1375705	36.0864287	1195.8165743
133	28.9390046	37.6758853	1090.3026159	31.3813504	36.8812929	1157.3847765	34.0281427	36.1158162	1228.9541448
134	29.6805666	37.7095774	1119.2416205	32.2051109	36.9123439	1188.7661270	34.9426490	36.1444345	1262.9822875
135	30.4411311	37.7424276	1148.9221870	33.0504950	36.9426006	1220.9712378	35.8817327	36.1723038	1297.9249365
136	31.2211851	37.7744572	1179.3633181	33.9180705	36.9720834	1254.0217328	36.8460543	36.1994438	1333.8066692
137	32.0212279	37.8056865	1210.5845031	34.6084199	37.0008121	1287.9398034	37.8362920	36.2258734	1370.6527234
138	32.8417719	37.8361355	1242.6057311	35.7221409	37.0288059	1322.7482232	38.8531423	36.2516114	1408.4890154
139	33.6833423	37.8658238	1275.4475029	36.6590647	37.0560338	1358.4703641	39.8973205	36.2766757	1447.3421577
140	34.5464779	37.8947703	1309.1308452	37.6221681	37.0825638	1395.1302112	40.9695610	36.3010841	1487.2394783
141	35.4317314	37.9229936	1343.6773232	38.1085640	37.1085640	1432.7523793	42.0706180	36.3248536	1528.2090393
142	36.3396696	37.9505117	1379.1090546	39.6232559	37.1338017	1471.3621293	43.2012658	36.3480011	1570.2796572
143	37.2708736	37.9773423	1415.4487242	40.6633664	37.1583939	1510.9853852	44.3622998	36.3705427	1613.4809231
144	38.2259397	38.0035025	1452.7195978	41.7307798	37.1823570	1551.6487516	45.5545367	36.3924945	1657.8432229
145	39.?054794	38.0290092	149?.9455375	42.8262127	37.2057072	1593.3795314	46.7788148	36.4138717	1703.3977596
146	40.2101198	38.0538785	1530.1510169	43.9504008	37.2284601	1636.2057441	48.0359955	36.4346894	1750.1765744
147	41.2405042	38.0781266	1570.3611368	45.1040988	37.2506310	1680.1561449	49.3269629	36.4549623	1798.2125699
148	42.2972921	38.1017687	1611.6016410	46.2850814	37.2722349	1725.2602438	50.6526250	36.4747046	1847.5395328
149	43.3811602	38.1248202	1653.8989330	47.5031436	37.2932861	1771.5483252	52.0139143	36.4939302	1898.1921577
150	44.4928024	38.1472958	1697.2800932	48.7501011	37.3137989	1819.0514688	53.4117882	36.5126527	1950.2060720
151	45.6329305	38.1692098	1741.7728957	50.0297913	37.3337870	1867.8015699	54.8472300	36.5308851	2003.6178603
152	46.8022743	38.1905762	1787.4058262	51.3430733	37.3532638	1917.8313612	56.3212494	36.5486404	2058.4650903
153	48.0015826	38.2114089	1834.2081005	52.6908290	37.3722424	1969.1744345	57.8348829	36.5659310	2114.7863397
154	49.2316232	38.2317210	1882.2096831	54.0739632	37.3907356	2021.8652634	59.3891954	36.5827691	2172.6212226
155	50.4931835	38.2515257	1931.4413063	55.4934048	37.4087558	2075.9392092	60.9852600	36.5991665	2232.0104180
156	51.7870714	38.2708355	1981.9340988	56.9501066	37.4263150	2131.4326314	62.6242594	36.6151347	2292.9956980
157	53.1141151	38.2896629	2033.7215612	58.4450469	37.4434251	2188.3827300	64.3072864	36.6306851	2355.6199375
158	54.4751643	38.3080099	2086.8356762	59.9792294	37.4600976	2246.8277849	66.0355447	36.6458284	2419.9272439
159	55.8710903	38.3259182	2141.3108405	61.5538842	37.4763435	2306.8070143	67.8102500	36.6605755	2485.9620086
160	57.3027870	38.3433694	2197.1819308	63.1699467	37.4921740	2368.3606985	69.6326505	36.6749366	255?.7730387
161	58.7711710	38.3603845	2254.4847179	64.8276669	37.5075995	2431.5301069	71.?.40280	36.6889218	2623.4056691
162	60.2771822	38.3769746	2313.2558888	66.5293932	37.5226304	2496.3578339	73.4256987	36.7025410	2694.9097171
163	61.8217850	38.3931501	2373.5330710	68.2757898	37.5372769	2562.8872271	75.3990144	36.7158038	2768.3354154
164	63.4059682	38.4089215	2435.3548560	70.0680293	37.5515408	2631.1630168	77.4253629	36.7287194	2843.7344302
165	65.0307462	38.4242988	2498.7608243	71.9073150	37.5654555	2701.2310461	79.5061695	36.7412971	2921.1597931
166	66.6971591	38.4392920	2563.7915095	73.7948820	37.5790066	2773.1383611	81.6428978	36.7535455	3000.6659626
167	68.4062738	38.4539105	2630.4887295	75.7319977	37.5922711	2846.9332432	83.8370507	36.7770892	3082.3088604
168	70.1591845	38.4681638	2698.8950033	77.7195626	37.6050778	2922.6652409	86.0901714	36.7884009	3166.1459111
169	71.9570136	38.4820610	2769.0541878	79.7601117	37.6176154	3000.3852035	88.4038448	36.7994166	3252.2360825
170	73.8009121	38.4956110	2841.0112015	81.8530146	37.6298323	3080.1453152	90.7795981	36.8101439	3340.6399273
171	75.6920605	38.5088224	2914.8121136	84.0024772	37.6417367	3161.9991298	93.2194025	36.8205906	3431.4196255
172	77.6316695	38.5217037	2990.5041740	86.2075423	37.6533366	3246.0016070	95.7246740	36.8307638	3524.6390280
173	79.6209811	38.5342632	3068.1358436	88.4704903	37.6646398	3332.2091493	98.2972746	36.8406708	3620.3637019
174	81.6612687	38.5465089	3147.7568246	90.7928406	37.6756539	3420.6796395	100.9390138	36.8503185	3718.6609765
175	83.7538387	38.5584487	3229.4180934	93.1761527	37.6863863	3511.4724802	103.6517498	36.8597137	3819.5999904
176	85.9000308	38.5700901	3313.1719321	95.6220267	37.6968441	3604.6486329	106.4373906	36.8688630	3923.2517402
177	88.1012191	38.5814407	3399.0719629	98.1321049	37.7070344	3700.2706596	109.2978955	36.8777728	4029.6891308
178	90.3588129	38.5925077	3487.1731821	100.7080727	37.7169641	3798.4027645	112.2352764	36.8864495	4138.9870263
179	92.6742575	38.6032982	3577.5319409	103.3516596	37.7266398	3899.1108371	115.2515995	36.8948991	4251.2223027
180	95.?790353	38.6138191	367?.2062524	106.0646406	37.7360680	4002.4624967	118.3469862	36.9031275	4366.4739022
181	97.?846668	38.6240771	3765.2552877	108.8488375	37.7452551	4108.5271373	121.5295152	36.9111406	4484.8228885
182	99.9827114	38.6340788	3862.7399545	111.7001194	37.7542072	4217.3759748	124.7957237	36.9189440	4606.3525037
183	102.5447684	38.6438307	3962.7226560	114.6384051	37.7629302	4329.0820942	128.1496087	36.9265431	4731.1482274
184	105.1724781	38.6533389	4065.2674344	117.6476632	37.7714302	4443.7204093	131.5936295	36.9339434	4859.2978361
185	107.8675229	38.6626095	4170.4399125	120.7359144	37.7797127	4561.3681625	135.1302083	36.9411500	4990.8914655
186	110.6316281	38.6716485	4278.3074354	123.9052321	37.7877834	4682.1040769	138.7618326	36.9481680	5126.0216738
187	113.4665636	38.6804617	4388.9390635	127.1577445	37.7956477	4806.0093091	142.4910569	36.9550023	5264.7835064
188	116.3741443	38.6890546	4502.4056271	130.4956353	37.8033038	4933.1670535	146.3205004	36.9616578	5407.2745633
189	119.3562318	38.6974329	4618.7797714	133.9211457	37.8107778	5063.6626608	150.2526676	36.9681390	5553.5950673
190	122.4147352	38.7056019	4738.1360032	137.4365758	37.8180535	5197.5838345	154.2909134	36.9744507	5703.8479349
191	125.5516128	38.7135667	4860.5507384	141.0442695	37.8251439	5335.0204103	158.4374817	36.9805971	5858.1388483
192	128.7688729	38.7213326	4986.1023512	144.7465984	37.8320525	5476.0646962	162.6954890	36.9865827	6016.5763300
193	132.0685752	38.7289044	5114.8712240	148.5462992	37.8387844	5620.8113946	167.0679303	36.9924116	6179.2718190
194	135.4528325	38.7362870	5246.9397993	152.4456396	37.8453441	5769.3576939	171.5578809	36.9980880	6346.3397493
195	138.9233113	38.7434852	5382.3926318	156.4473377	37.8517361	5921.8033335	176.1684990	37.0036158	6517.8976302
196	142.4837340	38.7505036	5521.3164431	160.5540803	37.8579645	6078.2506711	180.9030274	37.0089990	6694.0661292
197	146.1348797	38.7573466	5663.8001771	164.7686249	37.8640336	6238.8047514	185.7647963	37.0142413	6874.9691566
198	149.8795860	38.7640186	5809.9350568	169.0938013	37.8699475	6403.5733763	190.7572252	37.0193463	7060.7339528
199	153.7202504	38.7705239	5959.8146427	173.5325136	37.8757101	6572.6671776	195.8838256	37.0243178	7251.4911780
200	157.6593318	38.7768667	6113.5348931	178.?277421	37.8813253	674?.1996912	201.1482034	37.0243178	7447.3750036

Table 1

M	C(11.00,M,4)	A(11.00,M,4)	S(11.00,M,4)	M	C(11.25,M,4)	A(11.25,M,4)	S(11.25,M,4)	M	C(11.50,M,4)	A(11.50,M,4)	S(11.50,M,4)
1/3	1.0090839	.3273500	.3303236	1/3	1.0092885	.3272169	.3302563	1/3	1.0094929	.3270840	.3301890
1	1.0275000	.9732360	1.0000000	1	1.0281250	.9726444	1.0000000	1	1.0287500	.9720535	1.0000000
2	1.0557563	1.9204243	2.0275000	2	1.0570410	1.9186815	2.0281250	2	1.0583266	1.9169414	2.0287500
3	1.0847895	2.8422621	3.0832563	3	1.0867703	2.8388391	3.0851660	3	1.0867535	2.8354230	3.0870766
4	1.1146213	3.7394279	4.1680458	4	1.1173357	3.7338253	4.1719363	4	1.1200551	3.7282362	4.1753300
5	1.1452733	4.6125819	5.2826671	5	1.1487608	4.6043285	5.2892720	5	1.1522567	4.5960984	5.2958851
6	1.1767684	5.4623668	6.4279404	6	1.1810597	5.4510186	6.4380328	6	1.1853841	5.4397068	6.4481318
7	1.2091295	6.2894081	7.6047008	7	1.2142873	6.2745470	7.6191025	7	1.2194639	6.2597393	7.6335259
8	1.2423806	7.0943144	8.8138303	8	1.2484391	7.0755472	8.8333897	8	1.2545235	7.0568547	8.8529998
9	1.2765460	7.8776783	10.0562188	9	1.2835514	7.8546356	10.0818288	9	1.2905910	7.8316935	10.1075132
10	1.3116510	8.6400762	11.3327648	10	1.3195513	8.6124115	11.3653802	10	1.3276955	8.5848783	11.3981042
11	1.3477214	9.3820693	12.6444159	11	1.3567665	9.3494580	12.6850316	11	1.3658667	9.3170141	12.7257997
12	1.3847838	10.1042037	13.9921373	12	1.3949256	10.0663422	14.0417981	12	1.4051354	10.0288693	14.0916665
13	1.4228653	10.8070109	15.3769211	13	1.4341579	10.7636155	15.4367236	13	1.4455331	10.7204756	15.4968019
14	1.4619941	11.4910081	16.7997864	14	1.4744935	11.4418144	16.8708915	14	1.4870921	11.3929289	16.9423349
15	1.5021990	12.1566989	18.2617805	15	1.5159637	12.1014608	18.3453750	15	1.5298460	12.0465895	18.4294271
16	1.5435094	12.8045732	19.7639795	16	1.5585002	12.7430622	19.8613387	16	1.5738291	12.6819825	19.9592731
17	1.5859559	13.4351077	21.3074889	17	1.6024358	13.3671122	21.4199389	17	1.6190767	13.2996184	21.5331022
18	1.6295697	14.0487666	22.8934449	18	1.6475043	13.9740909	23.0223747	18	1.6655251	13.8999938	23.1521739
19	1.6743829	14.6460016	24.5230146	19	1.6938403	14.5644653	24.6690789	19	1.7135119	14.4835904	24.8178040
20	1.7204284	15.2272521	26.1973975	20	1.7414796	15.1386697	26.3637193	20	1.7627753	15.0508777	26.5313159
21	1.7677402	15.7929461	27.9178259	21	1.7904587	15.6972057	28.1051989	21	1.8134551	15.6023112	28.2940912
22	1.8163531	16.3434999	29.6855662	22	1.8403154	16.2404433	29.8956576	22	1.8655920	16.1383341	30.1075464
23	1.8663028	16.8793186	31.5019192	23	1.8925883	16.7688202	31.7364730	23	1.9192277	16.6593770	31.9731383
24	1.9176261	17.4007967	33.3682220	24	1.9458173	17.2827431	33.6290613	24	1.9744055	17.1658586	33.8923660
25	1.9703608	17.9083179	35.2858481	25	2.0005435	17.7826072	35.5748786	25	2.0311697	17.6581858	35.8667716
26	2.0245457	18.4022559	37.2562089	26	2.0568087	18.2687973	37.5754221	26	2.0895658	18.1367541	37.8979412
27	2.0802208	18.8829741	39.2807547	27	2.1146565	18.7416873	39.6322308	27	2.1493408	18.6019481	39.9875071
28	2.1374268	19.3508264	41.3609754	28	2.1741312	19.2016412	41.7468373	28	2.2114430	19.0541445	42.1371479
29	2.1962061	19.8061571	43.4984023	29	2.2352786	19.6490127	43.9210185	29	2.2750220	19.4936977	44.3485909
30	2.2566017	20.2493013	45.6946083	30	2.2981465	20.0841461	46.1562972	30	2.3404289	19.9209698	46.6236129
31	2.3186583	20.6805852	47.9512101	31	2.3627812	20.5073761	48.4544431	31	2.4077162	20.3363011	48.9640418
32	2.3824214	21.1003262	50.2693683	32	2.4292344	20.9190285	50.8172243	32	2.4769380	20.7400254	51.3717580
33	2.4479380	21.5086333	52.6522897	33	2.4975567	21.3194198	53.2464587	33	2.5481500	21.1324670	53.8486930
34	2.5152563	21.9064071	55.1002277	34	2.5678004	21.7038581	55.7440154	34	2.6214093	21.5139412	56.3963460
35	2.5844258	22.2933403	57.6154839	35	2.6400198	22.0876432	58.3118158	35	2.6967748	21.8847545	59.0182553
36	2.6554975	22.6699175	60.1999098	36	2.7142704	22.4560663	60.9518356	36	2.7743071	22.2452048	61.7150302
37	2.7285237	23.0364161	62.8554073	37	2.7905092	22.8144110	63.6661060	37	2.8540684	22.5955819	64.4893373
38	2.8035581	23.3931057	65.5839310	38	2.8690957	23.1629530	66.4567152	38	2.9361229	22.9361671	67.3434057
39	2.8806560	23.7402488	68.3874891	39	2.9497884	23.5019603	69.3258103	39	3.0205365	23.2672341	70.2795287
40	2.9598740	24.0781011	71.2681450	40	3.0327512	23.8316939	72.2755987	40	3.1073769	23.5890489	73.3000651
41	3.0412705	24.4069110	74.2280190	41	3.1180473	24.1524075	75.3083500	41	3.1967140	23.9018702	76.4074220
42	3.1249055	24.7269207	77.2692865	42	3.2057424	24.4643477	78.4263973	42	3.2885195	24.2059491	79.6041559
43	3.2108404	25.0383656	80.3941950	43	3.2959039	24.7677546	81.6321397	43	3.3831673	24.5015301	82.8927754
44	3.2991385	25.3414751	83.6050354	44	3.3886012	25.0628616	84.9280437	44	3.4804324	24.7888507	86.2759427
45	3.3896648	25.6364721	86.9041738	45	3.4839056	25.3498958	88.3166449	45	3.5804958	25.0681416	89.7563761
46	3.4830861	25.9235738	90.2940386	46	3.5818905	25.6290780	91.8005505	46	3.6834351	25.3396273	93.3368719
47	3.5788709	26.2029915	93.7771247	47	3.6825312	25.9006229	95.3824410	47	3.7893338	25.6035259	97.0203070
48	3.6772899	26.4749309	97.3559956	48	3.7862052	26.1647396	99.0650722	48	3.8982772	25.8600495	100.8096408
49	3.7784154	26.7395921	101.0332855	49	3.8926922	26.4216313	102.8512773	49	4.0103526	26.1094041	104.7079180
50	3.8823218	26.9971700	104.8117009	50	4.0021741	26.6714955	106.7439695	50	4.1256503	26.3517902	108.7182706
51	3.9890856	27.2478540	108.6940226	51	4.1147353	26.9145245	110.7461437	51	4.2442627	26.5874024	112.8439209
52	4.0987865	27.4918287	112.6831083	52	4.2304622	27.1509052	114.8608790	52	4.3662853	26.8164300	117.0881836
53	4.2115021	27.7292737	116.7818937	53	4.3494440	27.3808197	119.0913412	53	4.4918160	27.0390571	121.4544689
54	4.3273184	27.9603637	120.9933958	54	4.4717721	27.6044447	123.4407852	54	4.6209557	27.2554626	125.9462949
55	4.4463196	28.1852688	125.3207142	55	4.5975407	27.8219523	127.9125572	55	4.7538082	27.4658202	130.5672406
56	4.5685934	28.4041545	129.7670339	56	4.7269465	28.0335098	132.5100979	56	4.8904802	27.6702991	135.3210488
57	4.6942298	28.6171820	134.3356273	57	4.8597891	28.2392801	137.2369444	57	5.0310815	27.8690335	140.2115209
58	4.8233211	28.8245080	139.0298570	58	4.9964506	28.4394213	142.0967335	58	5.1757251	28.0622732	145.2426104
59	4.9555624	29.0262852	143.8531781	59	5.1369964	28.6340876	147.0932041	59	5.3245271	28.2500833	150.4183354
60	5.0922514	29.2226620	148.8091405	60	5.2814744	28.8234287	152.2302005	60	5.4776073	28.4326448	155.7428626
61	5.2322883	29.4137830	153.9013919	61	5.4300159	29.0075902	157.5116749	61	5.6350885	28.6101043	161.2204669
62	5.3751762	29.5997888	159.1336802	62	5.5827351	29.1867139	162.9416907	62	5.7970973	28.7826044	166.8555584
63	5.5240211	29.7808163	164.5059364	63	5.7397495	29.3609375	168.5244258	63	5.9637639	28.9502837	172.6526557
64	5.6759316	29.9569589	170.0338774	64	5.9011799	29.5303951	174.2641753	64	6.1352221	29.1132770	178.6164195
65	5.8320198	30.1284660	175.7098091	65	6.0671506	29.6952172	180.1653552	65	6.3116097	29.2717152	184.7516416
66	5.9924003	30.2953441	181.5418288	66	6.2377892	29.8555304	186.2325058	66	6.4930665	29.4257256	191.0632513
67	6.1571913	30.4577558	187.5342291	67	6.4132271	30.0114581	192.4702951	67	6.6797442	29.5754319	197.5563198
68	6.3265141	30.6158207	193.6914204	68	6.5935991	30.1631203	198.8835221	68	6.8717868	29.7209545	204.2360640
69	6.5004932	30.7696552	200.0179345	69	6.7790440	30.3106338	205.4771212	69	7.0693507	29.8624102	211.1078508
70	6.6792568	30.9193725	206.5184277	70	6.9697047	30.4541119	212.2561652	70	7.2725946	29.9999127	218.1772016
71	6.8629363	31.0650827	213.1976845	71	7.1657276	30.5936650	219.2258699	71	7.4816816	30.1335725	225.4497951
72	7.0516671	31.2068931	220.0606208	72	7.3672637	30.7294007	226.3915975	72	7.6967800	30.2634969	232.9314777
73	7.2455879	31.3449081	227.1122879	73	7.5744680	30.8614231	233.7588612	73	7.9180824	30.3897905	240.6282577
74	7.4448416	31.4792293	234.3578758	74	7.7874999	30.9898340	241.3333291	74	8.1457067	30.5125545	248.5463202
75	7.6495747	31.6099556	241.8027174	75	8.0065233	31.1147322	249.1208290	75	8.3798958	30.6318878	256.6920269
76	7.8599380	31.7371830	249.4522921	76	8.2317068	31.2362137	257.1273523	76	8.6208178	30.7478860	265.0719226
77	8.0760863	31.8610054	257.3122301	77	8.4632235	31.3543720	265.3590591	77	8.8686663	30.8606426	273.6927404
78	8.2981787	31.9815137	265.3883165	78	8.7012517	31.4692980	273.8222827	78	9.1235405	30.9702479	282.5614067
79	8.5263786	32.0987968	273.6864952	79	8.9459744	31.5810801	282.5235344	79	9.3859451	31.0767902	291.6850472
80	8.7603540	32.2129410	280.2128738	80	9.1975799	31.6898043	291.4695089	80	9.6557910	31.1803550	300.0709923
81	9.0017571	32.3240301	290.9737279	81	9.4562619	31.7955544	300.6670887	81	9.9333950	31.2810255	310.7267833
82	9.2493264	32.4321461	299.9755054	82	9.7222192	31.8984115	310.1233506	82	10.2189901	31.3788828	320.6601783
83	9.5036829	32.5373685	309.2248318	83	9.9955667	31.9984550	319.8455699	83	10.5127758	31.4740050	330.8791585
84	9.7650342	32.6397747	318.7285147	84	10.2767845	32.0957617	329.8412265	84	10.8150181	31.5664690	341.3919343
85	10.0335726	32.7394401	328.4935488	85	10.5658191	32.1904065	340.1180110	85	11.1259499	31.6563490	352.2069524
86	10.3094958	32.8364380	338.5271214	86	10.8629827	32.2824623	350.6838301	86	11.4458210	31.7437171	363.3329023
87	10.5930070	32.9308309	348.8366173	87	11.1685041	32.3719998	361.5468128	87	11.7748883	31.8286436	374.7787233
88	10.8843147	33.0227153	359.4296243	88	11.4826183	32.4590879	372.7153169	88	12.1134163	31.9111967	386.5536116
89	11.1836333	33.1121346	370.3139389	89	11.8055669	32.5437937	384.1979352	89	12.4616771	31.9914427	398.6670279
90	11.4911832	33.1991549	381.4975723	90	12.1375985	32.6261823	396.0035022	90	12.8199503	32.0694461	411.1287050
91	11.8071908	33.2838490	392.9887555	91	12.4780685	32.7063172	408.1411007	91	13.1885238	32.1452696	423.9486552
92	12.1318885	33.3662764	404.7959463	92	12.8299395	32.7842599	420.6200691	92	13.5676939	32.2189741	437.1371791
93	12.4655155	33.4464497	416.9278343	93	13.1907815	32.8600704	433.4500086	93	13.9577651	32.2906188	450.7048730
94	12.8083171	33.5245720	429.3933503	94	13.5617722	32.9338071	446.6407901	94	14.3590509	32.3602613	464.6626381
95	13.1605459	33.6005567	442.2016674	95	13.9431971	33.0055266	460.2025623	95	14.7718736	32.4279575	479.0216890
96	13.5224609	33.6745077	455.3622133	96	14.3353495	33.0752843	474.1457594	96	15.1965649	32.4937619	493.7935625
97	13.8943286	33.7464795	468.8846942	97	14.7385312	33.1431336	488.4811089	97	15.6334662	32.5577272	508.9901275
98	14.2764226	33.8165251	482.7790027	98	15.1530524	33.2091269	503.2196401	98	16.0829283	32.6199050	524.6235936
99	14.6690242	33.8846960	497.0554253	99	15.5792320	33.2733149	518.3726925	99	16.5453125	32.6803450	540.7065220
100	15.0724224	33.9510423	511.7244495	100	16.0173979	33.3357471	533.9519245	100	17.0209903	32.7390960	557.2518345

Table 1

M	C(11.00,M,4)	A(11.00,M,4)	S(11.00,M,4)	M	C(11.25,M,4)	A(11.25,M,4)	S(11.25,M,4)	M	C(11.50,M,4)	A(11.50,M,4)	S(11.50,M,4)
101	15.4869140	34.0156129	526.7968719	101	16.4678872	33.3964713	549.9693224	101	17.5103437	32.7962051	574.2728248
102	15.9128041	34.0784554	542.2837859	102	16.9310465	33.4555344	566.4372096	102	18.0137661	32.8517182	591.7831685
103	16.3504062	34.1396160	558.1965900	103	17.4072322	33.5129818	583.3662561	103	18.5316619	32.9056799	609.7969346
104	16.8000424	34.1991396	574.5469963	104	17.8968106	33.5688577	600.7754283	104	19.0644472	32.9581336	628.3285565
105	17.2620436	34.2570702	591.3470387	105	18.0001584	33.6232050	618.6722950	105	19.6125500	33.0091214	647.3930436
106	17.7357498	34.3134503	608.6090823	106	18.576629	33.6760657	637.0724574	106	20.1764108	33.0586842	667.0055937
107	18.2245104	34.3683215	626.3458320	107	19.4497221	33.7274803	655.9901203	107	20.7564826	33.1068619	687.1820045
108	18.7256844	34.4217241	644.5703424	108	19.5967456	33.7774884	675.4398424	108	21.3532315	33.1536932	707.9384871
109	19.2406408	34.4736974	663.2960269	109	20.5591541	33.8261286	695.4365080	109	21.9671369	33.1992158	729.2917187
110	19.7697584	34.5242797	682.5366676	110	21.1373903	33.8734381	715.9957421	110	22.5985921	33.2434661	751.2568556
111	20.3134267	34.5735082	702.3064260	111	21.7318691	33.9194535	737.1331223	111	23.2484045	33.2864798	773.8575477
112	20.8720460	34.6214192	722.6198527	112	22.5430779	33.9642101	758.8649914	112	23.9167961	33.3282914	797.1059522
113	21.4480272	34.6680479	743.4918987	113	22.9714770	34.0077423	781.2080693	113	24.6044040	33.3689346	821.0227484
114	22.0357930	34.7134286	764.9379259	114	23.6175498	34.0500087	804.1795463	114	25.3117807	33.4084419	845.6271524
115	22.6417773	34.7575947	786.9737189	115	24.2817933	34.0912668	827.7970960	115	26.0394943	33.4468451	870.9389331
116	23.2644262	34.8005788	809.6154962	116	24.9647188	34.1313234	852.0788894	116	26.7881298	33.4841750	896.9784274
117	23.9041979	34.8424125	832.8799224	117	25.6665515	34.1702841	877.0436082	117	27.5582885	33.5204618	923.7665572
118	24.5615633	34.8831265	856.7841202	118	26.3887317	34.2081791	902.7104597	118	28.3505893	33.5557344	951.3248458
119	25.2370063	34.9227508	881.3456836	119	27.1309148	34.2450374	929.0991914	119	29.1655688	33.5900213	979.6754351
120	25.9310240	34.9613147	906.5826899	120	27.8939718	34.2808874	956.2301062	120	30.0041818	33.6233500	1008.8411039
121	26.6441272	34.9986464	932.5137139	121	28.6784897	34.3157568	984.1240779	121	30.8669020	33.6557472	1038.8452856
122	27.3768407	35.0353736	959.1578410	122	29.4850722	34.3496722	1012.8025676	122	31.7542225	33.6872391	1069.7120876
123	28.1297038	35.0709232	986.5346817	123	30.3143399	34.3826599	1042.2876399	123	32.6671564	33.7178509	1101.4663102
124	28.9032706	35.1055214	1014.6643355	124	31.1669307	34.4147452	1072.6019798	124	33.6063372	33.7476072	1134.1334666
125	29.6981106	35.1391936	1043.5676561	125	32.0435006	34.4459528	1103.7689105	125	34.5725194	33.7765319	1166.7398033
126	30.5143036	35.1719645	1073.2657667	126	32.9447241	34.4763067	1135.8124111	126	35.5664793	33.8046483	1202.3123232
127	31.3513658	35.2038584	1103.7805753	127	33.8712945	34.5058302	1168.7571352	127	36.5930156	33.8319789	1237.8788025
128	32.2161999	35.2348987	1135.1345441	128	34.8239246	34.5345461	1202.6284297	128	37.6409498	33.8585457	1274.4678181
129	33.1021454	35.2651082	1167.3507410	129	35.8033475	34.5624764	1237.4523543	129	38.7231271	33.8843700	1312.1087679
130	34.0124544	35.2945092	1200.4528864	130	36.8103166	34.5896427	1273.2557018	130	39.8354170	33.9094727	1350.8318951
131	34.9477969	35.3231233	1234.4653408	131	37.8456068	34.6160659	1310.0660184	131	40.9817140	33.9338738	1390.6683121
132	35.9083613	35.3509716	1269.4131378	132	38.9100145	34.6417662	1347.9116252	132	42.1599383	33.9575930	1431.6500261
133	36.8963550	35.3780746	1305.3219991	133	40.0043587	34.6667635	1386.8216397	133	43.3720365	33.9806494	1473.9099644
134	37.9110048	35.4044521	1342.2183541	134	41.1294812	34.6910769	1426.8259983	134	44.6189326	34.0030613	1517.1820009
135	38.9535574	35.4301237	1380.1293589	135	42.2862479	34.7147253	1467.9554796	135	45.9017783	34.0248470	1561.8009834
136	40.0247802	35.4551083	1419.0829163	136	43.4755486	34.7377267	1510.2417275	136	47.2214544	34.0460238	1607.7027617
137	41.1254617	35.4794241	1459.1076965	137	44.6982984	34.7600989	1553.7172761	137	48.5790713	34.0666088	1654.9242162
138	42.2564119	35.5030891	1500.2331582	138	45.9554381	34.7816592	1598.4155745	138	49.9757196	34.0866185	1703.5032874
139	43.4184632	35.5261208	1542.4895701	139	47.2479348	34.8030241	1644.3710126	139	51.4125215	34.1060690	1753.4790070
140	44.6124710	35.5485361	1585.9080333	140	48.5767829	34.8230101	1691.6189474	140	52.8906315	34.1249760	1804.8915285
141	45.8393139	35.5703514	1630.5205042	141	49.9430050	34.8436329	1740.1957303	141	54.4112371	34.1433545	1857.7821600
142	47.0998950	35.5915829	1676.3598181	142	51.3476520	34.8631080	1790.1367353	142	55.9755602	34.1612195	1912.1933071
143	48.3951422	35.6122461	1723.4597132	143	52.7918047	34.8820503	1841.4863873	143	57.5848576	34.1785851	1968.1689573
144	49.7260086	35.6323563	1771.8548553	144	54.2765742	34.9004745	1894.2781919	144	59.2404222	34.1954655	2025.7538149
145	51.134738	35.6519283	1821.5808639	145	55.8031028	34.9183946	1948.5547661	145	60.9435844	34.2118741	2084.9942372
146	52.4985443	35.6709764	1872.6743377	146	57.3725651	34.9358246	2004.3578690	146	62.6957124	34.2278242	2145.9378215
147	53.9422543	35.6895148	1925.1728820	147	58.9816865	34.9527777	2061.7304341	147	64.4982142	34.2433285	2208.6335339
148	55.4255663	35.7075570	1979.1151363	148	60.6451545	34.9692670	2120.7166026	148	66.3525378	34.2583995	2273.1317481
149	56.9498721	35.7251163	2034.5408026	149	62.3507995	34.9853053	2181.3617571	149	68.2601733	34.2730493	2339.4842859
150	58.5159936	35.7422056	2091.4906748	150	64.1044157	35.0009049	2243.7125566	150	70.2226533	34.2872897	2407.7444592
151	60.1251384	35.7588376	2150.0066684	151	65.9073524	35.0160777	2307.8169723	151	72.2415545	34.3011322	2477.9671125
152	61.7786260	35.7750244	2210.1318518	152	67.7609967	35.0308034	2373.7243247	152	74.3184992	34.3145878	2550.2086670
153	63.4775382	35.7907780	2271.9104778	153	69.6667747	35.0451895	2441.4853214	153	76.4551561	34.3276674	2624.5271662
154	65.2231705	35.8061100	2335.3880160	154	71.6261528	35.0591509	2511.1520951	154	78.6532418	34.3403814	2700.9823223
155	67.0168077	35.8210316	2400.6111865	155	73.6406383	35.0727303	2582.7782489	155	80.9145225	34.3527401	2779.6355342
156	68.8597699	35.8355539	2467.6279942	156	75.7117813	35.0859383	2656.4188872	156	83.2408151	34.3647535	2860.5500367
157	70.7534136	35.8496875	2536.4877641	157	77.8411751	35.0987860	2732.1306685	157	85.6339885	34.3764311	2943.7909018
158	72.6991325	35.8634428	2607.2411776	158	80.0304582	35.1112802	2809.9718436	158	88.0959557	34.3877823	3029.4248903
159	74.6983586	35.8768300	2679.9403101	159	82.2813148	35.1234337	2890.0023018	159	90.6287247	34.3988163	3117.5208559
160	76.7525635	35.8893588	2754.6386687	160	84.5954768	35.1352546	2972.2836166	160	93.2343005	34.4095420	3207.1495806
161	78.8632590	35.9025350	2831.3912321	161	86.9747240	35.1467522	3056.8790934	161	95.947867	34.4199679	3301.3838812
162	81.039*9986	35.9148798	2910.2544911	162	89.4203887	35.1579353	3143.8538179	162	98.6723368	34.4301025	3397.2988678
163	83.2803785	35.9268900	2991.2864897	163	91.9355512	35.1688124	3233.2747066	163	101.5091665	34.4399538	3495.9710046
164	85.5500390	35.9335794	3074.5468682	164	94.5215470	35.1793920	3325.2105578	164	104.4275550	34.4495298	3597.4801711
165	87.9628650	35.9499556	3160.0969072	165	97.1799653	35.1896822	3419.7321049	165	107.4258472	34.4588382	3701.9077261
166	90.3195883	35.9610274	3247.9995722	166	99.9131521	35.1996809	3516.9120704	166	110.5184553	34.4678865	3809.3375733
167	92.8037880	35.9718008	3338.3195605	167	102.7232095	35.2094258	3616.8252225	167	113.6456809	34.4766819	3919.8560288
168	95.3358922	35.9822898	3431.1233485	168	105.6122997	35.2188944	3719.5484319	168	116.9646169	34.4852315	4033.5518095
169	97.9781792	35.9924962	3526.4792407	169	108.5825457	35.2281040	3825.1607317	169	120.3273497	34.4935421	4150.5165065
170	100.6725791	36.0024294	3624.4574199	170	111.6365326	35.2370616	3933.7433774	170	123.7867610	34.5016206	4270.8438561
171	103.4410751	36.0120057	3725.1299990	171	114.7763101	35.2457742	4045.3799909	171	127.3456304	34.5094732	4394.6306171
172	106.2857046	36.0215053	3828.5710741	172	118.0043938	35.2542485	4160.1562200	172	131.0068172	34.5171064	4521.9762475
173	109.2085615	36.0306621	3934.8567787	173	121.3224843	35.2624909	4278.1606138	173	134.7732632	34.5245263	4652.9830647
174	112.2117970	36.0395738	4044.0653402	174	124.7354843	35.2705079	4399.4838812	174	138.6479945	34.5317388	4787.7563279
175	115.2976214	36.0482470	4156.2771372	175	128.2428089	35.2783055	4524.2193654	175	142.6341244	34.5387497	4926.4043225
176	118.4683060	36.0566881	4271.5747586	176	131.8505230	35.2858899	4652.4630352	176	146.7348555	34.5455647	5069.0384469
177	121.7251844	36.0649033	4390.0430645	177	135.5563189	35.2932668	4784.3135582	177	150.9534826	34.5521893	5215.7733023
178	125.0736545	36.0728986	4511.7682489	178	139.3714107	35.3004418	4919.8723771	178	155.2933952	34.5586287	5366.7267849
179	128.5131800	36.0806799	4636.8429034	179	143.2912317	35.3074206	5059.2437879	179	159.7580800	34.5648882	5522.0201801
180	132.072924	36.0882923	4761.3560834	180	147.3212976	35.3142085	5202.5350195	180	164.3511251	34.5709727	5681.7782604
181	135.6785930	36.0956233	4897.4033758	181	151.4647997	35.3208107	5349.8563171	181	169.0762200	34.5768872	5846.1293855
182	139.4097543	36.1027964	5033.0819687	182	155.723540	35.3272323	5501.3210761	182	173.9371613	34.5826364	6015.2056055
183	143.2435225	36.1097775	5172.4917230	183	160.1044099	35.3334782	5657.0456801	183	178.9378547	34.5882249	6189.1427668
184	147.1827194	36.1165718	5315.7352455	184	164.6073464	35.3395533	5817.1500900	184	184.0823180	34.5936573	6368.0806215
185	151.2302442	36.1231842	5462.9175649	185	169.2369280	35.3454622	5981.7574365	185	189.3746847	34.5989378	6552.1629396
186	155.3890759	36.1296196	5614.1482090	186	173.9967617	35.3512094	6150.9943645	186	194.8192069	34.6040708	6741.5376242
187	159.6622755	36.1358829	5769.5372849	187	178.8903743	35.3567994	6324.9910812	187	200.4220250	34.6090603	6936.3568311
188	164.0525881	36.1419785	5929.1995604	188	183.9216661	35.3622365	6503.8814555	188	206.1823415	34.6139104	7136.7770902
189	168.5644452	36.1479109	6093.2525485	189	189.0946630	35.3675249	6687.8031216	189	212.1100838	34.6186249	7342.9594317
190	173.1999675	36.1536846	6261.8169937	190	194.4127447	35.3726686	6876.8975345	190	218.2062488	34.6232077	7555.0695155
191	177.9629666	36.1593037	6435.0169612	191	199.8806032	35.3776716	7071.3103293	191	224.4817359	34.6276624	7773.2777643
192	182.8569482	36.1647725	6612.9799278	192	205.5022452	35.3825377	7271.1909325	192	230.9355858	34.6319926	7997.5595002
193	187.8855143	36.1700949	6795.8368760	193	211.2819958	35.3872707	7476.6931776	193	237.5749839	34.6362018	8228.6950861
194	193.0523659	36.1752748	6983.7223902	194	217.2243019	35.3918742	7687.9751734	194	244.4052647	34.6402934	8466.2700700
195	198.3613060	36.1803161	7176.7747561	195	223.3337354	35.3963518	7905.1994754	195	251.4319161	34.6442706	8710.6753347
196	203.8162419	36.1852225	7375.1360621	196	229.6149968	35.4007069	8128.5332108	196	258.6605837	34.6481367	8962.1072508
197	209.4211885	36.1899976	7578.9523040	197	236.0729185	35.4049429	8358.1482076	197	266.0970755	34.6518947	9220.7678345
198	215.1802712	36.1946448	7788.3734925	198	242.7124694	35.4090630	8594.2211261	198	273.7473664	34.6555477	9486.8649100
199	221.0977287	36.1991677	8003.5537638	199	249.5387576	35.4130704	8836.9335955	199	281.6176032	34.6590986	9760.6122764
200	227.1779162	36.2035696	8224.6514925	200	256.5570352	35.4169682	9086.4723531	200	289.7141093	34.6625503	10042.2298795

Table 1

M	C(11.75,M,4)	A(11.75,M,4)	S(11.75,M,4)	M	C(12.00,M,4)	A(12.00,M,4)	S(12.00,M,4)	M	C(12.25,M,4)	A(12.25,M,4)	S(12.25,M,4)
1/3	1.0096973	.3269511	.3301217	1/3	1.0099016	.3268184	.3300545	1/3	1.0101059	.3266859	.3299873
1	1.0293750	.9714633	1.0000000	1	1.0300000	.9708738	1.0000000	1	1.0306250	.9702850	1.0000000
2	1.0596129	1.9152041	2.0293750	2	1.0609000	1.9134697	2.0300000	2	1.0621879	1.9117380	2.0306250
3	1.0907390	2.8320137	3.0889879	3	1.0927270	2.8286114	3.0909000	3	1.0947174	2.8252158	3.0928129
4	1.1227795	3.7226606	4.1797269	4	1.1255088	3.7170984	4.1836270	4	1.1282431	3.7115496	4.1875303
5	1.1557611	4.5878913	5.3025054	5	1.1592741	4.5797072	5.3091358	5	1.1627956	4.5715460	5.3157734
6	1.1897116	5.4284311	6.4582675	6	1.1940523	5.4171914	6.4684099	6	1.1984062	5.4059876	6.4785590
7	1.2248594	6.2449847	7.6479791	7	1.2293739	6.2302830	7.6624622	7	1.2351074	6.2158333	7.6769751
8	1.2606338	7.0382365	8.8726385	8	1.2667701	7.0196922	8.8923360	8	1.2729325	7.0012214	8.9120825
9	1.2976649	7.8088515	10.1332723	9	1.3047732	7.7861089	10.1591061	9	1.3119161	7.7634353	10.1850150
10	1.3357838	8.5574756	11.4309371	10	1.3439164	8.5302028	11.4638753	10	1.3520935	8.5030591	11.4969311
11	1.3750224	9.2847365	12.7667209	11	1.3842339	9.2526241	12.8077957	11	1.3935014	9.2206759	12.8490246
12	1.4154137	9.9912437	14.1417433	12	1.4257609	9.9540040	14.1920296	12	1.4361774	9.9169688	14.2425260
13	1.4569915	10.6775695	15.5571571	13	1.4685337	10.6349553	15.6177905	13	1.4801603	10.5925713	15.6787034
14	1.4997906	11.3443493	17.0141485	14	1.5125897	11.2960731	17.0863242	14	1.5254902	11.2480983	17.1583637
15	1.5438470	11.9920819	18.5139392	15	1.5579674	11.9379351	18.5989139	15	1.5722083	11.8841463	18.6843539
16	1.5891975	12.6213303	20.0577861	16	1.6047064	12.5611020	20.1568813	16	1.6203572	12.5012941	20.2565622
17	1.6356801	13.2326220	21.6469336	17	1.6528476	13.1661185	21.7615077	17	1.6699807	13.1001035	21.8769194
18	1.6839341	13.8264695	23.2828637	18	1.7024331	13.7535131	23.4144354	18	1.7211238	13.6811192	23.5469001
19	1.7333997	14.4033705	24.9667979	19	1.7535061	14.3237991	25.1168684	19	1.7739332	14.2448701	25.2680239
20	1.7843183	14.9638086	26.7001975	20	1.8061112	14.8774749	26.8703745	20	1.8281569	14.7916597	27.0418571
21	1.8367327	15.5082536	28.4845158	21	1.8602946	15.4150241	28.6764857	21	1.8841442	15.3226140	28.6700140
22	1.8906367	16.0371620	30.3212485	22	1.9161034	15.9369166	30.5367803	22	1.9418461	15.8375879	30.7541582
23	1.9462256	16.5509770	32.2119352	23	1.9735865	16.4436084	32.4526837	23	2.0013151	16.3372593	32.6960043
24	2.0033960	17.0501295	34.1581608	24	2.0327941	16.9355421	34.4264702	24	2.0625054	16.8220830	34.6973194
25	2.0622457	17.5350378	36.1615567	25	2.0937779	17.4131477	36.4592643	25	2.1257727	17.2925002	36.7599243
26	2.1209242	18.0061083	38.2238025	26	2.1565913	17.8768424	38.5530423	26	2.1908745	17.7489389	38.8855975
27	2.1851822	18.4637361	40.3466267	27	2.2212890	18.3270315	40.7096335	27	2.2579700	18.1918146	41.0765720
28	2.2493719	18.9080046	42.5318088	28	2.2879277	18.7641082	42.9309225	28	2.3271204	18.6215303	43.3345420
29	2.3154477	19.3401866	44.7811807	29	2.3565555	19.1884546	45.2188502	29	2.3983884	19.0384769	45.6616624
30	2.3834634	19.7597442	47.0966279	30	2.4272625	19.6004413	47.5754157	30	2.4718391	19.4430340	48.0600508
31	2.4534777	20.1673289	49.4800914	31	2.5000803	20.0004285	50.0026782	31	2.5475391	19.8355697	50.5318898
32	2.5255486	20.5632825	51.9335690	32	2.5750828	20.3887055	52.5027585	32	2.6255575	20.2164412	53.0794290
33	2.5997366	20.9479368	54.4591176	33	2.6523352	20.7657918	55.0778413	33	2.7055652	20.5859951	55.7049865
34	2.6761038	21.3216144	57.0588542	34	2.7319053	21.1318367	57.7301765	34	2.7883354	20.9445677	58.4109517
35	2.7547144	21.6846264	59.7349581	35	2.8138625	21.4872201	60.4620818	35	2.8742435	21.2924853	61.1997871
36	2.8356341	22.0372832	62.4896724	36	2.8982783	21.8322525	63.2759443	36	2.9622672	21.6300646	64.0740306
37	2.9189309	22.3798744	65.3253066	37	2.9852267	22.1672354	66.1742226	37	3.0529866	21.9576127	67.0362977
38	3.0046745	22.7126892	68.2442375	38	3.0747835	22.4924616	69.1594493	38	3.1464843	22.2754277	70.0892844
39	3.0929368	23.0360065	71.2489119	39	3.1670270	22.8082151	72.2342328	39	3.2423454	22.5837989	73.2357687
40	3.1837918	23.3500974	74.3418487	40	3.2620378	23.1147720	75.4012598	40	3.3421576	22.8830068	76.4786141
41	3.2773157	23.6552251	77.5256405	41	3.3598989	23.4124000	78.6632976	41	3.4445111	23.1733237	79.8207717
42	3.3735868	23.9516455	80.8029562	42	3.4608959	23.7013592	82.0231965	42	3.5499993	23.4550139	83.2652828
43	3.4726860	24.2396071	84.1765431	43	3.5645168	23.9819021	85.4838924	43	3.6587180	23.7283337	86.8152821
44	3.5746961	24.5193511	87.6492290	44	3.6714523	24.2542739	89.0484092	44	3.7707663	23.9933318	90.4740001
45	3.6797028	24.7911122	91.2239251	45	3.7815958	24.5187125	92.7198614	45	3.8862460	24.2508495	94.2447664
46	3.7877941	25.0551181	94.9036279	46	3.8950437	24.7754491	96.5014573	46	4.0052623	24.5005211	98.1310123
47	3.8990605	25.3115902	98.6914220	47	4.0118950	25.0247078	100.3965910	47	4.1279234	24.7427736	102.1362746
48	4.0135954	25.5607433	102.5904925	48	4.1322519	25.2667065	104.4083960	48	4.2543411	24.9778227	106.2641980
49	4.1314948	25.8027865	106.6040780	49	4.2562194	25.5016569	108.5406479	49	4.3846303	25.2058971	110.5185391
50	4.2528575	26.0379225	110.7355727	50	4.3839060	25.7297640	112.7968674	50	4.5189096	25.4271894	114.9031693
51	4.3777851	26.2663485	114.9884302	51	4.5154232	25.9512272	117.1807734	51	4.6573012	25.6419060	119.4220789
52	4.5063826	26.4882650	119.3662153	52	4.6508859	26.1662400	121.6961966	52	4.7999310	25.8502423	124.0793801
53	4.6387576	26.7036310	123.8725979	53	4.7904125	26.3749993	126.3470825	53	4.9469289	26.0523880	128.8793111
54	4.7750211	26.9132541	128.5113555	54	4.9341249	26.5776605	131.1374950	54	5.0984286	26.2485268	133.8262400
55	4.9152873	27.1167010	133.2863766	55	5.0821486	26.7744276	136.0716198	55	5.2545680	26.4388374	138.9246686
56	5.0596739	27.3143422	138.2016639	56	5.2346131	26.9654637	141.1537684	56	5.4154891	26.6234930	144.1792366
57	5.2083018	27.5063434	143.2613377	57	5.3916514	27.1509336	146.3883915	57	5.5813385	26.8026615	149.5947257
58	5.3612957	27.6928655	148.4696355	58	5.5534010	27.3310055	151.7800329	58	5.7522670	26.9765060	155.1760642
59	5.5187837	27.8740648	153.8309352	59	5.7200030	27.5058306	157.3334399	59	5.9284301	27.1451847	160.9283311
60	5.6808980	28.0500933	159.0306169	60	5.8916031	27.6755637	163.0534370	60	6.1099883	27.3088511	166.8567613
61	5.8477744	28.2210085	165.0306169	61	6.0683512	27.8403531	168.9450401	61	6.2971057	27.4676542	172.9667496
62	6.0115527	28.3872238	170.8873013	62	6.2504017	28.0003428	175.0133913	62	6.4899556	27.6217385	179.2638553
63	6.1963771	28.5486085	176.8979441	63	6.4379138	28.1556726	181.2637930	63	6.6887105	27.7712441	185.7538119
64	6.3783957	28.7053877	183.0943212	64	6.6310512	28.3064782	187.7017068	64	6.8935523	27.9163072	192.4425224
65	6.5657611	28.8576930	189.4727169	65	6.8299327	28.4528915	194.3327580	65	7.1046673	28.0570597	199.3360747
66	6.7536303	29.0056519	196.0384779	66	7.0348422	28.5950403	201.1627408	66	7.3222477	28.1936298	206.4407420
67	6.9571651	29.1493887	202.7971082	67	7.2459287	28.7330488	208.1976230	67	7.5464916	28.3261417	213.7629897
68	7.1615318	29.2890236	209.7542733	68	7.4633066	28.8670377	215.4435517	68	7.7776029	28.4547161	221.3094813
69	7.3719018	29.4246738	216.9158051	69	7.6872058	28.9971240	222.9068582	69	8.0157920	28.5794698	229.0870841
70	7.5884514	29.5564530	224.2877008	70	7.9178219	29.1234213	230.5940640	70	8.2612756	28.7005165	237.1028761
71	7.8113622	29.6844716	231.8761582	71	8.1553566	29.2460401	238.5118859	71	8.5142772	28.8179663	245.3641517
72	8.0408209	29.8088370	239.6875204	72	8.4000173	29.3650875	246.6672425	72	8.7750269	28.9319260	253.8764288
73	8.2770200	29.9296535	247.7283413	73	8.6520178	29.4806675	255.0672598	73	9.0437621	29.0424995	262.6534557
74	8.5201575	30.0470222	256.0053613	74	8.9115783	29.5928810	263.7192776	74	9.3207273	29.1497872	271.6972178
75	8.7704371	30.1610416	264.5255188	75	9.1789257	29.7018263	272.6308559	75	9.6061746	29.2538870	281.0179451
76	9.0280687	30.2718073	273.2959560	76	9.4542935	29.8075983	281.8097816	76	9.9003637	29.3548933	290.6241197
77	9.2932882	30.3794120	282.3240247	77	9.7379223	29.9102896	291.2640751	77	10.2035623	29.4528983	300.5244834
78	9.5662580	30.4839461	291.6172929	78	10.0300599	30.0099999	301.0019973	78	10.5160464	29.5479911	310.7280457
79	9.8472668	30.5854071	301.1835509	79	10.3309617	30.1067863	311.0320572	79	10.8381003	29.6402582	321.2440921
80	10.1365303	30.6841502	311.0308177	80	10.6408906	30.2007634	321.3630190	80	11.1700172	29.7297836	332.0821924
81	10.4342909	30.7799881	321.1673480	81	10.9601173	30.2920033	332.0039095	81	11.5120989	29.8166487	343.2522005
82	10.7407981	30.8730910	331.6016388	82	11.2809208	30.3805858	342.9640068	82	11.8645570	29.9009326	354.7643085
83	11.0563091	30.9635371	342.3424370	83	11.6275884	30.4665681	354.2529477	83	12.2280121	29.9827121	366.6289654
84	11.3810882	31.0514022	353.3987461	84	11.9764161	30.5500855	365.8805361	84	12.6024949	30.0620615	378.8569775
85	11.7154076	31.1367559	364.7798343	85	12.3357086	30.6311510	377.8569522	85	12.9884664	30.1390530	391.4594724
86	12.0595477	31.2196817	376.4952419	86	12.7057798	30.7098553	390.1926608	86	13.3862175	30.2137507	404.4479181
87	12.4137970	31.3002372	388.5547896	87	13.0869532	30.7862673	402.8984406	87	13.7961704	30.2862405	417.8341363
88	12.7784522	31.3784940	400.9685866	88	13.4795618	30.8604537	415.9853938	88	14.2186782	30.3565706	431.6303068
89	13.1538193	31.4545175	413.7470388	89	13.8839487	30.9324793	429.4649556	89	14.6541252	30.4248107	445.8489849
90	13.5402127	31.5283716	426.9008581	90	14.3004671	31.0024071	443.3489043	90	15.1029078	30.4910232	460.5031101
91	13.9379565	31.6001181	440.4410708	91	14.7294812	31.0702982	457.6493715	91	15.5654343	30.5552681	475.6060178
92	14.3473839	31.6698172	454.3790273	92	15.1713656	31.1362118	472.3788526	92	16.0476039	30.6176039	491.1714522
93	14.7688383	31.7375274	468.7264112	93	15.6265066	31.2002056	487.5502182	93	16.5334158	30.6780875	507.2135779
94	15.2026730	31.8033053	483.4952496	94	16.0953018	31.2623356	503.1767248	94	17.0397517	30.7367738	523.7469937
95	15.6492515	31.8672061	498.6979225	95	16.5781608	31.3226559	519.2720265	95	17.5615941	30.7937163	540.7867454
96	16.1089482	31.9292834	514.3471740	96	17.0755056	31.3812193	535.8501873	96	18.0994179	30.8489666	558.3483395
97	16.5821486	31.9895822	530.4561223	97	17.5877708	31.4380770	552.9256930	97	18.6537126	30.9025753	576.4477574
98	17.0692492	32.0481741	547.0382709	98	18.1154039	31.4932787	570.5134638	98	19.2249825	30.9545909	595.1014700
99	17.5706584	32.1050872	564.1075201	99	18.6588660	31.5468725	588.6288677	99	19.8137476	31.0050609	614.3264525
100	18.0867965	32.1603761	581.6781785	100	19.2186320	31.5989053	607.2877337	100	20.4205436	31.0540312	634.1402002

Table 1 383

M	C(11.75,M,4)	A(11.75,M,4)	S(11.75,M,4)	M	C(12.00,M,4)	A(12.00,M,4)	S(12.00,M,4)	M	C(12.25,M,4)	A(12.25,M,4)	S(12.25,M,4)
101	18.6180962	32.2140873	599.7649750	101	19.7951910	31.6494226	626.5063658	101	21.0459228	31.1015464	654.5607438
102	19.1650027	32.2662657	618.3830712	102	20.3890467	31.6984686	646.3015508	102	21.6904542	31.1476496	675.6066686
103	19.7279747	32.3169552	637.5480739	103	21.0007181	31.7460860	666.6905035	103	22.3547243	31.1923829	697.2971208
104	20.3074839	32.3661981	657.2760496	104	21.6307397	31.7923165	687.6913216	104	23.0393378	31.2357869	719.6518451
105	20.9040163	32.4140358	677.5835325	105	22.2793619	31.8372005	709.3220613	105	23.7449175	31.2779012	742.6911829
106	21.5160718	32.4805084	698.4875408	106	22.9380517	31.8807772	731.6017231	106	24.4721056	31.3187640	766.4361004
107	22.1501651	32.5056548	720.0056206	107	23.6364933	31.9230846	754.5497748	107	25.2215638	31.3584126	790.9082760
108	22.8008262	32.5495128	742.1557657	108	24.3455861	31.9641598	778.1862681	108	25.9939742	31.3968831	816.1297698
109	23.4705005	32.5921193	764.9566119	109	25.0759557	32.0040387	802.5318562	109	26.7900397	31.4342104	842.1237441
110	24.1600494	32.6335100	788.4272124	110	25.8282344	32.0427560	827.6078119	110	27.6104946	31.4704285	868.9137837
111	24.6697508	32.6737195	812.5872618	111	26.6030814	32.0803456	853.4360462	111	28.4560557	31.5055704	896.5242684
112	25.6002998	32.7127815	837.4570127	112	27.4011739	32.1168404	880.0391276	112	29.3275224	31.5396681	924.9803241
113	26.3523086	32.7507288	863.0573124	113	28.2232091	32.1522722	907.4403015	113	30.2256778	31.5727525	954.3078466
114	27.1264076	32.7875933	869.4096210	114	29.0699053	32.1866721	935.6635106	114	31.1513392	31.6048539	984.5335244
115	27.9232459	32.8234057	916.5360286	115	29.9420025	32.2200700	964.7334159	115	32.1053490	31.6360014	1015.6848636
116	28.7434912	32.8581952	944.4592745	116	30.6402626	32.2524951	994.6754184	116	33.0885753	31.6662233	1047.7902126
117	29.5878313	32.8919039	973.2027657	117	31.7654705	32.2839758	1025.5156810	117	34.1019129	31.6955471	1080.8787879
118	30.4569738	32.9248271	1002.7905970	118	32.7184346	32.3145397	1057.2811514	118	35.1462840	31.7239996	1114.9807008
119	31.3516474	32.9567234	1033.2475708	119	33.6993976	32.3442133	1089.9995660	119	36.2226389	31.7516067	1150.1269848
120	32.2726021	32.9977094	1054.5992182	120	34.7109372	32.3730226	1123.6995736	120	37.3319573	31.7783934	1186.3496237
121	33.2206097	33.0178112	1096.8718203	121	35.7523169	32.4009928	1158.4105609	121	38.4752484	31.8043841	1223.6815810
122	34.1954652	33.0470540	1130.0924300	122	36.8248864	32.4281483	1194.1628777	122	39.6535529	31.8296025	1262.1568294
123	35.2009363	33.0754623	1164.2888952	123	37.9296330	32.4545130	1230.9877641	123	40.8679430	31.8540716	1301.8103823
124	36.2350153	33.1030599	1199.4898815	124	39.0675219	32.4801097	1268.9173970	124	42.1195237	31.8778136	1342.6783253
125	37.2994189	33.1298700	1235.7248968	125	40.2395476	32.5049608	1307.9849190	125	43.4294342	31.9008500	1387.7978491
126	38.3950893	33.1559150	1273.0243157	126	41.4467340	32.5290882	1348.2244666	126	44.7368481	31.9232020	1428.2072832
127	39.5239451	33.1812167	1311.4194050	127	42.6901361	32.5525128	1389.6712006	127	46.1089753	31.9448397	1472.9461313
128	40.6839316	33.2057964	1350.9423500	128	43.9708401	32.5752552	1432.3613367	128	47.5210627	31.9659330	1519.0551066
129	41.8790221	33.2296747	1391.6262816	129	45.2899653	32.5973351	1476.3321768	129	48.9763952	31.9863510	1566.5761693
130	43.1092183	33.2528716	1433.5053037	130	46.6486643	32.6187719	1521.6221421	130	50.4762973	32.0061623	1615.5525645
131	44.3755516	33.2754066	1476.6145220	131	48.0481242	32.6395844	1568.2708064	131	52.0221339	32.0253849	1666.0288619
132	45.6790835	33.2972984	1520.9900736	132	49.4895680	32.6597907	1616.3189307	132	53.6153118	32.0440363	1718.0509958
133	47.0209065	33.3185656	1566.6691571	133	50.9742550	32.6794084	1665.8084986	133	55.2572807	32.0621334	1771.6663076
134	48.4021457	33.3392258	1613.6900636	134	52.5034827	32.6984548	1716.7827536	134	56.9495349	32.0796928	1826.9235883
135	49.8239587	33.3592665	1662.0922092	135	54.0785971	32.7169464	1769.2862353	135	58.6936144	32.0967305	1883.8731232
136	51.2875375	33.3787944	1711.9161679	136	55.7009447	32.7348994	1823.3648234	136	60.4911064	32.1132618	1942.5667377
137	52.7941089	33.3977359	1763.2037054	137	57.3719731	32.7523295	1879.0657682	137	62.3436465	32.1293020	2003.0578441
138	54.3449358	33.4161369	1815.9978143	138	59.0931323	32.7692520	1936.4377412	138	64.2529207	32.1448654	2065.4014906
139	55.9413183	33.4340127	1870.3427501	139	60.8659263	32.7856815	1995.5308735	139	66.2206664	32.1599665	2129.6544113
140	57.5845946	33.4513785	1926.2840685	140	62.6919040	32.8013325	2056.3967998	140	68.2486743	32.1746188	2195.8750777
141	59.2761420	33.4602487	1983.8686630	141	64.5725612	32.8171190	2119.0887038	141	70.3387900	32.1888357	2264.1237520
142	61.0173787	33.4846375	2043.1448051	142	66.5098410	32.8321543	2183.6613650	142	72.4929154	32.2026301	2334.4625420
143	62.8097642	33.5005586	2104.1621838	143	68.5051362	32.8467518	2250.1712060	143	74.7130109	32.2160147	2406.9554574
144	64.6548010	33.5160023	2166.9719480	144	70.5602903	32.8609241	2318.6763422	144	77.0010969	32.2290015	2481.6684685
145	66.7740358	33.5310507	2231.6267490	145	72.6770990	32.8746836	2389.2366326	145	79.3592555	32.2416024	2558.6695652
146	68.5090506	33.5456473	2299.1807848	146	74.8574120	32.8880423	2461.9137316	146	81.7896327	32.2538289	2630.0288027
147	70.5215143	33.5598274	2366.6898454	147	77.1031344	32.9010119	2536.7711436	147	84.2944402	32.2656921	2719.8184534
148	72.5930838	33.5736028	2437.2113597	148	79.4152286	32.9138028	2613.8742180	148	86.8759574	32.2772028	2804.1128936
149	74.7255056	33.5869851	2509.8044434	149	81.7907153	32.9258209	2693.2905064	149	89.5365336	32.2883714	2890.9888511
150	76.9205673	33.5999855	2584.5299490	150	84.2526767	32.9376980	2775.0892217	150	92.2785900	32.2992081	2980.5253847
151	79.1801090	33.6126150	2661.4505163	151	86.7802570	32.9492214	2859.3418984	151	95.1046218	32.3097229	3072.8039747
152	81.5060247	33.6248840	2740.6306253	152	89.3836647	32.9604091	2946.1221554	152	98.0172008	32.3199252	3167.9085965
153	83.9002642	33.6366029	2822.1366500	153	92.0651747	32.9712710	3035.5058201	153	101.0189776	32.3298243	3265.9257973
154	86.3648344	33.6483817	2906.0369142	154	94.8271239	32.9818165	3127.5709948	154	104.1126838	32.3394293	3366.9447040
155	88.9018014	33.6596301	2992.4017486	155	97.6715438	32.9920548	3222.3981247	155	107.3011348	32.3487488	3471.0574588
156	91.5132919	33.6705574	3081.3035500	156	100.6021431	33.0019950	3320.0700686	156	110.5872320	32.3577915	3578.3585915
157	94.2014948	33.6811730	3172.8168419	157	103.6201652	33.0116456	3420.6721707	157	113.9733660	32.3665654	3688.9458255
158	96.9388637	33.6914856	3267.0183307	158	106.7287702	33.0210151	3524.2923359	158	117.4644018	32.3750786	3802.9197915
159	99.8171182	33.7015039	3363.9870004	159	109.9305333	33.0301118	3631.0211061	159	121.0617665	32.3833389	3920.3842103
160	102.7492461	33.7112363	3462.8041186	160	113.2265088	33.0389435	3740.9517393	160	124.7603424	32.3913537	4041.4459768
161	105.7675052	33.7206910	3566.5533647	161	116.6254088	33.0475179	3854.1802916	161	128.5303424	32.3991303	4166.2152599
162	108.8771256	33.7298759	3672.3208699	162	120.1241711	33.0558427	3970.7057179	162	132.5286417	32.4066759	4294.8056024
163	112.0726119	33.7387490	3781.1952955	163	123.7278962	33.0639249	4090.9298716	163	136.5871046	32.4139972	4427.3340241
164	115.3647449	33.7474669	3893.2679074	164	127.4397331	33.0717718	4214.6577078	164	140.7700847	32.4211010	4563.9211266
165	118.7535843	33.7558887	4003.6326523	165	131.2629251	33.0793901	4342.0975010	165	145.0811685	32.4279937	4704.6912133
166	122.2419708	33.7640682	4127.3862366	166	135.2008129	33.0867865	4473.3604261	166	149.5242793	32.4346815	4849.7723819
167	125.8328287	33.7720152	4249.6282074	167	139.2566373	33.0939694	4608.5612390	167	154.1034604	32.4411707	4999.2966612
168	129.5291680	33.7797355	4375.4610361	168	143.4345424	33.1009393	4747.8180763	168	158.8228789	32.4474670	5153.4001215
169	133.3340874	33.7872355	4504.9907240	169	147.7375787	33.1077080	4891.2526187	169	163.6868295	32.4535762	5312.2230004
170	137.2507762	33.7945214	4638.3242915	170	152.1697060	33.1142796	5038.9901974	170	168.6997387	32.4595039	5475.9098299
171	141.2825177	33.8015991	4775.5750677	171	156.7347972	33.1206598	5191.1599034	171	173.8661682	32.4652555	5644.6095686
172	145.4326917	33.8084754	4916.8575854	172	161.4363412	33.1268542	5347.8947006	172	179.1908196	32.4708361	5818.4757368
173	149.7047770	33.8151553	5062.2902771	173	166.2799464	33.1328682	5509.3315418	173	184.6785384	32.4762509	5997.6665564
174	154.1023548	33.8216444	5211.9950541	174	171.2683448	33.1387070	5675.6114882	174	190.3343187	32.4815048	6182.3450948
175	158.6291115	33.8279485	5366.0974089	175	176.4063951	33.1443757	5846.8798330	175	196.1633072	32.4866026	6372.6794135
176	163.2889417	33.8340726	5524.7265205	176	181.6985870	33.1498793	6023.2862281	176	202.1708085	32.4915490	6568.8427207
177	168.0854514	33.8400219	5688.0153621	177	187.1495446	33.1552225	6204.9843151	177	208.3622895	32.4963483	6771.0135292
178	173.0229615	33.8458015	5856.1008136	178	192.7640310	33.1604103	6392.1343597	178	214.7433846	32.5010050	6979.3758187
179	178.1055110	33.8514162	6029.1237751	179	198.5469519	33.1654598	6584.8983097	179	221.3199008	32.5055234	7194.1192033
180	183.2073604	33.8568706	6208.2292861	180	204.5033604	33.1703368	6783.4453425	180	228.0978227	32.5099074	7415.4391041
181	188.7223954	33.8621694	6390.5466046	181	210.6384613	33.1750843	6987.9487030	181	235.0833186	32.5141612	7643.5369268
182	194.2653305	33.8673169	6579.2895420	182	216.9955151	33.1796935	7198.5871543	182	242.2827452	32.5182887	7878.6202454
183	199.9732127	33.8723176	6773.5561724	183	223.4466436	33.1841684	7415.5447794	183	249.7026543	32.5222934	8120.9029906
184	205.8474259	33.8771756	6973.5293852	184	230.1703339	33.1685130	7639.0111229	184	257.3497981	32.5261792	8370.6056449
185	211.8941940	33.8818949	7179.3768110	185	237.0754439	33.1927311	7869.1814568	185	265.2311357	32.5299495	8627.9554430
186	218.1185860	33.8864796	7391.2710050	186	244.1877072	33.1968263	8106.2569007	186	273.3538392	32.5336077	8893.1865786
187	224.5258194	33.8909334	7609.3895910	187	251.5133384	33.2008022	8350.4446079	187	281.7253005	32.5371573	9166.5404178
188	231.1212654	33.8952601	7833.9154104	188	259.0587386	33.2046624	8601.9579464	188	290.3531379	32.5406014	9448.2657183
189	237.9104526	33.8994634	8065.0366758	189	266.8305008	33.2084101	8861.0166950	189	299.2452027	32.5439431	9738.6188562
190	244.8990721	33.9035467	8302.9471284	190	274.8354158	33.2120486	9127.8471858	190	308.4095871	32.5471856	10037.8640589
191	252.0929824	33.9075135	8547.8462005	191	283.0804783	33.2155812	9402.6826016	191	317.8543037	32.5503317	10346.2736460
192	259.4982137	33.9113671	8799.9391828	192	291.5728926	33.2190108	9685.7630798	192	327.5889287	32.5533843	10664.1282766
193	267.1209737	33.9151107	9059.4373965	193	300.3200794	33.2223406	9977.3359725	193	337.6213397	32.5563462	10991.7172054
194	274.9676524	33.9187475	9326.5583703	194	309.3296818	33.2255734	10277.6560519	194	347.9609932	32.5592200	11329.3385451
195	283.0448272	33.9222805	9601.5260226	195	318.6095723	33.2287121	10586.9857337	195	358.6172987	32.5620085	11677.2995383
196	291.3592690	33.9257127	9884.5708498	196	328.1678595	33.2317593	10905.5953060	196	369.5999534	32.5647142	12035.9168369
197	299.9179475	33.9290469	10175.9301188	197	338.0128952	33.2347177	11233.7631654	197	380.9189520	32.5673394	12405.5167904
198	308.7280372	33.9322850	10475.8480662	198	348.1532821	33.2375900	11571.7760607	198	392.5845949	32.5698866	12786.4357424
199	317.7969233	33.9354327	10784.5761035	199	358.5978806	33.2403787	11919.9293428	199	404.6074982	32.5723581	13179.0203373
200	327.1322079	33.9384896	11102.3730268	200	369.3658170	33.2430861	12278.5272234	200	416.9986028	32.5747562	13583.6278355

M	C(12.50,M,4)	A(12.50,M,4)	S(12.50,M,4)	M	C(12.75,M,4)	A(12.75,M,4)	S(12.75,M,4)	M	C(13.00,M,4)	A(13.00,M,4)	S(13.00,M,4)
1/3	1.0103100	.3265534	.3299202	1/3	1.0105141	.3264211	.3298531	1/3	1.0107180	.3262889	.3297860
1	1.0312500	.9695970	1.0000000	1	1.0318750	.9691096	1.0000000	1	1.0325000	.9685230	1.0000000
2	1.0634766	1.9100092	2.0312500	2	1.0647660	1.9082831	2.0318750	2	1.0660563	1.9065598	2.0325000
3	1.0967102	2.8218271	3.0947266	3	1.0987054	2.8184452	3.0966410	3	1.1007031	2.8150700	3.0985563
4	1.1309824	3.7060141	4.1914368	4	1.1337267	3.7004920	4.1953464	4	1.1364759	3.6949831	4.1992593
5	1.1663256	4.5634077	5.3224192	5	1.1698642	4.5552921	5.3290731	5	1.1734114	4.5471991	5.3357353
6	1.2027733	5.3948195	6.4887448	6	1.2071536	5.3836870	6.4989373	6	1.2115473	5.3725899	6.5091167
7	1.2403599	6.2010371	7.6915180	7	1.2455316	6.1864926	7.7060809	7	1.2509226	6.1719999	7.7206939
8	1.2791212	6.9828239	8.9318780	8	1.2853362	6.9644992	8.9517226	8	1.2915775	6.9462469	8.9716165
9	1.3190937	7.7409201	10.2109902	9	1.3263062	7.7184728	10.2370588	9	1.3335538	7.6961229	10.2631940
10	1.3603154	8.4760438	11.5300929	10	1.3685823	8.4491560	11.5633650	10	1.3769943	8.4223951	11.5967478
11	1.4028253	9.1888909	12.8904083	11	1.4122058	9.1572681	12.9319473	11	1.4216434	9.1258064	12.9736421
12	1.4465635	9.8801367	14.2932336	12	1.4572199	9.8435063	14.3441531	12	1.4678468	9.8070764	14.3952855
13	1.4918718	10.5504355	15.7398971	13	1.5036688	10.5085464	15.8013730	13	1.5155518	10.4669021	15.8631323
14	1.5384928	11.2004223	17.2317689	14	1.5515982	11.1530431	17.3050417	14	1.5648072	11.1059584	17.3786841
15	1.5865707	11.8307126	18.7702617	15	1.6010554	11.7776312	18.8566399	15	1.6155635	11.7248992	18.9434913
16	1.6361510	12.4419031	20.3568323	16	1.6520890	12.3829254	20.4576953	16	1.6681725	12.3243576	20.5591548
17	1.6872807	13.0345727	21.9929834	17	1.7047494	12.9695219	22.1097844	17	1.7223881	12.9049468	22.2273273
18	1.7400083	13.6092826	23.6802641	18	1.7590883	13.5379982	23.8145337	18	1.7783658	13.4672608	23.9497154
19	1.7943835	14.1665771	25.4202723	19	1.8151592	14.0889141	25.5736220	19	1.8361626	14.0118749	25.7280912
20	1.8504580	14.7069838	27.2146558	20	1.8730174	14.6228119	27.3887812	20	1.8958379	14.5393461	27.5642438
21	1.9082848	15.2310146	29.0651138	21	1.9327198	15.1402175	29.2617986	21	1.9574527	15.0502142	29.4600817
22	1.9679187	15.7391657	30.9733987	22	1.9943253	15.6416402	31.1945184	22	2.0210699	15.5450016	31.4175344
23	2.0294162	16.2319183	32.9413174	23	2.0578944	16.1275738	33.1888437	23	2.0867546	16.0242147	33.4386043
24	2.0928354	16.7097389	34.9707335	24	2.1234898	16.5984967	35.2467381	24	2.1545742	16.4883435	35.5253589
25	2.1582365	17.1730302	37.0635690	25	2.1911760	17.0548727	37.3702279	25	2.2245978	16.9378629	37.6799331
26	2.2275814	17.6223808	39.2218055	26	2.2610198	17.4971510	39.5614039	26	2.2968973	17.3732329	39.9045309
27	2.2952340	18.0580662	41.4474869	27	2.3330898	17.9257671	41.8224237	27	2.3715464	17.7948987	42.2014282
28	2.3669600	18.4805490	43.7427209	28	2.4074570	18.3411432	44.1555134	28	2.4486217	18.2032917	44.5729746
29	2.4409275	18.8902294	46.1096809	29	2.4841947	18.7436881	46.5629704	29	2.5282019	18.5988297	47.0215963
30	2.5172065	19.2874951	48.5506084	30	2.5633784	19.1337983	49.0471651	30	2.6103684	18.9819174	49.5497981
31	2.5958692	19.6727226	51.0678149	31	2.6450861	19.5118578	51.6105435	31	2.6952054	19.3529466	52.1601666
32	2.6769901	20.0462764	53.6606842	32	2.7293982	19.8782390	54.2556296	32	2.7827996	19.7122970	54.8553720
33	2.7605461	20.4085105	56.3406743	33	2.8163978	20.2333025	56.9850277	33	2.8732406	20.0603361	57.6381716
34	2.8469163	20.7597677	59.1013204	34	2.9061704	20.5773979	59.8014255	34	2.9666209	20.3974199	60.5114122
35	2.9358824	21.1003808	61.9482366	35	2.9988046	20.9108641	62.7075959	35	3.0630361	20.7238934	63.4780331
36	3.0276287	21.4306723	64.8841190	36	3.0943915	21.2340294	65.7064008	36	3.1625847	21.0400904	66.5410691
37	3.1222421	21.7509550	67.9117477	37	3.1930252	21.5472120	68.8007921	37	3.2653688	21.3463346	69.7036539
38	3.2198122	22.0615321	71.0339899	38	3.2948029	21.8507203	71.9938173	38	3.3714932	21.6429390	72.9690226
39	3.3204313	22.3626978	74.2536021	39	3.3993248	22.1446531	75.2886203	39	3.4810668	21.9302073	76.3405159
40	3.4241948	22.6547373	77.5742334	40	3.5081942	22.4299001	78.6884450	40	3.5942014	22.2084332	79.8215826
41	3.5312009	22.9379270	80.9984282	41	3.6200179	22.7061418	82.1966392	41	3.7110130	22.4779014	83.4157841
42	3.6415509	23.2125353	84.5296290	42	3.7354059	22.9738503	85.8166571	42	3.8316209	22.7388876	87.1267971
43	3.7553444	23.4788221	88.1711800	43	3.8544720	23.2332892	89.5520631	43	3.9561496	22.9916587	90.9584180
44	3.8727040	23.7370396	91.9265293	44	3.9773333	23.4847140	93.4065351	44	4.0847234	23.2364733	94.9154655
45	3.9937260	23.9874324	95.7992334	45	4.1041108	23.7283721	97.3836584	45	4.2174769	23.4735819	98.9992900
46	4.1185300	24.2302374	99.7929594	46	4.2349293	23.9645036	101.4879792	46	4.3545449	23.7032270	103.2167669
47	4.2472340	24.4656848	103.9114894	47	4.3693177	24.1933408	105.7229085	47	4.4960676	23.9256436	107.5713118
48	4.3799601	24.6939974	108.1587235	48	4.5092088	24.4151092	110.0928262	48	4.6421898	24.1410592	112.0673795
49	4.5168339	24.9153914	112.5386836	49	4.6529399	24.6300271	114.6020351	49	4.7930610	24.3496941	116.7095693
50	4.6579849	25.1300765	117.0555174	50	4.8012523	24.8383061	119.2549749	50	4.9480355	24.5517618	121.5025303
51	4.8035470	25.3382560	121.7135023	51	4.9542922	25.0401513	124.0562273	51	5.1096726	24.7474691	126.4514658
52	4.9536578	25.5401270	126.5170493	52	5.1122103	25.2357614	129.0105195	52	5.2757307	24.9370161	131.5611384
53	5.1084596	25.7358808	131.4707071	53	5.2751620	25.4253290	134.1227298	53	5.4471985	25.1205967	136.8368754
54	5.2680990	25.9257025	136.5791667	54	5.4433078	25.6090408	139.3978919	54	5.6242324	25.2983997	142.2840739
55	5.4327271	26.1097722	141.8472657	55	5.6168132	25.7870777	144.8411997	55	5.8070200	25.4706041	147.9083063
56	5.6024998	26.2882639	147.2799927	56	5.7958492	25.9596150	150.4580129	56	5.9957481	25.6373889	153.7153262
57	5.7775779	26.4613468	152.8824925	57	5.9805919	26.1268225	156.2538621	57	6.1906099	25.7989239	159.7110743
58	5.9581272	26.6291848	158.6600704	58	6.1712232	26.2888650	162.2344539	58	6.3918047	25.9553743	165.9016843
59	6.1443187	26.7919368	164.6181976	59	6.3679310	26.4459018	168.4056771	59	6.5995384	26.1069000	172.2934890
60	6.3363286	26.9497559	170.7625163	60	6.5709008	26.5980878	174.7736081	60	6.8140234	26.2536562	178.8930274
61	6.5343389	27.1027945	177.0988449	61	6.7803565	26.7455727	181.3445169	61	7.0354792	26.3957929	185.7070508
62	6.7385770	27.2511947	183.6331938	62	6.9964803	26.8885017	188.1248733	62	7.2641322	26.5334556	192.7425300
63	6.9491163	27.3950979	190.3717208	63	7.2194932	27.0270155	195.1213537	63	7.5002165	26.6667851	200.0066622
64	7.1662762	27.5346404	197.3208371	64	7.4496145	27.1612507	202.3408468	64	7.7439736	26.7959178	207.5068787
65	7.3902223	27.6699543	204.4871133	65	7.6870710	27.2913392	209.7904613	65	7.9956527	26.9209857	215.2508523
66	7.6211667	27.8011678	211.8773355	66	7.9320963	27.4174093	217.4775323	66	8.2555114	27.0421169	223.2465050
67	7.8593282	27.9284052	219.4985023	67	8.1849319	27.5395850	225.4096287	67	8.5238155	27.1594353	231.5020164
68	8.1049322	28.0517868	227.3578305	68	8.4458266	27.6579807	233.5945606	68	8.8008395	27.2730608	240.0258319
69	8.3582113	28.1714296	235.4627627	69	8.7150373	27.7727309	242.0403872	69	9.0868668	27.3831097	248.8266715
70	8.6194054	28.2874469	243.8209740	70	8.9928292	27.8839306	250.7554245	70	9.3821900	27.4896947	257.9135383
71	8.8887619	28.3999485	252.4403795	71	9.2794756	27.9916953	259.7482537	71	9.6871112	27.5929246	267.2957283
72	9.1665357	28.5090410	261.3291413	72	9.5752589	28.0961312	269.0277293	72	10.0019423	27.6929052	276.9828395
73	9.4529899	28.6148276	270.4956770	73	9.8804703	28.1973409	278.6029882	73	10.3270054	27.7897387	286.9847818
74	9.7483958	28.7174096	279.9486669	74	10.1954102	28.2954243	288.4834584	74	10.6625331	27.8835241	297.3117872
75	10.0530332	28.8168811	289.6970628	75	10.5203889	28.3904778	298.6788687	75	11.0091687	27.9743575	307.9744203
76	10.3671905	28.9133392	299.7500960	76	10.8557263	28.4825951	309.1992576	76	11.3669666	28.0623317	318.9835890
77	10.6911652	29.0068744	310.1172865	77	11.2017526	28.5718668	320.0549840	77	11.7363951	28.1475368	330.3505556
78	11.0252641	29.0975752	320.8084517	78	11.5588085	28.6583809	331.2567366	78	12.1178258	28.2300598	342.0869487
79	11.3698036	29.1855274	331.8337158	79	11.9272455	28.7422226	342.8155451	79	12.5116522	28.3099853	354.2047745
80	11.7251100	29.2708145	343.2035195	80	12.3074265	28.8234743	354.7427906	80	12.9182840	28.3873950	366.7164297
81	12.0915197	29.3535171	354.9286295	81	12.6997257	28.9022162	367.0502170	81	13.3381292	28.4623680	379.6347117
82	12.4693797	29.4337135	367.0201491	82	13.1045294	28.9785257	379.7499727	82	13.7716174	28.5349311	392.9728419
83	12.8590478	29.5114798	379.4895288	83	13.5222363	29.0524779	392.8544722	83	14.2191949	28.6053086	406.7444592
84	13.2608930	29.5868895	392.3485766	84	13.9532576	29.1241458	406.3767085	84	14.6813188	28.6734224	420.9636542
85	13.6752959	29.6600141	405.6094696	85	14.3980177	29.1935998	420.3299661	85	15.1584616	28.7393921	435.6449729
86	14.1026469	29.7309227	419.2847656	86	14.8569545	29.2609083	434.7279837	86	15.6511116	28.8032854	450.8034346
87	14.5433567	29.7996826	433.3874145	87	15.3305199	29.3261377	449.5849382	87	16.1597728	28.8651674	466.4545402
88	14.9978366	29.8663689	447.9307712	88	15.8191802	29.3893521	464.9154581	88	16.6849654	28.9251016	482.6143190
89	15.4665190	29.9310147	462.9286078	89	16.3234166	29.4506138	480.7346384	89	17.2272268	28.9831493	499.2992843
90	15.9498477	29.9937112	478.3951268	90	16.8437255	29.5099831	497.0580550	90	17.7871116	29.0393697	516.5265111
91	16.4482805	30.0545079	494.3449746	91	17.3806193	29.5675184	513.9017805	91	18.3651928	29.0938206	534.3136227
92	16.9622892	30.1134622	510.7932550	92	17.9348265	29.6232765	531.2823998	92	18.9620615	29.1465575	552.6788155
93	17.4923608	30.1706300	527.7555443	93	18.5062927	29.6773122	549.2170263	93	19.5783285	29.1976343	571.6408770
94	18.0389970	30.2260654	545.2479050	94	19.0961808	29.7296787	567.7233190	94	20.2146242	29.2471035	591.2192055
95	18.6027157	30.2798210	563.2869021	95	19.7043716	29.7804275	586.8194998	95	20.8715995	29.2950155	611.4338297
96	19.1840506	30.3319447	581.8896178	96	20.3329644	29.8296088	606.5243714	96	21.5499265	29.3414193	632.3054292
97	19.7835522	30.3824947	601.0736683	97	20.9810776	29.8772707	626.8573357	97	22.2502991	29.3863626	653.8553557
98	20.4017882	30.4315100	620.8572205	98	21.6498494	29.9234604	647.8384133	98	22.9734338	29.4298911	676.1056547
99	21.0393440	30.4790400	641.2590087	99	22.3399384	29.9682233	669.4882628	99	23.7200704	29.4720495	699.0790885
100	21.6968235	30.5251297	662.2983527	100	23.0520239	30.0116035	691.8282012	100	24.4909727	29.5128809	722.7991589

Table 1   385

M	C(12.50,M,4)	A(12.50,M,4)	S(12.50,M,4)	M	C(12.75,M,4)	A(12.75,M,4)	S(12.75,M,4)	M	C(13.00,M,4)	A(13.00,M,4)	S(13.00,M,4)
101	22.3748493	30.5698227	683.9951762	101	23.7868072	30.0536436	714.8802251	101	25.2869293	29.5524270	747.2901316
102	23.0740633	30.6131614	706.3700255	102	24.5450117	30.0943850	738.6670323	102	26.1087545	29.5907283	772.5770909
103	23.7951278	30.6551859	729.4440888	103	25.3273839	30.1338680	763.2120440	103	26.9572890	29.6278240	798.6858154
104	24.5387255	30.6959388	753.2392166	104	26.1348943	30.1721313	788.5394279	104	27.8334009	29.6637521	825.6431044
105	25.3055607	30.7354558	777.7779421	105	26.9677377	30.2092127	81?.6741222	105	28.7379864	29.6985492	853.4765053
106	26.0963595	30.7737753	803.0835029	106	27.?.73343	30.2451486	841.6418598	106	29.6719710	29.7322511	882.2144918
107	26.9118707	30.8109336	829.1798623	107	28.7143306	30.2799744	869.4691941	107	30.6373101	29.7648931	911.8864328
108	27.7528567	30.8469659	856.0917331	108	29.6295999	30.3137244	898.1835247	108	31.6319901	29.7965056	942.5227728
109	28.6201438	30.8819064	883.8445997	109	30.5740434	30.3464319	927.8131246	109	32.6600298	29.8271241	974.1547630
110	29.5145233	30.9157880	912.4647435	110	31.5485910	30.3781290	958.3871680	110	33.7214808	29.8567788	1006.8147928
111	30.4363521	30.9486429	941.9792668	111	32.5542023	30.4088470	989.9357590	111	34.8174289	29.8855000	1040.5362736
112	31.2800037	30.9805022	972.4161189	112	33.5918675	30.4386161	1022.4899613	112	35.9489954	29.9133172	1075.3537025
113	32.3689789	31.0113961	1003.8041226	113	34.6626083	30.4674657	1056.0818289	113	37.1173377	29.9402588	1111.3026979
114	33.2804063	31.0413538	1036.1730015	114	35.7674790	30.4954240	1090.7444372	114	38.3236512	29.9663524	1148.4200356
115	34.4235440	31.0704037	1069.5534078	115	36.9075674	?0.5225187	1126.5119161	115	39.5691698	29.9916246	1186.7436068
116	35.4992798	31.0985732	1103.9769518	116	38.0839961	30.5467765	1163.4194835	116	40.8551579	30.0161013	1226.3128566
117	36.6083323	31.1258892	1139.4762316	117	39.2979234	30.5742231	1201.5034796	117	42.1829608	30.0398075	1267.1680245
118	37.7526520	31.1523774	1176.0848638	118	40.5504448	30.5988837	1240.8014030	118	43.5539971	30.0627676	1309.3509353
119	38.9324224	31.1780629	1213.8375159	119	41.8430934	30.6227825	1281.3519478	119	44.9654090	30.0850049	1352.9043924
120	40.1490606	31.2029701	1252.7699383	120	43.1768420	30.6459431	1323.1950411	120	46.4309148	30.1065423	1397.8742014
121	41.4037187	31.2271225	1292.9189989	121	44.5531038	30.6683882	1366.3718831	121	47.9399196	30.1274017	1444.3052162
122	42.6975850	31.2505431	1334.3227176	122	45.9732340	30.6901400	1410.9249869	122	49.4979670	30.1476046	1492.2451358
123	44.0318845	31.2732539	1377.0203026	123	47.4386308	30.7112199	1456.8982209	123	51.1036509	30.1671715	1541.7431027
124	45.4078809	31.2952765	1421.0521871	124	48.9507372	30.7316486	1504.3368517	124	52.7676170	30.1861225	1592.8497535
125	46.8268772	31.3166317	1466.4600680	125	50.5110419	30.7514462	1553.2875889	125	54.?025646	30.2044770	164?.6173707
126	48.2902171	31.3373399	1513.2869451	126	52.1210814	30.7706323	1603.7986308	126	56.2532479	30.2222538	1700.0993352
127	49.79?2864	31.3574205	1561.5771?22	127	53.7824409	30.7892257	1655.9197122	127	58.0814785	30.2394710	1756.3531832
128	51.3555141	31.3768926	1611.3764485	128	55.4967562	30.8072448	1709.7021531	128	59.9691265	30.2561462	1814.4346517
129	52.9803739	31.3957746	1662.7319626	129	57.2657153	30.8247073	1765.1989093	129	61.9181232	30.2722266	1874.4037682
130	54.6153856	31.4140845	1715.6923365	130	59.0910600	30.8416303	1822.4646246	130	63.9304622	30.2879386	1936.3219114
131	56.3221164	31.4318395	1770.3077220	131	60.9745875	30.8580305	1881.5556845	131	66.0082022	30.3030882	2000.2523736
132	58.0821825	31.4490565	1826.6298304	132	62.9181525	30.8739242	1942.5302720	132	68.1534688	30.3177610	2066.2605757
133	59.8972520	31.4657517	1884.7120209	133	64.9236686	30.8893269	2005.4484245	133	70.3684565	30.3319719	2134.4140445
134	61.7690398	31.4819411	1944.6092716	134	66.9931105	30.9042538	2070.3720930	134	72.6554313	30.3457355	2204.7825010
135	63.6993223	31.4976398	2006.3783114	135	69.1285159	30.9187197	2137.3652036	135	75.0167329	30.3590658	2277.4379324
136	65.6899261	31.5128629	2070.0776337	136	71.3319874	30.9327386	2206.4937195	136	77.4547767	30.3719766	2352.4546652
137	67.7427363	31.5276246	2135.7675598	137	73.6056945	30.9463245	2277.8257068	137	79.9720569	30.3844810	2429.9094419
138	69.8596968	31.5419390	2203.5102961	138	75.9518760	30.9594907	2351.4314013	138	82.5711488	30.3965917	2509.8814968
139	72.0428123	31.5558196	2273.3699929	139	78.3728420	30.9722503	2427.3832773	139	85.2547111	30.4083213	2592.4526476
140	74.2941502	31.5692797	2345.4128052	140	80.8709764	30.9846156	2505.7561193	140	88.0254892	30.4196816	2677.7073587
141	76.6158424	31.5823318	2419.7069554	141	83.4487387	30.9965990	2586.6270957	141	90.8863176	30.4306844	2765.7329479
142	79.0100875	31.5949884	2496.3227978	142	86.1086673	31.0082123	2670.0758344	142	93.8401230	30.4413408	2856.6191655
143	81.4791527	31.6072615	2575.3328853	143	88.8533811	31.0194668	2756.1845017	143	96.8899269	30.4516618	2950.4592805
144	84.0253763	31.6191626	265?.8120381	144	91.6855826	31.0303736	2845.0378828	144	100.0388496	30.4616597	3047.3492154
145	86.?11693	31.6307032	2740.8374143	145	94.6080605	31.0409435	2936.7234063	145	103.2901122	30.4713394	3147.3880650
146	89.3590183	31.6418940	2827.4885836	146	97.6236925	31.0511870	3031.3315259	146	106.6470408	30.4807161	3250.6781772
147	92.1514876	31.6527457	2916.8476019	147	100.7354477	31.0611139	3128.9552183	147	110.1130697	30.4897977	3357.3252181
148	95.0312216	31.6632685	3008.9990895	148	103.9403901	31.0707343	3229.6906?80	148	113.6917444	30.4985934	3467.4382877
149	98.0009473	31.6734725	3104.0303111	149	107.2596812	31.0800575	3333.6370561	149	117.3867261	30.5071123	3581.1300322
150	101.0634769	31.6833673	3202.0312584	150	110.6785836	31.0890926	3440.8967373	150	121.2017947	30.5153630	3698.5167583
151	104.2217106	31.6929622	3303.0947353	151	114.2064634	31.0978487	3551.5753209	151	125.1408531	30.5233540	3819.7185530
152	107.4786390	31.7022664	3407.3164459	152	117.8467945	31.1063343	3665.7817843	152	129.2079308	30.5310934	3944.8594061
153	110.8373465	31.7112886	3514.7950849	153	121.6031610	31.1145578	3783.6285788	153	133.4071886	30.5385893	4074.0673369
154	114.3010136	31.7200375	3625.6324314	154	125.4792618	31.1225272	3905.2317398	154	137.7429222	30.5458492	4207.4745255
155	117.8729202	31.7285212	3739.9234450	155	129.4789133	31.1302505	4030.7110017	155	142.2195672	30.5528806	4345.2174476
156	121.5564490	31.7367478	3857.8063652	156	133.6060536	31.1377352	4160.1899149	156	146.8417031	30.5596906	4487.4370148
157	125.3550880	31.7447251	3979.3628143	157	137.8647466	31.1449887	4293.7959686	157	151.6140584	30.5662853	4634.2787179
158	129.2724345	31.7524607	4104.7179023	158	142.2591854	31.1520181	4431.6607152	158	156.5415154	30.5726744	4785.8927763
159	133.3121981	31.7599619	4233.9903368	159	146.7936969	31.1588304	4573.9190906	159	161.6291146	30.5788614	4942.4342917
160	137.4782043	31.7672358	4367.3025350	160	151.4727460	31.1654322	4720.7135975	160	166.?820608	30.5848536	510?.0634063
161	141.7743982	31.7742893	4504.7807393	161	156.3009398	31.1718301	4872.1863436	161	172.?.57278	30.5906573	5270.9454671
162	146.20?9482	31.7811290	4646.5551375	162	161.2830323	31.1780304	5028.4872034	162	177.9053640	30.5962782	5443.2511949
163	150.7737497	31.7877614	4792.7599057	163	166.4239289	31.1840392	5189.7703157	163	183.6875981	30.6017223	5621.1568589
164	155.4854294	31.7941929	4943.5337354	164	171.7286917	31.1898623	5356.1942446	164	189.6574450	30.6069949	5804.8444570
165	160.3443490	31.8004295	5099.0191647	165	177.2025437	31.1955055	5527.9229363	165	195.8213120	30.6121016	5994.5019020
166	165.3551099	31.8064771	5259.3635137	166	182.8508748	31.2009745	5705.1254800	166	202.1855046	30.6170476	6190.3232139
167	170.5224571	31.8123414	5424.7186237	167	188.6792465	31.2062745	5887.9763549	167	208.7565335	30.6218378	6392.5087185
168	175.8512839	31.8180280	5595.2410808	168	194.6933974	31.2114108	6076.6556013	168	215.5411159	30.6264773	6601.2652520
169	181.3466365	31.8235423	5771.0923647	169	200.8992495	31.2163884	6271.3489988	169	222.5462073	30.6309708	6816.8063729
170	187.0137191	31.8288895	5952.4390013	170	207.3029131	31.2212122	6472.2482482	170	229.7789590	30.6353228	7039.3525802
171	192.8578977	31.8340747	6139.4527202	171	213.9106934	31.2258871	6679.5511613	171	237.2467752	30.6395378	7269.1315392
172	198.8347070	31.8391027	6332.3106179	172	220.7290968	31.2304175	6893.4618548	172	244.9572954	30.6436202	7506.3783144
173	205.0998541	31.8439784	6531.1953248	173	227.7648368	31.2348080	7114.1909515	173	252.9184075	30.6475740	7751.3356098
174	211.5092245	31.8487063	6736.2951789	174	235.0248409	31.2390629	7341.9557883	174	261.1382558	30.6514034	8004.2540173
175	218.1168878	31.8532910	6947.8044034	175	242.5162577	31.2431863	7576.9806292	175	269.6252491	30.6551122	8265.3922731
176	224.9351030	31.8577367	7165.9232912	176	250.2464635	31.2471824	7819.4968870	176	278.3880697	30.6587043	8535.0175222
177	231.9643250	31.8620477	7390.8583942	177	258.2230695	31.2510550	8069.7433505	177	287.4356620	30.6621834	8813.4055919
178	239.2132102	31.8662281	7622.8227192	178	266.4539298	31.2548080	8327.9664200	178	296.7773416	30.6655529	9100.8412738
179	246.6886230	31.8702818	7862.0359294	179	274.9471489	31.2584451	8594.4203498	179	306.4226052	30.6688164	9397.6186155
180	254.?376425	31.8742126	8108.?245524	180	283.7110872	31.2619698	8869.3674987	180	316.3813309	30.6719771	9704.0412207
181	262.3475688	31.8780244	8363.1221948	181	292.7543802	31.2653056	9153.0785879	181	326.6637335	30.6750384	10020.4225606
182	270.5459303	31.8817206	8625.4697636	182	302.08?3261	31.2686959	9445.8329781	182	337.2803048	30.6780033	10347.0862941
183	279.0004907	31.8853048	8896.0156939	183	311.7149150	31.2719040	9747.9188942	183	348.2419147	30.6808748	10684.3665989
184	287.7192560	31.8887804	9175.0161846	184	321.6508279	31.2750130	10059.6330002	184	359.5597770	30.6836560	11032.6085136
185	296.7104828	31.8921507	9462.7354406	185	331.9034481	31.2780259	10381.2846371	185	371.2454697	30.6863497	11392.1682906
186	305.9828853	31.8954189	9759.4459234	186	342.4828705	31.2809457	10713.1880082	186	383.3109915	30.6889585	11763.4137603
187	315.5446443	31.8985880	10065.4286087	187	353.3995120	31.2837754	11055.6709557	187	395.7665533	30.6914852	12146.7247078
188	325.4054144	31.9016611	10380.9732530	188	364.6641214	31.2865176	11409.0704677	188	408.6310313	30.6939324	12542.4932611
189	335.5743336	31.9046411	10706.3786674	189	376.2877903	31.2891752	11773.7345891	189	421.9115398	30.6963026	12951.1242924
190	346.0610316	31.9075307	11041.9530010	190	388.2819636	31.2917506	12150.0223794	190	435.6236649	30.6985981	13373.0358323
191	356.8754388	31.9103328	11388.0140326	191	400.6584512	31.2942465	12538.3043431	191	449.7814340	30.7008215	13803.6594972
192	368.0277963	31.9130500	11744.8894714	192	413.4294394	31.2966653	12938.9627442	192	464.3993306	30.7029748	14258.4409312
193	379.5286649	31.9156849	12112.9172677	193	426.6075028	31.2990094	13352.3922337	193	479.4923089	30.7050603	14722.8402618
194	391.3889357	31.9182399	12492.4459326	194	440.2056149	31.3012811	13778.9972655	194	495.0758089	30.7070802	15202.3325707
195	403.6198400	31.9207174	12883.8348683	195	454.2371710	31.3034825	14219.2053535	195	511.1657727	30.7090365	15697.4083796
196	416.2329600	31.9231200	13287.4547082	196	468.7159808	31.3056160	14673.4425245	196	527.7788604	30.7109312	16208.5741523
197	429.2402400	31.9254496	13703.6876682	197	483.6563027	31.3076836	15142.1585053	197	544.9314668	30.7127663	16736.3528127
198	442.6539975	31.9277087	14132.9279082	198	499.0728474	31.3096873	15625.8148080	198	562.6417395	30.7145437	17281.2842795
199	456.4869349	31.9298994	14575.5819057	199	514.9807944	31.3116292	16124.8876554	199	580.9275961	30.7162651	17843.9260190
200	470.7521516	31.9320237	15032.0688406	200	531.3?58073	31.3135110	16639.8684498	200	599.8077430	30.7179323	18424.8536151

Table 1

M	C(13.25,M,4)	A(13.25,M,4)	S(13.25,M,4)	M	C(13.50,M,4)	A(13.50,M,4)	S(13.50,M,4)	M	C(13.75,M,4)	A(13.75,M,4)	S(13.75,M,4)
1/3	1.0109219	.3261568	.3297190	1/3	1.0111258	.3260248	.3296521	1/3	1.0113295	.3258930	.3295852
1	1.0331250	.9679371	1.0000000	1	1.0337500	.9673519	1.0000000	1	1.0343750	.9667674	1.0000000
2	1.0673473	1.9048393	2.0331250	2	1.0686391	1.9031215	2.0337500	2	1.0699316	1.9014065	2.0343750
3	1.1027031	2.8117017	3.1004723	3	1.1047056	2.8083400	3.1023091	3	1.1067105	2.8049852	3.1043066
4	1.1392302	3.6894874	4.2031754	4	1.1419894	3.6840049	4.2070947	4	1.1447537	3.6785355	4.2110172
5	1.1769672	4.5391288	5.3424056	5	1.1805316	4.5310809	5.3490841	5	1.1841046	4.5230555	5.3557709
6	1.2159542	5.3615281	6.5193728	6	1.2203745	5.3505015	6.5296157	6	1.2248082	5.3395098	6.5398755
7	1.2562327	6.1575590	7.7353270	7	1.2615622	6.1431695	7.7499903	7	1.2669110	6.1288312	7.7646837
8	1.2978454	6.9280668	8.9915597	8	1.3041399	6.9099584	9.0115524	8	1.3104611	6.8919214	9.0315947
9	1.3408365	7.6738698	10.2894051	9	1.3481546	7.6517131	10.3156923	9	1.3555082	7.6296522	10.3420558
10	1.3852518	8.3957603	11.6302417	10	1.3936548	8.3692509	11.6638469	10	1.4021038	8.3428661	11.6975640
11	1.4311382	9.0945048	13.0154934	11	1.4408007	9.0633624	13.0575018	11	1.4503011	9.0323781	13.0996577
12	1.4785447	9.7708456	14.4466316	12	1.4893140	9.7348125	14.4981925	12	1.5001552	9.6989758	14.5499688
13	1.5275215	10.4255008	15.9251763	13	1.5395783	10.3843410	15.9875065	13	1.5517230	10.3434207	16.0501240
14	1.5781206	11.0591660	17.4526978	14	1.5915391	11.0126636	17.5270848	14	1.6050635	10.9664491	17.6018470
15	1.6303959	11.6725139	19.0308184	15	1.6452536	11.6204726	19.1186239	15	1.6602375	11.5687725	19.2069105
16	1.6844027	12.2661962	20.6612143	16	1.7007809	12.2084378	20.7638775	16	1.7173082	12.1510792	20.8671481
17	1.7401986	12.8408433	22.3456170	17	1.7581822	12.7772071	22.4646583	17	1.7763407	12.7140342	22.5844563
18	1.7978426	13.3970655	24.0858155	18	1.8175209	13.3274071	24.2228406	18	1.8374024	13.2582808	24.3607970
19	1.8573962	13.9354536	25.8836582	19	1.8788622	13.8596441	26.0403614	19	1.9005631	13.7844407	26.1981994
20	1.9189224	14.4565794	27.7410544	20	1.9422738	14.3745046	27.9192236	20	1.9658950	14.2931149	28.0987625
21	1.9824867	14.9609964	29.6599768	21	2.0076255	14.8725558	29.8614974	21	2.0334726	14.7848845	30.0646574
22	2.0481566	15.4492403	31.6424635	22	2.0755897	15.3543466	31.8693230	22	2.1033732	15.2603113	32.0981300
23	2.1160018	15.9218297	33.6906201	23	2.1456408	15.8204079	33.9449126	23	2.1756767	15.7199384	34.2015032
24	2.1860944	16.3792665	35.8066219	24	2.2180562	16.2712531	36.0905534	24	2.2504656	16.1642909	36.3771799
25	2.2585087	16.8220365	37.9927163	25	2.2929156	16.7073790	38.3086096	25	2.3278253	16.5938764	38.6276455
26	2.3373218	17.2506101	40.2512250	26	2.3703015	17.1292663	40.6015252	26	2.4078443	17.0091086	40.9554708
27	2.4106131	17.6654423	42.5845468	27	2.4502992	17.5373797	42.9718266	27	2.4906140	17.4106930	43.3633151
28	2.4904647	18.0669738	44.9951599	28	2.5329967	17.9321690	45.4221258	28	2.5762288	17.7988573	45.8539291
29	2.5729613	18.4556310	47.4856246	29	2.6184854	18.3140692	47.9551225	29	2.6647867	18.1741219	48.4301579
30	2.6581907	18.8318267	50.0585059	30	2.7065593	18.6835010	50.5736079	30	2.7563887	18.5369154	51.0949445
31	2.7462432	19.1959605	52.7167766	31	2.7932158	19.0408716	53.2804672	31	2.8511396	18.8876524	53.8513333
32	2.8372125	19.5484192	55.4630198	32	2.8926556	19.3865747	56.0786630	32	2.9491475	19.2267334	56.7024728
33	2.9311952	19.8895769	58.3002324	33	2.9902827	19.7209913	58.9713385	33	3.0505245	19.5545459	59.6516204
34	3.0282910	20.2197962	61.2314276	34	3.0912047	20.0444897	61.9616212	34	3.1553862	19.8714643	62.7021448
35	3.1286032	20.5394276	64.2597186	35	3.1955329	20.3574266	65.0528259	35	3.2638526	20.1778507	65.8575310
36	3.2322382	20.8488108	67.3883218	36	3.3033821	20.6601465	68.2483588	36	3.3760476	20.4740550	69.1213837
37	3.3393060	21.1482742	70.6205599	37	3.4148713	20.9529034	71.5517409	37	3.4920992	20.7604157	72.4974312
38	3.4499206	21.4381359	73.9598560	38	3.5301232	21.2352597	74.9666122	38	3.6121401	21.0372929	75.9895304
39	3.5641992	21.7187039	77.4097665	39	3.6492648	21.5102875	78.4967353	39	3.7363074	21.3049039	79.6016705
40	3.6822633	21.9902760	80.9739857	40	3.7724275	21.7753688	82.1460001	40	3.8647430	21.5636533	83.3379780
41	3.8042383	22.2531407	84.6562490	41	3.8997469	22.0317957	85.9184276	41	3.9975935	21.8138038	87.2027210
42	3.9302536	22.5075772	88.4604873	42	4.0313634	22.2798507	89.8181746	42	4.1350108	22.0556411	91.2003145
43	4.0604433	22.7538557	92.3907409	43	4.1674219	22.5199072	93.8495360	43	4.2771518	22.2894416	95.3353253
44	4.1949455	22.9922378	96.4511842	44	4.3080724	22.7519296	98.0169599	44	4.4241789	22.5154722	99.6124771
45	4.3339030	23.2229767	100.6461297	45	4.4534698	22.9764736	102.3250323	45	4.5762601	22.7339913	104.0366560
46	4.4774636	23.3463175	104.9800327	46	4.6037744	23.1936867	106.7785021	46	4.7335690	22.9452483	108.6129161
47	4.6257796	23.6624973	109.4574963	47	4.7591518	23.4038082	111.3822166	47	4.8962854	23.1494848	113.3464851
48	4.7790085	23.8717457	114.0832759	48	4.9197732	23.6070696	116.1414284	48	5.0645952	23.3469339	118.2427705
49	4.9373132	24.0742850	118.8622844	49	5.0858156	23.8036949	121.0612016	49	5.2386907	23.5378213	123.3073657
50	5.1008617	24.2703303	123.7995976	50	5.2574618	23.9939007	126.1470172	50	5.4187707	23.7223650	128.5460564
51	5.2698277	24.4600898	128.9004592	51	5.4349012	24.1778967	131.4044790	51	5.6050409	23.9007759	133.9648271
52	5.4443908	24.6437651	134.1702870	52	5.6183291	24.3558856	136.8393802	52	5.7977142	24.0732576	139.5698681
53	5.6247362	24.8215512	139.6146777	53	5.8079477	24.5280634	142.4577093	53	5.9970106	24.2400074	145.3675823
54	5.8110556	24.9936370	145.2394139	54	6.0039659	24.6946200	148.2656570	54	6.2031579	24.4012156	151.3645929
55	6.0035468	25.1602052	151.0504695	55	6.2065998	24.8557388	154.2696229	55	6.4163914	24.5570664	157.5677508
56	6.2024143	25.3214327	157.0540163	56	6.4160725	25.0115974	160.4762227	56	6.6369549	24.7077379	163.9841423
57	6.4078693	25.4774908	163.2564306	57	6.6326150	25.1623675	166.8922952	57	6.8651002	24.8534022	170.6210971
58	6.6201299	25.6285453	169.6642999	58	6.8584557	25.3082152	173.5249101	58	7.1010880	24.9942257	177.4861974
59	6.8394217	25.7747565	176.2844298	59	7.0878714	25.4493013	180.3813759	59	7.3451879	25.1303693	184.5872854
60	7.0659776	25.9162797	182.1238516	60	7.3270871	25.5857812	187.4692473	60	7.5976788	25.2619884	191.9324733
61	7.3000381	26.0532653	190.1898291	61	7.5743763	25.7178053	194.7963344	61	7.8588490	25.3892335	199.5301521
62	7.5438519	26.1858587	197.4898872	62	7.8300115	25.8455190	202.3707107	62	8.1289969	25.5122499	207.3890011
63	7.7916757	26.3142008	205.0317191	63	8.0942744	25.9690631	210.2007222	63	8.4084312	25.6311782	215.5179980
64	8.0497750	26.4384279	212.8233948	64	8.3674561	26.0885737	218.2949966	64	8.6974710	25.7461541	223.9264292
65	8.3164238	26.5586719	220.8731698	65	8.6493578	26.2041826	226.6624527	65	8.9964466	25.8573091	232.6239002
66	8.5919053	26.6750605	229.1895935	66	8.9417905	26.3160170	235.3123105	66	9.3056994	25.9647702	241.6203468
67	8.8765122	26.7877174	237.7814988	67	9.2435759	26.4242002	244.2541010	67	9.6255828	26.0686600	250.9260462
68	9.1705466	26.8967621	246.6580110	68	9.5555466	26.5288515	253.4976769	68	9.9584623	26.1690973	260.5516291
69	9.4743210	27.0023106	255.8285576	69	9.8780463	26.6300861	263.0532235	69	10.2987156	26.2661967	270.5080913
70	9.7981579	27.1044749	265.3028785	70	10.2114304	26.7280156	272.9312698	70	10.6527340	26.3600694	280.8068070
71	10.1123906	27.2033634	275.0910364	71	10.5560661	26.8227478	283.1427001	71	11.0189227	26.4508223	291.4595410
72	10.4473635	27.2990814	285.2034270	72	10.9123304	26.9143873	293.6987663	72	11.3976972	26.5385594	302.4784627
73	10.7934324	27.3917303	295.6507905	73	11.2806246	27.0030348	304.6110997	73	11.7894930	26.6233806	313.8761599
74	11.1509549	27.4814086	306.4442230	74	11.6613457	27.0887862	315.8917243	74	12.1947568	26.7053831	325.6656529
75	11.5203406	27.5682116	317.5951879	75	12.0549161	27.1717419	327.5530700	75	12.6139516	26.7846604	337.8604097
76	11.9019519	27.6522315	329.1155285	76	12.4617695	27.2519874	339.6079861	76	13.0475562	26.8613031	350.4743613
77	12.2962040	27.7335574	341.0174804	77	12.8823543	27.3296129	352.0697556	77	13.4960659	26.9353988	363.5219175
78	12.7035158	27.8122757	353.3136844	78	13.3171337	27.4047042	364.9521099	78	13.9599932	27.0070320	377.0179334
79	13.1243198	27.8884702	366.0172002	79	13.7665870	27.4773498	378.2692436	79	14.4393380	27.0762848	390.9779766
80	13.5590629	27.9622216	379.1415200	80	14.2312093	27.5476119	392.0358306	80	14.9382384	27.1432360	405.4178445
81	14.0082068	28.0336083	392.7005828	81	14.7115126	27.6155689	406.2670399	81	15.4493716	27.2079623	420.3540329
82	14.4722287	28.1027062	406.7087896	82	15.2009262	27.6813406	420.9774046	82	15.9807543	27.2705376	435.8037546
83	14.9516212	28.1695885	421.1810183	83	15.7212970	27.7449486	436.1865787	83	16.5300925	27.3310333	451.7845086
84	15.4468937	28.2343265	436.1326396	84	16.2518908	27.8064799	451.9078725	84	17.0983144	27.3895186	468.3146011
85	15.9583721	28.2969887	451.5795332	85	16.8003921	27.8660023	468.1597665	85	17.6860690	27.4460603	485.4129155
86	16.4871997	28.3576418	467.5381053	86	17.3674054	27.9235815	484.9601586	86	18.2940276	27.5007229	503.0989845
87	17.0333382	28.4163502	484.0253050	87	17.9535553	27.9792807	502.3275640	87	18.9223848	27.5535690	521.3930121
88	17.5975676	28.4731763	501.0586433	88	18.5594878	28.0331615	520.2811193	88	19.5733590	27.6046589	540.3158969
89	18.1804870	28.5281803	518.6562109	89	19.1853705	28.0852032	538.8406071	89	20.2461932	27.6540509	559.8892559
90	18.7827156	28.5814207	536.8366979	90	19.8333936	28.1357032	558.0264776	90	20.9421561	27.7018014	580.1354491
91	19.4048931	28.6329541	555.6194135	91	20.5027707	28.1844771	577.8598712	91	21.6620427	27.7479651	601.0776052
92	20.0476302	28.6828352	575.0243066	92	21.1947392	28.2316587	598.3626419	92	22.4066754	27.7925947	622.7396479
93	20.7117596	28.7311170	595.0719867	93	21.9100616	28.2772998	619.5573811	93	23.1769049	27.8357411	645.1463233
94	21.3978366	28.7778507	615.7837463	94	22.6495262	28.3214508	641.4674427	94	23.9736110	27.8774526	668.3232282
95	22.1066400	28.8230859	637.1815829	95	23.4139477	28.3641604	664.1169689	95	24.7977039	27.9177799	692.2968391
96	22.8389224	28.8668708	659.2882229	96	24.2041685	28.4054756	687.5309166	96	25.6501249	27.9567661	717.0945430
97	23.5954617	28.9092519	682.1271453	97	25.0210591	28.4454419	711.7350851	97	26.5318480	27.9944566	742.7446679
98	24.3770614	28.9502740	705.7226070	98	25.8655199	28.4841035	736.7561442	98	27.4438803	28.0308946	769.2765159
99	25.1845515	28.9899809	730.0996684	99	26.7384812	28.5215027	762.6216641	99	28.3872636	28.0661217	796.7203962
100	26.0187898	29.0284147	755.2842199	100	27.6409049	28.5576810	789.3601453	100	29.3630758	28.1001781	825.1076598

Table 1   387

M	C(13.25,M,4)	A(13.25,M,4)	S(13.25,M,4)	M	C(13.50,M,4)	A(13.50,M,4)	S(13.50,M,4)	M	C(13.75,M,4)	A(13.75,M,4)	S(13.75,M,4)
101	26.8806622	29.0656161	781.3030097	101	28.5737855	28.5926781	817.0010502	101	30.3724316	28.1331027	854.4707356
102	27.7710842	29.1016248	808.1836719	102	29.5381507	28.6265326	845.5748357	102	31.4164839	28.1649331	884.8431672
103	28.6910013	29.1364730	835.9547561	103	30.5350633	28.6592819	875.1129964	103	32.4964255	28.1957057	916.2596511
104	29.6413907	29.1702156	864.6457574	104	31.5656217	28.6909619	905.6480497	104	33.6134902	28.2254557	948.7560766
105	30.6232618	29.2028705	894.2871481	105	32.6309614	28.7216076	937.2136714	105	34.7689539	28.2542170	982.3695668
106	31.6376574	29.2344784	924.9104099	106	33.7322564	28.7512529	969.8446329	106	35.9641367	28.2820224	1017.1385207
107	32.6656548	29.2650728	956.5480673	107	34.8707200	28.7799302	1003.5768892	107	37.2004039	28.3089309	1053.1026573
108	33.7683671	29.2946664	989.2337220	108	36.0476068	28.8076713	1038.4476093	108	38.4791678	28.3348920	1090.3030612
109	34.8869442	29.3233604	1023.0020891	109	37.2642136	28.8345067	1074.4952161	109	39.8018891	28.3600164	1128.7822290
110	36.0425743	29.3510953	1057.8890333	110	38.5218808	28.8604660	1111.7594297	110	41.1700791	28.3843059	1168.5841181
111	37.2354845	29.3779507	1093.9316075	111	39.8219943	28.8855777	1150.2813105	111	42.5853006	28.4077882	1209.7541972
112	38.4695431	29.4039450	1131.1680921	112	41.1659866	28.9098696	1190.1033047	112	44.0491703	28.4304901	1252.3394978
113	39.7442599	29.4291059	1169.6380352	113	42.5553386	28.9333684	1231.2692913	113	45.5633605	28.4524375	1296.3886680
114	41.0607886	29.4534600	1209.3822951	114	43.9915813	28.9561001	1273.8246299	114	47.1296010	28.4736556	1341.9520285
115	42.4209272	29.4770333	1250.4430837	115	45.4762972	28.9780895	1317.8162112	115	48.7496810	28.4941686	1389.0816295
116	43.8261204	29.4998508	1292.8640109	116	47.0111222	28.9993611	1363.2925083	116	50.4254513	28.5139998	1437.6313106
117	45.2773606	29.5219366	1336.6901312	117	48.5977476	29.0199382	1410.3036305	117	52.1583262	28.5331720	1488.2567619
118	46.7778898	29.5433143	1381.9679919	118	50.2379215	29.0398435	1458.9013781	118	53.9517859	28.5517071	1540.4155881
119	48.3272007	29.5640066	1428.7456816	119	51.9334514	29.0590989	1509.1392997	119	55.8063785	28.5696262	1594.3673740
120	49.9280393	29.5840354	1477.0728924	120	53.6862054	29.0777255	1561.0727511	120	57.7247228	28.5869498	1650.1737526
121	51.5810056	29.6034221	1527.0009216	121	55.4981148	29.0957443	1614.7589564	121	59.7090101	28.6036977	1707.8984753
122	53.2905562	29.6221871	1578.5823272	122	57.3711762	29.1131746	1670.2570713	122	61.7615074	28.6198890	1767.6074855
123	55.0553059	29.6403505	1631.8733334	123	59.3074534	29.1300359	1727.6282475	123	63.8845592	28.6355422	1829.3689928
124	56.8795294	29.6579315	1686.9291893	124	61.3090799	29.1463467	1786.9357009	124	66.0805909	28.6506753	1893.2535520
125	58.7638539	29.6749488	1743.8087187	125	63.3782614	29.1621250	1848.2447808	125	68.3521112	28.6653054	1959.3341429
126	60.7102102	29.6914205	1802.5723826	126	65.5172777	29.1773281	1911.6230422	126	70.7017150	28.6794493	2027.6862541
127	62.7212359	29.7073641	1863.2825028	127	67.7284858	29.1921530	1977.1403199	127	73.1320865	28.6931232	2098.3879691
128	64.7988769	29.7227965	1926.0038287	128	70.0143222	29.2064358	2044.8688058	128	75.6460020	28.7063427	2171.5200556
129	66.9453397	29.7377340	1990.8027056	129	72.3773056	29.2202523	2114.8831280	129	78.2463333	28.7191228	2247.1660576
130	69.1629041	29.7521926	2057.7480453	130	74.8200397	29.2336177	2187.2604336	130	80.9360510	28.7314783	2325.4123909
131	71.4539252	29.7661877	2126.9109493	131	77.3452160	29.2465467	2262.0804733	131	83.7182277	28.7434231	2406.3484419
132	73.8208365	29.7797340	2198.3648746	132	79.9556171	29.2590536	2339.4256994	132	86.5960418	28.7549710	2490.0666696
133	76.2661517	29.7928460	2272.1857111	133	82.6541192	29.2711523	2419.3813064	133	89.5727808	28.7661351	2576.6627115
134	78.7924680	29.8055375	2348.4518628	134	85.4423957	29.2828559	2502.0354256	134	92.6518451	28.7769282	2666.2354902
135	81.4024685	29.8178222	2427.2443308	135	88.3274204	29.2941774	2587.4791213	135	95.8367523	28.7873626	2758.8873373
136	84.0589253	29.8297129	2508.6467994	136	91.3084708	29.3051293	2675.8065417	136	99.1311407	28.7974502	2854.7240086
137	86.8847022	29.8412224	2592.7457246	137	94.3901317	29.3157236	2767.1150125	137	102.5387736	28.8072026	2953.8552303
138	89.7627580	29.8523629	2679.6304268	138	97.5757987	29.3259720	2861.5051443	138	106.0635440	28.8166310	3056.3940039
139	92.7361493	29.8631462	2769.3931848	139	100.8669319	29.3358859	2959.0809429	139	109.7094783	28.8257459	3162.4575479
140	95.8080343	29.8735837	2862.1293341	140	104.2733100	29.345·761	3059.9499248	140	113.4807416	28.8345580	3272.1670262
141	98.9816754	29.8836866	2957.9373684	141	107.7925343	29.3547532	3164.2232349	141	117.3816421	28.8430772	3385.6477678
142	102.2604434	29.8934655	3056.9190438	142	111.4305323	29.3637274	3272.0157691	142	121.4163361	28.8513133	3503.0294099
143	105.6478206	29.9029310	3159.1794872	143	115.1913128	29.3724086	3383.4463014	143	125.5903329	28.8592757	3624.4460459
144	109.1474047	29.9120929	3264.8273078	144	119.0790106	29.3808063	3498.6376142	144	129.9075006	28.8669735	3750.0363788
145	112.7029124	29.9209611	3373.9747124	145	123.0979365	29.3889300	3617.7166338	145	134.3730710	28.8744155	3879.9438794
146	116.4981839	29.9295449	3486.7376249	146	127.2524918	29.3967884	3740.8145702	146	138.9921453	28.8816101	4014.3169054
147	120.3571863	29.9378535	3603.2358088	147	131.5472634	29.4043902	3868.0670621	147	143.7700003	28.8885657	4153.3090957
148	124.3440181	29.9458957	3723.5928950	148	135.9813836	29.4117438	3999.6143255	148	148.7120940	28.8952901	4297.0790959
149	128.4629137	29.9536800	3847.9370131	149	140.5765443	29.4188574	4135.6013091	149	153.8240723	28.9017910	4445.7911900
150	132.7182477	29.9612148	3976.3999267	150	145.5310027	29.4257387	4276.1778534	150	159.1117748	28.9080759	4599.6152622
151	137.1145396	29.9685080	4109.1181744	151	150.2255865	29.4323954	4421.4988561	151	164.5812420	28.9141519	4758.7270370
152	141.6564588	29.9755673	4246.2327140	152	155.2957001	29.4388347	4571.7244426	152	170.2387222	28.9200260	4923.3092790
153	146.3489290	29.9824003	4387.8891728	153	160.5369299	29.4450638	4727.0201426	153	176.0906783	28.9257049	5093.5470012
154	151.1966339	29.9890142	4534.2380017	154	165.9550513	29.4510895	4887.5570725	154	182.1437954	28.9311951	5269.6376795
155	156.2050224	29.9954160	4685.4346357	155	171.5560343	29.4569185	5053.5121239	155	188.4049883	28.9365028	5451.7814749
156	161.3793138	30.0016126	4841.6396581	156	177.3460505	29.4625572	5225.0681582	156	194.8814098	28.9416341	5640.1864632
157	166.7250036	30.0076105	5003.0189719	157	183.3314797	29.4680118	5402.4142286	157	201.5804583	28.9465949	5835.0678730
158	172.2477693	30.0134161	5169.7439755	158	189.5189171	29.4732883	5585.7456883	158	208.5097865	28.9513909	6036.6483313
159	177.9534767	30.0190356	5341.9917448	159	195.9151806	29.4783926	5775.2646054	159	215.6773105	28.9560274	6245.1581179
160	183.8481856	30.0244748	5519.9452214	160	202.5273179	29.4833302	5971.1797860	160	223.0912180	28.9605099	6460.8354283
161	189.9331568	30.0297397	5703.7934070	161	209.3626419	29.4881066	6173.7071039	161	230.7597980	28.9648434	6683.9266463
162	196.2273582	30.0348358	5893.7315538	162	216.4285032	29.4927270	6383.0697168	162	238.6923529	28.9690329	6914.6866250
163	202.7293723	30.0397684	6089.9614220	163	223.7330685	29.4971967	6599.4983220	163	246.8974025	28.9730832	7153.3789779
164	209.4454026	30.0445430	6292.6913943	164	231.2840596	29.5015203	6823.2213905	164	255.3845008	28.9769988	7400.2763304
165	216.3832816	30.0491644	6502.1367968	165	239.0863996	29.5057029	7054.5154501	165	264.1633430	28.9807844	7655.6608812
166	223.5509778	30.0536376	6718.5200784	166	247.1591806	29.5097489	7293.6053468	166	273.2439579	28.9844441	7919.8242241
167	230.9561039	30.0579675	6942.0710562	167	255.5008030	29.5136622	7540.7645274	167	282.6367190	28.9879822	8193.0681820
168	238.6065249	30.0621585	7173.0271601	168	264.1239551	29.5174488	7796.2653304	168	292.3523562	28.9914027	8475.7049010
169	246.5103660	30.0662151	7411.6336849	169	273.0361886	29.5211113	8060.3892855	169	302.4019684	28.9947098	8768.0572572
170	254.6760219	30.0701416	7658.1440509	170	282.2531758	29.5246542	8333.4274241	170	312.7970361	28.9979066	9070.4592256
171	263.1121651	30.0739423	7912.8200728	171	291.7792205	29.5280815	8615.6805998	171	323.5494342	29.0009973	9383.2562617
172	271.8277556	30.0776211	8175.9322379	172	301.6207692	29.5313968	8907.4598203	172	334.6714460	29.0039853	9706.8056960
173	280.8320500	30.0811820	8447.7599935	173	311.6026276	29.5346040	9209.0865895	173	346.1757770	29.0068740	10041.4771420
174	290.1346117	30.0846286	8728.5920435	174	322.3301478	29.5377064	9520.8932621	174	358.0755694	29.0096667	10387.6529190
175	299.7453207	30.0879648	9018.7266552	175	333.2087903	29.5407075	9843.2234099	175	370.3844171	29.0123666	10745.7284884
176	309.6743844	30.0911940	9318.4719758	176	344.4545870	29.5436106	10176.4322003	176	383.1163814	29.0149768	11116.1129054
177	319.9323484	30.0943197	9628.1463503	177	356.0799293	29.5464190	10520.8867873	177	396.2860070	29.0175002	11499.2292868
178	330.5301075	30.0973451	9948.0787087	178	368.0976270	29.5491357	10876.9667166	178	409.9083385	29.0199398	11895.5152938
179	341.4789173	30.1002735	10278.6088162	179	380.5209219	29.5517636	11245.0643436	179	423.9989377	29.0222983	12305.4236324
180	352.7804064	30.1031081	10620.0877335	180	393.3635030	29.5543058	11625.5852654	180	438.5739012	29.0245784	12729.4225700
181	364.4765887	30.1058517	10972.8781399	181	406.6395212	29.5567650	12018.9487684	181	453.6498790	29.0267827	13167.9964712
182	376.5498757	30.1085074	11337.3547286	182	420.3835015	29.5591439	12425.5882897	182	469.2440936	29.0289138	13621.6463502
183	389.0230903	30.1110780	11713.9046042	183	434.5508768	29.5614451	12845.9518948	183	485.3743594	29.0309741	14090.8904439
184	401.9094802	30.1135661	12102.9276945	184	449.2169689	29.5636712	13280.5027715	184	502.0591030	29.0329659	14576.2648032
185	415.2227317	30.1159744	12504.8371747	185	464.3780416	29.5658246	13729.7197404	185	519.3173847	29.0348915	15078.3239062
186	428.9769847	30.1183056	12920.0599064	186	480.0508005	29.5679077	14194.0977820	186	537.1689198	29.0367531	15597.6412908
187	443.1868474	30.1205620	13349.0368912	187	496.2525150	29.5699228	14674.1485625	187	555.6341014	29.0385528	16134.8102106
188	457.8674117	30.1227460	13792.2237385	188	513.0001034	29.5718722	15170.4010975	188	574.7340236	29.0402928	16690.4443120
189	473.0342697	30.1248600	14250.0911502	189	530.3148224	29.5737578	15683.4021349	189	594.4905057	29.0419749	17265.1783356
190	488.7035299	30.1269062	14723.1254199	190	548.2129477	29.5755819	16213.7169574	190	614.9261069	29.0436011	17859.6688414
191	504.8918343	30.1288869	15211.8289498	191	566.7151347	29.5773465	16761.9299051	191	636.0642022	29.0451733	18474.5949582
192	521.6163764	30.1308040	15716.7207841	192	585.8417705	29.5790534	17328.6450398	192	657.9289091	29.0466932	19110.6591684
193	538.8949188	30.1326596	16238.3371605	193	605.6139303	29.5807047	17914.4868103	193	680.5452154	29.0481626	19768.5880695
194	556.7458130	30.1344558	16777.2320794	194	626.0534005	29.5823020	18520.1007406	194	703.9389572	29.0495832	20449.1332849
195	575.1880181	30.1361943	17333.9778924	195	647.1827027	29.5838471	19146.1541411	195	728.1368588	29.0500565	21153.0722421
196	594.2411212	30.1378772	17909.1659105	196	669.0251190	29.5853418	19793.3368438	196	753.1665634	29.0522843	21881.2091009
197	613.9253584	30.1395060	18503.4070318	197	691.6047168	29.5867878	20462.3619628	197	779.0566640	29.0535679	22634.3756643
198	634.2616359	30.1410827	19117.3323902	198	714.9463760	29.5881865	21153.9666795	198	805.8367369	29.0548088	23413.4323283
199	655.2715526	30.1426087	19751.5940261	199	739.0758162	29.5895395	21868.9130555	199	833.5373747	29.0560085	24219.2690652
200	676.9774228	30.1440859	20406.8655787	200	764.0196250	29.5908484	22607.9888717	200	862.1902220	29.0571684	25052.8064399

M	C(5.00,M,12)	A(5.00,M,12)	S(5.00,M,12)	M	C(5.25,M,12)	A(5.25,M,12)	S(5.25,M,12)	M	C(5.50,M,12)	A(5.50,M,12)	S(5.50,M,12)
1	1.0041667	.9958506	1.0000000	1	1.0043750	.9956441	1.0000000	1	1.0045833	.9954376	1.0000000
2	1.0083507	1.9875691	2.0041667	2	1.0087691	1.9869511	2.0043750	2	1.0091877	1.9863335	2.0045833
3	1.0125522	2.9751725	3.0125174	3	1.0131825	2.9739402	3.0131441	3	1.0138131	2.9727086	3.0137710
4	1.0167711	3.9586780	4.0250695	4	1.0176152	3.9566209	4.0263266	4	1.0184598	3.9545835	4.0275841
5	1.0210077	4.9381028	5.0418406	5	1.0220672	4.9350391	5.0439418	5	1.0231277	4.9319786	5.0460439
6	1.0252619	5.9134632	6.0628483	6	1.0265388	5.9091864	6.0660091	6	1.0278170	5.9049144	6.0691716
7	1.0295338	6.8847766	7.0881102	7	1.0310299	6.8790904	7.0925479	7	1.0325279	6.8734112	7.0969986
8	1.0338235	7.8520597	8.1176440	8	1.0355407	7.8447695	8.1235778	8	1.0372603	7.8374894	8.1295165
9	1.0381311	8.8153292	9.1514675	9	1.0400711	8.8062422	9.1591184	9	1.0420144	8.7971690	9.1677768
10	1.0424567	9.7746017	10.1895986	10	1.0445215	9.7635268	10.1991896	10	1.0467903	9.7524702	10.2087912
11	1.0468002	10.7298938	11.2320553	11	1.0491917	10.7166415	11.2438110	11	1.0515881	10.7034129	11.2555815
12	1.0511619	11.6812220	12.2788555	12	1.0537819	11.6656045	12.2930027	12	1.0564079	11.6500170	12.3071695
13	1.0555417	12.6286028	13.3300174	13	1.0583922	12.6104338	13.3467846	13	1.0612497	12.5923023	13.3635774
14	1.0599398	13.5720528	14.3855591	14	1.0630226	13.5511475	14.4051768	14	1.0661138	13.5302885	14.4248271
15	1.0643562	14.5115877	15.4454990	15	1.0678734	14.4877636	15.4681994	15	1.0710001	14.4639952	15.4909409
16	1.0687911	15.4472242	16.5098552	16	1.0723444	15.4202998	16.5358728	16	1.0759089	15.3934419	16.5619411
17	1.0732444	16.3789785	17.5786463	17	1.0770360	16.3487739	17.6082172	17	1.0808401	16.3186481	17.6378500
18	1.0777162	17.3068665	18.6518906	18	1.0817480	17.2732036	18.6852532	18	1.0857940	17.2396331	18.7186300
19	1.0822067	18.2309044	19.7296068	19	1.0864806	18.1936066	19.7670011	19	1.0907706	18.1564162	19.8044841
20	1.0867159	19.1511081	20.8118135	20	1.0912340	19.1100003	20.8534818	20	1.0957699	19.0690165	20.8952547
21	1.0912439	20.0674936	21.8985294	21	1.0960081	20.0224023	21.9447158	21	1.1007922	19.9774523	21.9910246
22	1.0957907	20.9800766	22.9897733	22	1.1008032	20.9308299	23.0407239	22	1.1058375	20.8817452	23.0918168
23	1.1003565	21.8888730	24.0855640	23	1.1056192	21.8350005	24.1415271	23	1.1109059	21.7819114	24.1976543
24	1.1049413	22.7938984	25.1859205	24	1.1104563	22.7358312	25.2471462	24	1.1155976	22.6779707	25.3085602
25	1.1095453	23.6951685	26.2908619	25	1.1153145	23.6324393	26.3576025	25	1.1211126	23.5669418	26.4245577
26	1.1141684	24.5926989	27.4004071	26	1.1201940	24.5251418	27.4729170	26	1.1262510	24.4578434	27.5456703
27	1.1189107	25.4865052	28.5145755	27	1.1250949	25.4139558	28.5931110	27	1.1314130	25.3416940	28.6719213
28	1.1234724	26.3766027	29.6333862	28	1.1300172	26.2988981	29.7182059	28	1.1365986	26.2215120	29.8033343
29	1.1281536	27.2630068	30.7568587	29	1.1349610	27.1799856	30.8482230	29	1.1418080	27.0973160	30.9399329
30	1.1328542	28.1457329	31.8850122	30	1.1399264	28.0572352	31.9831840	30	1.1470413	27.9691242	32.0817409
31	1.1375744	29.0247963	33.0178665	31	1.1449136	28.9306636	33.1231104	31	1.1522986	28.8369548	33.2287822
32	1.1423143	29.9002120	34.1554409	32	1.1499226	29.8002873	34.2680241	32	1.1575800	29.7008260	34.3810808
33	1.1470740	30.7719954	35.2977552	33	1.1543535	30.6661230	35.4179457	33	1.1628855	30.5607559	35.5386608
34	1.1518535	31.6401614	36.4448292	34	1.1600064	31.5281872	36.5729002	34	1.1682154	31.4167624	36.7015463
35	1.1566528	32.5047250	37.5966827	35	1.1650815	32.3864963	37.7329066	35	1.1735697	32.2658634	37.8697617
36	1.1614722	33.3657013	38.7533355	36	1.1701787	33.2410666	38.8979981	36	1.1789486	33.1170768	39.0433315
37	1.1663117	34.2231050	39.9146078	37	1.1752982	34.0919145	40.0681668	37	1.1843521	33.9614203	40.2222801
38	1.1711713	35.0769501	41.0811195	38	1.1804402	34.9390561	41.2434350	38	1.1897804	34.8019116	41.4066322
39	1.1760512	35.9272542	42.2522908	39	1.1855046	35.7825077	42.4239052	39	1.1952336	35.6385681	42.5964126
40	1.1809514	36.7740290	43.4283420	40	1.1907916	36.6222852	43.6095098	40	1.2007117	36.4714075	43.7916461
41	1.1858721	37.6172903	44.6092934	41	1.1960013	37.4584047	44.8003014	41	1.2062150	37.3004471	44.9923578
42	1.1908132	38.4570526	45.7951655	42	1.2012338	38.2908020	45.9963027	42	1.2117435	38.1257043	46.1985728
43	1.1957749	39.2933304	46.9859787	43	1.2064892	39.1197332	47.1975365	43	1.2172973	38.9471963	47.4103163
44	1.2007573	40.1261381	48.1817536	44	1.2117676	39.9449739	48.4040257	44	1.2228766	39.7649403	48.6276136
45	1.2057605	40.9554903	49.3825109	45	1.2170691	40.7666200	49.6157933	45	1.2284814	40.5789535	49.8504901
46	1.2107845	41.7814011	50.5882714	46	1.2223938	41.5846870	50.8328624	46	1.2341120	41.3892527	51.0789715
47	1.2158294	42.6038849	51.7990558	47	1.2277447	42.3991905	52.0552562	47	1.2397683	42.1958551	52.3130835
48	1.2208954	43.4229559	53.0148852	48	1.2331131	43.2101461	53.2829980	48	1.2454506	42.9987773	53.5528518
49	1.2259824	44.2386283	54.2357806	49	1.2385080	44.0175693	54.5161111	49	1.2511589	43.7980363	54.7983024
50	1.2310907	45.0509162	55.4617630	50	1.2439265	44.8214753	55.7546191	50	1.2568934	44.5936488	56.0494612
51	1.2362202	45.8598335	56.6928537	51	1.2493486	45.6218796	56.9985455	51	1.2626541	45.3856313	57.3063546
52	1.2413711	46.6653544	57.9290739	52	1.2548346	46.4187973	58.2479142	52	1.2684413	46.1740005	58.5690087
53	1.2465435	47.4676127	59.1704450	53	1.2603245	47.2122438	59.5027488	53	1.2742550	46.9587728	59.8374500
54	1.2517375	48.2665022	60.4169886	54	1.2658384	48.0022340	60.7630733	54	1.2800953	47.7399666	61.1117050
55	1.2569530	49.0620769	61.6687220	55	1.2713765	48.7887831	62.0289118	55	1.2859624	48.5175923	62.3918003
56	1.2621903	49.8543504	62.9256790	56	1.2769388	49.5719060	63.3002882	56	1.2918564	49.2916721	63.6777627
57	1.2674495	50.6433365	64.1876694	57	1.2825254	50.3516177	64.5772270	57	1.2977774	50.0622203	64.9696191
58	1.2727305	51.4290488	65.4553188	58	1.2881364	51.1279330	65.8597524	58	1.3037256	50.8292529	66.2673966
59	1.2780335	52.2115009	66.7280493	59	1.2937720	51.9008667	67.1478888	59	1.3097010	51.5927859	67.5711221
60	1.2833587	52.9907063	68.0060829	60	1.2994323	52.6704335	68.4416608	60	1.3157038	52.3528354	68.8808231
61	1.2887060	53.7666785	69.2894415	61	1.3051175	53.4366482	69.7410931	61	1.3217341	53.1094173	70.1965269
62	1.2940756	54.5394309	70.5781475	62	1.3108272	54.1995253	71.0462104	62	1.3277920	53.8625473	71.5182610
63	1.2994676	55.3089768	71.8722232	63	1.3165620	54.9590793	72.3063703	63	1.3338777	54.6122412	72.8460530
64	1.3048820	56.0753296	73.1716908	64	1.3223220	55.7153247	73.6735996	64	1.3399913	55.3595146	74.1799307
65	1.3103191	56.8385025	74.4765728	65	1.3281072	56.4682760	74.9959216	65	1.3461330	56.1013833	75.5199321
66	1.3157787	57.5985087	75.7868919	66	1.3339176	57.2179475	76.3240287	66	1.3523028	56.8408627	76.8660551
67	1.3212611	58.3553614	77.1026706	67	1.3397525	57.9643535	77.6579463	67	1.3585008	57.5769682	78.2183578
68	1.3267664	59.1090735	78.4239317	68	1.3456149	58.7075081	78.9976999	68	1.3647273	58.3097154	79.5768586
69	1.3322946	59.8596583	79.7506981	69	1.3515020	59.4474256	80.3433148	69	1.3709823	59.0391194	80.9415859
70	1.3378458	60.6071286	81.0829927	70	1.3574148	60.1841201	81.6948168	70	1.3772659	59.7651956	82.3125682
71	1.3434202	61.3514974	82.4208385	71	1.3633535	60.9176056	83.0522316	71	1.3835784	60.4879595	83.6893341
72	1.3490177	62.0927775	83.7642506	72	1.3693182	61.6478960	84.4155851	72	1.3899198	61.2074265	85.0743125
73	1.3546387	62.8309317	85.1132764	73	1.3753090	62.3750054	85.7849033	73	1.3962903	61.9236085	86.4633323
74	1.3602830	63.5661229	86.4679150	74	1.3813259	63.0990475	87.1602123	74	1.4026905	62.6365245	87.8596226
75	1.3659508	64.2982136	87.8281900	75	1.3873692	63.8199361	88.5415382	75	1.4091189	63.3461878	89.2623125
76	1.3716423	65.0272667	89.1941488	76	1.3934390	64.5373851	89.9289074	76	1.4155774	64.0526133	90.6714315
77	1.3773575	65.7532946	90.5657911	77	1.3995353	65.2519080	91.3223464	77	1.4220655	64.7558158	92.0870089
78	1.3830965	66.4763100	91.9431486	78	1.4055582	65.9633185	92.7218817	78	1.4285833	65.4558100	93.5009743
79	1.3888594	67.1963253	93.3262450	79	1.4118080	66.6716301	94.1275399	79	1.4351309	66.1526105	94.9376576
80	1.3943463	67.9133530	94.7151044	80	1.4179846	67.3768563	95.5393479	80	1.4417086	66.8462223	96.3727865
81	1.4004573	68.6274055	96.1097507	81	1.4241683	68.0790107	96.9573325	81	1.4483164	67.5366888	97.8144971
82	1.4062925	69.3384951	97.5102000	82	1.4303492	68.7781064	98.3815209	82	1.4549546	68.2239955	99.2628136
83	1.4121521	70.0466341	98.9165005	83	1.4368772	69.4741570	99.8119400	83	1.4616231	68.9081664	100.7177681
84	1.4180361	70.7518348	100.3286526	84	1.4429627	70.1671756	101.2486173	84	1.4683222	69.5892158	102.1793932
85	1.4239445	71.4541093	101.7466886	85	1.4492757	70.8571755	102.6915800	85	1.4750520	70.2671580	103.6477135
86	1.4298776	72.1534699	103.1706332	86	1.4556162	71.5441697	104.1408556	86	1.4818127	70.9402072	105.1227655
87	1.4358355	72.8499285	104.6005108	87	1.4619846	72.2281715	105.5964719	87	1.4885043	71.6137773	106.6045781
88	1.4418181	73.5434973	106.0363463	88	1.4683807	72.9091938	107.0584564	88	1.4954071	72.2824826	108.0930825
89	1.4478257	74.2341882	107.4781644	89	1.4748049	73.5872495	108.5268372	89	1.5022811	72.9481370	109.5886096
90	1.4538583	74.9220131	108.9259901	90	1.4812572	74.2623517	110.0016421	90	1.5091665	73.6107264	111.0908907
91	1.4599160	75.6069840	110.3798484	91	1.4877377	74.9345132	111.4828993	91	1.5160836	74.2703486	112.6000573
92	1.4659990	76.2891127	111.8397644	92	1.4942465	75.6037469	112.9706370	92	1.5230323	74.9269335	114.1161409
93	1.4721073	76.9684110	113.3057634	93	1.5007839	76.2700653	114.4648835	93	1.5300129	75.5805228	115.6391732
94	1.4782411	77.6448906	114.7778708	94	1.5073498	76.9334813	115.9656674	94	1.5370254	76.2311301	117.1691861
95	1.4844005	78.3185633	116.2561119	95	1.5139445	77.5940076	117.4730172	95	1.5440701	76.8787691	118.7062115
96	1.4905855	78.9894406	117.7405124	96	1.5205680	78.2516568	118.9869616	96	1.5511471	77.5234322	120.2502816
97	1.4967962	79.6575342	119.2310978	97	1.5272204	78.9064409	120.5075296	97	1.5582565	78.1651961	121.8014288
98	1.5030329	80.3228556	120.7278941	98	1.5339022	79.5583730	122.0347500	98	1.5653986	78.8040110	123.3596853
99	1.5092955	80.9854164	122.2309270	99	1.5406129	80.2074653	123.5686521	99	1.5725733	79.4399114	124.9250839
100	1.5155843	81.6452279	123.7402225	100	1.5473530	80.8537303	125.1092649	100	1.5797809	80.0729106	126.4976572

Table 1 389

M	C(5.00,M,12)	A(5.00,M,12)	S(5.00,M,12)	M	C(5.25,M,12)	A(5.25,M,12)	S(5.25,M,12)	M	C(5.50,M,12)	A(5.50,M,12)	S(5.50,M,12)
101	1.5218992	82.3023017	125.2558067	101	1.5541227	81.4971801	126.6566180	101	1.5870216	80.7030218	128.0774381
102	1.5282404	82.9566490	126.7777059	102	1.5609220	82.1378271	128.2107407	102	1.5942954	81.3302581	129.6644597
103	1.5346081	83.6082811	128.3059464	103	1.5677510	82.7756835	129.7716626	103	1.6016026	81.9546327	131.2587551
104	1.5410023	84.2572094	129.8405545	104	1.5746099	83.4107614	131.3394137	104	1.6089433	82.5761586	132.8603378
105	1.5474232	84.9034451	131.3815558	105	1.5814989	84.0430730	132.9140236	105	1.6163176	83.1948489	134.4693011
106	1.5538708	85.5469992	132.9289800	106	1.5884179	84.6726302	134.4955225	106	1.6237258	83.8107164	136.0856187
107	1.5603452	86.1878831	134.4828507	107	1.5953672	85.2994451	136.0539404	107	1.6311678	84.4237741	137.7093144
108	1.5668467	86.8261076	136.0431959	108	1.6023470	85.9235297	137.6793076	108	1.6386440	85.0340348	139.3405123
109	1.5733752	87.4616839	137.6100426	109	1.6093572	86.5448958	139.2816546	109	1.6461545	85.6415112	140.9791563
110	1.5799309	88.0946230	139.1834178	110	1.6163982	87.1635552	140.8910118	110	1.6536993	86.2462161	142.6253108
111	1.5865140	88.7249358	140.7633487	111	1.6234699	87.7795198	142.5074100	111	1.6612788	86.8481620	144.2790101
112	1.5931244	89.3526331	142.3498628	112	1.6305726	88.3928013	144.1308799	112	1.6688930	87.4473616	145.9402889
113	1.5997624	89.9777259	143.9429870	113	1.6377064	89.0034114	145.7614525	113	1.6765421	88.0438274	147.6091819
114	1.6064281	90.6002250	145.5427495	114	1.6448713	89.6113617	147.3991589	114	1.6842262	88.6375718	149.2857240
115	1.6131216	91.2201411	147.1491776	115	1.6520676	90.2166638	149.0440302	115	1.6919456	89.2286074	150.9699502
116	1.6193429	91.8374849	148.7622992	116	1.6592954	90.8193292	150.6960978	116	1.6997004	89.8169464	152.6618958
117	1.6265923	92.4522671	150.3821421	117	1.6665548	91.4193695	152.3553933	117	1.7074907	90.4026011	154.3615962
118	1.6333697	93.0644984	152.0087344	118	1.6738460	92.0167960	154.0291481	118	1.7153166	90.9855839	156.0690868
119	1.6401754	93.6741892	153.6421041	119	1.6811691	92.6116201	155.6957941	119	1.7231785	91.5659068	157.7844035
120	1.6470095	94.2813503	155.2822795	120	1.6885242	93.2038533	157.3769632	120	1.7310764	92.1435820	159.5075920
121	1.6533720	94.8859920	156.9292690	121	1.6959115	93.7935067	159.0654875	121	1.7390105	92.7186217	161.2386584
122	1.6607632	95.4881248	158.5831611	122	1.7033311	94.3805916	160.7613990	122	1.7469810	93.2910378	162.9776689
123	1.6676830	96.0877591	160.2439242	123	1.7107832	94.9651192	162.4647301	123	1.7549880	93.8608422	164.7246499
124	1.6746317	96.6849054	161.9116073	124	1.7182679	95.5471006	164.1755133	124	1.7630317	94.4280470	166.4796379
125	1.6816093	97.2795738	163.5862390	125	1.7257853	96.1265470	165.8937812	125	1.7711122	94.9926640	168.2426696
126	1.6886160	97.8717747	165.2678483	126	1.7333356	96.7034693	167.6195664	126	1.7792298	95.5547049	170.0137818
127	1.6956519	98.4615184	166.9564543	127	1.7409189	97.2778786	169.3529020	127	1.7873846	96.1141816	171.7930116
128	1.7027172	99.0488150	168.6521163	128	1.7485355	97.8497858	171.0938210	128	1.7955768	96.6711057	173.5803963
129	1.7098118	99.6336747	170.3548334	129	1.7561853	98.4192018	172.8423565	129	1.8033065	97.2254888	175.3759731
130	1.7169360	100.2161076	172.0646452	130	1.7638686	98.9861374	174.5985418	130	1.8120740	97.7773427	177.1797796
131	1.7240899	100.7961237	173.7815812	131	1.7715855	99.5506035	176.3624104	131	1.8203793	98.3266787	178.9918536
132	1.7312736	101.3737332	175.5056712	132	1.7793362	100.1126109	178.1339959	132	1.8287227	98.8735085	180.8122330
133	1.7384873	101.9489459	177.2369448	133	1.7871208	100.6721701	179.9133322	133	1.8371044	99.4178434	182.6409557
134	1.7457310	102.5217719	178.9754321	134	1.7949395	101.2292920	181.7004530	134	1.8455244	99.9596948	184.4780601
135	1.7530048	103.0922209	180.7211630	135	1.8027923	101.7839870	183.4953925	135	1.8533831	100.4990740	186.3235845
136	1.7603090	103.6603030	182.4741679	136	1.8106796	102.3362658	185.2981848	136	1.8624805	101.0359924	188.1775876
137	1.7676437	104.2260279	184.2344769	137	1.8186013	102.8861390	187.1088644	137	1.8710169	101.5704611	190.0400481
138	1.7750088	104.7894054	186.0021206	138	1.8265577	103.4336169	188.9274557	138	1.8795924	102.1024914	191.9110650
139	1.7824047	105.3504452	187.7771294	139	1.8345489	103.9787101	190.7540233	139	1.8882072	102.6320943	193.7906574
140	1.7898314	105.9091570	189.5595341	140	1.8425750	104.5214288	192.5865722	140	1.8968615	103.1592809	195.6788646
141	1.7972890	106.4655506	191.3493655	141	1.8506363	105.0617835	194.4311472	141	1.9055554	103.6840623	197.5757261
142	1.8047777	107.0196354	193.1466545	142	1.8587328	105.5997344	196.2817835	142	1.9142892	104.2064494	199.4812815
143	1.8122976	107.5714212	194.9514323	143	1.8668648	106.1354419	198.1405163	143	1.9230630	104.7264531	201.3955707
144	1.8193489	108.1209173	196.7637299	144	1.8750323	106.6687660	200.0073810	144	1.9318771	105.2440844	203.3186337
145	1.8274316	108.6681334	199.5835788	145	1.8832356	107.1997670	201.8824133	145	1.9407315	105.7593540	205.2505108
146	1.8350459	109.2130789	200.4110104	146	1.8914747	107.7284551	203.7656489	146	1.9496265	106.2722728	207.1912423
147	1.8426919	109.7557633	202.2460562	147	1.8997499	108.2548401	205.6571236	147	1.9585623	106.7828514	209.1408088
148	1.8503698	110.2961958	204.0887481	148	1.9080613	108.7789323	207.5568735	148	1.9675391	107.2911005	211.0994311
149	1.8580797	110.8343658	205.9391179	149	1.9164091	109.3007416	209.4649348	149	1.9765569	107.7970308	213.0669702
150	1.8658217	111.3703627	207.7971976	150	1.9247934	109.8202778	211.3813439	150	1.9856162	108.3006528	215.0435272
151	1.8735959	111.9040758	209.6630192	151	1.9332144	110.3375511	213.3061373	151	1.9947169	108.8019770	217.0291433
152	1.8814026	112.4355941	211.5366152	152	1.9416722	110.8525711	215.2393517	152	2.0038594	109.3010141	219.0238602
153	1.8892417	112.9649070	213.4180177	153	1.9501670	111.3653497	217.1810238	153	2.0130437	109.7977743	221.0277196
154	1.8971136	113.4920236	215.3072595	154	1.9586990	111.8758906	219.1311908	154	2.0222702	110.2922680	223.0407633
155	1.9050182	114.0169529	217.2043730	155	1.9672683	112.3842097	221.0895898	155	2.0315389	110.7845057	225.0630335
156	1.9129558	114.5397042	219.1093913	156	1.9758751	112.8903146	223.0571581	156	2.0408501	111.2744976	227.0945724
157	1.9209264	115.0602663	221.0223471	157	1.9845195	113.3942149	225.0330331	157	2.0502040	111.7622539	229.1354225
158	1.9289303	115.5787084	222.9432735	158	1.9932018	113.8959202	227.0175526	158	2.0596008	112.2477849	231.1856265
159	1.9369675	116.0949793	224.8722038	159	2.0019221	114.3954402	229.0107544	159	2.0690406	112.7311007	233.2452273
160	1.9450382	116.6091080	226.8091713	160	2.0106805	114.8927843	231.0126765	160	2.0785237	113.2122114	235.3142679
161	1.9531425	117.1211034	228.7542096	161	2.0194772	115.3879619	233.0233569	161	2.0880503	113.6911271	237.3927917
162	1.9612806	117.6309743	230.7073521	162	2.0283124	115.8809826	235.0428341	162	2.0976205	114.1678577	239.4808420
163	1.9694526	118.1387296	232.6686327	163	2.0371863	116.3718558	237.0711465	163	2.1072346	114.6424133	241.5784625
164	1.9776587	118.6443780	234.6380854	164	2.0460990	116.8605907	239.1083328	164	2.1168928	115.1148038	243.6856971
165	1.9858989	119.1479283	236.6157441	165	2.0550506	117.3471967	241.1544318	165	2.1265952	115.5850300	245.8052899
166	1.9941735	119.6493892	238.6016430	166	2.0640415	117.8316831	243.2094824	166	2.1363421	116.0531289	247.9291851
167	2.0024826	120.1487693	240.5958165	167	2.0730717	118.3140591	245.2735239	167	2.1461337	116.5190831	250.0655272
168	2.0108262	120.6460774	242.5982991	168	2.0821414	118.7943338	247.3465956	168	2.1559701	116.9829114	252.2116509
169	2.0192047	121.1413218	244.6091253	169	2.0912507	119.2725165	249.4287369	169	2.1658516	117.4446235	254.3676310
170	2.0276180	121.6345114	246.6283300	170	2.1003999	119.7486164	251.5199876	170	2.1757785	117.9042292	256.5334826
171	2.0360665	122.1256545	248.6559481	171	2.1095892	120.2226423	253.6203376	171	2.1857508	118.3617379	258.7092611
172	2.0445501	122.6147597	250.6920145	172	2.1183187	120.6946034	255.7299768	172	2.1957688	118.8171592	260.8950119
173	2.0530690	123.1018353	252.7365646	173	2.1280885	121.1645087	257.8487954	173	2.2058327	119.2705027	263.0907807
174	2.0616235	123.5868900	254.7896336	174	2.1373989	121.6323671	259.9768839	174	2.2159428	119.7217779	265.2966134
175	2.0702136	124.0699319	256.8512571	175	2.1467500	122.0981875	262.1142828	175	2.2260992	120.1709942	267.5125562
176	2.0788395	124.5509695	258.9214707	176	2.1561420	122.5619789	264.2610328	176	2.2363022	120.6181610	269.7386555
177	2.0875013	125.0300112	261.0003101	177	2.1655751	123.0237500	266.4171748	177	2.2465519	121.0632876	271.9749576
178	2.0961992	125.5070651	263.0878114	178	2.1750495	123.4835096	268.5827499	178	2.2568486	121.5063833	274.2215095
179	2.1049334	125.9821395	265.1840106	179	2.1845654	123.9412666	270.7577995	179	2.2671925	121.9474574	276.4783581
180	2.1137039	126.4552428	267.2889440	180	2.1941228	124.3970296	272.9423649	180	2.2775838	122.3865192	278.7455506
181	2.1225110	126.9263827	269.4026479	181	2.2037221	124.8508073	275.1364877	181	2.2880227	122.8235778	281.0231344
182	2.1313548	127.3955678	271.5251590	182	2.2133634	125.3026084	277.3402098	182	2.2985095	123.2586424	283.3111571
183	2.1402355	127.8628061	273.6565138	183	2.2230469	125.7524414	279.5535733	183	2.3090443	123.6917220	285.6096665
184	2.1491531	128.3281057	275.7967493	184	2.2327727	126.2003151	281.7766201	184	2.3196274	124.1228257	287.9187109
185	2.1581079	128.7914745	277.9459024	185	2.2425411	126.6462378	284.0093929	185	2.3302591	124.5519625	290.2383383
186	2.1671000	129.2529207	280.1040103	186	2.2523522	127.0902181	286.2519340	186	2.3409394	124.9791415	292.5685973
187	2.1761296	129.7124522	282.2711104	187	2.2622063	127.5322644	288.5042862	187	2.3516687	125.4043714	294.9095367
188	2.1851968	130.1700763	284.4472400	188	2.2721034	127.9723852	290.7664924	188	2.3624472	125.8276613	297.2612055
189	2.1943018	130.6258027	286.6324369	189	2.2820439	128.4105889	293.0385958	189	2.3732751	126.2490200	299.6236526
190	2.2034447	131.0796375	288.8267387	190	2.2920278	128.8468838	295.3206397	190	2.3841526	126.6684562	301.9969277
191	2.2126258	131.5315892	291.0301834	191	2.3020554	129.2812782	297.6126675	191	2.3950800	127.0859788	304.3810803
192	2.2218450	131.9816656	293.2428092	192	2.3121269	129.7137804	299.9147229	192	2.4060574	127.5015965	306.7761603
193	2.2311027	132.4298745	295.4646542	193	2.3222425	130.1443986	302.2266498	193	2.4170852	127.9153180	309.1822177
194	2.2403990	132.8762235	297.6957570	194	2.3324023	130.5731411	304.5490923	194	2.4281635	128.3271519	311.5993028
195	2.2497340	133.3207205	299.9361559	195	2.3426065	131.0000161	306.8814946	195	2.4392926	128.7371068	314.0274663
196	2.2591079	133.7633731	302.1858899	196	2.3528554	131.4250316	309.2241011	196	2.4504726	129.1451913	316.4667589
197	2.2685208	134.2041890	304.4449978	197	2.3631492	131.8481957	311.5769566	197	2.4617040	129.5514140	318.9172315
198	2.2779730	134.6431758	306.7135186	198	2.3734880	132.2695166	313.9401058	198	2.4729868	129.9557833	321.3789355
199	2.2874646	135.0803410	308.9914916	199	2.3838720	132.6890022	316.3135937	199	2.4843213	130.3583077	323.8519223
200	2.2969957	135.5156923	311.2789562	200	2.3943014	133.1066605	318.6974657	200	2.4957078	130.7589957	326.3362436

Table 1

M	C(5.00,M,12)	A(5.00,M,12)	S(5.00,M,12)	M	C(5.25,M,12)	A(5.25,M,12)	S(5.25,M,12)	M	C(5.50,M,12)	A(5.50,M,12)	S(5.50,M,12)
201	2.3065665	135.9492371	313.5759518	201	2.4047765	133.5224996	321.0917671	201	2.5071464	131.1578555	328.8319514
202	2.3161772	136.3309831	315.8825163	202	2.4152974	133.9365273	323.4965436	202	2.5186375	131.5548956	331.3390978
203	2.3258279	136.8109375	318.1988955	203	2.4258643	134.3487515	325.9118410	203	2.5301813	131.9501242	333.8577354
204	2.3355189	137.2391079	320.5245234	204	2.4364775	134.7591801	328.3377053	204	2.5417780	132.3435496	336.3879167
205	2.3452502	137.6655016	322.8600422	205	2.4471371	135.1678209	330.7741827	205	2.5534278	132.7351800	338.9298946
206	2.3550221	138.0901261	325.2052924	206	2.4578433	135.5746816	333.2213198	206	2.5651310	133.1250236	341.4831224
207	2.3648346	138.5129886	327.5603145	207	2.4685963	135.9797701	335.6791631	207	2.5768978	133.5130886	344.0482534
208	2.3746881	138.9340956	329.9251491	208	2.4793965	136.3830941	338.1477594	208	2.5886986	133.8993831	346.6251412
209	2.3845827	139.3534571	332.2998372	209	2.4902438	136.7846612	340.6271559	209	2.6005634	134.2839152	349.2138398
210	2.3945184	139.7710777	334.6844199	210	2.5011386	137.1844791	343.1173997	210	2.6124827	134.6666928	351.8144032
211	2.4044956	140.1869653	337.0789383	211	2.5120811	137.5825554	345.6185383	211	2.6244566	135.0477241	354.4268859
212	2.4145143	140.6011273	339.4834339	212	2.5230715	137.9768978	348.1306194	212	2.6364853	135.4270169	357.0513424
213	2.4245748	141.0135707	341.8979482	213	2.5341099	138.3735136	350.6536909	213	2.6485692	135.8045793	359.6878278
214	2.4346772	141.4243028	344.3225230	214	2.5451966	138.7664106	353.1876008	214	2.6607085	136.1804190	362.3363970
215	2.4448217	141.8333306	346.7572002	215	2.5563319	139.1575961	355.7329974	215	2.6729034	136.5545440	364.9971055
216	2.4550084	142.2406612	349.2020218	216	2.5675158	139.5470776	358.2893293	216	2.6851542	136.9269621	367.6700089
217	2.4652376	142.6463016	351.6570303	217	2.5787487	139.9348626	360.8568451	217	2.6974612	137.2976811	370.3551631
218	2.4755095	143.0502588	354.1222679	218	2.5900307	140.3209584	363.4355938	218	2.7098245	137.6667087	373.0526242
219	2.4858241	143.4525399	356.5977773	219	2.6013621	140.7053724	366.0256245	219	2.7222446	138.0340526	375.7624488
220	2.4961817	143.8531518	359.0836014	220	2.6127431	141.0881119	368.6269866	220	2.7347215	138.3997205	378.4846933
221	2.5065824	144.2521013	361.5797831	221	2.6241738	141.4691842	371.2397297	221	2.7472557	138.7637202	381.2194148
222	2.5170265	144.6493955	364.0863655	222	2.6355546	141.8485966	373.8639035	222	2.7598472	139.1260591	383.9666705
223	2.5275141	145.0450412	366.6033920	223	2.6471856	142.2263563	376.4995581	223	2.7724965	139.4867448	386.7265177
224	2.5380454	145.4390452	369.1309062	224	2.6587670	142.6024705	379.1467437	224	2.7852038	139.8457850	389.4990143
225	2.5486206	145.8314143	371.6689516	225	2.6703991	142.9769464	381.8055107	225	2.7979693	140.2031870	392.2842181
226	2.5592399	146.2221553	374.2175723	226	2.6820821	143.3497910	384.4759098	226	2.8107934	140.5589585	395.0821874
227	2.5699034	146.6112750	376.7768121	227	2.6938162	143.7210116	387.1579919	227	2.8236762	140.9131057	397.8929908
228	2.5806113	146.9987801	379.3467155	228	2.7056017	144.0906152	389.8518081	228	2.8366180	141.2655392	400.7166570
229	2.5913639	147.3846772	381.9273269	229	2.7174387	144.4586087	392.5574098	229	2.8496192	141.6165633	403.5532750
230	2.6021612	147.7689732	384.5186907	230	2.7293275	144.8249994	395.2743464	230	2.8626799	141.9658863	406.4028942
231	2.6130036	148.1516745	387.1206519	231	2.7412683	145.1897940	398.0041759	231	2.8758006	142.3136156	409.2655741
232	2.6238911	148.5327879	389.7338555	232	2.7532613	145.5529996	400.7454442	232	2.8889813	142.6597583	412.1413747
233	2.6348239	148.9123199	392.3577436	233	2.7653068	145.9146232	403.4967055	233	2.9022225	143.0043219	415.0303560
234	2.6458024	149.2902771	394.9925705	234	2.7774051	146.2746715	406.2640123	234	2.9155243	143.3473133	417.9325784
235	2.6568266	149.6666660	397.6383729	235	2.7895562	146.6331514	409.0414174	235	2.9288871	143.6887399	420.8481027
236	2.6678967	150.0414931	400.2951994	236	2.8017605	146.9900699	411.8309736	236	2.9423112	144.0286088	423.7769899
237	2.6790129	150.4147649	402.9630361	237	2.8140182	147.3454336	414.6327341	237	2.9557968	144.3669271	426.7193011
238	2.6901755	150.7864879	405.6421090	238	2.8263295	147.6992494	417.4467523	238	2.9693442	144.7037018	429.6750979
239	2.7013845	151.1566684	408.3322845	239	2.8386947	148.0515240	420.2730819	239	2.9829537	145.0389400	432.6444421
240	2.7126403	151.5253129	411.0336690	240	2.8511140	148.4022641	423.1117766	240	2.9966256	145.3726409	435.6273958
241	2.7239430	151.8924278	413.7463093	241	2.8635877	148.7514764	425.9628906	241	3.0103601	145.7048648	438.6240214
242	2.7352927	152.2580194	416.4702522	242	2.8761158	149.0991675	428.8264783	242	3.0241576	146.0355054	441.6343815
243	2.7466898	152.6220940	419.2055450	243	2.8886989	149.4453441	431.7025941	243	3.0380183	146.3646674	444.6585390
244	2.7581343	152.9846579	421.9522347	244	2.9013369	149.7900128	434.5912930	244	3.0519426	146.6923275	447.6965574
245	2.7696265	153.3457175	424.7103690	245	2.9140303	150.1331801	437.4926299	245	3.0659306	147.0184928	450.7484999
246	2.7811667	153.7052788	427.4799956	246	2.9267791	150.4748527	440.4066602	246	3.0799828	147.3431699	453.8144305
247	2.7927548	154.0633482	430.2611622	247	2.9395838	150.8150369	443.3334393	247	3.0940994	147.6663637	456.8944134
248	2.8043913	154.4199318	433.0539171	248	2.9524445	151.1537393	446.2730231	248	3.1082807	147.9880870	459.9885128
249	2.8160763	154.7750358	435.8583064	249	2.9653614	151.4909663	449.2254676	249	3.1225270	148.3083404	463.0967934
250	2.8278099	155.1286664	438.6743847	250	2.9783349	151.8267244	452.1908290	250	3.1368386	148.6271327	466.2193204
251	2.8395925	155.4808296	441.5021946	251	2.9913651	152.1610199	455.1691639	251	3.1512157	148.9444706	469.3561590
252	2.8514241	155.8315315	444.3417871	252	3.0044523	152.4938593	458.1605290	252	3.1656588	149.2603606	472.5073747
253	2.8633051	156.1807783	447.1932112	253	3.0175968	152.8252488	461.1649913	253	3.1801681	149.5748094	475.6730335
254	2.8752355	156.5285759	450.0565163	254	3.0307988	153.1551948	464.1825781	254	3.1947438	149.8878235	478.8532016
255	2.8872156	156.8749303	452.9317518	255	3.0440585	153.4837036	467.2133769	255	3.2093864	150.1994096	482.0479454
256	2.8992457	157.2198476	455.8189674	256	3.0573763	153.8107815	470.2574354	256	3.2240961	150.5095740	485.2533183
257	2.9113259	157.5633337	458.7182131	257	3.0707523	154.1364346	473.3148117	257	3.2388732	150.8183234	488.4814280
258	2.9234564	157.9053946	461.6295390	258	3.0841868	154.4606691	476.3855640	258	3.2537181	151.1256640	491.7203012
259	2.9356375	158.2460361	464.5529954	259	3.0976802	154.7834913	479.4697509	259	3.2686309	151.4316025	494.9740192
260	2.9478693	158.5852642	467.4886329	260	3.1112325	155.1049074	482.5674310	260	3.2836122	151.7361452	498.2426501
261	2.9601521	158.9230847	470.4365022	261	3.1248442	155.4249233	485.6786635	261	3.2986620	152.0392904	501.5262023
262	2.9724861	159.2595034	473.3966543	262	3.1385154	155.7435453	488.8035077	262	3.3137809	152.3410685	504.8249243
263	2.9848714	159.5945262	476.3691404	263	3.1522464	156.0607794	491.9420230	263	3.3289591	152.6414618	508.1387052
264	2.9973084	159.9281589	479.3540118	264	3.1660374	156.3766316	495.0942694	264	3.3442268	152.9404846	511.4676743
265	3.0097972	160.2604072	482.3513202	265	3.1798888	156.6911080	498.2603068	265	3.3595546	153.2381431	514.8119012
266	3.0223380	160.5912768	485.3611174	266	3.1933009	157.0042146	501.4401957	266	3.3749525	153.5344436	518.1714497
267	3.0349311	160.9207736	488.3834554	267	3.2077737	157.3159573	504.6339965	267	3.3904210	153.8293922	521.5464082
268	3.0475766	161.2489032	491.4183864	268	3.2210077	157.6263420	507.8417703	268	3.4059605	154.1229951	524.9369293
269	3.0602749	161.5756712	494.4659630	269	3.2343032	157.9353748	511.0635780	269	3.4215711	154.4152585	528.3427897
270	3.0730260	161.9010834	497.5262379	270	3.2476605	158.2430614	514.2994812	270	3.4372553	154.7061885	531.7643609
271	3.0858303	162.2251453	500.5992839	271	3.2610800	158.5494077	517.5495414	271	3.4530074	154.9957911	535.2016142
272	3.0986879	162.5478625	503.6850904	272	3.2745618	158.8544196	520.8138207	272	3.4688327	155.2840725	538.6546216
273	3.1115991	162.8692407	506.7837820	273	3.2881063	159.1581029	524.0923811	273	3.4847325	155.5710385	542.1234553
274	3.1245641	163.1892853	509.8953811	274	3.3017138	159.4604634	527.3852853	274	3.5007042	155.8566953	545.6081878
275	3.1375831	163.5080020	513.0199452	275	3.3153846	159.7615068	530.6925959	275	3.5167491	156.1410489	549.1088920
276	3.1506564	163.8253962	516.1575283	276	3.3291189	160.0612389	534.0143760	276	3.5328675	156.4241051	552.6256411
277	3.1637841	164.1414733	519.3081847	277	3.3429171	160.3596654	537.3506889	277	3.5490598	156.7058698	556.1585086
278	3.1769665	164.4562390	522.4719898	278	3.3567795	160.6567919	540.7015982	278	3.5653261	156.9863491	559.7075664
279	3.1902039	164.7696986	525.6489354	279	3.3707064	160.9526242	544.0671677	279	3.5816674	157.2655486	563.2728948
280	3.2034964	165.0818575	528.8391349	280	3.3846980	161.2471678	547.4474616	280	3.5980834	157.5434744	566.8545622
281	3.2168443	165.3927212	532.0426357	281	3.3987547	161.5404284	550.8425442	281	3.6145746	157.8201321	570.4526456
282	3.2302478	165.7022950	535.2594800	282	3.4128766	161.8324116	554.2524204	282	3.6311414	158.0955276	574.0672203
283	3.2437072	166.0105842	538.4897278	283	3.4270641	162.1231230	557.6773350	283	3.6477842	158.3696666	577.6983617
284	3.2572227	166.3175942	541.7334350	284	3.4413174	162.4125680	561.1171733	284	3.6645032	158.6425549	581.3461459
285	3.2707944	166.6233303	544.9906577	285	3.4556368	162.7007522	564.5720609	285	3.6812988	158.9141982	585.0106640
286	3.2844227	166.9277978	548.2614521	286	3.4700225	162.9876811	568.0420637	286	3.6981714	159.1846021	588.6919479
287	3.2981078	167.2310020	551.5458748	287	3.4844750	163.2733601	571.5272477	287	3.7151214	159.4537723	592.3901193
288	3.3118499	167.5329480	554.8439826	288	3.4989945	163.5577948	575.0276795	288	3.7321490	159.7217144	596.1052407
289	3.3256493	167.8336412	558.1558326	289	3.5135812	163.8409904	578.5434256	289	3.7492547	159.9884341	599.8373697
290	3.3395062	168.1330867	561.4814819	290	3.5282356	164.1229525	582.0745531	290	3.7664388	160.2539369	603.5866444
291	3.3534208	168.4312896	564.8209881	291	3.5429580	164.4036864	585.6211292	291	3.7837016	160.5182283	607.3530832
292	3.3673934	168.7282552	568.1744089	292	3.5577486	164.6831497	589.1832217	292	3.8010436	160.7813140	611.1367848
293	3.3814242	169.0239886	571.5418022	293	3.5726078	164.9614909	592.7608983	293	3.8184651	161.0431993	614.9378284
294	3.3955134	169.3184949	574.9232264	294	3.5875358	165.2385721	596.3542272	294	3.8359664	161.3038898	618.7562935
295	3.4096614	169.6117791	578.3187399	295	3.6025330	165.5144464	599.9632770	295	3.8535479	161.5633909	622.5922598
296	3.4238683	169.9038464	581.7284013	296	3.6175997	165.7891190	603.5881163	296	3.8712100	161.8217081	626.4458077
297	3.4381345	170.1947019	585.1522696	297	3.6327361	166.0625952	607.2288143	297	3.8889530	162.0788467	630.3170177
298	3.4524600	170.4843504	588.5904041	298	3.6479426	166.3348801	610.8854404	298	3.9067774	162.3348122	634.2059707
299	3.4668453	170.7727971	592.0428641	299	3.6632195	166.6059789	614.5580642	299	3.9246834	162.5896098	638.1127480
300	3.4812905	171.0600469	595.5097094	300	3.6785670	166.8758968	618.2467557	300	3.9426716	162.8432449	642.0374315

M	C(5.00,M,12)	A(5.00,M,12)	S(5.00,M,12)	M	C(5.25,M,12)	A(5.25,M,12)	S(5.25,M,12)	M	C(5.50,M,12)	A(5.50,M,12)	S(5.50,M,12)
301	3.4957958	171.3461048	598.9909998	301	3.7210382	167.1446390	621.9515853	301	3.9607421	163.0957228	645.9801030
302	3.5103617	171.6309757	602.4867957	302	3.7373177	167.4122106	625.6726235	302	3.9768955	163.3470489	649.9408452
303	3.5249882	171.9146646	605.9971573	303	3.7536685	167.6766167	629.4095412	303	3.9971322	163.5972262	653.9197407
304	3.5396756	172.1971764	609.5221455	304	3.7700908	167.9438623	633.1638097	304	4.0154523	163.8462662	657.9168729
305	3.5544243	172.4735159	613.0618211	305	3.7865849	168.2079525	636.9337005	305	4.0338565	164.0941679	661.9323252
306	3.5692344	172.7596880	616.6162454	306	3.8031513	168.4708923	640.7202854	306	4.0523450	164.3409386	665.9661817
307	3.5841062	173.0376976	620.1854797	307	3.8197900	168.7326868	644.5234367	307	4.0709183	164.5865834	670.0185267
308	3.5990399	173.3155495	623.7695659	308	3.8365016	168.9933410	648.3432267	308	4.0895766	164.8311075	674.0894450
309	3.6140359	173.5922484	627.3685258	309	3.8532863	169.2520597	652.1797284	309	4.1083205	165.0745160	678.1790216
310	3.6290944	173.8677993	630.9826618	310	3.8701444	169.5112480	656.0330147	310	4.1271503	165.3168139	682.2873421
311	3.6442157	174.1422067	634.6117562	311	3.8870763	169.7685107	659.9031591	311	4.1460664	165.5580064	686.4144924
312	3.6593999	174.4154756	638.2559719	312	3.9040823	170.0246529	663.7902355	312	4.1650592	165.7980984	690.5605589
313	3.6746474	174.6876105	641.9153718	313	3.9211626	170.2796793	667.6943177	313	4.1841591	166.0370951	694.7256281
314	3.6899584	174.9586163	645.5900191	314	3.9383177	170.5335948	671.6154804	314	4.2033365	166.2750013	698.9097872
315	3.7053332	175.2284976	649.2799776	315	3.9555479	170.7864043	675.5537981	315	4.2226018	166.5118221	703.1131238
316	3.7207721	175.4972590	652.9853108	316	3.9728534	171.0281125	679.5093460	316	4.2419554	166.7475625	707.3357256
317	3.7362754	175.7649052	656.7060829	317	3.9902346	171.2887244	683.4821994	317	4.2613977	166.9822273	711.5776810
318	3.7518432	176.0314409	660.4423583	318	4.0076919	171.5382446	687.4724340	318	4.2809291	167.2156214	715.8390787
319	3.7674758	176.2968706	664.1942015	319	4.0252256	171.7866778	691.4801259	319	4.3005500	167.4483498	720.1200078
320	3.7831737	176.5611989	667.9616773	320	4.0428359	172.0340290	695.5053515	320	4.3202609	167.6798173	724.4205579
321	3.7989369	176.8244305	671.7448510	321	4.0605233	172.2803026	699.5481874	321	4.3400621	167.9102288	728.7408188
322	3.8147658	177.0865697	675.5437878	322	4.0782881	172.5255036	703.6087107	322	4.3599540	168.1395890	733.0808309
323	3.8306606	177.3476213	679.3585536	323	4.0961306	172.7696364	707.6869988	323	4.3799372	168.3679028	737.4408349
324	3.8466217	177.6075897	683.1892143	324	4.1140512	173.0127053	711.7831295	324	4.4000119	168.5951749	741.8207721
325	3.8626493	177.8664794	687.0358360	325	4.1320502	173.2547164	715.8971807	325	4.4201786	168.8214101	746.2207840
326	3.8787437	178.1242948	690.8984853	326	4.1501279	173.4956728	720.0292308	326	4.4404378	169.0466131	750.6405626
327	3.8949051	178.3810405	694.7772290	327	4.1682847	173.7355797	724.1793587	327	4.4607898	169.2707887	755.0814003
328	3.9111339	178.6367208	698.6721342	328	4.1865209	173.9744415	728.3476434	328	4.4812350	169.4939414	759.5421901
329	3.9274303	178.8913402	702.5832681	329	4.2048370	174.2122629	732.5341644	329	4.5017740	169.7160761	764.0234251
330	3.9437946	179.1449031	706.5106983	330	4.2232331	174.4490483	736.7390013	330	4.5224072	169.9371972	768.5251991
331	3.9602271	179.3974139	710.4544929	331	4.2417098	174.6848023	740.9622345	331	4.5431349	170.1573096	773.0476063
332	3.9767280	179.6488769	714.4147200	332	4.2602673	174.9195293	745.2039443	332	4.5639576	170.3764177	777.5907412
333	3.9932977	179.8992965	718.3914480	333	4.2789059	175.1532339	749.4642115	333	4.5848757	170.5945261	782.1546988
334	4.0099364	180.1486770	722.3847457	334	4.2976261	175.3859205	753.7431175	334	4.6058897	170.8116394	786.7395745
335	4.0266445	180.3970227	726.3946821	335	4.3164283	175.6175935	758.0407436	335	4.6270001	171.0277622	791.3454642
336	4.0434222	180.6443380	730.4213267	336	4.3353126	175.8482574	762.3571719	336	4.6482071	171.2428989	795.9724642
337	4.0602698	180.8906271	734.4647489	337	4.3542796	176.0779165	766.6924845	337	4.6695114	171.4570540	800.6206714
338	4.0771876	181.1358942	738.5250187	338	4.3733296	176.3065753	771.0467641	338	4.6909133	171.6702321	805.2901828
339	4.0941759	181.3801436	742.6022062	339	4.3924629	176.5342380	775.4200937	339	4.7124134	171.8824376	809.9810961
340	4.1112349	181.6233795	746.6963821	340	4.4115799	176.7609090	779.8125566	340	4.7340119	172.0936750	814.6935095
341	4.1283651	181.8656061	750.8076170	341	4.4309810	176.9865926	784.2242366	341	4.7557095	172.3039485	819.4275214
342	4.1455666	182.1068277	754.9359821	342	4.4503666	177.2112932	788.6552176	342	4.7775065	172.5132627	824.1832309
343	4.1628398	182.3470483	759.0815487	343	4.4698369	177.4350150	793.1055342	343	4.7994034	172.7216220	828.9607374
344	4.1801852	182.5862722	763.2443885	344	4.4893925	177.6577623	797.5754211	344	4.8214007	172.9290306	833.7601408
345	4.1976024	182.8245034	767.4245735	345	4.5090336	177.8795393	802.0648136	345	4.8434987	173.1354929	838.5815414
346	4.2150924	183.0617461	771.6221759	346	4.5287606	178.1003503	806.5738472	346	4.8656981	173.3410132	843.4250402
347	4.2326553	183.2980044	775.8372683	347	4.5485739	178.3201994	811.1026078	347	4.8879992	173.5455959	848.2907383
348	4.2502914	183.5332824	780.0699236	348	4.5684739	178.5390909	815.6511817	348	4.9104026	173.7492452	853.1787375
349	4.2680009	183.7675842	784.3202149	349	4.5884610	178.7570289	820.2196556	349	4.9329086	173.9519654	858.0891400
350	4.2857842	184.0009137	788.5882158	350	4.6085355	178.9740176	824.8081166	350	4.9555177	174.1537606	863.0220486
351	4.3036417	184.2332750	792.8740001	351	4.6286979	179.1900611	829.4166521	351	4.9782305	174.3546352	867.9775663
352	4.3215735	184.4646722	797.1776417	352	4.6489484	179.4051635	834.0453500	352	5.0010474	174.5545933	872.9557969
353	4.3395801	184.6951093	801.4992152	353	4.6692876	179.6193289	838.6942984	353	5.0239689	174.7536392	877.9568443
354	4.3576617	184.9245901	805.8387953	354	4.6897157	179.8325614	843.3635860	354	5.0469954	174.9517768	882.9908131
355	4.3758186	185.1531188	810.1964570	355	4.7102332	180.0448652	848.0533017	355	5.0701275	175.1490105	888.0278085
356	4.3940512	185.3806992	814.5722755	356	4.7308405	180.2562441	852.7635349	356	5.0933655	175.3453444	893.0979360
357	4.4123597	185.6073353	818.9663267	357	4.7515379	180.4667023	857.4943753	357	5.1167101	175.5407825	898.1913016
358	4.4307445	185.8330310	823.3786864	358	4.7723259	180.6762437	862.2459132	358	5.1401617	175.7353289	903.3060117
359	4.4492060	186.0577902	827.8094309	359	4.7932048	180.8848724	867.0182391	359	5.1637208	175.9289877	908.4481734
360	4.4677443	186.2816168	832.2586359	360	4.8141751	181.0925923	871.8114439	360	5.1873879	176.1217629	913.6118942
361	4.4863599	186.5045147	836.7263812	361	4.8352371	181.2994074	876.6256190	361	5.2111634	176.3136587	918.7992821
362	4.5050531	186.7264877	841.2127712	362	4.8563913	181.5053216	881.4608561	362	5.2350472	176.5046789	924.0104455
363	4.5238241	186.9475396	845.7177943	363	4.8776380	181.7103389	886.3172473	363	5.2590419	176.6948276	929.2454934
364	4.5426734	187.1676743	850.2416184	364	4.8989776	181.9144631	891.1948853	364	5.2831458	176.8841088	934.5045352
365	4.5616012	187.3868955	854.7842914	365	4.9204107	182.1176981	896.0938329	365	5.3073602	177.0725263	939.7876810
366	4.5806079	187.6052072	859.3458930	366	4.9419375	182.3200479	901.0142736	366	5.3316856	177.2600843	945.0950412
367	4.5996938	187.8226129	863.9265009	367	4.9635584	182.5215163	905.9562110	367	5.3561225	177.4467865	950.4267268
368	4.6188592	188.0391166	868.5261947	368	4.9852740	182.7221071	910.9197695	368	5.3806714	177.6326369	955.7828493
369	4.6381044	188.2547219	873.1450538	369	5.0070846	182.9218241	915.9050435	369	5.4053328	177.8176394	961.1635207
370	4.6574298	188.4694326	877.7831582	370	5.0289906	183.1206712	920.9121280	370	5.4301073	178.0017978	966.5688535
371	4.6768358	188.6832524	882.4405881	371	5.0509924	183.3186521	925.9411186	371	5.4549952	178.1851160	971.9989608
372	4.6963226	188.8961850	887.1174239	372	5.0730905	183.5157706	930.9921110	372	5.4799973	178.3675979	977.4539560
373	4.7158906	189.1082340	891.8137465	373	5.0952853	183.7120304	936.0652015	373	5.5051140	178.5492472	982.9339533
374	4.7355402	189.3194032	896.5296371	374	5.1175771	183.9074354	941.1604868	374	5.5303457	178.7300677	988.4390673
375	4.7552716	189.5296961	901.2651773	375	5.1399665	184.1019892	946.2780639	375	5.5556932	178.9100632	993.9694130
376	4.7750852	189.7391164	906.0204488	376	5.1624539	184.2956955	951.4180304	376	5.5811567	179.0892376	999.5251062
377	4.7949814	189.9476678	910.7955340	377	5.1850396	184.4885581	956.5804843	377	5.6067370	179.2675944	1005.1062629
378	4.8149605	190.1553538	915.5905154	378	5.2077242	184.6805805	961.7655240	378	5.6324346	179.4451375	1010.7130000
379	4.8350228	190.3621781	920.4054759	379	5.2305080	184.8717666	966.9732481	379	5.6582499	179.6218706	1016.3454346
380	4.8551688	190.5681442	925.2404988	380	5.2533914	185.0621198	972.2037561	380	5.6841836	179.7977974	1022.0036845
381	4.8753986	190.7732556	930.0956675	381	5.2763701	185.2516438	977.4571475	381	5.7102361	179.9729215	1027.6878681
382	4.8957128	190.9775159	934.9710661	382	5.2994592	185.4403423	982.7335226	382	5.7364080	180.1472466	1033.3981041
383	4.9161116	191.1809287	939.8667789	383	5.3226443	185.6282189	988.0329817	383	5.7626999	180.3207763	1039.1345121
384	4.9365954	191.3834975	944.7828905	384	5.3459309	185.8152770	993.3556260	384	5.7891122	180.4935144	1044.8972120
385	4.9571645	191.5852257	949.7194959	385	5.3693193	186.0015204	998.7015569	385	5.8156457	180.6654644	1050.6863242
386	4.9778194	191.7861169	954.6766504	386	5.3928101	186.1869525	1004.0708762	386	5.8423007	180.8366298	1056.5019599
387	4.9985603	191.9861745	959.6544698	387	5.4164036	186.3715768	1009.4636863	387	5.8690779	181.0070144	1062.3442706
388	5.0193876	192.1854020	964.6530301	388	5.4401004	186.5553970	1014.8800900	388	5.8959779	181.1766215	1068.2133485
389	5.0403017	192.3830028	969.6724177	389	5.4639008	186.7384164	1020.3201904	389	5.9230011	181.3454548	1074.1093263
390	5.0613030	192.5813804	974.7127195	390	5.4878054	186.9206388	1025.7840912	390	5.9501482	181.5135179	1080.0323274
391	5.0823918	192.7781382	979.7740225	391	5.5118146	187.1020670	1031.2718966	391	5.9774197	181.6808142	1085.9824756
392	5.1035684	192.9740795	984.8564143	392	5.5359287	187.2827052	1036.7837112	392	6.0048162	181.8473471	1091.9598953
393	5.1248333	193.1692078	989.9599827	393	5.5601484	187.4625565	1042.3196399	393	6.0323383	182.0131203	1097.9647115
394	5.1461867	193.3635264	995.0848159	394	5.5844741	187.6416244	1047.8797884	394	6.0599865	182.1781372	1103.9970498
395	5.1676292	193.5570388	1000.2310027	395	5.6089062	187.8199123	1053.4642624	395	6.0877614	182.3421012	1110.0570362
396	5.1891610	193.7497481	1005.3986319	396	5.6334451	187.9974236	1059.0731686	396	6.1156637	182.5059158	1116.1447977
397	5.2107825	193.9416579	1010.5877928	397	5.6580914	188.1741616	1064.7066137	397	6.1436938	182.6686843	1122.2604613
398	5.2324941	194.1327713	1015.7985753	398	5.6828456	188.3501298	1070.3647052	398	6.1718524	182.8307102	1128.4041551
399	5.2542961	194.3230918	1021.0310694	399	5.7077080	188.5253315	1076.0475508	399	6.2001400	182.9919969	1134.5760075
400	5.2761890	194.5126225	1026.2853655	400	5.7326793	188.6997700	1081.7552588	400	6.2285574	183.1525477	1140.7761476

M	C(5.00,M,12)	A(5.00,M,12)	S(5.00,M,12)	M	C(5.25,M,12)	A(5.25,M,12)	S(5.25,M,12)	M	C(5.50,M,12)	A(5.50,M,12)	S(5.50,M,12)
401	5.2981732	194.7013668	1031.5615545	401	5.7577597	188.8734486	1087.4879381	401	6.2571049	183.3123660	1147.0047049
402	5.3202489	194.8893260	1036.8597277	402	5.7829499	189.0463707	1093.2456978	402	6.2857833	183.4714552	1153.2618098
403	5.3424166	195.0765092	1042.1799766	403	5.8082503	189.2185396	1099.0286477	403	6.3145931	183.6298185	1159.5475931
404	5.3646766	195.2629137	1047.5223932	404	5.8336614	189.3899586	1104.8368991	404	6.3435350	183.7874593	1165.8621863
405	5.3870295	195.4485448	1052.8870698	405	5.8591837	189.5606308	1110.6705595	405	6.3726096	183.9443809	1172.2057213
406	5.4094754	195.6334056	1058.2740993	406	5.8848176	189.7305596	1116.5297432	406	6.4018174	184.1005065	1178.5783309
407	5.4320149	195.8174993	1063.6835747	407	5.9105637	189.8997482	1122.4145609	407	6.4311590	184.2560795	1184.9801782
408	5.4546483	196.0008292	1069.1155896	408	5.9364224	190.0681998	1128.3251246	408	6.4606352	184.4108631	1191.4113072
409	5.4773760	196.1833984	1074.5702379	409	5.9623943	190.2359177	1134.2615470	409	6.4902464	184.5649404	1197.8719424
410	5.5001984	196.3652100	1080.0476139	410	5.9884798	190.4029050	1140.2239413	410	6.5199934	184.7183148	1204.3621888
411	5.5231159	196.5462672	1085.5478123	411	6.0146794	190.5691649	1146.2124210	411	6.5498767	184.8709894	1210.8821822
412	5.5461289	196.7265732	1091.0709282	412	6.0409936	190.7347006	1152.2271004	412	6.5798969	185.0229675	1217.4320589
413	5.5692377	196.9061309	1096.6170571	413	6.0674229	190.8995152	1158.2680940	413	6.6100548	185.1742522	1224.0119558
414	5.5924429	197.0849437	1102.1862948	414	6.0939679	191.0636119	1164.3355169	414	6.6403509	185.3248466	1230.6220106
415	5.6157447	197.2630145	1107.7787347	415	6.1206290	191.2269938	1170.4294848	415	6.6707853	185.4747540	1237.2623615
416	5.6391437	197.4403463	1113.3944825	416	6.1474068	191.3896640	1176.5501138	416	6.7013603	185.6239774	1243.9331474
417	5.6626401	197.6169424	1119.0336261	417	6.1743017	191.5516256	1182.6975205	417	6.7320748	185.7725200	1250.6345076
418	5.6862345	197.7928057	1124.6962663	418	6.2013142	191.7128818	1188.8718222	418	6.7629302	185.9203849	1257.3665825
419	5.7099271	197.9679393	1130.3825007	419	6.2284450	191.8734355	1195.0731364	419	6.7939269	186.0675752	1264.1295126
420	5.7337185	198.1423462	1136.0924278	420	6.2556944	192.0332898	1201.3015814	420	6.8250658	186.2140940	1270.9234396
421	5.7576090	198.3160294	1141.8261463	421	6.2830631	192.1924479	1207.5572758	421	6.8563473	186.3599442	1277.7485054
422	5.7815990	198.4889919	1147.5637552	422	6.3105515	192.3509126	1213.8403389	422	6.8877723	186.5051290	1284.6048527
423	5.8056890	198.6612368	1153.3653542	423	6.3381602	192.5086871	1220.1508904	423	6.9193412	186.6496515	1291.4926249
424	5.8293794	198.8327669	1159.1710432	424	6.3658896	192.6657744	1226.4890506	424	6.9510549	186.7935145	1298.4115661
425	5.8541705	199.0035853	1165.0009226	425	6.3937404	192.8221773	1232.8549402	425	6.9829139	186.9367212	1305.3630210
426	5.8765629	199.1736949	1170.8550931	426	6.4217130	192.9778990	1239.2486806	426	7.0149189	187.0792745	1312.3459349
427	5.9000569	199.3430987	1176.7336560	427	6.4498080	193.1329424	1245.6703936	427	7.0470706	187.2211775	1319.3608537
428	5.9276530	199.5117995	1182.6367129	428	6.4780259	193.2873104	1252.1202015	428	7.0793697	187.3624330	1326.4079243
429	5.9523515	199.6798003	1188.5643659	429	6.5063673	193.4410060	1258.5982274	429	7.1118168	187.5030440	1333.4872940
430	5.9771530	199.8471041	1194.5167174	430	6.5348326	193.5940321	1265.1045947	430	7.1444126	187.6430136	1340.5991108
431	6.0020578	200.0137136	1200.4938704	431	6.5634225	193.7463917	1271.6394273	431	7.1771578	187.7823445	1347.7435234
432	6.0270664	200.1796318	1206.4959282	432	6.5921375	193.8980875	1278.2028498	432	7.2100531	187.9210397	1354.9206812
433	6.0521792	200.3448615	1212.5229946	433	6.6209781	194.0491226	1284.7949873	433	7.2430992	188.0591022	1362.1307343
434	6.0773966	200.5094057	1218.5751737	434	6.6499449	194.1994998	1291.4155854	434	7.2762967	188.1965347	1369.3738335
435	6.1027191	200.6732671	1224.6525703	435	6.6790384	194.3492220	1298.0659102	435	7.3096464	188.3333402	1376.6501303
436	6.1281470	200.8364485	1230.7552894	436	6.7082592	194.4982919	1304.7449486	436	7.3431490	188.4695216	1383.9597767
437	6.1536810	200.9989529	1236.8834364	437	6.7376078	194.6467126	1311.4532077	437	7.3768051	188.6050816	1391.3029257
438	6.1793213	201.1607829	1243.0371174	438	6.7670848	194.7944867	1318.1908155	438	7.4103154	188.7400232	1398.6797308
439	6.2050685	201.3219415	1249.2164387	439	6.7966908	194.9416171	1324.9579004	439	7.4445808	188.8743491	1406.0903463
440	6.2309230	201.4824314	1255.4215072	440	6.8264263	195.0881066	1331.7545912	440	7.4787018	189.0080621	1413.5349270
441	6.2568851	201.6422553	1261.6524302	441	6.8562920	195.2339581	1338.5810175	441	7.5129791	189.1411651	1421.0136028
442	6.2829555	201.8014161	1267.9093153	442	6.8862882	195.3791742	1345.4373095	442	7.5474136	189.2736608	1428.5266079
443	6.3091345	201.9599164	1274.1922708	443	6.9164158	195.5237577	1352.3235977	443	7.5820059	189.4055521	1436.0740216
444	6.3354225	202.1177591	1280.5014053	444	6.9466751	195.6677115	1359.2400135	444	7.6167568	189.5368415	1443.6560275
445	6.3618201	202.2749468	1286.8368278	445	6.9770668	195.8110382	1366.1866886	445	7.6516669	189.6675320	1451.2727843
446	6.3883277	202.4314823	1293.1986480	446	7.0075914	195.9537406	1373.1637553	446	7.6857371	189.7976262	1458.9244512
447	6.4149457	202.5873683	1299.5869757	447	7.0382497	196.0958214	1380.1713468	447	7.7213680	189.9271269	1466.6111883
448	6.4416747	202.7426074	1306.0019214	448	7.0690424	196.2372832	1387.2095064	448	7.7573603	190.0560367	1474.3331563
449	6.4685150	202.8972024	1312.4435961	449	7.0999691	196.3781289	1394.2786384	449	7.7929149	190.1843584	1482.0905166
450	6.4954671	203.0511559	1318.9121111	450	7.1310314	196.5183611	1401.3786075	450	7.8286324	190.3120946	1489.8834315
451	6.5225316	203.2044706	1325.4075782	451	7.1622297	196.6579824	1408.5096389	451	7.8645136	190.4392394	1497.7120639
452	6.5497088	203.3571492	1331.9301098	452	7.1935644	196.7969956	1415.6718686	452	7.9005593	190.5658214	1505.5765775
453	6.5769993	203.5091942	1338.4798186	453	7.2250363	196.9354032	1422.8654330	453	7.9367702	190.6918172	1513.4771308
454	6.6044034	203.6606083	1345.0568179	454	7.2566458	197.0732079	1430.0904693	454	7.9731471	190.8172382	1521.4139071
455	6.6319218	203.8113942	1351.6612213	455	7.2883936	197.2104123	1437.3471151	455	8.0095907	190.9420870	1529.3870542
456	6.6595548	203.9615544	1358.2931431	456	7.3202804	197.3470191	1444.6355088	456	8.0464018	191.0663661	1537.3967448
457	6.6873029	204.1110915	1364.9526978	457	7.3523066	197.4830309	1451.9557891	457	8.0832811	191.1900783	1545.4431466
458	6.7151667	204.2600081	1371.6400007	458	7.3844729	197.6184501	1459.3080957	458	8.1203295	191.3132260	1553.5264277
459	6.7431465	204.4083063	1378.3551674	459	7.4167800	197.7532795	1466.6925686	459	8.1575477	191.4358119	1561.6467572
460	6.7712430	204.5559902	1385.0983140	460	7.4492284	197.8875216	1474.1093486	460	8.1943364	191.5578384	1569.8043048
461	6.7994565	204.7030608	1391.8695570	461	7.4818188	198.0211790	1481.5585771	461	8.2312965	191.6793033	1577.9992412
462	6.8277876	204.8495121	1398.6690135	462	7.5145517	198.1542541	1489.0403958	462	8.2702288	191.8002239	1586.2317378
463	6.8562367	204.9953737	1405.4968010	463	7.5474279	198.2867496	1496.5549476	463	8.3081340	191.9205879	1594.5403075
464	6.8848043	205.1406211	1412.3530377	464	7.5804479	198.4186679	1504.1023755	464	8.3452130	192.0404027	1602.8101006
465	6.9134910	205.2852658	1419.2378420	465	7.6136124	198.5500116	1511.6828234	465	8.3844665	192.1596709	1611.1563136
466	6.9422972	205.4293104	1426.1513331	466	7.6469219	198.6807832	1519.2964358	466	8.4228953	192.2783949	1619.5407800
467	6.9712235	205.5727572	1433.0936303	467	7.6803772	198.8109851	1526.9433577	467	8.4615002	192.3965772	1627.9636753
468	7.0002702	205.7156089	1440.0648538	468	7.7139789	198.9406199	1534.6237349	468	8.5002821	192.5142204	1636.4251755
469	7.0294380	205.8578677	1447.0651240	469	7.7477275	199.0696900	1542.3377137	469	8.5392417	192.6313268	1644.9254575
470	7.0587274	205.9995363	1454.0945620	470	7.7816238	199.1981979	1550.0854413	470	8.5783799	192.7478989	1653.4646992
471	7.0981387	206.1406171	1461.1532894	471	7.8156684	199.3261460	1557.8670651	471	8.6176975	192.8639392	1662.0430791
472	7.1176726	206.2811125	1468.2414281	472	7.8498620	199.4535368	1565.6627335	472	8.6571952	192.9794501	1670.6607766
473	7.1473296	206.4210249	1475.3591007	473	7.8842051	199.5803726	1573.5325595	473	8.6968741	193.0944339	1679.3179718
474	7.1771101	206.5603567	1482.5064303	474	7.9186985	199.7066560	1581.4168006	474	8.7367347	193.2088932	1688.0148459
475	7.2070148	206.6991104	1489.6835405	475	7.9533428	199.8323893	1589.3354991	475	8.7767781	193.3228302	1696.7515306
476	7.2370440	206.8372884	1496.8905552	476	7.9881387	199.9575749	1597.2888419	476	8.8170050	193.4362474	1705.5283597
477	7.2671983	206.9748930	1504.1275992	477	8.0230868	200.0822152	1605.2769806	477	8.8574163	193.5491471	1714.3453637
478	7.2974783	207.1119266	1511.3947976	478	8.0581878	200.2063126	1613.3000674	478	8.8980128	193.6615318	1723.2027799
479	7.3278845	207.2483916	1518.6922759	479	8.0934424	200.3298694	1621.3582552	479	8.9387953	193.7734037	1732.1007927
480	7.3584173	207.3842904	1526.0201604	480	8.1288512	200.4528880	1629.4516976	480	8.9797648	193.8847652	1741.0395880
481	7.3890774	207.5196253	1533.3785777	481	8.1644149	200.5753708	1637.5805488	481	9.0209220	193.9956186	1750.0193528
482	7.4198652	207.6543987	1540.7676552	482	8.2001342	200.6973200	1645.7449037	482	9.0622679	194.1059662	1759.0402749
483	7.4507813	207.7886128	1548.1875204	483	8.2360098	200.8187380	1653.9450979	483	9.1038033	194.2158104	1768.1025428
484	7.4818263	207.9222700	1555.6383018	484	8.2720424	200.9396272	1662.1811078	484	9.1455291	194.3251535	1777.2063461
485	7.5130005	208.0553726	1563.1201280	485	8.3082325	201.0599897	1670.4531501	485	9.1874461	194.4339976	1786.3518752
486	7.5443047	208.1879229	1570.6331286	486	8.3445811	201.1798280	1678.7613827	486	9.2295552	194.5423452	1795.5399213
487	7.5757393	208.3199232	1578.1774333	487	8.3810886	201.2991442	1687.1059637	487	9.2718574	194.6501985	1804.7688766
488	7.6073049	208.4513758	1585.7531726	488	8.4177559	201.4179407	1695.4870523	488	9.3143534	194.7575597	1814.0407339
489	7.6390020	208.5822830	1593.3604775	489	8.4545836	201.5362197	1703.9048082	489	9.3570442	194.8644310	1823.3550873
490	7.6708312	208.7126470	1600.9994795	490	8.4915724	201.6539836	1712.3593918	490	9.3999306	194.9708148	1832.7121315
491	7.7027930	208.8424700	1608.6703107	491	8.5287230	201.7712344	1720.8509641	491	9.4430136	195.0767132	1842.1120621
492	7.7348879	208.9717544	1616.3731037	492	8.5660361	201.8879745	1729.3796871	492	9.4862941	195.1821284	1851.5550757
493	7.7671166	209.1005023	1624.1079916	493	8.6035126	202.0042061	1737.9457232	493	9.5297730	195.2870627	1861.0413599
494	7.7994796	209.2287159	1631.8751083	494	8.6411529	202.1199314	1746.5492358	494	9.5734511	195.3915183	1870.5711428
495	7.8319775	209.3563976	1639.6745879	495	8.6789580	202.2351526	1755.1903887	495	9.6173294	195.4954972	1880.1445939
496	7.8646107	209.4835495	1647.5065554	496	8.7169284	202.3498719	1763.8693467	496	9.6614088	195.5990018	1889.7619233
497	7.8973799	209.6101738	1655.3711761	497	8.7550650	202.4640915	1772.5862751	497	9.7056903	195.7020341	1899.4233321
498	7.9302857	209.7362726	1663.2685560	498	8.7933684	202.5778136	1781.3413401	498	9.7501747	195.8045964	1909.1292224
499	7.9633285	209.8618483	1671.1988416	499	8.8318394	202.6910403	1790.1347084	499	9.7948630	195.9066907	1918.8791971
500	7.9965091	209.9869028	1679.1621702	500	8.8704787	202.8037738	1798.9665478	500	9.8397561	196.0083193	1928.6740601

Table 1   393

M	C(5.75,M,12)	A(5.75,M,12)	S(5.75,M,12)	C(6.00,M,12)	A(6.00,M,12)	S(6.00,M,12)	C(6.25,M,12)	A(6.25,M,12)	S(6.25,M,12)
1	1.0047917	.9952312	1.0000000	1.0050000	.9950249	1.0000000	1.0052083	.9948187	1.0000000
2	1.0096063	1.9857163	2.0047917	1.0100250	1.9850994	2.0050000	1.0104438	1.9844828	2.0052083
3	1.0144440	2.9714750	3.0143980	1.0150751	2.9702481	3.0150250	1.0157065	2.9690192	3.0156521
4	1.0193049	3.9525387	4.0288420	1.0201505	3.9504957	4.0301001	1.0209967	3.9484543	4.0313596
5	1.0241890	4.9269210	5.0481468	1.0252513	4.9258663	5.0502506	1.0263144	4.9228146	5.0523553
6	1.0290966	5.9006470	6.0723359	1.0303775	5.8963844	6.0755019	1.0316597	5.8921265	6.0786697
7	1.0340277	6.8677391	7.1014325	1.0355294	6.8620740	7.1058794	1.0370330	6.8564160	7.1103294
8	1.0389824	7.8302193	8.1354602	1.0407070	7.8229592	8.1414088	1.0424342	7.8157092	8.1473624
9	1.0439609	8.7881096	9.1744426	1.0459106	8.7790039	9.1821158	1.0478635	8.7700319	9.1897965
10	1.0489632	9.7414319	10.2184034	1.0511401	9.7304119	10.2280264	1.0533211	9.7194100	10.2376601
11	1.0539895	10.6902080	11.2673686	1.0563958	10.6770267	11.2791665	1.0588072	10.6638690	11.2909312
12	1.0590398	11.6344596	12.3213561	1.0616778	11.6189321	12.3355624	1.0643218	11.6034344	12.3497884
13	1.0641144	12.5742081	13.3803959	1.0669862	12.5561513	13.3972402	1.0698652	12.5381317	13.4141102
14	1.0692133	13.5094752	14.4445103	1.0723211	13.4887078	14.4642264	1.0754374	13.4679859	14.4839754
15	1.0743366	14.4402822	15.5137236	1.0776827	14.4166246	15.5365475	1.0810386	14.3930223	15.5594127
16	1.0794845	15.3666504	16.5880602	1.0830712	15.3399250	16.6142303	1.0866690	15.3132657	16.6404514
17	1.0846570	16.2896008	17.6675446	1.0884865	16.2586319	17.6973014	1.0923288	16.2287410	17.7271204
18	1.0898543	17.2061547	18.7522016	1.0939289	17.1727680	18.7857879	1.0980180	17.1394729	18.8194491
19	1.0950765	18.1193329	19.8420559	1.0993986	18.0823562	19.8797169	1.1037368	18.0454860	19.9174671
20	1.1003238	19.0281563	20.9371325	1.1048956	18.9874191	20.9791154	1.1094854	18.9468047	21.0212039
21	1.1055961	19.9326457	22.0374562	1.1104201	19.8879792	22.0840110	1.1152640	19.8434534	22.1306893
22	1.1108938	20.8328217	23.1430524	1.1159722	20.7840590	23.1944311	1.1210727	20.7354562	23.2459533
23	1.1162168	21.7287050	24.2539461	1.1215520	21.6756806	24.3104032	1.1269116	21.6228373	24.3670260
24	1.1215654	22.6203160	25.3701630	1.1271598	22.5628662	25.4319552	1.1327809	22.5056205	25.4939376
25	1.1269395	23.5076751	26.4917283	1.1327956	23.4456380	26.5591150	1.1386808	23.3838297	26.6267185
26	1.1323395	24.3908025	27.6186679	1.1384596	24.3240179	27.6919106	1.1446115	24.2574886	27.7653994
27	1.1377652	25.2697184	28.7510073	1.1441519	25.1980278	28.8303701	1.1505730	25.1266208	28.9100108
28	1.1432170	26.1444430	29.8887726	1.1498726	26.0676894	29.9745220	1.1565655	25.9912497	30.0605838
29	1.1486950	27.0149961	31.0319896	1.1556220	26.9330242	31.1243946	1.1625893	26.8513987	31.2171493
30	1.1541991	27.8813977	32.1806846	1.1614001	27.7940540	32.2800166	1.1683445	27.7070909	32.3797387
31	1.1597297	28.7436677	33.3348837	1.1672071	28.6506000	33.4414167	1.1747312	28.5583495	33.5483831
32	1.1652867	29.6018256	34.4946133	1.1730431	29.5032835	34.6086237	1.1808496	29.4051974	34.7231143
33	1.1708704	30.4558911	35.6599000	1.1789083	30.3515259	35.7816589	1.1869998	30.2476576	35.9039638
34	1.1764808	31.3058837	36.8307704	1.1843029	31.1955482	36.9605752	1.1931821	31.0857526	37.0909637
35	1.1821181	32.1518229	38.0072511	1.1907269	32.0353713	38.1453781	1.1993966	31.9195052	38.2841458
36	1.1877824	32.9937280	39.1893692	1.1963805	32.8710162	39.3361050	1.2056435	32.7489378	39.4835423
37	1.1934739	33.8316181	40.3771516	1.2026439	33.7025037	40.5327855	1.2119228	33.5740728	40.6891858
38	1.1991926	34.6655126	41.5706255	1.2086772	34.5298544	41.7354494	1.2182349	34.3949326	41.9011006
39	1.2049387	35.4954303	42.7698180	1.2147206	35.3530800	42.9441267	1.2245799	35.2115391	43.1193426
40	1.2107124	36.3213903	43.9747568	1.2207942	36.1722279	44.1588473	1.2309579	36.0239146	44.3439235
41	1.2165137	37.1434114	45.1854691	1.2268982	36.9872914	45.3796415	1.2373692	36.8320808	45.5748814
42	1.2223428	37.9615125	46.4019828	1.2330327	37.7982999	46.6065397	1.2438138	37.6360597	46.8122506
43	1.2281999	38.7757122	47.6243257	1.2391979	38.6052735	47.8395724	1.2502920	38.4358728	48.0560644
44	1.2340850	39.5860292	48.8525256	1.2453939	39.4082324	49.0787703	1.2568039	39.2315419	49.3063564
45	1.2399983	40.3924419	50.0866106	1.2516208	40.2071964	50.3241642	1.2633498	40.0230883	50.5631604
46	1.2459400	41.1950887	51.3266089	1.2578789	41.0021855	51.5757850	1.2699297	40.8105334	51.8265101
47	1.2519101	41.9938681	52.5725489	1.2641683	41.7932194	52.8336339	1.2765440	41.5938985	53.0964399
48	1.2579089	42.7888383	53.8244591	1.2704892	42.5803178	54.0978322	1.2831926	42.3732048	54.3729838
49	1.2639363	43.5800174	55.0823679	1.2768416	43.3635003	55.3683214	1.2898759	43.1484731	55.6561765
50	1.2699927	44.3674234	56.3463043	1.2832258	44.1427863	56.6451630	1.2965940	43.9197246	56.9460524
51	1.2760781	45.1510745	57.6162970	1.2896419	44.9181954	57.9283888	1.3033471	44.6869799	58.2426464
52	1.2821926	45.9309886	58.8923751	1.2960902	45.6897466	59.2180308	1.3101354	45.4502598	59.5459935
53	1.2883365	46.7071833	60.1745677	1.3025706	46.4574593	60.5141209	1.3169590	46.2095849	60.8561289
54	1.2945097	47.4796765	61.4629042	1.3090835	47.2213526	61.8166915	1.3238182	46.9649756	62.1730879
55	1.3007126	48.2484859	62.7574139	1.3156289	47.9814453	63.1257750	1.3307131	47.7164524	63.4969061
56	1.3069452	49.0136289	64.0581255	1.3222070	48.7377566	64.4414039	1.3376439	48.4640356	64.8276191
57	1.3132076	49.7751231	65.3650717	1.3288181	49.4903050	65.7636109	1.3446107	49.2077452	66.1652630
58	1.3195001	50.5329859	66.6782794	1.3354621	50.2391095	67.0924289	1.3516139	49.9476015	67.5098737
59	1.3258227	51.2872345	67.9977794	1.3421395	50.9841885	68.4278911	1.3586536	50.6836243	68.8614877
60	1.3321756	52.0378663	69.3236021	1.3488502	51.7255607	69.7700305	1.3657299	51.4158535	70.2201412
61	1.3385589	52.7849584	70.6557777	1.3555944	52.4632445	71.1188807	1.3728421	52.1442488	71.5858711
62	1.3449729	53.5284678	71.9943367	1.3623724	53.1972582	72.4744751	1.3799933	52.8688900	72.9587142
63	1.3514175	54.2684316	73.3393095	1.3691842	53.9276201	73.8368475	1.3871808	53.5897766	74.3387075
64	1.3578931	55.0048666	74.6907271	1.3760302	54.6543484	75.2060317	1.3944057	54.3069280	75.7258883
65	1.3643996	55.7377897	76.0486201	1.3829103	55.3774611	76.5820619	1.4016682	55.0203635	77.1202940
66	1.3709374	56.4672176	77.4130198	1.3898249	56.0969762	77.9649722	1.4089686	55.7301027	78.5219622
67	1.3775065	57.1931670	78.7839572	1.3967740	56.8129116	79.3547970	1.4163069	56.4361643	79.9309307
68	1.3841070	57.9156645	80.1614636	1.4037579	57.5252852	80.7515710	1.4236835	57.1385676	81.3472377
69	1.3907392	58.6346966	81.5455706	1.4107766	58.2341146	82.1553289	1.4310985	57.8373315	82.7709212
70	1.3974032	59.3503097	82.9363098	1.4178305	58.9394175	83.5661055	1.4385522	58.5324749	84.2020197
71	1.4040990	60.0625102	84.3337130	1.4249197	59.6412115	84.9839360	1.4460446	59.2240165	85.6405719
72	1.4108270	60.7713143	85.7378120	1.4320443	60.3395139	86.4088557	1.4535761	59.9119749	87.0866166
73	1.4175872	61.4767382	87.1486390	1.4392045	61.0343422	87.8409000	1.4611468	60.5963688	88.5401927
74	1.4243798	62.1787982	88.5662263	1.4464005	61.7257136	89.2801045	1.4687570	61.2772167	90.0013395
75	1.4312050	62.8775101	89.9906061	1.4536325	62.4136454	90.7265050	1.4764068	61.9545368	91.4700965
76	1.4380628	63.5728900	91.4218111	1.4609007	63.0981546	92.1801376	1.4840964	62.6283475	92.9465033
77	1.4449536	64.2649538	92.8598739	1.4682052	63.7792583	93.6410382	1.4918260	63.2986669	94.4305996
78	1.4518773	64.9537172	94.3048275	1.4755462	64.4569735	95.1092434	1.4995960	63.9655132	95.9224257
79	1.4588342	65.6391960	95.7567048	1.4829239	65.1313169	96.5847897	1.5074064	64.6289043	97.4220216
80	1.4658245	66.3214060	97.2155390	1.4903386	65.8023054	98.0677136	1.5152574	65.2888582	98.9294280
81	1.4728482	67.0003626	98.6813635	1.4977903	66.4699556	99.5580522	1.5231494	65.9453926	100.4446854
82	1.4799056	67.6760813	100.1542177	1.5052792	67.1342846	101.0558424	1.5310825	66.5985253	101.9678348
83	1.4869968	68.3485777	101.6341173	1.5128056	67.7953076	102.5611216	1.5390569	67.2482739	103.4989173
84	1.4941220	69.0178671	103.1211141	1.5203696	68.4530424	104.0739273	1.5470728	67.8946559	105.0379742
85	1.5012813	69.6839648	104.6152361	1.5279715	69.1075049	105.5942968	1.5551305	68.5376887	106.5850470
86	1.5084750	70.3468860	106.1165174	1.5356113	69.7587113	107.1222684	1.5632301	69.1773898	108.1401774
87	1.5157031	71.0066458	107.6249924	1.5432894	70.4066779	108.6578797	1.5713719	69.8137764	109.7034075
88	1.5229658	71.6632593	109.1406955	1.5510058	71.0514208	110.2011691	1.5795561	70.4468656	111.2747794
89	1.5302634	72.3167416	110.6636613	1.5587609	71.6929561	111.7521750	1.5877830	71.0766746	112.8543356
90	1.5375959	72.9671076	112.1939247	1.5665547	72.3312996	113.3109358	1.5960527	71.7032203	114.4421186
91	1.5449635	73.6143720	113.7315206	1.5743875	72.9664672	114.8774905	1.6043655	72.3265197	116.0381713
92	1.5523665	74.2585498	115.2764841	1.5822595	73.5984748	116.4518780	1.6127215	72.9465896	117.6425367
93	1.5598049	74.8996556	116.8288505	1.5901707	74.2273382	118.0341374	1.6211211	73.5634466	119.2552583
94	1.5672790	75.5377041	118.3886555	1.5981215	74.8530728	119.6243081	1.6295645	74.1771075	120.8763794
95	1.5747889	76.1727099	119.9559345	1.6061121	75.4756943	121.2224296	1.6380518	74.7875888	122.5059439
96	1.5823347	76.8046874	121.5307234	1.6141427	76.0952182	122.8285417	1.6465833	75.3949070	124.1439957
97	1.5899167	77.4336512	123.1130581	1.6222134	76.7116599	124.4426845	1.6551593	75.9990785	125.7905790
98	1.5975351	78.0596155	124.7029748	1.6303245	77.3250348	126.0648979	1.6637799	76.6001195	127.4457383
99	1.6051899	78.6825948	126.3005099	1.6384761	77.9353580	127.6952224	1.6724454	77.1980464	129.1095182
100	1.6128815	79.3026031	127.9056998	1.6466685	78.5426447	129.3336985	1.6811561	77.7928751	130.7819636

Table 1

M	C(5.75,M,12)	A(5.75,M,12)	S(5.75,M,12)	M	C(6.00,M,12)	A(6.00,M,12)	S(6.00,M,12)	M	C(6.25,M,12)	A(6.25,M,12)	S(6.25,M,12)
101	1.6206099	79.9196548	129.5185813	101	1.6549018	79.1469102	130.9803670	101	1.6899121	78.3846219	132.4631196
102	1.6283753	80.5337638	131.1391912	102	1.6631763	79.7481693	132.6352688	102	1.6987137	78.9733026	134.1530317
103	1.6361779	81.1449443	132.7675665	103	1.6714922	80.3464372	134.2984452	103	1.7075612	79.5589332	135.8517454
104	1.6440179	81.7532102	134.4037444	104	1.6798497	80.9417285	135.9699374	104	1.7164547	80.1415294	137.5593066
105	1.6518955	82.3585753	136.0477624	105	1.6882489	81.5340582	137.6996579	105	1.7253946	80.7211069	139.2757013
106	1.6598109	82.9610538	137.6996579	106	1.6966902	82.1234410	139.3380360	106	1.7343810	81.2976815	141.0011559
107	1.6677641	83.5606588	139.3594637	107	1.7051736	82.7098916	141.0347262	107	1.7434143	81.8712687	142.7355369
108	1.6757555	84.1574045	141.0272329	108	1.7136995	83.2934244	142.7398998	108	1.7524945	82.4418838	144.4789512
109	1.6837852	84.7513045	142.7029984	109	1.7222680	83.8740542	144.4535993	109	1.7616221	83.0095425	146.2314457
110	1.6918533	85.3423723	144.3867735	110	1.7308793	84.4517952	146.1758673	110	1.7707972	83.5742599	147.9930678
111	1.6999601	85.9306215	146.0786268	111	1.7395337	85.0266619	147.9067467	111	1.7800201	84.1360513	149.7638651
112	1.7081057	86.5160653	147.7785689	112	1.7482314	85.5996585	149.6462804	112	1.7892911	84.6949318	151.5438852
113	1.7162904	87.0987173	149.4866926	113	1.7569726	86.1678294	151.3945118	113	1.7986103	85.2509166	153.3331763
114	1.7245143	87.6785907	151.2029830	114	1.7657574	86.7341586	153.1514844	114	1.8079781	85.8040207	155.1317866
115	1.7327776	88.2556988	152.9274973	115	1.7745862	87.2976702	154.9172418	115	1.8173946	86.3542589	156.9397646
116	1.7410805	88.8300548	154.6602749	116	1.7834591	87.8593783	156.6918280	116	1.8268602	86.9016462	158.7571592
117	1.7494232	89.4016718	156.4013554	117	1.7923764	88.4162969	158.4752871	117	1.8363751	87.4461972	160.5840194
118	1.7578058	89.9705628	158.1507786	118	1.8013383	88.9714397	160.2676636	118	1.8459396	87.9879268	162.4203945
119	1.7662286	90.5357410	159.9085844	119	1.8103450	89.5238206	162.0690019	119	1.8555538	88.5268495	164.2663341
120	1.7745918	91.1002191	161.6748130	120	1.8193967	90.0734533	163.8793469	120	1.8652182	89.0629798	166.1218879
121	1.7831955	91.6610101	163.4495048	121	1.8284937	90.6203515	165.6987436	121	1.8749328	89.5963322	167.9871061
122	1.7917400	92.2191267	165.2327004	122	1.8376362	91.1645289	167.5272374	122	1.8846981	90.1269212	169.8620389
123	1.8003254	92.7745819	167.0244404	123	1.8468244	91.7059939	169.3648735	123	1.8945143	90.6547609	171.7467371
124	1.8089520	93.3273881	168.8247658	124	1.8560585	92.2447750	171.2116979	124	1.9043815	91.1798658	173.6412513
125	1.8176199	93.8775582	170.6337178	125	1.8653388	92.7808707	173.0677564	125	1.9143002	91.7022499	175.5456328
126	1.8263293	94.4251045	172.4513377	126	1.8746655	93.3142992	174.9330952	126	1.9242705	92.2219274	177.4599330
127	1.8350805	94.9700393	174.2776971	127	1.8840388	93.8450738	176.8077607	127	1.9342927	92.7389122	179.3842035
128	1.8438736	95.5123763	176.1127476	128	1.8934590	94.3732078	178.6917995	128	1.9443672	93.2532184	181.3184962
129	1.8527088	96.0521265	177.9566211	129	1.9029263	94.8987142	180.5852585	129	1.9544941	93.7648597	183.2628634
130	1.8615864	96.5893028	179.8093300	130	1.9124409	95.4216061	182.4881848	130	1.9646737	94.2738501	185.2173575
131	1.8705065	97.1239173	181.6709163	131	1.9220031	95.9418967	184.4006257	131	1.9749306	94.7802032	187.1820312
132	1.8794693	97.6559824	183.5414228	132	1.9316131	96.4595987	186.3226288	132	1.9851924	95.2839327	189.1569376
133	1.8884757	98.1855102	185.4208921	133	1.9412712	96.9747250	188.2542420	133	1.9955319	95.7850522	191.1421300
134	1.8975241	98.7125127	187.3093672	134	1.9509776	97.4872886	190.1955132	134	2.0059253	96.2835793	193.1376619
135	1.9066164	99.2370021	189.2066913	135	1.9607325	97.9973021	192.1464907	135	2.0163729	96.7795153	195.1435873
136	1.9157522	99.7589903	191.1135076	136	1.9705361	98.5047782	194.1072232	136	2.0268748	97.2728857	197.1599601
137	1.9249319	100.2784892	193.0292599	137	1.9803888	99.0097295	196.0777593	137	2.0374314	97.7636997	199.1868349
138	1.9341555	100.7955107	194.9541917	138	1.9902907	99.5121687	198.0581481	138	2.0480431	98.2519707	201.2242663
139	1.9434233	101.3100666	196.8883472	139	2.0002422	100.0121082	200.0484338	139	2.0587099	98.7377118	203.2723094
140	1.9527356	101.8221687	198.8317706	140	2.0102434	100.5095604	202.0486810	140	2.0694324	99.2209361	205.3310193
141	1.9620924	102.3318287	200.7845061	141	2.0202946	101.0045377	204.0589245	141	2.0802107	99.7016566	207.4004517
142	1.9714941	102.8390582	202.7465996	142	2.0303961	101.4970524	206.0792191	142	2.0910451	100.1798864	209.4806624
143	1.9809409	103.3438688	204.7180927	143	2.0405461	101.9871168	208.1096152	143	2.1019360	100.6556383	211.5717076
144	1.9904329	103.8462721	206.6990335	144	2.0507508	102.4747431	210.1501633	144	2.1128836	101.1289253	213.6736435
145	1.9999704	104.3462795	208.6894664	145	2.0610046	102.9599434	212.2009141	145	2.1238882	101.5997597	215.7865271
146	2.0095536	104.8439025	210.6894368	146	2.0713096	103.4427297	214.2619186	146	2.1349501	102.0681547	217.9104153
147	2.0191827	105.3391524	212.6989903	147	2.0816661	103.9231142	216.3332282	147	2.1460696	102.5341228	220.0453653
148	2.0288579	105.8320405	214.7181730	148	2.0920745	104.4011086	218.4148944	148	2.1572471	102.9976766	222.1914349
149	2.0385795	106.3225782	216.7470309	149	2.1025348	104.8767250	220.5069689	149	2.1684827	103.4588285	224.3486620
150	2.0483477	106.8107765	218.7856104	150	2.1130475	105.3499751	222.6095037	150	2.1797769	103.9175911	226.5171647
151	2.0581627	107.2966468	220.8339582	151	2.1236128	105.8208708	224.7225512	151	2.1911299	104.3739766	228.6969416
152	2.0680247	107.7802000	222.8921209	152	2.1342308	106.2894236	226.8461640	152	2.2025420	104.8279795	230.8880715
153	2.0779340	108.2614472	224.9601456	153	2.1449020	106.7556454	228.9803948	153	2.2140136	105.2796659	233.0906136
154	2.0878908	108.7403995	227.0380767	154	2.1556265	107.2195477	231.1252968	154	2.2255449	105.7289940	235.3046272
155	2.0978953	109.2170677	229.1259705	155	2.1664046	107.6811420	233.2809233	155	2.2371363	106.1759941	237.5301721
156	2.1075477	109.6914628	231.2238857	156	2.1772366	108.1404398	235.4473279	156	2.2487881	106.6206780	239.7673084
157	2.1180483	110.1635955	233.3318134	157	2.1881228	108.5974525	237.6245645	157	2.2605005	107.0630579	242.0160965
158	2.1281973	110.6334768	235.4498617	158	2.1990634	109.0521915	239.8126873	158	2.2722739	107.5031417	244.2765970
159	2.1383949	111.1011173	237.5780590	159	2.2100588	109.5046682	242.0117508	159	2.2841087	107.9409533	246.5488710
160	2.1486413	111.5665276	239.7164538	160	2.2211090	109.9548937	244.2218095	160	2.2960051	108.3764929	248.8329797
161	2.1589369	112.0297186	241.8650952	161	2.2322146	110.4028793	246.4429186	161	2.3079635	108.8097748	251.1289848
162	2.1692818	112.4907006	244.0240321	162	2.2433757	110.8486362	248.6751332	162	2.3199841	109.2408122	253.4369482
163	2.1796763	112.9494044	246.1933139	163	2.2545925	111.2921753	250.9185089	163	2.3320674	109.6696163	255.7569323
164	2.1901206	113.4060802	248.3729922	164	2.2658655	111.7335077	253.1731014	164	2.3442135	110.0961986	258.0889997
165	2.2006149	113.8604987	250.5631108	165	2.2771948	112.1726445	255.4389669	165	2.3564230	110.5205706	260.4332132
166	2.2111595	114.3127501	252.7637237	166	2.2885808	112.6095965	257.7161617	166	2.3686960	110.9427438	262.7896362
167	2.2217547	114.7626448	254.9748852	167	2.3000237	113.0443747	260.0047426	167	2.3810330	111.3622796	265.1583323
168	2.2324006	115.2107931	257.1966399	168	2.3115238	113.4769897	262.3047663	168	2.3934342	111.7805393	267.5393652
169	2.2430975	115.6566052	259.4290404	169	2.3230815	113.9074524	264.6162901	169	2.4059000	112.1961842	269.9327994
170	2.2538457	116.1002913	261.6721379	170	2.3346969	114.3357736	266.9393716	170	2.4184307	112.6096754	272.3386994
171	2.2646453	116.5418615	263.9259836	171	2.3463703	114.7619638	269.2740684	171	2.4310267	113.0210243	274.7571302
172	2.2754968	116.9813260	266.1906369	172	2.3581022	115.1860336	271.6204388	172	2.4436883	113.4302418	277.1881569
173	2.2864002	117.4186947	268.4661257	173	2.3698927	115.6079936	273.9785410	173	2.4564159	113.8373390	279.6318452
174	2.2973559	117.8539778	270.7525259	174	2.3817422	116.0278543	276.3484337	174	2.4692097	114.2423268	282.0882611
175	2.3083640	118.2871850	273.0498817	175	2.3936509	116.4456262	278.7301758	175	2.4820702	114.6452163	284.5574708
176	2.3194249	118.7183263	275.3582458	176	2.4056191	116.8613196	281.1238267	176	2.4949976	115.0460183	287.0395509
177	2.3305388	119.1474117	277.6776707	177	2.4176472	117.2749449	283.5294459	177	2.5079924	115.4447436	289.5345365
178	2.3417060	119.5744508	280.0082065	178	2.4297355	117.6865123	285.9470931	178	2.5210549	115.8414030	292.0425309
179	2.3529267	119.9994534	282.3499155	179	2.4418841	118.0960322	288.3768286	179	2.5341853	116.2360071	294.5635858
180	2.3642011	120.4224292	284.7028422	180	2.4540936	118.5035146	290.8187127	180	2.5473842	116.6285667	297.0977711
181	2.3755296	120.8433880	287.0670433	181	2.4663640	118.9089697	293.2728063	181	2.5606519	117.0190922	299.6451553
182	2.3869123	121.2623393	289.4425729	182	2.4786959	119.3124077	295.7391703	182	2.5739886	117.4075943	302.2058072
183	2.3983496	121.6792927	291.8294968	183	2.4910893	119.7138385	298.2178662	183	2.5873948	117.7940835	304.7797958
184	2.4093417	122.0942577	294.2278349	184	2.5035448	120.1132721	300.7089555	184	2.6008708	118.1785701	307.3671906
185	2.4213889	122.5072438	296.6376766	185	2.5160625	120.5107186	303.2125003	185	2.6144170	118.5610645	309.9680613
186	2.4329914	122.9182605	299.0590655	186	2.5286428	120.9061876	305.7285628	186	2.6280337	118.9415772	312.5824783
187	2.4446494	123.3273171	301.4920768	187	2.5412860	121.2996890	308.2572056	187	2.6417214	119.3201182	315.2105121
188	2.4563634	123.7344230	303.9367063	188	2.5539925	121.6912330	310.7984916	188	2.6554804	119.6966979	317.8522335
189	2.4681335	124.1395374	306.3930696	189	2.5667624	122.0808289	313.3524841	189	2.6693110	120.0713264	320.5077139
190	2.4799599	124.5428199	308.8612031	190	2.5795962	122.4684864	315.9192465	190	2.6832137	120.4440138	323.1770249
191	2.4918431	124.9441291	311.3411630	191	2.5924942	122.8542153	318.4988427	191	2.6971887	120.8147702	325.8602386
192	2.5037832	125.3435248	313.8330061	192	2.6054567	123.2380252	321.0913369	192	2.7112366	121.1836056	328.5574273
193	2.5157805	125.7410157	316.3367893	193	2.6184840	123.6199256	323.6967936	193	2.7253576	121.5505300	331.2686639
194	2.5278352	126.1366111	318.8525697	194	2.6315764	123.9999260	326.3152776	194	2.7395522	121.9155531	333.9940215
195	2.5399478	126.5303200	321.3804050	195	2.6447343	124.3780358	328.9468540	195	2.7538207	122.2786850	336.7335737
196	2.5521184	126.9221514	323.9203527	196	2.6579579	124.7542645	331.5915883	196	2.7681635	122.6399353	339.4873944
197	2.5643473	127.3121142	326.4724711	197	2.6712477	125.1286213	334.2495462	197	2.7825810	122.9993139	342.2555580
198	2.5766348	127.7002173	329.0368183	198	2.6846040	125.5011158	336.9207939	198	2.7970736	123.3568304	345.0381390
199	2.5889811	128.0864696	331.6134531	199	2.6980270	125.8717570	339.6053979	199	2.8116417	123.7124945	347.8352126
200	2.6013867	128.4708800	334.2024342	200	2.7115171	126.2405542	342.3034249	200	2.8262857	124.0663157	350.6468544

Table 1

M	C(5.75,M,12)	A(5.75,M,12)	S(5.75,M,12)	M	C(6.00,M,12)	A(6.00,M,12)	S(6.00,M,12)	M	C(6.25,M,12)	A(6.25,M,12)	S(6.25,M,12)
201	2.6138516	128.8534572	336.8038209	201	2.7250747	126.6075166	345.0149420	201	2.8410059	124.4183037	353.4731401
202	2.6263764	129.2342099	339.4176725	202	2.7387001	126.9726534	347.7400168	202	2.8558028	124.7684680	356.3141460
203	2.6389611	129.6131469	342.0440489	203	2.7523936	127.3359735	350.4787168	203	2.8706768	125.1168179	359.1699489
204	2.6516061	129.9902768	344.6830100	204	2.7661556	127.6974861	353.2311104	204	2.8856283	125.4633629	362.0406257
205	2.6643117	130.3656083	347.3346161	205	2.7799863	128.0572001	355.9972660	205	2.9006576	125.8081123	364.9262539
206	2.6770782	130.7391499	349.9989278	206	2.7938863	128.4151244	358.7772523	206	2.9157652	126.1510754	367.8269115
207	2.6899059	131.1109101	352.6760060	207	2.8078557	128.7712681	361.5711386	207	2.9309514	126.4922616	370.7426767
208	2.7027950	131.4808974	355.3659118	208	2.8216950	129.1256399	364.3789943	208	2.9462168	126.8316799	373.6736201
209	2.7157459	131.8491204	358.0687068	209	2.8360044	129.4782486	367.2008893	209	2.9615617	127.1693396	376.6193449
210	2.7287588	132.2155874	360.7844527	210	2.8501845	129.8291031	370.0368937	210	2.9769865	127.5052497	379.5814066
211	2.7418341	132.5803067	363.5132116	211	2.8644354	130.1782121	372.8870782	211	2.9924916	127.8394194	382.5583931
212	2.7549721	132.9432868	366.2550457	212	2.8787576	130.5255841	375.7515136	212	3.0080775	128.1718597	385.5508948
213	2.7681730	133.3045359	369.0100178	213	2.8931514	130.8712280	378.6302711	213	3.0237446	128.5025734	388.5589623
214	2.7814372	133.6640623	371.7781908	214	2.9076171	131.2151522	381.5234225	214	3.0394933	128.8315756	391.5827069
215	2.7947649	134.0218741	374.5596280	215	2.9221552	131.5573654	384.4310396	215	3.0553240	129.1588732	394.6222002
216	2.8081565	134.3779797	377.3543929	216	2.9367660	131.8978760	387.3531948	216	3.0712371	129.4844749	397.6775241
217	2.8216122	134.7323870	380.1625493	217	2.9514498	132.2366926	390.2899608	217	3.0872331	129.8083895	400.7487612
218	2.8351324	135.0851042	382.9841615	218	2.9662071	132.5738235	393.2414106	218	3.1033125	130.1306258	403.8359944
219	2.8487175	135.4361393	385.8192940	219	2.9810381	132.9092771	396.2076177	219	3.1194756	130.4511925	406.9393068
220	2.8623676	135.7855005	388.6680114	220	2.9959433	133.2430618	399.1886557	220	3.1357228	130.7700983	410.0587824
221	2.8760831	136.1331956	391.5303790	221	3.0109230	133.5751858	402.1845990	221	3.1520547	131.0873516	413.1945052
222	2.8898643	136.4792326	394.4064621	222	3.0259776	133.9056575	405.1955220	222	3.1684717	131.4029612	416.3465599
223	2.9037116	136.8236194	397.2963264	223	3.0411075	134.2344851	408.2214996	223	3.1849741	131.7169355	419.5150316
224	2.9176252	137.1663639	400.2000379	224	3.0563130	134.5616767	411.2626071	224	3.2015625	132.0292830	422.7000057
225	2.9316055	137.5074739	403.1176631	225	3.0715946	134.8872405	414.3189202	225	3.2182373	132.3400121	425.9015683
226	2.9456527	137.8469573	406.0492686	226	3.0869526	135.2111846	417.3905148	226	3.2349990	132.6491312	429.1198056
227	2.9597673	138.1848217	408.9949213	227	3.1023873	135.5335170	420.4774674	227	3.2518479	132.9566487	432.3548046
228	2.9739496	138.5210748	411.9546887	228	3.1178993	135.8542458	423.5798547	228	3.2687847	133.2625728	435.6066525
229	2.9881997	138.8557245	414.9286382	229	3.1334888	136.1733789	426.6977540	229	3.2856096	133.5669118	438.8754372
230	3.0025182	139.1887783	417.9168380	230	3.1491562	136.4909243	429.8312428	230	3.3029232	133.8696739	442.1612468
231	3.0169053	139.5202438	420.9193561	231	3.1649020	136.8068898	432.9803990	231	3.3201259	134.1708673	445.4641699
232	3.0313613	139.8501286	423.9362614	232	3.1807265	137.1212834	436.1453010	232	3.3374182	134.4705001	448.7842958
233	3.0458865	140.1784402	426.9676227	233	3.1966301	137.4341128	439.3260275	233	3.3548006	134.7685804	452.1217140
234	3.0604814	140.5051862	430.0135092	234	3.2126133	137.7453859	442.5226576	234	3.3722735	135.0651162	455.4765146
235	3.0751462	140.8303740	433.0739906	235	3.2286764	138.0551103	445.7352709	235	3.3893374	135.3601156	458.8487882
236	3.0898813	141.1540110	436.1491368	236	3.2448197	138.3632939	448.9639473	236	3.4074928	135.6535865	462.2386256
237	3.1046870	141.4761047	439.2390181	237	3.2610438	138.6699442	452.2087670	237	3.4252402	135.9455369	465.6461184
238	3.1195636	141.7966623	442.3437050	238	3.2773491	138.9750688	455.4698108	238	3.4430800	136.2359745	469.0713586
239	3.1345115	142.1156913	445.4632686	239	3.2937358	139.2786754	458.7471599	239	3.4610127	136.5249073	472.5144386
240	3.1495310	142.4331989	448.5977801	240	3.3102045	139.5807716	462.0408957	240	3.4790388	136.8123430	475.9754513
241	3.1646225	142.7491923	451.7473112	241	3.3267555	139.8813647	465.3511002	241	3.4971588	137.0982094	479.4544902
242	3.1797864	143.0636789	454.9119337	242	3.3433893	140.1804624	468.6778557	242	3.5153732	137.3827542	482.9516490
243	3.1950228	143.3766657	458.0917201	243	3.3601062	140.4780721	472.0212450	243	3.5336824	137.6657451	486.4670221
244	3.2103323	143.6881599	461.2867429	244	3.3769068	140.7742011	475.3813512	244	3.5520870	137.9472698	490.0007046
245	3.2257152	143.9981687	464.4970752	245	3.3937913	141.0688568	478.7582580	245	3.5705875	138.2273357	493.5527916
246	3.2411717	144.3066991	467.7227903	246	3.4107603	141.3620465	482.1520493	246	3.5891843	138.5059506	497.1233790
247	3.2567023	144.6137582	470.9639621	247	3.4278141	141.6537777	485.5628095	247	3.6078779	138.7831218	500.7125633
248	3.2723074	144.9193529	474.2206644	248	3.4449531	141.9440574	488.9906236	248	3.6266690	139.0588569	504.3204412
249	3.2879872	145.2234904	477.4929717	249	3.4621779	142.2328929	492.4355767	249	3.6455579	139.3331634	507.9471102
250	3.3037421	145.5261774	480.7809589	250	3.4794888	142.5202914	495.8977546	250	3.6645452	139.6060485	511.5926681
251	3.3195725	145.8274211	484.0847010	251	3.4968862	142.8062601	499.3772433	251	3.6836313	139.8775198	515.2572132
252	3.3354788	146.1272281	487.4042735	252	3.5143707	143.0908061	502.8741296	252	3.7028169	140.1475844	518.9408445
253	3.3514613	146.4256054	490.7397523	253	3.5319425	143.3739364	506.3885002	253	3.7221024	140.4162498	522.6436614
254	3.3675204	146.7225598	494.0912137	254	3.5496022	143.6556581	509.9204427	254	3.7414884	140.6835231	526.3657639
255	3.3836564	147.0180981	497.4587341	255	3.5673502	143.9359782	513.4700049	255	3.7609753	140.9494116	530.1072522
256	3.3998698	147.3122270	500.8423905	256	3.5851870	144.2149037	517.0373952	256	3.7805637	141.2139224	533.8682275
257	3.4161608	147.6049532	504.2422603	257	3.6031129	144.4924415	520.6225822	257	3.8002541	141.4770627	537.6487912
258	3.4325299	147.8962836	507.6584211	258	3.6211285	144.7685935	524.2256951	258	3.8200471	141.7388396	541.4490453
259	3.4489775	148.1862246	511.0909511	259	3.6392341	145.0433816	527.8468235	259	3.8399432	141.9992601	545.2690924
260	3.4655038	148.4747829	514.5399285	260	3.6574303	145.3167976	531.4860577	260	3.8599429	142.2583313	549.1090356
261	3.4821094	148.7619651	518.0054324	261	3.6757174	145.5888534	535.1434880	261	3.8800468	142.5160601	552.9689785
262	3.4987945	149.0477779	521.4875417	262	3.6940960	145.8595556	538.8192054	262	3.9002553	142.7724536	556.8490253
263	3.5155595	149.3322276	524.9863362	263	3.7125665	146.1289110	542.5133014	263	3.9205692	143.0275186	560.7492806
264	3.5324049	149.6153209	528.5018957	264	3.7311293	146.3969264	546.2258680	264	3.9409888	143.2812620	564.6698498
265	3.5493310	149.8970641	532.0343007	265	3.7497850	146.6636083	549.9569973	265	3.9615148	143.5336907	568.6108386
266	3.5663382	150.1774637	535.5836317	266	3.7685339	146.9239635	553.7067823	266	3.9821476	143.7848115	572.5723534
267	3.5834269	150.4565262	539.1499699	267	3.7873766	147.1929985	557.4753162	267	4.0028880	144.0346311	576.5545011
268	3.6005975	150.7342579	542.7333969	268	3.8063135	147.4557199	561.2626928	268	4.0237364	144.2831564	580.5573891
269	3.6178504	151.0106651	546.3339944	269	3.8253450	147.7171343	565.0690063	269	4.0446934	144.5303939	584.5811255
270	3.6351859	151.2857542	549.9518448	270	3.8444718	147.9772480	568.8943513	270	4.0657595	144.7763504	588.6258189
271	3.6526045	151.5595315	553.5870302	271	3.8636941	148.2360677	572.7388231	271	4.0869353	145.0210325	592.6915784
272	3.6701066	151.8320031	557.2396353	272	3.8830126	148.4935997	576.6025172	272	4.1082214	145.2644469	596.7785137
273	3.6876925	152.1031754	560.9097418	273	3.9024277	148.7498504	580.4855298	273	4.1296184	145.5066000	600.8867351
274	3.7053627	152.3730545	564.5974344	274	3.9219398	149.0048263	584.3879574	274	4.1511268	145.7474984	605.0163535
275	3.7231176	152.6416466	568.3027971	275	3.9415495	149.2585336	588.3098072	275	4.1727473	145.9871487	609.1674804
276	3.7409575	152.9089559	572.0259146	276	3.9612572	149.5109787	592.2514467	276	4.1944804	146.2255573	613.3402277
277	3.7588829	153.1749943	575.7668722	277	3.9810635	149.7621679	596.2127039	277	4.2163266	146.4627305	617.5347080
278	3.7768942	153.4397622	579.5257551	278	4.0009688	150.0121073	600.1937675	278	4.2382866	146.6986749	621.7510346
279	3.7949919	153.7032673	583.3026493	279	4.0209737	150.2608033	604.1947363	279	4.2603611	146.9333968	625.9893213
280	3.8131762	153.9655155	587.0976412	280	4.0410786	150.5082620	608.2157100	280	4.2825504	147.1669025	630.2496823
281	3.8314477	154.2265139	590.9108174	281	4.0612839	150.7544896	612.2567885	281	4.3048554	147.3991984	634.5322328
282	3.8498067	154.4862672	594.7422651	282	4.0815904	150.9994921	616.3180725	282	4.3272765	147.6302906	638.8370881
283	3.8682537	154.7447817	598.5920718	283	4.1019983	151.2432757	620.3996629	283	4.3498144	147.8601855	643.1643646
284	3.8867891	155.0020635	602.4603255	284	4.1225083	151.4858465	624.5016612	284	4.3724697	148.0888892	647.5141790
285	3.9054133	155.2581184	606.3471145	285	4.1431209	151.7272104	628.6241695	285	4.3952430	148.3164079	651.8866840
286	3.9241267	155.5129521	610.2525278	286	4.1638365	151.9673736	632.7672903	286	4.4181349	148.5427477	656.2818917
287	3.9429298	155.7665707	614.1766545	287	4.1846556	152.2063419	636.9311268	287	4.4411460	148.7679148	660.7000266
288	3.9618230	156.0189797	618.1195843	288	4.2055789	152.4441213	641.1157824	288	4.4642769	148.9919153	665.1411725
289	3.9808067	156.2701851	622.0814073	289	4.2265068	152.6807177	645.3213614	289	4.4875284	149.2147551	669.6054495
290	3.9998814	156.5201925	626.0622141	290	4.2477398	152.9161370	649.5479682	290	4.5109009	149.4364403	674.0929779
291	4.0190475	156.7690076	630.0620955	291	4.2689785	153.1503850	653.7957080	291	4.5343952	149.6569769	678.6038788
292	4.0383055	157.0166363	634.0811430	292	4.2903234	153.3834677	658.0646866	292	4.5580118	149.8763708	683.1382740
293	4.0576557	157.2630840	638.1194485	293	4.3117751	153.6153908	662.3550100	293	4.5817515	150.0946279	687.6962859
294	4.0770986	157.5083564	642.1771042	294	4.3333339	153.8461600	666.6667851	294	4.6056148	150.3117542	692.2780374
295	4.0966347	157.7524592	646.2542029	295	4.3550006	154.0757810	671.0001190	295	4.6296024	150.5277555	696.8836521
296	4.1162644	157.9953980	650.3508376	296	4.3767756	154.3042597	675.3551196	296	4.6537149	150.7426376	701.5132545
297	4.1359882	158.2371781	654.4671020	297	4.3986595	154.5316017	679.7318952	297	4.6779530	150.9564063	706.1669694
298	4.1558065	158.4778053	658.6030902	298	4.4206528	154.7578127	684.1305547	298	4.7023173	151.1690674	710.8449223
299	4.1757197	158.7172850	662.7588967	299	4.4427560	154.9828982	688.5512075	299	4.7268085	151.3806266	715.5472397
300	4.1957284	158.9556226	666.9346164	300	4.4649698	155.2068639	692.9939635	300	4.7514273	151.5910897	720.2740482

Table 1

M	C(5.75,M,12)	A(5.75,M,12)	S(5.75,M,12)	M	C(6.00,M,12)	A(6.00,M,12)	S(6.00,M,12)	M	C(6.25,M,12)	A(6.25,M,12)	S(6.25,M,12)
301	4.2158329	159.1928237	671.1303448	301	4.4872947	155.4297153	697.4589333	301	4.7761744	151.8004623	725.0254755
302	4.2360338	159.4288936	675.3461777	302	4.5097311	155.6514580	701.9462280	302	4.8010503	152.0087501	729.8016499
303	4.2563314	159.6638377	679.5822115	303	4.5322798	155.8720975	706.4559591	303	4.8260557	152.2159586	734.6027002
304	4.2767264	159.8976614	683.8385429	304	4.5549412	156.0916393	710.9882389	304	4.8511914	152.4220935	739.4287559
305	4.2972190	160.1303700	688.1152693	305	4.5777159	156.3100389	715.5431801	305	4.8764581	152.6271604	744.2799473
306	4.3178098	160.3619689	692.4124683	306	4.6006045	156.5274516	720.1208960	306	4.9018563	152.8311648	749.1564054
307	4.3384994	160.5924634	696.7302981	307	4.6236075	156.7437329	724.7215005	307	4.9273868	153.0341121	754.0582617
308	4.3592880	160.8218585	701.0687975	308	4.6467255	156.9589382	729.3451000	308	4.9530503	153.2360079	758.9856485
309	4.3801762	161.0501599	705.4280855	309	4.6699592	157.1730729	733.9918336	309	4.9788474	153.4368576	763.9386987
310	4.4011646	161.2773725	709.8082617	310	4.6933090	157.3861422	738.6617928	310	5.0047789	153.6366666	768.9175461
311	4.4222535	161.5035016	714.2094263	311	4.7167755	157.5981514	743.3551017	311	5.0308454	153.8354404	773.9223250
312	4.4434435	161.7285523	718.6316798	312	4.7403594	157.8091059	748.0718772	312	5.0570478	154.0331842	778.9531705
313	4.4647350	161.9525297	723.0751233	313	4.7640612	158.0190108	752.8122366	313	5.0833866	154.2299034	784.0102182
314	4.4861285	162.1754391	727.5398583	314	4.7878815	158.2278715	757.5762978	314	5.1098625	154.4256034	789.0936048
315	4.5076245	162.3972854	732.0259868	315	4.8118209	158.4356930	762.3641793	315	5.1364764	154.6202894	794.2034673
316	4.5292236	162.6180738	736.5336113	316	4.8358800	158.6424806	767.1760002	316	5.1632289	154.8139667	799.3399437
317	4.5509261	162.8378093	741.0628348	317	4.8600594	158.8482394	772.0118802	317	5.1901207	155.0066404	804.5031726
318	4.5727326	163.0564969	745.6137609	318	4.8843597	159.0529745	776.8719396	318	5.2171526	155.1983158	809.6923933
319	4.5946436	163.2741417	750.1864935	319	4.9087815	159.2566911	781.7562993	319	5.2443252	155.3389981	814.9104459
320	4.6166596	163.4907485	754.7811372	320	4.9333254	159.4593941	786.6650809	320	5.2716394	155.5786925	820.1547711
321	4.6387811	163.7063224	759.3977968	321	4.9579922	159.6610886	791.5984063	321	5.2990959	155.7674039	825.4264106
322	4.6610086	163.9208682	764.0365779	322	4.9827820	159.8617797	796.5563983	322	5.3266954	155.9551375	830.7255065
323	4.6833426	164.1343909	768.6975865	323	5.0076959	160.0614724	801.5391803	323	5.3544386	156.1418985	836.0522018
324	4.7057836	164.3468954	773.3809291	324	5.0327344	160.2601715	806.5468762	324	5.3823263	156.3276918	841.4066404
325	4.7283322	164.5583864	776.0867127	325	5.0578981	160.4578821	811.5796106	325	5.4103592	156.5125224	846.7889666
326	4.7509888	164.7688689	782.8150449	326	5.0831876	160.6546091	816.6375087	326	5.4385382	156.6963953	852.1993258
327	4.7737539	164.9783477	787.5660337	327	5.1086035	160.8503573	821.7206962	327	5.4668639	156.8793155	857.6378640
328	4.7966282	165.1868275	792.3397876	328	5.1341465	161.0451316	826.8292997	328	5.4953371	157.0612880	863.1047279
329	4.8196120	165.3943131	797.1364157	329	5.1598172	161.2389369	831.9634462	329	5.5239587	157.2423176	868.6000650
330	4.8427060	165.6008092	801.9560277	330	5.1856163	161.4317780	837.1232634	330	5.5527293	157.4224092	874.1240237
331	4.8659106	165.8063206	806.7987337	331	5.2115444	161.6236597	842.3088798	331	5.5816498	157.6015677	879.6767530
332	4.8892264	166.0108519	811.6646443	332	5.2376021	161.8145868	847.5204242	332	5.6107209	157.7797979	885.2584028
333	4.9126540	166.2144079	816.5538708	333	5.2637901	162.0045640	852.7580263	333	5.6399434	157.9571047	890.8691236
334	4.9361938	166.4169931	821.4665247	334	5.2901091	162.1935960	858.0218164	334	5.6693181	158.1334927	896.5090670
335	4.9598464	166.6186122	826.4027185	335	5.3165596	162.3816876	863.3119255	335	5.6988458	158.3089669	902.1783350
336	4.9836123	166.8192699	831.3625649	336	5.3431424	162.5688433	868.6284852	336	5.7285273	158.4835318	907.8772308
337	5.0074921	167.0189707	836.3461772	337	5.3698581	162.7550680	873.9716276	337	5.7583633	158.6571923	913.6057581
338	5.0314863	167.2177191	841.3536693	338	5.3967074	162.9403662	879.3414857	338	5.7883548	158.8299529	919.3641214
339	5.0555955	167.4155197	846.3851556	339	5.4236910	163.1247425	884.7381932	339	5.8185025	159.0018184	925.1524762
340	5.0798203	167.6123771	851.4407511	340	5.4508094	163.3082014	890.1618841	340	5.8488072	159.1727935	930.9709787
341	5.1041611	167.8082957	856.5205714	341	5.4780635	163.4907477	895.6126936	341	5.8792697	159.3428826	936.8197859
342	5.1286185	168.0032800	861.6247325	342	5.5054538	163.6723858	901.0907570	342	5.9098909	159.5120905	942.6990556
343	5.1531931	168.1973344	866.7533510	343	5.5329811	163.8531202	906.5962108	343	5.9406716	159.6804216	948.6089465
344	5.1778855	168.3904634	871.9065442	344	5.5606460	164.0329554	912.1291919	344	5.9716126	159.8478806	954.5496181
345	5.2026962	168.5826715	877.0844297	345	5.5884492	164.2118959	917.6898379	345	6.0027148	160.0144719	960.5212307
346	5.2276258	168.7739629	882.2871259	346	5.6163914	164.3899462	923.2782871	346	6.0339789	160.1802000	966.5239455
347	5.2526749	168.9643421	887.5147517	347	5.6444734	164.5671106	928.8946785	347	6.0654059	160.3450694	972.5579244
348	5.2778439	169.1538134	892.7674266	348	5.6726958	164.7433937	934.5391519	348	6.0969965	160.5090846	978.6233302
349	5.3031336	169.3423811	898.0452705	349	5.7010592	164.9187997	940.2118477	349	6.1287517	160.6722500	984.7203268
350	5.3285444	169.5300496	903.3484041	350	5.7295645	165.0933330	945.9129069	350	6.1606723	160.8345699	990.8490785
351	5.3540771	169.7168232	908.6769486	351	5.7582124	165.2669980	951.6424715	351	6.1927591	160.9960488	997.0097508
352	5.3797320	169.9027061	914.0310256	352	5.7870034	165.4397990	957.4006838	352	6.2250131	161.1566911	1003.2025099
353	5.4055099	170.0877025	919.4107576	353	5.8159384	165.6117403	963.1876873	353	6.2574350	161.3165009	1009.4275230
354	5.4314113	170.2718167	924.8162675	354	5.8450181	165.7828262	969.0036277	354	6.2900258	161.4754828	1015.6849580
355	5.4574368	170.4550529	930.2476788	355	5.8742432	165.9530609	974.8486438	355	6.3227864	161.6336409	1021.9749838
356	5.4835870	170.6374153	935.7051156	356	5.9036144	166.1224486	980.7228871	356	6.3557176	161.7909796	1028.2977702
357	5.5098625	170.8189080	941.1887026	357	5.9331325	166.2909937	986.6265015	357	6.3888203	161.9475030	1034.6534978
358	5.5362640	170.9995352	946.6985652	358	5.9627982	166.4587001	992.5596340	358	6.4220954	162.1032154	1041.0423080
359	5.5627919	171.1793011	952.2348291	359	5.9926122	166.6255723	998.5224322	359	6.4555438	162.2581210	1047.4644034
360	5.5894469	171.3582097	957.7976210	360	6.0225752	166.7916142	1004.5150444	360	6.4891664	162.4122240	1053.9199472
361	5.6162297	171.5362651	963.3870680	361	6.0526881	166.9568301	1010.5376196	361	6.5229641	162.5655286	1060.4091136
362	5.6431408	171.7134713	969.0027077	362	6.0829515	167.1212239	1016.5903077	362	6.5569379	162.7180388	1066.9320777
363	5.6701809	171.8898326	974.6464385	363	6.1133663	167.2847999	1022.6732633	363	6.5910886	162.8697588	1073.4890156
364	5.6973505	172.0653527	980.3166194	364	6.1439331	167.4475621	1028.7866256	364	6.6254172	163.0206927	1080.0801042
365	5.7246503	172.2400359	986.0139698	365	6.1746528	167.6095146	1034.9305587	365	6.6599246	163.1708445	1086.7055215
366	5.7520809	172.4138860	991.7386201	366	6.2055261	167.7706612	1041.1052115	366	6.6946117	163.3202184	1093.3654461
367	5.7796430	172.5869071	997.4907010	367	6.2385537	167.9310062	1047.3107376	367	6.7294795	163.4688183	1100.0600578
368	5.8073371	172.7591031	1003.2704334	368	6.2677365	168.0905534	1053.5472913	368	6.7645288	163.6166482	1106.7895372
369	5.8351639	172.9304779	1009.0776810	369	6.2990751	168.2493069	1059.8150277	369	6.7997608	163.7637122	1113.5540661
370	5.8631241	173.1010354	1014.9128449	370	6.3305705	168.4072706	1066.1141029	370	6.8351762	163.9100143	1120.3538269
371	5.8912182	173.2707796	1020.7759690	371	6.3622234	168.5644483	1072.4446734	371	6.8707761	164.0555582	1127.1890031
372	5.9194469	173.4397143	1026.6667871	372	6.3940345	168.7208441	1078.8068968	372	6.9065614	164.2003481	1134.0597791
373	5.9478110	173.6078434	1032.5866341	373	6.4260047	168.8764618	1085.2009313	373	6.9425330	164.3443877	1140.9663405
374	5.9763109	173.7751707	1038.5344451	374	6.4581347	169.0313053	1091.6269359	374	6.9786921	164.4876810	1147.9088735
375	6.0049474	173.9417000	1044.5107560	375	6.4904254	169.1853784	1098.0850706	375	7.0150394	164.6302319	1154.8875656
376	6.0337211	174.1074352	1050.5157034	376	6.5228775	169.3386849	1104.5754960	376	7.0515761	164.7720442	1161.9026050
377	6.0626327	174.2723801	1056.5494244	377	6.5554919	169.4912288	1111.0983735	377	7.0883030	164.9131217	1168.9541811
378	6.0916828	174.4365383	1062.6120571	378	6.5882693	169.6430137	1117.6538653	378	7.1252213	165.0534682	1176.0424841
379	6.1208721	174.5999137	1068.7037399	379	6.6212107	169.7940435	1124.2421347	379	7.1623318	165.1930875	1183.1677054
380	6.1502013	174.7625100	1074.8246120	380	6.6543167	169.9443219	1130.8633454	380	7.1996356	165.3319834	1190.3300372
381	6.1796710	174.9243309	1080.9748133	381	6.6875883	170.0938526	1137.5176061	381	7.2371337	165.4701597	1197.5296728
382	6.2092819	175.0853802	1087.1544843	382	6.7210263	170.2426394	1144.2052504	382	7.2748272	165.6076200	1204.7668065
383	6.2390347	175.2456614	1093.3637662	383	6.7546314	170.3906860	1150.9262767	383	7.3127169	165.7443681	1212.0416337
384	6.2689301	175.4051782	1099.6028009	384	6.7884046	170.5379960	1157.6809081	384	7.3508039	165.8804076	1219.3543505
385	6.2989687	175.5639344	1105.8717310	385	6.8223466	170.6845731	1164.4693126	385	7.3890894	166.0157423	1226.7051544
386	6.3291513	175.7219334	1112.1706997	386	6.8564583	170.8304210	1171.2916592	386	7.4275742	166.1503758	1234.0942438
387	6.3594785	175.8791790	1118.4998510	387	6.8907406	170.9755433	1178.1481175	387	7.4662595	166.2843116	1241.5218180
388	6.3899510	176.0356748	1124.8593295	388	6.9251943	171.1199436	1185.0388581	388	7.5051462	166.4175535	1248.9880775
389	6.4205695	176.1914242	1131.2492804	389	6.9598203	171.2636255	1191.9640524	389	7.5442356	166.5501051	1256.4932237
390	6.4513347	176.3464309	1137.6698499	390	6.9946194	171.4065925	1198.9238727	390	7.5835284	166.6819698	1264.0374593
391	6.4822474	176.5006984	1144.1211846	391	7.0295925	171.5488483	1205.9184021	391	7.6230260	166.8131513	1271.6209877
392	6.5133081	176.6542302	1150.6034320	392	7.0647404	171.6903963	1212.9480845	392	7.6627292	166.9436531	1279.2440137
393	6.5445177	176.8070298	1157.1167401	393	7.1000641	171.8312401	1220.0128250	393	7.7026393	167.0734788	1286.9067429
394	6.5758769	176.9591008	1163.6612578	394	7.1355645	171.9713832	1227.1128891	394	7.7427572	167.2026317	1294.6093822
395	6.6073863	177.1104466	1170.2371347	395	7.1712423	172.1108290	1234.2484535	395	7.7830841	167.3311155	1302.3521395
396	6.6390467	177.2610706	1176.8445209	396	7.2070985	172.2495811	1241.4196958	396	7.8236210	167.4589335	1310.1352235
397	6.6708588	177.4109763	1183.4835676	397	7.2431340	172.3876429	1248.6267943	397	7.8643690	167.5860893	1317.9588445
398	6.7028233	177.5601672	1190.1544264	398	7.2793497	172.5250178	1255.8699283	398	7.9053292	167.7125863	1325.8232135
399	6.7349410	177.7086466	1196.8572497	399	7.3157464	172.6617093	1263.1492779	399	7.9465028	167.8384278	1333.7285427
400	6.7672126	177.8564179	1203.5921907	400	7.3523251	172.7977207	1270.4650243	400	7.9878909	167.9636173	1341.6750456

Table 1

M	C(5.75,M,12)	A(5.75,M,12)	S(5.75,M,12)	M	C(6.00,M,12)	A(6.00,M,12)	S(6.00,M,12)	M	C(6.25,M,12)	A(6.25,M,12)	S(6.25,M,12)
401	6.7996388	178.0034846	1210.3594033	401	7.3890868	172.9330554	1277.8173495	401	8.0294945	168.0881581	1349.6629364
402	6.8322204	178.1498499	1217.1590421	402	7.4260322	173.0677168	1285.2084362	402	8.0713148	168.2120537	1357.6924309
403	6.8649581	178.2955172	1223.9912625	403	7.4631624	173.2017082	1292.6304684	403	8.1133529	168.3353073	1365.7637457
404	6.8978527	178.4404898	1230.8562207	404	7.5004782	173.3350331	1300.0956308	404	8.1556099	168.4579223	1373.8770985
405	6.9309049	178.5847711	1237.7540734	405	7.5379806	173.4676945	1307.5961089	405	8.1980870	168.5799019	1382.0327084
406	6.9641155	178.7283644	1244.6849783	406	7.5756705	173.5996961	1315.1340895	406	8.2407854	168.7012496	1390.2307955
407	6.9974853	178.8712729	1251.6490939	407	7.6135488	173.7310409	1322.7097600	407	8.2837062	168.8219685	1398.4715809
408	7.0310149	179.0134998	1258.6465791	408	7.6516166	173.8617323	1330.3233088	408	8.3268505	168.9420619	1406.7552870
409	7.0647051	179.1550486	1265.6775940	409	7.6898740	173.9917734	1337.9749253	409	8.3702195	169.0615331	1415.0821375
410	7.0985569	179.2959223	1272.7422991	410	7.7283240	174.1211675	1345.6646000	410	8.4138144	169.1803853	1423.4523570
411	7.1325708	179.4361242	1279.8408560	411	7.7669656	174.2499180	1353.3931240	411	8.4576363	169.2986216	1431.8661713
412	7.1667477	179.5756575	1286.9734268	412	7.8058005	174.3780278	1361.1600896	412	8.5016865	169.4162453	1440.3238077
413	7.2010883	179.7145254	1294.1401745	413	7.8448295	174.5055003	1368.9658901	413	8.5459661	169.5332596	1448.8254942
414	7.2355936	179.8527310	1301.3412628	414	7.8840536	174.6323366	1376.8107195	414	8.5904764	169.6496676	1457.3714603
415	7.2702641	179.9902776	1308.5768564	415	7.9234739	174.7585459	1384.6947731	415	8.6352184	169.7654724	1465.9619367
416	7.3051008	180.1271683	1315.8471205	416	7.9630912	174.8841253	1392.6182470	416	8.6801935	169.8806772	1474.5971551
417	7.3401044	180.2634061	1323.1522213	417	8.0029067	175.0090799	1400.5813383	417	8.7254029	169.9952851	1483.2773486
418	7.3752757	180.3989943	1330.4923257	418	8.0429212	175.1334128	1408.5842450	418	8.7708477	170.1092992	1492.0027515
419	7.4106156	180.5339358	1337.8676014	419	8.0831358	175.2571272	1416.6271662	419	8.8165292	170.2227225	1500.7735992
420	7.4461248	180.6682339	1345.2782170	420	8.1235515	175.3802260	1424.7103020	420	8.8624486	170.3355581	1509.5901283
421	7.4818041	180.8018915	1352.7243418	421	8.1641693	175.5027125	1432.8338536	421	8.9086072	170.4478091	1518.4525769
422	7.5176545	180.9349117	1360.2061460	422	8.2049901	175.6245895	1440.9980228	422	8.9550062	170.5594785	1527.3611041
423	7.5536766	181.0672976	1367.7238004	423	8.2460151	175.7458602	1449.2030130	423	9.0016468	170.6705693	1536.3161903
424	7.5898713	181.1990521	1375.2774770	424	8.2872452	175.8665276	1457.4490280	424	9.0485304	170.7810845	1545.3178371
425	7.6262394	181.3301783	1382.8673482	425	8.3286814	175.9865946	1465.7362732	425	9.0956582	170.8910270	1554.3663676
426	7.6627818	181.4606792	1390.4935876	426	8.3703248	176.1060643	1474.0649546	426	9.1430314	171.0004000	1563.4620257
427	7.6994993	181.5905578	1398.1563694	427	8.4121764	176.2249396	1482.4352794	427	9.1906519	171.1092062	1572.6050571
428	7.7363927	181.7198170	1405.8558687	428	8.4542373	176.3432235	1490.8474558	428	9.2385193	171.2174486	1581.7957085
429	7.7734629	181.8484598	1413.5922614	429	8.4965085	176.4609189	1499.3016931	429	9.2866366	171.3251302	1591.0342278
430	7.8107108	181.9764891	1421.3657243	430	8.5389910	176.5780287	1507.7982015	430	9.3350045	171.4322539	1600.3208644
431	7.8481371	182.1039079	1429.1764351	431	8.5816860	176.6945559	1516.3371926	431	9.3836243	171.5388225	1609.6558689
432	7.8857428	182.2307190	1437.0245722	432	8.6245944	176.8105034	1524.9188785	432	9.4324974	171.6448390	1619.0394393
433	7.9235286	182.3569254	1444.9103150	433	8.6677174	176.9258740	1533.5434729	433	9.4816250	171.7503062	1628.4719906
434	7.9614955	182.4825300	1452.8338436	434	8.7110560	177.0406707	1542.2111903	434	9.5310084	171.8552269	1637.9536156
435	7.9996443	182.6075355	1460.7953391	435	8.7546112	177.1548962	1550.9222463	435	9.5806491	171.9596039	1647.4846240
436	8.0379760	182.7319450	1468.7949834	436	8.7983843	177.2685534	1559.6768575	436	9.6305483	172.0634402	1657.0652731
437	8.0764913	182.8557611	1476.8329594	437	8.8423762	177.3816452	1568.4752418	437	9.6807074	172.1667384	1666.6958215
438	8.1151911	182.9789868	1484.9094507	438	8.8865881	177.4941743	1577.3176181	438	9.7311278	172.2695014	1676.3765289
439	8.1540764	183.1016248	1493.0246418	439	8.9310210	177.6061436	1586.2042062	439	9.7818107	172.3717320	1686.1076566
440	8.1931480	183.2236781	1501.1787182	440	8.9756761	177.7175558	1595.1352272	440	9.8327577	172.4734328	1695.8894574
441	8.2324069	183.3451492	1509.3718663	441	9.0205545	177.8284138	1604.1109093	441	9.8839699	172.5746068	1705.7222250
442	8.2718538	183.4660411	1517.6042370	442	9.0656573	177.9387202	1613.1314579	442	9.9354489	172.6752565	1715.6061950
443	8.3114898	183.5863565	1525.8761270	443	9.1109856	178.0484778	1622.1971152	443	9.9871961	172.7753847	1725.5416439
444	8.3513157	183.7060981	1534.1876168	444	9.1565405	178.1576893	1631.3081008	444	10.0392127	172.8749341	1735.5288400
445	8.3913324	183.8252687	1542.5389324	445	9.2023232	178.2663575	1640.4641413	445	10.0915003	172.9740074	1745.5680527
446	8.4315409	183.9438710	1550.9302648	446	9.2483348	178.3744851	1649.6669645	446	10.1440602	173.0726672	1755.6595530
447	8.4719420	184.0619076	1559.3618057	447	9.2945765	178.4820747	1658.9153993	447	10.1968938	173.1707363	1765.8036132
448	8.5125367	184.1793814	1567.8337477	448	9.3410494	178.5891291	1668.2098759	448	10.2500027	173.2682973	1776.0005070
449	8.5533260	184.2962950	1576.3462844	449	9.3877546	178.6956508	1677.5509252	449	10.3033881	173.3653527	1786.2505097
450	8.5943106	184.4126511	1584.8996104	450	9.4346934	178.8016426	1686.9386799	450	10.3570516	173.4619053	1796.5538978
451	8.6354917	184.5284522	1593.4939210	451	9.4818669	178.9071071	1696.3733733	451	10.4109945	173.5579576	1806.9109493
452	8.6768701	184.6437012	1602.1294127	452	9.5292762	179.0120468	1705.8552402	452	10.4652185	173.6535122	1817.3219439
453	8.7184468	184.7584005	1610.8062829	453	9.5769226	179.1164645	1715.3845164	453	10.5197248	173.7485717	1827.7871063
454	8.7602227	184.8725528	1619.5247296	454	9.6248072	179.2203627	1724.9614430	454	10.5745151	173.8431387	1838.3068872
455	8.8021987	184.9861608	1628.2849523	455	9.6729312	179.3237440	1734.5862462	455	10.6295907	173.9372157	1848.8814022
456	8.8443759	185.0992270	1637.0871511	456	9.7212959	179.4266109	1744.2591774	456	10.6849531	174.0308053	1859.5109929
457	8.8867552	185.2117540	1645.9315270	457	9.7699024	179.5289661	1753.9804733	457	10.7406030	174.1239099	1870.1959460
458	8.9293376	185.3237444	1654.8182823	458	9.8187519	179.6308120	1763.7503757	458	10.7965445	174.2165321	1880.9365499
459	8.9721240	185.4352008	1663.7476199	459	9.8678457	179.7321513	1773.5691276	459	10.8527765	174.3086745	1891.7330944
460	9.0151155	185.5461256	1672.7197439	460	9.9171849	179.8329863	1783.4369976	460	10.9093014	174.4003394	1902.5858710
461	9.0583129	185.6565214	1681.7348593	461	9.9667708	179.9333197	1793.3541582	461	10.9661207	174.4915293	1913.4951724
462	9.1017173	185.7663908	1690.7931722	462	10.0166047	180.0331540	1803.3209290	462	11.0232359	174.5822468	1924.4612931
463	9.1453297	185.8757362	1699.8948895	463	10.0666877	180.1324915	1813.3375336	463	11.0806466	174.6724942	1935.4845290
464	9.1891511	185.9845602	1709.0402192	464	10.1170211	180.2313348	1823.4042213	464	11.1383603	174.7622740	1946.5651776
465	9.2331824	186.0928652	1718.2293703	465	10.1676062	180.3296864	1833.5212424	465	11.1963726	174.8515887	1957.7035379
466	9.2774247	186.2006537	1727.4625527	466	10.2184443	180.4275487	1843.6888487	466	11.2546871	174.9404405	1968.8999105
467	9.3218791	186.3079282	1736.7399774	467	10.2695365	180.5249240	1853.9072929	467	11.3133052	175.0288320	1980.1545976
468	9.3665464	186.4146912	1746.0618565	468	10.3208842	180.6218150	1864.1768294	468	11.3722287	175.1167655	1991.4679028
469	9.4114278	186.5209450	1755.4284029	469	10.3724886	180.7182238	1874.4977136	469	11.4314590	175.2042434	2002.8401315
470	9.4565242	186.6266921	1764.8398307	470	10.4243510	180.8141531	1884.8702021	470	11.4909979	175.2912681	2014.2715905
471	9.5018367	186.7319349	1774.2963549	471	10.4764728	180.9096050	1895.2945532	471	11.5508468	175.3778418	2025.7625884
472	9.5473663	186.8366758	1783.7981916	472	10.5283551	181.0045821	1905.7710259	472	11.6110075	175.4639670	2037.3134352
473	9.5931141	186.9409173	1793.3455580	473	10.5814994	181.0990867	1916.2998811	473	11.6714815	175.5496459	2048.9244427
474	9.6390812	187.0446616	1802.9386721	474	10.6344069	181.1931211	1926.8813805	474	11.7322705	175.6348809	2060.5959242
475	9.6852684	187.1479112	1812.5777533	475	10.6875790	181.2863876	1937.5157874	475	11.7933760	175.7196743	2072.3281947
476	9.7316770	187.2506684	1822.2630217	476	10.7410168	181.3797887	1948.2033664	476	11.8547999	175.8040283	2084.1215707
477	9.7783079	187.3529356	1831.9946987	477	10.7947219	181.4724266	1958.9443832	477	11.9165436	175.8879452	2095.9763706
478	9.8251623	187.4547151	1841.7730066	478	10.8486955	181.5646036	1969.7391052	478	11.9786309	175.9714274	2107.8929142
479	9.8722412	187.5560092	1851.5981690	479	10.9029390	181.6563219	1980.5878007	479	12.0409975	176.0544770	2119.8715231
480	9.9195457	187.6568202	1861.4704102	480	10.9574537	181.7475840	1991.4907397	480	12.1037111	176.1370963	2131.9125207
481	9.9670769	187.7571506	1871.3899559	481	11.0122410	181.8383921	2002.4481934	481	12.1657512	176.2192875	2144.0162317
482	10.0148358	187.8570024	1881.3570328	482	11.0673022	181.9287483	2013.4604434	482	12.2301197	176.3010528	2156.1829829
483	10.0628236	187.9563781	1891.3718686	483	11.1226387	182.0186550	2024.5277366	483	12.2938183	176.3823945	2168.4131027
484	10.1110412	188.0552779	1901.4346922	484	11.1782519	182.1081145	2035.6503753	484	12.3578486	176.4633148	2180.7069209
485	10.1594900	188.1537010	1911.5457334	485	11.2341432	182.1971288	2046.8286272	485	12.4222124	176.5438157	2193.0647695
486	10.2081709	188.2516708	1921.7052234	486	11.2903139	182.2857003	2058.0627704	486	12.4869114	176.6238996	2205.4869818
487	10.2570850	188.3491644	1931.9133943	487	11.3467654	182.3738312	2069.3530842	487	12.5519474	176.7035685	2217.9738932
488	10.3062336	188.4461930	1942.1704793	488	11.4034993	182.4615235	2080.6998497	488	12.6173221	176.7828246	2230.5259406
489	10.3556176	188.5427590	1952.4767129	489	11.4605168	182.5487796	2092.1033489	489	12.6830373	176.8616701	2243.1431627
490	10.4052383	188.6388644	1962.8323305	490	11.5178193	182.6356016	2103.5638657	490	12.7490948	176.9401070	2255.8262000
491	10.4550967	188.7345115	1973.2375688	491	11.5754084	182.7219917	2115.0816850	491	12.8154963	177.0181375	2268.5752948
492	10.5051940	188.8297025	1983.6926655	492	11.6332855	182.8079519	2126.6570935	492	12.8822437	177.0957638	2281.3907912
493	10.5555314	188.9244396	1994.1978595	493	11.6914519	182.8934845	2138.2903790	493	12.9493387	177.1729878	2294.2730349
494	10.6061100	189.0187249	2004.7533909	494	11.7499092	182.9785915	2149.9818309	494	13.0167832	177.2498117	2307.2223737
495	10.6569310	189.1125605	2015.3595009	495	11.8086587	183.0632751	2161.7317401	495	13.0845790	177.3263375	2320.2391569
496	10.7079954	189.2059487	2026.0164319	496	11.8677020	183.1475375	2173.5403998	496	13.1527278	177.4022674	2333.3237358
497	10.7593046	189.2988915	2036.7244273	497	11.9270405	183.2313806	2185.4081008	497	13.2212316	177.4779033	2346.4764636
498	10.8108596	189.3913911	2047.4837319	498	11.9866757	183.3148065	2197.3351413	498	13.2900922	177.5531473	2359.6976952
499	10.8626616	189.4834495	2058.2945914	499	12.0466091	183.3978174	2209.3218170	499	13.3593114	177.6280015	2372.9877874
500	10.9147119	189.5750690	2069.1572530	500	12.1068421	183.4804154	2221.3684261	500	13.4288912	177.7024678	2386.3470988

Table 1

M	C(6.50,M,12)	A(6.50,M,12)	S(6.50,M,12)	M	C(6.75,M,12)	A(6.75,M,12)	S(6.75,M,12)	M	C(7.00,M,12)	A(7.00,M,12)	S(7.00,M,12)
1	1.0054167	.9946125	1.0000000	1	1.0056250	.9944065	1.0000000	1	1.0058333	.9942005	1.0000000
2	1.0108627	1.9838666	2.0054167	2	1.0112816	1.9832507	2.0056250	2	1.0117007	1.9826351	2.0058333
3	1.0163382	2.9677910	3.0152793	3	1.0169701	2.9665638	3.0169066	3	1.0176023	2.9653373	3.0175340
4	1.0218433	3.9464146	4.0326175	4	1.0226906	3.9443766	4.0339767	4	1.0235383	3.9423403	4.0351363
5	1.0273783	4.9197659	5.0544609	5	1.0284432	4.9167201	5.0565673	5	1.0295089	4.9136772	5.0586746
6	1.0329433	5.8878732	6.0818392	6	1.0342282	5.8836247	6.0850105	6	1.0355144	5.8793808	6.0881835
7	1.0385384	6.8507649	7.1147825	7	1.0400457	6.8451209	7.1192387	7	1.0415549	6.8394838	7.1236979
8	1.0441638	7.8084691	8.1533209	8	1.0458960	7.8012389	8.1592844	8	1.0476306	7.7940187	8.1652528
9	1.0498197	8.7610136	9.1974847	9	1.0517791	8.7520089	9.2051804	9	1.0537418	8.7430178	9.2128835
10	1.0555062	9.7084263	10.2473044	10	1.0576954	9.6974607	10.2569595	10	1.0598886	9.6865131	10.2666253
11	1.0612236	10.6507348	11.3028107	11	1.0635449	10.6376240	11.3146549	11	1.0660713	10.6245367	11.3265140
12	1.0669719	11.5879666	12.3640342	12	1.0696279	11.5725286	12.3782998	12	1.0722901	11.5571201	12.3925853
13	1.0727513	12.5201492	13.4310061	13	1.0756440	12.5022037	13.4479278	13	1.0785451	12.4842951	13.4648754
14	1.0785620	13.4473096	14.5037574	14	1.0816951	13.4266786	14.5235724	14	1.0848366	13.4060929	14.5434205
15	1.0844042	14.3694749	15.5823149	15	1.0877796	14.3459824	15.6052675	15	1.0911648	14.3225447	15.6282571
16	1.0902781	15.2866721	16.6667236	16	1.0938984	15.2601441	16.6930471	16	1.0975300	15.2336816	16.7194219
17	1.0961838	16.1989279	17.7570017	17	1.1000456	16.1691924	17.7869455	17	1.1039322	16.1395343	17.8169519
18	1.1021214	17.1062689	18.8531854	18	1.1062394	17.0731559	18.8869970	18	1.1103718	17.0401335	18.9208841
19	1.1080912	18.0087217	19.9553069	19	1.1124620	17.9720631	19.9932364	19	1.1168490	17.9355097	20.0312559
20	1.1140934	18.9063125	21.0633981	20	1.1187196	18.8659421	21.1056984	20	1.1233639	18.8256931	21.1481049
21	1.1201281	19.7990676	22.1774915	21	1.1250124	19.7548213	22.2244179	21	1.1299169	19.7107140	22.2714689
22	1.1261954	20.6870129	23.2976196	22	1.1313405	20.6387284	23.3494303	22	1.1365081	20.5906021	23.4013858
23	1.1322957	21.5701745	24.4238150	23	1.1377043	21.5176914	24.4807708	23	1.1431377	21.4653874	24.5378939
24	1.1384289	22.4485780	25.5561107	24	1.1441039	22.3917379	25.6184751	24	1.1498060	22.3350993	25.6810316
25	1.1445954	23.3222491	26.6945396	25	1.1505395	23.2608953	26.7625791	25	1.1565132	23.1997673	26.8308376
26	1.1507953	24.1912134	27.8391351	26	1.1570113	24.1251911	27.9131186	26	1.1632595	24.0594207	27.9873508
27	1.1570288	25.0554961	28.9899304	27	1.1635195	24.9846525	29.0701299	27	1.1700452	24.9140885	29.1506104
28	1.1632960	25.9151226	30.1469592	28	1.1700643	25.8393064	30.2336494	28	1.1768705	25.7637997	30.3206556
29	1.1695972	26.7701178	31.3102552	29	1.1766459	26.6891797	31.4037136	29	1.1837356	26.6085829	31.4975261
30	1.1759325	27.6205067	32.4798524	30	1.1832645	27.5342993	32.5803595	30	1.1906407	27.4484569	32.6812616
31	1.1823022	28.4663141	33.6557849	31	1.1899204	28.3746917	33.7636240	31	1.1975861	28.2834799	33.8719023
32	1.1887063	29.3075648	34.6380871	32	1.1966137	29.2103833	34.9535444	32	1.2045720	29.1136503	35.0694884
33	1.1951451	30.1442833	36.0267934	33	1.2033446	30.0414004	36.1501581	33	1.2115987	29.9390061	36.2740605
34	1.2016188	30.9764940	37.2219385	34	1.2101135	30.8677692	37.3535028	34	1.2186663	30.7595752	37.4856591
35	1.2081276	31.8042211	38.4235574	35	1.2169203	31.6895157	38.5636162	35	1.2257752	31.5753855	38.7043255
36	1.2146716	32.6274889	39.6316850	36	1.2237655	32.5066657	39.7805365	36	1.2329256	32.3864644	39.9301007
37	1.2212511	33.4463213	40.8463566	37	1.2306492	33.3192449	41.0043021	37	1.2401177	33.1928395	41.1630263
38	1.2278662	34.2607423	42.0676077	38	1.2375716	34.1272790	42.2349513	38	1.2473517	33.9945389	42.4031440
39	1.2345172	35.0707756	43.2954739	39	1.2445329	34.9307932	43.4725229	39	1.2546279	34.7915872	43.6504956
40	1.2412041	35.8764448	44.5299911	40	1.2515334	35.7298130	44.7170558	40	1.2619466	35.5840137	44.9051235
41	1.2479273	36.6777735	45.7711952	41	1.2585733	36.5243635	45.9685892	41	1.2693079	36.3718446	46.1670701
42	1.2546869	37.4747851	47.0191225	42	1.2656528	37.3144696	47.2271626	42	1.2767122	37.1551065	47.4363780
43	1.2614831	38.2675028	48.2738094	43	1.2727721	38.1001562	48.4928154	43	1.2841597	37.9338259	48.7130902
44	1.2683162	39.0559498	49.5352925	44	1.2799314	38.8814481	49.7655874	44	1.2916506	38.7000200	49.9972499
45	1.2751862	39.8401489	50.8036087	45	1.2871310	39.6583698	51.0455189	45	1.2991853	39.4777422	51.2889005
46	1.2820935	40.6201233	52.0787949	46	1.2943712	40.4309457	52.3326499	46	1.3067638	40.2429914	52.5880858
47	1.2890381	41.3958955	53.3608864	47	1.3016520	41.1992002	53.6270211	47	1.3143866	41.0038026	53.8948496
48	1.2960204	42.1674883	54.6499265	48	1.3089738	41.9631574	54.9286731	48	1.3220539	41.7602014	55.2092362
49	1.3030405	42.9349241	55.9459470	49	1.3163368	42.7228414	56.2376469	49	1.3297659	42.5122135	56.5312901
50	1.3100987	43.6982254	57.2489875	50	1.3237412	43.4782761	57.5539836	50	1.3375228	43.2598643	57.8610560
51	1.3171951	44.4574144	58.5590062	51	1.3311872	44.2294853	58.8777248	51	1.3453250	44.0031791	59.1985788
52	1.3243299	45.2125133	59.8762813	52	1.3386751	44.9764925	60.2089120	52	1.3531728	44.7421830	60.5439038
53	1.3315033	45.9635441	61.2006111	53	1.3462052	45.7193213	61.5475871	53	1.3610663	45.4769011	61.8970766
54	1.3387156	46.7105287	62.5321144	54	1.3537776	46.4579951	62.8937923	54	1.3690058	46.2073582	63.2581429
55	1.3459667	47.4534890	63.8708301	55	1.3613926	47.1925371	64.2475699	55	1.3769917	46.9335789	64.6271487
56	1.3532577	48.1924466	65.2167971	56	1.3690504	47.9229704	65.6089524	56	1.3850242	47.6555980	66.0041404
57	1.3605878	48.9274230	66.5700547	57	1.3767513	48.6493190	66.9780129	57	1.3931035	48.3734098	67.3891646
58	1.3679576	49.6584398	67.9306425	58	1.3844955	49.3716027	68.3547642	58	1.4012299	49.0870686	68.7822680
59	1.3753674	50.3855183	69.2986001	59	1.3922833	50.0898473	69.7392597	59	1.4094037	49.7965885	70.1834979
60	1.3828173	51.1086796	70.6739676	60	1.4001149	50.8040744	71.1315431	60	1.4176263	50.5019935	71.5929017
61	1.3903076	51.8279449	72.0567849	61	1.4079906	51.5143064	72.5316580	61	1.4258947	51.2033075	73.0105269
62	1.3978384	52.5433351	73.4470925	62	1.4159105	52.2205657	73.9396486	62	1.4342125	51.9005543	74.4364217
63	1.4054100	53.2548713	74.8449309	63	1.4238750	52.9225746	75.3555591	63	1.4425787	52.5937574	75.8706341
64	1.4130227	53.9625740	76.2503409	64	1.4318843	53.6212550	76.7794341	64	1.4509937	53.2829402	77.3132128
65	1.4206766	54.6664640	77.6633636	65	1.4399387	54.3157290	78.2113184	65	1.4594579	53.9681262	78.7642066
66	1.4283719	55.3665618	79.0840402	66	1.4480383	55.0063485	79.6512571	66	1.4679714	54.6493383	80.2236644
67	1.4361089	56.0628878	80.5124121	67	1.4551835	55.6930451	81.0992954	67	1.4765345	55.3265998	81.6916358
68	1.4438878	56.7554624	81.9485210	68	1.4643746	56.3759200	82.5554790	68	1.4851477	55.9999336	83.1681704
69	1.4517089	57.4443057	83.3924088	69	1.4726117	57.0549961	84.0193535	69	1.4938110	56.6693623	84.6533180
70	1.4595723	58.1294379	84.8441177	70	1.4808951	57.7302634	85.4924652	70	1.5025249	57.3349087	86.1471290
71	1.4674783	58.8108790	86.3036900	71	1.4892252	58.4017535	86.9733603	71	1.5112896	57.9965952	87.6496540
72	1.4754272	59.4886488	87.7711683	72	1.4976020	59.0694877	88.4625655	72	1.5201055	58.6544443	89.1609436
73	1.4834191	60.1627671	89.2465954	73	1.5060261	59.7334869	89.9601875	73	1.5289728	59.3084781	90.6490491
74	1.4914542	60.8332537	90.7300145	74	1.5144975	60.3937718	91.4662136	74	1.5378918	59.9587189	92.2100219
75	1.4995330	61.5001280	92.2214688	75	1.5230165	61.0503635	92.9807110	75	1.5468628	60.6051887	93.7479137
76	1.5076554	62.1634095	93.7210017	76	1.5315835	61.7032826	94.5037275	76	1.5558862	61.2479092	95.2947765
77	1.5158219	62.8231176	95.2286571	77	1.5401986	62.3525495	96.0353110	77	1.5649622	61.8869023	96.6056627
78	1.5240326	63.4792716	96.7444790	78	1.5488622	62.9981847	97.5755096	78	1.5740911	62.5221895	98.4156249
79	1.5322878	64.1318905	98.2685116	79	1.5575746	63.6402085	99.1243719	79	1.5832733	63.1537924	99.9897161
80	1.5405877	64.7809935	99.8007994	80	1.5663359	64.2786412	100.6819465	80	1.5925091	63.7817323	101.5729894
81	1.5489325	65.4265994	101.3413871	81	1.5751466	64.9135027	102.2482824	81	1.6017997	64.4060304	103.1654985
82	1.5573226	66.0687271	102.8903196	82	1.5840068	65.5448131	103.8234290	82	1.6111426	65.0267080	104.7672973
83	1.5657581	66.7073954	104.4476421	83	1.5929168	66.1725923	105.4074358	83	1.6205409	65.6437859	106.3784398
84	1.5742393	67.3426228	106.0134002	84	1.6018770	66.7968600	107.0003526	84	1.6299941	66.2572850	107.9989807
85	1.5827664	67.9744280	107.5876395	85	1.6108875	67.4176358	108.6022296	85	1.6395004	66.8672262	109.6289748
86	1.5913397	68.6028294	109.1704058	86	1.6199488	68.0349392	110.2131171	86	1.6490661	67.4736300	111.2684771
87	1.5999595	69.2278452	110.7617455	87	1.6290610	68.6487898	111.8330659	87	1.6586857	68.0765170	112.9175433
88	1.6086259	69.8494938	112.3617050	88	1.6382245	69.2592068	113.4621269	88	1.6683613	68.6759076	114.5762289
89	1.6173393	70.4677932	113.9703309	89	1.6474395	69.8662093	115.1003514	89	1.6780934	69.2718219	116.2445903
90	1.6260999	71.0827616	115.5876702	90	1.6567063	70.4698166	116.7477909	90	1.6878823	69.8642803	117.9226837
91	1.6349079	71.6944168	117.2137701	91	1.6660253	71.0700476	118.4044972	91	1.6977283	70.4533027	119.6105660
92	1.6437637	72.3027768	118.8486780	92	1.6753967	71.6669212	120.0705225	92	1.7076317	71.0389091	121.3082943
93	1.6526674	72.9078592	120.4924417	93	1.6848208	72.2604561	121.7459192	93	1.7175929	71.6211192	123.0159261
94	1.6616193	73.5096818	122.1451091	94	1.6942979	72.8506711	123.4307400	94	1.7276122	72.1999528	124.7335190
95	1.6706198	74.1082620	123.8067284	95	1.7038283	73.4375847	125.1250379	95	1.7376899	72.7751295	126.4611312
96	1.6796690	74.7036174	125.4773482	96	1.7134124	74.0212153	126.8288662	96	1.7478265	73.3475687	128.1988211
97	1.6887672	75.2957654	127.1570171	97	1.7230503	74.6015811	128.5422786	97	1.7580221	73.9163897	129.9466475
98	1.6979147	75.8847231	128.8457843	98	1.7327425	75.1787012	130.2653289	98	1.7682772	74.4819119	131.7046697
99	1.7071117	76.4705079	130.5436990	99	1.7424892	75.7525929	131.9980714	99	1.7765922	75.0441543	133.4729469
100	1.7163586	77.0531367	132.2508107	100	1.7522907	76.3232745	133.7405606	100	1.7889673	75.6031360	135.2515391

Table 1

M	C(6.50,M,12)	A(6.50,M,12)	S(6.50,M,12)	C(6.75,M,12)	A(6.75,M,12)	S(6.75,M,12)	C(7.00,M,12)	A(7.00,M,12)	S(7.00,M,12)
101	1.7256555	77.6326267	133.9671693	1.7621473	76.8907639	135.4928512	1.7994030	76.1588759	137.0405064
102	1.7350028	78.2089946	135.6928248	1.7720594	77.4550791	137.2549965	1.8099995	76.7113928	138.8399094
103	1.7444007	78.7822574	137.4278276	1.7820272	78.0162378	139.0270579	1.8204572	77.2607054	140.6498088
104	1.7533496	79.3524317	139.1722283	1.7920511	78.5742576	140.8090851	1.8310766	77.8068322	142.4702660
105	1.7633496	79.9195342	140.9260779	1.8021314	79.1291561	142.6011362	1.8417578	78.3497917	144.3013426
106	1.7729011	80.4835815	142.6894275	1.8122684	79.6809507	144.4032676	1.8525014	78.8896024	146.1431004
107	1.7825043	81.0445900	144.4623285	1.8224626	80.2296589	146.2155359	1.8633077	79.4262824	147.9956019
108	1.7921595	81.6025760	146.2448328	1.8327137	80.7752978	148.0379983	1.8741770	79.9598499	149.8569095
109	1.8018670	82.1575559	148.0369923	1.8430228	81.3178847	149.8707121	1.8851097	80.4903230	151.7330865
110	1.8116272	82.7095459	149.8388594	1.8533898	81.8574366	151.7137348	1.8961061	81.0177197	153.6181962
111	1.8214401	83.2585620	151.6504865	1.8638151	82.3939706	153.5671246	1.9071668	81.5420577	155.5143023
112	1.8313063	83.8046203	153.4719266	1.8742990	82.9275034	155.4309397	1.9182919	82.0633548	157.4214691
113	1.8412258	84.3477367	155.3032329	1.8848420	83.4580518	157.3052387	1.9294819	82.5816286	159.3397610
114	1.8511992	84.8879271	157.1444588	1.8954442	83.9856326	159.1900807	1.9407373	83.0968967	161.2692429
115	1.8612265	85.4252072	158.9956579	1.9061061	84.5102624	161.0855249	1.9520582	83.6091765	163.2099802
116	1.8713081	85.9595928	160.8568844	1.9168279	85.0319576	162.9916310	1.9634452	84.1184853	165.1620384
117	1.8814444	86.4910993	162.7281925	1.9276101	85.5507348	164.9084589	1.9748987	84.6248404	167.1254836
118	1.8916355	87.0197424	164.6096369	1.9384529	86.0666101	166.8360690	1.9864189	85.1282589	169.1003823
119	1.9018819	87.5455374	166.5012724	1.9493567	86.5795998	168.7745219	1.9980063	85.6287578	171.0868012
120	1.9121838	88.0684997	168.4031543	1.9603218	87.0897201	170.7238785	2.0096614	86.1263541	173.0848075
121	1.9225414	88.5886445	170.3153381	1.9713486	87.5969871	172.6842004	2.0213344	86.6210646	175.0944689
122	1.9329552	89.1059871	172.2378795	1.9824375	88.1014166	174.6555490	2.0331758	87.1129052	177.1156533
123	1.9434254	89.6205425	174.1708347	1.9935887	88.6030246	176.6379865	2.0450362	87.6018949	179.1490291
124	1.9539522	90.1323257	176.1142600	2.0048026	89.1018268	178.6315751	2.0589654	88.0880475	181.1940651
125	1.9645362	90.6413517	178.0682123	2.0160796	89.5978390	180.6363777	2.0709643	88.5713815	18..2510305
126	1.9751774	91.1476354	180.0327484	2.0274201	90.0910767	182.6524574	2.0810333	89.0519121	185.3199949
127	1.9858763	91.6511914	182.0079258	2.0388243	90.5815554	184.6798774	2.0931727	89.5296557	187.4010282
128	1.9966331	92.1520346	183.9938021	2.0502927	91.0692907	186.7187018	2.1053828	90.0046287	189.4942008
129	2.0074482	92.6501794	185.9904352	2.0618256	91.5542977	188.7689945	2.1176842	90.4768471	191.5995837
130	2.0183219	93.1456405	187.9978834	2.0734234	92.0365919	190.8308200	2.1300173	90.9463269	193.7172479
131	2.0292544	93.6384324	190.0162052	2.0850864	92.5161884	192.9042434	2.1424424	91.4130939	195.8472652
132	2.0402462	94.1285693	192.0454597	2.0968150	92.9931022	194.9893298	2.1549400	91.8771339	197.9897076
133	2.0512976	94.6160656	194.0857059	2.1086096	93.4673483	197.0861448	2.1675104	92.3384927	200.1446475
134	2.0624088	95.1009355	196.1370035	2.1204705	93.9389418	199.1947543	2.1801543	92.7971759	202.3121580
135	2.0735802	95.5831932	198.1994123	2.1323981	94.4078973	201.3152248	2.1928718	93.2531989	204.4923122
136	2.0848120	96.0628528	200.2729924	2.1443929	94.8742298	203.4476230	2.2056636	93.7065772	206.6851841
137	2.0961048	96.5399282	202.3578045	2.1564551	95.3379538	205.5920158	2.2185299	94.1573261	208.8908476
138	2.1074587	97.0144333	204.4539093	2.1685852	95.7990840	207.7484709	2.2314714	94.6054609	211.1093776
139	2.1188741	97.4863821	206.5613679	2.1807834	96.2576348	209.9170561	2.2444883	95.0509968	213.3408489
140	2.1303513	97.9557882	208.6802420	2.1930503	96.7136206	212.0978395	2.2575811	95.4939487	215.5853372
141	2.1418907	98.4226654	210.8105933	2.2053863	97.1670560	214.2908899	2.2707504	95.9343318	217.8429184
142	2.1534926	98.8870274	212.9524840	2.2177916	97.6179550	216.4962761	2.2839964	96.3721609	220.1136687
143	2.1651574	99.3488876	215.1059767	2.2302666	98.0663318	218.7140677	2.2973197	96.8074507	222.3976651
144	2.1768853	99.8082595	217.2711340	2.2428119	98.5122007	220.9443343	2.3107207	97.2402161	224.6949848
145	2.1986768	100.2651566	219.4480193	2.2554277	98.9555756	223.1871462	2.3242000	97.6704717	227.0057056
146	2.2005321	100.7195921	221.6366961	2.2681145	99.3964705	225.4425739	2.3377578	98.0982320	229.3299055
147	2.2124517	101.1715794	223.8372282	2.2808726	99.8348991	227.7106884	2.3513947	98.5235115	231.6676633
148	2.2244358	101.6211316	226.0496799	2.2937025	100.2708755	229.9915610	2.3651112	98.9463246	234.0190580
149	2.2364848	102.0682618	228.2741156	2.3066046	100.7044131	232.2852635	2.3789077	99.3666856	236.3841592
150	2.2485991	102.5129832	230.5106004	2.3195793	101.1355258	234.5918682	2.3927846	99.7846088	238.7630769
151	2.2607790	102.9553086	232.7591995	2.3326269	101.5642270	236.9114474	2.4067425	100.2001081	241.1558615
152	2.2730249	103.3952510	235.0199785	2.3457479	101.9905303	239.2440743	2.4207319	100.6131978	243.5626040
153	2.2853371	103.8328232	237.2930034	2.3589428	102.4144490	241.5898222	2.4349031	101.0238919	245.9833659
154	2.2977160	104.2680380	239.5783405	2.3722118	102.8359965	243.9487650	2.4491067	101.4322039	248.4182890
155	2.3101620	104.7009081	241.8760565	2.3855555	103.2551861	246.3209768	2.4633931	101.8381481	250.8673956
156	2.3226754	105.1314461	244.1862185	2.3989742	103.6720309	248.7065323	2.4777629	102.2417379	253.3307888
157	2.3352565	105.5596645	246.5088039	2.4124685	104.0865441	251.1055065	2.4922166	102.6429872	255.8085517
158	2.3479058	105.9855760	248.8441504	2.4260386	104.4987387	253.5179750	2.5067545	103.0419093	258.3007683
159	2.3606236	106.4091929	251.1920682	2.4396852	104.9086277	255.9440136	2.5213772	103.4385180	260.8075228
160	2.3734104	106.8305275	253.5526798	2.4534083	105.3162239	258.3836987	2.5360853	103.8326265	263.3389000
161	2.3862663	107.2495922	255.9260907	2.4672087	105.7215403	260.8371070	2.5508791	104.2248482	265.8649952
162	2.3991919	107.6663992	258.3123265	2.4810868	106.1245895	263.3043157	2.5657592	104.6145964	268.4159643
163	2.4121816	108.0809607	260.7115484	2.4950429	106.5253842	265.7854025	2.5807261	105.0020842	270.9816235
164	2.4252536	108.4932887	263.1237360	2.5090775	106.9239370	268.2804454	2.5957804	105.3873249	273.5623497
165	2.4383904	108.9033053	265.5489896	2.5231911	107.3202606	270.7895229	2.6109224	105.7703313	276.1581300
166	2.4515983	109.3112925	267.9873799	2.5373840	107.7143672	273.3127140	2.6261528	106.1511164	278.7690525
167	2.4648778	109.7169921	270.4389782	2.5516568	108.1062695	275.8500080	2.6414720	106.5296932	281.3952053
168	2.4782292	110.1205060	272.9038560	2.5660099	108.4959796	278.4017548	2.6568806	106.9060744	284.0366773
169	2.4916530	110.5218460	275.3820853	2.5804437	108.8835098	280.9677647	2.6723791	107.2802728	286.6935579
170	2.5051494	110.9210238	277.8737382	2.5949587	109.2688724	283.5482083	2.6879680	107.6523011	289.3659370
171	2.5187190	111.3180510	280.3788876	2.6095553	109.6520709	286.1431670	2.7035478	108.0221717	292.0539050
172	2.5323620	111.7129393	282.8976066	2.6242341	110.0331431	288.7527223	2.7194191	108.3898973	294.7575528
173	2.5460790	112.1057001	285.4299687	2.6389954	110.4120751	291.3769564	2.7352823	108.7554903	297.4769718
174	2.5598703	112.4963449	287.9760477	2.6538397	110.7888876	294.0159518	2.7512382	109.1189630	300.2122542
175	2.5737362	112.8848851	290.5359179	2.6687676	111.1635924	296.6697915	2.7672870	109.4803278	302.9634923
176	2.5876773	113.2713320	293.1096541	2.6837794	111.5362013	299.3385591	2.7834295	109.8395968	305.7307794
177	2.6016939	113.6556970	295.6973314	2.6988757	111.9067260	302.0223385	2.7996662	110.1967822	308.5142089
178	2.6157864	114.0379912	298.2990253	2.7140568	112.2751781	304.7212142	2.8159976	110.5518962	311.3138751
179	2.6299552	114.4182258	300.9148117	2.7293234	112.6415693	307.4352710	2.8324243	110.9049506	314.1298727
180	2.6442008	114.7964119	303.5447669	2.7446758	113.0059110	310.1645944	2.8489467	111.2559575	316.9622970
181	2.6585236	115.1725606	306.1889678	2.7601146	113.3682148	312.9092702	2.8655656	111.6049288	319.8112437
182	2.6729239	115.5466827	308.8474913	2.7755403	113.7284920	315.6693749	2.8822814	111.9518762	322.6768093
183	2.6874023	115.9187892	311.5204153	2.7912533	114.0867540	318.4450252	2.8990947	112.2968114	325.5590907
184	2.7019590	116.2888911	314.2078175	2.8069541	114.4430121	321.2362784	2.9160061	112.6397463	328.4581854
185	2.7165946	116.6569990	316.9097765	2.8227432	114.7972774	324.0432325	2.9330161	112.9806922	331.3741915
186	2.7313095	117.0231238	319.6263711	2.8385211	115.1495601	326.8659757	2.9501254	113.3196609	334.3072076
187	2.7461041	117.3872760	322.3576807	2.8545884	115.4998743	329.7045968	2.9673344	113.6566637	337.2573330
188	2.7609788	117.7494664	325.1037848	2.8705454	115.8482280	332.5591852	2.9846439	113.9917120	340.2246674
189	2.7759341	118.1097055	327.8647636	2.8867928	116.1946332	335.4298306	3.0020543	114.3248172	343.2093113
190	2.7909704	118.4680038	330.6406977	2.9030310	116.5391008	338.3166234	3.0195663	114.6559906	346.2113657
191	2.8060882	118.8243718	333.4316682	2.9193606	116.8816416	341.2196544	3.0371804	114.9852434	349.2309320
192	2.8212878	119.1788198	336.2377564	2.9357820	117.2222663	344.1390150	3.0548973	115.3125866	352.2681124
193	2.8365698	119.5313583	339.0590442	2.9522957	117.5609858	347.0747969	3.0727176	115.6380314	355.3230097
194	2.8519346	119.8819975	341.8956141	2.9683024	117.8978106	350.0270927	3.0906417	115.9615888	358.3957273
195	2.8673826	120.2307476	344.7475486	2.9856025	118.2327513	352.9959951	3.1086705	116.2832697	361.4863690
196	2.8829142	120.5776188	347.6149312	3.0023965	118.5658186	355.9815975	3.1268044	116.6030851	364.5950395
197	2.8985300	120.9226213	350.4978454	3.0192850	118.8970229	358.9839940	3.1450441	116.9210456	367.7218439
198	2.9142304	121.2657651	353.3963754	3.0362684	119.2263745	362.0032790	3.1633902	117.2371622	370.8668880
199	2.9300158	121.6070602	356.3106058	3.0533475	119.5538839	365.0395474	3.1818433	117.5514454	374.0302782
200	2.9458867	121.9465165	359.2406216	3.0705225	119.8795614	368.0928949	3.2004040	117.8639060	377.2121215

Table 1

M	C(6.50,M,12)	A(6.50,M,12)	S(6.50,M,12)	M	C(6.75,M,12)	A(6.75,M,12)	S(6.75,M,12)	M	C(7.00,M,12)	A(7.00,M,12)	S(7.00,M,12)
201	2.9618436	122.2841441	362.1865083	201	3.0877942	120.2034171	371.1634174	201	3.2190731	118.1745544	380.4125255
202	2.9778869	122.6199527	365.1483519	202	3.1051631	120.5254614	374.2512117	202	3.2378510	118.4834012	383.6315986
203	2.9940171	122.9539521	368.1262388	203	3.1226296	120.8457043	377.3563747	203	3.2567385	118.7904569	386.8694496
204	3.0102347	123.2861521	371.1202559	204	3.1401944	121.1641560	380.4790043	204	3.2757361	119.0957318	390.1261881
205	3.0265402	123.6165624	374.1304906	205	3.1578580	121.4808263	383.6191987	205	3.2948446	119.3992363	393.4019242
206	3.0429339	123.9451926	377.1570308	206	3.1756209	121.7957254	386.7770567	206	3.3140645	119.7009805	396.6967687
207	3.0594165	124.2720525	380.1999647	207	3.1934838	122.1088630	389.9526777	207	3.3333965	120.0009748	400.0108332
208	3.0759883	124.5971511	383.2593812	208	3.2114472	122.4202491	393.1461615	208	3.3528413	120.2992293	403.3442297
209	3.0926499	124.9204984	386.3353595	209	3.2295116	122.7298934	396.3576087	209	3.3723996	120.5957541	406.6970711
210	3.1094018	125.2421037	389.4280194	210	3.2476776	123.0378058	399.5871202	210	3.3920719	120.8905592	410.0694707
211	3.1262444	125.5619763	392.5374212	211	3.2659457	123.3439958	402.8347978	211	3.4118590	121.1836545	413.4615426
212	3.1431782	125.8801256	395.6636656	212	3.2843167	123.6484731	406.1007435	212	3.4317615	121.4750501	416.8734016
213	3.1602037	126.1965609	398.8068438	213	3.3027910	123.9512474	409.3850602	213	3.4517801	121.7647557	420.3051631
214	3.1773215	126.5112914	401.9670475	214	3.3213692	124.2523280	412.6878512	214	3.4719155	122.0527811	423.7569432
215	3.1945320	126.8243263	405.1443690	215	3.3400519	124.5517246	416.0092203	215	3.4921683	122.3391361	427.2288587
216	3.2118357	127.1356747	408.3389010	216	3.3588397	124.8494464	419.3492722	216	3.5125393	122.6238305	430.7210271
217	3.2292332	127.4453458	411.5507367	217	3.3777331	125.1455030	422.7081119	217	3.5330291	122.9068737	434.2335664
218	3.2467248	127.7533485	414.7799699	218	3.3967329	125.4399035	426.0858450	218	3.5536385	123.1882754	437.7665955
219	3.2643113	128.0596918	418.0266947	219	3.4158395	125.7326573	429.4825779	219	3.5743680	123.4680452	441.3202340
220	3.2819930	128.3643847	421.2910060	220	3.4350536	126.0237736	432.8984174	220	3.5952185	123.7461924	444.8946020
221	3.2997704	128.6674361	424.5729990	221	3.4543758	126.3132615	436.3334710	221	3.6161906	124.0227265	448.4898206
222	3.3176442	128.9688548	427.8727694	222	3.4738066	126.6011301	439.7878468	222	3.6372851	124.2976568	452.1060112
223	3.3356147	129.2686496	431.1904135	223	3.4933468	126.8873886	443.2616534	223	3.6585026	124.5709927	455.7432963
224	3.3536827	129.5668293	434.5260283	224	3.5129969	127.1720458	446.7550002	224	3.6798438	124.8427433	459.4017988
225	3.3718484	129.8634025	437.8797109	225	3.5327575	127.4551108	450.2679971	225	3.7013096	125.1129180	463.0816427
226	3.3901126	130.1583780	441.2515594	226	3.5526292	127.7365925	453.8007546	226	3.7229006	125.3815257	466.7829522
227	3.4084757	130.4517643	444.6416720	227	3.5726128	128.0164997	457.3533838	227	3.7446175	125.6485757	470.5058528
228	3.4269383	130.7435699	448.0501477	228	3.5927087	128.2948412	460.9259966	228	3.7664611	125.9140769	474.2504703
229	3.4455009	131.0338035	451.4770860	229	3.6129177	128.5716258	464.5187053	229	3.7884321	126.1780384	478.0169314
230	3.4641640	131.3224734	454.9225869	230	3.6332404	128.8468622	468.1316231	230	3.8105313	126.4404690	481.8053635
231	3.4829282	131.6095881	458.3867509	231	3.6536774	129.1205591	471.7648634	231	3.8327594	126.7013776	485.6158947
232	3.5017941	131.8951560	461.8696792	232	3.6742293	129.3927250	475.4185408	232	3.8551172	126.9607731	489.4486541
233	3.5207622	132.1791853	465.3714733	233	3.6948968	129.6633685	479.0927701	233	3.8776053	127.2186642	493.3037713
234	3.5398329	132.4616847	468.8922354	234	3.7156806	129.9324982	482.7876669	234	3.9002247	127.4750597	497.1813766
235	3.5590070	132.7426619	472.4320684	235	3.7365813	130.2001225	486.5033476	235	3.9229760	127.7299682	501.0816013
236	3.5782850	133.0221254	475.9910754	236	3.7575996	130.4662499	490.2399289	236	3.9458600	127.9833984	505.0045773
237	3.5976674	133.3000833	479.5693604	237	3.7787361	130.7308886	493.9975285	237	3.9688776	128.2353588	508.9504374
238	3.6171547	133.5765437	483.1670278	238	3.7999915	130.9940471	497.7762646	238	3.9920293	128.4858580	512.9193149
239	3.6367477	133.8515146	486.7841825	239	3.8213664	131.2557336	501.5762561	239	4.0153162	128.7349044	516.9113443
240	3.6564467	134.1250042	490.4209302	240	3.8428616	131.5159564	505.3976225	240	4.0387389	128.9825064	520.9266605
241	3.6762525	134.3970203	494.0773769	241	3.8644777	131.7747235	509.2404842	241	4.0622982	129.2286725	524.9653993
242	3.6961655	134.6675710	497.7536293	242	3.8862154	132.0320433	513.1049619	242	4.0859949	129.4734109	529.0276975
243	3.7161864	134.9366640	501.4497948	243	3.9080754	132.2879237	516.9911773	243	4.1098299	129.7167300	533.1136924
244	3.7363157	135.2043074	505.1659812	244	3.9300583	132.5423729	520.8992527	244	4.1338039	129.9586379	537.2235223
245	3.7565541	135.4705088	508.9022970	245	3.9521649	132.7953987	524.8293110	245	4.1579177	130.1991429	541.3573261
246	3.7769021	135.7352760	512.8588511	246	3.9743958	133.0470093	528.7814759	246	4.1821723	130.4382531	545.5152439
247	3.7973603	135.9986169	516.4357532	247	3.9967518	133.2972125	532.7558717	247	4.2065683	130.6759766	549.6974161
248	3.8179294	136.2605389	520.2331135	248	4.0192335	133.5460162	536.7526235	248	4.2311066	130.9123214	553.9039844
249	3.8386098	136.5210499	524.0510429	249	4.0418417	133.7934281	540.7718570	249	4.2557880	131.1472955	558.1350910
250	3.8594023	136.7801574	527.8856527	250	4.0645771	134.0394562	544.8136987	250	4.2806135	131.3809069	562.3908790
251	3.8803074	137.0378689	531.7490550	251	4.0874403	134.2841081	548.8782757	251	4.3055837	131.6131634	566.6714925
252	3.9013257	137.2941921	535.6293624	252	4.1104322	134.5273915	552.9657160	252	4.3306996	131.8440730	570.9770762
253	3.9224579	137.5491343	539.5306881	253	4.1335533	134.7693141	557.0761482	253	4.3559620	132.0736434	575.3077758
254	3.9437045	137.8027030	543.4531460	254	4.1568046	135.0098835	561.2097015	254	4.3813718	132.3018824	579.6637379
255	3.9650663	138.0549055	547.3968506	255	4.1801866	135.2491073	565.3665081	255	4.4069298	132.5287978	584.0451097
256	3.9865437	138.3057494	551.3619168	256	4.2037002	135.4869929	569.5466927	256	4.4326369	132.7543971	588.4520395
257	4.0081375	138.5552418	555.3484606	257	4.2273460	135.7235480	573.7503929	257	4.4584940	132.9786881	592.8846764
258	4.0298482	138.8033901	559.3565980	258	4.2511248	135.9587798	577.9777388	258	4.4845018	133.2016783	597.3431703
259	4.0516765	139.0502016	563.3864463	259	4.2750374	136.1926959	582.2288636	259	4.5106614	133.4233753	601.8276722
260	4.0736232	139.2956833	567.4381229	260	4.2990844	136.4253036	586.5039010	260	4.5369736	133.6437865	606.3383326
261	4.0956886	139.5398425	571.5117461	261	4.3232668	136.6566102	590.8029854	261	4.5634393	133.8629195	610.8753072
262	4.1178736	139.7826862	575.6074347	262	4.3475852	136.8866229	595.1262522	262	4.5900594	134.0807816	615.4387465
263	4.1401788	140.0242217	579.7253083	263	4.3720403	137.1153491	599.4738374	263	4.6158347	134.2973802	620.0288059
264	4.1626047	140.2644559	583.8654870	264	4.3966331	137.3427958	603.8458777	264	4.6437662	134.5127227	624.6456406
265	4.1851522	140.5033958	588.0280918	265	4.4213641	137.5689704	608.2425108	265	4.6700549	134.7268162	629.2894068
266	4.2078217	140.7410485	592.2132439	266	4.4462343	137.7938798	612.6638749	266	4.6981015	134.9396682	633.9602617
267	4.2306141	140.9774208	596.4210657	267	4.4712444	138.0175312	617.1101092	267	4.7255071	135.1512857	638.6583632
268	4.2535299	141.2125196	600.6516798	268	4.4963951	138.2399316	621.5813536	268	4.7530726	135.3616759	643.3838703
269	4.2765699	141.4463519	604.9052097	269	4.5216873	138.4610880	626.0777487	269	4.7807988	135.5708459	648.1369429
270	4.2997346	141.6789244	609.1817796	270	4.5471218	138.6810073	630.5994924	270	4.8086868	135.7788029	652.9177418
271	4.3230249	141.9102439	613.4815143	271	4.5726994	138.8996965	635.1465579	271	4.8367375	135.9855039	657.7264286
272	4.3464413	142.1403172	617.8045391	272	4.5984208	139.1171625	639.7192573	272	4.8649518	136.1911057	662.5631661
273	4.3699845	142.3691509	622.1509804	273	4.6242869	139.3334120	644.3176781	273	4.8933307	136.3954655	667.4281179
274	4.3933552	142.5967519	626.5209669	274	4.6502986	139.5484520	648.9419651	274	4.9218751	136.5986401	672.3214486
275	4.4174542	142.8231268	630.9146201	275	4.6764565	139.7622891	653.5922636	275	4.9505861	136.8006364	677.2433237
276	4.4413821	143.0482817	635.3320743	276	4.7027616	139.9749301	658.2687201	276	4.9794645	137.0014612	682.1939098
277	4.4654396	143.2722239	639.7734564	277	4.7292146	140.1863817	662.9714817	277	5.0085114	137.2011273	687.1733743
278	4.4896274	143.4949595	644.2388960	278	4.7558164	140.3966505	667.7006963	278	5.0377207	137.3996235	692.1818856
279	4.5139462	143.7164951	648.7285233	279	4.7825679	140.6057432	672.4565127	279	5.0671144	137.5969745	697.2196133
280	4.5383967	143.9368373	653.2424695	280	4.8094698	140.8136664	677.2390806	280	5.0966726	137.7931810	702.2867277
281	4.5629797	144.1559923	657.7808662	281	4.8365231	141.0204265	682.0485504	281	5.1264032	137.9882495	707.3834003
282	4.5876958	144.3739667	662.3438459	282	4.8637285	141.2260300	686.8850735	282	5.1563072	138.1821868	712.5098035
283	4.6125459	144.5907667	666.9315417	283	4.8910870	141.4304836	691.7488020	283	5.1863857	138.3749993	717.6661107
284	4.6375305	144.8063987	671.5440876	284	4.9185994	141.6337935	696.6398891	284	5.2166396	138.5666935	722.8524963
285	4.6626504	145.0208690	676.1816181	285	4.9462665	141.8359662	701.5584884	285	5.2470700	138.7572761	728.0691359
286	4.6879065	145.2341838	680.8442685	286	4.9740893	142.0370080	706.5047549	286	5.2776779	138.9467534	733.3162058
287	4.7132993	145.4463494	685.5321750	287	5.0020685	142.2369253	711.4789442	287	5.3084643	139.1351318	738.5938837
288	4.7388297	145.6573720	690.2454743	288	5.0302051	142.4357243	716.4809127	288	5.3394304	139.3224177	743.9023480
289	4.7644983	145.8672577	694.9843039	289	5.0585000	142.6334114	721.5111178	289	5.3705770	139.5086174	749.2417784
290	4.7903060	146.0760126	699.7488022	290	5.0869541	142.8299927	726.5696179	290	5.4019054	139.6937373	754.6123555
291	4.8162535	146.2836429	704.5391082	291	5.1155682	143.0254744	731.6565720	291	5.4334165	139.8777835	760.0142609
292	4.8423415	146.4901545	709.3553618	292	5.1443433	143.2198627	736.7721402	292	5.4651115	140.0607624	765.4476774
293	4.8685709	146.6955536	714.1977033	293	5.1732802	143.4131636	741.9164835	293	5.4969913	140.2426801	770.9127889
294	4.8949423	146.8998461	719.0662747	294	5.2023799	143.6053833	747.0897637	294	5.5290571	140.4235428	776.4097801
295	4.9214566	147.1030380	723.9612165	295	5.2316433	143.7965279	752.2921437	295	5.5613099	140.6033555	781.9388372
296	4.9481145	147.3051352	728.8826731	296	5.2610713	143.9866032	757.5237870	296	5.5937509	140.7821274	787.5001471
297	4.9749168	147.5061436	733.8307876	297	5.2906648	144.1756154	762.7848583	297	5.6263811	140.9598616	793.0938979
298	5.0018642	147.7060690	738.8057044	298	5.3204248	144.3635703	768.0755231	298	5.6592016	141.1365650	798.7202790
299	5.0289577	147.9049174	743.8075686	299	5.3503522	144.5504739	773.3959479	299	5.6922136	141.3122435	804.3794807
300	5.0561979	148.1026944	748.8365263	300	5.3804479	144.7363320	778.7463002	300	5.7254182	141.4869033	810.0716943

Table 1

401

M	C(6.50,M,12)	A(6.50,M,12)	S(6.50,M,12)	M	C(6.75,M,12)	A(6.75,M,12)	S(6.75,M,12)	M	C(7.00,M,12)	A(7.00,M,12)	S(7.00,M,12)
301	5.0835856	148.2994060	753.8927241	301	5.4107130	144.9211505	784.1267481	301	5.7588165	141.6605500	815.7971125
302	5.1111217	148.4950578	758.9763097	302	5.4411482	145.1049353	789.5374611	302	5.7924096	141.8331898	821.5559290
303	5.1388069	148.6896555	764.0874314	303	5.4717547	145.2876920	794.9786093	303	5.8261986	142.0048283	827.3483386
304	5.1666421	148.8832048	769.2262384	304	5.5025333	145.4694265	800.4503640	304	5.8601848	142.1754714	833.1745373
305	5.1946281	149.0757113	774.3928805	305	5.5334851	145.6501444	805.9526973	305	5.8943692	142.3451248	839.0347221
306	5.2227657	149.2671808	779.5875086	306	5.5646109	145.8298515	811.4663823	306	5.9287530	142.5137943	844.9290913
307	5.2510557	149.4576187	784.8102743	307	5.5959118	146.0085534	817.0509932	307	5.9633374	142.6814857	850.8578443
308	5.2794989	149.6470306	790.0613299	308	5.6273388	146.1862557	822.6469051	308	5.9981236	142.8482045	856.8211818
309	5.3080962	149.8354220	795.3408288	309	5.6550429	146.3629640	828.2742939	309	6.0331126	143.0139564	862.8193053
310	5.3368484	150.0227986	800.6489250	310	5.6908750	146.5386839	833.9333368	310	6.0683058	143.1787470	868.8524180
311	5.3657563	150.2091656	805.9857733	311	5.7228862	146.7134209	839.6242119	311	6.1037042	143.3425820	874.9207237
312	5.3948208	150.3945285	811.3515296	312	5.7550774	146.8871805	845.3470981	312	6.1393092	143.5054667	881.0244280
313	5.4240427	150.5788929	816.7463504	313	5.7874497	147.0599682	851.1021755	313	6.1751218	143.6674069	887.1637371
314	5.4534230	150.7622639	822.1703931	314	5.8200041	147.2317894	856.8896252	314	6.2111434	143.8284078	893.3388589
315	5.4829623	150.9446471	827.6238161	315	5.8527417	147.4026495	862.7096294	315	6.2473750	143.9884750	899.5500023
316	5.5126617	151.1260477	833.1067784	316	5.8856633	147.5725539	868.5523711	316	6.2838180	144.1476140	905.7973773
317	5.5425220	151.3064710	838.6194402	317	5.9187702	147.7415079	874.4480344	317	6.3204736	144.3058300	912.0811954
318	5.5725440	151.4859222	844.1619621	318	5.9520633	147.9095169	880.3668046	318	6.3573431	144.4631284	918.4016690
319	5.6027286	151.6644067	849.7345061	319	5.9855436	148.0765861	886.3188679	319	6.3944276	144.6195145	924.7590121
320	5.6333767	151.8419296	855.3372347	320	6.0192123	148.2427208	892.3044115	320	6.4317284	144.7749937	931.1534397
321	5.6635892	152.0184960	860.9703114	321	6.0530704	148.4079262	898.3236239	321	6.4692468	144.9295712	937.5851681
322	5.6942670	152.1941113	866.6339006	322	6.0871189	148.5722075	904.3766943	322	6.5069841	145.0832523	944.0544149
323	5.7251109	152.3687804	872.3281675	323	6.1213590	148.7355699	910.4638132	323	6.5449415	145.2360420	950.5613990
324	5.7561219	152.5425084	878.0532785	324	6.1557916	148.8980186	916.5851721	324	6.5831203	145.3879457	957.1063405
325	5.7873009	152.7153006	883.8094004	325	6.1904179	149.0595586	922.7409637	325	6.6215219	145.5389683	963.6894608
326	5.8186488	152.8871618	889.5967013	326	6.2252390	149.2201950	928.9313817	326	6.6601474	145.6891152	970.3109827
327	5.8501665	153.0580971	895.4153501	327	6.2602560	149.3799328	935.1566207	327	6.6989983	145.8383912	976.9711301
328	5.8818549	153.2281115	901.2655166	328	6.2954699	149.5387772	941.4168767	328	6.7380758	145.9868015	983.6701283
329	5.9137149	153.3972099	907.1473715	329	6.3308820	149.6967331	947.7123466	329	6.7773812	146.1343512	990.4082041
330	5.9457476	153.5653973	913.0610864	330	6.3664932	149.8538054	954.0432286	330	6.8169159	146.2810451	997.1855853
331	5.9779537	153.7326787	919.0068340	331	6.4023047	150.0099992	960.4097217	331	6.8566813	146.4268882	1004.0025012
332	6.0103343	153.8990588	924.9847677	332	6.4383177	150.1653193	966.8120264	332	6.8956786	146.5718856	1010.8591825
333	6.0428903	154.0645425	930.9951220	333	6.4745332	150.3197706	973.2503441	333	6.9383092	146.7160420	1017.7558611
334	6.0756226	154.2291347	937.0380122	334	6.5109524	150.4733579	979.7248773	334	6.9773745	146.8593624	1024.6927703
335	6.1085322	154.3928401	943.1136348	335	6.5475766	150.6260862	986.2358297	335	7.0180759	147.0018516	1031.6701448
336	6.1416201	154.5556636	949.2221670	336	6.5844067	150.7779601	992.7834063	336	7.0590146	147.1435144	1038.6882206
337	6.1748872	154.7176099	955.3637871	337	6.6214440	150.9289846	999.3678129	337	7.1001922	147.2843556	1045.7472352
338	6.2083345	154.8786837	961.5386743	338	6.6586896	151.0791643	1005.9892569	338	7.1416100	147.4243801	1052.8474275
339	6.2419630	155.0388997	967.7470087	339	6.6961447	151.2285040	1012.6479465	339	7.1832694	147.5635925	1059.9890375
340	6.2757736	155.1982326	973.9889717	340	6.7338105	151.3770083	1019.3440912	340	7.2251718	147.7019975	1067.1723069
341	6.3097674	155.3567171	980.2647453	341	6.7716882	151.5246820	1026.0779017	341	7.2673186	147.8395998	1074.3974787
342	6.3439453	155.5143477	986.5745127	342	6.8097790	151.6715296	1032.8495899	342	7.3097113	147.9764041	1081.6647973
343	6.3783083	155.6711291	992.9184500	343	6.8480840	151.8175559	1039.6593689	343	7.3523513	148.1124150	1088.9745086
344	6.4128575	155.8270658	999.2967663	344	6.8866044	151.9627653	1046.5074528	344	7.3952400	148.2476372	1096.3268599
345	6.4475938	155.9821624	1006.7096238	345	6.9253416	152.1071625	1053.3940573	345	7.4383789	148.3820750	1103.7220999
346	6.4825163	156.1364234	1012.1572176	346	6.9642966	152.2507520	1060.3193988	346	7.4817695	148.5157333	1111.1604789
347	6.5176319	156.2898534	1018.6397359	347	7.0034708	152.3935384	1067.2836955	347	7.5254131	148.6486163	1118.6422483
348	6.5529358	156.4424568	1025.1573678	348	7.0428653	152.5355260	1074.2871663	348	7.5693114	148.7807288	1126.1676615
349	6.5884308	156.5942380	1031.7103035	349	7.0824814	152.6767195	1081.3300316	349	7.6134657	148.9120750	1133.7369728
350	6.6241182	156.7452015	1038.2987344	350	7.1223204	152.8171232	1088.4125130	350	7.6578776	149.0426595	1141.3504385
351	6.6599988	156.8953516	1044.9228525	351	7.1623834	152.9567415	1095.5348334	351	7.7025485	149.1724866	1149.0083161
352	6.6960738	157.0446929	1051.5828513	352	7.2026719	153.0955789	1102.6972169	352	7.7474801	149.3015609	1156.7108646
353	6.7323442	157.1932295	1058.2789251	353	7.2431869	153.2336396	1109.8998887	353	7.7926737	149.4298865	1164.4583447
354	6.7688111	157.3409660	1065.0112693	354	7.2839298	153.3709282	1117.1430756	354	7.8381310	149.5574679	1172.2510183
355	6.8054754	157.4879065	1071.7800803	355	7.3249019	153.5074488	1124.4270054	355	7.8835534	149.6843095	1180.0891493
356	6.8423384	157.6340554	1078.5855558	356	7.3661045	153.6432057	1131.7519073	356	7.9298425	149.8104154	1187.9730027
357	6.8794011	157.7794168	1085.4278942	357	7.4075388	153.7782033	1139.1180118	357	7.9760999	149.9357899	1195.9028452
358	6.9166645	157.9239952	1092.3072953	358	7.4492062	153.9124458	1146.5255506	358	8.0226272	150.0604374	1203.8789451
359	6.9541298	158.0677946	1099.2239598	359	7.4911080	154.0459374	1153.9747569	359	8.0694258	150.1843619	1211.9015723
360	6.9917980	158.2108194	1106.1780386	360	7.5332455	154.1786823	1161.4658649	360	8.1164975	150.3075678	1219.9709982
361	7.0296702	158.3530736	1113.1698376	361	7.5756200	154.3106847	1168.9991104	361	8.1638437	150.4300591	1228.0874949
362	7.0677476	158.4945613	1120.1995779	362	7.6182329	154.4419488	1176.5747304	362	8.2114662	150.5518400	1236.2513394
363	7.1060312	158.6352869	1127.2673055	363	7.6610854	154.5724786	1184.1929633	363	8.2593664	150.6729147	1244.4628056
364	7.1445223	158.7752542	1134.3733367	364	7.7041790	154.7022783	1191.8540487	364	8.3075460	150.7932872	1252.7221719
365	7.1832217	158.9144675	1141.5178590	365	7.7475150	154.8313519	1199.5582277	365	8.3560067	150.9129616	1261.0297180
366	7.2221309	159.0529308	1148.7010807	366	7.7910948	154.9597036	1207.3057428	366	8.4047501	151.0319419	1269.3857247
367	7.2612507	159.1906482	1155.9232116	367	7.8349197	155.0873373	1215.0968376	367	8.4537778	151.1502322	1277.7904747
368	7.3005825	159.3276235	1163.1844623	368	7.8789911	155.2142571	1222.9317573	368	8.5030915	151.2678365	1286.2442525
369	7.3401273	159.4638609	1170.4850448	369	7.9233105	155.3404670	1230.8107484	369	8.5526929	151.3847588	1294.7473440
370	7.3798864	159.5993544	1177.8251722	370	7.9678791	155.4659709	1238.7340589	370	8.6025836	151.5010029	1303.3000368
371	7.4198607	159.7341378	1185.2050585	371	8.0126984	155.5907728	1246.7019380	371	8.6527653	151.6165729	1311.9026204
372	7.4600517	159.8691851	1192.6249193	372	8.0577698	155.7148766	1254.7146364	372	8.7032398	151.7314726	1320.5553857
373	7.5004603	160.0015103	1200.0849709	373	8.1030948	155.8382862	1262.7724063	373	8.7540087	151.8457060	1329.2586255
374	7.5410878	160.1341172	1207.5854312	374	8.1486747	155.9610056	1270.8755011	374	8.8050737	151.9592769	1338.0126341
375	7.5819353	160.2660096	1215.1265190	375	8.1945110	156.0830385	1279.0241758	375	8.8564366	152.0721891	1346.8177078
376	7.6230041	160.3971915	1222.7084543	376	8.2406051	156.2043888	1287.2186868	376	8.9080992	152.1844465	1355.6741445
377	7.6642954	160.5276666	1230.3314564	377	8.2869585	156.3250603	1295.4592919	377	8.9600631	152.2960529	1364.5822437
378	7.7058103	160.6574388	1237.9957538	378	8.3335727	156.4450569	1303.7462504	378	9.0123301	152.4070120	1373.5423068
379	7.7475501	160.7865119	1245.7015642	379	8.3804490	156.5643822	1312.0798231	379	9.0649021	152.5173276	1382.5546369
380	7.7895160	160.9148896	1253.4491143	380	8.4275890	156.6830401	1320.4602721	380	9.1177807	152.6270034	1391.6195390
381	7.8317093	161.0425756	1261.2386304	381	8.4749942	156.8010343	1328.8878611	381	9.1709677	152.7360431	1400.7373196
382	7.8741310	161.1695737	1269.0703396	382	8.5226662	156.9183685	1337.3628054	382	9.2244650	152.8444505	1409.9082873
383	7.9167826	161.2958877	1276.9444706	383	8.5706061	157.0350464	1345.8855214	383	9.2782744	152.9522292	1419.1327523
384	7.9596651	161.4215211	1284.8612532	384	8.6188157	157.1510716	1354.4561275	384	9.3323977	153.0593828	1428.4110267
385	8.0027800	161.5464777	1292.8209183	385	8.6672966	157.2664478	1363.0749432	385	9.3868367	153.1659149	1437.7434244
386	8.0461284	161.6707611	1300.8236983	386	8.7160501	157.3811787	1371.7422398	386	9.4415932	153.2718293	1447.1302611
387	8.0897116	161.7943749	1308.8698267	387	8.7650779	157.4952678	1380.4582899	387	9.4966692	153.3771293	1456.5718543
388	8.1335308	161.9173227	1316.9595383	388	8.8143815	157.6087188	1389.2233678	388	9.5520664	153.4818187	1466.0685224
389	8.1775875	162.0396082	1325.0930691	389	8.8639624	157.7215351	1398.0377493	389	9.6077868	153.5859010	1475.6205898
390	8.2218827	162.1612348	1333.2706566	390	8.9138221	157.8337204	1406.9017116	390	9.6638322	153.6893796	1485.2283766
391	8.2664179	162.2822062	1341.4925393	391	8.9639624	157.9452782	1415.8155337	391	9.7202046	153.7922581	1494.8922088
392	8.3111944	162.4025258	1349.7589572	392	9.0143847	158.0562121	1424.7794961	392	9.7769058	153.8945399	1504.6124134
393	8.3562133	162.5221673	1358.0701516	393	9.0650906	158.1665253	1433.7938808	393	9.8339377	153.9962286	1514.3893191
394	8.4014762	162.6412240	1366.4263649	394	9.1160817	158.2762216	1442.8589714	394	9.8913023	154.0973275	1524.2232568
395	8.4469842	162.7596094	1374.8278411	395	9.1673597	158.3853043	1451.9750531	395	9.9490016	154.1978401	1534.1145592
396	8.4927386	162.8773571	1383.2748252	396	9.2189261	158.4937768	1461.1424128	396	10.0070375	154.2977698	1544.0635608
397	8.5387410	162.9944703	1391.7675639	397	9.2707825	158.6016425	1470.3613389	397	10.0654118	154.3971199	1554.0705983
398	8.5849925	163.1109527	1400.3063049	398	9.3229307	158.7089049	1479.6321214	398	10.1241267	154.4958939	1564.1360101
399	8.6314945	163.2268075	1408.8912974	399	9.3753722	158.8155674	1488.9550521	399	10.1831841	154.5940950	1574.2601368
400	8.6782485	163.3420381	1417.5227919	400	9.4281086	158.9216332	1498.3304243	400	10.2425861	154.6917266	1584.4433210

Table 1

M	C(6.50,M,12)	A(6.50,M,12)	S(6.50,M,12)	M	C(6.75,M,12)	A(6.75,M,12)	S(6.75,M,12)	M	C(7.00,M,12)	A(7.00,M,12)	S(7.00,M,12)
401	8.7252556	163.4566479	1426.2010404	401	9.4811418	159.0271057	1507.7585330	401	10.3023345	154.7887920	1594.6859070
402	8.7725174	163.5706403	1434.9262960	402	9.5344732	159.1319883	1517.2396747	402	10.3624314	154.8852944	1604.9882415
403	8.8200353	163.6840185	1443.6988135	403	9.5881046	159.2362842	1526.7741479	403	10.4228789	154.9812372	1615.3506729
404	8.8678104	163.7967859	1452.5188487	404	9.6420377	159.3399967	1536.3622525	404	10.4836791	155.0766235	1625.7735519
405	8.9158444	163.9089458	1461.3866592	405	9.6962741	159.4431291	1546.0042902	405	10.5448339	155.1714567	1636.2572309
406	8.9641386	164.0205014	1470.3025036	406	9.7508157	159.5456846	1555.7005643	406	10.6063454	155.2657399	1646.8020648
407	9.0126943	164.1314560	1479.2666422	407	9.8056640	159.6476665	1565.4513800	407	10.6682157	155.3594763	1657.4084102
408	9.0615131	164.2418129	1488.2793365	408	9.8608209	159.7490775	1575.2570441	408	10.7304470	155.4526690	1668.0766259
409	9.1105963	164.3515752	1497.3408496	409	9.9162880	159.8499221	1585.1178649	409	10.7930413	155.5453213	1678.8070729
410	9.1599453	164.4607461	1506.4514459	410	9.9720671	159.9502022	1595.0341529	410	10.8560007	155.6374363	1689.6001142
411	9.2095617	164.5693289	1515.6113912	411	10.0281600	160.0499214	1605.0062201	411	10.9193274	155.7290170	1700.4561149
412	9.2594468	164.6773267	1524.8209529	412	10.0845684	160.1490828	1615.0343801	412	10.9830234	155.8200666	1711.3754422
413	9.3096022	164.7847427	1534.0803998	413	10.1412941	160.2476896	1625.1189485	413	11.0470911	155.9105882	1722.3584656
414	9.3600292	164.8915800	1543.3900019	414	10.1983389	160.3457447	1635.2602426	414	11.1115324	156.0005848	1733.4055567
415	9.4107293	164.9978417	1552.7500311	415	10.2557045	160.4432515	1645.4585814	415	11.1763497	156.0900594	1744.5170391
416	9.4617041	165.1035309	1562.1607605	416	10.3133929	160.5402128	1655.7142860	416	11.2415451	156.1790152	1755.6934388
417	9.5129550	165.2086507	1571.6224646	417	10.3714057	160.6366317	1666.0276789	417	11.3071208	156.2674550	1766.9349839
418	9.5644835	165.3132042	1581.1354196	418	10.4297449	160.7325113	1676.3990846	418	11.3730790	156.3553820	1778.2421047
419	9.6162912	165.4171944	1590.6999032	419	10.4884122	160.8278546	1686.8288294	419	11.4394219	156.4427990	1789.6151836
420	9.6683794	165.5206243	1600.3161943	420	10.5474095	160.9226647	1697.3172416	420	11.5061519	156.5297090	1801.0546055
421	9.7207498	165.6234970	1609.9845737	421	10.6067387	161.0169443	1707.8646511	421	11.5732711	156.6161150	1812.5607574
422	9.7734038	165.7258155	1619.7053235	422	10.6664016	161.1106967	1718.4713898	422	11.6407818	156.7020199	1824.1340285
423	9.8263431	165.8275828	1629.4787274	423	10.7264001	161.2039246	1729.1377914	423	11.7086864	156.7874266	1835.7748104
424	9.8795691	165.9288018	1639.3050705	424	10.7867361	161.2966310	1739.8641915	424	11.7769871	156.8723379	1847.4834958
425	9.9330935	166.0294755	1649.1846396	425	10.8474115	161.3888189	1750.6509275	425	11.8456862	156.9567568	1859.2604839
426	9.9868877	166.1296068	1659.1177231	426	10.9084282	161.4804912	1761.4983390	426	11.9147860	157.0406862	1871.1061700
427	10.0409833	166.2291986	1669.1046108	427	10.9697881	161.5716506	1772.4067672	427	11.9842889	157.1241287	1883.0209560
428	10.0953720	166.3282509	1679.1455941	428	11.0314931	161.6623002	1783.3765553	428	12.0541973	157.2070874	1895.0052450
429	10.1500552	166.4267755	1689.2409661	429	11.0935453	161.7524427	1794.4080484	429	12.1245134	157.2895649	1907.0594422
430	10.2050347	166.5247664	1699.3910213	430	11.1559465	161.8420810	1805.5015937	430	12.1952398	157.3715641	1919.1839557
431	10.2603120	166.6222293	1709.5960560	431	11.2186987	161.9312179	1816.6575402	431	12.2663787	157.4530878	1931.3791954
432	10.3158887	166.7191671	1719.8563680	432	11.2818039	162.0198562	1827.8762389	432	12.3379325	157.5341386	1943.6455741
433	10.3717664	166.8155827	1730.1722567	433	11.3452640	162.1079987	1839.1580427	433	12.4099038	157.6147195	1955.9835066
434	10.4279468	166.9114789	1740.5440231	434	11.4090811	162.1956482	1850.5033067	434	12.4822949	157.6948329	1968.3934104
435	10.4844315	167.0068584	1750.9719699	435	11.4732572	162.2828074	1861.9123878	435	12.5551083	157.7744818	1980.8757053
436	10.5412222	167.1017241	1761.4564014	436	11.5377943	162.3694791	1873.3856450	436	12.6283464	157.8536687	1993.4308136
437	10.5983205	167.1960786	1771.9976364	437	11.6026944	162.4556659	1884.9234393	437	12.7020118	157.9323964	2006.0591601
438	10.6557280	167.2899249	1782.5959441	438	11.6679595	162.5413707	1896.5261337	438	12.7761069	158.0106675	2018.7611718
439	10.7134466	167.3832655	1793.2516721	439	11.7335918	162.6265961	1908.1940932	439	12.8503341	158.0884847	2031.5372787
440	10.7714777	167.4761033	1803.9651187	440	11.7995932	162.7113448	1919.9276850	440	12.9255962	158.1658505	2044.3879128
441	10.8298232	167.5684409	1814.7365965	441	11.8659660	162.7956195	1931.7272782	441	13.0009355	158.2427677	2057.3135090
442	10.8884848	167.6602810	1825.5664197	442	11.9327120	162.8794227	1943.5932442	442	13.0763346	158.3192388	2070.3145045
443	10.9474641	167.7516264	1836.4549019	443	11.9998335	162.9627572	1955.5259562	443	13.1531162	158.3952664	2083.3913391
444	11.0067628	167.8424796	1847.4023606	444	12.0673326	163.0456255	1967.5257897	444	13.2298427	158.4708531	2096.5444553
445	11.0663828	167.9328434	1858.4091114	445	12.1352113	163.1280304	1979.5931223	445	13.3070168	158.5460015	2109.7742980
446	11.1263257	168.0227203	1869.4755142	446	12.2034719	163.2099743	1991.7283336	446	13.3846410	158.6207140	2123.0813147
447	11.1865933	168.1121130	1880.6018400	447	12.2721164	163.2914598	2003.9318055	447	13.4627101	158.6949932	2136.4659557
448	11.2471874	168.2010242	1891.7884333	448	12.3411471	163.3724895	2016.2039219	448	13.5412506	158.7688416	2149.9286738
449	11.3081096	168.2894563	1903.0356206	449	12.4105660	163.4530660	2028.5450690	449	13.6202412	158.8422617	2163.4699244
450	11.3693619	168.3774120	1914.3437303	450	12.4803755	163.5331918	2040.9556350	450	13.6996927	158.9152561	2177.0910603
451	11.4309459	168.4648938	1925.7130921	451	12.5505776	163.6128695	2053.4360105	451	13.7796075	158.9878271	2190.7898583
452	11.4928636	168.5519043	1937.1440381	452	12.6211746	163.6921017	2065.9865881	452	13.8598886	159.0599772	2204.5694659
453	11.5551166	168.6384460	1948.6369014	453	12.6921687	163.7708901	2078.6077627	453	13.9403385	159.1317089	2218.4294544
454	11.6177068	168.7245215	1960.1920182	454	12.7635621	163.8492382	2091.2999313	454	14.0221601	159.2030246	2232.3702924
455	11.6806360	168.8101333	1971.8097252	455	12.8353572	163.9271479	2104.0634935	455	14.1039560	159.2739267	2246.3924530
456	11.7439061	168.8952839	1983.4903610	456	12.9075561	164.0046219	2116.8988506	456	14.1862291	159.3444176	2260.4964090
457	11.8075190	168.9799757	1995.2342671	457	12.9801611	164.0816626	2129.8064067	457	14.2668821	159.4144997	2274.6826381
458	11.8714764	169.0642112	2007.0417861	458	13.0531745	164.1582723	2142.7865678	458	14.3522178	159.4841753	2288.9516201
459	11.9357803	169.1479929	2018.9132645	459	13.1265986	164.2344535	2155.8397422	459	14.4359391	159.5534469	2303.3038379
460	12.0004323	169.2313232	2030.8490427	460	13.2004357	164.3102086	2168.9663408	460	14.5201487	159.6223167	2317.7397770
461	12.0654347	169.3142046	2042.8494750	461	13.2746881	164.3855399	2182.1667765	461	14.6048496	159.6907871	2332.2593257
462	12.1307891	169.3966395	2054.9149097	462	13.3493583	164.4604499	2195.4414646	462	14.6900445	159.7588604	2346.8647753
463	12.1964976	169.4786302	2067.0456988	463	13.4244484	164.5349408	2208.7908229	463	14.7757365	159.8265389	2361.5548199
464	12.2625619	169.5601793	2079.2421963	464	13.4999609	164.6090151	2222.2152713	464	14.8619283	159.8938429	2376.3305563
465	12.3289841	169.6412889	2091.5047582	465	13.5758902	164.6826751	2235.7152322	465	14.9486228	159.9607207	2391.1924846
466	12.3957661	169.7219616	2103.8337424	466	13.6522626	164.7559230	2249.2911304	466	15.0358321	160.0272286	2406.1411074
467	12.4629099	169.8021997	2116.2295085	467	13.7290566	164.8287612	2262.9433930	467	15.1235321	160.0933507	2421.1789306
468	12.5304173	169.8820055	2128.6924183	468	13.8062825	164.9011920	2276.6724496	468	15.2117527	160.1590893	2436.3004627
469	12.5982904	169.9613814	2141.2228356	469	13.8839429	164.9732177	2290.4787322	469	15.3004879	160.2244467	2451.5122154
470	12.6665311	170.0403296	2153.8211260	470	13.9620401	165.0448404	2304.3626750	470	15.3897408	160.2894251	2466.8127034
471	12.7351415	170.1188525	2166.4876571	471	14.0405765	165.1160626	2318.3247151	471	15.4795143	160.3540266	2482.2024442
472	12.8041235	170.1969523	2179.2227986	472	14.1195548	165.1868864	2332.3652917	472	15.5698141	160.4182534	2497.6819584
473	12.8734792	170.2746314	2192.0269221	473	14.1989773	165.2573140	2346.4848464	473	15.6606353	160.4821078	2513.2517699
474	12.9432105	170.3516920	2204.9004013	474	14.2788465	165.3273476	2360.6838237	474	15.7519891	160.5455919	2528.9124052
475	13.0133196	170.4287363	2217.8436118	475	14.3591650	165.3960896	2374.9626702	475	15.8438757	160.6087077	2544.6643943
476	13.0838084	170.5051667	2230.8569314	476	14.4399353	165.4662420	2389.3218353	476	15.9362983	160.6714575	2560.5082699
477	13.1546790	170.5811852	2243.9407398	477	14.5211600	165.5351070	2403.7617706	477	16.0292600	160.7338435	2576.4445094
478	13.2259335	170.6567942	2257.0954188	478	14.6028415	165.6035868	2418.2829306	478	16.1227640	160.7958676	2592.4738282
479	13.2975740	170.7319960	2270.3213524	479	14.6849825	165.6716636	2432.8857721	479	16.2166135	160.8575320	2608.5965922
480	13.3696025	170.8067925	2283.6189549	480	14.7675855	165.7393995	2447.5707546	480	16.3114116	160.9188387	2624.8134057
481	13.4420212	170.8811861	2296.9885289	481	14.8505532	165.8067366	2462.3383401	481	16.4065615	160.9797900	2641.1248173
482	13.5148322	170.9551789	2310.4303057	482	14.9341881	165.8736970	2477.1889933	482	16.5022664	161.0403877	2657.5313787
483	13.5880375	171.0287730	2323.9453823	483	15.0101929	165.9402829	2492.1231814	483	16.5985296	161.1006340	2674.0336451
484	13.6616394	171.1019707	2337.5334198	484	15.1026703	166.0064964	2507.1413743	484	16.6953544	161.1605309	2690.6321747
485	13.7356399	171.1747740	2351.1950592	485	15.1876228	166.0723395	2522.2440446	485	16.7927439	161.2200804	2707.3275291
486	13.8100413	171.2471850	2364.9305091	486	15.2730531	166.1378143	2537.4316673	486	16.8907016	161.2792846	2724.1202730
487	13.8848457	171.3192060	2378.7407404	487	15.3589641	166.2029228	2552.7047205	487	16.9892307	161.3381454	2741.0109047
488	13.9600553	171.3908390	2392.6255661	488	15.4453582	166.2676672	2568.0636846	488	17.0883346	161.3966649	2758.0002054
489	14.0356722	171.4620860	2406.5856414	489	15.5322384	166.3320494	2583.5090428	489	17.1880165	161.4548449	2775.0885399
490	14.1116988	171.5329492	2420.6213136	490	15.6196072	166.3960715	2599.0412812	490	17.2882799	161.5126876	2792.2765564
491	14.1881372	171.6034306	2434.7330124	491	15.7074675	166.4597355	2614.6608884	491	17.3891282	161.5701948	2809.5648364
492	14.2649896	171.6735323	2448.9210448	492	15.7958220	166.5230434	2630.3683560	492	17.4905648	161.6273685	2826.9539646
493	14.3422583	171.7432563	2463.1861392	493	15.8846735	166.5859971	2646.1641780	493	17.5925931	161.6842106	2844.4445294
494	14.4199455	171.8126047	2477.5283975	494	15.9740248	166.6485988	2662.0488515	494	17.6952166	161.7407230	2862.0371225
495	14.4980535	171.8815795	2491.9483430	495	16.0638787	166.7108502	2678.0228763	495	17.7984387	161.7969077	2879.7323391
496	14.5765847	171.9501827	2506.4463965	496	16.1542380	166.7727535	2694.0867550	496	17.9022629	161.8527666	2897.5307778
497	14.6555412	172.0184162	2521.0229812	497	16.2451056	166.8343105	2710.2409930	497	18.0066928	161.9083015	2915.4330407
498	14.7349254	172.0862822	2535.6785224	498	16.3364843	166.8955232	2726.4860986	498	18.1117318	161.9635143	2933.4397334
499	14.8147395	172.1537826	2550.4134477	499	16.4283771	166.9563935	2742.8225830	499	18.2173836	162.0184070	2951.5514652
500	14.8949860	172.2209192	2565.2281872	500	16.5207867	167.0169233	2759.2509600	500	18.3236516	162.0729812	2969.7688488

Table 1

403

M	C(7.25,M,12)	A(7.25,M,12)	S(7.25,M,12)	M	C(7.50,M,12)	A(7.50,M,12)	S(7.50,M,12)	M	C(7.75,M,12)	A(7.75,M,12)	S(7.75,M,12)
1	1.0060417	.9939946	1.0000000	1	1.0062500	.9937888	1.0000000	1	1.0064583	.9935831	1.0000000
2	1.0121198	1.9820199	2.0060417	2	1.0125391	1.9814050	2.0062500	2	1.0129584	1.9807905	2.0064583
3	1.0182347	2.9641117	3.0181615	3	1.0188674	2.9628870	3.0187891	3	1.0195004	2.9616631	3.0194167
4	1.0243866	3.9403057	4.0363962	4	1.0252354	3.9382728	4.0376565	4	1.0260847	3.9352415	4.0389171
5	1.0305756	4.9106373	5.0607828	5	1.0316431	4.9076003	5.0628918	5	1.0327115	4.9045662	5.0650018
6	1.0368020	5.8751416	6.0913584	6	1.0380908	5.8709071	6.0945349	6	1.0393811	5.8566773	6.0977133
7	1.0430660	6.8338538	7.1281603	7	1.0445789	6.8282307	7.1326258	7	1.0460937	6.8226145	7.1370943
8	1.0493678	7.7868085	8.1712263	8	1.0511075	7.7796081	8.1772047	8	1.0528498	7.7724177	8.1831881
9	1.0557078	8.7340403	9.2205941	9	1.0576770	8.7250764	9.2283122	9	1.0596494	8.7161260	9.2360378
10	1.0620860	9.6755837	10.2763019	10	1.0642874	9.6646722	10.2859892	10	1.0664930	9.6537787	10.2956872
11	1.0685028	10.6114727	11.3383878	11	1.0709392	10.5984320	11.3502766	11	1.0733807	10.5954146	11.3621802
12	1.0749583	11.5417413	12.4068906	12	1.0776326	11.5263920	12.4212158	12	1.0803130	11.5110722	12.4355509
13	1.0814528	12.4664234	13.4818489	13	1.0843678	12.4485884	13.4988484	13	1.0872900	12.4307920	13.5158739
14	1.0879866	13.3855523	14.5633017	14	1.0911451	13.3650568	14.5832162	14	1.0943121	13.3446061	14.6031640
15	1.0945599	14.2991615	15.6512884	15	1.0979648	14.2758328	15.6743613	15	1.1013795	14.2525584	15.6974761
16	1.1011728	15.2072842	16.7458482	16	1.1048270	15.1809519	16.7723261	16	1.1084926	15.1546844	16.7988556
17	1.1078258	16.1099532	17.8470211	17	1.1117322	16.0804491	17.8771531	17	1.1156516	16.0510215	17.9073482
18	1.1145189	17.0072014	18.9548468	18	1.1186805	16.9743593	18.9888853	18	1.1228569	16.9416070	19.0229998
19	1.1212524	17.8990612	20.0693657	19	1.1256723	17.8627173	20.1075659	19	1.1301087	17.8264776	20.1458567
20	1.1280267	18.7855651	21.1906181	20	1.1327077	18.7455576	21.2332381	20	1.1374073	18.7056702	21.2759654
21	1.1348418	19.6667452	22.3186447	21	1.1397872	19.6229144	22.3659459	21	1.1447530	19.5792210	22.4133726
22	1.1416981	20.5426334	23.4534866	22	1.1469108	20.4948217	23.5057330	22	1.1521462	20.4471664	23.5581257
23	1.1485959	21.4132617	24.5951847	23	1.1540790	21.3613135	24.6526439	23	1.1595872	21.3095423	24.7102719
24	1.1555353	22.2786614	25.7437806	24	1.1612920	22.2224234	25.8067229	24	1.1670762	22.1663844	25.8698591
25	1.1625167	23.1388641	26.8993160	25	1.1685501	23.0781847	26.9680149	25	1.1746135	23.0177282	27.0369352
26	1.1695402	23.9939009	28.0618327	26	1.1758535	23.9286308	28.1365650	26	1.1821996	23.8636091	28.2115488
27	1.1766062	24.8438030	29.2313729	27	1.1832026	24.7737946	29.3124185	27	1.1898346	24.7040620	29.3937484
28	1.1837149	25.6886010	30.4079791	28	1.1905976	25.6137089	30.4956212	28	1.1975190	25.5391219	30.5835830
29	1.1908665	26.5283257	31.5916940	29	1.1980369	26.4484063	31.6862188	29	1.2052530	26.3688232	31.7811020
30	1.1980613	27.3630075	32.7825605	30	1.2055266	27.2779194	32.8842577	30	1.2130369	27.1932005	32.9863549
31	1.2052996	28.1926768	33.9806218	31	1.2130612	28.1022801	34.0897843	31	1.2208711	28.0122878	34.1993918
32	1.2125816	29.0173635	35.1859214	32	1.2205428	28.9215206	35.3028454	32	1.2287559	28.8261191	35.4202629
33	1.2199076	29.8370977	36.3985030	33	1.2282718	29.7356726	36.5234882	33	1.2366916	29.6347281	36.6490187
34	1.2272779	30.6519091	37.6184106	34	1.2359485	30.5447678	37.7517600	34	1.2446785	30.4381484	37.8857103
35	1.2346927	31.4618273	38.8456885	35	1.2436732	31.3488376	38.9877085	35	1.2527171	31.2364132	39.1303889
36	1.2421523	32.2668815	40.0803812	36	1.2514461	32.1479131	40.2313817	36	1.2608076	32.0295557	40.3831060
37	1.2496570	33.0671011	41.3225335	37	1.2592677	32.9420255	41.4828278	37	1.2689503	32.8176086	41.6439135
38	1.2572070	33.8625151	42.5721905	38	1.2671381	33.7312055	42.7420955	38	1.2771456	33.6006047	42.9128638
39	1.2648026	34.6531523	43.8293975	39	1.2750577	34.5154837	44.0092336	39	1.2853938	34.3785764	44.1900094
40	1.2724441	35.4390414	45.0942001	40	1.2830268	35.2949906	45.2842913	40	1.2936953	35.1515560	45.4754032
41	1.2801318	36.2202110	46.3666442	41	1.2910457	36.0694565	46.5673181	41	1.3020504	35.9195754	46.7690985
42	1.2878659	36.9966893	47.6467760	42	1.2991148	36.8392114	47.8583639	42	1.3104595	36.6826665	48.0711489
43	1.2956468	37.7685046	48.9346419	43	1.3072342	37.6041853	49.1574786	43	1.3189229	37.4408609	49.3816084
44	1.3034747	38.5356848	50.2302887	44	1.3154045	38.3644077	50.4647129	44	1.3274409	38.1941901	50.7005313
45	1.3113498	39.2982578	51.5337634	45	1.3236257	39.1199083	51.7801173	45	1.3360140	38.9426853	52.0279722
46	1.3192726	40.0562513	52.8451132	46	1.3318984	39.8707163	53.1037431	46	1.3446424	39.6863774	53.3639862
47	1.3272432	40.8096928	54.1643858	47	1.3402228	40.6168609	54.4356415	47	1.3533266	40.4252974	54.7086286
48	1.3352619	41.5586095	55.4916289	48	1.3485992	41.3583711	55.7758642	48	1.3620668	41.1594758	56.0619552
49	1.3433291	42.3030287	56.8268909	49	1.3570279	42.0952757	57.1244634	49	1.3708635	41.8889430	57.4240220
50	1.3514451	43.0429774	58.1702200	50	1.3655093	42.8276031	58.4814913	50	1.3797170	42.6137293	58.7948855
51	1.3596101	43.7784824	59.5216651	51	1.3740438	43.5553820	59.8470006	51	1.3886276	43.3338648	60.1746024
52	1.3678244	44.5095904	60.8812751	52	1.3826315	44.2786405	61.2210443	52	1.3975959	44.0493792	61.5632301
53	1.3760883	45.2362679	62.2490995	53	1.3912730	44.9974067	62.6036759	53	1.4066220	44.7603023	62.9608259
54	1.3844022	45.9586014	63.6251878	54	1.3999684	45.7117085	63.9949489	54	1.4157064	45.4666634	64.3674479
55	1.3927663	46.6765970	65.0095900	55	1.4087182	46.4215737	65.3949173	55	1.4248495	46.1684919	65.7831544
56	1.4011809	47.3902807	66.4023563	56	1.4175227	47.1270268	66.8036355	56	1.4340517	46.8658168	67.2080039
57	1.4096464	48.0996784	67.8035372	57	1.4263822	47.8281041	68.2211582	57	1.4433133	47.5586671	68.6420556
58	1.4181630	48.8048160	69.2131835	58	1.4352971	48.5248239	69.6475405	58	1.4526347	48.2470714	70.0853689
59	1.4267311	49.5057190	70.6313465	59	1.4442677	49.2172163	71.0828376	59	1.4620163	48.9310583	71.5380036
60	1.4353509	50.2024127	72.0580776	60	1.4532944	49.9053082	72.5271053	60	1.4714585	49.6106562	73.0000198
61	1.4440228	50.8949226	73.4934285	61	1.4623775	50.5891261	73.9803998	61	1.4809616	50.2858931	74.4714783
62	1.4527471	51.5832736	74.9374513	62	1.4715174	51.2686968	75.4427773	62	1.4905262	50.9567971	75.9524399
63	1.4615241	52.2674909	76.3901984	63	1.4807143	51.9440465	76.9142946	63	1.5001525	51.6233960	77.4429661
64	1.4703542	52.9475991	77.8517225	64	1.4899688	52.6152015	78.3950090	64	1.5098410	52.2857174	78.9431166
65	1.4792375	53.6236231	79.3220766	65	1.4992811	53.2821878	79.8849778	65	1.5195920	52.9437888	80.4529596
66	1.4881746	54.2955872	80.8013142	66	1.5086516	53.9450314	81.3842589	66	1.5294061	53.5976374	81.9725516
67	1.4971657	54.9635160	82.2894888	67	1.5180807	54.6037579	82.8929105	67	1.5392835	54.2472903	83.5019577
68	1.5062110	55.6274336	83.7866545	68	1.5275687	55.2583929	84.4109912	68	1.5492247	54.8927745	85.0412411
69	1.5153111	56.2873641	85.2928655	69	1.5371160	55.9089619	85.9385599	69	1.5592301	55.5341166	86.5904658
70	1.5244661	56.9433314	86.8081766	70	1.5467230	56.5554901	87.4756759	70	1.5693001	56.1713434	88.1496959
71	1.5336764	57.5953595	88.3326426	71	1.5563900	57.1980026	89.0223989	71	1.5794352	56.8044811	89.7189960
72	1.5429423	58.2434718	89.8663190	72	1.5661174	57.8365243	90.5787888	72	1.5896357	57.4335561	91.2984312
73	1.5522643	58.8876920	91.4092613	73	1.5759057	58.4710800	92.1449063	73	1.5999021	58.0585943	92.8880669
74	1.5616426	59.5280434	92.9615256	74	1.5857551	59.1016945	93.7208119	74	1.6102348	58.6796217	94.4879690
75	1.5710775	60.1645493	94.5231682	75	1.5956660	59.7284920	95.3065670	75	1.6206342	59.2966641	96.0982038
76	1.5805694	60.7972327	96.0942457	76	1.6056390	60.3511970	96.9022331	76	1.6311008	59.9097470	97.7188381
77	1.5901187	61.4261165	97.6748151	77	1.6156742	60.9701337	98.5078720	77	1.6416350	60.5188958	99.3499389
78	1.5997256	62.0512237	99.2649337	78	1.6257722	61.5852260	100.1235462	78	1.6522372	61.1241358	100.9915739
79	1.6093907	62.6725769	100.8646594	79	1.6359332	62.1964979	101.7493184	79	1.6629079	61.7254920	102.6438112
80	1.6191141	63.2901986	102.4740500	80	1.6461578	62.8039731	103.3852516	80	1.6736476	62.3229893	104.3067191
81	1.6288962	63.9041113	104.0931641	81	1.6564463	63.4076751	105.0314094	81	1.6844565	62.9166526	105.9803667
82	1.6387374	64.5143372	105.7220603	82	1.6667991	64.0076274	106.6878558	82	1.6953353	63.5065064	107.6648232
83	1.6485382	65.1208984	107.3607977	83	1.6772166	64.6038533	108.3546549	83	1.7062844	64.0925752	109.3601585
84	1.6585987	65.7238170	109.0094359	84	1.6876992	65.1963760	110.0318714	84	1.7173041	64.6748832	111.0664429
85	1.6686194	66.3231149	110.6680346	85	1.6982473	65.7852481	111.7195706	85	1.7283950	65.2534547	112.7837470
86	1.6787006	66.9188137	112.3366539	86	1.7088614	66.3704034	113.4178180	86	1.7395576	65.8283135	114.5121420
87	1.6888428	67.5109351	114.0153546	87	1.7195417	66.9519536	115.1266793	87	1.7507922	66.3994835	116.2516996
88	1.6990462	68.0995006	115.7041973	88	1.7302889	67.5298919	116.8462211	88	1.7620994	66.9669884	118.0024918
89	1.7093113	68.6845316	117.4032435	89	1.7411032	68.1042403	118.5765100	89	1.7734797	67.5308516	119.7645913
90	1.7196384	69.2660492	119.1125548	90	1.7519851	68.6750214	120.3176131	90	1.7849334	68.0910966	121.5380709
91	1.7300278	69.8440746	120.8321931	91	1.7629350	69.2422573	122.0695982	91	1.7964611	68.6477466	123.3230043
92	1.7404801	70.4186287	122.5622210	92	1.7739533	69.8059700	123.8325332	92	1.8080632	69.2008246	125.1194654
93	1.7509955	70.9897324	124.3027011	93	1.7850405	70.3661814	125.6064856	93	1.8197403	69.7503535	126.9275286
94	1.7615744	71.5574064	126.0536965	94	1.7961970	70.9229132	127.3915271	94	1.8314928	70.2963562	128.7472689
95	1.7722173	72.1216713	127.8152710	95	1.8074233	71.4761870	129.1877241	95	1.8433212	70.8383553	130.5787617
96	1.7829244	72.6825476	129.5874882	96	1.8187197	72.0260244	130.9951474	96	1.8552260	71.3778732	132.4220828
97	1.7936962	73.2400556	131.3704126	97	1.8300867	72.5724466	132.8138671	97	1.8672076	71.9134323	134.2773088
98	1.8045332	73.7942155	133.1641089	98	1.8415247	73.1154740	134.6439538	98	1.8792667	72.4455547	136.1445164
99	1.8154355	74.3450475	134.9686420	99	1.8530342	73.6551303	136.4854785	99	1.8914036	72.9742626	138.0237831
100	1.8264038	74.8925716	136.7840776	100	1.8646157	74.1914338	138.3385127	100	1.9036189	73.4995779	139.9151867

Table 1

M	C(7.25,M,12)	A(7.25,M,12)	S(7.25,M,12)	M	C(7.50,M,12)	A(7.50,M,12)	S(7.50,M,12)	M	C(7.75,M,12)	A(7.75,M,12)	S(7.75,M,12)
101	1.8374383	75.4368075	138.6104814	101	1.8762696	74.7244063	140.2031284	101	1.9159131	74.0215222	141.8188056
102	1.8485395	75.9777752	140.4479197	102	1.8879962	75.2540683	142.0793980	102	1.9282867	74.5401173	143.7347187
103	1.8597078	76.5154940	142.2964592	103	1.8997962	75.7804406	143.9673942	103	1.9407402	75.0553846	145.6630054
104	1.8709435	77.0499837	144.1561670	104	1.9116699	76.3035434	145.8671904	104	1.9532742	75.5673455	147.6037457
105	1.8822471	77.5812636	146.0271105	105	1.9236179	76.8233972	147.7788604	105	1.9658891	76.0760212	149.5570199
106	1.8936190	78.1093529	147.9093576	106	1.9356405	77.3400221	149.7024782	106	1.9785855	76.5814327	151.5229089
107	1.9050597	78.6342709	149.8029767	107	1.9477382	77.8534381	151.6381187	107	1.9913638	77.0836012	153.5014944
108	1.9165694	79.1560365	151.7080363	108	1.9599116	78.3636652	153.5858570	108	2.0042247	77.5825472	155.4928582
109	1.9281487	79.6746687	153.6246057	109	1.9721611	78.8707232	155.5457686	109	2.0171687	78.0782916	157.4970829
110	1.9397979	80.1901863	155.5527544	110	1.9844871	79.3746317	157.5179296	110	2.0301962	78.5708548	159.5142516
111	1.9515175	80.7026080	157.4925523	111	1.9968901	79.8754104	159.5024167	111	2.0433079	79.0602573	161.5444478
112	1.9633079	81.2119525	159.4440698	112	2.0093707	80.3730787	161.4993068	112	2.0565043	79.5465194	163.5877557
113	1.9751696	81.7182381	161.4073777	113	2.0219292	80.8676558	163.5086775	113	2.0697858	80.0296611	165.6442600
114	1.9871029	82.2214833	163.3825473	114	2.0345663	81.3591610	165.5306067	114	2.0831532	80.5097026	167.7140458
115	1.9991083	82.7217064	165.3696502	115	2.0472823	81.8476135	167.5651730	115	2.0965069	80.9866638	169.7971990
116	2.0111863	83.2189254	167.3587585	116	2.0600778	82.3330320	169.6124553	116	2.1101475	81.4605643	171.8938059
117	2.0233372	83.7131584	169.3799447	117	2.0729533	82.8154355	171.6725332	117	2.1237755	81.9314238	174.0039534
118	2.0355615	84.2044233	171.4032819	118	2.0859093	83.2948428	173.7454865	118	2.1374916	82.3992619	176.1277290
119	2.0478597	84.6927380	173.4388434	119	2.0989462	83.7712723	175.8313958	119	2.1512962	82.8640980	178.2652205
120	2.0602322	85.1781202	175.4867031	120	2.1120646	84.2447427	177.9303420	120	2.1651900	83.3259512	180.4165168
121	2.0726794	85.6605875	177.5469352	121	2.1252650	84.7152722	180.0424067	121	2.1791735	83.7848408	182.5817068
122	2.0852018	86.1401574	179.6196146	122	2.1385479	85.1828792	182.1676717	122	2.1932474	84.2407587	184.7608803
123	2.0977999	86.6168472	181.7048165	123	2.1519139	85.6475818	184.3062197	123	2.2074121	84.6938049	186.9541276
124	2.1104741	87.0906744	183.8026164	124	2.1653633	86.1093981	186.4581335	124	2.2216683	85.1439171	189.1615397
125	2.1232249	87.5616561	185.9130905	125	2.1788969	86.5683459	188.6234969	125	2.2360166	85.5911410	191.3832080
126	2.1360527	88.0298093	188.0363155	126	2.1925150	87.0244432	190.8023937	126	2.2504575	86.0354951	193.6192246
127	2.1489581	88.4951511	190.1723682	127	2.2062182	87.4777075	192.9949087	127	2.2649917	86.4769978	195.8696820
128	2.1619413	88.9576984	192.3213263	128	2.2200070	87.9281565	195.2011269	128	2.2796198	86.9156674	198.1346737
129	2.1750031	89.4174678	194.4832676	129	2.2338821	88.3758077	197.4211339	129	2.2943423	87.3515222	200.4142935
130	2.1881437	89.8744762	196.6582707	130	2.2478439	88.8206785	199.6550160	130	2.3091599	87.7845801	202.7086358
131	2.2013638	90.3287400	198.8464144	131	2.2618929	89.2627861	201.9028599	131	2.3240733	88.2148591	205.0177968
132	2.2146637	90.7802759	201.0477782	132	2.2760297	89.7021476	204.1647527	132	2.3390829	88.6423771	207.3418690
133	2.2280439	91.2291001	203.2624418	133	2.2902549	90.1387803	206.4407824	133	2.3541895	89.0671518	209.6809519
134	2.2415050	91.6752289	205.4904858	134	2.3045690	90.5727009	208.7310373	134	2.3693936	89.4892007	212.0351414
135	2.2550474	92.1186785	207.7319908	135	2.3189725	91.0039263	211.0356063	135	2.3846960	89.9085413	214.4045350
136	2.2686717	92.5594651	209.9870382	136	2.3334661	91.4324734	213.3545789	136	2.4000971	90.3251911	216.7892310
137	2.2823782	92.9976046	212.2557099	137	2.3480503	91.8583586	215.6880450	137	2.4155977	90.7391674	219.1893281
138	2.2961676	93.4331129	214.5380882	138	2.3627256	92.2815986	218.0360953	138	2.4311985	91.1504871	221.6049259
139	2.3100403	93.8660057	216.8342558	139	2.3774926	92.7022098	220.3988209	139	2.4469000	91.5591675	224.0361244
140	2.3239968	94.2962989	219.1442961	140	2.3923520	93.1202085	222.7763135	140	2.4627029	91.9652254	226.4830243
141	2.3380376	94.7240080	221.4682929	141	2.4073042	93.5356110	225.1686665	141	2.4786078	92.3686777	228.9457272
142	2.3521632	95.1491486	223.8063305	142	2.4223498	93.9484332	227.5759896	142	2.4946155	92.7695411	231.4243350
143	2.3663742	95.5717360	226.1584937	143	2.4374895	94.3586914	229.9983194	143	2.5107266	93.1678322	233.9189505
144	2.3806711	95.9917857	228.5248680	144	2.4527238	94.7664014	232.4358089	144	2.5269417	93.5635675	236.4296771
145	2.3950543	96.4093127	230.9055390	145	2.4680533	95.1715790	234.8885327	145	2.5432615	93.9566764	238.9566187
146	2.4095244	96.8243324	233.3005933	146	2.4834787	95.5742400	237.3565861	146	2.5596867	94.3474362	241.4998802
147	2.4240820	97.2368597	235.7101178	147	2.4990004	95.9744000	239.8400647	147	2.5762180	94.7356021	244.0595670
148	2.4387275	97.6469096	238.1341997	148	2.5114192	96.3720746	242.3390051	148	2.5928561	95.1212772	246.6357850
149	2.4534614	98.0544970	240.5729272	149	2.5303355	96.7672791	244.8536843	149	2.6096016	95.5044774	249.2286411
150	2.4682844	98.4596367	243.0263886	150	2.5461501	97.1600289	247.3840198	150	2.6264553	95.8852187	251.8382428
151	2.4831970	98.8623434	245.4946730	151	2.5620636	97.5503393	249.9301700	151	2.6434178	96.2635168	254.4646981
152	2.4981996	99.2626317	247.9778700	152	2.5780765	97.9382254	252.4922335	152	2.6604899	96.6393874	257.1081159
153	2.5132929	99.6605160	250.4760697	153	2.5941894	98.3237022	255.0703100	153	2.6776722	97.0128461	259.7686058
154	2.5284774	100.0560110	252.9893626	154	2.6104031	98.7067848	257.6644994	154	2.6949655	97.3839084	262.4462781
155	2.5437536	100.4491308	255.5178400	155	2.6267181	99.0874880	260.2749025	155	2.7123705	97.7525896	265.1412436
156	2.5591221	100.8398898	258.0615936	156	2.6431351	99.4658266	262.9016207	156	2.7298879	98.1189050	267.8536142
157	2.5745835	101.2283021	260.6207157	157	2.6596547	99.8418153	265.5447558	157	2.7475185	98.4828698	270.5835021
158	2.5901383	101.6143819	263.1952992	158	2.6762776	100.2154686	268.2044105	158	2.7652628	98.8444991	273.3310206
159	2.6057870	101.9981431	265.7854375	159	2.6930043	100.5868011	270.8806881	159	2.7831218	99.2038078	276.0962834
160	2.6215303	102.3795997	268.3912245	160	2.7098356	100.9558272	273.5736924	160	2.8010962	99.5608109	278.8794052
161	2.6373687	102.7587655	271.0127548	161	2.7267721	101.3225611	276.2835280	161	2.8191866	99.9155232	281.6805014
162	2.6533028	103.1356543	273.6501236	162	2.7438144	101.6870173	279.0103001	162	2.8373938	100.2679592	284.4996880
163	2.6693332	103.5102707	276.3034264	163	2.7609632	102.0492097	281.7541144	163	2.8557187	100.6181338	287.3370818
164	2.6854604	103.8826553	278.9727596	164	2.7782192	102.4091525	284.5150776	164	2.8741618	100.9660613	290.1928004
165	2.7016851	104.2527946	281.6582200	165	2.7955831	102.7668596	287.2932969	165	2.8927241	101.3117562	293.0669623
166	2.7180078	104.6207112	284.3599051	166	2.8130555	103.1223450	290.0888800	166	2.9114063	101.6552328	295.9598864
167	2.7344291	104.9864182	287.0779129	167	2.8306371	103.4756223	292.9019355	167	2.9302091	101.9965054	298.8710927
168	2.7509496	105.3499291	289.8123419	168	2.8483286	103.8267054	295.7325726	168	2.9491334	102.3355881	301.8013019
169	2.7675695	105.7112569	292.5632915	169	2.8661306	104.1756079	298.5809012	169	2.9681799	102.6724949	304.7504353
170	2.7842906	106.0704148	295.3308614	170	2.8840440	104.5223432	301.4470318	170	2.9873494	103.0072398	307.7186152
171	2.8011124	106.4274158	298.1151520	171	2.9020692	104.8669250	304.3310758	171	3.0066427	103.3398367	310.7059646
172	2.8180358	106.7822729	300.9162644	172	2.9202072	105.2093664	307.2331450	172	3.0260606	103.6702993	313.7126073
173	2.8350614	107.1349990	303.7343002	173	2.9384585	105.5496809	310.1533521	173	3.0456039	103.9986414	316.7386678
174	2.8521899	107.4856068	306.5693616	174	2.9568238	105.8876817	313.0918106	174	3.0652734	104.3248765	319.7842717
175	2.8694219	107.8341090	309.4215515	175	2.9753040	106.2239818	316.0486344	175	3.0850700	104.6490184	322.8495452
176	2.8867580	108.1805184	312.2909733	176	2.9938996	106.5579943	319.0239384	176	3.1049944	104.9710801	325.9346152
177	2.9041988	108.5248475	315.1777313	177	3.0126115	106.8899322	322.0178380	177	3.1250475	105.2910753	329.0396095
178	2.9217450	108.8671087	318.0819301	178	3.0314403	107.2198084	325.0304495	178	3.1452301	105.6090170	332.1646570
179	2.9393972	109.2073145	321.0036751	179	3.0503868	107.5476357	328.0618898	179	3.1655430	105.9249186	335.3098871
180	2.9571561	109.5454772	323.9430723	180	3.0694517	107.8734268	331.1122766	180	3.1859872	106.2387931	338.4754301
181	2.9750222	109.8816092	326.9002284	181	3.0886358	108.1971943	334.1817284	181	3.2065633	106.5506534	341.6614173
182	2.9929963	110.2157225	329.8752506	182	3.1079398	108.5189509	337.2703642	182	3.2272724	106.8605125	344.8679806
183	3.0110790	110.5478294	332.8682469	183	3.1273644	108.8387089	340.3783039	183	3.2481152	107.1683835	348.0952530
184	3.0292709	110.8779418	335.8793259	184	3.1469104	109.1564809	343.5056683	184	3.2690926	107.4742787	351.3433682
185	3.0475728	111.2060718	338.9085968	185	3.1665786	109.4722792	346.6525788	185	3.2902055	107.7782111	354.6124608
186	3.0659852	111.5322312	341.9561696	186	3.1863697	109.7861160	349.8191574	186	3.3114547	108.0801932	357.9026662
187	3.0845089	111.8564319	345.0221548	187	3.2062845	110.0980034	353.0055271	187	3.3328412	108.3802375	361.2141210
188	3.1031444	112.1786857	348.1066636	188	3.2263238	110.4079537	356.2118117	188	3.3543658	108.6783565	364.5469622
189	3.1218926	112.4990042	351.2098081	189	3.2464883	110.7159789	359.4381355	189	3.3760294	108.9745624	367.9013280
190	3.1407540	112.8173991	354.3317007	190	3.2667789	111.0220908	362.6846238	190	3.3978329	109.2688676	371.2773574
191	3.1597294	113.1338819	357.4724547	191	3.2871963	111.3263041	365.9514027	191	3.4197773	109.5612843	374.6751903
192	3.1788194	113.4484641	360.6321841	192	3.3077412	111.6286225	369.2385990	192	3.4418633	109.8518246	378.0949676
193	3.1980248	113.7611571	363.8110035	193	3.3284146	111.9290658	372.5463403	193	3.4640920	110.1405006	381.5368309
194	3.2173462	114.0719723	367.0090284	194	3.3492172	112.2276431	375.8747549	194	3.4864643	110.4273241	385.0009229
195	3.2367843	114.3809209	370.2263746	195	3.3701498	112.5243658	379.2239721	195	3.5089810	110.7123071	388.4873872
196	3.2563399	114.6880141	373.4631589	196	3.3912133	112.8192455	382.5941219	196	3.5316432	110.9954614	391.9963683
197	3.2760136	114.9932632	376.7194988	197	3.4124083	113.1122937	385.9853352	197	3.5544517	111.2767988	395.5280115
198	3.2958062	115.2966791	379.9955125	198	3.4337359	113.4035217	389.3977436	198	3.5774076	111.5563308	399.0824632
199	3.3157184	115.5982728	383.2913187	199	3.4551967	113.6929408	392.8314795	199	3.6005117	111.8340691	402.6598708
200	3.3357509	115.8980554	386.6070371	200	3.4767917	113.9805623	396.2866762	200	3.6237650	112.1100252	406.2603825

Table 1

405

M	C(7.25,M,12)	A(7.25,M,12)	S(7.25,M,12)	M	C(7.50,M,12)	A(7.50,M,12)	S(7.50,M,12)	M	C(7.75,M,12)	A(7.75,M,12)	S(7.75,M,12)
201	3.3559043	116.1960377	389.9427880	201	3.4985217	114.2663973	399.7634679	201	3.6471685	112.3842105	409.8841475
202	3.3761796	116.4922304	393.2986923	202	3.5203874	114.5504569	403.2619896	202	3.6707231	112.6566364	413.5313159
203	3.3965774	116.7866445	396.6748719	203	3.5423899	114.8327522	406.7823771	203	3.6944298	112.9273142	417.2020390
204	3.4170983	117.0792904	400.0714493	204	3.5645298	115.1132941	410.3247669	204	3.7182897	113.1962550	420.8964669
205	3.4377433	117.3701789	403.4885476	205	3.5868081	115.3920935	41?.8892967	205	3.7423037	113.4634701	424.6147585
206	3.4585130	117.6593205	406.9262909	206	3.?92257	115.6691613	417.4761048	206	3.7664727	113.7289705	428.3570622
207	3.4794082	117.9467257	410.3848039	207	3.6317833	115.9445081	421.0853305	207	3.79?7978	113.9927672	432.1235249
208	3.5004296	118.2324049	413.8642121	208	3.6544820	116.2181447	424.7171138	208	3.8152801	114.2548712	435.9143327
209	3.5215780	118.5163686	417.3646417	209	3.6773225	116.4900817	428.3715958	209	3.8399204	114.5152932	439.7296128
210	3.5428542	118.7986268	420.8862198	210	3.7003057	116.7603296	432.0489182	210	3.8647199	114.7740442	443.5695332
211	3.5642590	119.0791901	424.4290740	211	3.7234327	117.0288990	435.7492240	211	3.8896796	115.0311348	447.4342531
212	3.5857931	119.3580684	427.9933330	212	3.7467041	117.2958003	439.4726566	212	3.9148004	115.2865756	451.3239327
213	3.6074572	119.6352720	431.5791261	213	3.7701210	117.5610437	443.2193607	213	3.9400035	115.5403774	455.2387331
214	3.6292523	119.9108108	435.1865833	214	3.7936843	117.8246397	446.9894818	214	3.9655299	115.7925505	459.1788166
215	3.6511790	120.1846950	438.8158356	215	3.8173948	118.0865985	450.7831660	215	3.9911406	116.0431054	463.1443464
216	3.6732382	120.4569343	442.4670146	216	3.8412535	118.3469302	454.6005608	216	4.0169167	116.2920526	467.1354870
217	3.6954307	120.7275388	446.1402528	217	3.8652613	118.6056449	458.4418143	217	4.0428593	116.5394023	471.1524037
218	3.7177573	120.9965181	449.8356835	218	3.8894192	118.8627527	462.3070757	218	4.0689694	116.7851647	475.1952630
219	3.7402187	121.2638822	453.5534408	219	3.9137281	119.1182635	466.1964949	219	4.0952482	117.0293502	479.2642324
220	3.7628159	121.5296406	457.2936595	220	3.9381889	119.3721874	470.1102230	220	4.1216966	117.2719687	483.3594806
221	3.7855495	121.7938030	461.0564753	221	3.9628026	119.6245340	474.0484119	221	4.1483159	117.5130304	487.4811772
222	3.8084206	122.0563791	464.8420249	222	3.9875701	119.8753133	478.0112145	222	4.1751071	117.7525452	491.6294931
223	3.8314298	122.3173782	468.6504454	223	4.0124924	120.1245350	481.9987846	223	4.2020714	117.9905231	495.8046003
224	3.8545780	122.5768100	472.4818752	224	4.0375705	120.3722087	486.0112770	224	4.2292098	118.2269739	500.0066717
225	3.8778661	122.8346838	476.3364532	225	4.0628053	120.6183440	490.0488474	225	4.?565234	118.4619074	504.2358814
226	3.9012948	123.0910090	480.2143193	226	4.0881978	120.8629506	494.1116527	226	4.2840135	118.6953334	508.4924048
227	3.9249652	123.3457940	484.1156142	227	4.1137491	121.1060378	498.1998506	227	4.3116810	118.9272615	512.7764183
228	3.9485779	123.5990505	488.0404793	228	4.1394600	121.3476152	502.3135997	228	4.3395273	119.1577013	517.0880993
229	3.9724339	123.8507854	491.9890572	229	4.1653316	121.5876922	506.4530597	229	4.3675534	119.3866624	521.4276266
230	3.9964340	124.1010084	495.9614911	230	4.1913649	121.8262779	510.6183913	230	4.3957605	119.6141544	525.7951801
231	4.0205791	124.3497288	499.9579251	231	4.2175610	122.0633818	514.8097562	231	4.4241498	119.8401865	530.1909406
232	4.0448701	124.5969555	503.9785043	232	4.2439207	122.2990130	519.0273172	232	4.4527225	120.0647682	534.6150904
233	4.0693079	124.8426976	508.0233744	233	4.2704452	122.5331806	523.2712379	233	4.4814796	120.2879088	539.0678129
234	4.0938933	125.0869638	512.0926823	234	4.2971355	122.7658937	527.5416832	234	4.5104225	120.5096175	543.5492925
235	4.1186272	125.3297632	516.1865756	235	4.3239926	122.9971615	531.8388187	235	4.5395523	120.7299035	548.0597151
236	4.1435106	125.5711044	520.3052028	236	4.3510176	123.2269928	536.1628113	236	4.5688703	120.9487760	552.5992674
237	4.1685443	125.8109963	524.4487134	237	4.3782114	123.4553965	540.5138289	237	4.5983776	121.1662440	557.1681377
238	4.1937293	126.0494476	528.6172577	238	4.4055753	123.6823817	544.8920403	238	4.6280754	121.3823166	561.7665152
239	4.2190664	126.2864668	532.8109870	239	4.4331101	123.9079569	549.2976156	239	4.6579651	121.5970026	566.3945906
240	4.2445566	126.5220627	537.0300534	240	4.4608170	124.1321311	553.7307277	240	4.6880478	121.8103110	571.0525557
241	4.2702008	126.7562437	541.2746100	241	4.4886971	124.3549129	558.1915427	241	4.7183247	122.0222506	575.7406035
242	4.2959999	126.9890184	545.5448107	242	4.5167515	124.5763110	562.6802399	242	4.7487972	122.2328303	580.4589282
243	4.3219549	127.2203952	549.8408106	243	4.5449812	124.7963339	567.1969914	243	4.7794666	122.4420586	585.2077254
244	4.3480667	127.4503825	554.1627655	244	4.5733873	125.0149902	571.7419726	244	4.8103340	122.6499444	589.9871920
245	4.3743363	127.6789886	558.5108323	245	4.6019710	125.2322884	576.3153599	245	4.8414007	122.8564962	594.7975260
246	4.4007646	127.9062218	562.8851685	246	4.6307333	125.4482369	580.9173309	246	4.8726681	123.0617225	599.6389267
247	4.4273525	128.1320904	567.2859331	247	4.6596754	125.6628441	585.5480643	247	4.9041374	123.2656320	604.5115947
248	4.4541011	128.3566026	571.7132856	248	4.6887984	125.8761184	590.2077297	248	4.9358099	123.4682330	609.4157321
249	4.4810113	128.5797665	576.1673867	249	4.7181034	126.0880680	594.8965380	249	4.9676870	123.6695340	614.3515421
250	4.5080841	128.8015903	580.6483980	250	4.7475915	126.2987011	599.6146414	250	4.9997700	123.8695432	619.3192291
251	4.5353204	129.0220818	585.1564821	251	4.7772640	126.5080259	604.3622329	251	5.0320602	124.0682689	624.3189991
252	4.5627213	129.2412493	589.6918025	252	4.8071219	126.7160506	609.1394969	252	5.0645589	124.2657195	629.3510593
253	4.5902878	129.4591006	594.2545238	253	4.8371664	126.9227832	613.9466187	253	5.0972675	124.4619030	634.4156183
254	4.6180207	129.6756435	598.8448116	254	4.8673987	127.1282317	618.7837851	254	5.1301874	124.6568277	639.5128858
255	4.6459213	129.8908861	603.4628323	255	4.8978199	127.3324042	623.6511838	255	5.1633199	124.8505015	644.6430732
256	4.6739904	130.1048361	608.1087536	256	4.9284313	127.5353085	628.5490037	256	5.1966663	125.0429326	649.8063931
257	4.7022291	130.3175012	612.7827440	257	4.9592340	127.7369526	633.4774350	257	5.2302281	125.2341288	655.0030594
258	4.7306384	130.5288891	617.4849731	258	4.9902292	127.9373442	638.4366689	258	5.2640067	125.4240982	660.2332875
259	4.7592193	130.7390076	622.2156115	259	5.0214191	128.1364911	643.4268981	259	5.2980034	125.6128486	665.4972941
260	4.7879729	130.9478643	626.9748308	260	5.0528020	128.3344011	648.4483162	260	5.3322196	125.8003877	670.7952975
261	4.8169003	131.1557818	631.7628037	261	5.0843820	128.5310818	653.5011182	261	5.3666569	125.9867235	676.1275171
262	4.8460024	131.3618223	636.5797040	262	5.1161594	128.7265410	658.5855002	262	5.4013165	126.1718635	681.4941740
263	4.8752803	131.5669387	641.4257064	263	5.1481354	128.9207860	663.7016556	263	5.4362000	126.3558155	686.8954905
264	4.9047351	131.7708233	646.3009867	264	5.1803112	129.1138246	668.8497950	264	5.4713088	126.5385872	692.3316906
265	4.9343679	131.9734835	651.2057218	265	5.2126882	129.3056642	674.0301062	265	5.5065444	126.7201859	697.8029994
266	4.9641797	132.1749267	656.1400898	266	5.2452675	129.4963123	679.2427944	266	5.5422081	126.9006194	703.3096438
267	4.9941716	132.3751601	661.1042695	267	5.2780504	129.6857762	684.4880618	267	5.5780015	127.0798951	708.8518519
268	5.0243448	132.5741910	666.0984411	268	5.3110382	129.8740633	689.7661122	268	5.6140261	127.2580204	714.4298535
269	5.0547002	132.7720267	671.1227859	269	5.3442322	130.0611809	695.0771504	269	5.6502834	127.4350027	720.0438796
270	5.0852390	132.9686743	676.1774860	270	5.3776336	130.2471363	700.4213826	270	5.6867748	127.6108493	725.6941630
271	5.1159623	133.1641409	681.2627250	271	5.4112439	130.4319367	705.7990163	271	5.7235019	127.7855675	731.3809378
272	5.1468712	133.3584337	686.3786873	272	5.4450641	130.6155893	711.2102601	272	5.7604662	127.9591645	737.1044397
273	5.1779669	133.5515597	691.5255586	273	5.4790958	130.7981011	716.6553243	273	5.7976692	128.1316477	742.8649059
274	5.2092505	133.7435259	696.7035255	274	5.5133401	130.9794794	722.1344201	274	5.8351125	128.3030240	748.6625751
275	5.2407230	133.9343393	701.9127759	275	5.5477985	131.1597311	727.6477062	275	5.8727976	128.4733006	754.4976876
276	5.2723857	134.1240067	707.1534990	276	5.5824722	131.3388632	733.1955587	276	5.9107261	128.6424845	760.3704851
277	5.3042397	134.3125352	712.4258847	277	5.6173627	131.5168826	738.7780309	277	5.9488995	128.8105828	766.2812112
278	5.3362862	134.4999314	717.7301244	278	5.6524712	131.6937964	744.3953936	278	5.9873195	128.9776025	772.2301107
279	5.3685262	134.6862023	723.0664106	279	5.6877992	131.8696115	750.0478649	279	6.0259876	129.1435504	778.2174302
280	5.4009611	134.8713545	728.4349368	280	5.7233479	132.0443343	755.7356640	280	6.0649054	129.3084334	784.2434177
281	5.4335919	135.0553948	733.8358979	281	5.7591188	132.2179719	761.4590119	281	6.1040746	129.4722584	790.3083231
282	5.4664198	135.2383299	739.2694898	282	5.7951133	132.3905311	767.2181208	282	6.1434967	129.6350322	796.4123977
283	5.4994461	135.4201664	744.7359097	283	5.8313328	132.5620185	773.0132441	283	6.1831735	129.7967614	802.5558945
284	5.5326719	135.6009109	750.2353558	284	5.8677786	132.7324407	778.8445769	284	6.2231065	129.9574529	808.7390680
285	5.5660985	135.7805700	755.7680277	285	5.9044522	132.9018045	784.7123555	285	6.2632974	130.1171332	814.9621745
286	5.5997270	135.9591501	761.3341262	286	5.9413551	133.0701162	790.6168077	286	6.3037478	130.2757490	821.2254718
287	5.6335587	136.1366578	766.9338533	287	5.9784885	133.2373826	796.5581628	287	6.3444596	130.4333668	827.5292197
288	5.6675948	136.3130995	772.5674120	288	6.0158541	133.4036100	802.5366513	288	6.3854342	130.5899732	833.8736792
289	5.7018365	136.4884816	778.2350067	289	6.0534532	133.5688050	808.5525044	289	6.4266734	130.7455747	840.2591134
290	5.7362851	136.6628104	783.9368433	290	6.0912872	133.7329739	814.6059585	290	6.4681790	130.9001777	846.6857869
291	5.7709418	136.8360924	789.6731284	291	6.1293578	133.8961231	820.6972458	291	6.5099527	131.0537887	853.1539659
292	5.8058079	137.0083337	795.4440702	292	6.1676663	134.0582590	826.8266036	292	6.5519961	131.2064139	859.6639186
293	5.8408847	137.1795406	801.2498781	293	6.2062142	134.2193878	832.9942698	293	6.5943111	131.3580598	866.2159148
294	5.8761734	137.3497194	807.0907628	294	6.2450030	134.3795159	839.2004840	294	6.6368994	131.5087325	872.8102259
295	5.9116752	137.5188762	812.9669362	295	6.2840343	134.5386493	845.4454871	295	6.6797627	131.6584385	879.4471253
296	5.9473916	137.6870171	818.8786114	296	6.3233095	134.6967943	851.7295214	296	6.7229028	131.8071837	886.1268880
297	5.9833238	137.8541483	824.8260030	297	6.3628302	134.8539571	858.0528309	297	6.7663216	131.9549745	892.8497908
298	6.0194730	138.0202758	830.8093268	298	6.4025979	135.0101437	864.4156611	298	6.8100207	132.1018170	899.6161124
299	6.0558407	138.1854056	836.8287998	299	6.4426141	135.1653602	870.8182590	299	6.8540021	132.2477171	906.4261331
300	6.0924280	138.3495438	842.8846405	300	6.4828805	135.3196126	877.2608731	300	6.8982675	132.3926810	913.2801352

M	C(7.25,M,12)	A(7.25,M,12)	S(7.25,M,12)	M	C(7.50,M,12)	A(7.50,M,12)	S(7.50,M,12)	M	C(7.75,M,12)	A(7.75,M,12)	S(7.75,M,12)
301	6.1292365	138.5126963	648.9770685	301	6.5233985	135.4729070	883.7437536	301	6.9428189	132.5367148	920.1784028
302	6.1662673	138.6748689	855.1063050	302	6.5641697	135.6252491	890.2671520	302	6.9876579	132.6798242	927.1212216
303	6.2035218	138.8360677	861.2725723	303	6.6051958	135.7766451	896.8313217	303	7.0327865	132.8220154	934.1088795
304	6.2410014	138.9962984	867.4760941	304	6.6464782	135.9271007	903.4365175	304	7.0782066	132.9632941	941.1416660
305	6.2787075	139.1555668	873.7170955	305	6.6880187	136.0766218	910.0829957	305	7.1239200	133.1036663	948.2198726
306	6.3166413	139.3138788	879.9958029	306	6.7298188	136.2252143	916.7710145	306	7.1699287	133.2431377	955.3437927
307	6.3548044	139.4712401	886.3124442	307	6.7718802	136.3728837	923.5008333	307	7.2162345	133.3817141	962.5137213
308	6.3931980	139.6276563	892.6672486	308	6.8142045	136.5196360	930.2727135	308	7.2628393	133.5194013	969.7299558
309	6.4318235	139.7831332	899.0604466	309	6.8567932	136.6654768	937.0869180	309	7.3097451	133.6562050	976.9927951
310	6.4708825	139.9376764	905.4922701	310	6.8996482	136.8104117	943.9437113	310	7.3569539	133.7921308	984.3025402
311	6.5097762	140.0912915	911.9629526	311	6.9427710	136.9544464	950.8433595	311	7.4044676	133.9271844	991.6594941
312	6.5491061	140.2439841	918.4727288	312	6.9861633	137.0975865	957.7861305	312	7.4522881	134.0613714	999.0639617
313	6.5886736	140.3957597	925.0218348	313	7.0298268	137.2398375	964.7722938	313	7.5004175	134.1946973	1006.5162498
314	6.6284802	140.5466239	931.6105084	314	7.0737633	137.3812050	971.8021206	314	7.5488577	134.3271676	1014.0166673
315	6.6685272	140.6965820	938.2389886	315	7.1179743	137.5216944	978.8758839	315	7.5976107	134.4587880	1021.5655249
316	6.7088162	140.8456396	944.9075158	316	7.1624616	137.6613112	985.9938582	316	7.6466786	134.5895637	1029.1631356
317	6.7493487	140.9938021	951.6163321	317	7.2072270	137.8000608	993.1563198	317	7.6960634	134.7195003	1036.8098142
318	6.7901260	141.1410748	958.3656808	318	7.2522722	137.9379486	1000.3635468	318	7.7457671	134.8486030	1044.5058776
319	6.8311497	141.2874630	965.1558068	319	7.2975989	138.0749800	1007.6158190	319	7.7957919	134.9768774	1052.2516447
320	6.8724212	141.4329721	971.9869564	320	7.3432089	138.2111602	1014.9134179	320	7.8461397	135.1043286	1060.0474366
321	6.9139421	141.5776074	978.8593776	321	7.3891039	138.3464947	1022.2566267	321	7.8968127	135.2309620	1067.8935763
322	6.9557138	141.7213741	985.7733197	322	7.4352858	138.4809885	1029.6457307	322	7.9478129	135.3567827	1075.7903890
323	6.9977379	141.8642774	992.7290335	323	7.4817564	138.6146469	1037.0810165	323	7.9991426	135.4817961	1083.7382019
324	7.0400159	142.0063226	999.7267714	324	7.5285173	138.7474752	1044.5627728	324	8.0508037	135.6060073	1091.7373445
325	7.0825493	142.1475147	1006.7667874	325	7.5755706	138.8794785	1052.0912902	325	8.1027985	135.7294215	1099.7881482
326	7.1253398	142.2878588	1013.8493367	326	7.6229179	139.0106618	1059.6668608	326	8.1551290	135.8520437	1107.8909467
327	7.1683887	142.4273602	1020.9746765	327	7.6705611	139.1410304	1067.2897786	327	8.2077976	135.9738791	1116.0460757
328	7.2116977	142.5660238	1028.1430651	328	7.7185021	139.2705892	1074.9603398	328	8.2608063	136.0949326	1124.2538733
329	7.2552684	142.7038547	1035.3547628	329	7.7667428	139.3993433	1082.6788419	329	8.3141573	136.2152094	1132.5146796
330	7.2991023	142.8408578	1042.6100312	330	7.8152849	139.5272977	1090.4455847	330	8.3678529	136.3347144	1140.8288369
331	7.3432010	142.9770382	1049.9091335	331	7.8641304	139.6544573	1098.2608696	331	8.4218953	136.4534525	1149.1966898
332	7.3875662	143.1124008	1057.2523345	332	7.9132813	139.7808272	1106.1250000	332	8.4762867	136.5714287	1157.6185851
333	7.4321994	143.2469505	1064.6399007	333	7.9627393	139.9064121	1114.0382813	333	8.5310294	136.6886478	1166.0948718
334	7.4771023	143.3806921	1072.0721001	334	8.0125064	140.0312170	1122.0010206	334	8.5861256	136.8051148	1174.6259012
335	7.5222764	143.5136306	1079.5492024	335	8.0625846	140.1552467	1130.0135269	335	8.6415777	136.9208344	1183.2120268
336	7.5677235	143.6457707	1087.0714788	336	8.1129757	140.2785060	1138.0761115	336	8.6973879	137.0358114	1191.8536045
337	7.6134452	143.7771173	1094.6392024	337	8.1636818	140.4009998	1146.1890872	337	8.7535585	137.1500507	1200.5509924
338	7.6594431	143.9076751	1102.2526476	338	8.2147048	140.5227327	1154.3527690	338	8.8100919	137.2635569	1209.3045509
339	7.7057189	144.0374489	1109.9120906	339	8.2660467	140.6437095	1162.5674738	339	8.8669904	137.3763347	1218.1146428
340	7.7522743	144.1664433	1117.6178095	340	8.3177095	140.7639349	1170.8335205	340	8.9242564	137.4883889	1226.9816332
341	7.7991109	144.2946630	1125.3700838	341	8.3696952	140.8834136	1179.1512301	341	8.9818922	137.5997240	1235.9058896
342	7.8462306	144.4221127	1133.1691947	342	8.4220058	141.0021501	1187.5209253	342	9.0399003	137.7103447	1244.8877818
343	7.8936349	144.5487971	1141.0154253	343	8.4746433	141.1201492	1195.9429310	343	9.0982830	137.8202555	1253.9276821
344	7.9413256	144.6747207	1148.9090602	344	8.5276098	141.2374154	1204.4175744	344	9.1570427	137.9294611	1263.0259650
345	7.9893044	144.7998880	1156.8503858	345	8.5809074	141.3539531	1212.9451842	345	9.2161819	138.0379659	1272.1830077
346	8.0375731	144.9243037	1164.8396902	346	8.6345381	141.4697671	1221.5260916	346	9.2757031	138.1457744	1281.3991896
347	8.0861335	145.0479722	1172.8772633	347	8.6885039	141.5848617	1230.1606297	347	9.3356087	138.2528912	1290.6748028
348	8.1349872	145.1708980	1180.9633968	348	8.7428071	141.6992415	1238.8491337	348	9.3959012	138.3593206	1300.0105014
349	8.1841361	145.2930856	1189.0983840	349	8.7974496	141.8129108	1247.5919408	349	9.4565830	138.4650670	1309.4046020
350	8.2335819	145.4145394	1197.2825201	350	8.8524337	141.9258740	1256.3893904	350	9.5176568	138.5701349	1318.8629856
351	8.2833265	145.5352639	1205.5161020	351	8.9077614	142.0381357	1265.2418241	351	9.5791250	138.6745286	1328.3806624
352	8.3333716	145.6552633	1213.7994284	352	8.9634349	142.1497001	1274.1495855	352	9.6409902	138.7782523	1337.9597674
353	8.3837190	145.7745421	1222.1328000	353	9.0194564	142.2605715	1283.1130204	353	9.7032549	138.8813105	1347.6007576
354	8.4343706	145.8931046	1230.5165190	354	9.0758280	142.3707543	1292.1324768	354	9.7659218	138.9837074	1357.3040125
355	8.4853283	146.0109551	1238.9508896	355	9.1325519	142.4802527	1301.2083048	355	9.8289933	139.0854472	1367.0699343
356	8.5365908	146.1280978	1247.4362179	356	9.1896304	142.5890710	1310.3408567	356	9.8924723	139.1865342	1376.8989276
357	8.5881691	146.2445371	1255.9728118	357	9.2470656	142.6972134	1319.5304871	357	9.9563611	139.2869725	1386.7913093
358	8.6400559	146.3602771	1264.5609809	358	9.3048597	142.8046841	1328.7775526	358	10.0206626	139.3867663	1396.7477610
359	8.6922563	146.4753220	1273.2010368	359	9.3630151	142.9114873	1338.0824214	359	10.0853794	139.4859197	1406.7684245
360	8.7447702	146.5896760	1281.8932931	360	9.4215339	143.0176272	1347.4454275	360	10.1505142	139.5844369	1416.8538030
361	8.7976050	146.7033433	1290.6380651	361	9.4804185	143.1231078	1356.8669614	361	10.2160696	139.6823219	1427.0043172
362	8.8507572	146.8163280	1299.4356700	362	9.5396711	143.2279332	1366.3473799	362	10.2820483	139.7795788	1437.2203868
363	8.9042305	146.9286342	1308.2864272	363	9.5992941	143.3321075	1375.8870510	363	10.3484532	139.8762116	1447.5024351
364	8.9580269	147.0402659	1317.1906577	364	9.6592897	143.4356348	1385.4863451	364	10.4152870	139.9722243	1457.8508883
365	9.0121483	147.1512273	1326.1486846	365	9.7196602	143.5385190	1395.1456348	365	10.4825524	140.0676209	1468.2661753
366	9.0665967	147.2615222	1335.1608329	366	9.7804081	143.6407643	1404.8652950	366	10.5502522	140.1624054	1478.7487277
367	9.1213741	147.3711548	1344.2274297	367	9.8415357	143.7423744	1414.6457031	367	10.6183893	140.2565817	1489.2989979
368	9.1764824	147.4801290	1353.3488037	368	9.9030453	143.8433535	1424.4872388	368	10.6869664	140.3501536	1499.9173692
369	9.2319236	147.5884488	1362.5252861	369	9.9649393	143.9437053	1434.3902840	369	10.7559863	140.4431251	1510.6043306
370	9.2876998	147.6961181	1371.7572097	370	10.0272202	144.0434338	1444.3552233	370	10.8254521	140.5355000	1521.3603219
371	9.3428130	147.8031408	1381.0449095	371	10.0898902	144.1425429	1454.3824435	371	10.8953665	140.6272821	1532.1857740
372	9.4002652	147.9095208	1390.3887225	372	10.1529521	144.2410365	1464.4723338	372	10.9657324	140.7184753	1543.0811405
373	9.4570585	148.0152619	1399.7889037	373	10.2164080	144.3389182	1474.6252859	373	11.0365527	140.8090833	1554.0468728
374	9.5141949	148.1203680	1409.2460462	374	10.2802606	144.4361920	1484.8416939	374	11.1078305	140.8991099	1565.0834256
375	9.5716765	148.2248429	1418.7602411	375	10.3445122	144.5328616	1495.1219545	375	11.1795685	140.9885587	1576.1912560
376	9.6295053	148.3286904	1428.3319176	376	10.4091654	144.6289308	1505.4664667	376	11.2517699	141.0774336	1587.3700246
377	9.6876836	148.4319143	1437.9614229	377	10.4742227	144.7244033	1515.8756322	377	11.3244376	141.1657383	1598.6225945
378	9.7462134	148.5345182	1447.6491065	378	10.5396866	144.8192828	1526.3498549	378	11.3975746	141.2534762	1609.9470321
379	9.8050967	148.6365060	1457.3953199	379	10.6055596	144.9135729	1536.8895415	379	11.4711839	141.3406512	1621.3446067
380	9.8643359	148.7378813	1467.2004166	380	10.6718444	145.0072775	1547.4951011	380	11.5452687	141.4272667	1632.8157906
381	9.9239329	148.8386478	1477.0647525	381	10.7385434	145.1004000	1558.1669455	381	11.6198319	141.5133265	1644.3610593
382	9.9838900	148.9388092	1486.9886854	382	10.8056593	145.1929441	1568.9054890	382	11.6948766	141.5988340	1655.9080912
383	10.0442093	149.0383690	1496.9725754	383	10.8731947	145.2849133	1579.7111483	383	11.7704060	141.6837929	1667.6757678
384	10.1048931	149.1373310	1507.0167847	384	10.9411522	145.3763114	1590.5843430	384	11.8464232	141.7682065	1679.4461738
385	10.1659435	149.2356986	1517.1216778	385	11.0095345	145.4671418	1601.5254951	385	11.9229314	141.8520785	1691.2925970
386	10.2273627	149.3334755	1527.2876213	386	11.0783439	145.5574080	1612.5350295	386	11.9999336	141.9354123	1703.2155284
387	10.2891530	149.4306653	1537.5149840	387	11.1475836	145.6471135	1623.6133734	387	12.0774332	142.0182114	1715.2154620
388	10.3513167	149.5272713	1547.8041370	388	11.2172560	145.7362619	1634.7609570	388	12.1554333	142.1004791	1727.2928952
389	10.4138559	149.6232972	1558.1554537	389	11.2873638	145.8248565	1645.9782130	389	12.2339371	142.1822190	1739.4483285
390	10.4767729	149.7187465	1568.5693096	390	11.3579099	145.9129009	1657.2655769	390	12.3129480	142.2634343	1751.6822656
391	10.5400701	149.8136225	1579.0460825	391	11.4288968	146.0003984	1668.6234867	391	12.3924691	142.3441284	1763.9952136
392	10.6037497	149.9079288	1589.5861526	392	11.5003274	146.0873524	1680.0523835	392	12.4725038	142.4243048	1776.3876827
393	10.6678140	150.0016687	1600.1899023	393	11.5722045	146.1737664	1691.5527109	393	12.5530554	142.5039667	1788.8601865
394	10.7322654	150.0948457	1610.8577163	394	11.6445307	146.2596436	1703.1249154	394	12.6341272	142.5831174	1801.4132419
395	10.7971062	150.1874631	1621.5899817	395	11.7173091	146.3449874	1714.7694461	395	12.7157226	142.6617602	1814.0473691
396	10.8623387	150.2795243	1632.3870878	396	11.7905422	146.4298012	1726.4867552	396	12.7978450	142.7398983	1826.7630917
397	10.9279653	150.3710326	1643.2494265	397	11.8642331	146.5140881	1738.2772974	397	12.8804977	142.8175351	1839.5609367
398	10.9939884	150.4619914	1654.1773918	398	11.9383846	146.5978516	1750.1415305	398	12.9636843	142.8946737	1852.4414344
399	11.0604104	150.5524040	1665.1713802	399	12.0129995	146.6810947	1762.0799151	399	13.0474081	142.9713172	1865.4051187
400	11.1272337	150.6422736	1676.2317906	400	12.0980807	146.7638208	1774.0929146	400	13.1316726	143.0474690	1878.4525268

Table 1

M	C(7.25,M,12)	A(7.25,M,12)	S(7.25,M,12)	M	C(7.50,M,12)	A(7.50,M,12)	S(7.50,M,12)	M	C(7.75,M,12)	A(7.75,M,12)	S(7.75,M,12)
401	11.1944608	150.7316035	1687.3590244	401	12.1636312	146.8460331	1786.1809953	401	13.2164813	143.1231321	1891.5841994
402	11.2620940	150.8203969	1698.5534852	402	12.2396539	146.9277348	1798.3446266	402	13.3018377	143.1983097	1904.8006807
403	11.3301359	150.9086571	1709.8155792	403	12.3161518	147.0089290	1810.5842805	403	13.3877454	143.2730048	1918.1025184
404	11.3985887	150.9963873	1721.1457150	404	12.3931277	147.0696189	1822.9004323	404	13.4742080	143.3472207	1931.4902639
405	11.4674552	151.0835906	1732.5443037	405	12.4705848	147.1698076	1835.2935600	405	13.5612289	143.4209603	1944.9644718
406	11.5367377	151.1702702	1744.0117589	406	12.5485259	147.2494982	1847.7641448	406	13.6488118	143.4942268	1958.5257007
407	11.6064388	151.2564293	1755.5484966	407	12.6269542	147.3286939	1860.3126707	407	13.7369604	143.5670231	1972.1745126
408	11.6765611	151.3420709	1767.1549354	408	12.7058727	147.4073976	1872.9396249	408	13.8256783	143.6393523	1985.9114730
409	11.7471070	151.4271983	1778.8314965	409	12.7852844	147.4856125	1885.6454976	409	13.9149691	143.7112173	1999.7371513
410	11.8180791	151.5118144	1790.5786035	410	12.8651924	147.5633416	1898.4307819	410	14.0048366	143.7826212	2013.6521204
411	11.8894800	151.5959223	1802.3966826	411	12.9455999	147.6405880	1911.2959743	411	14.0952845	143.8535670	2027.6569570
412	11.9613122	151.6795252	1814.2861625	412	13.0265099	147.7173545	1924.2415742	412	14.1863166	143.9240574	2041.7522415
413	12.0335785	151.7626260	1826.2474748	413	13.1079255	147.7936442	1937.2680841	413	14.2779365	143.9940955	2055.9385581
414	12.1062814	151.8452278	1838.2810533	414	13.1893501	147.8694601	1950.3760096	414	14.3701482	144.0636843	2070.2164946
415	12.1794235	151.9273335	1850.3873347	415	13.2722866	147.9448051	1963.5658597	415	14.4629554	144.1328264	2084.5866429
416	12.2530075	152.0089461	1862.5667582	416	13.3552384	148.0196821	1976.8381463	416	14.5553620	144.2015249	2099.0495983
417	12.3270361	152.0900686	1874.8197657	417	13.4387087	148.0940940	1990.1933847	417	14.6503718	144.2697826	2113.6059603
418	12.4015119	152.1707039	1887.1468018	418	13.5227006	148.1680437	2003.6320934	418	14.7449888	144.3376022	2128.2563321
419	12.4764377	152.2508550	1899.5483137	419	13.6072175	148.2415341	2017.1547940	419	14.8402169	144.4049867	2143.0013210
420	12.5518162	152.3305247	1912.0247515	420	13.6922626	148.3145681	2030.7620115	420	14.9360599	144.4719387	2157.8415378
421	12.6276501	152.4097160	1924.5765677	421	13.7778392	148.3871484	2044.4542741	421	15.0325220	144.5384612	2172.7775978
422	12.7039422	152.4884317	1937.2042178	422	13.8639507	148.4592779	2058.2321133	422	15.1296070	144.6045567	2187.8101198
423	12.7806951	152.5666748	1949.9081600	423	13.9506004	148.5309594	2072.0960640	423	15.2273191	144.6702282	2202.9397268
424	12.8579118	152.6444479	1962.6888551	424	14.0377917	148.6021957	2086.0466645	424	15.3256622	144.7354782	2218.1670459
425	12.9355951	152.7217539	1975.5467670	425	14.1255279	148.6729895	2100.0844561	425	15.4246404	144.8003095	2233.4927081
426	13.0137476	152.7985958	1988.4823620	426	14.2138124	148.7433436	2114.2099840	426	15.5242579	144.8647249	2248.9173485
427	13.0923723	152.8749761	2001.4961097	427	14.3026487	148.8132607	2128.4237964	427	15.6245187	144.9287268	2264.4416064
428	13.1714721	152.9508978	2014.5884820	428	14.3920403	148.8827435	2142.7264452	428	15.7254271	144.9923181	2280.0661252
429	13.2510497	153.0263635	2027.7599541	429	14.4819906	148.9517948	2157.1184855	429	15.8269871	145.0555013	2295.7915522
430	13.3311082	153.1013760	2041.0110038	430	14.5725030	149.0204172	2171.6004760	430	15.9292031	145.1182791	2311.6185394
431	13.4116503	153.1759381	2054.3421120	431	14.6635811	149.0886314	2186.1729790	431	16.0320792	145.1806540	2327.5477424
432	13.4926790	153.2500523	2067.7537623	432	14.7552285	149.1563860	2200.8365601	432	16.1355197	145.2426287	2343.5798216
433	13.5741973	153.3237215	2081.2464413	433	14.8474487	149.2237376	2215.5917887	433	16.2398289	145.3042057	2359.7154413
434	13.6562080	153.3969483	2094.8206386	434	14.9402453	149.2906709	2230.4392374	434	16.3447111	145.3653876	2375.9552703
435	13.7387143	153.4697353	2108.4768466	435	15.0336248	149.3571885	2245.3794826	435	16.4502707	145.4261769	2392.2999814
436	13.8217190	153.5420852	2122.2155609	436	15.1275819	149.4232929	2260.4131044	436	16.5565121	145.4865761	2408.7502521
437	13.9052253	153.6140006	2136.0372799	437	15.2221293	149.4889867	2275.5406863	437	16.6634395	145.5465877	2425.3067642
438	13.9892360	153.6854841	2149.9425052	438	15.3172676	149.5542725	2290.7628156	438	16.7710576	145.6062142	2441.9702037
439	14.0737543	153.7565384	2163.9317412	439	15.4130005	149.6191528	2306.0800832	439	16.8793707	145.6654581	2458.7412613
440	14.1587832	153.8271659	2178.0054954	440	15.5093318	149.6836301	2321.4930838	440	16.9883833	145.7243219	2475.6206320
441	14.2443259	153.8973693	2192.1642787	441	15.6062651	149.7477070	2337.0024156	441	17.0980999	145.7828079	2492.6090152
442	14.3303853	153.9671511	2206.4086045	442	15.7038043	149.8113858	2352.6086807	442	17.2085251	145.8409187	2509.7071152
443	14.4169647	154.0365138	2220.7389899	443	15.8019531	149.8746691	2368.3124850	443	17.3196635	145.8986565	2526.9156403
444	14.5040672	154.1054600	2235.1559546	444	15.9007153	149.9375594	2384.1144380	444	17.4315197	145.9560238	2544.2353038
445	14.5916960	154.1739921	2249.6600219	445	16.0000947	150.0000590	2400.0151533	445	17.5440983	146.0130231	2561.6668235
446	14.6798541	154.2421127	2264.2517179	446	16.1000953	150.0621704	2416.0152480	446	17.6574039	146.0696565	2579.2109218
447	14.7685449	154.3098242	2278.9315720	447	16.2007209	150.1238961	2432.1153433	447	17.7714413	146.1259266	2596.8683257
448	14.8577716	154.3771290	2293.7001169	448	16.3019708	150.1852383	2448.3160642	448	17.8862152	146.1818356	2614.6397670
449	14.9475373	154.4440297	2308.5578885	449	16.4038628	150.2461996	2464.6180397	449	18.0017303	146.2373858	2632.5259821
450	15.0378453	154.5105286	2323.5054258	450	16.5063869	150.3067822	2481.0219024	450	18.1179915	146.2925795	2650.5277125
451	15.1286989	154.5766281	2338.5432711	451	16.6095518	150.3669885	2497.5282893	451	18.2350035	146.3474191	2668.6457040
452	15.2201015	154.6423307	2353.6719700	452	16.7133615	150.4268209	2514.1378412	452	18.3527713	146.4019068	2686.8807075
453	15.3120563	154.7076387	2368.8920715	453	16.8178200	150.4862816	2530.8512027	453	18.4712996	146.4560449	2705.2334788
454	15.4045666	154.7725545	2384.2041278	454	16.9229314	150.5453731	2547.6690227	454	18.5905934	146.5098355	2723.7047783
455	15.4976359	154.8370805	2399.6086944	455	17.0286997	150.6040974	2564.5919541	455	18.7106576	146.5632810	2742.2953717
456	15.5912674	154.9012190	2415.1063303	456	17.1351291	150.6624571	2581.6206539	456	18.8314973	146.6163835	2761.0060293
457	15.6854647	154.9649722	2430.6975977	457	17.2422237	150.7204542	2598.7557830	457	18.9531174	146.6691453	2779.8375266
458	15.7802310	155.0283427	2446.3830624	458	17.3499876	150.7780912	2615.9980066	458	19.0755229	146.7215685	2798.7906440
459	15.8755699	155.0913325	2462.1632934	459	17.4584250	150.8353701	2633.3479942	459	19.1987190	146.7736553	2817.8661670
460	15.9714848	155.1539441	2478.0388633	460	17.5675401	150.8922993	2650.8064192	460	19.3227107	146.8254078	2837.0640990
461	16.0679792	155.2161797	2494.0103482	461	17.6773373	150.9488629	2668.3739593	461	19.4475033	146.8768283	2856.3875967
462	16.1650566	155.2780415	2510.0783274	462	17.7878206	151.0050811	2686.0512966	462	19.5731017	146.9279189	2875.8351000
463	16.2627205	155.3395319	2526.2433840	463	17.8989945	151.0609502	2703.8391172	463	19.6995113	146.9786815	2895.4082017
464	16.3609744	155.4006529	2542.5061044	464	18.0108632	151.1164722	2721.7381117	464	19.8267373	147.0291185	2915.1077130
465	16.4598220	155.4614069	2558.8670788	465	18.1234311	151.1716494	2739.7489750	465	19.9547850	147.0792318	2934.9344503
466	16.5592667	155.5217961	2575.3281083	466	18.2367026	151.2264839	2757.8724061	466	20.0836597	147.1290235	2954.8892354
467	16.6593123	155.5818225	2591.8861675	467	18.3506820	151.2809778	2776.1091086	467	20.2133666	147.1784957	2974.9728950
468	16.7599623	155.6414886	2608.5454798	468	18.4653737	151.3351332	2794.4597906	468	20.3439113	147.2276505	2995.1862617
469	16.8612204	155.7007962	2625.3054421	469	18.5807823	151.3889522	2812.9251643	469	20.4752991	147.2764898	3015.5301730
470	16.9630903	155.7597478	2642.1666625	470	18.6969122	151.4424370	2831.5059466	470	20.6075354	147.3250157	3036.0054740
471	17.0655756	155.8183453	2659.1297527	471	18.8137679	151.4955896	2850.2028568	471	20.7406257	147.3732303	3056.6130074
472	17.1686801	155.8765909	2676.1953284	472	18.9313539	151.5484120	2869.0166267	472	20.8745756	147.4211355	3077.3536331
473	17.2724076	155.9344867	2693.3640085	473	19.0496749	151.6009063	2887.9479806	473	21.0093905	147.4687332	3098.2282087
474	17.3767617	155.9920348	2710.6364161	474	19.1687354	151.6530744	2906.9976555	474	21.1450762	147.5160256	3119.2375992
475	17.4817463	156.0492373	2728.0131778	475	19.2885400	151.7049189	2926.1663909	475	21.2816381	147.5630144	3140.3826754
476	17.5873652	156.1060963	2745.4949241	476	19.4090933	151.7564411	2945.4549309	476	21.4190821	147.6097018	3161.6643135
477	17.6936222	156.1626139	2763.0822893	477	19.5304002	151.8076433	2964.8640242	477	21.5574136	147.6560895	3183.0833956
478	17.8005212	156.2187920	2780.7759114	478	19.6524652	151.8585275	2984.3944244	478	21.6966386	147.7021796	3204.6408092
479	17.9080660	156.2746327	2798.5764326	479	19.7752931	151.9090957	3004.0468896	479	21.8367627	147.7479739	3226.3374478
480	18.0162605	156.3301382	2816.4844986	480	19.8988887	151.9593499	3023.8221826	480	21.9777918	147.7934744	3248.1742105
481	18.1251088	156.3853102	2834.5007591	481	20.0232567	152.0092917	3043.7210713	481	22.1197317	147.8386829	3270.1520023
482	18.2346146	156.4401510	2852.6258679	482	20.1404021	152.0589234	3063.7443280	482	22.2625883	147.8836013	3292.2717340
483	18.3447821	156.4946624	2870.8604825	483	20.2743296	152.1082469	3083.8927301	483	22.4063675	147.9282315	3314.5343223
484	18.4556152	156.5488465	2889.2052646	484	20.4010441	152.1572640	3104.1670597	484	22.5510753	147.9725753	3336.9406898
485	18.5671178	156.6027051	2907.6608798	485	20.5285507	152.2059766	3124.5681038	485	22.6967177	148.0166345	3359.4917652
486	18.6792942	156.6562403	2926.2279976	486	20.6568541	152.2543867	3145.0966545	486	22.8433006	148.0604110	3382.1884828
487	18.7921482	156.7094540	2944.9072918	487	20.7859595	152.3024961	3165.7535086	487	22.9908303	148.1039066	3405.0317835
488	18.9056841	156.7623482	2963.6994401	488	20.9158717	152.3503067	3186.5394681	488	23.1393127	148.1471231	3428.0226138
489	19.0199060	156.8149247	2982.6051242	489	21.0465959	152.3978203	3207.4553398	489	23.2887541	148.1900623	3451.1619265
490	19.1348179	156.8671854	3001.6250302	490	21.1781371	152.4450388	3228.5019357	490	23.4391607	148.2327259	3474.4506807
491	19.2504241	156.9191323	3020.7598481	491	21.3105005	152.4919640	3249.6800728	491	23.5905386	148.2751158	3497.8898413
492	19.3667288	156.9707673	3040.0102722	492	21.4436911	152.5385978	3270.9905733	492	23.7428941	148.3172337	3521.4803799
493	19.4837361	157.0220921	3059.3770010	493	21.5777142	152.5849419	3292.4342644	493	23.8962337	148.3590813	3545.2232741
494	19.6014503	157.0731088	3078.8607370	494	21.7125749	152.6309982	3314.0119786	494	24.0505635	148.4006603	3569.1195077
495	19.7198757	157.1238190	3098.4621873	495	21.8482785	152.6767684	3335.7245535	495	24.2058901	148.4419726	3593.1700713
496	19.8390167	157.1742248	3118.1820631	496	21.9848302	152.7222543	3357.5728320	496	24.3622198	148.4830198	3617.3759613
497	19.9588774	157.2243278	3138.0210797	497	22.1222354	152.7674577	3379.5576622	497	24.5195591	148.5238035	3641.7381811
498	20.0794623	157.2741299	3157.9799571	498	22.2604994	152.8123803	3401.6798976	498	24.6779146	148.5643256	3666.2577402
499	20.2007757	157.3236330	3178.0594194	499	22.3996275	152.8570239	3423.9403970	499	24.8372928	148.6045876	3690.9356548
500	20.3228220	157.3728387	3198.2601951	500	22.5396252	152.9013902	3446.3400245	500	24.9977003	148.6445913	3715.7729476

Table 1

M	C(8.00,M,12)	A(8.00,M,12)	S(8.00,M,12)	M	C(8.25,M,12)	A(8.25,M,12)	S(8.25,M,12)	M	C(8.50,M,12)	A(8.50,M,12)	S(8.50,M,12)
1	1.0066667	.9933775	1.0000000	1	1.0068750	.9931719	1.0000000	1	1.0070833	.9929665	1.0000000
2	1.0133778	1.9801763	2.0066667	2	1.0137973	1.9795625	2.0068750	2	1.0142168	1.9789489	2.0070833
3	1.0201336	2.9604400	3.0200444	3	1.0207671	2.9592178	3.0206723	3	1.0214009	2.9579965	3.0213002
4	1.0269345	3.9342120	4.0401781	4	1.0277849	3.9321841	4.0414394	4	1.0286358	3.9301578	4.0427010
5	1.0337808	4.9015351	5.0671126	5	1.0348509	4.8985068	5.0692243	5	1.0359220	4.8954815	5.0713368
6	1.0406726	5.8624520	6.1008933	6	1.0419655	5.8582315	6.1040752	6	1.0432598	5.8540156	6.1072588
7	1.0476104	6.8170053	7.1415660	7	1.0491290	6.8114031	7.1460407	7	1.0506495	6.8058078	7.1505186
8	1.0545945	7.7652371	8.1891764	8	1.0563418	7.7580664	8.1951697	8	1.0580916	7.7509055	8.2011681
9	1.0616251	8.7071892	9.2437709	9	1.0636041	8.6982658	9.2515115	9	1.0655864	8.6893559	9.2592597
10	1.0687026	9.6429031	10.3053961	10	1.0709164	9.6320455	10.3151157	10	1.0731343	9.6212057	10.3248461
11	1.0758273	10.5724203	11.3740987	11	1.0782790	10.5594493	11.3860321	11	1.0807357	10.5465013	11.3979804
12	1.0829995	11.4957818	12.4499260	12	1.0856921	11.4805207	12.4643111	12	1.0883909	11.4652889	12.4787161
13	1.0902195	12.4130283	13.5329255	13	1.0931563	12.3953030	13.5500032	13	1.0961003	12.3776141	13.5671070
14	1.0974876	13.3242003	14.6231450	14	1.1006717	13.3038391	14.6431595	14	1.1038644	13.2835225	14.6632074
15	1.1048042	14.2293380	15.7206327	15	1.1082388	14.2061717	15.7438312	15	1.1116834	14.1830591	15.7670718
16	1.1121696	15.1284815	16.8254369	16	1.1158580	15.1023431	16.8520700	16	1.1195578	15.0762689	16.8787552
17	1.1195840	16.0216703	17.9376065	17	1.1235295	15.9923953	17.9679280	17	1.1274881	15.9631963	17.9983130
18	1.1270479	16.9089441	19.0571905	18	1.1312538	16.8763703	19.0914575	18	1.1354744	16.8438854	19.1258011
19	1.1345616	17.7903418	20.1842384	19	1.1390311	17.7543094	20.2227113	19	1.1435174	17.7183802	20.2612755
20	1.1421253	18.6659024	21.3188000	20	1.1468620	18.6262539	21.3617424	20	1.1516173	18.5867242	21.4047929
21	1.1497395	19.5356647	22.4609254	21	1.1547467	19.4922447	22.5086044	21	1.1597746	19.4489608	22.5564102
22	1.1574044	20.3996669	23.6106649	22	1.1626855	20.3523225	23.6633511	22	1.1679896	20.3051328	23.7161847
23	1.1651205	21.2579472	24.7680693	23	1.1706790	21.2065276	24.8260366	23	1.1762629	21.1552828	24.8841744
24	1.1728879	22.1105436	25.9331898	24	1.1787274	22.0549002	25.9967156	24	1.1845948	21.9994534	26.0604373
25	1.1807072	22.9574936	27.1060777	25	1.1868312	22.8974800	27.1754430	25	1.1929856	22.8376864	27.2450320
26	1.1885786	23.7988347	28.2867849	26	1.1949906	23.7343067	28.3622742	26	1.2014360	23.6700238	28.4380177
27	1.1965024	24.6346041	29.4753634	27	1.2032062	24.5654194	29.5572648	27	1.2099461	24.4965068	29.6394536
28	1.2044791	25.4648385	30.6718659	28	1.2114782	25.3908573	30.7604710	28	1.2185166	25.3171768	30.8493998
29	1.2125090	26.2895746	31.8763450	29	1.2198072	26.2106590	31.9719493	29	1.2271477	26.1320746	32.0679164
30	1.2205924	27.1088490	33.0888539	30	1.2281933	27.0248631	33.1917564	30	1.2358400	26.9412408	33.2950641
31	1.2287026	27.9226977	34.3094463	31	1.2366372	27.8335077	34.4199498	31	1.2445939	27.7447158	34.5309041
32	1.2369212	28.7311566	35.5381759	32	1.2451390	28.6366309	35.6565869	32	1.2534098	28.5425395	35.7754980
33	1.2451673	29.5342615	36.7750971	33	1.2536994	29.4342702	36.9017259	33	1.2622881	29.3347516	37.0289078
34	1.2534684	30.3320479	38.0202644	34	1.2623185	30.2264633	38.1554253	34	1.2712293	30.1213918	38.2911959
35	1.2618249	31.1245509	39.2737329	35	1.2709970	31.0132472	39.4177439	35	1.2802338	30.9024991	39.5624252
36	1.2702371	31.9118055	40.5355577	36	1.2797351	31.7946590	40.6887409	36	1.2893022	31.6781124	40.8426591
37	1.2787053	32.6938465	41.8057248	37	1.2885333	32.5707351	41.9684759	37	1.2984347	32.4482705	42.1319612
38	1.2872300	33.4707005	43.0845001	38	1.2973919	33.3415123	43.2570092	38	1.3076320	33.2130117	43.4303960
39	1.2958115	34.2424256	44.3717301	39	1.3063115	34.1070264	44.5544012	39	1.3168944	33.9723740	44.7380279
40	1.3044503	35.0090321	45.6675416	40	1.3152924	34.8673137	45.8607127	40	1.3262224	34.7263954	46.0549223
41	1.3131466	35.7705617	46.9719919	41	1.3243350	35.6224096	47.1760051	41	1.3356164	35.4751133	47.3811447
42	1.3219009	36.5270480	48.2851385	42	1.3334398	36.3723497	48.5003401	42	1.3450771	36.2185652	48.7167611
43	1.3307136	37.2785245	49.6070395	43	1.3426072	37.1171692	49.8337799	43	1.3546047	36.9567879	50.0618382
44	1.3395850	38.0250244	50.9377530	44	1.3518377	37.8569029	51.1763872	44	1.3641998	37.6898184	51.4164429
45	1.3485156	38.7665805	52.2773381	45	1.3611315	38.5915858	52.5282248	45	1.3738629	38.4176931	52.7806427
46	1.3575057	39.5032257	53.6258537	46	1.3704893	39.3212522	53.8893564	46	1.3835944	39.1404482	54.1545055
47	1.3665557	40.2349924	54.9833593	47	1.3799114	40.0459364	55.2598457	47	1.3933949	39.8581199	55.5381000
48	1.3756661	40.9619129	56.3499151	48	1.3893983	40.7656724	56.6397572	48	1.4032648	40.5707438	56.9314948
49	1.3848372	41.6840195	57.7255812	49	1.3989504	41.4804940	58.0291555	49	1.4132045	41.2783554	58.3347596
50	1.3940695	42.4013439	59.1104184	50	1.4085682	42.1904347	59.4281059	50	1.4232147	41.9809901	59.7479641
51	1.4033633	43.1139177	60.5044878	51	1.4182521	42.8955280	60.8366742	51	1.4332959	42.6786827	61.1711789
52	1.4127190	43.8217726	61.9078511	52	1.4280026	43.5958068	62.2549263	52	1.4434484	43.3714682	62.6044747
53	1.4221371	44.5249397	63.3205701	53	1.4378201	44.2913041	63.6829289	53	1.4536728	44.0593809	64.0479231
54	1.4316180	45.2234500	64.7427072	54	1.4477052	44.9820525	65.1207490	54	1.4639696	44.7424552	65.5015959
55	1.4411622	45.9173344	66.1743253	55	1.4576581	45.6680844	66.5684542	55	1.4743394	45.4207250	66.9655655
56	1.4507699	46.6066236	67.6154875	56	1.4676795	46.3494321	68.0261123	56	1.4847827	46.0942243	68.4399049
57	1.4604417	47.2913480	69.0662574	57	1.4777698	47.0261274	69.4937918	57	1.4952999	46.7629864	69.9246876
58	1.4701780	47.9715377	70.5266991	58	1.4879295	47.6982149	70.9715617	58	1.5058916	47.4270449	71.4199875
59	1.4799792	48.6472229	71.9968771	59	1.4981590	48.3656882	72.4594911	59	1.5165583	48.0864326	72.9258791
60	1.4898457	49.3184333	73.4768563	60	1.5084588	49.0286164	73.9576502	60	1.5273006	48.7411826	74.4424374
61	1.4997780	49.9851987	74.9667020	61	1.5188295	49.6870182	75.4661090	61	1.5381190	49.3913274	75.9697380
62	1.5097765	50.6475483	76.4664900	62	1.5292715	50.3409243	76.9849385	62	1.5490140	50.0368993	77.5078569
63	1.5198417	51.3055116	77.9762565	63	1.5397852	50.9903656	78.5142099	63	1.5599862	50.6779307	79.0568709
64	1.5299740	51.9591175	79.4960982	64	1.5503712	51.6353724	80.0539951	64	1.5710361	51.3144533	80.6168571
65	1.5401738	52.6083948	81.0260722	65	1.5610300	52.2759751	81.6043664	65	1.5821642	51.9464989	82.1878932
66	1.5504416	53.2533724	82.5662640	66	1.5717621	52.9122203	83.1653964	66	1.5933712	52.5740990	83.7700574
67	1.5607779	53.8940785	84.1166877	67	1.5825680	53.5440881	84.7371585	67	1.6046576	53.1972849	85.3634287
68	1.5711831	54.5305416	85.6774656	68	1.5934481	54.1716579	86.3197264	68	1.6160239	53.8160876	86.9680863
69	1.5816577	55.1627896	87.2486487	69	1.6044031	54.7949427	87.9131746	69	1.6274708	54.4305380	88.5841102
70	1.5922020	55.7908506	88.8303064	70	1.6154333	55.4139716	89.5175776	70	1.6389987	55.0406666	90.2115810
71	1.6028167	56.4147523	90.4225084	71	1.6265395	56.0287738	91.1330110	71	1.6506083	55.6465039	91.8505797
72	1.6135022	57.0345221	92.0253251	72	1.6377219	56.6393781	92.7595504	72	1.6623001	56.2480800	93.5011880
73	1.6242588	57.6501875	93.6388273	73	1.6489812	57.2458131	94.3972723	73	1.6740747	56.8454249	95.1634881
74	1.6350872	58.2617757	95.2630861	74	1.6603180	57.8481074	96.0462536	74	1.6859327	57.4385684	96.8375628
75	1.6459878	58.8693136	96.8981734	75	1.6717327	58.4462891	97.7065716	75	1.6978748	58.0275399	98.5234955
76	1.6569611	59.4728281	98.5441612	76	1.6832258	59.0403865	99.3783043	76	1.7099014	58.6123690	100.2213703
77	1.6680075	60.0723458	100.2011223	77	1.6947980	59.6304273	101.0615331	77	1.7220132	59.1930847	101.9312716
78	1.6791275	60.6678932	101.8691298	78	1.7064498	60.2164393	102.7563281	78	1.7342106	59.7697158	103.6532848
79	1.6903217	61.2594965	103.5482573	79	1.7181816	60.7984499	104.4627779	79	1.7464948	60.3422913	105.3874956
80	1.7015905	61.8471820	105.2385790	80	1.7299941	61.3764866	106.1809595	80	1.7588658	60.9108395	107.1339903
81	1.7129345	62.4309755	106.9401695	81	1.7418878	61.9505764	107.9109536	81	1.7713244	61.4753888	108.8928561
82	1.7243540	63.0109028	108.6531040	82	1.7538633	62.5207462	109.6528414	82	1.7838713	62.0359674	110.6641805
83	1.7358497	63.5869895	110.3774580	83	1.7659211	63.0870229	111.4067047	83	1.7965070	62.5926031	112.4480518
84	1.7474221	64.1592611	112.1133078	84	1.7780618	63.6494331	113.1726258	84	1.8092323	63.1453237	114.2445588
85	1.7590715	64.7277428	113.8607298	85	1.7902860	64.2080031	114.9506876	85	1.8220477	63.6941568	116.0537911
86	1.7707987	65.2924598	115.6198013	86	1.8025942	64.7627591	116.7409736	86	1.8349539	64.2391296	117.8758388
87	1.7826040	65.8534369	117.3906000	87	1.8149870	65.3137272	118.5435678	87	1.8479514	64.7802694	119.7107927
88	1.7944880	66.4106989	119.1732040	88	1.8274651	65.8609333	120.3585548	88	1.8610411	65.3176030	121.5587441
89	1.8064513	66.9642704	120.9676920	89	1.8400289	66.4044030	122.1860198	89	1.8742235	65.8511573	123.4197852
90	1.8184945	67.5141759	122.7741433	90	1.8526791	66.9441619	124.0260487	90	1.8874992	66.3809589	125.2940087
91	1.8306176	68.0604396	124.5926376	91	1.8654163	67.4802353	125.8787278	91	1.9008690	66.9070340	127.1815079
92	1.8428217	68.6030857	126.4232552	92	1.8782410	68.0126483	127.7441441	92	1.9143335	67.4294091	129.0823769
93	1.8551072	69.1421381	128.2660769	93	1.8911539	68.5414260	129.6223851	93	1.9278934	67.9481161	130.9967104
94	1.8674746	69.6776207	130.1211841	94	1.9041556	69.0665932	131.5135390	94	1.9415493	68.4631625	132.9246038
95	1.8799244	70.2095569	131.9886586	95	1.9172467	69.5881745	133.4176945	95	1.9553019	68.9745925	134.8661531
96	1.8924572	70.7379705	133.8685830	96	1.9304277	70.1061944	135.3349412	96	1.9691520	69.4824253	136.8214550
97	1.9050736	71.2628846	135.7610403	97	1.9436994	70.6206773	137.2653689	97	1.9831001	69.9866863	138.7906070
98	1.9177741	71.7843224	137.6661139	98	1.9570623	71.1316472	139.2090683	98	1.9971471	70.4874005	140.7737071
99	1.9305593	72.3023070	139.5838860	99	1.9705171	71.6391282	141.1661307	99	2.0112936	70.9845930	142.7708542
100	1.9434296	72.8168613	141.5144472	100	1.9840645	72.1431441	143.1366478	100	2.0255402	71.4782885	144.7821478

Table 1

409

M	C(8.00,M,12)	A(8.00,M,12)	S(8.00,M,12)	M	C(8.25,M,12)	A(8.25,M,12)	S(8.25,M,12)	M	C(8.50,M,12)	A(8.50,M,12)	S(8.50,M,12)
101	1.9563858	73.3280079	143.4578769	101	1.9977049	72.6437185	145.1207123	101	2.0398878	71.9685115	146.8076880
102	1.9694284	73.8357694	145.4142627	102	2.0114391	73.1408750	147.1184172	102	2.0543370	72.4552866	148.8475758
103	1.9825579	74.3401633	147.3836911	103	2.0252678	73.6346369	149.1298563	103	2.0688885	72.9386379	150.9019128
104	1.9957750	74.8412268	149.3662491	104	2.0391915	74.1250273	151.1551241	104	2.0835432	73.4185895	152.9708013
105	2.0090802	75.3389670	151.3420241	105	2.0532109	74.6120693	153.1943155	105	2.0983016	73.8951654	155.0543445
106	2.0224740	75.8334110	153.3711042	106	2.0673267	75.0957858	155.2475265	106	2.1131646	74.3683894	157.1526461
107	2.0359572	76.3245604	155.3935783	107	2.0815396	75.5761994	157.3148532	107	2.1281328	74.8382848	159.2658107
108	2.0495302	76.8124971	157.4295354	108	2.0958502	76.0533328	159.3963928	108	2.1432071	75.3048753	161.3939435
109	2.0631938	77.2971826	159.4790657	109	2.1102592	76.5272082	161.4922430	109	2.1583882	75.7681840	163.5371506
110	2.0769484	77.7786582	161.5422595	110	2.1247672	76.9978480	163.6025022	110	2.1736767	76.2282340	165.6955388
111	2.0907947	78.2569452	163.6192079	111	2.1393750	77.4652742	165.7272694	111	2.1890736	76.6850482	167.8692155
112	2.1047334	78.7320648	165.7100026	112	2.1540832	77.9295089	167.8666444	112	2.2045795	77.1386495	170.0582691
113	2.1187649	79.2040378	167.8147359	113	2.1688925	78.3905737	170.0207276	113	2.2201953	77.5890603	172.2628686
114	2.1328900	79.6728853	169.9335008	114	2.1838036	78.8484903	172.1896201	114	2.2359217	78.0363032	174.4830640
115	2.1471093	80.1386278	172.0663908	115	2.1988173	79.3032802	174.3734237	115	2.2517595	78.4804003	176.7189357
116	2.1614233	80.6012859	174.2135001	116	2.2139342	79.7549649	176.5722410	116	2.2677094	78.9213739	178.9707452
117	2.1758328	81.0608800	176.3749234	117	2.2291550	80.2035653	178.7861752	117	2.2837724	79.3592459	181.2384546
118	2.1903384	81.5174304	178.5507563	118	2.2444804	80.6491028	181.0153301	118	2.2999491	79.7940382	183.5222270
119	2.2049406	81.9709574	180.7410947	119	2.2599112	81.0915980	183.2598105	119	2.3162404	80.2257723	185.8221761
120	2.2196402	82.4214809	182.9460353	120	2.2754481	81.5310719	185.5197217	120	2.3326471	80.6544698	188.1384165
121	2.2344378	82.8690207	185.1656755	121	2.2910918	81.9675405	187.7951698	121	2.3491700	81.0801520	190.4710636
122	2.2493341	83.3135967	187.4001134	122	2.3068430	82.4010379	190.0862616	122	2.3658100	81.5028402	192.8202337
123	2.2643297	83.7552285	189.6494474	123	2.3227026	82.8315708	192.3931046	123	2.3825678	81.9225555	195.1860437
124	2.2794252	84.1939356	191.9137771	124	2.3386712	83.2591641	194.7158072	124	2.3994443	82.3393186	197.5686115
125	2.2946214	84.6297374	194.1932023	125	2.3547495	83.6838377	197.0544784	125	2.4164404	82.7531505	199.9680558
126	2.3099188	85.0626530	196.4878236	126	2.3709384	84.1056116	199.4092280	126	2.4335568	83.1640716	202.3844962
127	2.3253183	85.4927017	198.7977025	127	2.3872386	84.5245057	201.7801664	127	2.4507945	83.5721026	204.8180531
128	2.3408204	85.9199023	201.1230607	128	2.4036509	84.9405394	204.1674050	128	2.4681543	83.9772636	207.2688476
129	2.3564259	86.3442739	203.4638812	129	2.4201760	85.3537325	206.5710560	129	2.4856371	84.3795750	209.7370019
130	2.3721354	86.7658350	205.8203070	130	2.4368147	85.7641043	208.9912320	130	2.5032437	84.7790567	212.2226390
131	2.3879496	87.1846043	208.1924424	131	2.4535678	86.1716741	211.4280467	131	2.5209750	85.1757286	214.7258827
132	2.4038693	87.6006003	210.5803920	132	2.4704361	86.5764609	213.8816145	132	2.5388319	85.5696105	217.2468577
133	2.4198951	88.0138413	212.9842613	133	2.4874203	86.9784838	216.3520506	133	2.5568153	85.9607221	219.7856896
134	2.4360277	88.4243457	215.4041564	134	2.5045214	87.3777617	218.8394710	134	2.5749261	86.3490827	222.3425049
135	2.4522679	88.8321315	217.8401841	135	2.5217399	87.7743133	221.3439923	135	2.5931651	86.7347118	224.9174310
136	2.4686163	89.2372167	220.2924520	136	2.5390769	88.1681572	223.8657323	136	2.6115334	87.1176286	227.5105962
137	2.4850738	89.6396192	222.7610683	137	2.5565331	88.5593119	226.4048092	137	2.6300318	87.4978522	230.1221296
138	2.5016409	90.0393568	225.2461421	138	2.5741092	88.9477958	228.9613422	138	2.6486611	87.8754014	232.7521613
139	2.5183186	90.4364472	227.7477831	139	2.5918062	89.3336272	231.5354515	139	2.6674225	88.2502952	235.4008225
140	2.5351073	90.8309078	230.2661016	140	2.6096249	89.7168240	234.1272577	140	2.6863167	88.6225521	238.0682449
141	2.5520081	91.2227561	232.8012090	141	2.6275661	90.0974043	236.7368826	141	2.7053448	88.9921907	240.7545617
142	2.5690214	91.6120204	235.3532170	142	2.6456306	90.4753861	239.3644487	142	2.7245077	89.3592295	243.4599065
143	2.5861483	91.9986848	237.9222385	143	2.6638193	90.8507869	242.0100793	143	2.7438063	89.7236887	246.1844142
144	2.6033892	92.3827995	240.5083888	144	2.6821331	91.2236245	244.6738986	144	2.7632416	90.0855805	248.9282204
145	2.6207452	92.7643703	243.1117760	145	2.7005727	91.5939163	247.3560316	145	2.7828145	90.4449290	251.6914620
146	2.6382168	93.1434142	245.7325212	146	2.7191392	91.9616797	250.0566043	146	2.8025261	90.8017499	254.4742765
147	2.6558049	93.5199479	248.3707380	147	2.7378332	92.3269321	252.7757435	147	2.8223774	91.1560611	257.2768027
148	2.6735103	93.8939880	251.0265249	148	2.7566558	92.6896905	255.5135767	148	2.8423692	91.5078803	260.0991800
149	2.6913337	94.2655510	253.7000532	149	2.7756079	93.0499719	258.2702326	149	2.8625026	91.8572250	262.9415492
150	2.7092759	94.6346533	256.3913869	150	2.7946902	93.4077933	261.0458404	150	2.8827787	92.2041125	265.8040518
151	2.7273378	95.0013112	259.1006628	151	2.8139036	93.7631715	263.8405306	151	2.9031984	92.5485602	268.6868305
152	2.7455200	95.3655410	261.8280006	152	2.8332492	94.1161232	266.6544342	152	2.9237627	92.8905852	271.5900289
153	2.7638235	95.7273586	264.5735206	153	2.8527278	94.4666649	269.4876835	153	2.9444727	93.2302046	274.5137916
154	2.7822490	96.0867800	267.3373440	154	2.8723403	94.8148130	272.3404113	154	2.9653294	93.5674353	277.4582643
155	2.8007973	96.4438212	270.1195930	155	2.8920877	95.1605840	275.2127516	155	2.9863338	93.9022940	280.4235937
156	2.8194693	96.7984979	272.9203903	156	2.9119708	95.5039940	278.1048393	156	3.0074870	94.2347975	283.4099275
157	2.8382657	97.1508257	275.7398596	157	2.9319906	95.8450593	281.0168101	157	3.0287900	94.5649624	286.4174145
158	2.8571875	97.5008202	278.5781253	158	2.9521480	96.1837957	283.9488006	158	3.0502440	94.8928050	289.4462045
159	2.8762354	97.8434969	281.4353128	159	2.9724440	96.5202192	286.9009486	159	3.0718498	95.2183418	292.4964485
160	2.8954103	98.1938711	284.3115482	160	2.9928796	96.8543455	289.8733927	160	3.0936088	95.5415888	295.5582983
161	2.9147131	98.5369581	287.2069585	161	3.0134556	97.1861905	292.8662722	161	3.1155218	95.8625624	298.6519071
162	2.9341445	98.8777729	290.1216716	162	3.0341731	97.5157695	295.8797279	162	3.1375901	96.1812783	301.7774289
163	2.9537054	99.2163307	293.0558161	163	3.0550331	97.8430982	298.9139010	163	3.1598147	96.4977526	304.9150191
164	2.9733968	99.5526464	296.0095215	164	3.0760364	98.1681919	301.9689341	164	3.1821967	96.8120009	308.0748338
165	2.9932195	99.8867348	298.9829183	165	3.0971842	98.4910658	305.0449705	165	3.2047373	97.1240389	311.2570305
166	3.0131743	100.2186108	301.9761378	166	3.1184773	98.8117352	308.1421547	166	3.2274375	97.4338823	314.4617678
167	3.0332621	100.5482888	304.9893120	167	3.1399168	99.1302149	311.2606320	167	3.2502985	97.7415463	317.6892053
168	3.0534838	100.8757836	308.0225741	168	3.1615038	99.4465201	314.4005488	168	3.2733215	98.0470464	320.9395039
169	3.0738404	101.2011096	311.0760580	169	3.1832391	99.7606655	317.5620526	169	3.2965075	98.3503978	324.2128254
170	3.0943327	101.5242810	314.1498983	170	3.2051239	100.0726660	320.7452917	170	3.3198578	98.6516155	327.5093329
171	3.1149615	101.8453123	317.2442310	171	3.2271591	100.3825360	323.9504156	171	3.3433734	98.9507146	330.8291907
172	3.1357280	102.1642175	320.3591925	172	3.2493458	100.6902903	327.1775747	172	3.3670557	99.2477100	334.1725641
173	3.1566328	102.4810107	323.4949205	173	3.2716851	100.9959432	330.4269205	173	3.3909056	99.5426164	337.5396198
174	3.1776770	102.7957060	326.6515533	174	3.2941779	101.2995090	333.6986056	174	3.4149246	99.8354487	340.9305254
175	3.1988615	103.1083173	329.8292303	175	3.3168254	101.6010021	336.9927835	175	3.4391136	100.1262213	344.3454500
176	3.2201873	103.4188582	333.0280919	176	3.3396286	101.9004366	340.3096089	176	3.4634740	100.4149487	347.7845036
177	3.2416552	103.7273426	336.2482791	177	3.3625885	102.1978266	343.6492375	177	3.4880069	100.7016454	351.2480376
178	3.2632662	104.0337840	339.4899343	178	3.3857063	102.4931859	347.0118260	178	3.5127137	100.9863256	354.7360445
179	3.2850213	104.3381960	342.7532006	179	3.4089830	102.7865285	350.3975323	179	3.5375954	101.2690035	358.2487582
180	3.3069215	104.6405921	346.0382219	180	3.4324198	103.0778682	353.8065154	180	3.5626533	101.5496932	361.7863535
181	3.3289676	104.9409855	349.3451434	181	3.4560177	103.3672186	357.2389351	181	3.5878888	101.8284086	365.3490069
182	3.3511607	105.2393896	352.6741110	182	3.4797778	103.6545932	360.6949728	182	3.6133030	102.1051637	368.9368957
183	3.3735018	105.5358175	356.0252718	183	3.5037013	103.9400057	364.1747306	183	3.6388972	102.3799722	372.5501987
184	3.3959918	105.8302823	359.3987736	184	3.5277892	104.2234694	367.6784319	184	3.6646728	102.6528479	376.1890959
185	3.4186318	106.1227960	362.7947654	185	3.5520428	104.5049975	371.2062211	185	3.6906309	102.9238043	379.8537687
186	3.4414227	106.4133744	366.2133972	186	3.5764631	104.7846033	374.7582639	186	3.7167728	103.1928549	383.5443996
187	3.4643655	106.7020276	369.6548198	187	3.6010513	105.0623008	378.3347270	187	3.7431000	103.4600131	387.2611724
188	3.4874612	106.9887691	373.1191853	188	3.6258085	105.3381006	381.9357782	188	3.7696136	103.7252923	391.0042704
189	3.5107110	107.2736117	376.6066465	189	3.6507359	105.6120180	385.5615867	189	3.7963150	103.9887056	394.7738860
190	3.5341157	107.5565679	380.1173675	190	3.6758347	105.8840650	389.2123226	190	3.8232056	104.2502662	398.5702010
191	3.5576765	107.8376503	383.6514732	191	3.7011061	106.1542545	392.8881573	191	3.8502866	104.5099872	402.3934066
192	3.5813943	108.1168711	387.2091497	192	3.7265512	106.4225991	396.5892634	192	3.8775595	104.7678813	406.2436932
193	3.6052703	108.3942428	390.7905441	193	3.7521712	106.6891115	400.3158146	193	3.9050255	105.0239616	410.1212527
194	3.6293054	108.6697777	394.3958144	194	3.7779674	106.9538041	404.0679858	194	3.9326861	105.2782407	414.0262783
195	3.6535008	108.9434877	398.0251198	195	3.8039409	107.2166894	407.8459532	195	3.9605427	105.5307314	417.9589644
196	3.6778575	109.2153852	401.6786206	196	3.8300930	107.4777796	411.6498942	196	3.9885965	105.7814461	421.9195071
197	3.7023765	109.4854819	405.3564781	197	3.8564249	107.7370871	415.4799872	197	4.0168491	106.0303975	425.9081036
198	3.7270590	109.7537900	409.0588546	198	3.8829378	107.9946241	419.3364121	198	4.0453018	106.2775978	429.9249527
199	3.7519061	110.0203212	412.7859136	199	3.9096330	108.2504026	423.2193500	199	4.0739560	106.5230595	433.9702544
200	3.7769188	110.2850873	416.5378197	200	3.9365118	108.5044346	427.1289830	200	4.1028132	106.7667947	438.0442104

Table 1

M	C(8.00,M,12)	A(8.00,M,12)	S(8.00,M,12)	M	C(8.25,M,12)	A(8.25,M,12)	S(8.25,M,12)	M	C(8.50,M,12)	A(8.50,M,12)	S(8.50,M,12)
201	3.6020983	110.5481000	420.3147385	201	3.9635753	108.7567321	431.0654948	201	4.1318748	107.0088156	442.1470235
202	3.6274456	110.8093708	424.1168368	202	3.9908249	109.0073068	435.0290700	202	4.1611422	107.2491342	446.2788963
203	3.6529619	111.0689114	427.9442824	203	4.0182618	109.2561707	439.0198949	203	4.1906170	107.4877626	450.4400405
204	3.8766483	111.3257332	431.7972443	204	4.0455873	109.5033352	443.0381567	204	4.2203005	107.7247125	454.6306575
205	3.9045060	111.5828475	435.6758926	205	4.0737028	109.7488121	447.0840440	205	4.2501943	107.9599959	458.8509560
206	3.9305360	111.8372658	439.5803985	206	4.0017095	109.9926129	451.1577468	206	4.2802998	108.1936244	463.1011522
207	3.9567396	112.0899991	443.5109345	207	4.1299088	110.2347490	455.2594965	207	4.3105186	108.4256096	467.3814521
208	3.9831178	112.3410587	447.4676741	208	4.1583019	110.4752318	459.3893651	208	4.3411522	108.6559632	471.6920707
209	4.0096719	112.5904557	451.4507919	209	4.1868902	110.7140726	463.5476670	209	4.3719020	108.8846966	476.0332229
210	4.0364031	112.8382010	455.4604638	210	4.2156751	110.9512825	467.7345572	210	4.4028696	109.1118212	480.4051249
211	4.0633125	113.0843056	459.4968669	211	4.2446579	111.1868727	471.9502323	211	4.4340566	109.3373483	484.8079945
212	4.0904012	113.3287804	463.5601794	212	4.2738399	111.4208544	476.1948901	212	4.4654645	109.5612892	489.2420511
213	4.1176705	113.5716362	467.6505806	213	4.3032225	111.6532383	480.4687300	213	4.4970949	109.7836550	493.7075157
214	4.1451217	113.8128836	471.7682511	214	4.3328072	111.8840356	484.7719525	214	4.5289493	110.0044567	498.2046106
215	4.1727558	114.0525334	475.9133728	215	4.3625952	112.1132570	489.1047597	215	4.5610294	110.2237055	502.7335599
216	4.2005742	114.2905961	480.0861286	216	4.3925881	112.3409132	493.4673549	216	4.5933367	110.4414122	507.2945893
217	4.2285780	114.5270822	484.2867028	217	4.4227871	112.5670150	497.8599430	217	4.6258728	110.6575876	511.8879260
218	4.2567685	114.7620022	488.5152809	218	4.4531938	112.7915729	502.2827301	218	4.6586394	110.8722425	516.5137988
219	4.2851470	114.9953664	492.7720494	219	4.4838095	113.0145975	506.7359239	219	4.6916381	111.0853877	521.1724382
220	4.3137146	115.2271852	497.0571964	220	4.5146357	113.2360993	511.2197334	220	4.7248705	111.2970337	525.8640763
221	4.3424727	115.4574687	501.3709110	221	4.5456738	113.4560887	515.7343690	221	4.7583384	111.5071911	530.5889468
222	4.3714226	115.6862272	505.7133838	222	4.5769253	113.6745760	520.2800428	222	4.7920433	111.7158704	535.3472852
223	4.4005654	115.9134707	510.0848064	223	4.6083917	113.8915715	524.8569681	223	4.8259869	111.9230819	540.1393265
224	4.4299025	116.1392093	514.4853717	224	4.6400744	114.1070853	529.4653598	224	4.8601710	112.1288359	544.9553154
225	4.4594352	116.3634530	518.9152742	225	4.6719749	114.3211275	534.1054341	225	4.8945972	112.3331428	549.8254864
226	4.4891647	116.5862116	523.3747094	226	4.7040947	114.5337083	538.7774090	226	4.9292673	112.5360127	554.7200836
227	4.5190925	116.8074949	527.8638741	227	4.7364353	114.7448375	543.4815037	227	4.9641929	112.7374558	559.6493509
228	4.5492198	117.0273128	532.3829666	228	4.7689983	114.9545251	548.2179390	228	4.9993459	112.9374819	564.6135338
229	4.5795479	117.2456750	536.9321864	229	4.8017852	115.1627810	552.9869374	229	5.0347579	113.1361012	569.6128796
230	4.6100782	117.4625911	541.5117343	230	4.8347975	115.3696149	557.7887226	230	5.0704208	113.3333235	574.6476375
231	4.6408121	117.6780706	546.1218125	231	4.8680367	115.5750365	562.6235200	231	5.1063363	113.5291586	579.7180583
232	4.6717508	117.8921231	550.7626246	232	4.9015045	115.7790555	567.4915567	232	5.1425061	113.7236164	584.8243946
233	4.7028958	118.1047581	555.4343750	233	4.9352023	115.9816815	572.3930612	233	5.1789322	113.9167063	589.9669007
234	4.7342485	118.3159848	560.1372713	234	4.9691318	116.1829239	577.3262635	234	5.2156163	114.1084382	595.1458329
235	4.7658101	118.5258127	564.8715198	235	5.0032946	116.3827922	582.2973953	235	5.2525603	114.2988216	600.3614492
236	4.7975822	118.7342511	569.6373299	236	5.0376922	116.5812958	587.3006899	236	5.2897659	114.4878659	605.6140005
237	4.8295661	118.9413090	574.4349172	237	5.0723264	116.7784440	592.3383822	237	5.3272351	114.6755805	610.9037754
238	4.8617632	119.1469957	579.2644782	238	5.1071986	116.9742460	597.4107036	238	5.3649697	114.8619749	616.2310105
239	4.8941749	119.3513202	584.1262414	239	5.1423106	117.1687111	602.5179072	239	5.4029715	115.0470582	621.5959802
240	4.9268028	119.5542916	589.0204164	240	5.1776640	117.3618484	607.6602178	240	5.4412426	115.2308397	626.9989517
241	4.9596481	119.7559188	593.9472191	241	5.2132604	117.5536670	612.8378818	241	5.4797847	115.4133287	632.4401943
242	4.9927125	119.9562107	598.9068573	242	5.2491016	117.7441757	618.0511422	242	5.5185999	115.5945340	637.9199790
243	5.0259972	120.1551762	603.8995797	243	5.2851892	117.9333837	623.3002438	243	5.5576899	115.7744649	643.4385788
244	5.0595039	120.3528241	608.9255769	244	5.3215249	118.1212998	628.5854330	244	5.5970569	115.9531302	648.9962668
245	5.0932339	120.5491630	613.9850808	245	5.3581103	118.3079328	633.9069579	245	5.6367027	116.1305389	654.5933257
246	5.1271888	120.7442016	619.0783147	246	5.3949473	118.4932914	639.2650682	246	5.6766294	116.3066998	660.2300284
247	5.1613700	120.9379487	624.2055034	247	5.4320376	118.6773844	644.6600156	247	5.7168388	116.4816216	665.9066578
248	5.1957792	121.1304126	629.3668734	248	5.4693829	118.8602203	650.0920532	248	5.7573331	116.6553132	671.6234966
249	5.2304177	121.3216019	634.5626526	249	5.5069849	119.0418079	655.5614361	249	5.7981142	116.8277830	677.3808297
250	5.2652871	121.5115251	639.7930703	250	5.5448454	119.2221556	661.0684209	250	5.8391842	116.9990398	683.1789439
251	5.3003891	121.7001904	645.0583574	251	5.5829662	119.4012718	666.6132663	251	5.8805451	117.1690921	689.0181281
252	5.3357250	121.8876064	650.3587465	252	5.6213491	119.5791651	672.1962326	252	5.9221989	117.3379483	694.8986732
253	5.3712965	122.0737812	655.6944715	253	5.6599059	119.7556437	677.8175817	253	5.9641479	117.5056169	700.8208722
254	5.4071051	122.2587230	661.0657650	254	5.6909084	119.9313159	683.4775775	254	6.0063939	117.6721061	706.7850200
255	5.4431525	122.442A401	666.4728731	255	5.7380883	120.1055899	689.1764859	255	6.0489392	117.8374243	712.7914139
256	5.4794402	122.6249405	671.9160256	256	5.7775377	120.2786740	694.9145742	256	6.0917858	118.0015798	718.8403531
257	5.5159698	122.8062323	677.3954658	257	5.8172583	120.4505763	700.6921119	257	6.1349360	118.1645807	724.9321389
258	5.5527429	122.9863235	682.9114355	258	5.8572519	120.6213049	706.5093702	258	6.1783918	118.3264351	731.0670749
259	5.5897612	123.1652220	688.4641784	259	5.8975205	120.7908676	712.3666221	259	6.2221554	118.4871511	737.2454667
260	5.6270263	123.3429357	694.0539396	260	5.9380660	120.9592726	718.2641427	260	6.2662290	118.6467367	743.4676221
261	5.6645398	123.5194726	699.6809659	261	5.9788902	121.1265278	724.2022087	261	6.3506148	118.8051999	749.7338511
262	5.7023034	123.6948403	705.3455057	262	6.0199951	121.2926409	730.1810988	262	6.3553150	118.9625485	756.0444659
263	5.7403187	123.8690467	711.0478091	263	6.0613825	121.4576197	736.2010939	263	6.4003318	119.1187904	762.3997809
264	5.7785875	124.0420993	716.7881278	264	6.1030545	121.6214721	742.2624764	264	6.4456675	119.2739334	768.8001127
265	5.8171114	124.2140060	722.5667153	265	6.1450130	121.7842057	748.3655310	265	6.4913243	119.4279852	775.2457801
266	5.8558922	124.3847741	728.3838268	266	6.1872600	121.9458281	754.5105440	266	6.5373045	119.5809534	781.7371044
267	5.8949315	124.5544114	734.2397189	267	6.2297974	122.1063470	760.6978040	267	6.5836104	119.7328458	788.2744089
268	5.9342310	124.7229252	740.1346904	268	6.2726273	122.2657698	766.9276014	268	6.6302443	119.8836698	794.8560193
269	5.9737925	124.8903231	746.0688814	269	6.3157516	122.4241041	773.2002287	269	6.6772085	120.0334329	801.4882636
270	6.0136178	125.0566123	752.0426740	270	6.3591724	122.5813573	779.5159802	270	6.7245054	120.1821428	808.1654722
271	6.0537086	125.2218003	758.0562918	271	6.4028917	122.7375367	785.8751526	271	6.7721373	120.3298066	814.8899776
272	6.0940667	125.3858944	764.1100004	272	6.4469116	122.8926497	792.2780443	272	6.8201067	120.4764319	821.6621149
273	6.1346938	125.5489017	770.2040671	273	6.4912341	123.0467036	798.7249559	273	6.8684157	120.6220259	828.4822216
274	6.1755917	125.7108295	776.3387609	274	6.5358613	123.1997057	805.2161899	274	6.9170670	120.7665958	835.3506373
275	6.2167624	125.8716849	782.5143526	275	6.5807954	123.3516630	811.7520513	275	6.9660629	120.9101489	842.2677044
276	6.2582074	126.0314751	788.7311150	276	6.6260383	123.5025827	818.3328466	276	7.0154059	121.0526924	849.2337673
277	6.2999288	126.1902070	794.9893224	277	6.6715923	123.6524720	824.9588849	277	7.0650983	121.1942332	856.2491731
278	6.3419283	126.3478878	801.2892512	278	6.7174595	123.8013378	831.6304773	278	7.1151428	121.3347785	863.3142714
279	6.3842079	126.5045243	807.6311796	279	6.7636421	123.9491871	838.3479368	279	7.1655417	121.4743353	870.4294142
280	6.4267693	126.6601235	814.0153875	280	6.8101421	124.0960269	845.1115789	280	7.2162976	121.6129105	877.5949559
281	6.4696144	126.8146922	820.4421567	281	6.8569618	124.2418641	851.9217210	281	7.2674131	121.7505111	884.8112535
282	6.5127451	126.9682373	826.9117711	282	6.9041035	124.3867055	858.7786828	282	7.3183906	121.8871438	892.0786666
283	6.5561634	127.1207655	833.4245163	283	6.9515692	124.5305579	865.6827863	283	7.3707327	122.0228155	899.3975571
284	6.5998712	127.2722836	839.9806797	284	6.9993612	124.6734281	872.6343555	284	7.4229421	122.1575330	906.7682898
285	6.6438703	127.4227983	846.5805509	285	7.0474818	124.8153228	879.6337167	285	7.4755212	122.2913030	914.1912319
286	6.6881628	127.5723162	853.2244213	286	7.0959332	124.9562485	886.6811985	286	7.5284728	122.4241320	921.6667531
287	6.7327506	127.7208439	859.9125841	287	7.1447178	125.0962121	893.7771317	287	7.5817995	122.5560268	929.1952260
288	6.7776356	127.8683880	866.6453346	288	7.1938377	125.2352199	900.9218495	288	7.6355039	122.6869939	936.7770255
289	6.8223198	128.0149549	873.4229702	289	7.2432954	125.3732787	908.1156872	289	7.6895888	122.8170399	944.4125294
290	6.8683053	128.1605512	880.2457900	290	7.2930930	125.5103947	915.3589826	290	7.7440567	122.9461712	952.1021182
291	6.9140940	128.3051834	887.1140953	291	7.3432330	125.6465745	922.6520756	291	7.7989104	123.0743942	959.8461749
292	6.9601879	128.4488576	894.0281893	292	7.3937178	125.7818244	929.9953086	292	7.8541527	123.2017154	967.6450853
293	7.0065892	128.5915804	900.9883772	293	7.4445496	125.9161509	937.3890264	293	7.9097863	123.3281411	975.4992380
294	7.0532998	128.7333580	907.9949664	294	7.4957308	126.0495602	944.8335759	294	7.9658139	123.4536775	983.4090242
295	7.1003218	128.8741967	915.0482662	295	7.5472640	126.1820585	952.3293068	295	8.0222384	123.5783310	991.3748382
296	7.1476573	129.0141027	922.1485880	296	7.5991514	126.3136522	959.8765708	296	8.0790626	123.7021078	999.3970766
297	7.1953083	129.1530822	929.2962452	297	7.6513956	126.4443473	967.4757222	297	8.1362893	123.8250139	1007.4761393
298	7.2432770	129.2911412	936.4915535	298	7.7039989	126.5741500	975.1271178	298	8.1939214	123.9470556	1015.6124286
299	7.2915655	129.4282860	943.7348306	299	7.7569639	126.7030664	982.8311167	299	8.2519617	124.0682389	1023.8063500
300	7.3401760	129.5645225	951.0263961	300	7.8102931	126.8311026	990.5880807	300	8.3104130	124.1885699	1032.0583116

Table 1

M	C(8.00,M,12)	A(8.00,M,12)	S(8.00,M,12)	C(8.25,M,12)	A(8.25,M,12)	S(8.25,M,12)	C(8.50,M,12)	A(8.50,M,12)	S(8.50,M,12)
301	7.3891105	129.6998568	958.3665721	7.8639888	126.9582645	998.3983737	8.3692785	124.3080545	1040.3687247
302	7.4383712	129.8342948	965.7556026	7.9180538	127.0845582	1006.2623626	8.4285609	124.4266987	1048.7380031
303	7.4879604	129.9678425	973.1940538	7.9724904	127.2099895	1014.1804163	8.4862632	124.5445084	1057.1665640
304	7.5378801	130.1005058	980.6820142	8.0273012	127.3345644	1022.1529067	8.5483884	124.6614895	1065.6548272
305	7.5881326	130.2322905	988.2198943	8.0824889	127.4582686	1030.1802079	8.6089395	124.7776479	1074.2032155
306	7.6387202	130.3632025	995.8080269	8.1380560	127.5911681	1038.2628969	8.6699194	124.8929892	1082.8121550
307	7.6896450	130.4932475	1003.4467471	8.1940052	127.7032085	1046.4007529	8.7313314	125.0075193	1091.4820744
308	7.7409093	130.6224313	1011.1363921	8.2503390	127.8244157	1054.5947581	8.7931783	125.1212438	1100.2134058
309	7.7925154	130.7507596	1018.8773014	8.3070601	127.9447952	1062.8450971	8.8554633	125.2341684	1109.0065841
310	7.8444655	130.8782360	1026.6698167	8.3641711	128.0643528	1071.1521571	8.9181895	125.3462988	1117.8620474
311	7.8967619	131.0048722	1034.5142822	8.4216748	128.1830940	1079.5163282	8.9813600	125.4576405	1126.7802369
312	7.9494070	131.1306677	1042.4110441	8.4795738	128.3010245	1087.9380030	9.0449780	125.5681391	1135.7615970
313	8.0024030	131.2556302	1050.3604510	8.5378708	128.4181497	1096.4175768	9.1090466	125.6779801	1144.8065749
314	8.0557524	131.3797651	1058.3628541	8.5965987	128.5344752	1104.9554476	9.1735690	125.7869889	1153.9156215
315	8.1094574	131.5030779	1065.4166064	8.6556701	128.6500064	1113.5520163	9.2385484	125.8952310	1163.0891905
316	8.1635204	131.6255741	1074.5280638	8.7151779	128.7647487	1122.2076864	9.3039882	126.0027118	1172.3277390
317	8.2179439	131.7472590	1082.6915842	8.7750947	128.8787076	1130.9228643	9.3698914	126.1094366	1181.6317271
318	8.2727302	131.8681381	1090.9095281	8.8354235	128.9918884	1139.6979590	9.4362615	126.2154108	1191.0016165
319	8.3278817	131.9882167	1099.1822583	8.8961670	129.1042963	1148.5333825	9.5031017	126.3206396	1200.4378800
320	8.3834009	132.1075000	1107.5101401	8.9573282	129.2159368	1157.4295495	9.5704153	126.4251283	1209.9409817
321	8.4392903	132.2259934	1115.8935410	9.0183098	129.3268149	1166.3868777	9.6382057	126.5288820	1219.5113970
322	8.4955522	132.3437020	1124.3328313	9.0809148	129.4369360	1175.4057875	9.7064764	126.6319060	1229.1496027
323	8.5521892	132.4606312	1132.8283835	9.1433461	129.5463051	1184.4867022	9.7752306	126.7342054	1238.8560791
324	8.6092038	132.5767859	1141.3805727	9.2062066	129.6549275	1193.6300483	9.8444718	126.8357863	1248.6313096
325	8.6665985	132.6921714	1149.9897766	9.2694993	129.7628082	1202.8362549	9.9142035	126.9366507	1258.4757814
326	8.7243758	132.8067928	1158.6563751	9.3332271	129.8699523	1212.1057542	9.9844291	127.0368065	1268.3899849
327	8.7825383	132.9206551	1167.3807509	9.3973930	129.9763648	1221.4389813	10.0551521	127.1362581	1278.3744140
328	8.8410886	133.0337634	1176.1632893	9.4620001	130.0820507	1230.8363743	10.1263761	127.2350101	1288.4295661
329	8.9000292	133.1461225	1185.0043779	9.5270513	130.1870149	1240.2983744	10.1981046	127.3330676	1298.5559422
330	8.9593627	133.2577376	1193.9044071	9.5925498	130.2912625	1249.8254257	10.2703412	127.4304353	1308.7540468
331	9.0190918	133.3686135	1202.8637698	9.6584986	130.3947983	1259.4179755	10.3430894	127.5271182	1319.0243879
332	9.0792191	133.4787552	1211.4828546	9.7249008	130.4976271	1269.0764741	10.4163530	127.6231211	1329.3674774
333	9.1397472	133.5881674	1220.9620807	9.7917595	130.5997538	1278.8013749	10.4901355	127.7184488	1339.7838303
334	9.2006789	133.6968550	1230.1018279	9.8590778	130.7011831	1288.5931343	10.5644406	127.8131059	1350.2739658
335	9.2620167	133.8048229	1239.3025068	9.9268590	130.8019199	1298.4522121	10.6392721	127.9070973	1360.8384064
336	9.3237635	133.9120757	1248.5645235	9.9951061	130.9019689	1308.3790711	10.7146336	128.0004276	1371.4776785
337	9.3859219	134.0186182	1257.8852870	10.0638225	131.0013347	1318.3741772	10.7905289	128.0931015	1382.1923121
338	9.4484947	134.1244552	1267.2742089	10.1330113	131.1000221	1328.4379997	10.8669618	128.1851235	1392.9628409
339	9.5114847	134.2295912	1276.7227037	10.2026757	131.1980356	1338.5710110	10.9439361	128.2764983	1403.8498027
340	9.5743946	134.3340310	1286.2341884	10.2728191	131.2953798	1348.7736867	11.0214557	128.3672304	1414.7937389
341	9.6387272	134.4377792	1295.8090830	10.3434447	131.3920594	1359.0465058	11.0995243	128.4573244	1425.8151945
342	9.7029854	134.5408402	1305.4478102	10.4145559	131.4880789	1369.3899505	11.1781459	128.5467847	1436.9147188
343	9.7676720	134.6432188	1315.1507956	10.4861560	131.5834427	1379.8045064	11.2573245	128.6356157	1448.0928648
344	9.8327898	134.7449193	1324.9184676	10.5582483	131.6781554	1390.2906624	11.3370639	128.7238220	1459.3501892
345	9.8983417	134.8459463	1334.7512574	10.6308363	131.7722214	1400.8489108	11.4173681	128.8114078	1470.6872531
346	9.9643307	134.9463043	1344.6495991	10.7039233	131.8656451	1411.4797470	11.4982411	128.8983777	1482.1046211
347	10.0307595	135.0459977	1354.6139298	10.7775127	131.9584308	1422.1836703	11.5796870	128.9847358	1493.6028622
348	10.0976313	135.1450308	1364.6446893	10.8516081	132.0505831	1432.9611630	11.6617097	129.0704865	1505.1825492
349	10.1649488	135.2434081	1374.7422026	10.9262130	132.1421061	1443.8127912	11.7443135	129.1556341	1516.8442569
350	10.2327151	135.3411338	1384.9072694	11.0013307	132.2330042	1454.7390041	11.8275024	129.2401828	1528.5885724
351	10.3009332	135.4382124	1395.1399846	11.0769648	132.3232816	1465.7403348	11.9112805	129.3241368	1540.4160748
352	10.3696061	135.5346481	1405.4409178	11.1531189	132.4129427	1476.8172996	11.9956521	129.4075004	1552.3273554
353	10.4387368	135.6304451	1415.8105259	11.2297966	132.5019915	1487.9704186	12.0806213	129.4902776	1564.3230075
354	10.5083284	135.7256077	1426.2492608	11.3070015	132.5904322	1499.2002152	12.1661924	129.5724726	1576.4036288
355	10.5783839	135.8201401	1436.7575892	11.3847371	132.6782691	1510.5072167	12.2523696	129.6540894	1588.5698212
356	10.6489065	135.9140465	1447.3359731	11.4630072	132.7655063	1521.8919538	12.3391572	129.7351322	1600.8221908
357	10.7198992	136.0073310	1457.9848796	11.5418154	132.8521478	1533.3549810	12.4265596	129.8156050	1613.1613480
358	10.7913652	136.0999976	1468.7047788	11.6211654	132.9381977	1544.8967764	12.5145810	129.8955118	1625.5879075
359	10.8633076	136.1920506	1479.4961440	11.7010609	133.0236600	1556.5179417	12.6032260	129.9748566	1638.1024885
360	10.9357297	136.2834940	1490.3594517	11.7815057	133.1085388	1568.2190026	12.6924988	130.0536433	1650.7057145
361	11.0086346	136.3743318	1501.2951814	11.8625035	133.1928380	1580.0005083	12.7824040	130.1318758	1663.3982133
362	11.0820255	136.4645680	1512.3038159	11.9440582	133.2765617	1591.8630118	12.8729461	130.2095581	1676.1806174
363	11.1559056	136.5542066	1523.3856414	12.0261736	133.3597136	1603.8070700	12.9641294	130.2866940	1689.0535634
364	11.2302783	136.6432516	1534.5417470	12.1088536	133.4422978	1615.8332436	13.0559587	130.3632874	1702.0176928
365	11.3051468	136.7317069	1545.7720253	12.1921019	133.5243181	1627.9420972	13.1484384	130.4393421	1715.0736515
366	11.3805145	136.8195764	1557.0771722	12.2759226	133.6057784	1640.1341991	13.2415732	130.5148618	1728.2220899
367	11.4563846	136.9068640	1568.4576867	12.3603196	133.6866825	1652.4101217	13.3353676	130.5898504	1741.4636630
368	11.5327605	136.9935735	1579.9140713	12.4452968	133.7670341	1664.7704413	13.4298265	130.6643115	1754.7990307
369	11.6096456	137.0797087	1591.4468318	12.5308582	133.8468371	1677.2157381	13.5249544	130.7382489	1768.2288572
370	11.6870432	137.1652736	1603.0564773	12.6170079	133.9260952	1689.7465963	13.6207562	130.8116663	1781.7538116
371	11.7649568	137.2502718	1614.7435205	12.7037498	134.0048121	1702.3636042	13.7172365	130.8845672	1795.3745678
372	11.8433899	137.3347071	1626.5084773	12.7910881	134.0829915	1715.0673540	13.8144003	130.9569555	1809.0918043
373	11.9223458	137.4185832	1638.3518672	12.8790268	134.1606372	1727.8584421	13.9122523	131.0288346	1822.9062046
374	12.0018281	137.5019038	1650.2742130	12.9675701	134.2377526	1740.7374589	14.0107974	131.1002081	1836.8184569
375	12.0818403	137.5846727	1662.2760411	13.0567222	134.3143415	1753.7050390	14.1100406	131.1710796	1850.8292543
376	12.1623859	137.6668934	1674.3578814	13.1464871	134.3904076	1766.7617612	14.2099867	131.2414526	1864.9392949
377	12.2434685	137.7485696	1686.5202673	13.2368692	134.4659540	1779.9082483	14.3106408	131.3113307	1879.1492816
378	12.3250916	137.8297049	1698.7637357	13.3278727	134.5409848	1793.1451175	14.4120078	131.3807173	1893.4599223
379	12.4072589	137.9103028	1711.0888273	13.4195018	134.6155032	1806.4729802	14.5140929	131.4496159	1907.8719301
380	12.4899739	137.9903671	1723.4960862	13.5117609	134.6895128	1819.8924920	14.6169010	131.5180298	1922.3860230
381	12.5732404	138.0699011	1735.9860601	13.6046543	134.7630170	1833.4042529	14.7204374	131.5859626	1937.0029240
382	12.6570620	138.1489083	1748.5593005	13.6981863	134.8360194	1847.0089372	14.8247072	131.6534175	1951.7233514
383	12.7414424	138.2273924	1761.2163625	13.7923613	134.9085233	1860.7070934	14.9297155	131.7203980	1966.5480685
384	12.8263854	138.3053567	1773.9578050	13.8871834	134.9805321	1874.4994547	15.0354677	131.7869074	1981.4777840
385	12.9118946	138.3828046	1786.7841903	13.9826582	135.0520493	1888.3866385	15.1419689	131.8529491	1996.5132517
386	12.9979739	138.4597397	1799.6960850	14.0787889	135.1230781	1902.3692966	15.2492245	131.9185262	2011.6552206
387	13.0846271	138.5361653	1812.6940589	14.1755806	135.1936220	1916.4480856	15.3572398	131.9836420	2026.9044451
388	13.1718579	138.6120847	1825.7786859	14.2730377	135.2636842	1930.6236662	15.4660203	132.0482999	2042.2616849
389	13.2595703	138.6875014	1838.9505439	14.3711649	135.3332679	1944.8967039	15.5755713	132.1125030	2057.7277052
390	13.3480681	138.7624186	1852.2102142	14.4699666	135.4023766	1959.2678687	15.6858982	132.1762545	2073.3032764
391	13.4370552	138.8368396	1865.5582823	14.5694476	135.4710134	1973.7378353	15.7970067	132.2395577	2088.9891747
392	13.5266356	138.9107679	1878.9953375	14.6696126	135.5391815	1988.3072830	15.9089021	132.3024156	2104.7861813
393	13.6168132	138.9842065	1892.5219731	14.7704662	135.6068842	2002.9768956	16.0215902	132.3648313	2120.6950835
394	13.7075919	139.0571587	1906.1387863	14.8720131	135.6741246	2017.7473617	16.1350765	132.4268081	2136.7166737
395	13.7989759	139.1296279	1919.8463782	14.9742582	135.7409058	2032.6193749	16.2493666	132.4883490	2152.8517501
396	13.8909690	139.2016171	1933.6453541	15.0772062	135.8072311	2047.5936331	16.3644663	132.5494570	2169.1011167
397	13.9835755	139.2731296	1947.5363231	15.1808620	135.8731035	2062.6708393	16.4803812	132.6103866	2185.4655830
398	14.0767993	139.3441685	1961.5198986	15.2852305	135.9385262	2077.8517014	16.5971173	132.6703866	2201.9459642
399	14.1706447	139.4147369	1975.5966980	15.3903164	136.0035021	2093.1369318	16.7146802	132.7302143	2218.5430815
400	14.2651156	139.4848380	1989.7673426	15.4961248	136.0680343	2108.5272483	16.8330758	132.7896211	2235.2577616

Table 1

M	C(8.00,M,12)	A(8.00,M,12)	S(8.00,M,12)	C(8.25,M,12)	A(8.25,M,12)	S(8.25,M,12)	C(8.50,M,12)	A(8.50,M,12)	S(8.50,M,12)
401	14.3602164	139.5544748	2004.0324583	15.6026607	136.1321260	2124.0233731	16.9523101	132.8486101	2252.0908375
402	14.4559512	139.6236505	2018.3926747	15.7099290	136.1957800	2139.6260338	17.0723890	132.9071842	2269.0431476
403	14.5523242	139.6923680	2032.8485259	15.8179348	136.2589994	2155.3359628	17.1933184	132.9653464	2286.1155366
404	14.6493397	139.7606305	2047.4009500	15.9266831	136.3217871	2171.1538976	17.3151044	133.0230994	2303.3088550
405	14.7470019	139.8284409	2062.0502897	16.0361790	136.3841461	2187.0805306	17.4377531	133.0804462	2320.6239594
406	14.8453153	139.8958022	2076.7972917	16.1484277	136.4460793	2203.1167597	17.5612705	133.1373897	2338.0617125
407	14.9442841	139.9627174	2091.6426070	16.2574344	136.5075896	2219.2631874	17.6856628	133.1939327	2355.6229829
408	15.0439126	140.0291895	2106.5868900	16.3682043	136.5686799	2235.5206218	17.8109363	133.2500780	2373.3086458
409	15.1442054	140.0952213	2121.6308037	16.4817426	136.6293531	2251.6898261	17.9370971	133.3058284	2391.1195820
410	15.2451667	140.1608159	2136.7750090	16.5950546	136.6896120	2268.3715687	18.0641515	133.3611866	2409.0566791
411	15.3469012	140.2259760	2152.0201758	16.7091456	136.7494595	2284.9666232	18.1921059	133.4161555	2427.1208306
412	15.4491132	140.2907047	2167.3669770	16.8240209	136.8088983	2301.6757688	18.3209667	133.4707378	2445.3129365
413	15.5521073	140.3550046	2182.8160902	16.9396861	136.8679313	2318.4997897	18.4507402	133.5249362	2463.6339031
414	15.6557880	140.4188788	2198.3681975	17.0561464	136.9265612	2335.4394758	18.5814329	133.5787533	2482.0846433
415	15.7601599	140.4823299	2214.0239855	17.1734074	136.9847908	2352.4956222	18.7130514	133.6321920	2500.6660762
416	15.8352277	140.5453608	2229.7841454	17.2914746	137.0426227	2369.6690296	18.8456022	133.6852547	2519.3791276
417	15.9709958	140.6079743	2245.6493730	17.4103535	137.1000598	2386.9605042	18.9790919	133.7379443	2538.2247298
418	16.0774691	140.6701732	2261.6203689	17.5300497	137.1571047	2404.3708577	19.1135271	133.7902633	2557.2038216
419	16.1846523	140.7319601	2277.6978380	17.6505688	137.2137601	2421.9009074	19.2489146	133.8422143	2576.3173487
420	16.2925500	140.7933379	2293.8824903	17.7719164	137.2700287	2439.5514762	19.3852611	133.8937998	2595.5662633
421	16.4011670	140.8543091	2310.1750402	17.8940983	137.3259130	2457.3233926	19.5225733	133.9450226	2614.9515243
422	16.5105081	140.9148766	2326.5762072	18.0171203	137.3814158	2475.2174909	19.6608582	133.9958851	2634.4740977
423	16.6205781	140.9750430	2343.0867153	18.1409880	137.4365396	2493.2346112	19.8001226	134.0463898	2654.1349559
424	16.7313820	141.0348109	2359.7072934	18.2657073	137.4912870	2511.3755092	19.9403735	134.0965393	2673.9350785
425	16.8429245	141.0941830	2376.4386754	18.3912840	137.5456605	2529.6413064	20.0816178	134.1463361	2693.8754520
426	16.9552107	141.1531620	2393.2815909	18.5177241	137.5996629	2548.0325904	20.2233626	134.1957826	2713.9570698
427	17.0682454	141.2117503	2410.2368106	18.6450334	137.6532964	2566.5503145	20.3671150	134.2448814	2734.1809324
428	17.1820337	141.2699505	2427.3050560	18.7732180	137.7065638	2585.1953479	20.5113820	134.2936348	2754.5480474
429	17.2965806	141.3277655	2444.4870897	18.9022839	137.7594675	2603.9685660	20.6566710	134.3420453	2775.0594294
430	17.4118912	141.3851975	2461.7836703	19.0322371	137.8120099	2622.8708499	20.8029891	134.3901153	2795.7161004
431	17.5279704	141.4422492	2479.1955615	19.1630837	137.8641936	2641.9030870	20.9503436	134.4378473	2816.5190994
432	17.6448236	141.4989230	2496.7235319	19.2948299	137.9160209	2661.0661708	21.0987418	134.4852435	2837.4694330
433	17.7624557	141.5552216	2514.3683555	19.4274819	137.9674944	2680.3610007	21.2481913	134.5323063	2858.5681749
434	17.8808721	141.6111472	2532.1308112	19.5610458	138.0186164	2699.7884826	21.3986993	134.5790381	2879.8163661
435	18.0000779	141.6667026	2550.0116933	19.6955280	138.0693894	2719.3495284	21.5502734	134.6254412	2901.2150654
436	18.1200784	141.7218900	2568.0117612	19.8309348	138.1198156	2739.0450565	21.7029212	134.6715180	2922.7653388
437	18.2408790	141.7767119	2586.1318397	19.9672725	138.1698976	2758.8759913	21.8566502	134.7172706	2944.4682600
438	18.3624848	141.8311707	2604.3727186	20.1045475	138.2196376	2778.8432637	22.0114681	134.7627015	2966.3249102
439	18.4849014	141.8852689	2622.7352034	20.2427662	138.2690379	2798.9478112	22.1673827	134.8078128	2988.3363783
440	18.6081341	141.9390089	2641.2201048	20.3819352	138.3180010	2819.1905774	22.3244017	134.8526069	3010.5037610
441	18.7321883	141.9923929	2659.8282388	20.5220610	138.3668290	2839.5725127	22.4825328	134.8970858	3032.8281627
442	18.8570695	142.0454234	2678.5604271	20.6631502	138.4152244	2860.0945092	22.6417841	134.9412520	3055.3106955
443	18.9827833	142.0981028	2697.4174967	20.8052094	138.4632893	2880.7577239	22.8021634	134.9851074	3077.9524797
444	19.1093352	142.1504332	2716.4002800	20.9482452	138.5110260	2901.5629333	22.9636787	135.0286545	3100.7546431
445	19.2367308	142.2024171	2735.5096152	21.0922644	138.5584367	2922.5111785	23.1263381	135.0718952	3123.7183218
446	19.3649757	142.2540567	2754.7463460	21.2372737	138.6055237	2943.6034429	23.2901497	135.1148318	3146.8446600
447	19.4940755	142.3053543	2774.1113217	21.3832800	138.6522892	2964.8407166	23.4551216	135.1574664	3170.1348097
448	19.6240360	142.3563123	2793.6053972	21.5302900	138.6987354	2986.2239965	23.6212620	135.1998012	3193.5899313
449	19.7548629	142.4069327	2813.2294332	21.6783107	138.7448645	3007.7542865	23.7885793	135.2418382	3217.2111933
450	19.8865620	142.4572179	2832.9842961	21.8273491	138.7906786	3029.4325973	23.9570817	135.2835795	3240.9997726
451	20.0191391	142.5071701	2852.8708581	21.9774122	138.8361798	3051.2599464	24.1267777	135.3250272	3264.9568544
452	20.1526000	142.5567915	2872.8899972	22.1285069	138.8813704	3073.2373585	24.2976758	135.3661834	3289.0836321
453	20.2869507	142.6060843	2893.0425972	22.2806404	138.9262524	3095.3658654	24.4697843	135.4070501	3313.3813079
454	20.4221970	142.6550506	2913.3295478	22.4338198	138.9708280	3117.6465058	24.6431119	135.4476294	3337.8510922
455	20.5583450	142.7036926	2933.7517449	22.5880523	139.0150992	3140.0803255	24.8176673	135.4879233	3362.4942041
456	20.6954006	142.7520126	2954.3100898	22.7433451	139.0590681	3162.6683778	24.9934591	135.5279337	3387.3118714
457	20.8333700	142.8000125	2975.0054905	22.8997056	139.1027368	3185.4117229	25.1704961	135.5676628	3412.3053305
458	20.9722591	142.8476945	2995.8388604	23.0571411	139.1461073	3208.3114285	25.3487871	135.6071124	3437.4758266
459	21.1120742	142.8950608	3016.8111195	23.2155589	139.1891816	3231.3685696	25.5283410	135.6462846	3462.8246138
460	21.2528213	142.9421134	3037.9231937	23.3752666	139.2319619	3254.5842286	25.7091668	135.6851812	3488.3529548
461	21.3945068	142.9888543	3059.1760150	23.5359716	139.2744501	3277.9594952	25.8912734	135.7238043	3514.0621216
462	21.5371368	143.0352857	3080.5705218	23.6977814	139.3166481	3301.4954667	26.0746690	135.7621557	3539.9533550
463	21.6807178	143.0814097	3102.1076586	23.8607036	139.3585580	3325.1932481	26.2593655	135.8002373	3566.0280549
464	21.8252559	143.1272282	3123.7883764	24.0247459	139.4001818	3349.0539517	26.4453660	135.8380511	3592.2874304
465	21.9707576	143.1727432	3145.6136311	24.1899161	139.4415213	3373.0786976	26.6323907	135.8755989	3618.7327997
466	22.1172293	143.2179568	3167.5843898	24.3562217	139.4825786	3397.2686137	26.8213389	135.9128827	3645.3654904
467	22.2645775	143.2628710	3189.7016191	24.5236708	139.5233555	3421.6248355	27.0113234	135.9499042	3672.1868293
468	22.4131087	143.3074878	3211.9662966	24.6922710	139.5638540	3446.1465062	27.2026536	135.9866653	3699.1981527
469	22.5625294	143.3518090	3234.3794053	24.8620304	139.6040760	3470.8407772	27.3953391	136.0231679	3726.4008064
470	22.7129463	143.3958368	3256.9419347	25.0329568	139.6440233	3495.7028076	27.5893894	136.0594137	3753.7961454
471	22.8643659	143.4395730	3279.6548809	25.2050584	139.6836999	3520.7357644	27.7848142	136.0954046	3781.3855348
472	23.0167950	143.4830195	3302.5192468	25.3783432	139.7231016	3545.9408228	27.9816233	136.1311423	3809.1703491
473	23.1702403	143.5261783	3325.5360418	25.5528193	139.7622362	3571.3191660	28.1798265	136.1666287	3837.1519724
474	23.3247086	143.5690513	3348.7062821	25.7284949	139.8011036	3596.8719853	28.3794336	136.2018655	3865.3317989
475	23.4802066	143.6116404	3372.0309907	25.9053783	139.8397056	3622.6004803	28.5804546	136.2368544	3893.7112325
476	23.6367413	143.6539477	3395.5111973	26.0834778	139.8780441	3648.5058586	28.7828995	136.2715973	3922.2916871
477	23.7943196	143.6959742	3419.1479387	26.2628017	139.9161207	3674.5893364	28.9867784	136.3060958	3951.0745866
478	23.9529484	143.7377227	3442.9422583	26.4433585	139.9539374	3700.8521381	29.1921014	136.3403516	3980.0613649
479	24.1126347	143.7799448	3466.8952067	26.6251566	139.9914959	3727.2954966	29.3988788	136.3743665	4009.2534663
480	24.2733856	143.8203922	3491.0078415	26.8082045	140.0287999	3753.9206532	29.6071208	136.4081422	4038.6523451
481	24.4352082	143.8613167	3515.2812271	26.9925109	140.0658452	3780.7286577	29.8168379	136.4416803	4068.2594659
482	24.5961096	143.9019702	3539.7164353	27.1700484	140.1026396	3807.7213686	30.0280405	136.4749825	4098.0763038
483	24.7620970	143.9423545	3564.3145449	27.3649338	140.1391827	3834.8994531	30.2407391	136.5080505	4128.1043443
484	24.9271776	143.9824713	3589.0766419	27.5530677	140.1754763	3862.2643868	30.4549444	136.5408858	4158.3450835
485	25.0933588	144.0223226	3614.0038195	27.7424950	140.2115221	3889.8174545	30.6706669	136.5734903	4188.8000278
486	25.2606479	144.0619098	3639.0971784	27.9332247	140.2473217	3917.5599496	30.8879175	136.6058654	4219.4706947
487	25.4290522	144.1012349	3664.3578263	28.1252656	140.2828770	3945.4931742	31.1067069	136.6380128	4250.3586122
488	25.5985792	144.1402996	3689.7868785	28.3186268	140.3181894	3973.6184398	31.3270460	136.6699341	4281.4653191
489	25.7692364	144.1751056	3715.3854577	28.5133174	140.3532607	4001.9370667	31.5489460	136.7016309	4312.7923651
490	25.9410313	144.2176545	3741.1546941	28.7093464	140.3880926	4030.4503840	31.7724177	136.7331047	4344.3413111
491	26.1139715	144.2559482	3767.0957254	28.9067232	140.4226866	4059.1597304	31.9974723	136.7643572	4376.1137287
492	26.2880647	144.2939883	3793.2096970	29.1054569	140.4570444	4088.0664536	32.2241210	136.7953899	4408.1112010
493	26.4633184	144.3317765	3819.4977616	29.3055569	140.4911677	4117.1719105	32.4523752	136.8262042	4440.3353220
494	26.6397406	144.3693144	3845.9610801	29.5070326	140.5250579	4146.4774674	32.6822462	136.8568019	4472.7876973
495	26.8173388	144.4066037	3872.6008207	29.7098935	140.5587167	4175.9845001	32.9137455	136.8871843	4505.4699435
496	26.9961211	144.4436460	3899.4148806	29.9141490	140.5921447	4205.6943935	33.1468845	136.9173531	4538.3836890
497	27.1760952	144.4804431	3926.4142806	30.1198088	140.6253464	4235.6085425	33.3816749	136.9470596	4571.5305735
498	27.3572692	144.5169964	3953.5903758	30.3268825	140.6583205	4265.7283513	33.6181285	136.9770555	4604.9122484
499	27.5396510	144.5533077	3980.9476450	30.5353798	140.6910694	4296.0552337	33.8562569	137.0065921	4638.5303769
500	27.7232487	144.5893785	4008.4872960	30.7453105	140.7235947	4326.5906135	34.0960720	137.0359210	4672.3866337

Table 1

413

M	C(8.75,M,12)	A(8.75,M,12)	S(8.75,M,12)	M	C(9.00,M,12)	A(9.00,M,12)	S(9.00,M,12)	M	C(9.25,M,12)	A(9.25,M,12)	S(9.25,M,12)
1	1.0072917	.9927611	1.0000000	1	1.0075000	.9925558	1.0000000	1	1.0077083	.9923506	1.0000000
2	1.0146365	1.9783358	2.0072917	2	1.0150563	1.9777229	2.0075000	2	1.0154761	1.9771104	2.0077083
3	1.0220349	2.9567759	3.0219282	3	1.0226692	2.9555562	3.0225563	3	1.0233037	2.9543374	3.0231844
4	1.0294872	3.9281333	4.0439631	4	1.0303392	3.9261104	4.0452254	4	1.0311917	3.9240892	4.0464881
5	1.0369939	4.8924591	5.0734503	5	1.0380667	4.8894396	5.0755646	5	1.0391404	4.8864230	5.0776798
6	1.0445553	5.8498043	6.1104442	6	1.0458522	5.8455976	6.1136313	6	1.0471505	5.8413956	6.1168203
7	1.0521719	6.8002194	7.1549995	7	1.0536961	6.7946378	7.1594836	7	1.0552223	6.7890632	7.1639707
8	1.0598440	7.7437545	8.2071714	8	1.0615988	7.7366132	8.2131797	8	1.0633563	7.7294818	8.2191930
9	1.0675720	8.6804595	9.2670154	9	1.0695608	8.6715764	9.2747786	9	1.0715530	8.6627068	9.2825493
10	1.0753564	9.6103837	10.3345873	10	1.0775309	9.5995796	10.3443394	10	1.0798129	9.5887932	10.3541023
11	1.0831975	10.5335764	11.4099437	11	1.0853644	10.5206745	11.4219219	11	1.0881364	10.5077956	11.4339152
12	1.0910958	11.4500862	12.4931412	12	1.0935069	11.4349127	12.5075864	12	1.0965241	11.4197682	12.5220516
13	1.0990517	12.3599615	13.5842370	13	1.1020104	12.3423451	13.6013933	13	1.1049765	12.3247648	13.6185757
14	1.1070656	13.2632503	14.6832888	14	1.1102755	13.2430224	14.7034037	14	1.1134940	13.2228393	14.7235523
15	1.1151380	14.1600003	15.7903544	15	1.1186026	14.1369950	15.8136792	15	1.1220772	14.1140430	15.8370463
16	1.1232692	15.0502588	16.9054924	16	1.1269921	15.0243126	16.9322818	16	1.1307266	14.9984301	16.9591235
17	1.1314597	15.9340729	18.0287616	17	1.1354446	15.9050249	18.0592739	17	1.1394426	15.8760522	18.0898501
18	1.1397099	16.8114891	19.1602213	18	1.1439604	16.7791811	19.1947185	18	1.1482258	16.7469610	19.2292927
19	1.1480203	17.6825538	20.2999313	19	1.1525401	17.6468298	20.3386789	19	1.1570767	17.6112080	20.3775185
20	1.1563913	18.5473130	21.4479516	20	1.1611841	18.5080197	21.4912190	20	1.1659958	18.4688440	21.5345952
21	1.1648233	19.4058123	22.6043429	21	1.1698930	19.3627987	22.6524031	21	1.1749837	19.3199196	22.7005911
22	1.1733168	20.2580970	23.7691663	22	1.1786672	20.2112146	23.8222961	22	1.1840409	20.1644850	23.8755748
23	1.1818723	21.1042121	24.9424831	23	1.1875072	21.0533147	25.0009634	23	1.1931679	21.0025901	25.0596157
24	1.1904901	21.9442023	26.1243554	24	1.1964135	21.8891461	26.1884706	24	1.2023652	21.8342841	26.2527835
25	1.1991707	22.7781119	27.3148455	25	1.2053866	22.7187555	27.3848841	25	1.2116334	22.6596162	27.4551487
26	1.2079147	23.6059849	28.5140162	26	1.2144270	23.5421891	28.5902707	26	1.2209731	23.4786355	28.6667822
27	1.2167224	24.4278651	29.7219309	27	1.2235352	24.3594929	29.8046978	27	1.2303848	24.2913890	29.8877553
28	1.2255943	25.2437957	30.9386533	28	1.2327117	25.1707125	31.0282330	28	1.2398690	25.0979258	31.1181401
29	1.2345310	26.0538199	32.1642477	29	1.2419571	25.9758933	32.2609448	29	1.2494263	25.8982931	32.3580091
30	1.2435328	26.8579805	33.3987787	30	1.2512718	26.7750802	33.5029018	30	1.2590573	26.6925381	33.6074354
31	1.2526002	27.6563198	34.6423114	31	1.2606563	27.5683178	34.7541736	31	1.2687625	27.4807077	34.8664927
32	1.2617337	28.4488801	35.8949116	32	1.2701112	28.3556504	36.0148299	32	1.2785426	28.2628482	36.1352553
33	1.2709339	29.2357031	37.1566453	33	1.2796371	29.1371220	37.2849411	33	1.2883980	29.0390059	37.4137978
34	1.2802011	30.0168304	38.4275792	34	1.2892343	29.9127762	38.5645782	34	1.2983290	29.8092264	38.7021959
35	1.2895359	30.7923032	39.7077803	35	1.2989036	30.6826563	39.8538125	35	1.3083374	30.5735553	40.0005253
36	1.2989388	31.5621624	40.9973162	36	1.3085454	31.4468052	41.1527161	36	1.3184225	31.3320375	41.3088627
37	1.3084102	32.3264487	42.2962550	37	1.3184602	32.2052658	42.4613615	37	1.3285853	32.0847178	42.6272852
38	1.3179507	33.0852024	43.6046652	38	1.3283687	32.9580802	43.7798217	38	1.3388265	32.8316406	43.9558705
39	1.3275607	33.8384636	44.9226159	39	1.3383113	33.7052905	45.1081704	39	1.3491466	33.5728498	45.2946970
40	1.3372409	34.5862721	46.2501766	40	1.3483486	34.4469384	46.4464817	40	1.3595463	34.3083893	46.6438436
41	1.3469916	35.3286672	47.5874175	41	1.3584612	35.1830654	47.7948303	41	1.3700261	35.0383024	48.0033899
42	1.3568134	36.0656882	48.9344090	42	1.3686697	35.9137126	49.1532915	42	1.3805867	35.7626321	49.3734160
43	1.3667068	36.7973740	50.2912224	43	1.3789146	36.6389207	50.5219412	43	1.3912288	36.4814212	50.7540028
44	1.3766724	37.5237633	51.6579293	44	1.3892564	37.3587302	51.9008557	44	1.4019528	37.1947119	52.1452316
45	1.3867106	38.2448942	53.0346017	45	1.3996758	38.0731814	53.2901122	45	1.4127595	37.9025465	53.5471844
46	1.3968221	38.9608050	54.4213123	46	1.4101734	38.7823140	54.6897880	46	1.4236496	38.6049665	54.9599439
47	1.4070072	39.6715334	55.8181344	47	1.4207497	39.4861677	56.0999614	47	1.4346235	39.3020135	56.3835935
48	1.4172667	40.3771107	57.2251416	48	1.4314053	40.1847819	57.5207111	48	1.4456821	39.9937285	57.8182170
49	1.4276009	41.0775928	58.6424083	49	1.4421409	40.8781954	58.9521165	49	1.4568259	40.6801523	59.2638991
50	1.4380105	41.7729981	60.0700092	50	1.4529569	41.5664471	60.3942573	50	1.4680556	41.3613255	60.7207250
51	1.4484960	42.4633693	61.5080197	51	1.4638541	42.2495752	61.8472143	51	1.4793719	42.0372880	62.1887806
52	1.4590579	43.1487431	62.9565156	52	1.4748330	42.9276181	63.3110684	52	1.4907753	42.7080799	63.6681525
53	1.4696969	43.8291555	64.4155736	53	1.4858943	43.6006135	64.7859014	53	1.5022667	43.3737407	65.1589278
54	1.4804134	44.5046425	65.8852705	54	1.4970385	44.2685990	66.2717956	54	1.5138467	44.0343095	66.6611945
55	1.4912081	45.1752397	67.3656839	55	1.5082663	44.9316119	67.7688341	55	1.5255159	44.6898255	68.1750412
56	1.5020815	45.8409825	68.8568920	56	1.5195783	45.5896893	69.2771004	56	1.5372751	45.3403271	69.7005572
57	1.5130342	46.5019061	70.3589755	57	1.5309751	46.2428677	70.7966786	57	1.5491250	45.9858528	71.2378323
58	1.5240667	47.1580454	71.8720077	58	1.5424574	46.8911839	72.3276537	58	1.5610661	46.6264407	72.7869573
59	1.5351797	47.8094349	73.3960744	59	1.5540328	47.5346738	73.8701111	59	1.5730993	47.2621284	74.3480234
60	1.5463737	48.4561091	74.9312541	60	1.5656810	48.1733735	75.4241369	60	1.5952253	47.8929536	75.9211228
61	1.5576494	49.0981021	76.4776278	61	1.5774336	48.8073186	76.9898180	61	1.6074448	48.5189533	77.5063481
62	1.5690072	49.7354478	78.0352772	62	1.5892543	49.4365445	78.5672416	62	1.6197584	49.1401645	79.1037928
63	1.5804479	50.3681798	79.6042844	63	1.6011737	50.0610664	80.1564959	63	1.6221670	49.7566239	80.7135512
64	1.5919720	50.9963316	81.1847324	64	1.6131825	50.6809790	81.7576696	64	1.6346712	50.3683677	82.3357182
65	1.6035801	51.6199362	82.7767044	65	1.6252814	51.2962575	83.3708522	65	1.6472718	50.9754321	83.9703894
66	1.6152729	52.2390266	84.3802845	66	1.6374710	51.9069550	84.9961336	66	1.6599695	51.5778528	85.6176611
67	1.6270509	52.8536355	85.9955574	67	1.6497520	52.5131067	86.6336046	67	1.6727651	52.1756654	87.2776306
68	1.6389149	53.4637954	87.6226083	68	1.6621252	53.1147461	88.2833556	68	1.6856593	52.7689051	88.9503957
69	1.6508653	54.0695383	89.2615232	69	1.6745911	53.7119068	89.9454818	69	1.6986529	53.3576069	90.6360550
70	1.6629028	54.6708964	90.9123885	70	1.6871505	54.3046221	91.6200729	70	1.7117467	53.9418055	92.3347079
71	1.6750282	55.2679013	92.5752913	71	1.6998042	54.8929251	93.3072234	71	1.7249414	54.5215353	94.0464546
72	1.6872419	55.8605845	94.2503195	72	1.7125527	55.4768488	95.0070276	72	1.7382378	55.0968306	95.7713960
73	1.6995447	56.4489774	95.9375614	73	1.7253969	56.0564256	96.7195803	73	1.7516368	55.6677252	97.5096339
74	1.7119372	57.0331109	97.6371061	74	1.7383373	56.6316879	98.4449772	74	1.7651390	56.2342528	99.2612706
75	1.7244201	57.6130160	99.3490433	75	1.7513745	57.2026679	100.1833145	75	1.7787453	56.7964469	101.0264096
76	1.7369940	58.1887232	101.0734634	76	1.7645102	57.7693974	101.9346894	76	1.7924564	57.3543405	102.8051548
77	1.7496596	58.7602633	102.8104575	77	1.7777440	58.3319081	103.6991995	77	1.8062733	57.9079668	104.5976112
78	1.7624175	59.3276654	104.5601170	78	1.7910771	58.8902314	105.4769435	78	1.8201966	58.4573578	106.4038845
79	1.7752685	59.8909605	106.3225346	79	1.8045102	59.4443984	107.2680206	79	1.8342273	59.0025465	108.2240811
80	1.7882131	60.4501780	108.0978030	80	1.8180440	59.9944401	109.0725308	80	1.8483661	59.5435648	110.0583084
81	1.8012522	61.0053473	109.8860162	81	1.8316793	60.5403672	110.8905747	81	1.8626140	60.0804447	111.9066745
82	1.8143863	61.5564978	111.6872684	82	1.8454169	61.0822702	112.7222541	82	1.8769716	60.6132179	113.7692885
83	1.8276162	62.1036587	113.5016547	83	1.8592575	61.6201193	114.5676710	83	1.8914399	61.1419156	115.6462601
84	1.8409426	62.6468587	115.3292710	84	1.8732020	62.1539645	116.4269285	84	1.9060198	61.6665691	117.5377000
85	1.8543661	63.1861265	117.1702136	85	1.8872510	62.6838358	118.3001305	85	1.9207120	62.1872094	119.4437198
86	1.8678876	63.7214906	119.0245797	86	1.9014054	63.2097626	120.1873814	86	1.9355175	62.7038671	121.3644318
87	1.8815076	64.2529793	120.8924673	87	1.9156659	63.7317742	122.0887868	87	1.9504371	63.2165727	123.2999493
88	1.8952269	64.7806206	122.7739748	88	1.9300334	64.2499000	124.0044527	88	1.9654717	63.7253564	125.2503864
89	1.9090463	65.3044424	124.6692017	89	1.9445086	64.7641687	125.9344861	89	1.9806222	64.2302482	127.2158581
90	1.9229664	65.8244723	126.5782480	90	1.9590925	65.2746092	127.8789947	90	1.9958895	64.7312779	129.1964803
91	1.9369880	66.3407377	128.5012144	91	1.9737857	65.7812498	129.8380872	91	2.0112745	65.2284751	131.1923699
92	1.9511119	66.8532660	130.4382024	92	1.9885890	66.2841189	131.8118729	92	2.0267781	65.7218690	133.2036444
93	1.9653388	67.3620841	132.3893143	93	2.0035035	66.7832446	133.8004619	93	2.0424012	66.2114868	135.2304225
94	1.9796693	67.8672190	134.3546531	94	2.0185297	67.2786546	135.8039654	94	2.0581447	66.6973633	137.2728237
95	1.9941044	68.3686972	136.3343224	95	2.0336687	67.7703768	137.8224951	95	2.0740095	67.1795211	139.3309583
96	2.0086448	68.8665453	138.3284268	96	2.0489212	68.2584385	139.8561638	96	2.0899962	67.6579908	141.4049779
97	2.0232911	69.3607896	140.3370716	97	2.0642881	68.7428670	141.9050851	97	2.1061071	68.1328005	143.4949746
98	2.0380443	69.8514551	142.3603628	98	2.0797703	69.2236894	143.9693732	98	2.1223417	68.6039781	145.6010817
99	2.0529051	70.3385706	144.3984071	99	2.0953686	69.7009324	146.0491435	99	2.1387014	69.0715516	147.7234234
100	2.0678742	70.8221591	146.4513121	100	2.1110838	70.1746227	148.1445121	100	2.1551872	69.5355484	149.8621248

Table 1

M	C(8.75,M,12)	A(8.75,M,12)	S(8.75,M,12)	M	C(9.00,M,12)	A(9.00,M,12)	S(9.00,M,12)	M	C(9.25,M,12)	A(9.25,M,12)	S(9.25,M,12)
101	2.0829524	71.3022468	148.5191863	101	2.1269170	70.6447868	150.2555959	101	2.1718001	69.9959959	152.0173120
102	2.0981406	71.7788593	150.6021387	102	2.1428688	71.1114509	152.3825129	102	2.1885411	70.4529213	154.1891121
103	2.1134395	72.2520217	152.7002793	103	2.1589404	71.5746441	154.5253817	103	2.2054111	70.9063515	156.3776532
104	2.1288500	72.7217588	154.8137188	104	2.1751324	72.0343832	156.6843221	104	2.2224111	71.3563133	158.5830642
105	2.1443729	73.1880957	156.9425689	105	2.1914459	72.4907030	158.5830642	105	2.2395422	71.8028331	160.8054754
106	2.1600090	73.6510567	159.0869418	106	2.2078818	72.9436258	161.0509004	106	2.2568053	72.2459373	163.0450176
107	2.1757590	74.1106664	161.2469507	107	2.2244409	73.3931769	163.2587822	107	2.2742016	72.6856521	165.3018229
108	2.1916239	74.5669491	163.4227097	108	2.2411242	73.8393816	165.4832230	108	2.2917319	73.1220033	167.5760245
109	2.2076045	75.0199288	165.6143337	109	2.2579326	74.2822646	167.7243472	109	2.3093973	73.5550167	169.8677563
110	2.2237016	75.4696294	167.8219382	110	2.2748671	74.7216507	169.9822798	110	2.3271989	73.9847179	172.1771536
111	2.2399161	75.9160747	170.0455398	111	2.2919286	75.1581645	172.2571469	111	2.3451377	74.4111321	174.5043525
112	2.2562488	76.3592882	172.2855559	112	2.3091181	75.5912302	174.5490755	112	2.3632148	74.8342845	176.8494902
113	2.2727007	76.7992933	174.5418048	113	2.3264365	76.0210722	176.8581936	113	2.3814313	75.2542000	179.2127050
114	2.2892724	77.2361134	176.8145054	114	2.3438847	76.4477143	179.1846301	114	2.3997881	75.6709035	181.5941363
115	2.3059650	77.6697713	179.1037779	115	2.3614639	76.8711805	181.5285148	115	2.4182865	76.0844194	183.9939244
116	2.3227794	78.1002900	181.4097429	116	2.3791748	77.2914943	183.6899786	116	2.4369275	76.4947722	186.4122110
117	2.3397163	78.5276922	183.7325223	117	2.3970187	77.7086792	186.2691535	117	2.4557121	76.9019860	188.8491384
118	2.3567767	78.9520006	186.0722386	118	2.4149963	78.1227585	188.6661721	118	2.4746416	77.3060850	191.3048505
119	2.3739616	79.3732374	188.4290154	119	2.4331088	78.5337553	191.0811684	119	2.4937169	77.7070928	193.7794921
120	2.3912717	79.7914249	190.8029769	120	2.4513571	78.9416926	193.5142772	120	2.5129393	78.1050332	196.2732090
121	2.4087081	80.2065852	193.1942486	121	2.4697423	79.3465932	195.9656343	121	2.5323099	78.4999295	198.7861483
122	2.4262716	80.6187402	195.6029567	122	2.4882653	79.7484796	198.4353765	122	2.5518298	78.8918052	201.3184582
123	2.4439631	81.0279117	198.0292283	123	2.5069273	80.1473743	200.9236419	123	2.5715001	79.2806833	203.8702880
124	2.4617837	81.4341212	200.4731914	124	2.5257293	80.5432995	203.4305692	124	2.5913221	79.6665867	206.4417881
125	2.4797342	81.8373903	202.9349751	125	2.5446722	80.9362775	205.9562984	125	2.6112969	80.0495381	209.0331103
126	2.4978156	82.2377401	205.4147093	126	2.5637573	81.3263300	208.5009707	126	2.6314256	80.4295603	211.6444071
127	2.5160288	82.6351918	207.9125749	127	2.5829855	81.7134789	211.0647280	127	2.6517095	80.8066755	214.2758328
128	2.5343749	83.0297664	210.4285537	128	2.6023579	82.0977458	213.6477134	128	2.6721498	81.1809060	216.9275423
129	2.5528547	83.4214848	212.9629286	129	2.6218755	82.4791521	216.2500713	129	2.6927476	81.5522739	219.5996921
130	2.5714693	83.8103675	215.5157832	130	2.6415396	82.8577193	218.8719468	130	2.7135042	81.9208010	222.2924398
131	2.5902196	84.1964352	218.0872525	131	2.6613511	83.2334682	221.5134864	131	2.7344208	82.2865092	225.0059440
132	2.6091066	84.5797081	220.6774721	132	2.6813113	83.6064201	224.1748376	132	2.7554986	82.6494199	227.7403648
133	2.6281313	84.9602066	223.2865786	133	2.7014211	83.9765956	226.8561489	133	2.7767389	83.0095546	230.4958635
134	2.6472948	85.3379507	225.9147099	134	2.7216818	84.3440155	229.5575700	134	2.7981430	83.3669345	233.2726024
135	2.6665980	85.7129604	228.5620047	135	2.7420944	84.7087003	232.2792517	135	2.8197120	83.7215806	236.0707454
136	2.6860419	86.0852554	231.2286026	136	2.7626601	85.0706702	235.0213461	136	2.8414473	84.0735140	238.8904574
137	2.7056276	86.4548554	233.9146445	137	2.7833800	85.4299456	237.7840062	137	2.8633501	84.4227552	241.7319047
138	2.7253562	86.8217799	236.6202722	138	2.8042554	85.7865465	240.5673863	138	2.8854218	84.7693250	244.5952548
139	2.7452285	87.1860483	239.3456283	139	2.8252873	86.1404928	243.3716417	139	2.9076636	85.1132438	247.4808765
140	2.7652458	87.5476798	242.0908568	140	2.8464770	86.4910043	246.1969290	140	2.9300768	85.4545317	250.3883401
141	2.7854091	87.9066935	244.8561027	141	2.8678255	86.8405005	249.0434060	141	2.9526628	85.7932091	253.3184169
142	2.8057194	88.2631084	247.6415118	142	2.8893342	87.1866010	251.9112315	142	2.9754229	86.1292958	256.2710797
143	2.8261777	88.6169431	250.4472311	143	2.9110042	87.5301251	254.8005658	143	2.9983585	86.4628116	259.2465026
144	2.8467853	88.9982666	253.2734089	144	2.9328368	87.8710919	257.7115700	144	3.0214708	86.7937762	262.2448610
145	2.8675431	89.3169472	256.1201941	145	2.9548331	88.2095205	260.6444068	145	3.0447613	87.1222092	265.2683310
146	2.8884523	89.6631533	258.9877372	146	2.9769943	88.5454298	263.5992398	146	3.0682313	87.4481299	268.3110931
147	2.9095139	90.0068534	261.8761895	147	2.9993218	88.8788385	266.5762341	147	3.0918823	87.7715574	271.3793245
148	2.9307291	90.3480654	264.7857033	148	3.0218167	89.2097653	269.5755559	148	3.1157156	88.0925110	274.4712068
149	2.9520990	90.6868074	267.7164324	149	3.0444803	89.5382285	272.5973726	149	3.1397325	88.4110095	277.5869223
150	2.9736247	91.0230973	270.6685314	150	3.0673139	89.8642467	275.6418529	150	3.1639346	88.7270716	280.7266549
151	2.9953074	91.3569529	273.6421561	151	3.0903188	90.1878379	278.7091668	151	3.1883233	89.0407161	283.8905895
152	3.0171482	91.6883917	276.6374635	152	3.1134961	90.5090202	281.7994855	152	3.2129000	89.3519614	287.0789128
153	3.0391482	92.0174312	279.6546117	153	3.1368474	90.8278117	284.9129817	153	3.2376661	89.6608259	290.2918128
154	3.0613087	92.3440889	282.6937599	154	3.1603737	91.1442299	288.0498290	154	3.2626231	89.9673273	293.5294788
155	3.0836307	92.6688820	285.7550686	155	3.1840765	91.4582927	291.2102027	155	3.2877725	90.2714850	296.7921019
156	3.1061155	92.9903275	288.8386993	156	3.2079571	91.7700176	294.3942793	156	3.3131157	90.5733157	300.0998783
157	3.1287643	93.3099425	291.9448148	157	3.2320168	92.0794219	297.6022364	157	3.3386543	90.8728376	303.3929900
158	3.1515782	93.6272439	295.0735791	158	3.2582569	92.3865230	300.8342531	158	3.3643898	91.1700693	306.7316443
159	3.1745584	93.9422443	298.2251573	159	3.2803788	92.6913380	304.0905100	159	3.3903236	91.4650254	310.0960341
160	3.1977063	94.2549724	301.3997157	160	3.3052839	92.9938839	307.3711869	160	3.4164573	91.7577263	313.4863577
161	3.2210229	94.5654328	304.5974220	161	3.3300735	93.2941775	310.6764728	161	3.4427925	92.0481681	316.9028150
162	3.2445095	94.8736458	307.8184448	162	3.3550491	93.5922358	314.0065463	162	3.4693307	92.3364282	320.3456076
163	3.2681674	95.1796227	311.0629543	163	3.3802120	93.8880752	317.3615954	163	3.4960735	92.6224634	323.8149383
164	3.2919978	95.4833946	314.3311217	164	3.4055636	94.1817123	320.7418074	164	3.5230224	92.9063105	327.3110118
165	3.3160019	95.7849626	317.6231195	165	3.4311053	94.4731636	324.1473710	165	3.5501790	93.1879865	330.8340342
166	3.3401811	96.0843476	320.9391214	166	3.4568384	94.7624453	327.5784762	166	3.5775450	93.4675078	334.3842132
167	3.3645366	96.3815654	324.2790203	167	3.4827649	95.0496735	331.0353148	167	3.6051219	93.7448909	337.9617582
168	3.3890697	96.6766316	327.6433391	168	3.5088856	95.3345642	334.5180797	168	3.6329114	94.0201522	341.5668801
169	3.4137816	96.9695668	331.0320087	169	3.5352022	95.6174335	338.0269353	169	3.6609151	94.2933080	345.1997914
170	3.4386738	97.2603716	334.4466904	170	3.5617163	95.8981970	341.5621675	170	3.6891346	94.5643743	348.8607065
171	3.4637474	97.5490747	337.8853642	171	3.5884291	96.1768705	345.1238838	171	3.7175717	94.8333671	352.5498411
172	3.4890039	97.8356910	341.3491116	172	3.6153423	96.4534695	348.7123129	172	3.7462280	95.1003022	356.2674128
173	3.5144446	98.1202330	344.8381156	173	3.6424574	96.7280094	352.3276553	173	3.7751052	95.3651955	360.0136408
174	3.5400708	98.4027112	348.3525601	174	3.6697758	97.0005056	355.9701127	174	3.8042009	95.6280625	363.7887459
175	3.5658838	98.6831466	351.8926309	175	3.6972992	97.2709733	359.6398885	175	3.8335290	95.8889188	367.5922509
176	3.5918850	98.9615520	355.4585147	176	3.7250293	97.5394276	363.3371877	176	3.8630791	96.1477796	371.4264799
177	3.6180758	99.2379420	359.0503997	177	3.7529666	97.8058835	367.0622166	177	3.8928570	96.4046604	375.2895090
178	3.6444576	99.5123312	362.6684755	178	3.7811139	98.0703558	370.8151832	178	3.9228645	96.6595762	379.1824160
179	3.6710318	99.7847342	366.3129331	179	3.8094722	98.3328593	374.5962971	179	3.9531032	96.9125420	383.1052804
180	3.6977997	100.0551653	369.9839650	180	3.8380433	98.5934068	378.4057693	180	3.9835750	97.1635728	387.0583687
181	3.7247629	100.3236368	373.6817647	181	3.8668266	98.8520186	382.2438126	181	4.0142818	97.4126833	391.0419587
182	3.7519226	100.5901688	377.4065276	182	3.8958298	99.1087004	386.1106012	182	4.0452252	97.6598884	395.0562405
183	3.7792804	100.8547694	381.1584502	183	3.9250485	99.3634773	390.0064710	183	4.0764071	97.9052024	399.1014657
184	3.8068376	101.1174546	384.9377305	184	3.9544864	99.6163546	393.9315196	184	4.1078294	98.1486400	403.1778728
185	3.8345958	101.3782383	388.7445682	185	3.9841450	99.8673495	397.8860060	185	4.1394940	98.3902154	407.2857022
186	3.8625564	101.6371342	392.5791640	186	4.0140261	100.1164759	401.8701510	186	4.1714026	98.6299429	411.4251962
187	3.8907209	101.8941560	396.4417204	187	4.0441313	100.3637478	405.8841771	187	4.2035571	98.8678367	415.5965987
188	3.9190907	102.1493172	400.3324443	188	4.0744623	100.6091790	409.9263085	188	4.2359595	99.1039107	419.8001559
189	3.9476674	102.4026314	404.2515320	189	4.1050208	100.8527831	414.0027708	189	4.2686117	99.3381789	424.0361154
190	3.9764525	102.6541118	408.1991994	190	4.1358084	101.0945738	418.1077916	190	4.3015156	99.5706551	428.3047271
191	4.0054475	102.9037718	412.1756519	191	4.1668270	101.3345646	422.2436000	191	4.3346731	99.8013530	432.6062427
192	4.0346539	103.1516245	416.1810094	192	4.1980782	101.5727688	426.4104270	192	4.3680862	100.0302862	436.9409159
193	4.0640732	103.3976831	420.2157532	193	4.2295638	101.8091498	430.6085052	193	4.4017569	100.2574682	441.3090021
194	4.0937071	103.6419605	424.2798264	194	4.2612855	102.0438708	434.8380690	194	4.4356871	100.4829125	445.7107590
195	4.1235570	103.8844695	428.3735335	195	4.2932452	102.2767948	439.0993545	195	4.4698789	100.7065322	450.1464461
196	4.1536246	104.1252231	432.4970905	196	4.3254445	102.5079849	443.3925097	196	4.5043342	100.9286406	454.6163250
197	4.1839115	104.3642339	436.6507151	197	4.3578853	102.7374540	447.7180442	197	4.5390551	101.1489507	459.1206591
198	4.2144192	104.6015145	440.8346266	198	4.3905695	102.9652149	452.0759295	198	4.5740436	101.3675757	463.6597142
199	4.2451493	104.8370775	445.0490458	199	4.4234987	103.1912803	456.4664990	199	4.6093019	101.5645283	468.2337578
200	4.2761035	105.0709353	449.2941951	200	4.4566750	103.4156628	460.8899978	200	4.6448319	101.7998213	472.8430597

Table 1 415

M	C(8.75,M,12)	A(8.75,M,12)	S(8.75,M,12)	M	C(9.00,M,12)	A(9.00,M,12)	S(9.00,M,12)	M	C(9.25,M,12)	A(9.25,M,12)	S(9.25,M,12)
201	4.3072834	105.3031002	453.5702986	201	4.4901000	103.6383750	465.3466727	201	4.6806358	102.0134675	477.4878917
202	4.3386907	105.5335844	457.8775820	202	4.5237758	103.8594293	469.8367728	202	4.7167157	102.2254794	482.1685275
203	4.3703270	105.7624003	462.2162727	203	4.5577041	104.0788380	474.3605046	203	4.7530738	102.4358696	486.8852432
204	4.4021940	105.9895597	466.5865997	204	4.5918869	104.2966134	478.9182527	204	4.7897120	102.6446504	491.6383170
205	4.4342933	106.2150748	470.9887937	205	4.6263261	104.5127676	483.5101396	205	4.8266327	102.8518342	496.4280290
206	4.4658267	106.4389574	475.4230870	206	4.6610235	104.7273128	488.1364657	206	4.8638380	103.0574331	501.2546617
207	4.4991958	106.6612194	479.8897136	207	4.6959812	104.9402608	492.7974892	207	4.9013301	103.2614594	506.1184298
208	4.5320025	106.8818724	484.3889095	208	4.7312010	105.1516237	497.4934703	208	4.9391112	103.4639250	511.0198299
209	4.5650483	107.1009281	488.9209119	209	4.7666850	105.3614131	502.2246714	209	4.9771835	103.6648418	515.9589411
210	4.5983351	107.3183981	493.4859603	210	4.8024352	105.5696408	506.9913564	210	5.0155493	103.8642218	520.9361246
211	4.6318647	107.5342939	498.0842954	211	4.8384534	105.7763184	511.7937916	211	5.0542108	104.0620766	525.9516739
212	4.6655387	107.7486268	502.7161600	212	4.8747418	105.9814574	516.6322450	212	5.0931704	104.2584180	531.0058847
213	4.6993590	107.9614082	507.3817987	213	4.9113024	106.1850694	521.5069869	213	5.1324302	104.4532574	536.0990551
214	4.7339273	108.1726493	512.0814577	214	4.9481372	106.3871657	526.4182893	214	5.1719927	104.6466065	541.2314853
215	4.7684455	108.3823613	516.8153850	215	4.9852482	106.5877575	531.3664264	215	5.2118601	104.8384766	546.4034780
216	4.8032154	108.5905551	521.5838305	216	5.0226376	106.7868561	536.3516746	216	5.2520349	105.0288790	551.6153381
217	4.8382389	108.7972419	526.3870459	217	5.0603073	106.9844725	541.3743122	217	5.2925193	105.2178249	556.8673730
218	4.8735177	109.0024325	531.2252848	218	5.0982597	107.1806179	546.4346196	218	5.3333158	105.4053255	562.1598924
219	4.9090538	109.2061377	536.0988025	219	5.1364966	107.3753031	551.5328792	219	5.3744268	105.5913919	567.4932082
220	4.9448490	109.4083684	541.0078563	220	5.1750203	107.5685391	556.6693758	220	5.4158547	105.7760349	572.8676350
221	4.9809051	109.6091351	545.9527052	221	5.2138330	107.7603365	561.8443961	221	5.4576019	105.9592656	578.2834897
222	5.0172242	109.8084485	550.9336104	222	5.2529367	107.9507062	567.0582291	222	5.4996709	106.1410947	583.7410916
223	5.0538082	110.0063191	555.9508346	223	5.2923337	108.1396588	572.3111658	223	5.5420642	106.3215328	589.2407625
224	5.0906589	110.2027573	561.0046428	224	5.3320263	108.3272048	577.6034996	224	5.5847843	106.5005908	594.7828268
225	5.1277782	110.3977736	566.0953017	225	5.3720164	108.5133546	582.9355258	225	5.6278337	106.6782790	600.3676111
226	5.1651683	110.5913781	571.2230799	226	5.4123066	108.6981187	588.3075423	226	5.6712149	106.8546081	605.9954447
227	5.2028310	110.7835811	576.3882452	227	5.4528989	108.8815074	593.7198489	227	5.7149305	107.0295984	611.6666596
228	5.2407683	110.9743929	581.5910792	228	5.4937956	109.0635309	599.1727477	228	5.7589831	107.2032301	617.3815901
229	5.2789822	111.1638233	586.8318475	229	5.5349991	109.2441994	604.6665433	229	5.8033753	107.3755346	623.1405732
230	5.3174748	111.3518825	592.1108297	230	5.5765116	109.4235230	610.2015424	230	5.8481096	107.5465391	628.9439485
231	5.3562481	111.5385804	597.4283045	231	5.6183354	109.6015117	615.7780540	231	5.8931888	107.7162265	634.7920581
232	5.3953040	111.7239267	602.7845526	232	5.6604729	109.7781754	621.3963894	232	5.9386155	107.8846159	640.6852469
233	5.4346448	111.9079314	608.1798566	233	5.7029265	109.9535239	627.0568623	233	5.9843923	108.0517173	646.6238623
234	5.4742724	112.0906041	613.6145014	234	5.7456984	110.1275672	632.7597888	234	6.0305220	108.2175404	652.6082546
235	5.5141890	112.2719544	619.0887738	235	5.7887912	110.3003148	638.5054872	235	6.0770072	108.3820951	658.6387766
236	5.5543966	112.4519920	624.6029628	236	5.8322071	110.4717765	644.2942784	236	6.1238508	108.5453910	664.7157838
237	5.5948974	112.6307262	630.1573594	237	5.8759486	110.6419618	650.1264855	237	6.1710555	108.7074378	670.8396347
238	5.6356935	112.8081667	635.7522568	238	5.9200183	110.8108802	656.0024341	238	6.2186241	108.8682451	677.0106902
239	5.6767871	112.9843227	641.3879504	239	5.9644184	110.9785411	661.9224524	239	6.2665593	109.0278223	683.2293143
240	5.7181804	113.1592035	647.0647375	240	6.0091515	111.1449539	667.8868708	240	6.3148640	109.1861789	689.4958736
241	5.7598754	113.3328183	652.7829179	241	6.0542202	111.3101280	673.8960223	241	6.3635411	109.3433241	695.8107376
242	5.8018745	113.5051762	658.5427933	242	6.0996268	111.4740724	679.9502425	242	6.4125934	109.4992672	702.1742787
243	5.8441799	113.6762868	664.3446679	243	6.1453740	111.6367965	686.0498593	243	6.4620238	109.6540175	708.5868721
244	5.8867937	113.8461586	670.1888477	244	6.1914643	111.7983091	692.1952433	244	6.5118352	109.8075840	715.0488959
245	5.9297182	114.0148007	676.0756414	245	6.2379003	111.9586195	698.3867077	245	6.5620306	109.9599759	721.5607312
246	5.9729558	114.1822220	682.0053597	246	6.2846846	112.1177365	704.6246080	246	6.6126130	110.1112020	728.1227618
247	6.0165086	114.3484313	687.9783154	247	6.3318197	112.2756690	710.9092925	247	6.6635852	110.2612714	734.7353748
248	6.0603789	114.5134375	693.9948240	248	6.3793083	112.4324258	717.2411122	248	6.7149503	110.4101928	741.3989599
249	6.1045692	114.6772492	700.0552029	249	6.4271532	112.5880156	723.6204206	249	6.7667114	110.5579751	748.1139103
250	6.1490817	114.8398751	706.1597721	250	6.4753568	112.7424473	730.0475738	250	6.8188715	110.7046269	754.8806217
251	6.1939187	115.0013238	712.3088538	251	6.5239220	112.8957293	736.5229306	251	6.8714336	110.8501570	761.6994931
252	6.2390827	115.1616038	718.5027725	252	6.5728514	113.0478703	743.0468525	252	6.9244009	110.9945738	768.5709267
253	6.2845760	115.3207235	724.7418552	253	6.6221478	113.1988787	749.6197039	253	6.9777765	111.1378859	775.4953276
254	6.3304011	115.4786914	731.0264313	254	6.6718139	113.3487630	756.2418517	254	7.0315635	111.2801018	782.4731041
255	6.3765602	115.6355158	737.3568323	255	6.7218525	113.4975315	762.9136656	255	7.0857652	111.4212298	789.5046676
256	6.4230560	115.7912049	743.7333926	256	6.7722664	113.6451925	769.6355181	256	7.1403846	111.5612783	796.5904328
257	6.4698908	115.9457670	750.1564486	257	6.8230584	113.7917544	776.4077845	257	7.1954251	111.7002555	803.7308174
258	6.5170671	116.0992101	756.6263393	258	6.8742313	113.9372252	783.2308429	258	7.2508898	111.8381696	810.9264424
259	6.5645873	116.2515428	763.1434064	259	6.9257881	114.0816131	790.1050742	259	7.3067821	111.9750289	818.1771322
260	6.6124541	116.4027152	769.7079037	260	6.9777315	114.2249262	797.0308623	260	7.3631052	112.1108410	825.4839143
261	6.6606699	116.5529076	776.3204479	261	7.0300645	114.3671724	804.0085938	261	7.4198624	112.2456144	832.8470195
262	6.7092373	116.7019558	782.9811178	262	7.0827899	114.5083597	811.0386582	262	7.4770572	112.3793569	840.2668784
263	6.7581588	116.8499251	789.6903951	263	7.1359109	114.6484959	818.1214482	263	7.5346929	112.5120763	847.7439391
264	6.8074371	116.9968233	796.4485140	264	7.1894302	114.7875890	825.2573590	264	7.5927728	112.6437805	855.2786320
265	6.8570746	117.1426581	803.2559511	265	7.2433509	114.9256467	832.4467892	265	7.6513004	112.7744772	862.8714048
266	6.9070742	117.2874372	810.1130257	266	7.2976761	115.0626766	839.6901402	266	7.7102792	112.9041742	870.5227052
267	6.9574382	117.4311682	817.0200999	267	7.3524086	115.1986864	846.9878162	267	7.7697126	113.0328791	878.2329844
268	7.0081696	117.5738588	823.9775381	268	7.4075517	115.3336838	854.3402249	268	7.8296041	113.1605995	886.0026970
269	7.0592708	117.7155165	830.9857077	269	7.4631083	115.4676762	861.7477766	269	7.8899573	113.2873429	893.8323012
270	7.1107446	117.8561488	838.0449784	270	7.5190816	115.6006712	869.2108849	270	7.9507757	113.4131168	901.7222585
271	7.1625938	117.9957630	845.1557231	271	7.5754748	115.7326761	876.7299665	271	8.0120630	113.5379286	909.6730342
272	7.2148211	118.1343666	852.3183169	272	7.6322908	115.8636984	884.3054413	272	8.0738226	113.6617756	917.6850972
273	7.2674291	118.2719668	859.5331380	273	7.6895330	115.9937453	891.9377321	273	8.1360583	113.7846953	925.7589198
274	7.3204208	118.4085710	866.8005671	274	7.7472045	116.1228241	899.6272651	274	8.1987738	113.9066647	933.8949782
275	7.3737989	118.5441863	874.1209879	275	7.8053085	116.2509421	907.3744696	275	8.2619727	114.0277012	942.0937520
276	7.4275662	118.6788199	881.4947868	276	7.8638483	116.3781063	915.1797787	276	8.3256587	114.1478108	950.3557247
277	7.4817255	118.8124789	888.9223530	277	7.9229272	116.5043238	923.0436265	277	8.3898357	114.2670037	958.6813834
278	7.5362797	118.9451704	896.4040785	278	7.9822484	116.6296018	930.9664537	278	8.4545073	114.3852838	967.0712191
279	7.5912318	119.0769001	903.9403582	279	8.0421153	116.7539472	938.9487021	279	8.5196775	114.5026591	975.5257264
280	7.6465845	119.2076787	911.5315900	280	8.1024311	116.8773670	946.9908474	280	8.5853500	114.6191366	984.0454039
281	7.7023409	119.3375093	919.1781745	281	8.1631994	116.9998679	955.0932485	281	8.6515287	114.7347231	992.6307539
282	7.7585038	119.4664001	926.8805154	282	8.2244234	117.1214570	963.2564479	282	8.7182176	114.8494254	1001.2822826
283	7.8150762	119.5943579	934.6390191	283	8.2861065	117.2421410	971.4808712	283	8.7854205	114.9632504	1010.0005002
284	7.8720611	119.7213895	942.4540953	284	8.3482523	117.3619265	979.7669778	284	8.8531415	115.0762046	1018.7859207
285	7.9294616	119.8475014	950.3261565	285	8.4108642	117.4808204	988.1152301	285	8.9213844	115.1882949	1027.6390622
286	7.9872806	119.9727005	958.2556180	286	8.4739457	117.5988291	996.5260944	286	8.9901535	115.2995277	1036.5604467
287	8.0455211	120.0969293	966.2428986	287	8.5375003	117.7159594	1005.0000401	287	9.0594526	115.4099096	1045.5506001
288	8.1041864	120.2203863	974.2884197	288	8.6015316	117.8322178	1013.5375404	288	9.1292858	115.5194472	1054.6100527
289	8.1632794	120.3428861	982.3926061	289	8.6660430	117.9476107	1022.1390719	289	9.1998574	115.6281469	1063.7393385
290	8.2228033	120.4644991	990.5558856	290	8.7310384	118.0621446	1030.8051150	290	9.2705714	115.7360151	1072.9389959
291	8.2827613	120.5852318	998.7786889	291	8.7965212	118.1758259	1039.5361534	291	9.3420321	115.8430582	1082.2095673
292	8.3431564	120.7050905	1007.0614502	292	8.8624951	118.2886610	1048.3326745	292	9.4140436	115.9492825	1091.5515994
293	8.4039919	120.8240816	1015.4046066	293	8.9289638	118.4006561	1057.1951696	293	9.4866102	116.0546942	1100.9656430
294	8.4652710	120.9422113	1023.8085985	294	8.9959310	118.5118174	1066.1241334	294	9.5597361	116.1592996	1110.4522532
295	8.5269970	121.0594859	1032.2738696	295	9.0634005	118.6221513	1075.1200644	295	9.6334258	116.2631049	1120.0119893
296	8.5891730	121.1759115	1040.8008665	296	9.1313760	118.7316638	1084.1834649	296	9.7076834	116.3661160	1129.6454151
297	8.6518024	121.2914944	1049.3900395	297	9.1998612	118.8403611	1093.3148409	297	9.7825315	116.4683393	1139.3530985
298	8.7148884	121.4062405	1058.0418419	298	9.2688603	118.9482492	1102.5147022	298	9.8579204	116.5697805	1149.1356120
299	8.7784345	121.5201560	1066.7567303	299	9.3383767	119.0553342	1111.7835625	299	9.9339085	116.6704458	1158.9935323
300	8.8424439	121.6332469	1075.5351649	300	9.4084146	119.1616221	1121.1219392	300	10.0104824	116.7703411	1168.9274408

Table 1

M	C(8.75,M,12)	A(8.75,M,12)	S(8.75,M,12)	M	C(9.00,M,12)	A(9.00,M,12)	S(9.00,M,12)	M	C(9.25,M,12)	A(9.25,M,12)	S(9.25,M,12)
301	8.9069201	121.7455192	1084.3776088	301	9.4789777	119.2671187	1130.5303537	301	10.0876465	116.8694723	1178.9379232
302	8.9718664	121.6569787	1093.2845288	302	9.5500700	119.3718299	1140.0093314	302	10.1654054	116.9678451	1189.0255697
303	9.0372862	121.9676314	1102.2563952	303	9.6216955	119.4757617	1149.5594014	303	10.2437638	117.0654655	1199.1909751
304	9.1031831	122.0774831	1111.2936814	304	9.6933582	119.5789198	1159.1810969	304	10.3227261	117.1623391	1209.4347389
305	9.1695605	122.1865396	1120.3968645	305	9.7665622	119.6813100	1168.8749552	305	10.4022971	117.2584718	1219.7574650
306	9.2364219	122.2948066	1129.5664250	306	9.8393114	119.7829380	1178.6415173	306	10.4824815	117.3538690	1230.1597622
307	9.3037708	122.4022899	1138.8028469	307	9.9136100	119.8838094	1188.4813287	307	10.5632840	117.4485366	1240.6422437
308	9.3716108	122.5089952	1148.1066176	308	9.9879621	119.9839299	1198.3949387	308	10.6447093	117.5424799	1251.2055276
309	9.4399454	122.6149280	1157.4782284	309	10.0628718	120.0833051	1208.3829007	309	10.7267623	117.6357047	1261.8502369
310	9.5087784	122.7200940	1166.9181738	310	10.1383433	120.1819406	1218.4457725	310	10.8094477	117.7282164	1272.5769992
311	9.5781132	122.8244987	1176.4269522	311	10.2143809	120.2798418	1228.5841158	311	10.8927705	117.8200204	1283.3864469
312	9.6479536	122.9281476	1186.0050654	312	10.2909887	120.3770142	1238.7984967	312	10.9767356	117.9111221	1294.2792174
313	9.7183033	123.0310462	1195.6530190	313	10.3681712	120.4734632	1249.0894854	313	11.0613480	118.0015270	1305.2559531
314	9.7891659	123.1331999	1205.3713223	314	10.4459324	120.5691942	1259.4576556	314	11.1466125	118.0912404	1316.3173011
315	9.8605452	123.2346142	1215.1604882	315	10.5242769	120.6642126	1269.9035890	315	11.2325343	118.1802675	1327.4639136
316	9.9324450	123.3352944	1225.0210334	316	10.6032090	120.7585237	1280.4278659	316	11.3191185	118.2686136	1338.6964479
317	10.0048691	123.4352457	1234.9534785	317	10.6827331	120.8521327	1291.0310749	317	11.4063700	118.3562839	1350.0155664
318	10.0778213	123.5344735	1244.9583476	318	10.7628536	120.9450449	1301.7138080	318	11.4942941	118.4432836	1361.4219364
319	10.1513054	123.6329830	1255.0361689	319	10.8435750	121.0372654	1312.4766616	319	11.5828960	118.5296178	1372.9162305
320	10.2253253	123.7307794	1265.1874743	320	10.9249018	121.1287994	1323.3202366	320	11.6721808	118.6152916	1384.4991265
321	10.2998850	123.8278678	1275.4127996	321	11.0068385	121.2196520	1334.2451383	321	11.7621538	118.7003109	1396.1713072
322	10.3749883	123.9242535	1285.7126846	322	11.0893898	121.3098283	1345.2519769	322	11.8528204	118.7846781	1407.9334611
323	10.4506393	124.0199414	1296.0876730	323	11.1725603	121.3993333	1356.3413667	323	11.9441859	118.8684009	1419.7862815
324	10.5268419	124.1149367	1306.5383123	324	11.2563545	121.4881720	1367.5139270	324	12.0362557	118.9514832	1431.7304675
325	10.6036001	124.2092443	1317.0651541	325	11.3407771	121.5763494	1378.7702815	325	12.1290352	119.0339300	1443.7667232
326	10.6809180	124.3028692	1327.6687542	326	11.4258330	121.6638703	1390.1110586	326	12.2225298	119.1157461	1455.8957583
327	10.7507997	124.3958164	1338.3496722	327	11.5115267	121.7507398	1401.5368915	327	12.3167452	119.1969364	1468.1162881
328	10.8372493	124.4880907	1349.1084720	328	11.5978631	121.8369626	1413.0484162	328	12.4116867	119.2775056	1480.4350333
329	10.9162709	124.5796971	1359.9457212	329	11.6848471	121.9225435	1424.6462814	329	12.5073601	119.3574585	1492.8467200
330	10.9958687	124.6706403	1370.8619921	330	11.7724835	122.0074873	1436.3311285	330	12.6037710	119.4367999	1505.3540802
331	11.0760469	124.7609252	1381.8578608	331	11.8607771	122.0917988	1448.1036120	331	12.7009251	119.5155343	1517.9578512
332	11.1568098	124.8505566	1392.9393077	332	11.9497329	122.1754827	1459.9643891	332	12.7988281	119.5936664	1530.6587763
333	11.2381615	124.9395391	1404.0907175	333	12.0393559	122.2585436	1471.9141220	333	12.8974857	119.6712009	1543.4576044
334	11.3201064	125.0278775	1415.3288790	334	12.1296511	122.3409862	1483.9534779	334	12.9969038	119.7481423	1556.3550901
335	11.4026489	125.1155764	1426.6489854	335	12.2206235	122.4228151	1496.0831290	335	13.0970883	119.8244952	1569.3519940
336	11.4857932	125.2026405	1438.0516343	336	12.3122782	122.5040349	1508.3037525	336	13.1980450	119.9002640	1582.4490823
337	11.5695438	125.2890743	1449.5374275	337	12.4046202	122.5846500	1520.6160307	337	13.2997800	119.9754532	1595.6471273
338	11.6539050	125.3748825	1461.1069712	338	12.4975549	122.6646650	1533.0206509	338	13.4022991	120.0500673	1608.9469072
339	11.7368814	125.4600695	1472.7608762	339	12.5913873	122.7440844	1545.5183058	339	13.5056085	120.1241106	1622.3492063
340	11.8244774	125.5446398	1484.4997576	340	12.6858227	122.8229125	1558.1096931	340	13.6097142	120.1975875	1635.8548148
341	11.9106976	125.6285980	1496.3242350	341	12.7809664	122.9011539	1570.7955158	341	13.7146224	120.2705024	1649.4645290
342	11.9975464	125.7119483	1508.2349326	342	12.8768236	122.9788128	1583.5764822	342	13.8203393	120.3428595	1663.1791354
343	12.0850285	125.7946953	1520.2324790	343	12.9733998	123.0558936	1596.4533058	343	13.9268711	120.4146631	1676.9994907
344	12.1731485	125.8768434	1532.3175075	344	13.0707003	123.1324006	1609.4267056	344	14.0342241	120.4859175	1690.9263618
345	12.2619110	125.9583967	1544.4906560	345	13.1687306	123.2083380	1622.4974059	345	14.1424045	120.5566269	1704.9605859
346	12.3513208	126.0393597	1556.7525671	346	13.2674960	123.2837102	1635.6661365	346	14.2514189	120.6267953	1719.1029904
347	12.4413825	126.1197366	1569.1038879	347	13.3670023	123.3585213	1648.9336325	347	14.3612736	120.6964270	1733.3544093
348	12.5321009	126.1995317	1581.5452704	348	13.4672548	123.4327755	1662.3006948	348	14.4719751	120.7655261	1747.7156829
349	12.6234808	126.2787492	1594.0773713	349	13.5682592	123.5064769	1675.7678096	349	14.5835299	120.8340466	1762.1876580
350	12.7155271	126.3573932	1606.7008522	350	13.6700211	123.5796297	1689.3361488	350	14.6959446	120.9021426	1776.7711878
351	12.8082444	126.4354679	1619.4163792	351	13.7725463	123.6522379	1703.0061699	351	14.8092258	120.9696681	1791.4671324
352	12.9016379	126.5129774	1632.2246237	352	13.8758404	123.7243056	1716.7787162	352	14.9233803	121.0366770	1806.2763583
353	12.9957123	126.5899259	1645.1262616	353	13.9799092	123.7958358	1730.6545566	353	15.0384147	121.1031734	1821.1997365
354	13.0904727	126.6663173	1658.1219739	354	14.0847585	123.8668355	1744.6344658	354	15.1543358	121.1691611	1836.2381532
355	13.1859241	126.7421558	1671.2124467	355	14.1903942	123.9373058	1758.7192243	355	15.2711505	121.2346440	1851.3924890
356	13.2820715	126.8174452	1684.3983708	356	14.2968222	124.0072514	1772.9096185	356	15.3889656	121.2996261	1866.6636394
357	13.3789199	126.8921897	1697.6804422	357	14.4040483	124.0766763	1787.2064446	357	15.5074881	121.3641111	1882.0525050
358	13.4764745	126.9663931	1711.0593621	358	14.5120787	124.1455844	1801.6104889	358	15.6270250	121.4281028	1897.5599931
359	13.5747405	127.0400593	1724.5358367	359	14.6209193	124.2139796	1816.1225676	359	15.7474833	121.4916050	1913.1870180
360	13.6737230	127.1131923	1738.1105772	360	14.7305762	124.2818656	1830.7434869	360	15.8688701	121.5546214	1928.9345013
361	13.7734272	127.1857958	1751.7843001	361	14.8410555	124.3492462	1845.4740630	361	15.9911927	121.6171559	1944.8033715
362	13.8739584	127.2578738	1765.5577273	362	14.9523634	124.4161253	1860.3151185	362	16.1144581	121.6792119	1960.7945641
363	13.9750220	127.3294301	1779.4315858	363	15.0645061	124.4825065	1875.2674819	363	16.2386737	121.7407933	1976.9090222
364	14.0769232	127.4004683	1793.4066078	364	15.1774899	124.5483935	1890.3319881	364	16.3638468	121.8019036	1993.1476960
365	14.1795674	127.4709923	1807.4835310	365	15.2913211	124.6137901	1905.5094780	365	16.4899848	121.8625465	2009.5115428
366	14.2829601	127.5410058	1821.6630984	366	15.4060060	124.6786998	1920.8007991	366	16.6170951	121.9227255	2026.0015276
367	14.3871067	127.6105125	1835.9460585	367	15.5215511	124.7431264	1936.2068051	367	16.7451852	121.9824442	2042.6186228
368	14.4920127	127.6795160	1850.3331652	368	15.6379627	124.8070733	1951.7283562	368	16.8742627	122.0417060	2059.3638080
369	14.5976836	127.7480201	1864.8251779	369	15.7552474	124.8705443	1967.3663189	369	17.0043351	122.1005145	2076.2380707
370	14.7041250	127.8160282	1879.4228615	370	15.8734118	124.9335427	1983.1215663	370	17.1354102	122.1588732	2093.2424058
371	14.8113426	127.8835440	1894.1269865	371	15.9924624	124.9960722	1998.9949780	371	17.2674957	122.2167855	2110.3778161
372	14.9193420	127.9505711	1908.9383292	372	16.1124058	125.0581361	2014.9874404	372	17.4005993	122.2742548	2127.6453113
373	15.0281289	128.0171130	1923.8576712	373	16.2332489	125.1197381	2031.0998462	373	17.5347289	122.3312845	2145.0459111
374	15.1377090	128.0831732	1938.8658000	374	16.3549982	125.1808815	2047.3330951	374	17.6693925	122.3878779	2162.5806400
375	15.2480881	128.1487552	1954.0235090	375	16.4776607	125.2415697	2063.6880933	375	17.8060979	122.4440384	2180.2505324
376	15.3592721	128.2138624	1969.2715971	376	16.6012432	125.3018062	2080.1657540	376	17.9433532	122.4997694	2198.0566303
377	15.4712668	128.2784984	1984.6308692	377	16.7257525	125.3615942	2096.7669972	377	18.0816666	122.5550740	2215.9999835
378	15.5840781	128.3426666	2000.1021359	378	16.8511956	125.4209372	2113.4927497	378	18.2210461	122.6099556	2234.0816501
379	15.6977120	128.4063700	2015.6862140	379	16.9775796	125.4798384	2130.3439453	379	18.3615000	122.6644174	2252.3026961
380	15.8121745	128.4696124	2031.3839260	380	17.1049115	125.5383011	2147.3215249	380	18.5030365	122.7184626	2270.6641961
381	15.9274716	128.5323970	2047.1961005	381	17.2331983	125.5963287	2164.4264364	381	18.6456641	122.7720944	2289.1672326
382	16.0436004	128.5947271	2063.1235721	382	17.3634473	125.6539242	2181.6596247	382	18.7893911	122.8253159	2307.8128967
383	16.1605940	128.6566060	2079.1671815	383	17.4926656	125.7110910	2199.0220819	383	18.9342260	122.8781303	2326.6022378
384	16.2784317	128.7180370	2095.3277755	384	17.6253606	125.7678323	2216.5147476	384	19.0801772	122.9305407	2345.5365138
385	16.3971286	128.7790233	2111.6062073	385	17.7560396	125.8241512	2234.1386082	385	19.2272537	122.9825502	2364.6166751
386	16.5166910	128.8395681	2128.0033359	386	17.8892099	125.8800508	2251.8946478	386	19.3754638	123.0341619	2383.8439448
387	16.6371252	128.8996746	2144.5200269	387	18.0233790	125.9355343	2269.7838577	387	19.5248163	123.0853787	2403.2194066
388	16.7584376	128.9593461	2161.1571521	388	18.1585543	125.9906047	2287.8072366	388	19.6753201	123.1362038	2422.7442249
389	16.8806345	129.0185855	2177.9155897	389	18.2947435	126.0452652	2305.9657909	389	19.8269840	123.1866402	2442.4195500
390	17.0037225	129.0773962	2194.7962242	390	18.4319540	126.0995189	2324.2605344	390	19.9798170	123.2366907	2462.2465290
391	17.1277080	129.1357811	2211.7999467	391	18.5701937	126.1533686	2342.6924884	391	20.1338281	123.2863583	2482.2263460
392	17.2525975	129.1937434	2228.9276547	392	18.7094701	126.2068175	2361.2626821	392	20.2890264	123.3356460	2502.3601741
393	17.3783977	129.2512861	2246.1802522	393	18.8497912	126.2598684	2379.9721522	393	20.4454209	123.3845568	2522.6492005
394	17.5051152	129.3084123	2263.5586498	394	18.9911646	126.3125245	2398.8219434	394	20.6030211	123.4330933	2543.0946214
395	17.6327566	129.3651249	2281.0637650	395	19.1335983	126.3647886	2417.8131080	395	20.7618360	123.4812586	2563.6976425
396	17.7613288	129.4214270	2298.6965217	396	19.2771003	126.4166636	2436.9467063	396	20.9218752	123.5290555	2584.4594765
397	17.8908385	129.4773215	2316.4578505	397	19.4216786	126.4681525	2456.2238066	397	21.0831480	123.5764867	2605.3813536
398	18.0212925	129.5328114	2334.3486890	398	19.5673412	126.5192580	2475.6454852	398	21.2456639	123.6235552	2626.4645016
399	18.1526978	129.5878997	2352.3699815	399	19.7140962	126.5699832	2495.2128263	399	21.4094325	123.6702635	2647.7101655
400	18.2850612	129.6425891	2370.5226793	400	19.8619519	126.6203307	2514.9269226	400	21.5744636	123.7166146	2669.1195980

Table 1

417

M	C(8.75,M,12)	A(8.75,M,12)	S(8.75,M,12)	M	C(9.00,M,12)	A(9.00,M,12)	S(9.00,M,12)	M	C(9.25,M,12)	A(9.25,M,12)	S(9.25,M,12)
401	18.4183898	129.6968827	2388.8077406	401	20.0109166	126.6703034	2534.7888745	401	21.7407667	123.7626112	2690.6940616
402	18.5526906	129.7507832	2407.2261304	402	20.1609985	126.7199041	2554.7997911	402	21.9083518	123.8082559	2712.4348284
403	18.6879706	129.8042936	2425.7788209	403	20.3122059	126.7691356	2574.9607895	403	22.0772287	123.8535514	2734.3431802
404	18.8242307	129.8574166	2444.4667915	404	20.4545475	126.8180006	2595.2729955	404	22.2474073	123.8985005	2756.4204089
405	18.9614971	129.9101550	2463.2910285	405	20.6180316	126.8665018	261?.7375430	405	22.4188978	123.9431057	2778.6678162
406	19.0997580	129.9625117	2482.2525256	406	20.??3668	126.9146420	2636.3555745	406	22.5917101	123.9873697	2801.0867140
407	19.2390271	130.0144894	2501.3522837	407	20.9284618	126.9624238	2657.1282414	407	22.7659545	124.0312951	2823.6784741
408	19.3733117	130.0660908	2520.5913107	408	21.0854253	127.0098500	2678.0567032	408	22.9413413	124.0748846	2846.4442787
409	19.5206191	130.1173187	2539.9706224	409	21.2435660	127.0569230	2699.1421285	409	23.1181808	124.1181406	2869.3856200
410	19.6629570	130.1681758	2559.4912416	410	21.4028927	127.1036457	2720.3856945	410	23.2963835	124.1610657	2892.5038008
411	19.8083327	130.2186647	2579.1541985	411	21.5534144	127.1500205	2741.7885872	411	23.4759598	124.2036625	2915.8001843
412	19.9507539	130.2687881	2598.9605313	412	21.7051400	127.1960502	2763.3520017	412	23.6569203	124.2459334	2939.2761441
413	20.0962281	130.3185487	2618.9112652	413	21.8580786	127.2417371	2785.0771417	413	23.8392757	124.2878810	2962.9330644
414	20.2427631	130.3679490	2639.0075133	414	22.0122392	127.2870840	2806.9652203	414	24.0230368	124.3295077	2986.7723401
415	20.3903566	130.4169918	2659.2502764	415	22.2176310	127.3320933	2829.0174595	415	24.2082144	124.3708160	3010.7953770
416	20.5390464	130.4656798	2679.6406431	416	22.3842632	127.3767675	2851.2350904	416	24.3948194	124.4118083	3035.0035913
417	20.6838103	130.5140149	2700.1796894	417	22.5521452	127.4211092	2873.6193536	417	24.5825629	124.4524870	3059.3984107
418	20.8396662	130.5620003	2720.8684997	418	22.7212863	127.4651208	2896.1714988	418	24.7723557	124.4928546	3083.9812735
419	20.9916221	130.6096383	2741.7081659	419	22.8916959	127.5088049	2918.8927851	419	24.5633093	124.5329134	3108.7536292
420	21.1446860	130.6569315	2762.6997879	420	23.0633836	127.5521635	2941.7844810	420	25.1557348	124.5726658	3133.7169384
421	21.2988660	130.7038824	2783.8444739	421	23.2363590	127.5951996	2964.8478646	421	25.3498435	124.6121141	3158.8726732
422	21.4541702	130.7504934	2805.1433399	422	23.4106317	127.6379152	2988.0842236	422	25.5450471	124.6512606	3184.2223167
423	21.6106069	130.7967669	2826.5975101	423	23.5862114	127.6803128	3011.4948553	423	25.7419568	124.6901077	3209.7673638
424	21.7681842	130.8427056	2848.2081170	424	23.7631080	127.7223949	3035.0810668	424	25.9403844	124.7286575	3235.5093206
425	21.9269106	130.8883116	2869.9763012	425	23.9413313	127.7641636	3058.8441748	425	26.?03415	124.7669127	326?.4497049
426	22.0857943	130.9335875	2891.9032117	426	24.1208913	127.8056215	3082.7855061	426	26.3418400	124.8048751	3287.5900464
427	22.2479438	130.9785357	2913.9900060	427	24.3017980	127.8467707	3106.9063974	427	26.5448917	124.8425471	3313.9318364
428	22.4100677	131.0231585	2936.2378498	428	24.4840615	127.8876136	3131.2081954	428	26.7495085	124.8799310	3340.4767781
429	22.5734744	131.0674583	2958.6479175	429	24.6676920	127.9281525	3155.6922569	429	26.9557027	124.9170289	3367.2262866
430	22.7380727	131.1114374	2981.2213919	430	24.8525996	127.9683895	3180.3599409	430	27.1634862	124.9538430	3394.1819892
431	22.9038711	131.1550981	3003.9594646	431	25.0390949	128.0083271	3205.2126485	431	27.3723714	124.9903755	3421.3454754
432	23.0708785	131.1984428	3026.8633357	432	25.2268881	128.0479673	3230.2517434	432	27.5838706	125.0266286	3448.7183468
433	23.2391037	131.2414737	3049.9342142	433	25.4160898	128.0873125	3255.4786315	433	27.7954963	125.0626043	3476.3022175
434	23.4085555	131.2841932	3073.1733179	434	25.6067104	128.1263647	3280.8947213	434	28.0107609	125.0983049	3504.0987138
435	23.5792429	131.3266033	3096.5818734	435	25.7987608	128.1651263	3306.5014317	435	28.2263772	125.1337325	3532.1094747
436	23.7511748	131.3687065	3120.1611162	436	25.9922515	128.2035993	3332.3001925	436	28.4442579	125.1688889	3560.3361519
437	23.9243605	131.4105049	3143.9122911	437	26.1871934	128.2417859	3358.2924440	437	28.6635157	125.2037764	3588.7804098
438	24.0988089	131.4520008	3167.8366515	438	26.3835973	128.2796882	3384.4796373	438	28.8844636	125.2383971	3617.4439255
439	24.2745294	131.4931962	3191.9354605	439	26.5814743	128.3173084	3410.8632346	439	29.1071147	125.2727530	3646.3283891
440	24.4515312	131.5340934	3216.2099999	440	26.7808353	128.3546486	3437.4447089	440	29.3314820	125.3068460	3675.4355038
441	24.6298236	131.5746946	3240.6615211	441	26.9816916	128.3917107	3464.2255443	441	29.5575789	125.3406783	3704.7669858
442	24.8094161	131.6150019	3265.2913447	442	27.1840543	128.4284970	3491.2072039	442	29.7854186	125.3742518	3734.3245647
443	24.9903181	131.6550174	3290.1007608	443	27.3879347	128.4650094	3518.3912902	443	30.0150145	125.4075684	3764.1099833
444	25.1725391	131.6947432	3315.0910789	444	27.5933442	128.5012501	3545.7792249	444	30.2463802	125.4406302	3794.1249978
445	25.??60889	131.7341815	334?.2636180	445	27.8002943	128.5372209	3573.3725691	445	30.4795294	125.4734392	3824.3713780
446	25.5409771	131.7733343	3365.6197069	446	28.0087965	128.5729240	3601.1728634	446	30.7144758	125.5059971	3854.8509074
447	25.7272133	131.8122036	3391.1606840	447	28.2188625	128.6083613	3629.1816599	447	30.9512332	125.5383060	3885.5653832
448	25.9148076	131.8507916	3416.8878974	448	28.4305039	128.6435347	3657.4005224	448	31.1898156	125.5703677	3916.5166164
449	26.1037698	131.8891002	3442.8027050	449	28.6437327	128.6784464	3685.8310263	449	31.4302371	125.6021842	3947.7064320
450	26.2941097	131.9271316	3468.9064747	450	28.8585607	128.7130982	3714.4747591	450	31.6725119	125.6237573	3979.1366691
451	26.4858376	131.9648876	3495.2005845	451	29.0749999	128.7474920	3743.3333198	451	31.9166541	125.6650989	4010.8091809
452	26.6789635	132.0023703	3521.6864221	452	29.2930624	128.7816297	3772.4083197	452	32.1626783	125.6961809	4042.7258351
453	26.8734976	132.0395817	3548.3653856	453	29.5127604	128.8155134	3801.7013801	453	32.4105990	125.7270350	4074.8885134
454	27.0694502	132.0765237	3575.2388832	454	29.7341061	128.8491448	3831.2141425	454	32.6604307	125.7576531	4107.2991124
455	27.2668316	132.1131983	3602.3083335	455	29.9571119	128.8825259	3860.9482406	455	32.9121882	125.7880370	4139.9595461
456	27.4656523	132.1496074	3629.5751651	456	30.1817902	128.9156584	3890.9053605	456	33.1658863	125.8181884	4172.8717313
457	27.6659227	132.1857529	3657.0408174	457	30.4081537	128.9485443	3921.0871508	457	33.4215400	125.8481092	4206.0376176
458	27.8676533	132.2216368	3684.7067400	458	30.6362148	128.9811854	3951.4953044	458	33.6791644	125.8778012	4239.4591576
459	28.0708765	132.2572610	3712.5743934	459	30.8659864	129.0135836	3982.1315193	459	33.9387746	125.9072660	4273.1383220
460	28.2755383	132.2926272	3740.6452483	460	31.0974813	129.0457405	4012.9975057	460	34.2003860	125.9365055	4307.0770966
461	28.4817141	132.3277375	3768.9207866	461	31.3307124	129.0776581	4044.0949870	461	34.4640140	125.9655212	4341.2774926
462	28.6893933	132.3625936	3797.4025?07	462	31.5655928	129.1093380	4075.4256994	462	34.7295741	125.9943150	4375.7414565
463	28.8985688	132.3971973	3826.0918940	463	31.8024355	129.1407822	4106.9913922	463	34.9973820	126.0228886	4410.4711706
464	29.1093056	132.4315506	3854.9904808	464	32.0409537	129.1719922	4138.7938277	464	35.2671535	126.0512436	4445.4685526
465	29.3215610	132.4656552	3884.0997864	465	32.2812609	129.2029700	4170.8347814	465	35.5390044	126.0793817	4480.7357060
466	29.5353640	132.4995129	3913.4213474	466	32.5233704	129.2337171	4203.1160423	466	35.8129509	126.1073046	4516.2747105
467	29.7507261	132.5331256	3942.9567114	467	32.7672956	129.2642353	4235.6394127	467	36.0890091	126.1350138	4552.0876616
468	29.9676584	132.5664949	3972.7074374	468	33.0130503	129.2945264	4268.4067083	468	36.3671952	126.1625111	4588.1766705
469	30.1861726	132.5996228	4002.6750959	469	33.2606482	129.3245919	4301.4197587	469	36.6475257	126.1897981	4624.5408877
470	30.4062801	132.6325106	4032.8612685	470	33.5101031	129.3544337	4334.6804069	470	36.9300170	126.2168764	4661.1913914
471	30.6279926	132.6651604	4063.2675486	471	33.7614289	129.3840533	4368.1905100	471	37.2146809	126.2437475	4698.1214084
472	30.8513217	132.6975739	4093.8955412	472	34.0146396	129.4134524	4401.9519388	472	37.5015491	126.2704130	4735.3360943
473	31.0762792	132.7297528	4124.7468629	473	34.2697494	129.4426326	4435.9665784	473	37.7906235	126.2968746	4772.8376434
474	31.3028771	132.7616988	4155.8231421	474	34.5267725	129.4715957	4470.2363278	474	38.0819263	126.3231338	4810.6282669
475	31.5311273	132.7934135	4187.1260192	475	34.7857233	129.5003431	4504.7631003	475	38.3754744	126.3491921	4848.7101932
476	31.7610417	132.8248986	4218.6571465	476	35.0466162	129.5288765	4539.5488236	476	38.6712854	126.3750511	4887.0856676
477	31.9926327	132.8561558	4250.4181882	477	35.3094658	129.5571975	4574.5954398	477	38.9693766	126.4007123	4925.7569530
478	32.2259123	132.8871867	4282.4108209	478	35.5742868	129.5853077	4609.9049056	478	39.2697655	126.4261772	4964.7263296
479	32.4608929	132.9179930	4314.6367331	479	35.8410940	129.6132086	4645.4791925	479	39.5724699	126.4514472	5003.9960951
480	32.?075869	132.9485763	4347.0976260	480	36.1099022	129.6409019	4681.3202864	480	39.8775077	126.4765240	5043.5685650
481	32.9360068	132.9789382	4379.7952129	481	36.3807265	129.6683890	4717.4301886	481	40.1848995	126.5014090	5083.4460728
482	33.1761652	133.0090803	4412.7312197	482	36.6535819	129.6956714	4753.8109751	482	40.4946554	126.5261036	5123.6309696
483	33.4180747	133.0390043	4445.9073849	483	36.9284838	129.7227508	4790.4644970	483	40.8068017	126.5506093	5164.1256250
484	33.6617482	133.0687116	4479.3254596	484	37.2054474	129.7496286	4827.3929800	484	41.1213542	126.5749276	5204.9324268
485	33.9071984	133.0982038	4512.9872078	485	37.4844883	129.7763063	4864.5984282	485	41.4383313	126.5990599	5246.0537809
486	34.1544384	133.1274826	4546.8944062	486	37.7656219	129.8027854	4902.0829164	486	41.7577517	126.6230075	5287.4921122
487	34.4034812	133.1565494	4581.0488446	487	38.0488641	129.8290674	4939.8485383	487	42.0795344	126.6467720	5329.2498640
488	34.6543399	133.1854058	4615.4523258	488	38.3342306	129.8551537	4977.8974024	488	42.4039983	126.6703547	5371.3294584
489	34.9070278	133.2140534	4650.1066657	489	38.6217373	129.8810459	5016.2316330	489	42.7308624	126.6937569	5413.7334966
490	35.1615582	133.2424935	4685.0136935	490	38.9114003	129.9067453	5054.8533702	490	43.0602461	126.7169802	5456.4643590
491	35.4179446	133.2707278	4720.1752518	491	39.2032358	129.9322534	5093.7647706	491	43.3921689	126.7400258	5499.5246052
492	35.6762004	133.2987577	4755.5931964	492	39.4972601	129.9575715	5132.9680064	492	43.7266502	126.7628952	5542.9167741
493	35.9363394	133.3265847	4791.2693968	493	39.7934895	129.9827013	5172.4652665	493	44.0637098	126.7855896	5586.6434243
494	36.1983752	133.3542102	4827.2057362	494	40.0919407	130.0076440	5212.2587560	494	44.4033675	126.8081104	5630.7071340
495	36.4623217	133.3816358	4863.4041114	495	40.3926303	130.0324010	5252.3506967	495	44.7458435	126.8304590	5675.1105016
496	36.7281928	133.4088628	4899.8664331	496	40.6955750	130.0569737	5292.7433270	496	45.0905578	126.8526366	5719.8564101
497	36.9960025	133.4358928	4936.5946258	497	41.0007918	130.0813635	5333.4389020	497	45.4381309	126.8746445	5764.9467029
498	37.2657650	133.4627271	4973.5906284	498	41.3082977	130.1055717	5374.4396938	498	45.7883831	126.8964841	5810.3848338
499	37.5374946	133.4893671	5010.8563934	499	41.6181100	130.1295997	5415.7479916	499	46.1413353	126.9181567	5856.1732169
500	37.8112055	133.5158143	5048.3938880	500	41.?302458	130.1534488	545?.3661015	500	46.4970081	126.9396634	5902.3145522

418

Table 1

M	C(9.50,M,12)	A(9.50,M,12)	S(9.50,M,12)
1	1.0079167	.9921455	1.0000000
2	1.0159960	1.9764982	2.0079167
3	1.0239385	2.9531194	3.0238127
4	1.0320447	3.9220697	4.0477512
5	1.0402151	4.8834093	5.0797959
6	1.0484501	5.8371982	6.1200109
7	1.0567503	6.7834955	7.1684610
8	1.0651163	7.7223602	8.2252113
9	1.0735484	8.6538505	9.2903276
10	1.0820474	9.5780245	10.3638760
11	1.0906136	10.4949395	11.4459234
12	1.0992476	11.4046527	12.5365369
13	1.1079500	12.3072205	13.6357845
14	1.1167212	13.2026992	14.7437345
15	1.1255619	14.0911443	15.8604557
16	1.1344726	14.9726111	16.9860177
17	1.1434539	15.8471545	18.1204903
18	1.1525062	16.7148287	19.2639442
19	1.1616302	17.5756879	20.4164504
20	1.1708265	18.4297854	21.5780806
21	1.1800955	19.2771744	22.7489071
22	1.1894379	20.1179077	23.9290026
23	1.1988543	20.9520374	25.1184406
24	1.2083453	21.7796154	26.3172949
25	1.2179113	22.6006933	27.5256401
26	1.2275531	23.4153220	28.7435514
27	1.2372712	24.2235522	29.9711046
28	1.2470663	25.0254342	31.2083758
29	1.2569389	25.8210178	32.4554421
30	1.2668897	26.6103525	33.7123810
31	1.2769192	27.3934874	34.9792707
32	1.2870282	28.1704711	36.2561899
33	1.2972171	28.9413521	37.5432181
34	1.3074868	29.7061782	38.8404353
35	1.3178377	30.4649970	40.1479220
36	1.3282706	31.2178556	41.4657598
37	1.3387861	31.9648009	42.7940304
38	1.3493848	32.7058794	44.1328164
39	1.3600674	33.4411371	45.4822012
40	1.3708346	34.1706197	46.8422687
41	1.3816871	34.8943725	48.2131033
42	1.3926254	35.6124407	49.5947903
43	1.4036504	36.3248688	50.9874158
44	1.4147626	37.0317012	52.3910661
45	1.4259628	37.7329818	53.8058288
46	1.4372517	38.4287541	55.2317916
47	1.4486299	39.1190616	56.6690432
48	1.4600982	39.8039470	58.1176732
49	1.4716574	40.4834530	59.5777714
50	1.4833080	41.1576218	61.0494288
51	1.4950508	41.8264954	62.5327368
52	1.5068867	42.4901153	64.0277876
53	1.5188162	43.1485228	65.5346742
54	1.5308401	43.8017589	67.0534904
55	1.5429593	44.4498641	68.5843305
56	1.5551744	45.0928788	70.1272898
57	1.5674862	45.7308430	71.6824642
58	1.5798954	46.3637963	73.2499504
59	1.5924029	46.9917780	74.8298458
60	1.6050095	47.6148273	76.4222488
61	1.6177158	48.2329829	78.0272582
62	1.6305227	48.8462831	79.6449740
63	1.6434310	49.4547662	81.2754968
64	1.6564415	50.0584700	82.9189278
65	1.6695550	50.6574320	84.5753693
66	1.6827723	51.2516695	86.2449243
67	1.6960943	51.8412793	87.9276966
68	1.7095217	52.4262383	89.6237909
69	1.7230554	53.0066027	91.3333125
70	1.7366962	53.5824086	93.0563679
71	1.7504451	54.1536919	94.7930642
72	1.7643028	54.7204880	96.5435093
73	1.7782702	55.2828323	98.3078121
74	1.7923482	55.8407596	100.0860822
75	1.8065376	56.3943047	101.8784304
76	1.8208393	56.9435019	103.6849680
77	1.8352543	57.4883856	105.5058073
78	1.8497834	58.0289894	107.3410616
79	1.8644275	58.5653471	109.1908450
80	1.8791876	59.0974919	111.0552725
81	1.8940645	59.6254570	112.9344601
82	1.9090592	60.1492753	114.8285246
83	1.9241725	60.6689792	116.7375837
84	1.9394056	61.1846011	118.6617563
85	1.9547592	61.6961731	120.6011619
86	1.9702344	62.2037269	122.5559211
87	1.9858321	62.7072942	124.5261554
88	2.0015532	63.2069061	126.5119875
89	2.0173989	63.7025939	128.5135407
90	2.0333699	64.1943884	130.5309396
91	2.0494675	64.6823200	132.5643095
92	2.0656924	65.1664192	134.6137770
93	2.0820458	65.6467160	136.6794694
94	2.0985287	66.1232404	138.7615152
95	2.1151420	66.5960219	140.8600439
96	2.1318869	67.0650899	142.9751859
97	2.1487643	67.5304736	145.1070728
98	2.1657754	67.9922020	147.2558371
99	2.1829211	68.4503038	149.4216125
100	2.2002026	68.9048074	151.6045336

M	C(9.75,M,12)	A(9.75,M,12)	S(9.75,M,12)
1	1.0081250	.9919405	1.0000000
2	1.0163160	1.9758864	2.0081250
3	1.0245736	2.9519022	3.0244410
4	1.0328982	3.9200518	4.0490146
5	1.0412905	4.8803985	5.0819128
6	1.0497510	5.8330054	6.1232034
7	1.0582803	6.7779347	7.1729544
8	1.0668788	7.7152483	8.2312347
9	1.0755472	8.6450076	9.2981134
10	1.0842860	9.5672735	10.3736606
11	1.0930958	10.4821064	11.4579466
12	1.1019772	11.3895661	12.5510424
13	1.1109308	12.2897122	13.6530196
14	1.1199571	13.1826036	14.7639504
15	1.1290567	14.0682986	15.8839075
16	1.1382303	14.9468554	17.0129643
17	1.1474785	15.8183315	18.1511946
18	1.1568017	16.6827839	19.2986731
19	1.1662007	17.5402692	20.4554748
20	1.1756761	18.3908436	21.6216755
21	1.1852285	19.2345628	22.7973516
22	1.1948585	20.0714820	23.9825801
23	1.2045667	20.9016560	25.1774386
24	1.2143538	21.7251393	26.3820053
25	1.2242204	22.5419856	27.5963591
26	1.2341672	23.3522486	28.8205795
27	1.2441948	24.1559813	30.0547467
28	1.2543039	24.9532362	31.2989415
29	1.2644951	25.7440657	32.5532454
30	1.2747691	26.5285214	33.8177405
31	1.2851266	27.3066549	35.0925097
32	1.2955683	28.0785169	36.3776363
33	1.3060948	28.8441581	37.6732046
34	1.3167068	29.6036287	38.9792994
35	1.3274051	30.3569782	40.2960062
36	1.3381902	31.1042561	41.6234113
37	1.3490630	31.8455113	42.9616015
38	1.3600241	32.5807924	44.3106645
39	1.3710743	33.3101475	45.6706886
40	1.3822143	34.0336243	47.0417630
41	1.3934448	34.7512702	48.4239773
42	1.4047666	35.4631322	49.8174221
43	1.4161803	36.1692570	51.2221887
44	1.4276867	36.8696908	52.6383690
45	1.4392867	37.5644794	54.0660557
46	1.4509809	38.2536683	55.5053424
47	1.4627701	38.9373028	56.9563233
48	1.4746551	39.6154274	58.4190934
49	1.4866367	40.2880867	59.8937486
50	1.4987156	40.9553247	61.3803853
51	1.5108927	41.6171851	62.8791009
52	1.5231687	42.2737113	64.3899936
53	1.5355444	42.9249460	65.9131623
54	1.5480207	43.5709321	67.4487068
55	1.5605984	44.2117120	68.9967275
56	1.5732783	44.8473275	70.5573259
57	1.5860612	45.4778202	72.1306042
58	1.5989479	46.1032314	73.7166653
59	1.6119394	46.7236021	75.3156132
60	1.6250364	47.3389730	76.9275526
61	1.6382398	47.9493842	78.5525890
62	1.6515505	48.5548759	80.1908288
63	1.6649693	49.1554875	81.8423792
64	1.6784972	49.7512586	83.5073486
65	1.6921350	50.3422280	85.1858458
66	1.7058836	50.9284344	86.8779808
67	1.7197439	51.5099164	88.5838644
68	1.7337168	52.0867118	90.3036083
69	1.7478033	52.6588586	92.0373251
70	1.7620042	53.2263941	93.7851284
71	1.7763205	53.7893556	95.5471325
72	1.7907531	54.3477799	97.3234530
73	1.8053029	54.9017036	99.1142060
74	1.8199710	55.4511629	100.9195090
75	1.8347583	55.9961938	102.7394800
76	1.8496657	56.5368320	104.5742382
77	1.8646942	57.0731130	106.4239039
78	1.8798449	57.6050718	108.2885982
79	1.8951186	58.1327432	110.1684430
80	1.9105164	58.6561619	112.0635616
81	1.9260394	59.1753621	113.9740781
82	1.9416885	59.6903778	115.9001174
83	1.9574647	60.2012427	117.8418059
84	1.9733691	60.7079903	119.7992706
85	1.9894027	61.2106537	121.7726396
86	2.0055666	61.7092659	123.7620423
87	2.0218618	62.2038596	125.7676089
88	2.0382895	62.6944670	127.7894708
89	2.0548506	63.1811204	129.8277602
90	2.0715462	63.6638516	131.8826108
91	2.0883775	64.1426922	133.9541570
92	2.1053456	64.6176736	136.0425345
93	2.1224515	65.0888269	138.1478801
94	2.1396964	65.5561829	140.2703316
95	2.1570815	66.0197723	142.4100281
96	2.1746078	66.4796253	144.5671095
97	2.1922765	66.9357722	146.7417173
98	2.2100887	67.3882427	148.9339938
99	2.2280457	67.8370665	151.1440825
100	2.2461485	68.2822731	153.3721281

M	C(10.00,M,12)	A(10.00,M,12)	S(10.00,M,12)
1	1.0083333	.9917355	1.0000000
2	1.0167361	1.9752749	2.0083333
3	1.0252089	2.9506859	3.0250694
4	1.0337523	3.9180356	4.0502784
5	1.0423669	4.8773906	5.0840307
6	1.0510533	5.8288172	6.1263976
7	1.0598121	6.7723807	7.1774509
8	1.0686439	7.7081461	8.2372630
9	1.0775492	8.6361780	9.3059069
10	1.0865288	9.5565401	10.3834561
11	1.0955832	10.4692960	11.4699849
12	1.1047131	11.3745084	12.5655681
13	1.1139190	12.2722398	13.6702812
14	1.1232017	13.1625518	14.7842002
15	1.1325617	14.0455059	15.9074018
16	1.1419997	14.9211629	17.0399635
17	1.1515164	15.7895831	18.1819632
18	1.1611123	16.6508262	19.3334796
19	1.1707883	17.5049516	20.4945919
20	1.1805448	18.3520181	21.6653802
21	1.1903827	19.1920841	22.8459250
22	1.2003026	20.0252073	24.0363077
23	1.2103051	20.8514453	25.2366103
24	1.2203910	21.6708548	26.4469154
25	1.2305609	22.4834924	27.6673063
26	1.2408156	23.2894139	28.8978672
27	1.2511557	24.0886750	30.1366828
28	1.2615820	24.8813306	31.3898385
29	1.2720952	25.6674353	32.6514205
30	1.2826960	26.4470432	33.9235156
31	1.2933851	27.2202082	35.2062116
32	1.3041633	27.9869833	36.4995957
33	1.3150313	28.7474215	37.8037600
34	1.3259899	29.5015750	39.1187913
35	1.3370398	30.2494959	40.4447813
36	1.3481818	30.9912356	41.7818211
37	1.3594167	31.7268452	43.1300029
38	1.3707452	32.4563754	44.4894196
39	1.3821680	33.1798764	45.8601648
40	1.3936861	33.8973981	47.2423328
41	1.4053002	34.6089899	48.6360189
42	1.4170110	35.3147007	50.0413191
43	1.4288194	36.0145792	51.4583301
44	1.4407262	36.7086736	52.8871495
45	1.4527323	37.3970317	54.3278758
46	1.4648384	38.0797008	55.7806081
47	1.4770454	38.7567281	57.2454465
48	1.4893541	39.4281601	58.7224918
49	1.5017654	40.0940431	60.2118459
50	1.5142801	40.7544229	61.7136113
51	1.5268991	41.4093450	63.2278914
52	1.5396233	42.0588545	64.7547905
53	1.5524534	42.7029962	66.2944138
54	1.5653906	43.3418144	67.8468672
55	1.5784355	43.9753532	69.4122578
56	1.5915891	44.6036560	70.9906933
57	1.6048524	45.2267663	72.5822824
58	1.6182261	45.8447269	74.1871347
59	1.6317113	46.4575804	75.8053609
60	1.6453089	47.0653690	77.4370722
61	1.6590198	47.6681346	79.0823811
62	1.6728450	48.2659186	80.7414010
63	1.6867854	48.8587622	82.4142460
64	1.7008419	49.4467063	84.1010314
65	1.7150156	50.0297914	85.8018733
66	1.7293074	50.6080576	87.5168889
67	1.7437183	51.1815447	89.2461963
68	1.7582493	51.7502923	90.9899146
69	1.7729014	52.3143394	92.7481639
70	1.7876755	52.8737251	94.5210653
71	1.8025728	53.4284877	96.3087408
72	1.8175943	53.9786655	98.1113137
73	1.8327409	54.5242963	99.9289079
74	1.8480137	55.0654178	101.7616488
75	1.8634139	55.6020673	103.6096626
76	1.8789423	56.1342816	105.4730764
77	1.8946002	56.6620975	107.3520187
78	1.9103885	57.1855512	109.2466189
79	1.9263084	57.7046789	111.1570074
80	1.9423610	58.2195162	113.0833158
81	1.9585473	58.7300987	115.0256768
82	1.9748685	59.2364616	116.9842241
83	1.9913258	59.7386396	118.9590926
84	2.0079202	60.2366673	120.9504184
85	2.0246528	60.7305792	122.9583385
86	2.0415249	61.2204091	124.9829913
87	2.0585376	61.7061908	127.0245163
88	2.0756921	62.1879579	129.0830539
89	2.0929896	62.6657433	131.1587460
90	2.1104311	63.1395802	133.2517356
91	2.1280181	63.6095010	135.3621667
92	2.1457515	64.0755382	137.4901848
93	2.1636328	64.5377238	139.6359363
94	2.1816631	64.9960897	141.7995691
95	2.1998436	65.4506675	143.9812322
96	2.2181756	65.9014884	146.1810758
97	2.2366604	66.3485836	148.3992514
98	2.2552993	66.7919837	150.6359119
99	2.2740934	67.2317194	152.8912111
100	2.2930442	67.6678209	155.1653045

Table 1

419

M	C(9.50,M,12)	A(9.50,M,12)	S(9.50,M,12)	M	C(9.75,M,12)	A(9.75,M,12)	S(9.75,M,12)	M	C(10.00,M,12)	A(10.00,M,12)	S(10.00,M,12)
101	2.2176208	69.3557411	153.8047361	101	2.2643985	68.7238915	155.6182767	101	2.3121529	68.1003182	157.4583488
102	2.2351770	69.8031330	156.0223569	102	2.2827967	69.1619506	157.8826752	102	2.3314208	68.5292412	159.7705017
103	2.2528721	70.2470108	158.2575339	103	2.3013445	69.5964792	160.1654719	103	2.3508494	68.9546194	162.1019225
104	2.2707074	70.6874022	160.5104061	104	2.3200429	70.0275057	162.4669164	104	2.3704398	69.3764820	164.4527719
105	2.2886838	71.1243346	162.7811135	105	2.3388932	70.4550584	164.7868593	105	2.3901934	69.7948582	166.8232116
106	2.3068026	71.5578350	165.0697973	106	2.3578967	70.8791652	167.1257525	106	2.4101117	70.2097767	169.2134051
107	2.3250648	71.9879306	167.3765998	107	2.3770547	71.2998538	169.4636492	107	2.4301960	70.6212662	171.6235168
108	2.3434715	72.4146480	169.7016646	108	2.3963682	71.7171520	171.8607039	108	2.4504476	71.0293549	174.0537127
109	2.3620240	72.8380137	172.0451361	109	2.4158387	72.1310869	174.2570721	109	2.4708680	71.4340710	176.5041604
110	2.3807234	73.2580541	174.4071601	110	2.4354674	72.5416857	176.6729108	110	2.4914586	71.8354423	178.9750284
111	2.3995707	73.6747953	176.7878835	111	2.4552556	72.9489753	179.1083782	111	2.5122207	72.2334965	181.4664869
112	2.4185673	74.0882632	179.1874542	112	2.4752045	73.3529823	181.5636338	112	2.5331559	72.6282610	183.9787077
113	2.4377143	74.4984835	181.6060216	113	2.4953156	73.7537332	184.0388383	113	2.5542655	73.0197629	186.5118636
114	2.4570129	74.9054818	184.0437359	114	2.5155900	74.1512543	186.5341539	114	2.5755511	73.4080294	189.0661291
115	2.4764643	75.3092833	186.5007488	115	2.5360292	74.5455715	189.0497439	115	2.5970140	73.7930370	191.6416802
116	2.4960696	75.7099132	188.9772131	116	2.5566344	74.9367107	191.5857731	116	2.6186558	74.1749623	194.2386942
117	2.5158302	76.1073963	191.4732827	117	2.5774071	75.3246976	194.1424075	117	2.6404779	74.5536816	196.8573500
118	2.5357471	76.5017574	193.9891128	118	2.5983485	75.7095574	196.7198145	118	2.6624819	74.9292710	199.4978279
119	2.5558218	76.8930210	196.5248600	119	2.6194601	76.0913155	199.3181630	119	2.6846692	75.3017564	202.1603098
120	2.5760554	77.2812114	199.0806818	120	2.6407432	76.4699967	201.9376231	120	2.7070415	75.6711633	204.8449790
121	2.5964492	77.6663527	201.6567372	121	2.6621992	76.8456260	204.5783663	121	2.7296002	76.0375174	207.5520205
122	2.6170044	78.0484690	204.2531864	122	2.6838296	77.2182279	207.2405655	122	2.7523468	76.4008437	210.2816207
123	2.6377223	78.4275840	206.8701907	123	2.7056357	77.5878268	209.9243951	123	2.7752831	76.7611673	213.0339675
124	2.6586043	78.8037212	209.5079131	124	2.7276190	77.9544470	212.6300308	124	2.7984104	77.1185130	215.8092506
125	2.6796516	79.1769040	212.1665174	125	2.7497809	78.3181123	215.3576498	125	2.8217305	77.4729054	218.6076610
126	2.7008655	79.5471557	214.8461690	126	2.7721229	78.6788467	218.1074307	126	2.8452449	77.8243690	221.4293915
127	2.7222474	79.9144993	217.5470345	127	2.7946464	79.0366737	220.8795536	127	2.8689553	78.1729280	224.2746365
128	2.7437985	80.2789575	220.2692819	128	2.8173529	79.3916168	223.6742000	128	2.8928633	78.5186062	227.1435918
129	2.7655202	80.6405531	223.0130803	129	2.8402439	79.7436992	226.4915529	129	2.9169705	78.8614277	230.0364550
130	2.7874139	80.9993086	225.7786006	130	2.8633209	80.0929441	229.3317967	130	2.9412785	79.2014159	232.9534255
131	2.8094809	81.3552462	228.5660145	131	2.8865853	80.4393742	232.1951176	131	2.9657892	79.5385943	235.8947040
132	2.8317227	81.7083882	231.3754954	132	2.9100388	80.7830122	235.0817029	132	2.9905041	79.8729860	238.8604932
133	2.8541405	82.0587563	234.2072181	133	2.9336829	81.1238307	237.9917418	133	3.0154250	80.2046143	241.8509974
134	2.8767358	82.4063726	237.0613586	134	2.9575191	81.4620019	240.9254427	134	3.0405535	80.5335017	244.8664223
135	2.8995099	82.7512584	239.9380944	135	2.9815489	81.7973980	243.8829437	135	3.0658915	80.8596712	247.9069759
136	2.9224644	83.0934354	242.8376043	136	3.0057740	82.1300910	246.8644927	136	3.0914406	81.1831449	250.9728673
137	2.9456005	83.4329247	245.7600586	137	3.0301959	82.4601027	249.8702667	137	3.1172026	81.5039454	254.0643079
138	2.9689199	83.7697476	248.7056692	138	3.0548163	82.7874546	252.9004626	138	3.1431793	81.8220946	257.1815105
139	2.9924238	84.1039248	251.6745891	139	3.0796366	83.1121683	255.9552788	139	3.1693724	82.1376145	260.3246897
140	3.0161139	84.4354773	254.6670129	140	3.1046587	83.4343469	259.0349155	140	3.1957839	82.4505268	263.4940621
141	3.0399914	84.7644256	257.6831268	141	3.1298840	83.7537655	262.1395742	141	3.2224154	82.7608530	266.6898460
142	3.0640580	85.0907902	260.7231182	142	3.1553144	84.0706911	265.2694582	142	3.2492688	83.0686145	269.9122614
143	3.0883151	85.4145913	263.7871762	143	3.1809513	84.3850625	268.4247726	143	3.2763461	83.3738326	273.1615302
144	3.1127643	85.7358492	266.8754913	144	3.2067965	84.6969002	271.6057238	144	3.3036490	83.6765282	276.4378763
145	3.1374070	86.0545837	269.9882557	145	3.2328517	85.0062246	274.8125204	145	3.3311794	83.9767222	279.7415253
146	3.1622448	86.3708148	273.1256627	146	3.2591187	85.3130560	278.0453721	146	3.3589392	84.2744352	283.0727046
147	3.1872793	86.6845620	276.2879075	147	3.2855990	85.6174145	281.3044907	147	3.3869304	84.5696878	286.4316439
148	3.2125119	86.9958449	279.4751868	148	3.3122948	85.9193201	284.5900397	148	3.4151548	84.8625003	289.8185742
149	3.2379443	87.3046828	282.6876987	149	3.3392069	86.2187924	287.9023842	149	3.4436144	85.1528929	293.2337290
150	3.2635780	87.6110950	285.9256430	150	3.3663379	86.5158511	291.2415911	150	3.4723112	85.4408855	296.6773434
151	3.2894147	87.9151004	289.1892210	151	3.3936894	86.8105157	294.6079290	151	3.5012471	85.7264980	300.1496546
152	3.3154559	88.2167181	292.4786356	152	3.4212632	87.1028054	298.0016184	152	3.5304242	86.0097501	303.6509017
153	3.3417032	88.5159667	295.7940915	153	3.4490609	87.3927394	301.4228816	153	3.5598444	86.2906612	307.1813259
154	3.3681584	88.8128648	299.1357947	154	3.4770845	87.6803366	304.8719425	154	3.5895098	86.5692508	310.7411703
155	3.3948230	89.1074310	302.5039531	155	3.5053358	87.9656160	308.3490270	155	3.6194223	86.8455380	314.3306801
156	3.4216986	89.3996835	305.8987761	156	3.5338167	88.2485961	311.8543829	156	3.6495842	87.1195418	317.9501024
157	3.4487871	89.6896405	309.3204747	157	3.5625290	88.5292956	315.3881796	157	3.6799974	87.3912811	321.5996866
158	3.4760900	89.9773201	312.7692618	158	3.5914745	88.8077328	318.9507085	158	3.7106640	87.6607747	325.2796840
159	3.5035090	90.2627400	316.2453518	159	3.6206552	89.0839259	322.5421831	159	3.7415862	87.9280410	328.9903480
160	3.5313459	90.5459182	319.7489608	160	3.6500731	89.3578930	326.1628383	160	3.7727661	88.1930985	332.7319343
161	3.5593024	90.8268721	323.2803068	161	3.6797299	89.6296521	329.8129114	161	3.8042058	88.4559555	336.5047004
162	3.5874802	91.1056193	326.8396092	162	3.7096277	89.8992209	333.4926413	162	3.8359076	88.7166600	340.3089062
163	3.6158811	91.3821771	330.4270895	163	3.7397684	90.1666171	337.2022690	163	3.8678735	88.9752000	344.1448138
164	3.6445069	91.6565626	334.0429706	164	3.7701541	90.4318583	340.9420374	164	3.9001057	89.2316033	348.0126872
165	3.6733592	91.9287930	337.6874774	165	3.8007866	90.6949067	344.7121915	165	3.9326066	89.4858875	351.9127930
166	3.7024400	92.1988852	341.3608366	166	3.8316679	90.9559447	348.5129760	166	3.9653783	89.7380703	355.8453996
167	3.7317509	92.4668559	345.0632766	167	3.8628003	91.2148242	352.3446460	167	3.9984232	89.9881689	359.8107779
168	3.7612940	92.7327218	348.7950275	168	3.8941855	91.4716173	356.2074462	168	4.0317433	90.2362005	363.8092010
169	3.7910709	92.9964995	352.5563215	169	3.9258238	91.7263408	360.1016317	169	4.0653412	90.4821624	367.8409444
170	3.8210835	93.2582054	356.3473924	170	3.9577231	91.9790114	364.0274575	170	4.0992190	90.7261313	371.9062856
171	3.8513338	93.5178557	360.1684759	171	3.9898796	92.2296455	367.9851806	171	4.1333792	90.9680641	376.0055047
172	3.8818235	93.7754666	364.0198097	172	4.0222974	92.4782596	371.9750602	172	4.1678240	91.2079974	380.1388839
173	3.9125546	94.0310541	367.9016332	173	4.0549785	92.7248701	375.9973576	173	4.2025559	91.4459479	384.3067079
174	3.9435290	94.2846341	371.8141878	174	4.0879252	92.9694929	380.0523361	174	4.2375772	91.6819318	388.5092638
175	3.9747486	94.5362223	375.7577163	175	4.1211396	93.2121442	384.1402613	175	4.2728903	91.9159654	392.7468410
176	4.0062154	94.7858345	379.7324654	176	4.1546239	93.4528399	388.2614010	176	4.3084978	92.1480648	397.0197313
177	4.0379312	95.0334860	383.7386807	177	4.1883802	93.6915957	392.4160248	177	4.3444019	92.3782461	401.3282291
178	4.0699982	95.2791924	387.7766120	178	4.2224108	93.9284272	396.6044050	178	4.3806053	92.6065251	405.6726310
179	4.1021182	95.5229689	391.8465101	179	4.2567179	94.1633500	400.8268158	179	4.4171103	92.8329174	410.0532363
180	4.1345933	95.7648307	395.9486283	180	4.2913037	94.3963794	405.0835337	180	4.4539196	93.0574388	414.4703466
181	4.1673255	96.0047927	400.0832271	181	4.3261706	94.6275307	409.3748374	181	4.4910356	93.2801046	418.9242661
182	4.2003168	96.2428700	404.2505472	182	4.3613207	94.8568191	413.7010780	182	4.5284609	93.5009301	423.4153017
183	4.2335693	96.4790773	408.4508640	183	4.3967565	95.0842595	418.0623287	183	4.5661980	93.7199307	427.9437626
184	4.2670851	96.7134293	412.6844333	184	4.4324801	95.3098668	422.4590851	184	4.6042497	93.9371214	432.5099606
185	4.3008662	96.9459406	416.9515184	185	4.4684940	95.5336559	426.8915652	185	4.6426184	94.1525171	437.1142103
186	4.3349147	97.1766257	421.2523846	186	4.5048005	95.7556413	431.3600591	186	4.6813069	94.3661326	441.7568287
187	4.3692328	97.4054988	425.5872994	187	4.5414020	95.9758376	435.8648596	187	4.7203178	94.5779828	446.4381356
188	4.4038225	97.6325743	429.9565321	188	4.5783009	96.1942592	440.4062616	188	4.7596538	94.7880821	451.1584534
189	4.4386861	97.8578662	434.3603547	189	4.6154996	96.4109205	444.9845625	189	4.7993176	94.9964450	455.9181072
190	4.4738257	98.0813885	438.7990408	190	4.6530005	96.6258356	449.6000621	190	4.8393119	95.2030860	460.7174247
191	4.5092435	98.3031552	443.2728666	191	4.6908061	96.8390186	454.2530626	191	4.8796395	95.4080192	465.5567366
192	4.5449417	98.5231800	447.7821101	192	4.7289189	97.0504834	458.9438687	192	4.9203031	95.6112587	470.4363761
193	4.5809225	98.7414767	452.3270518	193	4.7673414	97.2602439	463.6727877	193	4.9613057	95.8128185	475.3566792
194	4.6171881	98.9580587	456.9079743	194	4.8060761	97.4683138	468.4401291	194	5.0026499	96.0127126	480.3179849
195	4.6537409	99.1729396	461.5251624	195	4.8451254	97.6747069	473.2462051	195	5.0443386	96.2109546	485.3206348
196	4.6905830	99.3861324	466.1789033	196	4.8844921	97.8794364	478.0913305	196	5.0863748	96.4075583	490.3649734
197	4.7277168	99.5976513	470.8694863	197	4.9241786	98.0825160	482.9758226	197	5.1287612	96.6025372	495.4513482
198	4.7651445	99.8075085	475.5972031	198	4.9641875	98.2839588	487.9000012	198	5.1715009	96.7959046	500.5801094
199	4.8028686	100.0157174	480.3623476	199	5.0045215	98.4837781	492.8641887	199	5.2145968	96.9876740	505.7516103
200	4.8408913	100.2222909	485.1652162	200	5.0451833	98.6819870	497.8687102	200	5.2580517	97.1778585	510.9662071

Table 1

M	C(9.50,M,12)	A(9.50,M,12)	S(9.50,M,12)	M	C(9.75,M,12)	A(9.75,M,12)	S(9.75,M,12)	M	C(10.00,M,12)	A(10.00,M,12)	S(10.00,M,12)
201	4.8792150	100.4272419	490.0061075	201	5.0861754	98.8785984	502.9136935	201	5.3018688	97.3664713	516.2242588
202	4.9178421	100.6305832	494.8853225	202	5.1275006	99.0736252	508.0000689	202	5.3400511	97.5505252	521.5261276
203	4.9567751	100.8323272	499.8031647	203	5.1691615	99.2670801	513.1275694	203	5.3800015	97.7380333	526.8721787
204	4.9960162	101.0324867	504.7599397	204	5.2111609	99.4589760	518.2967309	204	5.4000232	97.9220032	532.2627802
205	5.0355680	101.2310740	509.7559559	205	5.2535016	99.6493252	523.5078919	205	5.4200192	98.1054327	537.6983034
206	5.0754329	101.4281016	514.7915239	206	5.2961863	99.8381403	528.7613935	206	5.4600927	98.2834053	543.1791226
207	5.1156134	101.6235816	519.8669568	207	5.3392178	100.0254336	534.0575798	207	5.5715468	98.4655034	548.7056153
208	5.1561120	101.8175261	524.9825702	208	5.3825990	100.2112175	539.3967977	208	5.6150347	98.6422205	554.2781621
209	5.1969312	102.0099474	530.1386822	209	5.4263326	100.3955040	544.7793967	209	5.6650096	98.8203258	559.8971468
210	5.2380736	102.2008573	535.3356135	210	5.4704216	100.5763053	550.2057293	210	5.7130246	98.9953844	565.5629563
211	5.2795417	102.3902676	540.5736871	211	5.5148687	100.7596333	555.6761508	211	5.7665332	99.1699365	571.2759310
212	5.3213381	102.5781903	545.8532288	212	5.5595770	100.9394998	561.1910186	212	5.8000385	99.3411133	577.0366141
213	5.3634653	102.7646369	551.1745668	213	5.6048494	101.1179168	566.7506966	213	5.8570438	99.5115054	582.8452526
214	5.4059261	102.9496191	556.5380322	214	5.6503888	101.2948957	572.3555460	214	5.9000025	99.6811720	588.7022064
215	5.4487230	103.1331484	561.9439583	215	5.6962982	101.4704483	578.0059348	215	5.9350879	99.8490532	594.6081498
216	5.4918587	103.3152361	567.3926813	216	5.7425806	101.6445861	583.7022330	216	6.0050935	100.0150003	600.5532168
217	5.5353359	103.4958936	572.8845400	217	5.7892391	101.8173204	589.4448137	217	6.0547326	100.1807927	606.5679102
218	5.5791574	103.6751321	578.4198759	218	5.8362767	101.9886625	595.2340528	218	6.1051887	100.3445378	612.6226428
219	5.6233257	103.8529628	583.9990333	219	5.8833964	102.1586237	601.0703295	219	6.1550653	100.5070292	618.7278315
220	5.6678437	104.0293968	589.6223590	220	5.9315015	102.3272150	606.9540259	220	6.2070358	100.6801281	624.8833968
221	5.7127141	104.2044449	595.2902027	221	5.9796949	102.4944476	612.8855274	221	6.2590939	100.8270556	631.0912626
222	5.7579398	104.3781181	601.0029168	222	6.0282799	102.6603324	618.8652223	222	6.3112530	100.9883428	637.3503565
223	5.8035235	104.5504273	606.7608565	223	6.0772597	102.8248803	624.8935022	223	6.3500468	101.1434005	643.6616094
224	5.8494680	104.7213830	612.5643800	224	6.1265374	102.9881020	630.9707620	224	6.4163768	101.2993165	650.0254562
225	5.8957763	104.8909959	618.4138480	225	6.1764164	103.1500081	637.0973994	225	6.4703528	101.4533705	655.4423350
226	5.9424512	105.0592766	624.3096243	226	6.2265998	103.3106094	643.2738158	226	6.5242724	101.6071443	662.9126878
227	5.9894956	105.2262356	630.2520755	227	6.2771909	103.4699164	649.5004155	227	6.5750413	101.7591514	669.4369602
228	6.0369124	105.3918832	636.2415711	228	6.3281931	103.6279394	655.7776064	228	6.6334634	101.9090022	676.0156015
229	6.0847047	105.5562297	642.2784836	229	6.3796096	103.7846888	662.1057995	229	6.6837422	102.0594072	682.6490549
230	6.1328752	105.7192854	648.3631882	230	6.4314440	103.9401748	668.4854091	230	6.7440317	102.2073765	689.3378071
231	6.1814272	105.8810603	654.4960635	231	6.4836994	104.0944078	674.9168531	231	6.8000357	102.3547205	696.0822088
232	6.2303635	106.0415646	660.6774906	232	6.5363795	104.2473977	681.4005525	232	6.8373531	102.5005433	702.8829746
233	6.2796872	106.2008082	666.9078541	233	6.5894876	104.3991545	687.9369320	233	6.9143028	102.6451728	709.7403327
234	6.3294014	106.3588010	673.1875413	234	6.6430272	104.5496883	694.5264196	234	6.9721236	102.7886011	716.6548355
235	6.3795091	106.5155529	679.5169427	235	6.6970018	104.6990089	701.1694467	235	7.0302247	102.9303441	723.6269591
236	6.4300136	106.6710736	685.8964518	236	6.7514449	104.8471260	707.8664465	236	7.0850099	103.0719115	730.6571633
237	6.4809179	106.8253727	692.3264654	237	6.8062701	104.9940493	714.6178634	237	7.1470333	103.2110131	737.7459937
238	6.5322251	106.9784599	698.8073832	238	6.8615711	105.1397885	721.4241335	238	7.2074490	103.3505554	744.8938768
239	6.5839386	107.1303446	705.3396084	239	6.9173214	105.2843532	728.2857046	239	7.2675111	103.4801571	752.1013259
240	6.6360614	107.2810364	711.9235469	240	6.9735246	105.4277527	735.2030260	240	7.3220736	103.6247188	759.3688370
241	6.6885969	107.4305446	718.5596084	241	7.0301645	105.5699965	742.1765506	241	7.3831409	103.7599524	766.6969106
242	6.7415483	107.5788785	725.2482053	242	7.0873047	105.7110938	749.2067351	242	7.4507171	103.8941676	774.0660515
243	6.7949189	107.7260473	731.9897536	243	7.1448891	105.8510540	756.2940398	243	7.5120064	104.0272737	781.5367687
244	6.8487120	107.8720602	738.7846724	244	7.2029413	105.9898863	763.4389289	244	7.5754131	104.1592707	789.0495751
245	6.9029310	108.0169262	745.6333844	245	7.2614652	106.1275994	770.6418702	245	7.6355416	104.2901947	796.6249882
246	6.9575792	108.1606543	752.5363154	246	7.3204646	106.2642028	777.9033354	246	7.7021961	104.4203278	804.2635298
247	7.0126600	108.3032535	759.4938946	247	7.3799434	106.3997052	785.2238000	247	7.7600811	104.5487879	811.9657259
248	7.0681769	108.4447327	766.5065546	248	7.4399054	106.5341155	792.6037434	248	7.8511009	104.6764339	819.7321269
249	7.1241333	108.5851007	773.5747315	249	7.5003547	106.6674425	800.0436488	249	7.8963601	104.8031245	827.5632078
250	7.1805327	108.7243661	780.6988408	250	7.5612950	106.7996950	807.5440034	250	7.9521631	104.9287185	835.4595059
251	7.2373786	108.8625377	787.8793975	251	7.6227306	106.9308816	815.1052985	251	8.0025144	105.0532746	843.4217310
252	7.2946745	108.9996204	795.1166760	252	7.6846652	107.0610109	822.7280290	252	8.0554187	105.1766012	851.4502454
253	7.3524240	109.1356336	802.4114505	253	7.7471031	107.1900914	830.4126943	253	8.1650805	105.2993070	859.5456641
254	7.4106307	109.2705749	809.7638745	254	7.8100484	107.3181315	838.1597974	254	8.2300045	105.4200003	867.7085446
255	7.4692984	109.4044563	817.1745052	255	7.8735050	107.4451398	845.9698458	255	8.2954954	105.5412896	875.9394492
256	7.5284301	109.5372861	824.6438034	256	7.9374772	107.5711244	853.8433508	256	8.3800579	105.6507831	884.2389446
257	7.5880302	109.6690726	832.1722335	257	8.0019692	107.6960936	861.7809260	257	8.4383967	105.7792990	892.6076025
258	7.6481021	109.7998240	839.7602637	258	8.0669852	107.8200557	869.7827972	258	8.5007167	105.8958155	901.0459992
259	7.7066496	109.9295484	847.4083658	259	8.1325295	107.9430187	877.8497825	259	8.5732026	106.0133708	909.5547159
260	7.7696764	110.0582539	855.1170153	260	8.1986063	108.0649906	885.9823120	260	8.6511195	106.1233027	918.1343385
261	7.8311863	110.1859484	862.8866917	261	8.2652220	108.1859795	894.1809183	261	8.7232122	106.2435594	926.7854580
262	7.8931832	110.3126400	870.7178780	262	8.3323749	108.3059933	902.4461382	262	8.7950056	106.3572037	935.5086701
263	7.9556709	110.4383365	878.6110612	263	8.4000754	108.4250399	910.7785131	263	8.8592048	106.4700333	944.3045757
264	8.0186533	110.5630458	886.5667321	264	8.4683260	108.5431270	919.1785385	264	8.9431148	106.5816582	953.1737805
265	8.0821343	110.6857755	894.5853854	265	8.5371312	108.6602623	927.6469146	265	9.0178408	106.6927500	962.1168954
266	8.1461179	110.8095333	902.6675198	266	8.6064954	108.7764537	936.1840458	266	9.0327878	106.8027272	971.1345362
267	8.2106080	110.9313270	910.8136376	267	8.6764232	108.8917085	944.7905411	267	9.1303610	106.9117956	980.2273240
268	8.2756086	111.0521640	919.0242456	268	8.7469191	109.0060345	953.4669643	268	9.2440357	107.0195026	989.3958050
269	8.3411239	111.1720519	927.2998542	269	8.8179878	109.1194390	962.2138834	269	9.3220071	107.1272356	998.6408508
270	8.4071578	111.2909982	935.6409781	270	8.8896340	109.2319296	971.0318712	270	9.3600905	107.2335221	1007.9628579
271	8.4737144	111.4090102	944.0481358	271	8.9618622	109.3435136	979.9215052	271	9.4700212	107.3391293	1017.3625483
272	8.5407980	111.5260953	952.5218502	272	9.0346774	109.4541982	988.8833674	272	9.5570048	107.4437646	1026.8405696
273	8.6084126	111.6422607	961.0626482	273	9.1080841	109.5639908	997.9180448	273	9.6300465	107.5475252	1036.3975743
274	8.6765626	111.7575137	969.6710609	274	9.1820873	109.6728985	1007.0261289	274	9.7100518	107.6504481	1046.0342208
275	8.7452520	111.8718615	978.3476234	275	9.2566919	109.7809284	1016.2082162	275	9.7979264	107.7523105	1055.7511727
276	8.8144853	111.9853111	987.0928755	276	9.3319024	109.8880877	1025.4649080	276	9.8753758	107.8537294	1065.5490991
277	8.8842666	112.0978696	995.9073607	277	9.4077241	109.9943834	1034.7968104	277	9.9819056	107.9541118	1075.4286749
278	8.9546004	112.2095441	1004.7916274	278	9.4841619	110.0998223	1044.2045344	278	10.0440215	108.0536646	1085.3905806
279	9.0254901	112.3203414	1013.7462277	279	9.5612207	110.2044115	1053.6886963	279	10.1200292	108.1523547	1095.4355021
280	9.0969428	112.4302684	1022.7717187	280	9.6389056	110.3081577	1063.2499170	280	10.2130344	108.2503089	1105.5641313
281	9.1689560	112.5393320	1031.8686615	281	9.7172217	110.4110677	1072.8888225	281	10.2931431	108.3474137	1115.7771657
282	9.2415478	112.6475390	1041.0376218	282	9.7961741	110.5131484	1082.6060442	282	10.3975309	108.4437160	1126.0753088
283	9.3147101	112.7548961	1050.2791696	283	9.8757680	110.6144064	1092.4022184	283	10.4744939	108.5392225	1136.4592607
284	9.3884516	112.8614099	1059.5938797	284	9.9560086	110.7148482	1102.2779864	284	10.5577480	108.6339397	1146.9297636
285	9.4627768	112.9670872	1068.9823313	285	10.0369012	110.8144806	1112.2339950	285	10.6457293	108.7278741	1157.4875117
286	9.5376904	113.0719343	1078.4451081	286	10.1184510	110.9133099	1122.2708963	286	10.7344437	108.8210321	1168.1332409
287	9.6131972	113.1759580	1087.9827985	287	10.2006635	111.0113428	1132.3893473	287	10.8233974	108.9134203	1178.8676846
288	9.6893016	113.2791646	1097.5959957	288	10.2835438	111.1085055	1142.5900108	288	10.9140985	109.0050449	1189.6915820
289	9.7660086	113.3815606	1107.2852973	289	10.3670975	111.2050445	1152.8735546	289	11.0000473	109.0959123	1200.6056785
290	9.8433228	113.4831523	1117.0513059	290	10.4513303	111.3007261	1163.2406522	290	11.0937561	109.1860237	1211.6107259
291	9.9212492	113.5839461	1126.8946288	291	10.5362474	111.3956366	1173.6919826	291	11.1852290	109.2754004	1222.7074819
292	9.9997924	113.6839481	1136.8158779	292	10.6218544	111.4897821	1184.2282299	292	11.2824726	109.3640334	1233.8967109
293	10.0789574	113.7831648	1146.8156703	293	10.7081569	111.5831688	1194.8500843	293	11.3754932	109.4519340	1245.1791835
294	10.1587491	113.8816021	1156.8946277	294	10.7951607	111.6758029	1205.5582412	294	11.4712973	109.5391081	1256.5556767
295	10.2391726	113.9792662	1167.0533768	295	10.8828714	111.7676904	1216.3534020	295	11.5663915	109.6255617	1268.0269741
296	10.3202327	114.0761632	1177.2925494	296	10.9712947	111.8588374	1227.2362734	296	11.6632822	109.7113009	1279.5938655
297	10.4019345	114.1722992	1187.6127821	297	11.0604365	111.9492497	1238.2075681	297	11.7604762	109.7963315	1291.2571477
298	10.4842832	114.2676801	1198.0147167	298	11.1503025	112.0389334	1249.2680046	298	11.8554802	109.8806593	1303.0176240
299	10.5672838	114.3623118	1208.4989998	299	11.2408988	112.1278943	1260.4183071	299	11.9573009	109.9642902	1314.8761042
300	10.6509414	114.4562002	1219.0662836	300	11.3322311	112.2161381	1271.6592059	300	12.0569451	110.0472300	1326.8334051

Table 1   421

M	C(9.50,M,12)	A(9.50,M,12)	S(9.50,M,12)	M	C(9.75,M,12)	A(9.75,M,12)	S(9.75,M,12)	M	C(10.00,M,12)	A(10.00,M,12)	S(10.00,M,12)
301	10.7352614	114.5493512	1229.7172250	301	11.4243054	112.3036708	1282.9914370	301	12.1574196	110.1294843	1338.8903501
302	10.8202489	114.6417705	1240.4524864	302	11.5171279	112.3904980	1294.4157424	302	12.2587314	110.2110588	1351.0477697
303	10.9053092	114.7334639	1251.2727353	303	11.6107046	112.4766254	1305.9328703	303	12.3608875	110.2919591	1363.3065012
304	10.9924476	114.8244371	1262.1786444	304	11.7050416	112.5620587	1317.5435749	304	12.4633949	110.3721909	1375.6673887
305	11.0792696	114.9146957	1273.1708920	305	11.8001450	112.6468034	1329.2486165	305	12.5677607	110.4517595	1388.1312836
306	11.1653805	115.0042455	1284.2501616	306	11.8950212	112.7308651	1341.0487615	306	12.6724920	110.5306706	1400.6990443
307	11.2573857	115.0930918	1295.4171421	307	11.9926764	112.8142494	1352.9447827	307	12.7750961	110.6089295	1413.3715363
308	11.3444909	115.1812403	1306.6725278	308	12.0901169	112.8969618	1364.9374590	308	12.8845803	110.6865417	1426.1496325
309	11.4343014	115.2686965	1318.0170166	309	12.1803491	112.9790071	1377.0275759	309	12.9915518	110.7635124	1439.0342128
310	11.5248230	115.3554657	1329.4513200	310	12.2873794	113.0603914	1389.2159250	310	13.1002181	110.8398470	1452.0261646
311	11.6150611	115.4415534	1340.9761430	311	12.3672144	113.1411198	1401.5033044	311	13.2093865	110.9155508	1465.1263826
312	11.7050216	115.5269649	1352.5922041	312	12.4878605	113.2211976	1413.8905187	312	13.3194648	110.9906289	1478.3357691
313	11.8007101	115.6117058	1364.3002258	313	12.5833243	113.3006300	1426.3783792	313	13.4304603	111.0650865	1491.6552339
314	11.8941324	115.6957807	1376.1009359	314	12.6916126	113.3794222	1438.9677036	314	13.5423308	111.1389287	1505.0856942
315	11.9032943	115.7791954	1387.9950683	315	12.7847320	113.4575794	1451.6593162	315	13.6552340	111.2121607	1518.6280750
316	12.0832016	115.8619549	1399.9833626	316	12.8853392	113.5351056	1464.4540481	316	13.7690276	111.2847875	1532.2833090
317	12.1796603	115.9440644	1412.0665643	317	13.0034910	113.6120090	1477.3527373	317	13.8837695	111.3568140	1546.0523366
318	12.2752763	116.0255290	1424.2454246	318	13.1091444	113.6882917	1490.3562283	318	13.9994676	111.4282453	1559.9361060
319	12.3724556	116.1063537	1436.5207009	319	13.2158562	113.7639555	1503.4653726	319	14.1161298	111.4990863	1573.9355736
320	12.4704042	116.1865435	1448.8931564	320	13.3230334	113.8390175	1516.6810288	320	14.2337642	111.5693418	1588.0517034
321	12.5691282	116.2661035	1461.3635606	321	13.4312830	113.9134705	1530.0040622	321	14.3523789	111.6390166	1602.2854676
322	12.6853338	116.3450386	1473.9326888	322	13.5404122	113.9873235	1543.4353452	322	14.4719821	111.7081157	1616.6378465
323	12.7869271	116.4233539	1486.6013226	323	13.6504280	114.0605213	1556.9757574	323	14.5925919	111.7766436	1631.1098286
324	12.8700145	116.5010537	1499.3702497	324	13.7613378	114.1332497	1570.6261854	324	14.7141868	111.8446052	1645.7024105
325	12.9719021	116.5781434	1512.2402642	325	13.8731486	114.2053003	1584.3875232	325	14.8363050	111.9120052	1660.4165973
326	13.0745963	116.6546276	1525.2121663	326	13.9858680	114.2768311	1598.2606718	326	14.9604450	111.9788481	1675.2534023
327	13.1781036	116.7305111	1538.2867627	327	14.0955031	114.3477556	1612.2465798	327	15.0851154	112.0451386	1690.2138473
328	13.2824302	116.8057995	1551.4648662	328	14.2140616	114.4181084	1626.3460430	328	15.2108247	112.1108313	1705.2989627
329	13.3875828	116.8804948	1564.7472964	329	14.3295509	114.4878943	1640.5601046	329	15.3375816	112.1760806	1720.5097874
330	13.4935678	116.9546040	1578.1348792	330	14.4459785	114.5571177	1654.8896554	330	15.4653948	112.2407411	1735.8473690
331	13.6003919	117.0281313	1591.6284470	331	14.5633520	114.6257832	1669.3356339	331	15.5942730	112.3048672	1751.3127637
332	13.7000617	117.1010811	1605.2288389	332	14.6816793	114.6938953	1683.8989059	332	15.7242253	112.3684634	1766.9070368
333	13.8016838	117.1734578	1618.9369005	333	14.8009579	114.7614585	1698.5806652	333	15.8552605	112.4315339	1782.6312621
334	13.9253951	117.2452362	1632.7534843	334	14.9212258	114.8284771	1713.3816331	334	15.9873877	112.4940832	1798.4865226
335	14.0302123	117.3165104	1646.6794494	335	15.0424607	114.8949556	1728.3028589	335	16.1206159	112.5561156	1814.4739103
336	14.1473323	117.3871951	1660.7156618	336	15.1645807	114.9608983	1743.3453197	336	16.2549544	112.6176353	1830.5945263
337	14.2593321	117.4573247	1674.8629941	337	15.2875938	115.0263095	1758.5100004	337	16.3904124	112.6785466	1846.8494807
338	14.3722184	117.5269033	1689.1223262	338	15.4121079	115.0911936	1773.7978942	338	16.5269991	112.7391536	1863.2398930
339	14.4859985	117.5959355	1703.4945446	339	15.5373313	115.1555547	1789.2100021	339	16.6347241	112.7991606	1879.7668921
340	14.6003793	117.6644255	1717.9805431	340	15.6635721	115.2193971	1804.7473333	340	16.8035968	112.8585717	1896.4316163
341	14.7162580	117.7323775	1732.5812224	341	15.7900386	115.2827249	1820.4109054	341	16.9435268	112.9176909	1913.2352131
342	14.8327718	117.7997958	1747.2974904	342	15.9191392	115.3455424	1836.2017441	342	17.0843237	112.9762224	1930.1788339
343	14.9501979	117.8666845	1762.1302622	343	16.0484822	115.4078536	1852.1208833	343	17.2271972	113.0342701	1947.2636636
344	15.0685537	117.9330479	1777.0804602	344	16.1788761	115.4696626	1868.1693654	344	17.3707572	113.0918382	1964.4908608
345	15.1876064	117.9988900	1792.1490138	345	16.3103295	115.5309734	1884.3482416	345	17.5155135	113.1489304	1981.8616180
346	15.3080835	118.0642150	1807.3368602	346	16.4428509	115.5917901	1900.6585710	346	17.6614761	113.2055508	1999.3771315
347	15.4292725	118.1290268	1822.6449437	347	16.5764491	115.6521167	1917.1014219	347	17.8085551	113.2617033	2017.0386076
348	15.5514209	118.1933296	1838.0742162	348	16.7111327	115.7119570	1933.6778710	348	17.9553605	113.3173917	2034.8472236
349	15.6745363	118.2571274	1853.6256371	349	16.8469107	115.7713151	1950.3890037	349	18.1067027	113.3726199	2052.8043232
350	15.7986264	118.3204240	1869.3001734	350	16.9837918	115.8301948	1967.2359144	350	18.2575919	113.4273916	2070.9110259
351	15.9235988	118.3832235	1885.0987998	351	17.1217851	115.8885999	1984.2197062	351	18.4097385	113.4817107	2089.1686178
352	16.0497615	118.4455297	1901.0224986	352	17.2608996	115.9465343	2001.3414913	352	18.5631530	113.5355608	2107.5783663
353	16.1769221	118.5073466	1917.0722601	353	17.4011444	116.0040018	2018.6023910	353	18.7178459	113.5890058	2126.1415093
354	16.3048886	118.5696779	1933.2490821	354	17.5425287	116.0610061	2036.0053354	354	18.8735280	113.6419692	2144.8593552
355	16.4338690	118.6295274	1949.5539707	355	17.6850618	116.1175510	2053.5460642	355	19.0311099	113.6945347	2163.7331832
356	16.5640712	118.6898931	1965.9879397	356	17.8237529	116.1736402	2071.2311260	356	19.1897025	113.7466460	2182.7642952
357	16.6953034	118.7497955	1982.5520109	357	17.9733115	116.2292773	2089.0598789	357	19.3496166	113.7983266	2201.9539955
358	16.8273708	118.8092325	1999.2472143	358	18.1193471	116.2844660	2107.0334904	358	19.5103635	113.8495801	2221.3036122
359	16.9605905	118.8581837	2016.0745881	359	18.2663693	116.3392099	2125.1531375	359	19.6734540	113.9004100	2240.8144756
360	17.0943518	118.9256808	2033.0351786	360	18.4152876	116.3935126	2143.4200068	360	19.8373994	113.9508199	2260.4879296
361	17.2301962	118.9847185	2050.1300405	361	18.5649118	116.4473777	2161.8352944	361	20.0027111	114.0008131	2280.3253290
362	17.3663019	119.0423003	2067.3602366	362	18.7177517	116.5008088	2180.4002062	362	20.1694004	114.0503932	2300.3280401
363	17.5040875	119.0994298	2084.7268385	363	18.8678172	116.5538069	2199.1159578	363	20.3374787	114.0995635	2320.4974405
364	17.6423615	119.1561106	2102.2309260	364	19.0211182	116.6033321	2217.9837750	364	20.5085577	114.1483274	2340.8349192
365	17.7823326	119.2123461	2119.8735375	365	19.1750548	116.6585315	2237.0048932	365	20.6778490	114.1966883	2361.3418769
366	17.9231094	119.2631400	2137.6559201	366	19.3314671	116.7102606	2256.1805580	366	20.8501644	114.2446498	2382.0197259
367	18.0650007	119.3234957	2155.5790295	367	19.4935352	116.7615728	2275.5120250	367	21.0239158	114.2922145	2402.8698903
368	18.2050153	119.3784166	2173.6440302	368	19.6433796	116.8124715	2295.0005603	368	21.1991151	114.3393862	2423.8938060
369	18.3521620	119.4329061	2191.8520454	369	19.8065105	116.8629600	2314.6474398	369	21.3757744	114.3861632	2445.0929211
370	18.4974500	119.4839676	2210.2042075	370	19.9674384	116.9130415	2334.4539503	370	21.5535058	114.4325635	2466.4686955
371	18.6435881	119.5406044	2228.7016575	371	20.1253708	116.9627194	2354.4213387	371	21.7325217	114.4785753	2488.0226013
372	18.7914856	119.5938200	2247.3455456	372	20.2932274	117.0119969	2374.5510625	372	21.9146344	114.5242070	2509.7561230
373	18.9402515	119.6465176	2266.1370312	373	20.4531099	117.0608773	2394.8442809	373	22.0972563	114.5694614	2531.6707574
374	19.0901952	119.6990006	2285.0772827	374	20.6243320	117.1093637	2415.3023097	374	22.2814001	114.6143419	2553.7680137
375	19.2413259	119.7509720	2304.1674779	375	20.7919047	117.1574594	2435.9267018	375	22.4670785	114.6588515	2576.0494138
376	19.3935530	119.8025353	2323.4088038	376	20.9608389	117.2051674	2456.7186365	376	22.6543041	114.7029932	2598.5164923
377	19.5471861	119.8536935	2342.8024568	377	21.1311458	117.2524909	2477.6794744	377	22.8430900	114.7467701	2621.1707964
378	19.7019347	119.9044500	2362.3496430	378	21.3023363	117.2994330	2498.8106212	378	23.0334491	114.7901853	2644.0138864
379	19.8579083	119.9548078	2382.0515776	379	21.4759229	117.3459968	2520.1134575	379	23.2253945	114.8332416	2667.0473355
380	20.0151168	120.0047700	2401.9094860	380	21.6504137	117.3921853	2541.5893794	380	23.4189394	114.8759421	2690.2727300
381	20.1735698	120.0543398	2421.9246028	381	21.8253203	117.4380015	2563.2397931	381	23.6140973	114.9182696	2713.6916694
382	20.3332772	120.1035203	2442.0981726	382	22.0033622	117.4834485	2585.0661164	382	23.8109814	114.9602872	2737.3057667
383	20.4942490	120.1523144	2462.4314498	393	22.1824420	117.5235292	2607.0697786	383	24.0093016	115.0019378	2761.1167480
384	20.6564951	120.2007254	2482.9256988	384	22.3626743	117.5732465	2629.2522206	384	24.2093830	115.0432441	2785.1259535
385	20.8200257	120.2487550	2503.5821939	385	22.5443710	117.6176035	2651.6148949	385	24.4111278	115.0842200	2809.3353365
386	20.9848509	120.2964095	2524.4022196	386	22.7275441	117.6616030	2674.1592660	386	24.6145539	115.1248354	2833.7464643
387	21.1509810	120.3436920	2545.3870706	387	22.9122054	117.7052479	2696.8868100	387	24.8195752	115.1651260	2858.3610182
388	21.3184263	120.3905954	2566.5380516	388	23.0983370	117.7485410	2719.7990154	388	25.0265058	115.2050836	2883.1806934
389	21.4871971	120.4371357	2587.8564778	389	23.2800413	117.7914851	2742.8973324	389	25.2350600	115.2447110	2908.2071992
390	21.6573041	120.4833095	2609.3436750	390	23.4752403	117.8340832	2766.1834237	390	25.4453522	115.2840109	2933.4422592
391	21.8287578	120.5291206	2631.0009791	391	23.6659767	117.8763380	2789.6586640	391	25.6573968	115.3229860	2958.8876114
392	22.0015688	120.5745719	2652.8297369	392	23.8582627	117.9182522	2813.3246407	392	25.8712084	115.3316390	2984.5450082
393	22.1757479	120.6196663	2674.8313056	393	24.0521111	117.9598286	2837.1829034	393	26.0858018	115.3999726	3010.4162166
394	22.3513059	120.6644064	2697.0070535	394	24.2475345	118.0010699	2861.2350145	394	26.3041918	115.4379894	3036.5030184
395	22.5282537	120.7087951	2719.3583593	395	24.4445457	118.0419788	2885.4825490	395	26.5233934	115.4756919	3062.8072103
396	22.7063024	120.7528351	2741.8866130	396	24.6431577	118.0825560	2909.9270948	396	26.7444217	115.5130829	3089.3306037
397	22.8853530	120.7965293	2764.5932154	397	24.8433863	118.1228102	2934.5702524	397	26.9672919	115.5501649	3116.0750254
398	23.0675467	120.8398902	2787.4795784	398	25.0452358	118.1627379	2959.4136358	398	27.1920193	115.5869404	3143.0423173
399	23.2501648	120.8828907	2810.5471251	399	25.2487284	118.2023439	2984.4588716	399	27.4186195	115.6234119	3170.2343367
400	23.4342286	120.9255633	2833.7972899	400	25.4538743	118.2416306	3009.7075999	400	27.6471080	115.6595821	3197.6529562

Table 1

M	C(9.50,M,12)	A(9.50,M,12)	S(9.50,M,12)	M	C(9.75,M,12)	A(9.75,M,12)	S(9.75,M,12)	M	C(10.00,M,12)	A(10.00,M,12)	S(10.00,M,12)
401	23.6197495	120.9679007	2857.2315184	401	25.6606870	118.2806007	3035.1614742	401	27.8775006	115.6954533	3225.3000642
402	23.8067392	121.0039057	2880.8512680	402	25.8691801	118.3192568	3060.8221612	402	28.1098131	115.7310281	3253.1775647
403	23.9852092	121.0515806	2904.6580072	403	26.0793672	118.3576013	3086.6913413	403	28.3440615	115.7663088	3281.2873778
404	24.1951713	121.0929293	2928.6532164	404	26.2912620	118.3956367	3112.7707085	404	28.5802620	115.8012980	3309.6314393
405	24.3703373	121.1339512	2952.8383878	405	26.5048785	118.4333656	3139.0619705	405	28.8184309	115.8359980	3338.2117013
406	24.5600190	121.1746518	2977.2150250	406	26.7202307	118.4707904	3165.5668490	406	29.0585945	115.8704113	3367.0301322
407	24.7641285	121.2150328	3001.7846440	407	26.9373325	118.5079137	3192.2870797	407	29.3007393	115.9045401	3396.0887167
408	24.9601778	121.2550967	3026.5497725	408	27.1561984	118.5447377	3219.2244123	408	29.5449122	115.9383869	3425.3894560
409	25.1577792	121.2946458	3051.5089503	409	27.3768425	118.5812649	3246.3806106	409	29.7911198	115.9719539	3454.9343682
410	25.3569450	121.3342827	3076.6667295	410	27.5992793	118.6174977	3273.7574531	410	30.0393791	116.0052435	3484.7254879
411	25.5578374	121.3734099	3102.0236744	411	27.8235235	118.6534385	3301.3567325	411	30.2897073	116.0382581	3514.7648670
412	25.7600191	121.4122297	3127.5813319	412	28.0495096	118.6890897	3329.1802559	412	30.5421215	116.0709997	3545.0545743
413	25.9833526	121.4507447	3153.3413810	413	28.2774925	118.7244535	3357.2298456	413	30.7966392	116.1034708	3575.5966958
414	26.1853006	121.4889571	3179.3053337	414	28.5072472	118.7595323	3385.5073381	414	31.0522778	116.1356735	3606.3933349
415	26.3768758	121.5268694	3205.4748342	415	28.7388685	118.7943284	3414.0145852	415	31.3120551	116.1676101	3637.4466127
416	26.5834911	121.5644839	3231.8515100	416	28.9723718	118.8288440	3442.7534538	416	31.5729889	116.1992827	3668.7586679
417	26.7959596	121.6018029	3258.4370012	417	29.2077724	118.8630815	3471.7258256	417	31.8350972	116.2306936	3700.3316568
418	27.0060943	121.6388289	3285.2329608	418	29.4450055	118.8970430	3500.9335980	418	32.1013980	116.2618449	3732.1677540
419	27.2219084	121.6755640	3312.2410551	419	29.6843268	118.9307308	3530.3786835	419	32.3689096	116.2927388	3764.2691520
420	27.4374152	121.7120106	3339.4629635	420	29.9255120	118.9641471	3560.0630103	420	32.6366505	116.3233773	3796.6380616
421	27.6543280	121.7481707	3366.9003786	421	30.1686568	118.9972941	3589.9885223	421	32.9108393	116.3537626	3829.2767121
422	27.8735505	121.7840472	3394.5550067	422	30.4137771	119.0301739	3620.1571791	422	33.1843946	116.3839988	3862.1873514
423	28.0942262	121.8196417	3422.4285672	423	30.6605890	119.0627888	3650.5709562	423	33.4614354	116.4137819	3895.3722461
424	28.3166388	121.8549566	3450.5227934	424	30.9100088	119.0951407	3681.2318452	424	33.7402807	116.4434201	3928.8336815
425	28.5403122	121.8899942	3478.8394322	425	31.1611526	119.1272320	3712.1418540	425	34.0214497	116.4728133	3962.5739622
426	28.7687603	121.9247565	3507.3802444	426	31.4143370	119.1590646	3743.3030066	426	34.3049618	116.5019636	3996.5954119
427	28.9944971	121.9592458	3536.1470047	427	31.6695784	119.1906406	3774.7173436	427	34.5908365	116.5308730	4030.9003737
428	29.2240369	121.9934642	3565.1415018	428	31.9268938	119.2219622	3806.3869220	428	34.8790935	116.5595435	4065.4912102
429	29.4553993	122.0274138	3594.3655387	429	32.1862998	119.2530313	3838.3138158	429	35.1697526	116.5879770	4100.3703036
430	29.6885824	122.0610958	3623.8209326	430	32.4478135	119.2838500	3870.5001156	430	35.4623338	116.6161756	4135.5400562
431	29.9235170	122.0945152	3653.5095150	431	32.7114520	119.3144204	3902.9479290	431	35.7583575	116.6441410	4171.0028900
432	30.1605123	122.1276712	3683.4331320	432	32.9772325	119.3447443	3935.6593810	432	36.0583438	116.6718754	4206.7612475
433	30.3992030	122.1605667	3713.5936444	433	33.2451725	119.3748239	3968.6366135	433	36.3568133	116.6993306	4242.8175913
434	30.6393440	122.1932038	3743.9929274	434	33.5152649	119.4046610	4001.8817860	434	36.6597867	116.7266584	4279.1744045
435	30.8825103	122.2255846	3774.6328715	435	33.7878013	119.4342576	4035.3970756	435	36.9652950	116.7537108	4315.8341913
436	31.1269968	122.2577111	3805.5153817	436	34.0621255	119.4636158	4069.1846768	436	37.2733290	116.7805097	4352.7994763
437	31.3724189	122.2895852	3836.6423785	437	34.3388803	119.4927373	4103.2468024	437	37.5839401	116.8071468	4390.0728053
438	31.6217918	122.3212089	3868.0157974	438	34.6178837	119.5216241	4137.5856827	438	37.8971396	116.8335340	4427.6567453
439	31.8721309	122.3525843	3899.6375891	439	34.8991540	119.5502781	4172.2035664	439	38.2129491	116.8597031	4465.5538849
440	32.1244520	122.3837133	3931.5097201	440	35.1827096	119.5787011	4207.1027204	440	38.5313903	116.8856560	4503.7668340
441	32.3787706	122.4145977	3963.6341721	441	35.4685692	119.6068951	4242.2854300	441	38.8524952	116.9113944	4542.2982243
442	32.6351025	122.4452395	3996.0129426	442	35.7567513	119.6348618	4277.7539992	442	39.1762560	116.9369200	4581.1507096
443	32.8934637	122.4756407	4028.6480451	443	36.0472749	119.6626032	4313.5107505	443	39.5027248	116.9622347	4620.3269655
444	33.1533702	122.5058031	4061.5415089	444	36.3401590	119.6901210	4349.5580250	444	39.8319141	116.9873402	4659.8296903
445	33.4153385	122.5357286	4094.6953792	445	36.6354228	119.7174169	4385.8981843	445	40.1638467	117.0122383	4699.6616044
446	33.6800845	122.5654190	4128.1117176	446	36.9330856	119.7444929	4422.5336071	446	40.4985455	117.0369305	4739.8254511
447	33.9475248	122.5948763	4161.7926021	447	37.2331669	119.7713507	4459.4666927	447	40.8360333	117.0614187	4780.3239966
448	34.2162760	122.6241021	4195.7401269	448	37.5356864	119.7979920	4496.6998596	448	41.1763336	117.0857045	4821.1600299
449	34.4871549	122.6530984	4229.9564029	449	37.8406638	119.8244186	4534.2355460	449	41.5194697	117.1097896	4862.3363636
450	34.7601782	122.6818670	4264.4435578	450	38.1481192	119.8506322	4572.0762099	450	41.8654653	117.1336764	4903.8558333
451	35.0353629	122.7104096	4299.2037360	451	38.4580727	119.8766346	4610.2243291	451	42.2143442	117.1573642	4945.7212986
452	35.3127262	122.7387280	4334.2390991	452	38.7705446	119.9024274	4648.6824018	452	42.5661304	117.1808571	4987.9356428
453	35.5922853	122.7668239	4369.5518252	453	39.0855552	119.9280123	4687.4529464	453	42.9208482	117.2041558	5030.5017732
454	35.8740576	122.7946992	4405.1441105	454	39.4031254	119.9533910	4726.5385016	454	43.2785219	117.2272619	5073.4226214
455	36.1580605	122.8223556	4441.0181681	455	39.7232758	119.9785651	4765.9416270	455	43.6391762	117.2501771	5116.7011433
456	36.4443118	122.8497947	4477.1962287	456	40.0460274	120.0035364	4805.6649027	456	44.0028360	117.2729029	5160.3403195
457	36.7333293	122.8770183	4513.6205405	457	40.3714013	120.0283064	4845.7109301	457	44.3695263	117.2954409	5204.3431555
458	37.0238099	122.9040282	4550.3533698	458	40.6994190	120.0528768	4886.0823315	458	44.7392724	117.3177926	5248.7126819
459	37.3187346	122.9308257	4587.3770007	459	41.0301018	120.0772491	4926.7817504	459	45.1120997	117.3399597	5293.4519543
460	37.6121588	122.9574129	4624.6937353	460	41.3634713	120.1014250	4967.8118522	460	45.4880338	117.3619435	5338.5640539
461	37.9089217	122.9837912	4662.3058941	461	41.6995495	120.1254061	5009.1753235	461	45.8671008	117.3837456	5384.0520877
462	38.2100419	123.0099623	4700.2158158	462	42.0383584	120.1491939	5050.8748731	462	46.2493266	117.4053675	5429.9191885
463	38.5125381	123.0359279	4738.4258577	463	42.3799200	120.1727900	5092.9132315	463	46.6347377	117.4263108	5476.1685151
464	38.8174290	123.0616895	4776.9383958	464	42.7242569	120.1961959	5135.2931515	464	47.0233605	117.4480768	5522.8032528
465	39.1247337	123.0872488	4815.7558248	465	43.0713915	120.2194132	5178.0174084	465	47.4152218	117.4691671	5569.8266133
466	39.4344711	123.1126073	4854.8805584	466	43.4213465	120.2424433	5221.0887999	466	47.8103487	117.4900830	5617.2418351
467	39.7466607	123.1377567	4894.3150296	467	43.7741450	120.2652878	5264.5101464	467	48.2087682	117.5108261	5665.0521838
468	40.0613218	123.1627284	4934.0616903	468	44.1299099	120.2879483	5308.2842914	468	48.6105080	117.5313978	5713.2609520
469	40.3784704	123.1874941	4974.1230120	469	44.4883646	120.3104260	5352.4141013	469	49.0155955	117.5517995	5761.8714600
470	40.6981368	123.2120652	5014.5014859	470	44.8493326	120.3327227	5396.9024660	470	49.4240588	117.5720326	5810.8870556
471	41.0203304	123.2364434	5055.1996227	471	45.2142375	120.3548396	5441.7522985	471	49.8359260	117.5920984	5860.3111144
472	41.3450747	123.2606300	5096.2199531	472	45.5816032	120.3767783	5486.9665360	472	50.2512254	117.6119984	5910.1470404
473	41.6723398	123.2846267	5137.5650278	473	45.9519537	120.3985401	5532.5481392	473	50.6699556	117.6317340	5960.3982658
474	42.0022963	123.3084350	5179.2374176	474	46.3253133	120.4201266	5578.5000928	474	51.0922355	117.6513064	6011.0682514
475	42.3343144	123.3320562	5221.2397199	475	46.7017065	120.4415391	5624.8254061	475	51.5180041	117.6707171	6062.1604869
476	42.6689651	123.3554919	5263.5745283	476	47.0811578	120.4627790	5671.5271126	476	51.9473208	117.6899674	6113.6784910
477	43.0077690	123.3787435	5306.2444934	477	47.4638922	120.4838478	5718.6082704	477	52.3802151	117.7090585	6165.6258118
478	43.3462471	123.4018125	5349.2522623	478	47.8493347	120.5047467	5766.0719627	478	52.8167169	117.7279919	6218.0060269
479	43.6914207	123.4247003	5392.6005095	479	48.2517644	120.5254772	5813.9227439	479	53.2583563	117.7467689	6270.8227439
480	44.0373112	123.4474083	5436.2919302	480	48.6000452	120.5460406	5862.1594080	480	53.7005634	117.7653906	6324.0796001
481	44.3859399	123.4699379	5480.3292414	481	49.0251644	120.5664383	5910.7894533	481	54.1468199	117.7838585	6377.8025635
482	44.7373286	123.4922906	5524.7151812	482	49.4234938	120.5866716	5959.8146176	482	54.5981037	117.8021737	6431.9284324
483	45.0914991	123.5144678	5569.4525098	483	49.8254883	120.6067418	6009.2381114	483	55.0543987	117.8203375	6486.5278361
484	45.4484735	123.5364707	5614.5440089	484	50.2288883	120.6266503	6059.0631711	484	55.5131953	117.8383513	6541.5822348
485	45.8080627	123.5583008	5659.9924823	485	50.6350062	120.6463983	6109.2930595	485	55.9757952	117.8562161	6597.0954201
486	46.1709227	123.5799555	5705.8007562	486	51.0454400	120.6659871	6159.9310656	486	56.4422802	117.8739334	6653.0712154
487	46.5364425	123.6014480	5751.9716789	487	51.4642167	120.6854181	6210.9805056	487	56.9126124	117.8915042	6709.5134755
488	46.9040560	123.6227678	5798.5081214	488	51.8823634	120.7046925	6262.4447222	488	57.3863841	117.9089297	6766.4260879
489	47.2731861	123.6439201	5845.4129713	489	52.3039076	120.7238115	6314.3270857	489	57.8651082	117.9262113	6823.8129720
490	47.6504559	123.6649082	5892.6891535	490	52.7268769	120.7427765	6366.6309933	490	58.3473174	117.9433501	6881.6780802
491	48.0276887	123.6857275	5940.3396195	491	53.1572990	120.7615886	6419.3598702	491	58.8335450	117.9603472	6940.0253976
492	48.4079079	123.7063853	5988.3673082	492	53.5892021	120.7802490	6472.5171692	492	59.3233246	117.9772038	6998.8589426
493	48.7911372	123.7268808	6036.7752161	493	54.0246143	120.7987591	6526.1063712	493	59.8181898	117.9939211	7058.1827672
494	49.1774003	123.7472154	6085.5663532	494	54.4635643	120.8171200	6580.1309855	494	60.3166747	118.0105003	7118.0009570
495	49.5667214	123.7673902	6134.7437536	495	54.9068308	120.8353329	6634.5945498	495	60.8193137	118.0269424	7178.3176317
496	49.9591246	123.7874066	6184.3104750	496	55.3521927	120.8533991	6689.5006306	496	61.3261413	118.0432487	7239.1369453
497	50.3546344	123.8072657	6234.2695997	497	55.8019292	120.8713196	6744.8528233	497	61.8371924	118.0594202	7300.4630866
498	50.7532752	123.8269689	6284.6242341	498	56.2553199	120.8890957	6800.6547525	498	62.3525024	118.0754580	7362.3002790
499	51.1550720	123.8465173	6335.3775093	499	56.7123944	120.9067285	6856.9100725	499	62.8721066	118.0913633	7424.6527814
500	51.5600497	123.8659122	6386.5325813	500	57.1731826	120.9242192	6913.6224669	500	63.3960408	118.1071372	7487.5248880

Table 1   423

M	C(10.25,M,12)	A(10.25,M,12)	S(10.25,M,12)
1	1.0085417	.9915307	1.0000000
2	1.0171563	1.9746638	2.0085417
3	1.0258445	2.9494704	3.0256980
4	1.0346069	3.9160210	4.0515425
5	1.0434442	4.8743356	5.0861494
6	1.0523569	5.8246336	6.1295936
7	1.0613458	6.7666335	7.1819505
8	1.0704115	7.7010537	8.2432964
9	1.0795546	8.6273616	9.3137078
10	1.0887758	9.5458244	10.3932624
11	1.0980757	10.4565084	11.4820382
12	1.1074551	11.3594795	12.5801140
13	1.1169147	12.2548031	13.6875691
14	1.1264550	13.1425438	14.8044838
15	1.1360768	14.0227660	15.9309387
16	1.1457808	14.8955334	17.0670155
17	1.1555676	15.7609089	18.2127962
18	1.1654381	16.6189553	19.3683639
19	1.1753929	17.4697347	20.5338020
20	1.1854327	18.3133085	21.7091949
21	1.1955583	19.1497378	22.8946276
22	1.2057703	19.9790832	24.0901859
23	1.2160696	20.8014045	25.2959562
24	1.2264569	21.6167613	26.5120258
25	1.2369329	22.4252126	27.7384827
26	1.2474983	23.2268169	28.9754156
27	1.2581541	24.0216321	30.2229139
28	1.2689008	24.8097158	31.4810680
29	1.2797393	25.5911250	32.7499688
30	1.2906704	26.3659161	34.0297081
31	1.3016949	27.1341453	35.3203785
32	1.3128135	27.8956681	36.6220734
33	1.3240272	28.6511396	37.9348870
34	1.3353366	29.4000145	39.2589141
35	1.3467426	30.1425469	40.5942507
36	1.3582460	30.8787905	41.9409932
37	1.3698477	31.6087987	43.2992392
38	1.3815485	32.3326242	44.6690869
39	1.3933492	33.0503194	46.0506353
40	1.4052507	33.7619362	47.4439845
41	1.4172539	34.4675261	48.8492352
42	1.4293596	35.1671401	50.2664891
43	1.4415687	35.8608288	51.6958487
44	1.4538821	36.5486425	53.1374174
45	1.4663007	37.2306309	54.5912995
46	1.4788253	37.9068433	56.0576002
47	1.4914570	38.5773286	57.5364255
48	1.5041965	39.2421353	59.0278825
49	1.5170448	39.9013116	60.5320790
50	1.5300029	40.5549051	62.0491238
51	1.5430717	41.2029632	63.5791268
52	1.5562521	41.8455306	65.1221985
53	1.5695451	42.4826599	66.6784506
54	1.5829516	43.1143911	68.2479957
55	1.5964727	43.7407720	69.8309473
56	1.6101092	44.3618479	71.4274260
57	1.6238622	44.9776637	73.0375292
58	1.6377327	45.5882639	74.6613914
59	1.6517217	46.1936928	76.2991242
60	1.6658301	46.7939941	77.9508458
61	1.6800591	47.3892113	79.6166760
62	1.6944096	47.9793673	81.2967351
63	1.7088827	48.5645650	82.9911447
64	1.7234794	49.1447866	84.7000274
65	1.7382008	49.7200941	86.4235068
66	1.7530479	50.2905292	88.1617076
67	1.7680219	50.8561331	89.9147555
68	1.7831237	51.4169466	91.6827774
69	1.7983546	51.9730105	93.4659011
70	1.8137155	52.5243649	95.2642557
71	1.8292077	53.0710497	97.0779712
72	1.8448322	53.6131044	98.9071789
73	1.8605901	54.1505683	100.7520110
74	1.8764826	54.6834802	102.6126011
75	1.8925109	55.2118788	104.4890838
76	1.9086761	55.7358021	106.3815947
77	1.9249794	56.2552882	108.2902708
78	1.9414219	56.7703746	110.2152502
79	1.9580049	57.2810985	112.1566721
80	1.9747295	57.7874970	114.1146770
81	1.9915970	58.2896066	116.0894066
82	2.0086086	58.7874637	118.0810036
83	2.0257654	59.2811043	120.0896122
84	2.0430689	59.7705640	122.1153776
85	2.0605201	60.2558784	124.1584465
86	2.0781203	60.7370825	126.2189665
87	2.0958710	61.2142111	128.2970869
88	2.1137732	61.6872988	130.3929578
89	2.1318283	62.1563797	132.5067310
90	2.1500377	62.6214878	134.6385593
91	2.1684026	63.0826568	136.7885970
92	2.1859244	63.5399200	138.9569996
93	2.2056044	63.9933104	141.1439240
94	2.2244439	64.4428610	143.3495283
95	2.2434443	64.8886042	145.5739722
96	2.2626071	65.3305722	147.8174166
97	2.2819335	65.7687180	150.0800237
98	2.3014251	66.2033104	152.3619572
99	2.3210831	66.6341438	154.6633823
100	2.3409090	67.0613283	156.9844653

M	C(10.50,M,12)	A(10.50,M,12)	S(10.50,M,12)
1	1.0087500	.9913259	1.0000000
2	1.0175766	1.9740529	2.0087500
3	1.0264804	2.9482557	3.0263266
4	1.0354621	3.9140081	4.0528069
5	1.0445224	4.8713835	5.0882690
6	1.0536618	5.8204545	6.1327913
7	1.0628315	6.7612932	7.1864533
8	1.0721817	7.6939710	8.2493347
9	1.0815633	8.6185586	9.3215164
10	1.0910269	9.5351262	10.4030797
11	1.1005734	10.4437435	11.4941066
12	1.1102035	11.3444793	12.5946801
13	1.1199177	12.2374020	13.7048835
14	1.1297170	13.1225795	14.8248012
15	1.1396020	14.0000788	15.9545182
16	1.1495736	14.8699855	17.0941203
17	1.1595323	15.7323389	18.2436938
18	1.1697791	16.5871711	19.4033262
19	1.1800147	17.4346182	20.5731053
20	1.1903398	18.2747144	21.7531199
21	1.2007553	19.1075236	22.9434597
22	1.2112619	19.9331089	24.1442150
23	1.2218604	20.7515320	25.3554769
24	1.2325517	21.5628580	26.5773373
25	1.2433365	22.3671455	27.8098890
26	1.2542157	23.1644565	29.0532255
27	1.2651901	23.9548515	30.3074413
28	1.2762605	24.7383906	31.5726314
29	1.2874278	25.5151332	32.8488919
30	1.2986928	26.2851382	34.1363197
31	1.3100563	27.0484642	35.4350125
32	1.3215194	27.8051689	36.7450689
33	1.3330826	28.5553100	38.0665882
34	1.3447471	29.2989442	39.3996709
35	1.3565137	30.0361281	40.7444180
36	1.3683832	30.7669176	42.1009316
37	1.3803565	31.4913681	43.4693148
38	1.3924346	32.2095347	44.8496713
39	1.4046184	32.9214718	46.2421059
40	1.4169088	33.6272335	47.6467243
41	1.4293068	34.3268733	49.0636332
42	1.4418132	35.0204445	50.4929400
43	1.4544291	35.7079995	51.9347532
44	1.4671553	36.3895905	53.3891823
45	1.4799930	37.0652694	54.8563376
46	1.4929429	37.7350874	56.3363306
47	1.5060061	38.3990953	57.8292735
48	1.5191837	39.0573436	59.3352796
49	1.5324766	39.7098821	60.8544633
50	1.5458857	40.3567605	62.3869399
51	1.5594122	40.9980277	63.9328256
52	1.5730571	41.6337326	65.4922378
53	1.5868213	42.2639232	67.0652949
54	1.6007060	42.8886476	68.6521162
55	1.6147122	43.5079530	70.2528223
56	1.6288409	44.1218665	71.8675345
57	1.6430933	44.7304946	73.4963754
58	1.6574704	45.3338237	75.1394687
59	1.6719732	45.9319194	76.7969390
60	1.6866030	46.5248271	78.4689122
61	1.7013608	47.1125920	80.1555152
62	1.7162477	47.6952585	81.8568760
63	1.7312648	48.2728708	83.5731236
64	1.7464134	48.8454729	85.3043885
65	1.7616945	49.4131082	87.0508019
66	1.7771093	49.9758198	88.8124964
67	1.7926591	50.5336504	90.5896057
68	1.8083448	51.0866423	92.3822648
69	1.8241678	51.6348374	94.1906096
70	1.8401293	52.1782775	96.0147774
71	1.8562304	52.7170037	97.8549067
72	1.8724725	53.2510570	99.7111372
73	1.8888566	53.7804778	101.5836096
74	1.9053841	54.3053064	103.4724662
75	1.9220562	54.8255825	105.3778503
76	1.9389742	55.3413457	107.2999065
77	1.9559393	55.8526352	109.2387807
78	1.9729529	56.3594896	111.1946200
79	1.9902163	56.8619178	113.1675729
80	2.0076307	57.3600472	115.1577892
81	2.0251974	57.8538262	117.1654198
82	2.0429179	58.3433221	119.1906173
83	2.0607934	58.8285721	121.2335352
84	2.0783254	59.3096130	123.2943286
85	2.0970151	59.7864813	125.3731540
86	2.1153640	60.2592132	127.4701691
87	2.1338734	60.7278446	129.5855331
88	2.1525448	61.1924110	131.7194065
89	2.1713796	61.6529477	133.8719513
90	2.1903791	62.1094896	136.0433309
91	2.2095450	62.5620715	138.2337100
92	2.2288785	63.0107276	140.4432550
93	2.2483812	63.4554921	142.6721334
94	2.2680545	63.8963986	144.9205146
95	2.2879000	64.3334806	147.1885691
96	2.3079191	64.7667714	149.4764691
97	2.3281134	65.1963037	151.7843882
98	2.3484844	65.6221103	154.1125016
99	2.3690336	66.0442233	156.4609860
100	2.3897627	66.4626749	158.8300196

M	C(10.75,M,12)	A(10.75,M,12)	S(10.75,M,12)
1	1.0089583	.9911212	1.0000000
2	1.0179969	1.9734425	2.0089583
3	1.0271165	2.9470419	3.0269553
4	1.0363177	3.9119969	4.0540717
5	1.0455014	4.8683843	5.0903895
6	1.0549683	5.8162801	6.1359909
7	1.0644190	6.7557598	7.1909591
8	1.0739544	7.6868980	8.2553781
9	1.0835753	8.6097688	9.3293325
10	1.0932823	9.5244456	10.4129078
11	1.1030763	10.4310012	11.5061901
12	1.1129580	11.3295077	12.6092664
13	1.1229283	12.2200366	13.7222244
14	1.1329878	13.1026586	14.8451527
15	1.1431375	13.9774440	15.9781405
16	1.1533781	14.8444623	17.1212780
17	1.1637105	15.7037826	18.2746561
18	1.1741354	16.5554732	19.4383666
19	1.1846537	17.3996017	20.6125020
20	1.1952662	18.2362355	21.7971556
21	1.2059738	19.0654409	22.9924218
22	1.2167773	19.8872940	24.1983956
23	1.2276776	20.7018301	25.4151729
24	1.2386755	21.5091440	26.6428505
25	1.2497720	22.3092899	27.8815260
26	1.2609679	23.1023316	29.1312980
27	1.2722640	23.8883319	30.3922659
28	1.2836614	24.6673535	31.6645299
29	1.2951609	25.4394584	32.9481913
30	1.3067634	26.2047079	34.2433522
31	1.3184698	26.9631629	35.5501156
32	1.3302811	27.7148837	36.8685854
33	1.3421982	28.4599302	38.1988665
34	1.3542220	29.1983615	39.5410646
35	1.3663536	29.9302365	40.8952867
36	1.3785939	30.6556133	42.2616403
37	1.3909438	31.3745496	43.6402341
38	1.4034043	32.0871026	45.0311779
39	1.4159765	32.7933291	46.4345822
40	1.4286613	33.4934851	47.8505587
41	1.4414597	34.1870263	49.2792199
42	1.4543728	34.8746079	50.7206796
43	1.4674015	35.5560847	52.1750524
44	1.4805470	36.2315107	53.6424539
45	1.4938102	36.9009398	55.1230009
46	1.5071923	37.5644252	56.6168111
47	1.5206942	38.2220196	58.1240033
48	1.5343171	38.8737753	59.6446975
49	1.5480620	39.5197443	61.1790046
50	1.5619301	40.1599778	62.7270766
51	1.5759224	40.7945268	64.2890067
52	1.5900400	41.4234418	65.8649290
53	1.6042841	42.0467728	67.4549690
54	1.6188558	42.6645694	69.0592531
55	1.6331563	43.2768807	70.6779089
56	1.6477866	43.8837554	72.3110652
57	1.6625480	44.4852417	73.9588518
58	1.6774417	45.0813876	75.6213999
59	1.6924688	45.6722405	77.2988416
60	1.7076305	46.2576473	78.9913104
61	1.7229280	46.8382546	80.6989409
62	1.7383626	47.4135086	82.4218689
63	1.7539354	47.9836550	84.1602315
64	1.7696477	48.5487392	85.9141669
65	1.7855008	49.1088061	87.6838146
66	1.8014960	49.6639004	89.4693155
67	1.8176344	50.2140660	91.2708114
68	1.8339173	50.7593469	93.0884458
69	1.8503462	51.2997863	94.9223631
70	1.8669222	51.8354273	96.7727093
71	1.8836467	52.3663124	98.6396314
72	1.9005210	52.8924339	100.5232781
73	1.9175465	53.4139836	102.4237992
74	1.9347246	53.9308530	104.3413457
75	1.9520565	54.4431333	106.2760703
76	1.9695436	54.9508651	108.2281267
77	1.9871875	55.4540889	110.1976704
78	2.0049894	55.9528447	112.1848578
79	2.0229507	56.4471721	114.1898472
80	2.0410730	56.9371105	116.2127979
81	2.0593576	57.4226988	118.2538709
82	2.0775060	57.9039757	120.3132285
83	2.0964177	58.3809794	122.3910345
84	2.1152001	58.8537479	124.4874542
85	2.1341488	59.3223188	126.6026543
86	2.1532672	59.7867294	128.7368031
87	2.1725569	60.2470165	130.8900703
88	2.1920194	60.7032169	133.0626271
89	2.2116562	61.1553667	135.2546465
90	2.2314690	61.6035020	137.4663027
91	2.2514592	62.0476584	139.6977717
92	2.2716285	62.4878712	141.9492309
93	2.2919785	62.9241755	144.2208594
94	2.3125108	63.3566059	146.5128379
95	2.3332271	63.7851968	148.8253408
96	2.3541289	64.2099824	151.1585759
97	2.3752180	64.6309964	153.5127048
98	2.3964960	65.0482723	155.8879228
99	2.4179646	65.4618433	158.2844187
100	2.4396255	65.8717422	160.7023833

Table 1

M	C(10.25,M,12)	A(10.25,M,12)	S(10.25,M,12)	M	C(10.50,M,12)	A(10.50,M,12)	S(10.50,M,12)	M	C(10.75,M,12)	A(10.75,M,12)	S(10.75,M,12)
101	2.3609042	67.4848948	159.3253743	101	2.4106731	66.8774968	161.2197823	101	2.4614805	66.2780018	163.1420088
102	2.3810703	67.9048740	161.6862785	102	2.4317655	67.2887205	163.6304554	102	2.4835313	66.6806543	165.6034893
103	2.4014086	68.3212963	164.0673488	103	2.4530444	67.6963772	166.0622219	103	2.5057796	67.0797317	168.0870206
104	2.4219206	68.7341917	166.4687574	104	2.4745086	68.1004978	168.5152663	104	2.5282272	67.4752658	170.5928002
105	2.4426079	69.1435902	168.8906781	105	2.4961605	68.5011131	170.9897749	105	2.5508759	67.8672880	173.1210273
106	2.4634718	69.5495214	171.3332860	106	2.5180019	68.8982534	173.4859354	106	2.5737275	68.2556295	175.6719032
107	2.4845140	69.9520146	173.7967578	107	2.5400345	69.2919488	176.0039374	107	2.5967838	68.6409212	178.2456307
108	2.5057359	70.3510990	176.2812717	108	2.5622598	69.6822293	178.5439718	108	2.6200466	69.0225938	180.8424144
109	2.5271390	70.7468033	178.7870076	109	2.5845795	70.0691245	181.1062316	109	2.6435179	69.4008776	183.4624611
110	2.5487250	71.1391564	181.3141466	110	2.6072955	70.4526637	183.6909111	110	2.6671994	69.7758027	186.1059790
111	2.5704954	71.5281865	183.8628716	111	2.6301093	70.8328760	186.2982066	111	2.6910931	70.1473990	188.7731764
112	2.5924517	71.9139217	186.4333670	112	2.6531228	71.2097903	188.9283159	112	2.7152208	70.5156959	191.4642714
113	2.6145955	72.2963900	189.0258187	113	2.6763376	71.5834353	191.5814387	113	2.7395244	70.8807227	194.1794722
114	2.6369285	72.6756191	191.6404142	114	2.6997555	71.9538392	194.2577762	114	2.7640660	71.2425086	196.9189966
115	2.6594523	73.0516364	194.2773428	115	2.7253784	72.3210302	196.9575318	115	2.7883274	71.6010822	199.6830626
116	2.6821685	73.4244691	196.9367951	116	2.7472080	72.6850361	199.6809102	116	2.8133107	71.9564727	202.4718901
117	2.7050786	73.7941441	199.6189635	117	2.7712460	73.0458046	202.4281182	117	2.8390177	72.3087066	205.2857008
118	2.7281845	74.1606892	202.3240422	118	2.7954944	73.4036031	205.1993642	118	2.8644506	72.6578137	208.1247185
119	2.7514878	74.5241279	205.0522267	119	2.8199550	73.7582187	207.9948586	119	2.8901113	73.0038212	210.9891691
120	2.7749901	74.8844896	207.8037145	120	2.8446296	74.1097583	210.8148157	120	2.9160019	73.3467565	213.8792804
121	2.7986931	75.2417992	210.5787045	121	2.8695201	74.4582486	213.6594433	121	2.9421244	73.6866469	216.7952823
122	2.8225986	75.5960827	213.3773976	122	2.8946284	74.8037161	216.5289634	122	2.9684809	74.0235196	219.7374067
123	2.8467083	75.9473656	216.1999962	123	2.9199564	75.1461870	219.4235918	123	2.9950736	74.3574012	222.7058876
124	2.8710239	76.2956734	219.0467045	124	2.9455060	75.4856872	222.3435483	124	3.0219044	74.6883163	225.7009612
125	2.8955473	76.6410312	224.9177285	125	2.9712792	75.8222426	225.2890543	125	3.0489757	75.0162973	228.7228657
126	2.9202801	76.9934642	224.8132758	126	2.9972779	76.1558788	228.2603335	126	3.0762894	75.3413643	231.7718413
127	2.9452241	77.3229969	227.7335558	127	3.0235041	76.4866207	231.2576115	127	3.1038478	75.6635450	234.8481307
128	2.9703812	77.6596540	230.6787799	128	3.0499598	76.8144939	234.2811156	128	3.1316531	75.9826652	237.9519786
129	2.9957533	77.9934599	233.6491612	129	3.0768469	77.1395231	237.3310753	129	3.1597075	76.2993502	241.0836317
130	3.0213420	78.3244386	236.6449144	130	3.1035676	77.4617329	240.4077222	130	3.1880132	76.6130251	244.2433393
131	3.0471493	78.6526142	239.6662564	131	3.1307238	77.7811478	243.5112898	131	3.2165725	76.9239151	247.4313525
132	3.0731770	78.9780104	242.7134057	132	3.1581176	78.0977922	246.6420136	132	3.2453877	77.2320447	250.6479251
133	3.0994271	79.3006506	245.7865527	133	3.1857512	78.4116899	249.8001312	133	3.2744609	77.5374385	253.8933127
134	3.1259013	79.6205584	248.8860098	134	3.2136265	78.7226648	252.9858824	134	3.3037946	77.8401207	257.1677736
135	3.1528017	79.9377557	252.0119111	135	3.2417457	79.0313406	256.1995088	135	3.3333911	78.1401155	260.4715683
136	3.1795302	80.2522686	255.1645128	136	3.2701110	79.3371406	259.4412545	136	3.3632528	78.4374467	263.8049594
137	3.2063887	80.5641167	258.3440431	137	3.2987245	79.6402881	262.7113655	137	3.3933319	78.7321380	267.1682122
138	3.2340792	80.8733238	261.5507318	138	3.3275883	79.9408060	266.0100900	138	3.4237809	79.0242127	270.5615941
139	3.2617036	81.1799120	264.7848109	139	3.3567047	80.2387172	269.3376803	139	3.4544523	79.3136942	273.9853570
140	3.2895640	81.4839037	268.0465145	140	3.3860759	80.5340444	272.6943830	140	3.4853985	79.6005055	277.4398274
141	3.3176623	81.7853207	271.3360785	141	3.4157040	80.8268098	276.0804588	141	3.5166218	79.8849693	280.9252258
142	3.3450007	82.0841850	274.6537409	142	3.4455914	81.1170357	279.4961628	142	3.5481249	80.1668083	284.4418476
143	3.3745811	82.3805181	277.9997416	143	3.4757404	81.4047442	282.9417542	143	3.5799102	80.4461449	287.9899725
144	3.4034057	82.6743414	281.3743227	144	3.5061531	81.6899571	286.4174946	144	3.6119802	80.7230014	291.5698827
145	3.4324764	82.9656762	284.7777284	145	3.5368319	81.9726960	289.9236477	145	3.6443375	80.9973996	295.1818629
146	3.4617955	83.2545437	288.2102048	146	3.5677792	82.2529824	293.4604796	146	3.6769847	81.2693616	298.8262004
147	3.4913650	83.5409646	291.6720003	147	3.5969973	82.5308376	297.0282588	147	3.7099244	81.5389089	302.5031851
148	3.5211871	83.8249597	295.1633653	148	3.6304865	82.8062826	300.6272561	148	3.7431591	81.8060629	306.2131395
149	3.5512639	84.1065496	298.6845524	149	3.6622553	83.0793384	304.2577446	149	3.7766910	82.0700849	309.9562686
150	3.5815976	84.3857546	302.2358163	150	3.6943000	83.3500256	307.9199998	150	3.8105244	82.3332760	313.7329602
151	3.6121904	84.6625950	305.8174139	151	3.7266251	83.6183650	311.6142998	151	3.8446604	82.5933720	317.5434846
152	3.6430445	84.9370907	309.4296043	152	3.7592331	83.8843767	315.3409250	152	3.8791021	82.8511686	321.3881450
153	3.6741622	85.2092615	313.0726488	153	3.7921264	84.1480609	319.1001580	153	3.9138524	83.1066713	325.2672471
154	3.7055457	85.4791273	316.7468110	154	3.8253075	84.4094978	322.8922944	154	3.9489140	83.3599055	329.1810996
155	3.7371972	85.7467075	320.4523567	155	3.8587789	84.6686472	326.7175919	155	3.9842897	83.6108913	333.1300136
156	3.7691191	86.0120215	324.1895539	156	3.8925432	84.9255486	330.5763703	156	4.0199823	83.8596486	337.1143033
157	3.8013137	86.2750885	327.9586730	157	3.9266030	85.1802217	334.4689141	157	4.0559946	84.1061972	341.1342856
158	3.8337832	86.5359274	331.7599867	158	3.9609608	85.4326597	338.3955171	158	4.0923296	84.3505558	345.1902802
159	3.8665301	86.7945572	335.5937699	159	3.9956192	85.6829598	342.3564779	159	4.1289900	84.5927468	349.2826098
160	3.8995567	87.0509966	339.4603000	160	4.0305809	85.9310830	346.3520601	160	4.1659789	84.8327864	353.4115999
161	3.9328654	87.3052642	343.3596568	161	4.0653484	86.1770141	350.3826779	161	4.2032991	85.0706948	357.5775788
162	3.9664585	87.5573782	347.2927222	162	4.1014246	86.4208318	354.4485264	162	4.2409537	85.3064908	361.7808780
163	4.0003388	87.8073571	351.2591809	163	4.1373121	86.6625347	358.5499510	163	4.2789456	85.5401932	366.0218317
164	4.0345084	88.0552187	355.2595197	164	4.1735136	86.9021409	362.6872630	164	4.3172778	85.7718207	370.3007772
165	4.0689698	88.3009812	359.2940281	165	4.2100318	87.1396688	366.8607766	165	4.3559534	86.0013916	374.6180550
166	4.1037256	88.5446622	363.3629980	166	4.2438696	87.3751364	371.0708084	166	4.3949795	86.2289901	378.9740084
167	4.1387783	88.7862794	367.4667236	167	4.2840297	87.6085615	375.3176780	167	4.4343472	86.4544364	383.3689839
168	4.1741303	89.0258503	371.6055018	168	4.3215149	87.8399618	379.6017077	168	4.4740715	86.6779465	387.8033311
169	4.2097844	89.2633921	375.7796322	169	4.3593282	88.0693549	383.9232226	169	4.5141517	86.8994721	392.2774026
170	4.2457429	89.4989222	379.9894165	170	4.3974723	88.2967583	388.2825508	170	4.5545910	87.1190308	396.7915543
171	4.2820087	89.7324574	384.2351595	171	4.4359502	88.5221691	392.6800231	171	4.5953926	87.3366400	401.3461453
172	4.3185941	89.9640148	388.5171681	172	4.4747648	88.7456646	397.1159733	172	4.6365596	87.5523172	405.9415379
173	4.3554721	90.1936110	392.8357523	173	4.5139190	88.9672016	401.5907381	173	4.6780955	87.7660794	410.5780975
174	4.3928750	90.4212627	397.1912243	174	4.5534158	89.1868169	406.1046571	174	4.7200034	87.9779438	415.2561930
175	4.4301958	90.6469864	401.5838994	175	4.5932581	89.4045273	410.6580728	175	4.7622868	88.1879268	419.9761964
176	4.4680301	90.8707983	406.0140952	176	4.6334491	89.6203492	415.2513310	176	4.8049489	88.3960465	424.7384831
177	4.5062015	91.0927147	410.4821323	177	4.6739918	89.8342991	419.8847801	177	4.8479932	88.6023165	429.5434321
178	4.5446920	91.3127516	414.9883338	178	4.7148893	90.0463932	424.5587719	178	4.8914232	88.8067559	434.3914253
179	4.5835113	91.5309250	419.5330258	179	4.7561445	90.2566475	429.2736612	179	4.9352422	89.0093802	439.2828485
180	4.6223621	91.7472506	424.1165371	180	4.7977608	90.4650781	434.0298057	180	4.9794537	89.2102055	444.2180907
181	4.6621473	91.9617440	428.7391992	181	4.8397412	90.6717007	438.8275665	181	5.0240613	89.4092476	449.1975444
182	4.7019698	92.1744208	433.4013465	182	4.8820889	90.8765311	443.6673077	182	5.0692686	89.6065225	454.2216058
183	4.7421325	92.3852964	438.1033163	183	4.9248072	91.0795847	448.5493967	183	5.1144790	89.8020459	459.2906743
184	4.7826382	92.5943860	442.8454488	184	4.9678993	91.2808770	453.4742039	184	5.1602962	89.9958332	464.4051533
185	4.8234899	92.8017048	447.6280871	185	5.0113684	91.4604233	458.4421032	185	5.2065238	90.1878999	469.5654494
186	4.8648906	93.0072677	452.4515770	186	5.0552179	91.6782387	463.4534716	186	5.2531656	90.3782613	474.7719733
187	4.9062431	93.2110897	457.3162675	187	5.0994510	91.8743383	468.5086895	187	5.3002252	90.5669326	480.0251389
188	4.9481506	93.4131854	462.2225106	188	5.1440712	92.0687368	473.6081405	188	5.3477064	90.7539286	485.3253461
189	4.9904161	93.6135695	467.1706613	189	5.1890819	92.2614491	478.7522118	189	5.3956129	90.9392644	490.6730705
190	5.0330425	93.8122564	472.1610773	190	5.2344863	92.4524898	483.9412936	190	5.4439486	91.1229546	496.0686024
191	5.0760331	94.0092607	477.1941199	191	5.2802881	92.6418734	489.1757799	191	5.4927173	91.3050130	501.5126320
192	5.1193909	94.2045964	482.2701530	192	5.3264906	92.8296143	494.4560680	192	5.5419229	91.4854566	507.0053493
193	5.1631190	94.3982778	487.3895439	193	5.3730974	93.0157267	499.7825586	193	5.5915693	91.6642973	512.5472723
194	5.2072207	94.5903188	492.5526629	194	5.4201120	93.2002247	505.1556560	194	5.6416605	91.8415501	518.1388416
195	5.2516990	94.7807334	497.7598836	195	5.4675380	93.3831224	510.5757680	195	5.6922003	92.0172291	523.7805020
196	5.2965573	94.9695353	503.0115826	196	5.5153789	93.5644336	516.0433060	196	5.7431930	92.1913482	529.4727024
197	5.3417987	95.1567381	508.3081399	197	5.5636385	93.7441721	521.5586849	197	5.7946424	92.3639214	535.2158953
198	5.3874266	95.3423555	513.6499386	198	5.6123203	93.9223515	527.1223234	198	5.8465527	92.5349624	541.0105377
199	5.4334442	95.5264008	519.0373651	199	5.6614281	94.0989854	532.7346437	199	5.8989281	92.7044847	546.8570905
200	5.4798548	95.7088874	524.4708093	200	5.7109656	94.2740872	538.3960719	200	5.9517727	92.8725019	552.7560186

Table 1

M	C(10.25,M,12)	A(10.25,M,12)	S(10.25,M,12)	C(10.50,M,12)	A(10.50,M,12)	S(10.50,M,12)	C(10.75,M,12)	A(10.75,M,12)	S(10.75,M,12)
201	5.5266619	95.8898285	529.9506641	5.7609366	94.4476700	544.1070375	6.0050906	93.0390273	558.7077913
202	5.5738688	96.0692371	535.4773260	5.8113448	94.6197473	549.8679741	6.0583862	93.2040741	564.7128819
203	5.6214790	96.2471262	541.0511949	5.8621940	94.7903319	555.6793169	6.1131638	93.3676555	570.7717681
204	5.6694958	96.4235087	546.6726738	5.9134882	94.9594368	561.5415129	6.1679275	93.5297845	576.8849319
205	5.7179227	96.5983974	552.3421696	5.9652313	95.1270749	567.4550012	6.2231819	93.6904740	582.0526594
206	5.7667633	96.7718049	558.0600923	6.0174270	95.2932589	573.4202324	6.2789312	93.8497368	589.2760413
207	5.8160211	96.9437438	563.8268556	6.0700795	95.4580013	579.4376595	6.3351900	94.0075855	595.5549725
208	5.8656996	97.1142264	569.6428766	6.1231927	95.6213148	585.5077390	6.3919326	94.1640327	601.8901525
209	5.9158024	97.2832652	575.5085762	6.1767707	95.7832117	591.6309317	6.4491937	94.3190909	608.2820851
210	5.9663332	97.4508723	581.4243787	6.2308174	95.9437043	597.8077024	6.5069677	94.4727723	614.7312788
211	6.0172957	97.6170599	587.3907119	6.2853371	96.1028048	604.0385198	6.5652593	94.6250892	621.2382465
212	6.0686934	97.7818400	593.4080076	6.3403338	96.2605252	610.3238568	6.6240731	94.7760537	627.8035058
213	6.1205302	97.9452246	599.4767010	6.3958117	96.4168775	616.6641906	6.6834137	94.9256778	634.4275788
214	6.1728097	98.1072254	605.5972311	6.4517750	96.5718736	623.0600022	6.7432860	95.0739735	641.1109926
215	6.2255358	98.2678541	611.7700408	6.5082281	96.7255253	629.5117773	6.8033946	95.2209525	647.8542786
216	6.2787122	98.4271224	617.9955766	6.5651751	96.8778441	636.0200053	6.8645443	95.3666254	654.6579731
217	6.3323429	98.5850419	624.2742888	6.6225203	97.0288418	642.5851804	6.9261401	95.5110070	661.5226175
218	6.3864317	98.7416238	630.6066317	6.6805683	97.1785296	649.2078007	6.9831868	95.6541056	668.4487576
219	6.4409824	98.8968796	636.9930633	6.7390232	97.3269191	655.8883690	7.0507893	95.7959337	675.4369444
220	6.4959991	99.0508206	643.4340458	6.7979897	97.4740214	662.6273922	7.1139526	95.9365026	682.4877337
221	6.5514858	99.2034577	649.9300449	6.8574721	97.6198477	669.4253819	7.1775818	96.0758233	689.6016863
222	6.6074464	99.3548021	656.4815307	6.9174750	97.7644091	676.2828540	7.2419818	96.2139071	696.7793681
223	6.6638850	99.5048647	663.0889771	6.9780029	97.9077166	683.2003290	7.3068579	96.3507648	704.0213499
224	6.7208057	99.6536564	669.7528621	7.0390604	98.0497810	690.1783319	7.3723152	96.4864074	711.3282079
225	6.7782126	99.8011879	676.4736579	7.1005522	98.1906132	697.2173923	7.4383589	96.6208456	718.7005231
226	6.8361098	99.9474699	683.2518804	7.1627829	98.3302237	704.3180445	7.5049942	96.7540902	726.1388819
227	6.8945016	100.0925130	690.0879003	7.2274922	98.4686233	711.4800273	7.5722366	96.8861518	733.6438761
228	6.9533921	100.2363277	696.9824918	7.2888600	98.6058223	718.7062846	7.6400609	97.0170408	741.2161025
229	7.0127857	100.3789204	703.9358840	7.3524559	98.7418313	725.9949646	7.7085031	97.1467677	748.8561634
230	7.0726866	100.5203134	710.9486696	7.4167899	98.8766605	733.3474205	7.7775585	97.2753427	756.5646666
231	7.1330991	100.6605049	718.0213562	7.4816868	99.0103202	740.7642105	7.8472324	97.4027762	764.3422250
232	7.1940276	100.7995091	725.1544553	7.5471516	99.1428205	748.2458973	7.9175306	97.5290782	772.1894575
233	7.2554766	100.9373361	732.3484829	7.6131892	99.2741715	755.7930489	7.9884584	97.6542588	780.1069880
234	7.3174505	101.0739957	739.6039596	7.6798046	99.4043832	763.4062381	8.0600217	97.7783279	788.0954465
235	7.3799537	101.2094979	746.9214101	7.7470029	99.5334653	771.0860427	8.1322261	97.9012955	796.1554682
236	7.4429908	101.3438525	754.3013638	7.8147892	99.6614279	778.8330456	8.2050773	98.0231713	804.2876943
237	7.5065664	101.4770692	761.7443546	7.8831686	99.7882804	786.6478347	8.2785841	98.1439649	812.4927715
238	7.5706850	101.6091576	769.2509210	7.9521463	99.9140326	794.5310033	8.3527434	98.2636861	820.7713526
239	7.6353512	101.7401274	776.8216059	8.0217276	100.0386940	802.4831496	8.4275700	98.3823442	829.1240960
240	7.7005698	101.8699879	784.4569572	8.0919197	100.1622741	810.5048771	8.5030670	98.4999488	837.5516660
241	7.7663455	101.9987486	792.1575270	8.1627220	100.2847823	818.5967948	8.5792403	98.6165093	846.0547330
242	7.8323831	102.1264187	799.9238786	8.2341458	100.4052278	826.7595168	8.6560960	98.7320348	854.6339734
243	7.8989873	102.2530076	807.7565556	8.3061946	100.5266199	834.9936626	8.7336402	98.8465346	863.2900694
244	7.9670629	102.3785244	815.6561429	8.3788728	100.6459677	843.2998571	8.8118791	98.9600178	872.0237096
245	8.0351149	102.5029781	823.6232058	8.4521889	100.7642802	851.6787309	8.8908188	99.0724934	880.8355887
246	8.1037482	102.6263778	831.6583207	8.5261456	100.8815665	860.1309198	8.9704657	99.1839703	889.7264075
247	8.1729677	102.7487324	839.7620688	8.6007493	100.9978354	868.6570653	9.0508262	99.2944574	898.6968732
248	8.2427784	102.8700507	847.9350800	8.6760059	101.1130958	877.2578147	9.1319065	99.4039636	907.7476994
249	8.3131855	102.9903415	856.1778150	8.7519209	101.2273565	885.9338206	9.2137131	99.5124975	916.8796059
250	8.3841940	103.1096136	864.4910005	8.8285002	101.3406260	894.6857415	9.2962527	99.6200677	926.0933190
251	8.4558090	103.2278755	872.8751944	8.9057496	101.4529130	903.5142417	9.3795316	99.7266828	935.3895717
252	8.5280357	103.3451358	881.3310034	8.9837949	101.5642260	912.4199914	9.4635566	99.8323513	944.7691033
253	8.6008793	103.4614030	889.8590391	9.0622821	101.6745735	921.4036663	9.5483343	99.9370817	954.2326598
254	8.6743451	103.5766854	898.4599184	9.1415771	101.7839638	930.4659484	9.6338714	100.0408821	963.7809941
255	8.7484385	103.6909916	907.1342635	9.2215659	101.8924053	939.6075254	9.7201748	100.1437609	973.4148655
256	8.8231648	103.8043296	915.8827207	9.3022546	101.9999061	948.8290918	9.8072514	100.2457263	983.1350403
257	8.8985293	103.9167077	924.7058668	9.3836493	102.1064744	958.1313458	9.8951080	100.3467863	992.9422917
258	8.9745376	104.0281340	933.6043761	9.4657562	102.2121184	967.5149951	9.9837517	100.4469490	1002.8373998
259	9.0511951	104.1386167	942.5789336	9.5485816	102.3168460	976.9807513	10.0731895	100.5462225	1012.8211515
260	9.1285074	104.2481636	951.6308081	9.6321317	102.4206652	986.5293329	10.1634285	100.6446145	1022.9943410
261	9.2064800	104.3567828	960.7586350	9.7164128	102.5235838	996.1614646	10.2544759	100.7421329	1033.0577695
262	9.2851187	104.4644820	969.9651161	9.8014314	102.6256097	1005.8778774	10.3463389	100.8387854	1043.3122453
263	9.3644291	104.5712691	979.2502348	9.8871940	102.7267507	1015.6793089	10.4390248	100.9345798	1053.6585842
264	9.4444169	104.6771517	988.6146059	9.9737069	102.8270143	1025.5665028	10.5325401	101.0295236	1064.0976090
265	9.5250880	104.7821376	998.0590808	10.0609768	102.9264082	1035.5402097	10.6268951	101.1236245	1074.6301501
266	9.6064481	104.8862344	1007.5841688	10.1490104	103.0249398	1045.6011866	10.7220894	101.2168899	1085.2570452
267	9.6985032	104.9894495	1017.1906169	10.2378142	103.1226171	1055.7501970	10.8181465	101.3093271	1095.9791396
268	9.7712592	105.0917905	1026.8791201	10.3273951	103.2194469	1065.9880112	10.9150590	101.4009437	1106.7972861
269	9.8547220	105.1932647	1036.6503792	10.4177598	103.3154369	1076.3154063	11.0128398	101.4917468	1117.7123451
270	9.9388977	105.2938794	1046.5051012	10.5089152	103.4105942	1086.7331661	11.1114965	101.5817437	1128.7251849
271	10.0237925	105.3936421	1056.4439990	10.6008682	103.5049261	1097.2420813	11.2110369	101.6709415	1139.8366813
272	10.1094124	105.4925598	1066.4677915	10.6936258	103.5984397	1107.8429496	11.3114692	101.7593473	1151.0477183
273	10.1957636	105.5906397	1076.5772039	10.7871950	103.6911422	1118.5365754	11.4128011	101.8469682	1162.3591874
274	10.2928524	105.6878890	1086.7729675	10.8815830	103.7830406	1129.3237704	11.5150407	101.9338112	1173.7719885
275	10.3708651	105.7843147	1097.0554850	10.9767969	103.8741419	1140.2053534	11.6181963	102.0198831	1185.2870292
276	10.4592681	105.8799237	1107.4265051	11.0728438	103.9644525	1151.1821503	11.7222760	102.1051907	1196.9052255
277	10.5480077	105.9747229	1117.8857732	11.1697312	104.0539806	1162.2549941	11.8272880	102.1897410	1208.6275015
278	10.6387103	106.0687192	1128.4343808	11.2674664	104.1427317	1173.4247253	11.9332408	102.2735405	1220.4547896
279	10.7295827	106.1619195	1139.0730912	11.3650567	104.2307129	1184.6921917	12.0401428	102.3565960	1232.3880304
280	10.8212312	106.2543304	1149.8026738	11.4655097	104.3179310	1196.0582483	12.1480024	102.4389140	1244.4281732
281	10.9136625	106.3459587	1160.6239050	11.5658329	104.4043926	1207.5237580	12.2568282	102.5205012	1256.5761756
282	11.0068834	106.4368110	1171.5375675	11.6670339	104.4901042	1219.0895909	12.3666290	102.6013640	1268.8330038
283	11.1009005	106.5268937	1182.5444509	11.7691205	104.5750723	1230.7566248	12.4774134	102.6815088	1281.1996328
284	11.1957207	106.6162136	1193.6453515	11.8721003	104.6593034	1242.5257453	12.5891902	102.7609420	1293.6770462
285	11.2913508	106.7047769	1204.8410722	11.9759812	104.7428039	1254.3978456	12.7019684	102.8396700	1306.2662364
286	11.3877978	106.7925902	1216.1324230	12.0807712	104.8255800	1266.3738268	12.8157568	102.9176989	1318.9682048
287	11.4850686	106.8796598	1227.5202208	12.1864777	104.9076382	1278.4545978	12.9305647	102.9950351	1331.7839617
288	11.5831702	106.9659920	1239.0052894	12.2931094	104.9889346	1290.6410755	13.0464010	103.0716846	1344.7145263
289	11.6821098	107.0515929	1250.5884549	12.4006741	105.0696254	1302.9341849	13.1632750	103.1476535	1357.7609273
290	11.7818945	107.1364689	1262.2705693	12.5091800	105.1495666	1315.3348591	13.2811960	103.2229479	1370.9242023
291	11.8825315	107.2206261	1274.0524638	12.6186354	105.2288145	1327.8440391	13.4001734	103.2975738	1384.2053983
292	11.9840281	107.3040705	1285.9349953	12.7290484	105.3073750	1340.4626744	13.5202166	103.3715372	1397.6055716
293	12.0863917	107.3868082	1297.9190234	12.8404276	105.3852540	1353.1917228	13.6413352	103.4448438	1411.1257882
294	12.1896296	107.4688451	1310.0054150	12.9527813	105.4624575	1366.0321504	13.7635388	103.5174995	1424.7671234
295	12.2937494	107.5501872	1322.1950446	13.0661183	105.5389913	1378.9849318	13.8868372	103.5895101	1438.5306623
296	12.3987585	107.6308405	1334.4887940	13.1804467	105.6148613	1392.0510499	14.0112401	103.6608814	1452.4174995
297	12.5046645	107.7108106	1346.8875524	13.2957756	105.6900732	1405.2314966	14.1367575	103.7316190	1466.4287396
298	12.6114752	107.7901035	1359.3922170	13.4121136	105.7646326	1418.5272722	14.2633993	103.8017285	1480.5654970
299	12.7191982	107.8687248	1372.0036922	13.5294696	105.8385453	1431.9393859	14.3911755	103.8712155	1494.8288963
300	12.8278414	107.9466803	1384.7228904	13.6478525	105.9118170	1445.4688555	14.5200965	103.9400856	1509.2200718

426

Table 1

M	C(10.25,M,12)	A(10.25,M,12)	S(10.25,M,12)
301	12.9374125	108.0239755	1397.5507317
302	13.0479196	108.1006160	1410.4881443
303	13.1593706	108.1766075	1423.5360638
304	13.2717735	108.2519554	1436.6954344
305	13.3851366	108.3266651	1449.9672079
306	13.4994680	108.4007421	1463.3523445
307	13.6147759	108.4741917	1476.8518124
308	13.7310688	108.5470193	1490.4665883
309	13.8483550	108.6192300	1504.1976571
310	13.9666430	108.6908292	1518.0460121
311	14.0859414	108.7618220	1532.0126552
312	14.2062589	108.8322135	1546.0985966
313	14.3276040	108.9020083	1560.3048555
314	14.4499856	108.9712130	1574.6324595
315	14.5734126	109.0398311	1589.0824451
316	14.6978938	109.1078681	1603.6558576
317	14.8234383	109.1753288	1618.3537514
318	14.9500552	109.2422182	1633.1771897
319	15.0777536	109.3085411	1648.1272449
320	15.2065427	109.3743023	1663.2049985
321	15.3364319	109.4395065	1678.4115412
322	15.4674306	109.5041584	1693.7479731
323	15.5995483	109.5682629	1709.2154037
324	15.7327944	109.6318244	1724.8149520
325	15.8671787	109.6948475	1740.5477464
326	16.0027108	109.7573370	1756.4149251
327	16.1394007	109.8192971	1772.4176359
328	16.2772580	109.8807325	1788.5570365
329	16.4162929	109.9416476	1804.8342946
330	16.5565155	110.0020468	1821.2505875
331	16.6979357	110.0619344	1837.8071030
332	16.8405639	110.1213149	1854.5050387
333	16.9844104	110.1801924	1871.3456026
334	17.1294855	110.2385713	1888.3300129
335	17.2757999	110.2964557	1905.4594985
336	17.4233640	110.3538499	1922.7352984
337	17.5721886	110.4107580	1940.1586624
338	17.7222844	110.4671842	1957.7308510
339	17.8736622	110.5231324	1975.4531353
340	18.0263331	110.5786068	1993.3267976
341	18.1803080	110.6336114	2011.3531306
342	18.3355981	110.6881501	2029.5334386
343	18.4922147	110.7422269	2047.8690368
344	18.6501690	110.7958457	2066.3612515
345	18.8094726	110.8490104	2085.0114205
346	18.9701368	110.9017248	2103.8208931
347	19.1321734	110.9539928	2122.7910299
348	19.2955940	111.0058181	2141.9232033
349	19.4604106	111.0572045	2161.2187974
350	19.6266349	111.1081557	2180.6792079
351	19.7942791	111.1586753	2200.3058429
352	19.9633552	111.2087671	2220.1001220
353	20.1338756	111.2584346	2240.0634772
354	20.3058524	111.3076815	2260.1973527
355	20.4792982	111.3565113	2280.5032051
356	20.6542256	111.4049276	2300.9825034
357	20.8306471	111.4529338	2321.6367289
358	21.0085755	111.5005334	2342.4673760
359	21.1880238	111.5477298	2363.4759515
360	21.3690048	111.5945266	2384.6639753
361	21.5515317	111.6409270	2406.0329801
362	21.7356177	111.6869344	2427.5845118
363	21.9212761	111.7325522	2449.3201296
364	22.1085204	111.7777836	2471.2414057
365	22.2973640	111.8226320	2493.3499261
366	22.4878206	111.8671005	2515.6472900
367	22.6799041	111.9111924	2538.1351107
368	22.8736283	111.9549109	2560.8150147
369	23.0690072	111.9982591	2583.6886430
370	23.2660550	112.0412402	2606.7576502
371	23.4647858	112.0838572	2630.0237051
372	23.6652142	112.1261133	2653.4884910
373	23.8673546	112.1680116	2677.1537052
374	24.0712216	112.2095549	2701.0210598
375	24.2768299	112.2507465	2725.0922814
376	24.4841945	112.2915892	2749.3691113
377	24.6933303	112.3320859	2773.8533058
378	24.9042525	112.3722397	2798.5466361
379	25.1169764	112.4120534	2823.4508887
380	25.3315172	112.4515299	2848.5678651
381	25.5478906	112.4906721	2873.8993823
382	25.7661121	112.5294328	2899.4472728
383	25.9861977	112.5679647	2925.2133850
384	26.2081631	112.6061208	2951.1995827
385	26.4320245	112.6439537	2977.4077458
386	26.6577981	112.6814662	3003.8397703
387	26.8855001	112.7186609	3030.4975684
388	27.1151471	112.7555407	3057.3830685
389	27.3467556	112.7921081	3084.4982155
390	27.5803425	112.8283658	3111.8449712
391	27.8159246	112.8643164	3139.4253136
392	28.0535189	112.8999626	3167.2412382
393	28.2931427	112.9353068	3195.2947572
394	28.5348133	112.9703517	3223.5878999
395	28.7785482	113.0050999	3252.1227132
396	29.0243650	113.0395537	3280.9012614
397	29.2722814	113.0737157	3309.9256264
398	29.5223155	113.1075884	3339.1979078
399	29.7744853	113.1411742	3368.7202233
400	30.0288090	113.1744755	3398.4947086

M	C(10.50,M,12)	A(10,50,M,12)	S(10.50,M,12)
301	13.7672712	105.9844530	1459.1167080
302	13.8877348	106.0564590	1472.8839792
303	14.0092525	106.1278404	1486.7717140
304	14.1318335	106.1986026	1500.7809666
305	14.2554870	106.2687510	1514.9128000
306	14.3802225	106.3382910	1529.1682870
307	14.5060495	106.4072277	1543.5485096
308	14.6329774	106.4755665	1558.0545590
309	14.7610160	106.5433125	1572.6875364
310	14.8901748	106.6104709	1587.4485524
311	15.0204639	106.6770468	1602.3387272
312	15.1518929	106.7430451	1617.3591911
313	15.2844720	106.8084710	1632.5110841
314	15.4182111	106.8733294	1647.7955561
315	15.5531205	106.9376251	1663.2137672
316	15.6892103	107.0013632	1678.7668877
317	15.8264909	107.0645484	1694.4560979
318	15.9649727	107.1271855	1710.2825888
319	16.1046662	107.1892793	1726.2475615
320	16.2455820	107.2508345	1742.3522277
321	16.3877308	107.3118558	1758.5978097
322	16.5311235	107.3723477	1774.9855405
323	16.6757708	107.4323150	1791.5166640
324	16.8216838	107.4917621	1808.1924348
325	16.9688736	107.5506935	1825.0141187
326	17.1173512	107.6091138	1841.9829922
327	17.2671280	107.6670273	1859.1003434
328	17.4182154	107.7244384	1876.3674714
329	17.5706248	107.7813516	1893.7856868
330	17.7243677	107.8377711	1911.3563116
331	17.8794560	107.8937012	1929.0806793
332	18.0359012	107.9491462	1946.9601353
333	18.1937153	108.0041102	1964.9960365
334	18.3529103	108.0585975	1983.1897518
335	18.5134983	108.1126121	2001.5426622
336	18.6754914	108.1661583	2020.0561605
337	18.8389020	108.2192399	2038.7316519
338	19.0037424	108.2718611	2057.5705539
339	19.1700251	108.3240259	2076.5742962
340	19.3377628	108.3757382	2095.7443213
341	19.5069683	108.4270019	2115.0820842
342	19.6776542	108.4778210	2134.5890524
343	19.8498337	108.5281992	2154.2667067
344	20.0235197	108.5781405	2174.1165404
345	20.1987255	108.6276485	2194.1400601
346	20.3754644	108.6767272	2214.3387856
347	20.5537497	108.7253801	2234.7142500
348	20.7335950	108.7736110	2255.2679997
349	20.9150140	108.8214236	2276.0015948
350	21.0980203	108.8688214	2296.9166087
351	21.2826280	108.9158081	2318.0146291
352	21.4688510	108.9623872	2339.2972571
353	21.6567035	109.0085623	2360.7661081
354	21.8461996	109.0543368	2382.4228116
355	22.0373539	109.0997143	2404.2690112
356	22.2301807	109.1446982	2426.3063651
357	22.4246948	109.1892919	2448.5365458
358	22.6209109	109.2334988	2470.9612406
359	22.8188438	109.2773222	2493.5821515
360	23.0185087	109.3207655	2516.4009953
361	23.2199207	109.3638320	2539.4195040
362	23.4220950	109.4065249	2562.6394247
363	23.6280471	109.4488475	2586.0625197
364	23.8347925	109.4908029	2609.6905668
365	24.0433469	109.5323945	2633.5253593
366	24.2537262	109.5736253	2657.5687062
367	24.4659463	109.6144984	2681.8224324
368	24.6800233	109.6550170	2706.2883787
369	24.8959735	109.6951841	2730.9684020
370	25.1138133	109.7350029	2755.8643756
371	25.3335592	109.7744762	2780.9781889
372	25.5552278	109.8136071	2806.3117480
373	25.7788361	109.8523987	2831.8669759
374	26.0044009	109.8908537	2857.6458119
375	26.2319394	109.9289751	2883.6502128
376	26.4614689	109.9667659	2909.8821522
377	26.6930067	110.0042289	2936.3436210
378	26.9265705	110.0413670	2963.0366278
379	27.1621780	110.0781829	2989.9631983
380	27.3998471	110.1146794	3017.1253763
381	27.6395957	110.1508594	3044.5252234
382	27.8814422	110.1867256	3072.1648191
383	28.1254048	110.2222806	3100.0462613
384	28.3715021	110.2575272	3128.1716661
385	28.6197527	110.2924681	3156.5431682
386	28.8701756	110.3271060	3185.1629209
387	29.1227896	110.3614433	3214.0330965
388	29.3776140	110.3954829	3243.1558861
389	29.6346682	110.4292271	3272.5335002
390	29.8939715	110.4626787	3302.1681683
391	30.1555438	110.4958401	3332.0621398
392	30.4194048	110.5287138	3362.2176836
393	30.6855746	110.5613024	3392.6370883
394	30.9540733	110.5936084	3423.3226629
395	31.2249215	110.6256341	3454.2767362
396	31.4981395	110.6573820	3485.5016577
397	31.7737483	110.6888545	3516.9997972
398	32.0517686	110.7200540	3548.7735455
399	32.3322215	110.7509829	3580.8253140
400	32.6151285	110.7816435	3613.1575356

M	C(10.75,M,12)	A(10.75,M,12)	S(10.75,M,12)
301	14.6501724	104.0083442	1523.7401683
302	14.7814135	104.0759967	1538.3903407
303	14.9138303	104.1430486	1553.1717542
304	15.0474334	104.2095051	1568.0855845
305	15.1822333	104.2753715	1583.1330178
306	15.3182408	104.3406532	1598.3152511
307	15.4554667	104.4053552	1613.6334919
308	15.5939219	104.4694828	1629.0889587
309	15.7336175	104.5330409	1644.6828806
310	15.8745645	104.5960348	1660.4164981
311	16.0167741	104.6584693	1676.2910626
312	16.1602577	104.7203495	1692.3078367
313	16.3050267	104.7816803	1708.4680944
314	16.4510926	104.8424665	1724.7731211
315	16.5984669	104.9027131	1741.2242136
316	16.7471615	104.9624247	1757.8226806
317	16.8971882	105.0216061	1774.5698421
318	17.0485588	105.0802621	1791.4670303
319	17.2012855	105.1383973	1808.5155891
320	17.3553804	105.1960163	1825.7168746
321	17.5108556	105.2531238	1843.0722550
322	17.6677237	105.3097241	1860.5831106
323	17.8259971	105.3658220	1878.2508343
324	17.9856883	105.4214217	1896.0768314
325	18.1468101	105.4765279	1914.0625197
326	18.3093753	105.5311447	1932.2093298
327	18.4733967	105.5852766	1950.5187050
328	18.6388876	105.6389278	1968.9921018
329	18.8058610	105.6921028	1987.6309894
330	18.9743301	105.7448055	2006.4368503
331	19.1443085	105.7970404	2025.4111805
332	19.3158096	105.8488115	2044.5554890
333	19.4888471	105.9001228	2063.8712986
334	19.6634347	105.9509787	2083.3601456
335	19.8395863	106.0013829	2103.0235803
336	20.0173159	106.0513397	2122.8631666
337	20.1966377	106.1008529	2142.8804824
338	20.3775659	106.1499265	2163.0771201
339	20.5601149	106.1985643	2183.4546860
340	20.7442993	106.2467703	2204.0148009
341	20.9301336	106.2945483	2224.7591002
342	21.1176327	106.3419021	2245.6892338
343	21.3068115	106.3888355	2266.8068666
344	21.4976851	106.4353521	2288.1136781
345	21.6902685	106.4814557	2309.6113631
346	21.8845771	106.5271500	2331.3016316
347	22.0806265	106.5724386	2353.1862088
348	22.2784321	106.6173250	2375.2668352
349	22.4780097	106.6618130	2397.5452673
350	22.6793752	106.7059059	2420.0232770
351	22.8825446	106.7496073	2442.7026522
352	23.0875341	106.7929207	2465.5851968
353	23.2943599	106.8358496	2488.6727309
354	23.5030385	106.8783973	2511.9670908
355	23.7135866	106.9205672	2535.4701294
356	23.9260208	106.9623627	2559.1837160
357	24.1403581	107.0037871	2583.1097368
358	24.3566155	107.0448437	2607.2500948
359	24.5748101	107.0855358	2631.6067103
360	24.7949595	107.1258666	2656.1815204
361	25.0170810	107.1658393	2680.9764799
362	25.2411923	107.2054570	2705.9935609
363	25.4673114	107.2447231	2731.2347532
364	25.6954560	107.2836404	2756.7020646
365	25.9256445	107.3222123	2782.3975206
366	26.1578950	107.3604417	2808.3231651
367	26.3922262	107.3983316	2834.4810601
368	26.6286565	107.4358851	2860.8732863
369	26.8672049	107.4731052	2887.5019429
370	27.1078903	107.5099949	2914.3691478
371	27.3507318	107.5465570	2941.4770381
372	27.5957488	107.5827944	2968.8277699
373	27.8429607	107.6187101	2996.4235187
374	28.0923872	107.6543070	3024.2664794
375	28.3440482	107.6895878	3052.3588667
376	28.5979636	107.7245553	3080.7029149
377	28.8541537	107.7592123	3109.3008785
378	29.1126389	107.7935617	3138.1550322
379	29.3734396	107.8276060	3167.2676711
380	29.6365766	107.8613481	3196.6411107
381	29.9020710	107.8947906	3226.2776873
382	30.1699437	107.9279362	3256.1797583
383	30.4402161	107.9607875	3286.3497020
384	30.7129097	107.9933471	3316.7899181
385	30.9880462	108.0256176	3347.5028278
386	31.2656474	108.0576016	3378.4908740
387	31.5457355	108.0893016	3409.7565215
388	31.8283327	108.1207201	3441.3022570
389	32.1134616	108.1518597	3473.1305897
390	32.4011447	108.1827228	3505.2440513
391	32.6914049	108.2133119	3537.6451960
392	32.9842654	108.2436294	3570.3366009
393	33.2797495	108.2736777	3603.3208663
394	33.5778805	108.3034592	3636.6006157
395	33.8786824	108.3329763	3670.1784963
396	34.1821789	108.3622313	3704.0571787
397	34.4883943	108.3912266	3738.2393576
398	34.7973528	108.4199644	3772.7277519
399	35.1090791	108.4484470	3807.5251047
400	35.4235979	108.4766768	3842.6341838

Table 1

M	C(10.25,M,12)	A(10.25,M,12)	S(10.25,M,12)	M	C(10.50,M,12)	A(10.50,M,12)	S(10.50,M,12)	M	C(10.75,M,12)	A(10.75,M,12)	S(10.75,M,12)
401	30.2853051	113.2074948	3428.5235176	401	32.9005108	110.8120382	3645.7726640	401	35.7409343	108.5046559	3878.0577817
402	30.5439921	113.2402345	3458.8088227	402	33.1883903	110.8421692	3678.6731749	402	36.0611135	108.5323866	3913.7987160
403	30.8048887	113.2726969	3489.3528147	403	33.4787887	110.8720030	3711.8615652	403	36.3841610	108.5598711	3949.8598296
404	31.0680137	113.3048043	3520.1577034	404	33.7717281	110.9016494	3745.3403539	404	36.7101024	108.5871116	3986.2439906
405	31.3333864	113.3367992	3551.2257171	405	34.0672307	110.9310032	3779.1120320	405	37.0389638	108.6141102	4022.9540930
406	31.6010257	113.3684437	3582.5591035	406	34.3653190	110.9601023	3813.1793128	406	37.3707712	108.6408691	4059.9930568
407	31.8709511	113.3998202	3614.1601292	407	34.6660156	110.9889490	3847.5446318	407	37.7055510	108.6673903	4097.3630280
408	32.1431822	113.4309310	3646.0310803	408	34.9693432	111.0175454	3882.2106474	408	38.0433299	108.6936762	4135.0693790
409	32.4177385	113.4617783	3678.1742625	409	35.2753249	111.0458939	3917.1799906	409	38.3841347	108.7197288	4173.1127088
410	32.6945400	113.4923644	3710.5920010	410	35.5839840	111.0739964	3952.4553155	410	38.7279926	108.7455497	4211.4968436
411	32.9739068	113.5226914	3743.2866411	411	35.8953439	111.1018552	3988.0392995	411	39.0749309	108.7711416	4250.2248362
412	33.2555589	113.5527616	3776.2605478	412	36.2094282	111.1294723	4023.9346435	412	39.4249771	108.7965062	4289.2997670
413	33.5396168	113.5825770	3809.5161067	413	36.5252607	111.1568498	4060.1440716	413	39.7781592	108.8216456	4328.7247441
414	33.8261010	113.6121400	3843.0557235	414	36.8456654	111.1839899	4096.6703323	414	40.1345052	108.8465618	4368.5029033
415	34.1150323	113.6414526	3876.8818245	415	37.1682668	111.2108946	4133.5161977	415	40.4940435	108.8712568	4408.6374085
416	34.4064315	113.6705169	3910.9968568	416	37.4934891	111.2375659	4170.6844645	416	40.8568026	108.8957326	4449.1314520
417	34.7003198	113.6993351	3945.4032803	417	37.8215571	111.2640058	4208.1779536	417	41.2228115	108.9199910	4489.9882547
418	34.9957184	113.7279092	3980.1036081	418	38.1524958	111.2902165	4245.9995107	418	41.5920992	108.9440340	4531.2110661
419	35.2956487	113.7562413	4015.1003264	419	38.4863301	111.3161997	4284.1520065	419	41.9646951	108.9678636	4572.8031653
420	35.5971323	113.7843335	4050.3959751	420	38.8230855	111.3419576	4322.6383366	420	42.3406288	108.9914815	4614.7678604
421	35.9011912	113.8121877	4085.9931074	421	39.1627875	111.3674920	4361.4614220	421	42.7199303	109.0148898	4657.1084892
422	36.2078472	113.8398060	4121.8942985	422	39.5054619	111.3928050	4400.6242095	422	43.1026296	109.0380902	4699.8284194
423	36.5171225	113.8671904	4158.1021457	423	39.8511347	111.4178984	4440.1296714	423	43.4887574	109.0610847	4742.9310490
424	36.8290396	113.8943429	4194.6192682	424	40.1998321	111.4427741	4479.9808060	424	43.8783441	109.0838750	4786.4198064
425	37.1436210	113.9212655	4231.4483079	425	40.5515806	111.4674340	4520.1806381	425	44.2714210	109.1064629	4830.2981505
426	37.4608894	113.9479600	4268.5919289	426	40.9064070	111.4918801	4560.7322188	426	44.6680191	109.1288503	4874.5695715
427	37.7800679	113.9744284	4306.0528183	427	41.2633380	111.5161141	4601.6386257	427	45.0681701	109.1510389	4919.2375906
428	38.1035794	114.0006726	4343.8336861	428	41.6254010	111.5401399	4642.9029637	428	45.4719058	109.1730305	4964.3057608
429	38.4290475	114.0266946	4381.9372656	429	41.9893232	111.5639533	4684.5283647	429	45.8792583	109.1948268	5009.7776666
430	38.7572956	114.0524962	4420.3663131	430	42.3570324	111.5875621	4726.5179879	430	46.2902600	109.2164297	5055.6569249
431	39.0883475	114.0780793	4459.1236087	431	42.7276565	111.6109662	4768.8750204	431	46.7049436	109.2378407	5101.9471849
432	39.4222272	114.1034457	4498.2119563	432	43.1015235	111.6341672	4811.6026768	432	47.1233420	109.2590616	5148.6521284
433	39.7589587	114.1285973	4537.6341834	433	43.4786618	111.6571670	4854.7042003	433	47.5454886	109.2800941	5195.7754705
434	40.0985665	114.1535358	4577.3931421	434	43.8591001	111.6799673	4898.1828621	434	47.9714170	109.3009398	5243.3209591
435	40.4410750	114.1782631	4617.4917086	435	44.2428672	111.7025690	4942.0419622	435	48.4011609	109.3216005	5291.2923761
436	40.7865092	114.2027810	4657.9327836	436	44.6299923	111.7249762	4986.2849294	436	48.8347546	109.3420777	5339.6935370
437	41.1348940	114.2270913	4698.7192928	437	45.0205047	111.7471883	5030.9148217	437	49.2722327	109.3623731	5388.5282916
438	41.4852546	114.2511957	4739.8541868	438	45.4144341	111.7692078	5075.9353264	438	49.7136297	109.3824883	5437.8005243
439	41.8406163	114.2750959	4781.3404414	439	45.8118104	111.7910362	5121.3497606	439	50.1589810	109.4024249	5487.5141540
440	42.1980049	114.2987937	4823.1810577	440	46.2126638	111.8126753	5167.1615710	440	50.6083219	109.4221845	5537.6731350
441	42.5584462	114.3222908	4865.3790626	441	46.6170246	111.8341267	5213.3742348	441	51.0616881	109.4417887	5588.2814569
442	42.9219663	114.3455889	4907.9375088	442	47.0249236	111.8553920	5259.9912594	442	51.5191157	109.4611789	5639.3431450
443	43.2885914	114.3686997	4950.8594751	443	47.4363916	111.8764729	5307.0161830	443	51.9808411	109.4804169	5690.8622607
444	43.6583481	114.3915948	4994.1480665	444	47.8514601	111.8973709	5354.4525746	444	52.4463010	109.4994840	5742.8429019
445	44.0310603	114.4143059	5037.8064146	445	48.2701603	111.9180476	5402.3040347	445	52.9161325	109.5183818	5795.2892029
446	44.4073635	114.4368247	5081.8376777	446	48.6925243	111.9386246	5450.5741950	446	53.3901728	109.5371119	5848.2053354
447	44.7866764	114.4591528	5126.2450413	447	49.1185808	111.9589835	5499.2667193	447	53.8684598	109.5556756	5901.5955083
448	45.1692293	114.4812918	5171.0317177	448	49.5483714	111.9791658	5548.3853031	448	54.3510314	109.5740745	5955.4639681
449	45.5550498	114.5032432	5216.2009470	449	49.9819197	111.9991731	5597.9336746	449	54.8379261	109.5923101	6009.8149995
450	45.9441659	114.5250088	5261.7559968	450	50.4192615	112.0190068	5647.9155943	450	55.3291825	109.6103837	6064.6529256
451	46.3366056	114.5465900	5307.7001627	451	50.8604300	112.0386584	5698.3348558	451	55.8248398	109.6282969	6119.9821081
452	46.7323974	114.5679884	5354.0367683	452	51.3054589	112.0581595	5749.1952858	452	56.3249373	109.6450510	6175.8069479
453	47.1315700	114.5892056	5400.7691657	453	51.7543816	112.0774815	5800.5007446	453	56.8295149	109.6636475	6232.1318852
454	47.5341522	114.6102431	5447.9007357	454	52.2072324	112.0966360	5852.2551262	454	57.3386126	109.6810878	6288.9614000
455	47.9401730	114.6311024	5495.4348789	455	52.6640457	112.1156243	5904.4623586	455	57.8522710	109.6983732	6346.3000126
456	48.3496620	114.6517851	5543.3750609	456	53.1248561	112.1344478	5957.1264042	456	58.3705309	109.7155051	6404.1522936
457	48.7626487	114.6722925	5591.7242469	457	53.5896966	112.1531081	6010.2512603	457	58.8934336	109.7324849	6462.5228145
458	49.1791630	114.6926264	5640.4873717	458	54.0568084	112.1716066	6063.8409589	458	59.4210206	109.7493140	6521.4162481
459	49.5992350	114.7127880	5689.6668468	459	54.5316213	112.1899446	6117.8995673	459	59.9533339	109.7659936	6580.8372687
460	50.0223952	114.7327789	5730.2657697	460	55.0087730	112.2081235	6172.4311886	460	60.4904159	109.7825252	6640.7906027
461	50.4501741	114.7526004	5789.2886649	461	55.4900997	112.2261447	6227.4399616	461	61.0323092	109.7989909	6701.2810185
462	50.6811026	114.7722541	5839.7388389	462	55.9755381	112.2440096	6282.9300653	462	61.5790570	109.8151492	6762.3133277
463	51.3157121	114.7917413	5890.6199416	463	56.4654249	112.2617196	6338.9056994	463	62.1307027	109.8312443	6823.8923847
464	51.7540338	114.8110635	5941.9356536	464	56.9594974	112.2792759	6395.3711243	464	62.6872902	109.8471965	6886.0230873
465	52.1960995	114.8302220	5993.6896874	465	57.4578930	112.2966800	6452.3306217	465	63.2488239	109.8630071	6948.7103775
466	52.6419411	114.8492182	6045.8857868	466	57.9606496	112.3139331	6509.7885147	466	63.8154683	109.8786773	7011.9592414
467	53.0915911	114.8680536	6098.5277280	467	58.4678052	112.3310365	6567.7491642	467	64.3871485	109.8942083	7075.7747097
468	53.5450817	114.8867295	6151.6193190	468	58.9793985	112.3479916	6626.2169695	468	64.9639500	109.9096015	7140.1618582
469	54.0024460	114.9052471	6205.1644008	469	59.4954683	112.3647996	6685.1963680	469	65.5459798	109.9248579	7205.1258082
470	54.4637169	114.9236080	6259.1668468	470	60.0160536	112.3814618	6744.6918363	470	66.1331009	109.9399790	7270.6717270
471	54.9289278	114.9418133	6313.6305636	471	60.5411941	112.3979795	6804.7078899	471	66.7255433	109.9549657	7336.8046279
472	55.3981124	114.9598645	6368.5594914	472	61.0709295	112.4143539	6865.2490840	472	67.3232930	109.9698194	7403.5303712
473	55.8713046	114.9777628	6423.9576038	473	61.6053002	112.4305862	6926.3200135	473	67.9263075	109.9845412	7470.8536642
474	56.3485386	114.9955004	6479.8289094	474	62.1443466	112.4466778	6987.9253137	474	68.5349048	109.9991323	7538.7800617
475	56.8298491	115.0131058	6536.1774470	475	62.6881096	112.4626298	7050.0696603	475	69.1486363	110.0135939	7607.3149664
476	57.3152707	115.0305302	6593.0007290	476	63.2366305	112.4784436	7112.7577699	476	69.7683219	110.0279271	7676.4638297
477	57.8048386	115.0478528	6650.3225668	477	63.7899511	112.4941199	7175.9944004	477	70.3933298	110.0421329	7746.2321516
478	58.2985883	115.0650050	6708.1274055	478	64.3481131	112.5096603	7239.7843515	478	71.0239367	110.0562127	7816.6254814
479	58.7965554	115.0820137	6766.4259938	479	64.9111591	112.5250660	7304.1324646	479	71.6601928	110.0701075	7887.6494180
480	59.2987760	115.0988774	6825.2225492	480	65.4791318	112.5403380	7369.0436237	480	72.3021487	110.0839983	7959.3056108
481	59.8052864	115.1155983	6884.5213252	481	66.0520742	112.5554776	7434.5227555	481	72.9498554	110.0977064	8031.6117595
482	60.3161232	115.1321777	6944.3266116	482	66.6300298	112.5704859	7500.5748297	482	73.6030645	110.1112927	8104.5616149
483	60.8313234	115.1486166	7004.6427348	483	67.2130426	112.5853639	7567.2048595	483	74.2627280	110.1247584	8178.1649794
484	61.3509243	115.1649162	7065.4740582	484	67.8011501	112.6001129	7634.4179021	484	74.9297983	110.1381045	8252.4277074
485	61.8749635	115.1810779	7126.8249825	485	68.3944168	112.6147340	7702.2190588	485	75.5992283	110.1513322	8327.3557057
486	62.4034788	115.1971026	7188.6999459	486	68.9928680	112.6292283	7770.6134756	486	76.2764711	110.1644424	8402.9549340
487	62.9365095	115.2129916	7251.1034247	487	69.5965556	112.6435968	7839.6063436	487	76.9597814	110.1774362	8479.2314053
488	63.4740912	115.2287461	7314.0399332	488	70.2055254	112.6578407	7909.2028992	488	77.6492128	110.1903146	8556.1911867
489	64.0162657	115.2443671	7377.5140243	489	70.8198238	112.6719610	7979.4084246	489	78.3443203	110.2030787	8633.8403995
490	64.5630713	115.2598558	7441.5302900	490	71.4394972	112.6859589	8050.2282484	490	79.0468593	110.2157295	8712.1852198
491	65.1145475	115.2752134	7506.0933613	491	72.0645928	112.6998353	8121.6677456	491	79.7547857	110.2282679	8791.2318792
492	65.6707343	115.2904409	7571.2079088	492	72.6951580	112.7135914	8193.7323385	492	80.4692556	110.2406950	8870.9866648
493	66.2316718	115.3055394	7636.8786431	493	73.3312407	112.7272291	8266.4274965	493	81.1901260	110.2530118	8951.4559205
494	66.7974007	115.3205100	7703.1103149	494	73.9728890	112.7407466	8339.7580372	494	81.9174542	110.2652192	9032.6460465
495	67.3679618	115.3353539	7769.9077156	495	74.6201518	112.7541478	8413.7316262	495	82.6512981	110.2773182	9114.5635007
496	67.9433965	115.3500720	7837.2756774	496	75.2730931	112.7674328	8488.3517780	496	83.3917160	110.2893098	9197.2147988
497	68.5237463	115.3646655	7905.2190739	497	75.9317178	112.7806025	8563.6248561	497	84.1387668	110.3011949	9280.6065148
498	69.1090533	115.3791354	7973.7428202	498	76.5961201	112.7936580	8639.5565737	498	84.8925209	110.3129745	9364.7452816
499	69.6993598	115.3934827	8042.8518735	499	77.2663361	112.8066002	8716.1526938	499	85.6530053	110.3246495	9449.6377915
500	70.2947085	115.4077085	8112.5512333	500	77.9424166	112.8194302	8793.4190299	500	86.2203135	110.3362209	9535.2907968

Table 1

M	C(11.00,M,12)	A(11.00,M,12)	S(11.00,M,12)	M	C(11.25,M,12)	A(11.25,M,12)	S(11.25,M,12)	M	C(11.50,M,12)	A(11.50,M,12)	S(11.50,M,12)
1	1.0091667	.9909166	1.0000000	1	1.0093750	.9907121	1.0000000	1	1.0095833	.9905076	1.0000000
2	1.0184174	1.9728323	2.0091667	2	1.0188379	1.9722225	2.0093750	2	1.0192585	1.9716130	2.0095833
3	1.0277529	2.9458289	3.0275840	3	1.0283895	2.9446167	3.0282129	3	1.0290264	2.9434054	3.0288418
4	1.0371739	3.9099873	4.0553369	4	1.0380306	3.9079794	4.0566024	4	1.0388879	3.9059731	4.0578682
5	1.0466813	4.8653879	5.0925108	5	1.0477622	4.8623945	5.0946330	5	1.0488439	4.8594038	5.0967561
6	1.0562759	5.8121103	6.1391922	6	1.0575850	5.8079450	6.1423952	6	1.0588953	5.8037842	6.1456001
7	1.0659585	6.7502331	7.1954561	7	1.0674998	6.7447133	7.1999802	7	1.0690431	6.7392002	7.2044954
8	1.0757297	7.6798346	8.2614265	8	1.0775076	7.6727810	8.2674800	8	1.0792881	7.6657369	8.2735385
9	1.0855906	8.6009922	9.3371563	9	1.0876093	8.5922288	9.3449876	9	1.0895313	8.5834786	9.3528266
10	1.0955418	9.5137825	10.4227469	10	1.0978056	9.5031369	10.4325969	10	1.1000736	9.4925087	10.4424578
11	1.1055843	10.4182816	11.5182887	11	1.1080375	10.4055846	11.5304025	11	1.1106159	10.3929100	11.5425314
12	1.1157188	11.3145648	12.6238730	12	1.1184859	11.2995503	12.6385000	12	1.1212593	11.2847643	12.6531473
13	1.1259463	12.2027066	13.7395919	13	1.1289717	12.1854121	13.7569859	13	1.1320047	12.1681529	13.7744066
14	1.1362674	13.0827811	14.8655381	14	1.1395559	13.0629470	14.8859577	14	1.1428531	13.0431560	14.9064113
15	1.1466832	13.9548426	16.0018056	15	1.1502392	13.9323314	16.0255135	15	1.1538055	13.9098532	16.0492645
16	1.1571945	14.8190205	17.1484888	16	1.1610227	14.7936410	17.1757527	16	1.1648628	14.7683234	17.2030699
17	1.1678021	15.6753300	18.3056833	17	1.1719073	15.6469508	18.3367754	17	1.1760260	15.6186448	18.3679327
18	1.1785069	16.5238613	19.4734854	18	1.1828939	16.4923352	19.5086827	18	1.1872963	16.4608945	19.5439587
19	1.1893099	17.3646850	20.6519923	19	1.1939835	17.3298677	20.6915766	19	1.1986745	17.2951493	20.7312523
20	1.2002119	18.1978712	21.8413022	20	1.2051771	18.1596212	21.8855601	20	1.2101618	18.1214851	21.9299295
21	1.2112139	19.0234892	23.0415142	21	1.2164757	18.9816681	23.0907372	21	1.2217592	18.9399770	23.1400913
22	1.2223167	19.8416078	24.2527281	22	1.2278801	19.7960798	24.3072129	22	1.2334677	19.7506995	24.3618505
23	1.2335212	20.6522951	25.4750447	23	1.2393915	20.6029274	25.5350930	23	1.2452685	20.5537262	25.5953182
24	1.2448285	21.4556186	26.7085660	24	1.2510108	21.4022810	26.7744845	24	1.2572225	21.3491304	26.8406067
25	1.2562394	22.2516452	27.9533945	25	1.2627390	22.1942103	28.0254953	25	1.2692709	22.1369843	28.0978292
26	1.2677550	23.0404411	29.2096339	26	1.2745772	22.9787842	29.2882343	26	1.2814347	22.9173556	29.3671001
27	1.2793761	23.8220721	30.4773889	27	1.2865264	23.7560710	30.5628115	27	1.2937151	23.6903273	30.6485348
28	1.2911037	24.5966033	31.7567650	28	1.2985895	24.5261385	31.8493379	28	1.3061132	24.4559577	31.9422499
29	1.3029388	25.3640990	33.0478687	29	1.3107618	25.2890536	33.1479254	29	1.3186301	25.2143205	33.2483631
30	1.3148824	26.1246233	34.3508075	30	1.3230502	26.0448828	34.4586872	30	1.3312670	25.9654846	34.5669933
31	1.3269355	26.8782395	35.6656899	31	1.3354538	26.7936919	35.7817374	31	1.3440250	26.7095184	35.8982603
32	1.3390991	27.6250102	36.9926254	32	1.3479737	27.5355462	37.1171912	32	1.3569052	27.4464895	37.2422853
33	1.3513741	28.3649977	38.3317244	33	1.3606109	28.2705102	38.4651649	33	1.3699089	28.1764651	38.5991905
34	1.3637617	29.0982636	39.6830986	34	1.3733666	28.9986478	39.8257758	34	1.3830372	28.8995114	39.9690994
35	1.3762629	29.8248690	41.0468603	35	1.3862420	29.7200226	41.1991498	35	1.3962913	29.6156943	41.3521366
36	1.3888786	30.5448743	42.4231232	36	1.3992350	30.4346973	42.5853844	36	1.4096724	30.3250760	42.7484279
37	1.4016100	31.2583395	43.8120018	37	1.4123558	31.1427342	43.9846224	37	1.4231818	31.0277299	44.1581004
38	1.4144581	31.9653241	45.2136118	38	1.4255967	31.8441449	45.3969782	38	1.4368206	31.7237110	45.5812822
39	1.4274240	32.6658868	46.6280699	39	1.4389616	32.5391404	46.8225749	39	1.4505902	32.4130856	47.0181028
40	1.4405087	33.3600660	48.0554940	40	1.4524519	33.2276314	48.2615365	40	1.4644916	33.0959164	48.4686929
41	1.4537134	34.0479795	49.4960026	41	1.4660686	33.9097277	49.7139884	41	1.4785264	33.7722655	49.9331846
42	1.4670391	34.7296246	50.9497160	42	1.4798130	34.5854887	51.1800571	42	1.4926956	34.4421945	51.4117109
43	1.4804869	35.4050781	52.4167550	43	1.4936863	35.2549734	52.6598701	43	1.5070006	35.1057643	52.9044065
44	1.4940581	36.0743961	53.8972420	44	1.5076896	35.9182399	54.1535564	44	1.5214427	35.7630352	54.4114071
45	1.5077536	36.7376345	55.3913000	45	1.5218242	36.5753460	55.6612460	45	1.5360231	36.4140670	55.9328497
46	1.5215747	37.3948483	56.8990536	46	1.5360913	37.2263490	57.1830702	46	1.5507434	37.0589191	57.4688729
47	1.5355224	38.0460925	58.4206283	47	1.5504921	37.8713055	58.7191614	47	1.5656047	37.6976499	59.0196162
48	1.5495980	38.6914211	59.9561507	48	1.5650280	38.5102717	60.2696536	48	1.5806084	38.3303177	60.5852209
49	1.5638027	39.3308880	61.5057487	49	1.5797001	39.1433032	61.8346816	49	1.5957559	38.9569800	62.1658292
50	1.5781376	39.9645463	63.0695514	50	1.5945098	39.7704552	63.4143817	50	1.6110485	39.5776937	63.7615851
51	1.5926038	40.5924489	64.6476890	51	1.6094584	40.3917822	65.0088915	51	1.6264877	40.1925155	65.3726336
52	1.6072027	41.2146479	66.2402928	52	1.6245470	41.0073384	66.6183499	52	1.6420749	40.8015011	66.9991214
53	1.6219354	41.8311953	67.8474955	53	1.6397772	41.6171774	68.2428969	53	1.6578115	41.4047060	68.6411963
54	1.6368031	42.4421423	69.4694309	54	1.6551501	42.2213522	69.8826741	54	1.6736988	42.0021850	70.2990077
55	1.6518071	43.0475399	71.1062340	55	1.6706671	42.8199155	71.5378242	55	1.6897384	42.5939926	71.9727066
56	1.6669487	43.6474384	72.7580411	56	1.6863296	43.4129194	73.2084913	56	1.7059318	43.1801825	73.6624450
57	1.6822291	44.2418877	74.4249898	57	1.7021389	44.0004155	74.8948209	57	1.7222803	43.7608081	75.3683768
58	1.6976495	44.8309375	76.1072189	58	1.7180965	44.5824550	76.5969958	58	1.7387855	44.3359222	77.0906571
59	1.7132113	45.4146366	77.8048684	59	1.7342037	45.1590885	78.3150563	59	1.7554488	44.9055771	78.8294425
60	1.7289157	45.9930338	79.5180797	60	1.7504618	45.7303663	80.0492600	60	1.7722719	45.4698246	80.5848913
61	1.7447641	46.5661772	81.2469964	61	1.7668724	46.2963382	81.7997218	61	1.7892561	46.0287161	82.3571632
62	1.7607578	47.1341145	82.9917596	62	1.7834368	46.8570533	83.5665942	62	1.8064032	46.5823023	84.1464194
63	1.7768981	47.6968930	84.7525174	63	1.8001565	47.4125605	85.3500310	63	1.8237146	47.1306338	85.9528226
64	1.7931863	48.2545595	86.5294154	64	1.8170330	47.9629083	87.1501875	64	1.8411918	47.6737602	87.7765371
65	1.8096239	48.8071605	88.3226017	65	1.8340677	48.5081444	88.9672206	65	1.8583468	48.2117311	89.6177289
66	1.8262121	49.3547421	90.1322256	66	1.8512621	49.0483165	90.8012882	66	1.8760504	48.7445954	91.4765655
67	1.8429523	49.8973497	91.9584377	67	1.8686177	49.5834714	92.6525503	67	1.8946363	49.2724016	93.3532319
68	1.8598461	50.4350286	93.8013900	68	1.8861360	50.1136559	94.5211680	68	1.9127919	49.7951976	95.2478509
69	1.8768947	50.9678235	95.6612361	69	1.9038185	50.6389160	96.4073039	69	1.9311228	50.3130311	97.1606428
70	1.8940995	51.4957789	97.5381308	70	1.9216668	51.1592976	98.3111224	70	1.9496294	50.8259490	99.0917656
71	1.9114621	52.0189386	99.4322303	71	1.9396824	51.6748460	100.2327852	71	1.9683134	51.3339982	101.0413950
72	1.9289838	52.5373463	101.3436924	72	1.9578669	52.1856059	102.1724716	72	1.9871764	51.8372248	103.0097084
73	1.9466662	53.0510450	103.2726762	73	1.9762219	52.6916219	104.1303385	73	2.0062201	52.3356748	104.9968848
74	1.9645106	53.5600727	105.2193424	74	1.9947490	53.1929381	106.1065604	74	2.0254464	52.8293929	107.0031049
75	1.9825187	54.0644865	107.1838531	75	2.0134498	53.6895982	108.1013094	75	2.0448550	53.3184247	109.0285514
76	2.0006917	54.5643137	109.1663717	76	2.0323259	54.1816452	110.1147592	76	2.0644535	53.8028144	111.0734083
77	2.0190314	55.0596007	111.1670635	77	2.0513789	54.6691222	112.1470851	77	2.0842378	54.2826061	113.1378618
78	2.0375392	55.5503888	113.1860949	78	2.0706106	55.1520715	114.1984640	78	2.1042118	54.7578434	115.2220997
79	2.0562166	56.0367188	115.2236341	79	2.0900226	55.6305353	116.2690746	79	2.1243772	55.2285696	117.3263114
80	2.0750653	56.5186314	117.2798507	80	2.1096165	56.1045551	118.3590972	80	2.1447358	55.6948275	119.4506886
81	2.0940867	56.9961665	119.3549160	81	2.1293942	56.5741722	120.4687137	81	2.1652895	56.1566595	121.5954244
82	2.1132825	57.4693640	121.4490028	82	2.1493573	57.0394276	122.5981079	82	2.1860402	56.6141077	123.7607138
83	2.1326543	57.9382633	123.5622855	83	2.1695075	57.5003617	124.7474652	83	2.2069897	57.0672135	125.9467540
84	2.1522036	58.4029033	125.6949396	84	2.1898466	57.9570147	126.9169727	84	2.2281400	57.5160184	128.1537437
85	2.1719321	58.8633229	127.8471432	85	2.2103764	58.4094263	129.1068193	85	2.2494931	57.9605630	130.3818838
86	2.1918415	59.3195602	130.0190753	86	2.2310987	58.8576360	131.3171957	86	2.2710507	58.4008878	132.6313768
87	2.2119334	59.7716534	132.2109169	87	2.2520153	59.3016827	133.5482944	87	2.2928149	58.8370329	134.9024275
88	2.2322095	60.2196400	134.4228503	88	2.2731279	59.7416051	135.8003097	88	2.3147877	59.2689514	137.1952425
89	2.2526714	60.6635574	136.6550597	89	2.2944385	60.1774416	138.0734376	89	2.3369711	59.6969422	139.5100302
90	2.2733209	61.1034425	138.9077311	90	2.3159488	60.6092301	140.3678761	90	2.3593671	60.1207847	141.8470013
91	2.2941596	61.5393320	141.1810520	91	2.3376609	61.0370081	142.6838249	91	2.3819777	60.5406039	144.2063684
92	2.3151894	61.9712621	143.4752116	92	2.3595764	61.4608130	145.0214858	92	2.4048050	60.9564381	146.5883461
93	2.3364120	62.3992688	145.7904011	93	2.3816975	61.8906816	147.3810322	93	2.4278510	61.3683250	148.9931511
94	2.3578291	62.8233877	148.1268131	94	2.4040259	62.2966505	149.7627597	94	2.4511179	61.7763021	151.4210022
95	2.3794426	63.2435542	150.4846422	95	2.4265636	62.7087559	152.1667855	95	2.4746078	62.1804065	153.8721201
96	2.4012541	63.6601033	152.8640848	96	2.4493126	63.1170337	154.5933491	96	2.4983228	62.5806750	156.3467279
97	2.4232656	64.0727696	155.2653389	97	2.4722750	63.5215195	157.0426618	97	2.5222651	62.9771441	158.8450507
98	2.4454789	64.4816874	157.6886045	98	2.4954525	63.9222484	159.5149367	98	2.5464368	63.3698497	161.3673158
99	2.4678958	64.8868909	160.1340834	99	2.5188474	64.3192554	162.0103393	99	2.5708401	63.7588276	163.9137526
100	2.4905181	65.2884138	162.6019791	100	2.5424616	64.7125750	164.5292367	100	2.5954773	64.1441132	166.4845927

Table 1

M	C(11.00,M,12)	A(11.00,M,12)	S(11.00,M,12)
101	2.5133479	65.6862895	165.0924973
102	2.5363869	66.0805511	167.6058452
103	2.5596371	66.4712315	170.1422321
104	2.5831005	66.8583631	172.7018692
105	2.6067789	67.2419783	175.2849697
106	2.6306744	67.6221090	177.8917486
107	2.6547889	67.9987868	180.5224229
108	2.6791244	68.3720431	183.1772118
109	2.7036831	68.7419089	185.8563363
110	2.7284668	69.1084151	188.5600193
111	2.7534778	69.4715922	191.2884862
112	2.7787180	69.8314704	194.0419640
113	2.8041696	70.1880796	196.8206820
114	2.8298947	70.5414497	199.6248716
115	2.8558354	70.8916099	202.4547662
116	2.8820138	71.2385895	205.3106016
117	2.9084323	71.5824173	208.1926154
118	2.9350929	71.9231221	211.1010477
119	2.9619980	72.2607320	214.0361407
120	2.9891496	72.5952753	216.9981386
121	3.0165501	72.9267798	219.9872882
122	3.0442019	73.2552732	223.0038384
123	3.0721070	73.5807827	226.0480402
124	3.1002680	73.9033354	229.1201473
125	3.1286871	74.2229583	232.2204153
126	3.1573668	74.5396779	235.3491024
127	3.1863093	74.8535206	238.5064692
128	3.2155171	75.1645126	241.6927785
129	3.2449927	75.4726797	244.9082957
130	3.2747385	75.7780406	248.1532884
131	3.3047569	76.0806417	251.4280268
132	3.3350505	76.3804873	254.7327838
133	3.3656218	76.6776092	258.0678343
134	3.3964733	76.9720322	261.4334561
135	3.4276077	77.2637809	264.8299294
136	3.4590274	77.5528705	268.2575371
137	3.4907352	77.8393521	271.7165646
138	3.5227336	78.1232226	275.2072997
139	3.5550253	78.4045145	278.7300333
140	3.5876130	78.6832514	282.2850586
141	3.6204995	78.9594564	285.8726717
142	3.6536874	79.2331525	289.4931712
143	3.6871795	79.5043625	293.1468586
144	3.7209787	79.7731090	296.8340381
145	3.7550877	80.0394143	300.5550168
146	3.7895093	80.3033007	304.3101044
147	3.8242465	80.5647902	308.0996137
148	3.8593021	80.8239044	311.9238502
149	3.8946790	81.0806649	315.7831623
150	3.9303802	81.3350933	319.6778412
151	3.9664087	81.5872105	323.6082215
152	4.0027674	81.8370376	327.5746302
153	4.0394595	82.0845955	331.5773976
154	4.0764879	82.3299047	335.6168571
155	4.1133557	82.5729857	339.6933449
156	4.1515660	82.8138587	343.8072006
157	4.1896220	83.0525437	347.9587666
158	4.2280269	83.2690606	352.1483886
159	4.2667833	83.5234292	356.3764155
160	4.3055960	83.7556689	360.6431994
161	4.3453667	83.9857991	364.9490954
162	4.3851992	84.2138389	369.2944621
163	4.4253969	84.4398073	373.6796613
164	4.4659630	84.6637232	378.1050582
165	4.5069010	84.8856051	382.5710212
166	4.5482143	85.1054701	387.0779223
167	4.5899063	85.3233410	391.6261366
168	4.6319804	85.5392334	396.2160428
169	4.6744402	85.7531607	400.8480232
170	4.7172893	85.9651469	405.5224634
171	4.7605311	86.1752051	410.2397527
172	4.8041693	86.3833600	415.0002838
173	4.8482075	86.5896218	419.8044530
174	4.8925494	86.7940101	424.6526605
175	4.9374987	86.9965418	429.5453099
176	4.9827591	87.1972338	434.4828086
177	5.0254344	87.3961028	439.4655677
178	5.0745284	87.5931655	444.4940020
179	5.1210449	87.7884334	449.5685304
180	5.1679878	87.9819370	454.6895753
181	5.2153610	88.1736832	459.8575630
182	5.2631685	88.3636779	465.0729240
183	5.3114142	88.5519517	470.3360925
184	5.3601021	88.7385153	475.6475067
185	5.4092364	88.9233843	481.0076088
186	5.4588211	89.1065740	486.4168453
187	5.5088603	89.2890998	491.8756663
188	5.5593582	89.4679767	497.3845266
189	5.6103189	89.6462197	502.9438848
190	5.6617469	89.8220436	508.5542037
191	5.7136462	89.9978632	514.2159506
192	5.7660213	90.1712930	519.9295968
193	5.8188765	90.3431475	525.6956181
194	5.8722162	90.5134409	531.5144946
195	5.9260449	90.6822875	537.3867108
196	5.9803669	90.8494014	543.3127557
197	6.0351870	91.0150963	549.2931226
198	6.0905095	91.1792862	555.3283096
199	6.1463392	91.3419847	561.4188191
200	6.2026806	91.5032053	567.5651583

M	C(11.25,M,12)	A(11.25,M,12)	S(11.25,M,12)
101	2.5662972	65.1022415	167.0716983
102	2.5903562	65.4888888	169.6379954
103	2.6146408	65.8707505	172.2283517
104	2.6391531	66.2495599	174.8429925
105	2.6638951	66.6250501	177.4821455
106	2.6888691	66.9969536	180.1460406
107	2.7140773	67.3654030	182.8349098
108	2.7395218	67.7304302	185.5489870
109	2.7652048	68.0920671	188.2885088
110	2.7911286	68.4503451	191.0537136
111	2.8172954	68.8052954	193.8448421
112	2.8437075	69.1569491	196.6621375
113	2.8703673	69.5053365	199.5058451
114	2.8972770	69.8504882	202.3762124
115	2.9244390	70.1924341	205.2734894
116	2.9518556	70.5312041	208.1979283
117	2.9795292	70.8668276	211.1497839
118	3.0074623	71.1993338	214.1293131
119	3.0356573	71.5287518	217.1367754
120	3.0641166	71.8551101	220.1724327
121	3.0928427	72.1784373	223.2365493
122	3.1218381	72.4987614	226.3293919
123	3.1511053	72.8161103	229.4512300
124	3.1806469	73.1305118	232.6023353
125	3.2104655	73.4419931	235.7829822
126	3.2405636	73.7505814	238.9934476
127	3.2709439	74.0563036	242.2340112
128	3.3016090	74.3591862	245.5049550
129	3.3325615	74.6592557	248.8065640
130	3.3638043	74.9565381	252.1391255
131	3.3953400	75.2510594	255.5029298
132	3.4271713	75.5428453	258.8982698
133	3.4593010	75.8319210	262.3254411
134	3.4917320	76.1183118	265.7847421
135	3.5244669	76.4020427	269.2764741
136	3.5575088	76.6831383	272.8009410
137	3.5908605	76.9616230	276.3584498
138	3.6245248	77.2375213	279.9493103
139	3.6585047	77.5108570	283.5738351
140	3.6928032	77.7816540	287.2323398
141	3.7274232	78.0499358	290.9251430
142	3.7623678	78.3157259	294.6525662
143	3.7976400	78.5790473	298.4149340
144	3.8332429	78.8399231	302.2125740
145	3.8691795	79.0983758	306.0458169
146	3.9054531	79.3544280	309.9149964
147	3.9420667	79.6081021	313.8204465
148	3.9790236	79.8594200	317.7625163
149	4.0163269	80.1084037	321.7415399
150	4.0539800	80.3550749	325.5578668
151	4.0919861	80.5994550	329.8118468
152	4.1303468	80.8415653	333.9038329
153	4.1690705	81.0814269	338.0341813
154	4.2081555	81.3190607	342.2032517
155	4.2476069	81.5544874	346.4114072
156	4.2874283	81.7877275	350.6590142
157	4.3276229	82.0188012	354.9464424
158	4.3681944	82.2477288	359.2740653
159	4.4091462	82.4745300	363.6422597
160	4.4504819	82.6992248	368.0516409
161	4.4922052	82.9218326	372.5018878
162	4.5343196	83.1423729	376.9940030
163	4.5768289	83.3608648	381.5284127
164	4.6197366	83.5773273	386.1052415
165	4.6630467	83.7917794	390.7249782
166	4.7067627	84.0042396	395.3880248
167	4.7508886	84.2147266	400.0947876
168	4.7954282	84.4232585	404.8456762
169	4.8403854	84.6298537	409.6411044
170	4.8857640	84.8345299	414.4814898
171	4.9315680	85.0373052	419.3672538
172	4.9778015	85.2381971	424.2988218
173	5.0244683	85.4372231	429.2766232
174	5.0715727	85.6344006	434.3010916
175	5.1191187	85.8297467	439.3726643
176	5.1671105	86.0232785	444.4917830
177	5.2155521	86.2150128	449.6588935
178	5.2644479	86.4049662	454.8744456
179	5.3138021	86.5931554	460.1388936
180	5.3636189	86.7795967	465.4526957
181	5.4139030	86.9643063	470.8163147
182	5.4646583	87.1473003	476.2302177
183	5.5158895	87.3285948	481.6948760
184	5.5676009	87.5082053	487.2107654
185	5.6197972	87.6861477	492.7783664
186	5.6724828	87.8624374	498.3981636
187	5.7256623	88.0370896	504.0706464
188	5.7793404	88.2101198	509.7963087
189	5.8335217	88.3815428	515.5756491
190	5.8882110	88.5513737	521.4091708
191	5.9434130	88.7196272	527.2973818
192	5.9991325	88.8863179	533.2407947
193	6.0553673	89.0514605	539.2399272
194	6.1121435	89.2150692	545.2953015
195	6.1694448	89.3771584	551.4074450
196	6.2272833	89.5377420	557.5768898
197	6.2856661	89.6968342	563.8041731
198	6.3445922	89.8544487	570.0898372
199	6.4040728	90.0105994	576.4344295
200	6.4641110	90.1652997	582.8385022

M	C(11.50,M,12)	A(11.50,M,12)	S(11.50,M,12)
101	2.6203507	64.5257415	169.0800700
102	2.6454624	64.9037472	171.7004207
103	2.6708147	65.2781648	174.3458831
104	2.6964100	65.6490283	177.0166978
105	2.7222506	66.0163714	179.7131078
106	2.7483389	66.3802275	182.4353584
107	2.7746771	66.7406298	185.1836973
108	2.8012678	67.0976111	187.9583744
109	2.8281132	67.4512037	190.7596422
110	2.8552160	67.8014399	193.5877554
111	2.8825785	68.1483515	196.4429714
112	2.9102032	68.4919701	199.3255499
113	2.9380926	68.8323270	202.2357530
114	2.9662494	69.1694531	205.1738457
115	2.9946759	69.5033790	208.1400950
116	3.0233749	69.8341352	211.1347710
117	3.0523489	70.1617518	214.1581458
118	3.0816006	70.4862585	217.2104947
119	3.1111326	70.8076648	220.2920953
120	3.1409476	71.1260601	223.4032279
121	3.1710484	71.4414132	226.5441755
122	3.2014376	71.7537729	229.7152239
123	3.2321180	72.0631675	232.9166614
124	3.2630925	72.3696253	236.1487794
125	3.2943638	72.6731740	239.4118719
126	3.3259348	72.9738414	242.7062357
127	3.3578002	73.2716547	246.0321704
128	3.3899873	73.5666410	249.3899787
129	3.4224747	73.8588273	252.7799660
130	3.4552734	74.1482400	256.2024407
131	3.4883864	74.4349055	259.6577141
132	3.5218168	74.7188499	263.1461005
133	3.5555675	75.0000000	266.6679173
134	3.5896417	75.2786782	270.2234849
135	3.6240425	75.5546132	273.8131266
136	3.6587729	75.8279269	277.4371691
137	3.6938361	76.0986501	281.0959419
138	3.7292354	76.3668016	284.7897781
139	3.7649739	76.6324077	288.5190134
140	3.8010549	76.8954926	292.2839873
141	3.8374817	77.1560801	296.0850422
142	3.8742575	77.4141941	299.9225238
143	3.9113858	77.6698580	303.7967814
144	3.9488699	77.9230950	307.7081672
145	3.9867313	78.1739282	311.6570371
146	4.0249193	78.4223803	315.6437504
147	4.0634914	78.6684741	319.6686697
148	4.1024332	78.9122319	323.7321611
149	4.1417482	79.1536758	327.8345943
150	4.1814400	79.3928279	331.9763425
151	4.2215121	79.6297009	336.1577825
152	4.2615682	79.8643432	340.3792946
153	4.3028121	80.0967494	344.6412628
154	4.3440474	80.3269495	348.9440749
155	4.3856778	80.5549644	353.2881223
156	4.4277073	80.7808149	357.6738001
157	4.4701394	81.0045216	362.1015074
158	4.5129783	81.2261047	366.5716468
159	4.5552277	81.4455845	371.0846251
160	4.5998915	81.6629810	375.6408528
161	4.6439738	81.8783138	380.2407443
162	4.6884786	82.0916026	384.8847181
163	4.7334098	82.3028668	389.5731966
164	4.7787716	82.5121256	394.3066064
165	4.8245682	82.7193980	399.0853781
166	4.8708037	82.9247030	403.9099463
167	4.9174822	83.1280591	408.7807500
168	4.9646081	83.3294848	413.6982321
169	5.0121856	83.5289986	418.6623402
170	5.0602190	83.7266185	423.6750258
171	5.1087128	83.9223625	428.7352448
172	5.1576713	84.1162485	433.8439575
173	5.2070989	84.3082940	439.0016288
174	5.2570003	84.4985165	444.2087277
175	5.3073799	84.6869334	449.4657281
176	5.3582423	84.8735618	454.7731080
177	5.4095921	85.0584186	460.1313502
178	5.4614304	85.2415207	465.5409424
179	5.5137728	85.4228847	471.0023764
180	5.5666131	85.6025272	476.5161492
181	5.6199598	85.7804644	482.0827623
182	5.6737178	85.9567126	487.7027221
183	5.7281918	86.1312877	493.3765398
184	5.7830870	86.3042057	499.1047317
185	5.8385083	86.4754824	504.8878187
186	5.8944606	86.6451332	510.7263270
187	5.9509492	86.8131736	516.6207876
188	6.0079791	86.9796189	522.5717368
189	6.0655556	87.1444843	528.5797160
190	6.1236839	87.3077847	534.6452716
191	6.1823692	87.4695350	540.7689554
192	6.2416169	87.6297499	546.9513246
193	6.3014324	87.7884439	553.1929415
194	6.3618211	87.9456316	559.4943738
195	6.4227685	88.1013272	565.8561949
196	6.4843403	88.2555449	572.2789834
197	6.5464819	88.4082987	578.7633237
198	6.6092190	88.5596025	585.3098056
199	6.6725573	88.7094701	591.9190245
200	6.7365027	88.8579151	598.5915819

Table 1

M	C(11.00,M,12)	A(11.00,M,12)	S(11.00,M,12)	C(11.25,M,12)	A(11.25,M,12)	S(11.25,M,12)	C(11.50,M,12)	A(11.50,M,12)	S(11.50,M,12)
201	6.2595385	91.6629615	573.7678389	6.5247120	90.3185632	589.3026132	6.8010608	89.0049510	605.3280845
202	6.3169176	91.8212665	580.0273774	6.5858812	90.4704031	595.8273252	6.8662376	89.1505912	612.1291453
203	6.3748227	91.9781336	586.3442951	6.6476208	90.6208328	602.4132064	6.9320391	89.2948489	618.9953830
204	6.4332586	92.1335759	592.7191178	6.7099453	90.7698653	609.0608302	6.9984711	89.4377372	625.9274221
205	6.4922301	92.2376061	599.1523764	6.7728510	90.9175136	615.7707755	7.0655398	89.5792692	632.9258932
206	6.5517422	92.4402373	605.6446065	6.8363465	91.0637906	622.5436265	7.1332512	89.7194577	639.9914330
207	6.6117999	92.5914820	612.1963087	6.9004373	91.2087090	629.3799730	7.2016116	89.8583155	647.1246843
208	6.6724080	92.7413530	618.8081486	6.9651289	91.3522813	636.2804103	7.2705270	89.9958553	654.3262958
209	6.7335718	92.8898626	625.4805566	7.0304269	91.4945202	643.2455391	7.3403038	90.1320894	661.5969228
210	6.7952962	93.0370232	632.2141284	7.0963372	91.6354380	650.2759601	7.4106484	90.2670304	668.9372267
211	6.8575864	93.1828471	639.0094246	7.1626653	91.7750469	657.3723032	7.4816671	90.4006904	676.3478751
212	6.9204476	93.3273464	645.8670110	7.2300172	91.9133592	664.5351686	7.5533665	90.5330817	683.8295423
213	6.9830850	93.4705332	652.7874586	7.2977986	92.0503868	671.7651858	7.6257529	90.6642163	691.3829087
214	7.0479040	93.6124193	659.7713436	7.3662155	92.1861417	679.0629844	7.6938330	90.7941061	699.0086616
215	7.1125098	93.7530167	666.8192476	7.4352738	92.3206357	686.4291999	7.7723135	90.9227630	706.7074946
216	7.1777078	93.8923369	673.9317574	7.5049794	92.4538806	693.8644737	7.8471010	91.0501986	714.4801081
217	7.2435034	94.0303917	681.1094652	7.5753386	92.5858879	701.3694531	7.9223024	91.1764245	722.3272091
218	7.3099022	94.1671924	688.3529686	7.6463574	92.7166691	708.9447917	7.9982245	91.3014523	730.2495116
219	7.3769097	94.3027505	695.6628708	7.7180420	92.8462357	716.5911492	8.0749741	91.4252932	738.2477361
220	7.4445313	94.4370715	703.0397805	7.7903987	92.9745988	724.3091912	8.1522584	91.5479586	746.3226102
221	7.5127729	94.5701840	710.4843118	7.8634337	93.1017697	732.0995899	8.2303842	91.6694596	754.4748686
222	7.5816399	94.7020815	717.9970847	7.9371534	93.2277595	739.9630235	8.3092587	91.7898073	762.7052527
223	7.6511383	94.8327811	725.5787246	8.0115642	93.3525790	747.9001769	8.3888891	91.9090126	771.0145114
224	7.7212737	94.9622934	733.2298629	8.0866726	93.4762393	755.9117410	8.4692826	92.0270663	779.4034005
225	7.7920521	95.0906293	740.9511367	8.1624851	93.5987510	763.9984136	8.5504466	92.1440393	787.8726831
226	7.8634792	95.2177994	748.7431888	8.2390084	93.7201248	772.1608988	8.6323883	92.2598821	796.4231296
227	7.9355611	95.3438145	756.6066580	8.3152491	93.8403713	780.3999072	8.7151154	92.3746253	805.0555180
228	8.0083038	95.4686849	764.5422291	8.3942140	93.9595010	788.7161563	8.7986352	92.4882792	813.7706333
229	8.0817132	95.5924210	772.5505329	8.4729097	94.0775242	797.1103703	8.8829555	92.6008544	822.5692686
230	8.1557956	95.7150332	780.6322461	8.5523433	94.1944513	805.5832800	8.9680838	92.7123609	831.4522241
231	8.2305571	95.8365316	788.7880417	8.6325215	94.3102923	814.1356233	9.0540280	92.8228090	840.4203079
232	8.3060038	95.9569265	797.0185988	8.7134514	94.4250573	822.7681448	9.1407957	92.9322087	849.4743359
233	8.3821422	96.0762227	805.3246026	8.7951400	94.5387565	831.4815961	9.2283950	93.0405699	858.6151316
234	8.4589785	96.1944453	813.7067448	8.8775944	94.6513996	840.2767361	9.3168338	93.1479025	867.8435266
235	8.5365191	96.3115891	822.1657233	8.9608219	94.7629965	849.1543305	9.4061201	93.2542162	877.1603604
236	8.6147706	96.4276688	830.7022424	9.0448296	94.8735569	858.1151524	9.4962621	93.3595208	886.5664805
237	8.6937393	96.5426941	839.3170130	9.1296248	94.9830905	867.1599819	9.5872580	93.4638258	896.0627427
238	8.7734319	96.6566746	848.0107523	9.2152151	95.0916067	876.2896068	9.6791459	93.5671407	905.6500106
239	8.8538550	96.7696197	856.7841842	9.3016077	95.1991150	885.5048218	9.7719044	93.6694749	915.3291566
240	8.9350154	96.8815389	865.6380392	9.3888103	95.3056247	894.8064295	9.8655518	93.7708377	925.1010610
241	9.0169197	96.9924416	874.5730546	9.4768304	95.4111452	904.1952398	9.9600967	93.8712384	934.9666128
242	9.0995748	97.1023368	883.5899743	9.5656757	95.5156857	913.6720702	10.0555476	93.9706860	944.9267095
243	9.1829875	97.2112338	892.6895490	9.6553539	95.6192552	923.2377459	10.1519133	94.0691896	954.9822572
244	9.2671649	97.3191417	901.8725366	9.7458728	95.7218627	932.8930997	10.2492025	94.1667581	965.1341705
245	9.3521139	97.4260694	911.1397015	9.8272404	95.8235172	942.6389726	10.3474240	94.2634005	975.3833730
246	9.4378416	97.5320258	920.4918155	9.9294645	95.9242275	952.4762129	10.4465868	94.3591256	985.7307970
247	9.5243552	97.6370198	929.9296571	10.0225532	96.0240026	962.4056774	10.5466999	94.4539420	996.1773838
248	9.6116618	97.7410601	939.4540123	10.1165147	96.1228508	972.4282307	10.6447725	94.5478583	1006.7240037
249	9.5997687	97.8441553	949.0656741	10.2113570	96.2207810	982.5447453	10.7498136	94.6408832	1017.3718562
250	9.7886832	97.9463141	958.7654428	10.3070885	96.3178016	992.7561023	10.8528327	94.7330250	1028.1216698
251	9.8784128	98.0475450	968.5541260	10.4037174	96.4139211	1003.0631908	10.9568398	94.8242922	1038.9745025
252	9.9689649	98.1478563	978.4325388	10.5012523	96.5091478	1013.4669062	11.0618420	94.9146931	1049.9313415
253	10.0603471	98.2472564	988.4015038	10.5997015	96.6034901	1023.9681605	11.1678514	95.0042358	1060.9931835
254	10.1525670	98.3457537	998.4618509	10.6990737	96.6969562	1034.5678620	11.2743766	95.0929286	1072.1610349
255	10.2456322	98.4433562	1008.6144179	10.7993775	96.7895541	1045.2669357	11.3829275	95.1807795	1083.4359115
256	10.3395505	98.5400722	1018.8600501	10.9006217	96.8812920	1056.0663133	11.4920139	95.2677964	1094.8188389
257	10.4343297	98.6359097	1029.1996005	11.0028150	96.9721778	1066.9669300	11.6021457	95.3539874	1106.3108528
258	10.5299777	98.7308767	1039.6339302	11.1059664	97.0622195	1077.9697500	11.7133329	95.4393602	1117.9129935
259	10.6265025	98.8249810	1050.1639079	11.2100849	97.1514249	1089.0757164	11.8255867	95.5239226	1129.6263314
260	10.7239121	98.9182306	1060.7904104	11.3151799	97.2398018	1100.2858013	11.9389142	95.6076823	1141.4519171
261	10.8222146	99.0106331	1071.5143225	11.4212592	97.3273578	1111.6009806	12.0533288	95.6906469	1153.3908313
262	10.9214183	99.1021963	1082.3365371	11.5293335	97.4141006	1123.0222398	12.1603399	95.7728240	1165.4441601
263	11.0215313	99.1929278	1093.2579554	11.6364116	97.5000377	1134.5505734	12.2814211	95.8542211	1177.6130000
264	11.1225620	99.2828352	1104.2794867	11.7455030	97.5851767	1146.1869950	12.4031936	95.9348455	1189.8984579
265	11.2245188	99.3719258	1115.4020486	11.8556171	97.6695249	1157.9324880	12.5220575	96.0147045	1202.3016515
266	11.3274102	99.4602073	1126.6265674	11.9667635	97.7530897	1169.7881051	12.6420606	96.0938056	1214.8237090
267	11.4312448	99.5476868	1137.9539776	12.0769519	97.8358783	1181.7548686	12.7632136	96.1725787	1227.4657696
268	11.5360312	99.6343717	1149.3852224	12.1921921	97.9178980	1193.8338205	12.8855278	96.2497622	1240.2289832
269	11.6417782	99.7202693	1160.9212537	12.3064939	97.9991559	1206.0260125	13.0090141	96.3265310	1253.1145110
270	11.7484945	99.8053866	1172.5630318	12.4218673	98.0796591	1218.3325064	13.1336338	96.4027721	1266.1235250
271	11.8561890	99.8897307	1184.3115263	12.5383223	98.1594146	1230.7543737	13.2555483	96.4781894	1279.2572089
272	11.9648707	99.9733087	1196.1677153	12.6558690	98.2384293	1243.2926959	13.3866189	96.5528909	1292.5167571
273	12.0745487	100.0561275	1208.1325800	12.7745178	98.3167102	1255.9485650	13.5149074	96.6268832	1305.9033760
274	12.1852321	100.1381941	1220.2071348	12.8942789	98.3942640	1268.7230828	13.6444252	96.7001733	1319.4162834
275	12.2969300	100.2195152	1232.3923668	13.0151628	98.4710974	1281.6173617	13.7751843	96.7727649	1333.0627086
276	12.4096519	100.3000969	1244.6892969	13.1371799	98.5472173	1294.6325245	13.9071965	96.8446728	1346.8376929
277	12.5234070	100.3799481	1257.0989488	13.2603410	98.6226301	1307.7697044	14.0404738	96.9158655	1360.7450894
278	12.6382049	100.4590733	1269.6223558	13.3846570	98.6973425	1321.0300454	14.1750283	96.9864420	1374.7855632
279	12.7540552	100.5374797	1282.2605607	13.5101378	98.7713610	1334.4147021	14.3103723	97.0563190	1388.9605915
280	12.8709673	100.6151739	1295.0146159	13.6367954	98.8446920	1347.9248399	14.4480182	97.1255326	1403.2714639
281	12.9889512	100.6921624	1307.8855832	13.7646403	98.9173419	1361.5616353	14.5864784	97.1940893	1417.7198821
282	13.1080166	100.7684516	1320.8745344	13.8936838	98.9893171	1375.3262756	14.7262655	97.2619952	1432.3059604
283	13.2281734	100.8440479	1333.9825510	14.0239371	99.0606237	1389.2199595	14.8673922	97.3292564	1447.0322259
284	13.3494317	100.9189574	1347.2107244	14.1554115	99.1312681	1403.2438966	15.0093714	97.3958793	1461.8996181
285	13.4718014	100.9931865	1360.5560503	14.2881185	99.2012563	1417.3993082	15.1537160	97.4618697	1476.9094894
286	13.5952930	101.0667414	1374.0319575	14.4220696	99.2705945	1431.6874267	15.2989391	97.5272337	1492.0632054
287	13.7199165	101.1396282	1387.6272504	14.5572565	99.3392887	1446.1094963	15.4455539	97.5919772	1507.3621445
288	13.8455824	101.2118528	1401.3471669	14.6937510	99.4073448	1460.6667729	15.5935738	97.6561062	1522.8076984
289	13.9726011	101.2834215	1415.1928493	14.8315049	99.4747988	1475.3605239	15.7430122	97.7196265	1538.4012721
290	14.1006833	101.3543400	1429.1654504	14.9705503	99.5415667	1490.1920288	15.8938827	97.7825438	1554.1442843
291	14.2299396	101.4246144	1443.2661337	15.1108692	99.6077441	1505.1625791	16.0461991	97.8448638	1570.0381671
292	14.3603807	101.4942504	1457.4960733	15.2525639	99.6733068	1520.2734783	16.1999752	97.9065923	1586.0843662
293	14.4920175	101.5632539	1471.8564540	15.3955567	99.7382606	1535.5260421	16.3552250	97.9677348	1602.2843414
294	14.6248610	101.6316306	1486.3484715	15.5398900	99.8026111	1550.9215988	16.5119625	98.0282970	1618.6395663
295	14.7589222	101.6993863	1500.9733325	15.6855765	99.8663640	1566.4614888	16.6702022	98.0882843	1635.1515289
296	14.8942123	101.7665264	1515.7322547	15.8326288	99.9295247	1582.1470653	16.8299583	98.1477021	1651.8217310
297	15.0307426	101.8330568	1530.6264671	15.9810596	99.9920987	1597.9796940	16.9912454	98.2065560	1668.6516893
298	15.1685244	101.8989827	1545.6572097	16.1308821	100.0540916	1613.9607537	17.1540781	98.2648511	1685.6429347
299	15.3075692	101.9643099	1560.8257341	16.2821091	100.1155087	1630.0916358	17.3184714	98.3225930	1702.7970128
300	15.4478886	102.0290437	1576.1333034	16.4347539	100.1763554	1646.3737449	17.4944401	98.3797867	1723.1154842

Table 1   431

M	C(11.00,M,12)	A(11.00,M,12)	S(11.00,M,12)	M	C(11.25,M,12)	A(11.25,M,12)	S(11.25,M,12)	M	C(11.50,M,12)	A(11.50,M,12)	S(11.50,M,12)
301	15.5894943	102.0931894	1591.5811920	301	16.5883297	100.2366369	1662.8084987	301	17.6519993	98.4364375	1737.5999243
302	15.7323980	102.1567525	1607.1706863	302	16.7443500	100.2963586	1679.3973284	302	17.8211643	98.4925505	1755.2519236
303	15.8766116	102.2197383	1622.9030842	303	16.9013282	100.3555255	1696.1416784	303	17.9919504	98.5481309	1773.0730878
304	16.0221472	102.2821519	1638.7796958	304	17.0597782	100.4141429	1713.0430066	304	18.1643733	98.6031833	1791.0650383
305	16.1690169	102.3439986	1654.8018431	305	17.2197136	100.4722159	1730.1027848	305	18.3384485	98.6577140	1809.2294116
306	16.3172329	102.4052835	1670.9708600	306	17.3811484	100.5297495	1747.3224985	306	18.5141920	98.7117266	1827.5678601
307	16.4658075	102.4660117	1687.2880029	307	17.5440967	100.5867487	1764.7036469	307	18.6916197	98.7652265	1846.0820521
308	16.6177533	102.5261883	1703.7549004	308	17.7085726	100.6432186	1782.2477436	308	18.8707477	98.8182186	1864.7736718
309	16.7700827	102.5858183	1720.3726537	309	17.8745905	100.6991639	1799.9563162	309	19.0515924	98.8707077	1883.6444195
310	16.9238084	102.6449066	1737.1427364	310	18.0421648	100.7545896	1817.8309067	310	19.2341701	98.9226985	1902.6960119
311	17.0769433	102.7034583	1754.0665448	311	18.2113101	100.8095005	1835.8730715	311	19.4184976	98.9741958	1921.9301820
312	17.2355003	102.7614781	1771.1454881	312	18.3820411	100.8639015	1854.0843815	312	19.6045915	99.0252042	1941.3486796
313	17.3934924	102.8189708	1788.3809884	313	18.5543727	100.9177971	1872.4664226	313	19.7924689	99.0757285	1960.9532711
314	17.5529328	102.8759414	1805.7744809	314	18.7283200	100.9711922	1891.0207953	314	19.9821467	99.1257732	1980.7457400
315	17.7138346	102.9323944	1823.3274136	315	18.9038980	101.0240913	1909.7491153	315	20.1736423	99.1753428	2000.7278867
316	17.8762115	102.9883347	1841.0412483	316	19.0811220	101.0764992	1928.6530133	316	20.3669730	99.2244419	2020.9015290
317	18.0400767	103.0437668	1858.9174597	317	19.2600075	101.1284202	1947.7341353	317	20.5621565	99.2730749	2041.2685020
318	18.2054441	103.0986954	1876.9575364	318	19.4405701	101.1798590	1966.9941428	318	20.7592105	99.3212463	2061.8306585
319	18.3723273	103.1531251	1895.1629805	319	19.6222255	101.2308201	1986.4347129	319	20.9581529	99.3689604	2082.5898689
320	18.5407403	103.2070604	1913.5353079	320	19.8067894	101.2813078	2006.0575384	320	21.1590019	99.4162216	2103.5480219
321	18.7106971	103.2605058	1932.0760482	321	19.9924781	101.3313266	2025.8643278	321	21.3617757	99.4630342	2124.7070238
322	18.8822118	103.3134657	1950.7867453	322	20.1793076	101.3808809	2045.8568059	322	21.5664927	99.5094024	2146.0687994
323	19.0552988	103.3659445	1969.6689572	323	20.3690942	101.4299749	2066.0367135	323	21.7731716	99.5553305	2167.6352921
324	19.2299724	103.4179467	1988.7242560	324	20.5600545	101.4786129	2086.4058077	324	21.9818311	99.6008226	2189.4084637
325	19.4062471	103.4694765	2007.9542283	325	20.7528050	101.5267991	2106.9658622	325	22.1924903	99.6458629	2211.3902948
326	19.5841377	103.5205382	2027.3604755	326	20.9473625	101.5745378	2127.7186671	326	22.4051684	99.6905155	2233.5827851
327	19.7633590	103.5711361	2046.9446132	327	21.1437440	101.6218332	2148.6660297	327	22.6198846	99.7347244	2255.9879535
328	19.9443258	103.6212744	2066.7082721	328	21.3419666	101.6686892	2169.8097737	328	22.8366585	99.7785136	2278.6078361
329	20.1276534	103.6709573	2086.6530980	329	21.5420476	101.7151100	2191.1517403	329	23.0555098	99.8218872	2301.4444926
330	20.3121569	103.7201889	2106.7807514	330	21.7440043	101.7610997	2212.6937879	330	23.2764584	99.8648491	2324.5000063
331	20.4983517	103.7689733	2127.0920803	331	21.9478543	101.8066623	2234.4377922	331	23.4995245	99.9074031	2347.7764648
332	20.6862532	103.8173146	2147.5912600	332	22.1536155	101.8518016	2256.3856465	332	23.7247282	99.9495532	2371.2759892
333	20.8758772	103.8652168	2168.2775132	333	22.3613056	101.8965217	2278.5392620	333	23.9520902	99.9913032	2395.0007175
334	21.0672394	103.9126838	2189.1533904	334	22.5709428	101.9408265	2300.9005676	334	24.1816311	100.0326569	2418.9528077
335	21.2603558	103.9597197	2210.2206299	335	22.7825454	101.9847197	2323.4715104	335	24.4133717	100.0736181	2443.1344388
336	21.4552424	104.0063284	2231.4809857	336	22.9961318	102.0282053	2346.2540559	336	24.6473332	100.1141904	2467.5478105
337	21.6519154	104.0525137	2252.9362280	337	23.2117205	102.0712870	2369.2501876	337	24.8835368	100.1543777	2492.1951437
338	21.8503913	104.0982795	2274.5881435	338	23.4293304	102.1139685	2392.4619082	338	25.1220040	100.1941834	2517.0786805
339	22.0506866	104.1436295	2296.4385348	339	23.6489804	102.1562537	2415.8912366	339	25.3627566	100.2336113	2542.2006846
340	22.2528179	104.1885677	2318.4892214	340	23.8705896	102.1981460	2439.5402190	340	25.6058163	100.2726649	2567.5634412
341	22.4568020	104.2330976	2340.7420303	341	24.0944773	102.2396493	2463.4109085	341	25.8512054	100.3113478	2593.1692575
342	22.6626561	104.2772230	2363.1988413	342	24.3203630	102.2807671	2487.5053858	342	26.0989461	100.3496636	2619.0204629
343	22.8703971	104.3209477	2385.8614974	343	24.5483664	102.3215030	2511.8257408	343	26.3490610	100.3876156	2645.1194090
344	23.0800424	104.3642752	2408.7318945	344	24.7785074	102.3618606	2536.3741153	344	26.6015729	100.4252073	2671.4684701
345	23.2916094	104.4072091	2431.8119369	345	25.0108059	102.4018433	2561.1526226	345	26.8565046	100.4624423	2698.0700429
346	23.5051159	104.4497530	2455.1035463	346	25.2452822	102.4414547	2586.1634285	346	27.1138794	100.4993237	2724.9265475
347	23.7205794	104.4919105	2478.6008622	347	25.4819567	102.4806981	2611.4087106	347	27.3737208	100.5358551	2752.0404087
348	23.9380181	104.5336851	2502.3292416	348	25.7208500	102.5195771	2636.8906673	348	27.6360523	100.5720398	2779.4141477
349	24.1574499	104.5750802	2526.2672597	349	25.9619830	102.5580950	2662.6115173	349	27.9008978	100.6078809	2807.0502000
350	24.3788932	104.6160992	2550.4247096	350	26.2053766	102.5962551	2688.5735003	350	28.1682814	100.6433818	2834.9510978
351	24.6023664	104.6567457	2574.8036028	351	26.4510520	102.6340607	2714.7788769	351	28.4382274	100.6785458	2863.1193792
352	24.6278881	104.6970230	2599.4059691	352	26.6990306	102.6715153	2741.2299289	352	28.7107604	100.7133759	2891.5576066
353	25.0554770	104.7369345	2624.2338572	353	26.9493304	102.7086220	2767.9269595	353	28.9859052	100.7478756	2920.2683670
354	25.2851523	104.7764804	2649.2893343	354	27.2019840	102.7453840	2794.8782935	354	29.2636868	100.7820475	2949.2542722
355	25.5169328	104.8156730	2674.5744865	355	27.4570026	102.7818046	2822.0802776	355	29.5441305	100.8159651	2978.5179590
356	25.7508380	104.8545067	2700.0914193	356	27.7144120	102.8178869	2849.5372802	356	29.8272617	100.8494215	3008.0620895
357	25.9868874	104.8929877	2725.8422574	357	27.9742346	102.8536340	2877.2516922	357	30.1131063	100.8826296	3037.8893512
358	26.2251005	104.9311191	2751.8291447	358	28.2364931	102.8890492	2905.2259269	358	30.4016902	100.9155226	3068.0024575
359	26.4654973	104.9689041	2778.0542453	359	28.5012102	102.9241354	2933.4624199	359	30.6930398	100.9481032	3098.4041477
360	26.7080077	105.0063459	2804.5197425	360	28.7684901	102.9588958	2961.9636302	360	30.9871814	100.9803746	3129.0971875
361	26.9529219	105.0434477	2831.2278402	361	29.0381129	102.9933333	2990.7320392	361	31.2841419	101.0123397	3160.0843689
362	27.1999903	105.0802124	2858.1807061	362	29.3113452	103.0274509	3019.7701521	362	31.5839483	101.0440014	3191.3685108
363	27.4493236	105.1166432	2885.3807524	363	29.5851297	103.0612517	3049.0804973	363	31.8866278	101.0753625	3222.9524591
364	27.7009424	105.1527430	2912.8300760	364	29.8624903	103.0947385	3078.6656270	364	32.1922079	101.1064259	3254.8390868
365	27.9545677	105.1885150	2940.5310164	365	30.1424511	103.1279143	3108.5281173	365	32.5007166	101.1371945	3287.0312948
366	28.2111206	105.2239620	2968.4858861	366	30.4250366	103.1607820	3138.6705684	366	32.8121818	101.1676709	3319.5320114
367	28.4697226	105.2590870	2996.6970067	367	30.7102713	103.1933444	3169.0956050	367	33.1266319	101.1978581	3352.3441932
368	28.7306950	105.2938930	3025.1667293	368	30.9981801	103.2256043	3199.8058763	368	33.4440944	101.2277588	3385.4708250
369	28.9940597	105.3283828	3053.8974244	369	31.2887881	103.2575647	3230.8040564	369	33.7646013	101.2573756	3418.9149205
370	29.2598386	105.3625593	3082.8914841	370	31.5821204	103.2892282	3262.0928445	370	34.0881788	101.2867113	3452.6795218
371	29.5280538	105.3964254	3112.1513227	371	31.8782028	103.3205976	3293.6749649	371	34.4148572	101.3157685	3486.7677006
372	29.7987276	105.4299833	3141.6793766	372	32.1770610	103.3516756	3325.5531678	372	34.7446662	101.3445499	3521.1825578
373	30.0718826	105.4632376	3171.4781042	373	32.4787209	103.3824650	3357.7302287	373	35.0776359	101.3730581	3555.9272240
374	30.3475416	105.4961692	3201.5499869	374	32.7832089	103.4129684	3390.2089497	374	35.4137966	101.4012957	3591.0048599
375	30.6257274	105.5288415	3231.8975284	375	33.0905515	103.4431885	3422.9921566	375	35.7531788	101.4292652	3626.4186565
376	30.9064632	105.5611922	3262.5232558	376	33.4007764	103.4731281	3456.0827101	376	36.0958135	101.4569692	3662.1718333
377	31.1897725	105.5932589	3293.4297190	377	33.7139077	103.5027893	3489.4834856	377	36.4417317	101.4844103	3698.2676488
378	31.4756787	105.6250295	3324.6194915	378	34.0299766	103.5321752	3523.1973933	378	36.7909649	101.5115909	3734.7093804
379	31.7642058	105.6565115	3356.0951702	379	34.3490066	103.5612881	3557.2273689	379	37.1435450	101.5385135	3771.5003454
380	32.0553776	105.6877075	3387.8593759	380	34.6710066	103.5901306	3591.5763755	380	37.4995040	101.5651805	3808.6438494
381	32.3492186	105.7186201	3419.9147536	381	34.9960694	103.6187052	3626.2474040	381	37.8588742	101.5915944	3846.1433944
382	32.6457531	105.7492520	3452.2639722	382	35.3241668	103.6470145	3661.2434735	382	38.2216884	101.6177575	3884.0022586
383	32.9450058	105.7796056	3484.9097253	383	35.6553216	103.6750608	3696.5676311	383	38.5879796	101.6436723	3922.2239570
384	33.2470017	105.8096835	3517.8547311	384	35.9895902	103.7028466	3732.2229526	384	38.9577611	101.6693412	3960.8119363
385	33.5517659	105.8394882	3551.1017328	385	36.3269926	103.7303743	3768.2125428	385	39.3311265	101.6947663	3999.7697177
386	33.8593238	105.8690222	3584.6534988	386	36.6675582	103.7576464	3804.5395355	386	39.7080498	101.7199501	4039.1008442
387	34.1697009	105.8982879	3618.5128225	387	37.0113165	103.7846652	3841.2070936	387	40.0885853	101.7448949	4078.8088940
388	34.4829232	105.9272877	3652.6825234	388	37.3582976	103.8114330	3878.2184102	388	40.4727675	101.7696029	4118.8974793
389	34.7990166	105.9560242	3687.1654466	389	37.7085317	103.8379522	3915.5767078	389	40.8606316	101.7940763	4159.3702468
390	35.1180076	105.9844996	3721.9644632	390	38.0620492	103.8642251	3953.2852395	390	41.2522126	101.8183174	4200.2308784
391	35.4399227	106.0127164	3757.0824708	391	38.4188809	103.8902539	3991.3472886	391	41.6475463	101.8423284	4241.4830910
392	35.7647886	106.0406768	3792.5223935	392	38.7790579	103.9160401	4029.7661695	392	42.0466686	101.8661115	4283.1306374
393	36.0926325	106.0683893	3828.2871821	393	39.1426115	103.9415886	4068.5452274	393	42.4496159	101.8896689	4325.1773060
394	36.4234817	106.0958381	3864.3798147	394	39.5095735	103.9668990	4107.6878389	394	42.8564247	101.9130026	4367.6269219
395	36.7573636	106.1230436	3900.8032963	395	39.8799758	103.9919742	4147.1974124	395	43.2671321	101.9361148	4410.4833466
396	37.0943061	106.1500019	3937.5606599	396	40.2538505	104.0168166	4187.0773882	396	43.6817755	101.9590077	4453.7504787
397	37.4343372	106.1767153	3974.6549660	397	40.6312304	104.0414282	4227.3312387	397	44.1003925	101.9816832	4497.4322542
398	37.7774853	106.2031861	4012.0893032	398	41.0121482	104.0658112	4267.9624691	398	44.5230212	102.0041435	4541.5326466
399	38.1237789	106.2294165	4049.8667885	399	41.3966371	104.0899677	4308.9746173	399	44.9497002	102.0263906	4586.0556679
400	38.4732469	106.2554085	4087.9905675	400	41.7847305	104.1138999	4350.3712544	400	45.3804681	102.0484265	4631.0053681

Table 1

M	C(11.00,M,12)	A(11.00,M,12)	S(11.00,M,12)	C(11.25,M,12)	A(11.25,M,12)	S(11.25,M,12)	C(11.50,M,12)	A(11.50,M,12)	S(11.50,M,12)
401	38.8259183	106.2811645	4126.4638144	42.1764624	104.1376098	4392.1559849	45.8153643	102.0702532	4676.3858362
402	39.1818226	106.3066866	4165.2897327	42.5716667	104.1610995	4434.3324473	46.2544282	102.0918728	4722.2012005
403	39.5409893	106.3319768	4204.4715553	42.9709780	104.1843710	4476.9043141	46.6976998	102.1132871	4768.4556287
404	39.9034484	106.3570373	4244.0125446	43.3738309	104.2074264	4519.8752921	47.1452194	102.1344982	4815.1533285
405	40.2692300	106.3818701	4283.9159929	43.7804606	104.2302677	4563.2491230	47.5970278	102.1555079	4862.2985480
406	40.6383646	106.4064774	4324.1852229	44.1909024	104.2528968	4607.0295835	48.0531660	102.1763182	4909.8955758
407	41.0113829	106.4308612	4364.8235375	44.6051921	104.2753157	4651.2204859	48.5138755	102.1969309	4957.9487417
408	41.3868160	106.4550235	4405.8344704	45.0233658	104.2975264	4695.8256780	48.9785982	102.2173480	5006.4624172
409	41.7661952	106.4789663	4447.2212864	45.4454598	104.3195308	4740.8490438	49.4479764	102.2375713	5055.4410154
410	42.1490520	106.5026916	4488.9874816	45.8715110	104.3413508	4786.2945036	49.9218529	102.2576026	5104.8889919
411	42.5354183	106.5262014	4531.1365335	46.3015564	104.3629283	4832.1660146	50.4002706	102.2774437	5154.8108447
412	42.9253263	106.5494977	4573.6719518	46.7356335	104.3843253	4878.4675710	50.8832732	102.2970966	5205.2111154
413	43.3188084	106.5725824	4616.5972781	47.1737801	104.4055235	4925.2032045	51.3709046	102.3165628	5256.0943886
414	43.7158975	106.5954573	4659.9160865	47.6160343	104.4265248	4972.3769846	51.8632091	102.3358443	5307.4652932
415	44.1166266	106.6181245	4703.6319840	48.0624346	104.4473311	5019.9930189	52.3602315	102.3549428	5359.3285023
416	44.5210290	106.6405858	4747.7486105	48.5130199	104.4679441	5068.0554535	52.8620171	102.3738600	5411.6887338
417	44.9291384	106.6628431	4792.2696395	48.9678295	104.4883657	5116.5684734	53.3686114	102.3925976	5464.5507509
418	45.3409888	106.6848982	4837.1987779	49.4269029	104.5085976	5165.5363029	53.8800606	102.4111573	5517.9193623
419	45.7566146	106.7067530	4882.5397668	49.8902801	104.5286416	5214.9632058	54.3984112	102.4295409	5571.7994229
420	46.1760502	106.7284092	4928.2963813	50.3580015	104.5484994	5264.8534859	54.9177101	102.4477499	5626.1958341
421	46.5993307	106.7498687	4974.4724315	50.8301077	104.5681728	5315.2114874	55.4440048	102.4657862	5681.1135442
422	47.0264912	106.7711333	5021.0717622	51.3066400	104.5876634	5366.0415951	55.9753432	102.4836512	5736.5575491
423	47.4575674	106.7922048	5068.0982534	51.7876397	104.6069730	5417.3482351	56.5117736	102.5013466	5792.5328923
424	47.8925951	106.8130849	5115.5558208	52.2731489	104.6261033	5469.1358748	57.0533448	102.5188740	5849.0446659
425	48.3316105	106.8337752	5163.4484158	52.7632096	104.6450559	5521.4090237	57.6001060	102.5362351	5906.0980107
426	48.7746503	106.8542777	5211.7800263	53.2578647	104.6638325	5574.1722334	58.1521070	102.5534314	5963.6981167
427	49.2217512	106.8745939	5260.5546766	53.7571572	104.6824347	5627.4300981	58.7093980	102.5704645	6021.8502237
428	49.6729506	106.8947256	5309.7764279	54.2611306	104.7008641	5681.1872553	59.2720298	102.5873358	6080.5596217
429	50.1282860	106.9146744	5359.4493785	54.7698287	104.7191223	5735.4483859	59.8400534	102.6040470	6139.8316515
430	50.5877953	106.9344420	5409.5776645	55.2832958	104.7372109	5790.2182145	60.4135206	102.6205996	6199.6717048
431	51.0515168	106.9540301	5460.1654598	55.8015797	104.7551316	5845.5015103	60.9924835	102.6369951	6260.0852254
432	51.5194890	106.9734402	5511.2169766	56.3247165	104.7728858	5901.3030871	61.5769948	102.6532349	6321.0777088
433	51.9917510	106.9926740	5562.7364656	56.8527607	104.7904751	5957.6278035	62.1671076	102.6693206	6382.6547036
434	52.4683420	107.0117332	5614.7282166	57.3857553	104.8079010	6014.4805643	62.7628757	102.6852536	6444.8218112
435	52.9493018	107.0306191	5667.1965586	57.9237468	104.8251651	6071.8663196	63.3643533	102.7010353	6507.5846870
436	53.4346704	107.0493336	5720.1458604	58.4667819	104.8422688	6129.7900664	63.9715950	102.7166673	6570.9490403
437	53.9244882	107.0678780	5773.5805309	59.0149080	104.8592137	6188.2568483	64.5846561	102.7321508	6634.9206353
438	54.4187961	107.0862540	5827.5050191	59.5681728	104.8760012	6247.2717563	65.2035924	102.7474874	6699.5052915
439	54.9176350	107.1044631	5881.9238152	60.1266244	104.8926327	6306.8399291	65.8284602	102.7626784	6764.7088839
440	55.4210467	107.1225068	5936.8414502	60.6903115	104.9091098	6366.9665535	66.4593163	102.7777252	6830.5373441
441	55.9290729	107.1403866	5992.2624969	61.2592832	104.9254339	6427.6568650	67.0962181	102.7926292	6896.9956604
442	56.4417561	107.1581040	6048.1915698	61.8335889	104.9416063	6488.9161481	67.7392235	102.8073917	6964.0928784
443	56.9591389	107.1756604	6104.6333259	62.4132788	104.9576286	6550.7497371	68.3883910	102.8220140	7031.8321019
444	57.4812643	107.1930574	6161.5924648	62.9984033	104.9735020	6613.1630159	69.0437798	102.8364976	7100.2204929
445	58.0081759	107.2102963	6219.0737291	63.5890134	104.9892280	6676.1614192	69.7054493	102.8508437	7169.2642727
446	58.5399175	107.2273787	6277.0819050	64.1851604	105.0048079	6739.7504326	70.3734599	102.8650536	7238.9697220
447	59.0765334	107.2443059	6335.6218225	64.7868962	105.0202431	6803.9355930	71.0478722	102.8791286	7309.3431819
448	59.6180683	107.2610793	6394.6983559	65.3942734	105.0355350	6868.7224892	71.7287477	102.8930700	7380.3910542
449	60.1645673	107.2777004	6454.3164243	66.0073447	105.0506848	6934.1167626	72.4161482	102.9068791	7452.1198018
450	60.7160758	107.2941705	6514.4809915	66.6261636	105.0656939	7000.1241073	73.1101363	102.9205571	7524.5359096
451	61.2726398	107.3104910	6575.1970673	67.2507838	105.0805636	7066.7502709	73.8107751	102.9341052	7597.6460662
452	61.8343057	107.3266633	6636.4697072	67.8812599	105.0952952	7134.0010547	74.5181283	102.9475248	7671.4568613
453	62.4011202	107.3426886	6698.3040129	68.5176468	105.1098900	7201.8823147	75.2322604	102.9608169	7745.9749896
454	62.9731304	107.3585684	6760.7051331	69.1599997	105.1243492	7270.3999614	75.9532362	102.9739829	7821.2072500
455	63.5503841	107.3743040	6823.6782635	69.8083747	105.1386742	7339.5599611	76.6811214	102.9870240	7897.1604862
456	64.1329293	107.3896966	6887.2286476	70.4628282	105.1528660	7409.3683358	77.4159821	102.9999412	7973.8416076
457	64.7208145	107.4053476	6951.3615370	71.1234172	105.1669261	7479.8311640	78.1578853	103.0127358	8051.2575897
458	65.3140886	107.4206582	7016.0823915	71.7901993	105.1808556	7550.9545813	78.9068984	103.0254090	8129.4154750
459	65.9128011	107.4358297	7081.3964801	72.4632324	105.1946557	7622.7447805	79.6630895	103.0379618	8208.3223734
460	66.5170018	107.4508635	7147.3092812	73.1425752	105.2083276	7695.2080129	80.4285274	103.0503955	8287.9856429
461	67.1287410	107.4657607	7213.8262931	73.8282868	105.2218788	7768.3505861	81.1972816	103.0627112	8368.4119903
462	67.7420694	107.4805226	7280.9530240	74.5204270	105.2352917	7842.1788749	81.9754223	103.0749100	8449.6092719
463	68.3630384	107.4951504	7348.6950905	75.2190560	105.2485862	7916.6993019	82.7610201	103.0869930	8531.5846942
464	68.9896996	107.5096453	7417.0581319	75.9242347	105.2617572	7991.9183579	83.5541465	103.0989963	8614.3457143
465	69.6221052	107.5240085	7486.0478315	76.6360244	105.2748059	8067.8425926	84.3548737	103.1108160	8697.8998608
466	70.2603078	107.5382413	7555.6699367	77.3544871	105.2877334	8144.4786170	85.1632746	103.1225581	8782.2547345
467	70.9043606	107.5523448	7625.9302445	78.0796854	105.3005409	8221.8331041	85.9794227	103.1341888	8867.4180091
468	71.5543173	107.5663202	7696.8346052	78.8116825	105.3132293	8299.9127895	86.8033921	103.1457091	8953.3974318
469	72.2102319	107.5801687	7768.3889224	79.5505420	105.3257999	8378.7244720	87.6352580	103.1571200	9040.2008239
470	72.8721590	107.5938913	7840.5991543	80.2963283	105.3382538	8458.2750140	88.4750959	103.1684226	9127.8360819
471	73.5401538	107.6074893	7913.4713133	81.0491066	105.3505920	8538.5713423	89.3229822	103.1796180	9216.3111777
472	74.2142718	107.6209638	7987.0114670	81.8089418	105.3628156	8619.6204487	90.1789941	103.1907070	9305.6341559
473	74.8945693	107.6343159	8061.2257389	82.5759006	105.3749257	8701.4293905	91.0432095	103.2016908	9395.8131540
474	75.5811029	107.6475468	8136.1203082	83.3500497	105.3869233	8784.0052911	91.9157069	103.2125703	9486.8563635
475	76.2739297	107.6606574	8211.7014111	84.1314564	105.3988094	8867.3553408	92.7965658	103.2234466	9578.7720704
476	76.9731074	107.6736490	8287.9753408	84.9201688	105.4105852	8951.4867972	93.6858662	103.2340206	9671.5686362
477	77.6786942	107.6865225	8364.9484580	85.7163156	105.4222516	9036.4069860	94.5836891	103.2445932	9765.2545023
478	78.3907489	107.6992791	8442.6271423	86.5199060	105.4338096	9122.1233015	95.4901161	103.2550655	9859.8381914
479	79.1093307	107.7119198	8521.4778392	87.3310301	105.4452603	9208.6432076	96.4052297	103.2654384	9955.3283075
480	79.8344996	107.7244458	8600.1272219	88.1497586	105.4566046	9295.9742377	97.3291131	103.2757128	10051.7335422
481	80.5663159	107.7368575	8679.9617215	88.9761625	105.4678436	9384.1239963	98.2618505	103.2858897	10149.0626503
482	81.3048404	107.7491573	8760.5280374	89.8103141	105.4789782	9473.1001588	99.2035266	103.2959700	10247.3245008
483	82.0501348	107.7613449	8841.8328778	90.6522858	105.4900094	9562.9104729	100.1542270	103.3059546	10346.5280274
484	82.8022610	107.7734219	8923.8830126	91.5021500	105.5009381	9653.5627586	101.1140384	103.3159444	10446.6822544
485	83.5612817	107.7853892	9006.6852736	92.3599836	105.5117653	9745.0649096	102.0830479	103.3256404	10547.7962927
486	84.3272602	107.7972477	9090.2465554	93.2258585	105.5224919	9837.4248932	103.0613438	103.3353433	10649.8793406
487	85.1002601	107.8089986	9174.5738155	94.0998509	105.5331189	9930.6507516	104.0490150	103.3449150	10752.9406844
488	85.8803458	107.8206427	9259.6740756	94.9820370	105.5436472	10024.7506025	105.0461514	103.3544738	10856.9896994
489	86.6675823	107.8321810	9345.5544214	95.8724936	105.5540777	10119.7326395	106.0528437	103.3639021	10962.0358508
490	87.4620351	107.8436146	9432.2220036	96.7712982	105.5644114	10215.6051331	107.0691834	103.3732428	11068.0866944
491	88.2637704	107.8549442	9519.6840387	97.6785291	105.5746490	10312.3764313	108.0952631	103.3824939	11175.1578778
492	89.0728550	107.8661707	9607.9478092	98.5942653	105.5847916	10410.0549604	109.1311760	103.3916572	11283.2531409
493	89.8893562	107.8772958	9697.0206642	99.5185866	105.5948400	10508.6492258	110.1770165	103.4007335	11392.3843170
494	90.7133419	107.8883195	9786.9100203	100.4515733	105.6047950	10608.1678123	111.2328795	103.4097236	11502.5613334
495	91.5448809	107.8992431	9877.6233623	101.3933068	105.6146576	10708.6193057	112.2988613	103.4186285	11613.7942130
496	92.3840423	107.9100675	9969.1682432	102.3438691	105.6244286	10810.0126925	113.3750587	103.4274487	11726.0930743
497	93.2308960	107.9207936	10061.5522855	103.3033429	105.6341088	10912.3565616	114.4615697	103.4361853	11839.4681330
498	94.0855126	107.9314222	10154.7831815	104.2718117	105.6436991	11015.6599044	115.5584931	103.4448389	11953.9297027
499	94.9479631	107.9419543	10248.8686941	105.2493599	105.6532004	11119.9317161	116.6659286	103.4534104	12069.4881958
500	95.8183194	107.9523907	10343.8166572	106.2360727	105.6626134	11225.1810761	117.7839771	103.4619005	12180.1541244

Table 1 433

M	C(11.75,M,12)	A(11.75,M,12)	S(11.75,M,12)	M	C(12.00,M,12)	A(12.00,M,12)	S(12.00,M,12)	M	C(12.25,M,12)	A(12.25,M,12)	S(12.25,M,12)
1	1.0097917	.9903033	1.0000000	1	1.0100000	.9900990	1.0000000	1	1.0102083	.9898948	1.0000000
2	1.0196792	1.9710039	2.0097917	2	1.0201000	1.9703951	2.0100000	2	1.0205209	1.9697866	2.0102083
3	1.0295636	2.9421949	3.0294709	3	1.0303010	2.9409852	3.0301000	3	1.0309387	2.9397764	3.0307292
4	1.0397457	3.9039685	4.0591344	4	1.0406040	3.9019656	4.0604010	4	1.0414629	3.8999642	4.0616679
5	1.0499265	4.8564161	5.0988801	5	1.0510101	4.8534312	5.1010050	5	1.0520945	4.8504492	5.1031308
6	1.0602071	5.7996281	6.1488067	6	1.0615202	5.7954765	6.1520151	6	1.0628346	5.7913294	6.1552252
7	1.0705883	6.7336940	7.2090137	7	1.0721354	6.7281945	7.2135352	7	1.0736844	6.7227018	7.2180598
8	1.0810711	7.6587025	8.2796020	8	1.0828567	7.6516778	8.2856706	8	1.0846449	7.6446628	8.2917442
9	1.0916566	8.5747415	9.3606731	9	1.0936853	8.5660176	9.3685273	9	1.0957173	8.5573067	9.3763891
10	1.1023457	9.4818979	10.4523297	10	1.1046221	9.4713045	10.4622125	10	1.1069028	9.4607285	10.4721064
11	1.1131395	10.3802579	11.5546754	11	1.1156683	10.3676282	11.5668347	11	1.1182024	10.3550209	11.5790091
12	1.1240390	11.2699067	12.6678149	12	1.1268250	11.2550775	12.6825030	12	1.1296174	11.2402765	12.6972115
13	1.1350452	12.1509289	13.7918540	13	1.1380933	12.1337401	13.8093260	13	1.1411489	12.1165863	13.8268289
14	1.1461592	13.0234080	14.9268992	14	1.1494742	13.0037030	14.9474213	14	1.1527981	12.9840409	14.9679778
15	1.1573820	13.8874270	16.0730584	15	1.1609690	13.8650525	16.0968955	15	1.1645663	13.8427297	16.1207759
16	1.1687147	14.7430678	17.2304405	16	1.1725786	14.7178738	17.2578645	16	1.1764545	14.6927413	17.2853421
17	1.1801584	15.5904117	18.3991552	17	1.1843044	15.5622513	18.4304431	17	1.1884642	15.5341634	18.4617936
18	1.1917141	16.4295391	19.5793136	18	1.1951475	16.3982686	19.6147476	18	1.2005964	16.3670827	19.6502608
19	1.2033830	17.2605297	20.7710277	19	1.2071090	17.2260085	20.8108950	19	1.2123525	17.1915853	20.8508572
20	1.2151661	18.0834625	21.9744107	20	1.2201900	18.0455530	22.0190040	20	1.2252337	18.0077561	22.0637097
21	1.2270646	18.8984155	23.1895768	21	1.2323919	18.8569831	23.2391940	21	1.2377411	18.8156794	23.2889434
22	1.2390796	19.7054662	24.4166414	22	1.2447159	19.6603793	24.4715860	22	1.2503766	19.6154385	24.5266847
23	1.2512123	20.5046911	25.6557210	23	1.2571630	20.4558221	25.7163018	23	1.2631408	20.4071158	25.7770613
24	1.2634637	21.2961661	26.9069333	24	1.2697346	21.2433873	26.9734649	24	1.2760354	21.1907931	27.0402021
25	1.2758351	22.0799864	28.1703970	25	1.2824320	22.0231557	28.2431995	25	1.2890616	21.9665513	28.3162375
26	1.2883277	22.8561665	29.4462321	26	1.2952563	22.7952037	29.5256315	26	1.3022208	22.7344702	29.6052991
27	1.3009426	23.6248399	30.7345598	27	1.3082089	23.5596076	30.8208878	27	1.3155143	23.4946292	30.9075199
28	1.3136810	24.3860597	32.0355024	28	1.3212910	24.3164432	32.1290967	28	1.3289435	24.2471067	32.2230342
29	1.3265441	25.1396982	33.3491833	29	1.3345039	25.0657853	33.4503877	29	1.3425098	24.9919802	33.5519776
30	1.3395332	25.8864270	34.6757274	30	1.3478489	25.8077082	34.7848915	30	1.3562146	25.7293267	34.8944874
31	1.3526494	26.6257168	36.0152606	31	1.3613274	26.5422854	36.1327405	31	1.3700592	26.4592221	36.2507020
32	1.3658941	27.3578380	37.3679100	32	1.3749407	27.2695895	37.4940679	32	1.3840453	27.1817418	37.6207612
33	1.3792685	28.0828600	38.7338041	33	1.3886901	27.9896925	38.8690085	33	1.3981741	27.8969603	39.0048065
34	1.3927738	28.8008516	40.1130726	34	1.4025770	28.7026659	40.2576986	34	1.4124471	28.6049515	40.4029806
35	1.4064114	29.5118811	41.5058465	35	1.4166028	29.4085801	41.6602756	35	1.4268658	29.3057882	41.8154276
36	1.4201825	30.2160160	42.9122579	36	1.4307688	30.1075050	43.0768784	36	1.4414317	29.9995429	43.2422935
37	1.4340885	30.9133230	44.3324404	37	1.4450765	30.7995099	44.5076471	37	1.4561464	30.6862870	44.6837252
38	1.4481306	31.6038685	45.7665289	38	1.4595272	31.4846633	45.9527236	38	1.4710112	31.3660915	46.1398716
39	1.4623102	32.2877179	47.2146595	39	1.4741225	32.1630330	47.4122509	39	1.4860278	32.0390264	47.6108828
40	1.4766287	32.9649362	48.6769597	40	1.4888637	32.8346861	48.8863734	40	1.5011976	32.7051613	49.0969105
41	1.4910873	33.6355878	50.1535984	41	1.5037524	33.4996892	50.3752371	41	1.5165224	33.3645647	50.5981082
42	1.5056875	34.2997362	51.6446857	42	1.5187899	34.1581081	51.8789895	42	1.5320035	34.0173047	52.1146305
43	1.5204307	34.9574446	53.1503732	43	1.5339778	34.8100081	53.3977794	43	1.5476427	34.6634485	53.6466340
44	1.5353183	35.6087753	54.6708040	44	1.5493176	35.4554535	54.9317572	44	1.5634416	35.3030632	55.1942768
45	1.5503516	36.2537903	56.2061223	45	1.5648107	36.0945084	56.4810747	45	1.5794017	35.9362143	56.7577183
46	1.5655321	36.8925507	57.7564739	46	1.5804589	36.7272361	58.0458655	46	1.5955248	36.5629674	58.3371200
47	1.5808613	37.5251173	59.3220060	47	1.5962634	37.3536991	59.6263443	47	1.6118124	37.1833870	59.9326448
48	1.5963406	38.1515500	60.9028673	48	1.6122261	37.9739595	61.2226078	48	1.6282663	37.7975371	61.5444572
49	1.6119714	38.7719084	62.4992079	49	1.6283463	38.5880787	62.8348339	49	1.6448882	38.4054812	63.1727236
50	1.6277553	39.3862514	64.1111793	50	1.6446318	39.1961175	64.4631822	50	1.6616798	39.0072818	64.8176118
51	1.6436937	39.9946372	65.7389346	51	1.6610781	39.7981362	66.1078140	51	1.6786428	39.6030012	66.4792916
52	1.6597882	40.5971237	67.3826283	52	1.6776889	40.3941942	67.7688922	52	1.6957789	40.1927007	68.1579343
53	1.6760403	41.1937680	69.0424166	53	1.6944658	40.9843507	69.4465811	53	1.7130900	40.7764412	69.8537132
54	1.6924516	41.7846269	70.7184569	54	1.7114105	41.5686641	71.1410469	54	1.7305778	41.3542829	71.5668032
55	1.7090235	42.3697564	72.4109085	55	1.7285246	42.1471921	72.8524574	55	1.7482441	41.9262854	73.2973810
56	1.7257577	42.9492120	74.1199319	56	1.7458098	42.7199922	74.5809819	56	1.7660908	42.4925077	75.0456251
57	1.7426557	43.5230488	75.8456896	57	1.7632679	43.2871210	76.3267918	57	1.7841196	43.0530083	76.8117159
58	1.7597192	44.0913225	77.5883453	58	1.7809006	43.8486347	78.0900597	58	1.8023325	43.6078448	78.5958355
59	1.7769498	44.6540834	79.3480645	59	1.7987096	44.4045888	79.8709603	59	1.8207313	44.1570747	80.3981650
60	1.7943491	45.2113386	81.1250143	60	1.8166967	44.9550384	81.6696599	60	1.8393179	44.7007545	82.2188993
61	1.8119188	45.7632897	82.9193634	61	1.8348637	45.5000380	83.4863566	61	1.8580943	45.2389403	84.0582172
62	1.8296605	46.3098392	84.7312822	62	1.8532123	46.0396416	85.3212202	62	1.8770622	45.7716877	85.9163115
63	1.8475759	46.8510089	86.5609427	63	1.8717444	46.5739026	87.1744425	63	1.8962240	46.2990515	87.7933738
64	1.8656667	47.3870903	88.4085186	64	1.8904619	47.1028738	89.0461870	64	1.9155813	46.8210863	89.6895979
65	1.8839347	47.9178943	90.2741053	65	1.9093665	47.6266078	90.9366488	65	1.9351362	47.3378458	91.6051792
66	1.9023816	48.4435512	92.1581201	66	1.9284602	48.1451562	92.8460153	66	1.9548907	47.8493883	93.5403154
67	1.9210091	48.9641109	94.0605016	67	1.9477448	48.6585705	94.7744755	67	1.9748469	48.3557517	95.4952061
68	1.9398190	49.4796229	95.9815107	68	1.9672222	49.1669015	96.7222202	68	1.9950068	48.8570031	97.4700530
69	1.9588130	49.9901362	97.9213297	69	1.9868944	49.6701995	98.6894424	69	2.0153725	49.3531693	99.4650598
70	1.9779931	50.4956091	99.8801427	70	2.0067634	50.1685143	100.6763359	70	2.0359461	49.8443614	101.4804323
71	1.9973609	50.9963598	101.8581358	71	2.0268310	50.6618954	102.6831002	71	2.0567297	50.3305702	103.5163784
72	2.0169184	51.4921657	103.8554967	72	2.0470901	51.1503915	104.7099312	72	2.0777255	50.8118657	105.5731081
73	2.0366674	51.9831638	105.8724151	73	2.0675703	51.6340510	106.7570306	73	2.0989356	51.2882977	107.6508335
74	2.0566098	52.4694900	107.9090825	74	2.0882461	52.1129217	108.8246009	74	2.1203622	51.7599152	109.7497691
75	2.0767474	52.9509232	109.9656923	75	2.1091285	52.5870501	110.9128469	75	2.1420076	52.2267670	111.8701314
76	2.0970822	53.4277762	112.0424397	76	2.1302298	53.0564464	113.0219753	76	2.1638739	52.6889011	114.0121390
77	2.1176162	53.9000053	114.1395219	77	2.1515220	53.5212736	115.1521951	77	2.1859635	53.1463653	116.1760129
78	2.1383511	54.3676554	116.2571380	78	2.1730372	53.9814590	117.3037170	78	2.2082785	53.5992067	118.3619763
79	2.1592892	54.8307707	118.3954892	79	2.1947675	54.4370882	119.4767542	79	2.2308214	54.0474721	120.5702548
80	2.1804322	55.2893954	120.5547783	80	2.2167152	54.8882061	121.6715218	80	2.2535943	54.4912077	122.8010762
81	2.2017823	55.7435729	122.7352105	81	2.2388824	55.3348575	123.8882370	81	2.2765998	54.9304593	125.0546705
82	2.2233414	56.1933464	124.9369928	82	2.2612712	55.7770866	126.1271194	82	2.2998401	55.3652721	127.3312703
83	2.2451116	56.6387585	127.1603342	83	2.2838839	56.2149373	128.3883905	83	2.3233176	55.7956911	129.6311103
84	2.2670950	57.0798517	129.4054458	84	2.3067227	56.6484527	130.6722745	84	2.3470348	56.2217606	131.9544279
85	2.2892936	57.5166676	131.6725408	85	2.3297900	57.0776760	132.9789972	85	2.3709941	56.6435246	134.3014627
86	2.3117096	57.9492479	133.9618344	86	2.3530879	57.5026495	135.3087872	86	2.3951980	57.0610267	136.6724568
87	2.3343451	58.3776336	136.2735441	87	2.3766188	57.9234153	137.6618750	87	2.4196490	57.4743097	139.0676548
88	2.3572022	58.8018653	138.6078892	88	2.4003849	58.3400152	140.0384938	88	2.4443496	57.8834165	141.4873038
89	2.3802832	59.2219834	140.9650914	89	2.4243888	58.7524903	142.4388707	89	2.4693023	58.2883892	143.9316533
90	2.4035901	59.6380277	143.3453746	90	2.4486327	59.1608815	144.8632675	90	2.4945098	58.6892696	146.4009556
91	2.4271253	60.0500377	145.7489648	91	2.4731190	59.5652292	147.3119002	91	2.5199745	59.0860990	148.8954654
92	2.4503909	60.4580527	148.1760900	92	2.4978502	59.9655734	149.7850192	92	2.5455993	59.4789184	151.4154399
93	2.4748892	60.8621111	150.6269809	93	2.5228287	60.3619539	152.2828694	93	2.5716866	59.8677682	153.9611392
94	2.4996225	61.2622516	153.1018701	94	2.5480570	60.7544098	154.8056981	94	2.5979393	60.2526887	156.5328259
95	2.5235931	61.6587120	155.6009926	95	2.5735376	61.1429800	157.3537551	95	2.6244599	60.6337195	159.1307651
96	2.5483032	62.0509300	158.1245856	96	2.5992729	61.5277030	159.9272926	96	2.6512513	61.0108999	161.7552250
97	2.5732554	62.4395428	160.6728889	97	2.6252657	61.9086168	162.5265656	97	2.6783161	61.3842688	164.4064763
98	2.5984518	62.8243873	163.2461442	98	2.6515183	62.2857592	165.1518312	98	2.7056573	61.7538648	167.0847924
99	2.6238950	63.2055001	165.8445961	99	2.6780335	62.6591675	167.8033495	99	2.7332775	62.1197259	169.7904496
100	2.6495873	63.5829174	168.4684911	100	2.7048138	63.0288787	170.4813830	100	2.7611797	62.4818899	172.5237271

M	C(11.75,M,12)	A(11.75,M,12)	S(11.75,M,12)	C(12.00,M,12)	A(12.00,M,12)	S(12.00,M,12)	C(12.25,M,12)	A(12.25,M,12)	S(12.25,M,12)
101	2.6755312	63.9566750	171.1180784	2.7318620	63.3949295	173.1861969	2.7893688	62.8403943	175.2849069
102	2.7017291	64.3268083	173.7936096	2.7591806	63.7573559	175.9180588	2.8178415	63.1952758	178.0742736
103	2.7281835	64.6933526	176.4953387	2.7867724	64.1161940	178.6772394	2.8466070	63.5465712	180.8921152
104	2.7548970	65.0563425	179.2235222	2.8146401	64.4714792	181.4640118	2.8756661	63.8943167	183.7387222
105	2.7818720	65.4158127	181.9784192	2.8427865	64.8232467	184.2786519	2.9050219	64.2385482	186.6143083
106	2.8091112	65.7717972	184.7602912	2.8712144	65.1715314	187.1214385	2.9346773	64.5793012	189.5194102
107	2.8365171	66.1243298	187.5694724	2.8999265	65.5163677	189.9926528	2.9646355	64.9166108	192.4540875
108	2.8643923	66.4734440	190.4060195	2.9289258	65.8577898	192.8925754	2.9948995	65.2505118	195.4187230
109	2.8924394	66.8191729	193.2704117	2.9582151	66.1958315	195.8215052	3.0254724	65.5810387	198.4136224
110	2.9207613	67.1615494	196.1628512	2.9877972	66.5305262	198.7797202	3.0563574	65.9082256	201.4390948
111	2.9493604	67.5006060	199.0836124	3.0176752	66.8619072	201.7675174	3.0875577	66.2321062	204.4954523
112	2.9782395	67.8363748	202.0329728	3.0478519	67.1900071	204.7851926	3.1190766	66.5527139	207.5830100
113	3.0074015	68.1688878	205.0112123	3.0783304	67.5148585	207.8330445	3.1509171	66.8700818	210.7020866
114	3.0368489	68.4981765	208.0186138	3.1091138	67.8364936	210.9113750	3.1830827	67.1842426	213.8530037
115	3.0665847	68.8242721	211.0554627	3.1402049	68.1549441	214.0204887	3.2155767	67.4952289	217.0360865
116	3.0966117	69.1472057	214.1220475	3.1716069	68.4702417	217.1606936	3.2484024	67.8030725	220.2516632
117	3.1269327	69.4670080	217.2186592	3.2033230	68.7824175	220.3323005	3.2815632	68.1078053	223.5000656
118	3.1575506	69.7837091	220.3455919	3.2353562	69.0915025	223.5356236	3.3150625	68.4094587	226.7816287
119	3.1884683	70.0973394	223.5031425	3.2677098	69.3975272	226.7709798	3.3489037	68.7080639	230.0966912
120	3.2196887	70.4079284	226.6916108	3.3003869	69.7005220	230.0386896	3.3830905	69.0036517	233.4455949
121	3.2512148	70.7155057	229.9112994	3.3333908	70.0005168	233.3390765	3.4176262	69.2962524	236.8286854
122	3.2830496	71.0201006	233.1625143	3.3667247	70.2975414	236.6724673	3.4525144	69.5858964	240.2463115
123	3.3151961	71.3217419	236.4455639	3.4003919	70.5916252	240.0391919	3.4877589	69.8726135	243.6988260
124	3.3476574	71.6204582	239.7607600	3.4343958	70.8827972	243.4395839	3.5233631	70.1564332	247.1865848
125	3.3804366	71.9162780	243.1084175	3.4687398	71.1710863	246.8739797	3.5593307	70.4373849	250.7099479
126	3.4135367	72.2092293	246.4888541	3.5034272	71.4565211	250.3427195	3.5958656	70.7154975	254.2692786
127	3.4469609	72.4993399	249.9023908	3.5384615	71.7391298	253.8461467	3.6323713	70.9907998	257.8649442
128	3.4807124	72.7866374	253.3493517	3.5733461	72.0189404	257.3846082	3.6694518	71.2633200	261.4973155
129	3.5147944	73.0711491	256.8300641	3.6085845	72.2959806	260.9584542	3.7069108	71.5330865	265.1667672
130	3.5492101	73.3529019	260.3448584	3.6456804	72.5702778	264.5680388	3.7447521	71.8001268	268.8736780
131	3.5839628	73.6319227	263.8940685	3.6821372	72.8418592	268.2137192	3.7829790	72.0646487	272.6184301
132	3.6190557	73.9082378	267.4780313	3.7189586	73.1107517	271.8958564	3.8215977	72.3261394	276.4014099
133	3.6544923	74.1818737	271.0970870	3.7561482	73.3769819	275.6148149	3.8606099	72.5851658	280.2230076
134	3.6902759	74.4528561	274.7515793	3.7937096	73.6405761	279.3709631	3.9000203	72.8415747	284.0836175
135	3.7264098	74.7212109	278.4416552	3.8316467	73.9015605	283.1646727	3.9393330	73.0953926	287.9836378
136	3.7628976	74.9869636	282.1682650	3.8699632	74.1599609	286.9963195	3.9800521	73.3466465	291.9234708
137	3.7997426	75.2501393	285.9311626	3.9065628	74.4158029	290.8662826	4.0206818	73.5953596	295.9035229
138	3.8369484	75.5107631	289.7309053	3.9477495	74.6691118	294.7749455	4.0617263	73.8415604	299.9242047
139	3.8745186	75.7688596	293.5678537	3.9872270	74.9199126	298.7226949	4.1031897	74.0852732	303.9859309
140	3.9124566	76.0244535	297.4423723	4.0270992	75.1682303	302.7099219	4.1450764	74.3265233	308.0891206
141	3.9507660	76.2775690	301.3548289	4.0673707	75.4140894	306.7370211	4.1873908	74.5653355	312.2341971
142	3.9894506	76.5282301	305.3055949	4.1080439	75.6575143	310.8043913	4.2301370	74.8017344	316.4215878
143	4.0285140	76.7764606	309.2950455	4.1491244	75.8985290	314.9124352	4.2733197	75.0357445	320.6517249
144	4.0679599	77.0222840	313.3235595	4.1906156	76.1371574	319.0615596	4.3169432	75.2673899	324.9250446
145	4.1077920	77.2657238	317.3915194	4.2325218	76.3734232	323.2521752	4.3610120	75.4966945	329.2419877
146	4.1480141	77.5068030	321.4993113	4.2748470	76.6073497	327.4846969	4.4055306	75.7236819	333.6029997
147	4.1886301	77.7455446	325.6473254	4.3175954	76.8389601	331.7595439	4.4505037	75.9483756	338.0085303
148	4.2296437	77.9819711	329.8359555	4.3607714	77.0682773	336.0771394	4.4959360	76.1707987	342.4550341
149	4.2710590	78.2161051	334.0655992	4.4043791	77.2953241	340.4379108	4.5418320	76.3909741	346.9549700
150	4.3128798	78.4479687	338.3366582	4.4484229	77.5201229	344.8422899	4.5881965	76.6089247	351.4968020
151	4.3551101	78.6775841	342.6495380	4.4929071	77.7426959	349.2907128	4.6350344	76.8246728	356.0849986
152	4.3977538	78.9049729	347.0046460	4.5378362	77.9630652	353.7836199	4.6823503	77.0384308	360.7200329
153	4.4408152	79.1301567	351.4024019	4.5832146	78.1812527	358.3214561	4.7301493	77.2496506	365.4023033
154	4.4842982	79.3531571	355.8432171	4.6290467	78.3972799	362.9046707	4.7784363	77.4589241	370.1325326
155	4.5282069	79.5739950	360.3275153	4.6753372	78.6111682	367.5337174	4.8272161	77.6660828	374.9109689
156	4.5725456	79.7926916	364.8557222	4.7220905	78.8229388	372.2090546	4.8764940	77.8711482	379.7381850
157	4.6173185	80.0092675	369.4282678	4.7693115	79.0326127	376.9311451	4.9262749	78.0741413	384.6146790
158	4.6625297	80.2237434	374.0455862	4.8170046	79.2402106	381.7004556	4.9765639	78.2750832	389.5409538
159	4.7081836	80.4361395	378.7081159	4.8651746	79.4457531	386.5174611	5.0273663	78.4739945	394.5175177
160	4.7542846	80.6464761	383.4162996	4.9138264	79.6492605	391.3826357	5.0786874	78.6708958	399.5448841
161	4.8003370	80.8547731	388.1705842	4.9629646	79.8507529	396.2964621	5.1305323	78.8658073	404.6235714
162	4.8478462	81.0610503	392.9714212	5.0125943	80.0502504	401.2594767	5.1829065	79.0587493	409.7541037
163	4.8953137	81.2653273	397.8192663	5.0627202	80.2477727	406.2720210	5.2358153	79.2497415	414.9370102
164	4.9432469	81.4676235	402.7145800	5.1133474	80.4433393	411.3347412	5.2892643	79.4388037	420.1728255
165	4.9916496	81.6579581	407.6578269	5.1644809	80.6369696	416.4460886	5.3432588	79.6259554	425.4620898
166	5.0405241	81.8663501	412.6494765	5.2161257	80.8286828	421.6125695	5.3978046	79.8112159	430.8053466
167	5.0898813	82.0628183	417.6900026	5.2682870	81.0184978	426.8286952	5.4529072	79.9946043	436.2031532
168	5.1397197	82.2573914	422.7798839	5.3209698	81.2064335	432.0969022	5.5085723	80.1761396	441.6560604
169	5.1900461	82.4500580	427.9196036	5.3741795	81.3925084	437.4179520	5.5648056	80.3558403	447.1646327
170	5.2408653	82.6408661	433.1096497	5.4279213	81.5767410	442.7921315	5.6216130	80.5337252	452.7294363
171	5.2921821	82.8298241	438.3505150	5.4822005	81.7591495	448.2200528	5.6790003	80.7098126	458.3510514
172	5.3440014	83.0169498	443.6426972	5.5370225	81.9397520	453.7022534	5.7369734	80.8841205	464.0300517
173	5.3963281	83.2022610	448.9866986	5.5923928	82.1185663	459.2392759	5.7955384	81.0566670	469.7670251
174	5.4491671	83.3857753	454.3830267	5.6483167	82.2956102	464.8316687	5.8547012	81.2274699	475.5625635
175	5.5025236	83.5675101	459.8321938	5.7047999	82.4709012	470.4799854	5.9144679	81.3965465	481.4172647
176	5.5564024	83.7474827	465.3347174	5.7618479	82.6444566	476.1847852	5.9748448	81.5639152	487.3317326
177	5.6108089	83.9257101	470.8911198	5.8194663	82.8162937	481.9466331	6.0358380	81.7295923	493.3065774
178	5.6657481	84.1022093	476.5019287	5.8776610	82.9864294	487.7660994	6.0974538	81.8935952	499.3424154
179	5.7212252	84.2769970	482.1676768	5.9364376	83.1548806	493.6437604	6.1595987	82.0559408	505.4398092
180	5.7772455	84.4500809	487.8889019	5.9958020	83.3216639	499.5801980	6.2225789	82.2166459	511.5995679
181	5.8338144	84.6215043	493.6661474	6.0557600	83.4867960	505.5760000	6.2861011	82.3757270	517.8221468
182	5.8909371	84.7912566	499.4999918	6.1163176	83.6502931	511.6317600	6.3502717	82.5332005	524.1082479
183	5.9486192	84.9593628	505.3908989	6.1774808	83.8121713	517.7480776	6.4150974	82.6890828	530.4585196
184	6.0068661	85.1258390	511.3395182	6.2392556	83.9724469	523.9255584	6.4805848	82.8433899	536.8736170
185	6.0656834	85.2907009	517.3463843	6.3016481	84.1311355	530.1648140	6.5467408	82.9961376	543.3542018
186	6.1250765	85.4539641	523.4120676	6.3646646	84.2882530	536.4664621	6.6135721	83.1473419	549.9009426
187	6.1850512	85.6156443	529.5371441	6.4283113	84.4438148	542.8311267	6.6810857	83.2970181	556.5145147
188	6.2456132	85.7757567	535.7221953	6.4925944	84.5978365	549.2594380	6.7492884	83.4451819	563.1956004
189	6.3067681	85.9343165	541.9678085	6.5575203	84.7503331	555.7520324	6.8181874	83.5918485	569.9448889
190	6.3695219	86.0913388	548.2745766	6.6230955	84.9013199	562.3095527	6.8877897	83.7370329	576.7630763
191	6.4308803	86.2468385	554.6430985	6.6893265	85.0508118	568.9326483	6.9581026	83.8807502	583.6508660
192	6.4938494	86.4008304	561.0739789	6.7562198	85.1988236	575.6219747	7.0291332	84.0230153	590.6089686
193	6.5574350	86.5533290	567.5678283	6.8237819	85.3453699	582.3781945	7.1008390	84.1638427	597.6381018
194	6.6216432	86.7043489	574.1252632	6.8920198	85.4904652	589.2019764	7.1733772	84.3032471	604.7389908
195	6.6864801	86.8533045	580.7469064	6.9609400	85.6341240	596.0939962	7.2466054	84.4412427	611.9123680
196	6.7519519	87.0020098	587.4333866	7.0305494	85.7763604	603.0549362	7.3205812	84.5778439	619.1589734
197	6.8180648	87.1486790	594.1853385	7.1008549	85.9171885	610.0854856	7.3953121	84.7130647	626.4795546
198	6.8848250	87.2939259	601.0034033	7.1718634	86.0566223	617.1863404	7.4708059	84.8469191	633.8748667
199	6.9522389	87.4377645	607.8882283	7.2435820	86.1946755	624.3582038	7.5470704	84.9794208	641.3456727
200	7.0203129	87.5802083	614.8404672	7.3160179	86.3313619	631.6017859	7.6241134	85.1105836	648.8927431

Table 1 435

M	C(11.75,M,12)	A(11.75,M,12)	S(11.75,M,12)	M	C(12.00,M,12)	A(12.00,M,12)	S(12.00,M,12)	M	C(12.25,M,12)	A(12.25,M,12)	S(12.25,M,12)
201	7.0890535	87.7212708	621.8607801	201	7.3891780	86.4666949	638.9178037	201	7.7019429	85.2404210	656.5168565
202	7.1584671	87.8609656	628.9498336	202	7.4630698	86.6006881	646.3069818	202	7.7805669	85.3689463	664.2187994
203	7.2285604	87.9993057	636.1083007	203	7.5377005	86.7333545	653.7700516	203	7.8599935	85.4961729	671.9993663
204	7.2993401	88.1363044	643.3368611	204	7.6130775	86.8347074	661.3077521	204	7.9402310	85.6221138	679.8593599
205	7.3708128	88.2719746	650.6362012	205	7.6892083	86.9947598	668.9208296	205	8.0212875	85.7467821	687.7995908
206	7.4429854	88.4063293	658.0070141	206	7.7661004	87.1235246	676.6100379	206	8.1031715	85.8701905	695.8208783
207	7.51?8646	88.5393812	665.4499994	207	7.8437614	87.2510145	684.3761383	207	8.1858913	85.9923520	703.9240498
208	7.5894574	88.6711429	672.9658640	208	7.9221990	87.3772420	692.2198997	208	8.2694557	86.1132789	712.1099412
209	7.6637709	88.8016270	680.5553214	209	8.0014210	87.5022198	700.1420987	209	8.3533730	86.2329839	720.3793968
210	7.7388120	88.9308458	688.2190923	210	8.0814352	87.6259602	708.1435197	210	8.4391521	86.3514792	728.7332698
211	7.8145878	89.0588116	695.9579042	211	8.1622496	87.7484755	716.2249549	211	8.5253018	86.4687771	737.1724220
212	7.8911057	89.1855366	703.7724920	212	8.2436721	87.8697777	724.3872045	212	8.6123309	86.5848897	745.6977238
213	7.9683727	89.3110327	711.6635977	213	8.3263108	87.9598789	732.6310765	213	8.7002485	86.6998289	754.3100547
214	8.0463964	89.4353119	719.6319704	214	8.4095739	88.1087910	740.9573873	214	8.7890635	86.8136067	763.0103032
215	8.1251840	89.5583861	727.6783668	215	8.4936696	88.2265257	749.3669612	215	8.8787852	86.9262347	771.7993667
216	8.2047431	89.6802668	735.8035508	216	8.5786063	88.3430948	757.8606308	216	8.9694228	87.0377246	780.6781519
217	8.2850812	89.8009557	744.0082939	217	8.6643924	88.4585097	766.4392371	217	9.0609657	87.1480878	789.6475747
218	8.3662060	89.9204942	752.2933752	218	8.7510363	88.5727819	775.1036295	218	9.1534832	87.2573359	798.7085604
219	8.4481251	90.0388636	760.6595811	219	8.8385467	88.6859226	783.8546658	219	9.2469250	87.3654799	807.8620436
220	8.5308463	90.1560853	769.1077062	220	8.9269321	88.7979432	792.6932124	220	9.3413207	87.4725312	817.1089687
221	8.6143775	90.2721703	777.6385525	221	9.0162015	88.9088547	801.6201446	221	9.4366800	87.5785006	826.4502894
222	8.6987266	90.3871296	786.2529300	222	9.1063635	89.0186680	810.6363460	222	9.5330128	87.6833993	835.8869694
223	8.7830016	90.5009743	794.9516566	223	9.1974271	89.1273940	819.7427095	223	9.6303290	87.7872379	845.4199823
224	8.8699107	90.6137150	803.7355583	224	9.2894014	89.2350436	828.9401366	224	9.7288386	87.8900272	855.0503113
225	8.9567619	90.7253625	812.6054689	225	9.3822954	89.3416273	838.2295380	225	9.8279518	87.9917778	864.7789499
226	9.0444635	90.8359273	821.5622308	226	9.4761183	89.4471558	847.6118334	226	9.9282788	88.0925002	874.6069016
227	9.1330239	90.9454201	830.6066943	227	9.5713795	89.5516394	857.0879517	227	10.0295300	88.1922048	884.5351804
228	9.2224514	91.0538511	839.7397182	228	9.6665883	89.6550885	866.6588312	228	10.1320158	88.2909018	894.5648104
229	9.3127546	91.1612308	848.9621696	229	9.7632542	89.7575134	876.3254195	229	10.2354468	88.3886015	904.6968262
230	9.4039420	91.2675691	858.2749242	230	9.8603967	89.8589241	886.0886737	230	10.3399336	88.4853139	914.9322730
231	9.4960222	91.3728764	867.6788662	231	9.9594956	89.9593308	895.9495605	231	10.4454871	88.5810490	925.2722066
232	9.5890041	91.4771625	877.1748864	232	10.0590906	90.0587434	905.9090561	232	10.5521181	88.6758167	935.7176937
233	9.6828965	91.5804374	886.7638926	233	10.1595815	90.1571717	915.9681467	233	10.6598377	88.7696268	946.2698118
234	9.7777081	91.6827108	896.4467890	234	10.2612783	90.2546254	926.1278281	234	10.7685568	88.8624889	956.9296495
235	9.8734482	91.7839926	906.2244972	235	10.3638911	90.3511143	936.3891064	235	10.8785869	88.9544126	967.6983064
236	9.9701257	91.8842922	916.0979454	236	10.4675300	90.4466478	946.7529975	236	10.9896391	89.0454074	978.5768932
237	10.0677499	91.9836193	926.0680711	237	10.5722053	90.5412354	957.2205275	237	11.1018250	89.1354827	989.5665324
238	10.1663299	92.0819832	936.1358210	238	10.6779273	90.6348866	967.7927328	238	11.2151562	89.2246477	1000.6683574
239	10.2653752	92.1793933	946.3021509	239	10.7847066	90.7276105	978.4706601	239	11.3295442	89.3129118	1011.8835136
240	10.3663953	92.2758588	956.5680261	240	10.8925537	90.8194163	989.2553667	240	11.4453010	89.4002839	1023.2131578
241	10.4678996	92.3713890	966.9344214	241	11.0014792	90.9103132	1000.1479204	241	11.5621384	89.4867731	1034.6584588
242	10.5703977	92.4659928	977.4023209	242	11.1114940	91.0003101	1011.1493996	242	11.6801686	89.5723383	1046.2205972
243	10.6738995	92.5596793	987.9727187	243	11.2226089	91.0894159	1022.2608936	243	11.7994037	89.6571383	1057.9007658
244	10.7784148	92.6524573	998.6466182	244	11.3348350	91.1776395	103?.4835026	244	11.9198559	89.7410319	1069.7001695
245	10.8839535	92.7443357	1009.4250330	245	11.3?81834	91.2649896	1044.8183376	245	12.0415378	89.8240778	1081.6200254
246	10.9905255	92.8353231	1020.3089865	246	11.5626652	91.3514749	1056.2665210	246	12.1644618	89.9062845	1093.6615631
247	11.0981411	92.9254283	1031.2995120	247	11.6782919	91.4371038	1067.8291862	247	12.2886407	89.9876604	1105.8260249
248	11.2068104	93.0146598	1042.3976531	248	11.7950748	91.5218851	1079.5074781	248	12.4140782	90.0682141	1118.1146656
249	11.3165437	93.1030260	1053.6044634	249	11.9130255	91.6058267	1091.3025529	249	12.5408144	90.1479537	1130.5287528
250	11.4273515	93.1905350	1064.9210071	250	12.0321558	91.6889373	1103.2155784	250	12.6688352	90.2268876	1143.0695672
251	11.5392444	93.2771961	1076.3483587	251	12.1524774	91.7712251	1115.2477342	251	12.7981629	90.3050238	1155.7384024
252	11.6522328	93.3630166	1087.8876030	252	12.2740021	91.8526981	1127.4002115	252	12.9288108	90.3823704	1168.5365652
253	11.7663276	93.4480049	1099.5398358	253	12.3967421	91.9333644	1139.6742137	253	13.0607924	90.4589355	1181.4653760
254	11.8815395	93.5321690	1111.3061634	254	12.5207096	92.0132321	1152.0709558	254	13.1941213	90.5347268	1194.5261684
255	11.9978796	93.6155171	1123.1877029	255	12.6459167	92.0923090	1164.5916654	255	13.3288113	90.6097522	1207.7202897
256	12.1153588	93.6980570	1135.1855825	256	12.7723758	92.1706030	1177.2375820	256	13.4648762	90.6840195	1221.0491010
257	12.2339884	93.7797965	1147.3009413	257	12.9000996	92.2481218	1190.0099579	257	13.6023302	90.7575364	1234.5139773
258	12.3537795	93.8607433	1159.5349297	258	13.0291006	92.3248731	1202.9100575	258	13.7411873	90.8303103	1248.1163075
259	12.4747436	93.9409053	1171.8887093	259	13.1593916	92.4008644	1215.9391580	259	13.8814619	90.9023488	1261.8574948
260	12.5968922	94.0202900	118?.3634529	260	13.2909855	92.4761034	1229.0985496	260	14.0231685	90.9736594	1275.7389567
261	12.?202367	94.0989049	1196.9603450	261	13.4238954	92.5505974	1242.3895351	261	14.1663217	91.0442493	1289.7621252
262	12.8447890	94.1767574	1209.6805818	262	13.5581343	92.6243539	1255.8134205	262	14.3109362	91.1141259	1303.9284470
263	12.9705609	94.2538551	1222.5253708	263	13.6937157	92.6973601	1269.3715648	263	14.4570270	91.1832965	1318.2393832
264	13.0975643	94.3302052	1235.4959317	264	13.8306528	92.7696832	1283.0652805	264	14.6046092	91.2517680	1332.6964102
265	13.2258113	94.4058149	1248.5934961	265	13.9689593	92.8412705	1296.8959333	265	14.7536979	91.3195476	1347.3010194
266	13.3553141	94.4806915	1261.8193074	266	14.1086489	92.9121490	1310.8648926	266	14.9043086	91.3866423	1362.0547174
267	13.4860848	94.5548420	1275.1746215	267	14.2497354	92.9823258	1324.9735416	267	15.0564567	91.4530590	1376.9590259
268	13.6181361	94.6282735	1288.6607063	268	14.3922328	93.0518077	1339.2232770	268	15.2101581	91.5188045	1392.0154827
269	13.7514803	94.7009929	1302.2788424	269	14.5361551	93.1206017	1353.6155098	269	15.3654284	91.5838857	1407.2256407
270	13.8861303	94.7730072	1316.0303227	270	14.6815167	93.1887145	1368.1516649	270	15.5222838	91.6483092	1422.5910692
271	14.0220986	94.8443232	1329.9164530	271	14.8283318	93.2561530	1382.8331815	271	15.6807405	91.7120817	1438.1133530
272	14.1593983	94.9149477	1343.9385516	272	14.9765151	93.3229238	1397.6615134	272	15.8409147	91.7752098	1453.7940935
273	14.2980424	94.9848873	1358.0979499	273	15.1263813	93.3890034	1412.6381285	273	16.0025230	91.8376999	1469.6349062
274	14.4380441	95.0541488	1372.3959924	274	15.2776451	93.4544885	1427.7645098	274	16.1658821	91.8995586	1485.6374313
275	14.5794166	95.1227386	1386.8340365	275	15.4304216	93.5192956	1443.0421549	275	16.3309088	91.9607922	1501.8033134
276	14.7221734	95.1906634	1401.4134531	276	15.5847258	93.5834610	1458.4725765	276	16.4976202	92.0214070	1518.1342222
277	14.8663240	95.2579295	1416.1356265	277	15.7405730	93.6469911	1474.0573023	277	16.6660334	92.0814092	1534.6318424
278	15.0118942	95.3245433	1431.0019545	278	15.8979788	93.7098921	1489.7978753	278	16.8361658	92.1408052	1551.2978758
279	15.1588856	95.3905113	1446.0138487	279	16.0589586	93.7721704	1505.6958541	279	17.0080350	92.1996009	1568.1340416
280	15.3073164	95.4558395	1461.1727343	280	16.2?75281	93.8338321	1521.7528126	280	17.1816587	92.2578025	1585.1420767
281	15.4572005	95.5205343	1476.4800507	281	16.3797034	93.8948833	1537.9703408	281	17.3570548	92.3154160	1602.3237354
282	15.6095523	95.5846017	1491.9372512	282	16.5435005	93.9553300	1554.3500442	282	17.53?2414	92.3724473	1619.6807702
283	15.7613860	95.6480479	1507.5458034	283	16.7089355	94.0151782	1570.8935446	283	17.7132368	92.4289022	1637.2150316
284	15.9157162	95.7108780	1523.3071894	284	16.8760248	94.0744339	1587.6024801	284	17.8940594	92.4847867	1654.9282684
285	16.0715576	95.7731006	1539.2229057	285	17.0447851	94.1331028	1604.4785049	285	18.0767279	92.5401064	1672.8223278
286	16.2289250	95.8347190	1555.2944633	286	17.2152329	94.1911909	1621.5232900	286	18.2612612	92.5948672	1690.8990558
287	16.3878332	95.8957398	1571.5233883	287	17.3873852	94.2487039	1638.7385229	287	18.4476782	92.6490745	1709.1603170
288	16.5482974	95.9561690	1587.9112215	288	17.5612591	94.3056474	1656.1259081	288	18.6359983	92.7027341	1727.6079952
289	16.7103328	96.0160122	1604.4595189	289	17.7368717	94.3620271	1673.6871672	289	18.8262408	92.7558515	1746.2439935
290	16.8739548	96.0752752	1621.1698517	290	17.9142404	94.4178486	1691.4240389	290	19.0184253	92.8084320	1765.0702343
291	17.0391790	96.1339634	1638.0438065	291	18.0933828	94.4731175	1709.3382793	291	19.2125717	92.8604813	1784.0886596
292	17.2060209	96.1920826	1655.0829854	292	18.2743166	94.5278391	1727.4316621	292	19.4087001	92.9120046	1803.3012314
293	17.3744965	96.2496383	1672.2890063	293	18.4570598	94.5820189	1745.7059788	293	19.6068306	92.9630072	1822.7099315
294	17.5446218	96.3066358	1689.6635029	294	18.6416304	94.6356623	1764.1630386	294	19.8069836	93.0134945	1842.3167620
295	17.7164129	96.3630806	1707.2081247	295	18.8280467	94.6887745	1782.8046690	295	20.0091799	93.0634715	1862.1237456
296	17.8898861	96.4189781	1724.9245376	296	19.0163272	94.7413609	1801.6327157	296	20.2134403	93.1129436	1882.1329256
297	18.0650579	96.4743336	1742.8144237	297	19.2064904	94.7934266	1820.6490428	297	20.4197858	93.1619157	1902.3463659
298	18.2419449	96.5291523	1760.8794816	298	19.3985553	94.8449769	1839.8555333	298	20.6282378	93.2103929	1922.7661517
299	18.4205640	96.5834395	1779.1214266	299	19.5925409	94.8960167	1859.2540886	299	20.8388177	93.2583803	1943.3943895
300	18.6009320	96.6372002	1797.5419905	300	19.7884663	94.9465512	1878.8466295	300	21.0515473	93.3058827	1964.2332073

M	C(11.75,M,12)	A(11.75,M,12)	S(11.75,M,12)
301	18.7830661	96.6904397	1816.1429225
302	18.9669837	96.7431629	1834.9259887
303	19.1527020	96.7953748	1853.8929723
304	19.3402389	96.8470805	1873.0456744
305	19.5295121	96.8982848	1892.3859133
306	19.7208395	96.9489926	1911.9155254
307	19.9143394	96.9992086	1931.6363049
308	20.1089301	97.0489378	1951.5503043
309	20.3058300	97.0981847	1971.6592354
310	20.5046579	97.1469541	1991.9650644
311	20.7054327	97.1952506	2012.4697224
312	20.9081734	97.2430788	2033.1751551
313	21.1128993	97.2904432	2054.0833285
314	21.3196297	97.3373484	2075.1962278
315	21.5283845	97.3837987	2096.5158575
316	21.7391832	97.4297986	2118.0442420
317	21.9520461	97.4753524	2139.7834252
318	22.1669932	97.5204645	2161.7354712
319	22.3840450	97.5651392	2183.9024644
320	22.6032221	97.6093807	2206.2865094
321	22.8245453	97.6531932	2228.8897315
322	23.0480356	97.6965808	2251.7142768
323	23.2737143	97.7395477	2274.7623124
324	23.5016028	97.7820980	2298.0360268
325	23.?17226	97.8242357	2321.5376295
326	23.9640958	97.8659648	2345.2693522
327	24.1987442	97.9072893	2369.2334479
328	24.4355902	97.9482130	2393.4321921
329	24.6749564	97.9887399	2417.8678624
330	24.9165853	98.0288739	2442.5428387
331	25.1605400	98.0686166	2467.4594041
332	25.4069036	98.1079780	2492.6199441
333	25.6556796	98.1469558	2518.0268477
334	25.9069914	98.1855555	2543.6825273
335	26.1605631	98.2237810	2569.5894187
336	26.4167186	98.2616358	2595.7499816
337	26.6753823	98.2991236	2622.1667004
338	26.9365787	98.3362478	2648.8420827
339	27.2003327	98.3730121	2675.7786614
340	27.4666693	98.4094198	2702.9789942
341	27.7356138	98.4454745	2730.4456635
342	28.0071917	98.4811797	2758.1812773
343	28.2814288	98.5165386	2786.1884690
344	28.5583511	98.5515546	2814.4698978
345	28.8379850	98.5862311	2843.0282489
346	29.1203569	98.6205713	2871.8662339
347	29.4054937	98.6545786	2900.9665908
348	29.6934225	98.6882560	2930.3920845
349	29.9841706	98.7216070	2960.0855059
350	30.2777656	98.7546345	2990.0698776
351	30.5742354	98.7873418	3020.3474888
352	30.8736081	98.8197319	3050.9216787
353	31.1759122	98.8518080	3081.7952868
354	31.4811763	98.8835730	3112.9711990
355	31.7894293	98.9150300	3144.4523754
356	32.1007010	98.9461819	3176.2418049
357	32.4150204	98.9770318	3208.3425059
358	32.7324175	99.0075826	3240.7575263
359	33.0529224	99.0378371	3273.4899438
360	33.?765656	99.0677982	3306.5428862
361	33.?.33778	99.0974689	3339.9194318
362	34.0333900	99.1268518	3373.6228096
363	34.3666336	99.1559498	3407.6561996
364	34.7031403	99.1847656	3442.0228333
365	35.0429419	99.2133020	3476.7259735
366	35.3860707	99.2415621	3511.7689154
367	35.7325593	99.2695474	3547.1549360
368	36.0824406	99.2972621	3582.8875453
369	36.4357478	99.3247073	3618.9699859
370	36.7925145	99.3518867	3655.4057337
371	37.1527745	99.3788026	3692.1982482
372	37.5165621	99.4054575	3729.3510228
373	37.8839118	99.4318539	3766.8675849
374	38.2548584	99.4579944	3804.7514967
375	38.6294373	99.4838814	3843.0063551
376	39.0076938	99.5095174	3881.6357924
377	39.3896341	99.5349048	3920.6434762
378	39.7753242	99.5600460	3960.0331103
379	40.1647910	99.5849434	3999.8084345
380	40.5580712	99.6095994	4039.9732255
381	40.9552023	99.6340163	4080.5312967
382	41.3562220	99.6581965	4121.4864990
383	41.7611683	99.6821422	4162.8427210
384	42.1700798	99.7058557	4204.6038093
385	42.5829951	99.7293392	4246.7739691
386	42.9999536	99.7525951	4289.3569063
387	43.4209949	99.7756254	4332.3569179
388	43.8461588	99.7984324	4375.7779128
389	44.2754857	99.8210183	4419.6240715
390	44.7090160	99.8433851	4463.8995573
391	45.1467923	99.8655351	4508.6085738
392	45.5888547	99.8874703	4553.7553661
393	46.0352455	99.9091928	4599.3442208
394	46.4860073	99.9307046	4645.3794663
395	46.9411828	99.9520079	4691.8654736
396	47.4008152	99.9731046	4738.8066564
397	47.8649462	99.9939967	4786.2074717
398	48.3336258	100.0146862	4834.0724199
399	48.8068926	100.0351751	4882.4060457
400	49.2847934	100.0554654	4931.2129383

M	C(12.00,M,12)	A(12.00,M,12)	S(12.00,M,12)
301	19.9863510	94.9965853	1898.6350958
302	20.1862145	95.0461241	1918.6214468
303	20.3880766	95.0951724	1938.8076613
304	20.5919574	95.1437350	1959.1957379
305	20.7978770	95.1918168	1979.7876953
306	21.0058557	95.2394226	2000.5855723
307	21.2159143	95.2865570	2021.5914280
308	21.4280734	95.3332248	2042.8073423
309	21.6423542	95.3794305	2064.2354158
310	21.8587777	95.4251787	2085.8777699
311	22.0773655	95.4704740	2107.7365477
312	22.2981391	95.5153208	2129.8139132
313	22.5211205	95.5597235	2152.1120523
314	22.7463317	95.6036867	2174.6331728
315	22.9737951	95.6472145	2197.3795046
316	23.2035330	95.6903114	2220.3532997
317	23.4355683	95.7329816	2243.5568327
318	23.6699240	95.7752293	2266.9924010
319	23.9066233	95.8170587	2290.6623250
320	24.1456895	95.8584740	2314.5689483
321	24.3871464	95.8994792	2338.7146378
322	24.6310179	95.9400784	2363.1017842
323	24.8773280	95.9802756	2387.7328021
324	25.1261013	96.0200749	2412.6101301
325	25.3773623	96.0594801	2437.7362314
326	25.6311360	96.0984951	2463.1135938
327	25.8874443	96.1371239	2488.7447297
328	26.1463218	96.1753702	2514.6321770
329	26.4077860	96.2132378	2540.7784988
330	26.6718629	96.2507305	2567.1862838
331	26.9385815	96.2878520	2593.8581467
332	27.2079673	96.3246059	2620.7967282
333	27.4800470	96.3609960	2648.0046955
334	27.7548474	96.3970257	2675.4847425
335	28.0323959	96.4326987	2703.2395899
336	28.3127199	96.4680185	2731.2719858
337	28.5958471	96.5029886	2759.5847057
338	28.8818056	96.5376125	2788.1805528
339	29.1706268	96.5718936	2817.0623584
340	29.4623298	96.6058352	2846.2329820
341	29.7569531	96.6394408	2875.6953118
342	30.0545227	96.6727137	2905.4522649
343	30.3550679	96.7056571	2935.5067876
344	30.6586186	96.7382744	2965.8618555
345	30.??52048	96.7705687	2996.5204741
346	31.2748568	96.8025432	3027.4856789
347	31.5876054	96.8342012	3058.7605357
348	31.9034814	96.8655458	3090.3481411
349	32.2225163	96.8965800	3122.2516225
350	32.5447414	96.9273069	3154.4741388
351	32.8701888	96.9577296	3187.0188802
352	33.1988907	96.9878511	3219.8990690
353	33.5308796	97.0176743	3253.0879597
354	33.8661884	97.0472023	3286.6183393
355	34.2048503	97.0764379	3320.4850278
356	34.5463988	97.1053841	3354.6898781
357	34.8923678	97.1340437	3389.2367769
358	35.2412915	97.1624195	3424.1291447
359	35.5937044	97.1905143	3459.3704361
360	35.9496414	97.2183310	3494.9641405
361	36.3091378	97.2458723	3530.9137820
362	36.6722292	97.2731409	3567.2229198
363	37.0389515	97.3001395	3603.8951490
364	37.4093410	97.3268708	3640.9341006
365	37.7834344	97.3533374	3678.3434416
366	38.1612688	97.3795420	3716.1268760
367	38.5428815	97.4054871	3754.2881448
368	38.9283103	97.4311753	3792.8310263
369	39.3175934	97.4566093	3831.7593366
370	39.7107093	97.4817913	3871.0769300
371	40.1078770	97.5067241	3910.7876993
372	40.5089558	97.5314100	3950.8955764
373	40.9140454	97.5558515	3991.4045322
374	41.3231658	97.5800510	4032.3185775
375	41.7364177	97.6040109	4073.6417633
376	42.1538708	97.6277335	4115.3781810
377	42.5753197	97.6512213	4157.5319628
378	43.0010729	97.6744765	4200.1072825
379	43.4310836	97.6975015	4243.1083554
380	43.?653940	97.7202995	4286.5394390
381	44.3040484	97.7428698	4330.4048334
382	44.7470389	97.7652177	4374.7088817
383	45.1945597	97.7873442	4419.4559706
384	45.6465053	97.8092517	4464.6505303
385	46.1029704	97.8309423	4510.2970357
386	46.5640001	97.8524181	4556.4000061
387	47.0296401	97.8736813	4602.9640062
388	47.4999365	97.8947339	4649.9936463
389	47.9749359	97.9155782	4697.4935828
390	48.4546857	97.9362160	4745.4685186
391	48.9392321	97.9566495	4793.9232039
392	49.4286244	97.9768807	4842.8624360
393	49.9229106	97.9969116	4892.2910604
394	50.4221398	98.0167441	4942.2139710
395	50.9263611	98.0363803	4992.6361107
396	51.4356248	98.0558221	5043.5624719
397	51.9499810	98.0750714	5094.9980967
398	52.4694808	98.0941301	5146.9480777
399	52.9941756	98.1130001	5199.4175585
400	53.5241174	98.1316833	5252.4117341

M	C(12.25,M,12)	A(12.25,M,12)	S(12.25,M,12)
301	21.2664496	93.3529051	1985.2847546
302	21.4835435	93.3994524	2006.5512031
303	21.7028547	93.4455293	2028.0347467
304	21.9244047	93.4911406	2049.7376014
305	22.1482163	93.5362909	207?.6620061
306	22.?.43127	93.5809850	2093.8102224
307	22.6027171	93.6252275	2116.1645352
308	22.8334532	93.6690229	2138.7872523
309	23.0665447	93.7123757	2161.6207055
310	23.3020157	93.7552905	2184.6872502
311	23.5338904	93.7977715	2207.9892659
312	23.7801935	93.8398234	2231.5291564
313	24.0229496	93.8814502	2255.3093499
314	24.2681839	93.9226564	2279.3322995
315	24.5159216	93.9634452	2303.6004834
316	24.7661883	94.0038239	2328.1164050
317	25.0150098	94.0437935	2352.8825934
318	25.2744122	94.0833592	2377.9016032
319	25.5324218	94.1225251	2403.1760154
320	25.7930653	94.1612952	2428.7084372
321	26.0563695	94.1996735	2454.5015026
322	26.3223616	94.2376640	2480.5578721
323	26.5910691	94.2752706	2506.8802337
324	26.8625196	94.3124972	2533.4713028
325	27.1357411	94.3493476	2560.3338224
326	27.4137620	94.3858257	2587.4705635
327	27.6936108	94.4219351	2614.8843255
328	27.9763165	94.4576796	2642.5779364
329	28.2619080	94.4930629	2670.5542528
330	28.5504150	94.5280887	2698.8161608
331	28.8418672	94.5627605	2727.3665758
332	29.1362945	94.5970820	2756.2084430
333	29.4337276	94.6310566	2785.3447375
334	29.7341969	94.6646879	2814.7784651
335	30.0377334	94.6979794	2844.5126619
336	30.3443686	94.7309344	2874.5503954
337	30.6541341	94.7635564	2904.8947640
338	30.9670617	94.7958488	2935.5488981
339	31.2831838	94.8278149	2966.5159598
340	31.6025329	94.8591579	2997.7991436
341	31.9251421	94.8907812	3029.4016765
342	32.2510446	94.9217879	3061.3268187
343	32.5802740	94.9524813	3093.5778633
344	32.9128643	94.9828646	3126.1581373
345	33.2488498	95.0129408	3159.0710017
346	33.5882652	95.0427131	3192.3198515
347	33.9311454	95.0721846	3225.9081167
348	34.2775258	95.1013582	3259.8392821
349	34.6274422	95.1302370	3294.1167879
350	34.9809307	95.1588240	3328.7442301
351	35.3380277	95.1871222	3363.7251608
352	35.6937701	95.2151343	3399.0631086
353	36.0631950	95.2428634	3434.7619586
354	36.4313401	95.2703123	3470.8255137
355	36.8032434	95.2974830	3507.2564938
356	37.1789432	95.3243808	3544.0597372
357	37.5584782	95.3510059	3581.2386804
358	37.9418877	95.3773620	3618.7971585
359	38.3292111	95.4034518	3656.7390463
360	38.7204885	95.4292779	3695.0682574
361	39.1157601	95.4548431	3733.7887459
362	39.5150669	95.4801499	3772.9045061
363	39.9184498	95.5052009	3812.4195729
364	40.3259507	95.5299989	3852.3380228
365	40.7376114	95.5545462	3892.6639735
366	41.1534745	95.5788455	3933.4015849
367	41.5735829	95.6028992	3974.5550594
368	41.9979799	95.6267099	4016.1286424
369	42.4267093	95.6502800	4058.1266223
370	42.8558153	95.6736118	4100.5533316
371	43.2973426	95.6967079	4143.4131469
372	43.7393363	95.7195707	4186.7104895
373	44.1858420	95.7422023	4230.4498257
374	44.6369058	95.7646053	4274.8356677
375	45.0925742	95.7867819	4319.2725736
376	45.5523943	95.8087344	4364.3651478
377	46.0179134	95.8304651	4409.9180420
378	46.4876796	95.8519762	4455.5935554
379	46.9622413	95.8732699	4502.4236350
380	47.4416475	95.8943484	4549.3858763
381	47.9259477	95.9152139	4596.8275238
382	48.4151917	95.9358686	4644.7534471
383	48.9094301	95.9563145	4693.1686632
384	49.4087139	95.9765539	4742.0780934
385	49.9130945	95.9965887	4791.4868073
386	50.4226240	96.0164211	4841.3999018
387	50.9373550	96.0360530	4891.8225259
388	51.4573405	96.0554866	4942.7598808
389	51.9826342	96.0747238	4994.2172213
390	52.5132902	96.0937666	5046.1998555
391	53.0493634	96.1126170	5098.7131457
392	53.5909090	96.1312769	5151.7625092
393	54.1379829	96.1497482	5205.3534181
394	54.6906414	96.1680328	5259.4914010
395	55.2489417	96.1861327	5314.1820424
396	55.8129413	96.2040497	5369.4309842
397	56.3826985	96.2217857	5425.2439255
398	56.9582718	96.2393424	5481.6266239
399	57.5397209	96.2567217	5538.5848958
400	58.1271055	96.2739254	5590.1246166

Table 1   437

M	C(11.75,M,12)	A(11.75,M,12)	S(11.75,M,12)	M	C(12.00,M,12)	A(12.00,M,12)	S(12.00,M,12)	M	C(12.25,M,12)	A(12.25,M,12)	S(12.25,M,12)
401	49.7673737	100.0755588	4980.4977316	401	54.0593586	98.1501814	5305.9358515	401	58.7204864	96.2909552	5654.2517221
402	50.2546792	100.0954575	5030.2651053	402	54.5999521	98.1684965	5359.9952101	402	59.3199247	96.3078129	5712.9722085
403	50.7467563	100.1151632	5080.5197845	403	55.1459517	98.1866302	5414.5951622	403	59.9254822	96.3245003	5772.2921332
404	51.2436516	100.1346778	5131.2665408	404	55.6974112	98.2045843	5469.7411139	404	60.5372215	96.3410191	5632.2176154
405	51.7454123	100.1540032	5182.5101924	405	56.2543853	98.2223607	5525.4385251	405	61.1552057	96.3573709	589?.7548370
406	52.2520862	100.1731412	5234.2556047	406	56.8169292	98.2399611	5581.6929104	406	61.?794984	96.3735575	5953.9100427
407	52.7627212	100.1920936	5286.5076909	407	57.3850984	98.2573872	5638.5098395	407	62.4101641	96.3895805	6015.6895411
408	53.2803660	100.2108622	5339.2714121	408	57.9589494	98.2746408	5695.8949379	408	63.0472679	96.4054417	6078.0997052
409	53.8020695	100.2294489	5392.5517780	409	58.5385389	98.2917236	5753.8538874	409	63.6908754	96.4211425	3141.1469730
410	54.3268815	100.2478553	5446.3538476	410	59.1239243	98.3086372	5812.3924263	410	64.2410531	96.4366847	6204.8378484
411	54.8608518	100.2660832	5500.6827290	411	59.7151636	98.3253834	5871.5163506	411	64.5978680	96.4520693	6269.1789015
412	55.3980309	100.2841344	5555.5435808	412	60.3123152	98.3419637	5931.2315142	412	65.6613879	96.4672994	6334.1767695
413	55.9404700	100.3020106	5610.9416117	413	60.9154383	98.3583799	5991.5438294	413	66.3316812	96.4823752	6399.8381574
414	56.4882204	100.3197134	5666.8820817	414	61.5245927	98.3746336	6052.4592677	414	67.0008172	96.4972986	6466.1698387
415	57.0413343	100.3372445	5723.3703022	415	62.1398387	98.3907263	6113.9836604	415	67.6928655	96.5120712	6533.1786559
416	57.5990640	100.3546057	5780.4116364	416	62.7612370	98.4066597	6176.1236991	416	68.3838968	96.5266945	6600.8715214
417	58.1638627	100.3717985	5838.0115004	417	63.3888494	98.4224354	6239.6849361	417	69.0819824	96.5411701	6669.2554182
418	58.7333838	100.3888246	5896.1753631	418	64.0227379	98.4380548	6302.2737855	418	69.7871944	96.5554994	6738.3374006
419	59.3084815	100.4056855	5954.9087469	419	64.6625653	98.4535196	6366.2965234	419	70.4996053	96.5696838	6808.1245950
420	59.8892104	100.4223830	6014.2172284	420	65.3095949	98.4688313	6430.9594887	420	71.2192888	96.5837250	6878.6242003
421	60.4756256	100.4389186	6074.1064368	421	65.9626909	98.4839914	6496.2690037	421	71.9463190	96.5976242	6949.8434891
422	61.0677828	100.4552939	6134.5820644	422	66.6223178	98.4990014	6562.2317746	422	72.6807710	96.6113830	7021.7898081
423	61.6657381	100.4715103	6195.6498472	423	67.2805410	98.5138628	6628.8540924	423	73.4227206	96.6250028	7094.4705791
424	62.2695485	100.4875696	6257.3155853	424	67.9614264	98.5285770	6696.1426333	424	74.1722442	96.6384849	7167.8932996
425	62.8792712	100.5034730	631?.5851338	425	68.6410407	98.5431455	6764.1040597	425	74.9294192	96.6518308	7242.0655438
426	63.4949640	100.5192223	6382.4644050	426	69.3274511	98.5575698	6832.7451004	426	75.6943236	96.6650419	7316.9949629
427	64.1168855	100.5348189	6445.9593690	427	70.0257256	98.5710513	6902.0725514	427	76.4670365	96.6781194	7392.6692846
428	64.7444948	100.5502642	6510.0760545	428	70.7209328	98.5859914	6972.0932770	428	77.2476375	96.6910648	7469.1563231
429	65.3784513	100.5655598	6574.8205493	429	71.4281422	98.5999915	7042.8142098	429	78.0362072	96.7038793	7546.4039606
430	66.0186153	100.5807070	6640.1990005	430	72.1424236	98.6138530	7114.2423520	430	78.8328268	96.7165544	7624.4401678
431	66.6650475	100.5957074	6706.2176158	431	72.8630438	98.6275772	7186.3847756	431	79.6375786	96.7291213	7703.2729946
432	67.3173095	100.6105623	6772.8826634	432	73.5924863	98.6411655	7259.2466234	432	80.4505455	96.7415513	7782.9105731
433	67.9769630	100.6252732	6840.2004728	433	74.3284112	98.6546194	7332.8411097	433	81.2718115	96.7538557	7863.3611186
434	68.6425708	100.6398414	6908.1774358	434	75.0716953	98.6679399	7407.1695208	434	82.1014612	96.7660357	7944.6329301
435	69.3146960	100.6542683	6976.8200066	435	75.8224122	98.6811287	7482.2412161	435	82.9395803	96.7780927	8026.7343913
436	69.9934024	100.6685555	7046.1347026	436	76.5805363	98.6941868	7558.0638283	436	83.7862552	96.7900278	8109.6739717
437	70.6787544	100.6827032	7116.1281049	437	77.3464427	98.7071156	7634.6442647	437	84.6415732	96.8018424	8193.4602269
438	71.3709172	100.6967153	7186.8068594	438	78.1199071	98.7199165	7711.9907074	438	85.5055226	96.8135375	8278.1018001
439	72.0696565	100.7105907	7258.1776766	439	78.9011062	98.7325906	7790.1106145	439	86.3784925	96.8251144	8363.6074227
440	72.7753385	100.7243316	7330.2473331	440	79.6901173	98.7451392	7869.0117207	440	87.2602730	96.8365744	8449.9859152
441	73.4879304	100.7379393	7403.0226716	441	80.4870184	98.7575035	7948.7018380	441	88.1510549	96.8479186	8537.2461881
442	74.2074997	100.7514150	7476.5106020	442	81.2918886	98.7698649	8029.1888565	442	89.0509303	96.8591481	8625.3972431
443	74.9341148	100.7647601	7550.7181017	443	82.1048075	98.7820044	8110.4807451	443	89.9599918	96.8702642	8714.4481733
444	75.6678447	100.7779757	7625.6522165	444	82.9258556	98.7941034	8192.5855526	444	90.8783334	96.8812679	8804.4081652
445	76.4087590	100.7910633	7701.3200612	445	83.7551142	98.8060430	8275.5114082	445	91.8060497	96.8921604	8895.2864049
446	77.1569281	100.8040239	7777.7288202	446	84.5926653	98.8178643	8359.2665224	446	92.7432365	96.9029429	8987.0925483
447	77.9124230	100.8166588	7854.8857483	447	85.4385919	98.8295686	8443.8591877	447	93.6899849	96.9136164	9079.8357384
448	78.6753155	100.8295692	7932.7981713	448	86.2929779	98.8411571	8529.2977796	448	94.6454090	96.9241820	9173.5257752
449	79.4456780	100.8421565	8011.4734868	449	87.1559076	98.8526308	8615.5907575	449	95.6125911	96.9346409	9268.1728242
450	80.2235836	100.8546216	8090.9191647	450	88.0274667	98.8639909	8702.7466651	450	96.5886363	96.9449941	9363.7847754
451	81.0091061	100.8669659	8171.1427483	451	88.9077414	98.8752385	8790.7741318	451	97.5746453	96.9552426	9460.3734117
452	81.8023203	100.8791905	8252.1518544	452	89.7968188	98.8863747	8879.6818732	452	98.5707198	96.9653876	9557.9480570
453	82.6033014	100.8912966	8333.9541747	453	90.6947870	98.8974007	8969.4766920	453	99.5769626	96.9754301	9656.5187768
454	83.4121254	100.9032852	8416.5574761	454	91.6017344	98.9083175	9060.1734790	454	100.5934774	96.9853711	9756.0957394
455	84.2283691	100.9151576	8499.9696015	455	92.5177522	98.9191263	9151.7752139	455	101.6203692	96.9952117	9856.6892169
456	85.0533101	100.9269149	8584.1984706	456	93.4429297	98.9298280	9244.2929661	456	102.6577438	97.0049528	9958.3095060
457	85.8354267	100.9385582	8669.2520806	457	94.3773590	98.9404238	9337.7358959	457	103.7057082	97.0145954	10060.9673298
458	86.7273980	100.9500886	8755.1385073	458	95.3211326	98.9509146	9432.1132049	458	104.7643707	97.0241407	10164.6730381
459	87.5765037	100.9615072	8841.8659053	459	96.2743440	98.9613016	9527.4343875	459	105.8333403	97.0335894	10269.4374087
460	88.4341246	100.9728150	8920.4425090	460	97.2370374	98.9715857	9623.7087315	460	106.9142274	97.0429427	10375.2712490
461	89.3000421	100.9840132	9017.8766337	461	98.2094583	98.9817681	9720.9458189	461	108.0056435	97.0522015	10482.1854765
462	90.1744384	100.9951028	9107.1766758	462	99.1915529	98.9918496	9819.1552771	462	109.1082011	97.0613667	10590.1911199
463	91.0573964	101.0060849	9197.3511141	463	100.1834684	99.0018312	9918.3468300	463	110.2220140	97.0704393	10699.2993210
464	91.9490001	101.0169605	3288.4065105	464	101.1853031	99.0117141	10018.5302984	464	111.3471971	97.0794202	10809.5213350
465	92.8493340	101.0277307	9380.3575106	465	102.1971561	99.0214991	10119.7156014	465	112.4833664	97.0883104	10920.8685321
466	93.7584838	101.0383964	9473.2068447	466	103.2191297	99.0311872	10221.9127575	466	113.6321392	97.0971107	11033.3523899
467	94.6765356	101.0489588	9566.9653284	467	104.2513189	99.0407794	10325.1318852	467	114.7921339	97.1058221	11146.9845376
468	95.6035767	101.0594186	9661.6418640	468	105.2938321	99.0502767	10429.3832041	468	115.9639703	97.1144455	11261.7766715
469	96.5396950	101.0697769	9757.2454407	469	106.3467705	99.0596799	10534.6770363	469	117.1477691	97.1229817	11377.7406418
470	97.4849795	101.0800349	9853.7851357	470	107.4102382	99.0689900	10641.0238007	470	118.3436526	97.1314317	11494.8884140
471	98.4395200	101.0901934	9951.2701152	471	108.4843405	99.0782079	10748.4340449	471	119.5517441	97.1397963	11613.2320636
472	99.4034069	101.1002535	10049.7096352	472	109.5691839	99.0873345	10856.9183854	472	120.7721681	97.1480763	11732.7838077
473	100.3767320	101.1102159	10149.1130421	473	110.6649758	99.0963708	10966.4875694	473	122.0050507	97.1562727	11853.5559758
474	101.3595875	101.1200818	10249.4897741	474	111.7715245	99.1053177	11077.1524451	474	123.2505189	97.1643863	11975.5610265
475	102.3520668	101.1298520	10350.8493615	475	112.8892398	99.1141759	11188.9239697	475	124.5087013	97.1724178	12098.8115454
476	103.3542641	101.1395275	10453.2014283	476	114.0181322	99.1229464	11301.8132095	476	125.7797276	97.1803682	12223.3202467
477	104.3662746	101.1491091	10556.5556924	477	115.1583135	99.1316301	11415.8313417	477	127.0637290	97.1882383	12349.0999743
478	105.3881943	101.1585978	10660.9219669	478	116.3003006	99.1402279	11530.9896552	478	128.3608379	97.1960288	12476.1637033
479	106.4201204	101.1679945	10766.3101613	479	117.4729956	99.1487404	11647.2995518	479	129.6711881	97.2037407	12604.5245412
480	107.4621508	101.1773001	10872.7302817	480	118.6577256	99.1571688	11776.7725474	480	130.5949148	97.2113745	12734.1957295
481	108.5143843	101.1865155	10980.1924325	481	119.8542028	99.1655136	11883.4202730	481	132.5321546	97.2189313	12865.1906442
482	109.5769210	101.1956415	11088.7068168	482	121.0325449	99.1737759	12003.2544758	482	133.66?3453	97.2264117	12997.5227?88
483	110.6496617	101.2046790	11198.2837378	483	122.2428703	99.1819563	12124.2870207	483	135.0477264	97.2338164	13131.2058441
484	111.7333083	101.2136289	11308.9335995	484	123.4652990	99.1900507	12246.5298910	484	136.4263386	97.2411464	13266.2535706
485	112.8273636	101.2224920	11420.6669078	485	124.6999520	99.1980750	12369.9951900	485	137.8180242	97.2484023	13402.6799092
486	113.9321315	101.2312692	11533.4942713	486	125.9463515	99.2060148	12494.6951492	486	139.2259687	97.2555849	13540.4989334
487	115.0477170	101.2399612	11647.4264028	487	127.2046420	99.2138761	12620.6420935	487	140.6471914	97.2626949	13679.7248601
488	116.1742259	101.2485690	11762.4741198	488	128.4784853	99.2216595	12747.8485146	488	142.0829648	97.2697330	13820.3720515
489	117.3117652	101.2570933	11878.6483456	489	129.7632701	99.2293658	12876.3269998	489	143.5333951	97.2767000	13962.4550163
490	118.4604429	101.2655349	11995.9601108	490	131.0609028	99.2369959	13006.0902599	490	144.9986318	97.2835966	14105.9684114
491	119.6203680	101.2738947	12114.4205536	491	132.3715118	99.2445504	13137.1511727	491	146.4782262	97.2904236	14250.9870043
492	120.7916508	101.2821734	12234.0409217	492	133.6952270	99.2520301	13269.5226846	492	147.9741309	97.2971815	14397.4658694
493	121.9744024	101.2903718	12354.8325725	493	135.0321792	99.2594357	13403.2179115	493	149.4847001	97.3038712	14545.4400003
494	123.1687351	101.2984908	12476.8069748	494	136.3825010	99.2667680	13538.2500908	494	151.0106898	97.3104932	14694.9247004
495	124.3747623	101.3065310	12599.9757099	495	137.7463260	99.2740277	13674.6325918	495	152.5522572	97.3170483	14845.9353902
496	125.5925985	101.3144933	12724.3504722	496	139.1237893	99.2812156	13812.3789178	496	154.1095615	97.3235372	14998.4876474
497	126.8223593	101.3223783	12849.9430706	497	140.5150272	99.2883323	13951.5027071	497	155.6827533	97.3299605	15152.5972089
498	128.0641616	101.3301869	12976.7654300	498	141.9201775	99.2953785	14092.0177343	498	157.2720248	97.3363190	15308.2799722
499	129.3181232	101.3379198	13104.8295916	499	143.3393792	99.3023549	14233.9379118	499	158.8775101	97.3426131	15465.5519971
500	130.5843632	101.3455776	13234.1477148	500	144.7727730	99.3092623	14377.2772910	500	160.4993847	97.3488437	15624.4295072

M	C(12.50,M,12)	A(12.50,M,12)	S(12.50,M,12)	M	C(12.75,M,12)	A(12.75,M,12)	S(12.75,M,12)	M	C(13.00,M,12)	A(13.00,M,12)	S(13.00,M,12)
1	1.0104167	.9896907	1.0000000	1	1.0106250	.9894867	1.0000000	1	1.0108333	.9892828	1.0000000
2	1.0209418	1.9691784	2.0104167	2	1.0213629	1.9685706	2.0106250	2	1.0217840	1.9679632	2.0108333
3	1.0315767	2.9385684	3.0313585	3	1.0322149	2.9373612	3.0319879	3	1.0328534	2.9361548	3.0326174
4	1.0423222	3.8979646	4.0629352	4	1.0431822	3.8959665	4.0642028	4	1.0440426	3.8939701	4.0654707
5	1.0531798	4.8474701	5.1052574	5	1.0542660	4.8444938	5.1073849	5	1.0553531	4.8415203	5.1095133
6	1.0641504	5.7871369	6.1584372	6	1.0654675	5.7830489	6.1616509	6	1.0667861	5.7789154	6.1648664
7	1.0752353	6.7172159	7.2225976	7	1.0767881	6.7117367	7.2271184	7	1.0783429	6.7062642	7.2316524
8	1.0864357	7.6376570	8.2976228	8	1.0882290	7.6306609	8.3039066	8	1.0900249	7.6236744	8.3099953
9	1.0977527	8.5486089	9.3842585	9	1.0997914	8.5399242	9.3921356	9	1.1018336	8.5312525	9.4000203
10	1.1091876	9.4501697	10.4820112	10	1.1114767	9.4396282	10.4919270	10	1.1137701	9.4291039	10.5018538
11	1.1207417	10.3424360	11.5911988	11	1.1232862	10.3298733	11.6034037	11	1.1258359	10.3173328	11.6156239
12	1.1324160	11.2255036	12.7119405	12	1.1352211	11.2107590	12.7266899	12	1.1380325	11.1960423	12.7414598
13	1.1442120	12.0994875	13.8443565	13	1.1472828	12.0823836	13.8619110	13	1.1503612	12.0653345	13.8794923
14	1.1561309	12.9644215	14.9885686	14	1.1594727	12.9448447	15.0091938	14	1.1628234	12.9253103	15.0298535
15	1.1681740	13.8204584	16.1446995	15	1.1717921	13.7982384	16.1686665	15	1.1754207	13.7760696	16.1926769
16	1.1803424	14.6676701	17.3128734	16	1.1842424	14.6426601	17.3404565	16	1.1881544	14.6177111	17.3680976
17	1.1926377	15.5061478	18.4932159	17	1.1969249	15.4782042	18.5247009	17	1.2010261	15.4503325	18.5562520
18	1.2050610	16.3359813	19.6853535	18	1.2095412	16.3049639	19.7215259	18	1.2140372	16.2740305	19.7572780
19	1.2176137	17.1572598	20.8909145	19	1.2223926	17.1230317	20.9310671	19	1.2271892	17.0889007	20.9713152
20	1.2302972	17.9700714	22.1085282	20	1.2353805	17.9324989	22.1534597	20	1.2404838	17.8950378	22.1985045
21	1.2431128	18.7745038	23.3388254	21	1.2485064	18.7334560	23.3888402	21	1.2539224	18.6925353	23.4389882
22	1.2560619	19.5706430	24.5819381	22	1.2617718	19.5259923	24.6373466	22	1.2675065	19.4814859	24.6929106
23	1.2691458	20.3585745	25.8380000	23	1.2751781	20.3101965	25.8991184	23	1.2812379	20.2619811	25.9604172
24	1.2823661	21.1383830	27.1071458	24	1.2887269	21.0861560	27.1742965	24	1.2951179	21.0341116	27.2416550
25	1.2957241	21.9101522	28.3895119	25	1.3024196	21.8530577	28.4630234	25	1.3091484	21.7979669	28.5367729
26	1.3092212	22.6739651	29.6852360	26	1.3162578	22.6136873	29.7654431	26	1.3233308	22.5536359	29.8459213
27	1.3228589	23.4299036	30.9944572	27	1.3302431	23.3654296	31.0817009	27	1.3376669	23.3012061	31.1692521
28	1.3363387	24.1780489	32.3173161	28	1.3443769	24.1092687	32.4119440	28	1.3521583	24.0407645	32.5069190
29	1.3505620	24.9184814	33.6539548	29	1.3586609	24.8452875	33.7563209	29	1.3668067	24.7723969	33.8590773
30	1.3646304	25.6512806	35.0045169	30	1.3730967	25.5735683	35.1145818	30	1.3816137	25.4961882	35.2258840
31	1.3783453	26.3765251	36.3691473	31	1.3876858	26.2941925	36.4880785	31	1.3965812	26.2122224	36.6074977
32	1.3932083	27.0942929	37.7479925	32	1.4024300	27.0072406	37.8757643	32	1.4117109	26.9205828	38.0040790
33	1.4077208	27.8046610	39.1412008	33	1.4173308	27.7127922	39.2781943	33	1.4270044	27.6213515	39.4157898
34	1.4223846	28.5077057	40.5489216	34	1.4323900	28.4109261	40.6955251	34	1.4424636	28.3146099	40.8427942
35	1.4372011	29.2035026	41.9713062	35	1.4476091	29.1017203	42.1279151	35	1.4580903	29.0004384	42.2852578
36	1.4521720	29.8921263	43.4085073	36	1.4629899	29.7852520	43.5755242	36	1.4738863	29.6789169	43.7433481
37	1.4672987	30.5736507	44.8606793	37	1.4785342	30.4615975	45.0385141	37	1.4898534	30.3501238	45.2172344
38	1.4825831	31.2481492	46.3279780	38	1.4942436	31.1308324	46.5170483	38	1.5059935	31.0141374	46.7070877
39	1.4980267	31.9156940	47.8105611	39	1.5101200	31.7930315	48.0112920	39	1.5223084	31.6710345	48.2130812
40	1.5136311	32.5763570	49.3085878	40	1.5261650	32.4482686	49.5214119	40	1.5388001	32.3200915	49.7353896
41	1.5293981	33.2302090	50.8222190	41	1.5423805	33.0966171	51.0475769	41	1.5554704	32.9637838	51.2741896
42	1.5453293	33.8773202	52.3516171	42	1.5587683	33.7381492	52.5899574	42	1.5723213	33.5997861	52.8296600
43	1.5614265	34.5177062	53.8969464	43	1.5753302	34.3729368	54.1487257	43	1.5893548	34.2289723	54.4019813
44	1.5776914	35.1515977	55.4583729	44	1.5920681	35.0010506	55.7240560	44	1.6065728	34.8514153	55.9913361
45	1.5941257	35.7789009	57.0360643	45	1.6089838	35.6225609	57.3161240	45	1.6239773	35.4671874	57.5979089
46	1.6107311	36.3997369	58.6301900	46	1.6260793	36.2375371	58.9251079	46	1.6415704	36.0763602	59.2218863
47	1.6275066	37.0141726	60.2409211	47	1.6433564	36.8460478	60.5511871	47	1.6593541	36.6790043	60.8634567
48	1.6444628	37.6222739	61.8684307	48	1.6608170	37.4481611	62.1945435	48	1.6773305	37.2751897	62.5228108
49	1.6615928	38.2241062	63.5128936	49	1.6784632	38.0439442	63.8553605	49	1.6955015	37.8649857	64.2001413
50	1.6789009	38.8197339	65.1744862	50	1.6962969	38.6334636	65.5338237	50	1.7138695	38.4484607	65.8956428
51	1.6963894	39.4092212	66.8533871	51	1.7143200	39.2167853	67.2301206	51	1.7324364	39.0256825	67.6095123
52	1.7140602	39.9926313	68.5497765	52	1.7325347	39.7939743	68.9444406	52	1.7512044	39.5967181	69.3419487
53	1.7319150	40.5700269	70.2638367	53	1.7509429	40.3650952	70.6769753	53	1.7701758	40.1616337	71.0931531
54	1.7499557	41.1414699	71.9957517	54	1.7695466	40.9302117	72.4279182	54	1.7893527	40.7204950	72.8633289
55	1.7681845	41.7070277	73.7457074	55	1.7883481	41.4893869	74.1974648	55	1.8087374	41.2733669	74.6526817
56	1.7866030	42.2667432	75.5133919	56	1.8073493	42.0426834	75.9858129	56	1.8283320	41.8203135	76.4614191
57	1.8052135	42.8206943	77.3004949	57	1.8265523	42.5901629	77.7931621	57	1.8481390	42.3613983	78.2897511
58	1.8240178	43.3689345	79.1057084	58	1.8459595	43.1318866	79.6197145	58	1.8681605	42.8966842	80.1378901
59	1.8430180	43.9115228	80.9297262	59	1.8655728	43.6679151	81.4656740	59	1.8883989	43.4262364	82.0060505
60	1.8622161	44.4485174	82.7727442	60	1.8853945	44.1983080	83.3312467	60	1.9088565	43.9501072	83.8944494
61	1.8816142	44.9799760	84.6349603	61	1.9054268	44.7231248	85.2166412	61	1.9295358	44.4683666	85.8033060
62	1.9012143	45.5059557	86.5165745	62	1.9256720	45.2424241	87.1220681	62	1.9504391	44.9810716	87.7328418
63	1.9210186	46.0265128	88.4177868	63	1.9461322	45.7562638	89.0477400	63	1.9715685	45.4882819	89.6832809
64	1.9410292	46.5417034	90.3388074	64	1.9668099	46.2647013	90.9938723	64	1.9929275	45.9900563	91.6548498
65	1.9612483	47.0515828	92.2798366	65	1.9877072	46.7677935	92.9606822	65	2.0145176	46.4864531	93.6477773
66	1.9816780	47.5562056	94.2410849	66	2.0088266	47.2655965	94.9483894	66	2.0363415	46.9775298	95.6622949
67	2.0023204	48.0556262	96.2227629	67	2.0301704	47.7581660	96.9572161	67	2.0584019	47.4633436	97.6986364
68	2.0231780	48.5498981	98.2250834	68	2.0517410	48.2455570	98.9873365	68	2.0807012	47.9439508	99.7570383
69	2.0442527	49.0390744	100.2482613	69	2.0735407	48.7278239	101.0391275	69	2.1032422	48.4194072	101.8377396
70	2.0655470	49.5232076	102.2925140	70	2.0955721	49.2050205	103.1126682	70	2.1260273	48.8897681	103.9409817
71	2.0870631	50.0023498	104.3580611	71	2.1178376	49.6772003	105.2082403	71	2.1490593	49.3550879	106.0670091
72	2.1088034	50.4765524	106.4451242	72	2.1403396	50.1444158	107.3260778	72	2.1723407	49.8154209	108.2160683
73	2.1307701	50.9459663	108.5539276	73	2.1630807	50.6067194	109.4664174	73	2.1958744	50.2708203	110.3884091
74	2.1529656	51.4103419	110.6846977	74	2.1860634	51.0641627	111.6294981	74	2.2196631	50.7213392	112.5842835
75	2.1753923	51.8700291	112.8376633	75	2.2092903	51.5167963	113.8155615	75	2.2437094	51.1670297	114.8039466
76	2.1980527	52.3249772	115.0130556	76	2.2327641	51.9646721	116.0248519	76	2.2680163	51.6079436	117.0476560
77	2.2209490	52.7752352	117.2111082	77	2.2564872	52.4078388	118.2576159	77	2.2925865	52.0441322	119.3156723
78	2.2440839	53.2208513	119.4320573	78	2.2804623	52.8463464	120.5141031	78	2.3174228	52.4756460	121.6082587
79	2.2674598	53.6618735	121.6761412	79	2.3046923	53.2802438	122.7945654	79	2.3425282	52.9025352	123.9256815
80	2.2910792	54.0983490	123.9436010	80	2.3291796	53.7095795	125.0992577	80	2.3679056	53.3248493	126.2682097
81	2.3149446	54.5303248	126.2346802	81	2.3539271	54.1344015	127.4284373	81	2.3935579	53.7426374	128.6361153
82	2.3390586	54.9578472	128.5495248	82	2.3789326	54.5547521	129.7823645	82	2.4194881	54.1559480	131.0296733
83	2.3634238	55.3809622	130.8886834	83	2.4042138	54.9706936	132.1613021	83	2.4456992	54.5648290	133.4491614
84	2.3880428	55.7997152	133.2521072	84	2.4297586	55.3822071	134.5655159	84	2.4721943	54.9693280	135.8948606
85	2.4129182	56.2141511	135.6401500	85	2.4555748	55.7894937	136.9952745	85	2.4989764	55.3694918	138.3670550
86	2.4380528	56.6243145	138.0530682	86	2.4816653	56.1924490	139.4508493	86	2.5260487	55.7653670	140.8660314
87	2.4634492	57.0302494	140.4911210	87	2.5080330	56.5911678	141.9325146	87	2.5534142	56.1569995	143.3920801
88	2.4891101	57.4319994	142.9545702	88	2.5346808	56.9856948	144.4405476	88	2.5810762	56.5444348	145.9454943
89	2.5150383	57.8296076	145.4436803	89	2.5616118	57.3760740	146.9752284	89	2.6090378	56.9277178	148.5265705
90	2.5412367	58.2231168	147.9587186	90	2.5888289	57.7623491	149.5368402	90	2.6373024	57.3068932	151.1356083
91	2.5677079	58.6125692	150.4999553	91	2.6163352	58.1445631	152.1256691	91	2.6658732	57.6820048	153.7729107
92	2.5944548	58.9980007	153.0676621	92	2.6441338	58.5227588	154.7420043	92	2.6947535	58.0530962	156.4387839
93	2.6214804	59.3794705	155.6621179	93	2.6722277	58.8969784	157.3861381	93	2.7239467	58.4202106	159.1335374
94	2.6487875	59.7570018	158.2835983	94	2.7006201	59.2672637	160.0583659	94	2.7534561	58.7833906	161.8574841
95	2.6763790	60.1306409	160.9323858	95	2.7293142	59.6336561	162.7589860	95	2.7832852	59.1426782	164.6109402
96	2.7042580	60.5004081	163.6087649	96	2.7583132	59.9961965	165.4883002	96	2.8134374	59.4981153	167.3942253
97	2.7324273	60.8664031	166.3130228	97	2.7876203	60.3549254	168.2466134	97	2.8439163	59.8497431	170.2076628
98	2.7608901	61.2286051	169.0454501	98	2.8172387	60.7098829	171.0342337	98	2.8747254	60.1976024	173.0515791
99	2.7896494	61.5870731	171.8063402	99	2.8471719	61.0611086	173.8514724	99	2.9058683	60.5417336	175.9263046
100	2.8187082	61.9418455	174.5959896	100	2.8774231	61.4086418	176.6986443	100	2.9373485	60.8821767	178.8321729

Table 1   **439**

M	C(12.50,M,12)	A(12.50,M,12)	S(12.50,M,12)	M	C(12.75,M,12)	A(12.75,M,12)	S(12.75,M,12)	M	C(13.00,M,12)	A(13.00,M,12)	S(13.00,M,12)
101	2.8480698	62.2929605	177.4146979	101	2.9079957	61.7525213	179.5760674	101	2.9691698	61.2189712	181.7695214
102	2.8777372	62.6404558	180.2627676	102	2.9388932	62.0927854	182.4840631	102	3.0013358	61.5521561	184.7385912
103	2.9077136	62.9843686	183.1405048	103	2.9701189	62.4294723	185.4229563	103	3.0338503	61.8817703	187.7400271
104	2.9380023	63.3247360	186.0482184	104	3.0016764	62.7626194	188.3930752	104	3.0667170	62.2078519	190.7738774
105	2.9686065	63.6615943	188.9862207	105	3.0335692	63.0922641	191.3947516	105	3.0999398	62.5304388	193.8405944
106	2.9995295	63.9949800	191.9548271	106	3.0658009	63.4184432	194.4283209	106	3.1335225	62.8495685	196.9405341
107	3.0307745	64.3249286	194.9543566	107	3.0983750	63.7411930	197.4941218	107	3.1674689	63.1652780	200.0740566
108	3.0623451	64.6514758	197.9851311	108	3.1312953	64.0605497	200.5924968	108	3.2017832	63.4776039	203.2415255
109	3.0942445	64.9746564	201.0474762	109	3.1645653	64.3765488	203.7237921	109	3.2364692	63.7865826	206.4433087
110	3.1264763	65.2945053	204.1417208	110	3.1981888	64.6892258	206.8883574	110	3.2715309	64.0922499	209.6797779
111	3.1590437	65.6110568	207.2681970	111	3.2321696	64.9986155	210.0865462	111	3.3069725	64.3946413	212.9513088
112	3.1919504	65.9243449	210.4272408	112	3.2665114	65.3047525	213.3187158	112	3.3427980	64.6937919	216.2582814
113	3.2251999	66.2344032	213.6191912	113	3.3012180	65.6076710	216.5852271	113	3.3790117	64.9897364	219.6010794
114	3.2587957	66.5412650	216.8443911	114	3.3362935	65.9074048	219.8864452	114	3.4156177	65.2825092	222.9800911
115	3.2927415	66.8449633	220.1031868	115	3.3717416	66.2039875	223.2227386	115	3.4526202	65.5721443	226.3957088
116	3.3270409	67.1455307	223.3959284	116	3.4075664	66.4974520	226.5944802	116	3.4900236	65.8586753	229.8483289
117	3.3616976	67.4429994	226.7229693	117	3.4437717	66.7878313	230.0020466	117	3.5278322	66.1421355	233.3383525
118	3.3957153	67.7374015	230.0846669	118	3.4803618	67.0751578	233.4458183	118	3.5680503	66.4225578	236.8661847
119	3.4320977	68.0287685	233.4813822	119	3.5173407	67.3594635	236.9261802	119	3.6046825	66.6999748	240.4322350
120	3.4678488	68.3171317	236.9134799	120	3.5547124	67.6407802	240.4435208	120	3.6437333	66.9744186	244.0369175
121	3.5039722	68.6025221	240.3813287	121	3.5924812	67.9191393	243.9982332	121	3.6832071	67.2459211	247.6806508
122	3.5404719	68.8849703	243.8853008	122	3.6305513	68.1945272	247.5907145	122	3.7231085	67.5145139	251.3638579
123	3.5773518	69.1645067	247.4257727	123	3.6692270	68.4671090	251.2213658	123	3.7634421	67.7802281	255.0869663
124	3.6146159	69.4411613	251.0031245	124	3.7082126	68.7367807	254.8905928	124	3.8042128	68.0430945	258.8504085
125	3.6522681	69.7149638	254.6177404	125	3.7476123	69.0036172	258.5988054	125	3.8454251	68.3031438	262.6546212
126	3.6903126	69.9859435	258.2700085	126	3.7874307	69.2676485	262.3464177	126	3.8870838	68.5604061	266.5000463
127	3.7287533	70.2541297	261.9603211	127	3.8275721	69.5289039	266.1338484	127	3.9291939	68.8149112	270.3871301
128	3.7675945	70.5195510	265.6890745	128	3.8683412	69.7874126	269.9615205	128	3.9717602	69.0666887	274.3163240
129	3.8068403	70.7822360	269.4566690	129	3.9094423	70.0432036	273.8298617	129	4.0147876	69.3157679	278.2880842
130	3.8464949	71.0422130	273.2635093	130	3.9508801	70.2963053	277.7393040	130	4.0582811	69.5621777	282.3028718
131	3.8865625	71.2995098	277.1100042	131	3.9929593	70.5467462	281.6902841	131	4.1022458	69.8059466	286.3611529
132	3.9270476	71.5541540	280.9965668	132	4.0353845	70.7945540	285.6832433	132	4.1466868	70.0471030	290.4633987
133	3.9679543	71.8061730	284.9236143	133	4.0782504	71.0397566	289.7186278	133	4.1916093	70.2856748	294.6100856
134	4.0092872	72.0555939	288.8915686	134	4.1215919	71.2823813	293.7968882	134	4.2370184	70.5216898	298.8016948
135	4.0510506	72.3024435	292.9008558	135	4.1653839	71.5224552	297.9184802	135	4.2829194	70.7551754	303.0387132
136	4.0932490	72.5467482	296.9519064	136	4.2096411	71.7600052	302.0838640	136	4.3293177	70.9861587	307.3216326
137	4.1358870	72.7885343	301.0451554	137	4.2543685	71.9950577	306.2935051	137	4.3762181	71.2146665	311.6509503
138	4.1789692	73.0278277	305.1810425	138	4.2995722	72.2276390	310.5478736	138	4.4236277	71.4407253	316.0271689
139	4.2225001	73.2646543	309.3600117	139	4.3452541	72.4577751	314.8474447	139	4.4715503	71.6643614	320.4507966
140	4.2664845	73.4990393	313.5825118	140	4.3914224	72.6854918	319.1926988	140	4.5199921	71.8855007	324.9223469
141	4.3109270	73.7310079	317.8489963	141	4.4380813	72.9108144	323.5841213	141	4.5689587	72.1044690	329.4423390
142	4.3553325	73.9605852	322.1599233	142	4.4852359	73.1337681	328.0222026	142	4.6184557	72.3209916	334.0112976
143	4.4012058	74.1877956	326.5157559	143	4.5328915	73.3543778	332.5074385	143	4.6684890	72.5351936	338.6297534
144	4.4470517	74.4126637	330.9169617	144	4.5810535	73.5726682	337.0403300	144	4.7190643	72.7471000	343.2982424
145	4.4933751	74.6352136	335.3640134	145	4.6297272	73.7886637	34..6213835	145	4.7701875	72.9567354	348.0173067
146	4.5401811	74.8554691	339.8573885	146	4.6789187	74.0023883	346.2511107	146	4.8218645	73.1641241	352.7874941
147	4.5874747	75.0734540	344.3975696	147	4.7286316	74.2138660	350.9300288	147	4.8741014	73.3692901	357.6093587
148	4.6352609	75.2891915	348.9850443	148	4.7788733	74.4231203	355.6586603	148	4.9269002	73.5722573	362.4834601
149	4.6835448	75.5027050	353.6203052	149	4.8296488	74.6301747	360.4375336	149	4.9802789	73.7730493	367.4103642
150	4.7323318	75.7140173	358.3038050	150	4.8809638	74.8350523	365.2671824	150	5.0342320	73.9716893	372.3906432
151	4.7816269	75.9231512	363.0361818	151	4.9328241	75.0377759	370.1481462	151	5.0887695	74.1682005	377.4248751
152	4.8314355	76.1301290	367.8178087	152	4.9852353	75.2383683	375.0800703	152	5.1438978	74.3626056	382.5136446
153	4.8817630	76.3349730	372.6492442	153	5.0382034	75.4368517	380.0662056	153	5.1996234	74.5549272	387.6575424
154	4.9326147	76.5377053	377.5310072	154	5.0917343	75.6332484	385.1044090	154	5.2559526	74.7451876	392.8571658
155	4.9839961	76.7383475	382.4636219	155	5.1458340	75.8275804	390.1961434	155	5.3128921	74.9334090	398.1131184
156	5.0359127	76.9369212	387.4476179	156	5.2005085	76.0198893	395.3419774	156	5.3704485	75.1196132	403.4260106
157	5.0883701	77.1334478	392.4835306	157	5.2557639	76.2101366	400.5424859	157	5.4286283	75.3038218	408.7964590
158	5.1413740	77.3279483	397.5719007	158	5.3116064	76.3983547	405.7982498	158	5.4874384	75.4860552	414.2250873
159	5.1949299	77.5204437	402.7132747	159	5.3680422	76.5846912	411.1098562	159	5.5468857	75.6663376	419.7125258
160	5.2490438	77.7109546	407.9082046	160	5.4250777	76.7690204	416.4778984	160	5.6069770	75.8446868	425.2594115
161	5.3037213	77.8995015	413.1572484	161	5.4827191	76.9514116	421.9029761	161	5.6677192	76.0211246	430.8663884
162	5.3589684	78.0861045	418.4609698	162	5.5409730	77.1318853	427.3656552	162	5.7291195	76.1956715	436.5341076
163	5.4147910	78.2707839	423.8199382	163	5.5998459	77.3104617	432.9266683	163	5.7911850	76.3683477	442.2632271
164	5.4711951	78.4535593	429.2347292	164	5.6593442	77.4871606	438.5265141	164	5.8539228	76.5391734	448.0544121
165	5.5281867	78.6344504	434.7059243	165	5.7194747	77.6620018	444.1858583	165	5.9173403	76.7081682	453.9083349
166	5.5857720	78.8134767	440.2341111	166	5.7802442	77.8350049	449.9053331	166	5.9814448	76.8753519	459.8256752
167	5.6439571	78.9906574	445.8198831	167	5.8416593	78.0061891	455.6855772	167	6.0462438	77.0407438	465.8071200
168	5.7027483	79.1660114	451.4638402	168	5.9037269	78.1755737	461.5272365	168	6.1117448	77.2043632	471.8533638
169	5.7621520	79.3395577	457.1665885	169	5.9664540	78.3431774	467.4309634	169	6.1779553	77.3662291	477.9651086
170	5.8221744	79.5113148	462.9287405	170	6.0298476	78.5090191	473.3974174	170	6.2443832	77.5263602	484.1430640
171	5.8828220	79.6813013	468.7509149	171	6.0939147	78.6731172	479.4272650	171	6.3125361	77.6847751	490.3879472
172	5.9441014	79.8495353	474.6337369	172	6.1586625	78.8354901	485.5211796	172	6.3809219	77.8414923	496.7004833
173	6.0060192	80.0160349	480.5778383	173	6.2240983	78.9961560	491.6798422	173	6.4500486	77.9965299	503.0814052
174	6.0685819	80.1808181	486.5838575	174	6.2902294	79.1551327	497.9039405	174	6.5199241	78.1499059	509.5314537
175	6.1317962	80.3439024	492.6524393	175	6.3570363	79.3124380	504.1941699	175	6.5905566	78.3016381	516.0513778
176	6.1956691	80.5053055	498.7842356	176	6.4246069	79.4680396	510.5512329	176	6.6619543	78.4517442	522.6419344
177	6.2602073	80.6650446	504.9799047	177	6.4928683	79.6221047	516.9758398	177	6.7341255	78.6002416	529.3038887
178	6.3254178	80.8231369	511.2401121	178	6.5618550	79.7745006	523.4687081	178	6.8070785	78.7471475	536.0380142
179	6.3913076	80.9795994	517.5655299	179	6.6315747	79.9252994	530.0305631	179	6.8808218	78.8924790	542.8450027
180	6.4578837	81.1344489	523.9568375	180	6.7020352	80.0745028	536.6621979	180	6.9553641	79.0362529	549.7259145
181	6.5251534	81.2877020	530.4147212	181	6.7732443	80.2221425	543.3641731	181	7.0307139	79.1784860	556.6812785
182	6.5931237	81.4393752	536.9398746	182	6.8452101	80.3682301	550.1374174	182	7.1068799	79.3191947	563.7119724
183	6.6618021	81.5894847	543.5329983	183	6.9179404	80.5127818	556.9826275	183	7.1838711	79.4583954	570.8188724
184	6.7311958	81.7380467	550.1948003	184	6.9914435	80.6558138	563.9005679	184	7.2616964	79.5961043	578.0027435
185	6.8013125	81.8850772	556.9259962	185	7.0657276	80.7973420	570.8920115	185	7.3403648	79.7323373	585.2644399
186	6.8721595	82.0305919	563.7273086	186	7.1408010	80.9373823	577.9577391	186	7.4198854	79.8671103	592.6048046
187	6.9437445	82.1746064	570.5994681	187	7.2166720	81.0759503	585.0985401	187	7.5002675	80.0004380	600.0246900
188	7.0160751	82.3171362	577.5432126	188	7.2933491	81.2130616	592.3152121	188	7.5815204	80.1323385	607.5249575
189	7.0891593	82.4581967	584.5592877	189	7.3708410	81.3487315	599.6085612	189	7.6636535	80.2628246	615.1064779
190	7.1630047	82.5978029	591.6484470	190	7.4491562	81.4829747	606.9794022	190	7.7468764	80.3919122	622.7701314
191	7.2376195	82.7359699	598.8114516	191	7.5283034	81.6158067	614.4285583	191	7.8305988	80.5196164	630.5168078
192	7.3130112	82.8727124	606.0490709	192	7.6082917	81.7472423	621.9568617	192	7.9154302	80.6459519	638.3474066
193	7.3891884	83.0080453	613.3620821	193	7.6891298	81.8772960	629.5651534	193	8.0011807	80.7709334	646.2628368
194	7.4661591	83.1419830	620.7512704	194	7.7708268	82.0059824	637.2542832	194	8.0878602	80.8945755	654.2640176
195	7.5439316	83.2745398	628.2174295	195	7.8533918	82.1333160	645.0251099	195	8.1754787	81.0168925	662.3518778
196	7.6225142	83.4057302	635.7613611	196	7.9368341	82.2599108	652.8785017	196	8.2640464	81.1378986	670.5273564
197	7.7019154	83.5355685	643.3838753	197	8.0211629	82.3839810	660.8153358	197	8.3535735	81.2576079	678.7914028
198	7.7821437	83.6640673	651.0857906	198	8.1063878	82.5073405	668.8364988	198	8.4440706	81.3760342	687.1449764
199	7.8632077	83.7912419	658.8679343	199	8.1925182	82.6294031	676.9428866	199	8.5355480	81.4931913	695.5890469
200	7.9451161	83.9171053	666.7311419	200	8.2795637	82.7501824	685.1354047	200	8.9980165	81.6090928	704.1245949

Table 1

M	C(12.50,M,12)	A(12.50,M,12)	S(12.50,M,12)	M	C(12.75,M,12)	A(12.75,M,12)	S(12.75,M,12)	M	C(13.00,M,12)	A(13.00,M,12)	S(13.00,M,12)
201	8.0278777	84.0416713	674.6762580	201	8.3675340	82.8696919	693.4149684	201	8.7214866	81.7237521	712.7526114
202	8.1115014	84.1649530	682.7041357	202	8.4564391	82.9879450	701.7825025	202	8.8159694	81.8371826	721.4740980
203	8.1959962	84.2869638	690.8156371	203	8.5462888	83.1049549	710.2389416	203	8.9114757	81.9493975	730.2900674
204	8.2813712	84.4077167	699.0116334	204	8.6370931	83.2207345	718.7852303	204	9.0060167	82.0604097	739.2015432
205	8.3676355	84.5272248	707.2930045	205	8.7288622	83.3352970	727.4223234	205	9.1056036	82.1702322	748.2095599
206	8.4547983	84.6455008	715.6606400	206	8.8216064	83.4486551	736.1511856	206	9.2042476	82.2788777	757.3151635
207	8.5473692	84.7625575	724.1154284	207	8.9153359	83.5608213	744.9727920	207	9.3039603	82.3863588	766.5194111
208	8.6318574	84.8784075	732.6583075	208	9.0100614	83.6718084	753.8881279	208	9.4047532	82.4926880	775.8233714
209	8.7217726	84.9930631	741.2901649	209	9.1057933	83.7816286	762.8981892	209	9.5066380	82.5978777	785.2281246
210	8.8126244	85.1065366	750.0119374	210	9.2025423	83.8902942	772.0039825	210	9.6096266	82.7019400	794.7347626
211	8.9044225	85.2188404	758.8245618	211	9.3003193	83.9978174	781.2065248	211	9.7137309	82.8048871	804.3443892
212	8.9971769	85.3299864	767.7289843	212	9.3991352	84.1042101	790.5068442	212	9.8169630	82.9067308	814.0581201
213	9.0908975	85.4399865	776.7261612	213	9.4990010	84.2094844	799.9059794	213	9.9253351	83.0074831	823.8770830
214	9.1855944	85.5488526	785.8170588	214	9.5999279	84.3136518	809.4049004	214	10.0328595	83.1071556	833.8024181
215	9.2812776	85.6565964	795.0026531	215	9.7019272	84.4167241	819.0049083	215	10.1415488	83.2057598	843.8352777
216	9.3779576	85.7632294	804.2839308	216	9.8050101	84.5187128	828.7068355	216	10.2514156	83.3033073	853.9768265
217	9.4756447	85.8687631	813.6618884	217	9.9091884	84.6196292	838.5118456	217	10.3624726	83.3998094	864.2282421
218	9.5743493	85.9732089	823.1375331	218	10.0144735	84.7194847	848.4210340	218	10.4747328	83.4952772	874.5907148
219	9.6740821	86.0765779	832.7118824	219	10.1208773	84.8182904	858.4355075	219	10.5882090	83.5897219	885.0654475
220	9.7748538	86.1788812	842.3859645	220	10.2284116	84.9160573	868.5563848	220	10.7029146	83.6831544	895.6536565
221	9.8756752	86.2801298	852.1608183	221	10.3370885	85.0127963	878.7847904	221	10.8188629	83.7755855	906.3565712
222	9.9795572	86.3803347	862.0374935	222	10.4469200	85.1085183	889.1218848	222	10.9360672	83.8670261	917.1754340
223	10.0835110	86.4795065	872.0170507	223	10.5579186	85.2032339	899.5680049	223	11.0545413	83.9574867	928.1115012
224	10.1885475	86.5776559	882.1005617	224	10.6700964	85.2969538	910.1267234	224	11.1742988	84.0469777	939.1660425
225	10.2946782	86.6747935	892.2891092	225	10.7834662	85.3896884	920.7968199	225	11.2953537	84.1355097	950.3403413
226	10.4019145	86.7709296	902.5837874	226	10.8980405	85.4814480	931.5802861	226	11.4177200	84.2230929	961.6356950
227	10.5102617	86.8660747	912.9857019	227	11.0137322	85.5722429	942.4783766	227	11.5414120	84.3097374	973.0534150
228	10.6197497	86.9602388	923.4959696	228	11.1308542	85.6620833	953.4921589	228	11.6664440	84.3954533	984.5948270
229	10.7303721	87.0534323	934.1157193	229	11.2491195	85.7509791	964.6230131	229	11.7928304	84.4802506	996.2612710
230	10.8421468	87.1456649	944.8460914	230	11.3686414	85.8389404	975.8721326	230	11.9205861	84.5641391	1008.0541015
231	10.9550858	87.2369467	955.6882382	231	11.4894332	85.9259769	987.2407740	231	12.0497258	84.6471285	1019.9746876
232	11.0692013	87.3272875	966.6433240	232	11.6115685	86.0120983	998.7302072	232	12.1802645	84.7292285	1032.0244134
233	11.1845055	87.4166969	977.7125253	233	11.7348807	86.0973143	1010.3417157	233	12.3122174	84.8104487	1044.2046778
234	11.3010107	87.5051845	988.8970308	234	11.8595638	86.1816345	1022.0765964	234	12.4455997	84.8907984	1056.5168952
235	11.4187296	87.5927600	1000.1980415	235	11.9855717	86.2650681	1033.9361603	235	12.5804270	84.9702969	1068.9624949
236	11.5376747	87.6794325	1011.6167712	236	12.1129184	86.3476246	1045.9217320	236	12.7167150	85.0489236	1081.5429219
237	11.6578588	87.7652116	1023.1544459	237	12.2416182	86.4293132	1058.0346504	237	12.8544794	85.1267175	1094.2596369
238	11.7792948	87.8501063	1034.8123047	238	12.3716864	86.5101429	1070.2762686	238	12.9937363	85.2036776	1107.1141163
239	11.9019958	87.9341258	1046.5915995	239	12.5031345	86.5901228	1082.6479539	239	13.1345017	85.2798130	1120.1078526
240	12.0259750	88.0172792	1058.4935954	240	12.6359803	86.6692619	1095.1510885	240	13.2767922	85.3551324	1133.2423544
241	12.1512455	88.0995753	1070.5195703	241	12.7702376	86.7475690	1107.7870688	241	13.4206241	85.4296446	1146.5191465
242	12.2778210	88.1810229	1082.6708159	242	12.9059214	86.8250528	1120.5573064	242	13.5660142	85.5033582	1159.9397706
243	12.4057150	88.2616309	1094.9486369	243	13.0430468	86.9017220	1133.4632278	243	13.7129793	85.5762818	1173.5057848
244	12.5349412	88.3414079	1107.3543518	244	13.1816292	86.9775852	1146.5062744	244	13.8615366	85.6484239	1187.2187642
245	12.6655135	88.4203625	1119.8892930	245	13.3216840	87.0526508	1159.6879038	245	14.0117033	85.7197928	1201.0803008
246	12.7974465	88.4985031	1132.5548065	246	13.4632269	87.1269272	1173.0095877	246	14.1634967	85.7903968	1215.0920041
247	12.9307526	88.5758381	1145.3522524	247	13.6062737	87.2004227	1186.4728146	247	14.3169346	85.8602442	1229.2555008
248	13.0654480	88.6523759	1158.2830051	248	13.7508403	87.2731455	1200.0790883	248	14.4720347	85.9293430	1243.5724054
249	13.2015464	88.7281246	1171.3484530	249	13.8969430	87.3451038	1213.8299286	249	14.6288151	85.9977012	1258.0444701
250	13.3390625	88.8030924	1184.5499994	250	14.0445979	87.4163055	1227.7268716	250	14.7872939	86.0653268	1272.6732852
251	13.4780111	88.8772873	1197.8890619	251	14.1938219	87.4867587	1241.7714696	251	14.9474896	86.1322277	1287.4605792
252	13.6184070	88.9507173	1211.3670730	252	14.3446312	87.5564712	1255.9652915	252	15.1094208	86.1984116	1302.4080688
253	13.7602654	89.0233903	1224.9854800	253	14.4970429	87.6254508	1270.3099227	253	15.2731061	86.2638861	1317.5174895
254	13.9036015	89.0953141	1238.7457454	254	14.6510740	87.6937052	1284.8069657	254	15.4385648	86.3286590	1332.7905957
255	14.0484307	89.1664965	1252.6493470	255	14.8087417	87.7612420	1299.4580397	255	15.6058159	86.3927377	1348.2291605
256	14.1947685	89.2369449	1266.6977777	256	14.9680663	87.8280687	1314.2647814	256	15.7748789	86.4561296	1363.8349764
257	14.3426307	89.3066672	1280.8925462	257	15.1230565	87.8941929	1329.2288447	257	15.9457734	86.5188421	1379.6098553
258	14.4920331	89.3756706	1295.2351769	258	15.2837390	87.9596220	1344.3519012	258	16.1185193	86.5808826	1395.5556288
259	14.6429918	89.4439626	1309.7272100	259	15.4461287	88.0243631	1359.6356402	259	16.2931366	86.6422581	1411.6741481
260	14.7955229	89.5115507	1324.3702018	260	15.6102438	88.0884236	1375.0817688	260	16.4696456	86.7029759	1427.9672847
261	14.9496430	89.5784419	1339.1657247	261	15.7761026	88.1518106	1390.6920126	261	16.6480668	86.7630429	1444.4369301
262	15.1053684	89.6446435	1354.1153677	262	15.9407237	88.2145312	1406.4681153	262	16.8284208	86.8224662	1461.0849971
263	15.2627160	89.7101627	1369.2207361	263	16.1131258	88.2765924	1422.4118390	263	17.0107287	86.8812525	1477.9341179
264	15.4217026	89.7750063	1384.4834522	264	16.2843278	88.3380012	1438.5249648	264	17.1950116	86.9394090	1494.9241466
265	15.5823454	89.8391815	1399.9051548	265	16.4573487	88.3987643	1454.8092926	265	17.3812909	86.9969421	1512.1191582
266	15.7446615	89.9026951	1415.4875002	266	16.6322081	88.4588886	1471.2666413	266	17.5695882	87.0538587	1529.5004491
267	15.9086684	89.9655539	1431.2321616	267	16.8089253	88.5183808	1487.8988494	267	17.7599254	87.1101652	1547.0700373
268	16.0743837	90.0277647	1447.1408300	268	16.9875201	88.5772475	1504.7077747	268	17.9523246	87.1658683	1564.8299627
269	16.2418252	90.0893342	1463.2152137	269	17.1680125	88.6354954	1521.6952948	269	18.1468081	87.2209744	1582.7822873
270	16.4110108	90.1502669	1479.4570388	270	17.3504227	88.6931309	1538.8633073	270	18.3433985	87.2754899	1600.9290954
271	16.5819589	90.2105754	1495.8680497	271	17.5347709	88.7501604	1556.2137300	271	18.5421187	87.3294212	1619.2724940
272	16.7546876	90.2702602	1512.4500085	272	17.7210778	88.8065904	1573.7485009	272	18.7429917	87.3827745	1637.8146127
273	16.9292156	90.3293296	1529.2046961	273	17.9093643	88.8624271	1591.4695787	273	18.9460407	87.4355560	1656.5576043
274	17.1055616	90.3877902	1546.1339117	274	18.0996513	88.9176768	1609.3789430	274	19.1512895	87.4877718	1675.5036451
275	17.2837445	90.4456480	1563.2394733	275	18.2919601	88.9723456	1627.4785943	275	19.3587618	87.5394280	1694.6549346
276	17.4637835	90.5029093	1580.5232178	276	18.4863122	89.0264397	1645.7705544	276	19.5684817	87.5905306	1714.0136964
277	17.6456979	90.5595804	1597.9870014	277	18.6827202	89.0799651	1664.2568665	277	19.7804736	87.6410855	1733.5821781
278	17.8295073	90.6156672	1615.6326993	278	18.8812332	89.1329277	1682.9395957	278	19.9947621	87.6910986	1753.3626571
279	18.0152313	90.6711758	1633.4622066	279	19.0818463	89.1853335	1701.8203298	279	20.2113720	87.7405757	1773.3574138
280	18.2028900	90.7261121	1651.4774379	280	19.1045909	89.2371884	1720.9026753	280	20.4303285	87.7895225	1793.5687858
281	18.3925034	90.7804821	1669.6803279	281	19.4894897	89.2884981	1740.1872662	281	20.6516571	87.8379448	1813.9991143
282	18.5840920	90.8342915	1688.0728314	282	19.6955555	89.3392684	1759.6767559	282	20.8753834	87.8858481	1834.6507714
283	18.7776763	90.8875463	1706.6569234	283	19.9058416	89.3895049	1779.3733215	283	21.1015334	87.9332380	1855.5261548
284	18.9732771	90.9402520	1725.4345997	284	20.1173411	89.4392133	1799.2791630	284	21.3301333	87.9801200	1876.6276881
285	19.1709154	90.9924143	1744.4078768	285	20.3310879	89.4883990	1819.3965042	285	21.5612097	88.0264996	1897.9578214
286	19.3705124	91.0440389	1763.5787922	286	20.5471057	89.5370677	1839.7275920	286	21.7947895	88.0723821	1919.5190312
287	19.5723396	91.0951313	1782.9494046	287	20.7654187	89.5852247	1860.2746977	287	22.0308997	88.1177729	1941.3138207
288	19.7762687	91.1456970	1802.5217942	288	20.9860513	89.6328754	1881.0401164	288	22.2695678	88.1626773	1963.3447204
289	19.9822715	91.1957413	1822.2980629	289	21.2090280	89.6800251	1902.0261677	289	22.5108215	88.2071003	1985.6142882
290	20.1904202	91.2452698	1842.2803344	290	21.4343740	89.7266791	1923.2351957	290	22.7546887	88.2510473	2008.1251097
291	20.4007370	91.2942876	1862.4707546	291	21.6621142	89.7728427	1944.6695697	291	23.0011978	88.2945233	2030.8797984
292	20.6132447	91.3428001	1882.8714917	292	21.8922742	89.8185209	1966.3316839	292	23.2503775	88.3375334	2053.8809963
293	20.8279660	91.3908125	1903.4847364	293	22.1248796	89.8637189	1988.2239580	293	23.5022566	88.3800825	2077.1313737
294	21.0449240	91.4383299	1924.3127024	294	22.3599564	89.9084417	2010.3488376	294	23.7566643	88.4221758	2100.6336303
295	21.2641420	91.4853574	1945.3576264	295	22.5975310	89.9526943	2032.7087940	295	24.0142304	88.4638176	2124.3904946
296	21.4856434	91.5319001	1966.6217684	296	22.8376297	89.9964817	2055.3063250	296	24.2743845	88.5050132	2148.4047250
297	21.7094522	91.5779630	1988.1074118	297	23.0802750	90.0398087	2078.1439547	297	24.5373570	88.5457674	2172.6791096
298	21.9355924	91.6235510	2009.8168640	298	23.3255075	90.0826802	2101.2242342	298	24.8031784	88.5860848	2197.2164666
299	22.1640881	91.6686690	2031.7524564	299	23.5733410	90.1251010	2124.5497417	299	25.0718795	88.6259702	2222.0196450
300	22.3949640	91.7133219	2053.9165445	300	23.8238078	90.1670759	2148.1230827	300	25.3434915	88.6654280	2247.0915245

Table 1

M	C(12.50,M,12)	A(12.50,M,12)	S(12.50,M,12)	M	C(12.75,M,12)	A(12.75,M,12)	S(12.75,M,12)	M	C(13.00,M,12)	A(13.00,M,12)	S(13.00,M,12)
301	22.6282449	91.7575145	2076.3115085	301	24.0769357	90.2086094	2171.9468905	301	25.6180460	88.7044630	2272.4350160
302	22.8639558	91.8012514	2098.9397534	302	24.3327532	90.2497063	2196.0238263	302	25.8955749	88.7430796	2298.0530621
303	23.1021220	91.8445375	2121.8037092	303	24.5912887	90.2903711	2220.3565794	303	26.1761103	88.7812824	2323.9486369
304	23.3427801	91.8873773	2144.9056312	304	24.8525711	90.3306084	2244.9478681	304	26.4598848	88.8190755	2350.1247472
305	23.5859229	91.9297755	2168.2486002	305	25.1166297	90.3704226	2269.8004392	305	26.7463314	88.8564641	2376.5844320
306	23.8316096	91.9717366	2191.8345232	306	25.3834939	90.4098183	2294.9170689	306	27.0360833	88.8934517	2403.3307633
307	24.0799556	92.0132651	2215.6661328	307	25.6531935	90.4487998	2320.3005628	307	27.3289742	88.9300429	2430.3668466
308	24.3308874	92.0543654	2239.7458984	308	25.9257587	90.4873715	2345.9537563	308	27.6250381	88.9662419	2457.6959208
309	24.5841321	92.0950421	2264.0766758	309	26.2012199	90.5255376	2371.8795150	309	27.9243093	89.0020530	2485.3208589
310	24.8402168	92.1352994	2288.6608078	310	26.4796078	90.5633025	2398.0807348	310	28.2268227	89.0374803	2513.2451682
311	25.0989690	92.1751416	2313.5010246	311	26.7609537	90.6006704	2424.5603427	311	28.5326133	89.0725279	2541.4719909
312	25.3604166	92.2145732	2338.5999936	312	27.0452888	90.6376454	2451.3212953	312	28.8417166	89.1071999	2570.0046041
313	25.6245876	92.2535982	2363.9604103	313	27.3326450	90.6742317	2478.3665851	313	29.1541685	89.1415003	2598.8463207
314	25.8915104	92.2922209	2389.5849979	314	27.6230543	90.7104334	2505.6992301	314	29.4792637	89.1754331	2628.0004892
315	26.1612136	92.3304454	2415.4765083	315	27.9165493	90.7462544	2533.3222844	315	29.7892637	89.2090023	2657.4704945
316	26.4337263	92.3682759	2441.6377219	316	28.2131626	90.7816989	2561.2388337	316	30.1119907	89.2422117	2687.2597582
317	26.7090776	92.4057163	2468.0714482	317	28.5129275	90.8167707	2589.4519964	317	30.4381939	89.2750651	2717.3717390
318	26.9872972	92.4427708	2494.7805258	318	28.8158773	90.8514738	2617.9649238	318	30.7679410	89.3075665	2747.8099328
319	27.2684148	92.4794432	2521.7678230	319	29.1220460	90.8858120	2646.7808012	319	31.1012603	89.3397195	2778.5778738
320	27.5524608	92.5157376	2549.0362379	320	29.4314678	90.9197892	2675.9028472	320	31.4381906	89.3715013	2809.6791341
321	27.8394656	92.5516579	2576.5886987	321	29.7441771	90.9534093	2705.3343150	321	31.7787710	89.4029955	2841.1173248
322	28.1294601	92.5872078	2604.4281643	322	30.0602090	90.9866758	2735.0784921	322	32.1230411	89.4341258	2872.8960958
323	28.4224753	92.6223912	2632.5576244	323	30.3795987	91.0195927	2765.1387011	323	32.4710407	89.4649225	2905.0191369
324	28.7185427	92.6572119	2660.9800997	324	30.7023820	91.0521634	2795.5182998	324	32.8223103	89.4953891	2937.4901775
325	29.0176942	92.6916727	2689.6986424	325	31.0285948	91.0843918	2826.2206818	325	33.1783907	89.5255292	2970.3129878
326	29.3199619	92.7257801	2718.7163366	326	31.3582736	91.1162813	2857.2492766	326	33.5378233	89.5553463	3003.4913786
327	29.6253781	92.7595350	2748.0362985	327	31.6914552	91.1478355	2888.6075501	327	33.9011497	89.5848438	3037.0292018
328	29.9339758	92.7929418	2777.6616766	328	32.0281770	91.1790580	2920.2990054	328	34.2684122	89.6140252	3070.9303516
329	30.2457881	92.8260043	2807.5956524	329	32.3684763	91.2099523	2952.3271823	329	34.6396533	89.6428938	3105.1987637
330	30.5603484	92.8587259	2837.8414405	330	32.7123914	91.2405217	2984.6956587	330	35.0149162	89.6714531	3139.8384170
331	30.8791905	92.8911101	2868.4022888	331	33.0599606	91.2707698	3017.4080501	331	35.3942445	89.6997063	3174.8533332
332	31.2003488	92.9231606	2899.2614794	332	33.4112226	91.3006999	3050.4680106	332	35.7776821	89.7276567	3210.2475777
333	31.5253576	92.9548805	2930.4823282	333	33.7662169	91.3303153	3083.8792333	333	36.1652737	89.7553075	3246.0252598
334	31.8542520	92.9862735	2962.0081958	334	34.1249829	91.3596193	3117.6454502	334	36.5570641	89.7826620	3282.1905335
335	32.1860671	93.0173429	2993.8624377	335	34.4875609	91.3886153	3151.7704331	335	36.9530990	89.8097233	3318.7475976
336	32.5213386	93.0480919	3026.0485048	336	34.8539912	91.4173064	3186.2579940	336	37.3534242	89.8364946	3355.7006966
337	32.8601026	93.0785240	3058.5698434	337	35.2243149	91.4456959	3221.1119852	337	37.7580863	89.8629790	3393.0541209
338	33.2023953	93.1086423	3091.4299460	338	35.5985732	91.4737869	3256.3363000	338	38.1671323	89.8891796	3430.8122072
339	33.5482536	93.1384501	3124.6323413	339	35.9768081	91.5015826	3291.9348733	339	38.5806095	89.9150993	3468.9793395
340	33.8977146	93.1679506	3158.1805949	340	36.3590616	91.5290860	3327.9116813	340	38.9985651	89.9407413	3507.5599490
341	34.2508157	93.1971470	3192.0783094	341	36.7453767	91.5563003	3364.2707430	341	39.4210506	89.9661085	3546.5585152
342	34.6075951	93.2260424	3226.3291252	342	37.1357963	91.5832285	3401.0161196	342	39.8481120	89.9912038	3585.9795658
343	34.9680909	93.2546399	3260.9367202	343	37.5303641	91.6098736	3438.1519159	343	40.2797999	90.0160301	3625.8276778
344	35.3323418	93.2829425	3295.9048111	344	37.9291243	91.6362386	3475.6822801	344	40.7161644	90.0405904	3666.1074777
345	35.7003870	93.3109534	3331.2371529	345	38.3321212	91.6623264	3513.6114043	345	41.1572562	90.0648874	3706.8236420
346	36.0722661	93.3386756	3366.9375400	346	38.7394000	91.6881399	3551.9435255	346	41.6031264	90.0889241	3747.9808982
347	36.4480188	93.3661119	3403.0098060	347	39.1510061	91.7136820	3590.6829255	347	42.0538270	90.1127031	3789.5840246
348	36.8276857	93.3932654	3439.4578249	348	39.5669856	91.7389556	3629.8339316	348	42.5094101	90.1362273	3831.6378516
349	37.2113074	93.4201389	3476.2855106	349	39.9873848	91.7639635	3669.4009172	349	42.9699387	90.1594994	3874.1472617
350	37.5989252	93.4467355	3513.4968180	350	40.4122507	91.7887085	3709.3883020	350	43.4354363	90.1825221	3917.1171904
351	37.9905807	93.4730578	3551.0957432	351	40.8416309	91.8131933	3749.8005527	351	43.9059862	90.2052980	3960.5526266
352	38.3863159	93.4991087	3589.0863239	352	41.2755732	91.8374207	3790.6421836	352	44.3816350	90.2278299	4004.4586134
353	38.7861734	93.5248911	3627.4726358	353	41.7141262	91.8613934	3831.9177568	353	44.8624361	90.2501202	4048.8402485
354	39.1901960	93.5504077	3666.2588132	354	42.1573388	91.8851141	3873.6318830	354	45.3484458	90.2721717	4093.7026845
355	39.5984272	93.5756612	3705.4490092	355	42.6052605	91.9085853	3915.7892218	355	45.8397206	90.2939869	4139.0511303
356	40.0109108	93.6006544	3745.0474364	356	43.0579414	91.9318099	3958.3944623	356	46.3363176	90.3155682	4184.8908509
357	40.4276911	93.6253899	3785.0583472	357	43.5154320	91.9547902	4001.4524237	357	46.8382944	90.3369182	4231.2271685
358	40.8488129	93.6498704	3825.4860384	358	43.9777835	91.9775290	4044.9678558	358	47.3457092	90.3580395	4278.0654629
359	41.2743214	93.6740986	3866.3348513	359	44.4450475	92.0000267	4088.9456393	359	47.8586211	90.3789344	4325.4111721
360	41.7042622	93.6980769	3907.6091727	360	44.9172761	92.0222918	4133.3906867	360	48.3770895	90.3996053	4373.2697931
361	42.1386816	93.7218081	3949.3134349	361	45.3945221	92.0443209	4178.3079268	361	48.9011766	90.4200547	4421.6468826
362	42.5776262	93.7452946	3991.4521166	362	45.8770389	92.0661184	4223.7024049	362	49.4309373	90.4402850	4470.5480572
363	43.0211432	93.7685390	4034.0297428	363	46.3642804	92.0876867	4269.5793239	363	49.9664391	90.4602984	4519.9789945
364	43.4692801	93.7915438	4077.0508860	364	46.8589008	92.1090283	4315.9436042	364	50.5077422	90.4800973	4569.9454337
365	43.9220851	93.8143113	4120.5201661	365	47.3547554	92.1301455	4362.8005051	365	51.0549004	90.4996841	4620.4531759
366	44.3796068	93.8368442	4164.4422512	366	47.8578997	92.1510407	4410.1552605	366	51.6080043	90.5190609	4671.5080853
367	44.8418944	93.8591448	4208.8218580	367	48.3663899	92.1717162	4458.0131601	367	52.1670910	90.5382301	4723.1160896
368	45.3089975	93.8812155	4253.6637524	368	48.8802828	92.1921743	4506.3795500	368	52.7322345	90.5571938	4775.2831607
369	45.7809662	93.9030586	4298.9727499	369	49.3996358	92.2124174	4555.2598328	369	53.3035004	90.5759543	4828.0154152
370	46.2578512	93.9246765	4344.7537161	370	49.9245069	92.2324477	4604.6594685	370	53.8809550	90.5945138	4881.3189155
371	46.7397039	93.9460716	4391.0115673	371	50.4549548	92.2522673	4654.5839734	371	54.4646653	90.6128743	4935.1998705
372	47.2265758	93.9672462	4437.7512712	372	50.9910387	92.2718786	4705.0389302	372	55.0548992	90.6310380	4989.6645358
373	47.7185193	93.9882024	4484.9778469	373	51.5328185	92.2912837	4756.0299689	373	55.6511251	90.6490071	5044.7192350
374	48.2155872	94.0089424	4532.6963662	374	52.0803547	92.3104848	4807.5627873	374	56.2540123	90.6667836	5100.3703601
375	48.7178329	94.0294689	4580.9119534	375	52.6337084	92.3294840	4859.6431420	375	56.8634307	90.6843696	5156.6243723
376	49.2253103	94.0497837	4629.6297863	376	53.1929416	92.3482835	4912.2768504	376	57.4794512	90.7017672	5213.4878031
377	49.7380740	94.0698890	4678.8550966	377	53.7581166	92.3668854	4965.4697920	377	58.1021453	90.7189782	5270.9672543
378	50.2561789	94.0897870	4728.5931706	378	54.3292966	92.3852916	5019.2279086	378	58.7315852	90.7360048	5329.0693996
379	50.7796808	94.1094800	4778.8493495	379	54.9065453	92.4035044	5073.5572051	379	59.3678440	90.7528490	5387.8009848
380	51.3086358	94.1289669	4829.6290302	380	55.4899274	92.4215257	5128.4637505	380	60.0109957	90.7695125	5447.1688289
381	51.8431007	94.1482588	4880.9376660	381	56.0795079	92.4393575	5183.9536779	381	60.6611148	90.7859976	5507.1796246
382	52.3831330	94.1673489	4932.7807667	382	56.6753526	92.4570019	5240.0331857	382	61.3172769	90.8023060	5567.8409794
383	52.9287907	94.1862423	4985.1638998	383	57.2775283	92.4744607	5296.7085384	383	61.9825582	90.8184395	5629.1592163
384	53.4801322	94.2049408	5038.0926904	384	57.8860210	92.4917360	5353.9860667	384	62.6548082	90.8344002	5691.1417745
385	54.0372169	94.2234466	5091.5728227	385	58.5011418	92.5088297	5411.8721687	385	63.3327880	90.8501899	5753.7958104
386	54.6001046	94.2417615	5145.6100396	386	59.1227165	92.5257437	5470.3733105	386	64.0168932	90.8658102	5817.1285984
387	55.1688557	94.2598877	5200.2101442	387	59.7508953	92.5424798	5529.4960270	387	64.7124312	90.8812632	5881.1474916
388	55.7435313	94.2778270	5255.3789909	388	60.3857406	92.5590400	5589.2469223	388	65.4134825	90.8965505	5945.8599228
389	56.3241931	94.2955814	5311.1225312	389	61.0273472	92.5754261	5649.6326709	389	66.1221286	90.9116741	6011.2734054
390	56.9109034	94.3131527	5367.4467243	390	61.6757627	92.5916400	5710.6600181	390	66.8384517	90.9266355	6077.3955340
391	57.5037253	94.3305429	5424.3576277	391	62.3310677	92.6076833	5772.3357808	391	67.5625349	90.9414366	6144.2339856
392	58.1027225	94.3477538	5481.8613531	392	62.9933353	92.6235580	5834.6668485	392	68.2944624	90.9560791	6211.7965205
393	58.7079592	94.3647872	5539.9640755	393	63.6626395	92.6392658	5897.6601838	393	69.0343190	90.9705647	6280.0909829
394	59.3195004	94.3816451	5598.6720347	394	64.3390550	92.6548085	5961.3228233	394	69.7821908	90.9848950	6349.1253019
395	59.9374119	94.3983292	5657.9915351	395	65.0226575	92.6701877	6025.6618784	395	70.5381646	90.9990717	6418.9074928
396	60.5617599	94.4148412	5717.9289470	396	65.7135232	92.6854053	6090.6845359	396	71.3023280	91.0130965	6489.4456573
397	61.1926116	94.4311831	5778.4907069	397	66.4117294	92.7004629	6156.3980591	397	72.0747699	91.0269709	6560.7479853
398	61.8300346	94.4473564	5839.6833185	398	67.1173541	92.7153622	6222.8097886	398	72.8555799	91.0406967	6632.8227552
399	62.4740975	94.4633631	5901.5133531	399	67.8304759	92.7301048	6289.9271426	399	73.6448487	91.0542754	6705.6783351
400	63.1248693	94.4792047	5963.9874506	400	68.5511748	92.7446924	6357.7576186	400	74.4426679	91.0677086	6779.3231838

Table 1

M	C(12.50,M,12)	A(12.50,M,12)	S(12.50,M,12)	M	C(12.75,M,12)	A(12.75,M,12)	S(12.75,M,12)	M	C(13.00,M,12)	A(13.00,M,12)	S(13.00,M,12)
401	63.7824200	94.4948830	6027.1123199	401	69.2795310	92.7591267	6426.3087933	401	75.2491301	91.0809978	6853.7658517
402	64.4466203	94.5103997	6090.8947399	402	70.0156260	92.7734092	6495.5883243	402	76.0643290	91.0941445	6929.0149818
403	65.1181413	94.5257564	6155.3415602	403	70.7595420	92.7875416	6565.6039503	403	76.8883593	91.1071504	7005.0793108
404	65.7964553	94.5409548	6220.4597015	404	71.5113622	92.8015254	6636.3634923	404	77.7213165	91.1200169	7081.9676701
405	66.4819350	94.5559965	6286.2561568	405	72.2711704	92.8153622	6707.8748545	405	78.5632974	91.1327455	7159.6889966
406	67.1743541	94.5708831	6352.7379918	406	73.0390516	92.8290535	6780.1460249	406	79.4143998	91.1453376	7238.2522840
407	67.8740870	94.5856163	6419.9123159	407	73.8150915	92.8426009	6853.1850764	407	80.2747225	91.1577949	7317.6666838
408	68.5811087	94.6001975	6487.7864329	408	74.5993768	92.8560058	6927.0001679	408	81.1443653	91.1701186	7397.9414063
409	69.2954953	94.6146285	6556.3675417	409	75.3919952	92.8692698	7001.5995448	409	82.0234293	91.1823102	7479.0857716
410	70.0173234	94.6289107	6625.6630369	410	76.1933352	92.8823944	7076.9915400	410	82.9120164	91.1943712	7561.1092008
411	70.7468705	94.6430456	6695.6803603	411	77.0025862	92.8953809	7153.1845752	411	83.8102299	91.2063029	7644.0212172
412	71.4836150	94.6570343	6766.4270308	412	77.8207386	92.9082310	7230.1871613	412	84.7181741	91.2181068	7727.8314471
413	72.2282359	94.6708799	6837.9106457	413	78.6475840	92.9209459	7308.0079000	413	85.6359543	91.2297841	7812.5496212
414	72.9805134	94.6845821	6910.1366817	414	79.4832146	92.9335272	7386.6554840	414	86.5636771	91.2413363	7898.1855755
415	73.7403281	94.6981431	6983.1194951	415	80.3277237	92.9459762	7466.1386986	415	87.5014503	91.2527647	7984.7492526
416	74.5089618	94.7115643	7056.8603232	416	81.1812058	92.9582943	7546.4664223	416	88.4493327	91.2640706	8072.2507029
417	75.2850968	94.7248472	7131.3692850	417	82.0437561	92.9704829	7627.6476281	417	89.4075843	91.2752553	8160.7000856
418	76.0693165	94.7379931	7206.6543618	418	82.9154710	92.9825434	7709.6913842	418	90.3761665	91.2863202	8250.1076700
419	76.8617053	94.7510034	7282.7236983	419	83.7964479	92.9944771	7792.6068552	419	91.3552416	91.2972664	8340.4838365
420	77.6623480	94.7638797	7359.5854035	420	84.6867852	93.0062853	7876.4033031	420	92.3449234	91.3080954	8431.8390781
421	78.4713308	94.7766232	7437.2477516	421	85.5865823	93.0179694	7961.0900883	421	93.3453268	91.3188083	8524.1840015
422	79.2887405	94.7892353	7515.7190824	422	86.4959397	93.0295306	8046.6766706	422	94.3565678	91.3294064	8617.5293283
423	80.1145649	94.8017174	7595.0078229	423	87.4149591	93.0409703	8133.1726102	423	95.3787639	91.3398909	8711.8858960
424	80.9491926	94.8140709	7675.1224878	424	88.3437430	93.0522897	8220.5875693	424	96.4120339	91.3502631	8807.2646600
425	81.?24134	94.8262969	7755.0716804	425	89.2823953	93.0634902	8308.9313123	425	97.4564976	91.3605241	8903.6766939
426	82.6444177	94.8383970	7837.8640938	426	90.2310207	93.0745728	8398.2137076	426	98.5122763	91.3706751	9001.1331915
427	83.5052971	94.8503723	7920.5085115	427	91.1897253	93.0855390	8488.4447783	427	99.5794926	91.3807173	9099.6454678
428	84.3751439	94.8622241	9004.0138086	428	92.1586161	93.0963898	8579.6344536	428	100.6582705	91.3906519	9199.2249604
429	85.2540517	94.8739537	8088.3889525	429	93.1378014	93.1071266	8671.7930697	429	101.7487351	91.4004801	9299.8832309
430	86.1421147	94.8855625	8173.6430041	430	94.1273906	93.1177505	8764.9308712	430	102.8510130	91.4102029	9401.6319660
431	87.0394284	94.8970515	8259.7851188	431	95.1274941	93.1282627	8859.0582617	431	103.9652324	91.4196215	9504.4829790
432	87.9460891	94.9084221	8346.8245472	432	96.1382237	93.1386644	8954.1857558	432	105.0915224	91.4293370	9608.4482114
433	88.6621942	94.9196755	8434.7706363	433	97.1598924	93.1489567	9050.3239796	433	106.2300139	91.4387505	9713.5397338
434	89.7878421	94.9308129	8523.6328305	434	98.1920141	93.1591409	9147.4836719	434	107.3803390	91.4480632	9819.7697476
435	90.7231321	94.9418354	8613.4206726	435	99.2353042	93.1692179	9245.6756866	435	108.5441314	91.4572760	9927.1505866
436	91.6581647	94.9527443	8704.1438047	436	100.2896793	93.1791890	9344.9109903	436	109.7200262	91.4663901	10035.6947181
437	92.6230414	94.9635408	8795.8119694	437	101.3552572	93.1890553	9445.2006696	437	110.9086598	91.4754065	10145.4147443
438	93.5878648	94.9742209	8888.4350108	438	102.4321568	93.1988179	9546.5559268	438	112.1101703	91.4843263	10256.3234041
439	94.5627384	94.9848009	8982.0228755	439	103.5204985	93.2084778	9648.9880836	439	113.3246971	91.4931505	10368.4335744
440	95.5477669	94.9952669	9076.5856139	440	104.6204038	93.2180362	9752.5085821	440	114.5523814	91.5018802	10481.7582715
441	96.5430561	95.0056249	9172.1333808	441	105.7319956	93.2274940	9857.1289858	441	115.7933655	91.5105162	10596.3106529
442	97.5487130	95.0158762	9268.6764369	442	106.8553980	93.2360525	9962.8609814	442	117.0477936	91.5190598	10712.1040184
443	98.5648454	95.0260218	9366.2251499	443	107.9907366	93.2461125	10069.7163794	443	118.3158114	91.5275117	10829.1518120
444	99.5915625	95.0360628	9464.7899953	444	109.1381382	93.2552752	10177.7071160	444	119.5975660	91.5358731	10947.4676234
445	100.6289746	95.0460003	9564.3815578	445	110.?77309	93.2643416	10286.8452542	445	120.8932063	91.5441448	11067.0651894
446	101.6771931	95.0558354	9665.0105324	446	111.4696443	93.2733127	10397.1429851	446	122.2028827	91.5523280	11187.9583957
447	102.7363306	95.0655690	9766.6877256	447	112.6540093	93.2821894	10508.6126294	447	123.5267473	91.5604234	11310.1612784
448	103.8065007	95.0752023	9869.4240561	448	113.8509581	93.2909728	10621.2666387	448	124.8649537	91.5684320	11433.6880257
449	104.8878184	95.0847363	9973.2335059	449	115.0606246	93.2996639	10735.1175968	449	126.2176574	91.5763548	11558.5529794
450	105.9803988	95.0941721	10078.1183752	450	116.2831437	93.3082636	10850.1782214	450	127.5850153	91.5841928	11684.7706368
451	107.0843623	95.1035105	10184.0967750	451	117.5186521	93.3167729	10966.4613651	451	128.9671863	91.5919467	11812.3556521
452	108.1998244	95.1127526	10291.1831373	452	118.7672878	93.3251927	11083.9800172	452	130.3643308	91.5996175	11941.3022384
453	109.3269055	95.1218995	10399.3829618	453	120.0291902	93.3335240	11202.7473049	453	131.7766111	91.6072061	12071.6871693
454	110.4657279	95.1309521	10508.7098677	454	121.3045004	93.3417677	11322.7764952	454	133.2041911	91.6147133	12203.4637804
455	111.6164125	95.1399114	10619.1755956	455	122.5933607	93.3499248	11444.0809555	455	134.6472365	91.6221402	12336.6679714
456	112.7790835	95.1487783	10730.7920081	456	123.8959151	93.3579961	11566.6743562	456	136.1059149	91.6294874	12471.3152029
457	113.9538656	95.1575537	10843.5701944	457	125.2123209	93.3659825	11690.5702713	457	137.5803956	91.6367559	12607.4211228
458	115.1408851	95.1662387	10957.5249572	458	126.5426900	93.3738850	11815.7825805	458	139.0708499	91.6439464	12745.0015184
459	116.3402693	95.1748342	11072.6658423	459	127.8872061	93.3817044	11942.3252706	459	140.5774508	91.6510600	12884.0723683
460	117.5521471	95.1833411	11188.0061116	460	129.2460077	93.3894415	12070.2124767	460	142.1003731	91.6580972	13024.6498196
461	118.?.66486	95.1917602	11306.5582587	461	130.6192405	93.3970974	12199.4584843	461	143.6397939	91.6650591	13166.7501922
462	120.0139054	95.2000926	11425.3349073	462	132.0070760	93.4046727	12330.0777208	462	145.1958656	91.6719463	13310.3899304
463	121.2640502	95.2083391	11545.3488127	463	133.4096512	93.4121694	12462.0848068	463	146.7688471	91.6787598	13455.5858777
464	122.5272174	95.2165005	11666.6128629	464	134.8271287	93.4195853	12595.4944580	464	148.3588430	91.6855002	13602.3547264
465	123.8035426	95.2245778	11789.1400803	465	136.2596970	93.4269243	12730.3215667	465	149.9660638	91.6921684	13750.7135677
466	125.0931628	95.2325719	11912.9436229	466	137.7074259	93.4341860	12866.5812537	466	151.5906961	91.6987651	13900.6796315
467	126.3962166	95.2404835	12038.0367858	467	139.1705673	93.4413715	13004.2886796	467	153.2329287	91.7052911	14052.2703276
468	127.7128439	95.2483135	12164.4330024	468	140.6492546	93.4484814	13143.4592469	468	154.8929521	91.7117472	14205.5032563
469	129.0431860	95.2560629	12292.1458463	469	142.1433529	93.4555165	13284.1085015	469	156.5709590	91.7181340	14360.3962084
470	130.3873859	95.2637324	12421.1890323	470	143.6539293	93.4624777	13426.2521545	470	158.2671444	91.7244525	14516.9671674
471	131.7455878	95.2713228	12551.5764181	471	145.1802523	93.4693657	13569.9060837	471	159.9817052	91.7307032	14675.2343118
472	133.1179377	95.2788349	12683.3220059	472	146.7227924	93.4761812	13715.0863360	472	161.7148403	91.7368869	14835.2160707
473	134.5045829	95.2862696	12816.4399436	473	148.2817221	93.4829251	13861.8091284	473	163.4667511	91.7430044	14996.9308573
474	135.9058723	95.2936276	12950.9445264	474	149.8572154	93.4895982	14010.0908505	474	165.2376409	91.7490563	15160.3976084
475	137.3213563	95.3009098	13086.8501987	475	151.4494483	93.4962010	14159.9480059	475	167.0277153	91.7550433	15325.6352493
476	138.7517871	95.3081169	13224.1715550	476	153.0585987	93.5027345	14311.3975142	476	168.8371822	91.7609661	15492.6629646
477	140.1971183	95.3152498	13362.9233422	477	154.6845463	93.5091992	14464.4561130	477	170.6662517	91.7668255	15661.5001468
478	141.6575049	95.3223090	13503.1204604	478	156.3283728	93.5155960	14619.1409593	478	172.5151361	91.7726221	15832.1663986
479	143.1331039	95.3292955	13644.7779654	479	157.9893618	93.5219256	14775.4693321	479	174.3840501	91.7783566	16004.6815347
480	144.6240738	95.3362100	13787.9110693	480	159.6779987	93.5281886	14933.4586939	480	176.2732106	91.7840296	16179.0655684
481	146.1305745	95.3430532	13932.5351430	481	161.3644712	93.5343857	15093.1266926	481	178.1828371	91.7896418	16355.3387954
482	147.6527680	95.3498255	14078.6657175	482	163.0789687	93.5405177	15254.4911638	482	180.1?1512	91.7951939	16533.5216725
483	149.1903177	95.3565287	14226.3184856	483	164.8116828	93.5465852	15417.5701326	483	182.0643770	91.8006865	16713.6347837
484	150.7443987	95.3631624	14375.5093032	484	166.5628069	93.5525892	15582.3818154	484	184.0367410	91.8061201	16895.6991606
485	152.3151480	95.3697277	14526.2541919	485	168.3325367	93.5585296	15748.9446223	485	186.0304724	91.8114956	17079.7359017
486	153.9017641	95.3762254	14678.5693399	486	170.1210699	93.5644078	15917.2771590	486	188.0458025	91.8168135	17265.7663741
487	155.5049075	95.3826561	14832.4711040	487	171.9286063	93.5702241	16087.3982290	487	190.0829654	91.8220743	17453.8121766
488	157.1247502	95.3890204	14987.9760114	488	173.7553478	93.5759794	16259.3268353	488	192.1421975	91.8272788	17643.8951420
489	158.7614664	95.3953192	15145.1007617	489	175.6014983	93.5816741	16433.0821831	489	194.2237380	91.8324275	17836.0373395
490	160.4152317	95.4015530	15303.8622281	490	177.4672643	93.5873098	16608.6836814	490	196.3278285	91.8375210	18030.2610775
491	162.0862237	95.4077226	15464.2774597	491	179.3528539	93.5928845	16786.1509457	491	198.4547133	91.8425600	18226.5889600
492	163.7746218	95.4138285	15626.3636834	492	181.2584780	93.5984015	16965.5037996	492	200.6046394	91.8475449	18425.0436193
493	165.4806075	95.4198715	15790.1383052	493	183.1843493	93.6038605	17146.7622776	493	202.7778563	91.8524764	18625.6482587
494	167.2043638	95.4258522	15955.6189127	494	185.1306831	93.6092621	17329.9466269	494	204.9746164	91.8573550	18828.4261149
495	168.9460759	95.4317713	16122.8232765	495	187.0976966	93.6146069	17515.0773100	495	207.1951747	91.8621814	19033.4007313
496	170.7059309	95.4376293	16291.7693524	496	189.0856096	93.6198955	17702.1750066	496	209.4397891	91.8669561	19240.5959061
497	172.4841177	95.4434269	16462.4752833	497	191.0946442	93.6251285	17891.2606162	497	211.7087202	91.8716795	19450.0356952
498	174.2808272	95.4491648	16634.9594010	498	193.1250248	93.6303065	18082.3552604	498	214.0022313	91.8763524	19661.7444154
499	176.0962525	95.4548435	16809.2402282	499	195.1769782	93.6354300	18275.4802851	499	216.3205888	91.8809751	19875.7466468
500	177.9305885	95.4604637	16985.3364808	500	197.2507336	93.6404997	18470.6572633	500	218.?640619	91.8855484	20092.0672356

Table 1

443

M	C(13.25,M,12)	A(13.25,M,12)	S(13.25,M,12)	C(13.50,M,12)	A(13.50,M,12)	S(13.50,M,12)	C(13.75,M,12)	A(13.75,M,12)	S(13.75,M,12)
1	1.0110417	.9890789	1.0000000	1.0112500	.9888752	1.0000000	1.0114583	.9886715	1.0000000
2	1.0222053	1.9673560	2.0110417	1.0226266	1.9667492	2.0112500	1.0230480	1.9661428	2.0114583
3	1.0334921	2.9349493	3.0332469	1.0341311	2.9337446	3.0338766	1.0347704	2.9325407	3.0345063
4	1.0449036	3.8919754	4.0667390	1.0457651	3.8899823	4.0680077	1.0466271	3.8879908	4.0692767
5	1.0564411	4.8385498	5.1116426	1.0575299	4.8355820	5.1137728	1.0586197	4.8326171	5.1159038
6	1.0681059	5.7747865	6.1680837	1.0694272	5.7706621	6.1713027	1.0707497	5.7665421	6.1745235
7	1.0799996	6.7007985	7.2361896	1.0814582	6.6953395	7.2407299	1.0830188	6.6898872	7.2452733
8	1.0918235	7.6166975	8.3160892	1.0936246	7.6097300	8.3221881	1.0954283	7.6027721	8.3282920
9	1.1039790	8.5225938	9.4079127	1.1059279	8.5139481	9.4158127	1.1079801	8.5053153	9.4237204
10	1.1160677	9.4185968	10.5117917	1.1183696	9.4081069	10.5217406	1.1206757	9.3976341	10.5317005
11	1.1283909	10.3048145	11.6278594	1.1309512	10.2923183	11.6401102	1.1335168	10.2798442	11.6523763
12	1.1408503	11.1813537	12.7562503	1.1436744	11.1666930	12.7710614	1.1465050	11.1520602	12.7858931
13	1.1534472	12.0483202	13.8971006	1.1565408	12.0313404	13.9147358	1.1595421	12.0143953	13.9323981
14	1.1661831	12.9058184	15.0505478	1.1695519	12.8863688	15.0712766	1.1729296	12.8669613	15.0920402
15	1.1790597	13.7539519	16.2167309	1.1827093	13.7318851	16.2408285	1.1863694	13.7098691	16.2649698
16	1.1920785	14.5928228	17.3957906	1.1960148	14.5679951	17.4235378	1.1999633	14.5432279	17.4513392
17	1.2052411	15.4225323	18.5878691	1.2094700	15.3948036	18.6195526	1.2137128	15.3671460	18.6513025
18	1.2185489	16.2431805	19.7931102	1.2230765	16.2124139	19.8290226	1.2276200	16.1817304	19.8650153
19	1.2320037	17.0548664	21.0116591	1.2368361	17.0209285	21.0520991	1.2416864	16.9870867	21.0926353
20	1.2456071	17.8576878	22.2436629	1.2507505	17.8204485	22.2889352	1.2559141	17.7833195	22.3343217
21	1.2593607	18.6517414	23.4892700	1.2648215	18.6110739	23.5396857	1.2703048	18.5705321	23.5902358
22	1.2732661	19.4371232	24.7486307	1.2790507	19.3929037	24.8045072	1.2848604	19.3488268	24.8605406
23	1.2873251	20.2139278	26.0218968	1.2934400	20.1660358	26.0835579	1.2995827	20.1183046	26.1454010
24	1.3015393	20.9822488	27.3092219	1.3079912	20.9305669	27.3769979	1.3144738	20.8790653	27.4449837
25	1.3159105	21.7421789	26.6107612	1.3227061	21.6865928	28.6849891	1.3295355	21.6312077	28.7594575
26	1.3304403	22.4938097	29.9266717	1.3375866	22.4342079	30.0076953	1.3447697	22.3748295	30.0889929
27	1.3451306	23.2372320	31.2571120	1.3526344	23.1735060	31.3452818	1.3601785	23.1100271	31.4337626
28	1.3599831	23.9725352	32.6022427	1.3678516	23.9045795	32.6979163	1.3757639	23.8368960	32.7939412
29	1.3749996	24.6998082	33.9622258	1.3832399	24.6275199	34.0657678	1.3915279	24.5555305	34.1697051
30	1.3901819	25.4191385	35.3372253	1.3988013	25.3424177	35.4490077	1.4074725	25.2660240	35.5612330
31	1.4055318	26.1306130	36.7274072	1.4145379	26.0493623	36.8478090	1.4235397	25.9684686	36.9687054
32	1.4210512	26.8343174	38.1329390	1.4304514	26.7484424	38.2623469	1.4399118	26.6629556	38.3923052
33	1.4367420	27.5303366	39.5539902	1.4465440	27.4397452	39.6927983	1.4564108	27.3495750	39.8322170
34	1.4526060	28.2187545	40.9907322	1.4628176	28.1233974	41.1393423	1.4730989	28.0284161	41.2886278
35	1.4686452	28.8996542	42.4433382	1.4792743	28.7993646	42.6021599	1.4899781	28.6995669	42.7617267
36	1.4848615	29.5731177	43.9119834	1.4959161	29.4678513	44.0814342	1.5070508	29.3631145	44.2517048
37	1.5012568	30.2392262	45.3969448	1.5127452	30.1289011	45.5773503	1.5243191	30.0191452	45.7587556
38	1.5178332	30.8980601	46.8981017	1.5297636	30.7825969	47.0900955	1.5417852	30.6677439	47.2830747
39	1.5345926	31.5496989	48.4159349	1.5469734	31.4290204	48.6198591	1.5594515	31.3089950	48.8248599
40	1.5515371	32.1942210	49.9505275	1.5643769	32.0682526	50.1668325	1.5773202	31.9429817	50.3843114
41	1.5686686	32.8317043	51.5020646	1.5819761	32.7003734	51.7312094	1.5953392	32.5697862	51.9616316
42	1.5859893	33.4622255	53.0707332	1.5997733	33.3254619	53.3131855	1.6136742	33.1894900	53.5570253
43	1.6035013	34.0858608	54.6567225	1.6177708	33.9435965	54.9129588	1.6321643	33.8021734	55.1706996
44	1.6212066	34.7026853	56.2602239	1.6359707	34.5548544	56.5307296	1.6508661	34.4079160	56.8028693
45	1.6391075	35.3127735	57.8814305	1.6543754	35.1593121	58.1667003	1.6697823	35.0067965	58.4537300
46	1.6572059	35.9161988	59.5205380	1.6729871	35.7570454	59.8210757	1.6889152	35.5988925	60.1235123
47	1.6755043	36.5130340	61.1777439	1.6918082	36.3481289	61.4940628	1.7082674	36.1842810	61.8124276
48	1.6940046	37.1033512	62.8532481	1.7108410	36.9326367	63.1858710	1.7278413	36.7630378	63.5206950
49	1.7127092	37.6872214	64.5472528	1.7300880	37.5106420	64.8967120	1.7476395	37.3352382	65.2485363
50	1.7316204	38.2647152	66.2599620	1.7495515	38.0822171	66.6268000	1.7676645	37.9009564	66.9961757
51	1.7507404	38.8359021	67.9915824	1.7692340	38.6474334	68.3763515	1.7879190	38.4602659	68.7638403
52	1.7700715	39.4008511	69.7423228	1.7891378	39.2063619	70.1455855	1.8084056	39.0132392	70.5517593
53	1.7896160	39.9596301	71.5123943	1.8092656	39.7590723	71.9347233	1.8291269	39.5599481	72.3601648
54	1.8093764	40.5123068	73.3020103	1.8296199	40.3056339	73.7439890	1.8500856	40.1004636	74.1892917
55	1.8293549	41.0589475	75.1113867	1.8502031	40.8461151	75.5736088	1.8712845	40.6348559	76.0393774
56	1.8495540	41.5996184	76.9407416	1.8710179	41.3805836	77.4238119	1.8927263	41.1631943	77.9106619
57	1.8699762	42.1343846	78.7902956	1.8920668	41.9091061	79.2948298	1.9144138	41.6855474	79.8033882
58	1.8906238	42.6633105	80.6602718	1.9133526	42.4317489	81.1868967	1.9363498	42.2019830	81.7178020
59	1.9114995	43.1864600	82.5508956	1.9348778	42.9485774	83.1002493	1.9585372	42.7125682	83.6541519
60	1.9326056	43.7038962	84.4623091	1.9566452	43.4596563	85.0351271	1.9809787	43.2173692	85.6126890
61	1.9539448	44.2156814	86.3950007	1.9786574	43.9650495	86.9917722	2.0036774	43.7164515	87.5936678
62	1.9755196	44.7218773	88.3489455	2.0009173	44.4648203	88.9704297	2.0266362	44.2098799	89.5973452
63	1.9973326	45.2225450	90.3244651	2.0234277	44.9590312	90.9713470	2.0498581	44.6977186	91.6239815
64	2.0193865	45.7177449	92.3217977	2.0461921	45.4477441	92.9947747	2.0733441	45.1800307	93.6738396
65	2.0416839	46.2075367	94.3411843	2.0692109	45.9310201	95.0409659	2.0971032	45.6568790	95.7471857
66	2.0642275	46.6919794	96.3828682	2.0924885	46.4089197	97.1101768	2.1211325	46.1283253	97.8442288
67	2.0870200	47.1711315	98.4470957	2.1160300	46.8815028	99.2026662	2.1454371	46.5944307	99.9654213
68	2.1100642	47.6450508	100.5341157	2.1398353	47.3488285	101.3186962	2.1700203	47.0552559	102.1108584
69	2.1333628	48.1137943	102.6441799	2.1639085	47.8109553	103.4585316	2.1948851	47.5108607	104.2808787
70	2.1569187	48.5774186	104.7775427	2.1882525	48.2679409	105.6224401	2.2200348	47.9613040	106.4757637
71	2.1807347	49.0359797	106.9344614	2.2128703	48.7198427	107.8106925	2.2454727	48.4066446	108.6957985
72	2.2048136	49.4895328	109.1151961	2.2377651	49.1667171	110.0235628	2.2712021	48.8469401	110.9412712
73	2.2291584	49.9381325	111.3200097	2.2629399	49.6086201	112.2613279	2.2972263	49.2822476	113.2124733
74	2.2537721	50.3818331	113.5491682	2.2883980	50.0456071	114.5242678	2.3235483	49.7126238	115.5096996
75	2.2786575	50.8206880	115.8029402	2.3141425	50.4777326	116.8126658	2.3501726	50.1381245	117.8332482
76	2.3038176	51.2547502	118.0815977	2.3401766	50.9050508	119.1268083	2.3771017	50.5588408	120.1834208
77	2.3292556	51.6840719	120.3854153	2.3665036	51.3276151	121.4669949	2.4043393	50.9747195	122.5605225
78	2.3549745	52.1087049	122.7146710	2.3931267	51.7454785	123.8334885	2.4318890	51.3859225	124.9648619
79	2.3809773	52.5287005	125.0696455	2.4200494	52.1586932	126.2266152	2.4597544	51.7924671	127.3967509
80	2.4072673	52.9441093	127.4506228	2.4472750	52.5673109	126.6466647	2.4879391	52.1944062	129.8565053
81	2.4338475	53.3549814	129.8578901	2.4748068	52.9713828	131.0939396	2.5164468	52.5917919	132.3444445
82	2.4607213	53.7613663	132.2917376	2.5026484	53.3709596	133.5687465	2.5452810	52.9846759	134.8608912
83	2.4878917	54.1633131	134.7524589	2.5308032	53.7660910	136.0713949	2.5744457	53.3731090	137.4061723
84	2.5153622	54.5608701	137.2403506	2.5592747	54.1568267	138.6021981	2.6039446	53.7571417	139.9806180
85	2.5431360	54.9540854	139.7557128	2.5880666	54.5432156	141.1614728	2.6337814	54.1368240	142.5845626
86	2.5712165	55.3430064	142.2988488	2.6171823	54.9253059	143.7495394	2.6639602	54.5122049	145.2183440
87	2.5996070	55.7276799	144.8700653	2.6466252	55.3031455	146.3667217	2.6944847	54.8833334	147.8823042
88	2.6283110	56.1081524	147.4696723	2.6764002	55.6767817	149.0133473	2.7253950	55.2502576	150.5767890
89	2.6573319	56.4844697	150.0979832	2.7065007	56.0462612	151.6897475	2.7565871	55.6130250	153.3021460
90	2.6866733	56.8566772	152.7553151	2.7369579	56.4116304	154.3962571	2.7881730	55.9716828	156.0587351
91	2.7163386	57.2248109	155.4419884	2.7677487	56.7729349	157.1332150	2.8201208	56.3262775	158.8469081
92	2.7463315	57.5889420	158.1583270	2.7988858	57.1302199	159.9009637	2.8524347	56.6768552	161.6670289
93	2.7766556	57.9490875	160.9046585	2.8303733	57.4835302	162.6998495	2.8851189	57.0234614	164.5194636
94	2.8073145	58.3052998	163.6813142	2.8622150	57.8329100	165.5302228	2.9181775	57.3661410	167.4045825
95	2.8383119	58.6575219	166.4886287	2.8944149	58.1784029	168.3924378	2.9516150	57.7049386	170.3227600
96	2.8696516	59.0060962	169.3269406	2.9269771	58.5200523	171.2868528	2.9854355	58.0398981	173.2743750
97	2.9013374	59.3507649	172.1965922	2.9599056	58.8579009	174.2138299	3.0196437	58.3710630	176.2598105
98	2.9333730	59.6916693	175.0979296	2.9932045	59.1919910	177.1737355	3.0542437	58.6984763	179.2794542
99	2.9657623	60.0288508	178.0313026	3.0268781	59.5223644	180.1669400	3.0892403	59.0221805	182.3336979
100	2.9985093	60.3623498	180.9970649	3.0609305	59.8490625	183.1938181	3.1246378	59.3422176	185.4229382

Table 1

M	C(13.25,M,12)	A(13.25,M,12)	S(13.25,M,12)	M	C(13.50,M,12)	A(13.50,M,12)	S(13.50,M,12)	M	C(13.75,M,12)	A(13.75,M,12)	S(13.75,M,12)
101	3.0316178	60.6922067	183.9955742	101	3.0953659	60.1721261	186.2547485	101	3.1604410	59.6586291	188.5475761
102	3.0650919	61.0184612	187.0271920	102	3.1301888	60.4915956	189.3501144	102	3.1966554	59.9714562	191.7080170
103	3.0989356	61.3411526	190.0922839	103	3.1654034	60.8075111	192.4803032	103	3.2332827	60.2807394	194.9046714
104	3.1331531	61.6603199	193.?912195	104	3.2010142	61.1199121	195.6457066	104	3.2703307	60.5865188	198.1379541
105	3.1677483	61.9760016	196.3243726	105	3.2370256	61.4298377	198.8467208	105	3.3078033	60.8888343	20?.4082848
106	3.2027255	62.2882357	199.4921208	106	3.2734421	61.7343265	202.0837464	106	3.?.57052	61.1877249	204.7160881
107	3.23?0889	62.5970598	202.6948?63	107	3.3102684	62.0364168	205.3571886	107	3.3840414	61.4832296	208.0617933
108	3.2738428	62.9025112	205.9329353	108	3.3475089	62.3351464	208.6674570	108	3.4228169	61.7753866	211.4458346
109	3.3099915	63.2046268	209.2067781	109	3.3851684	62.6305527	212.0149659	109	3.4620366	62.0642339	214.8686515
110	3.3465393	63.5034430	212.5167696	110	3.4232515	62.9226726	215.4001342	110	3.5017058	62.3498090	218.3306981
111	3.3834907	63.7989957	215.8633089	111	3.4617631	63.2115428	218.8233857	111	3.5418295	62.6321490	221.8323939
112	3.4203501	64.0913207	219.2467996	112	3.5007079	63.4971993	222.2851488	112	3.5824130	62.9112905	225.3742234
113	3.4586220	64.3804532	222.6676497	113	3.5400909	63.7796779	225.7858568	113	3.6234615	63.1872697	228.9566364
114	3.4968109	64.6664285	226.1262717	114	3.5799169	64.0590140	229.3259476	114	3.6649803	63.4601224	232.5800979
115	3.5354215	64.9492798	229.6230826	115	3.6201910	64.3352425	232.9058646	115	3.7069749	63.7298842	236.2450782
116	3.5744585	65.2290424	233.1585042	116	3.6609181	64.6083980	236.5260555	116	3.7494506	63.9965899	239.9520530
117	3.6139265	65.5057498	236.7329626	117	3.7021035	64.8785148	240.1869737	117	3.7924131	64.2602743	243.7015036
118	3.6538302	65.7794352	240.3468891	118	3.7437521	65.1456265	243.8890771	118	3.8358678	64.5209715	247.4939167
119	3.6941746	66.0501316	244.0007193	119	3.7858693	65.4097666	247.6328292	119	3.8798204	64.7787153	251.3297845
120	3.7349645	66.3178718	247.6948939	120	3.8284604	65.6709682	251.4186986	120	3.9242767	65.0335394	255.2096050
121	3.7762047	66.5826879	251.4298584	121	3.8715305	65.9292640	255.2471589	121	3.9692424	65.2854766	259.1338817
122	3.8179003	66.8446120	255.2060631	122	3.9150853	66.1846862	259.1186895	122	4.0147233	65.5345598	263.1031241
123	3.8600563	67.1036756	259.0239634	123	3.9591300	66.4372670	263.0337747	123	4.0607253	65.7808212	267.1178474
124	3.9026777	67.3599099	26?.8840196	124	4.0036702	66.6870378	266.9929047	124	4.1072545	66.0242929	271.1785727
125	3.?.57698	67.6133459	266.7866974	125	4.0487115	66.9340300	270.9965749	125	4.1543168	66.2650063	275.2858272
126	3.9893377	67.8640141	270.7324671	126	4.0942595	67.1782744	275.0452863	126	4.2019183	66.5029929	279.4401440
127	4.0333866	68.1119447	274.7218048	127	4.14?3199	67.4198016	279.1395?58	127	4.2500653	66.7382834	283.6420623
128	4.0779219	68.3571676	278.7551914	128	4.1868985	67.6586419	283.2798657	128	4.2987640	66.9709084	287.8921276
129	4.1229490	68.5997125	282.8331133	129	4.2340011	67.8948251	287.4667642	129	4.3480206	67.2008981	292.1908916
130	4.1684732	68.8396085	286.9560623	130	4.2616336	68.1283808	291.7007653	130	4.3978417	67.4282823	296.5389122
131	4.2145001	69.0768845	291.1245355	131	4.3298020	68.3593383	295.9823989	131	4.4482336	67.6530907	300.9367539
132	4.2610352	69.3115693	295.3390355	132	4.3785123	68.5877264	300.3122009	132	4.4992030	67.8753523	305.3849875
133	4.3080841	69.5436910	299.6000707	133	4.4277705	68.8135736	304.6907132	133	4.5507564	68.0950960	309.8841905
134	4.3556525	69.7732777	303.9081548	134	4.4775829	69.0369084	309.1184837	134	4.6029004	68.3123503	314.4349469
135	4.4037462	70.0003571	308.2638074	135	4.5279558	69.2577588	313.5960666	135	4.6556420	68.5271434	319.0378473
136	4.4523709	70.2249566	312.6675536	136	4.5788953	69.4761519	318.1240224	136	4.7089879	68.7395033	323.6934893
137	4.5015305	70.4471031	317.1199245	137	4.6304078	69.6921156	322.7029176	137	4.7629451	68.9494574	328.4024772
138	4.5512369	70.6668236	321.6214570	138	4.6824999	69.9056768	327.3333255	138	4.8175205	69.1570331	333.1654223
139	4.6014902	70.8841445	326.1726939	139	4.7351780	70.1168621	332.0158254	139	4.8727212	69.3622572	337.9829427
140	4.6522983	71.0990921	330.7741841	140	4.7884488	70.3256980	336.7510034	140	4.9285545	69.5651565	342.8556639
141	4.7036674	71.3116921	335.4264824	141	4.8423188	70.5322106	341.5394522	141	4.9850275	69.7657572	347.7842184
142	4.7556037	71.5219704	340.1301498	142	4.8967949	70.7364258	346.3817711	142	5.0421476	69.9640854	352.7692459
143	4.8081135	71.7299521	344.8857535	143	4.9518839	70.9383692	351.2785660	143	5.0999222	70.1601668	357.8113936
144	4.8612031	71.9356625	349.6938671	144	5.0075926	71.1380659	35?.2304499	144	5.1583588	70.3540269	362.9113158
145	4.9148789	72.1391264	354.5550702	145	5.?39280	71.3355411	361.2380424	145	5.2174650	70.5456908	368.0696746
146	4.9691474	72.3403681	359.4699491	146	5.1208972	71.5308194	366.3019704	146	5.2772485	70.7351835	373.2871396
147	5.0240150	72.5394121	364.4390964	147	5.1785073	71.7239252	371.4228676	147	5.3377170	70.9225295	378.5643881
148	5.0794885	72.7362823	369.4631115	148	5.2367655	71.9148828	376.6013748	148	5.3988783	71.1077532	383.9021051
149	5.1355745	72.9310025	374.5426000	149	5.2956791	72.1037160	381.8381403	149	5.4607404	71.2908786	389.3009833
150	5.1922798	73.1235961	379.6781745	150	5.3552555	72.2904484	387.1338194	150	5.5233114	71.4719294	394.7617238
151	5.2496113	73.3140864	384.8704544	151	5.4155021	72.4751035	392.4890749	151	5.5865994	71.6509291	400.2850352
152	5.3075757	73.5024964	390.1200657	152	5.4764265	72.6577043	397.9045770	152	5.6506125	71.8279011	405.8716346
153	5.3661802	73.6888487	395.4276414	153	5.5380363	72.8382737	403.3810034	153	5.7153591	72.0028682	411.5222471
154	5.4254318	73.8731658	400.7938216	154	5.6003392	73.0168344	408.9190397	154	5.7808476	72.1758532	417.2376061
155	5.4853376	74.0554700	406.2192534	155	5.6633430	73.1934085	414.5193769	155	5.8470865	72.3468786	423.0184537
156	5.5459049	74.2357832	411.7045910	156	5.7270556	73.3680183	420.1827220	156	5.9140843	72.5159665	428.8655402
157	5.6071440	74.4141272	417.2504958	157	5.7914850	73.5406856	425.9097776	157	5.9818499	72.6831388	434.7795245
158	5.6690531	74.5905235	422.8576367	158	5.8566392	73.7114320	431.7012626	158	6.0503919	72.8484174	440.7614744
159	5.7316489	74.7649934	428.5266398	159	5.9225264	73.8802788	437.5579018	159	6.1197193	73.0118236	446.8118662
160	5.7949358	74.9375578	43?.2583387	160	5.9891548	74.0472473	443.4804282	160	6.1898411	73.1733786	452.9315836
161	5.8589216	75.1082377	440.0532745	161	6.0565328	74.2123583	449.4695330	161	6.2607664	73.3331035	459.1214256
162	5.9236138	75.2770536	445.9121961	162	6.12?5688	74.3756324	455.5261?58	162	6.3325043	73.4910189	465.3801930
163	5.9890204	75.4440258	451.8358099	163	6.1935713	74.5370901	461.6507846	163	6.4050642	73.6471453	471.7146973
164	6.0551492	75.6091745	457.8249303	164	6.2632490	74.6967517	467.8443560	164	6.4784556	73.8015031	478.1197615
165	6.1220081	75.7725196	463.8799795	165	6.3337106	74.8546370	474.1076050	165	6.5528879	73.9541122	484.5982171
166	6.1856053	75.9340808	470.0019876	166	6.4049648	75.0107659	480.4413155	166	6.6277708	74.1049925	491.1509050
167	6.2579468	76.0938775	476.1915929	167	6.4770207	75.1651579	486.8462803	167	6.7037140	74.2541636	497.7786758
168	6.3270470	76.2519292	482.4495417	168	6.5498871	75.3178323	493.3233010	168	6.7805274	74.4016447	504.4823898
169	6.3969002	76.4082547	488.7765888	169	6.6235734	75.4588082	499.8731891	169	6.8582209	74.5474551	511.2629172
170	6.4675407	76.5628730	495.1734969	170	6.6980886	75.6181045	506.4967615	170	6.9363047	74.6916137	518.1211382
171	6.5399531	76.7158026	501.6410376	171	6.7734421	75.7657399	513.1948501	171	7.0162889	74.8341392	525.0579429
172	6.6111541	76.8670622	508.1799908	172	6.8498433	75.9117329	519.9682921	172	7.0963839	74.9750501	532.0742318
173	6.6841522	77.0166698	514.7911448	173	6.9267018	76.0561018	526.8179354	173	7.1780001	75.1143647	539.1709157
174	6.7579564	77.1646435	521.4752971	174	7.0046272	76.1988646	533.7446372	174	7.2602480	75.2521010	546.3489158
175	6.8325755	77.3110012	528.2332535	175	7.0834292	76.3400391	540.7492644	175	7.3434383	75.3882770	553.6091638
176	6.9080185	77.4557605	535.0658290	176	7.1631178	76.4796431	547.8326936	176	7.4275819	75.5229103	560.9526021
177	6.9842946	77.5989389	541.9738475	177	7.2437029	76.6176941	554.9958114	177	7.5126896	75.6560185	568.3801840
178	7.0614128	77.7405536	548.9581421	178	7.3251945	76.7542092	562.2395143	178	7.5987725	75.7876187	575.8928736
179	7.1393826	77.8806217	556.0195549	179	7.4076030	76.8892056	569.5647088	179	7.6858418	75.9177280	583.4916462
180	7.2182133	78.0191602	563.1589375	180	7.?909385	77.0227003	576.9723118	180	7.7739087	76.0463634	591.1774879
181	7.2979144	78.1561856	570.3771508	181	7.5752116	77.1547098	584.4632503	181	7.8629848	76.1735446	598.9513967
182	7.3784955	78.2917146	577.6750651	182	7.6604327	77.2852507	592.0384619	182	7.9530815	76.2992790	606.8143214
183	7.4599664	78.4257635	585.0535607	183	7.7466126	77.4143394	599.6988946	183	8.0442105	76.4235920	614.7674629
184	7.5423369	78.5583484	592.5135271	184	7.8337620	77.5419920	607.4455072	184	8.1363838	76.5464968	622.8116734
185	7.6256168	78.6894853	600.0558639	185	7.9218918	77.6682245	615.2792691	185	8.2296132	76.6680072	630.9480572
186	7.7098164	78.8191907	607.6814808	186	8.0110131	77.7930526	623.2011609	186	8.3239108	76.7881450	639.1776703
187	7.7949456	78.9474705	615.3912971	187	8.1011370	77.9164921	631.2121740	187	8.4192890	76.9069199	647.5015811
188	7.8810148	79.0743656	623.1862427	188	8.1922748	78.0385583	639.3133109	188	8.5157600	77.0243492	655.9208701
189	7.9680343	79.1998670	631.0672575	189	8.2844378	78.1592665	647.5055587	189	8.6133364	77.1404482	664.4366301
190	8.0560147	79.3239979	639.0352918	190	8.3776378	78.2786319	655.7900235	190	8.7120309	77.2552320	673.0499665
191	8.1449665	79.4467731	647.0913065	191	8.4718882	78.3966694	664.1676613	191	8.8118562	77.3687155	681.7619973
192	8.2349005	79.5682075	655.2362730	192	8.5671949	78.5133937	672.6395475	192	8.9128254	77.4809134	690.5738536
193	8.3258275	79.6883156	663.4711735	193	8.6635759	78.6288195	681.2067424	193	9.0149515	77.5918402	699.4866790
194	8.4177586	79.8071121	671.7970010	194	8.7610411	78.7429612	689.8703183	194	9.1182479	77.7015104	708.5016305
195	8.5107046	79.9246112	680.2147596	195	8.8596028	78.8558331	698.6313594	195	9.2227278	77.8099382	717.6198784
196	8.6046770	80.0408271	688.7254642	196	8.9592733	78.9674493	707.4909622	196	9.3284049	77.9171376	726.8426061
197	8.6996870	80.1557737	697.3301412	197	9.0600652	79.0778237	716.4502355	197	9.4352928	78.0231227	736.1710110
198	8.7957460	80.2694651	706.0298282	198	9.1619909	79.1869703	725.5103007	198	9.5434056	78.1279071	745.6063038
199	8.8928657	80.3819147	714.8255743	199	9.2650633	79.2949027	734.6722915	199	9.6527571	78.2315044	755.1497094
200	8.9910578	80.4931364	723.7184400	200	9.3692952	79.4016343	743.9373548	200	9.7633616	78.3339282	764.8024665

Table 1

445

M C(13.25,M,12) A(13.25,M,12) S(13.25,M,12)

M	C(13.25,M,12)	A(13.25,M,12)	S(13.25,M,12)
201	9.0903340	80.6031433	732.7094978
202	9.1907065	80.7119489	741.7998318
203	9.2921872	80.8195662	750.9905383
204	9.3947884	80.9260082	760.2827255
205	9.4985226	81.0312877	769.6775139
206	9.6034021	81.1354175	779.1760365
207	9.7094396	81.2384100	788.7794385
208	9.8166480	81.3402778	798.4888782
209	9.9250402	81.4410330	808.3055262
210	10.0346292	81.5406879	818.2305664
211	10.1454262	81.6392545	828.2651956
212	10.2574506	81.7367446	838.4106238
213	10.3707100	81.8331700	848.6680744
214	10.4852199	81.9265424	859.0387844
215	10.6009942	82.0228732	869.5240044
216	10.7180469	82.1161737	880.1249986
217	10.8363920	82.2084554	890.8430455
218	10.9560438	82.2997292	901.6794374
219	11.0770168	82.3900062	912.6354812
220	11.1993255	82.4792973	923.7124900
221	11.3229847	82.5676132	934.9118235
222	11.4480093	82.6549647	946.2348082
223	11.5744145	82.7413621	957.6828176
224	11.7022153	82.8268160	969.2572320
225	11.8314272	82.9113367	980.9594473
226	11.9620659	82.9949343	992.7908745
227	12.0941471	83.0776189	1004.7529405
228	12.2276866	83.1594005	1016.8470875
229	12.3627006	83.2402890	1029.0747741
230	12.4992055	83.3202941	1041.4374748
231	12.6372175	83.3994254	1053.9366802
232	12.7767535	83.4776926	1066.5738977
233	12.9178301	83.5551050	1079.3506512
234	13.0604645	83.6316719	1092.2684813
235	13.2046738	83.7074027	1105.3289458
236	13.3504754	83.7823064	1118.5336196
237	13.4978869	83.8563920	1131.8840950
238	13.6469261	83.9296686	1145.3819819
239	13.7976109	84.0021449	1159.0289079
240	13.9499595	84.0738297	1172.8265188
241	14.1039903	84.1447317	1186.7764763
242	14.2597219	84.2148592	1200.8804686
243	14.4171729	84.2842210	1215.1401904
244	14.5763626	84.3528252	1229.5573634
245	14.7373099	84.4206802	1244.1337329
246	14.9000344	84.4877941	1258.8710358
247	15.0645556	84.5541751	1273.7710702
248	15.2308934	84.6198311	1288.8356258
249	15.3990678	84.6847701	1304.0665192
250	15.5690992	84.7489999	1319.4655870
251	15.7410080	84.8125283	1335.0346862
252	15.9148150	84.8753628	1350.7756942
253	16.0905411	84.9375111	1366.6905092
254	16.2682074	84.9989807	1382.7810502
255	16.4478356	85.0597790	1399.0492577
256	16.6294471	85.1199133	1415.4970932
257	16.8130639	85.1793908	1432.1265403
258	16.9987081	85.2382188	1448.9395042
259	17.1864022	85.2964044	1465.9383123
260	17.3761687	85.3539544	1483.1247146
261	17.5680306	85.4108760	1500.5008833
262	17.7620109	85.4671705	1518.0689139
263	17.9581331	85.5228610	1535.8309248
264	18.1564209	85.5779380	1553.7890580
265	18.3568980	85.6324134	1571.9454788
266	18.5595888	85.6862939	1590.3023769
267	18.7645176	85.7395860	1608.8619656
268	18.9717091	85.7922960	1627.6264831
269	19.1811884	85.8444304	1646.5981922
270	19.3929807	85.8959955	1665.7793806
271	19.6071115	85.9469974	1685.1723613
272	19.8236067	85.9974423	1704.7794728
273	20.0424924	86.0473363	1724.6030795
274	20.2637949	86.0966864	1744.6455718
275	20.4875409	86.1454955	1764.9093667
276	20.7137575	86.1937726	1785.3969077
277	20.9424719	86.2415225	1806.1106652
278	21.1737117	86.2887509	1827.0531371
279	21.4075048	86.3354635	1848.2268489
280	21.6438799	86.3816659	1869.6343537
281	21.8828638	86.4273638	1891.2782330
282	22.1244871	86.4725625	1913.1610969
283	22.3687783	86.5172677	1935.2855840
284	22.6157669	86.5614847	1957.6543623
285	22.8654827	86.6052187	1980.2701293
286	23.1179567	86.6484757	2003.1356120
287	23.3732165	86.6912591	2026.2535677
288	23.6312958	86.7335759	2049.6267842
289	23.8922246	86.7754305	2073.2580799
290	24.1560346	86.8168280	2097.1503046
291	24.4227575	86.8577735	2121.3063092
292	24.6924255	86.8982717	2145.7290967
293	24.9650710	86.9383227	2170.4215222
294	25.2407270	86.9779462	2195.3865932
295	25.5194267	87.0171320	2220.6273202
296	25.8012037	87.0558899	2246.1467468
297	26.0860920	87.0942245	2271.9479505
298	26.3741259	87.1321404	2298.0340425
299	26.6653402	87.1696423	2324.4081684
300	26.9597700	87.2067346	2351.0735086

M C(13.50,M,12) A(13.50,M,12) S(13.50,M,12)

M	C(13.50,M,12)	A(13.50,M,12)	S(13.50,M,12)
201	9.4746998	79.5071785	753.3066501
202	9.5812902	79.6115486	762.7813499
203	9.6890797	79.7145576	772.3626401
204	9.7980819	79.8168184	782.0517198
205	9.9083103	79.9177438	791.8498016
206	10.0197788	80.0175464	801.7581119
207	10.1325013	80.1162387	811.7778907
208	10.2464916	80.2138331	821.9103920
209	10.3617650	80.3103417	832.1568839
210	10.4783348	80.4057767	842.5186468
211	10.5962161	80.5001500	852.9969836
212	10.7154235	80.5934735	863.5931997
213	10.8359720	80.6857587	874.3086232
214	10.9578767	80.7770172	885.1445952
215	11.0811528	80.8672605	896.1024719
216	11.2058158	80.9564999	907.1836248
217	11.3318812	81.0447465	918.3894405
218	11.4593649	81.1320114	929.7213218
219	11.5882827	81.2183055	941.1806866
220	11.7186509	81.3036395	952.7689694
221	11.8504857	81.3880242	964.4876203
222	11.9833037	81.4714702	976.3381060
223	12.1186215	81.5539878	988.3219097
224	12.2549560	81.6355875	1000.4405312
225	12.3923242	81.7162793	1012.6954872
226	12.5322435	81.7960735	1025.0883114
227	12.6732313	81.8749800	1037.6205549
228	12.8158051	81.9530086	1050.2937062
229	12.9599829	82.0301692	1063.1095913
230	13.1057827	82.1064714	1076.0695742
231	13.2532228	82.1819248	1089.1753569
232	13.4023215	82.2565387	1102.4285797
233	13.5530976	82.3303226	1115.8309012
234	13.7055700	82.4032856	1129.3839989
235	13.8597577	82.4754369	1143.0895689
236	14.0156799	82.5467856	1156.9493265
237	14.1733563	82.6173405	1170.9650065
238	14.3328066	82.6871105	1185.1383628
239	14.4940507	82.7561044	1199.4711694
240	14.6571087	82.8243306	1213.9652201
241	14.8220012	82.8917979	1228.6223288
242	14.9887487	82.9585146	1243.4443300
243	15.1573721	83.0244861	1258.4330787
244	15.3278926	83.0897297	1273.5904509
245	15.5003314	83.1542444	1288.9183435
246	15.6747101	83.2180414	1304.4186748
247	15.8510506	83.2811287	1320.0933849
248	16.0293749	83.3435142	1335.9444355
249	16.2097054	83.4052056	1351.9738104
250	16.3920646	83.4662108	1368.1835158
251	16.5764753	83.5265372	1384.5755804
252	16.7629506	83.5861926	1401.1520557
253	16.9515493	83.6451842	1417.9150163
254	17.1422488	83.7035196	1434.8665603
255	17.3350991	83.7612061	1452.0086091
256	17.5301190	83.8182507	1469.3433082
257	17.7273328	83.8746693	1486.8740272
258	17.9267653	83.9304433	1504.6013600
259	18.1234414	83.9856053	1522.5281253
260	18.3323864	84.0401535	1540.6565667
261	18.5385257	84.0940990	1558.9889531
262	18.7471853	84.1474363	1577.5275768
263	18.9580911	84.2001842	1596.2747641
264	19.1713696	84.2523453	1615.2328552
265	19.3870475	84.3039262	1634.4042249
266	19.6051518	84.3549332	1653.7912724
267	19.8257098	84.4053727	1673.3964242
268	20.0487490	84.4552512	1693.2221340
269	20.2742974	84.5045747	1713.2708830
270	20.5023833	84.5533495	1733.5451805
271	20.7330351	84.6015817	1754.0475638
272	20.9662818	84.6492773	1774.7805989
273	21.2021524	84.6964424	1795.7468806
274	21.4406766	84.7430827	1816.9490331
275	21.6818842	84.7892041	1838.3897097
276	21.9258034	84.8348125	1860.0715940
277	22.1724708	84.8799135	1881.9973994
278	22.4219111	84.9245127	1904.1698702
279	22.6741576	84.9686158	1926.5917812
280	22.9292418	85.0122282	1949.2659388
281	23.1871958	85.0553555	1972.1951806
282	23.4480567	85.0980029	1995.3823764
283	23.7118423	85.1401759	2018.8304281
284	23.9785708	85.1818798	2042.5422705
285	24.2483598	85.2231197	2066.5208710
286	24.5211539	85.2639000	2090.7692309
287	24.7970168	85.3042282	2115.2903847
288	25.0759833	85.3441070	2140.0874016
289	25.3580881	85.3835422	2165.1633849
290	25.6433466	85.4225386	2190.5214729
291	25.9318545	85.4611012	2216.1648395
292	26.2235878	85.4992348	2242.0966940
293	26.5186032	85.5369442	2268.3202818
294	26.8169415	85.5742341	2294.8388850
295	27.1186280	85.6111091	2321.6558225
296	27.4237126	85.6475739	2348.7744505
297	27.7322294	85.6836330	2376.1981631
298	28.0442169	85.7192910	2403.9303925
299	28.3597144	85.7545523	2431.9746094
300	28.6787612	85.7894213	2460.3343238

M C(13.75,M,12) A(13.75,M,12) S(13.75,M,12)

M	C(13.75,M,12)	A(13.75,M,12)	S(13.75,M,12)
201	9.8752335	78.4351916	774.5658281
202	9.9883872	78.5353079	784.4410616
203	10.1028374	78.6342900	794.4294487
204	10.2185991	78.7321507	804.5322862
205	10.3356872	78.8289029	814.7508853
206	10.4541170	78.9245590	825.0865725
207	10.5739037	79.0191314	835.5406895
208	10.6950631	79.1126325	846.1145933
209	10.8176107	79.2050744	856.8096563
210	10.9415624	79.2964690	867.6272670
211	11.0669345	79.3868283	878.5688294
212	11.1937431	79.4751639	889.6357639
213	11.3220048	79.5644875	900.8295070
214	11.4517361	79.6518105	912.1515118
215	11.5829539	79.7381442	923.6032479
216	11.7156752	79.8235000	935.1862018
217	11.8499173	79.9078887	946.9018770
218	11.9856977	79.9913215	958.7517944
219	12.1230338	80.0738091	970.7374920
220	12.2619435	80.1553623	982.8605258
221	12.4024450	80.2359915	995.1224693
222	12.5445563	80.3157074	1007.5249143
223	12.6882960	80.3945202	1020.0694706
224	12.8336828	80.4724401	1032.7577666
225	12.9807354	80.5494774	1045.5914494
226	13.1294730	80.6256419	1058.5721848
227	13.2793148	80.7009436	1071.7016577
228	13.4320805	80.7753922	1084.9815726
229	13.5859898	80.8489974	1098.4136531
230	13.7416626	80.9217688	1111.9996429
231	13.8991191	80.9937158	1125.7413055
232	14.0583799	81.0648478	1139.6404246
233	14.2194655	81.1351739	1153.6989045
234	14.3823969	81.2047034	1167.9182609
235	14.5471922	81.2734451	1182.3006668
236	14.7138818	81.3414082	1196.8478619
237	14.8824783	81.4086001	1211.5617437
238	15.0530067	81.4750332	1226.4442220
239	15.2254891	81.5407125	1241.4972288
240	15.3999478	81.6056478	1256.7227178
241	15.5764056	81.6698475	1272.1226657
242	15.7543852	81.7333198	1287.6990712
243	15.9354909	81.7960732	1303.4539564
244	16.1180032	81.8581156	1319.3893663
245	16.3026886	81.9194552	1335.5073065
246	16.4894903	81.9800999	1351.8100581
247	16.6784323	82.0400575	1368.2995484
248	16.8695394	82.0993360	1384.9779607
249	17.0628362	82.1579429	1401.8475201
250	17.2583478	82.2158858	1418.9103563
251	17.4560997	82.2731724	1436.1687041
252	17.6561176	82.3298100	1453.6248039
253	17.8584272	82.3858060	1471.2809214
254	18.0630550	82.4411676	1489.1393487
255	18.2700276	82.4959021	1507.2024037
256	18.4793716	82.5500164	1525.4724313
257	18.6911144	82.6035178	1543.9518029
258	18.9052834	82.6564131	1562.6429173
259	19.1219065	82.7087091	1581.5482008
260	19.3410117	82.7604127	1600.6701072
261	19.5626274	82.8115306	1620.0111139
262	19.7867825	82.8620694	1639.5737463
263	20.0135061	82.9120356	1659.3605208
264	20.2423275	82.9614359	1679.3740349
265	20.4747766	83.0102764	1699.6168824
266	20.7093834	83.0585637	1720.0916390
267	20.9465784	83.1063040	1740.8010223
268	21.1866924	83.1535034	1761.7477007
269	21.4294566	83.2001682	1782.9343932
270	21.6750025	83.2463043	1804.3638498
271	21.9233619	83.2919177	1826.0388522
272	22.1745671	83.3370144	1847.9622141
273	22.4236506	83.3916002	1870.1367811
274	22.6850456	83.4256810	1892.5654318
275	22.9455853	83.4692624	1915.2510774
276	23.2085034	83.5123500	1938.1966626
277	23.4744342	83.5549495	1961.4051661
278	23.7434121	83.5970665	1984.8796003
279	24.0154720	83.6387063	2008.6230124
280	24.2906933	83.6798744	2032.6304844
281	24.5689797	83.7205761	2056.9291337
282	24.8514992	83.7608168	2081.4981134
283	25.1352445	83.8006016	2106.3486127
284	25.4232525	83.8399356	2131.4838572
285	25.7145607	83.8788241	2156.9071097
286	26.0092067	83.9172720	2182.6216704
287	26.3072288	83.9552844	2208.6308770
288	26.6086658	83.9928661	2234.9381059
289	26.9135568	84.0300221	2261.5467717
290	27.2219413	84.0667572	2288.4603285
291	27.5338594	84.1030761	2315.6822697
292	27.8493515	84.1389836	2343.2161291
293	28.1684587	84.1744843	2371.0654806
294	28.4912222	84.2095828	2399.2339393
295	28.8176842	84.2442837	2427.7251615
296	29.1478868	84.2785916	2456.5428457
297	29.4818730	84.3125107	2485.6907325
298	29.8196861	84.3460456	2515.1726054
299	30.1613700	84.3792006	2544.9922916
300	30.5069691	84.4119800	2575.1536616

Table 1

M	C(13.25,M,12)	A(13.25,M,12)	S(13.25,M,12)	M	C(13.50,M,12)	A(13.50,M,12)	S(13.50,M,12)	M	C(13.75,M,12)	A(13.75,M,12)	S(13.75,M,12)
301	27.2574508	87.2434218	2378.0332786	301	29.0013972	85.8239024	2489.0130849	301	30.8565281	84.4413880	2605.6606307
302	27.5564185	87.2797084	2405.2907294	302	29.3278629	85.6579999	2518.0144322	302	31.2100925	84.4764290	2636.5171507
303	27.8627094	87.3155985	2432.8491479	303	29.6575992	85.8917131	2547.3421451	303	31.5677081	84.5081069	2667.7272512
304	28.1703601	87.3510970	2460.7118573	304	29.9912471	85.9256611	2576.9997443	304	31.5294214	84.5394260	2699.2049593
305	28.4814078	87.3862076	2488.8822174	305	30.3235487	85.9506333	2606.9900914	305	32.2952794	84.5703902	273?.2243807
306	28.7953300	87.4209348	2517.3636252	306	30.6550460	85.9906356	2637.3196401	306	32.?.33295	84.6010037	2763.519C601
307	29.1123447	87.4552827	2546.1595'53	307	31.0143317	86.0228811	2667.9994060	307	33.0396197	84.6312704	2796.1649896
308	29.4353100	87.4892355	2575.2733600	308	31.3637992	86.0547650	2699.0043878	308	33.4181987	84.6611943	2829.2246093
309	29.7603249	87.5228573	2604.7086700	309	31.7183419	86.0862942	2730.3681669	309	33.8011155	84.6907791	2862.6429080
310	30.0883285	87.5560921	2634.4689949	310	32.0734541	86.1174727	2762.0849068	310	34.1884200	84.7200287	2896.4439235
311	30.4211604	87.5889639	2664.5579234	311	32.4343805	86.1483042	2794.1582930	311	34.5801623	84.7489471	2930.6323435
312	30.7570607	87.6214788	2694.9790838	312	32.7991661	86.1787928	2826.5925435	312	34.9763933	84.7775378	2935.2125058
313	31.0986700	87.6536346	2725.7361446	313	33.1681568	86.2089422	2859.3917096	313	35.3771645	84.8058046	3000.1868991
314	31.4400290	87.6854412	2756.8328145	314	33.5412985	86.2387562	2892.5598663	314	35.7825278	84.8337512	3035.5660636
315	31.7871793	87.7169004	2788.2728436	315	33.9185381	86.2632335	2926.1011649	315	36.1925360	84.8613812	3071.3485914
316	32.1381628	87.7480160	2820.0600229	316	34.3002228	86.2973929	2960.0198030	316	36.6072421	84.8886982	3107.5411274
317	32.4930217	87.7787919	2852.1981857	317	34.6261003	86.3262229	2994.3200258	317	37.0267001	84.9157057	3144.1483695
318	32.8517988	87.8092316	2884.6912073	318	35.0783189	86.3547321	3029.0061261	318	37.4509644	84.9424073	3181.1750696
319	33.2145374	87.8393389	2917.5430081	319	35.4709275	86.3829242	3064.0624451	319	37.8800900	84.9688064	3218.6260340
320	33.5812812	87.8691174	2950.7575435	320	35.8355753	86.4108027	3099.5533726	320	38.3141327	84.9949064	3256.5061240
321	33.5520745	87.8985707	2984.3388247	321	36.2735127	86.4383710	3135.4233481	321	38.7531488	85.0207108	3294.8202567
322	34.3288620	87.9277023	3018.2908993	322	36.6315097	86.4656326	3171.6963808	322	39.1971953	85.0462228	3333.5734055
323	34.7053389	87.9565158	3052.6178613	323	37.0942578	86.4925910	3208.3784505	323	39.6463296	85.0714458	3372.7706008
324	35.0892009	87.9850145	3087.3238502	324	37.5115680	86.5192494	3245.4727081	324	40.1008107	85.0963831	3412.4169306
325	35.?763441	88.0132021	312..4130511	325	37.9335731	86.5456113	3282.9842761	325	40.5600969	85.1210379	3452.5175413
326	35.8683554	88.0410819	3157.8896052	326	38.3803258	86.5716799	3320.9178492	326	41.0243480	85.1454134	3493.0776381
327	36.2644119	88.0686571	3193.7580606	327	38.7913795	86.5974585	3359.2781750	327	41.4943243	85.1695127	3534.1024061
328	36.6643315	88.0959312	3230.0224726	328	39.2283981	86.6229503	3398.0700545	328	41.9703870	85.1933390	3575.5974104
329	37.0698723	88.1229074	3266.6837041	329	39.6633064	86.6481565	3437.2983427	329	42.4512977	85.2168954	3617.5677975
330	37.4788833	88.1495980	3303.7569764	330	40.1155395	86.6730863	3476.9679490	330	42.9377188	85.2401850	3660.0190552
331	37.8923137	88.1759793	3341.2350597	331	40.5671992	86.7221130	3517.0838335	331	43.4297135	85.2632107	3702.9568140
332	38.3112136	88.2020813	3379.1287735	332	41.0235741	86.7462180	3557.6510317	332	43.9273457	85.2859755	3746.3865275
333	38.7342332	88.2278982	3417.4399870	333	41.4350893	86.7700549	3598.6746058	333	44.4303798	85.3084825	3790.3138732
334	39.1612237	88.2534333	3456.1742203	334	41.9517966	86.7700549	3640.1595952	334	44.9397814	85.3307345	3834.7445530
335	39.5943366	88.2786894	3495.3361440	335	42.4237543	86.8169331	3682.1114918	335	45.4547164	85.3527344	3879.6843344
336	40.0315241	88.3036697	3534.9304806	336	42.9010215	86.8403580	3724.5352451	336	45.9755517	85.3744651	3925.1390508
337	40.4735388	88.3233772	3574.9620047	337	43.3836580	86.8359862	3767.4362677	337	46.5023549	85.3959894	3971.1146024
338	40.9204342	88.3528149	3615.4355435	338	43.8717242	86.8627800	3810.8199257	338	47.0351943	85.4172501	4017.6163573
339	41.3722640	88.3750857	3656.3559777	339	44.3652811	86.8853201	3854.6916499	339	47.5741393	85.4382699	4064.6521516
340	41.8290827	88.4008925	3697.7282416	340	44.8643905	86.9076095	3899.0569310	340	48.1192596	85.4590514	4112.2262909
341	42.2909455	88.4245382	3739.5573243	341	45.3691149	86.9296509	3943.9213215	341	48.6706261	85.4795979	4160.3455505
342	42.7579080	88.4479257	3781.8482590	342	45.8795194	86.9514472	3989.2904354	342	49.2283104	85.4999114	4209.0161766
343	43.2300266	88.4710577	3824.6061778	343	46.3956620	86.9730009	4035.1695538	343	49.7923848	85.5199948	4258.2444870
344	43.7073581	88.4939372	3867.8362044	344	46.9176102	86.9943149	4081.5656158	344	50.3629225	85.5398507	4308.0368718
345	44.1899602	88.5165668	3911.5435525	345	47.?154364	87.0153917	412u.4832291	345	50.9399977	85.5594816	4358.3997943
346	44.6778910	88.5389492	3955.7335227	346	47.9791975	87.0362341	4175.9286654	346	51.5236852	85.5788902	4409.3397920
347	45.1712094	88.5610872	4000.4114137	347	48.5189635	87.0568446	4223.9078329	347	52.1140607	85.5980788	4460.8634772
348	45.6693748	88.5829834	4045.5826231	348	49.0648018	87.0772258	4272.4268264	348	52.7112010	85.6170501	4512.9775379
349	46.1742475	88.6046405	4091.2525979	349	49.6167809	87.0973802	4321.4916283	349	53.3151835	85.6358085	4565.6887389
350	46.6840881	88.6260611	4137.4268454	350	50.1749696	87.1173105	4371.1084091	350	53.9260866	85.6543504	4619.0039224
351	47.1995583	88.6472477	4184.1109335	351	50.7394380	87.1370190	4421.2833788	351	54.5439897	85.6726842	4672.9300090
352	47.7207200	88.6682302	4231.3104918	352	51.3102567	87.1565083	4472.0228168	352	55.1689729	85.6908104	4727.4739989
353	48.2476363	88.6889294	4279.0312118	353	51.8874971	87.1757808	4523.3330735	353	55.8011174	85.7087312	4782.6429717
354	48.7803707	88.7094294	4327.2789482	354	52.4712315	87.1948388	4575.2205707	354	56.4405052	85.7264489	4838.4440891
355	49.3189872	88.7297056	4376.0592188	355	53.0815328	87.2136843	4627.6918021	355	57.0872194	85.7439660	4894.8845943
356	49.8635511	88.7497603	4425.3782061	356	53.6594751	87.2323213	4680.7533349	356	57.7413437	85.7612846	4951.9718137
357	50.4141278	88.7695960	4475.2417571	357	54.1321329	87.2507803	4734.4118100	357	58.4029633	85.7784070	5009.7131574
358	50.9707838	88.7892151	4525.6553049	358	54.8725819	87.2689744	4788.6759429	358	59.0721639	85.7953355	5068.1161207
359	51.5335962	88.8086199	4576.6266587	359	55.4585984	87.2869957	4843.5485248	359	59.7490325	85.8120721	5127.1882847
360	52.1026029	88.8279128	4628.1802548	360	56.1141998	87.3048165	4899.0364232	360	60.4338568	85.8286192	5186.9373171
361	52.6779024	88.8467961	4680.2620577	361	56.7454441	87.3224390	4955.1505830	361	61.1261258	85.8449788	5247.3709739
362	53.2595543	88.8655721	4732.9407600	362	57.33.3303	87.3398655	5011.8960071	362	61.8265293	85.8611531	5308.4970997
363	53.8476285	88.8841430	4786.2003144	363	58.0293084	87.3570592	5069.2798575	363	62.5349983	85.8771442	5370.3233250
364	54.4421961	88.9025111	4840.0492688	364	58.6322292	87.3741391	5127.3092559	364	63.2515047	85.8929541	5432.8585873
365	55.0433287	88.9206786	4894.4901390	365	59.3424043	87.3909905	5135.9914351	365	63.9762615	85.9085849	5496.1100920
366	55.6510987	88.9386477	4949.5334676	366	60.0100063	87.4076544	5245.3330593	366	64.7093228	85.9240385	5560.0863535
367	56.2655796	88.9564206	5005.1845064	367	60.6851189	87.4241329	5305.3430290	367	65.4507838	85.9393172	5624.7956764
368	56.8883454	88.9739993	5061.4501460	368	61.1378265	87.4404281	5368.0290145	368	66.2007407	85.9544228	5690.2464602
369	57.5143710	88.9913861	5118.3399914	369	62.0582145	87.4565624	5427.3968410	369	66.9592909	85.9693573	5756.4472009
370	58.1530331	89.0085830	5175.8519624	370	62.7563694	87.4724766	5489.4550555	370	67.7265328	85.9841225	5823.4064918
371	58.7921054	89.0255921	5234.0019945	371	63.4623786	87.4892340	5552.2114249	371	68.5025660	85.9997205	5891.1330246
372	59.4412682	89.0424154	5292.7940999	372	64.1763303	87.5033160	5615.6738035	372	69.2874912	86.0131531	5959.6355906
373	60.0975989	89.0590550	5352.2353682	373	64.8983141	87.5192248	5679.8501338	373	70.0814104	86.0274223	6028.9203818
374	60.7611766	89.0755129	5412.3329871	374	65.6284201	87.5344621	5744.7404478	374	70.8844265	86.0415297	6099.0044921
375	61.4320812	89.0917911	5473.0941436	375	66.3667398	87.5495298	5810.3760379	375	71.6965439	86.0554774	6169.8889186
376	62.1103993	89.1078914	5534.5262248	376	67.1133856	87.5644300	5876.7435077	376	72.5181680	86.0692670	6241.5855626
377	62.7951960	89.1238160	5596.6366166	377	67.6683919	87.5791644	5943.8569734	377	73.3491053	86.0829005	6314.1037305
378	63.4605707	89.1395566	5659.4328147	378	68.6319104	87.5937349	6011.7253644	378	74.1885638	86.0963794	6387.4528358
379	64.1903014	89.1551452	5722.9223854	379	69.4040194	87.6081433	6080.3572748	379	75.0365525	86.1097057	6461.6423996
380	64.8993726	89.1705536	5787.1129967	380	70.?148146	87.6223914	6149.7612942	380	75.8994819	86.1228811	653C.6820522
381	65.6159698	89.1857938	5852.0123594	381	70.9743938	87.6364810	6219.9461058	381	76.7691635	86.1359071	6612.5815341
382	66.3404795	89.2008676	5917.6283292	382	71.7728557	87.6504138	6290.9205026	382	77.6473101	86.1487856	6689.3506075
383	67.0723890	89.2157767	5983.9088067	383	72.5803003	87.6641916	6362.6933503	383	78.5385361	86.1615182	6766.9995077
384	67.8125286	89.2305230	6051.0417977	384	73.3953287	87.6778162	6435.2736586	384	79.4384568	86.1741066	6845.5380437
385	68.5623616	89.2451083	6118.3555343	385	74.2225430	87.6912892	6508.6704873	385	80.3465891	86.1865523	6924.9765005
386	69.3194043	89.2595343	6187.4177459	386	75.0575466	87.7046123	6582.8930303	386	81.2693512	86.1988571	7005.3251897
387	70.0849061	89.2738027	6256.7371502	387	75.9019440	87.7177872	6657.9505770	387	82.2005625	86.2110225	7086.5945409
388	70.8503592	89.2879153	6326.8219563	388	76.7552409	87.7308155	6733.8525210	388	83.1424440	86.2230500	7168.7951034
389	71.6410568	89.3018738	6397.6806154	389	77.6193441	87.7436989	6810.6003520	389	84.0951178	86.2349413	7251.9375473
390	72.4320935	89.3156798	6469.3216723	390	78.4925618	87.7564390	6888.2277051	390	85.0587077	86.2466979	7336.0326651
391	73.2313846	89.3293351	6541.7537658	391	79.3753031	87.7690373	6966.7202678	391	86.0333387	86.2583213	7421.0913728
392	74.0404664	89.3428412	6614.9856303	392	80.2685786	87.7814955	7046.0958709	392	87.0191374	86.2698130	7507.1247115
393	74.8575965	89.3561998	6689.0260087	393	81.1716001	87.7938151	7126.3644455	393	88.0162317	86.2811746	7594.1438489
394	75.6845536	89.3694126	6763.8840933	394	82.0847806	87.8059976	7207.5360496	394	89.0247510	86.2924074	7682.1600805
395	76.5202372	89.3824810	6839.5685469	395	83.0082344	87.8180446	7289.6208303	395	90.0448263	86.3035130	7771.1848315
396	77.3651482	89.3954067	6916.0888841	396	83.9420770	87.8299576	7372.6290647	396	91.0765899	86.3144927	7861.2296578
397	78.2192883	89.4081913	6993.4540322	397	84.8864254	87.8417380	7456.5711417	397	92.1201758	86.3253481	7952.3062477
398	79.0830607	89.4208382	7071.6734205	398	85.8413977	87.8533874	7541.4575671	398	93.1757195	86.3360805	8044.4264235
399	79.9562695	89.4333430	7150.7564813	399	86.8071134	87.8649072	7627.2989648	399	94.2433580	86.3466914	8137.6021430
400	80.8391200	89.4457133	7230.7127508	400	87.7836934	87.8762988	7714.1060782	400	95.?232298	86.3571820	8231.8455010

Table 1

M	C(13.25,M,12)	A(13.25,M,12)	S(13.25,M,12)	C(13.50,M,12)	A(13.50,M,12)	S(13.50,M,12)	C(13.75,M,12)	A(13.75,M,12)	S(13.75,M,12)
401	81.7317186	69.4579484	7311.5518708	88.7712600	87.8875637	7801.8897717	96.4154751	86.3675538	8327.1687307
402	82.6341730	89.4700500	7393.2835895	89.7690367	87.8957033	7890.6610316	97.5202358	86.3778081	8423.5842058
403	83.5465920	89.4820193	7475.9177625	90.7790485	87.9097190	7980.4309383	98.6376551	86.3879462	8521.1044416
404	84.4650856	89.4938580	7559.4643545	91.8011218	87.9206121	8071.2108168	99.7678783	86.3979694	8619.7420967
405	85.4017651	89.5055673	7643.9334402	92.8333844	87.9313840	8163.0119385	100.9110519	86.4078792	871?.5099750
406	86.3447430	89.5171488	7729.3352053	93.8732856	87.9420361	8255.8458229	102.0?73243	86.4176766	8820.4210269
407	87.2??1328	89.5256038	7815.6799?33	94.9343961	87.9525697	8349.7240085	103.2368458	86.4273651	8922.4883512
408	88.2820497	89.5399337	7902.9780311	96.0024080	87.9629561	8444.6564846	104.4197680	86.4369398	9025.7251970
409	89.2383098	89.5511399	7991.2401308	97.0824351	87.9732866	8540.6609926	105.6162445	86.4464080	9130.1449649
410	90.2219307	89.5822237	8080.4767406	98.17?3125	87.5834726	8637.7433277	106.8264306	86.4557690	9235.7612094
411	91.2181312	89.5731864	8170.6985714	99.2790769	87.9935452	8735.9179402	108.0504835	86.4650240	9342.5876400
412	92.2253314	89.5840294	8261.9168026	100.3956665	88.0035058	8835.1970171	109.2885619	86.4741740	9450.6381235
413	93.2438528	89.5947540	8354.1421341	101.5254231	88.0133555	8935.5929336	110.5408267	86.4832205	9559.9266054
414	94.2732181	89.6053615	8447.3857869	102.6375321	88.0230957	9037.1184048	111.8074403	86.4921644	9670.4675120
415	95.3141516	89.6150531	8541.6590050	103.8225924	88.0327275	9139.7859869	113.0885672	86.5010070	9782.2749524
416	96.3655787	89.6262301	8636.9731556	104.9905966	88.0422522	9243.6085793	114.3843737	86.5097495	9895.3635196
417	97.4306263	89.6364938	8733.3397352	106.1717408	88.0516709	9348.5991759	115.6950280	86.5183929	10009.7478934
418	98.5064228	89.6465455	8830.7703616	107.3631729	88.0609048	9454.7709167	117.0207002	86.5269384	10125.4429214
419	99.5940979	89.6566062	8929.2767844	108.5740423	88.0701951	9562.1370896	118.3615624	86.5353871	10242.4636216
420	100.6937827	89.6666173	9028.8708823	109.7955003	88.0790029	9670.7111319	119.7177887	86.5437401	10360.8251840
421	101.6053099	89.6764400	9129.5646050	111.0305997	88.0883094	9780.5066323	121.0895550	86.5519984	10480.5429727
422	102.9297135	89.6861553	9231.3702749	112.2797951	88.0972158	9891.5373320	122.4770395	86.5601632	10601.6325277
423	104.0652291	89.6957646	9334.2999885	113.5429428	88.1060230	10003.8171270	123.8804222	86.5682355	10724.1095671
424	105.2152937	89.7052689	9438.3662176	114.8203009	88.1147323	10117.3600698	125.2998854	86.5762164	10847.9899893
425	106.??70459	89.7146694	954?.5815113	116.1120293	88.1233446	10232.1803706	126.7356132	86.5841068	10973.2898747
426	?07.5516258	89.7239673	9649.9585572	117.4182096	88.1318612	10348.2923999	128.1877921	86.5919079	11100.0254880
427	108.7391750	89.7331636	9757.5101831	118.73?2453	88.1402830	10465.7106095	129.6566106	86.5996206	11228.2132801
428	109.9363367	89.7422595	9866.2493581	120.07?0619	88.1486111	10584.4499348	131.1422593	86.6072455	11357.8696907
429	111.1537558	89.7512560	9976.1891948	121.4259063	88.1568466	10704.5249957	132.6449310	86.6147848	11489.0121500
430	112.3810785	89.7601543	10087.3429506	122.7919477	88.1649905	10825.9509030	134.1648208	86.6222383	11621.6570809
431	113.6219529	89.7689555	10199.7240291	124.1733572	88.1730437	10948.7428507	135.7021261	86.6296074	11755.8219018
432	114.8765286	89.7776605	10313.3459320	125.5703074	88.1810074	11072.9162079	137.2570463	86.6368930	11891.5420278
433	116.1449570	89.7862704	10428.2225106	126.9829734	88.1888825	11198.4865153	138.8297832	86.6440961	12028.7810741
434	117.4273909	89.7947863	10544.3674676	128.4115318	88.1966699	11325.4694937	140.4205412	86.6512175	12167.6108573
435	118.7239850	89.8032092	10661.7943595	129.8561616	88.2043703	11453.8810206	142.0295265	86.6582583	12308.0313985
436	120.0348957	89.8115401	10780.5186435	131.3170434	88.2119859	11583.7371821	143.6569482	86.6652193	12450.0609250
437	121.3602810	89.8197800	10900.5537391	132.7943601	88.2195164	11715.0542255	145.3030174	86.6721015	12593.7178732
438	122.7003007	89.8279300	11021.9140201	134.2882967	88.2269630	11847.8465857	146.9679478	86.6789057	12739.0208906
439	124.0551166	89.8359909	11144.6143208	135.7990400	88.2343268	11982.1368824	148.6519555	86.6856328	12885.9888384
440	125.4248918	89.8430638	11266.6694374	137.3267792	88.2416087	12117.9359224	150.3552592	86.6922887	13034.6407940
441	126.8097916	89.8516496	11394.0943292	138.8717055	88.2488095	12255.2627016	152.0780799	86.6988593	13184.9960532
442	128.2059831	89.8596493	11520.9041208	140.4340122	88.2559304	12394.1344071	153.8204612	86.7053604	13337.0741331
443	129.6235350	89.8673628	11649.1141039	142.0133948	88.2629720	12534.5684193	155.5831694	86.7117878	13490.8947743
444	131.0569180	89.8749941	11778.7397389	143.6115511	88.2699352	12676.5823141	157.3658892	86.7181424	13646.4779437
445	132.5040049	89.8825411	11909.7906570	145.??71811	88.2768210	1282..1938053	159.1690441	86.7244251	13803.8438369
446	133.9870699	89.8900056	12042.3003518	146.8609869	88.2836301	12965.4210463	160.9928560	86.7306365	13963.0128300
447	135.4462896	89.8973868	12176.2677317	148.5131730	88.2903635	13112.2820332	162.8375659	86.7367776	14124.0057370
448	136.9418424	89.9046910	12311.7140214	150.1839462	88.2970220	13260.7952062	164.70?4130	86.7428491	14286.8433329
449	138.4539086	89.9119136	12448.6558638	151.8735166	88.3036065	13410.9791524	166.5906396	86.7488519	14451.5467159
450	139.9826705	89.9190573	12587.1097724	153.5820926	88.3101176	13562.8526080	168.4594907	86.7547866	14618.1373554
451	141.5283125	89.9261230	12727.0924429	155.3098912	88.3165564	13716.4347606	170.4302140	86.7606541	14786.6368461
452	143.C910209	89.9331116	12868.6207554	157.0571274	88.3229235	13871.7446518	172.3830602	86.7664551	14957.0670601
453	144.6703943	89.9400238	13011.7117763	158.8240201	88.3292198	14028.8017792	174.3582828	86.7721905	15129.4501203
454	146.2683931	89.9468605	13156.3827606	160.6107904	88.3354450	14187.6257993	176.3561381	86.7778608	15303.8084030
455	147.8834399	89.9536227	13302.6511537	162.4176068	88.3416030	14348.2365097	178.3768855	86.7834669	15480.1645411
456	149.5163196	89.9603109	13450.5345037	164.2443304	88.3476914	14510.6542515	180.4207873	86.7890095	15658.5414266
457	151.1672689	89.9669261	13600.0509132	166.0923001	88.3537122	14674.8991119	182.4881088	86.7944893	15838.9622139
458	152.8363671	89.9734690	13751.2181422	167.9611571	88.3596659	14840.9917270	184.5791184	86.7999071	16021.4503227
459	154.5239353	89.9799405	13904.0545093	169.8507201	88.3655535	15008.9528341	186.6940875	86.8052634	16206.0294411
460	156.2301371	89.9863413	1405?.5784446	171.7615407	88.3713755	15178.8036042	188.8332906	86.8105591	16392.7235286
461	157.??51782	89.9926722	14214.8095317	173.6938360	88.3771327	15350.5651446	190.9970054	86.8157948	16581.5568192
462	159.6392666	89.9989340	14372.7637599	175.6479139	88.3828259	15524.2590028	193.1855127	86.8209711	16772.5538246
463	161.4628127	90.0051274	14532.4630266	177.6233659	88.3884091	15699.9069168	195.3990967	86.8260889	16965.7393373
464	163.2454291	90.0112531	.4693.9256393	179.6222224	88.3940231	15877.5308697	197.6380447	86.8311486	17161.1384340
465	165.0429704	90.0173340	14857.1710883	181.6429774	88.3995284	16057.1530921	199.9026473	86.8361511	17358.7764787
466	166.8703349	90.0233047	15022.2189990	183.6364559	88.4049724	16238.7960645	202.1931985	86.8410968	17558.6791260
467	168.7128515	90.0292319	15189.0093339	185.7529285	88.4103559	16422.4825204	204.5099955	86.8459866	17760.8723244
468	170.5757327	90.0350944	15357.8021554	187.8426489	88.4156795	16608.2354489	206.8533392	86.8508209	17965.3823200
469	172.4591731	90.0408929	15528.3779281	189.9553787	88.4209439	16796.0780978	209.2235337	86.8556005	18172.2356592
470	174.3634098	90.0466260	15700.8371012	192.0920324	88.4261497	16986.0339756	211.6208867	86.8603259	18381.4591930
471	176.2988724	90.0523205	15875.2005110	194.2539273	88.4312076	17178.1268569	214.0457094	86.8649978	18593.0800707
472	178.2351932	90.0579111	16051.4891634	196.4392940	88.4363862	17372.3807563	216.4983165	86.8696168	18807.1257891
473	180.2032068	90.0634804	16229.7243766	198.6422259	88.4414222	17568.8200702	218.9790264	86.8741834	19023.6241056
474	182.1922505	90.0889491	16409.9275834	200.8840297	88.4464002	17767.4692952	221.4881610	86.8786984	19242.6031320
475	184.2043544	90.0743778	16592.1205340	203.1439751	88.4513229	17968.3533259	224.0260462	86.8831621	19464.0912930
476	186.2388099	90.0797473	16776.3251983	205.4293448	88.4561007	18171.4973010	226.5930113	86.8875753	19688.1173392
477	188.2949753	90.0850581	16952.5637892	207.7404249	88.4610044	18376.9265458	229.1893896	86.8919385	19914.7103506
478	190.3740657	90.0903109	17150.8587645	210.0775047	88.4657646	18584.6670707	231.8155180	86.8962523	20143.8997402
479	192.4761126	90.0955064	17341.2328302	212.4403766	88.4704718	18794.7445754	234.4717175	86.9005172	20375.7152582
480	194.6013697	90.1006451	17533.7089028	214.??03365	88.4751200	1900..1854520	237.1583928	86.9047338	20610.1869957
481	196.7500932	90.1057277	17728.3103126	217.2478934	88.4797256	19222.0162585	239.8758328	86.9089026	20847.3453385
482	198.9225421	90.1107547	17925.0604058	219.6691178	88.4842815	19439.2639919	242.62?4100	86.9130242	21087.2212713
483	201.1189785	90.1157269	18123.9829479	222.1632517	88.4887925	19658.9555918	245.4044814	86.9170991	21329.8456310
484	203.3396673	90.1206448	18325.1019234	224.6625883	88.4932333	19881.1189434	248.2164077	86.9211279	21575.2501126
485	205.5843761	90.1255090	18523.4415937	227.1900424	88.4976354	20105.7815317	251.0605541	86.9251110	21823.4665204
486	207.8543758	90.1303200	18734.0264658	229.7459304	88.5019680	20332.9715741	253.9372896	86.9290489	22074.5270744
487	210.1499400	90.1350785	18941.8813455	232.3305721	88.5062922	20562.7175045	256.8469877	86.9329423	22328.4643640
488	212.4703456	90.1397851	19152.0312085	234.9442910	88.5105485	20795.0480768	259.7900261	86.9367916	22585.3113517
489	214.8163723	90.1444402	19364.5016311	237.5874143	88.5147575	21029.9923576	262.7657868	86.9405972	22845.1013778
490	217.1883001	90.1490445	19579.3180035	240.2602227	88.5189197	21267.5797820	265.7776562	86.9443598	23107.8681646
491	219.5864240	90.1535935	19796.5063066	242.9632008	88.5230355	21507.8400547	268.8230252	86.9480797	23373.6458208
492	222.0110241	90.1581028	20016.0927306	245.6965368	88.5271056	21750.8032555	271.9032891	86.9517575	23642.4688461
493	224.4623958	90.1625579	20238.1037546	248.4603228	88.5311304	21996.4997923	275.0188476	86.9553936	23914.3721351
494	226.9403347	90.1669643	20462.5661504	251.2558049	88.5351104	22244.9604151	278.1701052	86.9589885	24189.3909827
495	229.4456398	90.1713226	20689.5069852	254.0824327	88.5390461	22496.2162200	281.3574710	86.9625427	24467.5610879
496	231.9801131	90.1756334	20918.9536250	256.9408600	88.5429381	22750.2986626	284.5813587	86.9660566	24748.9185589
497	234.5415602	90.1798970	21150.9337381	259.8314447	88.5467867	23007.2395127	287.8421868	86.9695308	25033.4999176
498	237.1312899	90.1841141	21385.4752983	262.7545485	88.5505925	23267.0709574	291.1403785	86.9729655	25321.3421044
499	239.7493146	90.1882851	21622.6065882	265.7105371	88.5543560	23529.8255058	294.4763620	86.9763614	25612.4824829
500	242.3968499	90.1924105	21862.3562028	268.6997807	88.5580777	23795.5360430	297.?305703	86.9797188	25906.9588449

Table 2

MONTHLY PAYMENTS

This table lists the monthly payment (principal and interest) for level payment amortized loans (see Section 6.1). Payments are listed for loan amounts of from $10,000 to $100,000 in increments of $1,000, for terms of 5 to 30 years in increments of 5 years, and for interest rates of 5% to 13.75% in increments of ¼%. For instance, the monthly payment for a $27,000 loan at 5% for 25 years is $157.84.

Table 2

	5.00						5.25					
	TERM (YEARS)						TERM (YEARS)					
AMOUNT	5	10	15	20	25	30	5	10	15	20	25	30
10000	189.71	106.07	79.08	66.00	58.46	53.68	189.86	107.29	80.39	67.38	59.92	55.22
11000	207.58	116.67	86.99	72.60	64.30	59.05	208.85	118.02	88.43	74.12	65.92	60.74
12000	226.45	127.28	94.90	79.19	70.15	64.42	227.83	128.75	96.47	80.86	71.91	66.26
13000	245.33	137.89	102.80	85.79	76.00	69.79	246.82	139.48	104.50	87.60	77.90	71.79
14000	264.20	148.49	110.71	92.39	81.84	75.16	265.80	150.21	112.54	94.34	83.89	77.31
15000	283.07	159.10	118.62	98.99	87.69	80.52	284.79	160.94	120.58	101.08	89.89	82.83
16000	301.94	169.70	126.53	105.59	93.53	85.89	303.78	171.67	128.62	107.82	95.88	88.35
17000	320.81	180.31	134.43	112.19	99.38	91.26	322.76	182.40	136.66	114.55	101.87	93.87
18000	339.68	190.92	142.34	118.79	105.23	96.63	341.75	193.13	144.70	121.29	107.86	99.40
19000	358.55	201.52	150.25	125.39	111.07	102.00	360.73	203.85	152.74	128.03	113.86	104.92
20000	377.42	212.13	158.16	131.99	116.92	107.36	379.72	214.58	160.78	134.77	119.85	110.44
21000	396.30	222.74	166.07	138.59	122.76	112.73	398.71	225.31	168.81	141.51	125.84	115.96
22000	415.17	233.34	173.97	145.19	128.61	118.10	417.69	236.04	176.85	148.25	131.83	121.48
23000	434.04	243.95	181.88	151.79	134.46	123.47	436.68	246.77	184.89	154.98	137.83	127.01
24000	452.91	254.56	189.79	158.39	140.30	128.84	455.66	257.50	192.93	161.72	143.82	132.53
25000	471.78	265.16	197.70	164.99	146.15	134.21	474.65	268.23	200.97	168.46	149.81	138.05
26000	490.65	275.77	205.61	171.59	151.99	139.57	493.64	278.96	209.01	175.20	155.80	143.57
27000	509.52	286.38	213.51	178.19	157.84	144.94	512.62	289.69	217.05	181.94	161.80	149.09
28000	528.39	296.98	221.42	184.79	163.69	150.31	531.61	300.42	225.09	188.68	167.79	154.62
29000	547.27	307.59	229.33	191.39	169.53	155.68	550.59	311.15	233.12	195.41	173.78	160.14
30000	566.14	318.20	237.24	197.99	175.38	161.05	569.58	321.88	241.16	202.15	179.77	165.66
31000	585.01	328.80	245.15	204.59	181.22	166.41	588.57	332.60	249.20	208.89	185.77	171.18
32000	603.88	339.41	253.05	211.19	187.07	171.78	607.55	343.33	257.24	215.63	191.76	176.71
33000	622.75	350.02	260.96	217.79	192.91	177.15	626.54	354.06	265.28	222.37	197.75	182.23
34000	641.62	360.62	268.87	224.38	198.76	182.52	645.52	364.79	273.32	229.11	203.74	187.75
35000	660.49	371.23	276.78	230.98	204.61	187.89	664.51	375.52	281.36	235.85	209.74	193.27
36000	679.36	381.94	284.69	237.58	210.45	193.26	683.50	386.25	289.40	242.58	215.73	198.79
37000	698.24	392.44	292.59	244.18	216.30	198.62	702.48	396.98	297.43	249.32	221.72	204.32
38000	717.11	403.05	300.50	250.78	222.14	203.99	721.47	407.71	305.47	256.06	227.71	209.84
39000	735.98	413.66	308.41	257.38	227.99	209.36	740.45	418.44	313.51	262.80	233.71	215.36
40000	754.85	424.26	316.32	263.98	233.84	214.73	759.44	429.17	321.55	269.54	239.70	220.88
41000	773.72	434.87	324.23	270.53	239.68	220.10	778.43	439.90	329.59	276.28	245.69	226.40
42000	792.59	445.48	332.13	277.18	245.53	225.47	797.41	450.63	337.63	283.01	251.68	231.93
43000	811.46	456.08	340.04	283.78	251.37	230.83	816.40	461.35	345.67	289.75	257.68	237.45
44000	830.33	466.69	347.95	290.38	257.22	236.20	835.38	472.08	353.71	296.49	263.67	242.97
45000	849.21	477.29	355.86	296.98	263.07	241.57	854.37	482.81	361.74	303.23	269.66	248.49
46000	868.08	487.90	363.77	303.58	268.91	246.94	873.36	493.54	369.78	309.97	275.65	254.01
47000	886.95	498.51	371.67	310.18	274.76	252.31	892.34	504.27	377.82	316.71	281.65	259.54
48000	905.82	509.11	379.58	316.78	280.60	257.67	911.33	515.00	385.86	323.45	287.64	265.06
49000	924.69	519.72	387.49	323.38	286.45	263.04	930.31	525.73	393.90	330.18	293.63	270.58
50000	943.56	530.33	395.40	329.98	292.30	268.41	949.30	536.46	401.94	336.92	299.62	276.10
51000	962.43	540.93	403.30	336.58	298.14	273.78	968.29	547.19	409.98	343.66	305.62	281.62
52000	981.30	551.54	411.21	343.18	303.99	279.15	987.27	557.92	418.02	350.40	311.61	287.15
53000	1000.18	562.15	419.12	349.78	309.83	284.52	1006.26	568.65	426.06	357.14	317.60	292.67
54000	1019.05	572.75	427.03	356.38	315.68	289.88	1025.24	579.38	434.09	363.88	323.59	298.19
55000	1037.92	583.36	434.94	362.98	321.52	295.25	1044.23	590.10	442.13	370.61	329.59	303.71
56000	1056.79	593.97	442.84	369.58	327.37	300.62	1063.22	600.83	450.17	377.35	335.58	309.23
57000	1075.66	604.57	450.75	376.17	333.22	305.99	1082.20	611.56	458.21	384.09	341.57	314.76
58000	1094.53	615.18	458.66	382.77	339.06	311.36	1101.19	622.29	466.25	390.83	347.56	320.28
59000	1113.40	625.79	466.57	389.37	344.91	316.72	1120.17	633.02	474.29	397.57	353.56	325.80
60000	1132.27	636.39	474.48	395.97	350.75	322.09	1139.16	643.75	482.33	404.31	359.55	331.32
61000	1151.15	647.00	482.38	402.57	356.60	327.46	1158.15	654.48	490.37	411.04	365.54	336.84
62000	1170.02	657.61	490.29	409.17	362.45	332.83	1177.13	665.21	498.40	417.78	371.53	342.37
63000	1188.89	668.21	498.20	415.77	368.29	338.20	1196.12	675.94	506.44	424.52	377.53	347.89
64000	1207.76	678.82	506.11	422.37	374.14	343.57	1215.10	686.67	514.48	431.26	383.52	353.41
65000	1226.63	689.43	514.02	428.97	379.98	348.93	1234.09	697.40	522.52	438.00	389.51	358.93
66000	1245.50	700.03	521.92	435.57	385.83	354.30	1253.07	708.13	530.56	444.74	395.50	364.45
67000	1264.37	710.64	529.83	442.17	391.68	359.67	1272.06	718.85	538.60	451.48	401.50	369.98
68000	1283.24	721.25	537.74	448.77	397.52	365.04	1291.05	729.58	546.64	458.21	407.49	375.50
69000	1302.12	731.85	545.65	455.37	403.37	370.41	1310.03	740.31	554.68	464.95	413.48	381.02
70000	1320.99	742.46	553.56	461.97	409.21	375.78	1329.02	751.04	562.71	471.69	419.47	386.54
71000	1339.86	753.07	561.46	468.57	415.06	381.14	1348.00	761.77	570.75	478.43	425.47	392.06
72000	1358.73	763.67	569.37	475.17	420.90	386.51	1366.99	772.50	578.79	485.17	431.46	397.59
73000	1377.60	774.28	577.28	481.77	426.75	391.88	1385.98	783.23	586.83	491.91	437.45	403.11
74000	1396.47	784.88	585.19	488.37	432.60	397.25	1404.96	793.96	594.87	498.64	443.44	408.63
75000	1415.34	795.49	593.10	494.97	438.44	402.62	1423.95	804.69	602.91	505.38	449.44	414.15
76000	1434.21	806.10	601.00	501.57	444.29	407.98	1442.93	815.42	610.95	512.12	455.43	419.67
77000	1453.08	816.70	608.91	508.17	450.13	413.35	1461.92	826.15	618.99	518.86	461.42	425.20
78000	1471.96	827.31	616.82	514.77	455.98	418.72	1480.91	836.88	627.02	525.60	467.41	430.72
79000	1490.83	837.92	624.73	521.37	461.83	424.09	1499.89	847.60	635.06	532.34	473.41	436.24
80000	1509.70	848.52	632.63	527.96	467.67	429.46	1518.88	858.33	643.10	539.08	479.40	441.76
81000	1528.57	859.13	640.54	534.56	473.52	434.83	1537.86	869.06	651.14	545.81	485.39	447.28
82000	1547.44	869.74	648.45	541.16	479.36	440.19	1556.85	879.79	659.18	552.55	491.38	452.81
83000	1566.31	880.34	656.36	547.76	485.21	445.56	1575.84	890.52	667.22	559.29	497.38	458.33
84000	1585.18	890.95	664.27	554.36	491.06	450.93	1594.82	901.25	675.26	566.03	503.37	463.85
85000	1604.05	901.56	672.17	560.96	496.90	456.30	1613.81	911.98	683.30	572.77	509.36	469.37
86000	1622.93	912.16	680.08	567.56	502.75	461.67	1632.79	922.71	691.33	579.51	515.35	474.90
87000	1641.80	922.77	687.99	574.16	508.59	467.03	1651.78	933.44	699.37	586.24	521.35	480.42
88000	1660.67	933.38	695.90	580.76	514.44	472.40	1670.77	944.17	707.41	592.98	527.34	485.94
89000	1679.54	943.98	703.81	587.36	520.29	477.77	1689.75	954.90	715.45	599.72	533.33	491.46
90000	1698.41	954.59	711.71	593.96	526.13	483.14	1708.74	965.63	723.49	606.46	539.32	496.98
91000	1717.28	965.20	719.62	600.56	531.98	488.51	1727.72	976.35	731.53	613.20	545.32	502.51
92000	1736.15	975.80	727.53	607.16	537.82	493.88	1746.71	987.08	739.57	619.94	551.31	508.03
93000	1755.02	986.41	735.44	613.76	543.67	499.24	1765.70	997.81	747.61	626.68	557.30	513.55
94000	1773.90	997.02	743.35	620.36	549.51	504.61	1784.68	1008.54	755.65	633.41	563.29	519.07
95000	1792.77	1007.62	751.25	626.96	555.36	509.98	1803.67	1019.27	763.68	640.15	569.29	524.59
96000	1811.64	1018.23	759.16	633.56	561.21	515.35	1822.65	1030.00	771.72	646.89	575.28	530.12
97000	1830.51	1028.84	767.07	640.16	567.05	520.72	1841.64	1040.73	779.76	653.63	581.27	535.64
98000	1849.38	1039.44	774.98	646.76	572.90	526.09	1860.63	1051.46	787.80	660.37	587.26	541.16
99000	1868.25	1050.05	782.89	653.36	578.74	531.45	1879.61	1062.19	795.84	667.11	593.26	546.68
100000	1887.12	1060.66	790.79	659.96	584.59	536.82	1898.60	1072.92	803.88	673.84	599.25	552.20

5.50   5.75

AMOUNT	\<5.50\> 5	10	15	20	25	30	\<5.75\> 5	10	15	20	25	30
10000	191.01	108.53	81.71	68.79	61.41	56.78	192.17	109.77	83.04	70.21	62.91	58.36
11000	210.11	119.38	89.88	75.67	67.55	62.46	211.38	120.75	91.35	77.23	69.20	64.19
12000	229.21	130.23	98.05	82.55	73.69	68.13	230.60	131.72	99.65	84.25	75.49	70.03
13000	248.32	141.08	106.22	89.43	79.83	73.81	249.82	142.70	107.95	91.27	81.78	75.86
14000	267.42	151.94	114.39	96.30	85.97	79.49	269.03	153.68	116.26	98.29	88.07	81.70
15000	286.52	162.79	122.56	103.18	92.11	85.17	288.25	164.65	124.56	105.31	94.37	87.54
16000	305.62	173.64	130.73	110.06	98.25	90.85	307.47	175.63	132.87	112.33	100.66	93.37
17000	324.72	184.49	138.90	116.94	104.39	96.52	326.69	186.61	141.17	119.35	106.95	99.21
18000	343.82	195.35	147.08	123.82	110.54	102.20	345.90	197.58	149.47	126.38	113.24	105.04
19000	362.92	206.20	155.25	130.70	116.68	107.88	365.12	208.56	157.78	133.40	119.53	110.88
20000	382.02	217.05	163.42	137.58	122.82	113.56	384.34	219.54	166.08	140.42	125.82	116.71
21000	401.12	227.91	171.59	144.46	128.96	119.24	403.55	230.52	174.39	147.44	132.11	122.55
22000	420.23	238.76	179.76	151.34	135.10	124.91	422.77	241.49	182.69	154.46	138.40	128.39
23000	439.33	249.61	167.93	158.21	141.24	130.59	441.99	252.47	190.99	161.48	144.69	134.22
24000	458.43	260.46	196.10	165.09	147.38	136.27	461.20	263.45	199.30	168.50	150.99	140.06
25000	477.53	271.32	204.27	171.97	153.52	141.95	480.42	274.42	207.60	175.52	157.28	145.89
26000	496.63	282.17	212.44	178.85	159.66	147.63	499.64	285.40	215.91	182.54	163.57	151.73
27000	515.73	293.02	220.61	185.73	165.80	153.30	518.85	296.38	224.21	189.56	169.86	157.56
28000	534.83	303.87	228.78	192.61	171.94	158.98	538.07	307.35	232.51	196.58	176.15	163.40
29000	553.93	314.73	236.95	199.49	178.09	164.66	557.29	318.33	240.82	203.60	182.44	169.24
30000	573.03	325.58	245.13	206.37	184.23	170.34	576.50	329.31	249.12	210.63	188.73	175.07
31000	592.14	336.43	253.30	213.25	190.37	176.01	595.72	340.28	257.43	217.65	195.02	180.91
32000	611.24	347.28	261.47	220.12	196.51	181.69	614.94	351.26	265.73	224.67	201.31	186.74
33000	630.34	358.14	269.64	227.00	202.65	187.37	634.15	362.24	274.04	231.69	207.61	192.58
34000	649.44	368.99	277.81	233.88	208.79	193.05	653.37	373.22	282.34	238.71	213.90	198.41
35000	668.54	379.84	285.98	240.76	214.93	198.73	672.59	384.19	290.64	245.73	220.19	204.25
36000	687.64	390.69	294.15	247.64	221.07	204.40	691.80	395.17	298.95	252.75	226.48	210.09
37000	706.74	401.55	302.32	254.52	227.21	210.08	711.02	406.15	307.25	259.77	232.77	215.92
38000	725.84	412.40	310.49	261.40	233.35	215.76	730.24	417.12	315.56	266.79	239.06	221.76
39000	744.95	423.25	318.66	268.28	239.49	221.44	749.45	428.10	323.86	273.81	245.35	227.59
40000	764.05	434.11	326.83	275.15	245.63	227.12	768.67	439.08	332.16	280.83	251.64	233.43
41000	783.15	444.96	335.00	282.03	251.78	232.79	787.89	450.05	340.47	287.85	257.93	239.26
42000	802.25	455.81	343.18	288.91	257.92	238.47	807.10	461.03	348.77	294.88	264.22	245.10
43000	821.35	466.66	351.35	295.79	264.06	244.15	826.32	472.01	357.08	301.90	270.52	250.94
44000	840.45	477.52	359.52	302.67	270.20	249.83	845.54	482.98	365.38	308.92	276.81	256.77
45000	859.55	488.37	367.69	309.55	276.34	255.51	864.75	493.96	373.68	315.94	283.10	262.61
46000	878.65	499.22	375.86	316.43	282.48	261.18	883.97	504.94	381.99	322.96	289.39	268.44
47000	897.75	510.07	384.03	323.31	288.62	266.86	903.19	515.92	390.29	329.98	295.68	274.28
48000	916.86	520.93	392.20	330.19	294.76	272.54	922.40	526.89	398.60	337.00	301.97	280.11
49000	935.96	531.78	400.37	337.06	300.90	278.22	941.62	537.87	406.90	344.02	308.26	285.95
50000	955.06	542.63	408.54	343.94	307.04	283.89	960.84	548.85	415.21	351.04	314.55	291.79
51000	974.16	553.48	416.71	350.82	313.18	289.57	980.06	559.82	423.51	358.06	320.84	297.62
52000	993.26	564.34	424.88	357.70	319.33	295.25	999.27	570.80	431.81	365.08	327.14	303.46
53000	1012.36	575.19	433.05	364.58	325.47	300.93	1018.49	581.78	440.12	372.10	333.43	309.29
54000	1031.46	586.04	441.23	371.46	331.61	306.61	1037.71	592.75	448.42	379.13	339.72	315.13
55000	1050.56	596.89	449.40	378.34	337.75	312.28	1056.92	603.73	456.73	386.15	346.01	320.97
56000	1069.67	607.75	457.57	385.22	343.89	317.96	1076.14	614.71	465.03	393.17	352.30	326.80
57000	1088.77	618.60	465.74	392.10	350.03	323.64	1095.36	625.68	473.33	400.19	358.59	332.64
58000	1107.87	629.45	473.91	398.97	356.17	329.32	1114.57	636.66	481.64	407.21	364.88	338.47
59000	1126.97	640.31	482.08	405.85	362.31	335.00	1133.79	647.64	489.94	414.23	371.17	344.31
60000	1146.07	651.16	490.25	412.73	368.45	340.67	1153.01	658.62	498.25	421.25	377.46	350.14
61000	1165.17	662.01	498.42	419.61	374.59	346.35	1172.22	669.59	506.55	428.27	383.75	355.98
62000	1184.27	672.86	506.59	426.49	380.73	352.03	1191.44	680.57	514.85	435.29	390.05	361.82
63000	1203.37	683.72	514.76	433.37	386.88	357.71	1210.66	691.55	523.16	442.31	396.34	367.65
64000	1222.47	694.57	522.93	440.25	393.02	363.38	1229.87	702.52	531.46	449.33	402.63	373.49
65000	1241.58	705.42	531.10	447.13	399.16	369.06	1249.09	713.50	539.77	456.35	408.92	379.32
66000	1260.68	716.27	539.28	454.01	405.30	374.74	1268.31	724.48	548.07	463.38	415.21	385.16
67000	1279.78	727.13	547.45	460.88	411.44	380.42	1287.52	735.45	556.37	470.40	421.50	390.99
68000	1298.88	737.98	555.62	467.76	417.58	386.10	1306.74	746.43	564.68	477.42	427.79	396.83
69000	1317.98	748.83	563.79	474.64	423.72	391.77	1325.96	757.41	572.98	484.44	434.08	402.67
70000	1337.08	759.68	571.96	481.52	429.86	397.45	1345.17	768.38	581.29	491.46	440.37	408.50
71000	1356.18	770.54	580.13	488.40	436.00	403.13	1364.39	779.36	589.59	498.48	446.67	414.34
72000	1375.28	781.39	588.30	495.28	442.14	408.81	1383.61	790.34	597.90	505.50	452.96	420.17
73000	1394.38	792.24	596.47	502.16	448.28	414.49	1402.82	801.32	606.20	512.52	459.25	426.01
74000	1413.49	803.09	604.64	509.04	454.42	420.16	1422.04	812.29	614.50	519.54	465.54	431.84
75000	1432.59	813.95	612.81	515.92	460.57	425.84	1441.26	823.27	622.81	526.56	471.83	437.68
76000	1451.69	824.80	620.98	522.79	466.71	431.52	1460.47	834.25	631.11	533.58	478.12	443.52
77000	1470.79	835.65	629.15	529.67	472.85	437.20	1479.69	845.22	639.42	540.60	484.41	449.35
78000	1489.89	846.50	637.33	536.55	478.99	442.88	1498.91	856.20	647.72	547.63	490.70	455.19
79000	1508.99	857.36	645.50	543.43	485.13	448.55	1518.12	867.18	656.02	554.65	496.99	461.02
80000	1528.09	868.21	653.67	550.31	491.27	454.23	1537.34	878.15	664.33	561.67	503.29	466.86
81000	1547.19	879.06	661.84	557.19	497.41	459.91	1556.56	889.13	672.63	568.69	509.58	472.69
82000	1566.30	889.92	670.01	564.07	503.55	465.59	1575.77	900.11	680.94	575.71	515.87	478.53
83000	1585.40	900.77	678.18	570.95	509.69	471.26	1594.99	911.08	689.24	582.73	522.16	484.37
84000	1604.50	911.62	686.35	577.83	515.83	476.94	1614.21	922.06	697.54	589.75	528.45	490.20
85000	1623.60	922.47	694.52	584.70	521.97	482.62	1633.43	933.04	705.85	596.77	534.74	496.04
86000	1642.70	933.33	702.69	591.58	528.12	488.30	1652.64	944.02	714.15	603.79	541.03	501.87
87000	1661.80	944.18	710.86	598.46	534.26	493.98	1671.86	954.99	722.46	610.81	547.32	507.71
88000	1680.90	955.03	719.03	605.34	540.40	499.65	1691.08	965.97	730.76	617.83	553.61	513.54
89000	1700.00	965.88	727.20	612.22	546.54	505.33	1710.29	976.95	739.06	624.85	559.90	519.38
90000	1719.10	976.74	735.38	619.10	552.68	511.01	1729.51	987.92	747.37	631.88	566.20	525.22
91000	1738.21	987.59	743.55	625.98	558.82	516.69	1748.73	998.90	755.67	638.90	572.49	531.05
92000	1757.31	998.44	751.72	632.86	564.96	522.37	1767.94	1009.88	763.98	645.92	578.78	536.89
93000	1776.41	1009.29	759.89	639.74	571.10	528.04	1787.16	1020.85	772.28	652.94	585.07	542.72
94000	1795.51	1020.15	768.06	646.61	577.24	533.72	1806.38	1031.83	780.59	659.96	591.36	548.56
95000	1814.61	1031.00	776.23	653.49	583.38	539.40	1825.59	1042.81	788.89	666.98	597.65	554.39
96000	1833.71	1041.85	784.40	660.37	589.52	545.08	1844.81	1053.78	797.19	674.00	603.94	560.23
97000	1852.81	1052.70	792.57	667.25	595.66	550.76	1864.03	1064.76	805.50	681.02	610.23	566.07
98000	1871.91	1063.56	800.74	674.13	601.81	556.43	1883.24	1075.74	813.80	688.04	616.52	571.90
99000	1891.02	1074.41	808.91	681.01	607.95	562.11	1902.46	1086.72	822.11	695.06	622.82	577.74
100000	1910.12	1085.26	817.08	687.89	614.09	567.79	1921.68	1097.69	830.41	702.08	629.11	583.57

Table 2

		6.00							6.25			
	TERM (YEARS)						TERM (YEARS)					
AMOUNT	5	10	15	20	25	30	5	10	15	20	25	30
10000	193.33	111.02	84.39	71.64	64.43	59.96	194.49	112.28	85.74	73.09	65.97	61.57
11000	212.66	122.12	92.82	78.81	70.87	65.95	213.94	123.51	94.32	80.40	72.56	67.73
12000	231.99	133.22	101.26	85.97	77.32	71.95	233.39	134.74	102.89	87.71	79.16	73.89
13000	251.33	144.33	109.70	93.14	83.76	77.94	252.84	145.96	111.46	95.02	85.76	80.04
14000	270.66	155.43	118.14	100.30	90.20	83.94	272.29	157.19	120.04	102.33	92.35	86.20
15000	289.99	166.53	126.58	107.46	96.65	89.93	291.74	168.42	128.61	109.64	98.95	92.36
16000	309.32	177.63	135.02	1.4.63	103.09	95.93	311.19	179.65	137.19	116.95	105.55	98.51
17000	328.66	188.73	143.46	121.79	109.53	101.92	330.64	190.88	145.76	124.26	112.14	104.67
18000	347.99	199.84	151.89	128.96	115.97	107.92	350.09	202.10	154.34	131.57	118.74	110.83
19000	367.32	210.94	160.33	136.12	122.42	113.91	369.54	213.33	162.91	138.88	125.34	116.99
20000	386.66	222.04	168.77	143.29	129.86	119.91	388.99	224.56	171.48	146.19	131.93	123.14
21000	405.99	233.14	177.21	150.45	135.30	125.91	408.43	235.79	180.06	153.49	138.53	129.30
22000	425.32	244.25	185.65	157.61	141.75	131.90	427.88	247.02	188.63	160.80	145.13	135.46
23000	444.65	255.35	194.09	164.78	148.19	137.90	447.33	258.24	197.21	168.11	151.72	141.61
24000	463.99	266.45	202.53	171.94	154.63	143.89	466.78	269.47	205.78	175.42	158.32	147.77
25000	483.32	277.55	210.96	179.11	161.08	149.89	486.23	280.70	214.36	182.73	164.92	153.93
26000	502.65	288.65	219.40	186.27	167.52	155.88	505.68	291.93	222.93	190.04	171.51	160.09
27000	521.99	299.76	227.84	193.44	173.96	161.88	525.13	303.16	231.50	197.35	178.11	166.24
28000	541.32	310.86	236.28	200.60	180.40	167.87	544.58	314.38	240.08	204.66	184.71	172.40
29000	560.65	321.96	244.72	207.77	186.85	173.87	564.03	325.61	248.65	211.97	191.30	178.56
30000	579.98	333.06	253.16	214.93	193.29	179.87	583.48	336.84	257.23	219.28	197.90	184.72
31000	599.32	344.16	261.60	222.09	199.73	185.86	602.93	348.07	265.80	226.59	204.50	190.87
32000	618.65	355.27	270.03	229.26	206.18	191.86	622.38	359.30	274.38	233.90	211.09	197.03
33000	637.98	366.37	278.47	236.42	212.62	197.85	641.83	370.52	282.95	241.21	217.69	203.19
34000	657.32	377.47	286.91	243.59	219.06	203.85	661.27	381.75	291.52	248.52	224.29	209.34
35000	676.65	338.57	295.35	250.75	225.51	209.84	680.72	392.98	300.10	255.82	230.88	215.50
36000	695.98	399.67	303.79	257.92	231.95	215.84	700.17	404.21	308.67	263.13	237.48	221.66
37000	715.31	410.78	312.23	265.08	238.39	221.83	719.62	415.44	317.25	270.44	244.08	227.82
38000	734.65	421.88	320.67	272.24	244.83	227.83	739.07	426.66	325.82	277.75	250.67	233.97
39000	753.98	432.98	329.10	279.41	251.28	233.82	758.52	437.89	334.39	285.06	257.27	240.13
40000	773.31	444.08	337.54	286.57	257.72	239.82	777.97	449.12	342.97	292.37	263.87	246.29
41000	792.64	455.18	345.98	293.74	264.16	245.82	797.42	460.35	351.54	299.68	270.46	252.44
42000	811.98	466.29	354.42	300.90	270.61	251.81	816.87	471.58	360.12	306.99	277.06	258.60
43000	831.31	477.39	362.86	308.07	277.05	257.81	836.32	482.80	368.69	314.30	283.66	264.76
44000	850.64	488.49	371.30	315.23	283.49	263.80	855.77	494.03	377.27	321.61	290.25	270.92
45000	869.98	499.59	379.74	322.39	289.94	269.80	875.22	505.26	385.84	328.92	296.85	277.07
46000	889.31	510.69	388.17	329.56	296.38	275.79	894.67	516.49	394.41	336.23	303.45	283.23
47000	908.64	521.80	396.61	336.72	302.82	281.79	914.12	527.72	402.99	343.54	310.04	289.39
48000	927.97	532.90	405.05	343.89	309.26	287.78	933.56	538.94	411.56	350.85	316.64	295.54
49000	947.31	544.00	413.49	351.05	315.71	293.78	953.01	550.17	420.14	358.15	323.24	301.70
50000	966.64	555.10	421.93	358.22	322.15	299.78	972.46	561.40	428.71	365.46	329.83	307.86
51000	985.97	566.20	430.37	365.38	328.59	305.77	991.91	572.63	437.29	372.77	336.43	314.02
52000	1005.31	577.31	438.81	372.54	335.04	311.77	1011.36	583.86	445.86	380.08	343.03	320.17
53000	1024.64	588.41	447.24	379.71	341.48	317.76	1030.81	595.09	454.43	387.39	349.62	326.33
54000	1043.97	599.51	455.68	386.87	347.92	323.76	1050.26	606.31	463.01	394.70	356.22	332.49
55000	1063.30	610.61	464.12	394.04	354.37	329.75	1069.71	617.54	471.58	402.01	362.62	338.64
56000	1082.64	621.71	472.56	401.20	360.81	335.75	1089.16	628.77	480.16	409.32	369.41	344.80
57000	1101.97	632.82	481.00	408.37	367.25	341.74	1108.61	640.00	488.73	416.63	376.01	350.96
58000	1121.30	643.92	489.44	415.53	373.69	347.74	1128.06	651.22	497.31	423.94	382.61	357.12
59000	1140.64	655.02	497.88	422.69	380.14	353.73	1147.51	662.45	505.88	431.25	389.20	363.27
60000	1159.97	666.12	506.31	429.86	386.58	359.73	1166.96	673.68	514.45	438.56	395.80	369.43
61000	1179.30	677.23	514.75	437.02	393.02	365.73	1186.40	684.91	523.03	445.87	402.40	375.59
62000	1198.63	688.33	523.19	444.19	399.47	371.72	1205.85	696.14	531.60	453.18	409.00	381.74
63000	1217.97	699.43	531.63	451.35	405.91	377.72	1225.30	707.36	540.18	460.48	415.59	387.90
64000	1237.30	710.53	540.07	458.52	412.35	383.71	1244.75	718.59	548.75	467.79	422.19	394.06
65000	1256.63	721.63	548.51	465.68	418.80	389.71	1264.20	729.82	557.32	475.10	428.79	400.21
66000	1275.96	732.74	556.95	472.84	425.24	395.70	1283.65	741.05	565.90	482.41	435.38	406.37
67000	1295.30	743.84	565.38	480.01	431.68	401.70	1303.10	752.28	574.47	489.72	441.98	412.53
68000	1314.63	754.94	573.82	487.17	438.12	407.69	1322.55	763.50	583.05	497.03	448.58	418.69
69000	1333.96	766.04	582.26	494.34	444.57	413.69	1342.00	774.73	591.62	504.34	455.17	424.84
70000	1353.30	777.14	590.70	501.50	451.01	419.69	1361.45	785.96	600.20	511.65	461.77	431.00
71000	1372.63	788.25	599.14	508.67	457.45	425.68	1380.90	797.19	608.77	518.96	468.37	437.16
72000	1391.96	799.35	607.58	515.83	463.90	431.68	1400.35	808.42	617.34	526.27	474.96	443.32
73000	1411.29	810.45	616.02	522.99	470.34	437.67	1419.80	819.64	625.92	533.58	481.56	449.47
74000	1430.63	821.55	624.45	530.16	476.78	443.67	1439.25	830.87	634.49	540.89	488.16	455.63
75000	1449.96	832.65	632.89	537.32	483.23	449.66	1458.69	842.10	643.07	548.20	494.75	461.79
76000	1469.29	843.76	641.33	544.49	489.67	455.66	1478.14	853.33	651.64	555.51	501.35	467.95
77000	1488.63	854.86	649.77	551.65	496.11	461.65	1497.59	864.56	660.22	562.81	507.95	474.10
78000	1507.96	865.96	658.21	558.82	502.56	467.65	1517.04	875.78	668.79	570.12	514.54	480.26
79000	1527.29	877.06	666.65	565.98	509.00	473.64	1536.49	887.01	677.36	577.43	521.14	486.42
80000	1546.62	888.16	675.09	573.14	515.44	479.64	1555.94	898.24	685.94	584.74	527.74	492.57
81000	1565.96	899.27	683.52	580.31	521.88	485.64	1575.39	909.47	694.51	592.05	534.33	498.73
82000	1585.29	910.37	691.96	587.47	528.33	491.63	1594.84	920.70	703.09	599.36	540.93	504.89
83000	1604.62	921.47	700.40	594.64	534.77	497.63	1614.29	931.92	711.66	606.67	547.53	511.05
84000	1623.96	932.57	708.84	601.80	541.21	503.62	1633.74	943.15	720.24	613.98	554.12	517.20
85000	1643.29	943.67	717.28	608.97	547.66	509.62	1653.19	954.38	728.81	621.29	560.72	523.36
86000	1662.62	954.78	725.72	616.13	554.10	515.61	1672.64	965.61	737.38	628.60	567.32	529.52
87000	1681.95	965.88	734.16	623.30	560.54	521.61	1692.09	976.84	745.96	635.91	573.91	535.67
88000	1701.29	976.98	742.59	630.46	566.99	527.60	1711.54	988.06	754.53	643.22	580.51	541.83
89000	1720.62	988.08	751.03	637.62	573.43	533.60	1730.98	999.29	763.11	650.53	587.11	547.99
90000	1739.95	999.18	759.47	644.79	579.87	539.60	1750.43	1010.52	771.68	657.84	593.70	554.15
91000	1759.28	1010.29	767.91	651.95	586.31	545.59	1769.88	1021.75	780.25	665.14	600.30	560.30
92000	1778.62	1021.39	776.35	659.12	592.76	551.59	1789.33	1032.98	788.83	672.45	606.90	566.46
93000	1797.95	1032.49	784.79	666.28	599.20	557.58	1808.78	1044.20	797.40	679.76	613.49	572.62
94000	1817.28	1043.59	793.23	673.45	605.64	563.58	1828.23	1055.43	805.98	687.07	620.09	578.77
95000	1836.62	1054.69	801.66	680.61	612.09	569.57	1847.68	1066.66	814.55	694.38	626.69	584.93
96000	1855.95	1065.80	810.10	687.77	618.53	575.57	1867.13	1077.89	823.13	701.69	633.28	591.09
97000	1875.28	1076.90	818.54	694.94	624.97	581.56	1886.58	1089.12	831.70	709.00	639.88	597.25
98000	1894.61	1088.00	826.98	702.10	631.42	587.56	1906.02	1100.34	840.27	716.31	646.48	603.40
99000	1913.95	1099.10	835.42	709.27	637.86	593.56	1925.48	1111.57	848.85	723.62	653.07	609.56
100000	1933.28	1110.21	843.86	716.43	644.30	599.55	1944.93	1122.80	857.42	730.93	659.67	615.72

Table 2   453

	6.50						6.75					
	TERM (YEARS)						TERM (YEARS)					
AMOUNT	5	10	15	20	25	30	5	10	15	20	25	30
10000	195.66	113.55	87.11	74.56	67.52	63.21	196.83	114.82	88.49	76.04	69.09	64.86
11000	215.23	124.90	95.82	82.01	74.27	69.53	216.52	126.31	97.34	83.64	76.00	71.35
12000	234.79	136.26	104.53	89.47	81.02	75.85	236.20	137.79	106.19	91.24	82.91	77.83
13000	254.36	147.61	113.24	96.92	87.78	82.17	255.88	149.27	115.04	98.85	89.82	84.32
14000	273.93	158.97	121.96	104.38	94.53	88.49	275.57	160.75	123.89	106.45	96.73	90.80
15000	293.49	170.32	130.67	111.84	101.28	94.81	295.25	172.24	132.74	114.05	103.64	97.29
16000	313.06	181.68	139.38	119.29	108.03	101.13	314.94	183.72	141.59	121.66	110.55	103.78
17000	332.62	193.03	148.09	126.75	114.79	107.45	334.62	195.20	150.43	129.26	117.45	110.26
18000	352.19	204.39	156.80	134.20	121.54	113.77	354.30	206.68	159.28	136.87	124.36	116.75
19000	371.76	215.74	165.51	141.66	128.29	120.09	373.99	218.17	168.13	144.47	131.27	123.23
20000	391.32	227.10	174.22	149.11	135.04	126.41	393.67	229.65	176.98	152.07	138.18	129.72
21000	410.89	238.45	182.93	156.57	141.79	132.73	413.35	241.13	185.83	159.68	145.09	136.21
22000	430.46	249.81	191.64	164.03	148.55	139.05	433.04	252.61	194.68	167.28	152.00	142.69
23000	450.02	261.16	200.35	171.48	155.30	145.38	452.72	264.10	203.53	174.88	158.91	149.18
24000	469.59	272.52	209.07	178.94	162.05	151.70	472.40	275.58	212.38	182.49	165.82	155.66
25000	489.15	283.87	217.78	186.39	168.80	158.02	492.09	287.06	221.23	190.09	172.73	162.15
26000	509.72	295.22	226.49	193.85	175.55	164.34	511.77	298.54	230.08	197.69	179.64	168.64
27000	528.29	306.58	235.20	201.30	182.31	170.66	531.45	310.03	238.93	205.30	186.55	175.12
28000	547.85	317.93	243.91	208.76	189.06	176.98	551.14	321.51	247.77	212.90	193.46	181.61
29000	567.42	329.29	252.62	216.22	195.81	183.30	570.82	332.99	256.62	220.51	200.36	188.09
30000	5?6.98	340.64	261.33	223.67	202.56	189.62	590.50	344.47	265.47	228.11	207.27	194.58
31000	606.55	352.00	270.04	231.13	209.31	195.94	610.19	355.95	274.32	235.71	214.18	201.07
32000	626.12	363.35	278.75	238.56	216.07	202.26	629.8?	367.44	283.17	243.32	221.09	207.55
33000	645.68	374.71	287.47	246.04	222.82	208.58	649.55	378.92	292.02	250.92	228.00	214.04
34000	665.25	386.06	296.18	253.49	229.57	214.90	669.24	390.40	300.87	258.52	234.91	220.52
35000	684.82	397.42	304.89	260.95	236.32	221.22	688.92	401.88	309.72	266.13	241.82	227.01
36000	704.38	408.77	313.60	268.41	243.07	227.54	708.60	413.37	318.57	273.73	248.73	233.50
37000	723.95	420.13	322.31	275.86	249.83	233.87	728.29	424.85	327.42	281.33	255.64	239.98
38000	743.51	431.48	331.02	283.32	256.58	240.19	747.97	436.33	336.27	288.94	262.55	246.47
39000	763.08	442.84	339.73	290.77	263.33	246.51	767.65	447.81	345.11	296.54	269.46	252.95
40000	782.65	454.19	348.44	298.23	270.08	252.83	787.34	459.30	353.96	304.15	276.36	259.44
41000	802.21	465.55	357.15	305.68	276.83	259.15	807.02	470.78	362.81	311.75	283.27	265.93
42000	821.78	476.90	365.87	313.14	283.59	265.47	826.71	482.26	371.66	319.35	290.18	272.41
43000	841.34	488.26	374.58	320.60	290.34	271.79	846.39	493.74	380.51	326.96	297.09	278.90
44000	860.91	499.61	383.29	328.05	297.09	278.11	866.07	505.23	389.36	334.56	304.00	285.38
45000	880.48	510.97	392.00	335.51	303.84	284.43	885.76	516.71	398.21	342.16	310.91	291.87
46000	900.04	522.32	400.71	342.96	310.60	290.75	905.44	528.19	407.06	349.77	317.82	298.36
47000	919.61	533.68	409.42	350.42	317.35	297.07	925.12	539.67	415.91	357.37	324.73	304.84
48000	939.18	545.03	418.13	357.88	324.10	303.39	944.81	551.16	424.76	364.97	331.64	311.33
49000	958.74	556.39	426.84	365.33	330.85	309.71	964.49	562.64	433.61	372.58	338.55	317.81
50000	978.31	567.74	435.55	372.79	337.60	316.03	984.17	574.12	442.45	380.18	345.46	324.30
51000	997.87	579.09	444.26	380.24	344.36	322.35	1003.86	585.60	451.30	387.79	352.36	330.79
52000	1017.44	590.45	452.98	387.70	351.11	328.68	1023.54	597.09	460.15	395.39	359.27	337.27
53000	1037.01	601.80	461.69	395.15	357.86	335.00	1043.22	608.57	469.00	402.99	366.18	343.76
54000	1056.57	613.16	470.40	402.61	364.61	341.32	1062.91	620.05	477.85	410.60	373.09	350.24
55000	1076.14	624.51	479.11	410.07	371.36	347.64	1082.59	631.53	486.70	418.20	380.00	356.73
56000	1095.70	635.87	487.82	417.52	378.12	353.96	1102.27	643.02	495.55	425.80	386.91	363.21
57000	1115.27	647.22	496.53	424.98	384.87	360.28	1121.96	654.50	504.40	433.41	393.82	369.70
58000	1134.84	658.58	505.24	432.43	391.62	366.60	1141.64	665.98	513.25	441.01	400.73	376.19
59000	1154.40	669.93	513.95	439.89	398.37	372.92	1161.32	677.46	522.10	448.61	407.64	382.67
60000	1173.97	681.29	522.66	447.34	405.12	379.24	1181.01	688.94	530.95	456.22	414.55	389.16
61000	1193.54	692.64	531.38	454.80	411.88	385.56	1200.69	700.43	539.79	463.82	421.46	395.64
62000	1213.10	704.00	540.09	462.26	418.63	391.88	1220.37	711.91	548.64	471.43	428.37	402.13
63000	1232.67	715.35	548.80	469.71	425.38	398.20	1240.06	723.39	557.49	479.03	435.27	408.62
64000	1252.23	726.71	557.51	477.17	432.13	404.52	1259.74	734.87	566.34	486.63	442.18	415.10
65000	1271.80	738.06	566.22	484.62	438.88	410.84	1279.42	746.36	575.19	494.24	449.09	421.59
66000	1291.37	749.42	574.93	492.08	445.64	417.16	1299.11	757.84	584.04	501.84	456.00	428.07
67000	1310.93	760.77	583.64	499.53	452.39	423.49	1318.79	769.32	592.89	509.44	462.91	434.56
68000	1330.50	772.13	592.35	506.99	459.14	429.81	1338.48	780.80	601.74	517.05	469.82	441.05
69000	1350.06	783.48	601.06	514.45	465.89	436.13	1358.16	792.29	610.59	524.65	476.73	447.53
70000	1369.63	794.84	609.78	521.90	472.65	442.45	1377.84	803.77	619.44	532.25	483.64	454.02
71000	1389.20	806.19	618.49	529.36	479.40	448.77	1397.53	815.25	628.29	539.86	490.55	460.50
72000	1408.76	817.55	627.20	536.81	486.15	455.09	1417.21	826.73	637.13	547.46	497.46	466.99
73000	1428.33	828.90	635.91	544.27	492.90	461.41	1436.89	838.22	645.98	555.07	504.37	473.48
74000	1447.89	840.26	644.62	551.72	499.65	467.73	1456.58	849.70	654.83	562.67	511.27	479.96
75000	1467.46	851.61	653.33	559.18	506.41	474.05	1476.26	861.18	663.68	570.27	518.18	486.45
76000	1487.03	862.96	662.04	566.64	513.16	480.37	1495.94	872.66	672.53	577.88	525.09	492.93
77000	1506.59	874.32	670.76	574.09	519.91	486.69	1515.63	884.15	681.38	585.48	532.00	499.42
78000	1526.16	885.67	679.46	581.55	526.66	493.01	1535.31	895.63	690.23	593.08	538.91	505.91
79000	1545.73	897.03	688.17	589.00	533.41	499.33	1554.99	907.11	699.08	600.69	545.82	512.39
80000	1565.29	908.38	696.89	596.46	540.17	505.65	1574.68	918.59	707.93	608.29	552.73	518.88
81000	1584.86	919.74	705.60	603.91	546.92	511.98	1594.36	930.08	716.78	615.89	559.64	525.36
82000	1604.42	931.09	714.31	611.37	553.67	518.30	1614.04	941.56	725.63	623.50	566.55	531.85
83000	1623.99	942.45	723.02	618.83	560.42	524.62	1633.73	953.04	734.47	631.10	573.46	538.34
84000	1643.56	953.80	731.73	626.28	567.17	530.94	1653.41	964.52	743.32	638.71	580.37	544.82
85000	1663.12	965.16	740.44	633.74	573.93	537.26	1673.09	976.00	752.17	646.31	587.27	551.31
86000	1682.69	976.51	749.15	641.19	580.68	543.58	1692.78	987.49	761.02	653.91	594.18	557.79
87000	1702.25	987.87	757.86	648.65	587.43	549.90	1712.46	998.97	769.87	661.52	601.09	564.28
88000	1721.82	999.22	766.57	656.10	594.18	556.22	1732.14	1010.45	778.72	669.12	608.00	570.77
89000	1741.39	1010.58	775.29	663.56	600.93	562.54	1751.83	1021.93	787.57	676.72	614.91	577.25
90000	1760.95	1021.93	784.00	671.02	607.69	568.86	1771.51	1033.42	796.42	684.33	621.82	583.74
91000	1780.52	1033.29	792.71	678.47	614.44	575.18	1791.19	1044.90	805.27	691.93	628.73	590.22
92000	1800.09	1044.64	801.42	685.93	621.19	581.50	1810.88	1056.38	814.12	699.53	635.64	596.71
93000	1819.65	1056.00	810.13	693.38	627.94	587.82	1830.56	1067.86	822.97	707.14	642.55	603.20
94000	1839.22	1067.35	818.84	700.84	634.69	594.14	1850.25	1079.35	831.81	714.74	649.46	609.68
95000	1858.78	1078.71	827.55	708.29	641.45	600.46	1869.93	1090.83	840.66	722.35	656.37	616.17
96000	1878.35	1090.06	836.26	715.75	648.20	606.79	1889.61	1102.31	849.51	729.95	663.28	622.65
97000	1897.92	1101.42	844.97	723.21	654.95	613.11	1909.30	1113.79	858.36	737.55	670.18	629.14
98000	1917.48	1112.77	853.69	730.66	661.70	619.43	1928.98	1125.28	867.21	745.16	677.09	635.63
99000	1937.05	1124.12	862.40	738.12	668.46	625.75	1948.66	1136.76	876.06	752.76	684.00	642.11
100000	1956.61	1135.48	871.11	745.57	675.21	632.07	1968.35	1148.24	884.91	760.36	690.91	648.60

Table 2

	7.00						7.25					
	TERM (YEARS)						TERM (YEARS)					
AMOUNT	5	10	15	20	25	30	5	10	15	20	25	30
10000	198.01	116.11	89.88	77.53	70.68	66.53	199.19	117.40	91.29	79.04	72.28	68.22
11000	217.81	127.72	98.87	85.28	77.75	73.18	219.11	129.14	100.41	86.94	79.51	75.04
12000	237.61	139.33	107.86	93.04	84.81	79.84	239.03	140.88	109.54	94.85	86.74	81.86
13000	257.42	150.94	116.85	100.79	91.88	86.49	258.95	152.62	118.67	102.75	93.96	88.68
14000	277.22	162.55	125.84	108.54	98.95	93.14	278.87	164.36	127.80	110.65	101.19	95.50
15000	297.02	174.16	134.82	116.29	106.02	99.80	298.79	176.10	136.93	118.56	108.42	102.33
16000	316.82	185.77	143.81	124.05	113.08	106.45	318.71	187.84	146.06	126.46	115.65	109.15
17000	336.62	197.38	152.80	131.80	120.15	113.10	338.63	199.58	155.19	134.36	122.88	115.97
18000	356.42	209.00	161.79	139.55	127.22	119.75	358.55	211.32	164.32	142.27	130.11	122.79
19000	376.22	220.61	170.78	147.31	134.29	126.41	378.47	223.06	173.44	150.17	137.33	129.61
20000	396.02	232.22	179.77	155.06	141.36	133.06	398.39	234.80	182.57	158.08	144.56	136.44
21000	415.83	243.83	188.75	162.81	148.42	139.71	418.31	246.54	191.70	165.98	151.79	143.26
22000	435.63	255.44	197.74	170.57	155.49	146.37	438.23	258.28	200.83	173.88	159.02	150.08
23000	455.43	267.05	206.73	178.32	162.56	153.02	458.15	270.02	209.96	181.79	166.25	156.90
24000	475.23	278.66	215.72	186.07	169.63	159.67	478.06	281.76	219.09	189.69	173.47	163.72
25000	495.03	290.27	224.71	193.82	176.69	166.33	497.98	293.50	228.22	197.59	180.70	170.54
26000	514.83	301.88	233.70	201.58	183.76	172.98	517.90	305.24	237.34	205.50	187.93	177.37
27000	534.63	313.49	242.68	209.33	190.83	179.63	537.82	316.98	246.47	213.40	195.16	184.19
28000	554.43	325.10	251.67	217.08	197.90	186.28	557.74	328.72	255.60	221.31	202.39	191.01
29000	574.23	336.71	260.66	224.84	204.97	192.94	577.66	340.46	264.73	229.21	209.61	197.83
30000	594.04	348.33	269.65	232.59	212.03	199.59	597.58	352.20	273.86	237.11	216.84	204.65
31000	613.84	359.94	278.64	240.34	219.10	206.24	617.50	363.94	282.99	245.02	224.07	211.47
32000	633.64	371.55	287.63	248.10	226.17	212.90	637.42	375.68	292.12	252.92	231.30	218.30
33000	653.44	383.16	296.61	255.85	233.24	219.55	657.34	387.42	301.24	260.82	238.53	225.12
34000	673.24	394.77	305.60	263.60	240.30	226.20	677.26	399.16	310.37	268.73	245.75	231.94
35000	693.04	406.38	314.59	271.35	247.37	232.86	697.18	410.90	319.50	276.63	252.98	238.76
36000	712.84	417.99	323.58	279.11	254.44	239.51	717.10	422.64	328.63	284.54	260.21	245.58
37000	732.64	429.60	332.57	286.86	261.51	246.16	737.02	434.38	337.76	292.44	267.44	252.41
38000	752.45	441.21	341.55	294.61	268.58	252.81	756.94	446.12	346.89	300.34	274.67	259.23
39000	772.25	452.82	350.54	302.37	275.64	259.47	776.86	457.86	356.02	308.25	281.89	266.05
40000	792.05	464.43	359.53	310.12	282.71	266.12	796.77	469.60	365.15	316.15	289.12	272.87
41000	811.85	476.04	368.52	317.87	289.78	272.77	816.69	481.34	374.27	324.05	296.35	279.69
42000	831.65	487.66	377.51	325.63	296.85	279.43	836.61	493.08	383.40	331.96	303.58	286.51
43000	851.45	499.27	386.50	333.38	303.92	286.08	856.53	504.82	392.53	339.86	310.81	293.34
44000	871.25	510.88	395.48	341.13	310.98	292.73	876.45	516.56	401.66	347.77	318.04	300.16
45000	891.05	522.49	404.47	348.88	318.05	299.39	896.37	528.30	410.79	355.67	325.26	306.98
46000	910.86	534.10	413.46	356.64	325.12	306.04	916.29	540.04	419.92	363.57	332.49	313.80
47000	930.66	545.71	422.45	364.39	332.19	312.69	936.21	551.78	429.05	371.48	339.72	320.62
48000	950.46	557.32	431.44	372.14	339.25	319.35	956.13	563.52	438.17	379.38	346.95	327.44
49000	970.26	568.93	440.43	379.90	346.32	326.00	976.05	575.27	447.30	387.28	354.18	334.27
50000	990.06	580.54	449.41	387.65	353.39	332.65	995.97	587.01	456.43	395.19	361.40	341.09
51000	1009.86	592.15	458.40	395.40	360.46	339.30	1015.89	598.75	465.56	403.09	368.63	347.91
52000	1029.66	603.76	467.39	403.16	367.53	345.96	1035.81	610.49	474.69	411.00	375.86	354.73
53000	1049.46	615.37	476.38	410.91	374.59	352.61	1055.73	622.23	483.82	418.90	383.09	361.55
54000	1069.26	626.99	485.37	418.66	381.66	359.26	1075.65	633.97	492.95	426.80	390.32	368.38
55000	1089.07	638.60	494.36	426.41	388.73	365.92	1095.56	645.71	502.07	434.71	397.54	375.20
56000	1108.87	650.21	503.34	434.17	395.80	372.57	1115.48	657.45	511.20	442.61	404.77	382.02
57000	1128.67	661.82	512.33	441.92	402.86	379.22	1135.40	669.19	520.33	450.51	412.00	388.84
58000	1148.47	673.43	521.32	449.67	409.93	385.88	1155.32	680.93	529.46	458.42	419.23	395.66
59000	1168.27	685.04	530.31	457.43	417.00	392.53	1175.24	692.67	538.59	466.32	426.46	402.48
60000	1188.07	696.65	539.30	465.18	424.07	399.18	1195.16	704.41	547.72	474.23	433.68	409.31
61000	1207.87	708.26	548.29	472.93	431.14	405.83	1215.08	716.15	556.85	482.13	440.91	416.13
62000	1227.67	719.87	557.27	480.69	438.20	412.49	1235.00	727.89	565.97	490.03	448.14	422.95
63000	1247.48	731.48	566.26	488.44	445.27	419.14	1254.92	739.63	575.10	497.94	455.37	429.77
64000	1267.28	743.09	575.25	496.19	452.34	425.79	1274.84	751.37	584.23	505.84	462.60	436.59
65000	1287.08	754.71	584.24	503.94	459.41	432.45	1294.76	763.11	593.36	513.74	469.82	443.41
66000	1306.88	766.32	593.23	511.70	466.47	439.10	1314.68	774.85	602.49	521.65	477.05	450.24
67000	1326.68	777.93	602.21	519.45	473.54	445.75	1334.60	786.59	611.62	529.55	484.28	457.06
68000	1346.48	789.54	611.20	527.20	480.61	452.41	1354.52	798.33	620.75	537.46	491.51	463.88
69000	1366.28	801.15	620.19	534.96	487.68	459.06	1374.44	810.07	629.88	545.36	498.74	470.70
70000	1386.08	812.76	629.18	542.71	494.75	465.71	1394.36	821.81	639.00	553.26	505.96	477.52
71000	1405.89	824.37	638.17	550.46	501.81	472.36	1414.27	833.55	648.13	561.17	513.19	484.35
72000	1425.69	835.98	647.16	558.22	508.88	479.02	1434.19	845.29	657.26	569.07	520.42	491.17
73000	1445.49	847.59	656.14	565.97	515.95	485.67	1454.11	857.03	666.39	576.97	527.65	497.99
74000	1465.29	859.20	665.13	573.72	523.02	492.32	1474.03	868.77	675.52	584.88	534.88	504.81
75000	1485.09	870.81	674.12	581.47	530.08	498.98	1493.95	880.51	684.65	592.78	542.11	511.63
76000	1504.89	882.42	683.11	589.23	537.15	505.63	1513.87	892.25	693.78	600.69	549.33	518.45
77000	1524.69	894.04	692.10	596.98	544.22	512.28	1533.79	903.99	702.90	608.59	556.56	525.28
78000	1544.49	905.65	701.09	604.73	551.29	518.94	1553.71	915.73	712.03	616.49	563.79	532.10
79000	1564.29	917.26	710.07	612.49	558.36	525.59	1573.63	927.47	721.16	624.40	571.02	538.92
80000	1584.10	928.87	719.06	620.24	565.42	532.24	1593.55	939.21	730.29	632.30	578.25	545.74
81000	1603.90	940.48	728.05	627.99	572.49	538.90	1613.47	950.95	739.42	640.20	585.47	552.56
82000	1623.70	952.09	737.04	635.75	579.56	545.55	1633.39	962.69	748.55	648.11	592.70	559.38
83000	1643.50	963.70	746.03	643.50	586.63	552.20	1653.31	974.43	757.68	656.01	599.93	566.21
84000	1663.30	975.31	755.02	651.25	593.69	558.85	1673.23	986.17	766.80	663.92	607.16	573.03
85000	1683.10	986.92	764.00	659.00	600.76	565.51	1693.15	997.91	775.93	671.82	614.39	579.85
86000	1702.90	998.53	772.99	666.76	607.83	572.16	1713.07	1009.65	785.06	679.72	621.61	586.67
87000	1722.70	1010.14	781.98	674.51	614.90	578.81	1732.98	1021.39	794.19	687.63	628.84	593.49
88000	1742.51	1021.75	790.97	682.26	621.97	585.47	1752.90	1033.13	803.32	695.53	636.07	600.32
89000	1762.31	1033.37	799.96	690.02	629.03	592.12	1772.82	1044.87	812.45	703.43	643.30	607.14
90000	1782.11	1044.98	808.95	697.77	636.10	598.77	1792.74	1056.61	821.58	711.34	650.53	613.96
91000	1801.91	1056.59	817.93	705.52	643.17	605.43	1812.66	1068.35	830.71	719.24	657.75	620.78
92000	1821.71	1068.20	826.92	713.28	650.24	612.08	1832.58	1080.09	839.83	727.15	664.98	627.60
93000	1841.51	1079.81	835.91	721.03	657.30	618.73	1852.50	1091.83	848.96	735.05	672.21	634.42
94000	1861.31	1091.42	844.90	728.78	664.37	625.38	1872.42	1103.57	858.09	742.95	679.44	641.25
95000	1881.11	1103.03	853.89	736.53	671.44	632.04	1892.34	1115.31	867.22	750.86	686.67	648.07
96000	1900.92	1114.64	862.88	744.29	678.51	638.69	1912.26	1127.05	876.35	758.76	693.89	654.89
97000	1920.72	1126.25	871.86	752.04	685.58	645.34	1932.18	1138.79	885.48	766.66	701.12	661.71
98000	1940.52	1137.86	880.85	759.79	692.64	652.00	1952.10	1150.53	894.61	774.57	708.35	668.53
99000	1960.32	1149.47	889.84	767.55	699.71	658.65	1972.02	1162.27	903.73	782.47	715.58	675.35
100000	1980.12	1161.08	898.83	775.30	706.78	665.30	1991.94	1174.01	912.86	790.38	722.81	682.18

Table 2   455

| | 7.50 | | | | | | 7.75 | | | | | |
| | TERM (YEARS) | | | | | | TERM (YEARS) | | | | | |
AMOUNT	5	10	15	20	25	30	5	10	15	20	25	30
10000	200.38	118.70	92.70	80.56	73.90	69.92	201.57	120.01	94.13	82.09	75.53	71.64
11000	220.42	130.57	101.97	88.62	81.29	76.91	221.73	132.01	103.54	90.30	83.09	78.81
12000	240.46	142.44	111.24	96.67	88.68	83.91	241.88	144.01	112.95	98.51	90.64	85.97
13000	260.49	154.31	120.51	104.73	96.07	90.90	262.04	156.01	122.37	106.72	98.19	93.13
14000	280.53	166.18	129.78	112.78	103.46	97.89	282.20	168.01	131.78	114.93	105.75	100.30
15000	300.57	178.05	139.05	120.84	110.85	104.88	302.35	180.02	141.19	123.14	113.30	107.46
16000	320.61	189.92	148.32	128.89	118.24	111.87	322.51	192.02	150.60	131.35	120.85	114.63
17000	340.65	201.79	157.59	136.95	125.63	118.87	342.67	204.02	160.02	139.56	128.41	121.79
18000	360.68	213.66	166.86	145.01	133.02	125.86	362.83	216.02	169.43	147.77	135.96	128.95
19000	380.72	225.53	176.13	153.06	140.41	132.85	382.98	228.02	178.84	155.98	143.51	136.12
20000	400.76	237.40	185.40	161.12	147.80	139.84	403.14	240.02	188.26	164.19	151.07	143.28
21000	420.80	249.27	194.67	169.17	155.19	146.84	423.30	252.02	197.67	172.40	158.62	150.45
22000	440.83	261.14	203.94	177.23	162.58	153.83	443.45	264.02	207.08	180.61	166.17	157.61
23000	460.87	273.01	213.21	185.29	169.97	160.82	463.61	276.02	216.49	188.82	173.73	164.77
24000	480.91	284.88	222.48	193.34	177.36	167.81	483.77	288.03	225.91	197.03	181.28	171.94
25000	500.95	296.75	231.75	201.40	184.75	174.80	503.92	300.03	235.32	205.24	188.83	179.10
26000	520.99	308.62	241.02	209.45	192.14	181.80	524.08	312.03	244.73	213.45	196.39	186.27
27000	541.02	320.49	250.29	217.51	199.53	188.79	544.24	324.03	254.14	221.66	203.94	193.43
28000	561.06	332.36	259.56	225.57	206.92	195.78	564.39	336.03	263.56	229.87	211.49	200.60
29000	581.10	344.24	268.83	233.62	214.31	202.77	584.55	348.03	272.97	238.08	219.05	207.76
30000	601.14	356.11	278.10	241.68	221.70	209.76	604.71	360.03	282.38	246.28	226.60	214.92
31000	621.18	367.98	287.37	249.73	229.09	216.76	624.87	372.03	291.80	254.49	234.15	229.25
32000	641.21	379.85	296.64	257.79	236.48	223.75	645.02	384.03	301.21	262.70	241.71	236.42
33000	661.25	391.72	305.91	265.85	243.87	230.74	665.18	396.04	310.62	270.91	249.26	236.42
34000	681.29	403.59	315.18	273.90	251.26	237.73	685.34	408.04	320.03	279.12	256.81	243.58
35000	701.33	415.46	324.45	281.96	258.65	244.73	705.49	420.04	329.45	287.33	264.37	250.74
36000	721.37	427.33	333.72	290.01	266.04	251.72	725.65	432.04	338.86	295.54	271.92	257.91
37000	741.40	439.20	342.99	298.07	273.43	258.71	745.81	444.04	348.27	303.75	279.47	265.07
38000	761.44	451.07	352.26	306.13	280.82	265.70	765.96	456.04	357.68	311.96	287.02	272.24
39000	781.48	462.94	361.53	314.18	288.21	272.69	786.12	468.04	367.10	320.17	294.58	279.40
40000	801.52	474.81	370.80	322.24	295.60	279.69	806.28	480.04	376.51	328.38	302.13	286.56
41000	821.56	486.68	380.08	330.29	302.99	286.68	826.44	492.04	385.92	336.59	309.68	293.73
42000	841.59	498.55	389.35	338.35	310.38	293.67	846.59	504.04	395.34	344.80	317.24	300.89
43000	861.63	510.42	398.62	346.41	317.77	300.66	866.75	516.05	404.75	353.01	324.79	308.06
44000	881.67	522.29	407.89	354.46	325.16	307.65	886.91	528.05	414.16	361.22	332.34	315.22
45000	901.71	534.16	417.16	362.52	332.55	314.65	907.06	540.05	423.57	369.43	339.90	322.39
46000	921.75	546.03	426.43	370.57	339.94	321.64	927.22	552.05	432.99	377.64	347.45	329.55
47000	941.78	557.90	435.70	378.63	347.33	328.63	947.38	564.05	442.40	385.85	355.00	336.71
48000	961.82	569.77	444.97	386.68	354.72	335.62	967.53	576.05	451.81	394.06	362.56	343.88
49000	981.86	581.64	454.24	394.74	362.11	342.62	987.69	588.05	461.23	402.26	370.11	351.04
50000	1001.90	593.51	463.51	402.80	369.50	349.61	1007.85	600.05	470.64	410.47	377.66	358.21
51000	1021.94	605.38	472.78	410.85	376.89	356.60	1028.00	612.05	480.05	418.68	385.22	365.37
52000	1041.97	617.25	482.05	418.91	384.28	363.59	1048.16	624.06	489.46	426.89	392.77	372.53
53000	1062.01	629.12	491.32	426.96	391.67	370.58	1068.32	636.06	498.88	435.10	400.32	379.70
54000	1082.05	640.99	500.59	435.02	399.06	377.58	1088.48	648.06	508.29	443.31	407.88	386.86
55000	1102.09	652.86	509.86	443.08	406.45	384.57	1108.63	660.06	517.70	451.52	415.43	394.03
56000	1122.13	664.73	519.13	451.13	413.84	391.56	1128.79	672.06	527.11	459.73	422.98	401.19
57000	1142.16	676.60	528.40	459.19	421.22	398.55	1148.95	684.06	536.53	467.94	430.54	408.35
58000	1162.20	688.47	537.67	467.24	428.61	405.54	1169.10	696.06	545.94	476.15	438.09	415.52
59000	1182.24	700.34	546.94	475.30	436.00	412.54	1189.26	708.06	555.35	484.36	445.64	422.68
60000	1202.28	712.21	556.21	483.36	443.39	419.53	1209.42	720.06	564.77	492.57	453.20	429.85
61000	1222.31	724.08	565.48	491.41	450.78	426.52	1229.57	732.06	574.18	500.78	460.75	437.01
62000	1242.35	735.95	574.75	499.47	458.17	433.51	1249.73	744.07	583.59	508.99	468.30	444.18
63000	1262.39	747.82	584.02	507.52	465.56	440.51	1269.89	756.07	593.00	517.20	475.86	451.34
64000	1282.43	759.69	593.29	515.58	472.95	447.50	1290.05	768.07	602.42	525.41	483.41	458.50
65000	1302.47	771.56	602.56	523.64	480.34	454.49	1310.20	760.07	611.83	533.62	490.96	465.67
66000	1322.50	783.43	611.83	531.69	487.73	461.48	1330.36	792.07	621.24	541.83	498.52	472.83
67000	1342.54	795.30	621.10	539.75	495.12	468.47	1350.52	804.07	630.65	550.04	506.07	480.00
68000	1362.58	807.17	630.37	547.80	502.51	475.47	1370.67	816.07	640.07	558.25	513.62	487.16
69000	1382.62	819.04	639.64	555.86	509.90	482.46	1390.83	828.07	649.48	566.45	521.18	494.32
70000	1402.66	830.91	648.91	563.92	517.29	489.45	1410.99	840.07	658.89	574.66	528.73	501.49
71000	1422.69	842.78	658.18	571.97	524.68	496.44	1431.14	852.08	668.31	582.87	536.28	508.65
72000	1442.73	854.65	667.45	580.03	532.07	503.43	1451.30	864.08	677.72	591.08	543.84	515.82
73000	1462.77	866.52	676.72	588.08	539.46	510.43	1471.46	876.08	687.13	599.29	551.39	522.98
74000	1482.81	878.39	685.99	596.14	546.85	517.42	1491.62	888.08	696.54	607.50	558.94	530.15
75000	1502.85	890.26	695.26	604.19	554.24	524.41	1511.77	900.08	705.96	615.71	566.50	537.31
76000	1522.88	902.13	704.53	612.25	561.63	531.40	1531.93	912.08	715.37	623.92	574.05	544.47
77000	1542.92	914.00	713.80	620.31	569.02	538.40	1552.09	924.08	724.78	632.13	581.60	551.64
78000	1562.96	925.87	723.07	628.36	576.41	545.39	1572.24	936.08	734.20	640.34	589.16	558.80
79000	1583.00	937.74	732.34	636.42	583.80	552.38	1592.40	948.08	743.61	648.55	596.71	565.97
80000	1603.04	949.61	741.61	644.47	591.19	559.37	1612.56	960.09	753.02	656.76	604.26	573.13
81000	1623.07	961.48	750.88	652.53	598.58	566.36	1632.71	972.09	762.43	664.97	611.82	580.29
82000	1643.11	973.35	760.15	660.59	605.97	573.36	1652.87	984.09	771.85	673.18	619.37	587.46
83000	1663.15	985.22	769.42	668.64	613.36	580.35	1673.03	996.09	781.26	681.39	626.92	594.62
84000	1683.19	997.09	778.69	676.70	620.75	587.34	1693.18	1008.09	790.67	689.60	634.48	601.79
85000	1703.23	1008.97	787.96	684.75	628.14	594.33	1713.34	1020.09	800.08	697.81	642.03	608.95
86000	1723.26	1020.84	797.23	692.81	635.53	601.32	1733.50	1032.09	809.50	706.02	649.58	616.11
87000	1743.30	1032.71	806.50	700.87	642.92	608.32	1753.66	1044.09	818.91	714.23	657.14	623.28
88000	1763.34	1044.58	815.77	708.92	650.31	615.31	1773.81	1056.09	828.32	722.43	664.69	630.44
89000	1783.38	1056.45	825.04	716.98	657.70	622.30	1793.97	1068.09	837.74	730.64	672.24	637.61
90000	1803.42	1068.32	834.31	725.03	665.09	629.29	1814.13	1080.10	847.15	738.85	679.80	644.77
91000	1823.45	1080.19	843.58	733.09	672.48	636.29	1834.28	1092.10	856.56	747.06	687.35	651.94
92000	1843.49	1092.06	852.85	741.15	679.87	643.28	1854.44	1104.10	865.97	755.27	694.90	659.10
93000	1863.53	1103.93	862.12	749.20	687.26	650.27	1874.60	1116.10	875.39	763.48	702.46	666.26
94000	1883.57	1115.80	871.39	757.26	694.65	657.26	1894.75	1128.10	884.80	771.69	710.01	673.43
95000	1903.61	1127.67	880.66	765.31	702.04	664.25	1914.91	1140.10	894.21	779.90	717.56	680.59
96000	1923.64	1139.54	889.93	773.37	709.43	671.25	1935.07	1152.10	903.62	788.11	725.12	687.76
97000	1943.68	1151.41	899.20	781.43	716.82	678.24	1955.23	1164.10	913.04	796.32	732.67	694.92
98000	1963.72	1163.28	908.47	789.48	724.21	685.23	1975.3	1176.10	922.45	804.53	740.22	702.08
99000	1983.76	1175.15	917.74	797.54	731.60	692.22	1995.54	1188.11	931.86	812.74	747.78	709.25
100000	2003.79	1187.02	927.01	805.59	738.99	699.21	2015.70	1200.11	941.28	820.95	755.33	716.41

	8.00						8.25					
	TERM (YEARS)						TERM (YEARS)					
AMOUNT	5	10	15	20	25	30	5	10	15	20	25	30
10000	202.76	121.33	95.57	83.64	77.18	73.38	203.96	122.65	97.01	85.21	78.85	75.13
11000	223.04	133.46	105.12	92.01	84.90	80.71	224.36	134.92	106.72	93.73	86.73	82.64
12000	243.32	145.59	114.68	100.37	92.62	88.05	244.76	147.18	116.42	102.25	94.61	90.15
13000	263.59	157.73	124.23	108.74	100.34	95.39	265.15	159.45	126.12	110.77	102.50	97.66
14000	283.87	169.86	133.79	117.10	107.05	102.73	285.55	171.71	135.82	119.29	110.38	105.18
15000	304.15	181.99	143.35	125.47	115.77	110.06	305.94	183.98	145.52	127.81	118.27	112.69
16000	324.42	194.12	152.90	133.83	123.49	117.40	326.34	196.24	155.22	136.33	126.15	120.20
17000	344.70	206.26	162.46	142.19	131.21	124.74	346.74	208.51	164.92	144.85	134.04	127.72
18000	364.98	218.39	172.02	150.56	138.93	132.08	367.13	220.77	174.63	153.37	141.92	142.74
19000	385.25	230.52	181.57	158.92	146.65	139.42	387.53	233.04	184.33	161.89	149.81	142.74
20000	405.53	242.66	191.13	167.29	154.36	146.75	407.93	245.31	194.03	170.41	157.69	150.25
21000	425.80	254.79	200.69	175.65	162.08	154.09	428.32	257.57	203.73	178.93	165.57	157.77
22000	446.08	266.92	210.24	184.02	169.80	161.43	448.72	269.84	213.43	187.45	173.46	165.28
23000	466.36	279.05	219.80	192.38	177.52	168.77	469.11	282.10	223.13	195.98	181.34	172.79
24000	486.63	291.19	229.36	200.75	185.24	176.10	489.51	294.37	232.83	204.50	189.23	180.30
25000	506.91	303.32	238.91	209.11	192.95	183.44	509.91	306.63	242.54	213.02	197.11	187.82
26000	527.19	315.45	248.47	217.47	200.67	190.78	530.30	318.90	252.24	221.54	205.00	195.33
27000	547.46	327.58	258.03	225.84	208.39	198.12	550.70	331.16	261.94	230.06	212.88	202.84
28000	567.74	339.72	267.58	234.20	216.11	205.45	571.10	343.43	271.64	238.58	220.77	210.35
29000	588.02	351.85	277.14	242.57	223.83	212.79	591.49	355.69	281.34	247.10	228.65	217.87
30000	608.29	363.98	286.70	250.93	231.54	220.13	611.89	367.96	291.04	255.62	236.54	225.38
31000	628.57	376.12	296.25	259.30	239.26	227.47	632.28	380.22	300.74	264.14	244.42	232.89
32000	648.84	388.25	305.81	267.66	246.98	234.80	652.68	392.49	310.44	272.66	252.30	240.41
33000	669.12	400.38	315.37	276.03	254.70	242.14	673.08	404.75	320.15	281.18	260.19	247.92
34000	689.40	412.51	324.92	284.39	262.42	249.48	693.47	417.02	329.85	289.70	268.07	255.43
35000	709.67	424.65	334.48	292.75	270.14	256.82	713.87	429.28	339.55	298.22	275.96	262.94
36000	729.95	436.78	344.03	301.12	277.85	264.16	734.27	441.55	349.25	306.74	283.84	270.46
37000	750.23	448.91	353.59	309.48	285.57	271.49	754.66	453.81	358.95	315.26	291.73	277.97
38000	770.50	461.04	363.15	317.85	293.29	278.83	775.06	466.08	368.65	323.78	299.61	285.48
39000	790.78	473.18	372.70	326.21	301.01	286.17	795.45	478.35	378.35	332.31	307.50	292.99
40000	811.06	485.31	382.26	334.58	308.73	293.51	815.85	490.61	388.06	340.83	315.38	300.51
41000	831.33	497.44	391.82	342.94	316.44	300.84	836.25	502.88	397.76	349.35	323.26	308.02
42000	851.61	509.58	401.37	351.30	324.16	308.18	856.64	515.14	407.46	357.87	331.15	315.53
43000	871.88	521.71	410.93	359.67	331.88	315.52	877.04	527.41	417.16	366.39	339.03	323.04
44000	892.16	533.84	420.49	368.03	339.60	322.86	897.44	539.67	426.86	374.91	346.92	330.56
45000	912.44	545.97	430.04	376.40	347.32	330.19	917.83	551.94	436.56	383.43	354.80	338.07
46000	932.71	558.11	439.60	384.76	355.04	337.53	938.23	564.20	446.26	391.95	362.69	345.58
47000	952.99	570.24	449.16	393.13	362.75	344.87	958.62	576.47	455.97	400.47	370.57	353.10
48000	973.27	582.37	458.71	401.49	370.47	352.21	979.02	588.73	465.67	408.99	378.46	360.61
49000	993.54	594.51	468.27	409.86	378.19	359.54	999.42	601.00	475.37	417.51	386.34	368.12
50000	1013.82	606.64	477.83	418.22	385.91	366.88	1019.81	613.26	485.07	426.03	394.23	375.63
51000	1034.10	618.77	487.38	426.58	393.63	374.22	1040.21	625.53	494.77	434.55	402.11	383.15
52000	1054.37	630.90	496.94	434.95	401.34	381.56	1060.61	637.79	504.47	443.07	409.99	390.66
53000	1074.65	643.04	506.50	443.31	409.06	388.90	1081.00	650.06	514.17	451.59	417.88	398.17
54000	1094.93	655.17	516.05	451.68	416.78	396.23	1101.40	662.32	523.88	460.12	425.76	405.68
55000	1115.20	667.30	525.61	460.04	424.50	403.57	1121.79	674.59	533.58	468.64	433.65	413.20
56000	1135.48	679.43	535.17	468.41	432.22	410.91	1142.19	686.85	543.28	477.16	441.53	420.71
57000	1155.75	691.57	544.72	476.77	439.94	418.25	1162.59	699.12	552.98	485.68	449.42	428.22
58000	1176.03	703.70	554.28	485.14	447.65	425.58	1182.98	711.39	562.68	494.20	457.30	435.73
59000	1196.31	715.83	563.83	493.50	455.37	432.92	1203.38	723.65	572.38	502.72	465.19	443.25
60000	1216.58	727.97	573.39	501.86	463.09	440.26	1223.78	735.92	582.08	511.24	473.07	450.76
61000	1236.86	740.10	582.95	510.23	470.81	447.60	1244.17	748.18	591.79	519.76	480.95	458.27
62000	1257.14	752.23	592.50	518.59	478.53	454.93	1264.57	760.45	601.49	528.28	488.84	465.79
63000	1277.41	764.36	602.06	526.96	486.24	462.27	1284.96	772.71	611.19	536.80	496.72	473.30
64000	1297.69	776.50	611.62	535.32	493.96	469.61	1305.36	784.98	620.89	545.32	504.61	480.81
65000	1317.97	788.63	621.17	543.69	501.68	476.95	1325.76	797.24	630.59	553.84	512.49	488.32
66000	1338.24	800.76	630.73	552.05	509.40	484.28	1346.15	809.51	640.29	562.36	520.38	495.84
67000	1358.52	812.89	640.29	560.41	517.12	491.62	1366.55	821.77	649.99	570.88	528.26	503.35
68000	1378.79	825.03	649.84	568.78	524.84	498.96	1386.95	834.04	659.70	579.40	536.15	510.86
69000	1399.07	837.16	659.40	577.14	532.55	506.30	1407.34	846.30	669.40	587.93	544.03	518.37
70000	1419.35	849.29	668.96	585.51	540.27	513.64	1427.74	858.57	679.10	596.45	551.92	525.89
71000	1439.62	861.43	678.51	593.87	547.99	520.97	1448.13	870.83	688.80	604.97	559.80	533.40
72000	1459.90	873.56	688.07	602.24	555.71	528.31	1468.53	883.10	698.50	613.49	567.68	540.91
73000	1480.18	885.69	697.63	610.60	563.43	535.65	1488.93	895.36	708.20	622.01	575.57	548.42
74000	1500.45	897.82	707.18	618.97	571.14	542.99	1509.32	907.63	717.90	630.53	583.45	555.94
75000	1520.73	909.96	716.74	627.33	578.86	550.32	1529.72	919.89	727.61	639.05	591.34	563.45
76000	1541.01	922.09	726.30	635.69	586.58	557.66	1550.12	932.16	737.31	647.57	599.22	570.96
77000	1561.28	934.22	735.85	644.06	594.30	565.00	1570.51	944.43	747.01	656.09	607.11	578.48
78000	1581.56	946.36	745.41	652.42	602.02	572.34	1590.91	956.69	756.71	664.61	614.99	585.99
79000	1601.84	958.49	754.97	660.79	609.73	579.67	1611.30	968.96	766.41	673.13	622.88	593.50
80000	1622.11	970.62	764.52	669.15	617.45	587.01	1631.70	981.22	776.11	681.65	630.76	601.01
81000	1642.39	982.75	774.08	677.52	625.17	594.35	1652.10	993.49	785.81	690.17	638.64	608.53
82000	1662.66	994.89	783.63	685.88	632.89	601.69	1672.49	1005.75	795.52	698.69	646.53	616.04
83000	1682.94	1007.02	793.19	694.25	640.61	609.02	1692.89	1018.02	805.22	707.21	654.41	623.55
84000	1703.22	1019.15	802.75	702.61	648.33	616.36	1713.29	1030.28	814.92	715.74	662.30	631.06
85000	1723.49	1031.28	812.30	710.97	656.04	623.70	1733.68	1042.55	824.62	724.26	670.18	638.58
86000	1743.77	1043.42	821.86	719.34	663.76	631.04	1754.08	1054.81	834.32	732.78	678.07	646.09
87000	1764.05	1055.55	831.42	727.70	671.48	638.38	1774.47	1067.08	844.02	741.30	685.95	653.60
88000	1784.32	1067.68	840.97	736.07	679.20	645.71	1794.87	1079.34	853.72	749.82	693.84	661.11
89000	1804.60	1079.82	850.53	744.43	686.92	653.05	1815.27	1091.61	863.42	758.34	701.72	668.63
90000	1824.88	1091.95	860.09	752.80	694.63	660.39	1835.66	1103.87	873.13	766.86	709.61	676.14
91000	1845.15	1104.08	869.64	761.16	702.35	667.73	1856.06	1116.14	882.83	775.38	717.49	683.65
92000	1865.43	1116.21	879.20	769.52	710.07	675.06	1876.46	1128.40	892.53	783.90	725.37	691.17
93000	1885.70	1128.35	888.76	777.89	717.79	682.40	1896.85	1140.67	902.23	792.42	733.26	698.68
94000	1905.98	1140.48	898.31	786.25	725.51	689.74	1917.25	1152.93	911.93	800.94	741.14	706.19
95000	1926.26	1152.61	907.87	794.62	733.23	697.08	1937.64	1165.20	921.63	809.46	749.03	713.70
96000	1946.53	1164.74	917.43	802.98	740.94	704.41	1958.04	1177.47	931.33	817.98	756.91	721.22
97000	1966.81	1176.88	926.98	811.35	748.66	711.75	1978.44	1189.73	941.04	826.50	764.80	728.73
98000	1987.09	1189.01	936.54	819.71	756.38	719.09	1998.83	1202.00	950.74	835.02	772.68	736.24
99000	2007.36	1201.14	946.10	828.08	764.10	726.43	2019.23	1214.26	960.44	843.54	780.57	743.75
100000	2027.64	1213.28	955.65	836.44	771.82	733.76	2039.63	1226.53	970.14	852.07	788.45	751.27

Table 2 457

	8.50						8.75					
	TERM (YEARS)						TERM (YEARS)					
AMOUNT	5	10	15	20	25	30	5	10	15	20	25	30
10000	205.17	123.99	98.47	86.78	80.52	76.89	206.37	125.33	99.94	88.37	82.21	78.67
11000	225.68	136.38	108.32	95.46	88.57	84.58	227.01	137.86	109.94	97.21	90.44	86.54
12000	246.20	148.78	118.17	104.14	96.63	92.27	247.65	150.39	119.93	106.05	98.66	94.40
13000	266.71	161.18	128.02	112.82	104.68	99.96	268.28	162.92	129.93	114.88	106.88	102.27
14000	287.23	173.58	137.86	121.50	112.73	107.65	288.92	175.46	139.92	123.72	115.10	110.14
15000	307.75	185.98	147.71	130.17	120.78	115.34	309.56	187.99	149.92	132.56	123.32	118.01
16000	328.26	198.38	157.56	138.85	128.84	123.03	330.20	200.52	159.91	141.39	131.54	125.87
17000	348.78	210.78	167.41	147.53	136.89	130.72	350.83	213.06	169.91	150.23	139.76	133.74
18000	369.30	223.17	177.25	156.21	144.94	138.40	371.47	225.59	179.90	159.07	147.99	141.61
19000	389.81	235.57	187.10	164.89	152.99	146.09	392.11	238.12	189.90	167.91	156.21	149.47
20000	410.33	247.97	196.95	173.56	161.05	153.78	412.74	250.65	199.89	176.74	164.43	157.34
21000	430.85	260.37	206.80	182.24	169.10	161.47	433.38	263.19	209.88	185.58	172.65	165.21
22000	451.36	272.77	216.64	190.92	177.15	169.16	454.02	275.72	219.88	194.42	180.87	173.07
23000	471.88	285.17	226.49	199.60	185.20	176.85	474.66	288.25	229.87	203.25	189.09	180.94
24000	492.40	297.57	236.34	208.28	193.25	184.54	495.29	300.78	239.87	212.09	197.31	188.81
25000	512.91	309.96	246.18	216.96	201.31	192.23	515.93	313.32	249.86	220.93	205.54	196.68
26000	533.43	322.36	256.03	225.63	209.36	199.92	536.57	325.85	259.86	229.76	213.76	204.54
27000	553.95	334.76	265.88	234.31	217.41	207.61	557.21	338.38	269.85	238.60	221.98	212.41
28000	574.46	347.16	275.73	242.99	225.46	215.30	577.84	350.91	279.85	247.44	230.20	220.28
29000	594.98	359.56	285.57	251.67	233.52	222.98	598.48	363.45	289.84	256.28	238.42	228.14
30000	615.50	371.96	295.42	260.35	241.57	230.67	619.12	375.98	299.83	265.11	246.64	236.01
31000	636.01	384.36	305.27	269.03	249.62	238.36	639.75	388.51	309.83	273.95	254.86	243.88
32000	656.53	396.75	315.12	277.70	257.67	246.05	660.39	401.05	319.82	282.79	263.09	251.74
33000	677.05	409.15	324.96	286.38	265.72	253.74	681.03	413.58	329.82	291.62	271.31	259.61
34000	697.56	421.55	334.81	295.06	273.78	261.43	701.67	426.11	339.81	300.46	279.53	267.48
35000	718.08	433.95	344.66	303.74	281.83	269.12	722.30	438.64	349.81	309.30	287.75	275.35
36000	738.60	446.35	354.51	312.42	289.88	276.81	742.94	451.18	359.80	318.14	295.97	283.21
37000	759.11	458.75	364.35	321.09	297.93	284.50	763.58	463.71	369.80	326.97	304.19	291.08
38000	779.63	471.15	374.20	329.77	305.99	292.19	784.21	476.24	379.79	335.81	312.41	298.95
39000	800.14	483.54	384.05	338.45	314.04	299.88	804.85	488.77	389.78	344.65	320.64	306.81
40000	820.66	495.94	393.90	347.13	322.09	307.57	825.49	501.31	399.78	353.48	328.86	314.68
41000	841.18	508.34	403.74	355.81	330.14	315.25	846.13	513.84	409.77	362.32	337.08	322.55
42000	861.69	520.74	413.59	364.49	338.20	322.94	866.76	526.37	419.77	371.16	345.30	330.41
43000	882.21	533.14	423.44	373.16	346.25	330.63	887.40	538.91	429.76	380.00	353.52	338.28
44000	902.73	545.54	433.29	381.84	354.30	338.32	908.04	551.44	439.76	388.83	361.74	346.15
45000	923.24	557.94	443.13	390.52	362.35	346.01	928.68	563.97	449.75	397.67	369.96	354.02
46000	943.76	570.33	452.98	399.20	370.40	353.70	949.31	576.50	459.75	406.51	378.19	361.88
47000	964.28	582.73	462.83	407.88	378.46	361.39	969.95	589.04	469.74	415.34	386.41	369.75
48000	984.79	595.13	472.67	416.56	386.51	369.08	990.59	601.57	479.74	424.18	394.63	377.62
49000	1005.31	607.53	482.52	425.23	394.56	376.77	1011.22	614.10	489.73	433.02	402.85	385.48
50000	1025.83	619.93	492.37	433.91	402.61	384.46	1031.86	626.63	499.72	441.86	411.07	393.35
51000	1046.34	632.33	502.22	442.59	410.67	392.15	1052.50	639.17	509.72	450.69	419.29	401.22
52000	1066.86	644.73	512.06	451.27	418.72	399.84	1073.14	651.70	519.71	459.53	427.51	409.08
53000	1087.38	657.12	521.91	459.95	426.77	407.52	1093.77	664.23	529.71	468.37	435.74	416.95
54000	1107.89	669.52	531.76	468.62	434.82	415.21	1114.41	676.76	539.70	477.20	443.96	424.82
55000	1128.41	681.92	541.61	477.30	442.87	422.90	1135.05	689.30	549.70	486.04	452.18	432.69
56000	1148.93	694.32	551.45	485.98	450.93	430.59	1155.69	701.83	559.69	494.88	460.40	440.55
57000	1169.44	706.72	561.30	494.66	458.98	438.28	1176.32	714.36	569.69	503.72	468.62	448.42
58000	1189.96	719.12	571.15	503.34	467.03	445.97	1196.96	726.90	579.68	512.55	476.84	456.29
59000	1210.48	731.52	581.00	512.02	475.08	453.66	1217.60	739.43	589.67	521.39	485.06	464.15
60000	1230.99	743.91	590.84	520.69	483.14	461.35	1238.23	751.96	599.67	530.23	493.29	472.02
61000	1251.51	756.31	600.69	529.37	491.19	469.04	1258.87	764.49	609.66	539.06	501.51	479.89
62000	1272.02	768.71	610.54	538.05	499.24	476.73	1279.51	777.03	619.66	547.90	509.73	487.75
63000	1292.54	781.11	620.39	546.73	507.29	484.42	1300.15	789.56	629.65	556.74	517.95	495.62
64000	1313.06	793.51	630.23	555.41	515.35	492.10	1320.78	802.09	639.65	565.57	526.17	503.49
65000	1333.57	805.91	640.08	564.09	523.40	499.79	1341.42	814.62	649.64	574.41	534.39	511.36
66000	1354.09	818.31	649.93	572.76	531.45	507.48	1362.06	827.16	659.64	583.25	542.61	519.22
67000	1374.61	830.70	659.78	581.44	539.50	515.17	1382.69	839.69	669.63	592.09	550.84	527.09
68000	1395.12	843.10	669.62	590.12	547.55	522.86	1403.33	852.22	679.63	600.92	559.06	534.96
69000	1415.64	855.50	679.47	598.80	555.61	530.55	1423.97	864.75	689.62	609.76	567.28	542.82
70000	1436.16	867.90	689.32	607.48	563.66	538.24	1444.61	877.29	699.61	618.60	575.50	550.69
71000	1456.67	880.30	699.17	616.15	571.71	545.93	1465.24	889.82	709.61	627.43	583.72	558.56
72000	1477.19	892.70	709.01	624.83	579.76	553.62	1485.88	902.35	719.60	636.27	591.94	566.42
73000	1497.71	905.10	718.86	633.51	587.82	561.31	1506.52	914.89	729.60	645.11	600.16	574.29
74000	1518.22	917.49	728.71	642.19	595.87	569.00	1527.16	927.42	739.59	653.95	608.39	582.16
75000	1538.74	929.89	738.55	650.87	603.92	576.69	1547.79	939.95	749.59	662.78	616.61	590.03
76000	1559.26	942.29	748.40	659.55	611.97	584.37	1568.43	952.48	759.58	671.62	624.83	597.89
77000	1579.77	954.69	758.25	668.22	620.02	592.06	1589.07	965.02	769.58	680.46	633.05	605.76
78000	1600.29	967.09	768.10	676.90	628.08	599.75	1609.70	977.55	779.57	689.29	641.27	613.63
79000	1620.81	979.49	777.94	685.58	636.13	607.44	1630.34	990.08	789.56	698.13	649.49	621.49
80000	1641.32	991.89	787.79	694.26	644.18	615.13	1650.98	1002.61	799.56	706.97	657.71	629.36
81000	1661.84	1004.28	797.64	702.94	652.23	622.82	1671.62	1015.15	809.55	715.81	665.94	637.23
82000	1682.36	1016.68	807.49	711.62	660.29	630.51	1692.25	1027.68	819.55	724.64	674.16	645.09
83000	1702.87	1029.08	817.33	720.29	668.34	638.20	1712.89	1040.21	829.54	733.48	682.38	652.96
84000	1723.39	1041.48	827.18	728.97	676.39	645.89	1733.53	1052.74	839.54	742.32	690.60	660.83
85000	1743.91	1053.88	837.03	737.65	684.44	653.58	1754.16	1065.28	849.53	751.15	698.82	668.70
86000	1764.42	1066.28	846.88	746.33	692.50	661.27	1774.80	1077.81	859.53	759.99	707.04	676.56
87000	1784.94	1078.68	856.72	755.01	700.55	668.95	1795.44	1090.34	869.52	768.83	715.26	684.43
88000	1805.45	1091.07	866.57	763.68	708.60	676.64	1816.08	1102.88	879.51	777.67	723.49	692.30
89000	1825.97	1103.47	876.42	772.36	716.65	684.33	1836.71	1115.41	889.51	786.50	731.71	700.16
90000	1846.49	1115.87	886.27	781.04	724.70	692.02	1857.35	1127.94	899.50	795.34	739.93	708.03
91000	1867.00	1128.27	896.11	789.72	732.76	699.71	1877.99	1140.47	909.50	804.18	748.15	715.90
92000	1887.52	1140.67	905.96	798.40	740.81	707.40	1898.63	1153.01	919.49	813.01	756.37	723.76
93000	1908.04	1153.07	915.81	807.08	748.86	715.09	1919.26	1165.54	929.49	821.85	764.59	731.63
94000	1928.55	1165.47	925.66	815.75	756.91	722.78	1939.90	1178.07	939.48	830.69	772.82	739.50
95000	1949.07	1177.86	935.50	824.43	764.97	730.47	1960.54	1190.60	949.48	839.53	781.04	747.37
96000	1969.59	1190.26	945.35	833.11	773.02	738.16	1981.17	1203.14	959.47	848.36	789.26	755.23
97000	1990.10	1202.66	955.20	841.79	781.07	745.85	2001.81	1215.67	969.47	857.20	797.48	763.10
98000	2010.62	1215.06	965.04	850.47	789.12	753.54	2022.45	1228.20	979.46	866.04	805.70	770.97
99000	2031.14	1227.46	974.89	859.15	797.17	761.22	2043.09	1240.73	989.45	874.87	813.92	778.83
100000	2051.65	1239.86	984.74	867.82	805.23	768.91	2063.72	1253.27	999.45	883.71	822.14	786.70

458   **Table 2**

		9.00							9.25			
	TERM (YEARS)						TERM (YEARS)					
AMOUNT	5	10	15	20	25	30	5	10	15	20	25	30
10000	207.58	126.68	101.43	89.97	83.92	80.46	208.80	128.03	102.92	91.59	85.64	82.27
11000	228.34	139.34	111.57	98.97	92.31	88.51	229.68	140.84	113.21	100.75	94.20	90.49
12000	249.10	152.01	121.71	107.97	100.70	96.55	250.56	153.64	123.50	109.90	102.77	98.72
13000	269.86	164.68	131.85	116.96	109.10	104.60	271.44	166.44	133.79	119.06	111.33	106.95
14000	290.62	177.35	142.00	125.96	117.49	112.65	292.32	179.25	144.09	128.22	119.89	115.17
15000	311.38	190.01	152.14	134.96	125.88	120.69	313.20	192.05	154.38	137.38	128.46	123.40
16000	332.13	202.68	162.28	143.96	134.27	128.74	334.08	204.85	164.67	146.54	137.02	131.63
17000	352.89	215.35	172.43	152.95	142.66	136.79	354.96	217.66	174.96	155.70	145.58	139.85
18000	373.65	228.02	182.57	161.95	151.06	144.83	375.84	230.46	185.25	164.86	154.15	148.08
19000	394.41	240.68	192.71	170.95	159.45	152.88	396.72	243.26	195.55	174.01	162.71	156.31
20000	415.17	253.35	202.85	179.95	167.84	160.92	417.60	256.07	205.84	183.17	171.28	164.54
21000	435.93	266.02	213.00	188.94	176.23	168.97	438.48	268.87	216.13	192.33	179.84	172.76
22000	456.68	278.69	223.14	197.94	184.62	177.02	459.36	281.67	226.42	201.49	188.40	180.99
23000	477.44	291.35	233.28	206.94	193.02	185.06	480.24	294.48	236.71	210.65	196.97	189.22
24000	498.20	304.02	243.42	215.93	201.41	193.11	501.12	307.28	247.01	219.81	205.53	197.44
25000	518.96	316.69	253.57	224.93	209.80	201.16	522.00	320.08	257.30	228.97	214.10	205.67
26000	539.72	329.36	263.71	233.93	213.19	209.20	542.88	332.89	267.59	238.13	222.66	213.90
27000	560.48	342.02	273.85	242.93	226.58	217.25	563.76	345.69	277.88	247.28	231.22	222.12
28000	581.23	354.69	283.99	251.92	234.97	225.29	584.64	358.49	288.17	256.44	239.79	230.35
29000	601.99	367.36	294.14	260.92	243.37	233.34	605.52	371.29	298.47	265.60	248.35	238.58
30000	622.75	380.03	304.28	269.92	251.76	241.39	626.40	384.10	308.76	274.76	256.91	246.80
31000	643.51	392.69	314.42	278.92	260.15	249.43	647.28	396.90	319.05	283.92	265.48	255.03
32000	664.27	405.36	324.57	287.91	268.54	257.48	668.16	409.70	329.34	293.08	274.04	263.26
33000	685.03	418.03	334.71	296.91	276.93	265.53	689.04	422.51	339.63	302.24	282.61	271.48
34000	705.78	430.70	344.85	305.91	285.33	273.57	709.92	435.31	349.93	311.39	291.17	279.71
35000	726.54	443.37	354.99	314.90	293.72	281.62	730.80	448.11	360.22	320.55	299.73	287.94
36000	747.30	456.03	365.14	323.90	302.11	289.66	751.68	460.92	370.51	329.71	308.30	296.16
37000	768.06	468.70	375.28	332.90	310.50	297.71	772.56	473.72	380.80	338.87	316.86	304.39
38000	788.82	481.37	385.42	341.90	318.89	305.76	793.44	486.52	391.09	348.03	325.43	312.62
39000	809.58	494.04	395.56	350.89	327.29	313.80	814.32	499.33	401.38	357.19	333.99	320.84
40000	830.33	506.70	405.71	359.89	335.68	321.85	835.20	512.13	411.68	366.35	342.55	329.07
41000	851.09	519.37	415.85	368.89	344.07	329.90	856.08	524.93	421.97	375.51	351.12	337.30
42000	871.85	532.04	425.99	377.88	352.46	337.94	876.96	537.74	432.26	384.66	359.68	345.52
43000	892.61	544.71	436.13	386.88	360.85	345.99	897.84	550.54	442.55	393.82	368.24	353.75
44000	913.37	557.37	446.28	395.88	369.25	354.03	918.72	563.34	452.84	402.98	376.81	361.98
45000	934.13	570.04	456.42	404.88	377.64	362.08	939.60	576.15	463.14	412.14	385.37	370.20
46000	954.88	582.71	466.56	413.87	386.03	370.13	960.48	588.95	473.43	421.30	393.94	378.43
47000	975.64	595.38	476.71	422.87	394.42	378.17	981.36	601.75	483.72	430.46	402.50	386.66
48000	996.40	608.04	486.85	431.87	402.81	386.22	1002.24	614.56	494.01	439.62	411.06	394.88
49000	1017.16	620.71	496.99	440.87	411.21	394.27	1023.12	627.36	504.30	448.77	419.63	403.11
50000	1037.92	633.38	507.13	449.86	419.60	402.31	1043.99	640.16	514.60	457.93	428.19	411.34
51000	1058.68	646.05	517.28	458.86	427.99	410.36	1064.87	652.97	524.89	467.09	436.75	419.56
52000	1079.43	658.71	527.42	467.86	436.38	418.40	1085.75	665.77	535.18	476.25	445.32	427.79
53000	1100.19	671.38	537.56	476.85	444.77	426.45	1106.63	678.57	545.47	485.41	453.88	436.02
54000	1120.95	684.05	547.70	485.85	453.17	434.50	1127.51	691.38	555.76	494.57	462.45	444.24
55000	1141.71	696.72	557.85	494.85	461.56	442.54	1148.39	704.18	566.06	503.73	471.01	452.47
56000	1162.47	709.38	567.99	503.85	469.95	450.59	1169.27	716.98	576.35	512.89	479.57	460.69
57000	1183.23	722.05	578.13	512.84	478.34	458.63	1190.15	729.79	586.64	522.04	488.14	468.92
58000	1203.98	734.72	588.27	521.84	486.73	466.68	1211.03	742.59	596.93	531.20	496.70	477.15
59000	1224.74	747.39	598.42	530.84	495.13	474.73	1231.91	755.39	607.22	540.36	505.27	485.38
60000	1245.50	760.05	608.56	539.84	503.52	482.77	1252.79	768.20	617.52	549.52	513.83	493.61
61000	1266.26	772.72	618.70	548.83	511.91	490.82	1273.67	781.00	627.81	558.68	522.39	501.83
62000	1287.02	785.39	628.85	557.83	520.30	498.87	1294.55	793.80	638.10	567.84	530.96	510.06
63000	1307.78	798.06	638.99	566.83	528.69	506.91	1315.43	806.61	648.39	577.00	539.52	518.29
64000	1328.53	810.72	649.13	575.82	537.09	514.96	1336.31	819.41	658.68	586.15	548.08	526.51
65000	1349.29	823.39	659.27	584.82	545.48	523.00	1357.19	832.21	668.97	595.31	556.65	534.74
66000	1370.05	836.06	669.42	593.82	553.87	531.05	1378.07	845.02	679.27	604.47	565.21	542.97
67000	1390.81	848.73	679.56	602.82	562.26	539.10	1398.95	857.82	689.56	613.63	573.78	551.19
68000	1411.57	861.40	689.70	611.81	570.65	547.14	1419.83	870.62	699.85	622.79	582.34	559.42
69000	1432.33	874.06	699.84	620.81	579.05	555.19	1440.71	883.43	710.14	631.95	590.90	567.65
70000	1453.08	886.73	709.99	629.81	587.44	563.24	1461.59	896.23	720.43	641.11	599.47	575.87
71000	1473.84	899.40	720.13	638.81	595.83	571.28	1482.47	909.03	730.73	650.27	608.03	584.10
72000	1494.60	912.07	730.27	647.80	604.22	579.33	1503.35	921.84	741.02	659.42	616.59	592.33
73000	1515.36	924.73	740.41	656.80	612.61	587.37	1524.23	934.64	751.31	668.58	625.16	600.55
74000	1536.12	937.40	750.56	665.80	621.01	595.42	1545.11	947.44	761.60	677.74	633.72	608.78
75000	1556.88	950.07	760.70	674.79	629.40	603.47	1565.99	960.25	771.89	686.90	642.29	617.01
76000	1577.63	962.74	770.84	683.79	637.79	611.51	1586.87	973.05	782.19	696.06	650.85	625.23
77000	1598.39	975.40	780.99	692.79	646.18	619.56	1607.75	985.85	792.48	705.22	659.41	633.46
78000	1619.15	988.07	791.13	701.79	654.57	627.61	1628.63	998.66	802.77	714.38	667.98	641.69
79000	1639.91	1000.74	801.27	710.78	662.97	635.65	1649.51	1011.46	813.06	723.53	676.54	649.91
80000	1660.67	1013.41	811.41	719.78	671.36	643.70	1670.39	1024.26	823.35	732.69	685.11	658.14
81000	1681.43	1026.07	821.56	728.78	679.75	651.74	1691.27	1037.07	833.65	741.85	693.67	666.37
82000	1702.19	1038.74	831.70	737.78	688.14	659.79	1712.15	1049.87	843.94	751.01	702.23	674.59
83000	1722.94	1051.41	841.84	746.77	696.53	667.84	1733.03	1062.67	854.23	760.17	710.80	682.82
84000	1743.70	1064.08	851.98	755.77	704.92	675.88	1753.91	1075.47	864.52	769.33	719.36	691.05
85000	1764.46	1076.74	862.13	764.77	713.32	683.93	1774.79	1088.28	874.81	778.49	727.92	699.27
86000	1785.22	1089.41	872.27	773.76	721.71	691.98	1795.67	1101.08	885.11	787.65	736.49	707.50
87000	1805.98	1102.08	882.41	782.76	730.10	700.02	1816.55	1113.88	895.40	796.80	745.05	715.73
88000	1826.74	1114.75	892.55	791.76	738.49	708.07	1837.43	1126.69	905.69	805.96	753.62	723.95
89000	1847.49	1127.41	902.70	800.76	746.88	716.11	1858.31	1139.49	915.98	815.12	762.18	732.18
90000	1868.25	1140.08	912.84	809.75	755.28	724.16	1879.19	1152.29	926.27	824.28	770.74	740.41
91000	1889.01	1152.75	922.98	818.75	763.67	732.21	1900.07	1165.10	936.56	833.44	779.31	748.63
92000	1909.77	1165.42	933.13	827.75	772.06	740.25	1920.95	1177.90	946.86	842.60	787.87	756.86
93000	1930.53	1178.08	943.27	836.75	780.45	748.30	1941.83	1190.70	957.15	851.76	796.44	765.09
94000	1951.29	1190.75	953.41	845.74	788.84	756.35	1962.71	1203.51	967.44	860.91	805.00	773.31
95000	1972.04	1203.42	963.55	854.74	797.24	764.39	1983.59	1216.31	977.73	870.07	813.56	781.54
96000	1992.80	1216.09	973.70	863.74	805.63	772.44	2004.47	1229.11	988.02	879.23	822.13	789.77
97000	2013.56	1228.76	983.84	872.73	814.02	780.48	2025.35	1241.92	998.32	888.39	830.69	798.00
98000	2034.32	1241.42	993.98	881.73	822.41	788.53	2046.23	1254.72	1008.61	897.55	839.25	806.22
99000	2055.08	1254.09	1004.12	890.73	830.80	796.58	2067.11	1267.52	1018.90	906.71	847.82	814.45
100000	2075.84	1266.76	1014.27	899.73	839.20	804.62	2087.99	1280.33	1029.19	915.87	856.38	822.68

Table 2

459

<table>
<tr><th colspan="7">9.50</th><th colspan="6">9.75</th></tr>
<tr><th></th><th colspan="6">TERM (YEARS)</th><th colspan="6">TERM (YEARS)</th></tr>
<tr><th>AMOUNT</th><th>5</th><th>10</th><th>15</th><th>20</th><th>25</th><th>30</th><th>5</th><th>10</th><th>15</th><th>20</th><th>25</th><th>30</th></tr>
<tr><td>10000</td><td>210.02</td><td>129.40</td><td>104.42</td><td>93.21</td><td>87.37</td><td>84.09</td><td>211.24</td><td>130.77</td><td>105.94</td><td>94.85</td><td>89.11</td><td>85.92</td></tr>
<tr><td>11000</td><td>231.02</td><td>142.34</td><td>114.86</td><td>102.53</td><td>96.11</td><td>92.49</td><td>232.37</td><td>143.85</td><td>116.53</td><td>104.34</td><td>98.03</td><td>94.51</td></tr>
<tr><td>12000</td><td>252.02</td><td>155.28</td><td>125.31</td><td>111.86</td><td>104.84</td><td>100.90</td><td>253.49</td><td>156.92</td><td>127.12</td><td>113.82</td><td>106.94</td><td>103.10</td></tr>
<tr><td>13000</td><td>273.02</td><td>168.22</td><td>135.75</td><td>121.18</td><td>113.58</td><td>109.31</td><td>274.62</td><td>170.00</td><td>137.72</td><td>123.31</td><td>115.85</td><td>111.69</td></tr>
<tr><td>14000</td><td>294.03</td><td>181.16</td><td>146.19</td><td>130.50</td><td>122.32</td><td>117.72</td><td>295.74</td><td>183.08</td><td>148.31</td><td>132.79</td><td>124.76</td><td>120.28</td></tr>
<tr><td>15000</td><td>315.03</td><td>194.10</td><td>156.63</td><td>139.82</td><td>131.05</td><td>126.13</td><td>316.86</td><td>196.16</td><td>158.90</td><td>142.28</td><td>133.67</td><td>128.87</td></tr>
<tr><td>16000</td><td>336.03</td><td>207.04</td><td>167.08</td><td>149.14</td><td>139.79</td><td>134.54</td><td>337.99</td><td>209.23</td><td>169.50</td><td>151.76</td><td>142.58</td><td>137.46</td></tr>
<tr><td>17000</td><td>357.03</td><td>219.98</td><td>177.52</td><td>158.46</td><td>148.53</td><td>142.95</td><td>359.11</td><td>222.31</td><td>180.09</td><td>161.25</td><td>151.49</td><td>146.06</td></tr>
<tr><td>18000</td><td>378.03</td><td>232.92</td><td>187.96</td><td>167.78</td><td>157.27</td><td>151.35</td><td>380.24</td><td>235.39</td><td>190.69</td><td>170.73</td><td>160.40</td><td>154.65</td></tr>
<tr><td>19000</td><td>399.04</td><td>245.86</td><td>198.40</td><td>177.10</td><td>166.00</td><td>159.76</td><td>401.36</td><td>248.46</td><td>201.28</td><td>180.22</td><td>169.32</td><td>163.24</td></tr>
<tr><td>20000</td><td>420.04</td><td>258.80</td><td>208.84</td><td>186.43</td><td>174.74</td><td>168.17</td><td>422.48</td><td>261.54</td><td>211.87</td><td>189.70</td><td>178.23</td><td>171.83</td></tr>
<tr><td>21000</td><td>441.04</td><td>271.73</td><td>219.29</td><td>195.75</td><td>183.48</td><td>176.58</td><td>443.61</td><td>274.62</td><td>222.47</td><td>199.19</td><td>187.14</td><td>180.42</td></tr>
<tr><td>22000</td><td>462.04</td><td>284.67</td><td>229.73</td><td>205.07</td><td>192.21</td><td>184.99</td><td>464.73</td><td>287.69</td><td>233.06</td><td>208.67</td><td>196.05</td><td>189.01</td></tr>
<tr><td>23000</td><td>483.04</td><td>297.61</td><td>240.17</td><td>214.39</td><td>200.95</td><td>193.40</td><td>485.86</td><td>300.77</td><td>243.65</td><td>218.16</td><td>204.96</td><td>197.61</td></tr>
<tr><td>24000</td><td>504.04</td><td>310.55</td><td>250.61</td><td>223.71</td><td>209.69</td><td>201.61</td><td>506.98</td><td>313.85</td><td>254.25</td><td>227.64</td><td>213.87</td><td>206.20</td></tr>
<tr><td>25000</td><td>525.05</td><td>323.49</td><td>261.06</td><td>233.03</td><td>218.42</td><td>210.21</td><td>528.11</td><td>326.93</td><td>264.84</td><td>237.13</td><td>222.78</td><td>214.79</td></tr>
<tr><td>26000</td><td>546.05</td><td>336.43</td><td>271.50</td><td>242.35</td><td>227.16</td><td>218.62</td><td>549.23</td><td>340.00</td><td>275.43</td><td>246.61</td><td>231.70</td><td>223.38</td></tr>
<tr><td>27000</td><td>567.05</td><td>349.37</td><td>281.94</td><td>251.68</td><td>235.90</td><td>227.03</td><td>570.35</td><td>353.08</td><td>286.03</td><td>256.10</td><td>240.61</td><td>231.97</td></tr>
<tr><td>28000</td><td>588.05</td><td>362.31</td><td>292.38</td><td>261.00</td><td>244.64</td><td>235.44</td><td>591.48</td><td>366.16</td><td>296.62</td><td>265.58</td><td>249.52</td><td>240.56</td></tr>
<tr><td>29000</td><td>609.05</td><td>375.25</td><td>302.83</td><td>270.32</td><td>253.37</td><td>243.85</td><td>612.60</td><td>379.23</td><td>307.22</td><td>275.07</td><td>258.43</td><td>249.15</td></tr>
<tr><td>30000</td><td>630.06</td><td>388.19</td><td>313.27</td><td>279.64</td><td>262.11</td><td>252.26</td><td>633.73</td><td>392.31</td><td>317.81</td><td>284.55</td><td>267.34</td><td>257.75</td></tr>
<tr><td>31000</td><td>651.06</td><td>401.13</td><td>323.71</td><td>288.96</td><td>270.85</td><td>260.66</td><td>654.85</td><td>405.39</td><td>328.40</td><td>294.04</td><td>276.25</td><td>266.34</td></tr>
<tr><td>32000</td><td>672.06</td><td>414.07</td><td>334.15</td><td>298.28</td><td>279.58</td><td>269.07</td><td>675.97</td><td>418.46</td><td>339.00</td><td>303.53</td><td>285.16</td><td>274.93</td></tr>
<tr><td>33000</td><td>693.06</td><td>427.01</td><td>344.59</td><td>307.60</td><td>288.32</td><td>277.48</td><td>697.10</td><td>431.54</td><td>349.59</td><td>313.01</td><td>294.08</td><td>283.52</td></tr>
<tr><td>34000</td><td>714.06</td><td>439.95</td><td>355.04</td><td>316.92</td><td>297.06</td><td>285.89</td><td>718.22</td><td>444.62</td><td>360.18</td><td>322.50</td><td>302.99</td><td>292.11</td></tr>
<tr><td>35000</td><td>735.07</td><td>452.89</td><td>365.48</td><td>326.25</td><td>305.79</td><td>294.30</td><td>739.35</td><td>457.70</td><td>370.78</td><td>331.98</td><td>311.90</td><td>300.70</td></tr>
<tr><td>36000</td><td>756.07</td><td>465.83</td><td>375.92</td><td>335.57</td><td>314.53</td><td>302.71</td><td>760.47</td><td>470.77</td><td>381.37</td><td>341.47</td><td>320.81</td><td>309.30</td></tr>
<tr><td>37000</td><td>777.07</td><td>478.77</td><td>386.36</td><td>344.89</td><td>323.27</td><td>311.12</td><td>781.60</td><td>483.85</td><td>391.96</td><td>350.95</td><td>329.72</td><td>317.89</td></tr>
<tr><td>38000</td><td>798.07</td><td>491.71</td><td>396.81</td><td>354.21</td><td>332.00</td><td>319.52</td><td>802.72</td><td>496.93</td><td>402.56</td><td>360.44</td><td>338.63</td><td>326.48</td></tr>
<tr><td>39000</td><td>819.07</td><td>504.65</td><td>407.25</td><td>363.53</td><td>340.74</td><td>327.93</td><td>823.85</td><td>510.00</td><td>413.15</td><td>369.92</td><td>347.54</td><td>335.07</td></tr>
<tr><td>40000</td><td>840.07</td><td>517.59</td><td>417.69</td><td>372.85</td><td>349.48</td><td>336.34</td><td>844.97</td><td>523.08</td><td>423.75</td><td>379.41</td><td>356.45</td><td>343.66</td></tr>
<tr><td>41000</td><td>861.08</td><td>530.53</td><td>428.13</td><td>382.17</td><td>358.22</td><td>344.75</td><td>866.09</td><td>536.16</td><td>434.34</td><td>388.89</td><td>365.37</td><td>352.25</td></tr>
<tr><td>42000</td><td>882.08</td><td>543.47</td><td>438.57</td><td>391.50</td><td>366.95</td><td>353.16</td><td>887.22</td><td>549.24</td><td>444.93</td><td>398.38</td><td>374.28</td><td>360.84</td></tr>
<tr><td>43000</td><td>903.08</td><td>556.41</td><td>449.02</td><td>400.82</td><td>375.69</td><td>361.57</td><td>908.34</td><td>562.31</td><td>455.53</td><td>407.86</td><td>383.19</td><td>369.44</td></tr>
<tr><td>44000</td><td>924.08</td><td>569.35</td><td>459.46</td><td>410.14</td><td>384.43</td><td>369.98</td><td>929.47</td><td>575.39</td><td>466.12</td><td>417.35</td><td>392.10</td><td>378.03</td></tr>
<tr><td>45000</td><td>945.08</td><td>582.29</td><td>469.90</td><td>419.46</td><td>393.16</td><td>378.38</td><td>950.59</td><td>588.47</td><td>476.71</td><td>426.83</td><td>401.01</td><td>386.62</td></tr>
<tr><td>46000</td><td>966.09</td><td>595.23</td><td>480.34</td><td>428.78</td><td>401.90</td><td>386.79</td><td>971.72</td><td>601.54</td><td>487.31</td><td>436.32</td><td>409.92</td><td>395.21</td></tr>
<tr><td>47000</td><td>987.09</td><td>608.17</td><td>490.79</td><td>438.10</td><td>410.64</td><td>395.20</td><td>992.84</td><td>614.62</td><td>497.90</td><td>445.80</td><td>418.83</td><td>403.80</td></tr>
<tr><td>48000</td><td>1008.09</td><td>621.11</td><td>501.23</td><td>447.42</td><td>419.37</td><td>403.61</td><td>1013.96</td><td>627.70</td><td>508.49</td><td>455.29</td><td>427.75</td><td>412.39</td></tr>
<tr><td>49000</td><td>1029.09</td><td>634.05</td><td>511.67</td><td>456.74</td><td>428.11</td><td>412.02</td><td>1035.09</td><td>640.77</td><td>519.09</td><td>464.77</td><td>436.66</td><td>420.99</td></tr>
<tr><td>50000</td><td>1050.09</td><td>646.99</td><td>522.11</td><td>466.07</td><td>436.85</td><td>420.43</td><td>1056.21</td><td>653.85</td><td>529.68</td><td>474.26</td><td>445.57</td><td>429.58</td></tr>
<tr><td>51000</td><td>1071.09</td><td>659.93</td><td>532.55</td><td>475.39</td><td>445.59</td><td>428.84</td><td>1077.34</td><td>666.93</td><td>540.27</td><td>483.74</td><td>454.48</td><td>438.17</td></tr>
<tr><td>52000</td><td>1092.10</td><td>672.87</td><td>543.00</td><td>484.71</td><td>454.32</td><td>437.24</td><td>1098.46</td><td>680.01</td><td>550.87</td><td>493.23</td><td>463.39</td><td>446.76</td></tr>
<tr><td>53000</td><td>1113.10</td><td>685.81</td><td>553.44</td><td>494.03</td><td>463.06</td><td>445.65</td><td>1119.58</td><td>693.08</td><td>561.46</td><td>502.71</td><td>472.30</td><td>455.35</td></tr>
<tr><td>54000</td><td>1134.10</td><td>698.75</td><td>563.88</td><td>503.35</td><td>471.80</td><td>454.06</td><td>1140.71</td><td>706.16</td><td>572.06</td><td>512.20</td><td>481.21</td><td>463.94</td></tr>
<tr><td>55000</td><td>1155.10</td><td>711.69</td><td>574.32</td><td>512.67</td><td>480.53</td><td>462.47</td><td>1161.83</td><td>719.24</td><td>582.65</td><td>521.68</td><td>490.13</td><td>472.53</td></tr>
<tr><td>56000</td><td>1176.10</td><td>724.63</td><td>584.77</td><td>521.99</td><td>489.27</td><td>470.88</td><td>1182.96</td><td>732.31</td><td>593.24</td><td>531.17</td><td>499.04</td><td>481.13</td></tr>
<tr><td>57000</td><td>1197.11</td><td>737.57</td><td>595.21</td><td>531.31</td><td>498.01</td><td>479.29</td><td>1204.08</td><td>745.39</td><td>603.84</td><td>540.65</td><td>507.95</td><td>489.72</td></tr>
<tr><td>58000</td><td>1218.11</td><td>750.51</td><td>605.65</td><td>540.64</td><td>506.74</td><td>487.70</td><td>1225.21</td><td>758.47</td><td>614.43</td><td>550.14</td><td>516.86</td><td>498.31</td></tr>
<tr><td>59000</td><td>1239.11</td><td>763.45</td><td>616.09</td><td>549.96</td><td>515.48</td><td>496.10</td><td>1246.33</td><td>771.54</td><td>625.02</td><td>559.62</td><td>525.77</td><td>506.90</td></tr>
<tr><td>60000</td><td>1260.11</td><td>776.39</td><td>626.53</td><td>559.28</td><td>524.22</td><td>504.51</td><td>1267.45</td><td>784.62</td><td>635.62</td><td>569.11</td><td>534.68</td><td>515.49</td></tr>
<tr><td>61000</td><td>1281.11</td><td>789.33</td><td>636.98</td><td>568.60</td><td>532.95</td><td>512.92</td><td>1288.58</td><td>797.70</td><td>646.21</td><td>578.60</td><td>543.59</td><td>524.08</td></tr>
<tr><td>62000</td><td>1302.12</td><td>802.26</td><td>647.42</td><td>577.92</td><td>541.69</td><td>521.33</td><td>1309.70</td><td>810.78</td><td>656.80</td><td>588.08</td><td>552.51</td><td>532.68</td></tr>
<tr><td>63000</td><td>1323.12</td><td>815.20</td><td>657.86</td><td>587.24</td><td>550.43</td><td>529.74</td><td>1330.83</td><td>823.85</td><td>667.40</td><td>597.57</td><td>561.42</td><td>541.27</td></tr>
<tr><td>64000</td><td>1344.12</td><td>828.14</td><td>668.30</td><td>596.56</td><td>559.17</td><td>538.15</td><td>1351.95</td><td>836.93</td><td>677.99</td><td>607.05</td><td>570.33</td><td>549.86</td></tr>
<tr><td>65000</td><td>1365.12</td><td>841.08</td><td>678.75</td><td>605.89</td><td>567.90</td><td>546.56</td><td>1373.08</td><td>850.01</td><td>688.59</td><td>616.54</td><td>579.24</td><td>558.45</td></tr>
<tr><td>66000</td><td>1386.12</td><td>854.02</td><td>689.19</td><td>615.21</td><td>576.64</td><td>554.96</td><td>1394.20</td><td>863.08</td><td>699.18</td><td>626.02</td><td>588.15</td><td>567.04</td></tr>
<tr><td>67000</td><td>1407.12</td><td>866.96</td><td>699.63</td><td>624.53</td><td>585.38</td><td>563.37</td><td>1415.32</td><td>876.16</td><td>709.77</td><td>635.51</td><td>597.06</td><td>575.63</td></tr>
<tr><td>68000</td><td>1428.13</td><td>879.90</td><td>710.07</td><td>633.85</td><td>594.11</td><td>571.78</td><td>1436.45</td><td>889.24</td><td>720.37</td><td>644.99</td><td>605.97</td><td>584.23</td></tr>
<tr><td>69000</td><td>1449.13</td><td>892.84</td><td>720.52</td><td>643.17</td><td>602.85</td><td>580.19</td><td>1457.57</td><td>902.31</td><td>730.96</td><td>654.48</td><td>614.88</td><td>592.82</td></tr>
<tr><td>70000</td><td>1470.13</td><td>905.78</td><td>730.96</td><td>652.49</td><td>611.59</td><td>588.60</td><td>1478.70</td><td>915.39</td><td>741.55</td><td>663.96</td><td>623.80</td><td>601.41</td></tr>
<tr><td>71000</td><td>1491.13</td><td>918.72</td><td>741.40</td><td>661.81</td><td>620.32</td><td>597.01</td><td>1499.82</td><td>928.47</td><td>752.15</td><td>673.45</td><td>632.71</td><td>610.00</td></tr>
<tr><td>72000</td><td>1512.13</td><td>931.66</td><td>751.84</td><td>671.13</td><td>629.06</td><td>605.42</td><td>1520.95</td><td>941.55</td><td>762.74</td><td>682.93</td><td>641.62</td><td>618.59</td></tr>
<tr><td>73000</td><td>1533.14</td><td>944.60</td><td>762.28</td><td>680.46</td><td>637.80</td><td>613.82</td><td>1542.07</td><td>954.62</td><td>773.33</td><td>692.42</td><td>650.53</td><td>627.18</td></tr>
<tr><td>74000</td><td>1554.14</td><td>957.54</td><td>772.73</td><td>689.78</td><td>646.54</td><td>622.23</td><td>1563.19</td><td>967.70</td><td>783.93</td><td>701.90</td><td>659.44</td><td>635.77</td></tr>
<tr><td>75000</td><td>1575.14</td><td>970.48</td><td>783.17</td><td>699.10</td><td>655.27</td><td>630.64</td><td>1584.32</td><td>980.78</td><td>794.52</td><td>711.39</td><td>668.35</td><td>644.37</td></tr>
<tr><td>76000</td><td>1596.14</td><td>983.42</td><td>793.61</td><td>708.42</td><td>664.01</td><td>639.05</td><td>1605.44</td><td>993.85</td><td>805.12</td><td>720.87</td><td>677.26</td><td>652.96</td></tr>
<tr><td>77000</td><td>1617.14</td><td>996.36</td><td>804.05</td><td>717.74</td><td>672.75</td><td>647.46</td><td>1626.57</td><td>1006.93</td><td>815.71</td><td>730.36</td><td>686.18</td><td>661.55</td></tr>
<tr><td>78000</td><td>1638.15</td><td>1009.30</td><td>814.50</td><td>727.06</td><td>681.48</td><td>655.87</td><td>1647.69</td><td>1020.01</td><td>826.30</td><td>739.84</td><td>695.09</td><td>670.14</td></tr>
<tr><td>79000</td><td>1659.15</td><td>1022.24</td><td>824.94</td><td>736.38</td><td>690.22</td><td>664.27</td><td>1668.82</td><td>1033.08</td><td>836.90</td><td>749.33</td><td>704.00</td><td>678.73</td></tr>
<tr><td>80000</td><td>1680.15</td><td>1035.18</td><td>835.38</td><td>745.70</td><td>698.96</td><td>672.68</td><td>1689.94</td><td>1046.16</td><td>847.49</td><td>758.81</td><td>712.91</td><td>687.32</td></tr>
<tr><td>81000</td><td>1701.15</td><td>1048.12</td><td>845.82</td><td>755.03</td><td>707.69</td><td>681.09</td><td>1711.06</td><td>1059.24</td><td>858.08</td><td>768.30</td><td>721.82</td><td>695.92</td></tr>
<tr><td>82000</td><td>1722.15</td><td>1061.06</td><td>856.26</td><td>764.35</td><td>716.43</td><td>689.50</td><td>1732.19</td><td>1072.32</td><td>868.68</td><td>777.78</td><td>730.73</td><td>704.51</td></tr>
<tr><td>83000</td><td>1743.15</td><td>1074.00</td><td>866.71</td><td>773.67</td><td>725.17</td><td>697.91</td><td>1753.31</td><td>1085.39</td><td>879.27</td><td>787.27</td><td>739.64</td><td>713.10</td></tr>
<tr><td>84000</td><td>1764.16</td><td>1086.94</td><td>877.15</td><td>782.99</td><td>733.91</td><td>706.32</td><td>1774.44</td><td>1098.47</td><td>889.86</td><td>796.75</td><td>748.56</td><td>721.69</td></tr>
<tr><td>85000</td><td>1785.16</td><td>1099.88</td><td>887.59</td><td>792.31</td><td>742.64</td><td>714.73</td><td>1795.56</td><td>1111.55</td><td>900.46</td><td>806.24</td><td>757.47</td><td>730.28</td></tr>
<tr><td>86000</td><td>1806.16</td><td>1112.82</td><td>898.03</td><td>801.63</td><td>751.38</td><td>723.13</td><td>1816.68</td><td>1124.62</td><td>911.05</td><td>815.72</td><td>766.38</td><td>738.87</td></tr>
<tr><td>87000</td><td>1827.16</td><td>1125.76</td><td>908.48</td><td>810.95</td><td>760.12</td><td>731.54</td><td>1837.81</td><td>1137.70</td><td>921.65</td><td>825.21</td><td>775.29</td><td>747.46</td></tr>
<tr><td>88000</td><td>1848.16</td><td>1138.70</td><td>918.92</td><td>820.28</td><td>768.85</td><td>739.95</td><td>1858.93</td><td>1150.78</td><td>932.24</td><td>834.69</td><td>784.20</td><td>756.06</td></tr>
<tr><td>89000</td><td>1869.17</td><td>1151.64</td><td>929.36</td><td>829.60</td><td>777.59</td><td>748.36</td><td>1880.06</td><td>1163.86</td><td>942.83</td><td>844.18</td><td>793.11</td><td>764.65</td></tr>
<tr><td>90000</td><td>1890.17</td><td>1164.58</td><td>939.80</td><td>838.92</td><td>786.33</td><td>756.77</td><td>1901.18</td><td>1176.93</td><td>953.43</td><td>853.67</td><td>802.02</td><td>773.24</td></tr>
<tr><td>91000</td><td>1911.17</td><td>1177.52</td><td>950.24</td><td>848.24</td><td>795.06</td><td>765.18</td><td>1922.31</td><td>1190.01</td><td>964.02</td><td>863.15</td><td>810.94</td><td>781.83</td></tr>
<tr><td>92000</td><td>1932.17</td><td>1190.46</td><td>960.69</td><td>857.56</td><td>803.80</td><td>773.59</td><td>1943.43</td><td>1203.09</td><td>974.61</td><td>872.64</td><td>819.85</td><td>790.42</td></tr>
<tr><td>93000</td><td>1953.17</td><td>1203.40</td><td>971.13</td><td>866.88</td><td>812.54</td><td>781.99</td><td>1964.55</td><td>1216.16</td><td>985.21</td><td>882.12</td><td>828.76</td><td>799.01</td></tr>
<tr><td>94000</td><td>1974.17</td><td>1216.34</td><td>981.57</td><td>876.20</td><td>821.27</td><td>790.40</td><td>1985.68</td><td>1229.24</td><td>995.80</td><td>891.61</td><td>837.67</td><td>807.61</td></tr>
<tr><td>95000</td><td>1995.18</td><td>1229.28</td><td>992.01</td><td>885.52</td><td>830.01</td><td>798.81</td><td>2006.80</td><td>1242.32</td><td>1006.39</td><td>901.09</td><td>846.58</td><td>816.20</td></tr>
<tr><td>96000</td><td>2016.18</td><td>1242.22</td><td>1002.46</td><td>894.85</td><td>838.75</td><td>807.22</td><td>2027.93</td><td>1255.39</td><td>1016.99</td><td>910.58</td><td>855.49</td><td>824.79</td></tr>
<tr><td>97000</td><td>2037.18</td><td>1255.16</td><td>1012.90</td><td>904.17</td><td>847.49</td><td>815.63</td><td>2049.05</td><td>1268.47</td><td>1027.58</td><td>920.06</td><td>864.40</td><td>833.38</td></tr>
<tr><td>98000</td><td>2058.18</td><td>1268.10</td><td>1023.34</td><td>913.49</td><td>856.22</td><td>824.04</td><td>2070.18</td><td>1281.55</td><td>1038.18</td><td>929.55</td><td>873.31</td><td>841.97</td></tr>
<tr><td>99000</td><td>2079.18</td><td>1281.04</td><td>1033.78</td><td>922.81</td><td>864.96</td><td>832.45</td><td>2091.30</td><td>1294.63</td><td>1048.77</td><td>939.03</td><td>882.23</td><td>850.56</td></tr>
<tr><td>100000</td><td>2100.19</td><td>1293.98</td><td>1044.22</td><td>932.13</td><td>873.70</td><td>840.85</td><td>2112.42</td><td>1307.70</td><td>1059.36</td><td>948.52</td><td>891.14</td><td>859.15</td></tr>
</table>

		10.00							10.25			
		TERM (YEARS)							TERM (YEARS)			
AMOUNT	5	10	15	20	25	30	5	10	15	20	25	30
10000	212.47	132.15	107.46	96.50	90.87	87.76	213.70	133.54	109.00	98.16	92.64	89.61
11000	233.72	145.37	118.21	106.15	99.96	96.53	235.07	146.89	119.89	107.98	101.90	98.57
12000	254.96	158.58	128.95	115.80	109.04	105.31	256.44	160.25	130.79	117.80	111.17	107.53
13000	276.21	171.80	139.70	125.45	118.13	114.08	277.81	173.60	141.69	127.61	120.43	116.49
14000	297.46	185.01	150.44	135.10	127.22	122.86	299.18	186.95	152.59	137.43	129.69	125.45
15000	318.71	198.23	161.19	144.75	136.31	131.64	320.55	200.31	163.49	147.25	138.96	134.42
16000	339.95	211.44	171.94	154.40	145.39	140.41	341.92	213.66	174.39	157.06	148.22	143.38
17000	361.20	224.66	182.68	164.05	154.48	149.19	363.29	227.02	185.29	166.88	157.49	152.34
18000	382.45	237.87	193.43	173.70	163.57	157.96	384.66	240.37	196.19	176.70	166.75	161.30
19000	403.69	251.09	204.17	183.35	172.65	166.74	406.04	253.72	207.09	186.51	176.01	170.26
20000	424.94	264.30	214.92	193.00	181.74	175.51	427.41	267.08	217.99	196.33	185.28	179.22
21000	446.19	277.52	225.67	202.65	190.83	184.29	448.78	280.43	228.89	206.15	194.54	188.18
22000	467.43	290.73	236.41	212.30	199.91	193.07	470.15	293.79	239.79	215.96	203.80	197.14
23000	483.68	303.95	247.16	221.95	209.00	201.84	491.52	307.14	250.69	225.78	213.07	206.10
24000	509.93	317.16	257.91	231.61	218.09	210.62	512.89	320.49	261.59	235.59	222.33	215.06
25000	531.18	330.38	258.65	241.26	227.18	219.39	534.26	333.85	272.49	245.41	231.60	224.03
26000	552.42	343.59	279.40	250.91	236.26	228.17	555.63	347.20	283.39	255.23	240.86	232.99
27000	573.67	356.81	290.14	260.56	245.35	236.94	577.00	360.56	294.29	265.04	250.12	241.95
28000	594.92	370.02	300.89	270.21	254.44	245.72	598.37	373.91	305.19	274.86	259.39	250.91
29000	616.16	383.24	311.64	279.86	263.52	254.50	619.74	387.26	316.09	284.68	268.65	259.87
30000	637.41	396.45	322.38	289.51	272.61	263.27	641.11	400.62	326.99	294.49	277.91	268.83
31000	658.66	409.67	333.13	299.16	281.70	272.05	662.48	413.97	337.88	304.31	287.18	277.79
32000	679.91	422.88	343.87	308.81	290.78	280.82	683.85	427.32	348.78	314.13	296.44	286.75
33000	701.15	436.10	354.62	318.46	299.87	289.60	705.22	440.68	359.68	323.94	305.71	295.71
34000	722.40	449.31	365.37	328.11	308.96	298.37	726.59	454.03	370.58	333.76	314.97	304.67
35000	743.65	462.53	376.11	337.76	318.05	307.15	747.96	467.39	381.48	343.58	324.23	313.64
36000	764.89	475.74	386.86	347.41	327.13	315.93	769.33	480.74	392.38	353.39	333.50	322.60
37000	786.14	488.96	397.60	357.06	336.22	324.70	790.70	494.09	403.28	363.21	342.76	331.56
38000	807.39	502.17	408.35	366.71	345.31	333.48	812.07	507.45	414.18	373.02	352.03	340.52
39000	828.63	515.39	419.10	376.36	354.39	342.25	833.44	520.80	425.08	382.84	361.29	349.48
40000	849.88	528.60	429.84	386.01	363.48	351.03	854.81	534.16	435.98	392.66	370.55	358.44
41000	871.13	541.82	440.59	395.66	372.57	359.80	876.18	547.51	446.88	402.47	379.82	367.40
42000	892.38	555.03	451.33	405.31	381.65	368.58	897.55	560.86	457.78	412.29	389.08	376.36
43000	913.62	568.25	462.08	414.96	390.74	377.36	918.92	574.22	468.68	422.11	398.34	385.32
44000	934.87	581.46	472.83	424.61	399.83	386.13	940.29	587.57	479.58	431.92	407.61	394.28
45000	956.12	594.68	483.57	434.26	408.92	394.91	961.66	600.93	490.48	441.74	416.87	403.25
46000	977.36	607.89	494.32	443.91	418.00	403.68	983.03	614.28	501.38	451.56	426.14	412.21
47000	998.61	621.11	505.06	453.56	427.09	412.46	1004.40	627.63	512.28	461.37	435.40	421.17
48000	1019.86	634.32	515.81	463.21	436.18	421.23	1025.77	640.99	523.18	471.19	444.66	430.13
49000	1041.11	647.54	526.56	472.86	445.26	430.01	1047.14	654.34	534.08	481.01	453.93	439.09
50000	1062.35	660.75	537.30	482.51	454.35	438.79	1068.51	667.70	544.98	490.82	463.19	448.05
51000	1083.60	673.97	548.05	492.16	463.44	447.56	1089.88	681.05	555.87	500.64	472.46	457.01
52000	1104.85	687.18	558.79	501.81	472.52	456.34	1111.25	694.40	566.77	510.45	481.72	465.97
53000	1126.09	700.40	569.54	511.46	481.61	465.11	1132.62	707.76	577.67	520.27	490.98	474.93
54000	1147.34	713.61	580.29	521.11	490.70	473.89	1153.99	721.11	588.57	530.09	500.25	483.89
55000	1168.59	726.83	591.03	530.76	499.79	482.66	1175.36	734.46	599.47	539.90	509.51	492.86
56000	1189.83	740.04	601.78	540.41	508.87	491.44	1196.73	747.82	610.37	549.72	518.77	501.82
57000	1211.08	753.26	612.52	550.06	517.96	500.22	1218.11	761.17	621.27	559.54	528.04	510.78
58000	1232.33	766.47	623.27	559.71	527.05	508.99	1239.48	774.53	632.17	569.35	537.30	519.74
59000	1253.58	779.69	634.02	569.36	536.13	517.77	1260.85	787.88	643.07	579.17	546.57	528.70
60000	1274.82	792.90	644.76	579.01	545.22	526.54	1282.22	801.23	653.97	588.99	555.83	537.66
61000	1296.07	806.12	655.51	588.66	554.31	535.32	1303.59	814.59	664.87	598.80	565.09	546.62
62000	1317.32	819.33	666.26	598.31	563.39	544.09	1324.96	827.94	675.77	608.62	574.36	555.58
63000	1338.56	832.55	677.00	607.96	572.48	552.87	1346.33	841.30	686.67	618.44	583.62	564.54
64000	1359.81	845.76	687.75	617.61	581.57	561.65	1367.70	854.65	697.57	628.25	592.89	573.50
65000	1381.06	858.98	698.49	627.26	590.66	570.42	1389.07	868.00	708.47	638.07	602.15	582.47
66000	1402.30	872.19	709.24	636.91	599.74	579.20	1410.44	881.36	719.37	647.88	611.41	591.43
67000	1423.55	885.41	719.99	646.56	608.83	587.97	1431.81	894.71	730.27	657.70	620.68	600.39
68000	1444.80	898.63	730.73	656.21	617.92	596.75	1453.18	908.07	741.17	667.52	629.94	609.35
69000	1466.05	911.84	741.48	665.86	627.00	605.52	1474.55	921.42	752.07	677.33	639.20	618.31
70000	1487.29	925.06	752.22	675.52	636.09	614.30	1495.92	934.77	762.97	687.15	648.47	627.27
71000	1508.54	938.27	762.97	685.17	645.18	623.08	1517.29	948.13	773.87	696.97	657.73	636.23
72000	1529.79	951.49	773.72	694.82	654.26	631.85	1538.66	961.48	784.76	706.78	667.00	645.19
73000	1551.03	964.70	784.46	704.47	663.35	640.63	1560.03	974.83	795.66	716.60	676.26	654.15
74000	1572.28	977.92	795.21	714.12	672.44	649.40	1581.40	988.19	806.56	726.42	685.52	663.11
75000	1593.53	991.13	805.95	723.77	681.53	658.18	1602.77	1001.54	817.46	736.23	694.79	672.08
76000	1614.78	1004.35	816.70	733.42	690.61	666.95	1624.14	1014.90	828.36	746.05	704.05	681.04
77000	1636.02	1017.56	827.45	743.07	699.70	675.73	1645.51	1028.25	839.26	755.87	713.32	690.00
78000	1657.27	1030.78	838.19	752.72	708.79	684.51	1666.87	1041.60	850.16	765.68	722.58	698.96
79000	1678.52	1043.99	848.94	762.37	717.87	693.28	1688.25	1054.96	861.06	775.50	731.84	707.92
80000	1699.76	1057.21	859.68	772.02	726.96	702.06	1709.62	1068.31	871.96	785.31	741.11	716.88
81000	1721.01	1070.42	870.43	781.67	736.05	710.83	1730.99	1081.67	882.86	795.13	750.37	725.84
82000	1742.26	1083.64	881.18	791.32	745.13	719.61	1752.36	1095.02	893.76	804.95	759.63	734.80
83000	1763.50	1096.85	891.92	800.97	754.22	728.38	1773.73	1108.37	904.66	814.76	768.90	743.76
84000	1784.75	1110.07	902.67	810.62	763.31	737.16	1795.10	1121.73	915.56	824.58	778.16	752.73
85000	1806.00	1123.28	913.41	820.27	772.40	745.94	1816.47	1135.08	926.46	834.40	787.43	761.69
86000	1827.25	1136.50	924.16	829.92	781.48	754.71	1837.84	1148.44	937.36	844.21	796.69	770.65
87000	1848.49	1149.71	934.91	839.57	790.57	763.49	1859.21	1161.79	948.26	854.03	805.95	779.61
88000	1869.74	1162.93	945.65	849.22	799.66	772.26	1880.58	1175.14	959.16	863.85	815.22	788.57
89000	1890.99	1176.14	956.40	858.87	808.74	781.04	1901.95	1188.50	970.06	873.66	824.48	797.53
90000	1912.23	1189.36	967.14	868.52	817.83	789.81	1923.32	1201.85	980.96	883.48	833.74	806.49
91000	1933.48	1202.57	977.89	878.17	826.92	798.59	1944.69	1215.20	991.86	893.30	843.01	815.45
92000	1954.73	1215.79	988.64	887.82	836.00	807.37	1966.06	1228.56	1002.75	903.11	852.27	824.41
93000	1975.98	1229.00	999.38	897.47	845.09	816.14	1987.43	1241.91	1013.65	912.93	861.54	833.37
94000	1997.22	1242.22	1010.13	907.12	854.18	824.92	2008.80	1255.27	1024.55	922.74	870.80	842.34
95000	2018.47	1255.43	1020.87	916.77	863.27	833.69	2030.18	1268.62	1035.45	932.56	880.06	851.30
96000	2039.72	1268.65	1031.62	926.42	872.35	842.47	2051.55	1281.97	1046.35	942.38	889.33	860.26
97000	2060.96	1281.86	1042.37	936.07	881.44	851.24	2072.92	1295.33	1057.25	952.19	898.59	869.22
98000	2082.21	1295.08	1053.11	945.72	890.53	860.02	2094.29	1308.68	1068.15	962.01	907.86	878.18
99000	2103.46	1308.29	1063.86	955.37	899.61	868.80	2115.66	1322.04	1079.05	971.83	917.12	887.14
100000	2124.70	1321.51	1074.61	965.02	908.70	877.57	2137.03	1335.39	1089.95	981.64	926.38	896.10

Table 2

	10.50						10.75					
	TERM (YEARS)						TERM (YEARS)					
AMOUNT	5	10	15	20	25	30	5	10	15	20	25	30
10000	214.94	134.93	110.54	99.84	94.42	91.47	216.18	136.34	112.09	101.52	96.21	93.35
11000	236.43	148.43	121.59	109.82	103.86	100.62	237.80	149.97	123.30	111.68	105.83	102.68
12000	257.93	161.92	132.65	119.81	113.30	109.77	259.42	163.61	134.51	121.83	115.45	112.02
13000	279.42	175.42	143.70	129.79	122.74	118.92	281.03	177.24	145.72	131.98	125.07	121.35
14000	300.91	188.91	154.76	139.77	132.19	128.06	302.65	190.87	156.93	142.13	134.69	130.69
15000	322.41	202.40	165.81	149.76	141.63	137.21	324.27	204.51	168.14	152.28	144.31	140.02
16000	343.90	215.90	176.86	159.74	151.07	146.36	345.89	218.14	179.35	162.44	153.93	149.36
17000	365.40	229.39	187.92	169.72	160.51	155.51	367.51	231.78	190.56	172.59	163.56	158.69
18000	386.89	242.88	198.97	179.71	169.95	164.65	389.12	245.41	201.77	182.74	173.18	168.03
19000	408.38	256.38	210.03	189.69	179.39	173.80	410.74	259.04	212.98	192.89	182.80	177.36
20000	429.88	269.87	221.08	199.68	188.84	182.95	432.36	272.68	224.19	203.05	192.42	186.70
21000	451.37	283.36	232.13	209.66	198.28	192.10	453.98	286.31	235.40	213.20	202.04	196.03
22000	472.87	296.86	243.19	219.64	207.72	201.24	475.59	299.95	246.61	223.35	211.66	205.37
23000	494.36	310.35	254.24	229.63	217.16	210.39	497.21	313.58	257.82	233.50	221.28	214.70
24000	515.85	323.84	265.30	239.61	226.60	219.54	518.83	327.21	269.03	243.65	230.90	224.04
25000	537.35	337.34	276.35	249.59	236.05	228.68	540.45	340.85	280.24	253.81	240.52	233.37
26000	558.84	350.83	287.40	259.58	245.49	237.83	562.07	354.48	291.45	263.96	250.14	242.71
27000	580.34	364.32	298.46	269.56	254.93	246.98	583.68	368.11	302.66	274.11	259.77	252.04
28000	601.83	377.82	309.51	279.55	264.37	256.13	605.30	381.75	313.87	284.26	269.39	261.37
29000	623.32	391.31	320.57	289.53	273.81	265.27	626.92	395.38	325.07	294.42	279.01	270.71
30000	644.82	404.80	331.62	299.51	283.25	274.42	648.54	409.02	336.28	304.57	288.63	280.04
31000	666.31	418.30	342.67	309.50	292.70	283.57	670.16	422.65	347.49	314.72	298.25	289.38
32000	687.80	431.79	353.73	319.48	302.14	292.72	691.77	436.28	358.70	324.87	307.87	298.71
33000	709.30	445.29	364.78	329.47	311.58	301.86	713.39	449.92	369.91	335.03	317.49	308.05
34000	730.79	458.78	375.84	339.45	321.02	311.01	735.01	463.55	381.12	345.18	327.11	317.38
35000	752.29	472.27	386.89	349.43	330.46	320.16	756.63	477.19	392.33	355.33	336.73	326.72
36000	773.78	485.77	397.94	359.42	339.91	329.31	778.25	490.82	403.54	365.48	346.35	336.05
37000	795.27	499.26	409.00	369.40	349.35	338.45	799.86	504.45	414.75	375.63	355.97	345.39
38000	816.77	512.75	420.05	379.38	358.79	347.60	821.48	518.09	425.96	385.79	365.60	354.72
39000	838.26	526.25	431.11	389.37	368.23	356.75	843.10	531.72	437.17	395.94	375.22	364.06
40000	859.76	539.74	442.16	399.35	377.67	365.90	864.72	545.35	448.38	406.09	384.84	373.39
41000	881.25	553.23	453.21	409.34	387.11	375.04	886.34	558.99	459.59	416.24	394.46	382.73
42000	902.74	566.73	464.27	419.32	396.56	384.19	907.95	572.62	470.80	426.40	404.08	392.06
43000	924.24	580.22	475.32	429.30	406.00	393.34	929.57	586.26	482.01	436.55	413.70	401.40
44000	945.73	593.71	486.38	439.29	415.44	402.49	951.19	599.89	493.22	446.70	423.32	410.73
45000	967.23	607.21	497.43	449.27	424.88	411.63	972.81	613.52	504.43	456.85	432.94	420.07
46000	988.72	620.70	508.48	459.25	434.32	420.78	994.43	627.16	515.64	467.01	442.56	429.40
47000	1010.21	634.19	519.54	469.24	443.77	429.93	1016.04	640.79	526.85	477.16	452.18	438.74
48000	1031.71	647.69	530.59	479.22	453.21	439.07	1037.66	654.43	538.06	487.31	461.80	448.07
49000	1053.20	661.18	541.65	489.21	462.65	448.22	1059.28	668.06	549.26	497.46	471.43	457.41
50000	1074.70	674.67	552.70	499.19	472.09	457.37	1080.90	681.69	560.47	507.61	481.05	466.74
51000	1096.19	688.17	563.75	509.17	481.53	466.52	1102.52	695.33	571.68	517.77	490.67	476.08
52000	1117.68	701.66	574.81	519.16	490.97	475.66	1124.13	708.96	582.89	527.92	500.29	485.41
53000	1139.18	715.16	585.86	529.14	500.42	484.81	1145.75	722.60	594.10	538.07	509.91	494.75
54000	1160.67	728.65	596.92	539.13	509.86	493.96	1167.37	736.23	605.31	548.22	519.53	504.08
55000	1182.16	742.14	607.97	549.11	519.30	503.11	1188.99	749.86	616.52	558.38	529.15	513.41
56000	1203.66	755.64	619.02	559.09	528.74	512.25	1210.61	763.50	627.73	568.53	538.77	522.75
57000	1225.15	769.13	630.08	569.08	538.18	521.40	1232.22	777.13	638.94	578.68	548.39	532.08
58000	1246.65	782.62	641.13	579.06	547.63	530.55	1253.84	790.76	650.15	588.83	558.01	541.42
59000	1268.14	796.12	652.19	589.04	557.07	539.70	1275.46	804.40	661.36	598.99	567.63	550.75
60000	1289.63	809.61	663.24	599.03	566.51	548.84	1297.08	818.03	672.57	609.14	577.26	560.09
61000	1311.13	823.10	674.29	609.01	575.95	557.99	1318.70	831.67	683.78	619.29	586.88	569.42
62000	1332.62	836.60	685.35	619.00	585.39	567.14	1340.31	845.30	694.99	629.44	596.50	578.76
63000	1354.12	850.09	696.40	628.98	594.83	576.29	1361.93	858.93	706.20	639.59	606.12	588.09
64000	1375.61	863.58	707.46	638.96	604.28	585.43	1383.55	872.57	717.41	649.75	615.74	597.43
65000	1397.10	877.08	718.51	648.95	613.72	594.58	1405.17	886.20	728.62	659.90	625.36	606.76
66000	1418.60	890.57	729.56	658.93	623.16	603.73	1426.78	899.84	739.83	670.05	634.98	616.10
67000	1440.09	904.06	740.62	668.91	632.60	612.88	1448.40	913.47	751.04	680.20	644.60	625.43
68000	1461.59	917.56	751.67	678.90	642.04	622.02	1470.02	927.10	762.24	690.36	654.22	634.77
69000	1483.08	931.05	762.73	688.88	651.49	631.17	1491.64	940.74	773.45	700.51	663.84	644.10
70000	1504.57	944.54	773.78	698.87	660.93	640.32	1513.26	954.37	784.66	710.66	673.46	653.44
71000	1526.07	958.04	784.83	708.85	670.37	649.46	1534.87	968.00	795.87	720.81	683.09	662.77
72000	1547.56	971.53	795.89	718.83	679.81	658.61	1556.49	981.64	807.08	730.96	692.71	672.11
73000	1569.05	985.03	806.94	728.82	689.25	667.76	1578.11	995.27	818.29	741.12	702.33	681.44
74000	1590.55	998.52	818.00	738.80	698.69	676.91	1599.73	1008.91	829.50	751.27	711.95	690.78
75000	1612.04	1012.01	829.05	748.78	708.14	686.05	1621.35	1022.54	840.71	761.42	721.57	700.11
76000	1633.54	1025.51	840.10	758.77	717.58	695.20	1642.96	1036.17	851.92	771.57	731.19	709.45
77000	1655.03	1039.00	851.16	768.75	727.02	704.35	1664.58	1049.81	863.13	781.73	740.81	718.78
78000	1676.52	1052.49	862.21	778.74	736.46	713.50	1686.20	1063.44	874.34	791.88	750.43	728.12
79000	1698.02	1065.99	873.27	788.72	745.90	722.64	1707.82	1077.08	885.55	802.03	760.05	737.45
80000	1719.51	1079.48	884.32	798.70	755.35	731.79	1729.44	1090.71	896.76	812.18	769.67	746.79
81000	1741.01	1092.97	895.37	808.69	764.79	740.94	1751.05	1104.34	907.97	822.34	779.30	756.12
82000	1762.50	1106.47	906.43	818.67	774.23	750.09	1772.67	1117.98	919.18	832.49	788.92	765.45
83000	1783.99	1119.96	917.48	828.65	783.67	759.23	1794.29	1131.61	930.39	842.64	798.54	774.79
84000	1805.49	1133.45	928.54	838.64	793.11	768.38	1815.91	1145.24	941.60	852.79	808.16	784.12
85000	1826.98	1146.95	939.59	848.62	802.55	777.53	1837.53	1158.88	952.81	862.94	817.78	793.46
86000	1848.48	1160.44	950.64	859.61	812.00	786.68	1859.14	1172.51	964.02	873.10	827.40	802.79
87000	1869.97	1173.93	961.70	868.59	821.44	795.82	1880.76	1186.15	975.22	883.25	837.02	812.13
88000	1891.46	1187.43	972.75	878.57	830.88	804.97	1902.38	1199.78	986.43	893.40	846.64	821.46
89000	1912.96	1200.92	983.81	888.56	840.32	814.12	1924.00	1213.41	997.64	903.55	856.26	830.80
90000	1934.45	1214.41	994.86	898.54	849.76	823.27	1945.62	1227.05	1008.85	913.71	865.88	840.13
91000	1955.94	1227.91	1005.91	908.53	859.21	832.41	1967.23	1240.68	1020.06	923.86	875.50	849.47
92000	1977.44	1241.40	1016.97	918.51	868.65	841.56	1988.85	1254.32	1031.27	934.01	885.13	858.80
93000	1998.93	1254.90	1028.02	928.49	878.09	850.71	2010.47	1267.95	1042.48	944.16	894.75	868.14
94000	2020.43	1268.39	1039.07	938.48	887.53	859.85	2032.09	1281.58	1053.69	954.32	904.37	877.47
95000	2041.92	1281.88	1050.13	948.46	896.97	869.00	2053.71	1295.22	1064.90	964.47	913.99	886.81
96000	2063.41	1295.38	1061.18	958.44	906.41	878.15	2075.32	1308.85	1076.11	974.62	923.61	896.14
97000	2084.91	1308.87	1072.24	968.43	915.86	887.30	2096.94	1322.49	1087.32	984.77	933.23	905.48
98000	2106.40	1322.36	1083.29	978.41	925.30	896.44	2118.56	1336.12	1098.53	994.92	942.85	914.81
99000	2127.90	1335.86	1094.34	988.40	934.74	905.59	2140.18	1349.75	1109.74	1005.08	952.47	924.15
100000	2149.39	1349.35	1105.40	998.38	944.18	914.74	2161.80	1363.39	1120.95	1015.23	962.09	933.48

Table 2

11.00

11.25

	TERM (YEARS)						TERM (YEARS)				
AMOUNT	5	10	15	20	25	30	5	10	15	20	25	30
10000	217.42	137.75	113.66	103.22	98.01	95.23	218.67	139.17	115.23	104.93	99.82	97.13
11000	239.17	151.53	125.03	113.54	107.81	104.76	240.54	153.09	126.76	115.42	109.81	106.84
12000	260.91	165.30	136.39	123.86	117.61	114.28	262.41	167.00	138.28	125.91	119.79	116.55
13000	282.65	179.08	147.76	134.18	127.41	123.80	284.28	180.92	149.80	136.40	129.77	126.26
14000	304.39	192.85	159.12	144.51	137.22	133.33	306.14	194.84	161.33	146.90	139.75	135.98
15000	326.14	206.63	170.49	154.83	147.02	142.85	328.01	208.75	172.85	157.39	149.74	145.69
16000	347.88	220.40	181.86	165.15	156.82	152.37	349.88	222.67	184.38	167.88	159.72	155.40
17000	369.62	234.18	193.22	175.47	166.62	161.89	371.74	236.59	195.90	178.37	169.70	165.11
18000	391.36	247.95	204.59	185.79	176.42	171.42	393.61	250.50	207.42	188.87	179.68	174.83
19000	413.11	261.73	215.95	196.12	186.22	180.94	415.48	264.42	218.95	199.36	189.67	184.54
20000	434.85	275.50	227.32	206.44	196.02	190.46	437.35	278.34	230.47	209.85	199.65	194.25
21000	456.59	289.28	238.69	216.76	205.82	199.99	459.21	292.25	241.99	220.34	209.63	203.96
22000	478.33	303.05	250.05	227.08	215.62	209.51	481.08	306.17	253.52	230.84	219.61	213.68
23000	500.08	316.83	261.42	237.40	225.43	219.03	502.95	320.09	265.04	241.33	229.60	223.39
24000	521.82	330.60	272.78	247.73	235.23	228.56	524.82	334.01	276.56	251.82	239.58	233.10
25000	543.56	344.38	284.15	258.05	245.03	238.08	546.68	347.92	288.09	262.31	249.56	242.82
26000	565.30	358.15	295.52	268.37	254.83	247.60	568.55	361.84	299.61	272.81	259.54	252.53
27000	587.05	371.93	306.88	278.69	264.63	257.13	590.42	375.76	311.13	283.30	269.52	262.24
28000	608.79	385.70	318.25	289.01	274.43	266.65	612.28	389.67	322.66	293.79	279.51	271.95
29000	630.53	399.48	329.61	299.33	284.23	276.17	634.15	403.59	334.18	304.28	289.49	281.67
30000	652.27	413.25	340.98	309.66	294.03	285.70	656.02	417.51	345.70	314.78	299.47	291.38
31000	674.02	427.03	352.35	319.98	303.84	295.22	677.89	431.42	357.23	325.27	309.45	301.09
32000	695.76	440.80	363.71	330.30	313.64	304.74	699.75	445.34	368.75	335.76	319.44	310.80
33000	717.50	454.58	375.08	340.62	323.44	314.27	721.62	459.26	380.27	346.25	329.42	320.52
34000	739.24	468.35	386.44	350.94	333.24	323.79	743.49	473.17	391.80	356.75	339.40	330.23
35000	760.98	482.13	397.81	361.27	343.04	333.31	765.36	487.09	403.32	367.24	349.38	339.94
36000	782.73	495.90	409.17	371.59	352.84	342.84	787.22	501.01	414.84	377.73	359.37	349.65
37000	804.47	509.68	420.54	381.91	362.64	352.36	809.09	514.93	426.37	388.22	369.35	359.37
38000	826.21	523.45	431.91	392.23	372.44	361.88	830.96	528.84	437.89	398.72	379.33	369.08
39000	847.95	537.23	443.27	402.55	382.24	371.41	852.83	542.76	449.41	409.21	389.31	378.79
40000	869.70	551.00	454.64	412.88	392.05	380.93	874.69	556.68	460.94	419.70	399.30	388.50
41000	891.44	564.78	466.00	423.20	401.85	390.45	896.56	570.59	472.46	430.19	409.28	398.22
42000	913.18	578.55	477.37	433.52	411.65	399.98	918.43	584.51	483.98	440.69	419.26	407.93
43000	934.92	592.33	488.74	443.84	421.45	409.50	940.29	598.43	495.51	451.18	429.24	417.64
44000	956.67	606.10	500.10	454.16	431.25	419.02	962.16	612.34	507.03	461.67	439.23	427.36
45000	978.41	619.88	511.47	464.48	441.05	428.55	984.03	626.26	518.56	472.17	449.21	437.07
46000	1000.15	633.65	522.83	474.81	450.85	438.07	1005.90	640.18	530.08	482.66	459.19	446.78
47000	1021.89	647.43	534.20	485.13	460.65	447.59	1027.76	654.09	541.60	493.15	469.17	456.49
48000	1043.64	661.20	545.57	495.45	470.45	457.12	1049.63	668.01	553.13	503.64	479.15	466.21
49000	1065.38	674.98	556.93	505.77	480.26	466.64	1071.50	681.93	564.65	514.14	489.14	475.92
50000	1087.12	688.75	568.30	516.09	490.06	476.16	1093.37	695.84	576.17	524.63	499.12	485.63
51000	1108.86	702.53	579.66	526.42	499.86	485.69	1115.23	709.76	587.70	535.12	509.10	495.34
52000	1130.61	716.30	591.03	536.74	509.66	495.21	1137.10	723.68	599.22	545.61	519.08	505.06
53000	1152.35	730.08	602.40	547.06	519.46	504.73	1158.97	737.60	610.74	556.11	529.07	514.77
54000	1174.09	743.85	613.76	557.38	529.26	514.25	1180.83	751.51	622.27	566.60	539.05	524.48
55000	1195.83	757.63	625.13	567.70	539.06	523.78	1202.70	765.43	633.79	577.09	549.05	534.19
56000	1217.58	771.40	636.49	578.03	548.86	533.30	1224.57	779.35	645.31	587.58	559.01	543.91
57000	1239.32	785.18	647.86	588.35	558.66	542.82	1246.44	793.26	656.84	598.08	569.00	553.62
58000	1261.06	798.95	659.23	598.67	568.47	552.35	1268.30	807.18	668.36	608.57	578.98	563.33
59000	1282.80	812.73	670.59	608.99	578.27	561.87	1290.17	821.10	679.88	619.06	588.96	573.04
60000	1304.55	826.50	681.96	619.31	588.07	571.39	1312.04	835.01	691.41	629.55	598.94	582.76
61000	1326.29	840.28	693.32	629.63	597.87	580.92	1333.91	848.93	702.93	640.05	608.93	592.47
62000	1348.03	854.05	704.69	639.96	607.67	590.44	1355.77	862.85	714.45	650.54	618.91	602.18
63000	1369.77	867.83	716.06	650.28	617.47	599.96	1377.64	876.76	725.98	661.03	628.89	611.89
64000	1391.52	881.60	727.42	660.60	627.27	609.49	1399.51	890.68	737.50	671.52	638.87	621.61
65000	1413.26	895.38	738.79	670.92	637.07	619.01	1421.38	904.60	749.02	682.02	648.86	631.32
66000	1435.00	909.15	750.15	681.24	646.87	628.53	1443.24	918.52	760.55	692.51	658.84	641.03
67000	1456.74	922.93	761.52	691.57	656.68	638.06	1465.11	932.43	772.07	703.00	668.82	650.75
68000	1478.48	936.70	772.89	701.89	666.48	647.58	1486.98	946.35	783.59	713.49	678.80	660.46
69000	1500.23	950.48	784.25	712.21	676.28	657.10	1508.84	960.27	795.12	723.99	688.79	670.17
70000	1521.97	964.25	795.62	722.53	686.08	666.63	1530.71	974.18	806.64	734.48	698.77	679.88
71000	1543.71	978.03	806.98	732.85	695.88	676.15	1552.58	988.10	818.16	744.97	708.75	689.60
72000	1565.45	991.80	818.35	743.18	705.68	685.67	1574.45	1002.02	829.69	755.46	718.73	699.31
73000	1587.20	1005.58	829.72	753.50	715.48	695.20	1596.31	1015.93	841.21	765.96	728.71	709.02
74000	1608.94	1019.35	841.08	763.82	725.28	704.72	1618.18	1029.85	852.74	776.45	738.70	718.73
75000	1630.68	1033.13	852.45	774.14	735.08	714.24	1640.05	1043.77	864.26	786.94	748.68	728.45
76000	1652.42	1046.90	863.81	784.46	744.89	723.77	1661.92	1057.68	875.78	797.43	758.66	738.16
77000	1674.17	1060.68	875.18	794.79	754.69	733.29	1683.78	1071.60	887.31	807.93	768.64	747.87
78000	1695.91	1074.45	886.55	805.11	764.49	742.81	1705.65	1085.52	898.83	818.42	778.63	757.58
79000	1717.65	1088.23	897.91	815.43	774.29	752.34	1727.52	1099.43	910.35	828.91	788.61	767.30
80000	1739.39	1102.00	909.28	825.75	784.09	761.86	1749.38	1113.35	921.88	839.40	798.59	777.01
81000	1761.14	1115.78	920.64	836.07	793.89	771.38	1771.25	1127.27	933.40	849.90	808.57	786.72
82000	1782.88	1129.55	932.01	846.39	803.69	780.91	1793.12	1141.19	944.92	860.39	818.56	796.43
83000	1804.62	1143.33	943.38	856.72	813.49	790.43	1814.99	1155.10	956.45	870.88	828.54	806.15
84000	1826.36	1157.10	954.74	867.04	823.29	799.95	1836.85	1169.02	967.97	881.38	838.52	815.86
85000	1848.11	1170.88	966.11	877.36	833.10	809.47	1858.72	1182.94	979.49	891.87	848.50	825.57
86000	1869.85	1184.65	977.47	887.68	842.90	819.00	1880.59	1196.85	991.02	902.36	858.49	835.28
87000	1891.59	1198.43	988.84	898.00	852.70	828.52	1902.46	1210.77	1002.54	912.85	868.47	845.00
88000	1913.33	1212.20	1000.21	908.33	862.50	838.04	1924.32	1224.69	1014.06	923.35	878.45	854.71
89000	1935.08	1225.98	1011.57	918.65	872.30	847.57	1946.19	1238.60	1025.59	933.84	888.43	864.42
90000	1956.82	1239.75	1022.94	928.97	882.10	857.09	1968.06	1252.52	1037.11	944.33	898.42	874.14
91000	1978.56	1253.53	1034.30	939.29	891.90	866.61	1989.93	1266.44	1048.63	954.82	908.40	883.85
92000	2000.30	1267.30	1045.67	949.61	901.70	876.14	2011.79	1280.35	1060.16	965.32	918.38	893.56
93000	2022.05	1281.08	1057.04	959.94	911.51	885.66	2033.66	1294.27	1071.58	975.81	928.36	903.27
94000	2043.79	1294.85	1068.40	970.26	921.31	895.18	2055.53	1308.19	1083.20	986.30	938.35	912.99
95000	2065.53	1308.63	1079.77	980.58	931.11	904.71	2077.39	1322.10	1094.73	996.79	948.33	922.70
96000	2087.27	1322.40	1091.13	990.90	940.91	914.23	2099.26	1336.02	1106.25	1007.29	958.31	932.41
97000	2109.02	1336.18	1102.50	1001.22	950.71	923.75	2121.13	1349.94	1117.77	1017.78	968.29	942.12
98000	2130.76	1349.95	1113.86	1011.54	960.51	933.28	2143.00	1363.86	1129.30	1028.27	978.27	951.84
99000	2152.50	1363.73	1125.23	1021.87	970.31	942.80	2164.86	1377.77	1140.82	1038.76	988.26	961.55
100000	2174.24	1377.50	1136.60	1032.19	980.11	952.32	2186.73	1391.69	1152.34	1049.26	998.24	971.26

Table 2 463

	11.50						11.75					
	TERM (YEARS)						TERM (YEARS)					
AMOUNT	5	10	15	20	25	30	5	10	15	20	25	30
10000	219.93	140.60	116.82	106.64	101.65	99.03	221.18	142.03	118.41	108.37	103.48	100.94
11000	241.92	154.65	128.50	117.31	111.81	108.93	243.30	156.23	130.25	119.21	113.83	111.04
12000	263.91	168.71	140.18	127.97	121.98	118.83	265.42	170.44	142.10	130.04	124.18	121.13
13000	285.90	182.77	151.86	138.64	132.14	128.74	287.54	184.64	153.94	140.88	134.52	131.22
14000	307.90	196.83	163.55	149.30	142.31	138.64	309.66	198.84	165.78	151.72	144.87	141.32
15000	329.89	210.89	175.23	159.96	152.47	148.54	331.77	213.04	177.62	162.56	155.22	151.41
16000	351.88	224.95	186.91	170.63	162.64	158.45	353.89	227.25	189.46	173.39	165.57	161.51
17000	373.87	239.01	198.59	181.29	172.80	168.35	376.01	241.45	201.30	184.23	175.92	171.60
18000	395.87	253.07	210.27	191.96	182.96	178.25	398.13	255.65	213.14	195.07	186.26	181.69
19000	417.86	267.13	221.96	202.62	193.13	188.16	420.25	269.86	224.98	205.90	196.61	191.79
20000	439.85	281.19	233.64	213.29	203.29	198.06	442.37	284.06	236.83	216.74	206.96	201.88
21000	461.84	295.25	245.32	223.95	213.46	207.96	464.48	298.26	248.67	227.58	217.31	211.98
22000	483.84	309.31	257.00	234.61	223.62	217.86	486.60	312.46	260.51	238.42	227.66	222.07
23000	505.83	323.37	268.68	245.28	233.79	227.77	508.72	326.67	272.35	249.25	238.00	232.16
24000	527.82	337.43	280.37	255.94	243.95	237.67	530.84	340.87	284.19	260.09	248.35	242.26
25000	549.82	351.49	292.05	266.61	254.12	247.57	575.08	355.07	296.03	270.93	258.70	252.35
26000	571.81	365.55	303.73	277.27	264.28	257.48	597.19	383.48	319.72	292.60	279.40	272.54
27000	593.80	379.61	315.41	287.94	274.45	267.38	619.31	397.68	331.56	303.44	289.74	282.63
28000	615.79	393.67	327.09	298.60	284.61	277.28	641.43	411.89	343.40	314.28	300.09	292.73
29000	637.79	407.73	338.78	309.26	294.78	287.18	663.55	426.09	355.24	325.11	310.44	302.82
30000	659.78	421.79	350.46	319.93	304.94	297.09	685.67	440.29	367.08	335.95	320.79	312.92
31000	681.77	435.85	362.14	330.59	315.11	306.99	707.79	454.49	378.92	346.79	331.14	323.01
32000	703.76	449.91	373.82	341.26	325.27	316.89	729.90	468.70	390.76	357.62	341.48	333.11
33000	725.76	463.96	385.50	351.92	335.43	326.80	752.02	482.90	402.60	368.46	351.83	343.20
34000	747.75	478.02	397.18	362.59	345.60	336.70	774.14	497.10	414.45	379.30	362.18	353.29
35000	769.74	492.08	408.87	373.25	355.76	346.60	796.26	511.31	426.29	390.13	372.53	363.39
36000	791.73	506.14	420.55	383.91	365.93	356.50	818.38	525.51	438.13	400.97	382.88	373.48
37000	813.73	520.20	432.23	394.58	376.09	366.41	840.50	539.71	449.97	411.81	393.22	383.58
38000	835.72	534.26	443.91	405.24	386.26	376.31	862.61	553.91	461.81	422.65	403.57	393.67
39000	857.71	548.32	455.59	415.91	396.42	386.21	884.73	568.12	473.65	433.48	413.92	403.76
40000	879.70	562.38	467.28	426.57	406.59	396.12	906.85	582.32	485.49	444.32	424.27	413.86
41000	901.70	576.44	478.96	437.24	416.75	406.02	928.97	596.52	497.34	455.16	434.62	423.95
42000	923.69	590.50	490.64	447.90	426.92	415.92	951.09	610.73	509.18	465.99	444.96	434.05
43000	945.68	604.56	502.32	458.56	437.08	425.83	973.21	624.93	521.02	476.83	455.31	444.14
44000	967.67	618.62	514.00	469.23	447.25	435.73	995.32	639.13	532.86	487.67	465.66	454.23
45000	989.67	632.68	525.69	479.89	457.41	445.63	1017.44	653.34	544.70	498.51	476.01	464.33
46000	1011.66	646.74	537.37	490.56	467.58	455.53	1039.56	667.54	556.54	509.34	486.36	474.42
47000	1033.65	660.80	549.05	501.22	477.74	465.44	1061.68	681.74	568.38	520.18	496.70	484.52
48000	1055.65	674.86	560.73	511.89	487.91	475.34	1083.80	695.94	580.22	531.02	507.05	494.61
49000	1077.64	688.92	572.41	522.55	498.07	485.24	1105.92	710.15	592.07	541.85	517.40	504.70
50000	1099.63	702.98	584.09	533.21	508.23	495.15	1128.03	724.35	603.91	552.69	527.75	514.80
51000	1121.62	717.04	595.78	543.88	518.40	505.05	1150.15	738.55	615.75	563.53	538.10	524.89
52000	1143.62	731.10	607.46	554.54	528.56	514.95	1172.27	752.76	627.59	574.36	548.44	534.99
53000	1165.61	745.16	619.14	565.21	538.73	524.85	1194.39	766.96	639.43	585.20	558.79	545.08
54000	1187.60	759.22	630.82	575.87	548.89	534.76	1216.51	781.16	651.27	596.04	569.14	555.18
55000	1209.59	773.27	642.50	586.54	559.06	544.66	1238.63	795.36	663.11	606.88	579.49	565.27
56000	1231.59	787.33	654.19	597.20	569.22	554.56	1260.74	809.57	674.95	617.71	589.83	575.36
57000	1253.58	801.39	665.87	607.86	579.39	564.47	1282.86	823.77	686.80	628.55	600.18	585.46
58000	1275.57	815.45	677.55	618.53	589.55	574.37	1304.98	837.97	698.64	639.39	610.53	595.55
59000	1297.56	829.51	689.23	629.19	599.72	584.27	1327.10	852.18	710.48	650.22	620.88	605.65
60000	1319.56	843.57	700.91	639.86	609.88	594.17	1349.22	866.38	722.32	661.06	631.23	615.74
61000	1341.55	857.63	712.60	650.52	620.05	604.08	1371.34	880.58	734.16	671.90	641.57	625.83
62000	1363.54	871.69	724.28	661.19	630.21	613.98	1393.45	894.79	746.00	682.74	651.92	635.93
63000	1385.53	885.75	735.96	671.85	640.38	623.88	1415.57	908.99	757.84	693.57	662.27	646.02
64000	1407.53	899.81	747.64	682.51	650.54	633.79	1437.69	923.19	769.69	704.41	672.62	656.12
65000	1429.52	913.87	759.32	693.18	660.70	643.69	1459.81	937.39	781.53	715.25	682.97	666.21
66000	1451.51	927.93	771.01	703.84	670.87	653.59	1481.93	951.60	793.37	726.08	693.31	676.30
67000	1473.50	941.99	782.69	714.51	681.03	663.50	1504.05	965.80	805.21	736.92	703.66	686.40
68000	1495.50	956.05	794.37	725.17	691.20	673.40	1526.16	980.00	817.05	747.76	714.01	696.49
69000	1517.49	970.11	806.05	735.84	701.36	683.30	1548.28	994.21	828.89	758.59	724.36	706.59
70000	1539.48	984.17	817.73	746.50	711.53	693.20	1570.40	1008.41	840.73	769.43	734.71	716.68
71000	1561.48	998.23	829.41	757.17	721.69	703.11	1592.52	1022.61	852.57	780.27	745.05	726.78
72000	1583.47	1012.29	841.10	767.83	731.86	713.01	1614.64	1036.82	864.42	791.11	755.40	736.87
73000	1605.46	1026.35	852.78	778.49	742.02	722.91	1636.76	1051.02	876.26	801.94	765.75	746.96
74000	1627.45	1040.41	864.46	789.16	752.19	732.82	1658.87	1065.22	888.10	812.78	776.10	757.06
75000	1649.45	1054.47	876.14	799.82	762.35	742.72	1680.99	1079.42	899.94	823.62	786.45	767.15
76000	1671.44	1068.53	887.82	810.49	772.52	752.62	1703.11	1093.63	911.78	834.45	796.79	777.25
77000	1693.43	1082.58	899.51	821.15	782.68	762.52	1725.23	1107.83	923.62	845.29	807.14	787.34
78000	1715.42	1096.64	911.19	831.82	792.85	772.43	1747.35	1122.03	935.46	856.13	817.49	797.43
79000	1737.42	1110.70	922.87	842.48	803.01	782.33	1769.47	1136.24	947.31	866.97	827.84	807.53
80000	1759.41	1124.76	934.55	853.14	813.18	792.23	1791.58	1150.44	959.15	877.80	838.19	817.62
81000	1781.40	1138.82	946.23	863.81	823.34	802.14	1813.70	1164.64	970.99	888.64	848.53	827.72
82000	1803.39	1152.88	957.92	874.47	833.50	812.04	1835.82	1178.84	982.83	899.48	858.88	837.81
83000	1825.39	1166.94	969.60	885.14	843.67	821.94	1857.94	1193.05	994.67	910.31	869.23	847.90
84000	1847.38	1181.00	981.28	895.80	853.84	831.84	1880.06	1207.25	1006.51	921.15	879.58	858.00
85000	1869.37	1195.06	992.96	906.47	864.00	841.75	1902.18	1221.45	1018.35	931.99	889.93	868.09
86000	1891.36	1209.12	1004.64	917.13	874.17	851.65	1924.29	1235.66	1030.19	942.83	900.27	878.19
87000	1913.36	1223.18	1016.33	927.79	884.33	861.55	1946.41	1249.86	1042.04	953.66	910.62	888.28
88000	1935.35	1237.24	1028.01	938.46	894.49	871.46	1968.53	1264.06	1053.88	964.50	920.97	898.37
89000	1957.34	1251.30	1039.69	949.12	904.66	881.36	1990.65	1278.27	1065.72	975.34	931.32	908.47
90000	1979.33	1265.36	1051.37	959.79	914.82	891.26	2012.77	1292.47	1077.56	986.17	941.67	918.56
91000	2001.33	1279.42	1063.05	970.45	924.99	901.17	2034.89	1306.67	1089.40	997.01	952.01	928.66
92000	2023.32	1293.48	1074.73	981.12	935.15	911.07	2057.00	1320.87	1101.24	1007.85	962.36	938.75
93000	2045.31	1307.54	1086.42	991.78	945.32	920.97	2079.12	1335.08	1113.08	1018.68	972.71	948.85
94000	2067.31	1321.60	1098.10	1002.44	955.48	930.87	2101.24	1349.28	1124.92	1029.52	983.06	958.94
95000	2089.30	1335.66	1109.78	1013.11	965.65	940.78	2123.36	1363.48	1136.77	1040.36	993.41	969.03
96000	2111.29	1349.72	1121.46	1023.77	975.81	950.68	2145.48	1377.69	1148.61	1051.20	1003.75	979.13
97000	2133.28	1363.78	1133.14	1034.44	985.97	960.53	2167.60	1391.89	1160.45	1062.03	1014.10	989.22
98000	2155.28	1377.84	1144.83	1045.10	996.14	970.49	2189.71	1406.09	1172.29	1072.87	1024.45	999.32
99000	2177.27	1391.89	1156.51	1055.77	1006.30	980.39	2211.83	1420.29	1184.13	1083.71	1034.80	1009.41
100000	2199.26	1405.95	1168.19	1066.43	1016.47	990.29	2211.83	1420.29	1184.13	1083.71	1034.80	1009.41

Table 2

12.00

12.25

AMOUNT	TERM (YEARS) 5	10	15	20	25	30	5	10	15	20	25	30
10000	222.44	143.47	120.02	110.11	105.32	102.86	223.71	144.92	121.63	111.86	107.17	104.79
11000	244.69	157.82	132.02	121.12	115.85	113.15	246.08	159.41	133.79	123.04	117.89	115.27
12000	266.93	172.17	144.02	132.13	126.39	123.43	268.45	173.90	145.96	134.23	128.61	125.75
13000	289.18	186.51	156.02	143.14	136.92	133.72	290.82	188.40	158.12	145.41	139.33	136.23
14000	311.42	200.86	168.02	154.15	147.45	144.01	313.19	202.89	170.28	156.60	150.04	146.71
15000	333.67	215.21	180.03	165.16	157.98	154.29	335.56	217.38	182.44	167.78	160.76	157.18
16000	355.91	229.55	192.03	176.17	168.52	164.58	357.94	231.87	194.61	178.97	171.48	167.66
17000	378.16	243.90	204.03	187.18	179.05	174.86	380.31	246.36	206.77	190.16	182.20	178.14
18000	400.40	258.25	216.03	198.20	189.58	185.15	402.68	260.86	216.93	201.34	192.91	188.62
19000	422.64	272.59	228.03	209.21	200.11	195.44	425.05	275.35	231.10	212.53	203.63	199.10
20000	444.89	286.94	240.03	220.22	210.64	205.72	447.42	289.84	243.26	223.71	214.35	209.58
21000	467.13	301.29	252.04	231.23	221.18	216.01	469.79	304.33	255.42	234.90	225.07	220.06
22000	489.38	315.64	264.04	242.24	231.71	226.29	492.16	318.82	267.59	246.08	235.78	230.54
23000	511.62	329.98	276.04	253.25	242.24	236.58	514.53	333.32	279.75	257.27	246.50	241.02
24000	533.87	344.33	288.04	264.26	252.77	246.87	536.90	347.81	291.91	268.46	257.22	251.50
25000	556.11	358.68	300.04	275.27	263.31	257.15	559.27	362.30	304.07	279.64	267.94	261.97
26000	578.36	373.02	312.04	286.28	273.84	267.44	581.65	376.79	316.24	290.83	278.65	272.45
27000	600.60	387.37	324.05	297.29	284.37	277.73	604.02	391.28	328.40	302.01	289.37	282.93
28000	622.84	401.72	336.05	308.30	294.90	288.01	626.39	405.78	340.56	313.20	300.09	293.41
29000	645.09	416.07	348.05	319.31	305.44	298.30	648.76	420.27	352.73	324.38	310.81	303.89
30000	667.33	430.41	360.05	330.33	315.97	308.58	671.13	434.76	364.89	335.57	321.52	314.37
31000	689.58	444.76	372.05	341.34	326.50	318.87	693.50	449.25	377.05	346.76	332.24	324.85
32000	711.82	459.11	384.05	352.35	337.03	329.16	715.87	463.74	389.22	357.94	342.96	335.33
33000	734.07	473.45	396.06	363.36	347.56	339.44	738.24	478.24	401.38	369.13	353.68	345.81
34000	756.31	487.80	408.06	374.37	358.10	349.73	760.61	492.73	413.54	380.31	364.39	356.28
35000	778.56	502.15	420.06	385.38	368.63	360.01	782.98	507.22	425.70	391.50	375.11	366.76
36000	800.80	516.50	432.06	396.39	379.16	370.30	805.36	521.71	437.87	402.68	385.83	377.24
37000	823.04	530.84	444.06	407.40	389.69	380.59	827.73	536.20	450.03	413.87	396.55	387.72
38000	845.29	545.19	456.06	418.41	400.23	390.87	850.10	550.70	462.19	425.05	407.26	398.20
39000	867.53	559.54	468.07	429.42	410.76	401.16	872.47	565.19	474.36	436.24	417.98	408.68
40000	889.78	573.88	480.07	440.43	421.29	411.45	894.84	579.68	486.52	447.43	428.70	419.16
41000	912.02	588.23	492.07	451.45	431.82	421.73	917.21	594.17	498.68	458.61	439.41	429.64
42000	934.27	602.58	504.07	462.46	442.35	432.02	939.58	608.66	510.85	469.80	450.13	440.12
43000	956.51	616.93	516.07	473.47	452.89	442.30	961.95	623.16	523.01	480.98	460.85	450.60
44000	978.76	631.27	528.07	484.48	463.42	452.59	984.32	637.65	535.17	492.17	471.57	461.07
45000	1001.00	645.62	540.08	495.49	473.95	462.88	1006.69	652.14	547.33	503.35	482.28	471.55
46000	1023.24	659.97	552.08	506.50	484.48	473.16	1029.07	666.63	559.50	514.54	493.00	482.03
47000	1045.49	674.31	564.08	517.51	495.02	483.45	1051.44	681.12	571.66	525.73	503.72	492.51
48000	1067.73	688.66	576.08	528.52	505.55	493.73	1073.81	695.62	583.82	536.91	514.44	502.99
49000	1089.98	703.01	588.08	539.53	516.08	504.02	1096.18	710.11	595.99	548.10	525.15	513.47
50000	1112.22	717.35	600.08	550.54	526.61	514.31	1118.55	724.60	608.15	559.20	535.87	523.95
51000	1134.47	731.70	612.09	561.55	537.14	524.59	1140.92	739.09	620.31	570.47	546.59	534.43
52000	1156.71	746.05	624.09	572.56	547.68	534.88	1163.29	753.58	632.48	581.65	557.31	544.91
53000	1178.96	760.40	636.09	583.58	558.21	545.16	1185.66	768.08	644.64	592.84	568.02	555.39
54000	1201.20	774.74	648.09	594.59	568.74	555.45	1208.03	782.57	656.80	604.02	578.74	565.86
55000	1223.44	789.09	660.09	605.60	579.27	565.74	1230.40	797.06	668.96	615.21	589.46	576.34
56000	1245.69	803.44	672.09	616.61	589.81	576.02	1252.78	811.55	681.13	626.40	600.18	586.82
57000	1267.93	817.78	684.10	627.62	600.34	586.31	1275.15	826.04	693.29	637.58	610.89	597.30
58000	1290.18	832.13	696.10	638.63	610.87	596.60	1297.52	840.54	705.45	648.77	621.61	607.78
59000	1312.42	846.48	708.10	649.64	621.40	606.88	1319.89	855.03	717.62	659.95	632.33	618.26
60000	1334.67	860.83	720.10	660.65	631.93	617.17	1342.26	869.52	729.78	671.14	643.05	628.74
61000	1356.91	875.17	732.10	671.66	642.47	627.45	1364.63	884.01	741.94	682.32	653.76	639.22
62000	1379.16	889.52	744.10	682.67	653.00	637.74	1387.00	898.50	754.11	693.51	664.48	649.70
63000	1401.40	903.87	756.11	693.68	663.53	648.03	1409.37	913.00	766.27	704.70	675.20	660.17
64000	1423.64	918.21	768.11	704.70	674.06	658.31	1431.74	927.49	778.43	715.88	685.92	670.65
65000	1445.89	932.56	780.11	715.71	684.60	668.60	1454.11	941.98	790.59	727.07	696.63	681.13
66000	1468.13	946.91	792.11	726.72	695.13	678.88	1476.49	956.47	802.76	738.25	707.35	691.61
67000	1490.38	961.26	804.11	737.73	705.66	689.17	1498.86	970.96	814.92	749.44	718.07	702.09
68000	1512.62	975.60	816.11	748.74	716.19	699.46	1521.23	985.46	827.08	760.62	728.79	712.57
69000	1534.87	989.95	828.12	759.75	726.72	709.74	1543.60	999.95	839.25	771.81	739.50	723.05
70000	1557.11	1004.30	840.12	770.76	737.26	720.03	1565.97	1014.44	851.41	783.00	750.22	733.53
71000	1579.36	1018.64	852.12	781.77	747.79	730.31	1588.34	1028.93	863.57	794.18	760.94	744.01
72000	1601.60	1032.99	864.12	792.78	758.32	740.60	1610.71	1043.42	875.74	805.37	771.66	754.49
73000	1623.84	1047.34	876.12	803.79	768.85	750.89	1633.08	1057.92	887.90	816.55	782.37	764.96
74000	1646.09	1061.69	888.12	814.80	779.39	761.17	1655.45	1072.41	900.06	827.74	793.09	775.44
75000	1668.33	1076.03	900.13	825.81	789.92	771.46	1677.82	1086.90	912.22	838.92	803.81	785.92
76000	1690.58	1090.38	912.13	836.83	800.45	781.75	1700.20	1101.39	924.39	850.11	814.53	796.40
77000	1712.82	1104.73	924.13	847.84	810.98	792.03	1722.57	1115.88	936.55	861.29	825.24	806.88
78000	1735.07	1119.07	936.13	858.85	821.51	802.32	1744.94	1130.37	948.71	872.48	835.96	817.36
79000	1757.31	1133.42	948.13	869.86	832.05	812.60	1767.31	1144.87	960.88	883.67	846.68	827.84
80000	1779.56	1147.77	960.13	880.87	842.58	822.89	1789.68	1159.36	973.04	894.85	857.40	838.32
81000	1801.80	1162.11	972.14	891.88	853.11	833.18	1812.05	1173.85	985.20	906.04	868.11	848.80
82000	1824.04	1176.46	984.14	902.89	863.64	843.46	1834.42	1188.34	997.36	917.22	878.83	859.28
83000	1846.29	1190.81	996.14	913.90	874.18	853.75	1856.79	1202.83	1009.53	928.41	889.55	869.75
84000	1868.53	1205.16	1008.14	924.91	884.71	864.03	1879.16	1217.33	1021.69	939.59	900.26	880.23
85000	1890.78	1219.50	1020.14	935.92	895.24	874.32	1901.53	1231.82	1033.85	950.78	910.98	890.71
86000	1913.02	1233.85	1032.14	946.93	905.77	884.61	1923.90	1246.31	1046.02	961.97	921.70	901.19
87000	1935.27	1248.20	1044.15	957.94	916.31	894.89	1946.28	1260.80	1058.18	973.15	932.42	911.67
88000	1957.51	1262.54	1056.15	968.96	926.84	905.18	1968.65	1275.29	1070.34	984.34	943.13	922.15
89000	1979.76	1276.89	1068.15	979.97	937.37	915.47	1991.02	1289.79	1082.51	995.52	953.85	932.63
90000	2002.00	1291.24	1080.15	990.98	947.90	925.75	2013.39	1304.28	1094.67	1006.71	964.57	943.11
91000	2024.24	1305.59	1092.15	1001.99	958.43	936.04	2035.76	1318.77	1106.83	1017.89	975.29	953.59
92000	2046.49	1319.93	1104.15	1013.00	968.97	946.32	2058.13	1333.26	1118.99	1029.08	986.00	964.06
93000	2068.73	1334.28	1116.16	1024.01	979.50	956.61	2080.50	1347.75	1131.16	1040.27	996.72	974.54
94000	2090.98	1348.63	1128.16	1035.02	990.03	966.90	2102.87	1362.25	1143.32	1051.45	1007.44	985.02
95000	2113.22	1362.97	1140.16	1046.03	1000.56	977.18	2125.24	1376.74	1155.48	1062.64	1018.16	995.50
96000	2135.47	1377.32	1152.16	1057.04	1011.10	987.47	2147.61	1391.23	1167.65	1073.82	1028.87	1005.98
97000	2157.71	1391.67	1164.16	1068.05	1021.63	997.75	2169.99	1405.72	1179.81	1085.01	1039.59	1016.46
98000	2179.96	1406.02	1176.16	1079.06	1032.16	1008.04	2192.3	1420.21	1191.97	1096.19	1050.31	1026.94
99000	2202.20	1420.36	1188.17	1090.08	1042.69	1018.33	2214.73	1434.71	1204.14	1107.38	1061.03	1037.42
100000	2224.44	1434.71	1200.17	1101.09	1053.22	1028.61	2237.10	1449.20	1216.30	1118.56	1071.74	1047.90

<table>
<tr><td></td><td colspan="6">12.50</td><td colspan="6">12.75</td></tr>
<tr><td></td><td colspan="6">TERM (YEARS)</td><td colspan="6">TERM (YEARS)</td></tr>
<tr><td>AMOUNT</td><td>5</td><td>10</td><td>15</td><td>20</td><td>25</td><td>30</td><td>5</td><td>10</td><td>15</td><td>20</td><td>25</td><td>30</td></tr>
<tr><td>10000</td><td>224.98</td><td>146.38</td><td>123.25</td><td>113.61</td><td>109.04</td><td>106.73</td><td>226.25</td><td>147.84</td><td>124.88</td><td>115.38</td><td>110.91</td><td>108.67</td></tr>
<tr><td>11000</td><td>247.48</td><td>161.01</td><td>135.58</td><td>124.98</td><td>119.94</td><td>117.40</td><td>248.88</td><td>162.62</td><td>137.37</td><td>126.92</td><td>122.00</td><td>119.54</td></tr>
<tr><td>12000</td><td>269.98</td><td>175.65</td><td>147.90</td><td>136.34</td><td>130.84</td><td>128.07</td><td>271.50</td><td>177.41</td><td>149.86</td><td>138.46</td><td>133.09</td><td>130.40</td></tr>
<tr><td>13000</td><td>292.47</td><td>190.29</td><td>160.23</td><td>147.70</td><td>141.75</td><td>138.74</td><td>294.13</td><td>192.19</td><td>162.35</td><td>150.00</td><td>144.18</td><td>141.27</td></tr>
<tr><td>14000</td><td>314.97</td><td>204.93</td><td>172.55</td><td>159.06</td><td>152.65</td><td>149.42</td><td>316.75</td><td>206.98</td><td>174.84</td><td>161.53</td><td>155.27</td><td>152.14</td></tr>
<tr><td>15000</td><td>337.47</td><td>219.56</td><td>184.88</td><td>170.42</td><td>163.55</td><td>160.09</td><td>339.38</td><td>221.76</td><td>187.33</td><td>173.07</td><td>166.36</td><td>163.00</td></tr>
<tr><td>16000</td><td>359.97</td><td>234.20</td><td>197.20</td><td>181.78</td><td>174.46</td><td>170.76</td><td>362.00</td><td>236.54</td><td>199.81</td><td>184.61</td><td>177.45</td><td>173.87</td></tr>
<tr><td>17000</td><td>382.46</td><td>248.84</td><td>209.53</td><td>193.14</td><td>185.36</td><td>181.43</td><td>384.63</td><td>251.33</td><td>212.30</td><td>196.15</td><td>188.54</td><td>184.74</td></tr>
<tr><td>18000</td><td>404.96</td><td>263.48</td><td>221.85</td><td>204.51</td><td>196.26</td><td>192.11</td><td>407.26</td><td>266.11</td><td>224.79</td><td>207.69</td><td>199.63</td><td>195.60</td></tr>
<tr><td>19000</td><td>427.46</td><td>278.11</td><td>234.18</td><td>215.87</td><td>207.17</td><td>202.78</td><td>429.88</td><td>280.90</td><td>237.28</td><td>219.22</td><td>210.72</td><td>206.47</td></tr>
<tr><td>20000</td><td>449.96</td><td>292.75</td><td>246.50</td><td>227.23</td><td>218.07</td><td>213.45</td><td>452.51</td><td>295.68</td><td>249.77</td><td>230.76</td><td>221.81</td><td>217.34</td></tr>
<tr><td>21000</td><td>472.46</td><td>307.39</td><td>258.83</td><td>238.59</td><td>228.97</td><td>224.12</td><td>475.13</td><td>310.46</td><td>262.26</td><td>242.30</td><td>232.90</td><td>228.21</td></tr>
<tr><td>22000</td><td>494.95</td><td>322.03</td><td>271.15</td><td>249.95</td><td>239.88</td><td>234.80</td><td>497.76</td><td>325.25</td><td>274.74</td><td>253.84</td><td>243.99</td><td>239.07</td></tr>
<tr><td>23000</td><td>517.45</td><td>336.67</td><td>283.48</td><td>261.31</td><td>250.78</td><td>245.47</td><td>520.38</td><td>340.03</td><td>287.23</td><td>265.38</td><td>255.08</td><td>249.94</td></tr>
<tr><td>24000</td><td>539.95</td><td>351.30</td><td>295.81</td><td>272.67</td><td>261.68</td><td>256.14</td><td>543.01</td><td>354.82</td><td>299.72</td><td>276.91</td><td>266.17</td><td>260.81</td></tr>
<tr><td>25000</td><td>562.45</td><td>365.94</td><td>308.13</td><td>284.04</td><td>272.59</td><td>266.81</td><td>565.63</td><td>369.60</td><td>312.21</td><td>288.45</td><td>277.26</td><td>271.67</td></tr>
<tr><td>26000</td><td>584.95</td><td>380.58</td><td>320.46</td><td>295.40</td><td>283.49</td><td>277.49</td><td>588.26</td><td>384.38</td><td>324.70</td><td>299.99</td><td>288.35</td><td>282.54</td></tr>
<tr><td>27000</td><td>607.44</td><td>395.22</td><td>332.78</td><td>306.76</td><td>294.40</td><td>288.16</td><td>610.88</td><td>399.17</td><td>337.19</td><td>311.53</td><td>299.44</td><td>293.41</td></tr>
<tr><td>28000</td><td>629.94</td><td>409.85</td><td>345.11</td><td>318.12</td><td>305.30</td><td>298.83</td><td>633.51</td><td>413.95</td><td>349.67</td><td>323.07</td><td>310.53</td><td>304.27</td></tr>
<tr><td>29000</td><td>652.44</td><td>424.49</td><td>357.43</td><td>329.48</td><td>316.20</td><td>309.50</td><td>656.13</td><td>428.74</td><td>362.16</td><td>334.61</td><td>321.63</td><td>315.14</td></tr>
<tr><td>30000</td><td>674.94</td><td>439.13</td><td>369.76</td><td>340.84</td><td>327.11</td><td>320.18</td><td>678.76</td><td>443.52</td><td>374.65</td><td>346.14</td><td>332.72</td><td>326.01</td></tr>
<tr><td>31000</td><td>697.44</td><td>453.77</td><td>382.08</td><td>352.20</td><td>338.01</td><td>330.85</td><td>701.38</td><td>458.30</td><td>387.14</td><td>357.68</td><td>343.81</td><td>336.87</td></tr>
<tr><td>32000</td><td>719.93</td><td>468.40</td><td>394.41</td><td>363.56</td><td>348.91</td><td>341.52</td><td>724.01</td><td>473.09</td><td>399.63</td><td>369.22</td><td>354.90</td><td>347.74</td></tr>
<tr><td>33000</td><td>742.43</td><td>483.04</td><td>406.73</td><td>374.93</td><td>359.82</td><td>352.20</td><td>746.63</td><td>487.87</td><td>412.12</td><td>380.76</td><td>365.99</td><td>358.61</td></tr>
<tr><td>34000</td><td>764.93</td><td>497.68</td><td>419.06</td><td>386.29</td><td>370.72</td><td>362.87</td><td>769.26</td><td>502.66</td><td>424.60</td><td>392.30</td><td>377.08</td><td>369.48</td></tr>
<tr><td>35000</td><td>787.43</td><td>512.32</td><td>431.38</td><td>397.65</td><td>381.62</td><td>373.54</td><td>791.89</td><td>517.44</td><td>437.09</td><td>403.83</td><td>388.17</td><td>380.34</td></tr>
<tr><td>36000</td><td>809.93</td><td>526.95</td><td>443.71</td><td>409.01</td><td>392.53</td><td>384.21</td><td>814.51</td><td>532.22</td><td>449.58</td><td>415.37</td><td>399.26</td><td>391.21</td></tr>
<tr><td>37000</td><td>832.42</td><td>541.59</td><td>456.03</td><td>420.37</td><td>403.43</td><td>394.89</td><td>837.14</td><td>547.01</td><td>462.07</td><td>426.91</td><td>410.35</td><td>402.08</td></tr>
<tr><td>38000</td><td>854.92</td><td>556.23</td><td>468.36</td><td>431.73</td><td>414.33</td><td>405.56</td><td>859.76</td><td>561.79</td><td>474.56</td><td>438.45</td><td>421.44</td><td>412.94</td></tr>
<tr><td>39000</td><td>877.42</td><td>570.87</td><td>480.68</td><td>443.09</td><td>425.24</td><td>416.23</td><td>882.39</td><td>576.58</td><td>487.05</td><td>449.99</td><td>432.53</td><td>423.81</td></tr>
<tr><td>40000</td><td>899.92</td><td>585.50</td><td>493.01</td><td>454.46</td><td>436.14</td><td>426.90</td><td>905.01</td><td>591.36</td><td>499.53</td><td>461.52</td><td>443.62</td><td>434.68</td></tr>
<tr><td>41000</td><td>922.42</td><td>600.14</td><td>505.33</td><td>465.82</td><td>447.05</td><td>437.58</td><td>927.64</td><td>606.14</td><td>512.02</td><td>473.06</td><td>454.71</td><td>445.54</td></tr>
<tr><td>42000</td><td>944.91</td><td>614.78</td><td>517.66</td><td>477.18</td><td>457.95</td><td>448.25</td><td>950.26</td><td>620.93</td><td>524.51</td><td>484.60</td><td>465.80</td><td>456.41</td></tr>
<tr><td>43000</td><td>967.41</td><td>629.42</td><td>529.98</td><td>488.54</td><td>468.85</td><td>458.92</td><td>972.89</td><td>635.71</td><td>537.00</td><td>496.14</td><td>476.89</td><td>467.28</td></tr>
<tr><td>44000</td><td>989.91</td><td>644.06</td><td>542.31</td><td>499.90</td><td>479.76</td><td>469.59</td><td>995.51</td><td>650.50</td><td>549.49</td><td>507.68</td><td>487.98</td><td>478.15</td></tr>
<tr><td>45000</td><td>1012.41</td><td>658.69</td><td>554.63</td><td>511.26</td><td>490.66</td><td>480.27</td><td>1018.14</td><td>665.28</td><td>561.98</td><td>519.22</td><td>499.07</td><td>489.01</td></tr>
<tr><td>46000</td><td>1034.91</td><td>673.33</td><td>566.96</td><td>522.62</td><td>501.56</td><td>490.94</td><td>1040.76</td><td>680.06</td><td>574.47</td><td>530.75</td><td>510.16</td><td>499.88</td></tr>
<tr><td>47000</td><td>1057.40</td><td>687.97</td><td>579.29</td><td>533.99</td><td>512.47</td><td>501.61</td><td>1063.39</td><td>694.85</td><td>586.95</td><td>542.29</td><td>521.25</td><td>510.75</td></tr>
<tr><td>48000</td><td>1079.90</td><td>702.61</td><td>591.61</td><td>545.35</td><td>523.37</td><td>512.28</td><td>1086.01</td><td>709.63</td><td>599.44</td><td>553.83</td><td>532.35</td><td>521.61</td></tr>
<tr><td>49000</td><td>1102.40</td><td>717.24</td><td>603.94</td><td>556.71</td><td>534.27</td><td>522.96</td><td>1108.64</td><td>724.42</td><td>611.93</td><td>565.37</td><td>543.44</td><td>532.48</td></tr>
<tr><td>50000</td><td>1124.90</td><td>731.88</td><td>616.26</td><td>568.07</td><td>545.18</td><td>533.63</td><td>1131.27</td><td>739.20</td><td>624.42</td><td>576.91</td><td>554.53</td><td>543.35</td></tr>
<tr><td>51000</td><td>1147.39</td><td>746.52</td><td>628.59</td><td>579.43</td><td>556.08</td><td>544.30</td><td>1153.89</td><td>753.98</td><td>636.91</td><td>588.44</td><td>565.62</td><td>554.21</td></tr>
<tr><td>52000</td><td>1169.89</td><td>761.16</td><td>640.91</td><td>590.79</td><td>566.98</td><td>554.97</td><td>1176.52</td><td>768.77</td><td>649.40</td><td>599.98</td><td>576.71</td><td>565.08</td></tr>
<tr><td>53000</td><td>1192.39</td><td>775.79</td><td>653.24</td><td>602.15</td><td>577.89</td><td>565.65</td><td>1199.14</td><td>783.55</td><td>661.88</td><td>611.52</td><td>587.80</td><td>575.95</td></tr>
<tr><td>54000</td><td>1214.89</td><td>790.43</td><td>665.56</td><td>613.52</td><td>588.79</td><td>576.32</td><td>1221.77</td><td>798.33</td><td>674.37</td><td>623.06</td><td>598.89</td><td>586.81</td></tr>
<tr><td>55000</td><td>1237.39</td><td>805.07</td><td>677.89</td><td>624.88</td><td>599.69</td><td>586.99</td><td>1244.39</td><td>813.12</td><td>686.86</td><td>634.60</td><td>609.98</td><td>597.68</td></tr>
<tr><td>56000</td><td>1259.88</td><td>819.71</td><td>690.21</td><td>636.24</td><td>610.60</td><td>597.66</td><td>1267.02</td><td>827.90</td><td>699.35</td><td>646.13</td><td>621.07</td><td>608.55</td></tr>
<tr><td>57000</td><td>1282.38</td><td>834.34</td><td>702.54</td><td>647.60</td><td>621.50</td><td>608.34</td><td>1289.64</td><td>842.69</td><td>711.84</td><td>657.67</td><td>632.16</td><td>619.42</td></tr>
<tr><td>58000</td><td>1304.88</td><td>848.98</td><td>714.86</td><td>658.96</td><td>632.41</td><td>619.01</td><td>1312.27</td><td>857.47</td><td>724.33</td><td>669.21</td><td>643.25</td><td>630.28</td></tr>
<tr><td>59000</td><td>1327.38</td><td>863.62</td><td>727.19</td><td>670.32</td><td>643.31</td><td>629.68</td><td>1334.89</td><td>872.25</td><td>736.81</td><td>680.75</td><td>654.34</td><td>641.15</td></tr>
<tr><td>60000</td><td>1349.88</td><td>878.26</td><td>739.51</td><td>681.68</td><td>654.21</td><td>640.35</td><td>1357.52</td><td>887.04</td><td>749.30</td><td>692.29</td><td>665.43</td><td>652.02</td></tr>
<tr><td>61000</td><td>1372.37</td><td>892.89</td><td>751.84</td><td>693.05</td><td>665.12</td><td>651.03</td><td>1380.14</td><td>901.82</td><td>761.79</td><td>703.83</td><td>676.52</td><td>662.88</td></tr>
<tr><td>62000</td><td>1394.87</td><td>907.53</td><td>764.16</td><td>704.41</td><td>676.02</td><td>661.70</td><td>1402.77</td><td>916.61</td><td>774.28</td><td>715.36</td><td>687.61</td><td>673.75</td></tr>
<tr><td>63000</td><td>1417.37</td><td>922.17</td><td>776.49</td><td>715.77</td><td>686.92</td><td>672.37</td><td>1425.39</td><td>931.39</td><td>786.77</td><td>726.90</td><td>698.70</td><td>684.62</td></tr>
<tr><td>64000</td><td>1439.87</td><td>936.81</td><td>788.81</td><td>727.13</td><td>697.83</td><td>683.04</td><td>1448.02</td><td>946.17</td><td>799.26</td><td>738.44</td><td>709.79</td><td>695.48</td></tr>
<tr><td>65000</td><td>1462.37</td><td>951.45</td><td>801.14</td><td>738.49</td><td>708.73</td><td>693.72</td><td>1470.64</td><td>960.96</td><td>811.74</td><td>749.98</td><td>720.88</td><td>706.35</td></tr>
<tr><td>66000</td><td>1484.86</td><td>966.08</td><td>813.46</td><td>749.85</td><td>719.63</td><td>704.39</td><td>1493.27</td><td>975.74</td><td>824.23</td><td>761.52</td><td>731.97</td><td>717.22</td></tr>
<tr><td>67000</td><td>1507.36</td><td>980.72</td><td>825.79</td><td>761.21</td><td>730.54</td><td>715.06</td><td>1515.90</td><td>990.53</td><td>836.72</td><td>773.05</td><td>743.07</td><td>728.08</td></tr>
<tr><td>68000</td><td>1529.86</td><td>995.36</td><td>838.12</td><td>772.58</td><td>741.44</td><td>725.74</td><td>1538.52</td><td>1005.31</td><td>849.21</td><td>784.59</td><td>754.16</td><td>738.95</td></tr>
<tr><td>69000</td><td>1552.36</td><td>1010.00</td><td>850.44</td><td>783.94</td><td>752.34</td><td>736.41</td><td>1561.15</td><td>1020.09</td><td>861.70</td><td>796.13</td><td>765.25</td><td>749.82</td></tr>
<tr><td>70000</td><td>1574.86</td><td>1024.63</td><td>862.77</td><td>795.30</td><td>763.25</td><td>747.08</td><td>1583.77</td><td>1034.88</td><td>874.19</td><td>807.67</td><td>776.34</td><td>760.69</td></tr>
<tr><td>71000</td><td>1597.35</td><td>1039.27</td><td>875.09</td><td>806.66</td><td>774.15</td><td>757.75</td><td>1606.40</td><td>1049.66</td><td>886.67</td><td>819.21</td><td>787.43</td><td>771.55</td></tr>
<tr><td>72000</td><td>1619.85</td><td>1053.91</td><td>887.42</td><td>818.02</td><td>785.05</td><td>768.43</td><td>1629.02</td><td>1064.45</td><td>899.16</td><td>830.74</td><td>798.52</td><td>782.42</td></tr>
<tr><td>73000</td><td>1642.35</td><td>1068.55</td><td>899.74</td><td>829.38</td><td>795.96</td><td>779.10</td><td>1651.65</td><td>1079.23</td><td>911.65</td><td>842.28</td><td>809.61</td><td>793.29</td></tr>
<tr><td>74000</td><td>1664.85</td><td>1083.18</td><td>912.07</td><td>840.74</td><td>806.86</td><td>789.77</td><td>1674.27</td><td>1094.01</td><td>924.14</td><td>853.82</td><td>820.70</td><td>804.15</td></tr>
<tr><td>75000</td><td>1687.35</td><td>1097.82</td><td>924.39</td><td>852.11</td><td>817.77</td><td>800.44</td><td>1696.90</td><td>1108.80</td><td>936.63</td><td>865.36</td><td>831.79</td><td>815.02</td></tr>
<tr><td>76000</td><td>1709.84</td><td>1112.46</td><td>936.72</td><td>863.47</td><td>828.67</td><td>811.12</td><td>1719.52</td><td>1123.58</td><td>949.12</td><td>876.90</td><td>842.88</td><td>825.89</td></tr>
<tr><td>77000</td><td>1732.34</td><td>1127.10</td><td>949.04</td><td>874.83</td><td>839.57</td><td>821.79</td><td>1742.15</td><td>1138.37</td><td>961.60</td><td>888.43</td><td>853.97</td><td>836.75</td></tr>
<tr><td>78000</td><td>1754.84</td><td>1141.73</td><td>961.37</td><td>886.19</td><td>850.48</td><td>832.46</td><td>1764.77</td><td>1153.15</td><td>974.09</td><td>899.97</td><td>865.06</td><td>847.62</td></tr>
<tr><td>79000</td><td>1777.34</td><td>1156.37</td><td>973.69</td><td>897.55</td><td>861.38</td><td>843.13</td><td>1787.40</td><td>1167.93</td><td>986.58</td><td>911.51</td><td>876.15</td><td>858.49</td></tr>
<tr><td>80000</td><td>1799.84</td><td>1171.01</td><td>986.02</td><td>908.91</td><td>872.28</td><td>853.81</td><td>1810.02</td><td>1182.72</td><td>999.07</td><td>923.05</td><td>887.24</td><td>869.35</td></tr>
<tr><td>81000</td><td>1822.33</td><td>1185.65</td><td>998.34</td><td>920.27</td><td>883.19</td><td>864.48</td><td>1832.65</td><td>1197.50</td><td>1011.56</td><td>934.59</td><td>898.33</td><td>880.22</td></tr>
<tr><td>82000</td><td>1844.83</td><td>1200.28</td><td>1010.67</td><td>931.64</td><td>894.09</td><td>875.15</td><td>1855.27</td><td>1212.29</td><td>1024.05</td><td>946.13</td><td>909.42</td><td>891.09</td></tr>
<tr><td>83000</td><td>1867.33</td><td>1214.92</td><td>1022.99</td><td>943.00</td><td>904.99</td><td>885.82</td><td>1877.90</td><td>1227.07</td><td>1036.53</td><td>957.66</td><td>920.51</td><td>901.96</td></tr>
<tr><td>84000</td><td>1889.83</td><td>1229.56</td><td>1035.32</td><td>954.36</td><td>915.90</td><td>896.50</td><td>1900.53</td><td>1241.85</td><td>1049.02</td><td>969.20</td><td>931.60</td><td>912.82</td></tr>
<tr><td>85000</td><td>1912.32</td><td>1244.20</td><td>1047.64</td><td>965.72</td><td>926.80</td><td>907.17</td><td>1923.15</td><td>1256.64</td><td>1061.51</td><td>980.74</td><td>942.69</td><td>923.69</td></tr>
<tr><td>86000</td><td>1934.82</td><td>1258.84</td><td>1059.97</td><td>977.08</td><td>937.70</td><td>917.84</td><td>1945.78</td><td>1271.42</td><td>1074.00</td><td>992.28</td><td>953.78</td><td>934.56</td></tr>
<tr><td>87000</td><td>1957.32</td><td>1273.47</td><td>1072.29</td><td>988.44</td><td>948.61</td><td>928.51</td><td>1968.40</td><td>1286.21</td><td>1086.49</td><td>1003.82</td><td>964.88</td><td>945.42</td></tr>
<tr><td>88000</td><td>1979.82</td><td>1288.11</td><td>1084.62</td><td>999.80</td><td>959.51</td><td>939.19</td><td>1991.03</td><td>1300.99</td><td>1098.98</td><td>1015.35</td><td>975.97</td><td>956.29</td></tr>
<tr><td>89000</td><td>2002.32</td><td>1302.75</td><td>1096.94</td><td>1011.17</td><td>970.42</td><td>949.86</td><td>2013.65</td><td>1315.77</td><td>1111.46</td><td>1026.89</td><td>987.06</td><td>967.16</td></tr>
<tr><td>90000</td><td>2024.81</td><td>1317.39</td><td>1109.27</td><td>1022.53</td><td>981.32</td><td>960.53</td><td>2036.28</td><td>1330.56</td><td>1123.95</td><td>1038.43</td><td>998.15</td><td>978.02</td></tr>
<tr><td>91000</td><td>2047.31</td><td>1332.02</td><td>1121.60</td><td>1033.89</td><td>992.22</td><td>971.20</td><td>2058.90</td><td>1345.34</td><td>1136.44</td><td>1049.97</td><td>1009.24</td><td>988.89</td></tr>
<tr><td>92000</td><td>2069.81</td><td>1346.66</td><td>1133.92</td><td>1045.25</td><td>1003.13</td><td>981.88</td><td>2081.53</td><td>1360.13</td><td>1148.93</td><td>1061.51</td><td>1020.33</td><td>999.76</td></tr>
<tr><td>93000</td><td>2092.31</td><td>1361.30</td><td>1146.25</td><td>1056.61</td><td>1014.03</td><td>992.55</td><td>2104.15</td><td>1374.91</td><td>1161.42</td><td>1073.04</td><td>1031.42</td><td>1010.62</td></tr>
<tr><td>94000</td><td>2114.81</td><td>1375.94</td><td>1158.57</td><td>1067.97</td><td>1024.93</td><td>1003.22</td><td>2126.78</td><td>1389.69</td><td>1173.91</td><td>1084.58</td><td>1042.51</td><td>1021.49</td></tr>
<tr><td>95000</td><td>2137.30</td><td>1390.57</td><td>1170.90</td><td>1079.33</td><td>1035.84</td><td>1013.89</td><td>2149.40</td><td>1404.48</td><td>1186.40</td><td>1096.12</td><td>1053.60</td><td>1032.36</td></tr>
<tr><td>96000</td><td>2159.80</td><td>1405.21</td><td>1183.22</td><td>1090.69</td><td>1046.74</td><td>1024.57</td><td>2172.03</td><td>1419.26</td><td>1198.88</td><td>1107.66</td><td>1064.69</td><td>1043.23</td></tr>
<tr><td>97000</td><td>2182.30</td><td>1419.85</td><td>1195.55</td><td>1102.06</td><td>1057.64</td><td>1035.24</td><td>2194.65</td><td>1434.05</td><td>1211.37</td><td>1119.20</td><td>1075.78</td><td>1054.09</td></tr>
<tr><td>98000</td><td>2204.80</td><td>1434.49</td><td>1207.87</td><td>1113.42</td><td>1068.55</td><td>1045.91</td><td>2217.28</td><td>1448.83</td><td>1223.86</td><td>1130.74</td><td>1086.87</td><td>1064.96</td></tr>
<tr><td>99000</td><td>2227.30</td><td>1449.12</td><td>1220.20</td><td>1124.78</td><td>1079.45</td><td>1056.59</td><td>2239.90</td><td>1463.61</td><td>1236.35</td><td>1142.27</td><td>1097.96</td><td>1075.83</td></tr>
<tr><td>100000</td><td>2249.79</td><td>1463.76</td><td>1232.52</td><td>1136.14</td><td>1090.35</td><td>1067.26</td><td>2262.53</td><td>1478.40</td><td>1248.84</td><td>1153.81</td><td>1109.05</td><td>1086.69</td></tr>
</table>

Table 2

13.00

13.25

	TERM (YEARS)						TERM (YEARS)				
AMOUNT	5	10	15	20	25	30	5	10	15	20	25	30
10000	227.53	149.31	126.52	117.16	112.78	110.62	228.81	150.79	128.17	118.94	114.67	112.58
11000	250.28	164.24	139.18	128.87	124.06	121.68	251.69	165.87	140.99	130.84	126.14	123.84
12000	273.04	179.17	151.83	140.59	135.34	132.74	274.58	180.95	153.81	142.73	137.60	135.09
13000	295.79	194.10	164.48	152.30	146.62	143.81	297.46	196.03	166.63	154.63	149.07	146.35
14000	318.54	209.03	177.13	164.02	157.90	154.87	320.34	211.10	179.44	166.52	160.54	157.61
15000	341.30	223.97	189.79	175.74	169.18	165.93	343.22	226.18	192.26	178.41	172.01	168.87
16000	364.05	238.90	202.44	187.45	180.45	176.99	366.10	241.26	205.08	190.31	183.47	180.12
17000	386.80	253.83	215.09	199.17	191.73	188.05	388.98	256.34	217.90	202.20	194.94	191.38
18000	409.56	268.76	227.74	210.88	203.01	199.12	411.86	271.42	230.71	214.10	206.41	202.64
19000	432.31	283.69	240.40	222.60	214.29	210.18	434.74	286.50	243.53	225.99	217.87	213.90
20000	455.06	298.62	253.05	234.32	225.57	221.24	457.63	301.58	256.35	237.89	229.34	225.15
21000	477.81	313.55	265.70	246.03	236.85	232.30	480.51	316.66	269.16	249.78	240.81	236.41
22000	500.57	328.48	278.35	257.75	248.12	243.36	503.39	331.74	281.98	261.67	252.27	247.67
23000	523.32	343.41	291.01	269.46	259.40	254.43	526.27	346.81	294.80	273.57	263.74	258.93
24000	546.07	358.35	303.66	281.18	270.68	265.49	549.15	361.89	307.62	285.46	275.21	270.19
25000	568.83	373.28	316.31	292.89	281.96	276.55	572.03	376.97	320.43	297.36	286.68	281.44
26000	591.58	388.21	328.96	304.61	293.24	287.61	594.91	392.05	333.25	309.25	298.14	292.70
27000	614.33	403.14	341.62	316.33	304.52	298.67	617.79	407.13	346.07	321.15	309.61	303.96
28000	637.09	418.07	354.27	328.04	315.79	309.74	640.68	422.21	358.89	333.04	321.08	315.22
29000	659.84	433.00	366.92	339.76	327.07	320.80	663.56	437.29	371.70	344.93	332.54	326.47
30000	682.59	447.93	379.57	351.47	338.35	331.86	686.44	452.37	384.52	356.83	344.01	337.73
31000	705.35	462.86	392.23	363.19	349.63	342.92	709.32	467.45	397.34	368.72	355.48	348.99
32000	728.10	477.79	404.88	374.90	360.91	353.98	732.20	482.52	410.16	380.62	366.94	360.25
33000	750.85	492.73	417.53	386.62	372.19	365.05	755.08	497.60	422.97	392.51	378.41	371.51
34000	773.60	507.66	430.18	398.34	383.46	376.11	777.96	512.68	435.79	404.41	389.88	382.76
35000	796.36	522.59	442.83	410.05	394.74	387.17	800.84	527.76	448.61	416.30	401.35	394.02
36000	819.11	537.52	455.49	421.77	406.02	398.23	823.73	542.84	461.43	428.20	412.81	405.28
37000	841.86	552.45	468.14	433.48	417.30	409.29	846.61	557.92	474.24	440.09	424.28	416.54
38000	864.62	567.38	480.79	445.20	428.58	420.36	869.49	573.00	487.06	451.98	435.75	427.79
39000	887.37	582.31	493.44	456.91	439.86	431.42	892.37	588.08	499.88	463.88	447.21	439.05
40000	910.12	597.24	506.10	468.63	451.13	442.48	915.25	603.16	512.69	475.77	458.68	450.31
41000	932.88	612.17	518.75	480.35	462.41	453.54	938.13	618.23	525.51	487.67	470.15	461.57
42000	955.63	627.11	531.40	492.06	473.69	464.60	961.01	633.31	538.33	499.56	481.61	472.82
43000	978.38	642.04	544.05	503.78	484.97	475.67	983.89	648.39	551.15	511.46	493.08	484.08
44000	1001.14	656.97	556.71	515.49	496.25	486.73	1006.78	663.47	563.96	523.35	504.55	495.34
45000	1023.89	671.90	569.36	527.21	507.53	497.79	1029.66	678.55	576.78	535.24	516.02	506.60
46000	1046.64	686.83	582.01	538.92	518.80	508.85	1052.54	693.63	589.60	547.14	527.48	517.86
47000	1069.39	701.76	594.66	550.64	530.08	519.91	1075.42	708.71	602.42	559.03	538.95	529.11
48000	1092.15	716.69	607.32	562.36	541.36	530.98	1098.30	723.79	615.23	570.93	550.42	540.37
49000	1114.90	731.62	619.97	574.07	552.64	542.04	1121.18	738.87	628.05	582.82	561.88	551.63
50000	1137.65	746.55	632.62	585.79	563.92	553.10	1144.06	753.94	640.87	594.72	573.35	562.89
51000	1160.41	761.48	645.27	597.50	575.20	564.16	1166.94	769.02	653.69	606.61	584.82	574.14
52000	1183.16	776.42	657.93	609.22	586.47	575.22	1189.83	784.10	666.50	618.50	596.28	585.40
53000	1205.91	791.35	670.58	620.94	597.75	586.29	1212.71	799.18	679.32	630.40	607.75	596.66
54000	1228.67	806.28	683.23	632.65	609.03	597.35	1235.59	814.26	692.14	642.29	619.22	607.92
55000	1251.42	821.21	695.88	644.37	620.31	608.41	1258.47	829.34	704.96	654.19	630.69	619.18
56000	1274.17	836.14	708.54	656.08	631.59	619.47	1281.35	844.42	717.77	666.08	642.15	630.43
57000	1296.93	851.07	721.19	667.80	642.87	630.53	1304.23	859.50	730.59	677.98	653.62	641.69
58000	1319.68	866.00	733.84	679.51	654.14	641.60	1327.11	874.58	743.41	689.87	665.09	652.95
59000	1342.43	880.93	746.49	691.23	665.42	652.66	1349.99	889.65	756.22	701.76	676.55	664.21
60000	1365.18	895.86	759.15	702.95	676.70	663.72	1372.88	904.73	769.04	713.66	688.02	675.46
61000	1387.94	910.80	771.80	714.66	687.98	674.78	1395.76	919.81	781.86	725.55	699.49	686.72
62000	1410.69	925.73	784.45	726.38	699.26	685.84	1418.64	934.89	794.68	737.45	710.95	697.98
63000	1433.44	940.66	797.10	738.09	710.54	696.91	1441.52	949.97	807.49	749.34	722.42	709.24
64000	1456.20	955.59	809.75	749.81	721.81	707.97	1464.40	965.05	820.31	761.24	733.89	720.50
65000	1478.95	970.52	822.41	761.52	733.09	719.03	1487.28	980.13	833.13	773.13	745.36	731.75
66000	1501.70	985.45	835.06	773.24	744.37	730.09	1510.16	995.21	845.95	785.02	756.82	743.01
67000	1524.46	1000.38	847.71	784.96	755.65	741.15	1533.04	1010.29	858.76	796.92	768.29	754.27
68000	1547.21	1015.31	860.36	796.67	766.93	752.22	1555.93	1025.36	871.58	808.81	779.76	765.53
69000	1569.96	1030.24	873.02	808.39	778.21	763.28	1578.81	1040.44	884.40	820.71	791.22	776.78
70000	1592.72	1045.18	885.67	820.10	789.48	774.34	1601.69	1055.52	897.22	832.60	802.69	788.04
71000	1615.47	1060.11	898.32	831.82	800.76	765.40	1624.57	1070.60	910.03	844.50	814.16	799.30
72000	1638.22	1075.04	910.97	843.53	812.04	796.46	1647.45	1085.68	922.85	856.39	825.62	810.56
73000	1660.97	1089.97	923.63	855.25	823.32	807.53	1670.33	1100.76	935.67	868.28	837.09	821.81
74000	1683.73	1104.90	936.28	866.97	834.60	818.59	1693.21	1115.84	948.48	880.18	848.56	833.07
75000	1706.48	1119.83	948.93	878.68	845.88	829.65	1716.09	1130.92	961.30	892.07	860.03	844.33
76000	1729.23	1134.76	961.58	890.40	857.15	840.71	1738.98	1146.00	974.12	903.97	871.49	855.59
77000	1751.99	1149.69	974.24	902.11	868.43	851.77	1761.86	1161.07	986.94	915.86	882.96	866.85
78000	1774.74	1164.62	986.89	913.83	879.71	862.84	1784.74	1176.15	999.75	927.76	894.43	878.10
79000	1797.49	1179.55	999.54	925.54	890.99	873.90	1807.62	1191.23	1012.57	939.65	905.89	889.36
80000	1820.25	1194.49	1012.19	937.26	902.27	884.96	1830.50	1206.31	1025.39	951.54	917.36	900.62
81000	1843.00	1209.42	1024.85	948.98	913.55	896.02	1853.38	1221.39	1038.21	963.44	928.83	911.88
82000	1865.75	1224.35	1037.50	960.69	924.82	907.08	1876.26	1236.47	1051.02	975.33	940.29	923.13
83000	1888.51	1239.28	1050.15	972.41	936.10	918.15	1899.14	1251.55	1063.84	987.23	951.76	934.39
84000	1911.26	1254.21	1062.80	984.12	947.38	929.21	1922.03	1266.63	1076.66	999.12	963.23	945.65
85000	1934.01	1269.14	1075.46	995.84	958.66	940.27	1944.91	1281.71	1089.48	1011.02	974.70	956.91
86000	1956.76	1284.07	1088.11	1007.56	969.94	951.33	1967.79	1296.78	1102.29	1022.91	986.16	968.17
87000	1979.52	1299.00	1100.76	1019.27	981.22	962.39	1990.67	1311.86	1115.11	1034.80	997.63	979.42
88000	2002.27	1313.93	1113.41	1030.99	992.50	973.46	2013.55	1326.94	1127.93	1046.70	1009.10	990.68
89000	2025.02	1328.87	1126.07	1042.70	1003.77	984.52	2036.43	1342.02	1140.75	1058.59	1020.56	1001.94
90000	2047.78	1343.80	1138.72	1054.42	1015.05	995.58	2059.31	1357.10	1153.56	1070.49	1032.03	1013.20
91000	2070.53	1358.73	1151.37	1066.13	1026.33	1006.64	2082.19	1372.18	1166.38	1082.38	1043.50	1024.45
92000	2093.28	1373.66	1164.02	1077.85	1037.61	1017.70	2105.08	1387.26	1179.20	1094.28	1054.96	1035.71
93000	2116.04	1388.59	1176.68	1089.57	1048.89	1028.77	2127.96	1402.34	1192.01	1106.17	1066.43	1046.97
94000	2138.79	1403.52	1189.33	1101.28	1060.17	1039.83	2150.84	1417.42	1204.83	1118.06	1077.90	1058.23
95000	2161.54	1418.45	1201.98	1113.00	1071.44	1050.89	2173.72	1432.49	1217.65	1129.96	1089.37	1069.48
96000	2184.30	1433.38	1214.63	1124.71	1082.72	1061.95	2196.60	1447.57	1230.47	1141.85	1100.83	1080.74
97000	2207.05	1448.31	1227.28	1136.43	1094.00	1073.01	2219.48	1462.65	1243.28	1153.75	1112.30	1092.00
98000	2229.80	1463.25	1239.94	1148.14	1105.28	1084.08	2242.36	1477.73	1256.10	1165.64	1123.77	1103.26
99000	2252.55	1478.18	1252.59	1159.86	1116.56	1095.14	2265.24	1492.81	1268.92	1177.54	1135.23	1114.52
100000	2275.31	1493.11	1265.24	1171.58	1127.84	1106.20	2288.13	1507.89	1281.74	1189.43	1146.70	1125.77

Table 2 467

	13.50						13.75					
	TERM (YEARS)						TERM (YEARS)					
AMOUNT	5	10	15	20	25	30	5	10	15	20	25	30
10000	230.10	152.27	129.83	120.74	116.56	114.54	231.39	153.77	131.50	122.54	118.47	116.51
11000	253.11	167.50	142.82	132.81	123.22	126.00	254.53	169.14	144.65	134.79	130.31	128.16
12000	276.12	182.73	155.80	144.88	139.88	137.45	277.67	184.52	157.80	147.05	142.16	139.81
13000	299.13	197.96	168.78	156.96	151.53	148.90	300.80	199.90	170.95	159.30	154.01	151.46
14000	322.14	213.18	181.76	169.03	163.19	160.36	323.94	215.27	184.10	171.56	165.85	163.12
15000	345.15	228.41	194.75	181.11	174.85	171.81	347.08	230.65	197.25	183.81	177.70	174.77
16000	368.16	243.64	207.73	193.18	186.50	183.27	370.22	246.03	210.40	196.06	189.55	186.42
17000	391.17	258.87	220.71	205.25	198.16	194.72	393.36	261.40	223.55	208.32	201.39	198.07
18000	414.18	274.09	233.70	217.33	209.82	206.17	416.50	276.78	236.70	220.57	213.24	209.72
19000	437.19	289.32	246.68	229.40	221.47	217.63	439.64	292.16	249.85	232.83	225.09	221.37
20000	460.20	304.55	259.66	241.47	233.13	229.08	462.78	307.53	263.00	245.08	236.93	233.02
21000	483.21	319.78	272.65	253.55	244.79	240.54	485.92	322.91	276.15	257.34	248.78	244.67
22000	506.22	335.00	285.63	265.62	256.44	251.99	509.05	338.29	289.30	269.59	260.63	256.32
23000	529.23	350.23	298.61	277.70	268.10	263.44	532.19	353.66	302.45	281.84	272.47	267.98
24000	552.24	365.46	311.60	289.77	279.75	274.90	555.33	369.04	315.60	294.10	284.32	279.63
25000	575.25	380.69	324.58	301.84	291.41	286.35	578.47	384.42	328.75	306.35	296.17	291.28
26000	598.26	395.91	337.56	313.92	303.07	297.81	601.61	399.79	341.90	318.61	308.01	302.93
27000	621.27	411.14	350.55	325.99	314.72	309.26	624.75	415.17	355.05	330.86	319.86	314.58
28000	644.28	426.37	363.53	338.06	326.38	320.72	647.89	430.55	368.20	343.11	331.71	326.23
29000	667.29	441.60	376.51	350.14	338.04	332.17	671.03	445.92	381.35	355.37	343.55	337.88
30000	690.30	456.82	389.50	362.21	349.69	343.62	694.17	461.30	394.50	367.62	355.40	349.53
31000	713.31	472.05	402.48	374.29	361.35	355.08	717.30	476.68	407.65	379.88	367.25	361.18
32000	736.32	487.28	415.46	386.36	373.01	366.53	740.44	492.05	420.80	392.13	379.09	372.84
33000	759.32	502.51	428.45	398.43	384.66	377.99	763.58	507.43	433.95	404.38	390.94	384.49
34000	782.33	517.73	441.43	410.51	396.32	389.44	766.72	522.81	447.10	416.64	402.79	396.14
35000	805.34	532.96	454.41	422.58	407.98	400.89	809.86	538.18	460.25	428.89	414.63	407.79
36000	828.35	548.19	467.39	434.65	419.63	412.35	833.00	553.56	473.40	441.15	426.48	419.44
37000	851.36	563.41	480.38	446.73	431.29	423.80	856.14	568.94	486.55	453.40	438.33	431.09
38000	874.37	578.64	493.36	458.80	442.95	435.26	879.28	584.31	499.70	465.65	450.17	442.74
39000	897.38	593.87	506.34	470.88	454.60	446.71	902.41	599.69	512.85	477.91	462.02	454.39
40000	920.39	609.10	519.33	482.95	466.26	458.16	925.55	615.07	525.99	490.16	473.87	466.05
41000	943.40	624.32	532.31	495.02	477.91	469.62	948.69	630.44	539.14	502.42	485.71	477.70
42000	966.41	639.55	545.29	507.10	489.57	481.07	971.83	645.82	552.29	514.67	497.56	489.35
43000	989.42	654.78	558.28	519.17	501.23	492.53	994.97	661.20	565.44	526.92	509.41	501.00
44000	1012.43	670.01	571.26	531.24	512.88	503.98	1018.11	676.57	578.59	539.18	521.25	512.65
45000	1035.44	685.23	584.24	543.32	524.54	515.44	1041.25	691.95	591.74	551.43	533.10	524.30
46000	1058.45	700.46	597.23	555.39	536.20	526.89	1064.39	707.33	604.89	563.69	544.95	535.95
47000	1081.46	715.69	610.21	567.47	547.85	538.34	1087.53	722.70	618.04	575.94	556.79	547.60
48000	1104.47	730.92	623.19	579.54	559.51	549.80	1110.66	738.08	631.19	588.19	568.64	559.25
49000	1127.48	746.14	636.18	591.61	571.17	561.25	1133.80	753.46	644.34	600.45	580.49	570.91
50000	1150.49	761.37	649.16	603.69	582.82	572.71	1156.94	768.83	657.49	612.70	592.33	582.56
51000	1173.50	776.60	662.14	615.76	594.48	584.16	1180.08	784.21	670.64	624.96	604.18	594.21
52000	1196.51	791.83	675.13	627.83	606.14	595.61	1203.22	799.59	683.79	637.21	616.03	605.86
53000	1219.52	807.05	688.11	639.91	617.79	607.07	1226.36	814.95	696.94	649.46	627.87	617.51
54000	1242.53	822.28	701.09	651.98	629.45	618.52	1249.50	830.34	710.09	661.72	639.72	629.16
55000	1265.54	837.51	714.08	664.06	641.10	629.98	1272.64	845.72	723.24	673.97	651.57	640.81
56000	1288.55	852.74	727.06	676.13	652.76	641.43	1295.78	861.09	736.39	686.23	663.41	652.46
57000	1311.56	867.96	740.04	688.20	664.42	652.88	1318.91	876.47	749.54	698.48	675.26	664.11
58000	1334.57	883.19	753.02	700.28	676.07	664.34	1342.05	891.85	762.69	710.74	687.11	675.77
59000	1357.58	898.42	766.01	712.35	687.73	675.79	1365.19	907.22	775.84	722.99	698.95	687.42
60000	1380.59	913.65	778.99	724.42	699.39	687.25	1388.33	922.60	788.99	735.24	710.80	699.07
61000	1403.60	928.87	791.97	736.50	711.04	698.70	1411.47	937.98	802.14	747.50	722.65	710.72
62000	1426.61	944.10	804.96	748.57	722.70	710.16	1434.61	953.35	815.29	759.75	734.49	722.37
63000	1449.62	959.33	817.94	760.65	734.36	721.61	1457.75	968.73	828.44	772.01	746.34	734.02
64000	1472.63	974.56	830.92	772.72	746.01	733.06	1480.89	984.11	841.59	784.26	758.19	745.67
65000	1495.64	989.78	843.91	784.79	757.67	744.52	1504.02	999.48	854.74	796.51	770.03	757.32
66000	1513.65	1005.01	856.89	796.87	769.33	755.97	1527.16	1014.86	867.89	808.77	781.88	768.97
67000	1541.66	1020.24	869.87	808.94	780.98	767.43	1550.30	1030.24	881.04	821.02	793.73	780.63
68000	1564.67	1035.47	882.86	821.01	792.64	778.88	1573.44	1045.61	894.19	833.28	805.57	792.28
69000	1587.68	1050.69	895.84	833.09	804.29	790.33	1596.58	1060.99	907.34	845.53	817.42	803.93
70000	1610.69	1065.92	908.82	845.16	815.95	801.79	1619.72	1076.37	920.49	857.78	829.27	815.58
71000	1633.70	1081.15	921.81	857.24	827.61	813.24	1642.86	1091.74	933.64	870.04	841.11	827.23
72000	1656.71	1096.37	934.79	869.31	839.26	824.70	1666.00	1107.12	946.79	882.29	852.96	838.88
73000	1679.72	1111.60	947.77	881.38	850.92	836.15	1689.14	1122.50	959.94	894.55	864.81	850.53
74000	1702.73	1126.83	960.76	893.46	862.58	847.61	1712.27	1137.87	973.09	906.80	876.65	862.18
75000	1725.74	1142.06	973.74	905.53	874.23	859.06	1735.41	1153.25	986.24	919.05	888.50	873.83
76000	1748.75	1157.28	986.72	917.60	885.89	870.51	1758.55	1168.63	999.39	931.31	900.35	885.49
77000	1771.76	1172.51	999.71	929.68	897.55	881.97	1781.69	1184.00	1012.54	943.56	912.19	897.14
78000	1794.77	1187.74	1012.69	941.75	909.20	893.42	1804.83	1199.38	1025.69	955.82	924.04	908.79
79000	1817.78	1202.97	1025.67	953.83	920.86	904.88	1827.97	1214.76	1038.84	968.07	935.89	920.44
80000	1840.79	1218.19	1038.65	965.90	932.52	916.33	1851.11	1230.13	1051.99	980.32	947.73	932.09
81000	1863.80	1233.42	1051.64	977.97	944.17	927.78	1874.25	1245.51	1065.14	992.58	959.58	943.74
82000	1886.81	1248.65	1064.62	990.05	955.83	939.24	1897.39	1260.89	1078.29	1004.83	971.43	955.39
83000	1909.82	1263.88	1077.60	1002.12	967.49	950.69	1920.52	1276.26	1091.44	1017.09	983.27	967.04
84000	1932.83	1279.10	1090.59	1014.19	979.14	962.15	1943.66	1291.64	1104.59	1029.34	995.12	978.69
85000	1955.84	1294.33	1103.57	1026.27	990.80	973.60	1966.80	1307.02	1117.74	1041.59	1006.97	990.35
86000	1978.85	1309.56	1116.55	1038.34	1002.45	985.05	1989.94	1322.39	1130.89	1053.85	1018.81	1002.00
87000	2001.86	1324.79	1129.54	1050.42	1014.11	996.51	2013.08	1337.77	1144.04	1066.10	1030.66	1013.65
88000	2024.87	1340.01	1142.52	1062.49	1025.77	1007.96	2036.22	1353.15	1157.19	1078.36	1042.51	1025.30
89000	2047.88	1355.24	1155.50	1074.56	1037.42	1019.42	2059.36	1368.52	1170.34	1090.61	1054.35	1036.95
90000	2070.89	1370.47	1168.49	1086.64	1049.08	1030.87	2082.50	1383.90	1183.49	1102.86	1066.20	1048.60
91000	2093.90	1385.70	1181.47	1098.71	1060.74	1042.33	2105.63	1399.28	1196.64	1115.12	1078.05	1060.25
92000	2116.91	1400.92	1194.45	1110.78	1072.39	1053.78	2128.77	1414.65	1209.79	1127.37	1089.89	1071.90
93000	2139.92	1416.15	1207.44	1122.86	1084.05	1065.23	2151.91	1430.03	1222.94	1139.63	1101.74	1083.55
94000	2162.93	1431.38	1220.42	1134.93	1095.71	1076.69	2175.05	1445.41	1236.09	1151.88	1113.59	1095.21
95000	2185.94	1446.61	1233.40	1147.01	1107.36	1088.14	2198.19	1460.78	1249.24	1164.14	1125.43	1106.86
96000	2208.95	1461.83	1246.39	1159.08	1119.02	1099.60	2221.33	1476.16	1262.39	1176.39	1137.28	1118.51
97000	2231.96	1477.06	1259.37	1171.15	1130.68	1111.05	2244.47	1491.54	1275.54	1188.64	1149.13	1130.16
98000	2254.96	1492.29	1272.35	1183.23	1142.33	1122.50	2267.61	1506.91	1288.69	1200.90	1160.97	1141.81
99000	2277.97	1507.52	1285.34	1195.30	1153.99	1133.96	2290.75	1522.29	1301.84	1213.15	1172.82	1153.46
100000	2300.98	1522.74	1298.32	1207.37	1165.64	1145.41	2313.88	1537.67	1314.99	1225.41	1184.67	1165.11

Table 3

MONTHLY PAYMENTS
FOR FHA LOANS

This table lists the monthly payments for FHA loans (see Section 6.3). For these loans the borrower must pay an annual interest of ½% on the original loan amount. This charge is for the Mutual Mortgage Insurance Fund. Hence, on a monthly basis the usual principal and interest payment is increased by .005/12 of the original loan amount. The monthly payment for a $50,000 FHA loan for 25 years at 8½% is $423.45.

TABLE 3 (See Section 6.3) Monthly Payments for FHA Loans* 25 Year Term

ANNUAL INTEREST RATE

AMOUNT	7.50	7.75	8.00	8.25	8.50	8.75	9.00	9.25	9.50	9.75	10.00	10.25
10000	78.07	79.70	81.35	83.01	84.69	86.38	88.09	89.80	91.54	93.28	95.04	96.80
11000	85.87	87.67	89.48	91.31	93.16	95.02	96.89	98.79	100.69	102.61	104.54	106.49
12000	93.68	95.64	97.62	99.61	101.63	103.66	105.70	107.77	109.84	111.94	114.04	116.17
13000	101.49	103.61	105.75	107.92	110.10	112.30	114.51	116.75	119.00	121.26	123.55	125.85
14000	109.29	111.58	113.89	116.22	118.57	120.93	123.32	125.73	128.15	130.59	133.05	135.53
15000	117.10	119.55	122.02	124.52	127.03	129.57	132.13	134.71	137.30	139.92	142.56	145.21
16000	124.91	127.52	130.16	132.82	135.50	138.21	140.94	143.69	146.46	149.25	152.06	154.89
17000	132.71	135.49	138.29	141.12	143.97	146.85	149.75	152.67	155.61	158.58	161.56	164.57
18000	140.52	143.46	146.43	149.42	152.44	155.49	158.56	161.65	164.77	167.90	171.07	174.25
19000	148.32	151.13	154.56	157.72	160.91	164.12	167.36	170.63	173.92	177.23	180.57	183.93
20000	156.13	159.40	162.70	166.02	169.38	172.76	176.17	179.61	183.07	186.56	190.07	193.61
21000	163.94	167.37	170.83	174.32	177.85	181.40	184.98	188.59	192.23	195.89	199.58	203.29
22000	171.74	175.34	178.97	182.63	186.32	190.04	193.79	197.57	201.38	205.22	209.08	212.97
23000	179.55	183.31	187.10	190.93	194.79	198.68	202.60	206.55	210.53	214.54	218.58	222.65
24000	187.36	191.28	195.24	199.23	203.25	207.31	211.41	215.53	219.69	223.87	228.09	232.33
25000	195.16	199.25	203.37	207.53	211.72	215.95	220.22	224.51	228.84	233.20	237.59	242.01
26000	202.97	207.22	211.51	215.83	220.19	224.59	229.02	233.49	237.99	242.53	247.10	251.69
27000	210.78	215.19	219.64	224.13	228.66	233.23	237.83	242.47	247.15	251.86	256.60	261.37
28000	218.58	223.16	227.78	232.43	237.13	241.87	246.64	251.45	256.30	261.19	266.10	271.05
29000	226.39	231.13	235.91	240.73	245.60	250.50	255.45	260.43	265.46	270.51	275.61	280.73
30000	234.20	239.10	244.04	249.04	254.07	259.14	264.26	269.41	274.61	279.84	285.11	290.41
31000	242.00	247.07	252.18	257.34	262.54	267.78	273.07	278.40	283.76	289.17	294.61	300.10
32000	249.81	255.04	260.31	265.64	271.01	276.42	281.88	287.38	292.92	298.50	304.12	309.78
33000	257.62	263.01	268.45	273.94	279.47	285.06	290.68	296.36	302.07	307.83	313.62	319.46
34000	265.42	270.98	276.58	282.24	287.94	293.70	299.49	305.34	311.22	317.15	323.12	329.14
35000	273.3	278.95	284.72	290.54	296.41	302.33	308.30	314.32	320.38	326.48	332.63	338.82
36000	281.04	286.92	292.85	298.84	304.88	310.97	317.11	323.30	329.53	335.81	342.13	348.50
37000	288.84	294.89	300.99	307.14	313.35	319.61	325.92	332.28	338.68	345.14	351.64	358.18
38000	296.65	302.86	309.12	315.44	321.82	328.25	334.73	341.26	347.84	354.47	361.14	367.86
39000	304.46	310.83	317.26	323.75	330.29	336.89	343.54	350.24	356.99	363.79	370.64	377.54
40000	312.26	318.80	325.39	332.05	338.76	345.52	352.35	359.22	366.15	373.12	380.15	387.22
41000	320.07	326.77	333.53	340.35	347.23	354.16	361.15	368.20	375.30	382.45	389.65	396.90
42000	327.88	334.74	341.66	348.65	355.70	362.80	369.96	377.18	384.45	391.78	399.15	406.58
43000	335.68	342.71	349.80	356.95	364.16	371.44	378.77	386.16	393.61	401.11	408.66	416.26
44000	343.49	350.68	357.93	365.25	372.63	380.08	387.58	395.14	402.76	410.43	418.16	425.94
45000	351.30	358.65	366.07	373.55	381.10	388.71	396.39	404.12	411.91	419.76	427.67	435.62
46000	359.10	366.62	374.20	381.85	389.57	397.35	405.20	413.10	421.07	429.09	437.17	445.30
47000	366.91	374.59	382.34	390.15	398.04	405.99	414.01	422.08	430.22	438.42	446.67	454.98
48000	374.72	382.56	390.47	398.46	406.51	414.63	422.81	431.06	439.37	447.75	456.18	464.66
49000	382.52	390.53	398.61	406.76	414.98	423.27	431.62	440.04	448.53	457.07	465.68	474.34
50000	390.33	398.50	406.74	415.06	423.45	431.91	440.43	449.02	457.68	466.40	475.18	484.02
51000	398.14	406.47	414.88	423.36	431.92	440.54	449.24	458.00	466.84	475.73	484.69	493.71
52000	405.94	414.44	423.01	431.66	440.38	449.18	458.05	466.99	475.99	485.06	494.19	503.39
53000	413.75	422.41	431.15	439.96	448.85	457.82	466.86	475.97	485.14	494.39	503.69	513.07
54000	421.56	430.38	439.28	448.26	457.32	466.46	475.67	484.95	494.30	503.71	513.20	522.75
55000	429.36	438.35	447.42	456.56	465.79	475.10	484.47	493.93	503.45	513.04	522.70	532.43
56000	437.17	446.32	455.55	464.87	474.26	483.73	493.28	502.91	512.60	522.37	532.21	542.11
57000	444.97	454.29	463.69	473.17	482.73	492.37	502.09	511.89	521.76	531.70	541.71	551.79
58000	452.78	462.26	471.82	481.47	491.20	501.01	510.90	520.87	530.91	541.03	551.21	561.47
59000	460.59	470.23	479.95	489.77	499.67	509.65	519.71	529.85	540.06	550.35	560.72	571.15
60000	468.39	478.20	488.09	498.07	508.14	518.29	528.52	538.83	549.22	559.68	570.22	580.83
61000	476.20	486.17	496.22	506.37	516.61	526.92	537.33	547.81	558.37	569.01	579.72	590.51
62000	484.01	494.14	504.36	514.67	525.07	535.56	546.14	556.79	567.53	578.34	589.23	600.19
63000	491.81	502.11	512.49	522.97	533.54	544.20	554.94	565.77	576.68	587.67	598.73	609.87
64000	499.62	510.08	520.63	531.27	542.01	552.84	563.75	574.75	585.83	596.99	608.24	619.55
65000	507.43	518.05	528.76	539.58	550.48	561.48	572.56	583.73	594.99	606.32	617.74	629.23
66000	515.23	526.02	536.90	547.88	558.95	570.11	581.37	592.71	604.14	615.65	627.24	638.91
67000	523.04	533.99	545.03	556.18	567.42	578.75	590.18	601.69	613.29	624.98	636.75	648.59
68000	530.85	541.96	553.17	564.48	575.89	587.39	598.99	610.67	622.45	634.31	646.25	658.27
69000	538.65	549.93	561.30	572.78	584.36	596.03	607.80	619.65	631.60	643.63	655.75	667.95
70000	546.46	557.90	569.44	581.08	592.83	604.67	616.60	628.63	640.75	652.96	665.26	677.63
71000	554.27	565.87	577.57	589.38	601.29	613.31	625.41	637.61	649.91	662.29	674.76	687.32
72000	562.07	573.84	585.71	597.68	609.76	621.94	634.22	646.59	659.06	671.62	684.26	697.00
73000	569.88	581.81	593.84	605.99	618.23	630.58	643.03	655.58	668.22	680.95	693.77	706.68
74000	577.69	589.78	601.98	614.29	626.70	639.22	651.84	664.56	677.37	690.28	703.27	716.36
75000	585.49	597.75	610.11	622.59	635.17	647.86	660.65	673.54	686.52	699.60	712.78	726.04
76000	593.30	605.72	618.25	630.89	643.64	656.50	669.46	682.52	695.68	708.93	722.28	735.72
77000	601.11	613.69	626.38	639.19	652.11	665.13	678.26	691.50	704.83	718.26	731.78	745.40
78000	608.91	621.66	634.52	647.49	660.58	673.77	687.07	700.48	713.98	727.59	741.29	755.08
79000	616.72	629.63	642.65	655.79	669.05	682.41	695.88	709.46	723.14	736.92	750.79	764.76
80000	624.53	637.60	650.79	664.09	677.52	691.05	704.69	718.44	732.29	746.24	760.29	774.44
81000	632.33	645.57	658.92	672.39	685.98	699.69	713.50	727.42	741.44	755.57	769.80	784.12
82000	640.14	653.54	667.06	680.70	694.45	708.32	722.31	736.40	750.60	764.90	779.30	793.80
83000	647.95	661.51	675.19	689.00	702.92	716.96	731.12	745.38	759.75	774.23	788.80	803.48
84000	655.75	669.48	683.33	697.30	711.39	725.60	739.92	754.36	768.91	783.56	798.31	813.16
85000	663.56	677.45	691.46	705.60	719.86	734.24	748.73	763.34	778.06	792.88	807.81	822.84
86000	671.37	685.42	699.60	713.90	728.33	742.88	757.54	772.32	787.21	802.21	817.32	832.52
87000	679.17	693.39	707.73	722.20	736.80	751.51	766.35	781.30	796.37	811.54	826.82	842.20
88000	686.98	701.36	715.86	730.50	745.27	760.15	775.16	790.28	805.52	820.87	836.32	851.88
89000	694.79	709.33	724.00	738.80	753.74	768.79	783.97	799.26	814.67	830.20	845.83	861.56
90000	702.59	717.30	732.13	747.11	762.20	777.43	792.78	808.24	823.83	839.52	855.33	871.24
91000	710.40	725.27	740.27	755.41	770.67	786.07	801.59	817.22	832.98	848.85	864.83	880.93
92000	718.21	733.24	748.40	763.71	779.14	794.71	810.39	826.20	842.13	858.18	874.34	890.61
93000	726.01	741.21	756.54	772.01	787.61	803.34	819.20	835.19	851.29	867.51	883.84	900.29
94000	733.82	749.18	764.67	780.31	796.08	811.98	828.01	844.17	860.44	876.84	893.35	909.97
95000	741.62	757.15	772.81	788.61	804.55	820.62	836.82	853.15	869.60	886.16	902.85	919.65
96000	749.43	765.12	780.94	796.91	813.02	829.26	845.63	862.13	878.75	895.49	912.35	929.33
97000	757.24	773.09	789.08	805.21	821.49	837.90	854.44	871.11	887.90	904.82	921.86	939.01
98000	765.04	781.06	797.21	813.51	829.96	846.53	863.25	880.09	897.06	914.15	931.36	948.69
99000	772.85	789.03	805.35	821.82	838.42	855.17	872.05	889.07	906.21	923.48	940.86	958.37
100000	780.66	797.00	813.48	830.12	846.89	863.81	880.86	898.05	915.36	932.80	950.37	968.05

*Includes ½% for Mutual Mortgage Insurance.

Table 3　　　　　　　　　　　　　　　　　　　　　　　　　　　　471

TABLE 3 (See Section 6.3) Monthly Payments for FHA Loans* 30 Year Term

ANNUAL INTEREST RATE

AMOUNT	7.50	7.75	8.00	8.25	8.50	8.75	9.00	9.25	9.50	9.75	10.00	10.25
10000	74.09	75.81	77.54	79.29	81.06	82.84	84.63	86.43	88.25	90.08	91.92	93.78
11000	81.50	83.39	85.30	87.22	89.16	91.12	93.09	95.08	97.08	99.09	101.12	103.15
12000	88.91	90.97	93.05	95.15	97.27	99.40	101.55	103.72	105.90	108.10	110.31	112.53
13000	96.31	98.55	100.81	103.08	105.38	107.69	110.02	112.36	114.73	117.11	119.50	121.91
14000	103.72	106.13	108.56	111.01	113.48	115.97	118.48	121.01	123.55	126.11	128.69	131.29
15000	111.13	113.71	116.31	118.94	121.59	124.26	126.94	129.65	132.38	135.12	137.89	140.67
16000	118.54	121.29	124.07	126.87	129.69	132.54	135.41	138.29	141.20	144.13	147.08	150.04
17000	125.95	128.87	131.82	134.80	137.80	140.82	143.87	146.94	150.03	153.14	156.27	159.42
18000	133.36	136.45	139.58	142.73	145.90	149.11	152.33	155.58	158.85	162.15	165.46	168.80
19000	140.77	144.03	147.33	150.66	154.01	157.39	160.79	164.22	167.68	171.16	174.66	178.18
20000	148.18	151.62	155.09	158.59	162.12	165.67	169.26	172.87	176.50	180.16	183.85	187.55
21000	155.59	159.20	162.84	166.52	170.22	173.96	177.72	181.51	185.33	189.17	193.04	196.93
22000	162.99	166.78	170.59	174.45	178.33	182.24	186.18	190.16	194.15	198.18	202.23	206.31
23000	170.40	174.36	178.35	182.37	186.43	190.52	194.65	198.80	202.98	207.19	211.42	215.69
24000	177.81	181.94	186.10	190.30	194.54	198.81	203.11	207.44	211.81	216.20	220.62	225.06
25000	185.22	189.52	193.86	198.23	202.65	207.09	211.57	216.09	220.63	225.21	229.81	234.44
26000	192.63	197.10	201.61	206.16	210.75	215.38	220.04	224.73	229.46	234.21	239.00	243.82
27000	200.04	204.68	209.37	214.09	218.86	223.66	228.50	233.37	238.28	243.22	248.19	253.20
28000	207.45	212.26	217.12	222.02	226.96	231.94	236.96	242.02	247.11	252.23	257.39	262.58
29000	214.86	219.84	224.88	229.95	235.07	240.23	245.42	250.66	255.93	261.24	266.58	271.95
30000	222.26	227.42	232.63	237.88	243.17	248.51	253.89	259.30	264.76	270.25	275.77	281.33
31000	229.67	235.00	240.38	245.81	251.28	256.79	262.35	267.95	273.58	279.25	284.96	290.71
32000	237.08	242.59	248.14	253.74	259.39	265.08	270.81	276.59	282.41	288.26	294.16	300.09
33000	244.49	250.17	255.89	261.67	267.49	273.36	279.28	285.23	291.23	297.27	303.35	309.46
34000	251.90	257.75	263.65	269.60	275.60	281.64	287.74	293.88	300.06	306.28	312.54	318.84
35000	259.31	265.33	271.40	277.53	283.70	289.93	296.20	302.52	308.88	315.29	321.73	328.22
36000	266.72	272.91	279.16	285.46	291.81	298.21	304.66	311.16	317.71	324.30	330.93	337.60
37000	274.13	280.49	286.91	293.39	299.91	306.50	313.13	319.81	326.53	333.30	340.12	346.97
38000	281.53	288.07	294.66	301.31	308.02	314.78	321.59	328.45	335.36	342.31	349.31	356.35
39000	288.94	295.65	302.42	309.24	316.13	323.06	330.05	337.09	344.18	351.32	358.50	365.73
40000	296.35	303.23	310.17	317.17	324.23	331.35	338.52	345.74	353.01	360.33	367.70	375.11
41000	303.76	310.81	317.93	325.10	332.34	339.63	346.98	354.38	361.83	369.34	376.89	384.48
42000	311.17	318.39	325.68	333.03	340.44	347.91	355.44	363.02	370.66	378.34	386.08	393.86
43000	318.58	325.97	333.44	340.96	348.55	356.20	363.90	371.67	379.48	387.35	395.27	403.24
44000	325.99	333.55	341.19	348.89	356.66	364.48	372.37	380.31	388.31	396.36	404.46	412.62
45000	333.40	341.14	348.94	356.82	364.76	372.77	380.83	388.95	397.13	405.37	413.66	422.00
46000	340.81	348.72	356.70	364.75	372.87	381.05	389.29	397.60	405.96	414.38	422.85	431.37
47000	348.21	356.30	364.45	372.68	380.97	389.33	397.76	406.24	414.78	423.39	432.04	440.75
48000	355.62	363.88	372.21	380.61	389.08	397.62	406.22	414.88	423.61	432.39	441.23	450.13
49000	363.03	371.46	379.96	388.54	397.18	405.90	414.68	423.53	432.44	441.40	450.43	459.51
50000	370.44	379.04	387.72	396.47	405.29	414.18	423.14	432.17	441.26	450.41	459.62	468.88
51000	377.85	386.62	395.47	404.40	413.40	422.47	431.61	440.81	450.09	459.42	468.81	478.26
52000	385.26	394.20	403.22	412.33	421.50	430.75	440.07	449.46	458.91	468.43	478.00	487.64
53000	392.67	401.78	410.98	420.25	429.61	439.03	448.53	458.10	467.74	477.44	487.20	497.02
54000	400.08	409.36	418.73	428.18	437.71	447.32	457.00	466.74	476.56	486.44	496.39	506.39
55000	407.48	416.94	426.49	436.11	445.82	455.60	465.46	475.39	485.39	495.45	505.58	515.77
56000	414.89	424.52	434.24	444.04	453.92	463.89	473.92	484.03	494.21	504.46	514.77	525.15
57000	422.30	432.10	442.00	451.97	462.03	472.17	482.38	492.67	503.04	513.47	523.97	534.53
58000	429.71	439.69	449.75	459.90	470.14	480.45	490.85	501.32	511.86	522.48	533.16	543.91
59000	437.12	447.27	457.50	467.83	478.24	488.74	499.31	509.96	520.69	531.48	542.35	553.28
60000	444.53	454.85	465.26	475.76	486.35	497.02	507.77	518.61	529.51	540.49	551.54	562.66
61000	451.94	462.43	473.01	483.69	494.45	505.30	516.24	527.25	538.34	549.50	560.74	572.04
62000	459.35	470.01	480.77	491.62	502.56	513.59	524.70	535.89	547.16	558.51	569.93	581.42
63000	466.76	477.59	488.52	499.55	510.67	521.87	533.16	544.54	555.99	567.52	579.12	590.79
64000	474.16	485.17	496.28	507.48	518.77	530.15	541.63	553.18	564.81	576.53	588.31	600.17
65000	481.57	492.75	504.03	515.41	526.88	538.44	550.09	561.82	573.64	585.53	597.50	609.55
66000	488.98	500.33	511.78	523.34	534.98	546.72	558.55	570.47	582.46	594.54	606.70	618.93
67000	496.39	507.91	519.54	531.27	543.09	555.01	567.01	579.11	591.29	603.55	615.89	628.30
68000	503.80	515.49	527.29	539.19	551.19	563.29	575.48	587.75	600.11	612.56	625.08	637.68
69000	511.21	523.07	535.05	547.12	559.30	571.57	583.94	596.40	608.94	621.57	634.27	647.06
70000	518.62	530.66	542.80	555.05	567.41	579.86	592.40	605.04	617.76	630.57	643.47	656.44
71000	526.03	538.24	550.56	562.98	575.51	588.14	600.87	613.68	626.59	639.58	652.66	665.82
72000	533.43	545.82	558.31	570.91	583.62	596.42	609.33	622.33	635.42	648.59	661.85	675.19
73000	540.84	553.40	566.06	578.84	591.72	604.71	630.97	630.97	644.24	657.60	671.04	684.57
74000	548.25	560.98	573.82	586.77	599.83	612.99	626.25	639.61	653.07	666.61	680.24	693.95
75000	555.66	568.56	581.57	594.70	607.94	621.28	634.72	648.26	661.89	675.62	689.43	703.33
76000	563.07	576.14	589.33	602.63	616.04	629.56	643.18	656.90	670.72	684.62	698.62	712.70
77000	570.48	583.72	597.08	610.56	624.15	637.84	651.64	665.54	679.54	693.63	707.81	722.08
78000	577.89	591.30	604.84	618.49	632.25	646.13	660.11	674.19	688.37	702.64	717.01	731.46
79000	585.30	598.88	612.59	626.42	640.36	654.41	668.57	682.83	697.19	711.65	726.20	740.84
80000	592.70	606.46	620.34	634.35	648.46	662.69	677.03	691.47	706.02	720.66	735.39	750.21
81000	600.11	614.04	628.10	642.28	656.57	670.98	685.49	700.12	714.84	729.67	744.58	759.59
82000	607.52	621.62	635.85	650.21	664.68	679.26	693.96	708.76	723.67	738.67	753.78	768.97
83000	614.93	629.21	643.61	658.13	672.78	687.54	702.42	717.40	732.49	747.68	762.97	778.35
84000	622.34	636.79	651.36	666.06	680.89	695.83	710.88	726.05	741.32	756.69	772.16	787.73
85000	629.75	644.37	659.12	673.99	688.99	704.11	719.35	734.69	750.14	765.70	781.35	797.10
86000	637.16	651.95	666.87	681.92	697.10	712.40	727.81	743.33	758.97	774.71	790.54	806.48
87000	644.57	659.53	674.63	689.85	705.20	720.68	736.27	751.98	767.79	783.71	799.74	815.86
88000	651.98	667.11	682.38	697.78	713.31	728.96	744.73	760.62	776.62	792.72	808.93	825.24
89000	659.38	674.69	690.13	705.71	721.42	737.25	753.20	769.26	785.44	801.73	818.12	834.61
90000	666.79	682.27	697.89	713.64	729.52	745.53	761.66	777.91	794.27	810.74	827.31	843.99
91000	674.20	689.85	705.64	721.57	737.63	753.81	770.12	786.55	803.09	819.75	836.51	853.37
92000	681.61	697.43	713.40	729.50	745.73	762.10	778.59	795.19	811.92	828.76	845.70	862.75
93000	689.02	705.01	721.15	737.43	753.84	770.38	787.05	803.84	820.74	837.76	854.89	872.12
94000	696.43	712.59	728.91	745.36	761.95	778.67	795.51	812.48	829.57	846.77	864.08	881.50
95000	703.84	720.17	736.66	753.29	770.05	786.95	803.97	821.12	838.39	855.78	873.28	890.88
96000	711.25	727.76	744.41	761.22	778.16	795.23	812.44	829.77	847.22	864.79	882.47	900.26
97000	718.65	735.34	752.17	769.15	786.26	803.52	820.90	838.41	856.05	873.80	891.66	909.63
98000	726.06	742.92	759.92	777.07	794.37	811.80	829.36	847.06	864.87	882.80	900.85	919.01
99000	733.47	750.50	767.68	785.00	802.47	820.08	837.83	855.70	873.70	891.81	910.05	928.39
100000	740.88	758.08	775.43	792.93	810.58	828.37	846.29	864.34	882.52	900.82	919.24	937.77

*Includes ½% for Mutual Mortgage Insurance.

Table 4

ANNUAL MORTGAGE CONSTANT

This table lists the annual mortgage constant for a loan with monthly payments. The annual mortgage constant is the capitalization rate for the lender on his investment (i.e. the loan amount). For example, the annual mortgage constant for an 8% loan with monthly payments for 20 years is 10.04%. See Sections 6.5 and 7.7 for details.

Table 4

ANNUAL INTEREST RATE

TERM	5.00	5.25	5.50	5.75	6.00	6.25	6.50	6.75	7.00	7.25	7.50	7.75	8.00	8.25	8.50	8.75	9.00	9.25
2	52.65	52.78	52.91	53.05	53.18	53.32	53.46	53.59	53.73	53.86	54.00	54.14	54.27	54.41	54.55	54.68	54.82	54.96
3	35.97	36.10	36.24	36.37	36.51	36.64	36.78	36.92	37.05	37.19	37.33	37.47	37.60	37.74	37.88	38.02	38.16	38.30
4	27.64	27.77	27.91	28.04	28.18	28.32	28.46	28.60	28.74	28.87	29.01	29.15	29.30	29.44	29.58	29.72	29.86	30.00
5	22.65	22.78	22.92	23.06	23.20	23.34	23.48	23.62	23.76	23.90	24.05	24.19	24.33	24.48	24.62	24.76	24.91	25.06
6	19.33	19.47	19.61	19.75	19.89	20.03	20.17	20.32	20.46	20.60	20.75	20.89	21.04	21.19	21.33	21.48	21.63	21.78
7	16.96	17.10	17.24	17.39	17.53	17.67	17.82	17.96	18.11	18.26	18.41	18.55	18.70	18.85	19.00	19.15	19.31	19.46
8	15.19	15.34	15.48	15.62	15.77	15.92	16.06	16.21	16.36	16.51	16.66	16.81	16.96	17.12	17.27	17.43	17.58	17.74
9	13.82	13.97	14.11	14.26	14.41	14.56	14.71	14.85	15.01	15.16	15.31	15.47	15.62	15.78	15.94	16.09	16.25	16.41
10	12.73	12.88	13.02	13.17	13.32	13.47	13.63	13.78	13.93	14.09	14.24	14.40	14.56	14.72	14.88	15.04	15.20	15.36
11	11.84	11.99	12.14	12.29	12.44	12.59	12.75	12.90	13.06	13.22	13.38	13.54	13.70	13.86	14.02	14.19	14.35	14.52
12	11.10	11.25	11.40	11.56	11.71	11.87	12.02	12.18	12.34	12.50	12.66	12.83	12.99	13.15	13.32	13.49	13.66	13.83
13	10.48	10.63	10.78	10.94	11.10	11.25	11.41	11.57	11.74	11.90	12.06	12.23	12.40	12.56	12.73	12.90	13.08	13.25
14	9.95	10.10	10.26	10.42	10.57	10.74	10.90	11.06	11.22	11.39	11.56	11.73	11.90	12.07	12.24	12.41	12.59	12.76
15	9.49	9.65	9.81	9.96	10.13	10.29	10.45	10.62	10.79	10.95	11.12	11.30	11.47	11.64	11.82	11.99	12.17	12.35
16	9.09	9.25	9.41	9.57	9.74	9.90	10.07	10.24	10.41	10.58	10.75	10.92	11.10	11.28	11.45	11.63	11.81	12.00
17	8.74	8.90	9.07	9.23	9.40	9.56	9.73	9.90	10.08	10.25	10.42	10.60	10.78	10.96	11.14	11.32	11.51	11.69
18	8.44	8.60	8.76	8.93	9.10	9.27	9.44	9.61	9.79	9.96	10.14	10.32	10.50	10.68	10.87	11.05	11.24	11.43
19	8.16	8.33	8.49	8.66	8.83	9.00	9.18	9.35	9.53	9.71	9.89	10.07	10.25	10.44	10.63	10.81	11.00	11.19
20	7.92	8.09	8.25	8.43	8.60	8.77	8.95	9.12	9.30	9.48	9.67	9.85	10.04	10.22	10.41	10.60	10.80	10.99
21	7.70	7.87	8.04	8.21	8.39	8.56	8.74	8.92	9.10	9.28	9.47	9.66	9.85	10.04	10.23	10.42	10.61	10.81
22	7.50	7.67	7.85	8.02	8.20	8.38	8.56	8.74	8.92	9.11	9.29	9.48	9.67	9.87	10.06	10.26	10.45	10.65
23	7.32	7.50	7.67	7.85	8.03	8.21	8.39	8.57	8.76	8.95	9.14	9.33	9.52	9.72	9.91	10.11	10.31	10.51
24	7.16	7.34	7.51	7.69	7.87	8.05	8.24	8.42	8.61	8.80	9.00	9.19	9.38	9.58	9.78	9.98	10.18	10.39
25	7.02	7.19	7.37	7.55	7.73	7.92	8.10	8.29	8.48	8.67	8.87	9.06	9.26	9.46	9.66	9.87	10.07	10.28
26	6.88	7.06	7.24	7.42	7.60	7.79	7.98	8.17	8.36	8.56	8.75	8.95	9.15	9.35	9.56	9.76	9.97	10.18
27	6.76	6.94	7.12	7.30	7.49	7.68	7.87	8.06	8.25	8.45	8.65	8.85	9.05	9.26	9.46	9.67	9.88	10.09
28	6.64	6.82	7.01	7.19	7.38	7.57	7.76	7.96	8.16	8.35	8.55	8.76	8.96	9.17	9.37	9.58	9.80	10.01
29	6.54	6.72	6.91	7.09	7.28	7.48	7.67	7.87	8.07	8.27	8.47	8.67	8.88	9.09	9.30	9.51	9.72	9.94
30	6.44	6.63	6.81	7.00	7.19	7.39	7.58	7.78	7.99	8.19	8.39	8.60	8.81	9.02	9.23	9.44	9.66	9.87
31	6.35	6.54	6.73	6.92	7.11	7.31	7.51	7.71	7.91	8.11	8.32	8.53	8.74	8.95	9.16	9.38	9.60	9.81
32	6.27	6.46	6.65	6.84	7.04	7.23	7.43	7.64	7.84	8.05	8.25	8.46	8.68	8.89	9.11	9.32	9.54	9.76
33	6.19	6.38	6.58	6.77	6.97	7.17	7.37	7.57	7.78	7.99	8.20	8.41	8.62	8.84	9.05	9.27	9.49	9.71
34	6.12	6.31	6.51	6.70	6.90	7.10	7.31	7.51	7.72	7.93	8.14	8.35	8.57	8.79	9.01	9.23	9.45	9.67
35	6.06	6.25	6.44	6.64	6.84	7.04	7.25	7.45	7.67	7.88	8.09	8.31	8.52	8.74	8.96	9.18	9.41	9.63
36	5.99	6.19	6.39	6.59	6.79	6.99	7.20	7.41	7.62	7.83	8.05	8.26	8.48	8.70	8.92	9.15	9.37	9.60
37	5.94	6.13	6.33	6.53	6.74	6.94	7.15	7.35	7.57	7.79	8.00	8.22	8.44	8.66	8.89	9.11	9.34	9.57
38	5.88	6.08	6.28	6.48	6.69	6.90	7.10	7.32	7.53	7.75	7.96	8.18	8.41	8.63	8.85	9.08	9.31	9.54
39	5.83	6.03	6.23	6.44	6.64	6.85	7.06	7.28	7.49	7.71	7.93	8.15	8.37	8.60	8.82	9.05	9.28	9.51
40	5.79	5.99	6.19	6.39	6.60	6.81	7.03	7.24	7.46	7.68	7.90	8.12	8.34	8.57	8.80	9.03	9.26	9.49

Table 4 475

ANNUAL INTEREST RATE

TERM	9.50	9.75	10.00	10.25	10.50	10.75	11.00	11.25	11.50	11.75	12.00	12.25	12.50	12.75	13.00	13.25	13.50	13.75
2	55.10	55.24	55.37	55.51	55.65	55.79	55.93	56.07	56.21	56.35	56.49	56.63	56.77	56.91	57.05	57.19	57.33	57.47
3	38.44	38.58	38.72	38.86	39.00	39.14	39.29	39.43	39.57	39.71	39.86	40.00	40.14	40.29	40.43	40.58	40.72	40.87
4	30.15	30.29	30.44	30.58	30.72	30.87	31.01	31.16	31.31	31.45	31.60	31.75	31.90	32.04	32.19	32.34	32.49	32.64
5	25.20	25.35	25.50	25.64	25.79	25.94	26.09	26.24	26.39	26.54	26.69	26.85	27.00	27.15	27.30	27.46	27.61	27.77
6	21.93	22.08	22.23	22.38	22.53	22.69	22.84	22.99	23.15	23.30	23.46	23.62	23.77	23.93	24.09	24.25	24.41	24.57
7	19.61	19.77	19.92	20.08	20.23	20.39	20.55	20.71	20.86	21.02	21.18	21.34	21.51	21.67	21.83	21.99	22.16	22.32
8	17.89	18.05	18.21	18.37	18.53	18.69	18.85	19.01	19.18	19.34	19.50	19.67	19.83	20.00	20.17	20.34	20.51	20.68
9	16.57	16.73	16.89	17.06	17.22	17.39	17.55	17.72	17.88	18.05	18.22	18.39	18.56	18.73	18.90	19.08	19.25	19.43
10	15.53	15.69	15.86	16.02	16.19	16.36	16.53	16.70	16.87	17.04	17.22	17.39	17.57	17.74	17.92	18.09	18.27	18.45
11	14.69	14.85	15.02	15.19	15.37	15.54	15.71	15.89	16.06	16.24	16.41	16.59	16.77	16.95	17.13	17.31	17.50	17.68
12	14.00	14.17	14.34	14.51	14.69	14.87	15.04	15.22	15.40	15.58	15.76	15.94	16.13	16.31	16.50	16.68	16.87	17.06
13	13.42	13.60	13.77	13.95	14.13	14.31	14.49	14.67	14.86	15.04	15.22	15.41	15.60	15.79	15.97	16.16	16.36	16.55
14	12.94	13.12	13.30	13.48	13.66	13.84	14.03	14.21	14.40	14.59	14.78	14.97	15.16	15.35	15.54	15.74	15.93	16.13
15	12.53	12.71	12.90	13.08	13.26	13.45	13.64	13.83	14.02	14.21	14.40	14.60	14.79	14.99	15.18	15.38	15.58	15.78
16	12.18	12.36	12.55	12.74	12.93	13.12	13.31	13.50	13.69	13.89	14.08	14.28	14.48	14.68	14.88	15.08	15.28	15.49
17	11.88	12.07	12.25	12.45	12.64	12.83	13.02	13.22	13.42	13.62	13.81	14.02	14.22	14.42	14.62	14.83	15.03	15.24
18	11.61	11.81	12.00	12.19	12.39	12.58	12.78	12.98	13.18	13.38	13.58	13.79	13.99	14.20	14.41	14.61	14.82	15.03
19	11.39	11.58	11.78	11.97	12.17	12.37	12.57	12.77	12.97	13.18	13.38	13.59	13.80	14.01	14.22	14.43	14.64	14.86
20	11.19	11.38	11.58	11.78	11.98	12.18	12.39	12.59	12.80	13.00	13.21	13.42	13.63	13.85	14.06	14.27	14.49	14.70
21	11.01	11.21	11.41	11.61	11.82	12.02	12.23	12.43	12.64	12.85	13.06	13.28	13.49	13.71	13.92	14.14	14.36	14.58
22	10.85	11.06	11.26	11.46	11.67	11.88	12.09	12.30	12.51	12.72	12.94	13.15	13.37	13.58	13.80	14.02	14.24	14.46
23	10.72	10.92	11.13	11.33	11.54	11.75	11.96	12.18	12.39	12.61	12.82	13.04	13.26	13.48	13.70	13.92	14.14	14.37
24	10.59	10.80	11.01	11.22	11.43	11.64	11.86	12.07	12.29	12.51	12.72	12.94	13.17	13.39	13.61	13.84	14.06	14.29
25	10.48	10.69	10.90	11.12	11.33	11.55	11.76	11.98	12.20	12.42	12.64	12.86	13.08	13.31	13.53	13.76	13.99	14.22
26	10.39	10.60	10.81	11.03	11.24	11.46	11.68	11.90	12.12	12.34	12.56	12.79	13.01	13.24	13.47	13.70	13.92	14.15
27	10.30	10.51	10.73	10.95	11.16	11.38	11.60	11.83	12.05	12.27	12.50	12.72	12.95	13.18	13.41	13.64	13.87	14.10
28	10.22	10.44	10.66	10.87	11.09	11.32	11.54	11.76	11.99	12.21	12.44	12.67	12.90	13.13	13.36	13.59	13.82	14.06
29	10.15	10.37	10.59	10.81	11.03	11.26	11.48	11.71	11.93	12.16	12.39	12.62	12.85	13.08	13.31	13.55	13.78	14.02
30	10.09	10.31	10.53	10.75	10.98	11.20	11.43	11.66	11.88	12.11	12.34	12.57	12.81	13.04	13.27	13.51	13.74	13.98
31	10.03	10.26	10.48	10.70	10.93	11.15	11.38	11.61	11.84	12.07	12.30	12.54	12.77	13.01	13.24	13.48	13.71	13.95
32	9.98	10.21	10.43	10.66	10.88	11.11	11.34	11.57	11.80	12.04	12.27	12.50	12.74	12.97	13.21	13.45	13.69	13.93
33	9.94	10.16	10.39	10.62	10.84	11.07	11.30	11.54	11.77	12.00	12.24	12.47	12.71	12.95	13.18	13.42	13.66	13.90
34	9.90	10.12	10.35	10.58	10.81	11.04	11.27	11.51	11.74	11.97	12.21	12.45	12.68	12.92	13.16	13.40	13.64	13.87
35	9.86	10.09	10.32	10.55	10.78	11.01	11.24	11.48	11.71	11.95	12.19	12.42	12.66	12.90	13.14	13.38	13.62	13.85
36	9.83	10.05	10.29	10.52	10.75	10.98	11.22	11.45	11.69	11.93	12.17	12.40	12.64	12.88	13.12	13.37	13.61	13.85
37	9.80	10.03	10.26	10.49	10.72	10.96	11.19	11.43	11.67	11.91	12.15	12.39	12.63	12.87	13.11	13.35	13.59	13.84
38	9.77	10.00	10.23	10.47	10.70	10.94	11.17	11.41	11.65	11.89	12.13	12.37	12.61	12.85	13.10	13.34	13.59	13.83
39	9.74	9.98	10.21	10.45	10.68	10.92	11.16	11.39	11.63	11.87	12.12	12.36	12.60	12.84	13.08	13.33	13.57	13.82
40	9.72	9.95	10.19	10.43	10.66	10.90	11.14	11.38	11.62	11.86	12.10	12.34	12.59	12.83	13.07	13.32	13.56	13.81

Table 5

DEPRECIATION

This table lists the amount of annual and total (cumulative) depreciation that may be claimed on each $1 of a depreciable asset. Values for the five most commonly used types of depreciation are listed. The type(s) of depreciation that are available to you can be determined from the figure in Section 11.4.

Choose the useful life that agrees most nearly with your estimate of the useful life when you acquired the property. Find the year (column on the left) corresponding to the tax years (complete or partial) that have passed since you acquired the property. For instance, a depreciable asset whose estimated useful life was 10 years can be depreciated by .1093750 of its value in the second year if 125% declining balance is used.

Further details are available in Sections 11.1 through 11.7.

Table 5

10 YEAR USEFUL LIFE

YEAR n	Straight Line ANNUAL a_n	Straight Line TOTAL A_n	DECLINING BALANCE 125% ANNUAL a_n	125% TOTAL A_n	150% ANNUAL a_n	150% TOTAL A_n	200% ANNUAL a_n	200% TOTAL A_n	Sum of the Years Digits ANNUAL a_n	TOTAL A_n
1	.1000000	.1000000	.1250000	.1250000	.1500000	.1500000	.2000000	.2000000	.1818182	.1818182
2	.1000000	.2000000	.1093750	.2343750	.1275000	.2775000	.1600000	.3600000	.1636364	.3454545
3	.1000000	.3000000	.0957031X	.3300781	.1083750	.3858750	.1280000	.4880000	.1454545	.4909091
4	.1000000	.4000000	.0837402	.4138184	.0921187X	.4779938	.1024000	.5904000	.1272727	.6181818
5	.1000000	.5000000	.0732231	.4870911	.0783009	.5562947	.0819200	.6723200	.1090909	.7272727
6	.1000000	.6000000	.0641136	.5512047	.0665558	.6228505	.0655360X	.7378560	.0909091	.8181818
7	.1000000	.7000000	.0560994	.6073041	.0565724	.6794229	.0524288	.7902848	.0727273	.8909091
8	.1000000	.8000000	.0490870	.6563911	.0480866	.7275095	.0419430	.8322278	.0545455	.9454545
9	.1000000	.9000000	.0429511	.6993422	.0408735	.7683831	.0335544	.8657823	.0363636	.9818182
10	.1000000	1.0000000	.0375822	.7369244	.0347425	.8031256	.0268435	.8926258	.0181818	1.0000000

X INDICATES YEAR AFTER WHICH A SWITCH TO STRAIGHT LINE MIGHT BE ADVISABLE (IF SALVAGE VALUE IS ZERO). SEE SECTION 11.7

15 YEAR USEFUL LIFE

YEAR n	Straight Line ANNUAL a_n	Straight Line TOTAL A_n	DECLINING BALANCE 125% ANNUAL a_n	125% TOTAL A_n	150% ANNUAL a_n	150% TOTAL A_n	200% ANNUAL a_n	200% TOTAL A_n	Sum of the Years Digits ANNUAL a_n	TOTAL A_n
1	.0666667	.0666667	.0833333	.0833333	.1000000	.1000000	.1333333	.1333333	.1250000	.1250000
2	.0666667	.1333333	.0763889	.1597222	.0900000	.1900000	.1155556	.2488889	.1166667	.2416667
3	.0666667	.2000000	.0700231	.2297454	.0810000	.2710000	.1001481	.3490370	.1083333	.3500000
4	.0666667	.2666667	.0641879X	.2939333	.0729000	.3439000	.0867951	.4358321	.1000000	.4500000
5	.0666667	.3333333	.0588389	.3527722	.0656100	.4095100	.0752224	.5110545	.0916667	.5416667
6	.0666667	.4000000	.0539357	.4067078	.0590490X	.4685590	.0651927	.5762472	.0833333	.6250000
7	.0666667	.4666667	.0499410	.4561488	.0531441	.5217031	.0565004	.6327476	.0750000	.7000000
8	.0666667	.5333333	.0453209	.5014698	.0478297	.5695328	.0489670X	.6817146	.0666667	.7666667
9	.0666667	.6000000	.0415442	.5430139	.0430467	.6125795	.0424381	.7241526	.0583333	.8250000
10	.0666667	.6666667	.0380822	.5810961	.0387420	.6513216	.0367796	.7609323	.0500000	.8750000
11	.0666667	.7333333	.0349087	.6160048	.0348678	.6861894	.0318757	.7928080	.0416667	.9166667
12	.0666667	.8000000	.0319996	.6480044	.0313811	.7175705	.0276256	.8204336	.0333333	.9500000
13	.0666667	.8666667	.0293330	.6773373	.0282430	.7458134	.0239422	.8443758	.0250000	.9750000
14	.0666667	.9333333	.0268886	.7042259	.0254187	.7712321	.0207499	.8651257	.0166667	.9916667
15	.0666667	1.0000000	.0246478	.7288737	.0228768	.7941089	.0179832	.8831089	.0083333	1.0000000

X INDICATES YEAR AFTER WHICH A SWITCH TO STRAIGHT LINE MIGHT BE ADVISABLE (IF SALVAGE VALUE IS ZERO). SEE SECTION 11.7

Table 5   479

20 YEAR USEFUL LIFE

YEAR n	Straight Line ANNUAL a_n	Straight Line TOTAL A_n	125% ANNUAL a_n	125% TOTAL A_n	150% ANNUAL a_n	150% TOTAL A_n	200% ANNUAL a_n	200% TOTAL A_n	Sum of Years Digits ANNUAL a_n	Sum of Years Digits TOTAL A_n
1	.0500000	.0500000	.0625000	.0625000	.0750000	.0750000	.1000000	.1000000	.0952381	.0952381
2	.0500000	.1000000	.0585938	.1210938	.0693750	.1443750	.0900000	.1900000	.0904762	.1857143
3	.0500000	.1500000	.0549316	.1760254	.0641719	.2085469	.0810000	.2710000	.0857143	.2714286
4	.0500000	.2000000	.0514984	.2275238	.0593590	.2679059	.0729000	.3439000	.0809524	.3523810
5	.0500000	.2500000	.0482798X	.2758036	.0549071	.3228129	.0656100	.4095100	.0761905	.4285714
6	.0500000	.3000000	.0452623	.3210658	.0507830	.3736020	.0590490	.4685590	.0714286	.5000000
7	.0500000	.3500000	.0424334	.3634992	.0469799X	.4205818	.0531441	.5217031	.0666667	.5666667
8	.0500000	.4000000	.0397813	.4032805	.0434564	.4640382	.0478297	.5695328	.0619048	.6285714
9	.0500000	.4500000	.0372950	.4405755	.0401971	.5042353	.0430467	.6125795	.0571429	.6857143
10	.0500000	.5000000	.0349640	.4755395	.0371824	.5414177	.0387420	.6513216	.0523810	.7380952
11	.0500000	.5500000	.0327788	.5083183	.0343937	.5758113	.0348678X	.6861894	.0476190	.7857143
12	.0500000	.6000000	.0307301	.5390484	.0318141	.6076255	.0313811	.7175705	.0428571	.8285714
13	.0500000	.6500000	.0288095	.5678579	.0294281	.6370536	.0282430	.7458134	.0380952	.8666667
14	.0500000	.7000000	.0270089	.5948668	.0272210	.6642746	.0254187	.7712321	.0333333	.9000000
15	.0500000	.7500000	.0253208	.6201876	.0251794	.6894540	.0228768	.7941089	.0285714	.9285714
16	.0500000	.8000000	.0237383	.6439259	.0232910	.7127449	.0205991	.8146980	.0238095	.9523810
17	.0500000	.8500000	.0222546	.6661805	.0215441	.7342890	.0185302	.8332282	.0190476	.9714286
18	.0500000	.9000000	.0208637	.6870442	.0199283	.7542174	.0166772	.8499054	.0142857	.9857143
19	.0500000	.9500000	.0195597	.7066040	.0184337	.7726511	.0150095	.8649148	.0095238	.9952381
20	.0500000	1.0000000	.0183373	.7249412	.0170512	.7897022	.0135085	.8784233	.0047619	1.0000000

X INDICATES YEAR AFTER WHICH A SWITCH TO STRAIGHT LINE MIGHT BE ADVISABLE (IF SALVAGE VALUE IS ZERO). SEE SECTION 11.7

25 YEAR USEFUL LIFE

YEAR n	Straight Line ANNUAL a_n	Straight Line TOTAL A_n	125% ANNUAL a_n	125% TOTAL A_n	150% ANNUAL a_n	150% TOTAL A_n	200% ANNUAL a_n	200% TOTAL A_n	Sum of Years Digits ANNUAL a_n	Sum of Years Digits TOTAL A_n
1	.0400000	.0400000	.0500000	.0500000	.0600000	.0600000	.0800000	.0800000	.0769231	.0769231
2	.0400000	.0800000	.0475000	.0975000	.0564000	.1164000	.0736000	.1536000	.0738462	.1507692
3	.0400000	.1200000	.0451250	.1426250	.0530160	.1694160	.0677120	.2213120	.0707692	.2215385
4	.0400000	.1600000	.0428687	.1854938	.0498350	.2192510	.0622950	.2836070	.0676923	.2892308
5	.0400000	.2000000	.0407253	.2262191	.0468449	.2660960	.0573114	.3409185	.0646154	.3538462
6	.0400000	.2400000	.0386890X	.2649081	.0440342	.3101302	.0527265	.3936450	.0615385	.4153846
7	.0400000	.2800000	.0367546	.3016627	.0413922	.3515224	.0485084	.4421534	.0584615	.4738462
8	.0400000	.3200000	.0349169	.3365796	.0389087	.3904311	.0446277	.4867811	.0553846	.5292308
9	.0400000	.3600000	.0331710	.3697506	.0365741X	.4270052	.0410575	.5278386	.0523077	.5815385
10	.0400000	.4000000	.0315125	.4012631	.0343797	.4613849	.0377729	.5656115	.0492308	.6307692
11	.0400000	.4400000	.0299368	.4311999	.0323169	.4937018	.0347511	.6003626	.0461538	.6769231
12	.0400000	.4800000	.0284400	.4596399	.0303779	.5240797	.0319710	.6323336	.0430769	.7200000
13	.0400000	.5200000	.0270180	.4866579	.0285552	.5526349	.0294133X	.6617469	.0400000	.7600000
14	.0400000	.5600000	.0256671	.5123250	.0268419	.5794768	.0270602	.6888072	.0369231	.7969231
15	.0400000	.6000000	.0243837	.5367088	.0252314	.6047082	.0248954	.7137026	.0338462	.8307692
16	.0400000	.6400000	.0231646	.5598733	.0237175	.6284257	.0229038	.7366064	.0307692	.8615385
17	.0400000	.6800000	.0220063	.5818797	.0222945	.6507202	.0210715	.7576779	.0276923	.8892308
18	.0400000	.7200000	.0209060	.6027857	.0209568	.6716770	.0193858	.7770636	.0246154	.9138462
19	.0400000	.7600000	.0198607	.6226464	.0196994	.6913763	.0178349	.7948986	.0215385	.9353846
20	.0400000	.8000000	.0188807	.6415141	.0185174	.7098938	.0164081	.8113067	.0184615	.9538462
21	.0400000	.8400000	.0179243	.6594384	.0174064	.7273001	.0150955	.8264021	.0153846	.9692308
22	.0400000	.8800000	.0170281	.6764665	.0163620	.7436621	.0138879	.8402900	.0123077	.9815385
23	.0400000	.9200000	.0161767	.6926431	.0153803	.7590424	.0127768	.8530668	.0092308	.9907692
24	.0400000	.9600000	.0153678	.7080110	.0144575	.7734999	.0117547	.8648214	.0061538	.9969231
25	.0400000	1.0000000	.0145995	.7226104	.0135900	.7870899	.0108143	.8756357	.0030769	1.0000000

X INDICATES YEAR AFTER WHICH A SWITCH TO STRAIGHT LINE MIGHT BE ADVISABLE (IF SALVAGE VALUE IS ZERO). SEE SECTION 11.7

Table 5

30 YEAR USEFUL LIFE

YEAR n	Straight Line		DECLINING BALANCE						Sum of the Years Digits	
			125%		150%		200%			
	ANNUAL a_n	TOTAL A_n	ANNUAL a_n	TOTAL A_n	ANNUAL a_n	TOTAL A_n	ANNUAL a_n	TOTAL A_n	ANNUAL a_n	TOTAL A_n
1	.0333333	.0333333	.0416667	.0416667	.0500000	.0500000	.0666667	.0666667	.0645161	.0645161
2	.0333333	.0666667	.0399306	.0815972	.0475000	.0975000	.0622222	.1288889	.0623656	.1268817
3	.0333333	.1000000	.0382668	.1198640	.0451250	.1426250	.0580741	.1869630	.0602151	.1870968
4	.0333333	.1333333	.0366723	.1565363	.0428687	.1854938	.0542025	.2411654	.0580645	.2451613
5	.0333333	.1666667	.0351443	.1916807	.0407253	.2262191	.0505890	.2917544	.0559140	.3010753
6	.0333333	.2000000	.0336800	.2253606	.0386890	.2649081	.0472164	.3389708	.0537634	.3548387
7	.0333333	.2333333	.0322766X	.2576373	.0367546	.3016627	.0440686	.3830394	.0516129	.4064516
8	.0333333	.2666667	.0309318	.2885691	.0349169	.3365796	.0411307	.4241701	.0494624	.4559140
9	.0333333	.3000000	.0296430	.3182120	.0331710	.3697506	.0383887	.4625588	.0473118	.5032258
10	.0333333	.3333333	.0284078	.3466198	.0315125	.4012631	.0358294	.4983882	.0451613	.5483871
11	.0333333	.3666667	.0272242	.3738440	.0299368X	.4311999	.0334408	.5318290	.0430108	.5913978
12	.0333333	.4000000	.0260898	.3999338	.0284400	.4596399	.0312114	.5630404	.0408602	.6322581
13	.0333333	.4333333	.0250028	.4249366	.0270180	.4866579	.0291306	.5921710	.0387097	.6709677
14	.0333333	.4666667	.0239610	.4488976	.0256671	.5123250	.0271886	.6193596	.0365591	.7075269
15	.0333333	.5000000	.0229626	.4718602	.0243837	.5367088	.0253760	.6447356	.0344086	.7419355
16	.0333333	.5333333	.0220058	.4938660	.0231646	.5598733	.0236843X	.6684199	.0322581	.7741935
17	.0333333	.5666667	.0210889	.5149549	.0220063	.5818797	.0221053	.6905253	.0301075	.8043011
18	.0333333	.6000000	.0202102	.5351651	.0209060	.6027857	.0206316	.7111569	.0279570	.8322581
19	.0333333	.6333333	.0193681	.5545333	.0198607	.6226464	.0192562	.7304131	.0258065	.8580645
20	.0333333	.6666667	.0185611	.5730944	.0188677	.6415141	.0179725	.7483856	.0236559	.8817204
21	.0333333	.7000000	.0177877	.5908821	.0179243	.6594384	.0167743	.7651599	.0215054	.9032258
22	.0333333	.7333333	.0170466	.6079287	.0170281	.6764665	.0156560	.7808159	.0193548	.9225806
23	.0333333	.7666667	.0163363	.6242650	.0161767	.6926431	.0146123	.7954282	.0172043	.9397849
24	.0333333	.8000000	.0156556	.6399206	.0153678	.7080110	.0136381	.8090663	.0150538	.9548387
25	.0333333	.8333333	.0150033	.6549239	.0145995	.7226104	.0127289	.8217952	.0129032	.9677419
26	.0333333	.8666667	.0143782	.6693021	.0138695	.7364799	.0118803	.8336755	.0107527	.9784946
27	.0333333	.9000000	.0137791	.6830812	.0131760	.7496559	.0110883	.8447638	.0086022	.9870968
28	.0333333	.9333333	.0132050	.6962861	.0125172	.7621731	.0103491	.8551129	.0064516	.9935484
29	.0333333	.9666667	.0126547	.7089409	.0118913	.7740645	.0096591	.8647720	.0043011	.9978495
30	.0333333	1.0000000	.0121275	.7210683	.0112968	.7853612	.0090152	.8737872	.0021505	1.0000000

X INDICATES YEAR AFTER WHICH A SWITCH TO STRAIGHT LINE MIGHT BE ADVISABLE (IF SALVAGE VALUE IS ZERO). SEE SECTION 11.7

Table 5

35 YEAR USEFUL LIFE

YEAR n	Straight Line ANNUAL a_n	Straight Line TOTAL A_n	125% ANNUAL a_n	125% TOTAL A_n	150% ANNUAL a_n	150% TOTAL A_n	200% ANNUAL a_n	200% TOTAL A_n	Sum of the Years Digits ANNUAL a_n	Sum of the Years Digits TOTAL A_n
1	.0285714	.0285714	.0357143	.0357143	.0428571	.0428571	.0571429	.0571429	.0555556	.0555556
2	.0285714	.0571429	.0344388	.0701531	.0410204	.0838776	.0538776	.1110204	.0539683	.1095238
3	.0285714	.0857143	.0332088	.1033619	.0392624	.1231399	.0507988	.1618192	.0523810	.1619048
4	.0285714	.1142857	.0320228	.1353847	.0375797	.1607197	.0478960	.2097153	.0507937	.2126984
5	.0285714	.1428571	.0308791	.1662638	.0359692	.1966888	.0451591	.2548744	.0492063	.2619048
6	.0285714	.1714286	.0297763	.1960401	.0344276	.2311164	.0425786	.2974530	.0476190	.3095238
7	.0285714	.2000000	.0287129	.2247529	.0329522	.2640686	.0401455	.3375986	.0460317	.3555556
8	.0285714	.2285714	.0276874X	.2524403	.0315399	.2956085	.0378515	.3754501	.0444444	.4000000
9	.0285714	.2571429	.0266986	.2791389	.0301882	.3257967	.0356886	.4111386	.0428571	.4428571
10	.0285714	.2857143	.0257450	.3048839	.0288944	.3546911	.0336492	.4447879	.0412698	.4841270
11	.0285714	.3142857	.0248256	.3297095	.0276561	.3823472	.0317264	.4765143	.0396825	.5238095
12	.0285714	.3428571	.0239389	.3536485	.0264708X	.4088181	.0299135	.5064277	.0380952	.5619048
13	.0285714	.3714286	.0230840	.3767324	.0253364	.4341544	.0282041	.5346319	.0365079	.5984127
14	.0285714	.4000000	.0222596	.3989920	.0242505	.4584050	.0265925	.5612243	.0349206	.6333333
15	.0285714	.4285714	.0214646	.4204566	.0232112	.4816162	.0250729	.5862972	.0333333	.6666667
16	.0285714	.4571429	.0206980	.4411545	.0222164	.5038326	.0236102	.6099374	.0317460	.6984127
17	.0285714	.4857143	.0199588	.4611133	.0212643	.5250969	.0222893	.6322267	.0301587	.7285714
18	.0285714	.5142857	.0192460	.4803593	.0203530	.5454499	.0210156X	.6532423	.0285714	.7571429
19	.0285714	.5428571	.0185586	.4989179	.0194807	.5649306	.0198147	.6730570	.0269841	.7841270
20	.0285714	.5714286	.0178958	.5168137	.0186458	.5835765	.0186825	.6917395	.0253968	.8095238
21	.0285714	.6000000	.0172567	.5340703	.0178467	.6014232	.0176149	.7093544	.0238095	.8333333
22	.0285714	.6285714	.0166403	.5507107	.0170319	.6185051	.0166083	.7259627	.0222222	.8555556
23	.0285714	.6571429	.0160460	.5667567	.0163498	.6348548	.0156593	.7416220	.0206349	.8761905
24	.0285714	.6857143	.0154730	.5822297	.0156491	.6505039	.0147645	.7563864	.0190476	.8952381
25	.0285714	.7142857	.0149204	.5971500	.0149784	.6654823	.0139208	.7703072	.0174603	.9126984
26	.0285714	.7428571	.0143875	.6115375	.0143365	.6798188	.0131253	.7834325	.0158730	.9285714
27	.0285714	.7714286	.0138737	.6254112	.0137221	.6935409	.0123753	.7958078	.0142857	.9428571
28	.0285714	.8000000	.0133782	.6387894	.0131340	.7066748	.0116681	.8074759	.0126984	.9555556
29	.0285714	.8285714	.0129004	.6516898	.0125711	.7192459	.0110014	.8184773	.0111111	.9666667
30	.0285714	.8571429	.0124397	.6641294	.0120323	.7312782	.0103727	.8288500	.0095238	.9761905
31	.0285714	.8857143	.0119954	.6761248	.0115166	.7427949	.0097800	.8386300	.0079365	.9841270
32	.0285714	.9142857	.0115670	.6876918	.0110231	.7538179	.0092211	.8478512	.0063492	.9904762
33	.0285714	.9428571	.0111539	.6988456	.0105507	.7643686	.0086942	.8565454	.0047619	.9952381
34	.0285714	.9714286	.0107555	.7096011	.0100985	.7744671	.0081974	.8647428	.0031746	.9984127
35	.0285714	1.0000000	.0103714	.7199725	.0096657	.7841328	.0077290	.8724718	.0015873	1.0000000

X INDICATES YEAR AFTER WHICH A SWITCH TO STRAIGHT LINE MIGHT BE ADVISABLE (IF SALVAGE VALUE IS ZERO). SEE SECTION 11.7

Table 5

40 YEAR USEFUL LIFE

YEAR n	Straight Line		DECLINING BALANCE 125%		150%		200%		Sum of the Years Digits	
	ANNUAL a_n	TOTAL A_n	ANNUAL a_n	TOTAL A_n	ANNUAL a_n	TOTAL A_n	ANNUAL a_n	TOTAL A_n	ANNUAL a_n	TOTAL A_n
1	.0250000	.0250000	.0312500	.0312500	.0375000	.0375000	.0500000	.0500000	.0487805	.0487805
2	.0250000	.0500000	.0302734	.0615234	.0360937	.0735938	.0475000	.0975000	.0475610	.0963415
3	.0250000	.0750000	.0293274	.0908508	.0347402	.1083340	.0451250	.1426250	.0463415	.1428829
4	.0250000	.1000000	.0284109	.1192617	.0334375	.1417715	.0428687	.1854938	.0451220	.1878049
5	.0250000	.1250000	.0275231	.1467848	.0321836	.1739550	.0407253	.2262191	.0439024	.2317073
6	.0250000	.1500000	.0266630	.1734478	.0309767	.2049317	.0386890	.2649081	.0426829	.2743902
7	.0250000	.1750000	.0258298	.1992775	.0298151	.2347468	.0367546	.3016627	.0414634	.3158537
8	.0250000	.2000000	.0250226	.2243001	.0286970	.2634438	.0349169	.3365796	.0402439	.3560976
9	.0250000	.2250000	.0242406X	.2485407	.0276209	.2910646	.0331710	.3697506	.0390244	.3951220
10	.0250000	.2500000	.0234831	.2720238	.0265851	.3176497	.0315125	.4012631	.0378049	.4329268
11	.0250000	.2750000	.0227493	.2947731	.0255881	.3432378	.0299368	.4311999	.0365854	.4695122
12	.0250000	.3000000	.0220383	.3168114	.0246286	.3678664	.0284400	.4596399	.0353659	.5048780
13	.0250000	.3250000	.0213496	.3381611	.0237050	.3915714	.0270180	.4866559	.0341463	.5390244
14	.0250000	.3500000	.0206825	.3588435	.0228161X	.4143875	.0256671	.5123250	.0329268	.5719512
15	.0250000	.3750000	.0200361	.3788797	.0219605	.4363480	.0243837	.5367088	.0317073	.6036585
16	.0250000	.4000000	.0194100	.3982897	.0211370	.4574849	.0231646	.5598733	.0304878	.6341463
17	.0250000	.4250000	.0188034	.4170931	.0203443	.4778292	.0220063	.5818797	.0292683	.6634146
18	.0250000	.4500000	.0182158	.4353090	.0195814	.4974106	.0209060	.6027857	.0280488	.6914634
19	.0250000	.4750000	.0176466	.4529556	.0188471	.5162577	.0198607	.6226464	.0268293	.7182927
20	.0250000	.5000000	.0170951	.4700507	.0181403	.5343981	.0188677	.6415141	.0256098	.7439024
21	.0250000	.5250000	.0165609	.4866116	.0174601	.5518582	.0179243X	.6594384	.0243902	.7682927
22	.0250000	.5500000	.0160434	.5026550	.0168053	.5686635	.0170281	.6764665	.0231707	.7914634
23	.0250000	.5750000	.0155420	.5181970	.0161751	.5848386	.0161767	.6926431	.0219512	.8134146
24	.0250000	.6000000	.0150563	.5332534	.0155656	.6004071	.0153678	.7080110	.0207317	.8341463
25	.0250000	.6250000	.0145858	.5478392	.0149947	.6153919	.0145995	.7226104	.0195122	.8536585
26	.0250000	.6500000	.0141300	.5619692	.0144228	.6298147	.0138695	.7364799	.0182927	.8719512
27	.0250000	.6750000	.0136885	.5756577	.0138819	.6436966	.0131760	.7496559	.0170732	.8890244
28	.0250000	.7000000	.0132607	.5889184	.0133614	.6570580	.0125172	.7621731	.0158537	.9048780
29	.0250000	.7250000	.0128463	.6017647	.0128603	.6699183	.0118913	.7740645	.0146341	.9195122
30	.0250000	.7500000	.0124449	.6142096	.0123781	.6822964	.0112968	.7853612	.0134146	.9329268
31	.0250000	.7750000	.0120560	.6262655	.0119139	.6942103	.0107319	.7960932	.0121951	.9451220
32	.0250000	.8000000	.0116792	.6379447	.0114671	.7056774	.0101953	.8062885	.0109756	.9560976
33	.0250000	.8250000	.0113142	.6492589	.0110371	.7167145	.0096856	.8159741	.0097561	.9658537
34	.0250000	.8500000	.0109607	.6602196	.0106232	.7273377	.0092013	.8251754	.0085366	.9743902
35	.0250000	.8750000	.0106181	.6708377	.0102248	.7375625	.0087412	.8339166	.0073171	.9817073
36	.0250000	.9000000	.0102863	.6811241	.0098414	.7474039	.0083042	.8422208	.0060976	.9878049
37	.0250000	.9250000	.0099649	.6910889	.0094724	.7568763	.0078890	.8501097	.0048780	.9926829
38	.0250000	.9500000	.0096535	.7007424	.0091171	.7659934	.0074945	.8576043	.0036585	.9963415
39	.0250000	.9750000	.0093518	.7100942	.0087752	.7747687	.0071198	.8647240	.0024390	.9987805
40	.0250000	1.0000000	.0090596	.7191538	.0084462	.7832149	.0067638	.8714878	.0012195	1.0000000

X INDICATES YEAR AFTER WHICH A SWITCH TO STRAIGHT LINE MIGHT BE ADVISABLE (IF SALVAGE VALUE IS ZERO). SEE SECTION 11.7

Table 5 483

45 YEAR USEFUL LIFE

YEAR n	Straight Line		DECLINING BALANCE						Sum of the Years Digits	
			125%		150%		200%			
	ANNUAL a_n	TOTAL A_n	ANNUAL a_n	TOTAL A_n	ANNUAL a_n	TOTAL A_n	ANNUAL a_n	TOTAL A_n	ANNUAL a_n	TOTAL A_n
1	.0222222	.0222222	.0277778	.0277778	.0333333	.0333333	.0444444	.0444444	.0434783	.0434783
2	.0222222	.0444444	.0270062	.0547840	.0322222	.0655556	.0424691	.086913b	.0425121	.0859903
3	.0222222	.0666667	.0262560	.0810400	.0311481	.0967037	.0405816	.1274952	.0415459	.1275362
4	.0222222	.0888889	.0255267	.1065666	.0301099	.1268136	.0387780	.1662732	.0405797	.1681159
5	.0222222	.1111111	.0248176	.1313842	.0291062	.1559198	.0370545	.2033277	.0396135	.2077295
6	.0222222	.1333333	.0241282	.1555124	.0281360	.1840558	.0354077	.2387354	.0386473	.2463768
7	.0222222	.1555556	.0234580	.1789704	.0271981	.2112539	.0338340	.2725694	.0376812	.2840580
8	.0222222	.1777778	.0228064	.2017768	.0262915	.2375455	.0323303	.3048996	.0367150	.3207729
9	.0222222	.2000000	.0221729	.2239497	.0254152	.2629606	.0308934	.3357930	.0357488	.3565217
10	.0222222	.2222222	.0215570X	.2455066	.0245680	.2875286	.0295203	.3653133	.0347826	.3913043
11	.0222222	.2444444	.0209581	.2664648	.0237490	.3112777	.0282083	.3935216	.0338164	.4251208
12	.0222222	.2666667	.0203760	.2868407	.0229574	.3342351	.0269546	.4204762	.0328502	.4579710
13	.0222222	.2888889	.0198100	.3066507	.0221922	.3564272	.0257566	.4462328	.0318841	.4898551
14	.0222222	.3111111	.0192597	.3259104	.0214524	.3778797	.0246119	.4708447	.0309179	.5207729
15	.0222222	.3333333	.0187247	.3446351	.0207373	.3986170	.0235180	.4943627	.0299517	.5507246
16	.0222222	.3555556	.0182046	.3628397	.0200461X	.4186631	.0224728	.5168354	.0289865	.5797101
17	.0222222	.3777778	.0176989	.3805386	.0193779	.4380410	.0214740	.5383094	.0280193	.6077295
18	.0222222	.4000000	.0172073	.3977459	.0187320	.4567730	.0205196	.5588290	.0270531	.6347826
19	.0222222	.4222222	.0167293	.4144752	.0181076	.4748805	.0196076	.5784366	.0260870	.6608696
20	.0222222	.4444444	.0162646	.4307397	.0175040	.4923845	.0187362	.5971728	.0251208	.6859903
21	.0222222	.4666667	.0158128	.4465525	.0169205	.5093050	.0179034	.6150762	.0241546	.7101449
22	.0222222	.4688889	.0153735	.4619261	.0163565	.5256615	.0171077	.6321839	.0231884	.7333333
23	.0222222	.5111111	.0149465	.4768726	.0158113	.5414728	.0163474X	.6485313	.0222222	.7555556
24	.0222222	.5333333	.0145313	.4914039	.0152842	.5567571	.0156208	.6641521	.0212560	.7768116
25	.0222222	.5555556	.0141277	.5055315	.0147748	.5715318	.0149266	.6790787	.0202899	.7971014
26	.0222222	.5777778	.0137352	.5192668	.0142823	.5858141	.0142632	.6933419	.0193237	.8164251
27	.0222222	.6000000	.0133537	.5326205	.0138062	.5996203	.0136293	.7069711	.0183575	.8347826
28	.0222222	.6222222	.0129828	.5456032	.0133460	.6129663	.0130235	.7199946	.0173913	.8521739
29	.0222222	.6444444	.0126221	.5582254	.0129011	.6258674	.0124447	.7324393	.0164251	.8685990
30	.0222222	.6666667	.0122715	.5704969	.0124711	.6383385	.0118916	.7443309	.0154589	.8840580
31	.0222222	.6888939	.0119306	.5824275	.0120554	.6503939	.0113631	.7556940	.0144928	.8985507
32	.0222222	.7111111	.0115992	.5940268	.0116535	.6620474	.0108580	.7665520	.0135266	.9120773
33	.0222222	.7333333	.0112770	.6053038	.0112651	.6733125	.0103755	.7769275	.0125604	.9246377
34	.0222222	.7555556	.0109638	.6162676	.0108896	.6842021	.0099143	.7868418	.0115942	.9362319
35	.0222222	.7777778	.0106592	.6269268	.0105266	.6947287	.0094737	.7963155	.0106280	.9468599
36	.0222222	.8000000	.0103631	.6372900	.0101757	.7049044	.009·526	.8053682	.0096618	.9565217
37	.0222222	.8222222	.0100753	.6473652	.0098365	.7147409	.0086503	.8140185	.0086957	.9652174
38	.0222222	.8444444	.0097954	.6571607	.0095086	.7242495	.0082658	.8222843	.0077295	.9729469
39	.0222222	.8666667	.0095233	.6666840	.0091917	.7334412	.0078985	.8301828	.0067633	.9797101
40	.0222222	.8888889	.0092588	.6759427	.0088853	.7423265	.0075474	.8377302	.0057971	.9855072
41	.0222222	.9111111	.0090016	.6849443	.0085891	.7509156	.0072120	.8449422	.0048309	.9903382
42	.0222222	.9333333	.0087515	.6936959	.0083028	.7592184	.0068915	.8518337	.0038647	.9942029
43	.0222222	.9555556	.0085084	.7022043	.0080261	.7672445	.0065852	.8584188	.0028986	.9971014
44	.0222222	.9777778	.0082721	.7104764	.0077585	.7750030	.0062925	.8647113	.0019324	.9990338
45	.0222222	1.0000000	.0080423	.7185188	.0074999	.7825029	.0060128	.8707242	.0009662	1.0000000

X INDICATES YEAR AFTER WHICH A SWITCH TO STRAIGHT LINE MIGHT BE ADVISABLE (IF SALVAGE VALUE IS ZERO). SEE SECTION 11.7

50 YEAR USEFUL LIFE

YEAR n	Straight Line ANNUAL a_n	Straight Line TOTAL A_n	DECLINING BALANCE 125% ANNUAL a_n	125% TOTAL A_n	150% ANNUAL a_n	150% TOTAL A_n	200% ANNUAL a_n	200% TOTAL A_n	Sum of the Years Digits ANNUAL a_n	Sum of the Years Digits TOTAL A_n
1	.0200000	.0200000	.0250000	.0250000	.0300000	.0300000	.0400000	.0400000	.0392157	.0392157
2	.0200000	.0400000	.0243750	.0493750	.0291000	.0591000	.0384000	.0784000	.0384314	.0776471
3	.0200000	.0600000	.0237656	.0731406	.0282270	.0873270	.0368640	.1152640	.0376471	.1152941
4	.0200000	.0800000	.0231715	.0963121	.0273802	.1147072	.0353894	.1506534	.0368627	.1521569
5	.0200000	.1000000	.0225922	.1189043	.0265588	.1412660	.0339739	.1846273	.0360784	.1882353
6	.0200000	.1200000	.0220274	.1409317	.0257620	.1670280	.0326149	.2172422	.0352941	.2235294
7	.0200000	.1400000	.0214767	.1624084	.0249892	.1920172	.0313103	.2485525	.0345098	.2580392
8	.0200000	.1600000	.0209398	.1833482	.0242395	.2162566	.0300579	.2786104	.0337255	.2917647
9	.0200000	.1800000	.0204163	.2037645	.0235123	.2397689	.0288556	.3074660	.0329412	.3247059
10	.0200000	.2000000	.0199059	.2236704	.0228069	.2625759	.0277014	.3351674	.0321569	.3568627
11	.0200000	.2200000	.0194082X	.2430786	.0221227	.2846986	.0265933	.3617607	.0313725	.3882353
12	.0200000	.2400000	.0189230	.2620017	.0214590	.3061576	.0255296	.3872902	.0305882	.4188235
13	.0200000	.2600000	.0184500	.2804516	.0208153	.3269729	.0245084	.4117986	.0298039	.4486275
14	.0200000	.2800000	.0179887	.2984403	.0201908	.3471637	.0235281	.4353267	.0290196	.4776471
15	.0200000	.3000000	.0175390	.3159793	.0195851	.3667488	.0225869	.4579136	.0282353	.5058824
16	.0200000	.3200000	.0171005	.3330798	.0189975	.3857463	.0216935	.4795971	.0274510	.5333333
17	.0200000	.3400000	.0166730	.3497528	.0184276X	.4041740	.0208161	.5004132	.0266667	.5600000
18	.0200000	.3600000	.0162562	.3660090	.0178748	.4220487	.0199835	.5203967	.0258824	.5858824
19	.0200000	.3800000	.0158498	.3818588	.0173385	.4393873	.0191841	.5395808	.0250980	.6109804
20	.0200000	.4000000	.0154535	.3973123	.0168184	.4562057	.0184168	.5579976	.0243137	.6352941
21	.0200000	.4200000	.0150672	.4123795	.0163138	.4725195	.0176801	.5756777	.0235294	.6588235
22	.0200000	.4400000	.0146905	.4270700	.0158244	.4883439	.0169729	.5926506	.0227451	.6815686
23	.0200000	.4600000	.0143232	.4413933	.0153497	.5036936	.0162940	.6089445	.0219608	.7035294
24	.0200000	.4800000	.0139652	.4553584	.0148892	.5185828	.0156422	.6245868	.0211765	.7247059
25	.0200000	.5000000	.0136160	.4689745	.0144425	.5330253	.0150165X	.6396033	.0203922	.7450980
26	.0200000	.5200000	.0132756	.4822501	.0140092	.5470345	.0144159	.6540192	.0196078	.7647059
27	.0200000	.5400000	.0129437	.4951939	.0135890	.5606235	.0138392	.6678584	.0188235	.7835294
28	.0200000	.5600000	.0126202	.5078140	.0131813	.5738048	.0132857	.6811441	.0180392	.8015686
29	.0200000	.5800000	.0123046	.5201187	.0127859	.5865907	.0127542	.6938983	.0172549	.8188235
30	.0200000	.6000000	.0119970	.5321157	.0124023	.5989929	.0122441	.7061424	.0164706	.8352941
31	.0200000	.6200000	.0116971	.5438128	.0120302	.6110231	.0117543	.7178967	.0156863	.8509804
32	.0200000	.6400000	.0114047	.5552175	.0116693	.6226924	.0112841	.7291808	.0149020	.8658824
33	.0200000	.6600000	.0111196	.5663371	.0113192	.6340117	.0108328	.7400136	.0141176	.8800000
34	.0200000	.6800000	.0108416	.5771786	.0109796	.6449913	.0103995	.7504130	.0133333	.8933333
35	.0200000	.7000000	.0105705	.5877492	.0106503	.6556416	.0099835	.7603965	.0125490	.9058824
36	.0200000	.7200000	.0103063	.5980554	.0103308	.6659723	.0095841	.7699806	.0117647	.9176471
37	.0200000	.7400000	.0100486	.6081040	.0100208	.6759932	.0092008	.7791814	.0109804	.9286275
38	.0200000	.7600000	.0097974	.6179014	.0097202	.6857134	.0088327	.7880142	.0101961	.9388235
39	.0200000	.7800000	.0095525	.6274539	.0094286	.6951420	.0084794	.7964936	.0094118	.9482353
40	.0200000	.8000000	.0093137	.6367676	.0091457	.7042877	.0081403	.8046338	.0086275	.9568627
41	.0200000	.8200000	.0090808	.6458484	.0088714	.7131591	.0078146	.8124485	.0078431	.9647059
42	.0200000	.8400000	.0088538	.6547022	.0086052	.7217643	.0075021	.8199506	.0070588	.9717647
43	.0200000	.8600000	.0086324	.6633346	.0083471	.7301114	.0072020	.8271525	.0062745	.9780392
44	.0200000	.8800000	.0084166	.6717512	.0080967	.7382080	.0069139	.8340664	.0054902	.9835294
45	.0200000	.9000000	.0082062	.6799575	.0078538	.7460618	.0066373	.8407038	.0047059	.9882353
46	.0200000	.9200000	.0080011	.6879585	.0076181	.7536799	.0063718	.8470756	.0039216	.9921569
47	.0200000	.9400000	.0078010	.6957596	.0073896	.7610695	.0061170	.8531926	.0031373	.9952941
48	.0200000	.9600000	.0076060	.7033656	.0071679	.7682375	.0058723	.8590649	.0023529	.9976471
49	.0200000	.9800000	.0074159	.7107814	.0069529	.7751903	.0056374	.8647023	.0015686	.9992157
50	.0200000	1.0000000	.0072305	.7180119	.0067443	.7819346	.0054119	.8701142	.0007843	1.0000000

X INDICATES YEAR AFTER WHICH A SWITCH TO STRAIGHT LINE MIGHT BE ADVISABLE (IF SALVAGE VALUE IS ZERO). SEE SECTION 11.7

Table 5 485

60 YEAR USEFUL LIFE

YEAR n	Straight Line ANNUAL a_n	Straight Line TOTAL A_n	DECLINING BALANCE 125% ANNUAL a_n	125% TOTAL A_n	150% ANNUAL a_n	150% TOTAL A_n	200% ANNUAL a_n	200% TOTAL A_n	Sum of the Years Digits ANNUAL a_n	Sum of the Years Digits TOTAL A_n
1	.0166667	.0166667	.0208333	.0208333	.0250000	.0250000	.0333333	.0333333	.0327869	.0327869
2	.0166667	.0333333	.0203993	.0412326	.0243750	.0493750	.0322222	.0655556	.0322404	.0650273
3	.0166667	.0500000	.0199743	.0612070	.0237656	.0731406	.0311481	.0967037	.0316940	.0967213
4	.0166667	.0666667	.0195582	.0807651	.0231715	.0963121	.0301099	.1268136	.0311475	.1278689
5	.0166667	.0833333	.0191507	.0999159	.0225922	.1189043	.0291062	.1559198	.0306011	.1584699
6	.0166667	.1000000	.0187518	.1186676	.0220274	.1409317	.0281360	.1840558	.0300546	.1885246
7	.0166667	.1166667	.0183611	.1370287	.0214767	.1624084	.0271981	.2112539	.0295082	.2180328
8	.0166667	.1333333	.0179786	.1550073	.0209398	.1833482	.0262915	.2375455	.0289617	.2469945
9	.0166667	.1500000	.0176040	.1726113	.0204163	.2037645	.0254152	.2629606	.0284153	.2754098
10	.0166667	.1666667	.0172373	.1898486	.0199059	.2236704	.0245680	.2875286	.0278689	.3032787
11	.0166667	.1833333	.0168782	.2067267	.0194082	.2430786	.0237490	.3112777	.0273224	.3306011
12	.0166667	.2000000	.0165265	.2232532	.0189230	.2620017	.0229574	.3342351	.0267760	.3573770
13	.0166667	.2166667	.0161822X	.2394355	.0184500	.2804516	.0221922	.3564272	.0262295	.3836066
14	.0166667	.2333333	.0158451	.2552806	.0179887	.2984403	.0214524	.3778797	.0256831	.4092896
15	.0166667	.2500000	.0155150	.2707956	.0175390	.3159793	.0207373	.3986170	.0251366	.4344262
16	.0166667	.2666667	.0151918	.2859873	.0171005	.3330798	.0200461	.4186631	.0245902	.4590164
17	.0166667	.2833333	.0148753	.3008626	.0166730	.3497528	.0193779	.4380410	.0240437	.4830601
18	.0166667	.3000000	.0145654	.3154279	.0162562	.3660090	.0187320	.4567730	.0234973	.5065574
19	.0166667	.3166667	.0142619	.3296899	.0158498	.3818588	.0181076	.4748805	.0229508	.5295082
20	.0166667	.3333333	.0139648	.3436547	.0154535	.3973123	.0175040	.4923845	.0224044	.5519126
21	.0166667	.3500000	.0136739	.3573285	.0150672X	.4123795	.0169205	.5093050	.0218579	.5737705
22	.0166667	.3666667	.0133890	.3707175	.0146905	.4270700	.0163565	.5256615	.0213115	.5950820
23	.0166667	.3833333	.0131101	.3838276	.0143232	.4413933	.0158113	.5414728	.0207650	.6158470
24	.0166667	.4000000	.0128369	.3966645	.0139652	.4553584	.0152842	.5567571	.0202186	.6360656
25	.0166667	.4166667	.0125695	.4092340	.0136160	.4689745	.0147748	.5715318	.0196721	.6557377
26	.0166667	.4333333	.0123076	.4215416	.0132756	.4822501	.0142823	.5858141	.0191257	.6748634
27	.0166667	.4500000	.0120512	.4335928	.0129437	.4951939	.0138062	.5996203	.0185792	.6934426
28	.0166667	.4666667	.0118001	.4453930	.0126202	.5078140	.0133460	.6129663	.0180328	.7114754
29	.0166667	.4833333	.0115543	.4569473	.0123046	.5201187	.0129011	.6258674	.0174863	.7289617
30	.0166667	.5000000	.0113136	.4682609	.0119970	.5321157	.0124711	.6383385	.0169399	.7459016
31	.0166667	.5166667	.0110779	.4793388	.0116971	.5438128	.0120554X	.6503939	.0163934	.7622951
32	.0166667	.5333333	.0108471	.4901859	.0114047	.5552175	.0116535	.6620474	.0158470	.7781421
33	.0166667	.5500000	.0106211	.5008070	.0111196	.5663371	.0112651	.6733125	.0153005	.7934426
34	.0166667	.5666667	.0103999	.5112069	.0108416	.5771786	.0108896	.6842021	.0147541	.8081967
35	.0166667	.5833333	.0101832	.5213901	.0105705	.5877492	.0105266	.6947287	.0142077	.8224044
36	.0166667	.6000000	.0099710	.5313611	.0103063	.5980554	.0101757	.7049044	.0136612	.8360656
37	.0166667	.6166667	.0097633	.5411244	.0100486	.6081040	.0098365	.7147409	.0131148	.8491803
38	.0166667	.6333333	.0095599	.5506843	.0097974	.6179014	.0095086	.7242495	.0125683	.8617486
39	.0166667	.6500000	.0093607	.5600451	.0095525	.6274539	.0091917	.7334412	.0120219	.8737705
40	.0166667	.6666667	.0091657	.5692108	.0093137	.6367676	.0088853	.7423265	.0114754	.8852459
41	.0166667	.6833333	.0089748	.5781856	.0090808	.6458484	.0085891	.7509156	.0109290	.8961749
42	.0166667	.7000000	.0087878	.5869734	.0088538	.6547022	.0083028	.7592184	.0103825	.9065574
43	.0166667	.7166667	.0086047	.5955787	.0086324	.6633346	.0080261	.7672445	.0098361	.9163934
44	.0166667	.7333333	.0084255	.6040035	.0084166	.6717512	.0077585	.7750030	.0092896	.9256831
45	.0166667	.7500000	.0082499	.6122535	.0082062	.6799575	.0074999	.7825029	.0087432	.9344262
46	.0166667	.7666667	.0080781	.6203315	.0080011	.6879585	.0072499	.7897528	.0081967	.9426230
47	.0166667	.7833333	.0079098	.6282413	.0078010	.6957596	.0070082	.7967611	.0076503	.9502732
48	.0166667	.8000000	.0077450	.6359863	.0076060	.7033656	.0067746	.8035357	.0071038	.9573770
49	.0166667	.8166667	.0075836	.6435699	.0074159	.7107814	.0065488	.8100845	.0065574	.9639344
50	.0166667	.8333333	.0074256	.6509955	.0072305	.7180119	.0063305	.8164150	.0060109	.9699454
51	.0166667	.8500000	.0072709	.6582664	.0070497	.7250616	.0061195	.8225345	.0054645	.9754098
52	.0166667	.8666667	.0071194	.6653809	.0068735	.7319351	.0059155	.8284500	.0049180	.9803279
53	.0166667	.8833333	.0069711	.6723570	.0067016	.7386367	.0057183	.8341684	.0043716	.9846995
54	.0166667	.9000000	.0068259	.6791829	.0065341	.7451708	.0055277	.8396961	.0038251	.9885246
55	.0166667	.9166667	.0066837	.6858666	.0063707	.7515415	.0053435	.8450395	.0032787	.9918033
56	.0166667	.9333333	.0065444	.6924110	.0062115	.7577530	.0051653	.8502049	.0027322	.9945355
57	.0166667	.9500000	.0064081	.6988191	.0060562	.7638091	.0049932	.8551981	.0021858	.9967213
58	.0166667	.9666667	.0062746	.7050937	.0059048	.7697139	.0048267	.8600248	.0016393	.9983607
59	.0166667	.9833333	.0061439	.7112376	.0057572	.7754711	.0046658	.8646906	.0010929	.9994536
60	.0166667	1.0000000	.0060159	.7172535	.0056132	.7810843	.0045103	.8692009	.0005464	1.0000000

X INDICATES YEAR AFTER WHICH A SWITCH TO STRAIGHT LINE MIGHT BE ADVISABLE (IF SALVAGE VALUE IS ZERO). SEE SECTION 11.7

Table 6

CLASS LIFE SYSTEM
(ASSET DEPRECIATION RANGE)

(partial list of depreciable assets whose life is stated in years)

This table lists the guideline life and its upper and lower limit. Although this system (class life system) is generally not used for real property, it can be used for personal property. For example, an office desk (see office furniture, fixtures, and equipment) can be depreciated over any period of time from 8 years to 12 years.

Table 6

Description of Assets	Lower Limit	Guide- line Life	Upper Limit

Agriculture:

Includes only such assets as are identified below and that are used in the production of crops or plants, vines and trees (including forestry); the keeping, grazing, or feeding of livestock for animal products (including serums), for animal increase, or value increase; the operation of dry lot or farm dairies, nurseries, greenhouses, sod farms, mushroom cellars, cranberry bogs, apiaries, and fur farms; the production of bulb, flower, and vegetable seed crops; and the performance of agricultural, animal husbandry and horticultural services.

Machinery and equipment, including grain bins and fences but no other land improvements	8	10	12

Animals:

Cattle, breeding or dairy	5.5	7	8.5
Horses, breeding or work	8	10	12
Hogs, breeding	2.5	3	3.5
Sheep and goats, breeding	4	5	6
Farm buildings	20	25	30

Building services:

Provision of the services of buildings, whether for use by others or for taxpayer's own account. Assets in the classes listed below include the structural shells of buildings and all integral parts thereof; equipment that services normal heating, plumbing, air conditioning, illumination, fire prevention, and power requirements; equipment for the movement of passengers and freight within the building; and any additions to buildings or their components, capitalized remodeling costs, and partitions both permanent and semipermanent. Structures, closely related to the equipment they house, which are section 38 property, are not included. See section 1.48-1(e)(1) of the regulations.

Such structures are included in asset guideline classes appropriate to the equipment to which they are related. Depreciation periods for assets used in the provision of the services of buildings and which are not specified below shall be determined according to the facts and circumstances pertinent to each asset, except in the case of farm buildings and other building structures for which a specific class has otherwise been designated.

Shelter, space, and related building services for manufacturing and for machinery and equipment repair activities:

Factories		45	
Garages		45	
Machine shops		45	
Loft buildings		50	

Table 6   489

Description of Assets	Lower Limit	Guide-line Life	Upper Limit
Building services for the conduct of wholesale and retail trade, includes stores and similar structures		60	
Building services for residential purposes:			
Apartments		40	
Dwellings		45	
Building services relating to the provision of miscellaneous services to businesses and consumers:			
Office buildings..		45	
Storage:			
Warehouses..		60	
Grain elevators..		60	
Banks..		50	
Hotels		40	
Theaters..		40	
Contract construction:			
Includes such assets used by general building, special trade, heavy construction and marine contractors; does not include assets used by companies in performing construction services on their own account.			
Contract construction other than marine	4	5	6
Marine contract construction..	9.5	12	14.5
Includes floating, self-propelled and other drillings platforms used in offshore drilling for oil and gas.			

Land Improvements:

Improvements directly to or added to land that are more often than not directly related to one or another of the specific classes of economic activity specified below. Includes only those depreciable land improvements which have a limited period of use in the trade or business, the length of which can be reasonably estimated for the particular improvement. That is, general grading of land such as in the case of cemeteries, golf courses and general site grading and leveling costs not directly related to buildings or other structural improvements to be added, are not depreciable or included in this class but such costs are added to the cost basis of the land.

Includes paved surfaces such as sidewalks and roads, canals, waterways, drainage facilities and sewers; wharves and docks; bridges; all fences except those included in specific classes described below (i.e., farm and railroad fences); landscaping, shrubbery and similar improvements; radio and television transmitting towers, and other inherently permanent physical structures added to land except buildings and their structural components.

Excludes land improvements of electric, gas, steam and water utilities; telephone and telegraph companies; and pipeline, water and

Table 6

Description of Assets	Lower Limit	Guide-line Life	Upper Limit
rail carriers which are assets covered by asset guideline classes specific to their respective classes of economic activity............................		20	
Manufacture of cement:			
Includes assets used in the production of cement, but does not include any assets used in the manufacture of concrete and concrete products nor in any mining or extraction process	16	20	24
Manufacture of other stone and clay products:			
Includes assets used in the manufacture of products from materials in the form of clay and stone, such as brick, tile and pipe; pottery and related products, such as vitreous-china, plumbing fixtures, earthenware and ceramic insulating materials; and also includes assets used in manufacture of concrete products. Does not include assets used in any mining or extraction processes	12	15	18
Services:			
Administrative services:			
Includes assets used in administering normal business transactions and the maintenance of business records, their retrieval and analysis, whether these services are performed for others or for taxpayer's own account and whether the assets are located in a single location or widely dispersed.			
Office furniture, fixtures, and equipment:			
Includes furniture and fixtures which are not a structural component of a building. Includes such assets as desks, files, safes, and communications equipment (not to include communications equipment which is included in other ADR classes)...	8	10	12
Information systems:			
Includes computers and their peripheral equipment (does not include equipment that is an integral part of other capital equipment and which is included in other ADR classes of economic activity, i.e., computers used primarily for process or production control, switching and channeling)	5	6	7

Information systems defined:

(1) Computers: A computer is an electronically activated device capable of accepting information, applying prescribed processes to the information and supplying the results of these processes with or without human intervention.

It usually consists of a central processing unit containing extensive storage, logic, arithmetic and control capabilities. Excluded from this category are adding machines, electronic desk calculators, etc.

(2) Peripheral equipment consists of the auxiliary machines which may be placed under control of the central processing unit. Non-limiting examples are

Table 6 491

Description of Assets	Lower Limit	Guide-line Life	Upper Limit

Card readers, card punches, magnetic tape feeds, high speed printers, optical character readers, tape cassettes, mass storage units, paper tape equipment, keypunches, data entry devices, teleprinters, terminals, tape drives, disc drives, disc files, disc packs, visual image projector tubes, card sorters, plotters, collators.

Peripheral equipment may be used on-line or off-line.

Data handling equipment, except computers:
 Includes typewriters, calculators, adding and accounting machines, copiers and duplicating equipment... | 5 | 6 | 7

Personal and professional services:
 Includes assets used in the provision of personal services such as those offered by hotels and motels, laundry and dry cleaning establishments, beauty and barber shops, photographic studios and mortuaries. Includes assets used in the provision of professional services such as those offered by doctors, dentists, lawyers, accountants, architects, engineers, and veterinarians and which are not classified in other ADR classes. Includes assets used in the provision of repair and maintenance services and those assets used in providing fire and burglary protection services and which are not classified in other ADR classes.

 Includes equipment or facilities used by cemetery organizations, news agencies, teletype wire services, plumbing contractors, frozen food lockers, research laboratories, hotels, and motels and which are not classified in other ADR classes.. | 8 | 10 | 12

Personal and professional services service assets:
 Includes assets such as glassware, silverware, crockery, and linens (generally sheets, pillowcases and bath towels) used in qualified activities as defined in class 70.2 of the class life system .... | 2 | 2.5 | 3

Recreation:
 Includes assets used in the provision of entertainment services on payment of a fee or admission charge, as in the operation of bowling alleys, billiard and pool establishments, theaters, concert halls, and miniature golf courses. Does not include amusement and theme parks and assets which consist primarily of specialized land improvements or structures, such as golf courses, sports stadia, race tracks, ski slopes, and buildings which house the assets used in entertainment services .... | 8 | 10 | 12

Theme and amusement parks:
 Includes assets used in the provision of rides, attractions, and amusements in activities defined as theme and amusement parks, and includes appurtenances associated with a ride, attraction, amusement or theme setting within the park such as ticket booths, facades, shop interiors, and props, special purpose structures, and buildings other than warehouses, administration buildings, hotels, and motels. Includes all land improvements for or in support of park activities (e.g. parking lots,

Description of Assets	Lower Limit	Guide-line Life	Upper Limit
sidewalks, waterways, bridges, fences, landscaping, etc.) and support functions (e.g. food and beverage retailing, souvenir vending, and other nonlodging accommodations) if owned by the park and provided exclusively for the benefit of park patrons.			
Theme and amusement parks are defined as combinations of amusements, rides, and attractions which are permanently situated on park land and open to the public for the price of admission. This guideline class is a composite of all assets used in this industry except transportation equipment (general purpose trucks, cars, airplanes, etc. which are included in asset guideline classes with the prefix 00.2), assets used in the provision of administrative services in asset guideline classes with the prefix 70.1, and warehouses, administration buildings, hotels, and motels	10	12.5	15
Transportation Equipment:			
Aircraft (airframes and engines)			
except aircraft of air transportation companies	5	6	7
Automobiles, taxis	2.5	3	3.5
Buses	7	9	11
General purpose trucks, including concrete ready-mix trucks and ore trucks for use over-the-road:			
Light (actual unloaded weight less than 13,000 pounds)	3	4	5
Heavy (actual unloaded weight 13,000 pounds or more)	5	6	7
Railroad cars and locomotives, except those owned by railroad transportation companies	12	15	18
Tractor units used over-the-road...	3	4	5
Trailers and trailer-mounted containers	5	6	7
Vessels, barges, tugs and similar water transportation equipment, except those used in marine contract construction	14.5	18	21.5

Table 7

TIME CALCULATIONS FOR SIMPLE INTEREST AND DISCOUNT

Definitions of Time

For simple interest and discount, there are four methods that can be used to determine t, the time expressed as a fraction of a year. Ordinary interest uses a 360 day year, and exact interest uses a 365 day year (366 days in a leap year). For these two definitions of a year, there are also two methods used to determine the elapsed time. Exact time uses the exact number of days between the beginning and ending dates (determined from the following table). Approximate time uses a 30 day month. Hence, there are four possible definitions for t:

Example: Find t for the period from June 24 to September 28

Definition of t	Solution
Ordinary interest, exact time: (Banker's Rule, employed commercially). $$t = \frac{\left(\begin{array}{c}\text{number of}\\\text{the day}\\\text{debt ends}\end{array}\right) - \left(\begin{array}{c}\text{number of}\\\text{the day}\\\text{debt begins}\end{array}\right)}{360}$$	$$t = \frac{271 - 175}{360} = \frac{96}{360}$$
Ordinary interest, approximate time: $$t = \frac{\left(\begin{array}{c}\text{number of days}\\\text{remaining in the}\\\text{first month}\end{array}\right) + \left(\begin{array}{c}\text{number of}\\\text{full months}\end{array}\right) \times 30 + \left(\begin{array}{c}\text{number of days}\\\text{into the}\\\text{last month}\end{array}\right)}{360}$$	$$t = \frac{6 + 2 \times 30 + 28}{360} = \frac{94}{360}$$
Exact interest, exact time: (Employed for governmental obligations and foreign trade). $$t = \frac{\left(\begin{array}{c}\text{number of}\\\text{the day}\\\text{debt ends}\end{array}\right) - \left(\begin{array}{c}\text{number of}\\\text{the day}\\\text{debt begins}\end{array}\right)}{365}$$	$$t = \frac{271 - 175}{365} = \frac{96}{365}$$
Exact interest, approximate time: $$t = \frac{\left(\begin{array}{c}\text{number of days}\\\text{remaining in the}\\\text{first month}\end{array}\right) + \left(\begin{array}{c}\text{number of}\\\text{full months}\end{array}\right) \times 30 + \left(\begin{array}{c}\text{number of days}\\\text{into the}\\\text{last month}\end{array}\right)}{365}$$	$$t = \frac{6 + 2 \times 30 + 28}{365} = \frac{94}{365}$$

Table 7 495

Due Date

If time is stated in days, the due date is the exact number of days after the debt begins. If time is stated in months, the due date is the same day of the month as the beginning date (if the month in which the debt is due doesn't have that many days, use the last day of the month). A debt due on a non-business day is due on the next business day.

Examples:

Term of Loan	Date of Loan	Due Date
60 days	May 12	July 11
2 months	May 12	July 12
3 months	Aug 31	Nov 30

Table 7

Number of Each Day of the Year*
(Counting from January 1)

Day of Mo.	Jan.	Feb.	Mar.	Apr.	May	June	July	Aug.	Sept.	Oct.	Nov.	Dec.
1	1	32	60	91	121	152	182	213	244	274	305	335
2	2	33	61	92	122	153	183	214	245	275	306	336
3	3	34	62	93	123	154	184	215	246	276	307	337
4	4	35	63	94	124	155	185	216	247	277	308	338
5	5	36	64	95	125	156	186	217	248	278	309	339
6	6	37	65	96	126	157	187	218	249	279	310	340
7	7	38	66	97	127	158	188	219	250	280	311	341
8	8	39	67	98	128	159	189	220	251	281	312	342
9	9	40	68	99	129	160	190	221	252	282	313	343
10	10	41	69	100	130	161	191	222	253	283	314	344
11	11	42	70	101	131	162	192	223	254	284	315	345
12	12	43	71	102	132	163	193	224	255	285	316	346
13	13	44	72	103	133	164	194	225	256	286	317	347
14	14	45	73	104	134	165	195	226	257	287	318	348
15	15	46	74	105	135	166	196	227	258	288	319	349
16	16	47	75	106	136	167	197	228	259	289	320	350
17	17	48	76	107	137	168	198	229	260	290	321	351
18	18	49	77	108	138	169	199	230	261	291	322	352
19	19	50	78	109	139	170	200	231	262	292	323	353
20	20	51	79	110	140	171	201	232	263	293	324	354
21	21	52	80	111	141	172	202	233	264	294	325	355
22	22	53	81	112	142	173	203	234	265	295	326	356
23	23	54	82	113	143	174	204	235	266	296	327	357
24	24	55	83	114	144	175	205	236	267	297	328	358
25	25	56	84	115	145	176	206	237	268	298	329	359
26	26	57	85	116	146	177	207	238	269	299	330	360
27	27	58	86	117	147	178	208	239	270	300	331	361
28	28	59	87	118	148	179	209	240	271	301	332	362
29	29	..	88	119	149	180	210	241	272	302	333	363
30	30	..	89	120	150	181	211	242	273	303	334	364
31	31	..	90	...	151	...	212	243	...	304	...	365

*For leap years, add one to each number after 59; i.e., after February 28.

Table 8

INCOME TAX TABLES

Table 8

1977 Tax Rate Schedules

If you cannot use one of the Tax Tables, figure your tax on the amount on Schedule TC, Part I, line 3, by using the appropriate Tax Rate Schedule on this page. Enter tax on Schedule TC, Part I, line 4.
Note: Your zero bracket amount has been built into these Tax Rate Schedules.

SCHEDULE X—Single Taxpayers Not Qualifying for Rates in Schedule Y or Z

Use this schedule if you checked Box 1 on Form 1040—

If the amount on Schedule TC, Part I, line 3, is:
Not over $2,200............ 0

Enter on Schedule TC, Part I, line 4:

Over—	But not over—		of the amount over—
$2,200	$2,700	14%	$2,200
$2,700	$3,200	$70+15%	$2,700
$3,200	$3,700	$145+16%	$3,200
$3,700	$4,200	$225+17%	$3,700
$4,200	$6,200	$310+19%	$4,200
$6,200	$8,200	$690+21%	$6,200
$8,200	$10,200	$1,110+24%	$8,200
$10,200	$12,200	$1,590+25%	$10,200
$12,200	$14,200	$2,090+27%	$12,200
$14,200	$16,200	$2,630+29%	$14,200
$16,200	$18,200	$3,210+31%	$16,200
$18,200	$20,200	$3,830+34%	$18,200
$20,200	$22,200	$4,510+36%	$20,200
$22,200	$24,200	$5,230+38%	$22,200
$24,200	$28,200	$5,990+40%	$24,200
$28,200	$34,200	$7,590+45%	$28,200
$34,200	$40,200	$10,290+50%	$34,200
$40,200	$46,200	$13,290+55%	$40,200
$46,200	$52,200	$16,590+60%	$46,200
$52,200	$62,200	$20,190+62%	$52,200
$62,200	$72,200	$26,390+64%	$62,200
$72,200	$82,200	$32,790+66%	$72,200
$82,200	$92,200	$39,390+68%	$82,200
$92,200	$102,200	$46,190+69%	$92,200
$102,200	....	$53,090+70%	$102,200

SCHEDULE Y—Married Taxpayers and Qualifying Widows and Widowers

If you are a married person living apart from your spouse, see page 7 of the instructions to see if you can be considered to be "unmarried" for purposes of using Schedule X or Z.

Married Filing Joint Returns and Qualifying Widows and Widowers

Use this schedule if you checked Box 2 or Box 5 on Form 1040—

If the amount on Schedule TC, Part I, line 3, is:
Not over $3,200............ 0

Enter on Schedule TC, Part I, line 4:

Over—	But not over—		of the amount over—
$3,200	$4,200	14%	$3,200
$4,200	$5,200	$140+15%	$4,200
$5,200	$6,200	$290+16%	$5,200
$6,200	$7,200	$450+17%	$6,200
$7,200	$11,200	$620+19%	$7,200
$11,200	$15,200	$1,380+22%	$11,200
$15,200	$19,200	$2,260+25%	$15,200
$19,200	$23,200	$3,260+28%	$19,200
$23,200	$27,200	$4,380+32%	$23,200
$27,200	$31,200	$5,660+36%	$27,200
$31,200	$35,200	$7,100+39%	$31,200
$35,200	$39,200	$8,660+42%	$35,200
$39,200	$43,200	$10,340+45%	$39,200
$43,200	$47,200	$12,140+48%	$43,200
$47,200	$55,200	$14,060+50%	$47,200
$55,200	$67,200	$18,060+53%	$55,200
$67,200	$79,200	$24,420+55%	$67,200
$79,200	$91,200	$31,020+58%	$79,200
$91,200	$103,200	$37,980+60%	$91,200
$103,200	$123,200	$45,180+62%	$103,200
$123,200	$143,200	$57,580+64%	$123,200
$143,200	$163,200	$70,380+66%	$143,200
$163,200	$183,200	$83,580+68%	$163,200
$183,200	$203,200	$97,180+69%	$183,200
$203,200	....	$110,980+70%	$203,200

Married Filing Separate Returns

Use this schedule if you checked Box 3 on Form 1040—

If the amount on Schedule TC, Part I, line 3, is:
Not over $1,600............ 0

Enter on Schedule TC, Part I, line 4:

Over—	But not over—		of the amount over—
$1,600	$2,100	14%	$1,600
$2,100	$2,600	$70+15%	$2,100
$2,600	$3,100	$145+16%	$2,600
$3,100	$3,600	$225+17%	$3,100
$3,600	$5,600	$310+19%	$3,600
$5,600	$7,600	$690+22%	$5,600
$7,600	$9,600	$1,130+25%	$7,600
$9,600	$11,600	$1,630+28%	$9,600
$11,600	$13,600	$2,190+32%	$11,600
$13,600	$15,600	$2,830+36%	$13,600
$15,600	$17,600	$3,550+39%	$15,600
$17,600	$19,600	$4,330+42%	$17,600
$19,600	$21,600	$5,170+45%	$19,600
$21,600	$23,600	$6,070+48%	$21,600
$23,600	$27,600	$7,030+50%	$23,600
$27,600	$33,600	$9,030+53%	$27,600
$33,600	$39,600	$12,210+55%	$33,600
$39,600	$45,600	$15,510+58%	$39,600
$45,600	$51,600	$18,990+60%	$45,600
$51,600	$61,600	$22,590+62%	$51,600
$61,600	$71,600	$28,790+64%	$61,600
$71,600	$81,600	$35,190+66%	$71,600
$81,600	$91,600	$41,790+68%	$81,600
$91,600	$101,600	$48,590+69%	$91,600
$101,600	....	$55,490+70%	$101,600

SCHEDULE Z—Unmarried or legally separated taxpayers Who Qualify as Heads of Household

Use this schedule if you checked Box 4 on Form 1040—

If the amount on Schedule TC, Part I, line 3, is:
Not over $2,200............ 0

Enter on Schedule TC, Part I, line 4:

Over—	But not over—		of the amount over—
$2,200	$3,200	14%	$2,200
$3,200	$4,200	$140+16%	$3,200
$4,200	$6,200	$300+18%	$4,200
$6,200	$8,200	$660+19%	$6,200
$8,200	$10,200	$1,040+22%	$8,200
$10,200	$12,200	$1,480+23%	$10,200
$12,200	$14,200	$1,940+25%	$12,200
$14,200	$16,200	$2,440+27%	$14,200
$16,200	$18,200	$2,980+28%	$16,200
$18,200	$20,200	$3,540+31%	$18,200
$20,200	$22,200	$4,160+32%	$20,200
$22,200	$24,200	$4,800+35%	$22,200
$24,200	$26,200	$5,500+36%	$24,200
$26,200	$28,200	$6,220+38%	$26,200
$28,200	$30,200	$6,980+41%	$28,200
$30,200	$34,200	$7,800+42%	$30,200
$34,200	$38,200	$9,480+45%	$34,200
$38,200	$40,200	$11,280+48%	$38,200
$40,200	$42,200	$12,240+51%	$40,200
$42,200	$46,200	$13,260+52%	$42,200
$46,200	$52,200	$15,340+55%	$46,200
$52,200	$54,200	$18,640+56%	$52,200
$54,200	$66,200	$19,760+58%	$54,200
$66,200	$72,200	$26,720+59%	$66,200
$72,200	$78,200	$30,260+61%	$72,200
$78,200	$82,200	$33,920+62%	$78,200
$82,200	$90,200	$36,400+63%	$82,200
$90,200	$102,200	$41,440+64%	$90,200
$102,200	$122,200	$49,120+66%	$102,200
$122,200	$142,200	$62,320+67%	$122,200
$142,200	$162,200	$75,720+68%	$142,200
$162,200	$182,200	$89,320+69%	$162,200
$182,200	....	$103,120+70%	$182,200

Table 8   499

1977 Tax Table A—SINGLE (Box 1)

(For single persons with tax table income of $20,000 or less who claim fewer than 4 exemptions)

To find your tax: Read down the left income column until you find your income as shown on line 34 of Form 1040. Read across to the column headed by the total number of exemptions claimed on line 7 of Form 1040. The amount shown at the point where the two lines meet is your tax. Enter on Form 1040, line 35.

The $2,200 zero bracket amount, your deduction for exemptions and the general tax credit have been taken into account in figuring the tax shown in this table. **Do not take a separate deduction for them.**

Caution: *If you can be claimed as a dependent on your parent's return **AND** you have unearned income (interest, dividends, etc.) of $750 or more **AND** your earned income is less than $2,200, you must first use Schedule TC (Form 1040), Part II.*

If line 34, Form 1040 is—		1	2	3	If line 34, Form 1040 is—		1	2	3	If line 34, Form 1040 is—		1	2	3
Over	But not over	Your tax is—			Over	But not over	Your tax is—			Over	But not over	Your tax is—		
If $3,200 or less your tax is 0					5,800	5,850	419	264	100	8,400	8,450	890	748	580
					5,850	5,900	427	273	108	8,450	8,500	900	757	590
3,200	3,250	4	0	0	5,900	5,950	436	283	116	8,500	8,550	909	767	601
3,250	3,300	11	0	0	5,950	6,000	444	292	124	8,550	8,600	919	776	611
3,300	3,350	18	0	0										
3,350	3,400	25	0	0	6,000	6,050	453	302	133	8,600	8,650	928	786	622
					6,050	6,100	461	311	141	8,650	8,700	938	795	632
3,400	3,450	32	0	0	6,100	6,150	470	321	150	8,700	8,750	947	805	643
3,450	3,500	39	0	0	6,150	6,200	478	330	158	8,750	8,800	957	814	653
3,500	3,550	46	0	0										
3,550	3,600	54	0	0	6,200	6,250	487	340	167	8,800	8,850	966	824	664
					6,250	6,300	495	349	175	8,850	8,900	976	833	674
3,600	3,650	61	0	0	6,300	6,350	504	359	184	8,900	8,950	985	843	685
3,650	3,700	69	0	0	6,350	6,400	512	368	192	8,950	9,000	996	852	695
3,700	3,750	76	0	0										
3,750	3,800	84	0	0	6,400	6,450	521	378	201	9,000	9,050	1,007	862	706
					6,450	6,500	529	387	210	9,050	9,100	1,018	871	716
3,800	3,850	91	0	0	6,500	6,550	538	397	219	9,100	9,150	1,029	881	727
3,850	3,900	99	0	0	6,550	6,600	546	406	229	9,150	9,200	1,040	890	737
3,900	3,950	106	0	0										
3,950	4,000	114	0	0	6,600	6,650	555	416	238	9,200	9,250	1,051	900	748
					6,650	6,700	563	425	248	9,250	9,300	1,062	909	758
4,000	4,050	122	0	0	6,700	6,750	572	435	257	9,300	9,350	1,073	919	769
4,050	4,100	130	0	0	6,750	6,800	580	444	267	9,350	9,400	1,084	928	779
4,100	4,150	138	0	0										
4,150	4,200	146	0	0	6,800	6,850	589	454	276	9,400	9,450	1,095	938	790
					6,850	6,900	597	463	286	9,450	9,500	1,106	947	800
4,200	4,250	154	4	0	6,900	6,950	606	473	295	9,500	9,550	1,117	957	811
4,250	4,300	162	11	0	6,950	7,000	615	482	305	9,550	9,600	1,128	966	821
4,300	4,350	170	19	0										
4,350	4,400	178	26	0	7,000	7,050	624	492	314	9,600	9,650	1,139	976	832
					7,050	7,100	634	501	324	9,650	9,700	1,150	985	842
4,400	4,450	186	34	0	7,100	7,150	643	511	333	9,700	9,750	1,161	996	852
4,450	4,500	194	41	0	7,150	7,200	653	520	343	9,750	9,800	1,172	1,007	862
4,500	4,550	203	49	0										
4,550	4,600	211	56	0	7,200	7,250	662	529	352	9,800	9,850	1,183	1,018	871
					7,250	7,300	672	538	362	9,850	9,900	1,194	1,029	881
4,600	4,650	220	64	0	7,300	7,350	681	546	371	9,900	9,950	1,205	1,040	890
4,650	4,700	228	71	0	7,350	7,400	691	555	381	9,950	10,000	1,216	1,051	900
4,700	4,750	236	79	0										
4,750	4,800	244	87	0	7,400	7,450	700	563	390	10,000	10,050	1,227	1,062	909
					7,450	7,500	710	572	400	10,050	10,100	1,238	1,073	919
4,800	4,850	251	95	0	7,500	7,550	719	580	409	10,100	10,150	1,249	1,084	928
4,850	4,900	259	103	0	7,550	7,600	729	589	419	10,150	10,200	1,260	1,095	938
4,900	4,950	266	111	0										
4,950	5,000	274	119	0	7,600	7,650	738	597	428	10,200	10,250	1,271	1,106	947
					7,650	7,700	748	606	438	10,250	10,300	1,282	1,117	957
5,000	5,050	283	127	0	7,700	7,750	757	615	447	10,300	10,350	1,293	1,128	966
5,050	5,100	291	135	0	7,750	7,800	767	624	457	10,350	10,400	1,304	1,139	976
5,100	5,150	300	143	0										
5,150	5,200	308	151	0	7,800	7,850	776	634	466	10,400	10,450	1,315	1,150	985
					7,850	7,900	786	643	476	10,450	10,500	1,326	1,161	996
5,200	5,250	317	159	6	7,900	7,950	795	653	485	10,500	10,550	1,337	1,172	1,007
5,250	5,300	325	168	14	7,950	8,000	805	662	495	10,550	10,600	1,348	1,183	1,018
5,300	5,350	334	176	21										
5,350	5,400	342	185	29	8,000	8,050	814	672	504	10,600	10,650	1,359	1,194	1,029
					8,050	8,100	824	681	514	10,650	10,700	1,370	1,205	1,040
5,400	5,450	351	193	36	8,100	8,150	833	691	523	10,700	10,750	1,381	1,216	1,051
5,450	5,500	359	202	44	8,150	8,200	843	700	533	10,750	10,800	1,392	1,227	1,062
5,500	5,550	368	210	52										
5,550	5,600	376	219	60	8,200	8,250	852	710	542	10,800	10,850	1,403	1,238	1,073
					8,250	8,300	862	719	552	10,850	10,900	1,414	1,249	1,084
5,600	5,650	385	227	68	8,300	8,350	871	729	561	10,900	10,950	1,425	1,260	1,095
5,650	5,700	393	236	76	8,350	8,400	881	738	571	10,950	11,000	1,436	1,271	1,106
5,700	5,750	402	245	84										
5,750	5,800	410	254	92										
Continued next column					*Continued next column*					*Continued on next page*				

Table 8

1977 Tax Table A—SINGLE (Box 1) *(Continued)*

(If your income or exemptions are not covered, use Schedule TC (Form 1040), Part I to figure your tax)

If line 34, Form 1040 is—		And the total number of exemptions claimed on line 7 is—			If line 34, Form 1040 is—		And the total number of exemptions claimed on line 7 is—			If line 34, Form 1040 is—		And the total number of exemptions claimed on line 7 is—		
Over	But not over	1	2	3	Over	But not over	1	2	3	Over	But not over	1	2	3
		Your tax is—					Your tax is—					Your tax is—		
11,000	11,050	1,447	1,282	1,117	14,000	14,050	2,200	1,998	1,804	17,000	17,050	3,053	2,834	2,617
11,050	11,100	1,459	1,293	1,128	14,050	14,100	2,214	2,011	1,816	17,050	17,100	3,069	2,849	2,631
11,100	11,150	1,470	1,304	1,139	14,100	14,150	2,227	2,025	1,829	17,100	17,150	3,084	2,863	2,646
11,150	11,200	1,482	1,315	1,150	14,150	14,200	2,241	2,038	1,841	17,150	17,200	3,100	2,878	2,660
11,200	11,250	1,493	1,326	1,161	14,200	14,250	2,254	2,052	1,854	17,200	17,250	3,115	2,892	2,675
11,250	11,300	1,505	1,337	1,172	14,250	14,300	2,268	2,065	1,866	17,250	17,300	3,131	2,907	2,689
11,300	11,350	1,516	1,348	1,183	14,300	14,350	2,281	2,079	1,879	17,300	17,350	3,146	2,921	2,704
11,350	11,400	1,528	1,359	1,194	14,350	14,400	2,295	2,092	1,891	17,350	17,400	3,162	2,936	2,718
11,400	11,450	1,539	1,370	1,205	14,400	14,450	2,308	2,106	1,904	17,400	17,450	3,177	2,950	2,733
11,450	11,500	1,551	1,381	1,216	14,450	14,500	2,322	2,119	1,917	17,450	17,500	3,193	2,965	2,747
11,500	11,550	1,562	1,392	1,227	14,500	14,550	2,335	2,133	1,930	17,500	17,550	3,208	2,979	2,762
11,550	11,600	1,574	1,403	1,238	14,550	14,600	2,349	2,146	1,944	17,550	17,600	3,224	2,994	2,776
11,600	11,650	1,585	1,414	1,249	14,600	14,650	2,362	2,160	1,957	17,600	17,650	3,239	3,008	2,791
11,650	11,700	1,597	1,425	1,260	14,650	14,700	2,376	2,173	1,971	17,650	17,700	3,255	3,023	2,805
11,700	11,750	1,608	1,436	1,271	14,700	14,750	2,389	2,187	1,984	17,700	17,750	3,270	3,038	2,820
11,750	11,800	1,620	1,447	1,282	14,750	14,800	2,403	2,200	1,998	17,750	17,800	3,286	3,053	2,834
11,800	11,850	1,631	1,459	1,293	14,800	14,850	2,416	2,214	2,011	17,800	17,850	3,301	3,069	2,849
11,850	11,900	1,643	1,470	1,304	14,850	14,900	2,430	2,227	2,025	17,850	17,900	3,317	3,084	2,863
11,900	11,950	1,654	1,482	1,315	14,900	14,950	2,443	2,241	2,038	17,900	17,950	3,332	3,100	2,878
11,950	12,000	1,666	1,493	1,326	14,950	15,000	2,457	2,254	2,052	17,950	18,000	3,348	3,115	2,892
12,000	12,050	1,679	1,505	1,337	15,000	15,050	2,472	2,268	2,065	18,000	18,050	3,363	3,131	2,907
12,050	12,100	1,691	1,516	1,348	15,050	15,100	2,486	2,281	2,079	18,050	18,100	3,379	3,146	2,921
12,100	12,150	1,704	1,528	1,359	15,100	15,150	2,501	2,295	2,092	18,100	18,150	3,394	3,162	2,936
12,150	12,200	1,716	1,539	1,370	15,150	15,200	2,515	2,308	2,106	18,150	18,200	3,410	3,177	2,950
12,200	12,250	1,729	1,551	1,381	15,200	15,250	2,530	2,322	2,119	18,200	18,250	3,425	3,193	2,965
12,250	12,300	1,741	1,562	1,392	15,250	15,300	2,544	2,335	2,133	18,250	18,300	3,441	3,208	2,979
12,300	12,350	1,754	1,574	1,403	15,300	15,350	2,559	2,349	2,146	18,300	18,350	3,456	3,224	2,994
12,350	12,400	1,766	1,585	1,414	15,350	15,400	2,573	2,362	2,160	18,350	18,400	3,472	3,239	3,008
12,400	12,450	1,779	1,597	1,425	15,400	15,450	2,588	2,376	2,173	18,400	18,450	3,487	3,255	3,023
12,450	12,500	1,791	1,608	1,436	15,450	15,500	2,602	2,389	2,187	18,450	18,500	3,503	3,270	3,038
12,500	12,550	1,804	1,620	1,447	15,500	15,550	2,617	2,403	2,200	18,500	18,550	3,518	3,286	3,053
12,550	12,600	1,816	1,631	1,459	15,550	15,600	2,631	2,416	2,214	18,550	18,600	3,534	3,301	3,069
12,600	12,650	1,829	1,643	1,470	15,600	15,650	2,646	2,430	2,227	18,600	18,650	3,549	3,317	3,084
12,650	12,700	1,841	1,654	1,482	15,650	15,700	2,660	2,443	2,241	18,650	18,700	3,565	3,332	3,100
12,700	12,750	1,854	1,666	1,493	15,700	15,750	2,675	2,457	2,254	18,700	18,750	3,580	3,348	3,115
12,750	12,800	1,866	1,679	1,505	15,750	15,800	2,689	2,472	2,268	18,750	18,800	3,596	3,363	3,131
12,800	12,850	1,879	1,691	1,516	15,800	15,850	2,704	2,486	2,281	18,800	18,850	3,611	3,379	3,146
12,850	12,900	1,891	1,704	1,528	15,850	15,900	2,718	2,501	2,295	18,850	18,900	3,627	3,394	3,162
12,900	12,950	1,904	1,716	1,539	15,900	15,950	2,733	2,515	2,308	18,900	18,950	3,642	3,410	3,177
12,950	13,000	1,917	1,729	1,551	15,950	16,000	2,747	2,530	2,322	18,950	19,000	3,659	3,425	3,193
13,000	13,050	1,930	1,741	1,562	16,000	16,050	2,762	2,544	2,335	19,000	19,050	3,676	3,441	3,208
13,050	13,100	1,944	1,754	1,574	16,050	16,100	2,776	2,559	2,349	19,050	19,100	3,693	3,456	3,224
13,100	13,150	1,957	1,766	1,585	16,100	16,150	2,791	2,573	2,362	19,100	19,150	3,710	3,472	3,239
13,150	13,200	1,971	1,779	1,597	16,150	16,200	2,805	2,588	2,376	19,150	19,200	3,727	3,487	3,255
13,200	13,250	1,984	1,791	1,608	16,200	16,250	2,820	2,602	2,389	19,200	19,250	3,744	3,503	3,270
13,250	13,300	1,998	1,804	1,620	16,250	16,300	2,834	2,617	2,403	19,250	19,300	3,761	3,518	3,286
13,300	13,350	2,011	1,816	1,631	16,300	16,350	2,849	2,631	2,416	19,300	19,350	3,778	3,534	3,301
13,350	13,400	2,025	1,829	1,643	16,350	16,400	2,863	2,646	2,430	19,350	19,400	3,795	3,549	3,317
13,400	13,450	2,038	1,841	1,654	16,400	16,450	2,878	2,660	2,443	19,400	19,450	3,812	3,565	3,332
13,450	13,500	2,052	1,854	1,666	16,450	16,500	2,892	2,675	2,457	19,450	19,500	3,829	3,580	3,348
13,500	13,550	2,065	1,866	1,679	16,500	16,550	2,907	2,689	2,472	19,500	19,550	3,846	3,596	3,363
13,550	13,600	2,079	1,879	1,691	16,550	16,600	2,921	2,704	2,486	19,550	19,600	3,863	3,611	3,379
13,600	13,650	2,092	1,891	1,704	16,600	16,650	2,936	2,718	2,501	19,600	19,650	3,880	3,627	3,394
13,650	13,700	2,106	1,904	1,716	16,650	16,700	2,950	2,733	2,515	19,650	19,700	3,897	3,642	3,410
13,700	13,750	2,119	1,917	1,729	16,700	16,750	2,965	2,747	2,530	19,700	19,750	3,914	3,659	3,425
13,750	13,800	2,133	1,930	1,741	16,750	16,800	2,979	2,762	2,544	19,750	19,800	3,931	3,676	3,441
13,800	13,850	2,146	1,944	1,754	16,800	16,850	2,994	2,776	2,559	19,800	19,850	3,948	3,693	3,456
13,850	13,900	2,160	1,957	1,766	16,850	16,900	3,008	2,791	2,573	19,850	19,900	3,965	3,710	3,472
13,900	13,950	2,173	1,971	1,779	16,900	16,950	3,023	2,805	2,588	19,900	19,950	3,982	3,727	3,487
13,950	14,000	2,187	1,984	1,791	16,950	17,000	3,038	2,820	2,602	19,950	20,000	3,999	3,744	3,503

Continued next column   Continued next column

Table 8   501

1977 Tax Table B—MARRIED FILING JOINTLY (Box 2) and QUALIFYING WIDOW(ER)S (Box 5)

(For married persons filing joint returns or qualifying widow(er)s with tax table income of $40,000 or less who claim fewer than 10 exemptions)

To find your tax: Read down the left income column until you find your income as shown on line 34 of Form 1040. Read across to the column headed by the total number of exemptions claimed on line 7 of Form 1040. The amount shown at the point where the two lines meet is your tax. Enter on Form 1040, line 35.

The $3,200 zero bracket amount, your deduction for exemptions and the general tax credit have been taken into account in figuring the tax shown in this table. **Do not take a separate deduction for them.**

If line 34, Form 1040 is— Over	But not over	2	3	4	5	6	7	8	9
					Your tax is—				
If $5,200 or less your tax is 0									
5,200	5,250	4	0	0	0	0	0	0	0
5,250	5,300	11	0	0	0	0	0	0	0
5,300	5,350	18	0	0	0	0	0	0	0
5,350	5,400	25	0	0	0	0	0	0	0
5,400	5,450	32	0	0	0	0	0	0	0
5,450	5,500	39	0	0	0	0	0	0	0
5,500	5,550	46	0	0	0	0	0	0	0
5,550	5,600	53	0	0	0	0	0	0	0
5,600	5,650	60	0	0	0	0	0	0	0
5,650	5,700	67	0	0	0	0	0	0	0
5,700	5,750	74	0	0	0	0	0	0	0
5,750	5,800	81	0	0	0	0	0	0	0
5,800	5,850	89	0	0	0	0	0	0	0
5,850	5,900	96	0	0	0	0	0	0	0
5,900	5,950	104	0	0	0	0	0	0	0
5,950	6,000	111	0	0	0	0	0	0	0
6,000	6,050	119	0	0	0	0	0	0	0
6,050	6,100	126	0	0	0	0	0	0	0
6,100	6,150	134	0	0	0	0	0	0	0
6,150	6,200	141	0	0	0	0	0	0	0
6,200	6,250	149	4	0	0	0	0	0	0
6,250	6,300	156	11	0	0	0	0	0	0
6,300	6,350	164	18	0	0	0	0	0	0
6,350	6,400	171	25	0	0	0	0	0	0
6,400	6,450	179	32	0	0	0	0	0	0
6,450	6,500	186	39	0	0	0	0	0	0
6,500	6,550	194	46	0	0	0	0	0	0
6,550	6,600	201	54	0	0	0	0	0	0
6,600	6,650	209	61	0	0	0	0	0	0
6,650	6,700	216	69	0	0	0	0	0	0
6,700	6,750	224	76	0	0	0	0	0	0
6,750	6,800	232	84	0	0	0	0	0	0
6,800	6,850	240	91	0	0	0	0	0	0
6,850	6,900	248	99	0	0	0	0	0	0
6,900	6,950	256	106	0	0	0	0	0	0
6,950	7,000	264	114	0	0	0	0	0	0
7,000	7,050	272	121	0	0	0	0	0	0
7,050	7,100	280	129	0	0	0	0	0	0
7,100	7,150	288	136	0	0	0	0	0	0
7,150	7,200	296	144	0	0	0	0	0	0
7,200	7,250	304	151	4	0	0	0	0	0
7,250	7,300	312	159	11	0	0	0	0	0
7,300	7,350	320	166	19	0	0	0	0	0
7,350	7,400	328	174	26	0	0	0	0	0
7,400	7,450	336	181	34	0	0	0	0	0
7,450	7,500	344	189	41	0	0	0	0	0
7,500	7,550	352	197	49	0	0	0	0	0
7,550	7,600	360	205	56	0	0	0	0	0
7,600	7,650	368	213	64	0	0	0	0	0
7,650	7,700	376	221	71	0	0	0	0	0
7,700	7,750	384	229	79	0	0	0	0	0
7,750	7,800	393	237	86	0	0	0	0	0
7,800	7,850	401	245	94	0	0	0	0	0
7,850	7,900	410	253	101	0	0	0	0	0
7,900	7,950	418	261	109	0	0	0	0	0
7,950	8,000	427	269	116	0	0	0	0	0
8,000	8,050	435	277	124	0	0	0	0	0
8,050	8,100	444	285	131	0	0	0	0	0
8,100	8,150	452	293	139	0	0	0	0	0
8,150	8,200	461	301	146	0	0	0	0	0
8,200	8,250	469	309	154	6	0	0	0	0
8,250	8,300	476	317	162	14	0	0	0	0
8,300	8,350	484	325	170	21	0	0	0	0
8,350	8,400	491	333	178	29	0	0	0	0

Continued next column

If line 34, Form 1040 is— Over	But not over	2	3	4	5	6	7	8	9
					Your tax is—				
8,400	8,450	499	341	186	36	0	0	0	0
8,450	8,500	506	349	194	44	0	0	0	0
8,500	8,550	514	358	202	51	0	0	0	0
8,550	8,600	521	366	210	59	0	0	0	0
8,600	8,650	529	375	218	66	0	0	0	0
8,650	8,700	536	383	226	74	0	0	0	0
8,700	8,750	544	392	234	81	0	0	0	0
8,750	8,800	553	400	242	89	0	0	0	0
8,800	8,850	561	409	250	96	0	0	0	0
8,850	8,900	570	417	258	104	0	0	0	0
8,900	8,950	578	426	266	111	0	0	0	0
8,950	9,000	587	434	274	119	0	0	0	0
9,000	9,050	595	443	282	127	0	0	0	0
9,050	9,100	604	451	290	135	0	0	0	0
9,100	9,150	612	460	298	143	0	0	0	0
9,150	9,200	621	468	306	151	1	0	0	0
9,200	9,250	629	477	314	159	9	0	0	0
9,250	9,300	638	485	323	167	16	0	0	0
9,300	9,350	646	494	331	175	24	0	0	0
9,350	9,400	655	502	340	183	31	0	0	0
9,400	9,450	663	511	348	191	39	0	0	0
9,450	9,500	672	520	357	199	46	0	0	0
9,500	9,550	680	529	365	207	54	0	0	0
9,550	9,600	689	539	374	215	61	0	0	0
9,600	9,650	697	548	382	223	69	0	0	0
9,650	9,700	706	558	391	231	76	0	0	0
9,700	9,750	714	567	399	239	84	0	0	0
9,750	9,800	723	577	408	247	92	0	0	0
9,800	9,850	731	586	416	255	100	0	0	0
9,850	9,900	740	596	425	263	108	0	0	0
9,900	9,950	748	605	433	271	116	0	0	0
9,950	10,000	757	615	442	279	124	0	0	0
10,000	10,050	765	624	450	288	132	0	0	0
10,050	10,100	774	634	459	296	140	0	0	0
10,100	10,150	782	643	467	305	148	0	0	0
10,150	10,200	791	653	476	313	156	4	0	0
10,200	10,250	799	662	485	322	164	11	0	0
10,250	10,300	808	672	494	330	172	19	0	0
10,300	10,350	816	681	504	339	180	26	0	0
10,350	10,400	825	691	513	347	188	34	0	0
10,400	10,450	833	700	523	356	196	41	0	0
10,450	10,500	842	710	532	364	204	49	0	0
10,500	10,550	850	719	542	373	212	57	0	0
10,550	10,600	859	729	551	381	220	65	0	0
10,600	10,650	867	738	561	390	228	73	0	0
10,650	10,700	876	748	570	398	236	81	0	0
10,700	10,750	884	757	580	407	244	89	0	0
10,750	10,800	893	765	589	415	253	97	0	0
10,800	10,850	901	774	599	424	261	105	0	0
10,850	10,900	910	782	608	432	270	113	0	0
10,900	10,950	918	791	618	441	278	121	0	0
10,950	11,000	927	799	627	450	287	129	0	0
11,000	11,050	935	808	637	459	295	137	0	0
11,050	11,100	944	816	646	469	304	145	0	0
11,100	11,150	952	825	656	478	312	153	0	0
11,150	11,200	961	833	665	488	321	161	6	0
11,200	11,250	969	842	675	497	329	169	14	0
11,250	11,300	978	850	684	507	338	177	22	0
11,300	11,350	986	859	694	516	346	185	30	0
11,350	11,400	995	867	703	526	355	193	38	0
11,400	11,450	1,003	876	713	535	363	201	46	0
11,450	11,500	1,012	884	722	545	372	209	54	0
11,500	11,550	1,020	893	732	554	380	218	62	0
11,550	11,600	1,029	901	741	564	389	226	70	0

Continued on next page

Table 8

1977 Tax Table B—MARRIED FILING JOINTLY (Box 2) and QUALIFYING WIDOW(ER)S (Box 5)
(Continued)

(If your income or exemptions are not covered, use Schedule TC (Form 1040), Part I to figure your tax)

If line 34, Form 1040 is— Over	But not over	And the total number of exemptions claimed on line 7 is— 2	3	4	5	6	7	8	9
11,600	11,650	1,037	910	751	573	397	235	78	0
11,650	11,700	1,046	918	760	583	406	243	86	0
11,700	11,750	1,054	927	770	592	415	252	94	0
11,750	11,800	1,063	935	779	602	424	260	102	0
11,800	11,850	1,071	944	789	611	434	269	110	0
11,850	11,900	1,080	952	798	621	443	277	118	0
11,900	11,950	1,088	961	808	630	453	286	126	0
11,950	12,000	1,097	969	817	640	462	294	134	0
12,000	12,050	1,105	978	827	649	472	303	142	0
12,050	12,100	1,114	986	836	659	481	311	150	0
12,100	12,150	1,122	995	846	668	491	320	158	3
12,150	12,200	1,131	1,003	855	678	500	328	166	11
12,200	12,250	1,139	1,012	865	687	510	337	174	19
12,250	12,300	1,148	1,020	874	697	519	345	183	27
12,300	12,350	1,156	1,029	884	706	529	354	191	35
12,350	12,400	1,165	1,037	893	716	538	362	200	43
12,400	12,450	1,173	1,046	903	725	548	371	208	51
12,450	12,500	1,182	1,054	912	735	557	380	217	59
12,500	12,550	1,190	1,063	922	744	567	389	225	67
12,550	12,600	1,199	1,071	931	754	576	399	234	75
12,600	12,650	1,207	1,080	941	763	586	408	242	83
12,650	12,700	1,216	1,088	950	773	595	418	251	91
12,700	12,750	1,225	1,097	960	782	605	427	259	99
12,750	12,800	1,235	1,105	969	792	614	437	268	107
12,800	12,850	1,245	1,114	979	801	624	446	276	115
12,850	12,900	1,255	1,122	988	811	633	456	285	123
12,900	12,950	1,265	1,131	998	820	643	465	293	131
12,950	13,000	1,275	1,139	1,007	830	652	475	302	139
13,000	13,050	1,285	1,148	1,017	839	662	484	310	148
13,050	13,100	1,295	1,156	1,026	849	671	494	319	156
13,100	13,150	1,305	1,165	1,036	858	681	503	327	165
13,150	13,200	1,315	1,173	1,045	868	690	513	336	173
13,200	13,250	1,325	1,182	1,054	877	700	522	345	182
13,250	13,300	1,335	1,190	1,063	887	709	532	354	190
13,300	13,350	1,345	1,199	1,071	896	719	541	364	199
13,350	13,400	1,355	1,207	1,080	906	728	551	373	207
13,400	13,450	1,365	1,216	1,088	915	738	560	383	216
13,450	13,500	1,375	1,225	1,097	925	747	570	392	224
13,500	13,550	1,385	1,235	1,105	934	757	579	402	233
13,550	13,600	1,395	1,245	1,114	944	766	589	411	241
13,600	13,650	1,405	1,255	1,122	953	776	598	421	250
13,650	13,700	1,415	1,265	1,131	963	785	608	430	258
13,700	13,750	1,426	1,275	1,139	972	795	617	440	267
13,750	13,800	1,437	1,285	1,148	982	804	627	449	275
13,800	13,850	1,448	1,295	1,156	991	814	636	459	284
13,850	13,900	1,459	1,305	1,165	1,001	823	646	468	292
13,900	13,950	1,470	1,315	1,173	1,010	833	655	478	301
13,950	14,000	1,481	1,325	1,182	1,020	842	665	487	310
14,000	14,050	1,492	1,335	1,190	1,029	852	674	497	319
14,050	14,100	1,503	1,345	1,199	1,039	861	684	506	329
14,100	14,150	1,514	1,355	1,207	1,048	871	693	516	338
14,150	14,200	1,525	1,365	1,216	1,058	880	703	525	348
14,200	14,250	1,536	1,375	1,225	1,067	890	712	535	357
14,250	14,300	1,547	1,385	1,235	1,077	899	722	544	367
14,300	14,350	1,558	1,395	1,245	1,086	909	731	554	376
14,350	14,400	1,569	1,405	1,255	1,096	918	741	563	386
14,400	14,450	1,580	1,415	1,265	1,105	928	750	573	395
14,450	14,500	1,591	1,426	1,275	1,115	937	760	582	405
14,500	14,550	1,602	1,437	1,285	1,124	947	769	592	414
14,550	14,600	1,613	1,448	1,295	1,134	956	779	601	424
14,600	14,650	1,624	1,459	1,305	1,143	966	788	611	433
14,650	14,700	1,635	1,470	1,315	1,153	975	798	620	443
14,700	14,750	1,646	1,481	1,325	1,162	985	807	630	452
14,750	14,800	1,657	1,492	1,335	1,172	994	817	639	462
14,800	14,850	1,668	1,503	1,345	1,181	1,004	826	649	471
14,850	14,900	1,679	1,514	1,355	1,191	1,013	836	658	481
14,900	14,950	1,690	1,525	1,365	1,200	1,023	845	668	490
14,950	15,000	1,701	1,536	1,375	1,211	1,032	855	677	500
15,000	15,050	1,712	1,547	1,385	1,222	1,042	864	687	509
15,050	15,100	1,723	1,558	1,395	1,233	1,051	874	696	519
15,100	15,150	1,734	1,569	1,405	1,244	1,061	883	706	528
15,150	15,200	1,745	1,580	1,415	1,255	1,070	893	715	538

Continued next column

If line 34, Form 1040 is— Over	But not over	And the total number of exemptions claimed on line 7 is— 2	3	4	5	6	7	8	9
15,200	15,250	1,756	1,591	1,426	1,266	1,080	902	725	547
15,250	15,300	1,767	1,602	1,437	1,277	1,089	912	734	557
15,300	15,350	1,778	1,613	1,448	1,288	1,099	921	744	566
15,350	15,400	1,789	1,624	1,459	1,299	1,108	931	753	576
15,400	15,450	1,800	1,635	1,470	1,310	1,118	940	763	585
15,450	15,500	1,811	1,646	1,481	1,321	1,127	950	772	595
15,500	15,550	1,822	1,657	1,492	1,332	1,137	959	782	604
15,550	15,600	1,833	1,668	1,503	1,343	1,146	969	791	614
15,600	15,650	1,844	1,679	1,514	1,354	1,156	978	801	623
15,650	15,700	1,855	1,690	1,525	1,365	1,165	988	810	633
15,700	15,750	1,866	1,701	1,536	1,375	1,176	997	820	642
15,750	15,800	1,877	1,712	1,547	1,385	1,187	1,007	829	652
15,800	15,850	1,888	1,723	1,558	1,395	1,198	1,016	839	661
15,850	15,900	1,899	1,734	1,569	1,405	1,209	1,026	848	671
15,900	15,950	1,910	1,745	1,580	1,415	1,220	1,035	858	680
15,950	16,000	1,921	1,756	1,591	1,426	1,231	1,045	867	690
16,000	16,050	1,932	1,767	1,602	1,437	1,242	1,054	877	699
16,050	16,100	1,943	1,778	1,613	1,448	1,253	1,064	886	709
16,100	16,150	1,954	1,789	1,624	1,459	1,264	1,073	896	718
16,150	16,200	1,965	1,800	1,635	1,470	1,275	1,083	905	728
16,200	16,250	1,976	1,811	1,646	1,481	1,286	1,092	915	737
16,250	16,300	1,987	1,822	1,657	1,492	1,297	1,102	924	747
16,300	16,350	1,998	1,833	1,668	1,503	1,308	1,111	934	756
16,350	16,400	2,009	1,844	1,679	1,514	1,319	1,121	943	766
16,400	16,450	2,020	1,855	1,690	1,525	1,330	1,130	953	775
16,450	16,500	2,031	1,866	1,701	1,536	1,341	1,141	962	785
16,500	16,550	2,042	1,877	1,712	1,547	1,352	1,152	972	794
16,550	16,600	2,053	1,888	1,723	1,558	1,363	1,163	981	804
16,600	16,650	2,064	1,899	1,734	1,569	1,374	1,174	991	813
16,650	16,700	2,075	1,910	1,745	1,580	1,385	1,185	1,000	823
16,700	16,750	2,086	1,921	1,756	1,591	1,396	1,196	1,010	832
16,750	16,800	2,099	1,932	1,767	1,602	1,407	1,207	1,019	842
16,800	16,850	2,111	1,943	1,778	1,613	1,418	1,218	1,029	851
16,850	16,900	2,124	1,954	1,789	1,624	1,429	1,229	1,038	861
16,900	16,950	2,136	1,965	1,800	1,635	1,440	1,240	1,048	870
16,950	17,000	2,149	1,976	1,811	1,646	1,451	1,251	1,057	880
17,000	17,050	2,161	1,987	1,822	1,657	1,462	1,262	1,067	889
17,050	17,100	2,174	1,998	1,833	1,668	1,473	1,273	1,076	899
17,100	17,150	2,186	2,009	1,844	1,679	1,484	1,284	1,086	908
17,150	17,200	2,199	2,020	1,855	1,690	1,495	1,295	1,095	918
17,200	17,250	2,211	2,031	1,866	1,701	1,506	1,306	1,106	927
17,250	17,300	2,224	2,042	1,877	1,712	1,517	1,317	1,117	937
17,300	17,350	2,236	2,053	1,888	1,723	1,528	1,328	1,128	946
17,350	17,400	2,249	2,064	1,899	1,734	1,539	1,339	1,139	956
17,400	17,450	2,261	2,075	1,910	1,745	1,550	1,350	1,150	965
17,450	17,500	2,274	2,086	1,921	1,756	1,561	1,361	1,161	975
17,500	17,550	2,286	2,099	1,932	1,767	1,572	1,372	1,172	984
17,550	17,600	2,299	2,111	1,943	1,778	1,583	1,383	1,183	994
17,600	17,650	2,311	2,124	1,954	1,789	1,594	1,394	1,194	1,003
17,650	17,700	2,324	2,136	1,965	1,800	1,605	1,405	1,205	1,013
17,700	17,750	2,336	2,149	1,976	1,811	1,616	1,416	1,216	1,022
17,750	17,800	2,349	2,161	1,987	1,822	1,627	1,427	1,227	1,032
17,800	17,850	2,361	2,174	1,998	1,833	1,638	1,438	1,238	1,041
17,850	17,900	2,374	2,186	2,009	1,844	1,649	1,449	1,249	1,051
17,900	17,950	2,386	2,199	2,020	1,855	1,660	1,460	1,260	1,060
17,950	18,000	2,399	2,211	2,031	1,866	1,671	1,471	1,271	1,071
18,000	18,050	2,411	2,224	2,042	1,877	1,682	1,482	1,282	1,082
18,050	18,100	2,424	2,236	2,053	1,888	1,693	1,493	1,293	1,093
18,100	18,150	2,436	2,249	2,064	1,899	1,704	1,504	1,304	1,104
18,150	18,200	2,449	2,261	2,075	1,910	1,715	1,515	1,315	1,115
18,200	18,250	2,461	2,274	2,086	1,921	1,726	1,526	1,326	1,126
18,250	18,300	2,474	2,286	2,099	1,932	1,737	1,537	1,337	1,137
18,300	18,350	2,486	2,299	2,111	1,943	1,748	1,548	1,348	1,148
18,350	18,400	2,499	2,311	2,124	1,954	1,759	1,559	1,359	1,159
18,400	18,450	2,511	2,324	2,136	1,965	1,770	1,570	1,370	1,170
18,450	18,500	2,524	2,336	2,149	1,976	1,781	1,581	1,381	1,181
18,500	18,550	2,536	2,349	2,161	1,987	1,792	1,592	1,392	1,192
18,550	18,600	2,549	2,361	2,174	1,998	1,803	1,603	1,403	1,203
18,600	18,650	2,561	2,374	2,186	2,009	1,814	1,614	1,414	1,214
18,650	18,700	2,574	2,386	2,199	2,020	1,825	1,625	1,425	1,225
18,700	18,750	2,586	2,399	2,211	2,031	1,836	1,636	1,436	1,236
18,750	18,800	2,599	2,411	2,224	2,042	1,847	1,647	1,447	1,247

Continued on next page

Table 8   503

1977 Tax Table B—MARRIED FILING JOINTLY (Box 2) and QUALIFYING WIDOW(ER)S (Box 5)
(Continued)

(If your income or exemptions are not covered, use Schedule TC (Form 1040), Part I to figure your tax)

If line 34, Form 1040 is— Over	But not over	2	3	4	5	6	7	8	9
18,800	18,850	2,611	2,424	2,236	2,053	1,858	1,658	1,458	1,258
18,850	18,900	2,624	2,436	2,249	2,064	1,869	1,669	1,469	1,269
18,900	18,950	2,636	2,449	2,261	2,075	1,880	1,680	1,480	1,280
18,950	19,000	2,649	2,461	2,274	2,086	1,891	1,691	1,491	1,291
19,000	19,050	2,661	2,474	2,286	2,099	1,902	1,702	1,502	1,302
19,050	19,100	2,674	2,486	2,299	2,111	1,913	1,713	1,513	1,313
19,100	19,150	2,686	2,499	2,311	2,124	1,924	1,724	1,524	1,324
19,150	19,200	2,699	2,511	2,324	2,136	1,935	1,735	1,535	1,335
19,200	19,250	2,711	2,524	2,336	2,149	1,946	1,746	1,546	1,346
19,250	19,300	2,724	2,536	2,349	2,161	1,957	1,757	1,557	1,357
19,300	19,350	2,736	2,549	2,361	2,174	1,968	1,768	1,568	1,368
19,350	19,400	2,749	2,561	2,374	2,186	1,979	1,779	1,579	1,379
19,400	19,450	2,761	2,574	2,386	2,199	1,990	1,790	1,590	1,390
19,450	19,500	2,774	2,586	2,399	2,211	2,001	1,801	1,601	1,401
19,500	19,550	2,786	2,599	2,411	2,224	2,012	1,812	1,612	1,412
19,550	19,600	2,799	2,611	2,424	2,236	2,023	1,823	1,623	1,423
19,600	19,650	2,811	2,624	2,436	2,249	2,034	1,834	1,634	1,434
19,650	19,700	2,824	2,636	2,449	2,261	2,045	1,845	1,645	1,445
19,700	19,750	2,836	2,649	2,461	2,274	2,056	1,856	1,656	1,456
19,750	19,800	2,849	2,661	2,474	2,286	2,069	1,867	1,667	1,467
19,800	19,850	2,861	2,674	2,486	2,299	2,081	1,878	1,678	1,478
19,850	19,900	2,874	2,686	2,499	2,311	2,094	1,889	1,689	1,489
19,900	19,950	2,886	2,699	2,511	2,324	2,106	1,900	1,700	1,500
19,950	20,000	2,899	2,711	2,524	2,336	2,119	1,911	1,711	1,511
20,000	20,050	2,911	2,724	2,536	2,349	2,131	1,922	1,722	1,522
20,050	20,100	2,924	2,736	2,549	2,361	2,144	1,933	1,733	1,533
20,100	20,150	2,936	2,749	2,561	2,374	2,156	1,944	1,744	1,544
20,150	20,200	2,949	2,761	2,574	2,386	2,169	1,955	1,755	1,555
20,200	20,250	2,961	2,774	2,586	2,399	2,181	1,966	1,766	1,566
20,250	20,300	2,974	2,786	2,599	2,411	2,194	1,977	1,777	1,577
20,300	20,350	2,986	2,799	2,611	2,424	2,206	1,988	1,788	1,588
20,350	20,400	2,999	2,811	2,624	2,436	2,219	1,999	1,799	1,599
20,400	20,450	3,011	2,824	2,636	2,449	2,231	2,010	1,810	1,610
20,450	20,500	3,024	2,836	2,649	2,461	2,244	2,021	1,821	1,621
20,500	20,550	3,036	2,849	2,661	2,474	2,256	2,034	1,832	1,632
20,550	20,600	3,049	2,861	2,674	2,486	2,269	2,046	1,843	1,643
20,600	20,650	3,061	2,874	2,686	2,499	2,281	2,059	1,854	1,654
20,650	20,700	3,074	2,886	2,699	2,511	2,294	2,071	1,865	1,665
20,700	20,750	3,087	2,899	2,711	2,524	2,306	2,084	1,876	1,676
20,750	20,800	3,101	2,911	2,724	2,536	2,319	2,096	1,887	1,687
20,800	20,850	3,115	2,924	2,736	2,549	2,331	2,109	1,898	1,698
20,850	20,900	3,129	2,936	2,749	2,561	2,344	2,121	1,909	1,709
20,900	20,950	3,143	2,949	2,761	2,574	2,356	2,134	1,920	1,720
20,950	21,000	3,157	2,961	2,774	2,586	2,369	2,146	1,931	1,731
21,000	21,050	3,171	2,974	2,786	2,599	2,381	2,159	1,942	1,742
21,050	21,100	3,185	2,986	2,799	2,611	2,394	2,171	1,953	1,753
21,100	21,150	3,199	2,999	2,811	2,624	2,406	2,184	1,964	1,764
21,150	21,200	3,213	3,011	2,824	2,636	2,419	2,196	1,975	1,775
21,200	21,250	3,227	3,024	2,836	2,649	2,431	2,209	1,986	1,786
21,250	21,300	3,241	3,036	2,849	2,661	2,444	2,221	1,999	1,797
21,300	21,350	3,255	3,049	2,861	2,674	2,456	2,234	2,011	1,808
21,350	21,400	3,269	3,061	2,874	2,686	2,469	2,246	2,024	1,819
21,400	21,450	3,283	3,074	2,886	2,699	2,481	2,259	2,036	1,830
21,450	21,500	3,297	3,087	2,899	2,711	2,494	2,271	2,049	1,841
21,500	21,550	3,311	3,101	2,911	2,724	2,506	2,284	2,061	1,852
21,550	21,600	3,325	3,115	2,924	2,736	2,519	2,296	2,074	1,863
21,600	21,650	3,339	3,129	2,936	2,749	2,531	2,309	2,086	1,874
21,650	21,700	3,353	3,143	2,949	2,761	2,544	2,321	2,099	1,885
21,700	21,750	3,367	3,157	2,961	2,774	2,556	2,334	2,111	1,896
21,750	21,800	3,381	3,171	2,974	2,786	2,569	2,346	2,124	1,907
21,800	21,850	3,395	3,185	2,986	2,799	2,581	2,359	2,136	1,918
21,850	21,900	3,409	3,199	2,999	2,811	2,594	2,371	2,149	1,929
21,900	21,950	3,423	3,213	3,011	2,824	2,606	2,384	2,161	1,940
21,950	22,000	3,437	3,227	3,024	2,836	2,619	2,396	2,174	1,951
22,000	22,050	3,451	3,241	3,036	2,849	2,631	2,409	2,186	1,964
22,050	22,100	3,465	3,255	3,049	2,861	2,644	2,421	2,199	1,976
22,100	22,150	3,479	3,269	3,061	2,874	2,656	2,434	2,211	1,989
22,150	22,200	3,493	3,283	3,074	2,886	2,669	2,446	2,224	2,001
22,200	22,250	3,507	3,297	3,087	2,899	2,681	2,459	2,236	2,014
22,250	22,300	3,521	3,311	3,101	2,911	2,694	2,471	2,249	2,026
22,300	22,350	3,535	3,325	3,115	2,924	2,706	2,484	2,261	2,039
22,350	22,400	3,549	3,339	3,129	2,936	2,719	2,496	2,274	2,051
22,400	22,450	3,563	3,353	3,143	2,949	2,731	2,509	2,286	2,064
22,450	22,500	3,577	3,367	3,157	2,961	2,744	2,521	2,299	2,076
22,500	22,550	3,591	3,381	3,171	2,974	2,756	2,534	2,311	2,089
22,550	22,600	3,605	3,395	3,185	2,986	2,769	2,546	2,324	2,101
22,600	22,650	3,619	3,409	3,199	2,999	2,781	2,559	2,336	2,114
22,650	22,700	3,633	3,423	3,213	3,011	2,794	2,571	2,349	2,126
22,700	22,750	3,647	3,437	3,227	3,024	2,806	2,584	2,361	2,139
22,750	22,800	3,661	3,451	3,241	3,036	2,819	2,596	2,374	2,151
22,800	22,850	3,675	3,465	3,255	3,049	2,831	2,609	2,386	2,164
22,850	22,900	3,689	3,479	3,269	3,061	2,844	2,621	2,399	2,176
22,900	22,950	3,703	3,493	3,283	3,074	2,856	2,634	2,411	2,189
22,950	23,000	3,717	3,507	3,297	3,087	2,869	2,646	2,424	2,201
23,000	23,050	3,731	3,521	3,311	3,101	2,881	2,659	2,436	2,214
23,050	23,100	3,745	3,535	3,325	3,115	2,894	2,671	2,449	2,226
23,100	23,150	3,759	3,549	3,339	3,129	2,906	2,684	2,461	2,239
23,150	23,200	3,773	3,563	3,353	3,143	2,919	2,696	2,474	2,251
23,200	23,250	3,787	3,577	3,367	3,157	2,931	2,709	2,486	2,264
23,250	23,300	3,801	3,591	3,381	3,171	2,944	2,721	2,499	2,276
23,300	23,350	3,815	3,605	3,395	3,185	2,956	2,734	2,511	2,289
23,350	23,400	3,829	3,619	3,409	3,199	2,969	2,746	2,524	2,301
23,400	23,450	3,843	3,633	3,423	3,213	2,981	2,759	2,536	2,314
23,450	23,500	3,857	3,647	3,437	3,227	2,994	2,771	2,549	2,326
23,500	23,550	3,871	3,661	3,451	3,241	3,006	2,784	2,561	2,339
23,550	23,600	3,885	3,675	3,465	3,255	3,019	2,796	2,574	2,351
23,600	23,650	3,899	3,689	3,479	3,269	3,031	2,809	2,586	2,364
23,650	23,700	3,913	3,703	3,493	3,283	3,044	2,821	2,599	2,376
23,700	23,750	3,927	3,717	3,507	3,297	3,057	2,834	2,611	2,389
23,750	23,800	3,941	3,731	3,521	3,311	3,071	2,846	2,624	2,401
23,800	23,850	3,955	3,745	3,535	3,325	3,085	2,859	2,636	2,414
23,850	23,900	3,969	3,759	3,549	3,339	3,099	2,871	2,649	2,426
23,900	23,950	3,983	3,773	3,563	3,353	3,113	2,884	2,661	2,439
23,950	24,000	3,997	3,787	3,577	3,367	3,127	2,896	2,674	2,451
24,000	24,050	4,011	3,801	3,591	3,381	3,141	2,909	2,686	2,464
24,050	24,100	4,025	3,815	3,605	3,395	3,155	2,921	2,699	2,476
24,100	24,150	4,039	3,829	3,619	3,409	3,169	2,934	2,711	2,489
24,150	24,200	4,053	3,843	3,633	3,423	3,183	2,946	2,724	2,501
24,200	24,250	4,067	3,857	3,647	3,437	3,197	2,959	2,736	2,514
24,250	24,300	4,081	3,871	3,661	3,451	3,211	2,971	2,749	2,526
24,300	24,350	4,095	3,885	3,675	3,465	3,225	2,984	2,761	2,539
24,350	24,400	4,109	3,899	3,689	3,479	3,239	2,996	2,774	2,551
24,400	24,450	4,123	3,913	3,703	3,493	3,253	3,009	2,786	2,564
24,450	24,500	4,137	3,927	3,717	3,507	3,267	3,022	2,799	2,576
24,500	24,550	4,151	3,941	3,731	3,521	3,281	3,036	2,811	2,589
24,550	24,600	4,165	3,955	3,745	3,535	3,295	3,050	2,824	2,601
24,600	24,650	4,179	3,969	3,759	3,549	3,309	3,064	2,836	2,614
24,650	24,700	4,193	3,983	3,773	3,563	3,323	3,078	2,849	2,626
24,700	24,750	4,208	3,997	3,787	3,577	3,337	3,092	2,861	2,639
24,750	24,800	4,224	4,011	3,801	3,591	3,351	3,106	2,874	2,651
24,800	24,850	4,240	4,025	3,815	3,605	3,365	3,120	2,886	2,664
24,850	24,900	4,256	4,039	3,829	3,619	3,379	3,134	2,899	2,676
24,900	24,950	4,272	4,053	3,843	3,633	3,393	3,148	2,911	2,689
24,950	25,000	4,288	4,067	3,857	3,647	3,407	3,162	2,924	2,701
25,000	25,050	4,304	4,081	3,871	3,661	3,421	3,176	2,936	2,714
25,050	25,100	4,320	4,095	3,885	3,675	3,435	3,190	2,949	2,726
25,100	25,150	4,336	4,109	3,899	3,689	3,449	3,204	2,961	2,739
25,150	25,200	4,352	4,123	3,913	3,703	3,463	3,218	2,974	2,751
25,200	25,250	4,368	4,137	3,927	3,717	3,477	3,232	2,987	2,764
25,250	25,300	4,384	4,151	3,941	3,731	3,491	3,246	3,001	2,776
25,300	25,350	4,400	4,165	3,955	3,745	3,505	3,260	3,015	2,789
25,350	25,400	4,416	4,179	3,969	3,759	3,519	3,274	3,029	2,801
25,400	25,450	4,432	4,193	3,983	3,773	3,533	3,288	3,043	2,814
25,450	25,500	4,448	4,208	3,997	3,787	3,547	3,302	3,057	2,826
25,500	25,550	4,464	4,224	4,011	3,801	3,561	3,316	3,071	2,839
25,550	25,600	4,480	4,240	4,025	3,815	3,575	3,330	3,085	2,851
25,600	25,650	4,496	4,256	4,039	3,829	3,589	3,344	3,099	2,864
25,650	25,700	4,512	4,272	4,053	3,843	3,603	3,358	3,113	2,876
25,700	25,750	4,528	4,288	4,067	3,857	3,617	3,372	3,127	2,889
25,750	25,800	4,544	4,304	4,081	3,871	3,631	3,386	3,141	2,901
25,800	25,850	4,560	4,320	4,095	3,885	3,645	3,400	3,155	2,914
25,850	25,900	4,576	4,336	4,109	3,899	3,659	3,414	3,169	2,926
25,900	25,950	4,592	4,352	4,123	3,913	3,673	3,428	3,183	2,939
25,950	26,000	4,608	4,368	4,137	3,927	3,687	3,442	3,197	2,952

Continued next column

Continued on next page

Table 8

1977 Tax Table B—MARRIED FILING JOINTLY (Box 2) and
(Continued) QUALIFYING WIDOW(ER)S (Box 5)

(If your income or exemptions are not covered, use Schedule TC (Form 1040), Part I to figure your tax)

If line 34, Form 1040 is— Over	But not over	2	3	4	5	6	7	8	9	If line 34, Form 1040 is— Over	But not over	2	3	4	5	6	7	8	9
		Your tax is—										Your tax is—							
26,000	26,050	4,624	4,384	4,151	3,941	3,701	3,456	3,211	2,966	29,600	29,650	5,813	5,543	5,296	5,056	4,786	4,511	4,236	3,974
26,050	26,100	4,640	4,400	4,165	3,955	3,715	3,470	3,225	2,980	29,650	29,700	5,831	5,561	5,312	5,072	4,802	4,527	4,252	3,988
26,100	26,150	4,656	4,416	4,179	3,969	3,729	3,484	3,239	2,994	29,700	29,750	5,849	5,579	5,328	5,088	4,818	4,543	4,268	4,002
26,150	26,200	4,672	4,432	4,193	3,983	3,743	3,498	3,253	3,008	29,750	29,800	5,867	5,597	5,344	5,104	4,834	4,559	4,284	4,016
26,200	26,250	4,688	4,448	4,208	3,997	3,757	3,512	3,267	3,022	29,800	29,850	5,885	5,615	5,360	5,120	4,850	4,575	4,300	4,030
26,250	26,300	4,704	4,464	4,224	4,011	3,771	3,526	3,281	3,036	29,850	29,900	5,903	5,633	5,376	5,136	4,866	4,591	4,316	4,044
26,300	26,350	4,720	4,480	4,240	4,025	3,785	3,540	3,295	3,050	29,900	29,950	5,921	5,651	5,392	5,152	4,882	4,607	4,332	4,058
26,350	26,400	4,736	4,496	4,256	4,039	3,799	3,554	3,309	3,064	29,950	30,000	5,939	5,669	5,408	5,168	4,898	4,623	4,348	4,073
26,400	26,450	4,752	4,512	4,272	4,053	3,813	3,568	3,323	3,078	30,000	30,050	5,957	5,687	5,424	5,184	4,914	4,639	4,364	4,089
26,450	26,500	4,768	4,528	4,288	4,067	3,827	3,582	3,337	3,092	30,050	30,100	5,975	5,705	5,440	5,200	4,930	4,655	4,380	4,105
26,500	26,550	4,784	4,544	4,304	4,081	3,841	3,596	3,351	3,106	30,100	30,150	5,993	5,723	5,456	5,216	4,946	4,671	4,396	4,121
26,550	26,600	4,800	4,560	4,320	4,095	3,855	3,610	3,365	3,120	30,150	30,200	6,011	5,741	5,472	5,232	4,962	4,687	4,412	4,137
26,600	26,650	4,816	4,576	4,336	4,109	3,869	3,624	3,379	3,134	30,200	30,250	6,029	5,759	5,489	5,248	4,978	4,703	4,428	4,153
26,650	26,700	4,832	4,592	4,352	4,123	3,883	3,638	3,393	3,148	30,250	30,300	6,047	5,777	5,507	5,264	4,994	4,719	4,444	4,169
26,700	26,750	4,848	4,608	4,368	4,137	3,897	3,652	3,407	3,162	30,300	30,350	6,065	5,795	5,525	5,280	5,010	4,735	4,460	4,185
26,750	26,800	4,864	4,624	4,384	4,151	3,911	3,666	3,421	3,176	30,350	30,400	6,083	5,813	5,543	5,296	5,026	4,751	4,476	4,201
26,800	26,850	4,880	4,640	4,400	4,165	3,925	3,680	3,435	3,190	30,400	30,450	6,101	5,831	5,561	5,312	5,042	4,767	4,492	4,217
26,850	26,900	4,896	4,656	4,416	4,179	3,939	3,694	3,449	3,204	30,450	30,500	6,119	5,849	5,579	5,328	5,058	4,783	4,508	4,233
26,900	26,950	4,912	4,672	4,432	4,193	3,953	3,708	3,463	3,218	30,500	30,550	6,137	5,867	5,597	5,344	5,074	4,799	4,524	4,249
26,950	27,000	4,928	4,688	4,448	4,208	3,967	3,722	3,477	3,232	30,550	30,600	6,155	5,885	5,615	5,360	5,090	4,815	4,540	4,265
27,000	27,050	4,944	4,704	4,464	4,224	3,981	3,736	3,491	3,246	30,600	30,650	6,173	5,903	5,633	5,376	5,106	4,831	4,556	4,281
27,050	27,100	4,960	4,720	4,480	4,240	3,995	3,750	3,505	3,260	30,650	30,700	6,191	5,921	5,651	5,392	5,122	4,847	4,572	4,297
27,100	27,150	4,976	4,736	4,496	4,256	4,009	3,764	3,519	3,274	30,700	30,750	6,209	5,939	5,669	5,408	5,138	4,863	4,588	4,313
27,150	27,200	4,992	4,752	4,512	4,272	4,023	3,778	3,533	3,288	30,750	30,800	6,227	5,957	5,687	5,424	5,154	4,879	4,604	4,329
27,200	27,250	5,008	4,768	4,528	4,288	4,037	3,792	3,547	3,302	30,800	30,850	6,245	5,975	5,705	5,440	5,170	4,895	4,620	4,345
27,250	27,300	5,024	4,784	4,544	4,304	4,051	3,806	3,561	3,316	30,850	30,900	6,263	5,993	5,723	5,456	5,186	4,911	4,636	4,361
27,300	27,350	5,040	4,800	4,560	4,320	4,065	3,820	3,575	3,330	30,900	30,950	6,281	6,011	5,741	5,472	5,202	4,927	4,652	4,377
27,350	27,400	5,056	4,816	4,576	4,336	4,079	3,834	3,589	3,344	30,950	31,000	6,299	6,029	5,759	5,489	5,218	4,943	4,668	4,393
27,400	27,450	5,072	4,832	4,592	4,352	4,093	3,848	3,603	3,358	31,000	31,050	6,317	6,047	5,777	5,507	5,234	4,959	4,684	4,409
27,450	27,500	5,088	4,848	4,608	4,368	4,107	3,862	3,617	3,372	31,050	31,100	6,335	6,065	5,795	5,525	5,250	4,975	4,700	4,425
27,500	27,550	5,104	4,864	4,624	4,384	4,121	3,876	3,631	3,386	31,100	31,150	6,353	6,083	5,813	5,543	5,266	4,991	4,716	4,441
27,550	27,600	5,120	4,880	4,640	4,400	4,135	3,890	3,645	3,400	31,150	31,200	6,371	6,101	5,831	5,561	5,282	5,007	4,732	4,457
27,600	27,650	5,136	4,896	4,656	4,416	4,149	3,904	3,659	3,414	31,200	31,250	6,389	6,119	5,849	5,579	5,298	5,023	4,748	4,473
27,650	27,700	5,152	4,912	4,672	4,432	4,163	3,918	3,673	3,428	31,250	31,300	6,407	6,137	5,867	5,597	5,314	5,039	4,764	4,489
27,700	27,750	5,168	4,928	4,688	4,448	4,178	3,932	3,687	3,442	31,300	31,350	6,425	6,155	5,885	5,615	5,330	5,055	4,780	4,505
27,750	27,800	5,184	4,944	4,704	4,464	4,194	3,946	3,701	3,456	31,350	31,400	6,443	6,173	5,903	5,633	5,346	5,071	4,796	4,521
27,800	27,850	5,200	4,960	4,720	4,480	4,210	3,960	3,715	3,470	31,400	31,450	6,461	6,191	5,921	5,651	5,362	5,087	4,812	4,537
27,850	27,900	5,216	4,976	4,736	4,496	4,226	3,974	3,729	3,484	31,450	31,500	6,479	6,209	5,939	5,669	5,378	5,103	4,828	4,553
27,900	27,950	5,232	4,992	4,752	4,512	4,242	3,988	3,743	3,498	31,500	31,550	6,497	6,227	5,957	5,687	5,394	5,119	4,844	4,569
27,950	28,000	5,248	5,008	4,768	4,528	4,258	4,002	3,757	3,512	31,550	31,600	6,515	6,245	5,975	5,705	5,410	5,135	4,860	4,585
28,000	28,050	5,264	5,024	4,784	4,544	4,274	4,016	3,771	3,526	31,600	31,650	6,533	6,263	5,993	5,723	5,426	5,151	4,876	4,601
28,050	28,100	5,280	5,040	4,800	4,560	4,290	4,030	3,785	3,540	31,650	31,700	6,551	6,281	6,011	5,741	5,442	5,167	4,892	4,617
28,100	28,150	5,296	5,056	4,816	4,576	4,306	4,044	3,799	3,554	31,700	31,750	6,569	6,299	6,029	5,759	5,459	5,183	4,908	4,633
28,150	28,200	5,312	5,072	4,832	4,592	4,322	4,058	3,813	3,568	31,750	31,800	6,587	6,317	6,047	5,777	5,477	5,199	4,924	4,649
28,200	28,250	5,328	5,088	4,848	4,608	4,338	4,072	3,827	3,582	31,800	31,850	6,605	6,335	6,065	5,795	5,495	5,215	4,940	4,665
28,250	28,300	5,344	5,104	4,864	4,624	4,354	4,086	3,841	3,596	31,850	31,900	6,623	6,353	6,083	5,813	5,513	5,231	4,956	4,681
28,300	28,350	5,360	5,120	4,880	4,640	4,370	4,100	3,855	3,610	31,900	31,950	6,641	6,371	6,101	5,831	5,531	5,247	4,972	4,697
28,350	28,400	5,376	5,136	4,896	4,656	4,386	4,114	3,869	3,624	31,950	32,000	6,659	6,389	6,119	5,849	5,549	5,263	4,988	4,713
28,400	28,450	5,392	5,152	4,912	4,672	4,402	4,128	3,883	3,638	32,000	32,050	6,677	6,407	6,137	5,867	5,567	5,279	5,004	4,729
28,450	28,500	5,408	5,168	4,928	4,688	4,418	4,143	3,897	3,652	32,050	32,100	6,695	6,425	6,155	5,885	5,585	5,295	5,020	4,745
28,500	28,550	5,424	5,184	4,944	4,704	4,434	4,159	3,911	3,666	32,100	32,150	6,713	6,443	6,173	5,903	5,603	5,311	5,036	4,761
28,550	28,600	5,440	5,200	4,960	4,720	4,450	4,175	3,925	3,680	32,150	32,200	6,731	6,461	6,191	5,921	5,621	5,327	5,052	4,777
28,600	28,650	5,456	5,216	4,976	4,736	4,466	4,191	3,939	3,694	32,200	32,250	6,749	6,479	6,209	5,939	5,639	5,343	5,068	4,793
28,650	28,700	5,472	5,232	4,992	4,752	4,482	4,207	3,953	3,708	32,250	32,300	6,767	6,497	6,227	5,957	5,657	5,359	5,084	4,809
28,700	28,750	5,489	5,248	5,008	4,768	4,498	4,223	3,967	3,722	32,300	32,350	6,785	6,515	6,245	5,975	5,675	5,375	5,100	4,825
28,750	28,800	5,507	5,264	5,024	4,784	4,514	4,239	3,981	3,736	32,350	32,400	6,803	6,533	6,263	5,993	5,693	5,391	5,116	4,841
28,800	28,850	5,525	5,280	5,040	4,800	4,530	4,255	3,995	3,750	32,400	32,450	6,821	6,551	6,281	6,011	5,711	5,407	5,132	4,857
28,850	28,900	5,543	5,296	5,056	4,816	4,546	4,271	4,009	3,764	32,450	32,500	6,839	6,569	6,299	6,029	5,729	5,424	5,148	4,873
28,900	28,950	5,561	5,312	5,072	4,832	4,562	4,287	4,023	3,778	32,500	32,550	6,857	6,587	6,317	6,047	5,747	5,442	5,164	4,889
28,950	29,000	5,579	5,328	5,088	4,848	4,578	4,303	4,037	3,792	32,550	32,600	6,875	6,605	6,335	6,065	5,765	5,460	5,180	4,905
29,000	29,050	5,597	5,344	5,104	4,864	4,594	4,319	4,051	3,806	32,600	32,650	6,893	6,623	6,353	6,083	5,783	5,478	5,196	4,921
29,050	29,100	5,615	5,360	5,120	4,880	4,610	4,335	4,065	3,820	32,650	32,700	6,911	6,641	6,371	6,101	5,801	5,496	5,212	4,937
29,100	29,150	5,633	5,376	5,136	4,896	4,626	4,351	4,079	3,834	32,700	32,750	6,930	6,659	6,389	6,119	5,819	5,514	5,228	4,953
29,150	29,200	5,651	5,392	5,152	4,912	4,642	4,367	4,093	3,848	32,750	32,800	6,949	6,677	6,407	6,137	5,837	5,532	5,244	4,969
29,200	29,250	5,669	5,408	5,168	4,928	4,658	4,383	4,108	3,862	32,800	32,850	6,969	6,695	6,425	6,155	5,855	5,550	5,260	4,985
29,250	29,300	5,687	5,424	5,184	4,944	4,674	4,399	4,124	3,876	32,850	32,900	6,988	6,713	6,443	6,173	5,873	5,568	5,276	5,001
29,300	29,350	5,705	5,440	5,200	4,960	4,690	4,415	4,140	3,890	32,900	32,950	7,008	6,731	6,461	6,191	5,891	5,586	5,292	5,017
29,350	29,400	5,723	5,456	5,216	4,976	4,706	4,431	4,156	3,904	32,950	33,000	7,027	6,749	6,479	6,209	5,909	5,604	5,308	5,033
29,400	29,450	5,741	5,472	5,232	4,992	4,722	4,447	4,172	3,918	33,000	33,050	7,047	6,767	6,497	6,227	5,927	5,622	5,324	5,049
29,450	29,500	5,759	5,489	5,248	5,008	4,738	4,463	4,188	3,932	33,050	33,100	7,066	6,785	6,515	6,245	5,945	5,640	5,340	5,065
29,500	29,550	5,777	5,507	5,264	5,024	4,754	4,479	4,204	3,946	33,100	33,150	7,086	6,803	6,533	6,263	5,963	5,658	5,356	5,081
29,550	29,600	5,795	5,525	5,290	5,040	4,770	4,495	4,220	3,960	33,150	33,200	7,105	6,821	6,551	6,281	5,981	5,676	5,372	5,097

Continued next column

Continued on next page

Table 8

1977 Tax Table B—MARRIED FILING JOINTLY (Box 2) and QUALIFYING WIDOW(ER)S (Box 5)
(Continued)

(If your income or exemptions are not covered, use Schedule TC (Form 1040), Part I to figure your tax)

If line 34, Form 1040 is— Over	But not over	2	3	4	5	6	7	8	9	If line 34, Form 1040 is— Over	But not over	2	3	4	5	6	7	8	9
33,200	33,250	7,125	6,839	6,569	6,299	5,999	5,694	5,389	5,113	36,600	36,650	8,451	8,158	7,866	7,573	7,251	6,923	6,613	6,308
33,250	33,300	7,144	6,857	6,587	6,317	6,017	5,712	5,407	5,129	36,650	36,700	8,470	8,178	7,885	7,593	7,270	6,943	6,631	6,326
33,300	33,350	7,164	6,875	6,605	6,335	6,035	5,730	5,425	5,145	36,700	36,750	8,491	8,197	7,905	7,612	7,290	6,962	6,649	6,344
33,350	33,400	7,183	6,893	6,623	6,353	6,053	5,748	5,443	5,161	36,750	36,800	8,512	8,217	7,924	7,632	7,309	6,982	6,667	6,362
33,400	33,450	7,203	6,911	6,641	6,371	6,071	5,766	5,461	5,177	36,800	36,850	8,533	8,236	7,944	7,651	7,329	7,001	6,685	6,380
33,450	33,500	7,222	6,930	6,659	6,389	6,089	5,784	5,479	5,193	36,850	36,900	8,554	8,256	7,963	7,671	7,348	7,021	6,703	6,398
33,500	33,550	7,242	6,949	6,677	6,407	6,107	5,802	5,497	5,209	36,900	36,950	8,575	8,275	7,983	7,690	7,368	7,040	6,721	6,416
33,550	33,600	7,261	6,969	6,695	6,425	6,125	5,820	5,515	5,225	36,950	37,000	8,596	8,295	8,002	7,710	7,387	7,060	6,739	6,434
33,600	33,650	7,281	6,988	6,713	6,443	6,143	5,838	5,533	5,241	37,000	37,050	8,617	8,314	8,022	7,729	7,407	7,079	6,757	6,452
33,650	33,700	7,300	7,008	6,731	6,461	6,161	5,856	5,551	5,257	37,050	37,100	8,638	8,334	8,041	7,749	7,426	7,099	6,775	6,470
33,700	33,750	7,320	7,027	6,749	6,479	6,179	5,874	5,569	5,273	37,100	37,150	8,659	8,353	8,061	7,768	7,446	7,118	6,793	6,488
33,750	33,800	7,339	7,047	6,767	6,497	6,197	5,892	5,587	5,289	37,150	37,200	8,680	8,373	8,080	7,788	7,465	7,138	6,811	6,506
33,800	33,850	7,359	7,066	6,785	6,515	6,215	5,910	5,605	5,305	37,200	37,250	8,701	8,392	8,100	7,807	7,485	7,157	6,830	6,524
33,850	33,900	7,378	7,086	6,803	6,533	6,233	5,928	5,623	5,321	37,250	37,300	8,722	8,412	8,119	7,827	7,504	7,177	6,849	6,542
33,900	33,950	7,398	7,105	6,821	6,551	6,251	5,946	5,641	5,337	37,300	37,350	8,743	8,431	8,139	7,846	7,524	7,196	6,869	6,560
33,950	34,000	7,417	7,125	6,839	6,569	6,269	5,964	5,659	5,354	37,350	37,400	8,764	8,451	8,158	7,866	7,543	7,216	6,888	6,578
34,000	34,050	7,437	7,144	6,857	6,587	6,287	5,982	5,677	5,372	37,400	37,450	8,785	8,470	8,178	7,885	7,563	7,235	6,908	6,596
34,050	34,100	7,456	7,164	6,875	6,605	6,305	6,000	5,695	5,390	37,450	37,500	8,806	8,491	8,197	7,905	7,582	7,255	6,927	6,614
34,100	34,150	7,476	7,183	6,893	6,623	6,323	6,018	5,713	5,408	37,500	37,550	8,827	8,512	8,217	7,924	7,602	7,274	6,947	6,632
34,150	34,200	7,495	7,203	6,911	6,641	6,341	6,036	5,731	5,426	37,550	37,600	8,848	8,533	8,236	7,944	7,621	7,294	6,966	6,650
34,200	34,250	7,515	7,222	6,930	6,659	6,359	6,054	5,749	5,444	37,600	37,650	8,869	8,554	8,256	7,963	7,641	7,313	6,986	6,668
34,250	34,300	7,534	7,242	6,949	6,677	6,377	6,072	5,767	5,462	37,650	37,700	8,890	8,575	8,275	7,983	7,660	7,333	7,005	6,686
34,300	34,350	7,554	7,261	6,969	6,695	6,395	6,090	5,785	5,480	37,700	37,750	8,911	8,596	8,295	8,002	7,680	7,352	7,025	6,704
34,350	34,400	7,573	7,281	6,988	6,713	6,413	6,108	5,803	5,498	37,750	37,800	8,932	8,617	8,314	8,022	7,699	7,372	7,044	6,722
34,400	34,450	7,593	7,300	7,008	6,731	6,431	6,126	5,821	5,516	37,800	37,850	8,953	8,638	8,334	8,041	7,719	7,391	7,064	6,740
34,450	34,500	7,612	7,320	7,027	6,749	6,449	6,144	5,839	5,534	37,850	37,900	8,974	8,659	8,353	8,061	7,738	7,411	7,083	6,758
34,500	34,550	7,632	7,339	7,047	6,767	6,467	6,162	5,857	5,552	37,900	37,950	8,995	8,680	8,373	8,080	7,758	7,430	7,103	6,776
34,550	34,600	7,651	7,359	7,066	6,785	6,485	6,180	5,875	5,570	37,950	38,000	9,016	8,701	8,392	8,100	7,777	7,450	7,122	6,795
34,600	34,650	7,671	7,378	7,086	6,803	6,503	6,198	5,893	5,588	38,000	38,050	9,037	8,722	8,412	8,119	7,797	7,469	7,142	6,814
34,650	34,700	7,690	7,398	7,105	6,821	6,521	6,216	5,911	5,606	38,050	38,100	9,058	8,743	8,431	8,139	7,816	7,489	7,161	6,834
34,700	34,750	7,710	7,417	7,125	6,839	6,539	6,234	5,929	5,624	38,100	38,150	9,079	8,764	8,451	8,158	7,836	7,508	7,181	6,853
34,750	34,800	7,729	7,437	7,144	6,857	6,557	6,252	5,947	5,642	38,150	38,200	9,100	8,785	8,470	8,178	7,855	7,528	7,200	6,873
34,800	34,850	7,749	7,456	7,164	6,875	6,575	6,270	5,965	5,660	38,200	38,250	9,121	8,806	8,491	8,197	7,875	7,547	7,220	6,892
34,850	34,900	7,768	7,476	7,183	6,893	6,593	6,288	5,983	5,678	38,250	38,300	9,142	8,827	8,512	8,217	7,894	7,567	7,239	6,912
34,900	34,950	7,788	7,495	7,203	6,911	6,611	6,306	6,001	5,696	38,300	38,350	9,163	8,848	8,533	8,236	7,914	7,586	7,259	6,931
34,950	35,000	7,807	7,515	7,222	6,930	6,629	6,324	6,019	5,714	38,350	38,400	9,184	8,869	8,554	8,256	7,933	7,606	7,278	6,951
35,000	35,050	7,827	7,534	7,242	6,949	6,647	6,342	6,037	5,732	38,400	38,450	9,205	8,890	8,575	8,275	7,953	7,625	7,298	6,970
35,050	35,100	7,846	7,554	7,261	6,969	6,665	6,360	6,055	5,750	38,450	38,500	9,226	8,911	8,596	8,295	7,972	7,645	7,317	6,990
35,100	35,150	7,866	7,573	7,281	6,988	6,683	6,378	6,073	5,768	38,500	38,550	9,247	8,932	8,617	8,314	7,992	7,664	7,337	7,009
35,150	35,200	7,885	7,593	7,300	7,008	6,701	6,396	6,091	5,786	38,550	38,600	9,268	8,953	8,638	8,334	8,011	7,684	7,356	7,029
35,200	35,250	7,905	7,612	7,320	7,027	6,719	6,414	6,109	5,804	38,600	38,650	9,289	8,974	8,659	8,353	8,031	7,703	7,376	7,048
35,250	35,300	7,924	7,632	7,339	7,047	6,737	6,432	6,127	5,822	38,650	38,700	9,310	8,995	8,680	8,373	8,050	7,723	7,395	7,068
35,300	35,350	7,944	7,651	7,359	7,066	6,755	6,450	6,145	5,840	38,700	38,750	9,331	9,016	8,701	8,392	8,070	7,742	7,415	7,087
35,350	35,400	7,963	7,671	7,378	7,086	6,773	6,468	6,163	5,858	38,750	38,800	9,352	9,037	8,722	8,412	8,089	7,762	7,434	7,107
35,400	35,450	7,983	7,690	7,398	7,105	6,791	6,486	6,181	5,876	38,800	38,850	9,373	9,058	8,743	8,431	8,109	7,781	7,454	7,126
35,450	35,500	8,002	7,710	7,417	7,125	6,809	6,504	6,199	5,894	38,850	38,900	9,394	9,079	8,764	8,451	8,128	7,801	7,473	7,146
35,500	35,550	8,022	7,729	7,437	7,144	6,827	6,522	6,217	5,912	38,900	38,950	9,415	9,100	8,785	8,470	8,148	7,820	7,493	7,165
35,550	35,600	8,041	7,749	7,456	7,164	6,845	6,540	6,235	5,930	38,950	39,000	9,436	9,121	8,806	8,491	8,167	7,840	7,512	7,185
35,600	35,650	8,061	7,768	7,476	7,183	6,863	6,558	6,253	5,948	39,000	39,050	9,457	9,142	8,827	8,512	8,187	7,859	7,532	7,204
35,650	35,700	8,080	7,788	7,495	7,203	6,881	6,576	6,271	5,966	39,050	39,100	9,478	9,163	8,848	8,533	8,206	7,879	7,551	7,224
35,700	35,750	8,100	7,807	7,515	7,222	6,900	6,594	6,289	5,984	39,100	39,150	9,499	9,184	8,869	8,554	8,226	7,898	7,571	7,243
35,750	35,800	8,119	7,827	7,534	7,242	6,919	6,612	6,307	6,002	39,150	39,200	9,520	9,205	8,890	8,575	8,245	7,918	7,590	7,263
35,800	35,850	8,139	7,846	7,554	7,261	6,939	6,630	6,325	6,020	39,200	39,250	9,541	9,226	8,911	8,596	8,265	7,937	7,610	7,282
35,850	35,900	8,158	7,866	7,573	7,281	6,958	6,648	6,343	6,038	39,250	39,300	9,562	9,247	8,932	8,617	8,284	7,957	7,629	7,302
35,900	35,950	8,178	7,885	7,593	7,300	6,978	6,666	6,361	6,056	39,300	39,350	9,583	9,268	8,953	8,638	8,304	7,976	7,649	7,321
35,950	36,000	8,197	7,905	7,612	7,320	6,997	6,684	6,379	6,074	39,350	39,400	9,604	9,289	8,974	8,659	8,323	7,996	7,668	7,341
36,000	36,050	8,217	7,924	7,632	7,339	7,017	6,702	6,397	6,092	39,400	39,450	9,625	9,310	8,995	8,680	8,343	8,015	7,688	7,360
36,050	36,100	8,236	7,944	7,651	7,359	7,036	6,720	6,415	6,110	39,450	39,500	9,646	9,331	9,016	8,701	8,362	8,035	7,707	7,380
36,100	36,150	8,256	7,963	7,671	7,378	7,056	6,738	6,433	6,128	39,500	39,550	9,667	9,352	9,037	8,722	8,382	8,054	7,727	7,399
36,150	36,200	8,275	7,983	7,690	7,398	7,075	6,756	6,451	6,146	39,550	39,600	9,688	9,373	9,058	8,743	8,401	8,074	7,746	7,419
36,200	36,250	8,295	8,002	7,710	7,417	7,095	6,774	6,469	6,164	39,600	39,650	9,709	9,394	9,079	8,764	8,421	8,093	7,766	7,438
36,250	36,300	8,314	8,022	7,729	7,437	7,114	6,792	6,487	6,182	39,650	39,700	9,730	9,415	9,100	8,785	8,440	8,113	7,785	7,458
36,300	36,350	8,334	8,041	7,749	7,456	7,134	6,810	6,505	6,200	39,700	39,750	9,751	9,436	9,121	8,806	8,461	8,132	7,805	7,477
36,350	36,400	8,353	8,061	7,768	7,476	7,153	6,828	6,523	6,218	39,750	39,800	9,772	9,457	9,142	8,827	8,482	8,152	7,824	7,497
36,400	36,450	8,373	8,080	7,788	7,495	7,173	6,846	6,541	6,236	39,800	39,850	9,793	9,478	9,163	8,848	8,503	8,171	7,844	7,516
36,450	36,500	8,392	8,100	7,807	7,515	7,192	6,865	6,559	6,254	39,850	39,900	9,814	9,499	9,184	8,869	8,524	8,191	7,863	7,536
36,500	36,550	8,412	8,119	7,827	7,534	7,212	6,884	6,577	6,272	39,900	39,950	9,835	9,520	9,205	8,890	8,545	8,210	7,883	7,555
36,550	36,600	8,431	8,139	7,846	7,554	7,231	6,904	6,595	6,290	39,950	40,000	9,856	9,541	9,226	8,911	8,566	8,230	7,902	7,575

Continued next column

1977 Tax Table C—MARRIED FILING SEPARATELY (Box 3)

(For married persons filing separate returns with tax table income of $20,000 or less who claim fewer than 4 exemptions)

To find your tax: Read down the left income column until you find your income as shown on line 34 of Form 1040. Read across to the column headed by the total number of exemptions claimed on line 7 of Form 1040. The amount shown at the point where the two lines meet is your tax. Enter on Form 1040, line 35.

The $1,600 zero bracket amount, your deduction for exemptions and the general tax credit have been taken into account in figuring the tax shown in this table. **Do not take a separate deduction for them.**

Caution: *If you or your spouse itemize deductions, or if you can be claimed as a dependent on your parent's return AND you have unearned income (interests, dividends, etc.) of $750 or more AND your earned income is less than $1,600 you must first use Schedule TC (Form 1040), Part II.*

If line 34, Form 1040 is— Over	But not over	1	2	3	If line 34, Form 1040 is— Over	But not over	1	2	3	If line 34, Form 1040 is— Over	But not over	1	2	3
		Your tax is—					Your tax is—					Your tax is—		
If $2,600 or less your tax is 0					5,000	5,050	403	227	68	7,800	7,850	980	780	580
2,600	2,625	2	0	0	5,050	5,100	413	236	76	7,850	7,900	991	791	591
2,625	2,650	5	0	0	5,100	5,150	422	245	84	7,900	7,950	1,002	802	602
2,650	2,675	9	0	0	5,150	5,200	432	254	92	7,950	8,000	1,013	813	613
2,675	2,700	12	0	0	5,200	5,250	441	264	100	8,000	8,050	1,024	824	624
2,700	2,725	16	0	0	5,250	5,300	451	273	108	8,050	8,100	1,035	835	635
2,725	2,750	19	0	0	5,300	5,350	460	283	116	8,100	8,150	1,046	846	646
2,750	2,775	23	0	0	5,350	5,400	470	292	124	8,150	8,200	1,057	857	657
2,775	2,800	26	0	0	5,400	5,450	479	302	133	8,200	8,250	1,068	868	668
2,800	2,825	30	0	0	5,450	5,500	489	311	141	8,250	8,300	1,079	879	679
2,825	2,850	33	0	0	5,500	5,550	498	321	150	8,300	8,350	1,090	890	690
2,850	2,875	37	0	0	5,550	5,600	508	330	158	8,350	8,400	1,101	901	701
2,875	2,900	41	0	0	5,600	5,650	517	340	167	8,400	8,450	1,114	912	712
2,900	2,925	44	0	0	5,650	5,700	527	349	175	8,450	8,500	1,126	923	723
2,925	2,950	48	0	0	5,700	5,750	536	359	184	8,500	8,550	1,139	934	734
2,950	2,975	52	0	0	5,750	5,800	546	368	192	8,550	8,600	1,151	945	745
2,975	3,000	56	0	0	5,800	5,850	555	378	201	8,600	8,650	1,164	956	756
3,000	3,050	61	0	0	5,850	5,900	565	387	210	8,650	8,700	1,176	967	767
3,050	3,100	69	0	0	5,900	5,950	574	397	219	8,700	8,750	1,189	978	778
3,100	3,150	76	0	0	5,950	6,000	584	406	229	8,750	8,800	1,201	989	789
3,150	3,200	84	0	0	6,000	6,050	593	416	238	8,800	8,850	1,214	1,000	800
3,200	3,250	91	0	0	6,050	6,100	603	425	248	8,850	8,900	1,226	1,011	811
3,250	3,300	99	0	0	6,100	6,150	612	435	257	8,900	8,950	1,239	1,022	822
3,300	3,350	106	0	0	6,150	6,200	622	444	267	8,950	9,000	1,251	1,033	833
3,350	3,400	114	0	0	6,200	6,250	631	454	276	9,000	9,050	1,264	1,044	844
3,400	3,450	122	0	0	6,250	6,300	641	463	286	9,050	9,100	1,276	1,055	855
3,450	3,500	130	0	0	6,300	6,350	650	473	295	9,100	9,150	1,289	1,066	866
3,500	3,550	138	0	0	6,350	6,400	661	482	305	9,150	9,200	1,301	1,079	877
3,550	3,600	146	0	0	6,400	6,450	672	492	314	9,200	9,250	1,314	1,091	888
3,600	3,650	154	4	0	6,450	6,500	683	501	324	9,250	9,300	1,326	1,104	899
3,650	3,700	162	11	0	6,500	6,550	694	511	333	9,300	9,350	1,339	1,116	910
3,700	3,750	170	19	0	6,550	6,600	705	520	343	9,350	9,400	1,351	1,129	921
3,750	3,800	178	26	0	6,600	6,650	716	530	352	9,400	9,450	1,364	1,141	932
3,800	3,850	186	34	0	6,650	6,700	727	539	362	9,450	9,500	1,376	1,154	943
3,850	3,900	194	41	0	6,700	6,750	738	549	371	9,500	9,550	1,389	1,166	954
3,900	3,950	203	49	0	6,750	6,800	749	558	381	9,550	9,600	1,401	1,179	965
3,950	4,000	211	56	0	6,800	6,850	760	568	390	9,600	9,650	1,414	1,191	976
4,000	4,050	220	64	0	6,850	6,900	771	577	400	9,650	9,700	1,426	1,204	987
4,050	4,100	228	71	0	6,900	6,950	782	587	409	9,700	9,750	1,439	1,216	998
4,100	4,150	237	79	0	6,950	7,000	793	596	419	9,750	9,800	1,451	1,229	1,009
4,150	4,200	245	87	0	7,000	7,050	804	606	428	9,800	9,850	1,464	1,241	1,020
4,200	4,250	254	95	0	7,050	7,100	815	615	438	9,850	9,900	1,476	1,254	1,031
4,250	4,300	262	103	0	7,100	7,150	826	626	447	9,900	9,950	1,489	1,266	1,044
4,300	4,350	271	111	0	7,150	7,200	837	637	457	9,950	10,000	1,501	1,279	1,056
4,350	4,400	280	119	0	7,200	7,250	848	648	466	10,000	10,050	1,514	1,291	1,069
4,400	4,450	289	127	0	7,250	7,300	859	659	476	10,050	10,100	1,526	1,304	1,081
4,450	4,500	299	135	0	7,300	7,350	870	670	485	10,100	10,150	1,539	1,316	1,094
4,500	4,550	308	143	0	7,350	7,400	881	681	495	10,150	10,200	1,551	1,329	1,106
4,550	4,600	318	151	0	7,400	7,450	892	692	504	10,200	10,250	1,564	1,341	1,119
4,600	4,650	327	159	6	7,450	7,500	903	703	514	10,250	10,300	1,576	1,354	1,131
4,650	4,700	337	168	14	7,500	7,550	914	714	523	10,300	10,350	1,589	1,366	1,144
4,700	4,750	346	176	21	7,550	7,600	925	725	533	10,350	10,400	1,602	1,379	1,156
4,750	4,800	356	185	29	7,600	7,650	936	736	542	10,400	10,450	1,616	1,391	1,169
4,800	4,850	365	193	36	7,650	7,700	947	747	552	10,450	10,500	1,630	1,404	1,181
4,850	4,900	375	202	44	7,700	7,750	958	758	561	10,500	10,550	1,644	1,416	1,194
4,900	4,950	384	210	52	7,750	7,800	969	769	571	10,550	10,600	1,658	1,429	1,206
4,950	5,000	394	219	60										

Continued next column

Continued next column

Continued on next page